WHAT DO POLITICAL SCIENTISTS DO?

Influences on Bureaucratic Rule Making

Rule making is one of the most important functions of the federal bureaucracy. By creating and revising regulations, bureaucrats influence the behavior of everyone, from individual Americans to large corporations. In theory, rule making is controlled by congressional mandates, with bureaucrats limited to translating legislative directives into law. But as we show in this chapter, there are many factors, from expertise to asymmetric information, that give bureaucrats a measure of discretion when drawing up rules. Rule making is generally carried out by unelected bureaucrats, often involving highly technical questions that attract little press attention. The question is, How do bureaucrats use their discretion, and whose interests are served and whose are ignored?

This issue is particularly important with regard to some aspects of the rule-making process, particularly the notice and comment procedure. These are designed to democratize the process, facilitate participation from small groups and individuals, and give these actors a voice over rule making. Many have argued that even with these rule making is often biased

toward business interests, with little attempt to accommodate citizen preferences, regardless of whether they are expressed through the notice and comment procedure. Moreover, individuals may lack the technical resources to file a credible comment on a proposed regulation, or may fall victim to the free rider problem and fail to organize a joint effort.

This empirical question about rule making is the subject of a collaboration between two political scientists, Susan Webb Yackee and Jason Webb Yackee, both of whom teach at the University of Wisconsin. Their study focused on thirty rules issued by a range of government agencies from 1994 to 2001. These rules attracted almost 1,700 comments. The authors and their research assistants read each comment and noted the source (corporations, government agencies, individuals, public interest groups, etc.), what the comment asked for in the proposed regulation (for example, whether the authors of the comment wanted more or less government involvement), and the complexity and the salience of the proposed rules (complex rules were expected to attract fewer comments from individuals, whereas salient rules were expected to attract more comments).

The authors found, firstly, evidence of a high level of business participation in the rule-making process. Nearly 57 percent of the comments filed came from corporations or business groups. An additional 19 percent came from government agencies. Only 6 percent came from public interest groups and only a few from individuals. Thus, although the notice and comment procedure provides the opportunity for citizens to participate in the writing of regulations, either as individuals or as part of an organized group, it appears that most of the time, relatively few Americans take advantage of the opportunity.

The Yackees built on this finding by using statistical analysis to determine the relationship between what business groups are asking for in their comments (more or less government regulation on a particular activity) and the content of the rule ultimately issued by bureaucrats at the end of the rule-making process. The analysis controlled for other factors, such as the kind of rule, the number of comments from business in favor of the rule being proposed.

The results of the figure, which

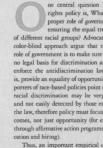

Susan Yackee

WHAT DO POLITICAL SCIENTISTS DO?

Evidence of Subtle Racism and Its Political Impact

One central question in civil rights policy is, What is the proper role of government in ensuring the equal treatment of different racial groups? Advocates for a color-blind approach argue that the only role of government is to make sure there is no legal basis for discrimination and then enforce the antidiscrimination laws: that is, provide an equality of opportunity. Supporters of race-based policies point out that racial discrimination may be very subtle and not easily detected by those enforcing the law, therefore policy must focus on outcomes, not just opportunity (for example, through affirmative action programs in education and hiring).

Thus, an important empirical question is, How can we measure discrimination? Obviously, overt discrimination is far less common today than it was a generation ago. Therefore, those who study this topic must be clever in designing their research to account for subtle forms of discrimination. One method to try to define the

extent of discrimination is through experiments that simulate real-world situations. Here we discuss two such examples that attempted to measure racially motivated behavior: one in hiring decisions and the other in political advertising.

Our first example comes from the field of economics (economists are interested in racial discrimination because of its impact on labor markets), but the approach described could be used by political scientists or any other type of social scientist. Two economists examined how a person's race could influence their chances of getting a job interview. In their experiment, they created résumés for job applicants, some of whom were well qualified and others of whom were not as well qualified for a particular job. They then assigned names to their fictitious applicants that are common among blacks and whites (based on the ratio of black newborns and white newborns that are given specific names). For example, African American names included Lakisha and Tyrone and

white names included Allison and Brad. Four résumés (high and low qualification for each race) were then sent to actual job openings in Boston and Chicago for sales, administrative support, clerical, and customer service jobs. The study found that résumés with white names received 50 percent more calls for interviews than résumés with black names. In addition, 8.4 percent of the employers contacted at least one more white applicant than black applicant, whereas only 3.5 percent of employers contacted at least one more black applicant than white applicant. The value of a high-quality résumé also varied between the two races. White résumés of high quality received 27 percent more calls than those of low quality, but for black résumés, the difference was only 8 percent in favor of the high-quality ones. This type of controlled experiment reveals that a person's race still matters for something as important as getting a job interview.

An experiment by political scientists Nicholas Valentino, Vincent Hutchings, and

American Politics Today

SECOND EDITION

American Politics Today

SECOND EDITION

William T. Bianco
INDIANA UNIVERSITY, BLOOMINGTON

David T. Canon
UNIVERSITY OF WISCONSIN, MADISON

W. W. NORTON & COMPANY
NEW YORK • LONDON

W. W. Norton & Company has been independent since its founding in 1923, when
William Warder Norton and Mary D. Herter Norton first published lectures delivered at
the People's Institute, the adult education division of New York City's Cooper Union. The
firm soon expanded its program beyond the Institute, publishing books by celebrated
academics from America and abroad. By midcentury, the two major pillars of Norton's
publishing program—trade books and college texts—were firmly established. In the
1950s, the Norton family transferred control of the company to its employees, and
today—with a staff of four hundred and a comparable number of trade, college, and
professional titles published each year—W. W. Norton & Company stands as the largest
and oldest publishing house owned wholly by its employees.

The text of this book is composed in Garamond with the display set in ITC Officina Sans.

Editor: Aaron Javsicas
Managing editor, College: Marian Johnson
Project editor: Christine D'Antonio
Copyeditor: JoAnn Simony/Dooen Books
Editorial assistants: Carly Fraser, Callinda Taylor, and Cait Callahan
Senior production manager, College: Benjamin Reynolds
Emedia editor: Pete Lesser
Marketing manager: Nicole Netherton
Ancillaries editor: Lorraine Klimowich
Design directors: Hope Miller Goodell and Rubina Yeh
Photo researchers: Trish Marx and Julie Tesser
Composition by Textech, Inc.—Brattleboro, VT
Manufacturing by R. R. Donnelley & Sons—Jefferson City, MO

Library of Congress Cataloging-in-Publication Data

Bianco, William T., 1960-
    American politics today / William T. Bianco, David T. Canon. — 2nd ed.
        p. cm.
    Includes bibliographical references and index.

    ISBN 978-0-393-93471-7 (hardcover : alk. paper)

    1. United States—Politics and government.   I. Canon, David T.   II. Title.
JK275.B53 2010
320.473—dc22

                                                              2010045043

W. W. Norton & Company, Inc., 500 Fifth Avenue, New York, N.Y 10110-0017
    www.wwnorton.com

W. W. Norton & Company, Ltd., Castle House, 75/76 Wells Street, London W1T3QT
1 2 3 4 5 6 7 8 9 0

For our families,
Regina, Anna, and Catherine,
Sarah, Neal, Katherine, and Sophia,
who encouraged, empathized, and
helped, with patience,
grace, and love.

About the Authors

WILLIAM T. BIANCO is professor of political science at Indiana University, Bloomington, and Co-Chair of the Working Group on the Political Economy of Sustainable Democracy at the Workshop in Political Theory and Policy Analysis. He is the author of *Trust: Representatives and Constituents; American Politics: Strategy and Choice*; and numerous articles on American politics. He has received three National Science Foundation Grants. He has also served as a consultant to congressional candidates and party campaign committees, as well as to the U.S. Department of Energy, the U.S. Department of Health and Human Services, and other state and local government agencies.

DAVID T. CANON is professor of political science at the University of Wisconsin, Madison. His teaching and research interests focus on American political institutions, especially Congress, and racial representation. He is the author of *Actors, Athletes, and Astronauts: Political Amateurs in the U.S. Congress; Race, Redistricting, and Representation: The Unintended Consequences of Black Majority Districts* (winner of the Richard F. Fenno Prize); *The Dysfunctional Congress?* (with Kenneth Mayer); and various articles and book chapters. He recently finished a term as the Congress editor of *Legislative Studies Quarterly*. He is an AP consultant and has taught in the University of Wisconsin Summer AP Institute for US Government & Politics since 1997. Professor Canon is the recipient of a University of Wisconsin Chancellor's Distinguished Teaching Award.

Contents in Brief

Contents

Part I: Foundations

3. Federalism 64

4. Civil Liberties 98

Part II: Politics

5. Public Opinion 142

6. The Media 184

7. Political Parties 218

Part III: Institutions

10. Congress 346

11. The Presidency 392

12. The Bureaucracy 428

13. The Courts 464

Part IV: Policy

14. Civil Rights 508

17. Foreign Policy 634

Appendix

Boxed Features

Nuts and Bolts

What Do Political Scientists Do?

Challenging Conventional Wisdom

You Decide

Comparing Ourselves to Others

Preface

This book is based on three simple premises: politics is conflictual, political process matters, and politics is everywhere. It reflects our belief that politics is explainable, that political outcomes can be understood in terms of decisions made by individuals—and that the average college undergraduate can make sense of the political world in these terms. It focuses on contemporary American politics, the events and outcomes that our students have lived through and know something about. The result, we believe, is a book that provides an accessible but rigorous account of the American political system.

The book is also the product of our dissatisfaction with existing texts. Twenty years ago we were assistant professors at the same university, assigned to teach the introductory class in alternate semesters. While our graduate training was quite different, we found that we shared a deep disappointment with available texts. Their wholesale focus on grand normative concepts such as civic responsibility, or their use of analytic themes such as collective action, left students with little idea of how American politics really works, how events in Washington affect their everyday lives, and how to piece together all the facts about American politics into a coherent explanation of why things happen as they do. These texts did not engender excitement, fascination, or even passing interest. What they did was put students to sleep.

The first edition of this book broke new ground in both approach and content. In the second edition, our themes continue to embody our belief that it is possible to make sense of American politics—that we can move beyond simply describing what happens in political life to predicting and explaining behavior and outcomes, and, moreover, that this task can be accomplished in the introductory class. In part we wish to counter the widespread belief among students that politics is too complicated, too chaotic, or too secretive to make sense of. More than that, we want to empower our students, to demonstrate that everyday American politics is relevant to their lives. This emphasis is also a response to the typical complaint about American Government textbooks—that they are full of facts but devoid of useful information, and that after students finish reading, they are no better able to answer "why" questions than they were before they cracked the book.

In this edition, we have focused our explanatory efforts on conflict in American politics—identifying what Americans agree and disagree about, and how the reality of conflict shapes American politics, from campaign platforms to policy outcomes. While this emphasis seems especially timely given the rise of the Tea Party movement and the strongly worded debates in Congress over bailouts, health care, immigration, and other issues, our aim is to go beyond these events to identify a fundamental constant in American politics, the reality that much of politics is driven by disagreements over scope and form of government policy, and that compromise is an essential component of virtually all significant changes in government policy. Indeed, it is impossible to imagine politics without conflict. Conflict was embedded in our political system by our Founders who set up a system of checks and balances to make sure that no single group could dominate. The Constitution's division of power guarantees that enacting and implementing laws will involve conflict and compromise. Accordingly, without stinting our attention to process and to the ubiquity of politics in our everyday lives, this edition places conflict and compromise at the core of our description of American politics.

Throughout the text, we emphasize common sense, showing students that politics inside the Beltway is often strikingly similar to their everyday interactions. For example, what sustains policy compromises made by members of Congress? The fact that the members typically have long careers, that they interact frequently with each other, and that they only deal with colleagues who have kept their word in the past. These strategies are not unique to the political world. Rather, they embody rules of thumb that most people follow (or are at least aware of) in their everyday interactions. In short, we try to help students understand American politics by emphasizing how it is not all that different from the world they know.

This focus on common sense is coupled with many references to the political science literature. We believe that contemporary research has something to say about prediction and explanation of events that students care about—and that these insights can be taught without turning students into formal theorists or statisticians. This emphasis has the secondary benefit of tying the introductory course to the wider political science discipline, including the American politics subfield and work on democracies more generally.

To this end, in this edition we have added a box in each chapter (What Do Political Scientists Do?) that talks about a specific piece of research, setting out the authors' research question and how they went about answering it. These boxes are augmented by videos where the authors discuss their research, as well as how they came to be interested in politics and political science. Together, the boxes and videos allow us to offer deeper explanations of political phenomena, as well as reinforce our argument that political science research is both understandable and relevant.

We do not frame the text in terms of any one theory or approach. We present the essential insights of contemporary research, motivated by real-world political phenomena and explained using text or simple diagrams. This approach gives students a set of tools for understanding politics, provides an introduction to the political science literature, and matches up well with students' common-sense intuitions about everyday life. Moreover, by showing that academic scholarship is not a blind alley or irrelevant, this approach helps to bridge the gap between an instructor's teaching and his or her research.

While we do not ignore American history, our stress is on contemporary politics—on the debates, actions, and outcomes that most college students are aware of. The text is, as one of us put it, "ruthlessly contemporary." Focusing on recent events emphasizes the utility of the concepts and insights that we develop in the text. It also goes a long way to establishing the relevance of the intro class.

Finally, our book offers an individual-level perspective on America's government. The essential message is that politics—elections, legislative proceedings, regulatory choices, and everything else we see—is a product of the decisions made by real flesh-and-blood people. This approach grounds our discussion of politics in the real world. Many texts focus on abstractions such as "the eternal debate," "the great questions," or "the pulse of democracy." The problem with these constructs is that they don't explain where the debate, the questions, or even democracy come from. Nor do they help students to understand what's going in Washington and elsewhere, as it's not obvious that the participants care much about these sorts of abstractions—quite the opposite, in fact.

We replace these constructs with a focus on real people and actual choices. The primary goal is to make sense of American politics by understanding why politicians, bureaucrats, judges, and citizens act as they do. That is, we are grounding our description of American politics at the most fundamental level—an individual facing a decision. How, for example, does a voter choose among candidates? Stated that way, it is reasonably easy to talk about where the choice came from, how the individual might evaluate different options, and why one choice might look better than the others. Voters' decisions may be understood by examining the different feasible strategies they employ (issue voting, retrospective evaluations, stereotyping, etc.), and why some voters use one strategy while others use a different one.

By focusing on individuals and choices, we can place students in the shoes of the decision makers, and in doing so, give them insight into why these people act as they do. We can discuss, for example, why a House member might favor enacting wasteful pork-barrel spending, even though a proposal full of such projects will make his constituents economically worse off—and why constituents might reward such behavior, even if they suspect the truth. By taking this approach, we are not trying to let legislators off the hook. Rather, we believe that any real understanding of the political process must begin with a sense of the decisions the participants make and why they make them.

Focusing on individuals also segues naturally into a discussion of consequences, allowing us to move from examining decisions to describing and evaluating outcomes. In this way, we can show students how large-scale outcomes in politics, such as inefficient programs, don't happen by accident or because of malfeasance. Rather, they are the predictable results of choices made by individuals (here, politicians and voters).

The policy chapters—on civil rights in both the Full and Core versions of the text, and on economic policy, social policy, and foreign policy in the Full version—also represent a distinctive feature of this book. The discussion of policy at the end of an intro class often fits awkwardly with the material covered earlier. It is supposed to be a culmination of the semester-long discussion of institutions, politicians, and political behavior, but instead it often becomes an afterthought that gets discarded when time runs out in the last few weeks of the class. Our policy chapters explicitly draw on previous chapters' discussions of the actors that shape policy: the president, Congress, the courts, interest groups, and parties. By doing so, they deliver on the promise of showing how all the pieces of the puzzle fit together.

Finally, this book reflects our experience as practicing scholars and teachers, as well as interactions with over fifteen thousand students in introductory classes at several universities. Rather than thinking of the intro class as a service obligation, we believe it offers a unique opportunity for faculty to develop a broader sense of American politics and American political science, while at the same time giving students the tools they need to behave as knowledgeable citizens or enthusiastic political science majors. We hope that it works for you as well as it does for us.

Features of the Text

THE BOOK'S "THREE KEY IDEAS"—politics is conflictual, political process matters, and politics is everywhere—are fully integrated throughout the text.

 Politics Is Conflictual and conflict and compromise are a normal, healthy part of politics. The questions debated in elections, and the policy options considered by people in government, are generally marked by disagreement at all levels. Making policy typically involves important issues on which people disagree, sometimes strongly; so compromise, bargaining, and tough choices about trade-offs are often necessary.

 Political Process Matters because it is the mechanism we have established to resolve conflicts and achieve compromise. Governmental actions result from conscious choices made by voters, elected officials, and bureaucrats. The media often cover political issues in the same way they do sporting events, and while this makes for entertaining news, it also leads citizens to overlook the institutions, rules, and procedures that have a decisive influence on American life. Politics really is not just a game.

 Politics Is Everywhere in that the results of the political process affect all aspects of Americans' everyday lives. Politics governs what people can and cannot do, their quality of life, and how they think about events, other people, and situations.

CONFLICT AND COMPROMISE CHAPTER OPENERS reflect our "politics is conflictual" emphasis. Each chapter in the second edition begins with an example of conflict in American politics, from debates over what the Constitution means to disagreements within the Democratic and Republican parties. Each of these examples poses a question that frames the chapter. Why, for example, is conflict often as prevalent within American political parties as between them? How does this conflict shape what parties do and don't do, in elections and in government? Throughout each chapter, we return to the examples, showing how disagreements and efforts to mitigate them shape every area of American politics.

BOXED FEATURES reinforce the three key ideas while introducing other important ways to think about American politics.

- *NEW* **What Do Political Scientists Do?** boxes put the research front and center, explaining in an engaging, journalistic style how political scientists identify research topics and conduct their studies, and what makes this work important to the lives of ordinary people. What Do Political Scientists Do? videos (available on the free and open student StudySpace and on a DVD for instructors) feature contemporary political scientists talking about the work discussed in the boxes.

- **Nuts and Bolts** boxes distill critical concepts.

- **Challenging Conventional Wisdom** boxes provoke students to think critically by presenting alternative perspectives on many issues that are taken for granted.

- **You Decide** boxes prompt students to think analytically by making their own poitical decisions.

- **Comparing Ourselves to Others** boxes introduce students to relevant political and governmental issues in other countries.

NEW **BIG QUESTIONS** chapter-opening outlines encourage student understanding and analysis, priming readers with the relevant "what," "why," and "how" questions; **ANSWERING THE BIG QUESTIONS** chapter summaries prompt review at the end of each chapter.

KEY IDEA SIDEBARS point out where a discussion in the text is relevant to one of the three key ideas. This feature allows students to quickly zero in on the key ideas when studying for an exam or reading the chapter for the first time.

CRITICAL THINKING is further encouraged with a set of questions at the end of each chapter, and the charts, figures, and tables are accompanied by analytical questions that encourage students to probe the deeper meaning of the data.

Acknowledgments

This edition of the text is again dedicated to our families. Our wives, Regina and Sarah, have continued to accommodate our deadlines and schedules and have again served as our most accurate critics and sources of insight and inspiration. Our five children, several of whom are now undergraduates themselves, have again been forced to contend with politics and textbook writing as a perennial topic of conversation and have responded with critiques and insights of their own, which appear throughout the text.

Our colleagues at Indiana University and the University of Wisconsin (and before that, Duke University for both of us) provided many opportunities to talk about American politics and teaching this course.

Bill thanks his colleagues at Indiana University and elsewhere, including Christine Barbour, Ted Carmines, Mike Ensley, Russ Hansen, Jeff Hill, Yanna Krupnikov, Lin Ostrom, Regina Smyth, and Gerry Wright, for sharp insights and encouragement at crucial moments. He is also grateful to the legion of teaching assistants who have helped him organize and teach the intro class at three universities.

David gives special thanks to Ken Mayer whose daily "reality checks" and consistently thoughtful professional and personal advice are greatly appreciated. John Coleman, Barry Burden, Ken Goldstein, Ben Marquez, Byron Shafer, Charles Franklin, John Witte, Dave Weimer, Kathy Walsh, and all the great people at Wisconsin have provided a wonderful community within which to teach and research American politics. David would also like to thank the students at the University of Debrecen in Hungary where he taught American politics as a Fulbright Scholar in 2003–2004. The Hungarian students' unique perspective on democracy, civil liberties, and the role of government required David to think about American politics in a different way.

Both of us are grateful to the political science faculty at Duke University who, in addition to providing us with our first academic jobs, worked to construct a hospitable and invigorating place to research and to teach. In particular, Rom Coles, Ruth Grant, John Aldrich, Tom Spragens, Taylor Cole, and David Barber were model colleagues and scholars. We both learned to teach by watching them, and we are the better teachers and scholars for it.

Special thanks as well to the authors of the book's supplementary materials. Peter Francia of East Carolina University and Lori Han of Chapman University revised our test bank, and Peter also selected the clips for the Norton American Politics DVD; Mike Wagner of the University of Nebraska wrote the instructor's manual; Jacob Samuel Bower-Bir and Nathaniel Birkhead of Indiana University created the content for the Student StudySpace.

The outstanding people at W. W. Norton made this a much better book than we could have produced on our own. Steve Dunn was responsible for getting the process started and providing good commentary and encouragement from beginning to end. Roby Harrington has been a source of constant encouragement and feedback. Aaron Javsicas has once again been a graceful taskmaster and insightful editor, with a deep knowledge of American politics and how to write about it. We were especially privileged to work with Pete Lesser, whose clear vision for the electronic media and for the textbook itself was a major help. Christine D'Antonio was a superb project editor, bringing an eye for clarity of both words and visuals.

JoAnn Simony improved the text significantly with her careful copyediting. Cait Callahan, Callinda Taylor, and Carly Fraser made sure everyone had the right versions of everything. Trish Marx and Julie Tesser put together an excellent photo program. Megan Jackson cleared reprint permissions for the figures and tables. Ben Reynolds handled production with efficiency and good humor. Rubina Yeh created a beautiful design, and Hope Miller Goodell and Lisa Buckley brought it gracefully into line with second edition changes. Debra Morton Hoyt oversaw the creation of our handsome cover. The entire crew at Norton has been incredibly professional and supportive. We feel very fortunate to work with them.

We are also indebted to the many reviewers who have commented on the text.

FIRST EDITION REVIEWERS

Dave Adler, Idaho State University
Rick Almeida, Francis Marion University
Jim Bailey, Arkansas State University, Mountain Home
Todd Belt, University of Hawaii, Hilo
Scott Buchanan, Columbus State University
Randy Burnside, Southern Illinois University, Carbondale
Carolyn Cocca, SUNY College at Old Westbury
Tom Dolan, Columbus State University
Dave Dulio, Oakland University
Matt Eshbaugh-Soha, University of North Texas
Kevin Esterling, University of California, Riverside
Peter Francia, East Carolina University
Scott Frisch, California State University, Channel Islands
Sarah Fulton, Texas A&M University
Keith Gaddie, University of Oklahoma
Joe Giammo, University of Arkansas, Little Rock
Kate Greene, University of Southern Mississippi
Steven Greene, North Carolina State University
Phil Habel, Southern Illinois University, Carbondale
Charles Hartwig, Arkansas State University, Jonesboro
Ted Jelen, University of Nevada, Las Vegas
Jennifer Jensen, Binghamton University (SUNY)
Terri Johnson, University of Wisconsin, Green Bay
Luke Keele, Ohio State University
Linda Keith, University of Texas, Dallas
Chris Kelley, Miami University
Jason Kirksey, Oklahoma State University
Jeffrey Kraus, Wagner College
Chris Kukk, Western Connecticut State University
Mel Kulbicki, York College
Joel Lieske, Cleveland State University
Steve Light, University of North Dakota
Baodong (Paul) Liu, University of Utah
Ken Long, Saint Joseph College, Connecticut
Michael Lynch, University of Kansas
Cherie Maestas, Florida State University
Tom Marshall, University of Texas, Arlington
Scott McClurg, Southern Illinois University, Carbondale
Jonathan Morris, East Carolina University

Jason Mycoff, University of Delaware
Sean Nicholson-Crotty, University of Missouri, Columbia
Timothy Nokken, Texas Tech University
Sandra O'Brien, Florida Gulf Coast University
John Orman, Fairfield University
L. Marvin Overby, University of Missouri, Columbia
Catherine Paden, Simmons College
Dan Ponder, Drury University
Paul Posner, George Mason University
David Redlawsk, University of Iowa
Russell Renka, Southeast Missouri State University
Travis Ridout, Washington State University
Andy Rudalevige, Dickinson College
Denise Scheberle, University of Wisconsin, Green Bay
Tom Schmeling, Rhode Island College
Pat Sellers, Davidson College
Dan Smith, Northwest Missouri State University
Dale Story, University of Texas, Arlington
John Vile, Middle Tennessee State University
Mike Wagner, University of Nebraska
Dave Wigg, St. Louis Community College
Maggie Zetts, Purdue University

SECOND EDITION REVIEWERS

Danny Adkison, Oklahoma State University
Hunter Bacot, Elon College
Tim Barnett, Jacksonville State University
Robert Bruhl, University of Illinois, Chicago
Daniel Butler, Yale University
Jennifer Byrne, James Madison University
Jason Casellas, University of Texas, Austin
Jeffrey Christiansen, Seminole State College
Richard Conley, University of Florida
Michael Crespin, University of Georgia
Brian DiSarro, California State University, Sacramento
Ryan Emenaker, College of the Redwoods
John Evans, California State University, Northridge
John Fliter, Kansas State University
Jimmy Gleason, Purdue University
Dana Glencross, Oklahoma City Community College
Jeannie Grussendorf, Georgia State University
Phil Habel, Southern Illinois University, Carbondale
Lori Han, Chapman University
Katy Harriger, Wake Forest University
Richard Himelfarb, Hofstra University
Doug Imig, University of Memphis
Daniel Klinghard, College of the Holy Cross
Eddie Meaders, University of North Texas
Kristy Michaud, California State University, Northridge
Kris Miler, University of Illinois, Urbana-Champaign
Melinda Mueller, Eastern Illinois University

Michael Mundt, Oakton Community College
Emily Neff-Sharum, University of North Carolina, Pembroke
David Nice, Washington State University
Tim Nokken, Texas Tech University
Stephen Nuño, Northern Arizona University
Richard Powell, University of Maine, Orono
Travis Ridout, Washington State University
Sara Rinfret, University of Wisconsin, Green Bay
Martin Saiz, California State University, Northridge
Gabriel Ramon Sanchez, University of New Mexico
Charles Shipan, University of Michigan
Dan Smith, Northwest Missouri State University
Rachel Sondheimer, United States Military Academy
Chris Soper, Pepperdine University
Walt Stone, University of California, Davis
Greg Streich, University of Central Missouri
Charles Walcott, Virginia Tech
Rick Waterman, University of Kentucky
Edward Weber, Washington State University
Jack Wright, Ohio State University

It is a humbling experience to have so many smart people helping us find our voice
and make our arguments. Their reviews were often critical, but always insightful,
and we have been fortunate to have them guide our revisions. Again, they have our
profound thanks.

William T. Bianco
David T. Canon
October 2010

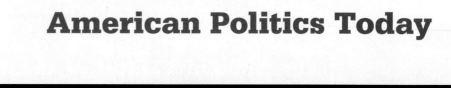

American Politics Today

The infamous "bridge to nowhere" would have cost hundreds of millions of dollars and connected Ketchikan, Alaska (population 8,600), to Gravina Island (population 50).

Understanding American Politics

The premise of this book is simple: *American Politics makes sense*. What happens in elections, in Congress, in the White House, and everywhere else in the political process has a logical and often simple explanation.

This claim may seem unrealistic or even naive. On the surface, American politics is full of bewildering complexities, from the enumerated powers in the Constitution to the unwritten rules that govern how Congress works. Many policy questions, from confronting economic crises to deciding what to do about climate change, seem hopelessly intractable. Politicians seem more interested in publicizing their disagreements than solving them. Election outcomes look random or even chaotic (how is it that the Democratic Party's resounding victories in 2006 and 2008 were followed by crushing defeat in 2010?).

Many people, we believe, have given up on American politics because they don't understand the political process, feel helpless to influence elections or policy making, and believe that politics is irrelevant to their lives. Since you are taking a class on American politics, we hope you have not given up on politics entirely. It is *not* our goal to turn you into a political junkie or a policy expert. And it isn't necessary to be completely immersed in politics to make sense of it, but we hope that you will have a basic understanding of the political process after finishing this book.

Much of that understanding will come from the central theme of this book: politics is about conflict and compromise. People naturally shy away from conflict in their personal lives and tend to see conflict in politics as a problem. Political compromise is often viewed as "selling out," "caving in," or basically giving up on one's core values and principles. However, because Americans (both inside and outside government) disagree about what should be done about most policy questions, conflict is an essential part of politics and compromise is usually needed to enact changes in government policy. We will discuss this theme in detail later in this chapter.

One goal of this book is to help you take an active role in the political process. A functioning democracy allows citizens to defer complicated policy decisions to their elected leaders, but it also requires citizens to monitor what politicians are doing and to hold those leaders accountable at the voting booth. This book will help you accomplish this important duty by providing the analytical skills you need to make sense of politics, even when it initially appears senseless.

Consider, for example, the congressional appropriation of $453 million made in 2005 for the construction of two bridges in Alaska. One of them, the infamous "bridge to nowhere," would have connected Ketchikan, Alaska, a town with 8,600 residents, to Gravina Island, population fifty. This bridge would have been nearly as long as the Golden Gate Bridge and taller than the Brooklyn Bridge. Assuming traffic of 1,000 cars a day (which is generous), the cost in tax dollars per trip would have been $43.15 for the projected life of the bridge. One commentator called the bridge a "national embarrassment" and said that it "has become an object of national ridicule and a symbol of . . . fiscal irresponsibility."[1] The bridge was funded as part of a $286.5 billion transportation bill, which passed by large margins in the House and Senate and included a record 6,371 earmarks—specific local projects identified in the legislation[2]—totaling $24 billion, so the "bridge to nowhere" was not alone.

If the story ended here, it could be seen as just another example of members of Congress taking care of their constituents by dishing out generous servings of federal spending. However, the story took on theatrical proportions when, shortly

---

FIGURE 1.1 THE BRIDGE TO NOWHERE

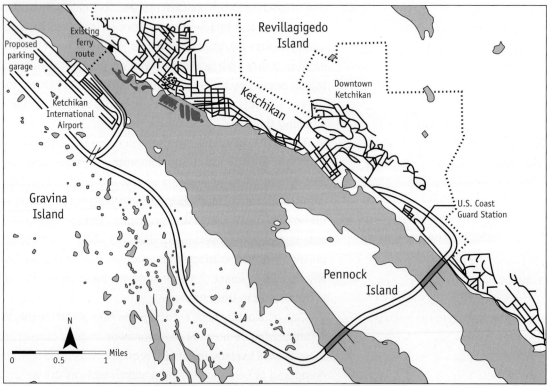

SOURCE: Taxpayers for Common Sense, "The Gravina Access Project: A Bridge to Nowhere," February 9, 2005, available at www.taxpayer.net/Transportation/gravinabridge.pdf.

▲ *The proposed "bridge to nowhere" is often held up as the most egregious example of wasteful government spending. Though the bridge was not built (this is a digitized image), many critics of the project were outraged that Congress considered funding the bridge in light of more pressing needs, such as rebuilding the areas devastated by Hurricane Katrina.*

after approving the transportation bill, the Senate was struggling to pay for rebuilding the highways and bridges destroyed by Hurricane Katrina. Senator Tom Coburn, a Republican from Oklahoma, proposed rescinding the $453 million earmarked for the Alaskan bridges and redirecting some of the money to highway repair projects in New Orleans. In response, Senator Ted Stevens of Alaska made an impassioned speech in defense of the spending, and the Senate rejected Coburn's proposal by an 82-to-15 vote.[3] The next development in the saga came a few weeks later when the House–Senate conference committee voted to eliminate the official earmarks for the two bridges but allotted the same amount of money to the governor of Alaska to spend on any transportation project in the state, including the bridges.[4] President Bush complained about the size of the bill but ultimately signed it. Nearly two years after the bill was signed into law—despite maintaining that the Gravina–Ketchikan bridge was necessary for local economic development and spending nearly $26 million on the initial phases of construction—Governor Sarah Palin announced that the bridge would not be built because of the controversy that surrounded it (the "bridge to nowhere" re-emerged as a political issue in 2008, when Palin was chosen as the Republican vice-presidential nominee).[5]

How did this happen? How did such a wasteful project get approved, then survive an effort to redirect spending to a seemingly more worthy cause, and waste nearly $26 million in taxpayers' money before it was canceled? The "bridge to nowhere" seems like a classic example of government waste, and it can certainly seem hard to understand how this project was approved by our elected leaders.

However, some supposed pork-barrel spending, which is the informal term given to wasteful spending of federal money on local projects, is more worthy

▲ One could certainly argue over whether Mormon cricket control is an appropriate task for the federal government, but there is no denying that these insects are a huge problem in some parts of the United States.

than it appears. The $410 billion spending bill Congress passed in March 2009 had more than 8,500 earmarks, including $1 million for eradicating "Mormon crickets" in Utah. As you might imagine, Jon Stewart of Comedy Central's *The Daily Show* had fun with that one.[6] Senator John McCain (R-AZ), who focused on eliminating earmarks in his 2008 presidential campaign, also ridiculed the spending. However, it turns out that Mormon crickets are a huge problem in the West: millions of the insects, which are about three inches long and have been described as cockroaches with grasshopper legs, destroy crops, literally cover homes and streets, and threaten the livelihoods of ranchers and farmers. Senator Robert Bennett (R-UT), the sponsor of the earmark, defended the program by saying, "It's good public policy, it's good economic policy, and it's the kind of thing a representative from the West should do."[7] As the old saying goes, one person's pork is another person's essential spending.

The "bridge to nowhere" may be more difficult to justify than Mormon cricket control, but the project had its defenders.[8] They pointed out that the bridge would bring much-needed economic development to Ketchikan, which is hemmed in by mountains and has nowhere to expand except to Gravina Island. The bridge also might have increased the traffic flow through Gravina's local airport, bringing jobs to the region. These proponents saw the bridge as an investment in the future and would probably argue that its critics ignored the potential long-term benefits. Indeed, in the governor's announcement that the bridge project was being canceled, she said, "Much of the public's attitude toward Alaska bridges is based on inaccurate portrayals of the projects here."[9]

The bridge also had friends in high places. At the time the bill was enacted, Alaska representative Don Young was chair of the House Transportation Committee, and Alaska senator Ted Stevens was chair of the Senate Commerce Committee. Of the $24 billion in earmarks in the transportation bill, nearly $1 billion went to Alaska. Only California and Illinois received more earmarked funds, despite Alaska's ranking as the forty-seventh state in terms of population (whereas California is first and Illinois is fifth).[10]

Finally, the "bridge to nowhere" can also be explained by two features of the legislative process. First, funding for the bridge was a relatively small part of a huge bill that included spending for all federal transportation projects for the next five years. The perception among members of Congress was that America's transportation infrastructure was in serious need of repair and that the bill was an important step toward addressing this problem. From this perspective, it would make little sense to vote against the bill over a single earmark of a few hundred million dollars.[11] Second, the congressional norm of reciprocity guarantees that some wasteful projects will be funded even though they could not stand on their own merits. This approach of "you scratch my back and I'll scratch yours" means that members can count on one another's support for their pet projects and to help get reelected.

This example shows how digging below the surface of political events can help to explain why things happen in American politics. While you may be relieved the bridge will not be built (and we agree), you now have a sense of why such a project gets approved in the first place. Our goal is to give you a similar understanding of the entire range of American politics. We are not going to spend much time talking about how American politics should be. Rather, our focus will be on explaining American politics as it is. Here are some other questions we will examine:

- Why do some people participate in the political system while others do not?
- How does the Constitution structure our rights and liberties and the broader political system?
- Why do people vote as they do?
- Why do so many people mistrust politicians and the political system?
- Why do most members of Congress get reelected?
- How do Supreme Court justices decide cases?
- Why do presidents sometimes appear all-powerful but look powerless at other times?
- How much do the media, interest groups, judges, and bureaucrats influence policy decisions and why?

We will answer these questions and many others by applying three key ideas about the nature of politics: politics is conflictual, political process matters, and politics is everywhere. But first, we begin with an even more basic question: Why do we have a government?

Why Do We Have a Government?

TO PROVIDE ORDER

At a basic level, the answer to this question seems obvious: without **government** there would be chaos. As the seventeenth-century British philosopher Thomas Hobbes said, life in the "state of nature" (that is, without government) would be "solitary, poor, nasty, brutish, and short."[12] Without government, there would be no laws—people could do whatever they wanted. Even if people tried to develop informal rules, there would be no way to guarantee that these rules would be enforced. This crucial governmental role was noted by the Founders in the preamble to the Constitution: two of the central goals of government are to "provide for the common defence" and to "insure domestic Tranquility." The former refers to military protection (by the Army and Navy at the time of the Founding; it now also includes the Marines, Coast Guard, and Air Force) against foreign invasion and the defense of our common security interests. The latter refers to law enforcement within the nation, which today includes the National Guard, FBI, Department of Homeland Security, state and local police, and courts. So at a minimal level, government is necessary to provide security.

However, there's more to it than that. The Founders also cited the desire to "establish Justice . . . , and secure the Blessings of Liberty to ourselves and our Posterity." But do we need government to do these things? It may be obvious that the police power of the state is required to prevent anarchy, but can't people have justice and liberty without government? In a utopian world, maybe, but the Founders had a more realistic view of human nature. As the Founder James Madison said, "But what is government itself, but the greatest of all reflections on human nature? If men were angels, no government would be necessary. If angels were

government The system for implementing decisions made through the political process.

▲ *Two important government functions are to "provide for the common defence" and "insure domestic Tranquility." The military and local police are two of the most commonly used forces the government maintains to fulfill those roles.*

to govern men, neither external nor internal controls on government would be necessary."[13] Furthermore, Madison continued, people have a variety of interests that have "divided mankind into parties, inflamed them with mutual animosity, and rendered them much more disposed to vex and oppress each other than to co-operate for their common good."[14] That is, without government, we would quickly be headed toward Hobbes's nasty and brutish state of nature. Madison's view of human nature might sound pessimistic, but it is also realistic. He assumes that people are self-interested: we want what is best for ourselves and our families, and to satisfy those interests, we tend to form groups with like-minded people. Madison saw these groups, which he called **factions**, as being opposed to the public good, and his greatest fear was of tyranny by a faction imposing its will on the rest of the nation. For example, if one group took power and established an official state religion, that faction would be tyrannizing people who practiced a different religion. This type of oppression is precisely why many of the early American colonists fled Europe in the first place.

So government is necessary to avoid the anarchy of the state of nature, and the right kind of government is needed to avoid oppression by whoever controls the policy-making process. As will be discussed in more detail in Chapters 2 and 3, America's government is set up to control the effects of factions by dividing government power in three main ways. First, the **separation of powers** divides the government into three branches—the judicial, executive, and legislative—and assigns distinct duties to each branch. Second, the system of **checks and balances** gives each branch some power over the other two. (For example, the president can veto legislation passed by Congress; Congress can impeach the president; and the Supreme Court has the power to interpret laws written by Congress to determine whether they are constitutional.) Third, **federalism** divides power yet again by allotting different responsibilities to local, state, and national government. With power divided in this fashion, Madison reasoned, no single faction could dominate the government.

TO PROMOTE THE GENERAL WELFARE

The preamble to the Constitution also states that the federal government exists to "promote the general Welfare," which means tackling the hard problems that Americans cannot solve on their own, such as taking care of the poor, the sick, or the aged, and dealing with global issues like climate change, terrorist threats, and poverty in other countries. However, government is not inevitable—people can

factions Groups of like-minded people who try to influence the government. American government is set up to avoid domination by any one of these groups.

separation of powers The division of government power across the judicial, executive, and legislative branches.

checks and balances A system in which each branch of government has some power over the others.

federalism The division of power across the local, state, and national levels of government.

decide that these problems aren't worth solving. But if people *do* want to address these large problems, government action is necessary because **public goods** such as these are not efficiently provided by the free market, either because of **collective action problems, positive externalities,** or other reasons.

The eighteenth-century Scottish philosopher David Hume explained the problem of collective action:

> Two neighbours may agree to drain a meadow which they possess in common [so they would be able to use it to grow crops] because 'tis easy for them to know each others mind and each must perceive that the immediate consequence of his failing in his part is the abandoning the whole project. But 'tis very difficult and indeed impossible that a thousand persons shou'd agree in any such action; it being difficult for them to concert so complicated a design and still more difficult for them to execute it while each seeks a pretext to free himself of the trouble and expence and wou'd lay the whole burden on others. Political society easily remedies both these inconveniences.[15]

That is, it is easy for two people to tackle a common problem without the help of government, but a thousand people, to say nothing of the more than 300 million in the United States today, would suffer from the **free rider problem**: because it is in everyone's interest to "lay the whole burden on others," and because everyone thinks this way, the meadow would never be drained. As Hume notes, "political society"—government—can "remedy those inconveniences" by draining the meadow and providing the desired public good. A government representing 300 million people can provide public goods, such as protecting the environment or defending the nation, that could not be provided by all those people acting on their own, so they elect leaders and pay taxes to provide those public goods.

Another reason why public goods are underproduced by the free market has to do with what economists call *positive externalities*, which means that the benefits from the good are shared by the primary consumer of the good and by society at large. Education is a great example. You benefit personally from your college education in terms of the knowledge and experience you gain, and perhaps from the higher salary you will earn because of your college degree. However, society also benefits from your education. Your employer will benefit from your knowledge and skills, as will people you interact with. If education were solely provided by the free market, those who could afford schooling would go, but the rest would not, leaving a large segment of society with little or no education and therefore unemployable. So, public education, like many important services, benefits all levels of society and must be provided by the government for the general welfare.

Now that we understand *why* we have a government, the next question is, *what* does the government do to "insure domestic Tranquility" and "promote the general Welfare"? Many visible components of the government promote these goals, from the police and armed services to the Internal Revenue Service, Post Office, Social Security Administration, National Aeronautics and Space Administration, Department of Education, and Food and Drug Administration. More generally, the government does several things:

- It creates and enforces laws and protects private property through the criminal justice system.
- It establishes a common currency and regulates commerce among the states and trade with other nations.
- It provides public goods that would not be produced or would be under-supplied by the free market, including national defense, an interstate highway system, and national parks.

public goods Services or actions (such as protecting the environment) that, once provided to one person, become available to everyone. Government is typically needed to provide public goods because they will be under-produced by the free market.

collective action problem A situation in which the members of a group would benefit by working together to produce some outcome, but each individual is better off refusing to cooperate and reaping benefits from those who do the work.

positive externalities Benefits created by a public good that are shared by the primary consumer of the good and by society more generally.

free rider problem The incentive to benefit from others' work without making a contribution, which leads individuals in a collective action situation to refuse to work together.

▲ *A lighthouse is a classic example of a public good—a service or product that could not be produced by private markets because once the good is provided, anyone can benefit from it without paying. Supplying public goods is one way that the government promotes the public welfare.*

Forms of Government

The Greek political philosopher Aristotle, writing in the fourth century B.C., developed a classification scheme for governments that is still surprisingly useful today. He distinguished three pure types of government based on the number of rulers versus the number ruled: monarchy (rule by one), aristocracy (rule by the few), and polity (rule by the many, more specifically the property-owning middle class). The only modifications to this typology in the past 2,000 years changed the last category to republicanism (representative democracy with a constitution) and expanded participation beyond the middle class.

Additional distinctions can be made within Aristotle's third type, constitutional republican governments, based on how they allocate power between the executive, legislative, and judicial branches. Presidential systems such as in the United States tend to follow a separation of power between the three branches, while parliamentary systems such as in the United Kingdom elect the chief executive from the legislature, so there is much closer coordination between those two branches.

Aristotle's third type can be further refined by considering the relationships between different levels of the government. In a federal system, power is shared between the local, state, and national levels of government. In a unitary system, all power is held at the national level. A confederation is a less common form of government in which states retain their sovereignty and autonomy but form a loose association at the national level.

- It regulates the market to promote the general good, specifically by addressing market failures in areas such as environmental pollution and product safety.
- It protects individual civil liberties, such as the freedom of speech and the free exercise of religion.

This book explains how political scientists study American politics to understand what the government, politicians, and citizens do, and why (see the What Do Political Scientists Do? box).

What Is Politics?

We define **politics** as the process that determines what government does. You may consider politics the same thing as government, but we view politics as being much broader; it includes ways of behaving and making decisions that are common in everyday life. Many aspects of our discussion of politics will probably sound familiar because your life involves politics on a regular basis. This may sound a little abstract, but it should become clear in light of the three key ideas of this book.

First, *politics is conflictual*. The questions debated in elections and the options considered by policy makers are generally marked by disagreement at all levels. The federal government does not spend much time resolving issues that everyone agrees should be decided in a particular way. Rather, making government policy involves issues on which people disagree, sometimes strongly, which makes compromise difficult—and this is a normal, healthy part of politics. Although compromise may be difficult, it is often necessary to produce an outcome that can be enacted and implemented.

Second, *political process matters*. Governmental actions don't happen by accident—they result from conscious choices made by elected officials and bureaucrats. Politics, as the process that determines what governments do, is also the process that puts certain individuals into positions of power and makes the rules that structure their choices. The media often cover political campaigns the way they would report on a boxing match or the Super Bowl, focusing exclusively on the competition, rivalries,

politics The process that determines what government does.

Designing and Conducting Research

One of the most important facts we want you to get out of this book is that political scientists have relevant and compelling things to say about American politics based on scientific research. This claim may come as a surprise. In our classes and our lives outside the university, both of us have found that many people think that politics is too random, too complicated, or too subjective to be studied in the same way as atoms, chemicals, or cells.

Research in political science, like research in all sciences, usually starts with an idea—a hypothesis. Hypotheses are statements about how one factor, a dependent variable, is affected or influenced by a second factor, an independent variable. (Hypotheses can also have multiple dependent and independent variables.) For example, a scholar interested in explaining election outcomes might develop a hypothesis that explains vote decisions in elections (dependent variable) based on voters' evaluations of the candidates' positions on health care reform (independent variable). In this case, the data used to test the hypothesis would probably be gathered from a mass survey of American citizens.

Where do hypotheses come from? Political scientists draw on a number of theories that make general statements about the motivations and actions of individuals. For example, in the chapter on Congress, we discuss research that assumes legislators have a variety of goals, but that getting reelected is generally their strongest motivation. In contemporary political science, no one theory of politics has proved to be superior to the others in all cases. Accordingly, you will read about many different theories in the chapters to come. Each chapter has a box called What Do Political Scientists Do? that explores how political scientists develop hypotheses from theories and how they test them with a variety of research methods.

The most common research method in the study of American politics is to gather data on the relevant variables of interest and conduct statistical analysis. So to continue the example of the impact of health care reform on voting, the researcher could do a national survey of 1,500 voters that reveals their views of candidates' positions on health care reform in the 2010 elections. The survey would also ask various questions about the voters' background (race, gender, age, and so on), other political variables (such as party affiliation and ideology—are they liberal, conservative, or moderate?), and how they voted in 2010. These responses would be included in a statistical analysis as controls for alternative explanations of how the person voted. That is, we know that someone who is liberal, nonwhite, and a woman is more likely to vote for a Democrat than someone who is conservative, white, and male. The question is whether a candidate's position on health care would influence voting after taking those other explanations into account.

A second approach is to use experiments to test hypotheses. Obviously, political scientists cannot conduct different versions of real elections the way that medical researchers can run various real-life trials when they are testing the effect of a drug. Instead, political scientists have to create experimental and control groups either in a laboratory setting, using clever "natural experiments," or with surveys. In each instance, the logic of the experiment is the same: the researcher holds everything else constant and varies the explanation of interest (the treatment). For example, one could examine the impact of negative advertising on assessments of candidates by exposing one group of subjects to negative ads and another group to positive ads in a laboratory setting.

Another approach is to conduct detailed case studies of the topic of interest. These could be based on historical analysis of archival documents, "participant observation," or interviews of politicians. One of the masters of this approach is political scientist Richard Fenno, who wrote many books based on what he called "soaking and poking." By hanging out with politicians and asking them questions about what they were doing and why, Fenno was able to gain keen insights into politics.

Finally, some scholars who study American politics are interested in normative questions such as the proper role of the Su-

Voters line up at a polling station near Lawrence, Kansas. Political scientists use scientific research to study voting and other political processes that matter to Americans' lives.

preme Court in a representative democracy, how politicians *should* represent their constituents, whether political deliberation can create a better understanding of what the public wants, or how the political system can be reformed to better serve the public good. These normative questions are the focus of democratic theory and theories of political representation. Typically there is a division of labor within political science between political philosophers who grapple with these normative questions and researchers who engage in empirical analysis, but empirical political scientists often tackle these normative questions as well.

This is by no means an exhaustive outline, but it provides an introduction to the type of research we will be discussing in the What Do Political Scientists Do? boxes. ■

ⓥ **Watch a video clip of William Bianco and David Canon discussing this topic at wwnorton.com/ studyspace.**

and entertaining stories, which can lead people to overlook the institutions, rules, and procedures that can have a decisive influence on politics. Indeed, the political process is the mechanism for resolving conflict. The most obvious example is elections, which democracies use to resolve the most basic conflict in society: deciding who should lead the country.

Third, *politics is everywhere.* Decisions about what government should do or who should be in charge are integral to society and they influence the everyday lives of all Americans. Politics helps to determine what people can and cannot do, their quality of life, and how they think about events, people, and situations. Moreover, people's political thought and behavior are driven by the same types of calculations and decision-making rules that shape beliefs and actions in other parts of life. For example, deciding which presidential candidate to vote for is similar to deciding which college to attend. In the first instance you might consider issue positions, character, and leadership ability, while in the latter you will weigh which school fits your academic goals, how much tuition you can afford, and where different schools are located. In both cases you are making a decision that will satisfy the criteria most important to you.

KEY IDEA 1: POLITICS IS CONFLICTUAL

Political scientists have long recognized the central role of conflict in politics. One prominent approach to studying political parties in the mid-twentieth century saw conflict between interest groups as explaining most outcomes in American politics. A famous political scientist, E. E. Schattschneider, argued that the scope of political conflict—that is, how many people are involved in the fight—determines who wins in politics. Others have argued that some conflict is essential for small-group decision making, otherwise group leaders will sink into a pathological "group-think" that threatens good decisions: if nobody challenges a widely shared but flawed view, people may convince themselves that the obvious flaws are not a problem. Bureaucratic politics, congressional politics, elections, and even Supreme Court decision making have all been studied through the lens of political conflict.

Despite this consensus among those who study politics that conflict is essential, most people do not like conflict, either in their personal lives or in politics. You probably have heard it said that the three topics one should not discuss in polite company are money, religion, and politics. Rather than talking about controversial subjects that may make people uncomfortable, many people simply avoid these topics. Indeed, since the 1950s political scientists have found strong evidence that people avoid discussing politics in order to maintain social harmony.[16] Diana Mutz's important work on this subject finds a trade-off between conflict in political discussions and participation in politics. That is, those who engage in more conflictual political debates are less likely to vote. It isn't surprising that only 23 percent of Americans could recall having a political conversation with someone who disagreed with them.[17]

Many people apply their disdain for conflict to politicians. "Why is there so much partisan bickering?" our students frequently ask. "Why can't they just get along?" This dislike of conflict, and of politics more generally, produces a desire for what political scientists John Hibbing and Elizabeth Theiss-Morse call "stealth democracy"—that is, nondemocratic practices such as running government like a business or taking action without political debate. In essence, this idea boils down to the nonsensical hope that everything would be better if we could just take the politics out of politics. Hibbing and Theiss-Morse argue that we need to do a better job of educating people about conflict and the policy differences that people have, and that the failure to do so "is encouraging students to conclude that real

▼ Conflict is inherent in American politics, a fact that was driven home by the national debate in 2009 and 2010 over health care reform.

democracy is unnecessary and stealth democracy will do just fine."[18] Conflict cannot be avoided in politics the way it can in polite company. Ignoring fundamental disagreements will not make them go away.

Instead of pretending that we agree on most policies and that conflict is unnecessary, Americans must recognize that the opposite is true: political conflict is inevitable because it is rooted in our disagreements on policy questions. It is wrongheaded to claim that there would be no conflict in politics if politicians would just listen to the public—Americans themselves are generally divided on what public policy should look like.

The recent debate over health care reform is a good example. On the surface, agreement appeared to be fairly broad (although not universal) that people in the United States should have access to affordable health care. But when the public heard the details—that taxes would be increased to pay for it, or that individuals would be required to buy insurance even if they didn't want it—support fell. Some people favored the status quo (no change), others wanted universal coverage through a government program, some favored a plan that required everyone to buy health insurance (with the poor subsidized by the government so they could afford it), and some people favored other options. It is much more difficult for members of Congress to arrive at consensus when, as in situations like this, there is no consensus among the American people. Moreover, in these kinds of situations, no matter what Congress does, many people will be unhappy with the result.

Abortion is another issue over which public opinion is fragmented. Abortion rights have been a perennial debate in elections and in Washington since a 1973 Supreme Court decision held that state laws banning abortion were unconstitutional. Surveys about abortion rights show public support is spread across a wide range of options, with little agreement about which policy is best. In Chapter 5, Public Opinion, we will look more closely at the political implications of this kind of broad disagreement. In such cases, the problem is not that citizens or politicians like to fight or are inherently unwilling to compromise. Rather, these conflicts reflect sharp, intense differences of opinion among both citizens and elected officials that are rooted in self-interest, ideology, and personal beliefs. You might expect that, given enough time, politicians will find ways to compromise, but this is not always true. Sometimes the problem is a lack of trade-offs. In many of these cases, no single policy choice satisfies even a slight majority of elected officials or citizens.

The idea that conflict is endemic to politics should be no surprise. Situations in which everyone (or almost everyone) agrees about what government should be doing are easy to resolve: either a popular new policy is enacted or an unpopular issue is avoided, and the policy debate naturally moves off the political agenda. For example, in the 1980s, a consensus emerged among scientists that chlorofluorocarbons (CFCs), chemicals used in aerosol cans, refrigerators, air conditioners, and other machinery, were damaging the atmosphere's ozone layer, which blocks the sun's harmful ultraviolet rays. After some debate (all but the most trivial policies have *some* opposition), a combination of international treaties, legislation, and regulations were enacted to strictly limit the use of CFCs and favor the available alternatives in most applications. The result? The ozone layer is recovering, and CFCs are now rarely discussed, either in government or in public debate.[19]

Whereas consensus issues are dealt with quickly and disappear, conflictual issues remain on the agenda as the winners try to extend their gains and the losers work to roll back policies. Thus, one reason that abortion rights is a perennial issue in campaigns and congressional debates is that there is no national consensus on when abortions should be allowed, no indication that the issue is becoming less important to citizens or elected officials, and no sign of a comprehensive compromise policy that would attract widespread support.

▼ When everyone (or almost everyone) agrees about what government should do to solve a given problem, the issue is generally dealt with quickly and without much conflict. In the 1980s general consensus was reached over how to deal with chlorofluorocarbons (chemicals once used for many applications, including in aerosol cans), and they were banned. Controversial issues, on the other hand, tend to stay with us and result in more visible political conflict.

While compromise can be very difficult, an important implication of the inevitable conflicts in American politics is that compromise and bargaining are essential to getting things done. A politician who bargains with opponents is not necessarily abandoning his principles; striking a deal may be the only way to make some of the policy changes he wants. Only in a limited set of circumstances can anyone in government act unilaterally. Enacting a law, for example, requires majority support in the House and Senate as well as the president's approval—or a two-thirds majority in both the House and Senate to override the president's veto. The president's power is also limited: the president can implement some policies through executive order, but most significant actions require congressional approval.

Finally, although conflict is an essential part of American politics, it is important to remember two more things about conflict. First, agreement sometimes exists in the midst of controversy. For example, the survey about abortion cited earlier found strong support for measures such as prohibiting government funding for abortions, requiring parental notification when a minor has an abortion, mandating a twenty-four-hour waiting period before an abortion, or requiring doctors who perform the procedure to present their patients with information on alternatives such as adoption. Similarly, despite the huge differences of opinion on health care, Congress did manage to pass significant health care reform in 2010. Second, we are not arguing that all conflict is good. The scream fests on cable news and obstruction for the sake of obstruction in Congress do not serve the greater public good. Our point is simply that conflict and compromise are inherent parts of politics.

KEY IDEA 2: POLITICAL PROCESS MATTERS

The political process is often described as though it were a version of a sporting event, with a focus on strategies and tactics and ultimately on "winning." In fact, a politics news show on CNN has a daily segment titled "The Play of the Day," which sounds a lot like the rundown of the best sports plays of the day on ESPN. This focus overlooks an important point: politics is the process that determines what government does, none of which is inevitable. Public policy—everything from defending the nation to building "bridges to nowhere"—is up for grabs. And the political process determines these government actions. It really is not just a game.

Elections are an excellent example of the importance of the political process. Elections allow voters to give fellow citizens the power to enact laws, write budgets, and appoint senior bureaucrats and federal judges, so it does matter who gets elected. George W. Bush, a Republican, was president from January 2001 to January 2009. Republicans held a majority of the seats in Congress for most of his first six years,[20] but the balance shifted when Democrats gained control of Congress in the 2006 elections. The shift to Democratic control was completed in November 2008, when Barack Obama was elected and Democrats strengthened their hold on Congress. Responding to the deepest economic crisis since the 1930s, Democrats quickly passed a $787 billion stimulus package designed to "create or save" 3.5 million jobs over two years. The mix of spending increases, tax cuts, and support for the states was very different from the Republican alternative, which was focused on tax cuts. The $3.4 trillion budget passed in April 2009 also had a very different mix of priorities than those of the previous eight years, with substantially new directions in alternative energy, global warming, education, health care, regulation of

▼ *The American Recovery and Reinvestment Act was signed into law by President Obama on February 17, 2009. Designed to create jobs and stimulate economic growth, the act is a good example of how process matters: without unified Democratic control of Congress and the presidency, Republican opponents would have been able to block enactment of the proposal.*

the mortgage and financial sectors, and the wars in Iraq and Afghanistan. All of this goes to show that political process matters: if the elections of 2006 and 2008 had gone to the other party, policies in all of these important areas would be significantly different.

Though election outcomes can be quite far-reaching, politics is more than elections. As you will see, many members of the federal bureaucracy have considerable influence over what government does by virtue of their roles in developing and implementing government policies. The same is true for federal judges, who review government actions to see if they are consistent with the Constitution and other federal laws. These individuals' decisions are part of the political process, even though they are not elected to their positions.

Ordinary citizens are also part of politics. They can vote; donate time or money to interest groups, party organizations, or individual candidates; or demand action from these groups or individuals. All of these actions can influence government policy, either by determining who holds the power to change policy directly or by signaling to policy makers which options have public support.

Another important element of politics is the web of rules and procedures that determine who has the power to make choices about government policy. These rules range from the requirement that the president has to have been born in the United States, to the rules that structure debates and voting in the House and the Senate, to the procedures for approving new federal regulations. Seemingly innocuous rules can have an enormous impact on what can happen or what does happen, which means that choices about these rules are actually disguised choices about outcomes. For example, the Constitution's rule that only natural-born citizens may become president means that former governor Arnold Schwarzenegger of California cannot run for the office, since he was born in Austria.

You can debate in the abstract whether this restriction is a good or bad idea. Perhaps those born in the United States are more likely to have its best interests at heart than those born outside the country, or perhaps not. However, abstract debates about rules do not capture their real impact on elections and policies. In the modern era, it's impossible to debate the merits of the presidential citizenship requirement without considering its impact on Schwarzenegger's political prospects, because many people have suggested that he would be a viable presidential candidate if he were allowed to run.

Another example is the cloture rule for ending debate in the Senate, which means that it takes 60 votes out of 100 to enact a new law, not just a simple majority of 51. During the period of George W. Bush's presidency when Democrats were the minority party in the Senate but the Republican majority fell short of sixty votes, cloture gave the Democrats real power over government policy. For the last half of 2009, the Democrats controlled the sixty Senate seats needed to stop a Republican filibuster (after an extremely close election in Minnesota and an eight-month-long recount and legal battle decided in favor of the Democrat Al Franken, and the party switch by former Republican Arlen Specter of Pennsylvania, gave the Democrats the two seats they needed). However, the filibuster-proof majority was short-lived as Republican Scott Brown won a surprising victory in the special election to fill the late senator Ted Kennedy's seat in Massachusetts, one of the most Democratic states in the nation. Of course, as we will discuss in Chapter 7, Political Parties, party unity is not guaranteed, meaning that a filibuster can still be a threat, even to a party with a sixty-vote majority.

The ability to determine political rules empowers the people who make those choices. To paraphrase a favorite saying of Representative John Dingell, a long-serving Democrat from Michigan, "If you let me decide procedure and I let you decide substance, I'll beat you every time."

▼ The election of Democrat Al Franken to a Senate seat from Minnesota provides additional illustrations that process matters. Franken was certified as the winner only after a months-long recount process involving numerous court challenges, and his eventual victory gave Senate Democrats the supermajority they needed to end Republican filibusters.

KEY IDEA 3: POLITICS IS EVERYWHERE

From coverage of campaigns, legislative proceedings, and presidential pronouncements, to debates over policy, most of us think about some aspect of politics every day. Even though most Americans have a relatively weak interest in politics, most of us absorb politics without really trying, simply by considering information that falls in our laps as we do other things. When you read the newspaper, watch TV, surf the Web, or listen to the radio, you'll almost surely encounter a political story. Similarly, when you walk down the street, you may see billboards, bumper stickers, posters, or T-shirts advertising a candidate, a political party, an interest group, or an issue position. Someone may ask you to sign a petition. You may walk past a vacant building or a homeless person and wonder whether the government is doing anything about these problems—or whether a winning candidate followed through on her promise to help. You may see an army recruiting office or glance at a newspaper headline about the war in Afghanistan, and wonder whether members of Congress and the president were right to pursue their current policy. Or you may be going to the post office to mail your tax return, and wonder what you're getting for your money.

Many people have an active interest in putting politics in front of us on a daily basis. Interest groups, political parties, and candidates work to raise public awareness of the political process and to shape what people know and want. The news media offer extensive coverage of politics in stories about elections and governing as well as about the consequences of government actions in the ways policies affect ordinary Americans.

The broad reach of politics can also be seen in the concerns that prompt ordinary Americans to look for information. Table 1.1 shows the top ten stories on Google News in March 2010. Of the ten stories, nine have a clear connection to the federal government, from health care legislation to support for nuclear power. The lone exception concerns the troubled marriage of golfer Tiger Woods—and even here, federal programs helped to create the Internet, which played an important role in informing the public about this scandal.

Politics is also a fundamental part of how Americans think about themselves. Although most people don't know a lot about politics and governing, virtually everyone can name their party identification, whether they are a Democrat, a Republican, or an independent.[21] Most Americans are able to place their own views on a continuum between liberal and conservative.[22] These beliefs shape our views; Americans often look at the world through a partisan or ideological lens. For example, surveys conducted after Hurricane Katrina found Democrats more likely than Republicans to give the federal government poor marks for its efforts to help people whose homes were damaged or lost due to the storm.[23] That is, a typical Democrat seeing the same events as a typical Republican would evaluate the situation differently.

Politics is everywhere in another important way: government actions touch virtually every aspect of your life. As the ironic saying goes, "No man's life, liberty, or property is safe while the legislature is in session."[24] Some people claim that "the personal is political," meaning that even our most private, personal rights and thoughts are affected by the political process and government actions.[25] The most obvious examples include abortion, gay marriage, and laws governing child custody and other aspects of divorce.

One measure of the government's capacity to influence our lives is its size. As Nuts and Bolts 1.2 shows, the federal government planned to spend about $3.5 trillion in 2011, accounting for 24 percent of the American economy. More than 12 million people receive a paycheck from the federal government, either directly, as a civil servant or member of the military, or because they work for a company funded

TABLE 1.1 POLITICS IS EVERYWHERE: TOP STORIES ON GOOGLE NEWS, MARCH 22, 2010

Story	Federal Government Involvement
House Passage of Health Care Legislation	New taxes, regulations, and benefits for Americans
Clinton Says Middle East Status Quo "Unacceptable"	Negotiating peace between Israel and Palestinians is high priority of U.S. foreign policy
Broad Coalition Packs Mall to Support Immigration Reform	Federal regulations determine who can immigrate to the United States
FEMA Chief to Survey Red River Flooding	Federal government provides disaster relief to communities affected by flooding
Tiger Woods: "Working on" Marriage with Elin	—
Last Haditha Defendant Seeks to Dismiss Charges	U.S. Marines accused of criminal behavior during military operation in Iraq
Michigan Loses New Request in Great Lakes Carp Case	Federal regulations prevent Michigan from removing carp from Great Lakes
NY's Cuomo Leads All in Governor's Contest	Cuomo is former U.S. Secretary of Housing and Urban Development
U.S. Senate Panel to Vote on Financial Reform Monday	Financial reform proposals would affect entire banking industry
Public Support for Nuclear Power at New Peak	Federal programs create incentive to build nuclear power plants

Source: Google News search, 3/22/10.

by a government contract, work for a project funded by a federal grant, or work for the Postal Service. Federal bureaucrats also issue thousands of pages of new regulations every year. Even in terms of these broad measures, the federal government's reach into the lives of ordinary Americans is extraordinary.

The impact of policy outcomes becomes clear when you think about your typical day. If you attend a public university, you might wake up in a dorm that was partially funded with taxpayers' money, or maybe your apartment was built with federal housing subsidies. Your breakfast was subject to regulation by the Food and Drug Administration. Your clothing was likely manufactured overseas and may have been subject to federal tariffs and other regulations before it was sold. The television you watch and the radio you listen to are regulated by the Federal Trade Commission, the Consumer Products Safety Commission, and the Federal Communications Commission. When you're checking your e-mail or an online weather report, remember that the Internet was developed under contract with an agency in the Department of Defense and that the National Weather Service provides the satellite imagery used to generate local weather forecasts.

As you walk out the door, consider that government regulations developed by bureaucrats in the Environmental Protection Agency determine how clean the air

The Size of the Federal Government

Federal Spending	$3.524 trillion (24.1% of GDP)
Federal Taxes	$2.175 trillion (14.9% of GDP)
Federal Workforce	2.1 million civil servants (1.35 million in civilian agencies, 750,000 in the Department of Defense)
	1.4 million military personnel
	5.1 million employees of government contractors
	2.9 million people paid through government grants
	800,000 Postal Service employees
Federal Regulations	69,000 new pages in 2009

SOURCES: Congressional Budget Office, "Current Budget Projections," available at www.cbo.gov/ftpdocs/108xx/doc10871/budgetprojections.pdf; The President's Budget for Fiscal Year 2011, "Total Executive Branch Civilian Full-Time Equivalent (FTE) Employees, 1981–2011", Table 17.1, available at www.whitehouse.gov/omb/budget/Historicals/; Department of Defense, "Military Personnel Active and Reserve Forces," available at www.whitehouse.gov/omb/budget/fy2011/assets/mil.pdf; Paul Light, "Fact Sheet on the New True Size of Government," Brookings Institution, September 5, 2003, available at www.brookings.edu/articles/2003/0905politics_light.aspx; *The Federal Register*, www.gpoaccess.gov/fr/.

is—and the costs that companies pay for environmental cleanup and protection. The design of your car was influenced by fuel economy legislation; the price you pay to fill your gas tank is affected by America's foreign policy. And if you drive on a highway, it was likely paid for, at least in part, by a federal highway bill. Suppose you are on your way to class. Most universities and colleges receive money from the federal government in the form of faculty research grants and funding for institutes and laboratories. And many college students receive direct governmental assistance as student loans or grants.

You can ignore what government does, refuse to participate in elections, and have nothing to do with any elected officials, bureaucrats, or judges, but the government's influence over your life is impossible to avoid. Opting out simply ensures that you have no influence over government policy—the decisions that affect your life still get made.

Finally, the idea that politics is everywhere has a deeper meaning: people's political behavior is similar to their behavior in the rest of their lives. You may think that politicians and bureaucrats may as well be a separate species or that the political world operates according to its own unique set of rules. In fact, the opposite is true. The more you learn about politics, the more you see politics embedded in your everyday life.

As we discuss in Chapter 8, Elections, many voters form judgments about candidates by focusing on a candidate's appearance, including race, gender, or age. Such stereotyping also shapes people's judgments about individuals who they meet in other areas of life. Inside politics and out, the same mechanisms apply.

Similarly, in Chapter 9, Interest Groups, we examine one of the biggest problems faced by groups from the Sierra Club to the National Rifle Association: getting organized. Convincing like-minded individuals to contribute time or money to a group's lobbying efforts is no easy task. Each would-be contributor also has the opportunity to be a free rider who refuses to participate yet reaps the benefits of others' participation.

▼ The idea that "politics is everywhere" is evident when government policies influence highly personal decisions, such as those pertaining to marriage, divorce, and abortion. Gay marriage has been controversial, and many states have passed laws and constitutional amendments defining marriage as being between a man and a woman.

Because of these difficulties, some groups of people with common goals remain unorganized, as in David Hume's example of the failure to drain a meadow for farm land when the cooperation of a large number of people is required. College students, many of whom want more student aid and lower interest rates on government-subsidized student loans but fail to organize politically toward those ends, are a good example.

The same kinds of collective action problems occur in everyday life as well. For example, when you live with roommates, keeping common areas neat and clean presents a collective action problem, since everyone has an interest in a clean area, but each person is also inclined to let someone else do the work. The same principles help us to understand campus protests of tuition hikes, alcohol bans, or changes in graduation requirements in terms of which kinds of issues and circumstances foster cooperation. In each case, individual free riders acting in their own self-interest may undermine the outcome that most people prefer.

This similarity between behavior in political situations and in the rest of life is no surprise; everything that happens in politics is the result of individuals' choices. And the connections between politics and everyday life mean you know more about politics than you realize.

▲ *The price of gasoline is largely beyond government control, but policies can have some impact on the price. A foreign policy that creates instability in oil-producing regions can cause gas prices to rise, while domestic policies encouraging more exploration and oil production may stabilize oil and gas prices.*

Sources of Conflict in American Politics

Where does political conflict come from? As mentioned earlier, most people avoid conflict, so you might think politicians would try to minimize it. The reality is that conflict must be dealt with in order to find compromise and enact policy; sometimes, however, disagreements are intractable because of inherent differences between people and their opinions about government and politics.

ECONOMIC INTERESTS

Relative economic equality was a defining characteristic of our nation's early history, at least among white men, since small landowners, businessmen, craftsmen, and their families comprised a large majority of the nation's population. Compared to our European counterparts, the United States has been relatively free from class-based politics. Over time, our nation became more stratified by class, to the point that the United States now ranks about ninety-first among the world's 194 countries in terms of income equality, but a commitment to the **free market** and **economic individualism** remain central parts of our national identity.

Despite this basic consensus on economic principles and a history relatively free of class-based politics, there are important differences among American citizens, interest groups, and political parties in terms of their economic interests and favored economic policies. As we discuss in Chapter 7, Political Parties, Democratic politicians and activists tend to favor more **redistributive tax policies** and social spending on programs for the poor. Democrats are also more inclined to regulate industry to protect the environment and worker and product safety. Republicans favor lower taxes and less spending on social policies. They are also more supportive than Democrats of the free market and less inclined to interfere with business interests.

free market An economic system based on competition among businesses without government interference.

economic individualism The autonomy of individuals to manage their own financial decisions without government interference.

redistributive tax policies Policies, generally favored by Democratic politicians, that use taxation to attempt to create greater social equality (i.e., higher taxation of the rich to provide programs for the poor).

▲ *The importance of cultural values in politics is evident in the influence of Americans who hold strong religious beliefs. Here, presidential candidate Barack Obama participates in a discussion with Pastor Rick Warren at a forum held in August 2008.*

CULTURAL VALUES

Political analysts often focus considerable attention on the **culture wars** in the United States between "red-state" Americans, who tend to have strong religious beliefs, and "blue-state" Americans, who tend to be more secular. (The color coding of the states comes from the election-night maps on television that show the states carried by Republican candidates in red and those won by Democrats in blue—but see Figure 1.2, "Purple America," for a more nuanced take on this). After George W. Bush was reelected in 2004, leaders of the Christian right claimed that they had delivered the election for Bush and demanded action on their issues, which raised the level of national conflict on a broad range of issues.[26] Cultural issues did not have as much traction in the 2008 elections (they were overwhelmed by economic concerns), but Barack Obama did not fare well in culturally conservative parts of the country.

Although the precise makeup and impact of "values voters" is still being debated, there is no doubt that many Americans disagree on cultural and moral issues, including the broad category of "family values" (such as whether and how to regulate pornography, gambling, and media obscenity and violence); whether to supplement the teaching of evolution in public schools with the perspectives of intelligent design and creationism; gay marriage; abortion; stem cell research; school prayer; the war on drugs; gun control; school vouchers; and religious displays in public places. These are all hot-button issues that interest groups and activists on both sides attempt to keep at the top of the policy agenda. Gay marriage and intelligent design have become high-profile, controversial issues more recently than many of the others, but all of them are sure to elicit strong opinions.

IDENTITY POLITICS

Racial, ethnic, and gender differences can also contribute to groups' political interests. Over the last generation, about 90 percent of African Americans have been strong supporters of Democratic candidates; in 2008, 95 percent voted for Obama. Other racial groups have been less cohesive in their voting than blacks, with their support for a particular party falling in the 55 to 70 percent range. Whites tend to vote Republican; Latinos tend to vote Democratic, with the exception of Cuban Americans, who tend to vote Republican; Asian Americans tend to vote Democratic but less consistently than Latinos. A gender gap in national politics is also evident, with women somewhat more likely to vote for Democrats and men for Republicans. Of course, these tendencies are not fixed. In the nineteenth century, African Americans were enthusiastic supporters of Republicans, the "party of Lincoln."[27] Southern whites solidly voted Democratic from the mid-nineteenth century until the 1960s, and now they solidly vote Republican. The gender gap did not consistently appear until 1980. Clearly the political implications of racial, ethnic, and gender differences change over time.

One of the enduring debates in American politics concerns whether ethnic and racial differences *should* be tied to political interests. One perspective is rooted in the **melting pot** image of America, which holds that as different racial and ethnic groups come to this country, they should mostly leave their native languages, customs, and traditions behind. This perspective focuses on the assimilation of various groups into American culture, with the belief that while groups will maintain some

culture wars Political conflict in the United States between "red-state" Americans, who tend to have strong religious beliefs, and "blue-state" Americans, who tend to be more secular.

melting pot The idea that as different racial and ethnic groups come to America, they should assimilate into American culture, leaving their native languages, customs, and traditions behind.

native traditions, our common bonds as Americans are more important. Supporters of this view advocate making English the country's official language and oppose bilingual public education.[28]

The alternatives to the melting pot view range from racial separatists, such as the Nation of Islam who see white-dominated society as oppressive and discriminatory, to multiculturalists, who argue that there is strength in diversity. The latter perspective advocates mutual tolerance and respect for different traditions and backgrounds.[29] Though debates will continue about the policies best suited to our nation's diverse population, our multiracial makeup is clear, as shown in Table 1.2. By 2042, whites will no longer comprise a majority of the U.S. population (this is already true in several states). The extent to which this racial and ethnic diversity continues to be a source of political conflict depends on the broader role of race in our society. As long as there are racial differences in employment, education, health, housing, and crime, and as long as racial discrimination is present in our society, race will continue to matter for politics. The long-running debate over immigration

▲ *Civil and voting rights policies contributed to the realignment of the South in the second half of the twentieth century, as more whites began supporting the Republican Party and the Democratic Party came to be seen as the champion of minority rights. Here, blacks and whites in Alabama wait in line together to vote at a city hall after enactment of the 1965 Voting Rights Act.*

TABLE 1.2 THE RACIAL COMPOSITION OF THE UNITED STATES

These census data show the racial diversity of the United States. Only 75 percent of Americans describe themselves as white. Moreover, the proportion of Hispanics and Latinos in the population is 15.1 percent and rising, although this category contains many distinct subgroups.

Race	Number	Percent
Total U.S. population	301,237,703	100
White	223,965,009	74.8
Hispanic or Latino (any race)	45,432,158	15.1
Mexican	29,318,971	9.7
Puerto Rican	4,127,728	1.4
Cuban	1,572,138	0.5
Dominican	1,249,471	0.4
Other, Hispanic or Latino	9,163,850	3.0
Black or African American	37,131,771	12.3
Asian	13,164,169	4.4
American Indian and Alaska Native	2,419,895	0.8
Native Hawaiian and Other Pacific Islander	446,164	0.1
Some other race	17,538,990	5.8
Two or more races	6,571,705	2.1

SOURCE: U.S. Census Bureau, 2006–2008 American Community Survey.

▶ *Debate continues between the advocates of the American cultural "melting pot" and those favoring a multicultural perspective on ethnic heritage. Should our diverse cultures be assimilated into a single, uniquely American identity? Does our diversity make us stronger, or do our differences push us apart?*

reform is strong evidence that racial and ethnic issues in politics are not going to disappear any time soon.

Many of the same observations apply to gender and politics. The women's movement is usually viewed as beginning in 1848 at the first Women's Rights Convention at Seneca Falls, New York. The fight for women's suffrage and legal rights dominated the movement through the late nineteenth and early twentieth centuries. In the 1960s and 1970s, feminism and the women's liberation movement called attention to a broad range of issues: workplace issues such as maternity leave, equal pay, and sexual harassment; reproductive rights and abortion; domestic violence; and sexual violence. While much progress has been made on many fronts, gender remains an important source of political disagreement and identity politics.

IDEOLOGY

One other source of differences in interests that we will discuss is **ideology**—a cohesive set of ideas and beliefs that allows you to organize and evaluate the political world. Ideology may seem most obviously related to political interests through political parties since Republicans tend to be **conservative** and Democrats tend to be **liberal**. While this is true in a relative sense (most Republicans are more conservative than most Democrats), few Americans consider their own views ideologically extreme. On a 7-point scale, with 1 being extremely liberal and 7 extremely conservative, fewer than 10 percent of all Americans placed themselves at either 1 or 7, and more than half identified themselves as moderates (a 3, 4, or 5 on the scale).[30]

Ideology shapes specific beliefs; conservatives promote traditional social practices and favor lower taxes, a free market, and more limited government, where as liberals support social tolerance, stronger government programs, and more market regulation. However, the picture gets a little cloudier if you look more closely. **Libertarians**, for example, prefer very limited government providing only national defense and a few other narrowly defined responsibilities. Because they are at the extreme end of the ideological continuum on this issue, libertarians are generally conservative on issues such as social welfare policy, environmental policy, and government funding for education, and generally liberal on issues involving personal

ideology A cohesive set of ideas and beliefs used to organize and evaluate the political world.

conservative One side of the ideological spectrum defined by support for lower taxes, a free market, and a more limited government; generally associated with Republicans.

liberal One side of the ideological spectrum defined by support for stronger government programs and more market regulation; generally associated with Democrats.

libertarians Those who prefer very limited government and therefore tend to be conservative on issues such as welfare policy, environmental policy, and public support for education, but liberal on issues of personal liberty such as free speech, abortion, and the legalization of drugs.

liberty such as free speech, abortion, and the legalization of drugs. For libertarians, the consistent ideological theme is limiting the role of government in our lives.

Also, personal ideologies are not always consistent. Someone could be a fiscal conservative (favoring balanced budgets) and a social liberal (favoring the pro-choice position on abortion and marital rights for gays), or a liberal on foreign policy issues (supporting humanitarian aid and opposing the war in Afghanistan) and a conservative on moral issues (pro-life on abortion and opposing stem cell research). Ideology is a significant source of conflict in politics, and it does not always operate in a straightforward manner. In Chapter 5, Public Opinion, we address the question of whether America is becoming more ideological and polarized, deepening our conflicts and making compromise more difficult. You may be surprised to find that the American public has fairly centrist views, and there are relatively few systematic differences between residents of blue states and red states on a broad range of policies. For example, political scientist Morris Fiorina finds that red-state and blue-state residents have very similar views on immigration, English as the official language, environmental policy, school vouchers, affirmative action, equal rights for women, and tolerance of others' views. Although politics is conflictual (a lack of extreme polarization does not mean reaching agreement on specific policies is easy), and differences are somewhat larger on gay rights, abortion, gun control, and the death penalty, even on these issues, views are not as polarized as you might think. (Out of thirteen issues, only two—gay rights and abortion—showed differences of 10 percent or more between red-state and blue-state respondents).[31]

Figure 1.2 illustrates this finding with data from the 2008 presidential election. The map shows the relative strength by state of John McCain and Barack Obama, with the reddest states showing the strongest Republican support and the bluest

---

FIGURE 1.2 PURPLE AMERICA: THE 2008 PRESIDENTIAL ELECTION

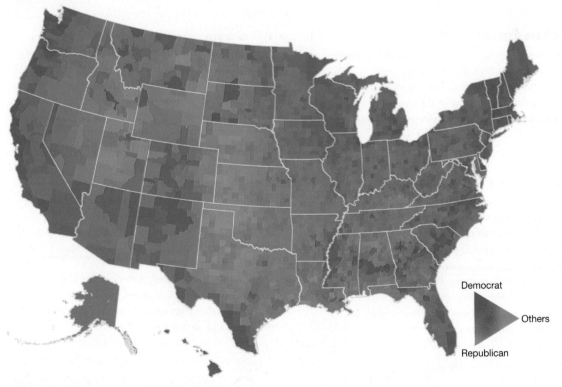

SOURCE: Provided by Robert J. Vanderbei, Princeton University.

states showing the Democratic strongholds. As you can see, most of the country is purple, which indicates a geographic intermixing between the parties and their associated ideological beliefs. One of the themes of Barack Obama's 2008 presidential campaign was that we should focus less on blue states and red states and recognize that we are all Americans rather than partisans. This appeal may have had some effect, as Obama made significant inroads in states that had been solidly red, such as Indiana, Virginia, and North Carolina.

Conclusion

By understanding that politics is conflictual, that it is rooted in process, and that it is everywhere, you will see that modern American political life makes more sense than you might have thought. Along the way, you will learn important "nuts and bolts" of the American political process as well as some political history. In general, though, we focus on real, contemporary questions, debates, and examples to illustrate broader points about our political system. After all, American politics in its current form is the politics that will have the greatest impact on your life.

Though you will disagree with some aspects of American politics, and some will make you angry, our goal is to provide you with the tools you need to understand *why* government operates as it does. We are not arguing that the federal government is perfect, or that policy failures such as the initial funding of the "bridge to nowhere" are inevitable. Rather, we believe that any attempt to explain these outcomes, or to devise ways to prevent similar problems in the future, requires an understanding of why they happened in the first place. After reading this book, you will have a better sense of how American politics works.

Why do we have a government?

- Government is necessary to establish justice, promote the general welfare, and secure liberty.
- The separation of powers and the system of checks and balances prevent the tyranny of the majority.
- Government is necessary to provide public goods and overcome collective action problems.

What is politics?

- Politics is conflictual. Making government policy typically involves issues on which people disagree, sometimes strongly, about what should be done. Although this may mean that compromises are hard to find, conflict is a normal and healthy part of politics.
- The political process matters. Politics is the process that determines what governments do. Governmental actions are the result of conscious choices made by elected officials and bureaucrats.

- Politics is everywhere. This key idea has two components: politics is a fundamental part of everyone's life, and the ways people think and act politically are driven by the same types of calculations and decision-making rules that govern beliefs and actions in other parts of their lives.

What are the sources of conflict in American politics?

- Some disagreements in politics are intractable because of strong differences between people and their attitudes toward government and politics.
- American political conflicts are rooted in citizens' different economic interests; cultural values; racial, ethnic, and gender identities; and ideologies.
- Despite these differences, Americans tend toward moderate views on most issues, producing a "purple America" rather than clear divisions between so-called red states and blue states.

CRITICAL THINKING

1. What are your views on the role of conflict in politics? What types of issues are most likely to be resolved through political conflict and compromise, and which issues are more resistant to compromise?
2. Consider the observation by Representative John Dingell (D-MI) that "If you let me decide procedure and I let you decide substance, I'll beat you every time." Do you think Dingell is right? What are some instances in which process was more important than substance in determining an outcome?
3. What are some examples from your life that illustrate that "politics is everywhere"? How do government policies affect the things you do every day? Can you think of past decisions or experiences that you may not have seen as political, but that illustrate this idea as well?

KEY TERMS

checks and balances (p. 8)
collective action problem (p. 9)
conservative (p. 22)
culture wars (p. 20)
economic individualism (p. 19)
factions (p. 8)
federalism (p. 8)

free market (p. 19)
free rider problem (p. 9)
government (p. 7)
ideology (p. 22)
liberal (p. 22)
libertarians (p. 22)
melting pot (p. 20)

politics (p. 10)
positive externalities (p. 9)
public goods (p. 9)
redistributive tax policies (p. 19)
separation of powers (p. 8)

SUGGESTED READING

Dahl, Robert. *On Democracy*. New Haven, CT: Yale University Press, 1998.

Fiorina, Morris P., with Samuel J. Abrams and Jeremy C. Pope. *Culture War? The Myth of a Polarized America,* 2nd ed. New York: Pearson, Longman, 2006.

Gutman, Amy. *Identity in Democracy*. Princeton, NJ: Princeton University Press, 2003.

Schattschneider, E. E. *The Semi-Sovereign People: A Realist's View of Democracy in America*. New York: Holt, Reinhart, and Winston, 1960.

Understanding the Constitution is crucial for understanding the American political system.

The Constitution and the Founding

One of our graduate students was known for carrying around a pocket-sized copy of the Constitution. He would whip it out to settle classroom disputes or consult it during political discussions in the student lounge. Though the framers of the Constitution surely did not expect citizens to carry this document at all times, they *did* anticipate (or at least hoped) that it would serve as the basis for an enduring government. One reason the Constitution has been so successful is because it provides the institutional foundation for resolving the conflict inherent in politics.

CONFLICT AND COMPROMISE
in American Politics

During your lifetime, three critical events have displayed the Constitution's conflict-resolution powers: President Clinton's 1998 impeachment, the disputed 2000 presidential election, and the struggle against terrorism since September 11, 2001. In each instance, the Constitution provided the legitimacy needed to resolve the problem and allow all sides to accept the outcome.

On January 21, 1998, the *Washington Post* revealed that President Bill Clinton had participated in an inappropriate sexual relationship with White House intern Monica Lewinsky and lied about it under oath. When physical evidence linking Clinton to Lewinsky surfaced, Clinton admitted the relationship and apologized to the nation. Two weeks later, Independent Counsel Kenneth Starr sent his report to Congress that claimed grounds for impeachment.[1] Republicans believed the public would agree with their disgust at Clinton's conduct and support removing him from office.

Although the public thought Clinton's conduct was immoral, most did not consider it a "high crime or misdemeanor" specified by the Constitution as grounds for impeachment. Congressional Republicans pressed ahead with the impeachment case despite strong public support for the president. The political backlash produced Democratic gains in the 1998 midterm election, but the House still approved articles of impeachment on December 19, 1998—the same day Clinton's public approval rating peaked at 73 percent! The Senate took the hint and voted to acquit.

In the second example, the constitutional and legal questions were more complex and the most important interpreter of the Constitution was the Supreme Court rather than the American people. November 7, 2000 was not a typical election

BIG QUESTIONS

✪ What were the sources of conflict at the Constitutional Convention?

✪ How was compromise achieved at the Constitutional Convention?

✪ How was the Constitution ratified?

✪ How is the Constitution a framework for government?

✪ Is the Constitution a "living document"?

night: the close battle between Vice President Al Gore and Texas governor George W. Bush only got tighter as votes started rolling in. The nation woke up on Wednesday to find that Gore had a national popular vote lead of several hundred thousand votes, while Bush led in Florida by 1,210 votes. With Florida's twenty-five electoral votes still officially up for grabs, Gore also led in the electoral college, but neither candidate had the 270 electoral votes needed to win.

Over the next month, the recount process in Florida narrowed Bush's lead to a few hundred votes. The dispute bounced between the state and federal courts as the Republican legal team tried to stop the recounts and certify Bush's lead while the Democratic lawyers tried to buy more time to recount votes. After two Florida state supreme court rulings favorable to Gore, the U.S. Supreme Court stepped in and gave the election to Bush. Democrats fumed that the Court had acted in a blatantly partisan fashion while Republicans argued that only the Supreme Court could legitimately decide what was basically a tied election.

More recently, the terrorist attacks of September 11 produced an outpouring of public support for strengthening our ability to prevent another attack. Congress responded by passing the USA PATRIOT Act, which gave the president the power to create military tribunals to try suspected terrorists, defined "enemy combatants," and expanded the government's surveillance powers. Although some members of Congress and political observers worried about the implications of these expanded executive powers for civil liberties, most saw them as necessary. However, when news leaked out that the president had approved enhanced interrogation methods (which critics called torture), domestic surveillance and secret renditions of suspected terrorists to other nations, the majority on the Supreme Court and in Congress determined that the executive branch had gone too far in its efforts to fight terrorism. Once again our constitutional system provided the self-corrective mechanism of checks and balances, restoring a better balance between protecting civil liberties and fighting terrorism. When one branch of government becomes too powerful (in this case the presidency), the other two branches fight back to restore the balance by striking down presidential actions as unconstitutional (the Supreme Court) or passing new laws (Congress).

What do these events show about the Constitution's ability to resolve conflict? When the Supreme Court decided to stop the 2000 recount, making Bush president, Americans accepted the decision because of their faith in the Constitution and the Supreme Court. Many Democratic partisans were outraged, but there were no riots, no one stormed the Capitol, and neither Gore nor other Democratic

▼ Election officials in Broward County, Florida, examine ballots during the 2000 presidential election recount. The election outcome remained in doubt until the Supreme Court ended the recount, giving George W. Bush a razor-thin 537-vote win in a state that cast nearly 6 million votes.

leaders contested the Court's decision. The impeachment example illustrates a very different relationship between the people, political officials, and the Constitution. Rather than deferring, the people imposed their interpretation of the Constitution on the experts. While most Americans did not have a good grasp of the congressional debates over the meaning of "high crimes and misdemeanors," their gut-level interpretation of the framers' intent—that impeachment should be used for *political* abuses of power rather than personal failings—kept Clinton in office. The last case illustrates the Constitution's system of checks and balances. If Congress or the Supreme Court believe the executive branch has taken the interpretation of its constitutional powers too far, it can be challenged by the other two branches. These examples also highlight a central point of this chapter: there are multiple interpreters of the Constitution.

The Constitutional Convention demonstrated that politics is conflictual, as many competing interests battled over which topics to include and how to resolve future political differences. The sweeping influence of the Constitution also shows that politics is everywhere. The document shapes every aspect of national politics, which in turn influences many parts of your life. The Constitution establishes the basic rules for our institutions of government, prevents the government from doing certain things to citizens (such as denying them freedom of speech), and guarantees specific individual rights. In other words, the Constitution determines the ground rules for the process that guides politics. We will return to these themes throughout this chapter.

Finally, and perhaps surprisingly, the Constitution is highly readable. You do not have to be a lawyer or a political philosopher to understand it. It contains only 4,543 words, about the length of a fifteen-page term paper, and although the writing is somewhat old-fashioned in places, it uses everyday language rather than the legalese that one would confront in a modern document of this type. If you haven't read it recently (or at all) turn to the Appendix and read it now.

▲ *The Constitution attempts to strike a balance between protecting our civil liberties from government intrusion and providing for a strong enough government to protect our national security. One consequence of the terrorist attacks of September 11 was more rigorous screening at airports and more widespread surveillance to try to stop the next terrorist attack.*

Conflict at the Constitutional Convention

The Constitution was created through conflict and compromise, and it is important to understand the historical context within which that process took place. Therefore we focus on the interests and ideas that were at stake for the framers and the compromises and decisions that they made. Understanding the historical context can help clarify *why* specific choices were made. And exploring the consequences of alternative choices is one way of seeing how politics matters.

Key historical events shaped the Constitutional Convention, including the Revolutionary War and problems with the first form of government in the United States, the Articles of Confederation. The events leading up to the Revolutionary War and the war itself led to widespread support for popular control of government through a **republican democracy**, a rejection of **monarchy**, and limitations on government power that would protect against tyranny. Although there were a few Tories (supporters of the British monarchy) in the Revolutionary and post-Revolutionary era,

republican democracy A form of government in which the interests of the people are represented through elected leaders.

monarchy A form of government in which power is held by a single person, or monarch, who comes to power through inheritance rather than election.

most Americans were eager to sever ties with the oppressive British government and establish a new nation that rejected the trappings of royalty.

ARTICLES OF CONFEDERATION: THE FIRST ATTEMPT AT GOVERNMENT

The first attempt to structure an American government, the **Articles of Confederation**, swung too far in the direction of **limited government**. The Articles were written in the summer of 1776 during the Second Continental Congress, which also authorized and approved the Declaration of Independence. The Articles were submitted to all thirteen states in 1777 for approval, but they did not formally go into effect until the last state ratified them in 1781. However, in the absence of any alternative, the Articles of Confederation served as the basis for organizing the government during the Revolutionary War.

In their zeal to reject monarchy, the authors of the Articles did not even include a president or any other executive leader. All national power was given to a Congress in which each state had a single vote. Members of Congress were elected by state legislatures rather than directly by the people. There was no judicial branch; all legal matters were left to the states, with the exception of disputes among the states, which would be resolved by special panels of judges appointed on an as-needed basis by Congress. In their eagerness to limit the power of government, the authors of the Articles gave each state veto power over any changes to the Articles and required approval from nine of the thirteen states on any legislation. Even more importantly, the states maintained autonomy and did not sacrifice any significant power to the national government. Powers granted to the national government, such as making treaties and coining money, were not exclusive powers; that is, they were not denied to the states. Congress also lacked any real authority over the states. For example, Congress could suggest the amount of money each state owed to support the Revolutionary army but could not enforce payment. General Washington's troops were in very bad shape, lacking food and clothing to say nothing about the arms and munitions they needed to defeat the British. The severe winter of 1780 led to an attempted mutiny in Morristown, New Jersey. At first Congress tried to compel the states to support their own troops, but this appeal failed. Desperate for funds, in 1781 Congress tried to give itself the power to raise taxes, but the measure was vetoed by Rhode Island, which represented less than 2 percent of the nation's population! If France had not come to the aid of the American army with much-needed funds and troops, the weakness of the national government could have led to defeat.[2]

After the Revolutionary War ended, the same weaknesses continued to plague Congress. The new government owed millions of dollars in war debts to foreign governments and domestic creditors, so Congress came up with a plan to repay the debts over twenty-five years, but again had no way to make the states pay their share. Instead, Congress proposed an amendment to the Articles that would allow it to collect import duties—but New York, which had the busiest port in the nation, did not want to share its revenue and vetoed the amendment. Foreign trade also suffered because of the weak national government. If a foreign government negotiated a trade arrangement with Congress, it could be vetoed or amended by a state government, so that a foreign country wanting to conduct business with the United States might have to negotiate separate agreements with Congress and each state legislature. Disputes with foreign countries about land boundaries also were complex and contentious because of the Articles. When Spain threatened to close trade routes on the Mississippi River and Great Britain disputed the U.S.–Canadian border, it was not clear whether state governments or Congress could resolve the

NUTS AND BOLTS

Comparing the Articles of Confederation and the Constitution

ISSUE	ARTICLES OF CONFEDERATION	CONSTITUTION
Legislature	Unicameral Congress	Bicameral Congress divided into the House of Representatives and the Senate
Members of Congress	Between two and seven per state	Two senators per state; representatives apportioned according to population of each state
Voting in Congress	One vote per state	One vote per representative or senator
Selection of members	Appointed by state legislatures	Representatives elected by popular vote; senators appointed by state legislatures
Term of legislative office	One year	Two years for representatives; six years for senators
Term limit for legislative office	No more than three out of every six years	None
Congressional pay	Paid by states	Paid by the federal government
Executive	None	President
National judiciary	Maritime judiciary established, no general federal courts	Supreme Court; Congress authorized to establish national judiciary
Settle disputes between states	Congress	Supreme Court
New states	Admitted with approval of nine states	Admitted with approval of Congress
Amendments to the document	When approved by all states	When approved by three-fourths of the states
Power to coin money	Federal government and the states	Federal government only
Taxes	Apportioned by Congress, collected by the states	Apportioned and collected by Congress
Ratification	Unanimous consent required	Consent of nine states required

disputes. Even trade among the states was complicated and inefficient. Each state could make its own currency, exchange rates varied, and many states charged tolls and fees to export goods across state lines. Just imagine how difficult interstate commerce would be today if you had to exchange currency at every state line.

A small group of leaders decided that something must be done. A group from Virginia urged state legislatures to send delegates to a convention on interstate commerce in Annapolis, Maryland, in September 1786. Eight states agreed, but only five ended up sending delegates. Alexander Hamilton and James Madison salvaged something from the convention by getting those delegates to agree to convene again in Philadelphia the following May. They also proposed expanding the scope of the next convention to examine the defects of the current government and "devise such

FIGURE 2.1 CONSTITUTIONAL TIMELINE

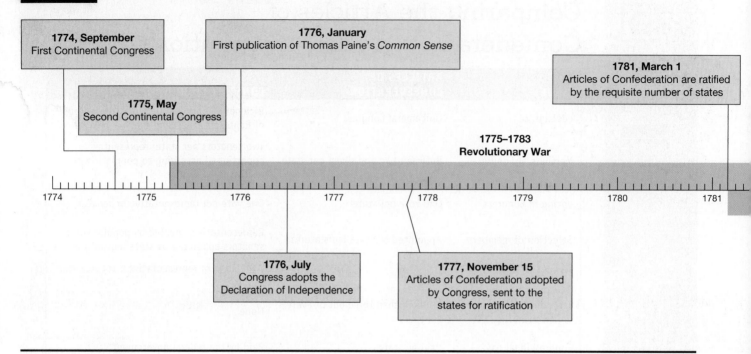

further provisions as shall appear to them necessary to render the Constitution of the Federal Government adequate to the exigencies of the Union."³

The issues that motivated the Annapolis Convention gained new urgency as events unfolded over the next several months. In the years after the war, economic chaos led to a depression, and many farmers lost their land because they could not pay their debts or state taxes. Frustration mounted, and early in 1787, a former captain in the Revolutionary army, Daniel Shays, led a force of a thousand farmers in an attempt to take over the Massachusetts state government arsenal in Springfield. Their goal was to force the state courts to stop prosecuting debtors and taking their land, but they were repelled by a state militia. Similar protests on a smaller scale happened at the same time in Pennsylvania and Virginia. Some state legislatures gave in to the debtors' demands, causing national leaders to fear that Shays's Rebellion had exposed fundamental discontent with the new government. The very future of the fledgling nation was at risk.

POLITICAL THEORIES OF THE FRAMERS

Although the leaders who gathered in Philadelphia in the summer of 1787 to write the Constitution were chastened by the failure of the Articles of Confederation, they still shared many of the principles that motivated the Revolution.

Republicanism First among these principles was rejection of monarchy in favor of a form of government based on self-rule. In its broadest sense, **republicanism** is the ideology of any state that is not a monarchy. As understood by the framers, it is a government in which elected leaders would represent the views of the people. Thomas Paine, an influential political writer of the Revolutionary era, wrote a pamphlet entitled *Common Sense* in 1776 that was a widely read⁴ and influential indictment of monarchy and an endorsement of the principles that fueled the Revolution and

republicanism As understood by James Madison and the framers, the belief that a form of government in which the interests of the people are represented through elected leaders is the best form of government.

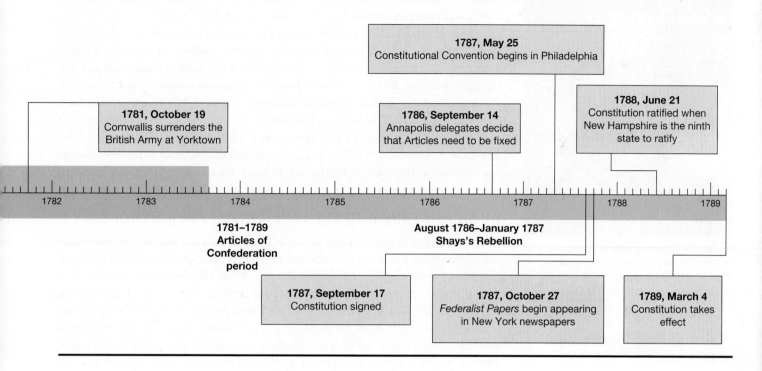

1787, May 25
Constitutional Convention begins in Philadelphia

1781, October 19
Cornwallis surrenders the British Army at Yorktown

1786, September 14
Annapolis delegates decide that Articles need to be fixed

1788, June 21
Constitution ratified when New Hampshire is the ninth state to ratify

1782 1783 1784 1785 1786 1787 1788 1789

1781–1789
Articles of Confederation period

August 1786–January 1787
Shays's Rebellion

1787, September 17
Constitution signed

1787, October 27
Federalist Papers begin appearing in New York newspapers

1789, March 4
Constitution takes effect

underpinned the thinking of the framers. Paine wrote that a monarchy was the "most bare-faced falsity ever imposed on mankind" and that the common interests of the community would be served by elected representatives. The best expression of these core principles is found in the Declaration of Independence:

> We hold these truths to be self-evident, that all men are created equal, that they are endowed by their Creator with certain unalienable Rights, that among these are Life, Liberty, and the pursuit of Happiness. That to secure these rights, Governments are instituted among Men, deriving their just powers from the consent of the governed. That whenever any Form of Government becomes destructive of these ends, it is the Right of the People to alter or to abolish it, and to institute new Government.

Three crucial ideas are packed into this passage: equality, self-rule, and natural rights. Equality was not given much attention in the Constitution (later chapters discuss how the problem of slavery was handled), but the notion that a government gains its legitimacy from the "**consent of the governed**" and that its central purpose is to uphold the "unalienable" or **natural rights** of the people were central to the framers. The "right of the people to alter or abolish" a government that did not protect these rights served both to justify the revolt against the British and to remind the framers of their continuing obligation to make sure that those needs were met. The leaders who met in Philadelphia thought the Articles of Confederation had become "destructive to those ends" and therefore had to be altered.

Paine, Jefferson, Madison, and the other political thinkers of the American Founding broke new ground in laying out the principles of republican democracy, but they also built on the ideas of political philosophers of their era. As mentioned in Chapter 1, the philosopher Thomas Hobbes argued that government was necessary to prevent people from living in an anarchic "state of nature" in which life would be "nasty, brutish, and short." However, Hobbes's central conclusion was undemocratic: he believed that a single king must rule because any other form of government

"consent of the governed" The idea that government gains its legitimacy through regular elections in which the people living under that government participate to elect their leaders.

natural rights Also known as "unalienable rights," the Declaration of Independence defines them as "Life, Liberty, and the pursuit of Happiness." The Founders believed that upholding these rights should be the government's central purpose.

▲ *Seventeenth-century political philosopher John Locke had a great influence on the Founders. Many ideas discussed in Locke's writing appear in the Declaration of Independence and the Constitution.*

Federalist Papers A series of eighty-five articles written by Alexander Hamilton, James Madison, and John Jay that sought to sway public opinion toward the Federalists' position.

would produce warring factions. Another seventeenth-century philosopher, John Locke, took this same notion of the consent of the governed in determining a government's legitimacy in a more democratic direction. A great influence on the framers, Locke discussed many of the ideas that appeared in the Declaration of Independence and Constitution, including natural rights, property rights, the need for a vigorous executive branch that would be checked by a legislative branch, and self-rule through elections.[5] Baron de Montesquieu, an eighteenth-century political thinker, also influenced the framers, especially Madison. Although he did not use the term "separation of powers," Montesquieu argued in *The Spirit of the Laws* (1748) that no two, let alone three, functions of government (judicial, legislative, and executive) should be controlled by one branch. He also argued that in order to preserve liberty, one branch of government should be able to check the excesses of the other branches.

HUMAN NATURE AND ITS IMPLICATIONS FOR DEMOCRACY

The most comprehensive statement of the framers' political philosophy and democratic theory was a series of essays written by James Madison, Alexander Hamilton, and John Jay entitled the **Federalist Papers**. As we discuss below in the section on ratification, these essays explained and justified the framework of government created by the Constitution. The essays also revealed the framers' view of human nature and its implications for democracy. The framers' view of human nature as basically self-interested led to James Madison's assessment that, "In framing a government which is to be administered by men over men, the great difficulty lies in this: you must first enable the government to control the governed; and in the next place oblige it to control itself." This analysis, which comes from *Federalist 51*, is often considered the clearest articulation of the need for republican government and a system of separated powers. In *Federalist 10* Madison described the central problem for government as the need to control factions, which he defined as, "A number of citizens, whether amounting to a majority or a minority of the whole, who are united and actuated by some common . . . interest, adverse to the rights of other citizens, or to the permanent and aggregate interests of the community." In today's terms this would refer to an interest group that works for self-serving goals rather than the broader interests of the community.

Madison goes on to argue that governments cannot control the causes of factions, because such differences of opinion—based on the fallibility of reason; differences in wealth, property, and native abilities; and attachments to different leaders—are part of human nature. The only way to eliminate factions would be to either remove liberty or try to make everyone the same. The first remedy Madison called "worse than the disease" and the second he found "as impracticable as the first would be unwise." The experiences of communist nations such as China and the former Soviet Union demonstrate the wisdom of Madison's insight. Forced collectivization of agriculture in which farmers work for the state rather than themselves; abolition of private property; strict limits on citizens' speech, travel, and religion; and the "reeducation" programs that led to the torture and death of millions are strong testimonies to the costs of trying to eliminate factions. Because people are driven by self-interest, which sometimes conflicts with the common good, government must, however, try to control the effects of factions. This was the task facing the framers at the Constitutional Convention.

ECONOMIC INTERESTS

Political ideas were clearly central in shaping the framers' thinking at the Constitutional Convention, but economic interests were equally important. Both the economic status of the framers themselves and the broader economic context of late eighteenth-century America are relevant here. One constitutional scholar addressed the relative importance of economic interests and political ideas for the framers, noting they "did not promote a new form of government to satisfy an abstract political theory. The framers were men of affairs who sought to advance their fortunes and careers as well as the interests of the states." This view was most famously expressed by Charles Beard nearly 100 years ago in his economic interpretation of the Constitution. Beard argued that the framers wanted to revise the Articles of Confederation and strengthen the national government largely to protect their property holdings and investments.[6] Some undemocratic features of the Constitution probably can be explained by the relatively privileged position of the framers. After all, broad political participation and control are more popular among the lower classes, who see an equal voice in government as a path to improved economic standing, whereas the privileged class tends to be more concerned with solidifying its own political position. However, Beard's argument has been countered by research showing, among other things, that the opponents of the Constitution also came from the upper class. (If both the supporters and opponents of the document shared the same economic background, it is difficult to claim that the framers' wealth explains the nature of the new system.) Most constitutional scholars now view the Constitution as the product of both ideas and interests. This balanced perspective is summarized by political scientist David Robertson, who says, "The delegates who made the Constitution were first and foremost politicians, not philosophers or real estate investors."[7]

▲ The economic context of the American Founding had an important impact on the Constitution. Most Americans worked on small farms or as artisans or business owners, which meant that economic power was broadly distributed. This woodcut shows New York City (in the distance, upper right) around the time the Constitution was written, viewed from upper Manhattan, probably about where Harlem is today.

The broader economic context of the American Founding was more important than the individual interests of the delegates. First, while there were certainly class differences among Americans in the late eighteenth century, they were insignificant compared to class distinctions in Europe. Most importantly, America did not have the history of feudalism that created tremendous levels of inequality in Europe between landowners and propertyless serfs who worked the land. In some European nations a few families owned as much as a third of the land. In contrast, most Americans owned small farms or worked as middle-class artisans and craftsmen. Thus, while political equality did not figure prominently in the Constitution, citizens' relative economic equality influenced the overall context of debates at the Constitutional Convention.

Second, despite Americans' general economic equality, there were significant regional economic differences. The southern part of the country was largely agricultural with large cotton and tobacco plantations that depended on slave labor. The South favored free trade because of its export-based economy (bolstered by westward expansion) and the slave trade. The middle Atlantic and northern states had smaller farms and a broad economic base that included manufacturing, fishing, and trade. These states favored government-managed trade and commercial development. Other economic divisions cut across regional lines, such as debtors versus creditors and states that had large property claims on western territories (such as Connecticut, Massachusetts, and Virginia) and those that did not. States with large port cities, such as New York, Massachusetts, and Pennsylvania, also were at odds with neighboring states when it came to national control of tariffs. States with ports wanted to maintain control over this important source of revenue.

Despite these regional and sector-based economic differences, a diverse population with various economic interests favored a stronger national government and reform of the Articles of Confederation. Creditors wanted a government that could pay off its debts to them, southern farmers wanted free trade that could

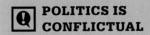
only be efficiently promoted by a central government, and manufacturers and traders desperately wanted a single national currency and uniform interstate commerce regulations to promote trade across state lines. However, there was a deep division between the supporters of empowering the national government to a greater degree and those who still favored relatively strong state governments. These two groups came to be known as the **Federalists** and the **Antifederalists**. The stage was set for a productive but contentious convention.

POLITICAL PROCESS MATTERS

The Politics of Compromise at the Constitutional Convention

The central players at the convention were James Madison, Gouverneur Morris, Edmund Randolph, James Wilson, Benjamin Franklin, and George Washington, the unanimous choice to preside over the convention. Several of the important leaders of the Revolution were not present. Patrick "Give me Liberty, or give me Death!" Henry was selected to attend, but he opposed any changes in the Articles, saying he "smelled a rat," and Thomas Jefferson and John Adams were working overseas as U.S. diplomats. Thomas Paine was back in England, and John Hancock and Samuel Adams were not selected to attend. The delegates met in secret to encourage open, uncensored debate, and convention proceedings were not published until more than thirty years later. James Madison's notes provide the best record of the debates and offer insight into the delegates' compromises and decisions.

Although there was broad consensus among the convention delegates that the Articles of Confederation needed to be changed, there were many tensions surrounding the nature of these changes that required political compromise:

- majority rule versus minority rights,
- large states versus small states,
- legislative power versus executive power (and how to elect the executive),
- national power versus state and local power, and
- slave states versus nonslave states.

This complex set of competing interests meant that the delegates had to focus on pragmatic solutions that *could* be accomplished rather than on proposals that represented particular groups' ideals but could not gain majority support. Robert Dahl, a leading democratic theorist of the twentieth century, argues that it was impossible for the Constitution to "reflect a coherent, unified theory of government" because so much compromising and vote-trading was required to find common ground.[8] Instead, the delegates tackled the problems one at a time, holding lengthy debates and multiple votes on most issues.

MAJORITY RULE VERSUS MINORITY RIGHTS

A central problem for any representative democracy is protecting minority rights within a system ruled by the majority. Today we often think of this issue in terms of racial and ethnic minorities, but these groups clearly were not the concern of the framers. Instead, they thought in terms of regional and economic minorities' interests. How could they be sure that small landowners and poorer people would not impose onerous taxes on the wealthier minority? How could they guarantee that the

Federalists Those at the Constitutional Convention who favored a strong national government and a system of separated powers.

Antifederalists Those at the Constitutional Convention who favored strong state governments and feared that a strong national government would be a threat to individual rights.

dominant agricultural interests would not impose punitive tariffs on manufacturing while allowing free export of farmed commodities? The answers to these questions can be found in Madison's writings on the problem of factions.

Recall that Madison defined a faction as a group motivated by selfish interests against the common good. If these interests prevailed, it could produce the very kind of tyranny that the Americans fought to escape during the Revolutionary War. Madison was especially concerned about tyranny by majority factions because, in a democracy, minority tyranny would be controlled by the republican principle: the majority could simply vote out the minority faction. If, on the other hand, the majority always rules, majority tyranny could be a real problem. Given the understanding of selfish human nature that Madison so clearly outlined, a populist, majoritarian democracy would not necessarily produce the common good. On the other hand, if too many protections were provided to minority and regional interests, the collective interest would not be served because constructive changes could be vetoed too easily, as under the Articles of Confederation.

Madison's solution to this problem provided the justification for our form of government. To control majority tyranny, he argued that factions must be set against one another to counter each other's ambitions and prevent the tyranny of any single majority faction. This was to be accomplished through what Madison called the "double protection" of the separation of powers within the national government in the form of checks and balances, and also by further dividing power across the levels of the state and local governments. Madison also argued that additional protection against majority tyranny came from the "size principle." That is, the new nation would be a large and diverse republic in which majority interests would be less likely to organize, and therefore less able to dominate. In a small territory, such as a state, "the more frequently will a majority be found of the same party," and "the more easily will they concert and execute their plans of oppression." However, in a large republic this was less likely to happen. According to Madison, "Extend the sphere, and you take in a greater variety of parties and interests; you make it less probable that a majority of the whole will have a common motive to invade the rights of other citizens; or if such a common motive exists, it will be more difficult for all who feel it to discover their own strength, and to act in unison with each other."[9] This insight provides the basis for modern **pluralism**, a political theory that makes the same argument about the cross-cutting interests of groups today.

The precise contours of Madison's solution still had to be hammered out at the convention, but the general principle pleased both the Antifederalists and the Federalists because state governments maintained some autonomy, but the national government would become stronger than it had been under the Articles. The issue here was striking the appropriate balance: none of the framers favored a pure populist majoritarian democracy, and few wanted to protect minority rights to the extent that the Articles had.

SMALL STATES VERSUS LARGE STATES

The question of the appropriate balance came to an immediate head in a debate between small states and large states over representation in the national legislature. Under the Articles every state had a single vote, but this did not seem fair to large states that instead were pushing for representation based on population. This proposal, along with other proposals to strengthen the national government, was formally made in the **Virginia Plan**. The small states countered with the **New Jersey Plan**, which proposed maintaining equal representation for every state. Rhode Island, the smallest state in the nation, was so concerned about small-state

pluralism The idea that having a variety of parties and interests within a government will strengthen the system, ensuring that no group possesses total control.

Virginia Plan A plan proposed by the larger states during the Constitutional Convention that based representation in the national legislature on population. The plan also included a variety of other proposals to strengthen the national government.

New Jersey Plan In response to the Virginia Plan, smaller states at the Constitutional Convention proposed that each state should receive equal representation in the national legislature, regardless of size.

Small States, Big States, and Crafting a Constitution

The European Union (EU) is tackling some of the same issues the Founders faced concerning how to represent states of dramatically different sizes. The EU expanded from fifteen to twenty-five members in May 2004, added two more members in January 2007, and is trying to ratify a new constitution. The first attempt failed when France and the Netherlands rejected the proposed constitution and seven other nations refused to vote on it (ratification was required by all twenty-seven nations). In December 2007, the EU member nations came up with a new draft, the Treaty of Lisbon, that was ratified by member nations and went into effect on December 1, 2009, but the proposed voting system (discussed below) will not be implemented until 2014.

In many ways the EU faces a far more difficult task than the Founders, but the issue of state size is equally vexing. Clearly, tiny states like Luxembourg, with its population of 453,000, cannot receive the same representation on the Council of the European Union as the 82.5 million Germans, just as Delaware and Rhode Island could not demand representation on par with New York and Virginia. However, the current allocation of voting rights favors the small and medium-sized EU member states. As the table shows, all nations smaller than Romania receive a disproportionately large share of votes, while large nations—especially Germany—do not receive their fair share.

The current proposal, the Treaty of Lisbon, would change this by allowing most kinds of measures to pass the Council with the support of 55 percent of the nations, as long as they have at least 65 percent of the EU population (although some issues, including taxation and most foreign policy matters, would require a unanimous vote). This rule would prevent the smaller nations from passing legislation not supported by the larger nations. In fact, the "big four"—United Kingdom, Germany, France, and Italy—would have nearly enough votes between them to block any measure proposed under the new 55/65 rule, while Poland, Spain, and the other middle-sized and smaller countries would lose voting power.

Many other complicated issues must also be resolved, including proposals for a common defense policy, enhancing the powers of the European Parliament, and revamping the European Commission. The sheer length of the rejected constitution is a testament to the complexity of the issues: the failed draft was 69,196 words and about 263 pages long (depending on what language you read it in), compared to the 4,543 words of the U.S. Constitution.[a]

VOTING WEIGHTS IN THE COUNCIL OF THE EUROPEAN UNION

	Accession Date	Population (millions)	Percentage of EU Population	Percentage of Council	Votes
Germany	1957	82	16.7	8.4	29
France	1957	63	12.8	8.4	29
United Kingdom	1973	60	12.3	8.4	29
Italy	1957	59	11.9	8.4	29
Spain	1986	44	8.9	7.8	27
Poland	2004	38	7.7	7.8	27
Romania	2007	22	4.4	4.1	14
Netherlands	1957	16	3.3	3.8	13
Greece	1981	11	2.3	3.5	12
Portugal	1986	11	2.1	3.5	12
Belgium	1957	11	2.1	3.5	12
Czech Republic	2004	10	2.1	3.5	12
Hungary	2004	10	2.0	3.5	12
Sweden	1995	9.0	1.8	2.9	10
Austria	1995	8.3	1.7	2.9	10
Bulgaria	2007	7.7	1.6	2.9	10
Denmark	1973	5.4	1.1	2.0	7
Slovakia	2004	5.4	1.1	2.0	7
Finland	1995	5.3	1.1	2.0	7
Ireland	1973	4.2	0.9	2.0	7
Lithuania	2004	3.4	0.7	2.0	7
Latvia	2004	2.3	0.5	1.2	4
Slovenia	2004	2.0	0.4	1.2	4
Estonia	2004	1.3	0.3	1.2	4
Cyprus	2004	0.77	0.2	1.2	4
Luxembourg	1957	0.46	0.1	1.2	4
Malta	2004	0.40	0.1	0.9	3
EU total		493	100	100	345

SOURCE: The Council of the European Union, available at http://europa.eu/institutions/inst/council/index_en.htm.

power that it boycotted the process and did not even send delegates to the convention. Tensions were running high; this issue appeared to have all the elements of a deal breaker, and there seemed to be no way to break the impasse.

Just as it appeared that the convention might grind to a halt before it really got started, Connecticut proposed what came to be known as the **Great Compromise**, or Connecticut Compromise, which suggested establishing a Congress with two houses: the Senate would have two senators from each state, and in the House of Representatives each state's number of representatives would be based on its population. Interestingly, Connecticut's population was ranked seventh of the thirteen states. Therefore it was in a perfect position to offer a compromise because it did not have strong vested interests in the plans offered by either the small states or the large states.

LEGISLATIVE POWER VERSUS EXECUTIVE POWER

An equally difficult task facing the framers was how to divide power at the national level. Here the central issues revolved around the executive, which in our system is the president. How much power should the president have relative to the legislative branch? (The courts also figured into the discussions, but they were less central.) And how would the president be elected? One of the central problems was that the delegates did not have any positive role models for the executive. Recall that under the Articles of Confederation there was no chief executive, and for the most part, the state governors were very weak. The delegates knew what they did not want: the king of England and his colonial governors were viewed as tramplers of liberty. The only one who actually favored a monarchy was Alexander Hamilton. He said that "the English model was the only good one" and proposed that a single executive and the Senate should "hold their places for life, or at least in good behavior."[10] Hamilton's extreme views on this topic meant that he was largely marginalized at the convention.

Many delegates rejected outright the idea of a single executive because they were not convinced it was possible to have an executive who would not be oppressive. When the idea of including an executive was first raised at the convention, Madison's notes reveal the strong reservations:

> Charles Pinckney rose to urge a "vigorous executive." James Wilson followed Pinckney by moving that the executive consist of a single person, Pinckney seconded him. A sudden silence followed. A considerable pause. A single executive . . . There was menace in the words, some saw monarchy in them. A single executive for the national government conjured up visions from the past—royal governors who could not be restrained, a crown, ermine, a scepter.

Edmund Randolph proposed a three-person executive for this reason, arguing that a single executive would be the "fetus of monarchy." The Virginia Plan envisioned a single executive who would share some legislative power with federal judges in a Council of Revision with the power to veto legislation passed by Congress (however, the veto could be overridden by a simple majority vote in Congress). The delegates finally agreed on the single executive because he would have the most "energy, dispatch, and responsibility for the office," but they constrained the president's power through the system of checks and balances. One significant power they granted to the executive was the veto. The presidential veto could be overridden by Congress, but this could only be done with the support of two-thirds of both chambers. This requirement gave the president a significant role in the legislative process.

Great Compromise A compromise between the large and small states, proposed by Connecticut, in which Congress would have two houses: a Senate with two legislators per state and a House of Representatives in which each state's representation would be based on population (also known as the Connecticut Compromise).

In addition to Hamilton, the other New Yorkers—Morris, William Livingston, and John Jay—also favored a strong executive. This was probably because the governor of New York closely resembled the type of executive that the Constitution envisioned. He was elected by the people rather than the legislature, served for three years, and was eligible for reelection. The New York governor also had a legislative veto power and considerable control over appointments to politically controlled jobs. The arguments the New Yorkers made on behalf of the strong executive relied heavily on the philosophy of John Locke. Locke saw the general superiority of a government of laws created by legislatures, but he also saw the need for an executive with more flexible leadership powers, or what he called "prerogative powers." Legislatures are unable, Locke wrote, "to foresee, and so by laws to provide for all accidents and necessities." They also are, by virtue of their size and unwieldiness, too slow to alter and adapt the law in a time of crisis. In these circumstances, the executive can step in to pursue policies in the public's interest. Prerogative power, then, is "the people's permitting their rulers to do several things of their own free choice where the law was silent, and sometimes too, against the direct letter of the law, for the public good, and their acquiescing in it when so done." The check on the use of such power was to be whether the legislature would decide to go along with it.[11]

Although there was support for this view, the Antifederalists were concerned that if such powers were viewed as open-ended, they could give rise to the type of oppressive leader the framers were trying to avoid. Madison attempted to reassure the opponents of executive power, arguing that any prerogative powers would have to be clearly enumerated in the Constitution. In fact, the Constitution explicitly provides only one extraordinary executive power: the right to grant reprieves and pardons, which means the president can forgive any crimes against the federal government.

The second contentious issue concerning the executive was the method of selecting a president. As one delegate, James Wilson, explained, "This subject has greatly divided the House [the convention], and will also divide the people out of doors. It is in truth the most difficult of all on which we have had to decide."[12] The problem was so severe because it cut across many of the other central tensions facing the framers. The way the president was elected incorporated the issues of majority rule and minority rights, state versus national power, and the nature of executive power itself. Would the president be elected by the nation as a whole, by the states, or by coalitions within Congress? If the state-level governments played a central role, would this mean that the president could not speak for national interests? If the president were elected by Congress, could the executive still provide a check on the legislative branch?

Most Americans do not realize how unique our presidential system is and how close we came to having a parliamentary system, which is the form of government in most other established democracies. In a **parliamentary system**, the executive branch depends on the support of the legislative branch. The Virginia Plan proposed that the president be elected by Congress, just as the British prime minister is elected by Parliament, and this was the preferred solution for the first two months of the convention. However, there were lingering concerns that the president would be too beholden to Congress, so the matter was referred back to a committee in late August. On September 4, the committee recommended that the president be selected by an electoral college, representation in which would be based on the number of representatives and senators each state has in Congress, and that each state's legislature would determine the method for choosing their state's electors.[13] Ten days before the convention adjourned, the delegates approved this recommendation by a vote of 9 to 2.

Why did the delegates favor this complicated, indirect way of electing the president? One prominent political scientist argues that they had simply run out of

parliamentary system A system of government in which legislative and executive power are closely joined. The legislature (parliament) selects the chief executive (prime minister) who forms the cabinet from members of the parliament.

alternatives and this was the only widely acceptable solution. He says, "What this strange record suggests to me is a group of baffled and confused men who finally settle on a solution more out of desperation than confidence."[14] As with all good compromises, all sides could claim victory to some extent. Advocates of state power were happy because state legislatures played a central role in presidential elections; those who worried about the direct influence of the people liked the indirect manner of election; and the proponents of strong executive power were satisfied that the president would not simply be an agent of Congress. However, the solution had its flaws and clearly did not work out the way the framers intended. First, if the electoral college was supposed to provide an independent check on the voters, it never played this role because the framers did not anticipate the quick emergence of political parties. Electors quickly became agents of the parties, as they remain today, rather than independent actors who would use their judgment to pick the most qualified candidate for president. Second, the emergence of parties also created what was arguably the biggest technical error in the Constitution: the provision that gave each elector two votes and elected the candidate with the most votes as president and the second-place finisher as vice president. With electors acting as agents of parties, they ended up casting one vote each for the presidential and vice presidential candidate of their own party. This created a tie in the 1800 presidential election when Thomas Jefferson and Aaron Burr each received seventy-three electoral votes. The problem was easily fixed by the 12th Amendment, which required that electors cast separate ballots for president and vice president.

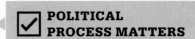

NATIONAL POWER VERSUS STATE AND LOCAL POWER

Tensions over the balance of power cut across virtually every debate at the convention: presidential versus legislative power, whether the national government could supercede state laws, apportionment in the legislature, slavery, regulation of commerce and taxation, and the amending process. The overall compromise that addressed these tensions was the second of Madison's "double protections," the system of federalism, which divided power between autonomous levels of government that controlled different areas of policy.

Federalism is such an important topic that we devote the entire next chapter to it, but two brief points about it should be made here. First, federalism is an example of how nuanced and careful compromises can alter the Constitution's meaning by changing a single word. The 10th Amendment, which was added to the Constitution as part of the Bill of Rights shortly after ratification, was a concession to the Antifederalists who were concerned about the national government gaining too much power in the new political system. The 10th Amendment says, "The powers not delegated to the United States by the Constitution, nor prohibited by it to the States, are reserved to the States respectively, or to the people." This definition of **reserved powers** was viewed as setting outer limits on the reach of national power. However, the Antifederalists were not happy with this wording because of the removal of a single word; they wanted the 10th Amendment to read, "The powers not *expressly* delegated to the United States," which would have more explicitly restricted national power. With the word "expressly" removed, the amendment became much more ambiguous and less restrictive of national power. Indeed, the Supreme Court did not use the amendment to strike down an act of Congress until 1871. However, between 1918 and 1937 and then again starting in the 1990s, the Supreme Court frequently invoked the 10th Amendment to nullify various laws passed by Congress as unconstitutional instrusions on the reserved powers of the states. (See the discussion in Chapter 3 of the Supreme Court's recent preference for state-centered federalism.) Second, the **national supremacy clause** of the

reserved powers As defined in the 10th Amendment, powers that are not given to the national government by the Constitution, or not prohibited to the states, are reserved by the states or the people.

national supremacy clause Part of Article VI, Section 2, of the Constitution stating that the Constitution and the laws and treaties of the United States are the "supreme Law of the Land," meaning national laws take precedent over state laws if the two conflict.

Constitution (Article VI) says that any national law is the supreme law of the land and takes precedence over any state law that conflicts with it. This is especially important in areas where the national and state governments have overlapping responsibilities for policy.

SLAVE STATES VERSUS NONSLAVE STATES

Slavery was another nearly insurmountable issue for the delegates. Southern states would not agree to any provisions limiting slavery. Although the nonslave states opposed the practice, they were not willing to scuttle the entire Constitution by taking a principled stand. Even after these basic divisions had been recognized, many unresolved issues remained between the slave and nonslave states. Could the importation of slaves be restricted in the future? How would northern states deal with runaway slaves? And most importantly, how would the slave population be counted for the purpose of slave states' representation in Congress?

The deals that the delegates cut on the issue of slavery illustrate the two most common forms of compromise: splitting the difference and logrolling (trading votes). Splitting the difference is familiar to anyone who has haggled over the price of a car or bargained for something at a flea market. Let's say the list price on the car is $20,000. You walk into the car dealership armed with the dealer invoice price, which is $18,500. You also know that there is a factory–dealer incentive of $500, which goes directly to the dealer, reducing its costs to $18,000. The highest price you are willing to pay is $18,500, so you start with an offer of $18,000 and the dealer counters with $19,000. You end up meeting halfway, or splitting the difference, and you buy the car for $18,500. Logrolling is when politicians trade votes for one another's pet projects.

The delegates went through similar negotiations over how slaves would be counted for purposes of states' congressional representation. The states had been through this debate once before, when they addressed the issue of taxation under the Articles of Confederation. At that point, the slave states argued that slaves should not be counted because they did not receive the same benefits as citizens and were not the same burden to the government. Nonslave states countered that slaves should be counted the same way as citizens when determining a state's fair share of the tax burden. They reached a compromise by agreeing that slaves would count as three-fifths of a person for purposes of taxation. The arguments over the issue of representation were even more contentious at the Constitutional Convention. Here the positions were precisely reversed, with slave states arguing that slaves should count like everyone else for the purposes of determining the number of House representatives for each state. Once again both sides managed to agree on the **Three-fifths Compromise** (it passed by a vote of 6 to 2, with two states divided evenly, so their votes did not count; a motion to count slaves the same as citizens was voted down 8 to 2).

The other two issues, the importation of slaves and dealing with runaway slaves, were handled by logrolling with an element of splitting the difference as well. Logrolling is more likely than splitting the difference when the issue cannot be neatly divided. For example, northern states either would be obligated to return runaway slaves to their southern owners or they would not. There was no way to split the difference. On issues with no clear middle ground, opposing sides will look for other issues on which they can trade votes. The nonslave states wanted more national government control

Three-fifths Compromise The states' decision during the Constitutional Convention to count each slave as three-fifths of a person in a state's population for the purposes of determining the number of House members and the distribution of taxes.

▼ A slave auction in Virginia. Slavery created several problems at the Constitutional Convention: Would there be limits on the importation of slaves? How would runaway slaves be dealt with by nonslave states? And how would slaves be counted for the purposes of congressional representation?

over commerce and trade than under the Articles, a change that slave states opposed. So a logroll, or vote trade, developed as a way to compromise the competing regional interests of slavery and regulation of commerce. Northern states agreed to return runaway slaves, and the southern states agreed to allow Congress to regulate commerce and tax imports with a simple majority vote (rather than the super-majority required under the Articles).

The importation of slaves was also included as part of this logroll, along with some split-the-difference negotiating. Northern states wanted to allow future Congresses to ban the importation of slaves (a likely prospect because the southern states did not control a House or Senate majority). Southern states wanted to allow the importation of slaves to continue indefinitely, arguing that slavery was essential to produce their labor-intensive crops. The committee that examined this issue recommended that the slave trade not be restricted until after 1800, but this was extended to 1808 after further negotiations between the states. The final language resulting from this part of the logroll was inserted in Article I, Section 9, and was included in Article V, which prevented a constitutional amendment from banning the slave trade until 1808.[15]

From a modern perspective it is difficult to understand how the framers could have taken such a purely political approach to the moral issue of slavery. Many of the

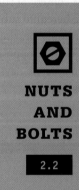

NUTS AND BOLTS

2.2

Major Compromises at the Constitutional Convention

	POSITION OF THE LARGE STATES	POSITION OF THE SMALL STATES	COMPROMISE
Apportionment in Congress	By population	State equality	Great Compromise created the Senate and House
Method of election to Congress	By the people	By the states	House elected by the people; Senate elected by the state legislatures
Electing the executive (president)	By the states	By Congress	By the electoral college
Who decides federal–state conflicts?	Some federal authority	State courts	State courts to decide[a]
	POSITION OF THE SLAVE STATES	**POSITION OF THE NONSLAVE STATES**	**COMPROMISE**
Control over commerce	By the states	By Congress	By Congress, but with twenty-year exemption for the importation of slaves
Counting slaves toward apportionment	Counted 1:1 like citizens	Not counted	Three-fifths Compromise
	POSITION OF THE FEDERALISTS	**POSITION OF THE ANTIFEDERALISTS**	**COMPROMISE**
Protection for individual rights	Secured by state constitutions; national Bill of Rights not needed	National Bill of Rights needed	Bill of Rights passed by the 1st Congress; ratified by all states as of December 1791

[a] This was changed by the Judiciary Act of 1789, which provided for appeals from state to federal courts.

▲ Union and Confederate troops clash in close combat in the Battle of Cold Harbor, Virginia, in June 1864. The inability of the framers to resolve the issue of slavery allowed tensions over the issue to grow throughout the early nineteenth century, culminating in the Civil War.

delegates believed slavery was immoral, yet they were willing to negotiate for southern states' support of the Constitution. Some southern delegates were apologetic about slavery, even as they argued for protecting their interests. Madison's notes give this example of a delegate from Virginia:

He urged strenuously that express security ought to be provided for including slaves in the ratio of Representation [this refers to the Three-fifths Compromise]. He lamented that such a species of property existed. But as it did exist the holders of it would require this security.[16]

Many constitutional scholars view the convention's treatment of slavery as its central failure. In fairness to the delegates, it is not clear that they could have done much better if the goal was to create a document that all states would support. However, the delegates' inability to resolve this issue meant that it would simmer below the surface for the next seventy years, finally boiling over into the bloodiest of all American wars, the Civil War.

The convention ended on a relatively harmonious note with Benjamin Franklin moving adoption. Franklin's motion was worded ambiguously to allow those who still had reservations to sign the Constitution anyway. Franklin's motion was in the "following convenient form," "Done in Convention by the unanimous consent of the States present the 17th of September . . . In Witness whereof we have hereunto subscribed our names." His clever wording meant that the signers were only bearing witness to the approval by the states and therefore could still, in good faith, oppose substantial parts of the document. Franklin's motion passed with ten ayes, no nays, and one delegation divided. All but three of the remaining delegates signed.

Ratification

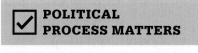

POLITICAL PROCESS MATTERS

Article VII of the Constitution, which described the process for ratifying the document, was also designed to maximize its chance of success. Only nine states were needed to ratify, rather than the unanimity rule that had applied to changing the Articles of Confederation. Equally important, ratification votes would be taken in state conventions set up specifically for that purpose, bypassing the state legislatures, which would be more likely to resist some of the Constitution's state–federal power-sharing arrangements.

The near-unanimous approval at the Constitutional Convention's end masked the very strong opposition that remained. Many delegates simply left the convention when it became clear that things were not going their way. Rhode Island sent no delegates and refused to appoint a ratification convention; more ominously, New York seemed dead set against the Constitution, and Pennsylvania, Virginia, and Massachusetts were split. The ratifying conventions in each state subjected the Constitution to intense scrutiny, as attendees examined every sentence for possible objections. A national debate raged over the next nine months.

The Antifederalists had many concerns about the Constitution, but they were most worried about the role of the president, the transfer of power from the states to the national government, and the lack of specific guarantees of civil liberties. In short, they feared that the national government would become tyrannical. The doubts about the single central executive were expressed by Patrick Henry, a leading Antifederalist.

Speaking to the Virginia ratifying convention, Henry was mocking in his indictment, "Your president may easily become a king. . . . There will be no checks, no real balances in this government. What can avail your specious, imaginary balances, your rope dancing, chain rattling, ridiculous ideal checks and contrivances."[17] Even Thomas Jefferson complained that the president seems like a "bad edition of a Polish King," in that he would control the armed forces and also could be reelected indefinitely.[18] State power and the ability to regulate commerce were also central concerns. States such as New York would lose substantial revenue if they could no longer charge states tariffs on goods that came into their ports. Other states were especially concerned that they would pay a disproportionate share of national taxes.

The Antifederalists' most important objection was the lack of protections for civil liberties in the new political system. During the last week of the convention, Elbridge Gerry and George Mason offered a resolution "to prepare a Bill of Rights." However, the resolution was unanimously defeated by the state delegations for a variety of reasons. Some believed that the national government posed no threat to liberties such as freedom of the press because it did not have the power to restrict them in the first place. Others thought that because it would be impossible to enumerate all rights, it was better to list none at all. Federalists such as Roger Sherman argued that state constitutions, most of which protected freedom of speech, freedom of the press, right to a trial by jury, and other civil liberties, would be sufficient to protect liberty. However, many Antifederalists still wanted assurances that the *national* government would not trample their rights.

The Federalists counterattacked on several fronts. First, supporters of the Constitution gained the upper hand in the debate by claiming the term "federalist." It is a common tactic in debates to co-opt a strong point of the opposing side as a positive for your side. The opponents to the Constitution probably had a stronger claim than its supporters to being federalists—that is, those who favor and emphasize the autonomous power of the state governments. Today, for example, the Federalist Society is a conservative group organized around the principles of states' rights and limited government. By calling themselves Federalists, the supporters of the Constitution asserted that they were the true protectors of states' interests, which irritated the Antifederalists to no end. The Antifederalists also had the rhetorical disadvantage of having "anti" attached to their name, defining them in terms of their opponents' position rather than their own. But the problem was more than just rhetorical—the Federalists were quick to point out that the Antifederalists did not have their own plan to solve the problems created by the Articles.

Second, the Federalists published a series of eighty-five articles that came to be known as the *Federalist Papers*. Because these articles were aimed at convincing New Yorkers to ratify the Constitution, they were originally published in New York newspapers, but they were widely read throughout the nation. The *Federalist Papers* should be viewed as political propaganda because they were one-sided arguments aimed at changing public opinion; the authors downplayed potentially unpopular aspects of the new system, such as the power of the president, while emphasizing points they knew would appeal to the opposition. Despite their biased arguments, the *Federalist Papers* are the best comprehensive discussion of the political theory underlying the Constitution and the framers' interpretations of many of its key provisions.

Third, the Federalists agreed that the new Congress's first order of business would be to add a **Bill of Rights** to the Constitution to protect individual rights and liberties. This promise was essential for securing the support of New York, Massachusetts, and Virginia. The ninth state, New Hampshire, ratified the Constitution on June 21, 1788, but New York and Virginia were still dragging their

Bill of Rights The first ten amendments to the Constitution; they protect individual rights and liberties.

necessary and proper clause Part of Article I, Section 8, of the Constitution that grants Congress the power to pass all laws related to one of its expressed powers; also known as the elastic clause.

heels, and their support was widely viewed as necessary for the legitimacy of the United States, even if it technically was not needed. By the end of the summer, both Virginia and New York finally voted for ratification, the latter by a narrow 30-to-27 vote. Two remaining states, Rhode Island and North Carolina, refused to ratify until Congress made good on its promise of a Bill of Rights. The 1st Congress submitted twelve amendments to the states, and ten were ratified by all the states as of December 15, 1791.

The Constitution: A Framework for Government

The Constitution certainly has its flaws, primarily its undemocratic qualities such as the indirect election of senators and the president, the compromises that suppressed the issue of slavery, and the absence of any general statement about citizens' right to vote. However, given the delegates' political context and the various factions that had to be satisfied, the Constitution's accomplishments are substantial. The document's longevity is testimony to the framers' foresight in crafting a flexible framework for government. Perhaps its most important feature is the system of separation of powers and checks and balances that prevent majority tyranny, while maintaining sufficient flexibility for decisive leadership during times of crisis, such as the Civil War, the Great Depression, and World War II. At the national level, the system of checks and balances means that each branch of government has certain exclusive powers, some shared powers, and the ability to check the other two branches (see Nuts and Bolts 2.3).

EXCLUSIVE POWERS

The framers viewed Congress as the "first branch" of government and granted it significant exclusive powers. With the popularly elected House of Representatives and the Senate indirectly elected by state legislatures, Congress was designed to be both the voice of the people and an institution more removed from the people, with a significant role in domestic and foreign policy. Congress was given the power to raise revenue for the federal government through taxes and borrowing, regulate interstate and foreign commerce, coin money, establish post offices and roads, grant patents and copyrights, declare war, "raise and support armies," make rules for the military, and create and maintain a navy. The most important of these powers is the so-called power of the purse—control over taxation and spending—given to Congress in Article I, Section 8, of the Constitution: "No money shall be drawn from the Treasury, but in consequence of appropriations made by law." Or as Madison put it, "the legislative department alone has access to the pockets of the people." Congress's exclusive powers take on additional significance through the **necessary and proper clause**, also known as the elastic clause, which gives Congress the power to "make all Laws which shall be necessary and proper for carrying into Execution the foregoing Powers, and all other

▼ *Two of Congress's exclusive powers are to raise and support armies and the power of the purse. The war in Iraq produced congressional struggles over whether the power to deny war funding should be used to force the executive branch to agree to a timetable for bringing troops home. Here, U.S. tanks patrol Sadr City, a Shiite stronghold in Baghdad, Iraq.*

Checks and Balances

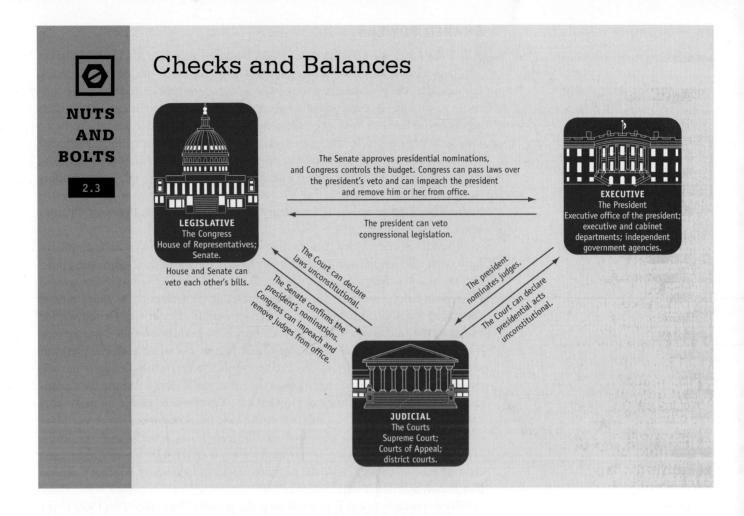

The Senate approves presidential nominations, and Congress controls the budget. Congress can pass laws over the president's veto and can impeach the president and remove him or her from office.

The president can veto congressional legislation.

LEGISLATIVE
The Congress
House of Representatives;
Senate.

House and Senate can veto each other's bills.

The Court can declare laws unconstitutional.

The Senate confirms the president's nominations. Congress can impeach and remove judges from office.

The president nominates judges.

The Court can declare presidential acts unconstitutional.

EXECUTIVE
The President
Executive office of the president; executive and cabinet departments; independent government agencies.

JUDICIAL
The Courts
Supreme Court;
Courts of Appeal;
district courts.

Powers vested by this Constitution in the Government of the United States, or in any Department or Officer thereof." This broad grant of power meant that Congress could pass laws related to any of its exclusive powers. For example, while the Constitution did not explicitly mention Congress's right to compel people to serve in the military, its power to enact a draft was clearly given by the necessary and proper clause, in conjunction with its power to "raise and support armies."

Congress's exclusive powers are far more numerous and specific than the limited powers granted to the president. The president, as the commander in chief of the armed forces, has power to receive ambassadors and foreign ministers and to issue pardons. The president's most important powers are contained in the executive powers clause that says, "The executive power shall be vested in a President of the United States of America," and in the directive to ensure "that the laws are faithfully executed." As we see later in the chapter, these Article II clauses have given the president most of his power.

The courts did not receive nearly as much attention in the Constitution as either Congress or the president. The framers devoted only six short paragraphs to the third branch of government. Alexander Hamilton argued in *Federalist* 78 that the Supreme Court would be the "least dangerous branch," because it had "neither the power of the purse nor the sword." The most important positive powers that the framers gave the Supreme Court were lifetime tenure for justices in good behavior and relative independence from the other two branches. The critical negative power of judicial review, the ability to strike down the laws and actions of other branches, will be discussed below.

SHARED POWERS

Along with dividing the exclusive powers between branches, checks and balances also designate some shared powers, areas where no branch has exclusive control. For example, the president has the power to negotiate treaties and make appointments to the federal courts and other government offices, but these executive actions are to be undertaken with the "advice and consent" of the Senate, which means they were intended to be shared powers. In the twentieth century, these particular powers became executive-centered, with the Senate providing almost no advice to the president and routinely giving its consent (often disapprovingly called "rubber stamping"). However, the Senate can assert its shared power, as shown by the Senate's blocking of several of President George W. Bush's and President Obama's lower court nominees.

The war powers, which include decisions about when and how to use military force, were also intended to be shared but have become executive-dominated powers. The framers disagreed about who should control the war powers. Some wanted to keep the arrangement set up by the Articles of Confederation in which nine of the thirteen states had to agree before Congress could declare war. Others wanted to follow the British system in which the executive branch controlled war powers. The resulting compromise shows checks and balances at work, with the president serving as the commander in chief of the armed forces, while Congress has the power to declare war and to appropriate the funds to conduct a war. At the Constitutional Convention, the original proposal gave Congress the power to "make war" rather than "declare war." Clearly this would have been a far more significant grant of power, suggesting an ongoing role for Congress in the conduct of a war. Rufus King argued that the conduct of war was an executive function, while others argued that the president should have the power to repel a sudden attack but that Congress should have the power to declare war.

Since very early in our nation's history, the president has taken a lead role in the war powers, relegating Congress to the role of sideline critic or supporter. Presidents have authorized the use of American troops on hundreds of occasions, but Congress has declared war only five times. Of these five, Congress debated the merits of entering only one war, the War of 1812. The other "declarations" of war recognized a state of war that already existed. For example, after Japan bombed Pearl Harbor, Hawaii, in 1941 Congress's subsequent declaration of war formally recognized what everyone already knew. Instead, the president usually takes the lead in the decision to use military force. As the 2003 invasion of Iraq demonstrated, if a president is intent on going to war, Congress must go along or get out of the way.

▼ *Sonia Sotomayor is sworn in before the Senate Judiciary Committee at her confirmation hearings to become a justice of the Supreme Court. The president and the Senate share the appointment power to the federal courts: the president makes the nominations, and the Senate provides its "advice and consent."*

In a few instances, however, Congress wanted to declare war and the president resisted. For example, in 1895 and 1896 when Grover Cleveland was president, tensions were mounting in the United States over Cuba's struggle for independence from Spain. Congressional leaders tried to convince Cleveland of the merits of entering the war to help Cuba, but he refused. When a congressman reminded him that Congress had the power to declare war, Cleveland countered that he was the commander in chief, saying, "I will not mobilize the army. I happen to know that we can buy the Island of Cuba from Spain for $100 million and a war will cost vastly more than that. . . . It would be an outrage to declare war."[19]

Examples such as this are interesting because they are unusual. It would be impossible today for Congress to declare war without a willing commander in chief. However, since the Vietnam War, Congress has tried to redress the imbalance in the war powers in other ways. In 1970, during the Vietnam War, Congress passed a resolution that prevented any funds from supporting ground troops in Laos or Cambodia (nations that bordered Vietnam). In 1973 Congress attempted to gain more control over the use of U.S. troops in "undeclared wars" by passing the War Powers Resolution. This attempt largely failed and will be discussed in more detail in later chapters. Then in the 1980s, Democrats in Congress prevented President Ronald Reagan from using any appropriated funds to support the Contra rebels in their fight against the Sandinista government in Nicaragua.[20] These examples show that while the president continues to dominate the war powers, Congress can assert its power when it has the will, just as it can by advising the president in treaty negotiations or withholding approval of the president's nominees for appointed positions.

NEGATIVE OR CHECKING POWERS

The last leg of the system of checks and balances is the negative power that the branches have over each other. Congress has two important negative checks on the other two branches: impeachment and the power of the purse. **Impeachment** was based on the British practice of removing unpopular or corrupt ministers of the king through a vote of no confidence, but the framers made one important change. The president, vice president, or other "officers of the United States" (including federal judges) could not be removed for political reasons, but rather only for abuses of power, specifically "Treason, Bribery, or other High Crimes or Misdemeanors." Some framers wanted impeachment to be a political vote of no confidence that could be initiated by a majority of the state legislatures or, in another proposed version, the state governors. Instead, they decided to place this central check with Congress as part of the overall move toward centralizing power at the national level.

The **power of the purse** can be an important check as well. Congress can punish executive agencies by freezing or cutting their funding or holding hearings on, investigations of, or audits of their operations to make sure money is being spent properly. Though the Constitution prevents Congress from lowering judges' salaries, they can freeze salaries to show displeasure with court decisions. Congress also has the power to alter the jurisdiction of the federal courts, limiting the issues they can consider, an extreme step that it has taken on several occasions. Congress can limit the discretion of judges in other ways, such as setting federal sentencing guidelines that recommend a range of years in prison that should be served for various crimes. Frustrated that some federal judges are ignoring the guidelines and handing out too many sentences more lenient than the recommendations, in 2003 Congress passed a law that requires the Justice Department to keep information on the sentencing record of every federal judge and forward this information to the House and Senate Judiciary Committees. This law drew a strong rebuke from then–chief justice William Rehnquist, who saw it as a threat to judicial independence. In his 2003 year-end report, Rehnquist said the law "could appear to be an unwarranted and ill-considered effort to intimidate individual judges in the performance of their judicial duties."[21] Even today the system of checks and balances is not fixed in stone but evolves according to the changing political climate.

The framers placed important checks on congressional power as well, and the president's most important check on Congress is the veto. Again there was very little agreement among the framers on this topic. The Antifederalists argued that it was "a political error of the greatest magnitude, to allow the executive power a negative, or in fact any kind of control over the proceedings of the legislature." On the other hand, the Federalists worried that Congress would slowly strip away

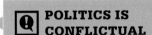

POLITICS IS CONFLICTUAL

impeachment A negative or checking power over the other branches that allows Congress to remove the president, vice president, or other "officers of the United States" (including federal judges) for abuses of power.

power of the purse The constitutional power of Congress to raise and spend money. Congress can use this as a negative or checking power over the other branches by freezing or cutting their funding.

presidential powers and leave the president too weak. Addressing this fear, Madison argued that the veto would "restrain the legislature from encroaching on the other coordinate departments, or on the rights of the people at large, or from passing laws unwise in their principle or incorrect in their form." Hamilton argued in *Federalist 73* that the veto was "chiefly designed" to counter "an immediate attack upon the constitutional rights of the Executive, or in a case in which the public good was evidently and palpably sacrificed." In the end, the Federalist view that the president needed some protections against the "depredations" of the legislature won the day. However, the veto has developed into a major policy-making tool for the president, which is probably broader than the check against "depredations" envisioned by the framers.

The president does not have any formal check on the courts other than the power to appoint judges (which does not always work out the way that presidents plan). However, presidents have, at various times, found unconventional ways to try to influence the courts. For example, Franklin D. Roosevelt tried to "pack the Court" by expanding the size of the Supreme Court with justices who would be sympathetic with his New Deal policies. More recently, George W. Bush attempted to expand the reach of executive power in the War on Terror by taking over some functions within the executive branch that previously had been performed by the courts. However, the Supreme Court struck down some of these policies as unconstitutional violations of defendants' due process rights. President Obama changed many of Bush's policies, such as harsh interrogation methods and excessive secrecy. But other Bush-era policies were either more difficult to change than Obama anticipated, such as the detainment of enemy combatants in the prison at Guantánamo Bay, or deemed necessary to fight terrorism, such as indefinite detention without trial for suspected terrorists who were arrested outside combat areas.[22] Critics are concerned that the expansion of executive power in order to fight terrorism has threatened the institutional balance of power by giving the president too much control over functions previously carried out by the courts.

The Constitution did not provide the Supreme Court with any negative checks on the other two branches. Instead, the practice of **judicial review**, the ability of the Supreme Court to strike down a law or an executive branch action as unconstitutional, was asserted by the Court much later, in the landmark decision of *Marbury v. Madison* in 1803. According to Madison's notes, nine of the eleven framers who spoke on the topic clearly favored explicitly granting the Supreme Court the power of judicial review, but the issue was not resolved at the convention. In several states, aggressive courts had struck down state laws, and delegates from those states resisted giving an unelected national court similar power over the entire country. While judicial review is not explicitly mentioned in the Constitution, supporters of the practice point to the supremacy clause, which states that the "Constitution, and the Laws of the United States which shall be made in Pursuance thereof . . . shall be the supreme Law of the Land." As Chief Justice John Marshall argued in *Marbury v. Madison*, in order to enforce the Constitution as the supreme law of the land, the Court must determine which laws are "in pursuance thereof." Critics of judicial review argue that the Constitution is supreme because it gains its legitimacy from the people, and therefore elected officials—Congress and the president—should be the primary interpreters of the Constitution rather than the courts. This dispute may never fully be resolved, but Marshall's bold assertion of judicial review made the Supreme Court an equal partner in the system of separate powers and checks and balances rather than "the least dangerous branch" that the framers described.

judicial review The Supreme Court's power to strike down a law or executive branch action that it finds unconstitutional.

The Question of Relevance: Is the Constitution a "Living Document"?

W. E. Gladstone, a great British prime minister of the late nineteenth century, called the American Constitution "the most wonderful work ever struck off at a given time by the brain and purpose of man."[23] On the other hand, Robert Dahl takes a more pragmatic view in asking, "Why should we feel bound today by a document produced more than two centuries ago by a group of fifty-five mortal men, actually signed by only thirty-nine, a fair number of whom were slaveholders, and adopted in only thirteen states by the votes of fewer than two thousand men, all of whom are long since dead and mainly forgotten?"[24]

Can the Constitution provide the blueprint for modern democratic governance? If so, how has it remained relevant after more than 200 years? The answer to the first question, in our opinion, is clearly yes. While the United States falls short on many measures of an ideal democracy, the Constitution remains relevant in part because it embodies many of the central values of American citizens: liberty and freedom, majority rule and minority rights, equal protection for all citizens under the laws, and a division of power across and within levels of government. The Constitution presents a list of substantive values, largely within the Bill of Rights, aimed at legally protecting certain individual rights that we still consider basic and necessary. The Constitution also sets out the institutional framework within which the government operates.

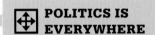

POLITICS IS EVERYWHERE

But these observations beg the question of *why* the Constitution remains relevant today. Why does this framework of government still work? How can the framers' values still be meaningful to us? There are at least four reasons that the Constitution continues to be a "living document": a willingness over the years to simply ignore the parts that become irrelevant, ambiguity in central passages that allows for flexible interpretation, the amending process, and the document's own designation of multiple interpreters of the Constitution. These factors have allowed the Constitution to evolve with the changing values and norms of the nation.

TURNING A BLIND EYE

Some parts of the Constitution are ignored today because they have no meaning in a modern context. For example, Article I, Section 4, says that "Congress shall assemble at least once in every Year," but the modern Congress is in session throughout the year (with various recesses). Nobody pays attention to this passage anymore because it simply does not matter. Another example is the 3rd Amendment's prohibition against the quartering of troops in someone's house without their consent. Today the idea that National Guard officers would roll up to your house and ask to sleep on your couch (or worse, kick you out of your bed) is absurd, but this was a real concern when the Constitution was written.

The tendency to ignore (or at least flexibly interpret) relevant passages can come into play in more meaningful ways as well. In the 2000 presidential election, George W. Bush and Dick Cheney nearly ran afoul of part of the 12th Amendment, which says that electors in the electoral college shall "vote by ballot for President

WHAT DO POLITICAL SCIENTISTS DO?

A Living Constitution?

Debates about how to interpret the Constitution are almost as old as the document itself. One question that dates back to the late nineteenth century is whether the document is a living Constitution—that is, should the Constitution be viewed as a flexible framework or a structural document that has fixed meaning? Those who think the former argue that a dynamic and modern society cannot be bound by ideas rooted in the late eighteenth century. Proponents of the other side of the debate fear that flexibility is a recipe for arbitrary law based on Supreme Court justices' individual preferences and biases. They offer an alternative perspective, called "originalism," that says constitutional interpretation must be based on the original meaning of the document and its amendments.

Political scientists, jurists, and legal scholars began articulating a vision of the living Constitution during the Progressive Era of the late nineteenth and early twentieth centuries. Woodrow Wilson, political scientist and president of the United States, described the Constitution as "the charter of a living government" and "the vehicle of a nation's life." One of the great Supreme Court justices, Oliver Wendell Holmes, wrote, "The provisions of the Constitution are not mathematical formulas. . . . They are organic, living institutions." [a]

This view gathered force during the Great Depression when the Supreme Court struck down as unconstitutional much of the early New Deal legislation proposed by Franklin D. Roosevelt and the Democratic Congress. One of the great constitutional scholars of the twentieth century, Edward Corwin, warned that if the Constitution did not meet the people's needs, its legitimacy would be undermined: "We shall value it [the Constitution] for the aid it lends to considered social purpose, not as a lawyer's document." [b]

Speaking forty years later, during the bicentennial of the Constitution, Thurgood Marshall, the first African American Supreme Court justice said, "I do not believe that the meaning of the Constitution was forever 'fixed' at the Philadelphia Convention." Noting the inability of the framers to deal with slavery, and the role of the Civil War, the civil rights movement, and the legislation of the 1950s and 1960s in bringing about legal equality for African Americans, Marshall said that he would celebrate a living Constitution that was "nurtured through two turbulent centuries of our own making." [c] Those on the other side of the debate include Supreme Court Justices Antonin Scalia and Clarence Thomas, who strongly reject the notion of a living Constitution and support a strict interpretation of the text of the document.

Political scientists who engage in this debate about the living Constitution

and Vice-President, one of whom, at least, shall not be an inhabitant of the same state with themselves." This would have put the Texas electors in a bind because both Bush and Cheney lived in Dallas, but Cheney changed his official state of residence to Wyoming. The courts dismissed legal challenges to this move, allowing the Texas electors to cast their votes for both Bush and Cheney. Whether this example demonstrates the courts' willingness to be flexible in their interpretation of the Constitution or a biased reading of the facts in Cheney's favor depends on your own interpretation.

executive powers clause Part of Article II, Section 1, of the Constitution that states, "The executive Power shall be vested in a President of the United States of America." This broad statement has been used to justify many assertions of presidential power.

AMBIGUITY

The second and far more important characteristic of the Constitution that has kept the document relevant is its ambiguity. Key passages were written in very general and therefore indeterminate language, which has allowed the Constitution to grow and evolve along with changing norms, values, and political contexts. This

are doing a type of research—normative theory—that is different from other work discussed in the What Do Political Scientists Do? boxes. Rather than examining empirical questions (what happened and why), they explore normative questions of right and wrong, just and unjust, or in this instance, the proper method for interpreting the Constitution. The method of these scholars is primarily textual analysis: they look at the text of the Constitution, Supreme Court decisions, and relevant historical documents to develop their arguments. For example, supporters of the living Constitution try to argue that their perspective is also consistent with the framers' intent, pointing out that the framers designed the document to be general and flexible so it would be relevant for many generations to come. They point to Edmund Randolph's advice to the Committee on Detail at the Constitutional Convention that it should "insert essential principles only; lest the operations of government should be clogged by rendering those provisions permanent and unalterable, which ought to be accommodated to times and events."[d] That is, essential principles were flexible enough to apply to times and events that could not be foreseen by the framers.

Bruce Ackerman, a law professor and political scientist at Yale University, is one of the most famous defenders of the living Constitution approach. He argues that the Constitution, the "official canon," is not as relevant for understanding the most important issues of the day as the "operational canon" based on landmark statutes and "superprecedents" (important Supreme Court decisions that shape other decisions on that topic). For example, he argues that *Brown v. Board of Education*, the Court decision that desegregated public schools, is more important than the Constitution's reference to a "republican form of government." According to Ackerman, "the living Constitution is organized on the basis of an operational canon that does not even assign primacy, much less exclusivity, to the official canon."[e]

Scholars and jurists from the originalist side of the debate strongly disagree. Political scientist Keith E. Whittington argues that "judges should not feel free to pour their own political values and ideals into the Constitution. . . . [T]he constant touchstone of constitutional law should be the purposes and values of those who had the authority to *make* the Constitution—not of those who are charged with governing under it and abiding by it."[f] Whittington goes on to argue that especially when striking down laws passed by Congress, the justification for the Court's decision must be found in an original understanding of the Constitution. Other scholars such as Yale law professor Akhil Reed Amar apply an originalist understanding to interpreting civil liberties.[g]

Although these normative questions concerning the living Constitution will never be resolved, research by political scientists plays an important role in shaping the debates. Answering the question about how justices *should* interpret the Constitution ultimately depends on one's broader views of the proper role of the Court within a representative democracy, but having the necessary tools and concepts is important for being able to engage that debate. ▪

Watch a video clip of political scientist Mark Graber discussing this topic at wwnorton.com/studyspace.

---

ambiguity was by design and political necessity, since the framers were well aware that the document would need to survive for generations, but in many instances the specific language that was written down was simply the wording that could be agreed upon.

Three of the most important parts of the Constitution are also among its most ambiguous: the necessary and proper (or elastic) clause, the **executive powers clause**, and the **commerce clause**. As discussed earlier, the necessary and proper clause gives Congress an extremely open-ended power to enact laws that are related to its **enumerated powers**, or those that are explicitly granted. But what does "necessary and proper" mean? Congress for the most part gets to answer that question. The executive powers clause is even more sparse in its language. Article II of the Constitution begins, "The executive Power shall be vested in a President of the United States of America." While it may not seem like much, this sentence has been used to justify a broad range of presidential actions, such as issuing executive orders or forming executive agreements with other nations. It is a broad delegation

commerce clause Part of Article I, Section 8, of the Constitution that gives Congress "the power to regulate Commerce . . . among the several States." The Supreme Court's interpretation of this clause has varied, but today it serves as the basis for much of Congress's legislation.

enumerated powers Powers explicitly granted to Congress, the president, or the Supreme Court in the first three articles of the Constitution. Examples include Congress's power to "raise and support armies" and the president's power as commander in chief.

of power because it does not define any boundaries for the "executive powers" it grants. This vague wording was necessary because the convention delegates could not agree on a definition of executive power. While this general wording was expedient for the framers, it also had the desirable consequence of making Article II flexible enough to serve the country, both in times that require strong presidential action, such as the Civil War, the Great Depression, or World War II, and also in times when the president was not as central, like the "golden age of Congress" in the late nineteenth century.

Perhaps the best illustration of the importance of ambiguity in the Constitution is the commerce clause, which gives Congress "the power to regulate commerce . . . among the several States." Again, the key words are not defined. What is "commerce," and what exactly does "among the states" mean? This ambiguity has allowed for different interpretations reflecting the prevailing norms of the time. In the nineteenth century, when the national government was relatively weak and more power was held at the state level, the Supreme Court interpreted the clause to mean that Congress could not regulate commerce that was entirely within the boundaries of a single state (intrastate commerce, as opposed to interstate commerce between states). Because manufacturing typically occurred within the boundaries of a given state, this ruling led to a distinction between manufacturing and commerce, which had significant implications. For example, Congress could not regulate working hours, worker safety, or child labor given that these were defined as part of manufacturing rather than commerce. In the New Deal era of the mid-1930s, the Court adopted a more expansive interpretation of the commerce clause that largely obliterated the distinction between intrastate and interstate commerce. This view was strengthened in the 1960s when the Supreme Court upheld a civil rights law that, among other things, prevented owners of hotels from discriminating against African Americans. As we discuss more fully in Chapter 3, Federalism, for nearly sixty years this interpretation held, but more recently the Supreme Court has tightened the scope of Congress's powers to regulate commerce. The commerce clause has been unchanged since 1789, but its ambiguous wording has been used to justify or restrict a varying array of legislation.

POLITICS IS EVERYWHERE

CHANGING THE CONSTITUTION

The most obvious way that the Constitution keeps up with the times is by allowing for changes to its language. The idea behind Article V, which lays out the formal process for amending the Constitution, was broadly supported by the framers: the people must control their own political system, which included the ability to change it through a regular, nonviolent process. George Washington called constitutional amendments "explicit and authentic acts" and Thomas Jefferson was adamant that each generation needed to have the power to change the Constitution. Toward the end of his life, he wrote in a letter to James Madison:

> Some men look at constitutions with sanctimonious reverence, and deem them like the ark of the covenant, too sacred to be touched. They ascribe to the men of the preceding age a wisdom more than human, and suppose what they did to be beyond amendment. I knew that age well; I belonged to it and labored with it. . . . It was very like the present . . . Let us not weakly believe that one generation is not as capable as another of taking care of itself.[25]

While there was strong consensus on including in the Constitution a set of provisions for amending it, there was no agreement on exactly how this should be done.

The U.S. Constitution as a Model for Other Nations

Albert P. Blaustein, a Rutgers law professor who helped draft more than forty constitutions worldwide, called the Constitution "America's most important export." He argues, "Since that seventeenth day of September 1787, a one-document constitution has been deemed an essential characteristic of nationhood. Today, of the 192 independent nations of the world, all but a very few have such a constitution or are committed to having one." Many of those that do not have constitutions, such as the United Kingdom, New Zealand, and Israel, are democratic nations with "sophisticated constitutional jurisprudence but no one specific document that can be called a constitution." Blaustein also argues that the American Constitution influenced the development of federalism in Latin America:

Venezuela, Argentina, Mexico, and Brazil are federal states.[a]

Though this conventional view is correct in a limited sense—most nations do have constitutions, and our nation led the way—it is profoundly incorrect to view the United States as a model for the democracies around the world. As political scientist Graham Wilson points out, "No other advanced industrial democracy has emulated the American system."[b] Nearly every other democracy has some version of parliamentary government, in which the chief executive is a prime minister who is selected by the majority party (or coalition of parties) in the legislature. Very few nations have our system of congressional single-member district elections and none share our unique institution of the electoral college. Instead, most have some version of

proportional representation in which a broader range of parties compete for votes. Even the practice of judicial review that allows the courts to strike down actions taken by the legislative and executive branches is almost unique to the United States. (Germany, France, and Italy are among the few nations that have judicial review.)

The Iraqi people's extreme difficulties establishing a democracy illustrate the problems associated with exporting two important features of our political system. The separation of church and state was crucial to the American settlers who were fleeing religious persecution in Europe. But in many democracies around the world, the state embraces a specific religion, including Islam, Catholicism, and the Anglican Church of England. Religious leaders in Iraq have as much power as elected leaders. Placing control of the armed services in the hands of elected leaders is a foreign concept in many parts of the world where military leaders and elected officials operate with rival power bases. Sectarian militias in Iraq clashing with Iraq's government are a stark reminder that civilian control of the military is another American export that does not always travel well. ■

Many countries have no separation of church and state. Religious leaders are powerful political players in Iraq's fledgling democracy. This picture shows Iraqis holding posters of radical Shiite cleric Muqtada al-Sadr during a service in Kufa, Iraq, on March 28, 2008.

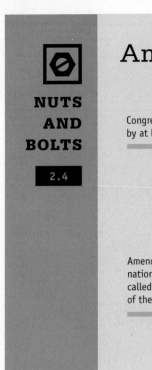

Amending the Constitution

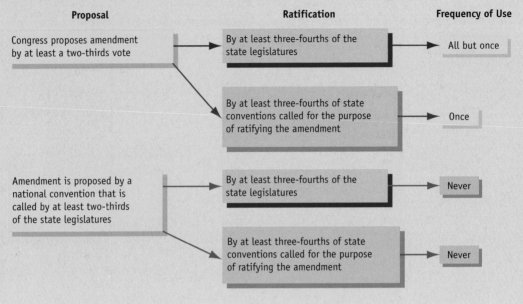

Proposal	Ratification	Frequency of Use
Congress proposes amendment by at least a two-thirds vote	By at least three-fourths of the state legislatures	All but once
	By at least three-fourths of state conventions called for the purpose of ratifying the amendment	Once
Amendment is proposed by a national convention that is called by at least two-thirds of the state legislatures	By at least three-fourths of the state legislatures	Never
	By at least three-fourths of state conventions called for the purpose of ratifying the amendment	Never

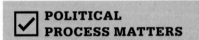

POLITICAL
PROCESS MATTERS

The Virginia Plan envisioned a relatively easy process of changing the Constitution "whensoever it shall seem necessary" by means of ratification by the people, while the New Jersey Plan proposed a central role for state governments. James Madison suggested the plan that was eventually adopted, which once again accommodated the views of those who wanted a stronger national government and those who favored the states. Article V describes the two steps necessary to change the Constitution: proposal and ratification. Congress may propose an amendment that has the approval of two-thirds of the members in both houses, or an amendment may be proposed by a national convention that has been called by two-thirds of the states' legislatures. In either case, the amendment must be ratified by three-fourths of the states' legislatures or state conventions (see Nuts and Bolts 2.4). A national convention has never been used to propose an amendment, and every amendment except for the twenty-first, which repealed Prohibition, has been ratified by state legislatures rather than state conventions.

Article V was a brilliant compromise that struck a balance between opposing views at the convention and made it neither too difficult nor too easy to amend the Constitution. However, the amending process has its flaws. First, one reason that a new constitutional convention has never been called is fear of a "runaway convention." Some scholars argue that nothing in Article V would constrain the convention to consider only a single issue, so it is possible that the convention could start from scratch, the way the framers did, even proposing a new method of ratification. Others dispute this view, but we have come close to finding out on several occasions. In the 1960s, thirty-five states—one short of the necessary two-thirds—called for a convention to propose a constitutional amendment that would overturn a Supreme Court decision concerning legislative redistricting. In the late 1970s, thirty states called for a convention to propose an amendment requiring a balanced federal budget. Even more troubling, Article V also does not specify voting procedures for a constitutional convention. Would votes be apportioned equally so that each state would have one vote (as was true at the 1787 convention), or would the voting power be based on population, or perhaps some mixture of the two, as in the electoral college? Article V is also silent on the mechanism for choosing delegates to attend the state conventions. Thus, there is a wide range in the different states' methods of selection. Delegates may be appointed by the governor, elected by the people, or comprised of the current state legislators.

Article V also does not address the question of time limits on amendments; rather, this issue has been left up to Congress. The 18th Amendment (Prohibition) was the first to have a time limit (it had to be ratified within seven years). All amendments before the 18th and some after have been approved by Congress and sent to the states for ratification without time limits. This led to the odd situation surrounding the 27th Amendment, which required that no legislation granting a congressional pay raise could go into effect until after the following election. This amendment was originally proposed in 1789 as part of the original Bill of Rights. It sat unratified for more than eighty years until Ohio ratified it to protest a congressional pay hike; however, no other states followed Ohio's lead. It sat for another 100 years until 1978, when Wyoming ratified the amendment. Then, in the early 1980s, the amendment gained national attention. From 1983 to 1992, enough states ratified the amendment to add it to the Constitution on May 7, 1992, after a lag of more than 202 years!

Most amendments have been wider-reaching than the 27th Amendment, but they have ranged from fairly narrow, technical corrections of errors in the original document (11th and 12th Amendments), to important topics such as the abolition of slavery (13th), mandating equal protection of the laws for all citizens (14th), providing for the popular election of senators (17th), giving blacks and then women the right to vote (15th and 19th), and allowing a national income tax (16th). Potential constitutional amendments have addressed many other issues, with more than 10,000 proposed; of those, thirty-three were sent to the states and twenty-seven have made it through the amending process (with the first ten coming at once in the Bill of Rights). Table 2.1 shows several amendments that were introduced but not ratified. The You Decide box outlines the debate over when it is appropriate to amend the Constitution.

MULTIPLE INTERPRETERS

The final way that the Constitution maintains its relevance is through changing interpretations of the document by multiple interpreters. As the discussion of the commerce clause pointed out, there have been significant changes over time in the way that the Constitution structures the policy-making process, even though the pertinent text of the Constitution has not changed.[26] This point is best understood by examining the concept of **implied powers**—that is, powers not explicitly stated in the Constitution but which can be inferred from an enumerated power. The Supreme Court often defines the boundaries of implied powers, but Congress, the president, and the public can also play key roles.

Three of the earliest examples of implied powers show the president, the Supreme Court, and Congress each interpreting the Constitution and contributing to its evolving meaning. The first involved the question of how active the president should be in stating national foreign policy principles. In issuing his famous proclamation of neutrality in 1793, George Washington unilaterally set forth a national foreign policy, even though the president's power to do so is not explicitly stated in the Constitution. Alexander Hamilton defended the presidential power to make such a proclamation as implied in both the executive powers clause and the

implied powers Powers supported by the Constitution that are not expressly stated in it.

TABLE 2.1   AMENDMENTS INTRODUCED IN CONGRESS THAT DID NOT PASS

Many proposed constitutional amendments have almost no chance of passing. Indeed, most of those listed here did not even make it to the floor of the House or Senate for a vote. Why do you think a member of Congress would propose an amendment that he or she knew would fail?

111th Congress (2009–2010)

Abolish the electoral college and provide for the direct election of the president and vice president

Provide a high-quality education to all citizens of the United States

Repeal the 16th Amendment (prohibit an income tax)

110th Congress (2007–2008)

Repeal the 22nd Amendment (abolish term limits for the president)

Provide the right to a clean, safe, and sustainable environment for all persons

Permit voluntary school prayer

Impose twelve-year term limits for the House and Senate

109th Congress (2005–2006)

Make the filibuster in the Senate a part of the Constitution

Provide for continuity of government in case of a catastrophic event

Prohibit desecration of the U.S. flag

108th Congress (2003–2004)

Include use of the word "God" in the Pledge of Allegiance and the national motto as protected speech

Define marriage in all states as a union between a man and a woman

Prohibit courts from protecting child pornography

107th Congress (2001–2002)

Include incarceration for minor traffic offenses in the 8th Amendment's definition of "cruel and unusual punishment"

Specify a right to "equal, high-quality" health care

Limit pardons granted between October 1 and January 21 of any presidential election year

Require a balanced budget without use of Social Security Trust Fund monies

SOURCE: The U.S. Constitution Online: Some Proposed Amendments, available at www.usconstitution.net/constamprop.html; http://thomas.loc.gov.

president's explicitly granted powers in the area of foreign policy (receiving ambassadors, negotiating treaties, and serving as commander in chief). Thomas Jefferson, on the other hand, thought it was a terrible idea for presidents to have that kind of power, preferring that such general policy statements be left to Congress.

The Supreme Court made its mark on the notion of implied powers in an early landmark case involving the creation of a national bank. In *McCulloch v. Maryland* (1819) the Court ruled that the federal government had the power to create a national bank and denied the state of Maryland the right to tax a branch of that bank.

Amending the Constitution

In a typical Congress there are between 50 and 100 proposals to amend the Constitution. Some of the proposed amendments reflect efforts to overturn particularly controversial Supreme Court decisions. Recent examples include amendments to prohibit abortion, guarantee the right to obtain an abortion, make flag desecration a crime, and permit prayer in public school. Some amendments are designed to change the government's basic structure and process, such as proposals to replace the electoral college with a direct popular vote, choose presidential electors at the congressional-district level, repeal the 22nd Amendment (which limits presidents to two terms), require a two-thirds congressional vote to raise taxes, impose term limits on representatives and senators, or repeal the 16th Amendment (which permitted a federal income tax). And some proposed amendments would guarantee specific benefits or create new classes of constitutionally guaranteed rights like affordable housing, quality health care, a clean environment, or full employment. Perhaps the most specific proposal is the one that would replace the 8th Amendment with, "Excessive bail shall not be required, nor excessive fines imposed, nor cruel and unusual punishments (including incarceration, before or after trial, for minor traffic offenses) inflicted." This proposed amendment was specifically designed to overturn the 2001 Supreme Court decision *Atwater v. Lago Vista*, in which the Court held by a 5–4 margin that the police can arrest and detain individuals for minor violations, such as not wearing a seatbelt, even if the violation itself would not result in a jail sentence. The amendment died in committee.

The only thing that cannot be changed in the Constitution is the equal apportionment of states' votes in the Senate (two senators per state).[a] Anything short of that is fair game, but many constitutional scholars argue that the amending process should not be used to address short-term, narrow policy issues such as term limits, burning the flag, the Pledge of Allegiance, or whether a person may be detained for not wearing a seatbelt. The only adopted amendments that fall into this category are Prohibition (which was subsequently repealed with another amendment) and the long-delayed 27th Amendment regarding congressional pay raises. The other amendments address broader policy concerns, expand or protect individual rights and liberties, modify electoral laws and institutions, or address basic concerns about the working of government. Constitutional scholar Kathleen Sullivan is critical of efforts to alter the Constitution. Constitutional principles should not, she concludes, be "up for grabs" or politicized but should be slow to change; amendments should be reserved for setting out the basic structure of government and defining "a few fundamental political ideals."[b] The alternative perspective chides those who "treat the Constitution like an untouchable religious text and the republic's founders as omniscient," and maintains that "meaningful democratic politics requires an aggressive constitutional politics."[c]

One area of debate concerns gay marriage. Many states have amended their constitutions to define marriage to exclude same-sex couples. Advocates of this view are pushing for an amendment to the Constitution to define marriage the same way at the national level. Would you support such an amendment? Try to separate your view on the specific issue, gay marriage, from your position on the question of amending the Constitution. If you oppose gay marriage, is it possible that the better path of action would be through the state legislatures? What kinds of policies would you favor addressing through constitutional amendments? Do you agree that amendments should be reserved for a "few fundamental political ideas"— things like the right to vote and the structure of government—or that more frequent amendments are necessary for "meaningful democratic politics"? ■

Some people argue that the Constitution should not be used to make policy, except for broader purposes such as expanding political rights or protecting equality. The 18th Amendment, ratified in 1919, prohibited the consumption of alcohol and is often upheld as an example of a failed policy attempt. In this 1933 photo, a beer distributor readies his first shipment following ratification of the 21st Amendment, which repealed Prohibition.

▲ The 8th Amendment's ban on "cruel and unusual punishment" is generally viewed as excluding capital punishment, but the execution of juveniles and the mentally retarded has been found unconstitutional. This picture shows the electric chair in the Southern Ohio Correctional Facility in Lucasville, Ohio.

The Court said it was not necessary for the Constitution to expressly grant Congress the power to create the bank; rather, it was implied in Congress's power over financial matters and from the necessary and proper clause of the Constitution.

Congress got into the act with an early debate over the president's implied power to remove appointed officials. The Constitution clearly gives the president the power to make appointments to cabinet positions and other top executive branch offices, but it is silent on how these people can be removed. This was one of the most difficult issues in the first Congress, and members spent more than a month debating the topic. The record of the debate is the most thorough examination of implied powers ever conducted in Congress. However, Congress ended up not taking any action on the issue, which left the president's removal power implicit in the Constitution.

Issues concerning implied powers have continued to surface frequently. The president's appointment powers have recently evolved as the Senate has played a much more aggressive role in providing its "advice and consent" on presidential nominations to the federal courts. As we explore more fully in Chapter 14, in the past twenty years the Senate has blocked court appointments at a significantly higher rate than it did in the first half of the twentieth century. Although this trend reversed when the Democrats gained unified control of the government and sixty seats in the Senate in 2009, those conditions only held until January 2010 when Republican Scott Brown won the special election to fill Ted Kennedy's seat. The relevant language in the Constitution is the same, yet the Senate's understanding of its role in this important process has changed.

Public opinion and social norms also influence the prevailing interpretation of the Constitution, as is evident in the evolving meanings of capital punishment and the freedom of speech. When the Constitution was written, capital punishment was broadly accepted, even for horse thieves. The framers were only concerned that people not be "deprived of life, liberty, or property without the due process of law." Therefore the prohibition in the 8th Amendment against "cruel and unusual punishment" certainly did not mean to the framers that the death penalty was unconstitutional. However, in 1972 the Supreme Court struck down capital punishment as unconstitutional because it was being applied arbitrarily.[27] Subsequently, after procedural changes were made, the Court once again upheld the practice. However, the Court has since decided that capital punishment for a mentally retarded man constituted cruel and unusual punishment—a decision that reflects modern sensibilities but not the thinking of the framers. Similarly, the text of the 1st Amendment protections for freedom of speech has never changed, but the Supreme Court has been willing to uphold significant limitations on free speech, especially in wartime. However, when external threats are less severe, the Court has been more tolerant of controversial speech.

The line between a new interpretation of the Constitution and constitutional change is difficult to define. Clearly not every new direction taken by the Court or new interpretation of the constitutional roles of the president or Congress is comparable to a constitutional amendment. In one respect, a constitutional amendment is much more permanent than a new interpretation by the Court. For example, the Supreme Court could not unilaterally decide that eighteen-year-olds, women, and African Americans no longer have the right to vote. Constitutional amendments expanded the right to vote to include these groups, and only further amendments could either expand or restrict the right to vote. However, gradual changes in constitutional interpretation are probably just as important as the amending process in explaining the Constitution's ability to keep pace with the times. Even the large "revolutions" in constitutional change have occurred by both means: the Civil War led to a **constitutional revolution** that was accomplished through three important amendments, whereas the New Deal constitutional revolution happened without changing a single word of the document.

constitutional revolution A significant change in the Constitution that may be accomplished either through amendments (as after the Civil War) or shifts in the Supreme Court's interpretation of the Constitution (as in the New Deal era).

Conclusion

To return to Dahl's challenge on the relevance of the Constitution, why should we pay attention to this document? Recent polls suggest that many Americans do not pay much attention to the Constitution and are even unfamiliar with its basic provisions. Indeed, a national poll found that only 42 percent of the public could name the three branches of government, although 73 percent could identify the Three Stooges (Larry, Moe, and Curly). Another survey was equally depressing: 24 percent of the public could not name any 1st Amendment rights, 52 percent did not know that the Senate has 100 members, and one-sixth thought that the Constitution created a Christian nation.[28]

To answer questions about the Constitution's relevance today, we only need to look at the examples discussed at the beginning of this chapter. In the first instance, the public's interpretation of the Constitution's grounds for impeachment was that Clinton's sexual transgressions and his lying about them did not rise to the level of a "high crime or misdemeanor." In the second case, the Supreme Court interpreted the Constitution in a manner that allowed the 2000 electoral crisis to be resolved. And although the fight against terrorism is still unfolding, the Constitution's self-corrective system of checks and balances means that when one branch of government gains too much power, the other two branches of government will fight back to restore the balance. In each example, the Constitution provided the basis for resolving the conflict.

A leading constitutional scholar, Walter Murphy, addresses the relevance issue this way: "The ideals that it enshrines, the processes it prescribes, and the actions it legitimizes must either help to change its citizenry or, at a minimum, reflect their current values. If a constitution does not articulate at least in general terms, the ideals that form or will reform its people and express the political character they have, it will soon be replaced or atrophy." The Constitution's ability to change with the times and reflect its citizens' values has allowed it to remain relevant and important today.

What were the sources of conflict at the Constitutional Convention?

- After the failed Articles of Confederation, the framers knew they had to create a stronger national government that could better deal with the economic problems of the new nation.
- While the framers agreed that the new government should be a representative democracy with the consent of the governed, their concerns about the self-interested nature of people and about individual and regional economic interests set the stage for a contentious Constitutional Convention.

How was compromise achieved at the Constitutional Convention?

- Five central tensions required political compromise between competing interests at the Constitutional Convention: majority rule versus minority rights; small states versus large states; legislative power versus executive power; national power versus state and local power; and slave states versus nonslave states.
- Each of these tensions had to be resolved through discussion, debate, and compromise, which included splitting the difference and logrolling.

How was the Constitution ratified?

- Despite the hard work of the framers at the Constitutional Convention, ratification of the document was far from assured.
- The Antifederalists worried that the president would be too powerful, that too much power was being transferred from the states to the national government, and that the document lacked specific guarantees of civil liberties.
- The *Federalist Papers*, written by James Madison, Alexander Hamilton, and John Jay, helped convince the skeptics, and by June 1788 the Constitution was ratified.

How is the Constitution a framework for government?

- The most important feature of the Constitution is the system of separation of powers and checks and balances. These arrangements prevent majority tyranny while maintaining sufficient flexibility for decisive leadership during times of crisis.
- At the national level, the system of checks and balances gives each branch of government certain exclusive powers, some shared powers, and the ability to check the power of the other two branches.

Is the Constitution a "living document"?

- The Constitution embodies many of the central values of American citizens: liberty and freedom, majority rule and minority rights, equal protection under the laws, and a division of power across and within levels of government.
- The Constitution has remained a "living document" that evolves with the changing values and norms of the nation for four main reasons: willingness to ignore the parts that become irrelevant, ambiguity in central passages that allows for flexible interpretation, the amending process, and multiple interpreters of its meaning.

STUDENT STUDYSPACE

Find quizzes and other review material at wwnorton.com/studyspace.

CRITICAL THINKING

1. Should the Constitution be a "living document" that evolves with the values and norms of our society, or should interpretation of the Constitution follow more closely the original intentions of the framers?
2. If you had been at the Constitutional Convention, which part of the document would you have worked to change? How would you have negotiated a compromise to make that change possible?

3. The Clinton impeachment scandal can be considered an example of how the public's interpretation of the Constitution influenced the way an event played out. What are some other examples of events changed by the public's interpretation of the Constitution?

KEY TERMS

Antifederalists (p. 36)
Articles of Confederation (p. 30)
Bill of Rights (p. 45)
commerce clause (p. 53)
"consent of the governed" (p. 33)
constitutional revolution (p. 60)
enumerated powers (p. 53)
executive powers clause (p. 53)
Federalist Papers (p. 34)
Federalists (p. 36)

Great Compromise (p. 39)
impeachment (p. 49)
implied powers (p. 57)
judicial review (p. 50)
limited government (p. 30)
monarchy (p. 29)
national supremacy clause (p. 41)
natural rights (p. 33)
necessary and proper clause (p. 46)

New Jersey Plan (p. 37)
parliamentary system (p. 40)
pluralism (p. 37)
power of the purse (p. 49)
republican democracy (p. 29)
republicanism (p. 32)
reserved powers (p. 41)
Three-fifths Compromise (p. 42)
Virginia Plan (p. 37)

SUGGESTED READING

Balkin, Jack M., ed. *The Constitution in 2020*. New York: Oxford University Press, 2009.

Currie, David P. *The Constitution of the United States: A Primer for the People*, 2nd ed. Chicago: University of Chicago Press, 2000.

Dahl, Robert A. *How Democratic Is the American Constitution?* New Haven, CT: Yale University Press, 2001.

Davis, Sue. *Corwin and Peltason's Understanding the Constitution*, 17th ed. Boston: Wadsworth Publishing, 2007.

Hamilton, Alexander, James Madison, and John Jay. *The Federalist Papers*. 1788. Reprint, 2nd ed., edited by Roy P. Fairfield. Baltimore, MD: Johns Hopkins University Press, 1981.

Ketcham, Ralph. *The Anti-Federalist Papers and the Constitutional Convention Debates*. New York: Signet Classics, 2003.

Kurland, Philip B., and Ralph Lerner, eds. *The Founders' Constitution*. Chicago: University of Chicago Press, 1987.

Rossiter, Clinton. *1787: The Grand Convention*. New York: MacMillan, 1966.

Sunstein, Cass R. *Designing Democracy: What Constitutions Do*. New York: Oxford University Press, 2001.

Wood, Gordon S. *The Creation of the American Republic*. New York: W. W. Norton, 1969.

In 1984, Congress decided to withhold federal highway funds from states that refused to raise the drinking age to twenty-one. Battles over the balance between federal and state power are inherent in our federalist system.

Federalism

In 1981, twenty-nine states and the District of Columbia allowed people over the age of either eighteen or nineteen to drink some types of alcohol. However, under intense lobbying from Mothers Against Drunk Driving and other organizations, Congress passed a law in 1984 that would withhold 5 percent of federal highway funds in 1986 and 10 percent for every year after from any state that did not raise the drinking age to twenty-one. Why didn't Congress simply pass a law making the national drinking age twenty-one? Establishing the drinking age had been viewed as a state power since the ratification of the 21st Amendment in 1933, which repealed Prohibition. Therefore, the only way that Congress could get states to change their laws was by using its "power of the purse" to induce them.

Several states challenged the law. However, in 1987 the Supreme Court ruled that although Congress did not have the power to directly implement a national drinking age, it was acceptable for Congress to "encourage" the states to adopt one.[1] It took twelve years for every state to fall in line.

CONFLICT AND COMPROMISE
in American Politics

Statistics suggest that the law is in the nation's interest. According to the National Highway Traffic Safety Administration (NHTSA), 50 percent of fatalities from car accidents in 1988 were alcohol-related. That number fell to 38 percent ten years later. From 1988 until 1998, the NHTSA showed that drivers who were between sixteen and twenty years old experienced the largest decrease in intoxication rates in fatal crashes (33 percent) for any age group in that period. Before 1986, young adults who lived in states with a drinking age of twenty-one drove to nearby states with lower age limits. As these intoxicated teens drove home, thousands were killed in accidents. Eliminating these age discrepancies helped reduce alcohol-related fatalities, saving as many as 1,250 lives a year.

Drinking laws illustrate the importance of our federal system. First, they are an example of the expansion of national power in the twentieth century to areas of policy previously reserved to the states. Second, they are evidence of the powerful political incentive to find national solutions to problems, even among politicians who normally prefer state power (many Republicans—typically supporters of states' rights—voted for the 1984 law). Finally, they remind us that disagreements between states can lead to intervention from the national government to resolve

SCHOOL OF EDUCATION
CURRICULUM LABORATORY
UM-DEARBORN

the dispute (states that already had a drinking age of twenty-one resented losing business to states with a drinking age of eighteen and were also upset because of the additional traffic deaths caused by the age discrepancies).

Before continuing, we should define some key terms and discuss how drinking laws and federalism more generally relate to our three themes. Federalism can be defined as a form of government that divides sovereign power across at least two political units. Sovereign power simply means that each unit of government (in the U.S. context, the national and state governments) has some degree of authority and autonomy, so states can do some things that the national government would not agree with, and in other areas, the national government holds sway over the states.

As discussed in Chapter 2, this division of power across levels of government is central to our system of separated powers. Though the concept of dividing power across levels of government is simple, the political battles over *how* that power is divided have been intense.

Disagreement over the proper distribution of power across levels of government is one way in which politics is conflictual. Recent examples include whether the national government should be able to prevent states from allowing marijuana use for medical purposes, allowing assisted suicides, or discriminating against their employees based on age or disability, or to compel states to ban guns within or around public schools or to require Americans to buy health insurance even if their state governments say they cannot be required to do so. These questions involve defining the frequently disputed boundaries between what the states and national government are allowed to do. Much of U.S. history has been rooted in this struggle to define American federalism. In some cases, disagreements are solved through compromise. Other cases are not so easily resolved and remain central to American politics.

The drinking laws, like many other examples in this chapter, also illustrate how much the political process matters. Congress's indirect route to affect changes in state laws through a combination of coercive penalties and incentive grants shows how the process of changing policy in a federal system can be quite slow and cumbersome. Because states control policy in many areas, it is difficult for the national government to get the states to change. If we had a single national government that could decide policy for the entire country, changes could be made much more easily.

Other than its impact on when you can legally start drinking, how does federalism affect your life? Answering this question illustrates that politics is everywhere. The results of these battles have tremendous consequences for all citizens. Not only must politicians and judges choose between emphasizing national power or state power, but decentralizing power across levels of government provides a much broader range of *individual-level* choices than a unitary system. For example, a retiree trying to decide where to live could choose between low-tax, low-service states such as Texas and high-tax, high-service states such as New York. Business owners often decide where to locate a new office or factory based on the balance between statewide income and education levels and an attractive "business climate," which depends on the corporate tax structure, environmental laws, regulatory policy, and levels of unionization of the workforce. States differ in these factors because our federal system gives states autonomy to choose policies that meet their residents' needs.

This chapter begins by defining federalism and showing how the balance between state and national power has evolved throughout our history, culminating with an examination of the particular tensions that have emerged in the past twenty years. We will also consider how the Supreme Court has shaped recent battles over federalism.

concurrent powers Responsibilities for particular policy areas, such as transportation, that are shared by federal, state, and local governments.

What Is Federalism?

A distinguishing feature of federalism is that each level of government has some degree of autonomy from the other levels; that is, each level can carry out some policies that may not be preferred by the other. In the United States, this means that the national and state governments have distinct powers and responsibilities. The national government, for example, is responsible for national defense and foreign policy. State and local governments have primary responsibility for conducting elections and promoting public safety. In other areas, such as transportation, the different levels of government share responsibilities in what are typically called the **concurrent powers** (see Nuts and Bolts 3.1). The national government has also taken on additional responsibilities through implied powers that are inferred from the powers explicitly granted in the Constitution (this will be discussed in more detail later in the chapter).

Local governments—cities, towns, school districts, and counties—are not autonomous units of government and therefore have a different place within our federal system than the national and state governments. Local governments are creatures of the state government. That is, state governments create local governments and control the types of activities they can engage in, by specifying in the state charter either what they *can* do or only what they *cannot* do—that is, they are allowed to do anything not specifically prohibited in the charter. This lack of autonomy does not imply that local governments are unimportant. Indeed they play the central role in providing public education, police and fire departments, and land use policies. They raise money through property taxes, user fees, and in some cases local sales taxes. But overall, local governments do not directly share power within our federal system with the state and national governments because of their lack of autonomy.

POLITICS IS EVERYWHERE

▼ *In unitary governments, power is centralized at the national level. For example, the British Parliament (the House of Commons is shown here) has complete authority over England, Scotland, Wales, and Northern Ireland.*

FEDERALISM IN COMPARATIVE PERSPECTIVE

This same observation about the place of local governments within our system may be made with respect to state governments by comparing U.S. federalism to forms of government in other countries. Just because a nation is comprised of states

National and State Responsibilities

NATIONAL GOVERNMENT POWERS	STATE GOVERNMENT POWERS	CONCURRENT POWERS
• Print money • Regulate interstate commerce and international trade • Make treaties and conduct foreign policy • Declare war • Provide an army and navy • Establish post offices • Make laws necessary and proper to carry out these powers	• Issue licenses • Regulate intrastate (within the state) businesses • Conduct elections • Establish local governments • Ratify amendments to the Constitution • Promote public health and safety • May exert powers the Constitution does not delegate to the national government or prohibit the states from using	• Collect taxes • Build roads • Borrow money • Establish courts • Make and enforce laws • Charter banks and corporations • Spend money for the general welfare • Take private property for public purposes, with just compensation

POWERS DENIED TO THE NATIONAL GOVERNMENT AND STATE GOVERNMENTS

DENIED TO THE NATIONAL GOVERNMENT	DENIED TO STATE GOVERNMENTS
• May not violate the Bill of Rights • May not impose export taxes among states • May not use money from the Treasury without an appropriation from Congress • May not change state boundaries	• May not enter into treaties with other countries • May not print money • May not tax imports or exports • May not interfere with contracts • May not suspend a person's rights without due process

SOURCE: GPO Access: Guide to the U.S. Government, available at http://bensguide.gpo.gov/3-5/government/federalism/html.

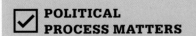
POLITICAL PROCESS MATTERS

unitary government A system in which the national, centralized government holds ultimate authority. It is the most common form of government in the world.

confederal government A form of government in which states hold power over a limited national government.

does not mean that it is a federal system. The key point again is the autonomy of the political subunit. The United Kingdom, for example, is comprised of England, Scotland, Wales, and Northern Ireland. In 1998, the British Parliament created a new Scottish government and gave it authority in a broad range of areas. However, Parliament could unilaterally dissolve the Scottish government; therefore the subunit (Scotland) is not autonomous. This type of government in which power is centralized within the national government is called a **unitary government**. Unitary governments are the most common in the modern world (about 80 percent); other examples include Israel, Italy, France, Japan, and Sweden. Although federalism is not as common, Australia, Austria, Canada, Germany, and Switzerland, among others, share this form of government with the United States (see Comparing Ourselves to Others).

At the opposite end of the spectrum from a unitary government is a **confederal government**, in which the states have most of the power and often even have veto power over the actions of the central government. This was the first type of government in the United States under the Articles of Confederation. As discussed in Chapter 2, there are many problems associated with having such a weak national government, thus there are few modern examples. The Commonwealth of Independent States (CIS), which was formed on December 21, 1991, after the breakup of the former Soviet Union, has had some success in coordinating the economic activity and security needs of twelve independent states.[2] The Commonwealth has a Council

Unitary versus Federal Systems

Unitary systems are about four times more common than federal systems. Why is this the case? The simplest reason is that federal systems are much more complicated and often involve disagreements over the division of power between the central and regional governments (in the United States, these disputes usually must be resolved in the courts). Second, some economists argue that decentralized federal systems undermine prudent financial management, producing slower economic growth and larger budget deficits than unitary systems. However, there is conflicting evidence on the impact of federalism on growth and budget deficits. One study found that if federal systems become more reliant on intergovernmental transfers (that is, grants from the central government to the states) and if states retain the ability to borrow independently, budget deficits tend to be higher. In contrast, if the central government in a federal system imposes borrowing restrictions on the states, or if states have a strong degree of autonomy for both taxing and borrowing, balanced budgets are more common. Unitary systems do not have to worry as much about lower levels of government as a source of national debt because the states have less fiscal autonomy.[a]

Federalism helps democracies deal with ethnic and national differences within their populations. For example, Canada's federal system provides French Canadians with autonomy in Quebec province.

Another potential drawback of federalism is that it promotes regional and ethnic separation. The former communist states of Eastern Europe demonstrate this point. Of those nine states, six were unitary and three were federal. The six unitary states have remained intact (in fact, they are now five states because East Germany has reunited with the Federal Republic of Germany), while the three federal states—Yugoslavia, the Soviet Union, and Czechoslovakia—have fractured into twenty-two independent states! Furthermore, most of the armed conflict in this region has occurred in these states.[b]

On the other hand, federalist systems are a useful tool for dealing with ethnic and national differences within countries. There are many multi-ethnic countries in the world, but very few of them are democracies—usually the iron fist of totalitarianism keeps these different factions together. In Iraq, for example, the Sunnis, Shiites, and Kurds were held together as one nation by Saddam Hussein's oppressive rule. When he was removed from power, the nation degenerated into sectarian violence as these groups struggled for power. Federalism made the fledgling democracy possible (the Kurds would never have agreed with the constitution without substantial autonomy), but the country may still split apart. There are several success stories of multinational or multi-ethnic democracies and all are federal: Switzerland, Canada, Belgium, Malaysia, India, and Spain.[c] Federalism allows each group, such as the French Canadians in Quebec, to have autonomy while remaining part of the larger country. ■

of Heads of State and Council of Heads of Government that produced hundreds of treaties and agreements in its first five years.[3] Over time, however, rifts among the member states have created problems, and today the CIS is viewed as largely ineffective.

Although true confederations are rare, intergovernmental organizations have proliferated in the past several decades. More than 1,200 multilateral organizations have been created by member nations seeking to coordinate their policies on, for example, economic activity, security, or environmental protection. The United Nations (UN), International Monetary Fund (IMF), and North Atlantic Treaty Organization (NATO) are some important examples. The European Union is an example of an intergovernmental organization that began as a loose confederation, but it is becoming more federalist in its decision-making process and structure.

Its relative success, compared to the failure of the CIS, can be explained in part by this move toward a more federal structure, while the CIS maintained its confederal structure.

Balancing National and State Power in the Constitution

Though the Founders wanted a national government that was stronger than it had been under the Articles of Confederation, they also wanted to preserve the autonomy of the states. These goals are reflected in different parts of the Constitution, which provides ample evidence for advocates of both state-centered and nation-centered federalism. The nation-centered position can point to the preamble of the Constitution, which begins, "We the People of the United States," compared to the Articles of Confederation that began, "We the undersigned delegates of the States." The Constitution's phrasing emphasizes the nation as a whole over the separate states.

Other aspects of the Constitution also support the nation-centered perspective. The Founders wanted a strong national government to provide national security and a healthy and efficient economy. As discussed in the previous chapter, Congress was granted the power to raise and support armies, declare war, and "suppress Insurrections and repel Invasion," while the president, as commander in chief of the armed forces, would oversee the conduct of war. Giving Congress the power to regulate interstate commerce centralized an important economic power at the national level, and many restrictions on state power had similar effects. States were *prohibited* from entering into "any Treaty, Alliance, or Confederation" or keeping troops or "Ships of War" during peacetime. They also could not coin money or impose duties on imports or exports (see Article I, Section 10). These provisions ensured that states would not interfere with the smooth operation of interstate commerce or create problems for national defense. Imagine, for example, that Texas had the power to tax oil produced in other states or that California decided to create its own army. This would create inefficiencies and potential danger for the rest of the country.

The necessary and proper clause of the Constitution, Article I, Section 8, which says that Congress has the power "To make all Laws which shall be necessary and proper for carrying into Execution the foregoing Powers," was a broad grant of power to the national government. The national supremacy clause, Article VI of the Constitution, says that the Constitution and all laws and treaties that are made under the Constitution shall be the "supreme Law of the Land" and "the Judges in every State shall be bound thereby, any Thing in the Constitution or Laws of any State to the Contrary notwithstanding." This is perhaps the clearest statement of the nation-centered focus of the Constitution. If any state law or constitution conflicts with national law or the Constitution, the national perspective wins.

Despite these clear examples of the Founders' nation-centered bias, many parts of the Constitution also address state powers and limits on national power. Article II gives the states the power to choose the electors for the electoral college, and Article V grants the states a central role in the process of amending the Constitution. Three-fourths of the states must ratify any constitutional amendment (either through conventions or the state legislatures, as specified by Congress), but the states can also bypass Congress in proposing amendments if two-thirds of the states call for a convention. This route to amending the Constitution has never been used, but the Founders clearly wanted to provide an additional check on national power. There are also limitations on Congress's authority to regulate interstate commerce. For example, it cannot favor one state over another in regulating commerce, and it cannot impose a tax on any good that is shipped from one state to another. Also Congress could not prohibit slavery until 1808, but it was allowed to impose a duty of up to $10 per slave.

Article I of the Constitution enumerates many specific powers for Congress, but the list of state powers is much shorter. This could be interpreted as more evidence for the nation-centered perspective, but at the time of the Founding, the default position was to keep most power at the state level. Therefore, the federal powers that were exceptions to this rule had to be clearly specified while state governments were given authority over all other matters. This view is supported by the 10th Amendment, which says, "The powers not delegated to the United States by the Constitution, nor prohibited by it to the states, are reserved to the states respectively, or to the people."

The 11th Amendment, the first one passed after the Bill of Rights, was another important affirmation of state sovereignty. Antifederalists were concerned that the part of Article III that gave the Supreme Court authority over cases involving a "State and Citizens of another State" would undermine state sovereignty by giving the Court too much power over state laws. Federalists, including Hamilton and Madison, assured them this would not happen, but the Supreme Court ruled in *Chisholm v. Georgia* (1793) that citizens of one state could sue the government of another state. The majority opinion ridiculed the "haughty notions of state independence, state sovereignty, and state supremacy." The states struck back by adopting the 11th Amendment, which made such lawsuits unconstitutional. While the Supreme Court lost this skirmish over state power, it continued to serve as the umpire in disputes between the national and state governments.

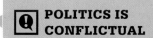

POLITICS IS CONFLICTUAL

Lastly, the **full faith and credit clause** of the Constitution is also very important for federalism and has elements that favor both the state- and nation-centered perspectives. Article IV specifies that states must respect each other's laws, granting citizens the "Full Faith and Credit" of their state's laws if they go to another state. For example, if you have a New York driver's license and are traveling to California, you do not need to stop at every state line to get a new license; each state will honor your New York license. Similarly, a legal marriage in one state must be honored by another state. However, divorce is a bit more complicated. If a divorce is granted in a state in which the couple does not have a legal residence, that divorce does not have to be honored by their home state. Article IV has also fueled the ongoing controversy over same-sex marriage. In 1996, after Hawaii courts gave homosexual marriages most of the same legal rights as heterosexual marriages, many states passed laws saying they would not have to honor those marriages. In response, Congress passed the Defense of Marriage Act in 1996, which said that states would not have to recognize same-sex marriages. Hawaii courts have since overturned the decision to recognize same-sex marriages, but as of this writing, eight states recognize civil unions between homosexual partners and five (Massachusetts, New Hampshire, Iowa, Vermont, and Connecticut, plus the District of Columbia) allow gay marriages.[4] Nancy Wilson and Paula Schoenwether, who married in Massachusetts then moved to Florida where gay marriage is banned, asked a federal court to overturn the act. However, the court ruled that the full faith and credit clause did not apply, citing the "policy exception."[5]

Under the **privileges and immunities clause** of Article IV, the citizens of each state are also "entitled to all Privileges and Immunities" of citizens in the other states, which means that states must treat visitors from other states the same as their own residents. This part of the Constitution favors a nation-centered perspective

full faith and credit clause Part of Article IV of the Constitution requiring that each state's laws be honored by the other states. For example, a legal marriage in one state must be recognized across state lines.

privileges and immunities clause Part of Article IV of the Constitution requiring that states must treat nonstate residents within their borders as they would treat their own residents. This was meant to promote commerce and travel between states.

because it was intended to promote free travel and economic activity between the states. For example, Michigan could not charge the owner of a lake cabin different property taxes depending on whether she lived in Chicago or in Detroit. States also may not deny new residents welfare benefits or deny police protection to visitors even though they do not pay state taxes. For example, a 1992 law in California limited the cash welfare benefit to new residents to the same level of benefits they had been receiving in the state from which they had just moved. The law was intended to save California's government money and also discourage people from moving to California just to get the higher benefit—particularly since California's cash benefit for a mother and one child was $456 a month in 1992, but in the neighboring state of Arizona it was only $275.[6] The Supreme Court ruled that the state law violated the privileges and immunities clause and the right to travel freely between the states.

However, states are allowed to make some distinctions between residents and nonresidents. For example, states do not have to permit nonresidents to vote in state elections, and public colleges and universities may charge out-of-state residents higher tuition than in-state residents. Therefore, the privileges and immunities clause cuts both ways on the question of the balance of power because it allows the states to determine and uphold these laws autonomously, but it also emphasizes that national citizenship is more important than state citizenship.

The Constitution sets the boundaries for the battles over federalism. For example, no state can decide to print its own currency, and the U.S. government cannot take over any public school district in the country. But within those broad boundaries, the balance between national and state power at any given point in history is a political decision, the product of choices made by elected leaders and the courts. Decisions by the Supreme Court have figured prominently in this evolution.

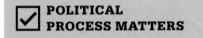

POLITICAL PROCESS MATTERS

The Evolving Concept of Federalism

FEDERALISM IN THE EARLY YEARS: ESTABLISHING NATIONAL SUPREMACY

As the United States gained its footing, several clashes between the advocates of state-centered and nation-centered federalism quickly evolved into a partisan struggle. The Federalists, the party of George Washington and Alexander Hamilton, controlled the new government for its first twelve years and favored strong national power. Their opponents, the Democratic-Republicans, led by Thomas Jefferson and James Madison, favored state power. The first confrontation came when the Federalists established a national bank in 1791, over the objections of Jefferson. This controversy did not come to a head until Congress chartered the second national bank in 1816. The state of Maryland, which was controlled by the Democratic-Republicans, tried to tax the National Bank's Baltimore branch out of existence, but the head cashier of the bank refused to pay the tax and the case eventually ended up at the Supreme Court. The Court had to decide whether Congress had the power to create the bank, and if it did, whether Maryland had the right to tax the bank. In the landmark decision *McCulloch v. Maryland* (1819) the Court ruled in favor of the national government on both counts. In deciding whether Congress could create the bank, the Court held that even though the word "bank" does not appear in the Constitution, Congress's power to create one is implied through its enumerated powers—such as the power to coin money, levy taxes, and borrow money. They also ruled that Maryland did not have the right to tax the bank because of the national supremacy clause of the Constitution, which says the Constitution and national laws take precedent over state laws if there is a conflict. Both the concept of implied powers and the validation of national supremacy were critical for establishing the centrality of the national government.

A few years later, the Supreme Court decided another case that cemented Congress's power to act based on the commerce clause in the Constitution. In *Gibbons v. Ogden* (1824) the Supreme Court said that Congress has broad power to regulate interstate commerce and struck down a New York law that had granted a monopoly to a private company operating steamboats on the Hudson River between New York and New Jersey. By granting this monopoly, the ruling stated, New York was interfering with interstate commerce.

Another important, early clash over federalism concerned the Sedition Act[7] of 1798 passed by a majority-Federalist Congress. The act banned "any false, scandalous writing against the government of the United States." The stated purpose of the law was to prevent the rejection of authority and mass political movements that were sweeping through France from taking hold in the United States. But Jeffersonians argued, rightly, that the law was an attempt to silence dissent and criticism of the government and was a clear violation of the 1st Amendment protection of freedom of speech. Indeed, under this law ten Democratic-Republican newspaper editors were arrested, fined, and jailed. The issue was important in the 1800 presidential election, and when Jefferson was elected he pardoned everyone convicted under the law.

The Sedition Act is important for our purposes because of a political tactic that Jefferson devised to try to overturn the law before he became president. His opponents controlled Congress and the Supreme Court, so there was not much hope of using the normal political channels to change the law. Thus, he and Madison came up with an idea to circumvent the national government by working through the states. They convinced the Kentucky and Virginia legislatures to pass resolutions challenging the national government's power to pass the Sedition Act through an idea they called the **doctrine of interposition**. Under this doctrine, if the national government passes an unconstitutional law, the people of the states can interpose or insert themselves between the law and the national government and declare the law void. This doctrine views the Constitution as a compact between the states. Although the tension over the Sedition Act was defused when Jefferson was elected president in 1800, this approach to federalism had important implications for national power.[8]

The idea of interposition regained significance as the basis for the southern states' push for broader **states' rights** on issues such as tariffs and slavery. John Calhoun, an important South Carolina senator, used the term "nullification" to refer to the same principle, urging South Carolina to ignore a tariff law passed by Congress in 1832. The states' rights perspective was at the center of the dispute between southern and northern states over slavery, which ultimately led to the secession of the states of the Confederacy and subsequently the Civil War. The stakes were enormous in the battles over federalism: about 528,000 died in the bloodiest of American wars (including battle deaths and soldiers who died from disease and infection).[9] As Abraham Lincoln so forcefully argued, concepts such as nullification and states' rights, when taken to their logical extremes, were too divisive to be allowed to stand. If states were allowed to ignore national laws, the basis of the United States would fall apart.

doctrine of interposition The idea that if the national government passes an unconstitutional law, the people of the states (through their state legislatures) can declare the law void. This idea provided the basis for southern secession and the Civil War.

states' rights The idea that states are entitled to a certain amount of self-government, free of federal government intervention. This became a central issue in the period leading up to the Civil War.

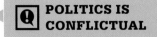
POLITICS IS CONFLICTUAL

▲ *In ruling on Dred Scott's petition to become a free man, the Supreme Court said that slaves were property, not U.S. citizens, and that Congress did not have the power to prohibit slavery in any state. This decision, which was rooted in a view of state-centered federalism, hastened the start of the Civil War.*

DUAL FEDERALISM

The ideas of states' rights and nullification did not produce the Civil War by themselves. They had some help from the Supreme Court's infamous *Dred Scott* decision, but before explaining the significance of that case, we will take a brief look at some key players in the evolution of the Court's approach to federalism. The first two-thirds of the nineteenth century saw an incredible period of stability in the leadership of the Court, because only two chief justices served during this time: John Marshall from 1801 to 1835, and Roger Taney from 1835 to 1864, although they had very different ideas about federalism. Marshall was a Federalist and a thorn in the side of states' rights advocates while Taney was a supporter of states' rights. The series of decisions under Marshall's leadership outlined earlier secured the place of the national government within our federal system, but in the years that followed, Taney was able to limit the reach of the national government through his vision of federalism, which is known as dual federalism.

Under **dual federalism** the national and state governments were viewed as distinct, with little overlap in their activities or the services they provided. In this view, the national government's activities are confined to powers strictly enumerated in the Constitution, despite the necessary and proper clause and the implied powers endorsed in *McCulloch v. Maryland*. While Taney developed the idea of dual federalism, one decision toward the end of Marshall's tenure endorsed a notion of "dual citizenship" in which an individual's rights as a U.S. citizen under the Bill of Rights did not apply to that same person under state law. That decision, *Barron v. Baltimore* (1833), held that a man whose wharf in the Baltimore harbor had been ruined by the city's dumping of sand and gravel could not sue the city for violating the 5th Amendment's prohibition of taking property without due process. The Court ruled that the 5th Amendment only applied to the U.S. Congress and not to state and local governments.

The Taney Court expanded the power of the states over commerce in ways that would not be accepted today, including giving the mayor of New York City the right to control immigration by requiring shipmasters to post bonds for foreign passengers who might later go on welfare[10] and allowing the city of Philadelphia to require ships to use local captains when entering the harbor.[11] The state-centered views of the Taney Court also produced a tragic decision, *Dred Scott v. Sandford*, (1857). Dred Scott was a slave who had lived for many years with his owner in the free Wisconsin Territory but was living in Missouri, a slave state, when his master died. Scott petitioned for his freedom under the Missouri Compromise, which said that slavery was illegal in any free state. The majority decision held that slaves were not citizens but private property, and therefore the Missouri Compromise violated the 5th Amendment because it deprived people (slave owners) of property without the due process of law. This unfortunate decision contributed to the Civil War, which started four years later, because it indicated that there could not be a political solution to the problem of slavery.

The Civil War ended the dispute over slavery, but it did not resolve the basic questions about the balance of power between the national and state systems. Right after the Civil War, the Constitution was amended to ensure that the Union's views on states' rights were the law of the land. The Civil War Amendments banned slavery (the 13th), prohibited states from denying citizens due process or equal protection of the laws (14th), and gave newly freed male slaves the right to vote (15th). The 14th Amendment was the most important in terms of federalism because it was the constitutional basis for many of the civil rights laws passed by Congress during Reconstruction.

However, the Supreme Court soon stepped in again to limit the power of the national government. In 1873 the Supreme Court reinforced the notion of dual

dual federalism The form of federalism favored by Chief Justice Roger Taney in which national and state governments are seen as distinct entities providing separate services. This model limits the power of the national government.

Early Landmark Supreme Court Decisions on Federalism

CASE	HOLDING AND SIGNIFICANCE
Chisholm v. Georgia (1793)	Citizens of one state could sue another state; led to the 11th Amendment, which prohibited such lawsuits.
McCulloch v. Maryland (1819)	Upheld the national government's right to create a bank and reaffirmed the idea of "national supremacy."
Gibbons v. Ogden (1824)	Congress, rather than the states, has broad power to regulate interstate commerce.
Barron v. Baltimore (1833)	Endorsed a notion of "dual federalism" in which the rights of a U.S. citizen under the Bill of Rights did not apply to that same person under state law.
Dred Scott v. Sandford (1857)	Sided with southern states' view that slaves were property and ruled that the Missouri Compromise violated the 5th Amendment, since making slavery illegal in some states deprived slave owners of property. Contributed to the start of the Civil War.
National Labor Relations Board v. Jones & Laughlin Steel Corporation (1937)	Upheld the National Labor Relations Act of 1935 as consistent with Congress's commerce clause powers, reversing the Court's more narrow interpretation of that clause.

federalism, ruling that the 14th Amendment did not change the balance of power between the national and state governments, despite its clear language aimed at state action. Endorsing the notion of dual citizenship, the Court ruled that the 14th Amendment right to due process and equal treatment under the law only applied to individuals' rights as citizens of the United States, not to their state citizenship.[12] By extension, freedom of speech, freedom of the press, and the other liberties protected in the Bill of Rights only applied to laws passed by Congress, not to state laws. This distinction between state and national citizenship sounds odd today partly because the 14th Amendment has long been viewed as the basis for making sure that states do not violate basic rights.

Ten years later, the Court overturned the 1875 Civil Rights Act, which guaranteed equal treatment in public accommodations, arguing that the 14th Amendment did not give Congress the power to regulate private conduct, such as whether a white restaurant owner had to serve a black customer, but only the conduct of state governments.[13] This narrow view of the 14th Amendment left the national government powerless to prevent southern states from implementing state and local laws that led to complete segregation of the races in the South (called Jim Crow laws) and the denial of many basic rights to blacks after the northern troops left the South at the end of Reconstruction.

The other area in which the Supreme Court limited the reach of the national government concerned Congress's power to regulate the economy through its **commerce clause powers**. In a series of cases in the late nineteenth and early twentieth centuries, the Supreme Court endorsed a view of laissez-faire capitalism—French for "leave alone"—aimed at protecting business from regulation by the national government. To this end, the Court defined clear boundaries between *inter*state and

commerce clause powers The powers of Congress to regulate the economy granted in Article I, Section 8, of the Constitution.

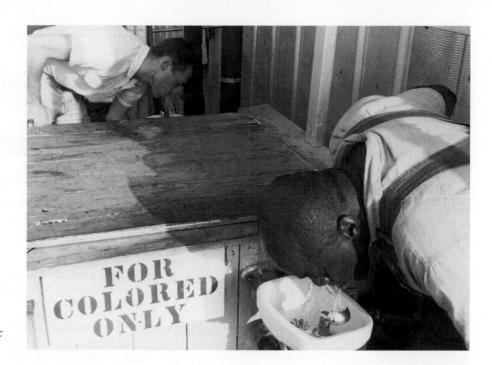

▶ *After the Supreme Court struck down the 1875 Civil Rights Act, southern states were free to impose Jim Crow laws. These state and local laws led to complete racial segregation, even for public drinking fountains.*

*intra*state commerce, ruling that Congress could not regulate any economic activity that occurred *within* a state. The Supreme Court allowed some national legislation that was connected to interstate commerce, such as limiting monopolies through the Sherman Antitrust Act (1890). However, when the national government tried to use this act to break up a cartel of four sugar companies that controlled 98 percent of the nation's sugar production, the Court ruled that Congress did not have this power. According to the decision, the commerce clause only dealt with the transportation of goods, not their manufacture, and the sugar in question was made within a single state. Even if the sugar was sold throughout the country, this was seen as "incidental" to its manufacture.[14] On the same grounds the Court also struck down attempts by Congress to regulate child labor.[15] In some instances, the Court's laissez-faire perspective also led them to strike down state laws, as in one case that ruled unconstitutional a New York law limiting working hours of bakers to no more than sixty hours a week or ten hours a day.[16] Therefore, the limits that the Court placed on Congress during this antiregulation phase did not necessarily tip the balance to the state governments. Rather, big business was the clear winner over both national and state government.

COOPERATIVE FEDERALISM

The Progressive Era policies of the early twentieth century and the New Deal policies of the 1930s ushered in a new era of American federalism in which the national government became much more involved in activities formerly reserved for the states, such as education, transportation, civil rights, agriculture, social welfare, and management–labor relations. At first, the Supreme Court resisted this broader reach of national power, clinging to its nineteenth-century conception of dual federalism.[17] But as commerce became more national, the distinction between interstate and intrastate commerce, and between manufacture and transportation, became increasingly difficult to sustain. Starting in 1937, the Supreme Court largely discarded these distinctions and gave Congress far more latitude in shaping economic and social policy for the nation.[18]

A few years later, the Court made it clear that there was virtually no limit on what could be construed as interstate commerce. The case involved a law that limited the number of acres of grains a farmer could grow. Congress's intent was to increase the price of farm commodities by limiting supply. A farmer who exceeded his quota challenged the law by saying that he fed all of his excess wheat to his own livestock and therefore was not engaged in interstate commerce (given that he did not buy or sell the wheat). The Court ruled that the farmer was undermining Congress's ability to regulate interstate commerce because if he had not exceeded his acreage quota, he would have had to buy more wheat to support his livestock.[19]

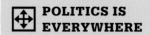

POLITICS IS EVERYWHERE

The type of federalism that emerged in the Progressive Era and blossomed in the late 1930s is called **cooperative federalism**, or "marble cake" federalism, as opposed to the "layer cake" model of dual federalism.[20] As the image of a marble cake suggests, the boundaries of state and national responsibilities are not as well-defined under cooperative federalism as under dual federalism. With the increasing industrialization and urbanization of the late 1930s and the 1940s, more complex problems arose that could not be solved at one level of government. Cooperative federalism adopts a more practical focus on intergovernmental relations and how to efficiently provide services. State and local governments maintained a level of influence as the implementers of national programs, but the national government played an enhanced role as the initiator of key policies.

Cooperative federalism accurately describes this important shift in national–state relations in the first half of the twentieth century, but it does not begin to capture the complexity of modern federalism. The marble cake metaphor falls short in one important way: the lines of authority and patterns of cooperation are not as messy as implied by the gooey flow of chocolate through white cake. Instead, the metaphor of **picket fence federalism**, which became popular in the 1960s, is a better description of cooperative federalism in action. As shown in Figure 3.1, each picket of the fence represents a different policy area, and the horizontal boards that hold the pickets together represent the different levels of government. This is certainly a much more orderly image than the marble cake, and it has important implications about how policy is made across levels of government. The most important point is that activity within the cooperative federal system occurs *within* pickets of the fence—that is, within policy areas. Policy makers within a given policy area will have more in common with others in that area at different levels of government than with people at the same level of government who work on different issues. For example, someone working in a state's education department will have more contact with people working in local school districts and the national Department of Education than with people who also work at the state level but focus on transportation policy.

Cooperative federalism, then, is most likely to emerge within policy areas rather than across them. This may create problems for the chief executives who are trying to run the show (mayors, governors, and the president) as rivalries develop between policy areas competing for funds. Also, contact within policy areas is not always cooperative. Everyone is familiar with detective shows in which the FBI arrives to investigate a local crime and pulls rank on the town sheriff, creating tension and provoking resentment from the local law enforcement officials who would rather handle their problems without interference from the Feds. This is the inefficient side of picket fence federalism in action. But overall, this version of federalism provides great opportunities for coordination and the development of expertise within policy areas.

cooperative federalism A form of federalism in which national and state governments work together to provide services efficiently. This form emerged in the late 1930s, representing a profound shift toward less concrete boundaries of responsibility in national–state relations.

picket fence federalism A more refined and realistic form of cooperative federalism in which policy makers within a particular policy area work together across the levels of government.

FIGURE 3.1 VERSIONS OF FEDERALISM

The layer cake and picket fence versions of federalism illustrate two very different relationships among local, state, and national levels of government. Which version seems more efficient?

Layer Cake and Marble Cake Federalism

Layer cake: No interactions between the levels of government.

Marble cake: Interactions between the levels of government are common.

Picket Fence Federalism

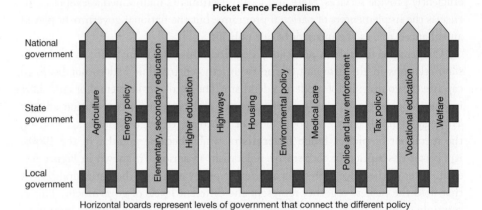

Horizontal boards represent levels of government that connect the different policy areas (pickets).

Federalism Today

This overview of the evolution of federalism within U.S. political history will help you understand federalism today, which is a complex mix of all the elements we have experienced in the past. Our system is predominantly characterized by cooperative federalism, but it has retained strong elements of national supremacy, dual federalism, and states' rights. So, rather than categorizing types of federalism into neat time periods, it makes sense to characterize the dominant tendency within each period, keeping in mind that competing versions of federalism have always been just below the surface; see Table 3.1. In the past twenty years, the competing versions are so evident that this period could be considered the "era of balanced federalism."[21]

COOPERATIVE FEDERALISM LIVES ON: GRANTS IN AID AND FISCAL FEDERALISM

fiscal federalism A form of federalism in which federal funds are allocated to the lower levels of government through transfer payments or grants.

The cooperative relationship between the national and state governments is rooted in the system of transfer payments or grants from the national government to lower levels of government, which is called **fiscal federalism**. However, just because

TABLE 3.1 COMPETING VERSIONS OF FEDERALISM

Type of Federalism	Period	Characteristics
Dual federalism (layer cake)	1789–1937	The national and state governments were viewed as very distinct with little overlap in their activities or the services they provided. Within this period, federalism could have been state-centered or nation-centered, but relations between levels of government were limited.
Cooperative federalism (marble cake)	1937–present	Greater cooperation and collaboration between the levels of government, but with policy changes typically coming from the national government in large bursts (the New Deal and Great Society programs).
Picket fence federalism	1961–present	A version of cooperative federalism emphasizing that policy makers within a given policy area have more in common with others in their area at different levels of government than with people at the same level of government who work on different issues.
Fiscal federalism	1937–present	The system of transfer payments or grants from the national government to lower-level governments involves varying degrees of national control over how the money is spent. Categorical grants give the national government a great deal of control, block grants involve less national control, and revenue sharing was a "no strings attached" grant of funds to the states.
New Federalism	1969–present	An attempt to shift power to the states by consolidating categorical grants into block grants and giving the states authority over programs such as welfare.
Coercive federalism	1970s–present	A system of federal preemptions of state and local authority and unfunded mandates on state and local governments to force the states to change their policies to match national goals or policies established by Congress.

money flows from Washington does not ensure cooperation. That is, depending on how the money is transferred, the national government can either help local and state governments achieve their own goals or use its fiscal power to impose its will. This may sound familiar. When your parents let you use the car or lent you $50, did they expect something in return, such as help with the yard work or washing the car—or was it "no strings attached"? Even in the era of dual federalism these kinds of questions arose between different levels of government, but they were far less frequent simply because the national government provided very little aid to the states.

Today, most aid to the states comes in one of two forms. **Categorical grants** are provided for specific purposes—they have strings attached—and therefore are discussed below in the section on coercive federalism. **Block grants** are financial aid to states to be used within a specific policy area, but within that area the states have a fair amount of discretion on how the money is spent.

A third type of grant, **general revenue sharing (GRS)**, was tried briefly in the 1970s and 1980s and was preferred by the states because it came with _no_ strings attached at all. GRS was started by President Richard Nixon in 1972 as part of his New Federalism program to return more control over programs to the states. At its peak in 1979, the federal government granted $6.8 billion (1.4 percent of federal spending) to the states through this program, which would be more than $25 billion in today's budget. However, the state component of the program was phased out beginning in 1980, and it was terminated in 1986 when Treasury Secretary James Baker reported that the federal government had no more revenue to share (it was a period of large national budget deficits). The political support for GRS was difficult to sustain because it was opposed by conservatives who wanted a smaller national government and by liberals who preferred more targeted spending.[22]

categorical grants Federal aid to state or local governments that is provided for a specific purpose, such as a mass transit program within the transportation budget or a school lunch program within the education budget.

block grants Federal aid provided to a state government to be spent within a certain policy area, but the state can decide how to spend the money within that area.

general revenue sharing (GRS) A type of grant used in the 1970s and 1980s in which the federal government provided state governments with funds to be spent at each state's discretion. These grants provided states with more control over programs.

Instead, advocates of cooperative federalism promoted block grants as the best way for the levels of government to work together to solve problems: the national government identified problem areas, then provided money to the states to help solve them. Between 1966, when the first block grant was created, and 1994, twenty-three block grants were established.[23] For example, Community Development Block Grants were started in 1974 to help state and local governments revitalize their communities; such grants may support ongoing programs or help with large capital expenditures, such as building a waste treatment plant or a highway. Since the 1970s, grants to the states as a proportion of the size of the national economy (gross domestic product, or GDP) has been relatively constant, while the rate of state and local spending has continued to inch up (see Figure 3.2). Even including those that were part of the 2009 stimulus package, grants to states were only 4 percent of the GDP in 2009.

New Federalism Richard Nixon's New Federalism seemed to be a brief experiment in state-centered fiscal federalism, but then it was revived during the presidency of Ronald Reagan in the 1980s. In his 1981 inaugural address, Reagan emphasized, "All of us need to be reminded that the federal government did not create the states. The states created the federal government." This classic statement of the states' rights position is similar to the Antifederalists' position at the Constitutional Convention. Reagan's goal of returning more power to the states was centered around consolidating seventy-seven categorical grants into nine general block grants that gave local politicians more control over how money was spent. This change was based on the belief that because state and local politicians were closer to the people, they would know better how to spend the money. However, this increase in state control came with a 25 percent cut in the amount of federal money granted to the states. Critics of this process dubbed it "shift and shaft," but it did have the effect

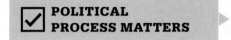

POLITICAL PROCESS MATTERS

FIGURE 3.2 **FEDERAL AND STATE/LOCAL GOVERNMENT SPENDING (INCLUDING GRANTS) AS A PERCENTAGE OF GROSS DOMESTIC PRODUCT (GDP), 1946–2009**

Since the early 1950s, federal spending as a percentage of the overall size of the economy has been flat, while the share of state and local spending has more than doubled. What does this say about the debates between nation-centered and state-centered federalism?

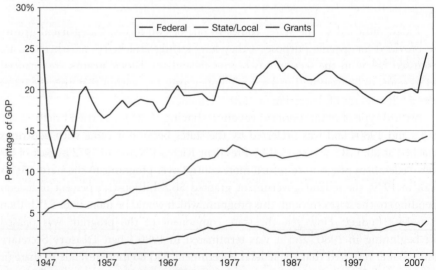

SOURCE: Statistical Abstract of the United States, Table 4.19, and the Bureau of Economic Analysis, Table 3.2 and Table 3.3.

of giving state and local governments more control. A second part of his proposal that was not adopted, because it was seen as too radical, was to give responsibility for welfare programs to the states while taking over responsibility for Medicaid, the program that funds health care for the poor, at the national level. As it turns out, this would have been a great deal for the states because the costs of Medicaid have risen much faster than welfare costs in recent years.

The next phase of New Federalism came when Republicans won control of Congress in 1994. Working with President Clinton, a moderate Democrat, Republicans passed several pieces of significant legislation that shifted power toward the states in what came to be known as the Devolution Revolution—that is, devolving power to the states. In 1996 the Personal Responsibility and Work Opportunity Act reformed welfare by creating a block grant to the states, Temporary Assistance to Needy Families (TANF), to replace the largest nationally administered welfare program. The 1996 Prison Litigation Reform Act ended federal court supervision of state and local prison systems. And the Unfunded Mandate Reform Act of 1995 made it more difficult for Congress to impose **unfunded mandates** on the states by requiring a separate vote on mandates that imposed costs of more than $50 million and requiring a Congressional Budget Office estimate of exactly how much such mandates would cost the states. Although this law could not prevent unfunded mandates, Republicans hoped that bringing more attention to the practice would create political pressure against them.

The shift from categorical grants to block grants was an important part of New Federalism after Reagan, but it has not substantially affected the balance of power between the national and state governments. The amount of money going to the states through block grants has been surpassed by categorical grants since 1982, despite shifting welfare spending to the states through the sizable TANF block grant. The reason for this should be clear, and we will look more closely at it in the next section: Congress prefers categorical grants because they have more control over how the money is spent.

NATIONAL SUPREMACY REIGNS? THE RISE OF COERCIVE FEDERALISM

Despite the overall shift toward cooperative federalism, strong overtones of national government supremacy remain. Three important characteristics of American politics in the past forty years have reinforced the role of the national government: (1) reliance on the national government in times of crisis and war, (2) the "rights revolution" of the 1950s and 1960s, and the Great Society programs of the 1960s, and (3) the rise of coercive federalism.

The first point is the most obvious and has always been a characteristic of American politics. Even in the 1800s, during the period of dual federalism and strong state power, the national government's strong actions were needed during the Civil War to hold the nation together. More recently, following the September 11 terrorist attacks, most Americans expected the national government to improve national security and retaliate for the attacks. Even Republicans, who normally oppose increasing the size of government, largely stood behind President Bush's proposal to create a new cabinet-level Department of Homeland Security.

Second, the "rights revolution" created by the Supreme Court and Lyndon Johnson's Great Society programs contributed to more national control over state policies. Landmark Court decisions thrust the national government into policy areas that had typically been reserved to the states. In the school desegregation and busing cases of the 1950s and 1960s, the Court upheld the national goal of promoting racial equality and fighting discrimination over the earlier norm of local control

unfunded mandates Federal laws that require the states to do certain things but do not provide state governments with funding to implement these policies.

coercive federalism A form of federalism in which the federal government pressures the states to change their policies by using regulations, mandates, and conditions (often involving threats to withdraw federal funding).

federal preemptions Impositions of national priorities on the states through national legislation that is based on the Constitution's supremacy clause.

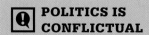

POLITICS IS CONFLICTUAL

▼ *The Americans with Disabilities Act of 1990 requires that public accommodations and commercial facilities be handicapped accessible, and recent Supreme Court rulings have held that the law applies to state and local government buildings. Disabled activists are shown in front of the White House lobbying for stronger legislation.*

of school districts.[24] The "one person, one vote" decisions, which required that the populations of legislative districts be equalized when district lines were redrawn, put the federal courts at the center of another policy area that had always been left to the states.[25] The rights revolution also applied to police powers, another area of traditional state control, including protection against self-incrimination and preventing illegally obtained evidence from being used in a criminal trial.[26]

These Court actions were paralleled by a burst of legislation from Congress and the president. Often dubbed the Great Society legislation, these laws tackled civil rights, education, the environment, medical care for the poor, and housing. These policies gave the national government much more leverage over policy areas previously controlled by state and local governments. In some cases, the national powers were far-reaching. For example, the 1965 Voting Rights Act sent federal marshals to the South to make sure that African Americans were allowed to vote. Another part of this act required local governments to submit any changes in their electoral practices, including the boundaries of their voting districts, to the Justice Department to make sure they did not have a discriminatory impact.

During this period, the national government also expanded its reach through an explosion in categorical grants, which the states sorely needed even though they came with strings attached. For example, the 1964 Civil Rights Act required nondiscrimination as a condition for receiving any kind of federal grants. The Elementary and Secondary Education Act of 1965 gave the federal government more control over public education than ever before by attaching federal grant money to certain conditions. Requiring a state drinking age of twenty-one before granting federal highway funds, as discussed at the beginning of this chapter, is another example.

Categorical grants aimed at a broad national goal are part of the third trend that has reinforced national supremacy in the past several decades, **coercive federalism**. As the name implies, this version of federalism refers to the use of federal regulations, mandates, or conditions to force or entice the states to change their policies to match national goals or policies established by Congress. The Clean Air and Water Acts, the Americans with Disabilities Act that promoted handicapped access to public buildings and commercial facilities, and the "Motor Voter Act" that required states to provide voter registration services at motor vehicle departments are all laws that forced states to change their policies. The laws most objectionable to the states are unfunded mandates, which require states to do certain things but force them to come up with the money on their own.

Along with these mandates, federal preemption is the other most direct method of coercive federalism. Derived directly from the Constitution's national supremacy clause, **federal preemptions** are the imposition of national priorities on the states. One study found that more than half of the 439 explicit preemptions of state laws between 1789 and 1991 occurred after 1969 (233, or 53 percent). Many of the preemptions also include unfunded mandates, making the state and local governments pick up the tab for policies that the national government wants them to implement. Although the 1995 unfunded mandate reform may have slowed the trend, it certainly has not eliminated mandates. The U.S. Conference on Mayors has identified ten federal mandates that consume 11.3 percent of cities' budgets, and the National Association of Counties estimates that twelve mandates account for 12.3 percent of their budgets. Many of the most expensive items are environmental laws aimed at goals that a majority of Americans share. However, state and local governments complain that they should not have to shoulder so much of the burden.[27] These are among the most

State versus National Power in the War on Terror

Do state and local governments still matter in a post–September 11 world? The conventional view is that the War on Terror and the wars in Iraq and Afghanistan have caused Americans to look increasingly to the national government to solve problems rather than to the states. The swift passage of the USA PATRIOT Act, the creation of the Department of Homeland Security, and executive orders concerning enemy combatants, military tribunals, and domestic surveillance certainly seem to support that view. These changes resemble policy responses to the other major crises of the twentieth century—the Great Depression's New Deal policies and the massive mobilization for World War II—which dramatically shifted the balance of power toward Washington.

However, the War on Terror and the wars in Iraq and Afghanistan appear to differ from these earlier crises. An initial focus on centralizing power in Washington in response to the terrorist attacks has not been sustained. Instead, as a 2002 study of all levels of government responses to the terrorist attacks found, national, state, and local governments "demonstrated a capacity and energy to marshal resources in a time of urgency."[a] States did not sit back and wait for Washington to take charge, but acted independently to ensure the safety of their citizens, suggesting that a successful homeland security policy is likely to be rooted in cooperation between

An antiterrorism training drill in Hillsborough County, Florida.

levels of government. One study found that "regional organizational structures" that promoted communication across levels of governments "are most effective in promoting intergovernmental cooperation and preparedness."[b]

Public perceptions of the different levels of government appear to be relatively unchanged from pre–September 11 levels. On the basic question of "trust and confidence in government" to handle problems, 59 percent of Americans have a "great deal" or a "fair amount" of trust in local government, 51 percent in state government, and 51 percent in national government for domestic policy and 62 percent for international policy.[c] Though polls showed a spike in support for the national government after September 11, more

recent numbers are quite similar to those before September 11. In general, polls show that, as they did before the attacks, more people think they "get the least for their money" from the federal government (36.4 percent) than the number who feel this way about state or local government (29.3 percent and 20.9 percent, respectively). The number of respondents with this negative view of the national government dipped a bit following September 11, but has now returned to the 1989 level (which is still a bit lower than in the 1990s). Similarly, people are much more likely to think that the national government "has too much power today" than to hold this belief about state and local government (the numbers are 51 percent for national government compared with 15 percent for state and 7 percent for local government). Soon after the attacks, this question registered a similar temporary increase of support for national power, which has since subsided.[d]

Overall then, despite the threat posed by terrorism most Americans still trust their state and local governments more than the national government, think that the national government is relatively more likely to waste their money, and believe the national government has too much power. Furthermore, rather than focusing exclusively on strengthening power at the national level, homeland security policies have involved efforts across levels of government. ■

controversial assertions of national power because they impose such high costs on state and local governments.

The presidency of George W. Bush provides strong evidence of this shift toward national power. Beyond the apparent centralization of power associated with fighting terrorism (see the Challenging Conventional Wisdom box for a more nuanced take on this), President Bush pushed the national government into more areas that had been dominated by the states, including significant mandates and preemptions in education testing, sales tax collection, emergency management, infrastructure, and elections administration. This is particularly noteworthy because it happened when Republicans, who have traditionally supported states' rights, controlled the presidency and Congress (in the House for six of Bush's eight years and in the Senate for four and a half years).[28]

President Obama continued the shift toward national power with one of the most active domestic policy agendas since the New Deal in the 1930s. A $787 billion economic stimulus package of tax cuts and spending designed to address the financial collapse of 2008–2009, a $938 billion health care reform law, ambitious cap-and-trade legislation, efforts to prop up and stimulate the battered housing industry, and strengthened regulations of finance and banking all were on the agenda in Obama's first two years. Health care reform was especially controversial with state governments—many of which saw the law as an unwarranted expansion of federal power.

THE STATES FIGHT BACK

Most Americans support the national policies that have been imposed on the states: racial equality, clean air and water, a fair legal process, safer highways, and equal access to the voting booth. At the same time, there has always been strong support for state and local governments. In fact, in most national surveys, Americans typically say that they trust state and local government more than the national government, and they believe their tax dollars are spent more efficiently at the lower levels of government. Though it would be impossible to apply the nineteenth-century concept of dual federalism in the twenty-first century, the popular preference for government that is "closer to the people" has always created political support for state-centered federalism, such as New Federalism and other devolution policies. The shift in public opinion toward favoring national power after the terrorist attacks of September 11 was temporary, and it appears that state and local governments quickly reasserted their position as the more trusted level of government (see Challenging Conventional Wisdom).

States appear to be reversing their traditional role of resisting change and protecting the status quo. In recent years, states have taken the lead on environmental policy, refusing to accept national pollution standards that are too lenient and a lack of national action on issues such as global warming. Many policies to address climate change, including development of renewable energy sources, carbon emissions limits, and carbon cap-and-trade programs, have been advocated at the state level. States have been out in front on fighting electronic waste, mercury emissions, and air pollution more generally.[29] States have also taken a lead role on health care policy, immigration, and stem cell research. States are also willing to challenge unpopular federal laws: more than thirty states have introduced legislation voiding the federal requirement that individuals purchase health insurance. While such limitation on federal power probably will not stand up in court, the challenges are an illustration of states' willingness to fight back.

States have one important advantage over the national government when it comes to experimenting with new policies: their numbers. The fact that there are fifty states potentially trying a mix of different policies is another reason that advocates of state-centered federalism see states as the proper repository of government power. In this view, such a mix of policies produces **competitive federalism**—the competition between states to provide the best policies to attract businesses, create jobs, and maintain a healthy social fabric. Supporters point out that competitive federalism is also a check on tyranny because people will "vote with their feet"— that is, move to a different state—if they do not like a given state's policies. One advocate of this view argues that it "disciplines government and forces the states to compete for the citizens' business, talents, and assets," which makes government act more like a free market (see What Do Political Scientists Do?).[30]

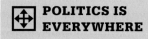

POLITICS IS EVERYWHERE

competitive federalism A form of federalism in which states compete to attract businesses and jobs through the policies they adopt.

States as Laboratories of Democracy: The Diffusion of Innovation

One strength of American federalism is the policy innovation that comes from having fifty states simultaneously experimenting to see which policy ideas work best. This feature of American federalism was famously described by Supreme Court Justice Louis Brandeis as the "laboratories of democracy." He wrote, "It is one of the happy incidents of the federal system that a single courageous state may, if its citizens choose, serve as a laboratory; and try novel social and economic experiments without risk to the rest of the country." [a] When states produce innovative policies, they spread across the nation to other states and even the national government, in a process called "policy diffusion." In recent years, policy diffusion has happened in areas such as environmental policy, welfare policy, regulation of electric power, and most recently, health care. The health care reform adopted by the federal government in 2010 was quite similar to a policy enacted by Massachusetts in 2006.

Political scientists Craig Volden and Charles Shipan explain how policies diffuse across state and local governments.[b] They identify and conduct a statistical analysis on the incidence of four mechanisms of diffusion—learning, economic competition, imitation, and coercion—for antismoking laws across the 675 largest U.S. cities between 1975 and 2000. *Learning* is the most obvious mechanism and mirrors the "laboratories of democracy" idea: states and cities adopt the policy that works best. *Economic competition* may encourage states and cities to adopt certain policies (or fail to adopt them) in response to economic forces from their neighbors. The most commonly cited example is welfare policy. States fearful of becoming "welfare magnets" will cut their welfare payments to match their neighboring states in a "race to the bottom." The economic competition mechanism for diffusion also applies to policies concerning education,

The manager of a truck stop in Jamestown, North Dakota, smiles after a state ban on indoor smoking went into effect. Political science research suggests policies may diffuse among states and cities through a variety of mechanisms.

the environment, infrastructure, minimum wages, and antismoking policies. *Imitation* happens when a state or city adopts a policy in an effort to be like another state or city it would like to emulate. Imitation may look like learning, but learning is based on the policy itself (a desire to implement the best policy), while imitation is generally done for other reasons (a city that attracts few tourists, for example, may want to imitate a city that many tourists visit). Finally, *coercion* may lead to diffusion when the national government requires states to adopt certain policies in order to qualify for federal funds, or when states adopt laws that apply to cities.

Volden and Shipan find support for all four mechanisms in the diffusion of smoking policy. The learning mechanism is supported by strong evidence that as more cities within a state adopt smoking restrictions, it becomes likelier that other cities within that state that don't have restrictions will change course and adopt them. They also show that cities are reluctant to adopt antismoking

laws if neighboring cities within ten miles do not yet have such laws, which is consistent with the economic competition variable. Bars and taverns were typically the most outspoken critics of the laws. Bar owners make an economic competition argument, saying that they would lose business to surrounding towns if their competitors still allowed smoking. That the likelihood of a city adopting antismoking laws increased when the nearest bigger city had already adopted such a law supports the imitation hypothesis. The coercion mechanism is supported by evidence showing that the adoption of a preemptive state-level law decreases the odds of a local antismoking restriction by 94 percent. In other words, if that state has already placed restrictions on smoking, it is unlikely cities will pass additional restrictions.

This study also has important implications for figuring out which type of policy diffusion is the best. Policy adoption based on learning about effective policies is clearly the preferred approach: good policies spread and bad ones die, just as the "laboratories" idea expects. On the other hand, competition can produce bad outcomes if states are forced to change policies that may harm vulnerable populations (a city may decline to restrict smoking because of worries about economic competition and thus fail to reduce its incidence of lung cancer). Imitating other governments may also lead to bad policy choices—simply trying to be like a bigger nearby city is not a valid reason for adopting a policy. Coercion by other governments can produce policy that is in the public interest (such as state-wide bans on smoking), but it also may lead to suboptimal policies. Understanding how and why policy ideas spread can help encourage better policy making. ■

Ⓖ **Watch a video clip of Craig Volden discussing this topic at wwnorton .com/studyspace.**

But just as competitive federalism can produce a good mix of policies, it can also create a "race to the bottom" as states compete in a negative way. Cass Sunstein, a University of Chicago law professor and head of the Office of Information and Regulatory Affairs in the Obama administration, points out that when states compete for businesses and jobs, they may do so by eliminating more environmental or occupational regulations than would be desirable. A priority to keep taxes low may lead to cuts in benefits to those who can least afford it, such as welfare or Medicaid recipients.[31]

There is no doubt that competition between states provides citizens with a broad range of choices about the type of government they prefer. Choices by different state leaders about tax policies, levels of support for public schools and parks, and how much to regulate business all provide a range of options for businesses deciding where to locate or expand, and to citizens considering a move. Because different citizens prefer different policies, this is generally viewed as an overall advantage to American democracy.

Fighting for States' Rights: The Role of the Modern Supreme Court

Just as the Supreme Court played a central role in defining the boundaries of dual federalism in the nineteenth and early twentieth centuries and in opening the door to a more nation-centered cooperative federalism in the late 1930s, today's Court is once again reshaping federalism. But this time the move is decidedly in the direction of state power. In the *New York Times*, Linda Greenhouse summarized the rising tension in the Court over federalism in these terms: "There are dissenting opinions at the Supreme Court, and then there are declarations of war. These days, federalism means war."[32] This "war" has had clear consequences for the balance of power between the national and state governments. As the next sections show, in little more than a decade (the late 1980s to the late 1990s), the Supreme Court invalidated more national laws on federalist grounds than in the previous two centuries.[33]

THE 10TH AMENDMENT

On paper, it seems that the 10th Amendment would be at the center of any resurgence of state power since it ensures that all powers not delegated to the national government are reserved to the states or to the people. In practice, however, the amendment has had little significance except during the early 1930s and in the recent era. Thirty-five years ago, a leading text on the Constitution said the 10th Amendment "does not alter the distribution of power between the national and state governments. It adds nothing to the Constitution."[34] To understand why, consider the following example. State and local governments have always controlled their own public schools. Thus, public education is a power reserved to the states under the 10th Amendment. However, a state law concerning public education is void if it conflicts with the Constitution—as racial segregation conflicted with the equal protection clause of the 14th Amendment—or with a national law that is based on an enumerated power. For example, a state could not compel an eighteen-year-old to attend school if the student had been drafted to serve in the army. Under

▼ The 10th Amendment provides some protection for states against mandates from the national government. For example, Congress cannot overturn state regulatory policy regarding the disposal of low-level radioactive waste. Here, containers of radioactive waste from nuclear power plants and other sources wait to be buried at a site near Clive, Utah, where state law does allow such disposal.

the 10th Amendment, the constitutionally enumerated national power to "raise and support armies" would trump the reserved state power to support public education.

This view was validated as recently as 1985 when the Court ruled that Congress had the power to impose a national minimum wage law on state governments, even if this was an area of traditional state power.[35] How times change! With the appointment of three conservative justices who favored a stronger role for the states (Antonin Scalia in 1986, Anthony Kennedy in 1988, and Clarence Thomas in 1991), the Court started to limit Congress's reach. One technique was to require that Congress provide an unambiguous statement of their intent to overrule state authority. For example, the Court ruled that the Missouri constitution, which requires state judges to retire by age seventy, did not violate the Age Discrimination in Employment Act because Congress did not make their intentions "unmistakably clear in the language of the statute."[36] In another case showing that the 10th Amendment still had some life, the Court ruled that Congress may not "commandeer" state regulatory processes by ordering states to dispose of low-level radioactive waste (under the Low-Level Radioactive Waste Policy Act).[37] The Court also ruled that Congress cannot require local law enforcement officers to perform background checks on prospective handgun purchasers, thus striking down part of the 1993 Brady Handgun Violence Prevention Act (Brady Bill).[38]

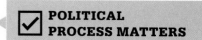

POLITICAL PROCESS MATTERS

THE 14TH AMENDMENT

As we noted earlier, the 14th Amendment was intended to give the national government broad control over the potentially discriminatory laws of southern states after the Civil War. Specifically, Section 1 guarantees that no state shall make or enforce any law depriving any person of "life, liberty, or property, without due process of law," or denying any person the "equal protection of the laws," while Section 5 empowers Congress "to enforce" those guarantees by "appropriate legislation." The Supreme Court narrowly interpreted the 14th Amendment in the late nineteenth century, severely limiting Congress's ability to affect state policy. However, throughout most of the twentieth century, the Court interpreted Section 5 to give Congress broad discretion to pass legislation to remedy bad state laws. For example, discriminatory application of literacy tests prevented millions of African Americans from voting in the South before the Voting Rights Act was passed in 1965. As part of the federalism revolution of the 1990s, the Court started to chip away at Congress's 14th Amendment powers.

In one important case in 1997 the Supreme Court struck down the Religious Freedom Restoration Act as an overly broad attempt to curtail state-sponsored harassment based on religion. This case established a new standard to justify **remedial legislation**—that is, national legislation that fixes discriminatory state law—under Section 5, saying, "There must be a congruence and proportionality between the injury to be prevented or remedied and the means adopted to that end."[39] Two applications of this logic also applied to the 11th Amendment, which originally was interpreted to mean that state governments could not be sued by residents of other states. More recently, the Supreme Court has expanded the reach of the 11th Amendment through the concept of **states' sovereign immunity**. States are now immune from a much broader range of lawsuits in state and federal court (see Nuts and Bolts 3.3 for some examples). In one application of the new standard for remedial legislation, the Court ruled that the Age Discrimination in Employment Act of 1967 could not be applied to state employees because it was not "appropriate legislation."[40] The Supreme Court also struck down the portion of the Americans with Disabilities Act (ADA) that applied to the states. Passed in 1990 with nearly unanimous support to protect the 45 million Americans who have some type of

remedial legislation National laws that address discriminatory state laws. Authority for such legislation comes from Section 5 of the 14th Amendment.

states' sovereign immunity Based on the 11th Amendment, immunity that prevents state governments from being sued by private parties in federal court unless the state consents to the suit.

Recent Important Supreme Court Decisions on Federalism

CASE	HOLDING AND SIGNIFICANCE
Gregory v. Ashcroft (1991)	The Missouri constitution's requirement that state judges retire by age seventy did not violate the Age Discrimination in Employment Act.
United States v. Lopez (1995)	Carrying a gun in a school did not fall within "interstate commerce," thus Congress could not prohibit the possession of guns on school property.
Seminole Tribe v. Florida (1996)	Used the 11th Amendment to strengthen states' sovereign immunity, ruling that Congress could not compel a state to negotiate with Indian tribes about gaming and casinos.
Printz v. United States (1997)	Struck down part of the Brady Handgun Violence Prevention Act by saying that Congress cannot require local law enforcement officers to perform background checks on prospective handgun purchasers.
City of Boerne v. Flores (1997)	Struck down the Religious Freedom Restoration Act as an overly broad attempt to curtail the state-sponsored harassment of religion, saying that national legislation aimed at remedying states' discrimination must be "congruent and proportional" to the harm.
Alden v. Maine (1999)	State employees could not sue the state of Maine for violating the overtime pay provisions of the federal Fair Labor Standards Act.
United States v. Morrison (2000)	Struck down the Violence Against Women Act, saying that Congress did not have the power under the commerce clause to provide a national remedy for gender-based crimes.
Kimel et al. v. Florida Board of Regents (2000)	The Age Discrimination in Employment Act of 1967 could not be applied to state employees because it was not considered "appropriate legislation" under Section 5 of the 14th Amendment.
Alabama v. Garrett (2001)	Struck down the portion of the Americans with Disabilities Act that applied to the states, saying that state governments are not required to make special accommodations for the disabled.
Federal Maritime Commission v. South Carolina Ports Authority (2002)	The 11th Amendment prevents the Federal Maritime Commission from pursuing a claim on behalf of a gambling boat owner denied access to a marina owned by the state of South Carolina.
Nevada Department of Human Resources v. Hibbs (2003)	Upheld Congress's power to apply the 1993 Family Leave Act to state employees as "appropriate legislation" under Section 5 of the 14th Amendment.

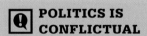

POLITICS IS CONFLICTUAL

disability, the ADA required employers, including state agencies, to make "reasonable accommodations" for a "qualified individual with a disability." However, the majority opinion said that states could refuse to hire people in wheelchairs, or deaf or blind people, as "States are not required . . . to make special accommodations for the disabled."[41] Three years later, the Court made a narrow exception to this ruling, saying that states did need to provide access for the disabled to courthouses.[42]

In another exception to the federalism revolution, the Court upheld Congress's power to apply the 1993 Family Leave Act to state employees as "appropriate legislation" under Section 5 of the 14th Amendment.[43] The key difference between this case and the age or disability cases is that in passing the Family Leave Act, Congress explicitly recognized the gender inequality of family care. That is, when a family member gets sick, the mother or wife typically bears the burden. Constitutional protections for discrimination based on age or disability are much weaker than discrimination based on gender or race.

THE COMMERCE CLAUSE

Another category of cases leading to more state power concerns the commerce clause of the Constitution. The first Court case to limit Congress's commerce powers since the New Deal of the 1930s came in 1995. The case involved the Gun-Free School Zones Act of 1990, which Congress passed in response to the increase in school shootings around the nation. The law made it a federal offense to have a gun within 1,000 feet of a school. Congress assumed that it had the power to pass this legislation, given the Court's expansive interpretation of the commerce clause over the previous fifty-five years, even though it concerned a traditional area of state power. Although it was a bit of a stretch to claim that carrying a gun in or around a school was related to interstate commerce, Congress might have been able to demonstrate the point by showing that most guns are made in one state and sold in another (thus commercially crossing state lines), that crime affects the economy and commerce, and that the quality of education, which is also crucial to the economy, is harmed if students and teachers are worrying about guns in their schools. However, they did not present this evidence because they did not think it was necessary.

Alfonso Lopez, a senior at Edison High School in San Antonio, Texas, was arrested for carrying a concealed .38 caliber handgun with five bullets in it. Lopez moved to dismiss the charges, arguing that the law was unconstitutional because carrying a gun in a school could not be regulated as "interstate commerce." The Court agreed in *United States v. Lopez*,[44] and the ruling was widely viewed as a warning shot over Congress's bow. If Congress wanted to encroach on the states' turf in the future, they would have to demonstrate that the law in question was a legitimate exercise of the commerce clause powers.

Congress learned its lesson. The next time it passed legislation that affected law enforcement at the state level, they were careful to document the impact on interstate commerce. The Violence Against Women Act was passed in 1994 with strong bipartisan support (unanimously in the House and by an overwhelming margin in the Senate) after weeks of testimony and thousands of pages of evidence were entered into the record showing the links between violence against women and commerce. Despite the evidence Congress presented, the Supreme Court ruled that Congress did not have the power under the commerce clause to make a national law regarding gender-based crimes.[45]

Another far-reaching case that limited Congress's power relative to the states upheld an Alabama law requiring applicants for drivers' licenses to take the written examination in English. This means that individuals who believe they have been subjected to a state law that has a discriminatory effect (rather than one inflicting direct, intentional discrimination) based on race, color, or national origin can no longer sue a state under Title VI of the 1964 Civil Rights Act. Instead, the Court concluded that Congress intended these regulations to be directly enforceable only by the Office for Civil Rights—a political body with very limited resources.

The significance of this line of federalism cases is enormous. Not only has the Supreme Court set new limits on Congress's ability to address national problems (the "congruence and proportionality" test), but it has also clearly stated

▼ The Lopez *decision struck down the 1990 Gun-Free School Zones Act, ruling that Congress did not have the power to forbid people to carry guns near schools. After the shooting of twelve students and one teacher at Columbine High School in Jefferson County, Colorado, on April 20, 1999, there were renewed calls nationwide for strengthening gun control laws.*

that the Court alone will determine which rights warrant protection by Congress. The cases have also been quite controversial on the bench. The introduction to this section mentioned that on the Court, federalism means "war." Nearly all of the cases mentioned here were decided by 5–4 margins, with extremely intense and persistent dissents. In many instances the dissenters took the unusual step of reading their opinions from the bench.

This account of recent federalism cases is consistent with the views of many constitutional experts, who see these rulings as an important shift of power from the national government to the states. However, it is important to recognize that the Court does not consistently rule against Congress; it often rules against the states because of broader Constitutional principles or general public consensus behind a specific issue. The clearest example of the Court ruling against the states for constitutional reasons was *U.S. Term Limits v. Thornton*, which struck down Arkansas's three-term limit for members of Congress.[46] In a narrow reading of the Constitution, the Court ruled by a 5–4 margin that states could not impose any additional limits on the qualifications for being a member of Congress beyond those in the Constitution. Another ruling against a state was *Romer v. Evans*, which struck down a state-wide initiative passed by a small majority of Colorado voters in 1992. The law banned state and local action of any type (executive, judicial, or legislative) that prohibited discrimination against lesbians and gays based on their sexual orientation.[47] The Court held that the initiative violated the equal protection clause of the 14th Amendment. Our final example of a case decided against the states is more difficult to ground in the Constitution. Instead it is an example of the "living Constitution" approach to the law, which will be discussed further in Chapter 13. This approach recognizes public consensus on important issues even when that consensus is not consistent with a narrow reading of the Constitution. In two separate cases, the Court ruled that the death penalty for those under eighteen years old and the mentally retarded is "cruel and unusual punishment" and thus prohibited by the 8th Amendment, despite the fact that the Constitution clearly recognizes the death penalty as legitimate if due process is followed.[48] The ruling struck down the practices, which previously were allowed by twenty states (but states may still allow the death penalty for mentally competent adults).

Based on these cases, some would argue that the shift in power toward the states has been relatively marginal. Furthermore, the national government still has the upper hand in the balance of power and has many tools at its disposal to blunt the impact of a Court decision. First, Congress can pass new laws to clarify their legislative intent and overturn any of the Court cases that involved statutory interpretation. Second, they can use their financial power to impose their will on the states, as they did with raising the drinking age. So, for example, Congress could pass a law stating that before a state could receive money from the federal government, it had to agree to abide by the Americans with Disabilities Act or the Age Discrimination in Employment Act.

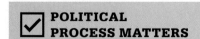

POLITICAL PROCESS MATTERS

Assessing Federalism

Issues concerning federalism seem to break down along traditional liberal and conservative lines. Liberals generally favor strong national power to fight discrimination against women, minorities, disabled people, gays, and the elderly, and they push for progressive national policies on issues such as protecting the environment and supporting the poor. Conservatives tend to favor limited intrusion from the national government and allowing the states to decide their own mix of social welfare and regulatory policies, including how aggressively they will protect various groups from discrimination.

However, assessing federalism is not so simple. In recent years the tables have turned, and in many cases liberals are suddenly arguing for states' rights while conservatives advocate the virtues of uniform national laws. On a broad range of new issues, such as medical uses of marijuana, gay marriage, cloning, and assisted suicide, state governments are passing socially liberal legislation.[49] And the Court's earlier, state-centered rulings give it little precedent for striking down these laws. The Court's conservative majority will either have to continue applying its state-centered federalism and uphold these liberal state laws, or strike them down on ideological grounds, which would undermine the Court's credibility. One potential solution, from a socially conservative perspective, involves passing congressional legislation banning, for example, cloning or gay marriage. This approach would also be difficult for the Court to sustain, however, given its earlier, narrow definition of "economic activity" under the commerce clause. The most interesting of these cases in many ways pertain to the medical use of marijuana and assisted suicide (see You Decide). In these cases, political ideology and policy views about the drug laws and the right to die were apparently more important for most of the justices than consistency on questions of federalism.[50]

In addition to pointing out the ideological complexities of federalism, any assessment of federalism today must consider the advantages and disadvantages for our political system. The advantages of a strong role for the states can be summarized in four main points: states can be laboratories of democracy, state and local government is closer to the people, states provide more access to the political system, and states provide an important check on national power.

The first point refers to the role that states play as the source of policy diversity and innovation. If many states are trying to solve problems creatively, they can complement the efforts of the national government. Successful policies first adopted at the state level often percolate up to the national level. One of the most important recent examples is welfare reform. Many states had great success in helping people get off of welfare by providing worker training, education assistance, health benefits, and child care. The national government decided that states were doing a better job than it was doing and, through the TANF block grant mentioned earlier, devolved welfare funding and responsibility to the states. Health care and environmental policy, especially on climate change, are other areas in which states have innovated.

Second, government that is closer to the people encourages participation in the political process. Local politicians know better what their constituents want than farther-removed national politicians do. If the voters want higher taxes to pay for more public benefits, such as public parks and better schools, they can enact these changes at the state and local levels. Also, local government provides a broad range of opportunities for direct involvement in politics, from working on local political campaigns to attending school board or city council meetings. When citizens are able to directly affect policies, they are more likely to get involved in the political process.

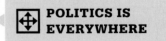

POLITICS IS EVERYWHERE

Third, our federalist system provides more potential paths to address problems. The court system allows citizens to pursue complaints under state or federal law. Likewise, cooperative federalism can draw on the strengths of different levels of government to solve problems. A local government may recognize a need and respond to it more quickly than the national government, but if it needs additional resources to address the problem, it may be able to turn to the state or national government

Medical Marijuana and Assisted Suicide

The debate over devolving power from the national government to the states has grown increasingly complicated in the past several years. The partisan nature of the debate has shifted, the courts have played a larger but inconsistent role, and issues of states' rights increasingly cut across normal ideological and partisan divisions. In the 1990s, Republicans continued to favor greater state control, and Democratic president Bill Clinton also supported devolution to the states in several areas, including welfare policy. Since the mid-1990s, the Supreme Court has played a central role in the shift of power to the states, but two recent cases involving medical marijuana (*Gonzales v. Raich*, 2005) and assisted suicide (*Gonzales v. Oregon*, 2006) show how the typical debate between national and state power can shift when a moral dimension is introduced.

In both cases, state voters supported liberal policies. In 1996, California voters passed the Compassionate Use Act, by a margin of 56 to 44 percent. This law allowed seriously ill Californians, typically AIDS and cancer patients, to use marijuana as part of their medical treatment with the permission of a doctor. Oregon voters approved the Death with Dignity Act in 1994 by a margin of 51 to 49 percent. This law allows physicians to prescribe a lethal drug dosage for terminally ill patients who wish to end their lives. A court order delayed implementation of the law until 1997, the same year that the matter was put before the voters again, but they rejected repealing the law by a margin of 60 to 40 percent. Both of these states' laws were challenged in

Federal drug enforcement agents raid a medical marijuana club.

federal court in classic confrontations between the states' rights and national power perspectives. Surprisingly, the Supreme Court ruled against medical marijuana and in favor of assisted suicide (this oversimplifies the legal arguments, but these were the bottom-line outcomes).

Should Congress be able to tell a state that it cannot allow the use of medical marijuana? Can the attorney general interpret a congressional law as a prohibition of assisted suicide? Unlike most of the cases discussed in this chapter, the states' rights position in these cases represented the liberal perspective, rather than the conservative position typically associated with state-centered federalism. Social liberals tended to support both the medical marijuana law and the assisted suicide law, while social conservatives tended to oppose them both. However, if you examine these cases in terms of the question of federal versus state power, a central ideological divide in this nation since the Constitutional Convention, the traditional liberal and conservative perspectives both look more complex. That is, a national-power liberal and a

social conservative would agree that the national government should regulate medical marijuana and assisted suicide. Likewise, states' rights conservatives and social liberals would share the view that the states should decide these issues on their own.

Somewhat surprisingly, there was almost no consistency among the eight justices who voted on both cases (Chief Justice William Rehnquist was replaced by John Roberts between the two cases). Only Justice Sandra Day O'Connor supported the states' rights position in both cases while Justice Antonin Scalia voted as a moral conservative against both laws—and counter to his previously articulated views on national power and federalism. The other six justices mixed their views, voting to uphold one of the laws and to strike down the other. The resulting rulings were inconsistent on the question of federalism as well. In the medical marijuana case, the Court upheld Congress's power to regulate the medical use of marijuana under the Controlled Substances Act. But in the assisted suicide case, the Court said that under that same congressional law, the U.S. attorney general did not have the power to limit the drugs that doctors in Oregon could prescribe for use in an assisted suicide.

As a matter of policy, should doctors be able to prescribe marijuana to alleviate pain? Should they be able to prescribe lethal drugs to terminally ill patients? Do you tend to support a state-centered or nation-centered perspective on federalism? Now revisit your answers to the first two questions. Are your positions more consistent with your views on federalism or with your policy concerns? ■

for help. Finally, federalism can provide a check on national tyranny. Competitive federalism ensures that Americans have a broad range of social policies, levels of taxation and regulation, and public services to choose from (Figure 3.3). When people "vote with their feet" by deciding whether to move and where to live, they encourage healthy competition between states that would be impossible under a unitary government.

On the other hand, there are problems with a federalist system that gives too much power to the states—unequal distribution of resources across the states, unequal protection for civil rights, and competitive federalism that produces a "race to the bottom." Also, one puzzle that will be considered in more detail in other chapters is that more people vote in national elections than state and local elections. Turnout at the local level is often ridiculously low. If people support local government so strongly, why aren't they more interested?

One central problem of giving too much responsibility to the states is the huge variation in the distribution of resources. Without federal funding, poor states simply cannot provide an adequate level of benefits because they have the greatest needs

---

FIGURE 3.3 **TYPES OF TAXES PER CAPITA BY STATE**

Tax rates vary dramatically by state. What are some of the advantages and disadvantages of living in a low-tax state or in a high-tax state? Which type of state would you rather live in?

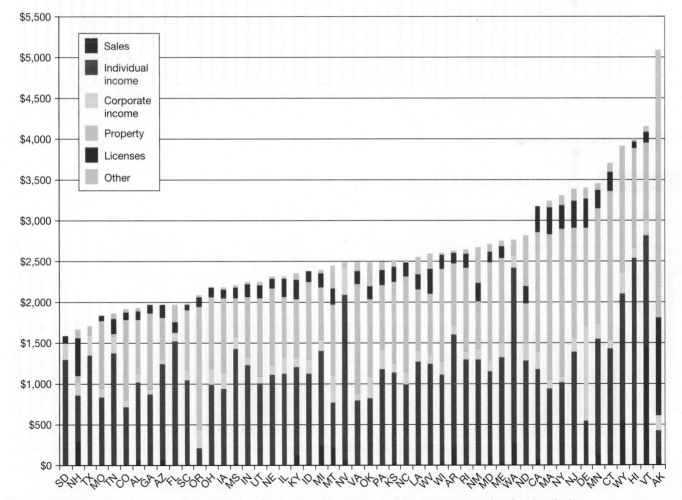

SOURCE: Calculated from U.S. Census Bureau, Quarterly Summary of State and Local Tax Revenue, available at www.census.gov/govs/www/qtax.html.

(Figure 3.4a) and the lowest incomes (Figure 3.4b), which leads to great disparities in important areas. For example, the wealthiest states spend more than twice as much per capita on education as the poorest states. Citizens of poor states are still citizens of the United States, and one important role for the national government is to ensure that all people have some kind of safety net. The resource problem becomes more acute in dealing with national-level problems that are intractable at the local or state level. For example, pollution spills across state lines and the

---

FIGURE 3.4A **POVERTY RATES BY STATE, 2008**

There are huge differences between the wealthiest states and the poorest states in terms of their income levels and poverty rates. What do these disparities imply about the role of the national government in terms of supporting a "social safety net"? How do recent developments in federalism support or undermine the notion of a social safety net?

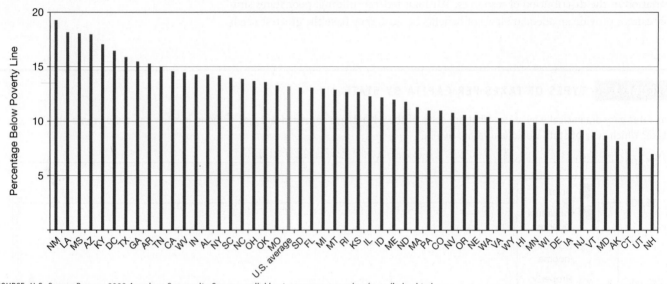

SOURCE: U.S. Census Bureau, 2008 American Community Survey, available at www.census.gov/acs/www/index.html.

FIGURE 3.4B **PER CAPITA INCOME BY STATE, 2009**

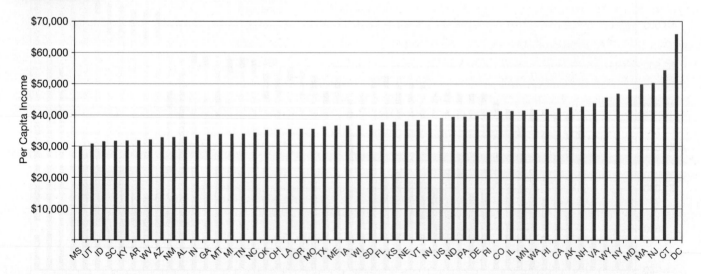

SOURCE: U.S. Dept. of Commerce, Bureau of Economic Analysis, State Annual Personal Income, March 25, 2010, www.bea.gov/regional/spi/default.cfm?selTable-summary.

deteriorating public infrastructure, like the highway system, crosses state boundaries. One study estimated that 45 percent of U.S. bridges are structurally deficient and 126,000 are seriously unsafe; two-thirds of the highway system is in need of major repair and 25 percent of mass transit needs to be updated. Solving these problems will cost hundreds of billions of dollars, vastly outstripping the resources of state and local governments. As part of the economic stimulus package that Congress enacted early in 2009, more than $30 billion was allocated to rebuilding the infrastructure, which is a good start, but much more is needed.

▲ Thirteen people died and about 100 more were injured when a bridge in Minneapolis, Minnesota, collapsed on August 1, 2007. Necessary repairs on bridges and highways will cost hundreds of billions of dollars over the next decade, requiring significant financial assistance from the national government.

The second problem, unequal civil rights protection, was evident in the discussion of the various federalism cases before the Supreme Court, which clearly show that states are not uniformly willing to protect the civil liberties and civil rights of their citizens. Without national laws, there will be large differences in the levels of protection against discrimination based on age, disability, and sexual orientation. Finally, as discussed earlier in the chapter, competitive federalism can create a "race to the bottom" as states attempt to lure businesses by keeping taxes and social spending low. This can create an unfair burden on states that take a more generous position toward the poor.

Conclusion

Alexis de Tocqueville, a French observer of American politics in the early nineteenth century, noted the tendency of democratic governments to centralize. This is especially true during wartime or times of crisis, as in the aftermath of the September 11 attacks, but it is also true during normal political times. Powerful interest groups have an incentive to claim national importance for their causes to increase their likelihood of success. As the political scientist E. E. Schattschneider noted more than a half-century ago, any participant in a conflict who is losing has an incentive to expand the scope of conflict. He uses the example of a street fight in which the person suffering the beating will have an incentive to expand the scope of conflict—that is, bring in his three friends who are down the alley. Placing this more directly in the context of federalism, political scientist Michael Greve explains, "Interest groups and parties thrive on redistribution, which is best accomplished at a highly centralized level of government—because it spreads the costs over a larger number of losers and eliminates exit options for them."[51] That is, when interest groups get a national law passed that benefits their group, say for example the dairy price support legislation for dairy farmers, which increases the price of milk by 26 percent for the average consumer, the costs are paid by the entire country. These groups win by expanding the conflict to the entire nation rather than keeping it contained within a specific state.

The drinking age example at the beginning of the chapter also illustrates this point. Mothers Against Drunk Driving would have had a much more difficult task going to all twenty-nine states that allowed drinking at age eighteen or nineteen and convincing each state legislature to change its law. Instead, they were able to convince Congress to pressure the states, and they accomplished their objective more efficiently. This scenario is repeated again and again across a broad range of issues and creates a powerful centralizing force. Within that general pattern of government centralization, however, there have been lengthy periods when the states' rights held sway over the national government.

But this evolving balance of power between the national government and the states obscures a broader reality of federalism: we are citizens of several levels of government simultaneously. Martha Derthick, a leading scholar of American federalism, says that the basic question of federalism involves choices about how many communities we will be.[52] If you asked most people in our nation about their primary geopolitical community, they would probably not say, "I am a Montanan" or "I am a Arizonan." Most people would likely say, "I am an American." Yet, we have strong attachments to our local communities and state identities. Most Texans would not be caught dead wearing a styrofoam cheesehead, but thousands of football fans in Green Bay, Wisconsin, regularly don the funny-looking things in Lambeau Field to watch their beloved Packers. We are members of multiple communities, which has had an indelible impact on our political system. The beauty of our federal system is that despite its complex and evolving nature, it makes a lot of sense.

What is federalism?

- Federalism divides certain powers and responsibilities between the national and state governments, but some concurrent powers are shared.
- Under federalism, each level of government has some degree of autonomy and independence.
- This federal system is in contrast to the more common unitary system and the less common confederal system.

How did the Founders balance national and state power in the Constitution?

- The Founders wanted a national government that was stronger than it had been under the Articles of Confederation, but they also wanted to preserve the autonomy of the states.
- The necessary and proper clause, supremacy clause, and extensive specific powers granted to Congress in Article I demonstrate the nation-centered focus of the Constitution.
- The 10th Amendment, which grants all undelegated powers to the states; the 11th Amendment, which prohibits citizens from suing the government of a state other than their own; and other specific state powers demonstrate the state-centered focus of the Constitution.

How has the concept of federalism evolved?

- From our nation's early history through the early 1930s, the country operated under dual federalism in which the national and state governments were viewed as very distinct. There was little overlap in their activities or the services they provided.
- The more active role for the national government that started with the New Deal policies of the 1930s ushered in a period of cooperative federalism based on

a more practical focus on intergovernmental relations and how to efficiently provide services.
- Picket fence federalism is a version of cooperative federalism emphasizing that policy makers within a given area have more in common with others in their area at different levels of government than with people at the same level of government who work on different issues.

What is federalism today?

- Cooperative federalism lives on today through fiscal federalism, the system of transfer payments or grants from the national government to lower levels of government.
- New Federalism attempted to return more policy control to the states by giving them more control over spending money and implementing programs.
- Coercive federalism involves the national government's attempts to compel the states to follow national policy priorities through unfunded mandates and other techniques. However, the states have been fighting back in recent years, attempting to assert their own priorities in some policy areas.

What is the role of the modern Supreme Court?

- The Supreme Court has enhanced state sovereignty by resurrecting the 10th Amendment's limitation against congressional encroachments on states' turf and by revitalizing and expanding the 11th Amendment's grant of state immunity from lawsuits.
- The Supreme Court has limited Congress's power to use the 14th Amendment and the commerce clause to achieve its goals. This line of cases does not enhance the power of the states, but it prevents the national government from encroaching on traditional areas of state power or imposing a state responsibility to protect new national-level rights.

How should we assess federalism?

- In recent years traditional positions on federalism have sometimes been reversed, with liberals suddenly arguing for states' rights while conservatives advocate the virtues of uniform national laws, as the cases concerning the medical use of marijuana and assisted suicide demonstrate.
- The advantages of a strong role for the states are that states are "laboratories of democracy," state and local government is "closer to the people," states provide more access to the political system, and states provide an important check on national power.
- On the other hand, giving too much power to the states may produce unequal protection for civil rights and competitive federalism that produces a "race to the bottom." Unequal distribution of resources across the states means that states are not equally able to deal with problems.

⊚ STUDENT STUDYSPACE

Find quizzes and other review material at wwnorton.com/studyspace.

CRITICAL THINKING

1. On which issues is the national government particularly well-suited to serve the people's interests? Which issues are the states better suited to handle? Explain the reasons for your choices.

2. How would our country be different if it were a unitary system? Do you think we would be better or worse off?

KEY TERMS

block grants (p. 79)
categorical grants (p. 79)
coercive federalism (p. 82)
commerce clause powers (p. 75)
competitive federalism (p. 84)
concurrent powers (p. 67)
confederal government (p. 68)

cooperative federalism (p. 77)
doctrine of interposition (p. 73)
dual federalism (p. 74)
federal preemptions (p. 82)
fiscal federalism (p. 78)
full faith and credit clause (p. 71)
general revenue sharing (GRS) (p. 79)

picket fence federalism (p. 77)
privileges and immunities clause (p. 71)
remedial legislation (p. 87)
states' rights (p. 73)
states' sovereign immunity (p. 87)
unfunded mandates (p. 81)
unitary government (p. 68)

SUGGESTED READING

Beer, Samuel. *To Make a Nation: The Rediscovery of American Federalism.* Cambridge, MA: Harvard University Press, 1993.

Conlan, Timothy. *From New Federalism to Devolution: Twenty-Five Years of Intergovernmental Reform.* Washington, DC: Brookings Institution, 1998.

Derthick, Martha. *Keeping the Compound Republic: Essays on American Federalism.* Washington, DC: Brookings Institution, 2001.

Elkins, Stanley, and Eric McKitrick. *The Age of Federalism: The Early American Republic, 1788–1800.* New York: Oxford University Press, 1993.

Grodzins, Martin. *The American System: A New View of Government in the United States.* Chicago: Rand McNally, 1966.

LaCroix, Alison L. *The Ideological Origins of American Federalism.* Cambridge, MA: Harvard University Press, 2010.

Manna, Paul. *School's In: Federalism and the National Education Agenda.* Washington, DC: Georgetown University Press, 2006.

McDonald, Forrest. *States' Rights and the Union: Imperium in Imperia, 1776–1876.* Lawrence, KS: University Press of Kansas, 2000.

Nagel, Robert F. *The Implosion of American Federalism.* New York: Oxford University Press, 2001.

Peterson, Paul E. *The Price of Federalism.* Washington, DC: Brookings Institution, 1995.

Posner, Paul L. *The Politics of Unfunded Mandates: Whither Federalism?* Washington, DC: Georgetown University Press, 1998.

Scheberle, Denise. *Federalism and Environmental Policy: Trust and the Politics of Implementation*, 2nd ed. Washington, DC: Georgetown University Press, 2004.

Students at Georgetown Law School protest during a speech by George W. Bush's attorney general Alberto Gonzales.

Civil Liberties

The claim is often made that "everything changed" after the terrorist attacks of September 11, 2001. Although the breadth of that claim can certainly be challenged, Americans did become less concerned about civil liberties in the wake of the attacks and more worried about security. Sixty percent of respondents in a national survey taken shortly after the terrorist attacks said that high school teachers do not have the "right to criticize America's policies toward terrorism" and instead should "defend America's policies in order to promote loyalty to our country." Forty-five percent of respondents said they would be willing to "give up some civil liberties" in order to curb terrorism.[1] Another survey showed that 49 percent of the public thought that "the 1st Amendment goes too far in the rights that it guarantees," an increase of 10 percent from the previous year.[2]

CONFLICT AND COMPROMISE
in American Politics

The government's position toward suspected terrorists also changed dramatically after the attacks. An internal memo by then–White House counsel Alberto Gonzales, who became attorney general during George W. Bush's second term, outlined a "new paradigm" that "places a high premium on . . . the ability to quickly obtain information from captured terrorists and their sponsors in order to avoid further atrocities against American civilians." Vice President Dick Cheney expanded on these sentiments on the television news show *Meet the Press* five days after the attacks, saying that the government needed to "work through, sort of, the dark side." Cheney said,

> A lot of what needs to be done here will have to be done quietly, without any discussion, using sources and methods that are available to our intelligence agencies, if we're going to be successful. That's the world these folks operate in. And so it's going to be vital for us to use any means at our disposal, basically, to achieve our objective.[3]

Former Supreme Court justice Sandra Day O'Connor predicted this shift in a speech shortly after the attacks, saying, "We're likely to experience more restrictions on our personal freedom than has ever been the case in our country."[4]

Despite these warnings and the expectation that our government should aggressively pursue suspected terrorists, it still came as a surprise when disturbing stories surfaced about the extent to which our government was willing to

BIG QUESTIONS

- ✪ What are the origins of civil liberties?

- ✪ How are the freedoms of speech, assembly, and the press protected by the 1st Amendment?

- ✪ How is the freedom of religion protected by the 1st Amendment?

- ✪ How are criminal defendants' rights balanced against the need for law and order?

- ✪ What are our privacy rights?

sacrifice civil liberties: surveillance of U.S. citizens without court orders including collecting data on millions of phone calls and emails, the abuse of Iraqi prisoners at Abu Ghraib and suspected terrorists at Guantánamo Bay, and a process called "extraordinary rendition" in which suspected terrorists were arrested in the United States and taken to a foreign country that is less protective of civil liberties, such as Egypt, Syria, Jordan, or Morocco, to be interrogated through torture.[5]

President Obama ended the practice of rendition, and domestic surveillance without a court order was stopped in 2007, but fulfilling Obama's pledge to quickly close the detention facility in Guantánamo Bay, where about 175 suspected terrorists are detained, proved to be very difficult because of disagreements over what do with the remaining detainees. In May 2009, the Senate blocked funds for the transfer or release of the detainees by a vote of 90 to 6. Possible sites for holding the suspected terrorists in Montana, Michigan, and Illinois have all met with local opposition, putting plans for closing the detention facility on hold. Another complication is whether to try the suspects in federal court or before a military tribunal. Convictions are much more likely before the latter because the rules of evidence and the standard for a conviction favor the prosecution (compared with federal court). However, the Obama administration believes that in the interest of a fair trial the detainees should be tried in federal court, and several high-profile cases have been successfully prosecuted.

Closing the detention facility at Guantánamo is an excellent illustration of our central theme that politics is conflictual. In a June 2009 poll, the public was split evenly, with 47 percent in favor of and 47 percent opposed to Obama's decision to close the military prison. Later polls showed less support for closing the prison, suggesting that this conflict would not be easily resolved. Unlike some issues, Guantánamo cannot easily be dealt with through compromise: either the prison is closed or it isn't—we cannot split the difference. The decision to try some of the suspected terrorists in federal court and some in military courts was an effort to compromise on the issue, but that decision was not met with much public support.

Public debate over revelations about the rendition program, domestic spying, torture at Guantánamo, and the compilation of the phone records of millions of Americans also demonstrates the resilience of support for **civil liberties**, the political freedoms that protect against arbitrary and abusive government actions. Figure 4.1 shows that the percentage of respondents saying civil liberties should not be sacrificed to fight terrorism hit a low of 35 percent after the terrorist attacks, but by early 2009 it was up to 65 percent. About three-fourths of Americans have consistently opposed government monitoring of Americans' phone calls, e-mail, and credit records.[6] On the other hand, more people are

civil liberties Basic political freedoms that protect citizens from governmental abuses of power.

FIGURE 4.1 SUPPORT FOR CIVIL LIBERTIES, 1996–2010

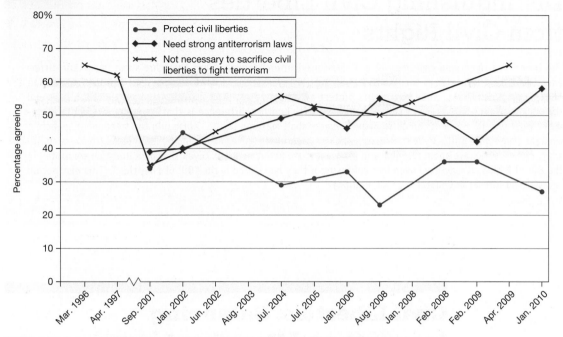

SOURCE: Poll data from several surveys conducted by the Pew Research Center, http://people-press.org.

concerned that "the government will fail to enact strong, new antiterrorism laws" than laws that "excessively restrict the average person's civil liberties," and this percentage has grown since September 2001, spiking to 58 percent shortly after the attempted bombing of an airplane on Christmas Day in 2009.

While Americans tend to support specific civil liberties, such as privacy for phone calls, the abuse of detainees at Guantánamo raises a critical point about civil liberties: *there are no absolutes.* Even the strongest critic of state-sponsored torture would have to admit that in some instances it might be justified. For example, if a nuclear device was set to detonate in Manhattan in three hours, few would insist on protecting the civil liberties of someone who knew where the bomb was hidden.

Because there are no absolutes, the Supreme Court has continually engaged in balancing interests and drawing lines to define and redefine the freedoms and liberties at the core of the American political system. Most of this chapter describes this process. Every time the Supreme Court decides whether a national security concern outweighs a particular freedom of speech or of the press, it makes a political decision with broad implications. The evolution of the meaning of civil liberties, as largely defined by the courts, is a great example that the political process matters. Civil liberties also are an excellent example that politics is everywhere. Freedom of speech, religion, and assembly; privacy rights; and the rights of criminal defendants generate great public interest because they are so obviously central to our political system and the daily lives of millions of Americans.

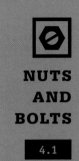
Distinguishing Civil Liberties from Civil Rights

The terms *civil rights* and *civil liberties* are often used interchangeably, but there are some important differences. Civil liberties refer to the freedoms guaranteed in the Bill of Rights and the "due process" protection of the 14th Amendment, while civil rights protect all persons from discrimination and are rooted in laws and the "equal protection" clause of the 14th Amendment. Another difference is that civil liberties primarily restrict what the government can do to you ("*Congress* shall make no law . . . abridging the freedom of speech"), whereas civil rights protect you from discrimination both by the government and by individuals. To oversimplify a bit, civil liberties are about freedom and civil rights are about equality. Given that civil liberties are rooted in the Bill of Rights, it may have been less confusing if they had called it the "Bill of Liberties." (This distinction is discussed further in Chapter 14, Civil Rights.)

Civil Liberties: Balancing Interests and Drawing Lines

POLITICS IS CONFLICTUAL

Civil liberties are deeply rooted in our key idea that politics is conflictual and involves trade-offs. When the Supreme Court rules on civil liberties cases, it must balance an individual's freedom with government interests and the public good. In some cases, the Court must not only balance these interests but "draw a line" between permissible and illegal conduct concerning a specific liberty.

BALANCING INTERESTS

Attempting to close the detention facility at Guantánamo and the War on Terror provide particularly contentious examples of balancing civil liberties against competing interests: to what extent should we sacrifice liberties to enhance our security? Other interests that compete with civil liberties include public safety or public health. For example, in the mid-twentieth century some Christian fundamentalist churches regularly handled dangerous snakes in their services, but many states and cities have laws against "the handling of poisonous reptiles in such manner as to endanger the public health, safety, and welfare." These conflicting interests collided in a 1947 case in which members of the Zion Tabernacle Church in Durham, North Carolina, were each fined $50 for handling a poisonous copperhead snake in a church service. They appealed all the way to the North Carolina Supreme Court, arguing that the local ordinance "impinges on the freedom of religious worship." The court rejected this view saying that "public safety is superior to religious practice."[7] Similarly, in some states Amish people are forced to place reflective "slow-moving vehicle" triangles on their horse-drawn carriages, even if it violates their religious beliefs, because of the paramount concern for public safety.[8] On the other hand, the Amish were not forced to send their children to public schools despite a state law requiring all children to attend school through age sixteen. The Court said this law presented "a very real threat of undermining the Amish community and religious practice as it exists today." However the majority opinion made it clear that this ruling would *not* apply to "faddish new sects or communes."[9]

▲ *How can conflicts between civil liberties and other legitimate interests, such as public safety and public health, be resolved? Sometimes freedom is forced to give way. Courts have upheld bans on the religious practice of snake handling and laws requiring the Amish to display reflective triangles when driving slow-moving buggies on public roads, despite religious objections to doing so.*

DRAWING LINES

Along with balancing competing interests, court rulings draw the lines defining the limits of permissible conduct by the government or an individual in the context of a specific civil liberty. For example, despite the 1st Amendment protection of freedom of speech it is obvious that some speech cannot be permitted; the classic example is falsely yelling "fire" in a crowded theater. Therefore, the courts must interpret the law to draw the line between protected speech and impermissible speech. The same can be said of other civil liberties such as the establishment of religion, freedom of the press, freedom from illegal searches, or other due process rights. For example, the 1st Amendment prohibits the government from establishing an official religion, which has been carefully interpreted by the Court over the years to avoid "excessive entanglement" between any religion and the government. On these grounds, government-sponsored prayer in public schools has been banned since the early 1960s (we examine these important cases later in the chapter). But sometimes it is difficult to draw the line between acceptable and impermissible government involvement concerning religion in schools. One such ruling allowed taxpayer subsidies to fund parochial schools for buying books but not maps. This odd hair-splitting led the late senator Daniel Patrick Moynihan to quip, "What about atlases?"[10] Another difficult issue is the 4th Amendment prohibition against "unreasonable searches and seizures" and the role of drug-sniffing dogs. Here the line-drawing involves deciding whether a sniff is a search, and if so, under what circumstances it is reasonable (see You Decide). Search and seizure cases also involve balancing interests: in this case, the individual freedoms of the target of police action and the broader interests in public order and security.

The Origins of Civil Liberties

Courts define the boundaries of civil liberties, but the other branches of government and the public often get involved as well. Skirmishes between President Obama and Congress over what to do with the Guantánamo detainees are recent examples of

Drawing Lines and the 4th Amendment

The Supreme Court has ruled that police do not need a search warrant to have drug-sniffing dogs search luggage at an airport or a car that has been stopped for a traffic violation unrelated to drugs. Lower courts have also ruled that sniffs are not considered searches in a hotel hallway, school locker, outside a passenger train's sleeper compartments, or outside an apartment door. However, lower courts have been split on whether drug-sniffing dogs may be used outside a home without a warrant, due, in part, to a Supreme Court precedent giving homes stronger 4th Amendment protection than cars, lockers, or other areas. For example, in 2001 the Court ruled that police needed a warrant to use a thermal imaging device outside a home in an attempt to detect marijuana growing under heat lamps inside.

Another case provided an opportunity for the Court to sort out the lower court conflict by determining which precedent from its own decisions was most relevant (the thermal imaging case

Federal agents use a drug-sniffing dog to inspect a car.

involving homes or the dog-sniffing cases about airports and cars). The case involved a Houston man, David Smith, who was arrested when a trained dog smelled methamphetamine in his garage. Based on the dog's positive indication, the police obtained a search warrant and found the meth and other evidence of criminal activity. Smith was sentenced to thirty-seven years in prison but has appealed the conviction on the grounds that the evidence against him was illegally obtained. His lawyers ar-

gued to the Supreme Court that the thermal imaging case was the relevant precedent and that the charges should be thrown out, saying, "No distinction exists between a thermal imaging device and drug sniffing dog in that they are both sense-enhancing and permit information regarding the interior of a home to be gathered which could not otherwise be obtained without a physical intrusion into a constitutionally protected area." The district attorney, urging the Court to reject the appeal, said the thermal imaging case was not relevant because the Court's ruling in that case was focused on protecting the original meaning of the 4th Amendment from erosion by new technology. He said that in contrast to thermal imaging devices, "The use of a drug detection dog does not constitute the use of any technology, let alone advanced technology."[a] The Supreme Court declined to hear the case, which means the conviction stands, and offered no explanation why. If you had to decide this case, how would you have ruled? ■

this broad political debate. The earliest debates during the American Founding also illustrate the basic questions involved in defining civil liberties. Should government be limited by an explicit statement of individual liberties? Would these limitations apply to the state governments or just the national government? How should these freedoms evolve as our society changes?

ORIGINS OF THE BILL OF RIGHTS

As we discussed in Chapter 2, the Founders did not include protection of civil liberties in the Constitution. There were a couple of attempts to do so, including one by George Mason and Elbridge Gerry five days before the Constitutional Convention adjourned. Mason said, "It would give great quiet to the people; and with the aid of the State declarations, a bill might be prepared in a few hours." But their motion to appoint a committee to draft a bill of rights was rejected. Two days later Charles Pinckney and Gerry tried to add a provision to protect the freedom of the press, but that too was rejected.[11]

Mason and Gerry opposed ratification of the Constitution, in part because it did not include a bill of rights, and many Antifederalists echoed this view as the battle for ratification raged in the thirteen states. In a letter to James Madison, Thomas Jefferson predicted that four states would withhold ratification until a bill of rights was added.[12] Some states ratified the Constitution but urged Congress to draft specific protections for individuals' and states' rights. In some states, the Antifederalists who lost the ratification battle continued making their case to the public and Congress. One of the most famous statements opposing the Constitution came from the Antifederalists on the losing side of Pennsylvania's 46-to-23 vote for ratification. Their address was printed in local papers, reprinted in various states, and became "a semi-official statement of anti-federalist objections to the new Constitution."[13] One key passage complained about the omission of a bill of rights, which was needed to "fundamentally establish those unalienable and personal rights of men, without the full, free, and secure enjoyment of which there can be no liberty, and over which it is not necessary for a good government to have the control."[14] Their statement went on to outline many of those civil liberties that became the basis for the Bill of Rights.

Madison and other supporters of the Constitution agreed that the first Congress would take up the issue. State conventions submitted 124 amendments to Congress for their consideration. That list was whittled down to seventeen by the House and then further reduced to twelve by the Senate. This even dozen was approved by the House and sent to the states, which ratified the ten amendments that became the Bill of Rights.[15]

Despite the profound significance of the Bill of Rights, one important point limited its reach: it applied only to the national government and not the states. For example, the 1st Amendment says that "*Congress* shall make no law" infringing on freedom of religion, speech, and the press, among others. Madison submitted another amendment, which he characterized as "the most valuable of the whole list," requiring states to protect some civil liberties: "The equal rights of conscience, the freedom of speech or of the press, and the right of trial by jury in criminal cases shall not be infringed by any State."[16] Antifederalists feared another power grab by the Federalists in limiting states' rights, so it was voted down in Congress as the amendments were being written. This decision proved consequential because the national government was quite weak for the first half of our nation's history and had much less impact on the daily lives of citizens than did state and local governments. Therefore, protecting civil liberties from the national government's actions protected citizens less than limits on state power would have.

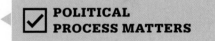

POLITICAL PROCESS MATTERS

CIVIL LIBERTIES BEFORE THE CIVIL WAR

When the Bill of Rights was ratified, the common understanding was that it applied only to the national government. However, Madison and others soon came to believe that these restrictions should also apply to the states.[17] Ultimately, the Supreme Court had to sort this out. In the last decision of his thirty-three years on the Court, the great chief justice John Marshall wrote in *Barron v. Baltimore* that indeed the Bill of Rights only applied to the national government and not to the states (see Chapter 3). In this case, John Barron sued the city of Baltimore when its street-paving project diverted streams and sent sand and gravel into the harbor area he owned, making it impossible for ships to use his once-valuable

The Bill of Rights: A Statement of Our Civil Liberties

1st Amendment	Freedom of religion, speech, press, and assembly; the separation of church and state; and the right to petition the government.
2nd Amendment	Right to bear arms.
3rd Amendment	Protection against the forced quartering of troops in one's home.
4th Amendment	Protection from unreasonable searches and seizures; requirement of "probable cause" for search warrants.
5th Amendment	Protection from forced self-incrimination or double jeopardy (being tried twice for the same crime); no person can be deprived of life, liberty, or property without due process of law; private property cannot be taken for public use without just compensation; and no person can be tried for a serious crime without the indictment of a grand jury.
6th Amendment	Right of the accused to a speedy and public trial by an impartial jury, to an attorney, to confront witnesses, to a compulsory process for obtaining witnesses in his or her favor, and to counsel in all felony cases.
7th Amendment	Right to a trial by jury in civil cases involving common law.
8th Amendment	Protection from excessive bail, excessive fines, and cruel and unusual punishment.
9th Amendment	The enumeration of specific rights in the Constitution shall not be construed to deny other rights retained by the people. This has been interpreted to include a general right to privacy and other fundamental rights.
10th Amendment	Powers not delegated by the Constitution to the national government, nor prohibited by it to the states, are reserved to the states or to the people.

wharf. Barron claimed that the city owed him the lost value of his property because the 5th Amendment says that private property may not be "taken for public use without just compensation." The Maryland state constitution did not have a similar provision, so Barron sued under the U.S. Constitution. He won in district court but lost on appeal. The Supreme Court agreed with the appeals court, saying that the Bill of Rights "demanded security against the apprehended encroachments of the General Government—not against those of the local governments," and "contain no expression indicating an intention to apply them to the state governments."[18]

As a consequence, the Bill of Rights played a surprisingly small role for more than a century. The Supreme Court used it only once before 1866 to invalidate a federal action—in the infamous *Dred Scott* case that contributed to the onset of the Civil War. Further evidence that the Bill of Rights was relatively insignificant in our nation's early history comes from a review of newspapers published in 1841 that could not find a single mention of the fiftieth anniversary of the Bill of Rights.[19]

SELECTIVE INCORPORATION AND THE 14TH AMENDMENT

The significance of the Bill of Rights increased somewhat with the ratification of the 14th Amendment in 1868. It was one of the three **Civil War Amendments** that attempted to guarantee the newly freed slaves equal rights as citizens of the United States. (The other two Civil War Amendments were the 13th, which abolished slavery, and the 15th, which gave male former slaves the right to vote.) Northern politicians were concerned that southerners would deny basic rights to

Civil War Amendments The 13th, 14th, and 15th Amendments to the Constitution, which abolished slavery and granted civil liberties and voting rights to freed slaves after the Civil War.

the former slaves, so the sweeping language of the 14th Amendment was adopted. Section 1 says:

> All persons born or naturalized in the United States, and subject to the jurisdiction thereof, are citizens of the United States and of the State wherein they reside. No State shall make or enforce any law which shall abridge the privileges or immunities of citizens of the United States; nor shall any State deprive any person of life, liberty, or property, without due process of law; nor deny to any person within its jurisdiction the equal protection of the laws.

The authors of this amendment and its supporters intended this language to require all states to protect civil liberties as guaranteed by the Bill of Rights.[20] The **due process clause**, which forbids any state from denying "life, liberty, or property, without due process of law," was an especially important expansion of civil liberties because the similar clause of the 5th Amendment had previously been interpreted by the Court to only apply to the federal government.

However, in its first opportunity to interpret the 14th Amendment, the Court disagreed. The case involved a group of approximately 1,000 butchers and slaughterhouse owners in Louisiana who were about to be run out of business by a law passed by the corrupt state legislature, which effectively gave a slaughterhouse monopoly to a single firm. The owners of rival slaughterhouses sued the state under the "privileges and immunities" clause of the 14th Amendment, arguing that the state government was denying their basic rights. Despite the clear language of the amendment saying that "no State shall make or enforce any law" limiting citizens' legal "privileges or immunities," the Court embraced the "dual citizenship" idea set forth in *Barron v. Baltimore* and stated that the 14th Amendment only protected U.S. citizens against the actions of the national government, not the state governments. The Court also rejected the plaintiffs' claim that the state was denying them "the equal protection of the laws" on the grounds that the 14th Amendment was intended to strike down laws that discriminated against blacks.[21] One constitutional scholar observed that all that remained of the 14th Amendment after this decision was a vague, general understanding that it was intended to give citizenship to the newly freed slaves.[22] In other words, all that remained was the first sentence!

Over the next fifty years a minority of justices tried mightily to restore the power of the 14th Amendment and use it to protect civil liberties against state government action. The first step was an 1897 case in which the Court ruled that the 14th Amendment's due process clause forbade the state of Illinois from taking private property without just compensation. However, the decision did not specifically mention the 5th Amendment's compensation clause.[23] The next step came about ten years later in a self-incrimination case in which a state judge gave jury instructions that included references to the fact that the accused did not take the stand in his defense. The Supreme Court upheld his conviction but said, "It is possible that some of the personal rights safeguarded in the first eight amendments against National action may also be safeguarded against state action, because a denial of them would be a denial of the due process of law."[24] Thus, in both the property and self-incrimination cases, the Supreme Court started to use the 14th Amendment to prohibit state governments from violating individual rights but without specific reference to the Bill of Rights.

This logical progression finally culminated in the 1925 case *Gitlow v. New York*, in which the Court said for the first time that the 14th Amendment incorporated one of the amendments in the Bill of Rights and applied it to the states. The case involved Benjamin Gitlow, a radical Socialist convicted under New York's Criminal

due process clause Part of the 14th Amendment that forbids states from denying "life, liberty, or property" to any person without due process of law. (A nearly identical clause in the 5th Amendment applies only to the national government.)

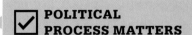
POLITICAL PROCESS MATTERS

selective incorporation The process through which the civil liberties granted in the Bill of Rights were applied to the states on a case-by-case basis through the 14th Amendment.

POLITICS IS EVERYWHERE

Anarchy Act of 1902 for advocating the overthrow of the government. The Court upheld his conviction, arguing that his writings were the "language of direct incitement," but also warned state governments that there were limits on such suppression of speech:

> For present purposes we may and do assume that freedom of speech and of the press—which are protected by the First Amendment from abridgement of Congress—are among the fundamental personal rights and "liberties" protected by the due process clause of the Fourteenth Amendment from impairment by the states.[25]

Slowly over the next fifty years, most civil liberties covered in the Bill of Rights were applied to the states on a case-by-case basis through the 14th Amendment. However, this process of **selective incorporation** was not smooth and incremental; rather it progressed in surges. The first flurry of activity came in the 1930s when most of the 1st Amendment was incorporated, requiring the states to allow a free press, the right to assemble, free exercise of religion, and the right to petition. The next flurry came in the 1960s with a series of cases on criminal defendants' rights and due process. Why the gap of nearly a quarter century (with only two exceptions)?[26] A case involving the double jeopardy clause of the 5th Amendment determined that some rights were so fundamental that they could not be denied by the states, while if others were denied, such as being tried twice for the same crime, it would not undermine our sense of "ordered liberty."[27] The example the Court gave of these fundamental rights was the "freedom of thought and speech." By elevating certain rights later referred to as the Honor Roll of Superior Rights, this ruling meant that civil liberties would be *selectively* incorporated by the 14th Amendment rather than applied as a group to the states. Thus, for the next twenty-five years, the Court largely confined selective incorporation to the 1st Amendment. However, this did not allow the states to ignore the due process of law. By choosing which cases to hear, the Court continued to monitor the states for conduct that, in the words of Justice Felix Frankfurter, "shocked the conscience," or in the blunt language of Justice Oliver Wendell Holmes, "[makes] you vomit."[28]

The second flurry of activity moved away from this idea of fundamental rights and more broadly applied the 14th Amendment to the Bill of Rights. Indeed, with the incorporation of the 2nd Amendment's right to bear arms in 2010, all of the significant amendments now apply to state and local governments (see Nuts and Bolts 4.3). As a result, the Bill of Rights has evolved from the nineteenth century's limitations that affected only national government action to a robust set of protections for freedom and liberty.

Freedom of Speech, Assembly, and the Press

The 1st Amendment's ringing words are the most famous statement of personal freedoms in the Constitution: "Congress shall make no law respecting an establishment of religion, or prohibiting the free exercise thereof; or abridging the freedom of speech, or of the press; or the right of the people peaceably to assemble, and to petition the Government for a redress of grievances." You may think that the 1st Amendment's position reflects its importance, but it actually ended up first through an accident of history. Twelve amendments were submitted to the states for ratification, but the first two were not ratified, so the original 3rd Amendment became the

Selective Incorporation

AMENDMENT	ISSUE	CASE
1st Amendment	Freedom of speech	*Gitlow v. New York* (1925)
	Freedom of the press	*Near v. Minnesota* (1931)
	Freedom of assembly	*DeJonge v. Oregon* (1937)
	Right to petition the government	*Hague v. CIO* (1939)
	Free exercise of religion	*Hamilton v. Regents of the University of California* (1934), *Cantwell v. Connecticut* (1940)
	Separation of church and state	*Everson v. Board of Education of Ewing Township* (1947)
2nd Amendment	Right to bear arms	*McDonald v. Chicago* (2010)
4th Amendment	Protection from unreasonable search and seizure	*Wolf v. Colorado (1949), Mapp v. Ohio (1961)*[a]
5th Amendment	Protection from forced self-incrimination	*Malloy v. Hogan* (1964)
	Protection from double jeopardy	*Benton v. Maryland* (1969)
6th Amendment	Right to a public trial	*In re Oliver 333 U.S. 257* (1948)
	Right to a fair trial and an attorney in death-penalty cases	*Powell v. Alabama* (1932)
	Right to an attorney in all felony cases	*Gideon v. Wainwright* (1963)
	Right to an attorney in cases involving jail time	*Argersinger v. Hamlin* (1972)
	Right to a jury trial in a criminal case	*Duncan v. Louisiana* (1968)
	Right to cross-examine a witness	*Pointer v. Texas* (1965)
	Right to compel witnesses to testify who are vital for the defendant's case	*Washington v. Texas* (1967)
8th Amendment	Protection from cruel and unusual punishment	*Robinson v. California* (1962)[b]
	Protection from excessive bail	*Schilb v. Kuebel* (1971)[c]
9th Amendment	Right to privacy and other non-enumerated, fundamental rights	*Griswold v. Connecticut* (1965)[d]

NOT INCORPORATED		
3rd Amendment	Prohibition against the quartering of troops in private homes	
5th Amendment	Right to indictment by a grand jury	
7th Amendment	Right to a jury trial in a civil case	
8th Amendment	Prohibition against excessive fines	

[a] *Wolf v. Colorado* applied the 4th Amendment to the states (which meant that states could not engage in unreasonable searches and seizures); *Mapp v. Ohio* applied the exclusionary rule to the states (which excludes the use of illegally obtained evidence in a trial).
[b] Some sources list *Louisiana ex rel. Francis v. Resweber* (1947) as the first case that incorporated the 8th Amendment. While the decision mentioned the 5th and 8th Amendments in the context of the due process clause of the 14th Amendment, this argument was not included in the majority opinion that upheld as constitutional the bizarre double-electrocution of Willie Francis (the electric chair malfunctioned on the first attempt but was successful on the second attempt; see Abraham and Perry, *Freedom and the Court*, pp. 71–72).
[c] Justice Blackmun "assumed" in this case that "the 8th Amendment's proscription of excessive bail [applies] to the states through the 14th Amendment," but later decisions did not seem to share this view. However, Justices Stevens and O'Connor agreed with Blackmun's view in *Browning-Ferris v. Kelco Disposal* (1989). Some sources argue that the excessive bail clause of the 8th Amendment is unincorporated.
[d] Justice Goldberg argued for explicit incorporation of the 9th Amendment in a concurring opinion joined by Justices Warren and Brennan. The opinion of the Court referred more generally to a privacy right rooted in five amendments, including the 9th, but did not explicitly argue for incorporation.

first.[29] As we noted earlier, defining the scope of our civil liberties depends on balancing interests and drawing lines. This is especially true of 1st Amendment freedoms, which can best be envisioned on a continuum from most to least protected, based on the Supreme Court cases that have tested their limits.

PROTECTED EXPRESSION

Any time you attend a religious service, go to a political rally, write an article for your student paper, or express a political idea, you are being protected by the 1st Amendment. However, the nature of this protection is not set in stone but is continually evolving due to political forces and shifting constitutional interpretations. For much of our nation's history, the freedom of speech and press were not strongly protected. Only recently have the courts developed a complex continuum ranging from strongly protected political speech (including symbolic speech such as flag burning) to less protected speech such as obscenity, commercial speech, libel, and fighting words.

Political Speech Freedom of speech got off to a rocky start when in 1798, just a few years after the Bill of Rights was ratified, Congress passed the Alien and Sedition Acts. The especially controversial Sedition Act made it a crime to "write, print, utter or publish . . . any false, scandalous and malicious writing or writings against the government of the United States." Supporters of the four acts claimed they were necessary to strengthen the national government in response to the French Revolution. In reality they were an attempt by the governing Federalist Party to neutralize the opposition Democratic-Republican Party. As many as twenty-five people, mostly newspaper editors, were tried under the law and ten were jailed, including Benjamin Franklin's grandson. The outcry against the laws helped propel Thomas Jefferson to the presidency in 1800. Jefferson pardoned the convicted editors, Congress repealed one of the acts in 1802, and the others were allowed to expire before the Supreme Court had a chance to rule them unconstitutional.

The next big challenge to freedom of speech came from the states rather than the national government. During the battles over slavery in the first half of the nineteenth century, northern states outlawed positive statements about slavery, while southern states prohibited criticism of slavery. By the end of the nineteenth century, such sedition laws prohibiting behavior considered subversive were quite common at the state level, and hundreds of people had been jailed for criticizing the government and its policies (recall that the 1st Amendment did not apply to the states in the nineteenth century).

World War I prompted the harshest crackdowns on free speech since the Sedition Act of 1798. The most important case from this period involved the general secretary of the Socialist Party, Charles Schenk. Schenk strongly opposed U.S. involvement in the war and had printed 15,000 leaflets that he was in the process of mailing to young men who had been drafted to serve in the army. The leaflet advocated resisting the draft, saying that it was unconstitutional under the 13th Amendment prohibition of "involuntary servitude" and that the war was a "monstrous wrong against humanity, in the interest of Wall Street's chosen few." Schenk was arrested under the Espionage Act of 1917 that prohibited "interfering with military or naval operations," including the draft. He appealed all the way to the Supreme Court, arguing that the 1st Amendment permitted him to protest the war and urge others to resist the draft, but the Court sustained his conviction, noting that free speech is not an absolute right:

> The most stringent protection of free speech would not protect a man in falsely shouting fire in a theatre and causing a panic. . . . The question in every case is whether the

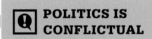

◀ *Many American socialists opposed U.S. involvement in World War I. Socialist leader Charles Schenk was prosecuted for encouraging young men to resist the draft, and another socialist, Eugene Debs, was jailed merely for speaking out against the war.*

words used are used in such circumstances and are of such a nature as to create a clear and present danger that they will bring about the substantive evils that Congress has a right to prevent.[30]

This **clear and present danger test** meant that the government could suppress speech they thought was dangerous (in this instance, preventing the government from fighting the war). Critics of this decision argue that Schenk's actions were not dangerous for the country and certainly not equivalent to shouting fire in a theater, which does not allow people a chance to think before panicking.[31] While Schenk's actions would have been legal under the current standard for protecting speech, things would get worse for supporters of the 1st Amendment before they got better. Another socialist leader, Eugene V. Debs, was sentenced to ten years in federal prison for making a speech in 1918 that condemned U.S. involvement in World War I, and two newspaper publishers were jailed for publishing articles critical of the war. Both high-profile convictions were sustained by the Court.[32] Then Congress passed the even more restrictive Sedition Act of 1918, which outlawed any "disloyal, profane, scurrilous, or abusive language about the form of government, the Constitution, soldiers and sailors, flag or uniform of the armed forces" and any words that favored the cause of the German empire or opposed the cause of the United States. In the first test case for the new law, the Court upheld the conviction of six anarchists who supported the cause of the Bolsheviks in Russia and urged the "workers of the world" to strike.

The great Justice Oliver Wendell Holmes, author of the *Schenk* decision and the clear and present danger test, had had enough. He dissented in the anarchists' case, arguing that the "surreptitious publishing of a silly leaflet by an unknown man" posed no danger to the country. In one of the most famous statements of the importance of the freedom of speech, he touted the "free trade in ideas" saying, "The best test of truth is the power of the thought to get itself accepted in the competition of the market . . . we should be eternally vigilant against attempts to

Q **POLITICS IS CONFLICTUAL**

clear and present danger test Established in *Schenk v. United States*, this test allows the government to restrict certain types of speech deemed dangerous.

▲ *Senator Joseph McCarthy stands in front of a map purporting to show communist activity in the United States. McCarthy was a central figure in the post–World War II Red Scare, during which Americans suspected of supporting communism were persecuted and imprisoned.*

check the expression of opinion that we loathe and believe to be fraught with death."[33] This notion of the marketplace of ideas in which good ideas triumph over bad is still central to modern defenses of the 1st Amendment. Holmes correctly pointed out that if freedom of speech is to have any meaning, we must protect the right to utter "words that we loathe" and that are "fraught with death" as well as those that we agree with and that pose no danger.

Over the next several decades the Court struggled to draw the line between dangerous speech and words that were simply unpopular. For example, during the Red Scare of the late 1940s and early 1950s, Senator Joseph McCarthy and others roused the nation against the communist threat, presenting the Court with many opportunities to defend unpopular speech. But for the most part they declined. The communist threat was real but exaggerated, and hundreds of innocent Americans had their careers and lives ruined by false accusations and guilt by association. The legal issue facing the Court was whether the Smith Act, which attempted to restrict the Communist Party by banning the advocacy of force or violence against the United States, violated the 1st Amendment. In 1951 the Court upheld the conviction of eleven members of the Communist Party under the Smith Act.[34]

The strongest protection for free speech, and the one that remains in force today, was put into place in 1969. This case involved a leader of the Ku Klux Klan, Clarence Brandenburg, who made a threatening speech at a cross-burning rally that was subsequently shown on television. Twelve hooded figures were shown on the film, many with weapons. The speech said that "revengence" [sic] might be taken if "our president, our Congress, our Supreme Court continues to suppress the white, Caucasian race." He continued, "We are marching on Congress July the Fourth, four hundred thousand strong." Brandenburg was convicted under the Ohio law banning "sabotage, violence, or unlawful methods of terrorism as a means of accomplishing industrial or political reform," but the Court unanimously reversed his conviction, arguing that threatening speech could not be suppressed just because it sounded dangerous. Specifically, the **direct incitement test** holds that speech is protected "except where such advocacy is directed to inciting or producing imminent lawless action and is likely to incite or produce such action."[35] Under this standard, most, if not all, of the sedition convictions during World War I and the Red Scare would have been overturned.

Symbolic Speech The use of signs, symbols, or other unspoken acts or methods to communicate in a political manner—**symbolic speech**—enjoys many of the same protections as regular speech. For example, during the Vietnam War the Court protected the 1st Amendment right of a war protestor to wear an American flag patch sewn on the seat of his pants,[36] high school students' right to wear an armband to protest the war[37] or tape a peace symbol on the flag and fly it upside-down outside an apartment window.[38] Lower courts convicted these protestors under state laws that protected the American flag, or in the armband case, under a school policy that explicitly prohibited wearing armbands to protest the Vietnam War. In the flag desecration case involving the peace symbol, the Court clearly stated that protected "speech" need not be verbal, saying that even though the appellant did not use words, "there can be little doubt that appellant communicated through the use of symbols."[39]

A 1989 case provided the strongest protection for symbolic speech yet. The case involved a man, Gregory Johnson, who burned a flag outside the 1984 Republican

direct incitement test Established in *Brandenberg v. Ohio*, this test protects threatening speech under the 1st Amendment unless that speech aims to and is likely to cause imminent "lawless action."

symbolic speech Nonverbal expression, such as the use of signs or symbols. It benefits from many of the same constitutional protections of verbal speech.

national convention in Texas, chanting along with a group of protestors, "America the red, white, and blue, we spit on you. You stand for plunder, you will go under." The Court refrained from critiquing Johnson's jingle, but its 5–4 decision overturned his conviction under Texas's flag desecration law on the grounds that symbolic political speech is protected by the 1st Amendment.[40] In response to this extremely unpopular decision, Congress passed the Flag Protection Act of 1989, which the Court also struck down as an unconstitutional infringement on political expression.[41] Congress then attempted to pass a constitutional amendment to overturn the Court decision; the House passed the amendment in 1995, 2000, and 2005, but each time the measure failed by a narrow margin in the Senate.

Although flag burning and other forms of symbolic speech have been protected by the Court, there are limits, especially when the symbolic speech conflicts with another substantial governmental interest. For example, Vietnam War protestors who burned their draft cards were not protected by the 1st Amendment because their actions interfered with Congress's constitutional authority to "raise and support" armies through the draft. Just because someone is expressing an idea doesn't mean the symbolic action associated with that idea will be protected speech.[42] Another important exception involved Joseph Frederick, a high school student from Juneau, Alaska, who was suspended from school for unfurling a fourteen-foot banner on a public sidewalk that said "Bong Hits 4 Jesus." The incident occurred just outside school grounds, as the Olympic torch relay passed through Juneau on its way to the 2002 Winter Games in Salt Lake City, Utah. Frederick sued the school claiming his 1st Amendment rights were violated, but the Supreme Court agreed with the school, saying "It was reasonable for [the principal] to conclude that the banner promoted illegal drug use—and that failing to act would send a powerful message to the students in her charge." The dissenters lamented the invention of "a special 1st Amendment rule permitting the censorship of any student speech that mentions drugs," based on "a silly, nonsensical banner."[43]

According to the Court, spending money in political campaigns can also be considered symbolic speech since it provides the means for more conventional types of political speech. Here the central question is whether the government can control campaign contributions and spending or whether such laws violate the 1st Amendment rights of candidates or their supporters. You probably have heard the old saying "Money talks," which implies that money is speech. Given the importance of advertising in modern campaigns, limitations on raising and spending money could limit the ability of candidates and groups to reach voters with their message. The Court has walked a tightrope on this one, balancing the public interest in honest and ethical elections and the 1st Amendment rights of candidates and their advocates. The Court has upheld individual candidates' right to spend their own money in federal elections, but presidential candidates give up that right if they accept federal campaign funds (taxpayers' money) in a presidential election. Also, candidates in federal elections are subject to limits on the types and size of contributions they can receive, and they must report all contributions and spending to the Federal Election Commission. The Bipartisan Campaign Reform Act, which went into effect for the 2004 elections, included a "Millionaires' Amendment" that lifted restrictions on campaign contributions for candidates whose opponent spent more than $350,000 of their own money in the election. This attempt to level the campaign finance playing field was struck down by the Supreme Court in 2008 as a violation of wealthy candidates' 1st Amendment rights.[44] In 2010, the Court also extended 1st Amendment rights to corporations that want to spend money on campaign ads (these cases are discussed in more detail in Chapter 8). However, the Court upheld a ban on so-called soft money (this term will be discussed in more detail in Chapter 8; at this point it is sufficient to note that it was seen by the Court as

▲ The American flag is a popular target for protesters: it has been spat upon, shredded, turned into underwear, and burned, as it was during this 2004 demonstration at the Democratic National Convention in Boston. Despite multiple efforts in Congress to ban flag desecration, these activities remain constitutionally protected symbolic speech.

hate speech Expression that is offensive or abusive, particularly in terms of race, gender, or sexual orientation. It is currently protected under the 1st Amendment.

the type of contribution with the most potential for corruption because soft money contributions were previously unlimited).[45]

Spending as a form of symbolic speech struck closer to home in a case in 2000 involving student activity fees at the University of Wisconsin. A group of students argued that they should not have to pay student fees to fund groups whose activities they opposed, including a student environmental group, a gay and bisexual student center, a community legal office, an AIDS support network, a campus women's center, and the Wisconsin Student Public Interest Research Group. In a unanimous opinion, the Court ruled that mandatory student fees could continue to support the full range of groups as long as the process for allocating money was "viewpoint neutral." The Court also said that student referendums that could add, cut, or even eliminate money for specific groups violated viewpoint neutrality. The potential for the majority to censor unpopular views was unacceptable to the Court, since "the whole theory of viewpoint neutrality is that minority views are treated with the same respect as are majority views."[46]

Hate Speech Free speech has been a hot topic on many college campuses since the mid-1980s in the context of **hate speech**. Do people have a right to say things that are offensive or abusive, especially in terms of race, gender, and sexual orientation? By the mid-1990s more than 350 public colleges and universities said no by regulating some forms of hate speech.[47] One example was a speech code adopted at the University of Michigan that prohibited "any behavior, verbal or physical, that stigmatizes or victimizes an individual on the basis of race, ethnicity, religion, sex, sexual orientation, creed, national origin, ancestry, age, marital status, handicap, or Vietnam veteran status," and "creates an intimidating, hostile, or demeaning environment for educational pursuits, employment or participation in University-sponsored extra-curricular activities."[48] The Supreme Court has yet to rule definitively on this issue, but lower courts struck down the University of Michigan's speech code as well as similar rules at the University of Wisconsin and several other universities. If the Court took up any of these cases, they would be likely to strike down the speech codes because they are not "content neutral" regulations and they do not meet the direct incitement test of targeting only expressions that would spur imminent violence.

One final significant issue combines the topics of symbolic speech and hate speech. Can a person who burned a cross on a black family's lawn be convicted under a city ordinance that prohibited conduct "arous[ing] anger, alarm, or resentment in others on the basis of race, color, creed, religion, or gender"? Or is the ordinance an unconstitutional limit on 1st Amendment rights? In a unanimous decision the Court said the cross burner could be punished for arson, terrorism, trespassing, or other violations of the law, but he could not be convicted under this St. Paul, Minnesota, ordinance because it was overly broad and vague. The Court said, "Let there be no mistake about our belief that burning a cross in someone's front yard is reprehensible. But St. Paul has sufficient means at its disposal to prevent such behavior without adding the First Amendment to the fire."[49] The city ordinance was unconstitutional because it took selective aim at a disfavored message, or in the legal jargon of the Court, it constituted "viewpoint discrimination." However, the Court has since upheld more carefully worded bans of cross burning. Eleven years after the St. Paul case, the Court ruled that Virginia could prohibit cross burning if there was an intent to intimidate, but that determining intent depends on the

▼ Are laws banning hate speech constitutional? Sometimes yes, but the threshold is relatively high. These Ku Klux Klan members are free to hold rallies, preach racism and xenophobia, and burn crosses, as long as they do not directly incite violence or display an "intent to intimidate."

context. For example, burning a cross on a black family's front lawn would be illegal under this law, but burning a cross at a Ku Klux Klan rally to symbolize white supremacist political views would still be protected by the 1st Amendment.[50]

Freedom of Assembly The right to assemble peaceably has been consistently protected by the Supreme Court. In an important 1937 case that applied this part of the 1st Amendment to the states for the first time, the Court upheld the right to teach communist doctrine in public meetings, saying that the right to assemble is "one that cannot be denied without violating those fundamental principles which lie at the base of all civil and political institutions."[51] Peaceful civil rights protestors who were arrested for disturbing the peace had their convictions overturned when the Court said the state of South Carolina could not "make criminal the peaceful expression of unpopular views."[52] Perhaps the most famous assembly case involved a neo-Nazi group that wanted to march in Skokie, Illinois, a suburb of Chicago that then had about 70,000 residents of whom nearly 60 percent were Jewish. Many of the residents were Holocaust survivors and strongly opposed the march. The village passed three ordinances that effectively banned the group from marching. In defense of these laws, the village government argued that residents would be so upset by the Nazi marchers that they might become violent, and the local government could not ensure the safety of the marchers. But the lower courts did not accept this argument, ruling that as long as the marchers engaged in protected speech (that is, they didn't incite imminent violence among *their* followers), then the village had to protect the marchers. They ruled that if "the audience is so offended by the ideas being expressed that it becomes disorderly and attempts to silence the speaker, it is the duty of the police to attempt to protect the speaker, not to silence his speech."[53] The Court elaborated on this responsibility to protect expressions of unpopular views by striking down another town's ordinance that allowed them to charge a higher permit fee to groups whose march would likely require more police protection.[54]

While broad protection is provided for peaceable assemblies, governments may regulate the time, manner, and place of expression as long as the regulation is content-neutral, not favoring certain groups or messages over others. For example, anti-abortion protestors were not allowed to picket a doctor's home in Brookfield, Wisconsin. The Court ruled that the ordinance banning all residential picketing was content-neutral and that there was a government interest in preserving the "sanctity of the home, the one retreat to which men and women can repair to escape from the tribulations of their daily pursuits."[55] "Time, manner, and place" restrictions also may be invoked for practical reasons. If the Ku Klux Klan planned to hold a march around the football stadium on the day of a game, the city council could deny them a permit and suggest they choose another day that would be more convenient. The legal standard for these regulations is that they are "reasonable." While vague, this standard allows the courts to balance the right to assemble against other practical considerations.

Freedom of the Press The task of balancing interests is central to many 1st Amendment cases involving the freedom of the press. Which is more important, the 1st Amendment freedom of the press to disclose details about current events or the 6th Amendment right to a fair trial, which may require keeping important information out of the public eye? When do national security concerns prevail over journalists' right to keep citizens informed? The general issue here is **prior restraint,** the government's right to prevent the media from publishing something. When applied to information concerning a ongoing trail, the prohibition to publish is called a **gag order.** Prior restraint has never been clearly defined by the Court, but

> ◄ Q **POLITICS IS CONFLICTUAL**

prior restraint A limit on freedom of the press that allows the government to prohibit the media from publishing certain materials.

gag order An aspect of prior restraint that allows the government to prohibit the media from publishing anything related to an ongoing trial.

▲ In July 1971, Daniel Ellsberg testified before Congress that he had leaked the classified Pentagon Papers to reporters, revealing Department of Defense plans and strategies for conducting the Vietnam War. The Supreme Court determined that the government could not prevent publication of the papers, despite their classified status.

several landmark cases have set a very high bar for applying it. The first involved a Minnesota law that banned "obscene, lewd and lascivious" publications or "malicious, scandalous and defamatory" content. Under this law, the state shut down a racist, bigoted publication by Jay Near that railed against many groups of people. The Court subsequently struck down the law saying, "The fact that the liberty of the press may be abused by miscreant purveyors of scandal does not make any less necessary the immunity of the press from previous restraint."[56] However, the Court did not specify when prior restraint would be acceptable (it simply said that there would have to be "exceptional circumstances").

The next major opportunity to clarify the issue came in 1971 with the Pentagon Papers case, which involved disclosure of parts of the top-secret report on internal planning for the Vietnam War. The incredibly divided case had nine separate written opinions! By a 6–3 margin the Court decided that the government could not prevent the publication of the Pentagon Papers, but at least five justices supported the view that, under some circumstances, the government could use prior restraint—though they could not agree on the standard. For some of the justices, a crucial consideration was that the papers revealed the U.S. government had lied about its involvement in and the progress of the Vietnam War. Justice Hugo Black noted the importance of this point saying, "Only a free and unrestrained press can effectively expose deception in government."[57] This ended up being an amazing prediction of the role of the press in uncovering the Watergate scandal that brought down the Nixon presidency.

Prior restraint has taken on new significance in the War on Terror. The media, especially the *New York Times*, skirmished with the Bush administration over publishing stories on various classified programs, including extraordinary rendition of suspected terrorists, domestic surveillance, and the Terrorist Finance Tracking Program, which monitors all large financial transactions in the international banking system. The sensational leaking of more than 91,000 reports concerning the war in Afghanistan by WikiLeaks ratcheted up the stakes. Some members of Congress called the leaks "treason" and urged for prosecution. However supporters of an unrestrained press point to the Pentagon Papers case as precedent for the role of journalists in holding the government accountable. They argue that the conduct of war and programs such as warrantless wiretapping of U.S. citizens may violate international or domestic law and the public has the right to know about them. Furthermore, these stories are not published without serious consideration of the consequences; the *New York Times* sat on the domestic telephone surveillance story for a year before publishing it. Critics of the media argue that revealing classified programs is irresponsible and may threaten national security. The Justice Department investigated leaks from the National Security Administration believed to be the source of some of the *New York Times* stories and promised to prosecute the leakers and the journalists. Congress responded by trying to pass the Free Flow of Information Act, which would have given journalists some protection of confidential sources and information. The bill passed the House in 2007 and 2009 but was killed both times when the Senate failed to get enough votes to prevent a filibuster.

Keeping sources confidential has always been an important aspect of the freedom of the press since many sources would not talk to reporters if they thought their names would appear on the front page the next day. But the need to protect sources sometimes conflicts with criminal investigations or trials. For example, Judith Miller, a *New York Times* reporter, was jailed for eighty-five days in 2005 for refusing to reveal her sources for several articles to the grand jury investigating the leak of a CIA operative's name by White House officials. She was released when she agreed to provide limited testimony to the grand jury concerning conversations with Dick Cheney's aide, Lewis "Scooter" Libby, without revealing her other sources.

Prior restraint also may be an issue in media coverage of a trial, but gag orders are allowed only when media coverage would make it impossible for the defendant to have a fair trial. In a 1976 case involving a multiple murder in Nebraska, the Court struck down a gag order that prevented the press from describing the facts of the case. The Court said, "The protection against prior restraint should have particular force as applied to reporting of criminal proceedings."[58] Gag orders that prohibit participants in a trial (jury members, witnesses, lawyers, law enforcement officials) from talking to the media operate under more complicated precedents that depend on whether this media contact would undermine a fair trail.[59]

LESS PROTECTED SPEECH AND PUBLICATIONS

Some forms of speech do not warrant the same level of protection as political speech because they do not contribute to public debate or express ideas that have important social value. Four categories of speech may be more easily regulated by the government than political speech: fighting words, slander and libel, commercial speech, and obscenity.

Fighting Words Governments may regulate **fighting words**, "which by their very utterance inflict injury or tend to incite an immediate breach of the peace."[60] Such laws must be narrowly written; it is not acceptable to ban all foul language, and the prohibited speech must target a single person rather than a group. At first the question of whether certain words provoke a backlash doesn't seem like a very logical test because it depends on the reaction of the targeted person. Inflammatory words directed at Archbishop Emeritus Desmond Tutu would not be fighting words because he would turn the other cheek, whereas the same words yelled at musician Busta Rhymes or actor Sean Penn *would* be fighting words because they would probably deck you. The Court has further clarified the test, based on "what persons of common intelligence would understand to be words likely to cause an average addressee to fight,"[61] but the fighting words doctrine has still been difficult to apply and is not widely used by the Court.

Slander and Libel A more extensive line of cases prohibiting speech concerns **slander**, spoken false statements that damage someone's reputation, and **libel**, written statements that do the same thing. As in many areas of 1st Amendment law, it is difficult to draw the line between permissible speech and slander or libel. One text on the subject calls the topic a "veritable public-law snake pit." The current legal standard distinguishes between speech about a public figure, such as a politician or celebrity, and about a regular person. In short, public figures must have much thicker skin than the average person because it is much more difficult for them to prove libel. To win a libel suit, a public figure has to demonstrate that the defamatory statement was made with "actual malice" and "with knowledge that it was false or with reckless disregard of whether it was false or not."[62] One of the most famous libel cases was brought against *Hustler* magazine by Reverend Jerry Falwell, a famous televangelist and political activist. Falwell sued *Hustler* for libel and emotional distress after the magazine published a parody of a liquor advertisement depicting him in a "drunken incestuous rendezvous with his mother in an outhouse" (this quote is from the Supreme Court case).[63] The lower court said that the parody wasn't believable, so *Hustler* couldn't be sued for libel, but they awarded Falwell damages for emotional distress. The Court unanimously overturned this decision saying that public figures and public officials have to put up with such things and compared the parody to outrageous political cartoons, which have always been protected by the 1st Amendment. Though the Court sided with the magazine in this case, other rulings have narrowed the definition of a "public figure," making it easier for a broader range of citizens to prove libel.[64]

fighting words Forms of expression that "by their very utterance" can incite violence. These can be regulated by the government but are often difficult to define.

slander and **libel** Spoken false statements (slander) and written false statements (libel) that damage a person's reputation. Both can be regulated by the government but are often difficult to distinguish from permissible speech.

▲ *Joe Camel peddles his wares on a New York City billboard. Commercial speech, as a general category, is not as strongly protected by the 1st Amendment as political speech, but advertising can be limited by the government only in specific circumstances.*

commercial speech Public expression with the aim of making a profit. It has received greater protection under the 1st Amendment in recent years but remains less protected than political speech.

***Miller* test** Established in *Miller v. California*, the Supreme Court uses this three-part test to determine whether speech meets the criteria for obscenity. If so, it can be restricted by the government.

Commercial Speech Commercial speech, which mostly refers to advertising, has evolved from having almost no protection under the 1st Amendment to having quite strong protection. One early case involved a business owner who distributed leaflets to advertise rides on his submarine that was docked in New York City. Under city ordinances, leafleting was only permitted if it was devoted to "information or a public protest," but not for a commercial purpose. The plaintiff changed the leaflet to have his advertisement on one side and a statement protesting a city policy on the other side (clever guy!). He was arrested anyway, and the Court upheld his conviction saying that the city council had the right to regulate the distribution of leaflets.[65] The Court became much more sympathetic to commercial speech starting in the 1970s when it struck down a law against advertising prescription drug prices and one prohibiting placing newspaper racks on city streets to distribute commercial publications such as real estate guides.[66] The key decision came in 1980 and established a test that is still central today. The Court ruled that the government may regulate commercial speech if it concerns an illegal activity, if the advertisement is misleading, or if regulating speech directly advances a substantial government interest and the regulation is not excessive. In practice, this test means that commercial speech can be regulated but that the government has to have a very good reason to do it. Even public health concerns have not been allowed to override commercial speech rights. For example, the Court struck down a Massachusetts regulation that limited the content of advertisements aimed at children (the ban on R. J. Reynolds's Joe Camel character is the classic example) in a manner that was more restrictive than federal law.[67]

Obscenity One area in which the press has never experienced complete freedom is in the publication of pornography and material considered obscene. The difficulty, once again, arises in deciding where to draw the line. Nearly everyone would agree that child pornography should not be published,[68] and that pornography should not be available to minors. However, beyond these points there is not much consensus. Some people are offended by nude paintings in art museums, while others enjoy watching hardcore X-rated movies. For example, George W. Bush's first attorney general, John Ashcroft, disliked giving press conferences under the bare breast of the Spirit of Justice statue that has decorated the Great Hall of the Department of Justice since the building opened in 1936. So the statue (and her more modest male counterpart, Majesty of Law, who already wore a loincloth) were hidden behind a blue velvet curtain at a cost of $8,650.[69]

Defining obscenity has proven difficult for the courts. In an often-quoted moment of frustration, Justice Potter Stewart wrote that he could not define obscenity, but "I know it when I see it."[70] In its first attempt to provide a framework for limiting obscenity, the Court ruled that a particular publication could be banned if an "average person, applying contemporary community standards" would find that the material appeals to prurient interests and was "utterly without redeeming social importance."[71] This standard proved unworkable because lower courts differed in their interpretation of both "redeeming social importance" and the "community standard" (some assumed a single national community and others applied local standards). The Court took another stab at it in 1973 in *Miller v. California,* the case that gave rise to the *Miller* test, which is still applied today. The test has three standards that must all be met in order for material to be banned as obscene. Using the same average person/contemporary community point of reference, material can be banned if it appeals to prurient interests, is "patently offensive," and the work as a whole lacks serious literary, artistic, political, or scientific value. The Court also clarified that *local* community standards were to apply rather than a single national standard, reasoning that what passes for obscenity in Sioux City, Iowa, probably

would be considered pretty tame in Las Vegas. Despite providing a more solid foundation for subsequent cases on this topic, there are still some difficulties with the test. As Kathleen Sullivan, the former dean of Stanford University Law School points out, "The first two parts of this test are incoherent: to put it crudely, they require the audience to be turned on and grossed out at the same time."[72]

Congress and the president also get in on the act of controlling obscenity. In general, Congress and the president take a more conservative approach—seeking legislation to limit obscenity, whereas the Court focuses on whether certain speech is protected. Furthermore, the Court tends to rein in Congress and the president when they try to limit obscene speech. In 1967, Congress created a Commission on Obscenity and Pornography that completed its work in 1970 and concluded that there was no link between sexually explicit materials and criminal behavior. President Nixon, who inherited the commission from the previous administration, was upset with the report, saying, "So long as I am in the White House there will be no relaxation of the national effort to control and eliminate smut from our national life . . . I totally reject this report."[73] Sixteen years later President Reagan established the Meese Commission on the same subject. The commission issued strong warnings about the negative effects of pornography on society, but the report was widely criticized for its bias and lack of scientific evidence to back up its claims.

One interesting aspect of the Meese Commission and other attempts to ban obscenity is the odd political coalition of the extreme right and left, between Christian conservatives and feminists, who both hate pornography but for very different reasons. Having failed in the courts to limit pornography as much as they would like, this coalition continued to press its case in Congress. They have tried novel approaches, such as pushing for the Pornography Victims' Compensation Act of 1991. Rather than banning pornography outright, this law would have allowed victims of sexual crimes to sue publishers, if it could be shown that the criminal was a consumer of the publishers' pornographic material. The bill did not become law.

More recent efforts have focused on the newest pornography medium, the Internet. Congress passed the Communications Decency Act in 1996, which criminalized the use of any computer network to display "indecent" material, unless the provider could offer an effective way of screening out potential users under the age of eighteen. The Court struck down the law in 1997 because it was overly vague, and because it is technically impossible to limit access to Web sites based on age. This ruling gives the Internet the same free speech protection as print,[74] but Congress wasn't going to give up without a fight. In 1998 the Child Online Protection Act (COPA) was signed into law by President Clinton. It prohibited commercial Web sites from distributing material that is "harmful to minors," using the language of the *Miller* test to specify what this means. The law bounced around in federal courts for six years, twice making it to the Supreme Court, which ultimately struck it down, arguing that the government could achieve the same goals using "less restrictive alternatives" to COPA and that the law carried a potential for "extraordinary harm and a serious chill upon protected speech."[75]

The Supreme Court recently addressed an area of the law that it had not touched for more than thirty years: regulating vulgar language that does not rise to the level of obscenity on broadcast television and radio (but not cable or other paid-subscription services). In 1978 the Court ruled that the Federal Communications Commission (FCC) had the power to regulate indecent language, but the FCC had always interpreted that power to only cover repeated use of vulgar words, as with comedian George Carlin's "Filthy Words" routine that was the target of the 1978 lawsuit.[76] After the use of vulgar words by Bono during the 2003 Golden Globe Awards and by Cher and Nicole Richie during the 2002 and 2003 Billboard Music Awards, the FCC announced that it would no longer tolerate even "isolated uses of sexual and

Q POLITICS IS CONFLICTUAL

POLITICS IS EVERYWHERE

excretory words." Fox Television challenged this new rule, but in 2009 the Supreme Court upheld the ban on "fleeting expletives" as "entirely rational" under existing law, while taking a swipe at the "foul-mouthed glitteratae from Hollywood."[77] The Court also ruled the following week that the FCC had not acted capriciously in fining CBS $550,000 for Janet Jackson's infamous "wardrobe malfunction" during the halftime show of the 2004 Super Bowl. However, in both cases the Court did not address the broader constitutional questions, holding open the possibility of stronger 1st Amendment protections for broadcast radio and television in the future.[78] In 2010 the Second Circuit Court struck down the "fleeting expletives" policy as unconstitutionally vague.

Freedom of Religion

The 1st Amendment has two parts that deal with religion: the **establishment clause**, which says that Congress cannot sponsor or endorse any particular religion, and the **free exercise clause**, which states that Congress cannot interfere in the practice of religion. The establishment clause is primarily concerned with drawing lines. Does a prayer at a public high school football game or a nativity scene on government property constitute state sponsorship of religion? The free exercise clause has more to do with balancing interests; recall the earlier examples of balancing public safety concerns against snake handling in religious services and the use of Amish buggies on highways. The combination of the establishment and free exercise clauses results in a general policy of noninterference and government neutrality toward religion. As Thomas Jefferson put it in 1802, the 1st Amendment provides a "wall of eternal separation between church and state." Though this language is not part of any law, it continues to be cited frequently in Court cases[79] in which religion and politics intersect. Since both of these areas tend to carry great moral weight and emotional charge, it's no wonder that vehement debates continue over the appropriateness of the saying "In God We Trust" on our currency, the White House Christmas tree, and whether public schools should teach evolution and "intelligent design." Since politics is everywhere, the boundaries of religious expression remain difficult to draw.

THE ESTABLISHMENT CLAUSE AND SEPARATION OF CHURCH AND STATE

Determining the boundaries between church and state—the central issue of the establishment clause—is very difficult. As a leading text on civil liberties puts it, the words of the establishment clause—"Congress shall make no law respecting an establishment of religion"—are commanding and clear, but their meaning is entirely unclear. What does the clause allow or forbid?[80] We know that the Founders did not want an official state religion nor for the government to favor one religion over another, but beyond that, it's hard to say. Jefferson's "eternal wall of separation" comment has been used in Court decisions that prohibit state aid for religious activities, but lately the Court has been moving toward a more "accommodationist" perspective that sometimes allows religious activity in public institutions.

The prohibition of prayer in public schools has proven to be the most controversial establishment clause issue. It exploded onto the political scene in 1962 when the Court ruled that the following prayer, written by the New York Board of State Regents and read every day in the state's public schools,[81] violated the separation of church and state: "Almighty God, we acknowledge our dependence upon Thee, and

we beg Thy blessing upon us, our parents, our teachers, and our country." Banning the prayer caused a huge public outcry protesting the perceived attack on religion.

Over the next forty years Congress repeatedly tried to amend the Constitution to allow school prayer, but these amendments never received the two-thirds vote in both houses necessary to send them to the states for ratification. Meanwhile, the Court continued to take a hard line on school-sponsored prayer. In 1985 the Court struck down the practice of observing a one-minute moment of silence for "meditation or voluntary prayer" in the Alabama public schools.[82] More recently the Court said that benedictions or prayers at public school graduations and a school policy that allowed an elected student representative to lead a prayer at a high school football game also violated the establishment clause.[83] On the other hand, the Court upheld the practice of opening every session of Congress with a prayer and let stand without comment a lower court ruling that allowed a prayer that was planned and led by students (rather than being school policy) at a Texas high school graduation.[84]

The Court has had an even more difficult time coming up with principles to govern aid to religious organizations, either directly, through tax dollars, or indirectly, through the use of public space. One early attempt was known as the *Lemon test*, after one of the parties in a 1971 case involving government support for religious schools. This case said that a practice violated the establishment clause if it (1) did not have a "secular legislative purpose," (2) either advanced or inhibited religion, or (3) fostered "an excessive government entanglement with religion."[85] The first two parts of the test are pretty straightforward, but the third was open to interpretation by lower courts and therefore led to conflicting rulings.

Though the *Lemon* test has not been completely abandoned, the Court started to move away from it in a 1984 case involving a creche owned by the city of Pawtucket, Rhode Island, and displayed in a park owned by a nonprofit corporation. The Court allowed the nativity display, saying, "The Constitution does not require complete separation of church and state; it affirmatively mandates accommodation, not merely tolerance, of all religions, and forbids hostility toward any."[86] Later rulings upheld similar religious displays, especially if they conformed to what observers have labeled the "three plastic animals rule"—if the baby Jesus is surrounded by Rudolph the red-nosed reindeer and other secular symbols, the overall display is considered sufficiently nonreligious to pass constitutional muster.[87] This picture became even more muddled in 2005 when the Court said that the Ten Commandments could not be posted in two Kentucky courthouses but could be displayed on a monument outside the capitol in Austin, Texas. However, there was some consistency between the seemingly contradictory rulings on the commandments and the "three plastic animals rule." Justice Breyer noted that Austin's monument was one of forty on the capitol grounds, so the display served a "mixed but primarily non-religious purpose," whereas the Kentucky courthouses' displays were clearly religious.[88]

The Court has also applied the accommodationist perspective to funding for religious schools by looking more favorably on providing tax dollars to students' families to subsidize tuition costs rather than funding the parochial schools directly. For example, a 2002 case upheld an Ohio school voucher program that distributed scholarships to needy students so they could attend the Cleveland school of their choice, including private, religious schools. The Court said the program did not

Lemon **test** Established in *Lemon v. Kurtzman*, the Supreme Court uses this test to determine whether a practice violates the 1st Amendment's establishment clause.

▼ *The establishment clause of the Constitution requires the separation of church and state. However, the Supreme Court has ruled that religious symbols are permitted on government property as long as they are part of larger, secular displays. Here, the Ten Commandments are displayed on one of the forty monuments outside the Texas state capitol in Austin.*

violate the establishment clause because it allowed students and their families "to exercise genuine choice among options public and private, secular and religious."[89] Critics of the decision pointed out that 96 percent of the students participating in the scholarship program were enrolled in religiously affiliated schools, which amounted to state-sponsorship of religious education, something that the Court had not previously allowed. There are several cases in which the Court has approved direct public support for specific programs in religious schools or organizations. One case involved tax-dollar support for a sign language interpreter for a deaf student who attended a parochial school. A deeply divided Court ruled that this was acceptable because the benefit given to the school was minimal. The dissenters pointed out that this was the first time tax dollars had directly paid for an instructional employee at a religious school.[90] The Court also ruled that it was acceptable to use federal funds to buy computers and other educational equipment to be used in public and private schools for "secular, neutral, and nonideological programs."[91]

Another important case involved a clash between the 1st Amendment's free speech and establishment clauses. The University of Virginia denied a student's request for $5,862 from student fees to fund his Christian newspaper, *Wide Awake*, because of its religious content (despite funding 118 other student organizations with a broad range of views), and the student sued the university for violating his freedom of speech. The Court ruled that free speech concerns trumped possible establishment issues, so that refusing to fund the Christian paper while funding so many others amounted to "viewpoint discrimination." The school was not obligated under the establishment clause to deny funding (as the dissenters claimed) because the student activity fund in question was neutral toward religion.[92]

THE FREE EXERCISE CLAUSE

While the freedom of belief is absolute, freedom of religious conduct cannot be unrestricted. That is, you can believe whatever you want without government interference but if you *act* on those beliefs, the government may regulate your behavior. And while the government has restricted religious conduct in dozens of cases, the freedom of religion has been among the most consistently protected civil liberties.

There is one prominent example of when the Court restricted the free exercise of religion but then quickly corrected its error. This 1940 case concerned the children in a Jehovah's Witness family, twelve-year-old Lillian Gobitis and her ten-year-old brother William, who were kicked out of a public school in Minersville, Pennsylvania, for refusing to recite the Pledge of Allegiance.[93] The children cited Exodus 20:3, "you shall have no other Gods before Me," in explaining why they refused to recite the pledge and salute the flag. The Court surprised the experts by siding with the school—until, three years later, they reversed course and ruled that the school could not force anyone to say the pledge, especially when it served no important government interest, such as protecting public safety.[94]

There are literally dozens of different topics and hundreds of cases that have come before the Court in the area of the free exercise of religion. Here are a smattering of the important questions:[95] May Amish parents be forced to send their children to schools beyond the eighth grade? (no); may religion serve as the basis for attaining "conscientious objector" status and avoiding the draft? (generally yes, but with many qualifications); is animal sacrifice as part of a religious ceremony protected by the 1st Amendment? (generally yes); may Christian Scientists be committed to a mental institution and compelled to take drugs? (no); may Mormons have multiple wives? (no); may the Amish be compelled to follow traffic laws and put license plates on their buggies? (yes); may people be forced to work on Friday night

POLITICS IS EVERYWHERE

and Saturday if those are their days of worship? (no); may a city levy licensing fees that target the selling of religious books? (no); may a city ban or tax door-to-door religious canvassing and proselytizing? (no); does the 1st Amendment protect distributing religious leaflets on public streets? (yes), and religious meetings in public parks? (yes, subject to "time, manner, and place" restrictions); may religious dress be regulated? (generally not, but in some contexts, such as the military, yes); are all prison inmates entitled to hold religious services? (apparently yes, but this is still an open question); and are religious organizations subject to child labor laws? (yes). Whew! Keep in mind, this list is by no means exhaustive.

One case addressing a seemingly minor question ended up having broad implications that defined the general basis for government restrictions of religious expression. The 1990 case addressed whether the state may deny unemployment benefits to someone who is fired for taking illegal drugs as part of a religious ceremony. The plaintiffs practiced a Native American religion in which peyote, a hallucinogenic cactus, is consumed during some services. The Court ruled that the state of Oregon had not violated the free exercise clause in denying unemployment benefits to the plaintiffs because they were fired from their jobs in a drug rehabilitation clinic for using peyote. If the case had ended with this simple ruling, it would be just another example of religious conduct that the government had an interest in regulating (in this case, consuming an illegal drug). The broader significance of the ruling came with the Court's announcement of a new interpretation of the free exercise clause: the government does not need a "compelling interest" in regulating a particular behavior to justify a law that limits a religious practice.[96] In other words, after this decision, it would be easier for the government to limit the exercise of religion because the Court would no longer require a "compelling" reason for the restrictions, just a good one.

The case caused an uproar, and Congress responded by passing the Religious Freedom Restoration Act in 1993, reinstating the need to demonstrate a "compelling state interest" before limiting religious freedoms; the act also specified exceptions to the Controlled Substances Act to allow the use of peyote in religious ceremonies. The Court replied in a 1997 decision that Congress could not usurp its power to define the constitutional protections for religion and that the 1993 law did not apply to the states.[97] Congress wouldn't give up and in 2000 passed another more narrowly written law, the Religious Land Use and Institutionalized Persons Act, that only concerned zoning and the religious rights of people in prisons and government-run mental institutions. Under their power to regulate commerce and control spending, Congress told states that if they accepted federal tax dollars, they would have to reinstate the "compelling interest" standard when restricting religious practices in these two areas.

The Supreme Court gave partial support to this law in the context of a case involving the religious freedoms of prison inmates in Ohio, without ruling on some of the underlying questions.[98] The Court also upheld the law in allowing a small religion in New Mexico, União do Vegetal, to use a hallucinogenic tea in their services even though the tea is considered a controlled substance by the federal government. The Court unanimously ruled that the government had not demonstrated a compelling interest in barring the sacramental use of the tea, indicating a shift back toward the stricter standard for justifying limits on religious practices. This case also reaffirmed the "*Sherbert* test," which requires the state to use the least restrictive means when regulating religious practices.[99] The struggle between Congress and the Court in

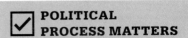

POLITICAL PROCESS MATTERS

▼ *Whether prison inmates should be able to freely exercise their religious beliefs is a contested area of the law. In 2000 Congress passed the Religious Land Use and Institutionalized Persons Act in an effort to partially control the standard states can use when restricting religious practices. Here, inmates pray with a chaplain at the West County Detention Facility in Richmond, California.*

defining civil liberties illustrates the importance of the political process. When Congress decides to tackle an important civil liberty such as religious freedom, they can influence outcomes in an area that is usually dominated by the courts.

The Right to Bear Arms

Until recently, the right to bear arms was the only civil liberty that the Supreme Court had played a relatively minor role in defining. Between 1791 (when the 2nd Amendment was ratified) and 2007, the Court issued only four rulings directly pertaining to the 2nd Amendment. The federal courts had always interpreted the 2nd Amendment's somewhat awkward phrasing—"A well regulated Militia, being necessary to the security of a free State, the right of the people to keep and bear Arms, shall not be infringed"—as a right to bear arms within the context of serving in a militia, rather than an individual right to own a gun. For example, the Court decided in 1939 that the right to own a sawed-off shotgun was not protected by the 2nd Amendment because it was not related to "the preservation or efficiency of a well regulated militia."[100] In thirty-two instances since the 1939 ruling, appeals courts affirmed this focus on a collective right (in the context of a militia) rather than an individual right to bear arms, recognizing an individual right only twice.[101]

This all changed with the landmark ruling in June 2008 that recognized for the first time an individual right to bear arms for self-defense and hunting.[102] The decision struck down the District of Columbia's ban on handguns, while noting that state and local governments could enforce ownership restrictions, such as preventing felons or the mentally impaired from buying guns. The Court did not apply the 2nd Amendment to the states in this decision but did so two years later in striking down a gun control ordinance in Chicago.[103] The dissenters in both strongly divided 5–4 decision, lamented the Court's activism in reopening a legal question considered settled since 1939 and pointed out that defining the new limits on gun control would require a flood of litigation.

Although legal conflict over gun ownership has intensified only recently, battles over guns have always been intense in the broader political realm.[104] Interest groups such as the National Rifle Association have long asserted that the 2nd Amendment guarantees an individual right to bear arms. Critics of this view emphasize the first clause of the amendment and point to the frequent mentions of state militias in congressional debates at the time the Bill of Rights was adopted. They argue that the 2nd Amendment was adopted to reassure Antifederalist advocates of states' rights that state militias, not a national standing army, would provide national security. In this view, the national armed forces and the National Guard have made the 2nd Amendment obsolete.

Before the Court's recent entry into this debate, Congress and state and local lawmakers had largely defined gun ownership and carrying rights, creating a great deal of variation among the states. Wyoming and Montana have virtually no restrictions on gun ownership, including allowing sales to minors and carrying concealed weapons, whereas California and Connecticut have many ownership restrictions. At the national level, Congress tends to respond to crime waves or high-profile assassinations by passing new gun control laws. One of the first was passed in 1934 in response to the upsurge of organized crime during Prohibition. The broadest federal gun control law, the Gun Control Act of 1968, was passed in the wake of the assassinations of Robert F. Kennedy and Martin Luther King Jr. and remains in effect today. The law set standards for gun dealers, banned the sale

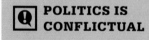

POLITICS IS CONFLICTUAL

◀ The attempted assassination of President Ronald Reagan by John Hinckley outside the Washington Hilton Hotel prompted calls for stronger gun control laws. Nearly thirteen years later, Congress passed the Brady Bill, which mandated a background check and five-day waiting period before purchasing a handgun. The law was revised in 1998 to require a computerized background check that can usually be done in minutes.

of weapons through the mail, restricted the sale of new machine guns, and included many other provisions.

Following the assassination attempt on President Reagan in 1981, the push for stronger gun control laws intensified, led by the Brady Campaign to Prevent Gun Violence. The head of this group was Sarah Brady, whose husband, James Brady, was Reagan's press secretary and was wounded and disabled in the assassination attempt. It took nearly thirteen years for the campaign to bear fruit, but in 1993 Congress passed and President Clinton signed the Brady Bill, which mandated a background check and a five-day waiting period for any handgun purchase. The next year Congress passed a major crime bill that included a provision banning the sale of nineteen kinds of semi-automatic weapons. This part of the law was allowed to expire in 2004. Given the strong public support for gun ownership—there are about 195 million privately owned guns in the United States—and the Supreme Court's endorsement of an individual right to bear arms, stronger gun control at the national level is essentially dead. However, as noted above, extensive litigation will be necessary to define the acceptable boundaries of gun control and which state and local restrictions will be allowed to stand.

Law, Order, and the Rights of Criminal Defendants

Every advanced democracy protects the rights of people who have been accused of a crime. In the United States, the **due process rights** of the 4th, 5th, 6th, and 8th Amendments include the right to a fair trial, right to consult a lawyer, freedom from self-incrimination, knowing what crime you are accused of, the right to confront the accuser in court, and freedom from unreasonable police searches, all of which are routinely ignored in nondemocratic countries. But even in the United States, many people support these civil liberties more in the abstract than in practice. For example, most people recognize the value of such principles as "innocent until proven guilty" and agree that the state should have the burden of proving guilt "beyond all reasonable doubt" in a criminal case. Similarly, most people endorse

due process rights The idea that laws and legal proceedings must be fair. The Constitution guarantees that the government cannot take away a person's "life, liberty, or property, without due process of law." Other specific due process rights are found in the 4th, 5th, 6th, and 8th Amendments, such as protection from self-incrimination and freedom from illegal searches.

the abstract principle of "due process of law" and general ideas such as requiring that police legally obtain any evidence used in court. However, when the Supreme Court started more aggressively protecting the rights of the accused during the Warren Court years of the late 1950s and early 1960s, there was public outrage. An "Impeach Earl Warren" movement started in part because of rulings seen as "soft on criminals"; his critics believed too many suspects were going free on "legal technicalities," such as having to inform a suspect of his right to talk to an attorney before being questioned by the police. Is this a legal technicality or a fundamental civil liberty? What does it mean to value due process but reject specific examples of adherence to due process procedures?

The difficulty in applying abstract principles of due process to concrete situations is not a failure of the American public. It *is* hard to define precisely what due process is, especially in a way that protects civil liberties without jeopardizing order. The roots of the idea of due process go all the way back to the Magna Carta of 1215, one of the earliest statements of legal rights, which stated, "No free man shall be taken, outlawed, banished, or in any way destroyed, nor will we proceed against or prosecute him, except by the lawfull [sic] judgement of his peers and by the law of the land." The 5th and 14th Amendments specify that life, liberty, and property may not be denied "without due process of law." In general, this language refers to *procedural* restrictions on what government can do and is based on the idea of fairness and justice. The difficulty comes, of course, in defining what is fair or just. The first aspect of due process discussed in the next section is a perfect example: the 4th Amendment protection against *unreasonable* searches and seizures.

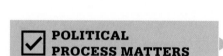

POLITICAL PROCESS MATTERS

THE 4TH AMENDMENT: UNREASONABLE SEARCHES AND SEIZURES

The 4th Amendment says, "The right of the people to be secure in their persons, houses, papers, and effects, against unreasonable searches and seizures, shall not be violated." Defining "unreasonable" puts us back in the familiar position of drawing lines and balancing interests. Police searches inherently involve a clash between public safety and the private freedom from government intrusions. These issues came to the fore with the passage of the USA PATRIOT Act of 2001 after the terrorist attacks of September 11. (The act's name is capitalized this way because it is actually an acronym for "Uniting and Strengthening America by Providing Appropriate Tools Required to Intercept and Obstruct Terrorism.") Several of the most controversial parts of the act strengthen police surveillance powers; make it easier to conduct "sneak and peek" searches (which means that the police enter a home with a warrant, look for evidence, and do not tell the suspect of their search until many months later); broaden Internet surveillance; increase the government's access to library, banking, and medical records; and permit roving wiretaps for suspected terrorists (by which a single warrant legalizes surveillance of all possible forms of communication for that individual). Congress extended the Patriot Act in 2006 with some stronger protections for civil liberties, such as providing more limits on roving wiretaps and requiring that targets of sneak-and-peek searches be notified within thirty days in most instances. Congress recently extended three provisions of the law that were set to expire at the end of 2009, including government access to business records and roving wiretaps, through February 28, 2011.

▼ *The USA PATRIOT Act strengthened the government's ability to conduct surveillance. This cartoon expresses concern that civil liberties have been weakened to pursue the War on Terror.*

Given the abusive practices of the British governors in the colonies, the Founders had strong opinions about the "right of the people to be secure in their persons, houses, papers, and effects." Over the years the Court provided strong protections against searches within a person's physical space, typically defined as his or her home. With the introduction of new technology—first telephones and wiretapping, and then more sophisticated listening and searching devices—the Court had to confront a broad array of complicated questions. The Court has attempted to achieve a balance between security and privacy by requiring court approval for search warrants, while carving out limited exceptions to this general rule. Under most circumstances, a law enforcement official seeking a search warrant must provide the court with "personal knowledge" of a "probable cause" of specific criminal activity and outline the evidence that is the target of the search. In other words, broad, general "fishing expeditions" for evidence are not allowed. School searches may be permitted with a weaker "reasonable suspicion," but there are limits. In 2003 school administrators in Safford, Arizona, responding to a tip that a student was in possession of prescription-strength ibuprofen pills, subjected thirteen-year-old Savana Redding to a strip search to find the contraband. After searching her backpack and outer clothing and finding nothing, the majority opinion describes what happened next: "Savana was told to pull her bra out and to the side and shake it, and to pull out the elastic on her underpants, thus exposing her breasts and pelvic area to some degree." The Court ruled that this search violated her 4th Amendment rights because "the content of the suspicion failed to match the degree of intrusion."[105] The exceptional cases in which the Court will allow a warrantless search include:

- A search that happens at the time of a legal arrest and "is confined to the immediate vicinity of the arrest."
- Collecting evidence that was not included in the search warrant but is out in the open in plain view.
- Setting up police roadblocks as long as they stop all drivers, not just those who fit a particular profile.
- Searching containers in cars, if the officer has probable cause to suspect criminal activity. For example, police saw a man drive away from a known drug dealer's apartment after putting a brown paper bag in his trunk that resembled a typical marijuana package. This would give the police grounds, without a warrant, to stop the car and order the suspect to open the trunk and the bag.
- Searching the passenger area of a car if the driver has been stopped for a traffic offense, and passengers may also be searched. Automobiles do not have the same 4th Amendment protections as homes.
- Searches conducted using aerial photography are legal.
- Searching an area where the officer thinks there is either a crime in progress or an "armed and dangerous" suspect.
- Searching school lockers, with probable cause.
- Searching for weapons and/or to prevent the destruction of evidence.[106]

A second set of cases are concerned with figuring out what to do if the police illegally obtain evidence. Here the need to balance security and privacy becomes quite concrete. Either you exclude the evidence from a criminal trial to protect privacy rights, or you allow the evidence to support conviction of the suspect.

In 1961 the 4th Amendment was incorporated (applied to the states through the 14th Amendment) in a case that established the **exclusionary rule** for all courts, which had previously applied only at the national level.[107] The rule states that illegally obtained evidence cannot be used in a criminal trial. In the landmark case, police broke into Dollree Mapp's residence without a warrant looking for a suspect thought to be hiding in the house. The officers did not find him, but in searching the

exclusionary rule The principle that illegally or unconstitutionally acquired evidence cannot be used in a criminal trial.

house they found some illegal pornographic material, and Mapp was convicted of possessing it. Her lawyer tried to defend her on 1st Amendment grounds, claiming she had the right to own the pornography, but instead the Court used the opportunity to apply the 4th Amendment to the states. The Court threw out Mapp's conviction not because of any right to own the material but because the police did not have a search warrant, arguing that applying the 4th Amendment only to the national government and not the states didn't make any sense: Why should a state's attorney be able to use illegally obtained evidence while a federal prosecutor could not? They ruled that in order for the exclusionary rule to deter illegal searches and seizures, it must apply to law enforcement at both state and national levels.

As part of the backlash against the Warren Court decisions that strictly upheld suspects' due process rights, subsequent Courts started weakening the exclusionary rule. The public was concerned that too many criminals were being set free because of the limits on obtaining and using evidence, and a majority of justices agreed. In 1974 the Court allowed the use of illegally obtained evidence in grand jury testimony.[108] Several years later it relaxed the general rule to allow the use of evidence if the "totality of circumstances" suggests that the police officer's action was justified.[109] The following year the Court established a "good faith exception" to the exclusionary rule, allowing evidence to be used as long as the officer believed that he conducted a legal search. In the specific case, the officer had a warrant that turned out to have errors on it, such as the wrong address.[110] In another case, an officer pulled over a suspect and called in the license plate to find out whether any warrants were outstanding. The answer was yes, and the officer searched the car, finding methamphetamine and a gun. Within fifteen minutes, the sheriff's office called back to say that the arrest warrant was out of date and should have been removed from the computer system five months earlier. However, the Court ruled that the evidence was still admissible because the officer *thought* he had a legitimate arrest warrant when he made the search.[111] Yet another case established an exception allowing the use of evidence that was initially obtained in an illegal search but subsequently acquired with a valid warrant.[112] The bottom line is that the exclusionary rule remains in effect, but in the last several decades it has become easier for prosecutors to use evidence obtained under questionable circumstances.

Another area of 4th Amendment law concerns drug testing. The clause granting people the right "to be secure in their persons" certainly seems to cover drug testing. On the other hand, the courts have long recognized the right of private companies to test their employees for illegal drugs, and in professional sports, testing for performance-enhancing drugs is increasingly common. Tour de France winner Floyd Landis was stripped of his title in 2006 after testing positive for artificially elevated testosterone levels, and major league baseball has struggled to rein in steroid and human growth hormone use by many of its players, including stars such as Mark McGwire, Manny Ramirez, and Alex Rodriguez. What about drug testing by the state? The Court has upheld random drug testing for high school athletes and mandatory drug testing for any junior high or high school students involved in extracurricular activities.[113] In the case of athletes, proponents of the policy were able to make the case that safety concerns should preclude a 260-pound lineman or a pitcher with a 90-mile-per-hour fastball from using drugs. However, the same arguments could not be made for members of the choir, band, debate club, social dance, or the chess club, so this decision to include all extracurricular activities was a particularly strong endorsement of schools' anti-drug policies.

Federal employees first became subject to drug testing in 1986, when President Ronald Reagan issued an executive order requiring all employees to refrain from using illegal drugs, on or off duty, as a condition of federal employment, and directed each agency to implement drug testing for sensitive positions. Two years later, Con-

▼ *Drug testing is generally allowed in the workplace and has become increasingly common in professional sports. Here, baseball slugger Mark McGwire testifies at the House Committee on Government Reform hearing on drug use in baseball in March 2005. He later admitted to using illegal steroids.*

gress passed the Drug-Free Workplace Act to apply the same rule to all executive agencies, the uniformed services, and any service providers under contract with the federal government. Despite these broad prohibitions, drug testing of federal employees is actually limited to about 400,000 people who hold security clearances, carry firearms, or work in public safety or national security. Some employees receive random tests, while others are tested only when they apply for a job, are involved in a workplace accident, or show signs of drug use. Many states have adopted similar drug-testing policies,[114] and the Court has upheld drug testing of public employees, with one exception. It struck down a Georgia law that would have required all candidates for state office to pass a drug test within thirty days of announcing a run for office because candidates are not public employees.[115] Rather than appealing to the courts, former senator Ernest Hollings of South Carolina had a different approach to avoid drug testing. When his opponent, Representative Tommy Hartnett, challenged him to take a drug test, the senator shot back, "I'll take a drug test if you take an I.Q. test."

The Post–September 11 Politics of Domestic Surveillance The debate over the trade-off between civil liberties and security intensified late in 2005 when a White House–approved domestic surveillance program was revealed (see What Do Political Scientists Do?). Since the terrorist attacks of September 11, the National Security Agency (NSA) had been monitoring the phone calls of many U.S. citizens who have had contact with suspected terrorists overseas (thus, the Bush administration's preferred label for the program was "terrorist surveillance" rather than "domestic spying"). These calls were intercepted without the approval of the Foreign Intelligence Surveillance Court (FISA), which was created by Congress in 1978 specifically for the purpose of approving the interception of calls. A few months later, another more extensive NSA program aimed at creating a database of every phone call made within the borders of the United States was revealed. Phone companies AT&T, Verizon, and BellSouth were reported to have turned over records of millions of customers' phone calls to the government.[116] Not much is known about the details of these programs, but critics in Congress wanted to know more.

At the center of this controversy is the NSA, which was created during the Korean War in 1952 by President Harry Truman. The agency was initially kept so secret that for many years the government even denied its existence. Insiders joked that the NSA stood for "No Such Agency." Today the NSA is responsible for surveillance that is aimed at national security (while the FBI is in charge of spying related to criminal activity, and the CIA oversees foreign intelligence gathering). The Bush administration argued that their activities were legal and that the appropriate members of Congress had been briefed.

Critics warn that phone surveillance may be the tip of the iceberg because the government may be monitoring travel, credit card, and banking records on a more widespread basis than is commonly believed. Government agencies have previously skirted the restrictions in the Privacy Act of 1974 and the 4th Amendment by purchasing this information from businesses, since the Privacy Act only requires disclosure of how the government is using personal information when the government itself collects the data. The Justice Department, which includes the FBI, spent $19 million in 2005 to purchase commercially gathered data on American citizens, according to a report by the Government Accountability Office. These data are then used to search for suspicious patterns of behavior in a process known as data mining.[117]

The debate over domestic surveillance has generated intense disagreement. At one extreme, critics of the surveillance program conjure up images of George Orwell's classic novel *1984* in which Big Brother, a reclusive totalitarian ruler, watches the characters' every move. They see the surveillance as a threat to civil liberties and to

The Trade-off between Security and Civil Liberties

Since the terrorist attacks of 9/11, we are regularly reminded of the trade-off between security and civil liberties. With every exposed terror cell and arrested would-be bomber, the nation breathes a collective sigh of relief that we dodged another attack. But heightened airport security and the resultant delays in travel are a regular reminder of the personal costs of the additional security. While nearly everyone is willing to surrender some personal privacy and bear some inconvenience to prevent terrorist attacks, the more difficult question is how to achieve the proper balance between protecting our security and preserving civil liberties.

Specific events sharpen the contours of this debate. The White House–approved domestic surveillance program discussed in the text raised concerns about how much privacy was being sacrificed in the search for terrorists. More recently, the Obama administration's efforts to close the detention facility for suspected terrorists in Guantánamo and to try five suspected terrorists in federal court in New York City have been met with NIMBY politics ("not in my backyard"). Everyone wants to fight terrorism as long as the suspected terrorists are not detained or put to trial in his hometown.

Studying the trade-off between security and civil liberties is a job for political scientists as well as scholars and practitioners in other fields, including law professors and federal judges. Research in this area involves examining relevant court cases and situating the debates within the context of the relevant parts of the Constitution. Two important recent contributions to this debate are by Bruce Ackerman, Yale political scientist and law professor, and Richard Posner, federal appeals court judge and lecturer at the University of Chicago law school.[a]

In a chilling passage from his book *Before the Next Attack: Preserving Civil Liberties in an Age of Terrorism*, Ackerman warns,

"The next major attack may kill and maim one hundred thousand innocents, dwarfing the pain and anguish suffered by those who lost family and friends on 9/11. The resulting political panic threatens to leave behind a wave of repressive legislation far more drastic than any imagined by the Patriot Act."[b] While the threat of terrorist attacks is real, according to Ackerman the more serious threat to our freedom comes from within. Terrorist groups do not have the ability to invade and take over our country, therefore, "If anybody destroys our legacy of freedom, it will be us."[c]

Ackerman's advice is to plan ahead so a devastating attack will not produce a police state. He argues that Congress should enact an "emergency constitution" that would be implemented after a terrorist attack. It would contain unilateral presidential power through repeated congressional authorizations, including "escalating supermajorities" in which 60 percent, then 70 percent, and then 80 percent majorities in both houses of Congress would be required to extend emergency powers to the president. Ackerman emphasizes that fighting terrorism is neither a war nor fighting crime, but an emergency. If we deal with terrorism on this basis, the threat to civil liberties will be short term, rather than a permanent part of the police state that could be implemented in the wake of a devastating terrorist attack.

Richard Posner is more willing to limit civil liberties to protect the country, at least in the short run. While Posner accepts Ackerman's view that fighting terrorism fits the model of neither a war nor crime, he argues more strongly for limiting the civil liberties of suspected terrorists, and he is not as concerned as Ackerman about concentrating power in the presidency. Posner examines the costs and benefits of different outcomes in cases involving detention, interrogation, radical speech, privacy, and searches based on less than probable cause. He argues that in some cases the president

Since September 11, 2001, Americans have been more directly confronted with trade-offs between security and civil liberties.

will need to act in an unconstitutional manner to protect the country (similar to Locke's "prerogative powers" discussed in Chapter 2). Posner's solution to this trade-off is that public officials (especially the president) should engage in civil disobedience: "While the term is usually applied to private individuals who deem it their moral duty to disobey positive law, there is no reason why it cannot also be used of public officials who do the same thing."[d] As long as the president was acting in the nation's interest, breaking the law would be justified.

These authors provide contrasting views on how we should balance protecting civil liberties and the need for national security, while bringing attention to a central debate that is sure to occupy constitutional scholars and politicians for the next generation. ∎

Ⓥ **Watch a video clip of political scientist Howard Schweber discussing this topic at wwnorton/studyspace.com.**

our system of checks and balances and separation of powers. By refusing to obtain warrants through the FISA court, the surveillance programs place too much power in the hands of the executive branch to determine what is in the nation's interests. On the other side, supporters of the program argue that getting a court order is too burdensome and may take too long, jeopardizing the surveillance necessary to protect the country. Congress tried to strike a balance between these two positions when it enacted the FISA Amendments Act of 2008. This law continued the ban on monitoring the purely domestic communications of Americans without a court order (this part of the surveillance program ended in 2007), gave the government broad authority to intercept international communications, and provided legal immunity to the telecommunications companies that cooperated in the original wiretapping program. However, the *New York Times* revealed that the NSA had been engaged in "overcollection" of domestic communication between Americans under the new law, including an attempt to wiretap a member of Congress without a court order. Although the Obama administration has vowed to stop purely domestic surveillance without a court order, technical problems make it difficult to distinguish between communications made within the United States or overseas.[118]

The idea that politics is everywhere may take on ominous overtones in this case if you are concerned about protecting your civil liberties, or it may provide comforting reassurance if you are more concerned about national security. Either way, this issue will remain significant in your daily life for the foreseeable future.

POLITICS IS EVERYWHERE

THE 5TH AMENDMENT: SELF-INCRIMINATION

The familiar phrase "I plead the 5th" has been part of our criminal justice system since the Bill of Rights was ratified, ensuring that a suspect cannot be compelled to provide court testimony that would cause her to be prosecuted for a crime. However, what about outside a court of law? If a police officer coerces a confession out of a suspect, does that amount to self-incrimination? Such police interrogations were allowed until a landmark case in 1966. Ernesto Miranda had been convicted in an Arizona

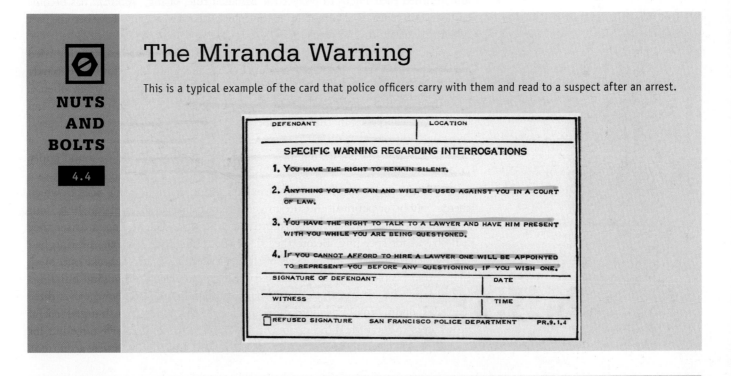

NUTS AND BOLTS

4.4

The Miranda Warning

This is a typical example of the card that police officers carry with them and read to a suspect after an arrest.

DEFENDANT		LOCATION

SPECIFIC WARNING REGARDING INTERROGATIONS

1. YOU HAVE THE RIGHT TO REMAIN SILENT.

2. ANYTHING YOU SAY CAN AND WILL BE USED AGAINST YOU IN A COURT OF LAW.

3. YOU HAVE THE RIGHT TO TALK TO A LAWYER AND HAVE HIM PRESENT WITH YOU WHILE YOU ARE BEING QUESTIONED.

4. IF YOU CANNOT AFFORD TO HIRE A LAWYER ONE WILL BE APPOINTED TO REPRESENT YOU BEFORE ANY QUESTIONING, IF YOU WISH ONE.

SIGNATURE OF DEFENDANT	DATE
WITNESS	TIME

☐ REFUSED SIGNATURE   SAN FRANCISCO POLICE DEPARTMENT   PR.9.1.4

court of kidnapping and rape, on the basis of a confession extracted after two hours of questioning in which he was not read his rights. The Court overturned the conviction, saying that a police interrogation "is inherently intimidating" and in these circumstances, "no statement obtained from the defendant can truly be the product of his free choice."[119] To make sure a confession is truly a free choice, the Court came up with the well-known **Miranda rights** described in Nuts and Bolts 4.4. If police do not read a suspect these rights, nothing the suspect says can be used in court.

Just as we saw with the exclusionary rule about illegally obtained evidence, the Court has carved out exceptions to the Miranda rights requirement because the practice was viewed by the public as "coddling criminals" and letting too many people go free on legal technicalities. In one case, police failed to read a suspect his Miranda rights until after frisking him, finding an empty holster, and asking him where his gun was. The suspect led police to a gun. The lower court dismissed the charges because the gun had been used as incriminating evidence in the trial, but the Supreme Court reinstated the conviction because, "concern for public safety must be paramount to adherence to the literal language of the Miranda rule."[120] A second case created an "inevitable discovery" exception to the Miranda rule. In this case, a murder suspect had been read his rights and had consulted by phone with his lawyer, who advised him not to answer any questions until the lawyer was present. While taking the suspect to meet with his lawyer, the detectives in the squad car appealed to the suspect's conscience, saying that the "parents of this little girl should be entitled to a Christian burial for the little girl who was snatched away from them on Christmas {E]ve and murdered."[121] After thinking about it, the suspect led them to the body. The Court said that this conversation did not violate the Miranda rule because a search party of 200 people was already in the vicinity of the body and would have found it anyway. In 2010, the Court ruled that once a suspect has invoked his or her Miranda rights, the prohibition on police questioning is not "eternal." Instead, if the suspect voluntarily changes his or her mind, police may resume questioning fourteen days after release from custody.[122] Although the Court has been willing to carve out limited exceptions to the Miranda rule, in 2000 the Court rejected Congress's attempt to overturn *Miranda* by designating all voluntary confessions as legally admissible evidence; the Court ruled that it, and not Congress, had the power to determine constitutional protections for criminal defendants. They also affirmed their intent to protect the Miranda rule, saying, "*Miranda* has become embedded in routine police practice to the point where the warnings have become part of our national culture."[123]

Another 5th Amendment right for defendants is protection against being tried more than once for a particular crime, a circumstance known as **double jeopardy** because the suspect is "twice put in jeopardy of life or limb" for a single offense. This prohibition was extended to the states in 1969.[124] However, prosecutors can exploit two loopholes in this civil liberty: (1) a suspect may be tried in federal court and state court for the same crime, and (2) if a suspect is found innocent of one set of *criminal* charges brought by the state, he or she may still be found guilty of the same or closely related offenses based on *civil* charges brought by a private individual. Usually these loopholes are exploited only in high-profile cases in which there is public or political pressure to get a conviction. For example, in 1992, four Los Angeles police officers were acquitted of beating Rodney King, a driver they had chased for speeding. Before the trial, a bystander's video of the beating had been widely broadcast, and at news of the acquittal massive riots broke out. More than 2,000 people were hurt, about sixty killed, more than a thousand buildings were destroyed, and Los Angeles saw about $1 billion in property damage over three days. Responding to political pressure, President George H. W. Bush urged federal prosecutors to retry the officers not for the *criminal* use of excessive force but for violating Rodney King's *civil* rights (two were found guilty and two were acquitted).

Property Rights, "Takings," and the 5th Amendment

Anyone who has watched television courtroom dramas is familiar with the phrase "I plead the 5th," which refers to the 5th Amendment's protection against self-incrimination. Another part of the amendment that is not well-known is at the heart of a hot legal debate over property rights; the clause says, "nor shall private property be taken for public use, without just compensation." For most of American history, this civil liberty has been noncontroversial. When the government needs private property for a public use such as building a highway or a park, the 5th Amendment states that it may take the property by the practice of eminent domain, but it must pay the property owner the fair market value. This bit of conventional wisdom has never been challenged.

A new, controversial interpretation of the 5th Amendment's "takings" clause has attempted to expand the principle of just compensation to cover not only "physical takings," but also "regulatory takings." For example, if the Endangered Species Act protects an animal whose habitat is on your land, you would not be able to develop that property. Thus, its market value would probably be lower than if the endangered species did not live on your land. Therefore, the argument goes, because of this law the government has "taken" some of the value of your land by legally protecting the species, so it should compensate you for your loss.

One key Court case decided that if a regulation "deprives a property owner of all beneficial use of his property," the owner must receive compensation. This case involved a man who bought two residential lots on the Isle of Palms, a South Carolina barrier island. His plan was to build single-family homes on the lots, but shortly after his purchase the state legislature enacted a law banning "permanent habitable structures" on this part of the barrier islands to prevent further erosion and destruction of the vulnerable land. The owner sued in state court and won a large monetary judgment, and the Supreme Court upheld this ruling.[a] Another

Greenpeace activists suspend themselves above the forest floor in Alaska's Tongass National Forest to call attention to logging of old-growth forests. Logging is forbidden if it threatens endangered species, raising questions about whether the economic loss this causes should be compensated under the takings clause of the 5th Amendment.

case concerned a takings claim based on a regulation that limited development in a coastal wetlands area in Rhode Island. Here the key legal issue was whether it mattered that the regulation was on the books *before* the plaintiff purchased the land. In a divisive 5–4 ruling, the Court said that a regulatory takings claim could still be made despite the argument that market forces would have already factored in the regulatory loss.[b]

A more controversial interpretation of the 5th Amendment challenges a long-standing practice of deferring to elected leaders' decisions about government takings of privately owned land for public use (of course, with compensation). This new challenge to the conventional wisdom urges the Court to prohibit certain takings, even with compensation, if they do not meet a more narrow definition of public use than the previous standard of "plausible public use." The issue was raised in a case involving a development project in New London, Connecticut, in which a ninety-acre working-class neighborhood would be sold to a private developer with a ninety-nine-year lease, to build a waterfront hotel, office space, and higher-end housing. One home owner sued the city to stop the development, saying that she shouldn't have to sell her home just because the city wants to develop the area, because transferring property from one private owner to another is not "public use." However, the Court ruled in a 5–4 decision that these issues

should be decided by the local government rather than the Court. Justice John Paul Stevens noted that "promoting economic development is a traditional and long accepted function of government" so a "plausible public use" is satisfied. Justice O'Connor wrote a strong dissent, saying that the "specter of condemnation hangs over all property. Nothing is to prevent the State from replacing any Motel 6 with a Ritz-Carlton, any home with a shopping mall, or any farm with a factory."[c]

These property rights cases reflect the broader "Constitution in Exile" movement that would like to return constitutional interpretation to the pre–New Deal era in which Congress's power to regulate commerce through laws and regulations was much more restricted.[d] Expanding the definition of regulatory taking would make it much more expensive to pass many laws, because any time a public policy imposed a cost on someone—say an employer who had to pay a higher wage—that person would have to be compensated. Therefore, it would likely become impossible to maintain a broad range of social and environmental legislation, including parts of the Clean Air Act, Clean Water Act, rent control, workplace safety regulations, and even minimum wage laws and Social Security, if the argument is taken to its logical extreme. In this area, the stakes in debating the conventional wisdom are much higher than in a typical academic dispute. ■

A similar pattern of prosecution followed in the trial of football star O. J. Simpson for the murder of his wife and her friend. Simpson was acquitted of first-degree murder but found guilty on civil charges brought by the victims' families.

THE 6TH AMENDMENT: THE RIGHT TO LEGAL COUNSEL AND A JURY TRIAL

When it comes to criminal law, the right to an attorney is one of the key civil liberties, because the legal system is too complicated for a layperson to navigate. An old expression among lawyers is "Only a fool has himself for a client." However, at one time poor people accused of a felony were forced to defend themselves in court because they could not afford the lawyer they had a right to (except in cases involving the death penalty).[125] This changed in 1963 with the celebrated case of *Gideon v. Wainwright*. Clarence Gideon was accused of breaking into a pool hall and stealing beer, wine, and money from a vending machine. He could not afford an attorney, so he tried to defend himself. He did a pretty good job—calling witnesses, cross-examining the prosecutor's witnesses, and providing a good summary argument. However, he was convicted and sentenced to five years in jail, based largely on the testimony of the person who turned out to be the guilty party. The Court unanimously overturned his conviction, saying, "In our adversary system of criminal justice, any person haled into court who is too poor to hire a lawyer cannot be assured a fair trial unless counsel is provided for him."[126]

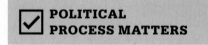

POLITICAL PROCESS MATTERS

Unlike the exclusionary rule and the protection against self-incrimination, the right to an attorney has been strengthened over time, both through legislation and subsequent Court rulings. One year after *Gideon*, Congress passed the Criminal Justice Act, which provided better legal representation for criminal defendants in federal court, and within two years twenty-three states had taken similar action. The Court has defined a general right to *effective* counsel and more recently mandated that defense attorneys must conduct any reasonable investigation into possible lines of defense when presenting evidence that could help the defendant.[127]

The 6th Amendment also protects the right to a speedy and public trial by an impartial jury in criminal cases. The Court affirmed the right to a speedy trial in 1967,[128] and in 1974 Congress strengthened the protection of this right when they passed, and then amended in 1979, the Federal Speedy Trial Act. The law requires that a trial begin within seventy days of the defendant's arrest or first appearance in court. This law was further strengthened by a more recent Court decision stating that a defendant may not waive the right to a speedy trial.[129] The most important legal disputes over the other key 6th Amendment issue, defining an "impartial jury," concern the process of jury selection and peremptory challenges, in which lawyers from each side are allowed to eliminate a certain number of people from the jury pool without providing any reason. Specifically, the Court has ruled that race and gender may not be the basis for a peremptory challenge.[130]

THE 8TH AMENDMENT: CRUEL AND UNUSUAL PUNISHMENT

The Founders would be surprised by the intense debates over whether the 8th Amendment prohibition against "cruel and unusual punishment" applies to the death penalty. Clearly, the death penalty was accepted in their time (even stealing a horse was a capital offense!) and the language of the Constitution reflects that. Both the 5th and 14th Amendments say that a person may not be deprived of "life, liberty, or property, without due process of law," which implies that someone *could* be deprived of life as long as the state follows due process. The death penalty remains popular in the United States, with support from about two-thirds of the public, and thirty-five states still allowing capital punishment. However, times change, and dozens of countries have now abolished the death penalty (see Comparing Ourselves to Others).

The Supreme Court remained silent in the death penalty debate for nearly two centuries. But in 1972, in one of the longest opinions in its history (243 pages), the Court said that the death penalty was unconstitutional because the process of applying it was far too inconsistent (two justices held that capital punishment was always "cruel and unusual" while three others took this more procedural position). Congress and thirty-five states rushed to make their laws compliant with the Court decision. The typical fix was to say more explicitly which crimes were punishable by death and to make capital sentencing a two-step process: first the determination of guilt or innocence and then a separate sentencing phase if the suspect was found guilty. Four years later, the Court approved these changes and allowed states to bring back the death penalty.[131]

While never again challenging the basic constitutionality of the death penalty, the Court has been chipping away at its edges for two decades. The Court struck down state laws that mandated the death penalty in murder cases and another law requiring a death sentence for rape, prohibited the execution of insane prisoners, and then abolished the death penalty for the mildly retarded (2002), for juveniles under the age of eighteen (2005), and for child rapists (2008).[132] The ruling on juveniles canceled the death sentences of seventy-three people for crimes committed before age eighteen, changing them to sentences of life in prison.

These recent cases have shown that the Court responds to public opinion and political change (this is sometimes called the "living Constitution" perspective, as discussed in Chapters 2 and 13). In his opinion in the juvenile death penalty case, Justice Anthony Kennedy noted that thirty states forbid the death penalty for offenders younger than eighteen, which was an increase of five states since the Court upheld the juvenile death penalty in 1989. Similarly, the number of states banning the death penalty for the mildly retarded grew from fourteen in 1989 (when the practice was upheld) to twenty-five in 2002 (when it was struck down). One observer noted that the Court shows sensitivity to the "'evolving standards of decency that mark the progress of a maturing society,' and looks to state legislation and jury verdicts to decide whether a 'national consensus' has developed against a previously accepted practice."[133] However, in 2008, the Court signaled that there are limits on how far they would go to restrict the death penalty, ruling that execution by lethal injection was not necessarily "cruel and unusual punishment."[134]

One unsettled area of 8th Amendment law concerns "proportionality"—the idea that some punishments may be so disproportionate to the crime, they constitute "cruel and unusual punishment." The principle was first cited in a 1910 case that overturned a punishment that required shackling and "hard and painful labor" for the full prison term.[135] Since then, the Court has applied proportionality (disallowed these punishments) to taking away citizenship as a punishment for a crime,[136] incarceration for drug addiction,[137] the beating of prison inmates,[138] and a disproportionate prison sentence.[139] In the latter case, the Court ruled that a life sentence without the possibility of parole for a seventh nonviolent felony (cashing a $100 check on a closed account) was unconstitutional. In 1991, however, the Court began to limit application of the principle to cases with a "gross disproportionality," saying that "the Eighth Amendment contains no proportionality guarantee."[140]

Are Our Civil Liberties Outside the Mainstream?

The United States prides itself on its strong protection of individual liberties and freedom, and in many instances that pride is well deserved. Our protections for the freedom of speech, freedom of the press, free exercise of religious beliefs, and criminal defendant rights are among the strongest in the world. So for most civil liberties, we may be outside the mainstream, but that's a good thing.

However, the United States is outside the global mainstream on the side of restricting civil liberties when it comes to the death penalty. As of early 2005, eighty-five nations had abolished the death penalty for all crimes, eleven countries only have the death penalty for exceptional crimes such as treason during wartime, and twenty-four countries have abolished the death penalty in practice (the law is still on the books, but these countries have had no executions in at least ten years). Japan and South Korea are the only other developed nations that have maintained the death penalty. In contrast, the death penalty is still used in China, Cuba, Liberia, Libya, North Korea, Saudi Arabia, Sudan, Syria, Uganda, Vietnam, and Yemen. This is not a lineup of countries with which the United States is usually associated; indeed, these are some of the worst human rights violators in the world.

In March 2005, the Supreme Court took note of the United States' international standing when it overturned a sixteen-year-old precedent that allowed the execution of minors. The case involved Christopher Simmons, who, at the age of seventeen, murdered a woman by tying her up with electrical wire,

Christopher Simmons was removed from death row when the Supreme Court ruled that executing people who were convicted as juveniles is not permitted under the 8th Amendment.

wrapping her head with duct tape, and throwing her off a bridge into a river. He was tried and sentenced to death as an adult under Missouri law. The Missouri Supreme Court overturned the sentence, and the U.S. Supreme Court upheld the ruling, saying that the decision "finds confirmation in the stark reality that the United States is the only country in the world that continues to give official sanction to the juvenile death penalty."[a] One Court observer noted, "For the Supreme Court itself, perhaps the most significant effect of yesterday's decision is to reaffirm the role of international law in constitutional interpretation."[b] The European Union, human rights lawyers from Great Britain, and several Nobel Peace Prize winners had filed briefs urging the Court to strike down the juvenile death penalty. The majority opinion recognized this expression of international opinion, saying that it "provide[s] respected and significant confirmation for our own

conclusions."[c] The three dissenters, led by Justice Antonin Scalia, strongly objected to the role played by international opinion. They criticized the majority for "proclaim[ing] itself sole arbiter of our Nation's moral standards—and in the course of discharging that awesome responsibility purport[ing] to take guidance from the views of foreign courts and legislatures." Scalia also chastised the majority for selectively paying attention to international opinion while ignoring it on other issues (such as abortion). "To invoke alien law when it agrees with one's own thinking, and ignore it otherwise, is not reasoned decisionmaking," he thundered, "but sophistry."[d]

Conservatives in Congress were also outraged that a Court decision would give such weight to international law and opinion, and several have introduced legislation that would ban such practices. Scalia rose to defend his institution, essentially telling Congress to back off. "It's none of your business," he told Congress. "No one is more opposed to the use of foreign law than I am, but I'm darned if I think it's up to Congress to direct the Court how to make its decisions." He went on to say that the proposed legislation "is like telling us not to use certain principles of logic. Let us make our mistakes just as we let you make yours."[e]

Whether the Supreme Court should pay attention to international opinion and law is certainly a matter of debate. However, it illustrates the importance of "comparing ourselves to others" and being aware of how our political system may be in step with or outside of the mainstream. ■

More recently, the Court ruled in two cases that California's "three strikes and you're out" law (which mandates very harsh sentences for third felony convictions) did not violate the 8th Amendment. In the first case, Gary Ewing stole three golf clubs, each valued at $399, and received twenty-five years to life. In the other case, Leandro Andrade stole nine videotapes valued at $150 from two different K-Marts and received two consecutive terms of twenty-five years to life (because there were two crimes), meaning that he would not be eligible for parole until he is eighty-seven years old.[141] In each case, the defendants' previous felony convictions were for nonviolent crimes.

Privacy Rights

You may be surprised to learn that there are no explicit **privacy rights** in the Constitution. The right was first developed in a 1965 case that questioned the constitutionality of an 1879 Connecticut law against using birth control. Estelle Griswold, the director of Planned Parenthood in Connecticut, was arrested nine days after opening a clinic that dispensed contraceptives. She was fined $100 and appealed her conviction. Though she lost in state court, she appealed all the way to the Supreme Court, which overturned her conviction. In a very fractured decision (there were six different opinions), the Court agreed the law was outdated—even the dissenters called it an "an uncommonly silly law" that was "obviously unenforceable"—but the justices agreed on little else. Even those who based their opinions on an implied constitutional right to privacy cited various constitutional roots. Justice William O. Douglas wrote the main opinion, but his reasoning was endorsed in its entirety by only one other justice. Douglas argued that the "penumbras" (the surrounding fringes or shadows) of the Bill of Rights create "zones of privacy." Specifically, he found privacy implicit in the 1st Amendment right of association, the 3rd's protection against the quartering of troops, the 4th's prohibition against unreasonable searches and seizures, the 5th's protection against self-incrimination, and the 9th's catch-all statement, "The enumeration in the Constitution, of certain rights, shall not be construed to deny or disparage others retained by the people."[142] These all seem like reasonable grounds for implicit privacy rights except the 1st Amendment right of association—since the Founders clearly meant political association, not an association with your spouse in bed.

The *Griswold* case was significant for establishing the constitutional basis for a right to privacy, but the dissenters in the case were concerned about where this right would lead. Justice Black warned that privacy "is a broad, abstract and ambiguous concept" that can be shrunken or expanded in subsequent decisions. He said that Douglas's argument required

> judges to determine what is or is not constitutional on the basis of their own appraisal of what laws are unwise or unnecessary. The power to make such decisions is of course that of a legislative body. Surely it has to be admitted that no provision of the Constitution specifically gives such blanket power to courts to exercise such a supervisory veto over the wisdom and value of legislative policies and to hold unconstitutional those laws which they believe unwise or dangerous.[143]

Justice Black's prediction came true eight years later in the landmark ruling in *Roe v. Wade*, which struck down laws in forty-six states that limited abortion. Twelve of those states allowed abortions for pregnancies due to rape or incest, to protect the

privacy rights Liberties protected by several amendments in the Bill of Rights that shield certain personal aspects of citizens' lives from governmental interference, such as the 4th Amendment's protection against unreasonable searches and seizures.

life of the mother, and in cases of severe fetal handicap. The much-criticized trimester analysis in the *Roe* ruling said that states could not limit abortions in the first trimester; in the second trimester, states could regulate abortions in the interests of the health of the mother; and in the third trimester, states could forbid all abortions except those necessary to protect the health or life of the mother. The justices cited a constitutional basis for abortion rights in the general right to privacy outlined in *Griswold*; the concept of "personal liberty" in the 14th Amendment's due process clause; and the "rights reserved to the people" by the 9th Amendment.[144] Subsequent decisions have upheld *Roe* but endorsed various state restrictions on abortion, such as requiring parental consent, a waiting period, or counseling sessions aimed at convincing the woman not to have an abortion.[145] Since *Roe*, most political action concerning abortion has taken place in the courts, but that could all change if the Supreme Court overturns this decision. Such a possibility became more likely when Justice Sandra Day O'Connor retired from the Court in 2006 and was replaced by Justice Samuel Alito. For example, in 2007 Alito voted to uphold a national ban on "partial-birth abortion" while O'Connor had previously voted to strike down a similar law.[146] Opponents of abortion are hoping that *Roe* will be overturned, which would shift the politics of abortion back to state legislatures and make it an even more contested political issue.

🅠 **POLITICS IS CONFLICTUAL**

Privacy rights have also become central in debates over the right to die, in which two types of political issues have been hotly debated. The first involves the right of a person who is brain dead or in a persistent vegetative state to refuse medical treatment so he may die. Courts have approved living wills in which a person can document his or her wishes in advance about end-of-life medical care. The problem comes when a person who can no longer communicate has not left instructions on how much medical intervention she should receive. Every month thousands of families have to make these decisions during the last few weeks of a patient's life, in consultation with their doctors. Most of the time the decisions are extremely difficult but without legal conflict. The high-profile case of Terri Schiavo illustrated how complicated these issues can get. After a heart failure that resulted in severe brain damage, Schiavo remained in a persistent vegetative state for fifteen years. Her husband said she would not have wanted to be kept alive in that condition, but Schiavo's parents wanted to do everything possible to keep her alive. After the federal courts refused to intervene, she was taken off life support at her husband's request. Given this precedent, the courts seem unlikely to get involved in matters traditionally resolved between a family and their doctor.

The second right-to-die issue is more complicated: May states allow assisted suicide for people with terminal illnesses, even if that practice conflicts with federal law? The case involved Oregon's Death with Dignity Act, discussed in Chapter 3, which allows a terminally ill patient to get a prescription from his doctor to end his life. The law was approved twice by the state's voters (first by a 51-to-49 margin in 1994 and then by a 60-to-40 margin in 1997, when it went into effect). In the law's first seven years, 166 people ended their lives through this procedure.[147] Oregon, Montana, and Washington are the only states with such a law, and it has been highly controversial; Attorney General John Ashcroft attempted to revoke the medical licenses of doctors who prescribed the drugs. According to Ashcroft's interpretation of the federal Controlled Substances Act, use of prescription drugs in doctor-assisted suicide is not a "legitimate medical purpose" of the drugs, and therefore not allowed under the law. However, the Supreme Court upheld the Oregon law in a

▼ *Privacy rights are not clearly articulated in the Constitution, but the federal courts are increasingly asked to rule on questions concerning intensely personal decisions such as abortion and the right to die. Terri Schiavo's case drew national attention in 2005 when her husband and her parents disagreed about whether she should be removed from life support after living in a vegetative state for fifteen years.*

recent case, ruling that the attorney general should not be given the "extraordinary authority" to "criminalize even the actions of registered physicians, whenever they engage in conduct he deems illegitimate."[148]

Conclusion

There probably isn't a day that goes by in which you are not affected in some way by your civil liberties, whether speaking in a public place, going to church, being searched at an airport, participating in a political demonstration, writing or reading an article in your school newspaper, or being free from illegal police searches in your home. Because civil liberties are defined as those things the government *cannot* do to us, defining our civil liberties is a political process. Often this process is confined to the courts, but on many issues, including free speech, freedom of the press, pornography, criminal rights, abortion, and gun control, these debates take place in the broader political world where defining civil liberties involves balancing competing ideals and interests and drawing lines by interpreting and applying the law. To return to the example discussed in the introduction, How should we balance national security and personal liberties? Debates over the boundaries of these freedoms—whether newspapers should publish stories about classified programs that may threaten civil liberties; whether government surveillance powers should be strengthened to fight terrorism—will rage for years to come. As with all political questions, there are no easy answers. These continually evolving liberties lie at the core of our political system.

What are the origins of civil liberties?

- Civil liberties are those freedoms that define what the government cannot do to its citizens.
- The battle over ratification of the Constitution led to the adoption of the Bill of Rights, which outlines Americans' basic freedoms.
- Early interpretation of the Constitution protected citizens only against the relatively weak national government, not the states, which limited the significance of the Bill of Rights.
- Through the process of selective incorporation, the Supreme Court's interpretation of the 14th Amendment has gradually broadened to apply most of the civil liberties in the Bill of Rights to state governments as well.

How are the freedoms of speech, assembly, and the press protected by the 1st Amendment?

- Determining the specific meaning of the freedom of speech, assembly, and the press involves balancing interests and drawing lines. Balancing interests means the Court must choose between competing constitutional rights, such as the right to protest against the Vietnam War by burning your draft card or Congress's right to raise and support armies. Drawing lines refers to the Court defining the range of permissable conduct concerning a specific liberty, such as the freedom of speech.
- The Court has drawn lines in various places throughout history and those lines will continue to evolve over the coming decades in important areas such as national security and regulation of the Internet.
- Political speech, the right of assembly, and freedom of the press have received stronger protection from the courts than commercial or other nonpolitical activity.

How is the freedom of religion protected by the 1st Amendment?

- The freedom of religion in the United States is protected by the establishment clause and the free exercise clause of the 1st Amendment.
- In interpreting the establishment clause, the Court has moved from a strict separation between church and state to allowing them to intermingle in many areas.
- Defining the free exercise clause often involves balancing different interests, illustrating our key idea that politics is conflictual and involves trade-offs.
- Congress has required that the government show a "compelling interest" in regulating a particular behavior before religious practices may be limited.

How are criminal defendants' rights balanced against the need for law and order?

- The civil liberties described in this section are central to defining the nature of criminal law.
- The Constitution protects the accused's right to the due process of law, including freedom from unreasonable police searches, the right to a fair trial, the right to consult a lawyer, freedom from self-incrimination and from being tried twice for the same crime, the right to know what crime you are accused of and to confront the accuser in court, and freedom from cruel and unusual punishment.

- These civil liberties, like all others, are continually evolving as the courts and Congress respond to different political forces.

What are our privacy rights?

- There is no explicit privacy right in the Constitution, but the Court has cited implied privacy protections in their rulings allowing access to birth control, abortion rights, and the right to die.
- If the Supreme Court overruled *Roe v. Wade*, the controversial decision protecting the right to an abortion, political debates over abortion laws would instead play out in the state legislatures.

⊚ STUDENT STUDYSPACE

Find quizzes and other review material at wwnorton.com/studyspace.

CRITICAL THINKING

1. What is the proper balance between national security and civil liberties? Is it appropriate to restrict civil liberties during a time of war? If so, how much? And if not, why?
2. Do you support complete freedom of speech for the most despicable group you can think of? When should speech be limited, if at all?
3. Has the Supreme Court balanced protection for the free exercise of religion without allowing the state establishment of religion, or have they swung too far in one direction? Which rulings support your conclusion?
4. Do you support due process rights for defendants in criminal cases, even if it means that some potentially guilty people go free? If so, why? If not, are you concerned about convicting innocent people?

KEY TERMS

civil liberties (p. 100)
Civil War Amendments (p. 106)
clear and present danger test (p. 111)
commercial speech (p. 118)
direct incitement test (p. 112)
double jeopardy (p. 132)
due process clause (p. 107)
due process rights (p. 125)

establishment clause (p. 120)
exclusionary rule (p. 127)
fighting words (p. 117)
free exercise clause (p. 120)
gag order (p. 115)
hate speech (p. 114)
Lemon test (p. 121)
libel (p. 117)

Miller test (p. 118)
Miranda rights (p. 132)
prior restraint (p. 115)
privacy rights (p. 137)
selective incorporation (p. 108)
slander (p. 117)
symbolic speech (p. 112)

SUGGESTED READING

Abraham, Henry J., and Barbara A. Perry. *Freedom and the Court: Civil Rights and Liberties in the United States*, 8th ed. Lawrence, KS: University Press of Kansas, 2003.

Amar, Akhil Reed. *The Bill of Rights*. New Haven, CT: Yale University Press, 1998.

Bondenhamer, David J., and James W. Ely, eds. *The Bill of Rights in Modern America*. Bloomington, IN: Indiana University Press, 2008.

Lewis, Anthony. *Gideon's Trumpet*. New York: Random House, 1964.

Moynihan, Daniel Patrick. *Secrecy: The American Experience*. New Haven, CT: Yale University Press, 1998.

Posner, Richard A. *Not a Suicide Pact: The Constitution in a Time of National Emergency*. New York: Oxford University Press, 2006.

Pritchett, C. Herman. *Constitutional Civil Liberties*. Englewood Cliffs, NJ: Prentice Hall, 1984.

Schweber, Howard. *Speech, Conduct, and the First Amendment*. New York: Peter Lang Publishing, 2003.

Protesters for and against health care reform make their views known at a Delray Beach, Florida, town hall meeting in August 2009.

Public Opinion

How much do Americans know about what government does? How much do they care about it? News coverage during the 2009–2010 health care reform debate showed anti- and pro-reform advocates loudly expressing their opinions at raucous town hall meetings across the country, suggesting that citizens on both sides of the issue hold passionate, often extreme views. In recent years, debates over issues such as abortion, gun control, and the wars in Iraq and Afghanistan have also provoked intense and vocal responses from many people, reflecting apparent sharp differences of opinion and unsuccessful attempts at compromise in Washington. At the same time, and paradoxically, on many issues Americans are reputed to have only a minor interest

CONFLICT AND COMPROMISE
in American Politics

in politics and public policy, and we often hear reports of misperceptions among the public about government. For example, as we will discuss later in the chapter, the average American believes that the government spends about ten times more on foreign aid than it actually spends. And yet, the fundamental assumption of democracy is that citizens have an idea of what they want government to do, and that they incorporate this information into their voting decisions. Do voters form valid opinions—with some basis in fact—to guide their behavior?

It turns out that the average American knows more than you might think. Consider Figure 5.1, which shows data from Pew Research Center surveys conducted between 2004 and 2010 on the percentages of Americans who defined the economy and the wars in Iraq and Afghanistan as the "most important problem" facing the United States. The percentage of Americans who believed the wars were the most important problems was relatively low at the time Iraqi leader Saddam Hussein was captured, then trended upward after photographs showing American troops abusing prisoners at Abu Ghraib prison were published in 2004 and after increases in attacks on American troops in 2005 and 2006, then began a steady decline after the 2007 "surge" of additional American troops and the resulting decrease in insurgent attacks.

As the Iraq war faded in importance, economic troubles, including the bankruptcies of investment banks on Wall Street and the collapse of stock prices, were reflected in a sharp increase in the percentage of Americans who defined the economy as the most important problem. These percentages began to decline

BIG QUESTIONS

✪ What is public opinion?

✪ Where do opinions come from?

✪ How is public opinion measured?

✪ What are the characteristics of U.S. public opinion?

✪ How does public opinion matter?

with the enactment of economic stimulus legislation in early 2009, along with a recovery in the stock market and improvements in the overall economy, although they remained high as of February 2010.

The figure also suggests the political consequences of these opinions. At the time then-president George W. Bush successfully ran for reelection in 2004, the percentage of Americans who listed the war as the most important problem was fairly low. However, by November 2006, the percentage had grown substantially, and many Republican representatives and senators who had strongly supported the war lost their races for reelection. One argument about these elections is that many Americans voted for Democratic congressional candidates *because* they opposed the war in Iraq.[1] Similarly, Democrat Barack Obama won the presidency in 2008 and Democrats gained additional seats in the House and Senate, a result attributed by many observers to Republicans being blamed for economic woes. These conclusions make sense only if a large fraction of American voters held opinions about the war and the economy that shaped their voting decisions. Although these

FIGURE 5.1 **TRACKING EVENTS AND PUBLIC OPINION, 2004–2010**

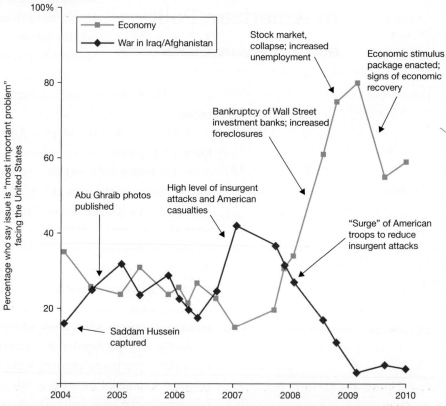

SOURCE: Pew Research Center, "Midterm Election Challenges for Both Parties," February 12, 2010, available at http://people-press.org/reports/pdf/589.pdf.

examples may suggest that Americans know something about political events and that their opinions can influence elections, we still must ask whether they are the exception or the rule. That is, in general, does public opinion matter in American politics?

In every election, candidates, political parties, journalists, and political scientists take thousands of polls. For the politicians and their allies, these polls are aimed at determining who is likely to vote; what sorts of arguments, slogans, and platforms would find favor with these voters; and which candidates are likely to win. News organizations, foundations, political scientists, and others conduct polls addressing these same questions, as well as where these opinions and preferences come from.[2] And yet some scholars have argued that most Americans make up their responses to survey questions, have no firm opinions about government policy, and are easily swayed by candidates, advocacy groups, or the media.[3]

This chapter shows that Americans really do hold measurable opinions on a wide range of topics, and these opinions shape their political behavior. We examine the sources of public opinion, from everyday events to what politicians say and do, as well as group characteristics such as race, gender, and ethnicity. We look at how politicians take account of public opinion—how their campaign strategies, as well as their actions in office, in particular their willingness to compromise policy differences, are shaped by information about what the public wants or might want in the future. As you will see, process matters: the way individual opinions are formed and the tools used to measure public opinion shape what people demand from government and how politicians respond to those demands. Studying public opinion reveals a new angle on the idea that politics is everywhere. That is, most Americans are not policy experts, but people do tend to think about politics the same way they think about most things in their lives. Aside from a few broad principles, such as party identification, that are typically formed early in life, opinions take form only when they are needed, such as when people vote on Election Day or answer a survey question.

Finally, opinion data show that Americans disagree about government policy. Examining American public opinion allows us to describe these disagreements in detail and better understand the political conflicts they raise. Perhaps surprisingly, we will also see that although Americans disagree about some important issues, *profound* polarization is relatively rare, meaning the compromise is sometimes easier to arrive at than you might think. Moreover, on a wide range of policy questions, most Americans hold opinions that are squarely in the middle of the political spectrum. Thus, although we spend considerable time in this chapter detailing how Americans disagree, it is important to remember that disagreement does not always exist, and when it does, acceptable compromises often can be found.

What Is Public Opinion?

Public opinion describes what the population thinks about politics and government—what government should be doing, evaluations of what government *is* doing, and judgments about elected officials and others who participate in the political process, as well as the wider set of beliefs that shape these opinions.

public opinion Citizens' views on politics and government actions.

Calvin and Hobbes   by Bill Watterson

▲ Politicians read public opinion polls closely to gauge whether their behavior will anger or please constituents. Few politicians always follow survey results—but virtually none would agree with Calvin's father that polls should be ignored entirely.

Public opinion matters for three reasons. First, citizens' political actions—including voting, contributing to campaigns, writing letters to senators, and other kinds of activism—are driven by their opinions.[4] For example, as we discuss in more detail in Chapter 7, party identification shapes voting decisions. A voter who thinks of herself as a Democrat is more likely to vote for Democratic candidates than a voter who identifies as a Republican.[5] Similarly, a voter who believes in small government would likely oppose new programs such as the health care proposals debated in the House and Senate during 2009 and 2010. Therefore, if we want to explain either an individual's behavior or broader political outcomes, such as who wins an election or the fate of a legislative proposal, we need good data on public opinion.

The second reason for examining public opinion is to explain the behavior of candidates, political parties, and other political actors. Other chapters in this book, particularly Chapter 8, Elections, and Chapter 10, Congress, show that the link between citizens' opinions and candidates' campaign strategies and actions in office is very strong. Politicians look to public opinion to determine what citizens want them to do and to determine how happy citizens are with their behavior in office. For example, in Chapter 10 we see how the opinions of ordinary citizens exert a strong influence on the ways that their representatives in the House and Senate choose to vote. Legislators are reluctant to cast votes that are inconsistent with what their constituents want, especially on issues that constituents consider important. Therefore, to explain a legislator's votes, you need to begin with data on constituents' opinions.

Third, because public opinion is a key to understanding what motivates both citizens and political officials, it can also shed light on the reasons for specific policy outcomes. For example, changes in the policy mood—the public's demand for new policies—are linked to changes in government spending.[6] When people want government to do more, spending increases faster; when people want less from the government, spending goes down (or increases more slowly). Thus, to explain what government does and why, we need to measure and understand public opinion.

EARLY THEORIES OF PUBLIC OPINION

Though it may sound strange, early studies of public opinion, based on surveys conducted during the 1950s, found little evidence that the public's political opinions existed at all.[7] The surveys revealed high levels of inconsistency; many people expressed liberal responses to some questions and conservative responses to others.

▲ *Are Americans poorly informed about politics? One survey found that more Americans could identify characters on* The Simpsons *than could list which liberties the Bill of Rights guarantees, and another found most respondents unable to name any Supreme Court justices.*

Responses also varied across time: many people who said in one survey that they favored an activist government switched to favoring a limited government when asked two years later. Few respondents could say why they liked a particular candidate, or why they were conservative, liberal, or moderate. Americans also had low levels of factual information, such as knowing which party held majorities in the House and Senate. One author estimated that up to 70 percent of survey respondents were either completely making up their responses—in other words, they answered more or less at random—or were unable to say anything meaningful. As he put it, "Large portions of the electorate do not have meaningful beliefs, even on issues that have formed the basis for intense political controversy among elites for substantial periods of time."[8] Only a small fraction of the electorate, perhaps 5 percent or less, was categorized as having the highest **level of conceptualization**, which required holding principles and preferences that were consistent with one another and stable over time.

Some modern studies seem to support these claims. One study found that people are more likely to know the names of characters on *The Simpsons* than to know which individual liberties are guaranteed by the Bill of Rights.[9] Another found that a majority of Americans could not name any members of the Supreme Court.[10] And in a 2007 survey, nearly 20 percent of college students thought that Martin Luther King's 1963 "I have a dream" speech was aimed at abolishing slavery rather than securing voting rights and ending the "separate but equal" system of public accommodations in southern states.[11] If these early studies and modern examples were the last word, there would be little need to study public opinion, because most people would have little to say, many others would make up their responses, and, most important, what little public opinion you might discern would have little impact on individual behavior or government actions.

THE NEW THEORY OF PUBLIC OPINION

Three arguments forced changes in the old view of public opinion. Some scholars argued that it was no surprise to find that people have trouble talking about politics.[12] After all, even if politics is everywhere, only a few Americans monitor political events or think about politics every day. Another important factor in interpreting survey results is that some survey questions are ambiguous and open to interpretation.[13] As a result, people may have trouble answering even seemingly simple questions about politics or public policy.

level of conceptualization The amount of complexity in an individual's beliefs about government and policy, and the extent to which those beliefs are consistent with each other and remain consistent over time.

liberal–conservative ideology A way of describing political beliefs in terms of a position on the spectrum running from liberal to moderate to conservative.

latent opinion An opinion formed on the spot, when it is needed (as distinct from a deeply held opinion that is stable over time).

POLITICS IS EVERYWHERE

A second critique focused on the timing of the early public opinion studies of the 1950s. Analysis of surveys taken in the 1960s and afterward found that many opinions remained stable over time.[14] Later surveys also found higher levels of factual knowledge in the American electorate.[15] Both findings suggest that even if the early findings about public opinion were true, at best they described only the American public of the 1950s, not contemporary public opinion.

The third and most important argument was that in order to accurately capture public opinion, scholars needed to expand their picture of what it might look like. Early surveys looked for evidence that citizens had beliefs that were internally consistent, stable, and based on a rationale that allowed them to explain why they held those beliefs. The new work began with the premise that none of these conditions were necessary, and that earlier scholars failed to find evidence of public opinion because they were looking for the wrong thing, rather than because it didn't exist.[16]

Describing Public Opinion Modern theories of public opinion distinguish between two types of opinions. The first are broad expressions such as how a person thinks about politics, what a citizen wants from government, or principles that apply across a range of issues. These kinds of beliefs are typically formed early in life and remain stable over time. Nuts and Bolts 5.1 shows part of a Pew Research Center survey that lists a number of such opinions. Some of these beliefs are obviously political, such as party identification, ideology, and judgments about whether elected officials lose touch with citizens. Others, such as beliefs about homosexuality or religion, may seem irrelevant to politics, but their presence on the Pew questionnaire illustrates an important finding: Americans' political opinions are shaped by a wide range of beliefs and ideas, including many influences that are not inherently political.

One important opinion measured by the Pew survey is **liberal–conservative ideology**, which describes whether a respondent identifies as a liberal, moderate, conservative, or something between these categories. As the responses in Figure 5.2 show, Americans are spread out across the ideological range, with most people identifying as either liberal or conservative, but not strongly so. Liberal–conservative ideology is a good example of a stable opinion: the best way to predict an American's ideology at age forty is to assume it will match his ideology at age twenty, and the same is true for party identification. However, even these typically stable opinions sometimes change in response to events. For example, although party identification is formed during early adulthood and adolescence, and often persists throughout an individual's life, it can change as new issues arise or when candidates' positions contradict a citizen's notion of the differences between parties.[17] In a later section, we look more closely at how such opinions are formed and why they change.

Many Opinions Are Latent The most important thing to understand about public opinion is that although ideology and party identification are largely consistent over time, they are the exceptions to the rule.[18] The average person does not maintain a set of fully formed opinions on all political topics, such as evaluations of all the state- or citywide candidates for office or assessments of the entire range of government programs. Instead, most Americans' political judgments are **latent opinions** constructed only when they are needed, such as when answering a survey question or deciding just before Election Day how to vote. For example, when an individual is first asked about his opinions on global warming, he will probably not have a specific response in mind. He simply will not have thought much about the question, and might have, at best, some vague ideas about the subject. His opinions

Surveying Political Principles

This is a portion of a Pew Research Center questionnaire that asks about a range of public opinion principles, from the government's role in protecting morality to party identification and liberal–conservative ideology. For each topic, two opposing statements are given, and respondents are asked to agree with the one that comes closest to their views, including options in the middle of the two extremes.

Statement 1	Strongly agree	Agree		Agree	Strongly agree	Statement 2
The government should do more to protect morality in society.	☐	☐		☐	☐	I worry the government is getting too involved in the issue of morality.
Homosexuality is a way of life that should be accepted by society.	☐	☐		☐	☐	Homosexuality is a way of life that should be discouraged by society.
The government should do more to help needy Americans, even if it means going deeper into debt.	☐	☐		☐	☐	The government today can't afford to do much more to help the needy.
Religion is a very important part of my life.	☐	☐		☐	☐	Religion is not that important to me.
Elected officials in Washington lose touch with the people pretty quickly.	☐	☐		☐	☐	Elected officials in Washington try hard to stay in touch with voters back home.

In politics today, do you consider yourself a Republican, Democrat, or Independent?

Strong Democrat	Democrat	Independent, lean Democrat	Independent, no leaning	Independent, lean Republican	Republican	Strong Republican
☐	☐	☐	☐	☐	☐	☐

In general, would you describe your political views as very conservative, conservative, moderate, liberal, or very liberal?

Very liberal	Liberal	Moderate	Conservative	Very conservative
☐	☐	☐	☐	☐

SOURCE: Pew Research Center, "Beyond Red vs. Blue," available at http://typology.people-press.org/typology.

on global warming become more specific and concrete only when he is asked to describe them.

People who follow politics closely have more pre-formed opinions than the average American, whose interest in politics is relatively low. But very few people are so informed that they have ready opinions, judgments, and evaluations across a wide range of political questions. Moreover, even when people do form opinions in advance, they may not remember every factor that influenced them. Thus, an individual may identify as a liberal or a conservative, or as a supporter of a particular party, but may be unable to explain specific reasons for these ideological leanings.[19]

When opinions are formed on the spot, they are based on **considerations**, the pieces of relevant information—such as ideology, party identification, religious beliefs, personal circumstances, or other factors—that come to mind when the opinion is requested.[20] The process of forming an opinion usually is not thorough or systematic, since most people don't take into account everything they know about the issue.[21] Rather, they only use considerations that come to mind immediately.[22] Highly informed people who follow politics use this process, as do those with low levels of political interest and knowledge.[23]

considerations The many pieces of information a person uses to form an opinion.

FIGURE 5.2 LIBERAL–CONSERVATIVE IDEOLOGY IN AMERICA

Many commentators describe politics in America as highly conflictual, with most Americans holding either liberal or conservative points of view and very few people in between. Do opinion data confirm or disprove this description?

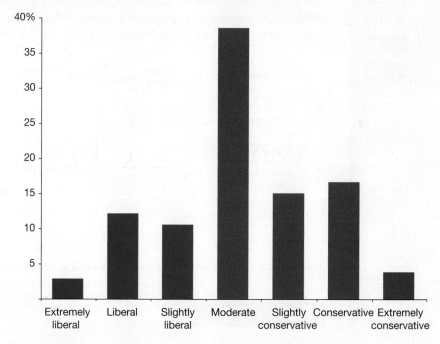

SOURCE: Data from 2008 General Social Survey, available at http://sda.berkeley.edu/archive.htm.

To see this process at work, consider how people decide whether they approve of the job the president is doing. Surveys on this topic typically ask respondents whether they approve or disapprove of the president's performance, although their wording varies. Figure 5.3 shows approval and disapproval percentages for President Obama from the time he assumed office in 2009 through the 2010 midterm elections. The data show a pattern that is typical for most presidents: initially high approval percentages, then a gradual decline during their first year or two in office. In the main, when a new president takes office, many voters hold high and often contradictory expectations about what the president will be able to do during his term. In the case of Obama, for example, some Americans expected a speedy economic recovery and enactment of many new programs, from health care reform to climate change legislation and repeal of regulations banning homosexuals from military service. Others opposed these initiatives from the beginning, so they never approved of Obama's performance. The downward trend in approval for Obama reflects that some voters switched their positive responses during 2009 and 2010 as they became disillusioned either with Obama's failure to satisfy their policy demands or the weak state of the American economy.

Many studies of public opinion support the idea that opinions are mostly formed on the spot using a wide range of considerations. Attitudes about immigration are shaped by evaluations of the state of the economy.[24] People judge government spending proposals differently depending on whether a Republican or a Democrat made the proposal, using their own party identification as a consideration.[25] Evaluations of affirmative action programs vary depending on whether the survey

FIGURE 5.3
APPROVAL RATINGS FOR PRESIDENT BARACK OBAMA, 2009–2010

The dots show presidential approval and disapproval as measured in a particular poll; the lines track the average ratings in all the polls taken at a particular time. Scholars claim that presidential approval is shaped by major national and international events. Are these influences evident in these data on approval of President Obama?

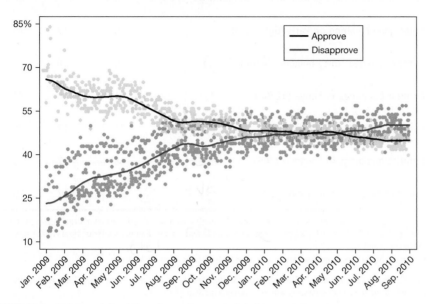

SOURCE: "National Job Approval, Barack Obama," www.pollster.com/polls/us/jobapproval-obama.php.

question reminds respondents that they may be hurt by these programs—that is, these preferences are influenced by considerations of personal economic well-being.[26] Voters' party identification and ideology influence their evaluations of candidates.[27] Individuals' willingness to allow protests and other expressions of opinions they disagree with depends on their belief in tolerance.[28] And if people feel obligated to help others in need, they are more likely to support government programs that benefit the poor.[29]

Sometimes competing or contradictory considerations influence the opinion-formation process. In the case of abortion laws, for example, many people believe in protecting human life but also value allowing women to make their own medical decisions.[30] When someone with both of these beliefs is asked for her opinion about abortion laws, her response will depend on which of these considerations comes to mind and seems most relevant as she is answering the question. Opinions about other morally complex issues such as right-to-die legislation, or race-related issues such as affirmative action are also often based on competing considerations.[31]

Events can also become considerations. Following the September 11 attacks, the Pew Research Center began surveying Americans about their fears of another terrorist attack. As Table 5.1 shows, every time a terrorist attack occurred in the next few years, regardless of its location, the percentage

▼ Images of intense confrontation between pro-life and pro-choice protesters may conceal the more nuanced, conflicting considerations that underlie many Americans' opinions about abortion. Most Americans believe that the decision to have an abortion should be left up to the woman but are uncomfortable allowing unrestricted access to the procedure.

TABLE 5.1 FEARS OF TERRORIST ATTACK

In this chapter, we argue that opinions are often sensitive to new information or events. Is this true of worries about a future terrorist attack?

	Followed Very Closely	Very Worried[a]	
		Before	After
Terrorist attacks in New York and Washington, DC (9/01)	74%	—	28%
Failed shoe bombing on Paris flight (1/02)	20	13	20
Arrest of alleged "dirty bomber" (6/02)	30	20	32
Terrorist bombings in Kenya (12/02)	21	20	31
Terrorist bombings in Madrid (3/04)	34	13	20
Terrorist bombings in London (7/05)	48	17	26
Thwarted British terrorist plot (8/06)	54	17	25[b]

[a] Percentage of respondents very worried there will soon be another terrorist attack on the United States. "Before" figures from closest available survey prior to incident; "after" and news interest from closest survey following incident.

[b] "Before" figure from August 9; "after" and news interest from August 10–13.

SOURCE: Pew Research Center, "American Attitudes Hold Steady in Face of Foreign Crises," August 16, 2006, available at http://people-press.org/reports/display.php3?ReportID=285.

of Americans answering that they were "very worried" about a future attack rose significantly. After the July 2005 bombings in London, the "very worried" segment of the U.S. population increased from 17 to 26 percent, an increase of almost 50 percent.

Most Americans form opinions—legitimate, meaningful opinions—when they are needed. Though they don't usually seek out new information or take account of everything they know, their opinions reflect at least some of their knowledge of politics, as well as their bedrock ideological beliefs, and ideas about what they want from government.

One of the most appealing features of this description of public opinions about politics is how closely it resembles the way most people think about other aspects of their lives. Do you prefer blue or black jeans? Coke or Pepsi? Jon Stewart or Stephen Colbert? Facebook or MySpace? These decisions are probably easy precisely because you face them every day and, as a result, are likely to have highly accessible opinions about which option you prefer. You don't have to think much to form your opinion. Now think about a different question: What kind of house would you like to own? If you are in your late teens or early twenties, you probably have not thought much about this one. New or old? Ranch, split-level, colonial, bungalow, Victorian, or contemporary? Granite counters, slate, Formica, or Corian? Oil, gas, or electric heat—or solar? How do you feel about walkout basements, decks, wall color, floor coverings, and appliances? The list is virtually endless.

If someone asked you to describe your preferred house, you probably could only begin to answer the question. You'd probably base your response on a relatively small set of ideas, using a few mental snapshots of your image of the perfect house. You would probably say something very different if you had time to think, or

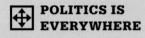

POLITICS IS EVERYWHERE

even if you were asked on a different day, or especially if you were asked when you are ready to buy a house. This strategy is exactly how most Americans form their opinions about politics. When someone is asked for an opinion on a political question she knows little about, her response is based on a few general, simple considerations. A question about who should provide health insurance—government or private insurers—may call to mind a fight with an insurance company over a medical claim, recent dealings with government bureaucrats, or how a good insurance plan helped a family member survive cancer. These considerations may not lead to the most thoughtful answer, but they may be all that people use to form their opinions.

This description of how most people think about politics explains many of the anomalies in early studies of public opinion. People have trouble expressing their opinions because they are often devising these opinions on the spot. Although people cannot often provide a rationale for their beliefs, this doesn't mean the beliefs are baseless; rather, such information may not be remembered. And it makes sense that opinions change over time, as people vary the considerations they use.

Thinking about opinions in terms of considerations implies that public opinion cannot simply be measured once and for all. Even if nothing major happens—no big events, new proposals, or other high-profile political activity—opinions may change as people call up different considerations to form them. Such variation does not mean that people are indecisive or that they do not understand what they are being asked. Rather, it reflects how the average person thinks and develops opinions.

Where Do Opinions Come From?

This section describes the sources of public opinion. Some of these influences come from early life experiences, such as exposure to the beliefs of parents, relatives, or teachers, while others result from later life events. Politicians also play a critical role in the opinion-formation process.

SOCIALIZATION: FAMILIES AND COMMUNITIES

Theories of **political socialization** show that many people's political opinions start with what they learned from their parents. These principles include a liberal–conservative ideology, level of trust in others, class identity, and ethnic identity.[32] There is also a high correlation between both the party identification and the liberal–conservative ideology of parents and those of their children.[33] These principles are not necessarily permanent; in fact, people sometimes respond to events by modifying their opinions, even those developed early in life. Even so, for many people, ideas learned during childhood continue to shape the way they think about politics throughout their lives.[34]

People are also socialized by their communities, the people they interact with while growing up, such as neighbors, teachers, clergy, and others.[35] Support for democracy as a system of government and for American political institutions is higher for individuals who took a civics class in high school.[36] Growing up in a

political socialization The process by which an individual's political opinions are shaped by other people and the surrounding culture.

homogenous community, one where many people share the same cultural, ethnic, or political beliefs, increases an adult's sense of civic duty—his belief that voting or other forms of political participation are things that people ought to do.[37] Volunteering in community organizations as a child also shapes political beliefs and participation in later life.[38] Engaging in political activity as a teenager, such as volunteering in a presidential campaign, generates higher levels of political interest as an adult; it also strengthens the belief that people should care about politics and participate in political activities.[39]

EVENTS

Although socialization often influences individuals' fairly stable core beliefs, public opinion is not fixed. People can revise their opinions in response to what happens to them and in the world around them. All kinds of events, from everyday interactions to traumatic, life-changing disasters, can capture a person's attention and force him to revise his fundamental understanding of politics and the role of government. For example, though an individual's initial partisan affiliation is likely to reflect the leanings of her parents, this starting point will change as a function of subsequent events, such as who runs for office, what platforms they campaign on, and their performance in office.[40]

Some events that shape beliefs are specific, individual experiences. For example, someone who believes that he managed to get a college degree only because he received government grants and guaranteed student loans might believe that it is a good thing to have a large, activist government that provides a wide range of benefits to its citizens. Other events shape the beliefs of large numbers of people in similar ways. Political realignments are a good example. A realignment is a nationwide shift in which large numbers of people move from identifying with one political party to identifying with another (see Chapter 7). Beginning in the early 1960s, large numbers of white southerners shifted their party identification from Democratic to Republican. This gradual change in principles was driven by national events, including support of civil rights and voting rights legislation by many Democratic elected officials in Washington.[41]

▲ Although events such as wars, economic upheavals, and major policy changes certainly influence public opinion, research shows that most Americans acquire some political opinions early in life from parents, friends, teachers, and others in their community.

Many observers have argued that military service during World War II also shaped the opinions of many Americans, giving veterans higher levels of trust in government and greater satisfaction with the performance of the federal government.[42] Others have suggested that the change in opinions was not the result of military service, but of the government's efforts to help veterans after the war through programs such as the GI Bill, which funded college education for veterans after they left the military.[43]

Recent events have also shaped beliefs. Scholars have shown that after the September 11 terrorist attacks, many citizens became more willing to restrict civil liberties to reduce the chances of future attacks.[44] Support for restrictions increased soon after September 11 and remained elevated even five years later, suggesting a long-term change in public opinion. Similarly, many Americans responded to the financial crisis of 2008 by reducing their expectations about future income and changing their spending patterns, becoming less willing to incur debt for new homes, cars, and vacations.[45]

Events hold a similar sway over other opinions, such as presidential approval, which is driven by factors such as changes in the economy. Presidents are more likely to have high approval ratings when economic growth is high and inflation and unemployment are low, whereas approval ratings fall when growth is negative and unemployment and inflation are high. Many of these factors shape attachments to political parties, both at the level of individual citizens and when partisanship is measured in the aggregate.[46]

Some events have a greater impact on public opinion than others, and some people are more likely than others to change their views. Political scientist John Zaller showed that opinion changes generated by an event or some other piece of new information are more likely when an individual considers the event or information important and when it is unfamiliar, meaning that the individual does not have a set of preexisting principles or other considerations with which to interpret the event. Changes in opinions are also more likely for people who do not have strong feelings about what they believe than for people with strong opinions.[47]

◀ POLITICS IS EVERYWHERE

Laid Off from the Auto Industry? Don't Worry. There's Work for Everyone.

Lathe Operator

Chemical Engineer

JOB APPLICATION AND A HAPPY MEAL...

Systems Analyst

Precision Welder

Structural Metallurgist

HEAVY DUTY FRIES

DANZIGER
NYTS/CWS Jan 27 2006 (2666)

◀ *Although few Americans are economic policy experts, most people's judgments about economic conditions, based on everyday events and their personal economic circumstances, are remarkably accurate.*

GROUP IDENTITY

Another influence on an individual's opinions are social categories or groups, such as gender, race, or education level. These characteristics might shape opinions in three ways. First, as noted in the discussion of socialization, people learn about politics from the people around them. Therefore, people who live in the same region or who were born in the same era might have similar beliefs because they experienced the same historical events at similar points in their lives or learned political viewpoints from each other. In the United States, opinions on many issues are highly correlated with the state or region where a person grew up. For example, until the 1970s relatively few native white southerners identified with the Republican Party.[48] Even today, native white southerners tend to have distinctly different attitudes about many issues, such as support for affirmative action policies, and hold different principles, such as lower support for government involvement in creating racial equality, when compared to people of other races and from different regions of the country.[49]

People also may rely on others who "look like" them as a source of opinions. Political scientists Donald Green, Bradley Palmquist, and Eric Schickler, for example, argue that group identities shape partisanship: when someone is trying to decide between being a Republican or a Democrat, she thinks about which demographic groups are associated with each party, and picks the party that has more members from the groups she thinks she is a part of.[50]

A more practical reason for looking at group variations in public opinion is that candidates and political consultants often formulate their campaign strategies in terms of groups. For example, analyses of the 2008 election argued that Obama's presidential win and Democratic gains in the House and Senate were driven by high levels of support from young Americans, African Americans, and people with advanced degrees. Similarly, Democratic losses in 2009 and 2010 special elections were the result of lower turnout among the same groups and strong support for Republican candidates by people who live in suburbs and those with strong religious beliefs.[51]

Table 5.2 reports data on the variation in opinions across different groups of Americans, as measured in the General Social Survey. The table shows group differences on three broad questions: an individual's feelings about the Bible, the role of women in politics, and whether government should redistribute income (tax some people and give the money to others as credits or benefits). These data reveal two important facts about group affiliations and public opinion. First, they show sharp differences between groups on some questions. People of different education levels tend to respond very differently to the question about the Bible: of the people with a high school education about a third agree with the statement shown in the table, compared with only 14 percent of the people with an advanced degree. Similar disparities arise between racial groups on the income redistribution question.

These data also show a great deal of consensus. There is little variation between men and women on the role of women in politics although there are relatively sharp regional and educational differences. Moreover, no one group holds strong views on all three issues. For example, the table shows that opinions on the Bible vary with a person's education level but shows only a weak correlation to opinions about redistribution.

These data show that group characteristics can be important predictors of some of an individual's opinions, but they are not the whole story.[52] The opinions that Americans hold are a product of their socialization and their life experiences as well as their group characteristics. A person's group characteristics may tell us something about their opinions on some issues but reveal little about their thoughts on

POLITICS IS EVERYWHERE

TABLE 5.2 THE IMPORTANCE OF GROUPS

Knowing an individual's group characteristics often allows scholars to predict some of that person's opinions. For other opinions, however, these characteristics provide very little information. Can you find an example of both statements in this table?

		"The Bible is the actual Word of God and is to be taken literally, word for word." (percentage who agree)	"Men are better suited [than women] for politics." (percentage who agree)	"Government should reduce the income differences between the rich and the poor." (percentage who strongly agree)
Gender	Male	28%	24%	22%
	Female	35	22	25
Age	18–30	27%	27%	28%
	31–40	29	29	24
	41–55	35	35	24
	Over 55	34	34	21
Education	High school	34%	34%	24%
	Bachelor's degree	19	19	14
	Advanced degree	14	14	17
Race	White	28%	23%	18%
	African American	62	21	34
	Other	38	22	25
Family income	Less than $15,000	48%	48%	39%
	$15,000–$20,000	35	35	24
	$20,000–$25,000	48	48	49
	More than $25,000	27	27	18
Region	New England	22%	22%	19%
	Middle Atlantic	20	20	18
	Midwest	32	21	30
	South	51	51	27
	Mountain	34	34	20
	Pacific	23	23	22

SOURCE: Data from 2008 General Social Survey, available at http://sda.berkeley.edu/archive.htm.

other issues, and these group memberships are only one factor that influences public opinion.

POLITICIANS AND OTHER POLITICAL ACTORS

Opinions and changes in opinion are also influenced by politicians and other political actors, such as political parties and party leaders, interest groups, and even the leaders of religious, civic, and other large organizations. In part, this link exists because Americans look to these individuals for information due to their presumed expertise. You may not know what to think about the war in Afghanistan or health care reform, so you might seek out someone who knows more about the issues than you do, and if that person's opinions seem reasonable, you might adopt them as your own.[53] Of course, people do not search haphazardly for advice; they only take account of a particular expert's opinions on an issue when they believe they generally agree with the expert, perhaps because they are both conservatives, or Democrats, or the individual has some other basis for thinking their preferences are alike.

Politicians and other political actors also work to shape public opinion. Political scientists Lawrence Jacobs and Robert Shapiro argue that politicians describe proposals using arguments and images designed to tap the public's strong opinions, with the goal of winning support for these proposals.[54] These authors argue that public opposition in 1994 to President Bill Clinton's health care reform proposals did not arise because Americans opposed health care reform or because they disliked what the Clinton plan would do; rather, opposition arose in reaction to the way the proposal was described by legislators who opposed it.

Similarly, in 2009 and 2010 President Obama and his staff expended much time and effort to promote health care reform, giving dozens of public speeches, holding rallies across the nation, briefing legislators, and expressing their willingness to negotiate with lawmakers on the issue. While health care reform was eventually enacted in April 2010, all of these efforts to mobilize public opinion had a minimal effect. In fact, depending on how the question was asked, support for reform might have even been weaker at the end of the process compared to the beginning.

Measuring Public Opinion

For the most part, information about public opinion comes from **mass surveys**, in-person or phone interviews with hundreds or even thousands of voters. The aim of a mass survey is to measure the attitudes of a particular **population or group of people**, such as the residents of a particular congressional district, evangelicals, senior citizens, or even the entire adult population in America. For large groups such as these, it would be impossible to survey everyone. So, surveys typically involve **samples** of between a few hundred and several thousand individuals.

Large-scale surveys such as the American National Election Study (NES), which is conducted every election year, use various types of questions to measure citizens' opinions and preferences. In presidential election years, participants in the NES are first asked whether they voted for president. If they say they did, they are asked which candidate they voted for: a major party candidate (Barack Obama or John McCain in 2008), an independent candidate, or some other candidate.

Another type of survey question measures people's preferences using an **issue scale**. In a recent National Election Study, for example, respondents were asked to express their opinions about health insurance: Should government provide insurance, or should Americans buy insurance on their own? These views were placed at opposite ends of a 7-point scale, and the person being surveyed was asked to choose a position on the scale that reflects his opinion. If he strongly believes in government-provided insurance, he takes position 1; if he believes in private

mass survey A way to measure public opinion by interviewing a large sample of the population.

population The group of people that a researcher or pollster wants to study, such as evangelicals, senior citizens, or Americans.

sample Within a population, the group of people surveyed in order to gauge the whole population's opinion. Researchers use samples because it would be impossible to interview the entire population.

issue scale A survey response format in which respondents select their answers from a range of positions between two extremes.

sampling error A calculation that describes what percentage of the people surveyed may not accurately represent the population being studied. Increasing the number of respondents lowers the sampling error.

random sample A subsection of a population chosen to participate in a survey through a selection process in which every member of the population has an equal chance of being chosen. This kind of sampling improves the accuracy of public opinion data.

Sampling Error in Mass Surveys

The **sampling error** in a survey (the predicted difference between the average opinion expressed by survey respondents and the average opinion in the population) using a random sample depends on the sample size. It is large for small samples of around 100 or less, but decreases rapidly as sample size increases. When the sample is about 1,000 people, the sampling error is only about 2 percentage points.

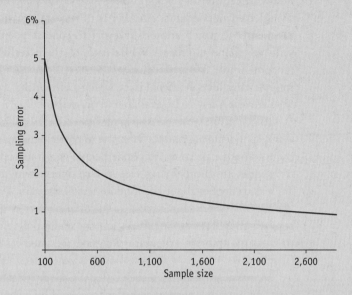

Surveys are composed of **random samples**, small subsets of the population being studied, in which every member of the population under study has an equal chance of being surveyed. Statistical analysis shows that even small random samples can provide very precise estimates of the opinions held by people in a large population.

The graph shows how the sampling error or margin of error for a random sample decreases as the size of the sample increases. These errors result from using samples to measure the beliefs of an entire population. Increasing the sample size lowers the sampling error, but the only way to eradicate sampling error is to survey the whole population.

For example, in surveys with 1,000 respondents the sampling error is 2 percent, meaning that 95 percent of the time, the results of a 1,000-person survey will fall within the range of 2 percentage points above or below the actual percentage in the population that holds a particular opinion surveyed. If the sample size was increased to 5,000 people, the sampling error would decline to 0.5 percent.

Sampling errors need to be taken into account when interpreting what a poll says about public opinion. For example, suppose a 1,000-person survey about a congressional race finds that 60 percent of the sample favor candidate Smith, while 40 percent support candidate Jones. Since the difference in support for the two candidates (twenty points) exceeds the sampling error (four points), it is reasonable to conclude that Smith has more supporters in the population compared to Jones and should be considered the favorite to win the election. In addition, the fact that the sampling error is four points means that there is a 95 percent chance that the actual level of support for Smith in the population falls between 62 and 58 percent—and that Jones's true level of support is between 38 and 42 percent.

In contrast, suppose the poll found a narrow 51 to 49 percent split slightly favoring Smith over Jones. Since the difference in support is smaller than the sampling error, it would be a mistake to conclude that Smith is the likely winner. Even though Smith is ahead among the sample surveyed in the poll, Jones may have more supporters in the population. Put another way, given the sampling error, the survey results tell us that there is a 95 percent chance that Smith's support in the population is between 49 and 53 percent, and Jones is between 47 and 51 percent. In other words, when a poll shows a difference in support smaller than the sampling error, the only thing that poll tells us is that neither candidate is the clear favorite.

insurance, he takes position 7; and if his position is somewhere in the middle, he picks an intermediate position on the scale.

PROBLEMS MEASURING PUBLIC OPINION

Survey results need to be read with caution. The problems begin with the difficulty in building a random sample. One standard tactic is to choose households at random from census data and send interviewers out for face-to-face meetings with the selected respondents. Another is to contact people by telephone using random digit dialing, which allows surveyors to contact people who have either listed or unlisted phone numbers. While each of these techniques in theory produces a random sample, in practice they may deviate from this ideal. For example, face-to-face interviewing loses households in which both adults work during the day, because they are less likely to be available to participate.

To keep costs down, many organizations use Internet polling, which has volunteer respondents log on to a Web site to participate in a survey, or robo-polls, which use a computer program to phone people and interview them. While these survey techniques are cheaper than face-to-face interviewing or calling respondents, there are serious doubts about the randomness of the samples these techniques produce.[55] (Push polls, in which a campaign uses biased survey questions as a way of driving support away from an opponent, are not really polls, in that they are not designed to measure opinion—they are designed to shape it. Push polls are discussed in Chapter 8.)

Question wording can also influence survey results. Table 5.3 shows Americans' opinions on abortion rights as measured by several surveys taken in 2005 and reveals that regardless of how the question is asked, about a quarter to a third of Americans take a strong position in favor of access to abortion, and about a fifth to a quarter take a strong anti-abortion position. For the rest of the population, almost a majority, opinions depend on how the question is asked and which considerations are called to mind.[56] In particular, support for abortion rights goes up if a question mentions medical conditions, economic hardship, or consultation with a doctor. Support goes down if abortion rights are described as a purely personal choice. Although these results do not reflect the trends in support for abortion rights discussed later in the chapter, the impact of question wording is likely to persist regardless of these trends.

Another problem with surveys is that people are sometimes reluctant to reveal their opinions. Rather than speaking truthfully, people often give socially acceptable answers or the ones that they believe the interviewer wants to hear. In the case of voter turnout in elections, up to one-fourth of the people who say they voted when surveyed actually did not vote at all[57] (the percentage of survey respondents who say they voted for the winning candidate is generally higher than the actual percentage of votes counted for the winner). A significant percentage of the population, probably 10 to 20 percent, are reluctant to express their racial prejudices or to admit that they would not vote for a female or minority or gay political candidate.

Pollsters use various techniques to address the problem of unreliable respondents. One is to verify answers whenever possible. The NES used to check with County Boards of Election to see if respondents who said they voted had actually gone to the polls, although they stopped doing so because of cost. When there is concern that respondents will try to hide their prejudices, pollsters sometimes frame a question in terms of the entire country rather than the respondent's own

TABLE 5.3 THE IMPACT OF QUESTION WORDING: ATTITUDES ON ABORTION

In many cases, the way people respond to survey questions depends on how the question is asked. How does question wording shape how people respond to surveys concerning abortion rights?

NBC/*Wall Street Journal* (May 2005)

Which of the following best represents your views about abortion . . . The choice on abortion should be left up to the woman and her doctor, abortion should be legal only in cases in which pregnancy results from rape or incest or when the life of the woman is at risk, or abortion should be illegal in all circumstances.

Should be left up to woman and her doctor	Legal only in cases of rape/ incest/risk to woman's life	Illegal in all circumstances	Not sure
55%	29%	14%	2%

CBS News (April 2005)

Which of these comes closest to your view—abortion should be generally available to those who want it, OR abortion should be available but under stricter limits than it is now, OR abortion should not be permitted?

Generally available to those who want it	Available, but under stricter limits than now	Should not be permitted	Don't know
36%	38%	24%	2%

CBS News (July 2005)

What is your personal feeling about abortion? It should be permitted in all cases. It should be permitted, but subject to greater restrictions than it is now. It should be permitted only in cases such as rape, incest, and to save the woman's life, or it should only be permitted to save the woman's life.

Permitted in all cases	Permitted, but greater restrictions than now	Permitted only if rape, incest, or to save woman's life	Only permitted to save the woman's life/Not permitted at all	Don't know
25%	15%	38%	18%	5%

ABC News/*Washington Post* (April 2005)

Do you think abortion should be legal in all cases, legal in most cases, illegal in most cases, or illegal in all cases?

Legal in all cases	Legal in most cases	Illegal in most cases	Illegal in all cases	No opinion
20%	36%	27%	14%	3%

SOURCE: Pew Research Center, "Abortion, the Court, and the Public," October 3, 2005, available at http://people-press.org/commentary/display.php3?AnalysisID=119.

beliefs. For example, during the 2008 presidential primaries, rather than asking respondents whether they were willing to vote for a Mormon candidate (such as Republican Mitt Romney), pollsters asked the question in a variety of indirect ways, including whether a respondent believed that the country was ready for a Mormon president.

Opinion researchers also have to contend with the opinion-formation process discussed earlier. Since many people develop their opinions on the fly, their answers will depend on the considerations that come to mind at the moment they are asked. As a result, the answer a person gives may change a day, a week, or a month later. This problem often arises in polls taken early in a presidential campaign; the results vary from week to week not necessarily because of what the candidates have done, but because opinions are based on very little information and can shift based on very small changes in what people know.[58]

THE ACCURACY OF PUBLIC OPINION

As noted earlier, early theories of public opinion held that the average American's opinions and beliefs about politics were incomplete at best, and at worst wildly inaccurate. Modern theories have revised these conclusions. It is true that many Americans have significant gaps in factual information, like which party controls the House or the Senate, or the name of the chief justice of the Supreme Court.[59] Americans also routinely overestimate the amount of federal money spent on government programs such as foreign aid. The amount of error in opinions about foreign aid is extremely large: typically, people believe that the government spends more than ten times the amount that it actually does. Other surveys show that many Americans overestimate the amount of money spent on other programs such as NASA or distributive benefits ("pork barrel" spending). However, rather than reflecting ignorance, these misperceptions often result from survey design or how people interpret survey questions.

In some cases, inaccurate or outlandish survey results are due to the fact that some people don't take surveys seriously. They agree to participate but are distracted and not really interested in explaining their beliefs to a stranger. So, faced with a long list of questions, they give quick, thoughtless responses, saying anything they can to end the interview as quickly as possible. Misperceptions may also result from forming opinions based on whatever considerations come to mind. This strategy means that in many cases, people exclude important pieces of information from the opinion-formation process.

Consider claims about health care reform. In an August 2009 survey, the Pew Research Center found that 86 percent of respondents had heard that reform legislation would create so-called death panels (the question asked about "government organizations that will make decisions about who will and will not receive health services when they are critically ill").[60] Moreover, 30 percent of these respondents (and 47 percent of Republican respondents) believed these claims, despite the fact that no such provision was included in any of the proposals offered by President Obama or by members of the House and Senate.

How can these findings be squared with our statement that, in the main, Americans hold opinions that have some basis in reality? For one thing, for many respondents, these questions are not something they have thought about in detail— probably only a very few had read through all the proposals, which were each hundreds of pages long. When asked for an opinion as part of a survey, there is no time for respondents to do research or think things through, so they guessed. Thus, it's no surprise that a significant percentage of respondents say that death panels were part of the bill: some people who guess an answer say yes, and some say no.

Incomplete or inaccurate responses to survey questions may also result from a respondent's unwillingness to say they don't know about something. There is good evidence that survey participants sometimes make up responses in order to not appear ill-informed.[61] Thus, when asked about death panels and health care reform, a respondent might affirm that a link existed even if they know little or nothing about the situation.

Moreover, leaving aside all of these factors, opinions about health care proposals could be influenced by politicians and others. At the same time health care was being debated, some Republican politicians claimed that death panels *were* part of reform proposals or that reforms might lead to death panels being instated in the future. Thus, when survey respondents mention death panels, their response might reflect opinions formed after listening (or half-listening) to these public figures. (The fact that Republican respondents were more likely to say that claims about death panels were true supports this conclusion—after all, Republican legislators were by far the more vocal proponents of this claim.)

▼ There are many ways for Americans to become well-informed about policy proposals, but there is no guarantee they will choose to systematically gather information. Most prefer instead to make snap judgments based on very little information. The resulting opinions reflect strong emotions rather than dispassionate appraisal, as shown in this protest against President Obama's health care proposals.

A final response to claims about errors in public opinion is that many supposed facts are actually "contested truths," meaning that it is reasonable for individuals to hold a wide range of views.[62] In the case of death panels, a person might know that the proposals did not contain this provision but respond in the affirmative because they think that reforms might lead to such panels being established at some future time. Since it is impossible to be sure either way, we cannot say that such respondents are mistaken in their beliefs.

Such problems do not arise in all areas of public opinion. Studies show that a respondent's ability to express an opinion, as well as the accuracy of her opinions, rises if the questions being asked have something to do with her everyday life.[63] Thus, the average American would be more likely to have an accurate sense of the state of the economy than the situation in Afghanistan. Everyday life gives us information about the economy; we learn about Afghanistan only if we take time to gather information.

HOW USEFUL ARE SURVEYS?

Mass opinion surveys are a powerful tool for measuring public opinion, but, as discussed earlier, their results must be interpreted carefully. Surveys often ask about complex issues that respondents may not have thought about. Samples may be biased, despite considerable efforts to randomize them. People may also be reluctant to admit some opinions to an interviewer, and many opinions change from day to day. The way people respond to a survey may reflect the wording of the questions, the timing of the survey (including events on the day the survey was carried out), and how familiar people are with the topics of the questions. Even if all of these problems could be solved, surveys that use a sample of the population can only measure public opinion within a margin of error, as we have seen. For all of these reasons, survey data may not give an accurate picture of what a population thinks. These issues also raise a fundamental question: How seriously should you (and political scientists and the media) take poll results? When should you believe these results?

Survey results are most likely to be accurate when they are based on a simple, easily understood question about a topic familiar to most Americans, such as their evaluation of the president or their opinion on the state of the economy. You can be even more confident if multiple surveys that ask about the same topic in slightly different ways produce similar findings, since no one survey or survey question provides a complete and accurate picture of public opinion. If a survey asks about a complex, unfamiliar topic—replacing the income tax with a national sales tax, for example—then the results may not provide much insight into public opinion, especially without data from other surveys that ask the same question in different ways or at different points in time. The same is true if a survey asks a hypothetical question or tries to get people to express unpopular or immoral opinions.

Characteristics of American Public Opinion

This section describes American public opinion in detail, including what people think of the federal government, their ideological beliefs, and many other opinions, along with their positions on public policy questions, such as abortion rights and

ideological polarization The effect on public opinion when many citizens move away from moderate positions and toward either end of the political spectrum, identifying themselves as either liberals or conservatives.

what to do about global warming. These opinions drive public demands for government action, from spending to regulation and other types of public policy. So, if we want to understand what America's national government does and why, we have to start by determining what Americans ask of it. The other priority is to describe the differences of opinion that divide Americans, from specific questions of public policy to general statements of belief.

IDEOLOGICAL POLARIZATION

We begin our discussion by examining liberal–conservative ideology and party identification to see if historical data show evidence of polarization. Are there fewer moderates and more strong liberals and conservatives compared to a generation ago? Figure 5.4 shows data from the General Social Survey on Americans' ideological opinions from the 1970s to 2008, aggregated (grouped) by decade. The liberals category in the figure combines people who said they were either "extremely liberal" or "liberal." Similarly, the group of conservatives includes respondents calling themselves either "extremely conservative" or "conservative." Finally, moderates said they were either "moderate," "slightly liberal," or "slightly conservative." The plots in Figure 5.4 show no evidence of **ideological polarization**. Over the last several decades, a strong majority of Americans have continued to say they are moderates, with less than 40 percent saying they are liberal or conservative. There is also no evidence that the degree of ideological polarization has increased; the percentage of liberals and of conservatives has remained relatively constant.[64]

Next, Figure 5.5 shows decade-by-decade data about how citizens describe their party identification using General Social Survey data and combining "strong Democrats" with "Democrats," "strong Republicans" with "Republicans," and classifying everyone else as an independent. Here again, there is little evidence of polarization. Since 1970, the percentage of Republicans has increased slightly, while the percentage of Democrats has declined significantly, with some increase in 2008. The number of independents, people who have no strong attachment to either party, also increased. As with the plots for ideology, the long-term trend for party identification is toward moderation and no strong attachments to parties.

FIGURE 5.4 LIBERAL–CONSERVATIVE IDEOLOGY IN AMERICA, 1970–2008

Many observers claim that American public opinion is increasingly polarized—with more liberals and conservatives, and fewer moderates. Does survey evidence back up this claim?

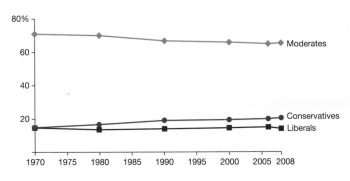

SOURCE: Data from General Social Survey, available at http://sda.berkeley.edu/archive.htm.

FIGURE 5.5 PARTY IDENTIFICATION IN AMERICA, 1970–2008

Party identification is another place to look for evidence of an increasingly polarized America. Do these data show evidence of polarization?

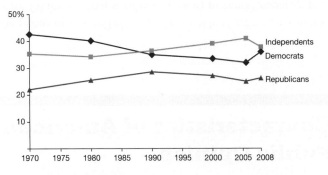

SOURCE: Data from General Social Survey, available at http://sda.berkeley.edu/archive.htm.

Looking more closely at opinion polarization, Table 5.4 shows responses to questions that tap a set of important principles, from foreign policy to domestic issues, civil liberties, and morality, all taken from a Pew Research Center survey. Principles such as these form the basis for opinions people express in surveys or act on when they vote or engage in other political behavior.

Although the responses in Table 5.4 show considerable conflict in American public opinion, it is important to understand that this particular survey was *designed* to divide people into categories based on what they believe and what they want from government. Moreover, on each principle, the survey asked people to choose between two reasonable points of view described in neutral language, and all of the questions tap subjects of impassioned debate during recent political campaigns. Like most surveys, this one did not ask about the many noncontroversial issues in American politics.

Until 1998, the General Social Survey (GSS) asked people whether they believed that "women should take care of home not country."[65] In 1974, more than a third of respondents agreed, but by 1998, agreement had declined to only about 15 percent, which is why the question isn't asked anymore. There is no reason to

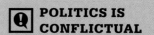

Q POLITICS IS CONFLICTUAL

TABLE 5.4 MEASURING AMERICAN PUBLIC OPINION: EXAMPLES OF PRINCIPLES

If polarization is not evident in ideological or party identification, perhaps it can be found in responses to specific questions about principles. Do responses to these questions show consistent evidence of polarization? Why might opinion surveys overstate the amount of polarization in the population?

	Strongly Agree	Agree	Neither, Don't Know	Agree	Strongly Agree	
Government regulation of business is necessary to protect the public interest.	32%	17%	10%	11%	30%	Government regulation of business usually does more harm than good.
This country should do whatever it takes to protect the environment.	63	14	5	12	18	This country has gone too far in its efforts to protect the environment.
Racial discrimination is the main reason why many black people can't get ahead these days.	18	9	12	16	44	Blacks who can't get ahead in this country are mostly responsible for their own condition.
The growing number of newcomers from other countries threatens traditional American values and customs.	29	11	10	16	34	The growing number of newcomers from other countries strengthens American society.
Homosexuality is a way of life that should be accepted by society.	35	14	7	6	38	Homosexuality is a way of life that should be discouraged by society.
We should all be willing to fight for our country, whether it is right or wrong.	39	7	8	8	38	It's acceptable to refuse to fight in war if you believe it is morally wrong.
Americans need to be willing to give up more privacy and freedom in order to be safe from terrorism.	24	11	5	9	51	Americans shouldn't have to give up privacy and freedom in order to be safe from terrorism.

SOURCE: Pew Research Center, "Beyond Red and Blue," May 10, 2005, available at http://people-press.org/reports/display.php3?ReportID=242.

gather data on issues about which the vast majority of Americans hold the same opinion. Around the same time, the GSS also stopped asking whether people believed that white people had the right to a segregated neighborhood—not out of moral considerations, but because American public opinion data showed an almost universally antisegregation perspective, whether everyone truly thought that way or not.

Finally, survey responses that reveal public opinion about broad principles do not tell us whether differences in these opinions translate into conflicts over specific policy questions. As we have discussed, public opinion about specific policy questions reflects multiple considerations and principles assembled into a response or evaluation of a policy option. Though the data on broad principles show some evidence of disagreement in American public opinion, they do not suggest deep, profound polarization. In some cases, the data even reveal considerable, widespread consensus.

EVALUATIONS OF GOVERNMENT AND OFFICEHOLDERS

Another set of opinions that are important for American politics address how people view their government: how well or poorly they think government is doing, whether they trust the government, and their evaluations of individual politicians, most notably their own representatives in the House and the Senate. These opinions matter for several reasons. A citizen's judgments about the government's overall performance may shape their evaluations of specific policies, especially if the citizen does not know much about the program.[66] Evaluations of specific policies may also be shaped by how much a citizen trusts the government, and as you would expect, more trust brings higher evaluations.[67] Trust in government and overall evaluations might also influence a citizen's willingness to vote for incumbent congressional representatives or a president seeking reelection.[68]

Table 5.5 shows citizen evaluations of government as measured in a Pew Research Center survey, revealing that the average American is fairly disenchanted with his government. A majority believes that elected officials lose touch with the people and don't care what average people think, and that corporations have too much power. A near-majority believes that government is almost always wasteful and inefficient. These evaluations are nothing new; many surveys over the last two generations show similar responses.[69]

This impression of a disenchanted and disapproving public is amplified by Figure 5.6, which shows levels of trust in government declining since the 1960s. All-time lows in trust were recorded in the mid-1970s during the Watergate scandal and impeachment of then-president Nixon, and in the early 1990s. Levels of trust have approached these lows during the recent financial crisis. As noted earlier, many scholars have argued that low levels of trust make it harder for elected officials to enact new policies, especially those that require large expenditures.[70] More profoundly, some scholars argue that low levels of trust raise questions about the future of democracy in America.[71] How can we say that American democracy is a good or popular form of government when so many people are unhappy with the performance of elected officials and bureaucrats?

One important response is that although Americans don't like their government in general, they tend to be far happier with their own representatives in Washington (see Chapter 10). One possibility is that putting a human face on government by asking about specific individuals improves evaluations because it calls to mind different considerations. Asking about "the government" may call to mind a vast room of bureaucrats pushing paperwork from one desk to another, whereas asking

▼ Trust in government reached its lowest recorded levels during the mid-1970s. The decline partly reflected the economic downturn and conflict over the Vietnam War, but opinions were also shaped by the discovery that then-president Richard Nixon lied about his involvement in the Watergate scandal. Here, Nixon resigns from office to avoid impeachment.

TABLE 5.5 MEASURING AMERICAN PUBLIC OPINION: BELIEFS ABOUT GOVERNMENT

Surveys show that Americans generally like their elected representatives in Congress. Presidents are sometimes extremely popular. Do Americans have positive feelings about government itself?

	Strongly Agree	Agree	Neither, Don't Know	Agree	Strongly Agree	
Government is almost always wasteful and inefficient.	39%	49%	8%	17%	28%	Government often does a better job than people give it credit for.
Too much power is concentrated in the hands of a few large companies.	46	7	8	14	25	The largest companies do not have too much power.
Elected officials in Washington lose touch with the people pretty quickly.	54	12	8	11	15	Elected officials in Washington try hard to stay in touch with voters back home.
Most elected officials care about what people like me think.	19	13	8	52	11	Most elected officials don't care about what people like me think.

SOURCE: Pew Research Center, "Beyond Red and Blue," May 10, 2005, available at http://people-press.org/reports/display.php3?ReportID=242.

FIGURE 5.6 TRUST IN GOVERNMENT

In America, trust in government varies widely over time. What factors drive these changes?

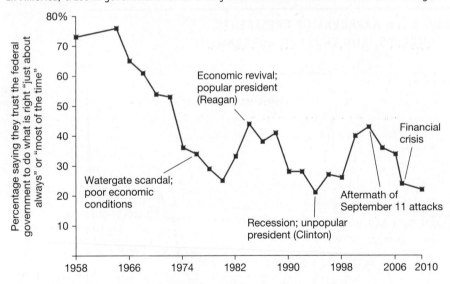

SOURCE: Pew Research Center, "The People and Their Government. Distrust, Discontent, Anger, and Partisan Rancor," April 18, 2010, available at http://people-press.org/reports/pdf/606.pdf.

about "your representative" may lead people to think of someone working on their behalf.

In addition, members of Congress work hard to convince their constituents that they are doing everything they can to satisfy their demands. Sometimes, members blame the institution of Congress and the government bureaucracy for shortcomings, setting themselves up as standing between their constituents and an inept,

What Ties Opinions Together?

Most scholars who study public opinion believe that most of the opinions expressed by the average American, when answering a survey question or when deciding how to vote, are arrived at only when needed, using whatever considerations (facts, ideas, other opinions, etc.) happen to be called to mind at the time.

One interpretation of this argument is that public opinion is wildly variable—opinions and the information used to construct them vary dramatically across people. For example, if we were looking at trust in government, one person might form opinions based on recent scandals, another might focus on the war in Iraq, and a third might recall a candidate's promises. If people behaved this way, it would be hard

to interpret data in public opinion—people holding the same opinions might be doing so for very different reasons.

However, work by political scientist James Stimson at the University of North Carolina at Chapel Hill shows that in many cases, people use similar or the same considerations to arrive at their beliefs about opinions such as trust in government.[a] In fact, a small set of considerations, most notably the state of the economy, shapes a wide range of disparate evaluations of both incumbent politicians and about government itself.

Stimson's analysis begins by showing how approval ratings for the president, Congress, senators, and governors varied over a twenty-five-year period, as well as the average level of trust in government over the same period. These ratings are

shown in the first figure. Each line gives approval ratings averaged across the entire population. For example, the line for presidential approval gives the average approval rating for whoever happened to be president at the time the survey was taken. The line for Congress gives the average rating for the institution over time. Similarly, the average rating for senators and governors averages responses at each point in time for all the individuals who happened to hold these offices.

The striking feature of this figure is the degree to which these approval lines move up and down together over time. In the main, all of the lines trend downward in the early 1980s, move upward in the late 1980s, then sharply downward in the early 1990s, reaching a low point around 1992, then move upward until the end of the time period.

GENERIC APPROVAL, ALONG WITH APPROVAL OF PRESIDENTS, SENATORS, GOVERNORS, CONGRESS, AND TRUST IN GOVERNMENT

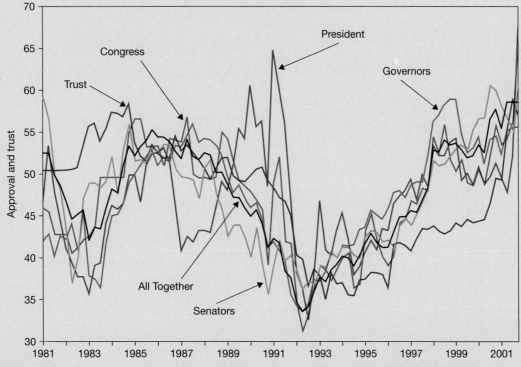

SOURCE: James Stimson, *Tides of Consent: How Public Opinion Shapes American Politics* (New York: Cambridge University Press, 2004), Figure 5.7, p. 155.

There are some exceptions—the line for presidential approval moves sharply upward in the early 1990s, which is the result of the "rally round the flag" effect caused by the first Gulf war. Leaving this exception aside, most of the trends in each kind of opinion are close to the dark line that represents the average across all of the opinions.

These data suggest two things about how Americans form these opinions. First, it appears that a small set of considerations, perhaps only one, is being used by many Americans to form most if not all of these opinions. Of course, some people might use an entirely different set of considerations or add their own idiosyncratic information. However, the fact that the average evaluation for each kind of opinion moves up and down largely in unison means that many people are using the same or similar considerations. Stimson's analysis identifies this critical consideration as evaluations of economic conditions.

The second figure compares the average opinion line from the first figure with a measure of consumer sentiment (the Michigan Index of Consumer Sentiment, a national survey) that asks whether people think economic conditions are good or bad. (Again, the sentiment line shows the average level of sentiment over time.) As you see, the two lines move up and down virtually in unison. In other words, one consideration—individual evaluations of economic conditions—plays a critical role in shaping a wide range of opinions.

Stimson's analysis tells us three critical things about public opinion in America. First, although the information people use to evaluate individual officeholders and government in general is idiosyncratic to some extent, most people rely at least in part on the same consideration, the state of the economy. Thus, the process of opinion formation helps to make democracy work—it connects the performance of people in government (as measured by the state of the economy), evaluations of their performance (as measured by approval ratings), and their prospects for reelection (since approval shapes vote decisions).

This finding also tells us that incumbents are to some extent the beneficiaries

GENERIC APPROVAL AND CONSUMER SENTIMENT

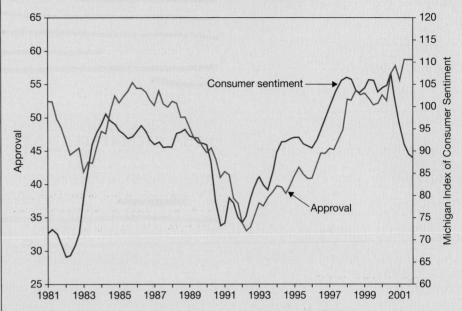

SOURCE: James Stimson, *Tides of Consent: How Public Opinion Shapes American Politics* (New York: Cambridge University Press, 2004), Figure 5.8, p. 156.

or victims of factors that are beyond their control. An individual governor or senator, for example, may be unable to do much about the state of the economy. As we argue in Chapter 11, even presidents have only a limited ability to influence economic conditions. Even so, the electoral fate of these individuals rests to some extent on economic conditions.

You may wonder, does this finding mean that politicians are unable to shape the public's evaluation of their performance in office—does their political fate rest exclusively on the state of the economy? No. Stimson's findings reflect the impact of economic considerations averaged across the entire electorate (and, in the case of senators, governors, and Congress, across many different officeholders). A voter's impression of a particular officeholder could also be shaped by other considerations, most notably the officeholder's performance in office. Everything we know about American politics (in particular, the factors discussed in Chapters 8 [Elections], 10 [Congress], and 11 [Presidency]) indicates that politicians work very hard to shape these perceptions and that their efforts are successful at least

some of the time. Nevertheless, Stimson's work suggests that because of how public opinion is formed, despite their best efforts, politicians are only partially successful at escaping blame for poor economic conditions.

Finally, Stimson's work helps to explain variation in levels of trust in government. Low levels of trust are often seen as a signal that Americans are weary of gridlock in Washington or upset about financial or personal scandals involving elected officials. However, in the main, trust in government appears to be driven by what people think about the state of the economy. If so, then attempts to restore trust by establishing new ethics requirements for elected officials or making procedural changes that make the government more open and transparent may have little impact on trust. Levels of trust in government revive only when the economy does. ■

Watch a video clip of James Stimson discussing this topic at wwnorton.com/studyspace.

inefficient government. As one scholar put it, "House members run for Congress by running against Congress."[72] In fact, members who deviate from this strategy while running for reelection by trying to convince their constituents that Congress does a good job are more likely to be defeated—not because they do a worse job than their colleagues, but because their statements call to mind unfavorable impressions of government that constituents consider when deciding whether to vote for the representative.[73]

POLICY PREFERENCES

In a diverse country of more than 300 million, people care about a wide range of government policies. One useful summary measure of Americans' policy preferences is the **policy mood** mentioned earlier, which captures the public's collective demands for government action on domestic policies.[74] Policy mood measures are constructed from surveys that ask about opinions on a wide range of policy questions.[75] Changes in the policy mood in America have led to changes in defense spending, environmental policy, and race-related policies, among others—and have influenced elections.[76] Figure 5.7 shows that when the policy mood leans in a liberal direction, such as in the early 1960s, conditions are ripe for an expansion of the federal government involving more spending and new programs. On the other hand, when the American policy mood leans toward the conservative, such as in the late 1970s and early 1980s, elected officials are likely to enact smaller increases in government spending and fewer new programs. Thus, the Democratic takeover of Congress in the 2006 elections and the election of Barack Obama in 2008 make sense in light of the increase in support for government action that preceded them.

Turning to specific issues, surveys conducted in the past few years show that most Americans are focused on the same set of issues: the wars in Iraq and Afghanistan,

---

FIGURE 5.7 POLICY MOOD

As the labels in the figure indicate, sharp changes in the policy mood often precede changes in the composition of Congress or the party that holds the presidency. Could you have used the recent policy mood data to predict the outcomes of the 2008 presidential and congressional elections?

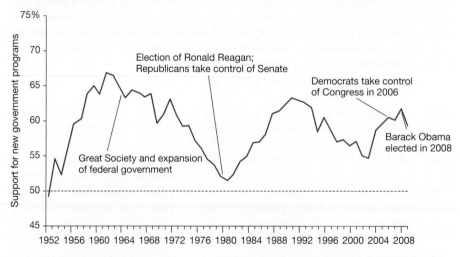

SOURCE: James Stimson, University of North Carolina, Chapel Hill, available at www.unc.edu/~jstimson.

What Do Citizens in Other Countries Think about American Democracy?

Americans may not be happy with their government, but they stand by the idea of democracy. Even though many Americans don't bother to vote and few people pay attention to politics on a daily or even weekly basis, support for our democratic system of government is nearly universal, to the extent that most surveys have stopped asking the question. Most Americans consider the advantages of democracy obvious.

Of course, Americans' enthusiasm for democracy does not imply that people elsewhere feel the same way. Many of us were born into this democracy and have known no other system of government. For us, support for democracy may be more a matter of habit or socialization than a firm, informed preference. People who have not experienced free and fair elections, or the slow, conflictual process of policy making by elected officials, may have very different views on the merits and disadvantages of a democratic system.

In 2003, the Pew Charitable Trust funded a survey of public opinion in more than forty countries to find out what people elsewhere thought about some of the values generally associated with American democracy. In particular, respondents were asked whether it was "very important" to live in a country that permitted citizens to freely criticize the government, had a trustworthy two-party system, and allowed the media to report without censorship. The table below shows that there is majority support in these regions for all three elements of democracy. Importantly, the differences between predominantly Muslim countries and others in the sample are fairly small. Even among those countries, few of which have strong, stable democracies or a tradition of democratic elections, nearly seven in ten respondents see freedom of speech and honest elections as critical. Of course, put another way, about a third of the population in those nations does not see these factors as very important.

It is also important not to over-read these survey findings. The respondents who favor these particular democratic institutions are not expressing support for America or American-style democracy, and a substantial fraction of the respondents are not strong supporters of democracy in any form. Thus, it would be a mistake for Americans to believe that everyone in other countries wants to copy the American model of democracy or that other countries would either accept the imposition of democracy or express gratitude for American attempts to change their political system. ■

OPINIONS ABOUT DEMOCRACY IN OTHER NATIONS

Surveys of Americans show strong support for democracy and civil liberties. Is this support something unique to established democracies such as the United States or is it shared by people throughout the world?

VERY IMPORTANT TO LIVE IN A COUNTRY WHERE . . .

	People can openly criticize the government	There are honest, two-party elections	The media can report without censorship
Latin America	71%	66%	67%
Sub-Saharan Africa	71	73	63
Eastern Europe	57	60	60
Muslim countries	67	71	53

SOURCE: Pew Research Center, "World Publics Welcome Global Trade–But Not Immigration," Pew Global Attitudes Project, available at http://pewglobal.org/reports/pdf/258.pdf.

terrorism, economic conditions, energy policy, health care, immigration, global warming, abortion, and gay rights.[77] The remainder of this section presents opinion data on these issues, some of which show significant levels of conflict, with large numbers of people on both sides of the question. In other cases, either most people hold similar opinions or the level of conflict depends on how the question is asked, meaning that most people's opinions are not very strong.

Iraq and Afghanistan The wars in Iraq and Afghanistan have influenced American politics since American troops invaded these countries in March 2003 and October

2001, respectively, and public opinion on both conflicts has changed profoundly since they began. Given the pessimistic tone of public opinion at the time of the 2006 midterm elections, it makes sense that the wars were a central issue in many congressional campaigns, and that Democratic candidates, who generally took anti-war positions, gained support. By the 2008 election, with public opinion on these conflicts less negative and many Americans worried about the economy, candidates' positions on the wars were not a decisive factor in most races.

Trends in opinion concerning the wars in Iraq and Afghanistan tell us a lot about where public opinion comes from and how it should be interpreted. Consider Figure 5.8, which shows the percentage of respondents in a series of surveys from 2007 to 2009 who believed that the wars in Iraq or Afghanistan were going well or very well for the United States.

The first thing to note, particularly in 2008 and 2009, is that the percentages are very different for the two wars—by late 2008, about 50 percent more people believed that the war in Iraq was going well compared to the percentage for Afghanistan. Thus, when forming opinions, most people weren't just making an automatic response based on their feelings about wars in general—they were distinguishing between the two conflicts.

Second, the data reveal the complexity of political calculations about America's involvement in Afghanistan. Clearly, in 2009, with a majority of respondents believing that the war was not going well, public support for sending additional troops was limited. Thus, when the Obama administration debated sending additional troops to Afghanistan, it worked hard to explain the decision to the public, because officials knew that support for this move would not be automatic.

FIGURE 5.8 **PERCEPTIONS OF THE WARS IN IRAQ
AND AFGHANISTAN**

Assessments of the wars in Iraq and Afghanistan have varied considerably over time. What factors do you think shaped these assessments and caused them to change?

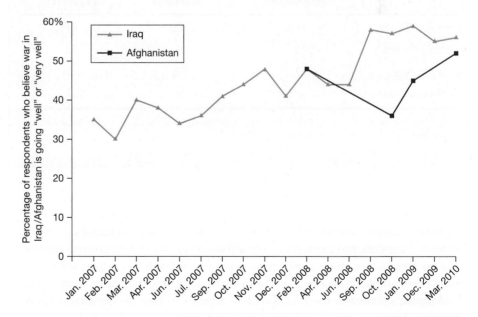

SOURCE: Pew Research Center, "Gloomy Americans Bash Congress, Are Divided on Obama," March 18, 2010, available at http://people-press.org/reports/pdf/598.pdf.

Terrorism As we discussed earlier, since the September 11 attacks, Americans have become more concerned about the possibility of a terrorist attack. In addition, a majority supports restricting civil liberties as a tactic for fighting terrorism. However, the extent of this support depends on the specific restriction. There is majority support for national identification cards and profiling at airports—but majority opposition to government monitoring of phone calls, e-mails, and credit card transactions.

These data highlight the difficulty of measuring public opinion using non-specific questions. When people are asked a general question about whether they favor restrictions of civil liberties to fight terrorism, a majority says no. When they are asked about specific restrictions, however, they favor some but not others. Thus, the way people respond to general questions about government policy may have little to do with their opinions on implementing specific policies.

Economic Conditions We have discussed how Americans' evaluations of the state of the economy relate to actual economic conditions. However, it is no exaggeration to say that Americans are always worried about the economy. Even when other pressing issues, such as the war in Iraq or terrorism, surpass the economy as the most important problem to Americans, the economy is typically listed second or third.

Recent history shows evidence of this pattern. As discussed in the introduction to this chapter, throughout 2006 and 2007, more than one-third of Americans rated the wars in Iraq and Afghanistan as the most important problem, while the economy ranked a distant second, cited by only 10 percent of respondents.[78] However, conditions began to change in late 2007 and worsened severely in September 2008: the combination of a collapse in housing prices and the near meltdown of the global financial system, along with improving conditions in Iraq, led many Americans to revise their opinions.

It is important to understand that not everyone who mentions "the economy" as a problem means the same thing. Consider Table 5.6, which shows the answers that Pew survey respondents gave in February 2008 and February 2010 when asked to be specific about their diagnoses of economic problems. These data from the first survey show little consensus about particular economic difficulties. One of the most frequently cited problems, prices, was mentioned by only one-fourth of the sample—and even within this category, respondents expressed concern about price increases in several different industries, such as energy and health care. However, as the financial crisis deepened and unemployment rose, attention focused on job losses and general economic conditions as the main symptoms of economic hard times.

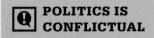

POLITICS IS CONFLICTUAL

These data make sense given what we know about the opinion-formation process. Most Americans base their judgments about the economy on whatever considerations come to mind when they are asked for an opinion—from personal circumstances to long-held values or information from a recent news broadcast. Since these individual considerations vary, so do people's judgments about the economy and their diagnoses of the problems. Only in extreme situations do most Americans see events in the same way.

These differences in opinion have an important policy implication: policies designed to improve economic conditions may prove widely unpopular if they do not address the considerations that lead individuals to worry. For example, policies that reduce energy prices will find favor with people who see the high price of energy as a drag on the American economy—but these changes will not satisfy

TABLE 5.6 AMERICANS' DIAGNOSES OF THE MOST IMPORTANT ECONOMIC PROBLEMS

Opinion data from early 2008 show little consensus about the most important economic problems facing the country. By early 2010 polls showed more agreement. What might explain this change?

	February 2008	February 2010
Prices	**24%**	**13%**
Gasoline/oil/energy	10	—
Health care/medical	9	13
Cost of living/inflation	4	—
Jobs	**18%**	**33%**
Unemployment/lack of jobs/low wages	14	31
Jobs moving overseas/outsourcing	4	2
Housing	**13%**	**0%**
Affordable housing/real estate	9	—
Mortgage problems/foreclosures	6	—
Government	**11%**	**13%**
Budget/deficit/government spending	4	11
Taxes	3	1
Government officials	2	1
Other government	1	—
Spending on war in Iraq	10	—
Economy (general)	**3%**	**24%**
Financial Crisis	**27%**	**0%**
Corporate greed	6	—
Bailout of financial firms	6	—
Problems with banks	8	—
Credit crunch	—	—
Other	**5%**	**11%**

SOURCE: Pew Research Center, "Obama's Ratings Are Flat, Wall Street's Are Abyssmal," February 12, 2010, available at http://people-press.org/reports/pdf/589.pdf.

people who consider high taxes or the cost of the war in Iraq and Afghanistan to be the culprit.

Health Care Health care is another important concern for Americans. Surveys taken in 2008 and 2009 showed that many Americans were worried about losing their health coverage and complained about the high cost of health care. This raises a puzzling question: if a majority of Americans were unhappy with the health care system, why had it stayed in place, despite many reform proposals?[79] An October 2009 Pew Research Center survey shows that these fears do not translate into strong support

for reforms to America's health care system. The survey asked respondents whether they supported different elements of various health care reform proposals, then asked whether respondents supported the various reform proposals being debated in Congress at the time. As you can see in Table 5.7, although majorities supported the specific provisions, only about a third approved of the reform proposals—proposals that include some or all of the specific reforms that respondents were asked about. By April 2010, a month after the Obama proposal was enacted, opinion was almost evenly split with a substantial portion of survey respondents continuing to be uncertain.

How can we explain the apparently anomalous responses in the early survey? Respondents might have believed that the reform proposals included other provisions, such as the infamous "death panels" mentioned earlier. Another possibility is that respondents were aware that the provisions they supported were in the proposals but believed that enacting them would lead to other problems in the future, such as increased health care costs.

In any case, these data explain the difficulties that politicians faced in 2009 and 2010 when trying to build support for health care reform. The obvious strategy was to emphasize the specific reforms in the proposals, particularly those that attracted strong support, such as requiring coverage for preexisting conditions, which was supported by more than 80 percent of respondents in the survey. The problem is that many of the respondents who knew that this reform was in the congressional proposals opposed them regardless, which means that providing this information might not change anyone's mind. As a result, these efforts had only modest effects, as seen in the survey results.

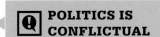

POLITICS IS CONFLICTUAL

| TABLE 5.7 | PUBLIC OPINION ON HEALTH CARE REFORM, 2009–2010 |

The table shows that close to a majority of Americans opposed congressional health care reforms in 2009, even as strong majorities supported many of the provisions included in these reforms. By the time the program was enacted, support had increased but only slightly. How are these patterns explained by the theories of opinion formation described in the chapter?

Proposals in Congress	October 2009	April 2010
Generally favor	34%	40%
Generally oppose	47	44
Don't know	19	16

Percentage Who Favor...	October 2009
Requiring insurance companies to cover preexisting conditions	82%
Requiring all to have insurance; government aid for those unable to afford	66
Requiring employers to provide or pay into a government fund	59
Raising taxes on high-income families to fund health overhaul	58
Government health insurance to compete with private plans	55

SOURCE: Pew Research Center, "Support for Health Care Principles, Opposition to Package," October 8, 2009, available at http://people-press.org/reports/pdf/551.pdf (accessed 11/11/09); Pew Research Center, "Distrust, Discontent, Anger and Partisan Rancor," April 18, 2010, available at http://people-press.org/reports/pdf/606.pdf (accessed 6/21/10).

Immigration Immigration is a good example of an issue on which the level of conflict among political elites, such as elected officials, is much higher than among the general public. In recent years, many immigration reform proposals have been debated in Congress but none have been enacted, as representatives and senators could not compromise on a proposal.[80] However, there is broad consensus among the American public for specific reforms. In a recent survey, more than two-thirds of the sample favored guest worker programs that would allow illegal immigrants to become citizens after several years—and a comparable number favored fining businesses that hired illegal workers as well. The question, then, is why immigration reform has been stymied in Congress. The problem is not partisan divisions in the electorate. Other research has found that similar percentages of Republicans, Democrats, and independents support this kind of program, at least in the general public.[81] These data suggest that the failure to reform immigration laws may have more to do with conflict within Congress, pressures from a small number of voters who have intense preferences, or the fact that, in recent years, economic concerns have overshadowed immigration for most Americans.

Global Warming Although most Americans agree that global warming is happening, the public is split on what is causing it. And on this issue, unlike immigration reform, grouping respondents by their partisanship reveals sharp differences in opinion, as shown in Table 5.8. If you are a Democrat, you are much more likely to believe that global warming is real and being caused by humans. If you are a Republican, you are more likely to believe that global warming isn't happening, or if it is, that it is a natural phenomenon that humans have no decisive role in influencing. Given this split and the decline since 2006 in the overall percentage of people who see "solid evidence" of global warming, it is no surprise that members of Congress and the president have been unable to agree on policies to combat climate change.

Social Issues Social issues are among the most divisive in American politics. Typically these issues involve the question of whether the government should restrict an individual's behavior in line with a particular moral code.

We looked at opinion data on abortion earlier in this chapter and saw that support for abortion rights, as measured in opinion surveys, varies substantially with small changes in question wording (see Table 5.3). Some Americans oppose abortion under any circumstances, while others view abortion as a personal choice that government should not control. But most people are in the middle, favoring access

---

TABLE 5.8 THE PARTISAN SPLIT OVER GLOBAL WARMING

The data reveal sharp position splits in voter attitudes on global warming. To what extent are these divisions reflected in congressional consideration of measures to fight global warming?

	Solid Evidence of Warming	Because of Human Activity	Because of Natural Patterns	No Warming	Don't Know/ Mixed
Republicans	35%	18%	13%	57%	11%
Democrats	75	50	18	17	15
Independents	53	33	15	35	17

SOURCE: Pew Research Center, "Fewer Americans See Solid Evidence of Global Warming," October 22, 2009, available at http://people-press.org/reports/pdf/556.pdf (accessed 11/11/09).

Responding to Public Opinion on Access to Abortion

As we discuss in Chapter 10, elected officials in America work hard to cast votes and take other actions that their constituents will like. At first glance, this behavior seems easy. All a politician needs to do is take a poll, measure public opinion in her state or district, and comply with the demands expressed in the survey responses.

Actually, it is not easy for a representative to find out what her constituents want, because public opinion is hard to measure. Everything you have learned in this chapter suggests that taking a poll doesn't necessarily tell the whole story. Poll results need interpretation and may not provide clear guidance to elected officials.

Consider public opinion on abortion rights. Suppose a member of the House represents a district where public opinion on abortion is the same as the national data in Table 5.3. Also assume that this representative believes the most important thing she can do is to behave in accordance with opinion in her district. What sort of guide does the survey data provide to the representative? How would you interpret these survey results, and what would you tell the representative to do?

The first problem is that the survey provides different guidance depending on which question the representative looks at. As the table shows, small differences in question wording can produce large changes in responses. Our representative could find data showing support for just about any interpretation—that her district is sharply divided or that it is in favor of current policies, of supporting additional restrictions, or even of demanding increased access.

These data reveal two problems with reading public opinion for guidance. For one thing, sometimes the American public, either in a district or across the entire nation, is so divided that survey responses give a representative little guidance about what to do. Moreover, in many cases, opinions are sensitive to question wording, so a representative cannot be sure that survey results are indicative of actual feelings or are an artifact of how the questions were asked.

Another issue with interpreting surveys stems from how opinions are formed—typically on the spot, based on relatively little information. As a result, the representative cannot use one survey as a fully accurate guide to what her constituents think. Even if the survey questions were not changed, opinions might look very different if the survey was taken a day, a month, or a year later.

Even in the case of abortion rights, which receives considerable media coverage, public opinion is hard to measure. Though a representative may want to act according to her constituents' opinions, the simple fact is that surveys may provide little guidance for her decisions. How should representatives behave in this situation? You decide. ∎

to abortion under some circumstances but not others. For these people, support for abortion laws depends on how the question is asked. This distribution of opinion has stayed roughly the same for more than a generation.

Another social issue, gay rights, shows a distribution of opinion that is similar to views on global warming. Survey data show that a majority of Americans favor allowing gay couples to form civil unions (partnerships that confer the same legal standing as marriage), but only about one-third of Americans support allowing gay couples to marry.[82] Taking a closer look, Table 5.9 shows that the conflict splits Americans in partisan terms, with a majority of Republicans opposing gay marriage and a majority of Democrats favoring civil unions or marriage rights. Thus, while the data show high levels of conflict, they suggest that disagreements over gay rights may be driven to a large extent by partisan identification. The data on opinions by age show that support for gay marriage and civil unions is higher for younger voters than older voters. If these differences persist, support for both policy changes should increase significantly in the years to come.

While these figures show how partisanship may affect positions on issues, it is also possible, particularly over time, that issue positions could cause changes in an

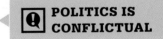

POLITICS IS CONFLICTUAL

TABLE 5.9 GENERATIONAL AND PARTISAN DIFFERENCES ON GAY RIGHTS

	Gay Marriage			Civil Unions		
	Favor	Oppose	Don't Know	Favor	Oppose	Don't Know
Total	39%	53%	8%	57%	37%	6%
Age 18–29	58	37	5	68	29	3
Age 30–49	38	53	9	56	39	5
Age 50–64	35	58	7	53	40	7
Age 65+	22	67	11	49	42	8
Conservative Republican	14	81	5	43	53	3
Moderate/liberal Republican	36	54	10	59	37	3
Independent	44	47	9	63	33	5
Conservative/ moderate Democrat	41	53	6	54	40	6
Liberal Democrat	72	24	3	76	21	3

SOURCE: Pew Research Center, "Most Still Support Civil Unions: Majority Continues to Oppose Gay Marriage," October 9, 2009, available at http://people-press.org/reports/pdf/553.pdf (accessed 11/12/09).

individual's party identification. For example, suppose a Republican decides that he favors gay marriage and supports an aggressive government effort to combat global warming, positions supported by more Democrats than Republicans. This inconsistency between his party identification and his preferences may lead the individual to identify as a Democrat, for the simple reason that Democratic candidates are more likely to share his position on these issues.

Does Public Opinion Matter?

As we discussed at the beginning of this chapter, some observers of American politics have argued that most Americans have no real opinions about candidates, policies, or anything else. Others have claimed that these opinions exist but are ignored by government officials. Having described what political scientists know about American public opinion, we can now analyze these claims.

To begin with, one of the most important pieces of evidence that public opinion remains highly relevant in American politics is the amount of time and effort politicians, journalists, and political scientists spend trying to find out what Americans think. If people were just making up their opinions, there would be no point to carrying out elaborate, expensive public opinion surveys. The intense effort to find out what people think, as well as the importance given to these data by candidates, party leaders, and political strategists, provide the best evidence that these opinions matter.

How Many Americans Are Consistently Liberal or Conservative?

As Tables 5.4 and 5.5 show, Americans hold polarized opinions on several important political principles and policy questions, but there are also issues on which most people hold moderate opinions. On the whole, the data do not support claims of a polarized America divided into two opposing camps, regardless of the issue.

Additional evidence against polarization comes from looking at a series of opinion questions in order to determine the percentage of Americans who consistently answer on the same ideological side of these questions, either liberal or conservative.

As we discussed in the beginning of the chapter, early studies of public opinion found little evidence of such consistency. Has this property of American public opinion changed over the last thirty years?

A 2006 Pew Research Center survey tested just this point by asking a series of questions about five politically divisive social issues: gay marriage, adoption of children by gay couples, abortion, stem cell research, and the morning-after pill. The researchers then calculated the number of times each respondent gave a socially conservative response to these questions. If Americans hold consistently liberal or conservative views, most people should give either no conservative responses or all conservative responses. The first column in the graph shows that 22 percent of respondents expressed consistently liberal views on the five questions. Similarly, the right-hand column shows that 12 percent expressed consistent conservatism. In other words, only about a third of the sample held beliefs that aligned with only one of these ideological positions. The rest gave liberal responses on some issues and conservative responses on others. These findings demonstrate the limits of the "liberal" and "conservative" labels that are often used to describe the beliefs held by individual Americans. Although many people lean to the liberal or conservative ends of the ideological spectrum, very few are liberal or conservative on all issues. ■

THE CONSISTENCY OF AMERICAN PUBLIC OPINION

Figure 5.4 showed that self-described moderates outnumber both conservatives and liberals. Is this label consistent with citizens' positions on specific issues?

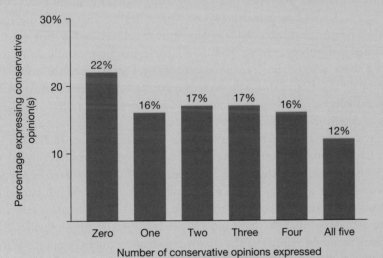

SOURCE: Pew Research Center, "Most Want Middle Ground on Abortion," August 3, 2006, available at http://people-press.org/reports/pdf/283.pdf.

Of course, it is easy to come up with examples in which public opinion appears to be ignored in the political process because policy has stayed the same despite a clear majority supporting change. And in other cases, new policies have been enacted even though a majority preferred the status quo. But these examples do not mean that public opinion is irrelevant. Rather, they reflect the complexities of the policy-making process. As we have seen, it's not always possible to please a majority of citizens; politicians' willingness to do so depends on whether the majority is organized into interest groups, how much they care about the issue (and the intensity

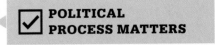

POLITICAL PROCESS MATTERS

of the opposition), whether their demands are shared by elected officials, and many other factors. Moreover, the American system of checks and balances between the branches of government deliberately makes it hard to change most government policies.

Many of the arguments about the irrelevance of public opinion also hinge on misreading poll results. On many of the issues discussed here, an individual's support for a particular policy option hinges on how survey questions are worded. For example, the percentage of people who say they favor abortion rights depends on whether the question describes the motivations for the procedure. Thus, depending on which poll results we use, the results of a particular policy can be made to look closely aligned with or completely contradictory to the opinions of a majority of Americans.

It is also important to remember that for most people, opinions are not predetermined, firm ideas. If you went out today and asked people what they want government to do, there is no guarantee that they would give the same answer the next day, week, or month. These shifts in opinion mean that it is often difficult to connect aggregate-level opinions (what Americans think as a group) with outcomes such as who wins an election or whether a proposal is enacted in Congress. In trying to connect outcomes to opinions, we are aiming at a moving target.

Even with all of these difficulties, it is clear that public opinion is the wellspring of politics in America, exerting conspicuous influence in widespread areas of government. The data on Americans' policy mood, for example, show that significant policy mood changes were often followed by changes in government policy. Chapter 10, Congress, shows how legislators spend a great deal of time trying to determine what their constituents want and how constituents will respond to different actions. In Chapter 8, Elections, we see how voters use retrospective evaluations to form opinions about who to vote for, and how candidates incorporate the public's views into campaign platforms that will attract support from the electorate. And Chapter 7, Political Parties, discusses how voters use candidates' party affiliations like brand names to determine how each party's candidates will behave if elected.

Recent events also speak to the influence of public opinion. In the case of the war in Iraq, as long as public support remained high, members of Congress voiced few criticisms of military strategy or reconstruction efforts. However, as public support waned, more and more House members and senators from both parties began to express reservations, disagree with President Bush's claims that conditions were getting better, and suggest that Congress needed to revise the war policy.[83] These comments no doubt reinforced the downward trend in public support for the war and may have directly influenced the pro-Democratic shift in the 2006 election, in which Democrats gained majority control of the House and Senate (see Chapter 8). By 2008, voters' concerns over Iraq were overshadowed by worries about the economy, and the war receded significantly as an electoral issue.

The debate over global warming shows the same pattern. Despite considerable media attention and legislative efforts over the last few years, the lack of consensus on the causes of global warming and the partisan split in opinion meant that success for these efforts has been hard to come by.[84]

In fact, it is hard to find a major policy change that did not have majority support (and significant opposition) in the electorate at the time it was made. From relief and reconstruction efforts after Hurricane Katrina to the enactment of a prescription drug benefit for Medicare recipients to the enactment of economic stimulus legislation in 2009—all of these efforts reflected the demands of a majority of Americans, which is exactly what we should expect if public opinion is real and relevant to what happens in politics. The one exception is the enactment of health care reform legislation, although support was very close to a majority at the time of enactment.

Conclusion

Public opinion is real, and it matters. Americans have ideas about what they want government to do and use these ideas to guide their political choices. American politicians are also extraordinarily sensitive to public opinion and reluctant to take actions that contradict the beliefs of large numbers of their constituents.

To put it another way, the role of public opinion in shaping the policy response to the financial crisis or the military strategy in Iraq and Afghanistan is not an exception but an example of how much public opinion matters in American politics. The average American is not an expert on government policies and knows relatively little about possible alternatives. But even a small amount of information is enough to inform beliefs about what policies should be enacted. And the changes in the last few years in government policy, politicians' statements, and election outcomes all reflect changes in the policy mood.

Likewise, very few Americans are experts about abortion rights, health care reform, or international conflict. Their responses to questions about these issues may vary from day to day, but most Americans know enough to decide what they want government to do about these problems—and to act on these opinions. Politicians, in turn, take public opinion very seriously, as it provides the yardstick that measures citizens' judgments of their behavior in office.

What is public opinion?

- Public opinion describes what Americans think about current government policies, evaluations of elected officials, and demands for policy change, as well as the wider set of beliefs and ideas that shape these evaluations.
- For most Americans, opinions are latent. They are formed only when people are required to make a decision or to express a preference.
- The considerations that are used to construct opinions can vary from day to day, depending on events, statements by politicians, personal experiences, and other factors. As a result, the opinions a person expresses often depend on when she is asked.

Where do opinions come from?

- An individual's opinions come from a variety of sources, including socialization, historical events and personal experiences, group identities, and the actions and statements of politicians and other national figures.

- Although socialization and early life events play a key role in shaping political opinions, most political opinions continually evolve throughout a person's life.
- An individual's group characteristics, such as race, gender, age, and religious beliefs, are an important predictor of his political opinions.

How is public opinion measured?

- Mass surveys are a powerful tool for measuring public opinion. Even relatively small random samples (1,000 people) can, in theory, provide accurate estimates of public opinion in the entire nation.
- People's responses to survey questions are often influenced by the timing of the survey, the wording of the questions, people's knowledge about the topic, and whether they hold unpopular opinions.
- While surveys sometimes reveal voters' misinformation and ignorance, particularly about the details of many public policies, they show that in many other areas, Americans have good information about the problems facing the nation.

What are the characteristics of U.S. public opinion?

- Americans disagree about how the government should address many policy questions, from immigration to global warming.
- However, in many areas, policy conflict reflects question wording or a disagreement on principles such as party affiliation. Thus, while conflict is a fact of American politics, it is easy to overstate its reach and its intensity.

How does public opinion matter?

- On big issues that most Americans care about deeply, government policy generally reflects the opinions held by ordinary Americans.
- Cases in which government policy appears to conflict with public opinion generally involve narrow splits in public opinion, a lack of consensus on what government should do, or a minority of the electorate that cares intensely about the issue.

⊚ STUDENT STUDYSPACE

Find quizzes and other review material at wwnorton.com/studyspace.

CRITICAL THINKING

1. Given that many Americans cannot answer basic political questions, and many of the opinions they express vary from day to day without anything changing in the political world, how can we say that public opinion exists?

2. In light of the many problems with measuring public opinion, how should you read survey results?
3. How much conflict is there in American public opinion?

KEY TERMS

considerations (p. 149)
ideological polarization (p. 164)
issue scale (p. 158)
latent opinion (p. 148)
level of conceptualization (p. 147)

liberal–conservative ideology (p. 148)
mass survey (p. 158)
policy mood (p. 170)
political socialization (p. 153)
population (p. 158)

public opinion (p. 145)
random sample (p. 159)
sample (p. 158)
sampling error (p. 159)

SUGGESTED READING

Alvarez, R. Michael, and John Brehm. *Hard Choices, Easy Answers.* Princeton, NJ: Princeton University Press, 2002.

Campbell, David. *Why We Vote: How Schools and Communities Shape Our Civic Life.* Princeton, NJ: Princeton University Press, 2006.

Carmines, Edward G., and James A. Stimson. *Issue Evolution: Race and the Transformation of American Politics.* Princeton, NJ: Princeton University Press, 1990.

Converse, Phillip E. "The Nature of Belief Systems in Mass Publics." In *Ideology and Discontent,* edited by David E. Apter, 206–61. Glencoe, IL: The Free Press of Glencoe, 1964.

Delli Carpini, Michael X., and Scott Keeter. *What Americans Know about Politics and Why It Matters.* New Haven, CT: Yale University Press, 1997.

Green, Donald P., Bradley Palmquist, and Eric Schickler. *Partisan Hearts and Minds.* New Haven, CT: Yale University Press, 2002.

Hibbing, John R., and Elizabeth Theiss-Morse. *Congress as Public Enemy: Public Attitudes toward American Political Institutions.* New York: Cambridge University Press, 1995.

Jacobs, Lawrence R., and Robert Y. Shapiro. *Politicians Don't Pander: Political Manipulation and the Loss of Democratic Responsiveness.* Chicago: University of Chicago Press, 2000.

Lupia, Arthur, and Mathew D. McCubbins. *The Democratic Dilemma*. New York: Cambridge University Press, 1998.

Marcus, George E., John L. Sullivan, Elizabeth Theiss-Morse, and Sandra L. Wood. *With Malice toward Some: How People Make Civil Liberties Judgments*. New York: Cambridge University Press, 1995.

Peffley, Mark, and Jon Hurwitz. *Justice in America: The Separate Realities of Blacks and Whites*. New York: Cambridge University Press, 2010.

Zaller, John. *The Nature and Origins of Mass Opinion*. New York: Cambridge University Press, 1992.

Child abductions receive extensive media coverage that causes citizens to demand action from their elected leaders. The Amber Alert program is one significant policy response to this perceived threat.

The Media

Child abductions are a perennial news story. Events such as the discovery in August 2009 of Jaycee Dugard, a twenty-nine-year-old woman who was abducted at age eleven and held captive along with her two children fathered by the alleged kidnapper, are front-page news. Television programs such as the *Nancy Grace* show (broadcast nightly on CNN's Headline News channel) give extensive coverage to abduction cases. Pundits demand better training for law enforcement and tougher laws.[1] Stories also cite the statistic that 800,000 children are reported missing every year.[2]

With all of this attention being paid to obviously horrific crimes, it is no surprise to find that a significant number of Americans are worried that their child will become the victim of a kidnapping, particularly by a sexual predator. It is also no surprise that politicians have responded with proposals that attract strong support and little conflict. All fifty states have laws requiring sex offenders to register with local police departments for the rest of their lives; many forbid offenders from living near schools or other places where children congregate. As of late 2009, these registries contained the names of more than 600,000 individuals. Congress has also passed legislation mandating a nationwide registry of sex offenders, as well as an Amber Alert system that distributes information about kidnappings to local media, electronic road signs, and Web sites. Such proposals are enacted quickly, with general agreement that they are a useful response to a pressing problem, despite the fact that the cost of these programs is significant and the lack of any evidence that these measures significantly reduce abductions of children.

There is no doubt that child abduction is one of the worst crimes imaginable and should be prosecuted vigorously. However, media coverage of these events gives at best an incomplete picture of the problem. For one thing, of the 800,000 children reported missing each year, the overwhelming majority are runaway teenagers or child custody cases that range from overstaying a visit with a noncustodial parent to cases in which one parent moves without notice to cut off contact with the other parent. In 2002, only 115 of the 800,000 reported abductions were kidnappings by a stranger. Moreover, though a lifetime requirement for registering sex offenders may seem like a good idea, many individuals are forced to register for relatively minor offenses that have nothing to do with children, such as public indecency.[3] There is little evidence that these

CONFLICT AND COMPROMISE
in American Politics

BIG QUESTIONS

✪ Who are the media, and how do they cover politics?

✪ How is the Internet affecting both the media business and what Americans know about politics?

✪ How do reporters do their jobs?

✪ How do people use the media to learn about politics?

✪ How does media coverage influence public opinion and policy?

✪ Why is media coverage of American politics the way it is?

registries reduce crime: Jaycee Dugard's kidnapper, Phillip Garrido, was listed on California's sex offender registry for more than a decade because of a prior conviction for rape, even as Dugard and their two children were living in a shed in his backyard.

In short, although the media may sometimes thrive on reporting on, or even promoting, conflict and controversy—in the form of political and celebrity scandals, election year "horse races," and similar stories—the issue of child abduction is one for which we might like to see more conflict in politics, not less. Although any abduction is a terrible thing, it is a leap to say that an epidemic of kidnapping is occuring in America or that nationwide registries, alert systems, and similar innovations will do much to reduce the likelihood of future abductions. In fact, one study of media coverage of childhood abductions found that elected officials often responded to these events by enacting new legislation that increased penalties or set up new warning systems—even if the news story was about a single, unique event.[4] This is not to say that legislators and bureaucrats should not consider new measures; rather, the point is to ask whether government is responding thoughtfully and debating these proposals in an objective manner, rather than responding reflexively.

Could the media do a better job of accurately portraying the issue of child abduction and the trade-offs involved in confronting it? Would it help if they did? The issue highlights the role of the media in American politics. Clearly, public fears and government's response to those fears are to some extent the result of the extensive publicity given to rare cases of actual kidnapping—and the relative lack of attention to the details mentioned above. This relationship between news coverage, public response, and government policy makes child abduction a political issue, and one of the principal reasons politics is everywhere is that so much air time and countless printed pages and Web sites are devoted to covering political issues and events. Thus, examining what the media report and how they report it is a crucial component of understanding what Americans know about their government.

Not only is politics influenced by the content of many news stories, political processes and outcomes also influence the news industry. Coverage is shaped by federal regulations that affect what can be printed or broadcast, as well as by the structure and ownership of media corporations, many of which need to make a profit to survive. These political influences on the media can, in turn, affect how Americans view officeholders, candidates, and events.

Complaints about media coverage of political events and stories are common. Studies show that Americans learn a great deal from media coverage of politics,[5] but many observers blame the media for gaps in Americans' political knowledge, low levels of civic engagement, and distrust of the federal government.[6] These observers want coverage that gives Americans a detailed appreciation of the complex policy questions facing elected officials and bureaucrats and that holds elected officials accountable for their campaign promises and behavior in office—rather than a steady stream of scandals, failures, and poll results.[7]

Our discussion of the news media addresses these arguments. Who are the media, and how do they cover politics? Who determines which stories make the news and how they are reported? Is media coverage politically biased? Where do people get their political information? How are Internet-based information sources affecting both the traditional media business and what Americans know about politics?

mass media Sources that provide information to the average citizen, such as newspapers, television networks, radio stations, and Web sites.

The News Media in America

This section describes the **mass media**, the many sources of political information available to the average American. It also describes the dramatic changes occurring in new forms of media and how these changes affect not only the amount of political information available and how it is delivered, but also how people use this information.

HISTORY OF THE NEWS MEDIA IN AMERICA

The role of the media as an information source and the controversy over how they report about politics are nothing new. Since the Founding, politicians have understood that Americans learn about politics largely from the media; and they have complained about coverage and sought to influence both the media's selection of stories and the way they report on them.

The Early Days Long before there was a United States, the news media were active in colonial America. One of the earliest newspapers, the *Pennsylvania Gazette*, was published by Ben Franklin beginning in 1729. For the most part, newspapers had relatively low circulations, due partly to their cost and partly to the fact that they were available only in major cities.[8] During the Revolutionary War, many newspapers offered a rationale for separation from Britain and chronicled the course of the conflict. Afterward, newspapers became the venue for debates over the proposed federal government.[9]

Despite the guarantee of freedom of the press included in the 1st Amendment of the Constitution, in 1798 Congress and President John Adams enacted the Alien and Sedition Acts, which made it a crime to criticize the president or Congress.[10] While these press restrictions were later repealed or allowed to expire, they serve as a reminder that the American media have never been free of government regulation, both in terms of what is published and who can own a newspaper or other media source.

▼ In colonial America, newspapers like the Pennsylvania Gazette *reported on government policy, elections, and scandals.*

▲ The New York Journal's *advocacy of war with Spain did not cause the conflict—but its steady stream of pro-war coverage did shape public opinion.*

penny press Newspapers sold for one cent in the 1830s, when more efficient printing presses made reduced-price newspapers available to a larger segment of the population.

wire service An organization that gathers news and sells it to other media outlets. The invention of the telegraph in the early 1800s made this type of service possible.

yellow journalism A style of newspaper popular in the late 1800s that featured sensationalized stories, bold headlines, and illustrations to increase readership.

investigative journalists Reporters who dig deeply into a particular topic of public concern, often targeting government failures and inefficiencies.

Federal Communications Commission (FCC) A government agency created in 1934 to regulate American radio stations and later expanded to regulate television, wireless communications technologies, and other broadcast media.

▼ *With the development of national radio networks in the 1920s and 1930s, Americans throughout the nation could hear coverage of important events as they occurred.*

Penny Press, Yellow Journalism, and Muckrakers Beginning in the 1830s, a combination of new technologies, entrepreneurs, and political ambition transformed the news media. In 1833, the *New York Sun* began selling papers for a penny a copy, rather than the standard price of six cents—thus earning the label **penny press**. The price reduction, which was made possible by cheaper, faster printing presses, made the newspaper available to the mass public for the first time, and this increase in circulation made it possible, even with the lower price, to hire larger staffs of reporters.[11] The development of the telegraph also aided newspapers by allowing reporters on assignment throughout the country to quickly send stories back home for publication. The Associated Press, the first **wire service**, was formed in the 1840s by a group of newspapers in New York to share the benefits and costs of this new technology.[12]

Many other newspapers soon appeared. Many were unabashedly partisan, using their coverage of events to support a particular political party or position. Some were even published by party organizations. For example, the *New York Tribune*, published by Horace Greeley, was strongly antislavery. By 1860, the *Tribune*'s circulation was larger than any other newspaper in the world, and its articles "helped to add fuel to the fires of slavery and sectionalism that divided North and South."[13]

The period after the Civil War saw the beginning of **yellow journalism**, a new type of newspaper reporting that appealed to a wider audience by using bold headlines, illustrations, and sensational stories (the name came from the fact that they were printed on yellow paper). The best example of yellow journalism was the *New York Journal*, published by William Randolph Hearst. During the months before the Spanish-American War, Hearst's reporter in Cuba cabled that there were no signs of war and asked whether he should return home. Hearst cabled back, "Please remain. You furnish the pictures and I'll furnish the war."[14] Of course, America did not fight the Spanish-American War just because Hearst's newspaper published daily articles calling for the conflict—but it appears that the paper had a significant impact on public opinion.

At the same time, other authors and reporters used newspapers and books to call for reforms to federal, state, and local governments. These **investigative journalists**, known as muckrakers, included Lincoln Steffens, who criticized corruption in municipal governments, and Upton Sinclair, who raised concerns about food safety and public health.[15] The year 1896 saw the purchase of a small New York newspaper by Arthur Ochs, who wanted to rebuild it around the goal of journalistic impartiality, accuracy, and complete coverage of events. He gave the *New York Times* a new motto: "All the News That's Fit to Print."[16] The first schools of journalism were also formed during this period.

New Technologies and Federal Regulation After World War I, new communications technology made it possible to broadcast news and entertainment programs over radio—and for many Americans to buy radios to hear these programs.[17] During the 1920s, hundreds of small, local stations were built, along with some larger stations that could broadcast across the country, eventually leading to the development of networks, groups of local radio (and later, TV) stations owned by one company that broadcast a common set of programs.

The Communications Act of 1934 authorized the **Federal Communications Commission (FCC)** to regulate **broadcast media**, which at the time meant radio stations and has since come to include television stations, cable TV, and other communications technologies. FCC regulations reflected the assumption that the airways were public property, so no one had an inherent right to operate a radio or TV station. Rather, the owners of these stations were expected to serve the public interest, as defined by the FCC.

A central concern of the FCC was that one company or organization might buy enough stations to dominate the airwaves in a particular city or state, so that only one set of programs or one network's point of view would be available. Over the next two generations, the FCC developed regulations to limit the number of radio and TV stations a company could own in a community and the total nationwide audience that a company's TV stations could reach. As new technologies such as cable and satellite TV developed, these regulations were expanded to include them.[18]

The 1940s saw the rise of TV as Americans' primary news source. As we discuss later, television made it possible to report on stories using instantly accessible visual footage rather than printed words, a crucial distinction given that many citizens are not highly motivated to learn about political events and issues. One frequently cited argument about public opinion during the Vietnam War was that the decline in public support for the war was driven by the fact that, for the first time in American history, stories depicting the horror of the war first-hand were a staple on nightly news broadcasts.[19] Such images were not new (previous wars saw graphic photos in magazines and many newsreels) but they became commonplace with the advent of television.

In the late 1940s, the FCC also developed the **fairness doctrine** (no longer in place), which required TV and radio stations to offer a variety of political views in their programming.[20] This rule did not mean that stations sent two reporters, one Republican and one Democrat (or one liberal and one conservative), to cover each political event. Rather, stations offered debates and presentations supporting different political positions as part of their news programs, as well as talk shows and interviews featuring a wide range of political figures.

The FCC also created the **equal time provision**, which states that if a radio or television station gives air time or space to a candidate outside its news coverage— such as during an entertainment show or a cooking program—they have to give equal time to other candidates running for the same office. For example, some observers argued that Republican Fred Thompson's entry into the 2008 presidential primaries meant that some reruns of *Law and Order* would have to be taken off the air, as Thompson had played a district attorney on the show for several seasons. However, since no one made a formal complaint to the FCC, the episodes featuring Thompson continued to be broadcast, although actor Sam Waterston took over Thompson's role in new episodes.[21] TV satirist Stephen Colbert's brief (and sarcastic) presidential

broadcast media Communications technologies, such as television and radio, that transmit information over airwaves.

fairness doctrine An FCC regulation requiring broadcast media to present several points of view to ensure balanced coverage. It was created in the late 1940s and eliminated in 1987.

equal time provision An FCC regulation requiring broadcast media to provide equal airtime on any non-news programming to all candidates running for an office.

▲ As these stark images from Vietnam (left) and Iraq (right) illustrate, photos and televised images of war have the potential to capture attention and shape public opinion.

▲ Under the FCC's equal time regulations, if comedian Stephen Colbert had campaigned for president while remaining host of The Colbert Report, other presidential candidates could have forced the Comedy Central cable channel to give them free airtime.

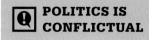

POLITICS IS CONFLICTUAL

concentration The trend toward single-company ownership of several media sources in one area.

cross-ownership The trend toward single-company ownership of several kinds of media outlets.

media conglomerates Companies that control a large number of media sources across several types of media outlets.

candidacy in 2007 also raised the question of whether *The Colbert Report* would have to go off the air during the campaign, since news and interview shows are normally exempted from the equal time provision. The issue became moot when Colbert was not allowed to compete in the South Carolina primaries.

Deregulation The FCC's limits on ownership and content assumed that radio and TV stations were public trustees who had a responsibility to provide full, fair, and unbiased coverage of political events. This assumption changed over time with the development of new communications technologies such as cable TV, satellite TV, and the Internet because, with so many sources of information, if one broadcaster ignored a candidate or an issue, citizens could still find out what they wanted to know from another source. Pressure for deregulation also came from the owners of media companies, who wanted to buy more TV, radio, and cable stations, as well as book and magazine publishers, Internet service providers, and newspapers, in order to increase efficiencies and profits.[22] After much debate, Congress enacted the Telecommunications Act of 1996, which gave the FCC the power to revise all of the ownership and content restrictions enacted over the last two generations; since then, the FCC has abolished most ownership restrictions. (The equal time provision is still in place, but the fairness doctrine was eliminated in 1987.)[23]

These regulatory changes accelerated two trends in American news media. The first is **concentration**, which refers to one company owning more than one media source in a town or community. For example, Clear Channel Communications owns multiple AM and FM radio stations in more than thirty different cities. The second trend is **cross-ownership**, one company owning several different kinds of media outlets, often in the same community. The Tribune Company in Chicago owns the WGN radio station, the WGN TV station, and the *Chicago Tribune* daily newspaper. These trends in turn have given rise to **media conglomerates**, companies that control a wide range of news sources.[24] All four major television networks (ABC, NBC, CBS, and Fox) are part of larger companies that each own many other broadcast and cable stations, movie production and distribution companies, radio stations, newspapers, and other media outlets. Nuts and Bolts 6.1 shows the diverse holdings of one such company, News Corporation.

One pro-deregulation FCC commissioner, Kathleen Abernathy, argued for deregulation, saying, "Democracy and civic discourse were not dead in America when there were only three to four stations in most markets in the 1960s and 1970s, and they will surely not be dead in this century when there are, at a minimum, four to six independent broadcasters in most markets, plus hundreds of cable channels and unlimited Internet voices."[25] Other commissioners disagreed, arguing that concentration would limit citizens' choices and force programming to become increasingly homogenized. As one commissioner put it, "As big media companies get bigger, they're likely to broadcast even more homogenized programming that increasingly appeals to the lowest common denominator. If [television] is [like] the toaster with pictures, soon only Wonder Bread will pop out."[26] As of now, it is not clear which viewpoint is correct, although many organizations, including the FCC, are researching the implications of deregulation.[27]

The deregulation of the news media stands in sharp contrast to the FCC's ongoing and strong regulation of entertainment broadcasts. For example, the FCC fined CBS Broadcasting for Janet Jackson's "wardrobe malfunction," which momentarily exposed her breast during broadcast of the 2004 Super Bowl halftime show. (A court later threw out the regulation that the fine was based on.)[28] A more

NUTS AND BOLTS

6.1

Holdings of News Corporation

News Corporation is an example of a media conglomerate, a company that controls a variety of different media outlets throughout the world. It owns cable television networks, TV and radio stations, newspapers, movie production companies, magazines, and even sports teams. This structure allows the company to operate more efficiently, as it can rebroadcast or reprint stories in different outlets, but opponents are concerned that conglomerates might expand to control most or even all of the sources that are available to the average citizen, making it impossible to access alternate points of view.

FOX TELEVISION STATIONS	FILM COMPANIES	BOOKS AND MAGAZINES
35 U.S. stations	20th Century Fox	*The Weekly Standard*
	Fox Searchlight Pictures	*TV Guide* (partial)
	Fox Television Studios	3 other magazines
	Blue Sky Studios	45 book publishers worldwide

SATELLITE AND CABLE HOLDINGS	NEWSPAPERS	OTHER HOLDINGS
DirecTV	*New York Post*	Los Angeles Kings (40 percent ownership)
Fox News Channel	*Wall Street Journal*	Los Angeles Lakers (10 percent ownership)
17 other cable channels worldwide	5 UK newspapers	MySpace.com
	20 Australian newspapers	15 other businesses

extreme example of the FCC's regulatory actions concerns radio personality Howard Stern, whose talk radio program specializes in outrageous behavior, featuring "strippers, porn stars, and dwarves," among other things.[29] By the 1990s, the show was a nationwide hit, producing over $100 million per year in revenue and $50 million per year in profits for the owner, Infinity Broadcasting. Although the show was the subject of repeated FCC investigations and fines,[30] the large profits it generated made the fines just a tolerable cost of doing business.

The situation changed in 2004, when members of Congress and FCC commissioners threatened to review and possibly cancel the broadcast licenses of radio stations that played Stern's show, on the grounds that broadcasting obscene material was not in the public interest.[31] In response, Stern moved his show to Sirius Satellite Radio, receiving a large salary increase and placing the show beyond FCC regulations, as the FCC has no jurisdiction over satellite radio.[32] On these unregulated airwaves, the show has become even more outrageous—but listeners have to buy a radio capable of receiving Sirius's signal and purchase a subscription. Stern's experience illustrates how pervasive politics is, in that defining obscenity is not a matter of abstract debate. The FCC's decisions about what qualifies as obscene determine what can be broadcast on free radio. Moreover, political processes also yielded the decision to keep satellite radio outside of the FCC's jurisdiction, meaning that while broadcasting on Sirius, Stern can say whatever he wants without fearing fines or other punishments.

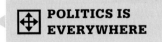

POLITICS IS EVERYWHERE

MEDIA SOURCES

There are many sources of political information—both from **mainstream media** such as newspapers, TV and radio stations, books, and magazines, and from countless Internet-based sources.

Print Media: Newspapers, Magazines, and Books National newspapers, such as the *New York Times*, *Washington Post*, *Los Angeles Times*, or *Wall Street Journal*, cover American politics using a large, worldwide staff. Foreign publications such as the United Kingdom's *Financial Times* also cover American politics. Smaller regional and local papers are published in medium- to large-sized cities and smaller towns. They differ from national papers in their staffing (fewer or no reporters based in other cities or outside the country) and in their coverage (focusing on local news and using more articles reprinted from other sources, such as the wire services). Across the nation and worldwide, publications and freelance journalists sell their articles to wire services, which resell them to newspapers and magazines for reprinting. Two of the best known wire services are the Associated Press and Reuters.

Recent years have seen significant declines in newspaper readership as Americans shift to other information sources, most notably the Internet. The newspaper business has also seen many corporate changes. In recent years, companies that owned newspapers in Chicago, Philadelphia, and Minneapolis have gone bankrupt, and one major U.S. city, Seattle, now has no hometown daily newspaper. It is too early to say that newspapers are "dead," as some do, but the drop in newspapers' circulation and their decreasing advertising revenues are forcing many newspapers to cut foreign bureaus, some local reporters, and the amount of news in every edition.[33] Even so, as we discuss later, newspapers remain a widely used information source.

Of the many magazines that cover politics, national weeklies such as *Time* and *Newsweek* often feature political events as front-page news. The British publication *The Economist* has a small but influential audience for its coverage of politics and business worldwide. Many other magazines occasionally cover political topics. Even *Reader's Digest*, *GQ*, or *Ladies' Home Journal* sometimes runs an article about political issues or a profile of a politician.

A small number of magazines offer extensive coverage of political events, including the *National Journal*, *The New Republic*, *The Nation*, and *The National Review*. These publications typically have minuscule circulations. In fact, the list of the top 100 magazines in America (based on circulation) includes publications on just about every topic, from *Sports Illustrated* to *Vogue*, but none focused on politics and government.[34] In contrast, on the *New York Times* Hardcover Nonfiction best-seller list in June 2010, a wide range of political books ranked among the most popular, including the autobiography of past First Lady Laura Bush, two books about President Barack Obama, and a book by former House Speaker (and possible presidential candidate) Newt Gingrich.

Television The four major national networks (ABC, CBS, Fox, and NBC) and many cable channels, such as CNN, offer nightly news as well as **prime-time news programs**. Some cable stations offer news coverage throughout the day and night, creating what is known as the twenty-four-hour **news cycle**—no matter when something happens, these stations are able to report the news to their audience. Local TV stations also cover some local political events in addition to running the national networks' programming. News coverage varies from the "talking head" format of a person behind a desk reading copy to the camera, to investigative reporting that involves reporters and camera crews gathering information in the field and assembling it for broadcast, to talk shows that air interviews with political figures

mainstream media Media sources that predate the Internet, such as newspapers, magazines, television, and radio.

prime time Evening hours when television viewership is at its highest and networks often schedule news programs.

news cycle The time between the release of information and its publication, like the twenty-four hours between issues of a daily newspaper.

or other people of interest. Some programs combine these formats; one popular example is *The O'Reilly Factor*, a nightly show on the Fox News Network hosted by conservative commentator Bill O'Reilly. In a typical episode, O'Reilly reports news stories, offers political commentary, and interviews elected officials, party officials, journalists, and other prominent people in the news.

Radio The major radio networks, such as ABC, CBS, and Clear Channel Communications, offer brief news programs throughout the day, but most political content on the radio consists of talk radio programs that include a host discussing politics with listeners who phone in. The major nationwide talk radio shows, such as *The Rush Limbaugh Show*, generally offer a politically conservative point of view—and openly advertise this orientation.[35] Liberal talk radio programs also are broadcast, but their audience is just a small fraction of the size of conservative programs' audience. Other political programs are aired on National Public Radio, an organization funded by the government and private donations. Overall, there are more than 13,000 radio stations in America. Just as with other media sources, only a fraction focus on delivering news or political coverage.

The Internet Political news sources on the Internet vary widely. Some are electronic versions of sources that originated in other kinds of media, while other Internet providers offer content that does not appear in other media. You can read most of the *New York Times* for free on its Web site, listen to Rush Limbaugh's radio program, or read many blogs or Web-only news providers that report on politics. Sometimes Internet sites for television news shows or print publications feature stories that are unavailable in the broadcast or print formats, which reflects a trend described throughout this chapter: as more and more people use the Internet, companies that own newspapers, magazines, TV stations, and radio networks are moving their content to the Web in an attempt to keep their audience and stay in business.

▲ *Rush Limbaugh exemplifies the conservative dominance of AM talk radio in America.*

ARE ALL MEDIA THE SAME?

From how they look to how they cover the news, media sources are not the same. One difference is timeliness. Newspapers in particular are prisoners of the news cycle because they publish only once per day. Publishing a book can take months or even years from the time writing begins to the day it's available for sale. Radio and TV coverage is somewhat easier to produce and rearrange on short notice, but Internet sites are even faster. Just write some new content, upload pictures, and the information is out.

A second difference is breadth. Nightly news programs on the major networks have only thirty minutes to deliver their report (twenty-three minutes excluding commercials). As a result, even an important political event like the president's State of the Union address receives only a brief discussion. Many radio programs face similar constraints, although some, such as NPR's *All Things Considered* and many talk radio programs, run for several hours every day, allowing them to spend more time on in-depth coverage. Newspapers may have more flexibility in the depth of their coverage, although they aim to print a set number of pages per section and per issue, while Internet outlets are the least constrained.

A final difference is resources. Major newspapers and television networks have offices and reporters stationed throughout the world. Local TV and radio stations, most newspapers, and many Internet sites depend on stories first published elsewhere, or they may hire freelance reporters from different regions as needed.

Similarly, during a presidential campaign, reporters from the major newspapers and TV networks accompany the presidential candidates throughout the campaign, while smaller newspapers and local TV stations generally rely on stories, photos, and video generated by others.

These differences mean that media sources are not interchangeable—what you learn about politics depends on where you look. People who get their political information exclusively from the nightly local news learn less about politics than people who thoroughly read a major paper such as the *New York Times*.

What Difference Does the Internet Make?

The evolution of the Internet has made new kinds of political information available to the average citizen. Many sites offer the full text of government reports and analyses; anyone can download the president's annual budget request, new regulations published in The Federal Register, or evaluations of government programs released by the Government Accountability Office.[36] Twenty years ago, these documents were available only at major libraries.

The Internet also contains a wealth of analytic information. For example, the Brookings Institution, a Washington-based think tank, publishes a regular report on Iraq that includes hundreds of charts that detail the attacks, casualties, oil production and other economic indicators, surveys of the population, and additional information.[37] If such a compilation had existed before the Internet, it would have been available only by subscription or circulated only among a small number of scholars and policy makers. Similarly, the proliferation of videos on the Internet allows average Americans to see politics at first hand. For example, you can watch online videos of President Obama's February 2010 health care roundtable with Democratic and Republican members of Congress or just about any other political event of significance.

Another type of Internet site collects links to political information. The Center for Responsive Politics, for example, offers a searchable database of contributions to candidates and political organizations.[38] The Pollster site collects and analyzes public opinion surveys, including presidential election polls, and offers interpretations of the results as well as discussions of possible sources of bias.[39] Other Web sites offer somewhat less useful but entertaining political information. For example, when U.S. Senator Larry Craig was arrested for lewd conduct in an airport restroom, The Smoking Gun published his police mug shot.[40]

Most American newspapers, television networks, radio stations, and cable stations offer free access to most or all of their daily news via Internet sites as well as providing some Web-only information. They also post blogs written by their reporters. For example, Chris Matthews, who anchors MSNBC's politics show *Hardball*, also writes the daily blog Hardblogger.[41] Similarly, one of the most influential conservative weekly magazines, *National Review*, has a Web version, National Review Online, where many of the magazine's reporters publish Web-exclusive stories.[42]

Other Internet-only news providers, such as ABC News's The Note, offer collections of links to daily political coverage throughout the nation or a preview of upcoming political events in Washington.[43] SCOTUSblog (Supreme Court of the United States blog) analyzes Supreme Court decisions, judicial nominations, and other legal questions.[44]

Search engines such as Bing or Google allow you to search through thousands of newspapers, wire service stories, and other information sources. Other Internet news sites that concentrate on political coverage include Politico and Slate.[45] Some news sites are expressly partisan—Salon and The Huffington Post lean in the liberal direction, while Power Line and Town Hall offer a conservative point of view.[46] Finally, an enormous amount of professional and amateur video coverage of politics is available on YouTube. Various political organizations and candidates use MySpace, Facebook, and other social networking sites to recruit and organize supporters.

The Internet has lowered the barriers to publication. In 1960, journalist A. J. Liebling wrote that "freedom of the press is guaranteed only to those who own one," meaning that it was all but impossible for average citizens to report on what they knew or present their analyses to the general public.[47] The Internet has created more opportunities for home-grown media, allowing a would-be political reporter to easily set up a Web site or blog, or post videos online. For example, a large number of civilians and military personnel in Iraq and Afghanistan have chronicled their experiences on blogs.[48] These sites provide information that would have been completely unavailable to most people even a few years ago.

Similarly, YouTube has many videos of campaign events and even some campaign ads, many prepared by people with no official connections to the candidates. These videos have the potential to change elections: in the 2006 Virginia Senate race, a volunteer for challenger James Webb recorded incumbent George Allen using a Tunisian racial slur, "macaca," to refer to the volunteer, who was of Indian descent.[49] The episode, which was later picked up by the mainstream media, dogged Allen for the entire campaign. After initially seeming a shoo-in for reelection, Allen lost by more than 9,000 votes.

The Internet creates new opportunities for two-way interaction between citizens, reporters, and government officials. Many reporters respond to comments posted by readers or host live chat sessions, allowing people to ask follow-up questions about published stories.[50]

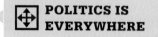

The Internet also allows ordinary citizens to report on events as they happen. For example, when a U.S. Airways jet ditched in the Hudson River in January 2009, the first reports and videos of the event appeared as Twitter posts. Politicians must now assume that anything they say or do (good or bad) will be instantly publicized using the same technology.

How much of a difference does all this information make? Some pundits argue that the Internet will transform American politics, leading to a better-informed, more politically active citizenry.[51] And it may—someday. Some studies show that Internet usage is associated with higher levels of political participation, yet others show no such association.[52] Moreover, there is no clear evidence that surfing the Web makes people more politically informed.[53]

Why hasn't the Internet created a better-informed citizenry? One answer is that not everyone uses the Internet. A December 2009 Pew Research Center survey found that about 20 percent of adults were not regular users of the Internet.[54] A second problem is that, to some extent, finding information on the Internet still requires doing your own research. Despite the availability of search engines, it is not always obvious where to look for political information. Suppose you wanted to learn more about the conflict in Afghanistan. A Google search in early 2010 on the terms "America," "Afghanistan," and "war" returned over 64 million Web pages, from reports on America's military strategy to pictures of Afghani civilian casualties. Thus, the problem is not finding information but deciding which of the 64 million pages will help you to learn about the conflict.

Third, some of the vast quantity of information on the Internet is of questionable reliability. Though this problem also arises for major publications, these

▲ During Virginia senator George Allen's 2006 reelection campaign, he was videotaped at a rally calling an opposition tracker "macaca." Millions saw the clip on YouTube, and many interpreted the term as a racial slur. Before the Internet, the incident would never have come to light, but it became one factor in Allen's defeat. Here, Allen concedes the race to Democratic challenger Jim Webb.

This fabricated photo shows President Obama apparently talking into a telephone he is holding upside down. The easy availability of doctored photos of many elected officials on the Internet highlights the dangers of relying on unvetted Web sites as a primary source of political information.

publications are so widely read that when mistakes show up in print, they are typically spotted and corrected. Most major publications also have extensive fact-checking operations, because their ability to attract an audience depends on upholding a reputation for accuracy. On the other hand, citizen-reporters who post information on lesser-known Web sites are unlikely to get the benefit of these correction mechanisms. For example, it is easy to find fake photographs of Presidents Barack Obama and George Bush speaking on the phone while holding the receiver upside down, or a fake photo of former vice-presidential candidate Sarah Palin in an American flag bikini. Some Web sites identify these pictures as the fabrications that they are, but others do not. In a world where Web sites come and go, and when citizens do not take the time to carefully investigate what they see or read, false information may easily be accepted as true.

Finally, the Internet's minimal impact on what Americans know also reflects a lack of demand for information. There is no requirement that Americans attain some baseline level of knowledge about politics. Thus, despite the wealth of information on the Internet, there is no guarantee that people will sit down, search for what they want or need to know, distinguish true from false information, and assemble what they find into coherent conclusions. In fact, people may prefer to focus on events that catch their attention, such as a new celebrity scandal or viral video, and avoid "boring" stories such as current events in politics.[55]

How Political Reporters Work: Sources, Leaks, and Shield Laws

The reality of reporting on politics is that many people involved in the political process don't want the public to know everything they are doing—or only want their own version of events to see print. Politicians want media coverage that highlights their achievements in order to build public support and secure election (or reelection), bureaucrats want favorable attention for their programs, and interest groups want publicity to further their causes. The result is that coverage of American politics reflects complex trade-offs between reporters who want complete, accurate information and sources who want favorable coverage.

Reporters also face legal hurdles as they research stories. Notwithstanding the freedom of the press guaranteed in the Bill of Rights, reporters are subject to legal limitations, including the clear and present danger test and prior restraint. If the government can convince a judge that publication of a particular story would lead to immediate harm to a person or persons, a judge can halt publication; this action is called prior restraint. But the clear and present danger test sets the bar extremely high for stopping publication of a story. The Supreme Court has held that such attempts carry "a presumption of unconstitutionality." Thus, as we discussed in Chapter 4, most attempts to prevent publication have been unsuccessful.

In late 2005, the *Washington Post* ran a story that described a network of secret prisons run by the Central Intelligence Agency (CIA) that were being used to hold suspected terrorists.[56] A month later, the *New York Times* published a story revealing that the National Security Agency (NSA), under orders from President Bush, had wiretapped thousands of international phone calls without court authorization.[57] Both stories relied on classified information, so how did the reporters learn

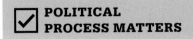

☑ POLITICAL
PROCESS MATTERS

about these secret programs? This information was **leaked** by people inside the government—their identities remain a mystery to this day.

Government officials have two tactics to deter leaks or influence the media's coverage of a story. First, there are laws prohibiting the disclosure of classified information. In the case of the NSA wiretaps, after the *New York Times* article was published, the Justice Department began an investigation to find and prosecute whomever had disclosed classified information about the program, intending to use the threat of prosecution to stop other officials from giving information to reporters.[58] In the mid-1980s, a government employee was convicted of giving classified pictures of a new Soviet aircraft carrier to a defense publication.[59] Ironically, the new carrier was identical to one already in service (and well-photographed). Even so, the employee was jailed until being pardoned by President Clinton in 2001.

Government officials also try to persuade reporters and editors to voluntarily refrain from publishing sensitive stories. In the case of the NSA wiretaps, the *New York Times* sat on the story for a full year, publishing only when it was rumored that another paper was ready to release its own version of the story.[60] And when the story of the secret CIA prisons broke, it did not name any of the countries in Eastern Europe where the prisons were allegedly located. The reporters had this information but agreed to keep it out of the story.

Why do reporters restrain their stories this way? Sometimes they agree that keeping secrets is in the national interest. Other times, reporters are rewarded for cooperating—they may get information about another government policy or future access to officials. Alternately, reporters may be coerced to back down from a story through threats, such as the possibility that if they go ahead with a story, they may lose access to people in government for future stories or even go to jail.

▲ The threat of prosecution is one way to deter government employees from leaking secret information to the press. U.S. intelligence analyst Samuel Morrison was convicted of espionage for giving this satellite image of a Soviet naval shipyard, and several other photos, to a reporter.

STAGING THE NEWS

People inside the federal government, from the president to the large numbers of bureaucrats, work to shape media coverage to suit their personal goals. Larry Speakes, the press secretary to President Reagan, had a sign in his office that said, "You don't tell us how to stage the news, and we won't tell you how to cover it."

Politicians and others in government try to influence coverage by providing select information to reporters. Sometimes they hold **press conferences** where they take questions from the media. Other times, they speak to single reporters or to a group **on background or off the record**, meaning that the reporter can use the information but cannot attribute it to the politician by name. Another strategy is to hold events aimed, at least in part, at securing favorable press coverage. In October 2007, officials at the Federal Emergency Management Agency (FEMA) held a press conference to detail its response to massive wildfires outside San Diego, California. The conference was attended only by television camera crews; FEMA allowed reporters to listen to the conference by phone, but they could not ask questions. So, who asked the questions? Other FEMA employees. Clearly, the event was designed to showcase the scope and effectiveness of FEMA's relief efforts, but the effort collapsed when the circumstances of the press conference came to light. A variation on this approach occurred at a press conference in 2009, when President Obama's staff

leak The release of either classified or politically embarrassing information by a government employee to a member of the press.

press conference An event at which a politician speaks to journalists and, in most cases, answers their questions afterward.

on background or **off the record** Comments a politician makes to the press on the condition that they can be reported only if they are not attributed to that politician.

Prior Restraint of Secret Information

The conflict between reporters and government officials is particularly sharp in the case of intelligence agencies. The Central Intelligence Agency (CIA), National Security Agency (NSA), and other government organizations need to keep their operations secret to operate effectively. For example, during the 1970s, one NSA operation involved using submarines to install recording equipment on Soviet underwater communications cables used to relay secret military data. Obviously, if the operation became public, the Soviets would stop using the cables until they could find and remove the recording equipment. (As it happened, the operation ended when a Soviet spy working for the CIA found out about it.) Intelligence agencies also need to keep the identities of their covert operatives secret. As Porter Goss, former director of the CIA argued, if someone living abroad is found to be an employee of the CIA, their ability to gather information will surely be compromised—in some places, their life might be in danger.[a]

Both of these arguments speak to the need for prior restraint, which gives the government the power to keep the details of secret operations and the names of covert operatives out of the newspapers and other media sources. But as we discussed in Chapter 4, attempts to invoke prior restraint are almost never successful. Why isn't keeping secrets an easy call?

The problem is accountability. If the media are restrained from publication, then there is a risk government officials will be able to do whatever they want, because the public, and most elected officials, will not find out. Put another way, without media watchdogs, the small number of unelected bureaucrats who make decisions about secret operations will never have to answer for those decisions to the public or to elected representatives. Moreover, these same bureaucrats would decide which operations would be considered secret in the first place. In some cases, the ability to keep operations secret has allowed intelligence agencies to carry out programs that might have been prohibited had they been publicized from the start, such as the network of CIA prisons in Eastern Europe that was revealed in 2005.

In sum, decisions about prior restraint are difficult, precisely because they involve balancing two important goals: allowing the government to carry out covert operations, and informing the public about government actions so that citizens can evaluate and respond to them. If you had to evaluate an intelligence agency's request for prior restraint, how would you decide whether to grant it? ■

---

apparently coordinated with a Huffington Post reporter to ask a specific question on Iran—and made sure that the reporter was able to ask the question early in the press conference.[61]

Of course, people who leak information to the media also have their own agendas. Consider the Watergate scandal. In 1972, 1973, and 1974, reporters for the *Washington Post* published a series of articles revealing that many senior members of the Nixon administration, including the president, had covered up a series of illegal programs run by the Committee to Reelect the President, including money laundering, provision of hush-money to potential witnesses, and break-ins to the Democratic Party headquarters. These stories were possible only because someone in the administration leaked information to the *Post*'s reporters. The informant's identity remained unknown for more than thirty years, but in 2005 he came forward as senior FBI official W. Mark Felt.[62] The authors of the stories, Bob Woodward and Carl Bernstein, were not sure why Felt was giving them information, although they suspected part of his motivation was resentment at not being promoted to a more senior position in the FBI. They believed his revelations only because they could confirm some of the details with other sources.

REVEALING SOURCES

Reporters covering important or controversial stories often promise their sources that they will remain anonymous in any coverage based on the information they provide. These assurances are an important factor in the decision to leak information, especially classified information. However, this assurance is not absolute. Reporters and their editors can, under certain circumstances, be compelled by a court to reveal the sources for their stories. While some states have **shield laws** that allow reporters to refuse to name their sources, there is no such law at the federal level—although there have been attempts to enact such a law in recent years. As a result, federal prosecutors can ask a judge to force reporters to name their sources, on the grounds that the identity of the source is fundamental to their case. If the judge agrees, the reporter can be jailed for contempt for an indefinite period of time unless he or she provides the information.

In 2005, a high-profile federal case brought public attention to this process, and to the lack of a federal shield law. The complex case was rooted in a news story in which a veteran journalist revealed that Valerie Plame, supposedly a mid-level employee for a private firm, secretly worked as an undercover employee of the CIA. The leak of Plame's CIA employment to the press—and the decision to publish the information—became all the more significant because of Plame's husband, former ambassador Joseph Wilson. Before the invasion of Iraq, Wilson had been hired by the CIA to determine whether the country of Niger had supplied Iraq with uranium. Wilson found no evidence of such exports, which detracted from the Bush administration's claims that Iraq was working to produce nuclear weapons. Thus, Wilson's CIA-based connection to Plame was leaked in what appeared to be an attempt to discredit his findings with the implication of a conflict of interest.

Regardless of the complex political circumstances surrounding the case, leaking Plame's identity broke the law: it is illegal to reveal the name of a clandestine CIA employee. The same source who originally leaked Plame's name for publication had also served as a source for another veteran journalist, *New York Times* reporter Judith Miller. Even though Miller did not publish information from this source, she was subpoenaed to reveal the name and ultimately jailed for over three months for refusing to do so. At that point, and with encouragement from her source, she decided to tell the special prosecutor that her source was I. Lewis Libby, then–vice president Dick Cheney's chief of staff. Libby was later convicted of lying to the grand jury about his role in the Plame case. President Bush commuted his prison sentence but did not issue a full pardon.

▲ *The journalists who revealed Valerie Plame's status as a covert CIA employee received the information from White House officials. By leaking it to the press, the officials apparently aimed to discredit a report Plame's husband wrote, which contradicted White House claims about Iraq purchasing nuclear bomb–making materials.*

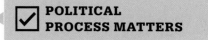
POLITICAL PROCESS MATTERS

How Do Americans Use the Media to Learn about Politics?

Americans now have many more ways to learn about politics than they did a generation or two ago. Imagine yourself in the 1940s. Suppose you want to learn about President Truman's State of the Union speech. You can't go to Washington to hear

shield laws Legislation, which exists in some states but not at the federal level, that gives reporters the right to refuse to name the sources of their information.

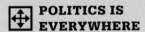

POLITICS IS EVERYWHERE

the speech in person. Where do you get your information? If you live in a big city, the speech will probably be covered in tomorrow's newspaper. If you live in a small town, your local paper may or may not have a story, and if they don't, you will need a subscription to either a big-city paper (arriving a week later) or a weekly or monthly news magazine, or a radio that can pick up a station broadcasting the speech.

Now consider the modern era in which major political events saturate the media, even if each event makes headlines only briefly. You can tune in to one of the four major television networks, numerous cable news channels, public TV stations, or radio stations, or listen to live streaming of the speech on the Internet. Most TV stations will feature pundits' commentary on the speech and will interview prominent politicians and commentators about it. Jay Leno and David Letterman will make jokes about the speech in their opening monologues on late-night TV, and Jon Stewart and Stephen Colbert will skewer it on their shows. Miss the speech? Tomorrow it will be front-page news in most newspapers, and larger, national papers will publish the full text. Countless Internet sites will offer information and analyses. And you will be able to watch a video of the speech on YouTube and many other sites.

The fact that there are many sources of political information in the modern era does not imply that the average American uses most of them. For the most part, Americans learn about politics in the same way as they become aware of other things, a process explained by the **by-product theory**.[63] This theory posits that for many Americans, political information is acquired accidentally. People read the sports pages of a newspaper and glance at front page stories along the way. They watch *The Daily Show* and learn about politics while laughing at Jon Stewart's reports. They read a story on a political blog or Internet news site because the title catches their eye as they're looking for something else.

After encountering new information, the question of whether an individual either remembers that information later, or uses it to modify her thoughts about politicians or policies, depends on her level of interest. John Zaller's work on information processing shows that highly interested people are unlikely to change their minds when they learn something new, as they have already decided what they think. On the other hand, people who are uninterested in politics are less likely to encounter new political information in the first place. Thus, media coverage is most likely to affect the beliefs of people who take a moderate interest in politics.[64]

MEDIA USAGE TRENDS

Even though there are many news sources, none of them is used by everyone (Table 6.1). As of 2008, about half of those surveyed watched local news and between a quarter and a third watched cable news, nightly network broadcasts, or got their news online. This table also highlights some important trends in media usage.[65] The percentage of people who read newspapers declined by almost half in fifteen years, and the percentage watching TV news has also declined, with the number watching nightly news broadcasts showing the largest drop, from 60 percent to only 29 percent. Use of online sources has increased from 2 percent of those surveyed in 1996 to more than a third. Moreover, other parts of the survey revealed that about 10 percent of Americans consult online blogs for political information. Table 6.2 shows that all age groups use Internet-based sources, but usage is most prevalent among younger Americans, as is the decline in traditional sources such as newspapers.

TABLE 6.1 **THE CHANGING NEWS LANDSCAPE**

The growth of the Internet has made a wide variety of new information sources available to the average American. Has this development changed the types of news sources that Americans regularly use?

	1993	1996	2000	2002	2004	2006	2008
Regularly watch . . .							
Local TV news	77%	65%	56%	57%	59%	54%	52%
Cable TV news	—	—	—	33	38	34	39
Nightly network news	60	42	30	32	34	28	29
Network morning news	—	—	20	22	22	23	22
Listened/read yesterday . . .							
Radio	47[a]	44	43	41	40	36	35
Newspaper	58[a]	50	47	41	42	40	34
Seek online news three or more days per week	—	2[b]	23	25	29	31	37

[a] From 1994.
[b] From 1995.

SOURCE: Pew Research Center, "Maturing Internet News Audience—Broader Than Deep," July 30, 2006, available at http://people-press.org/reports/pdf/282.pdf; Pew Research Center, "Key News Audiences Now Blend Online and Traditional Sources," August 17, 2008, available at http://people-press.org/reports/pdf/444.pdf.

TABLE 6.2 **TRADITIONAL NEWS SOURCES FACE STIFF COMPETITION**

Older Americans grew up without cable channels, the Internet, or even color TV. Are there generational differences in the use of different media sources?

	Age 18–29	30–49	50–64	65+
News yesterday . . .				
Watched TV news	41%	54%	64%	75%
Read a newspaper	19	28	40	55
Listened to radio news	31	41	37	29
Got news online	37	36	29	13

SOURCE: Pew Research Center, "Key News Audiences Now Blend Online and Traditional Sources," August 17, 2008, available at http://people-press.org/reports/pdf/444.pdf.

DOES THE SOURCE MATTER?

As we have discussed, people acquire different kinds of information in different formats from each type of media source. A newspaper can report on a Taliban attack in Afghanistan in a fair amount of detail and may have a few pictures—whereas a TV news show can include footage of the attack and the aftermath, even in a less detailed story. Do people who rely on different kinds of media sources learn different things about politics? And do most people tend to accumulate broad, general political knowledge, or information about specific topics?

In 2007, the Pew Trust asked people twenty-three questions about contemporary politics, defining "high-knowledge" individuals as those who answered fifteen or more questions correctly. They then divided people according to their principal source of political information, and calculated the percentage of high-knowledge people who used each news source. The results are shown in Table 6.3. For each source, the table also gives the percentage of people who answered four of the survey's specific political questions correctly: those who could identify Sunnis as a religious group in Iraq, "Scooter" Libby as the person convicted in the Valerie Plame case, Vladimir Putin as the president of Russia, and those who knew the approximate number of American combat deaths in Iraq. Regardless of the type of news source, the percentage of high-knowledge people rarely creeps above 50 percent, and the same is true for the percentage who could answer each of these four questions correctly. In other words, Americans are learning from news coverage, but very few learn enough to be considered current-events experts.

Table 6.3 also shows differences in the percentage of high-knowledge people who use the different media sources. *The Daily Show* and *The Colbert Report*, along with major online news sites, *NewsHour* (a PBS nightly newscast), *The O'Reilly Factor*, National Public Radio, and *The Rush Limbaugh Show* were among those drawing the highest percentages of high-knowledge individuals. At the other extreme were

---

TABLE 6.3 | KNOWLEDGE LEVELS BY NEWS SOURCE

One of the most important questions about media usage is whether people who know a lot about politics get their information from different sources than people who don't know as much. Does this table show differences between high-information and low-information?

	High-Knowledge Group	Percentage who could . . .			
		Identify Sunnis	Identify Libby	Identify Putin	Approximate U.S. Deaths in Iraq
Nationwide	35%	32%	29%	36%	55%
The audience of . . .					
The Daily Show/The Colbert Report	54%	50%	44%	52%	59%
Major newspaper Web sites	54	52	42	58	64
NewsHour	53	46	45	54	67
The O'Reilly Factor	51	43	44	53	64
National Public Radio	51	49	43	51	66
The Rush Limbaugh Show	50	40	42	52	70
Local daily newspaper	43	36	35	43	60
News from Google, Yahoo, etc.	41	44	33	44	60
CNN	41	38	36	41	60
Network evening news	38	31	33	37	61
Online news discussion blogs	37	35	32	36	57
Fox News Channel	35	32	29	38	58
Local TV news	35	30	30	35	57
Network morning shows	34	30	30	35	57

Entries show the percentage of regular viewers, readers, or listeners of each outlet who fall in the high-knowledge group (correctly answered at least 15 of 23 questions about politics and world affairs) and the percentage who correctly answered some of the individual questions on the test.

SOURCE: Pew Research Center, "What Americans Know: 1989–2007," April 15, 2007, available at http://people-press.org/reports/pdf/319.pdf.

groups who get their information from network evening news, blogs, the Fox News Channel, local TV news and, at the bottom, network morning news. Of course, some of these differences may be due to other factors, such as variation in the education levels of those who prefer particular media sources, or some survey respondents' use of multiple sources.

Studying the Impact of Media Coverage on American Citizens and Government Policy

This section details what political scientists know about whether exposure to media coverage of politics changes what people think or do, the study of **media effects**. There is considerable evidence that media coverage influences its audience. However, much of the impact stems not from what is contained in stories about political events but from what is left out, how information is presented, or even whether a story is reported at all. Political scientists label these mechanisms as priming, filtering (also called agenda-setting), slant, and framing.[66] In the remainder of this section, we will consider what political scientists know about each of these effects.

Among the first wave of scholars studying the media's impact on public opinion, there was little doubt of the media's power. Writing in the 1920s, Walter Lippman argued that by reading or listening to news coverage, Americans learned which issues they should care about, what government could do about these concerns, and the consequences of different policy choices.[67] This certainty was reversed beginning in the 1950s, when scholars began to test claims about media effects using survey data. The early studies yielded extremely negative results—as one scholar put it, media effects were governed by the "law of minimal consequences," meaning that they appeared to have little influence on what Americans knew about politics or their political behavior.[68] By the 1980s, however, these findings about the nonexistence of media effects were found to be incorrect: the result of bad surveys, inadequate statistics, and a narrow conception of what media effects would look like.[69]

Modern theories of media influence distinguish between the several ways coverage can affect media consumers' beliefs and judgments. The most obvious mechanism is the use of the media as a forum for persuasion, in which an overt effort is made to talk people into changing their minds about a candidate or an issue. However, people are not always conscious of the ways media reports shape their beliefs. Theorists describe four media effects that work largely without consumers' awareness of their influence.

- **Filtering** results from journalists' and editors' decisions about which of many potential news stories to report.
- **Slant** in a story gives favorable coverage to one candidate or policy without providing "balanced" favorable coverage of the other side.
- **Priming** happens when a story changes public opinion by publicizing a new argument or concern, such as when coverage of a candidate's background changes people's general impressions of a candidate.
- **Framing** refers to the way the description or presentation of a story, including the details, explanations, and context offered in the report, can influence public opinion.

media effects The influence of media coverage on average citizens' opinions and actions.

filtering The influence on public opinion that results from journalists' and editors' decisions about which of many potential news stories to report.

slant The imbalance in a story that covers one candidate or policy favorably without providing similar coverage of the other side.

priming The influence on the public's general impressions caused by positive or negative coverage of a candidate or issue.

framing The influence on public opinion caused by the way a story is presented or covered, including the details, explanations, and context offered in the report.

▲ The way a story is reported—which information is included in an article or which images are used—makes a big difference in what people learn from it. A story about the Palestinian–Israeli conflict, for example, might emphasize Israeli forces' destruction of Palestinians' homes (left) or suicide bombings by Palestinians in Israel (right).

The existence of these media effects does not imply that reporters or editors try to mislead the public or sway public opinion to conform to their own ideas about a story. If you read an article about a particular issue and decide to change your position, this doesn't suggest that the story was inaccurate or biased. Your decision may well be justified by the facts of the situation. Similarly, when slanted campaign coverage praises one candidate and dismisses the other as unqualified, you might conclude that the author agrees with the first candidate's positions and wrote the story to help the candidate get elected. But what if the first candidate is actually more qualified? If so, then slanted coverage of the campaign might be objective.

The same is true for other media effects. Space limitations mean that some filtering is inevitable as reporters and editors decide which stories to cover. Similar kinds of decisions about what to report and how to present the information lead to priming and framing effects. Even if everyone in the political media adhered to the highest standards of accuracy, these influences would still exist.

The modern conception of media effects is exemplified by James Druckman and Michael Parkin's 2005 study of a Senate race in Minnesota, which found that different newspapers covered the candidates differently, both in the amount of coverage they gave to each candidate and the percentage of positive versus negative stories they ran. They showed that a given paper's slant in coverage was correlated with endorsements, such that papers gave more coverage and more positive coverage to the candidates they endorsed. Voters who were regular readers of a paper that endorsed a particular candidate were more likely to hold a positive opinion of that candidate and more likely to vote for him.[70]

A study of priming by Jon Krosnick and Laura Brannon found that exposure to press coverage of the Persian Gulf War in 1990 and 1991 moved citizens to evaluate then-president George H. W. Bush based on his effectiveness in managing the war rather than other factors such as the state of the economy.[71] Such priming is more likely when citizens are politically knowledgeable about the issues being discussed and trust the authors of the related news stories.[72]

The concept of filtering is illustrated by Project Censored's annual list of Top Censored Stories.[73] Their list for 2010 included stories about nuclear waste pools in North Carolina and how private corporations benefit from Israel's policies toward the Palestinians. Their point is not that the government forces reporters to keep quiet; rather, the claim is that reporters and their editors are deciding against

TABLE 6.4 HOW FRAMING WORKS: ALTERNATIVE QUESTIONS ABOUT ECONOMIC STIMULUS

News stories sometimes exhibit framing effects: the way they describe a political event shapes the judgments formed by citizens, even though the story presents the same facts it otherwise would and the author has no conscious or unconscious bias. These data illustrate framing by showing how responses to poll questions vary with the specific wording of the question.

	Favor	Oppose	Unsure
Rasmussen Reports			
Do you favor or oppose the economic recovery package proposed by Barack Obama?	45%	34%	21%
Gallup			
Do you favor or oppose Congress passing a new $775 billion economic stimulus program as soon as possible after Barack Obama takes office?	53	36	11
ABC News/*Washington Post*			
Would you support or oppose new federal spending of about $800 billion on tax cuts, construction projects, energy, education, and health care to try to stimulate the economy?	70	27	3

SOURCE: Mark Blumenthal, "Economic Stimulus and the Many Faces of 'Public Opinion,'" January 27, 2009, available at www.pollster.com/blogs/economic_stimulus_and_the_many.php, (accessed 11/20/09).

covering these stories, sometimes for political or self-serving reasons. Of course, everyone can come up with a list of stories that they believe deserve more attention. However, because no media source can report on everything—due to the lack of space, time, and staff—some events or problems can easily fall through the cracks, receiving little or no attention despite their significance.

An example of framing can be found in a comparison of polling questions used to measure support for President Obama's economic stimulus package that was enacted in early 2009 (Table 6.4). Looking across the three poll questions, it appears that including Obama's name reduced support for the package, whereas adding details about how the money would be spent and omitting mention of Obama increased support. Presumably, the inferences that people drew from stories about the stimulus package—and their judgments about whether they supported the package or opposed it—depended on which details were emphasized in these stories.

HOW MEDIA COVERAGE AFFECTS PUBLIC POLICY

Although most politicians and political scientists would say that media coverage shapes public policy, it is very difficult to prove that this link exists. In part, the problem is that the chain of events is very complex: the media report on a situation, thereby informing citizens, who demand a policy response from politicians, who then enact appropriate legislation. (Alternatively, politicians or bureaucrats may learn about a story on their own and be moved to act without citizen pressures.) But as we have seen in this chapter, the average citizen has many sources of information, chooses to be exposed to only a few of them, and may or may not demand government action. Moreover, as we describe in subsequent chapters, citizen pressures are only one of the things that lead politicians or bureaucrats to develop policy solutions

Measuring Media Effects

One of the biggest problems with measuring media effects is that it is hard to determine causality—to be sure that exposure to a story, image, or Web site actually led people to change their minds about some issue. For example, one study found that when the Fox News network began broadcasting in a community, voting for Republican candidates in the next election increased significantly.[a] Does this mean that some viewers became pro-Republican after listening to allegedly pro-Republican broadcasts on Fox News? Perhaps, but the study did not directly measure the behavior of individuals in these communities, so there is no way to be sure that new Republican supporters were actually Fox News viewers. It may be that Fox News viewers are no more likely to vote Republican than anyone else, and that the relationship observed in the study is due to the fact that Fox News executives look for communities that are trending Republican when deciding where to enter new cable markets. If so, the apparent connection observed in the study may be an artifact of how Fox News executives site new markets, and say nothing about the effects of watching Fox News programming.

Given the problems with real-world data on media effects, one solution is to develop an experiment in which the experimenters first measure the political beliefs of their subjects, expose the subjects to different versions of a political story, and then measure their beliefs again, to see if different stories caused different beliefs. This is the strategy used by Thomas Nelson, Rosalee Clawson, and Zoe Oxley for their study on media effects.[b]

The authors focused on one kind of media effect, framing. They recruited a group of people who live in Columbus, Ohio, divided them randomly into two groups, and had the members of each group watch one of two television news stories that had run on two different local TV stations.

Both news stories described a rally that a local chapter of the Ku Klux Klan planned to hold in a nearby town. The different frames for these stories are shown in the first table. The first version of the story emphasized the threat to public safety posed by the rally—that members of the Klan might incite others to violence, or that there might be fights between Klan members and people who were holding

FRAMING THE NEWS: TWO REPORTS ON A KU KLUX KLAN RALLY

	Public Order Frame	Free Speech Frame
Theme	KKK rallies have the potential for disorder and physical violence between KKK supporters and those protesting their appearance.	Members of the KKK and those protesting their appearance were determined to get out their message.
Quotes	"Here you have a potential for some real sparks in the crowd," spoken by an observer.	"No free speech for racists," on sign held by protester.
	"The tension between Klan protesters and supporters came within seconds of violence," spoken by a reporter.	"I came down here to hear what they have to say and I think I should be able to listen if I want to," spoken by a supporter of the KKK.
Images	Police officers standing in front of Klan members protecting them from the protesters.	Chanting of protesters. KKK leaders speaking before a microphone.
Interviews	All three people interviewed emphasized the violence and disruption of public order that they had witnessed.	Three of the four people interviewed were Klan supporters who wanted to hear the Klan's message.

to societal problems. As a result, tracing changes in government policy back to media coverage is a difficult task.

Nevertheless, two important regularities in American politics are consistent with the idea that a link exists between media coverage and public policy. For one thing, both politicians and bureaucrats work very hard to get coverage that's in line with their preferred policy outcomes. For example, during the early days of the Iraq war, the Department of Defense implemented a new plan of "embedding" news reporters with military units, allowing reporters to view military operations at first hand. Though this practice seems designed to give the media maximum leeway, in fact it imposed new constraints on coverage. During the Vietnam War, for example, reporters could travel freely and make their own choices about which

MEASURING FRAMING EFFECTS

	Public Order Frame	Free Speech Frame
Tolerance for rallies	3.31	3.96
Tolerance for speeches	3.54	4.17
Importance of free speech	5.25	5.49
Importance of public order	5.43	4.75

Higher numbers indicate greater tolerance.

SOURCE: Thomas E. Nelson, Rosalee A. Clawson, and Zoe M. Oxley, "Media Framing of a Civil Liberties Conflict and Its Effect on Tolerance," *American Political Science Review* 91 (1997): 567–83.

a rally to protest against the Klan. The second story was almost identical except it omitted safety concerns, focusing instead on the free speech issues raised by the rally—that is, that our constitutional rights of free speech mean something only if we allow the expression of beliefs and attitudes that a majority (even a large majority) find hateful and distasteful.

After watching one of the two stories, people answered a series of questions that measured their tolerance for the rally and for free speech, as well as how important they considered free speech and public order. The authors' hypothesis was that the group who viewed the story emphasizing the threat to safety would give a higher priority to public order over free speech, and that the ordering would be reversed for the group who had viewed the story that emphasized the importance of free speech. Moreover, the safety-story group was also expected to have a lower tolerance for the rally. (By dividing people into the two groups at random, the researchers ensured that the two groups started the experiment with approximately the same beliefs about the trade-off between public safety

and free speech, as well as their tolerance for the rally, and that any differences measured after the experiment were due to the variation in the content of the stories that the groups were exposed to.)

The results for the two groups, shown in the second table, provided clear evidence of framing. The group who saw the story that emphasized free speech had a far greater tolerance for the rally and speeches than the people who saw the safety-focused story; they also placed a higher importance on free speech and a lower importance on public order.

Additional research shows that frames work most effectively at shaping what people think when the frames are simple and easy to understand and when a citizen is exposed to only one account of a particular political event and therefore doesn't see competing frames.[c] In particular, news stories on television, which are short and simple and present strong visual images, can have especially significant framing effects on their viewers, effects that are larger than what might be observed for an equivalent story in a newspaper or on a Web page.[d]

These findings do not necessarily imply that real-world stories on TV or elsewhere have strong framing effects, or if they do, that the effects are long-lasting. It may be that the writers of these stories take pains to present balanced coverage or that even when they present stories that have framing effects, viewers soon forget whatever inferences they might have learned. Even so, the important contribution of this study is to show that framing effects can really occur. Having established this point, the next step is to measure the extent and longevity of framing effects in the real world.

Experiments are not a perfect way to measure media effects, because it is impossible to be sure that subjects will respond to real-world stories in the same way they do in an experiment. After all, because they are in an experiment, people may pay closer attention to a story than they might otherwise. Moreover, knowing their responses are being analyzed, subjects may be reluctant to give what they perceive to be a "wrong" response, such as refusing to support free speech in this example. However, because experiments allow researchers to measure how individuals respond to a carefully specified dose of information, they remain a valuable tool for studying media effects as well as many other political phenomena. ■

🎦 **Watch a video clip of Zoe Oxley discussing this topic at wwnorton .com/studyspace.**

stories to investigate. In contrast, embedded reporters traveled with a particular unit and could be steered away from embarrassing or sensitive stories. More recently, President Obama traveled to Afghanistan in March 2010 to meet with Afghani officials and spur them to reduce official corruption and increase government services to the population. Reporters and photographers were allowed to accompany Obama and to file stories on his meeting with Afghani leaders and with U.S. troops. Of course, the trip wasn't taken solely to generate favorable press reports, but Obama's staff worked to maximize the amount of favorable press coverage, with the goal of sustaining public support of Obama's policies in Afghanistan.

Second, there are numerous cases in which the link between media coverage and public policy appears to be extremely strong. As we discuss elsewhere in this chapter, the development of the Amber Alert system and other policies directed at reducing the number of child abductions appear to have been driven by sensational stories about a very small number of actual kidnappings. Along these same lines, the government's response to the damage caused by Hurricane Katrina in 2005 increased significantly after early media coverage emphasized foot-dragging and inaction by the leaders of the Federal Emergency Management Agency (FEMA). And efforts by politicians and bureaucrats to put limits on the compensation of senior Wall Street executives were probably a response to stories that noted how firms receiving bailout funding from the federal government were granting large bonuses to senior management.

IS MEDIA COVERAGE BIASED?

Surveys of the American electorate routinely find that many people believe that media coverage of politics is biased to some extent. Interestingly, Democrats generally think the media favors Republican candidates, while Republicans have the opposite belief.[74] In the main, a majority of Americans, regardless of their party affiliation, do not have great confidence in any of the mainstream media, as shown in Table 6.5.

It is easy to find examples of suspicious decisions by reporters and their editors. In the fall of 2009, editors at Fox News used video footage of a 2008 presidential campaign rally to illustrate a story about a book signing event by former vice-presidential candidate Sarah Palin. The story as broadcast gave the impression that Palin's book event had attracted much larger crowds than was actually the case. Although Fox attributed the mix-up to an honest mistake, critics charged that the

TABLE 6.5 PARTISANSHIP AND NEWS SOURCE CREDIBILITY

Do Americans consider all media sources equally reliable for learning about politics? Are there partisan differences in the sources people choose?

Believe All or Most of What Organization Says	Republicans	Democrats	Gap
NewsHour	16%	34%	−18
National Public Radio	18	34	−16
Daily newspaper	19	29	−10
CBS News	18	26	−8
Local TV news	27	32	−5
CNN	22	35	−13
ABC News	19	28	−9
NBC News	16	31	−15
New York Times	10	24	−14
USA Today	16	15	+1
Time	12	26	−14
Wall Street Journal	29	24	+5
Fox News Channel	34	19	+15

Percentages are based on those who could rate each.

SOURCE: Pew Research Center, "Key News Audiences Now Blend Online and Traditional Sources," August 17, 2008, available at http://people-press.org/reports/pdf/444.pdf.

campaign footage was spliced in as part of a deliberate effort to support Palin because of Fox's presumed preference for Republicans.[75]

Similarly, the politically conservative Media Research Center argued in early 2006 that major news organizations were refusing to report good news about Iraq, instead offering "defeatist coverage" that exhibited a "pessimistic bias."[76] The Center's study found that 61 percent of the stories aired on the ABC, NBC, and CBS evening news programs during 2005 had a "negative or pessimistic bias," only 24 percent were "balanced or neutral," and only 15 percent were "positive or optimistic."[77] They concluded, "TV journalists have spent much of their time following the terrorists' agenda of violence and mayhem, pushing the accomplishments of our soldiers off the public's radar screen."[78] These claims were echoed by the *Washington Times*, which began a series of editorials in 2005 highlighting "underreported news from Iraq," such as increases in primary school enrollment and increases in Iraq's gross domestic product (GDP). They found few mentions of these topics in other publications, leading them to conclude that most reporters were focusing on bad news from Iraq.[79]

Many journalists and commentators readily admit that they take an ideological or partisan perspective. Rush Limbaugh, the previously mentioned talk radio host, describes himself as a strong conservative. Many of the commentators on the Fox News Channel make no secret of their conservative viewpoint. Similarly, the political news magazine *The Nation* describes itself as "a weekly journal of left/liberal opinion, covering national and international affairs as well as the arts."[80] These journalists' and organizations' points of view are well known and easy to see. Some people might even find the bias useful. A liberal, for example, could use *The Nation*'s endorsements as a guide to which candidates they should support, and a conservative might listen to Rush Limbaugh to get the same information.

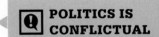

POLITICS IS CONFLICTUAL

More generally, claims about media bias make strong assumptions about what fair coverage would look like, presuming, for example, that some of the news stories about Iraq should necessarily be optimistic or report positive developments along with negative ones. But what if critical coverage is justified? Suppose the Media Research Center's study is accurate, and some 61 percent of the stories they analyzed about Iraq were truly negative or pessimistic. Does that percentage mean the coverage was inaccurate? During 2005, hundreds of American troops and large numbers of civilians were killed in Iraq, and there were thousands of bombings, kidnappings, and other attacks by insurgent forces. Moreover, though some improvements were noted in school enrollments and the country's GDP, many other indicators, such as levels of oil exports, showed little change or even declined.[81] In other words, if the expectation is that the media should give an accurate picture of what's happening in Iraq, it is not clear that optimism was appropriate in 2005. In fact, after two stories, the *Washington Times* stopped publishing its "underreported news from Iraq" series.

It is hard to find a scholarly study that presents strong evidence of systematic media bias. A 2006 study found that bias in news reporting is not *pervasive*, and to the extent that it exists, it is driven by market forces—reporters trying to offer coverage that will catch the attention of their audience.[82]

Similarly, the evidence for priming, filtering, and framing does not support claims of either liberal or conservative media bias. Reporters move beyond "just the facts" because much of what happens in American politics requires interpretation. They must choose what to report because so many things happen every day, and they decide how to report staged news, whether to reveal secrets, and which sources to rely on. Thus, filtering and framing of the news are virtually inevitable. There is no way to cover American politics, or any other topic, without choosing which

The Liberal Media?

One of the central criticisms of journalists in America is that a disproportionate number of them are liberals who, because of their own political leanings, tend to favor liberal politicians and liberal causes in their news coverage. As the late Michael Kelly, a well-known newspaper columnist, once wrote in the *Washington Post*: "Does a largely liberal news media still exhibit a largely liberal bias? [This question] can be answered both as a matter of logic and as a matter of fact, and the answer is: sure."[a]

Are these claims of liberal media bias true? On the surface, the answer seems to be yes. The first figure below gives the results of a 1997 survey conducted by the American Society of Newspaper Editors (ASNE), focusing on the party affiliations of newspaper reporters.[b] Reporters in this survey were much more likely to be Democrats rather than Republicans. Note that a majority said they were Democrats or liberals, or leaned in this direction, compared to only 15 percent who claimed a Republican or conservative affiliation.

A deeper look suggests a problem with this conclusion. The ASNE surveyed all journalists, not just those who cover politics. If you are interested in whether political reporting is biased in a liberal direction, it doesn't matter if restaurant reviewers are liberals, if the sports pages are dominated by Democrats, or even if the TV weather forecasters hate the Republican Party. The real question is whether an ideological bias exists among reporters who cover politics.

When you look at the ideological leanings of political reporters in particular, evidence for a liberal or pro-Democrat bias is weak. One survey sampled reporters based in Washington, DC, who cover national politics or the economy. The second figure shows their responses to a question about their ideological leanings. The figures reveal a complex ideological picture among political reporters. On social issues, there are more liberals than conservatives—but the pattern is reversed for economic issues. More important, on both sets of issues, the vast majority of reporters defined themselves as moderates.

These data suggest that the conventional wisdom about liberal reporters is only partly true. Although reporters in general are predominately liberal or Democratic, those who cover politics and the economy look very different, with a much higher percentage of moderates, conservatives, and Republicans. These data do not prove that the media cover politics without bias, but they suggest that the people who write about politics have a range of political views. ∎

ALL JOURNALISTS' SELF-REPORTED IDEOLOGIES

Allegations of a liberal bias in media coverage of politics center on the claim that reporters are predominantly liberals. Based on these data, what would you tell someone who made this claim?

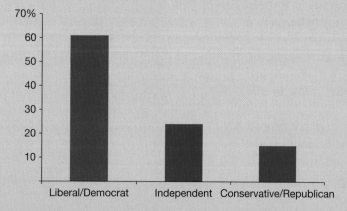

SOURCE: American Society of Newspaper Editors, "The Newspaper Journalists of the 90s," June 17, 1997, www.asne.org/kiosk/reports/97reports/journalists90s/survey19.html.

SELF-REPORTED IDEOLOGIES OF WASHINGTON REPORTERS WHO COVER POLITICS AND THE ECONOMY

This graph presents a more refined view of reporter ideology, focusing on Washington-based reporters who cover business, economics, or politics. Do these data support or refute claims of liberal media bias in political coverage?

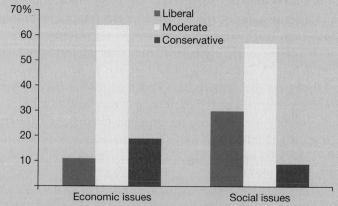

SOURCE: Fairness and Accuracy in Reporting, "Examining the 'Liberal Media' Claim," June 1, 1998, www.fair.org/reports/journalist-survey.html.

stories to report and how to cover them. You may disagree with the decisions of a particular reporter or publication, but there is no such thing as completely objective journalism; your preferred coverage would just involve a different frame, a different filter, and different kinds of priming.

Finally, it would be a mistake to argue that an overall media bias toward either liberal or conservative views must exist simply because so many Americans think it does. Analyses that compare media coverage to citizens' perceptions have found a **hostile media phenomenon**, in which people tend to view balanced coverage as biased against their preferred candidates. One study found that many Republicans believed that the newspapers and TV shows consistently gave favorable treatment to then-president Bill Clinton—even when a content analysis of these programs showed they were either balanced or only slightly favorable.[83] This hostile media phenomenon suggests that even though many Americans consider the media biased, the problem is not media coverage itself, so much as how this coverage is perceived.

hostile media phenomenon The idea that supporters of a candidate or issue tend to feel that media coverage is biased against their position, regardless of whether coverage is actually unfair.

attack journalism A type of increasingly popular media coverage focused on political scandals and controversies, which causes a negative public opinion of political figures.

horse race A description of the type of election coverage that focuses more on poll results and speculation about a likely winner than on substantive differences between the candidates.

soft news Media coverage that aims to entertain or shock, often through sensationalized reporting or by focusing on a candidate or politician's personality.

hard news Media coverage focused on facts and important issues surrounding a campaign.

Assessing Media Coverage of American Politics

In a democracy, the media's job is to provide citizens with information about politicians, government actions, and policy debates. Beginning with our discussion of how the media cover abductions of children, and continuing through many examples of reporting on politics, we have uncovered instances in which the media fall far short of this goal. We will examine some of the reasons for journalists' and editors' choices and the impact of those decisions on coverage and on what Americans know.

Scholars such as Thomas Patterson have documented the rise of **attack journalism**, where "bad news makes for good news," "the mere whiff of a controversy or scandal is grounds for a story," and "public officials are [portrayed as] an ineffective and untrustworthy lot."[84] Other researchers have argued that campaign coverage overemphasizes the **horse race** aspects of the campaign, such as which candidates are ahead and which are falling behind, rather than offering a complete description of each candidate's promises and analysis of how they are likely to behave in office.[85]

Media coverage of politics also emphasizes **soft news** (stories that are sensational or entertaining) over **hard news** (stories that focus on important issues and emphasize facts and figures).[86] At the same time, talk shows and those focused on entertainment have increased their political coverage mainly by reporting stories that emphasize scandals, personalities, and other topics that attract an audience rather than hard facts.[87] An oft-heard truism about local TV news is that "if it bleeds, it leads." An overemphasis on crime stories, coupled with a focus on the victims of crimes rather than on the causes and context of criminal events, leads people to overestimate the chances of being the victim of a violent crime.[88]

Moreover, citizens' perceptions of government may mirror press coverage. Many authors have suggested that citizens' low level of trust in government, as well as high levels of disapproval and dissatisfaction discussed in Chapter 5, may have more to do with how the media reports on American politics than with how government actually works.[89] The lack of hard information in much of the political coverage

FIGURE 6.1 HOW JOURNALISTS VIEW THEIR PROFESSION

Many observers complain about the quality of reporting on American politics. Do journalists share these concerns?

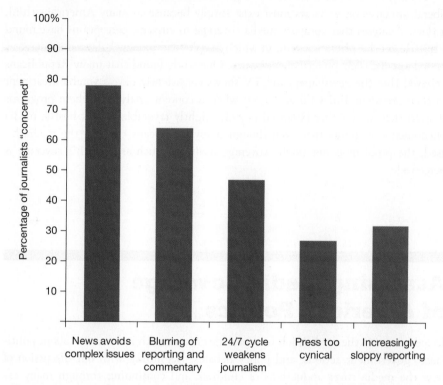

SOURCE: Pew Research Center, "Financial Woes Now Overshadow All Other Concerns for Journalists," March 17, 2008, available at http://people-press.org/reports/pdf/403.pdf.

also fails to address the profound ignorance that many Americans have about the structure of the federal government, particular government policies, and how decisions are made.

Many journalists agree with these broad criticisms of their field. Figure 6.1 shows that a majority of journalists believe the media avoid complex stories and are too timid, and that the line between reporting and commentary is becoming blurred. Similarly, a 2000 survey of journalists found that 53 percent avoided stories that they thought were too complex for their target audience and more than 70 percent avoided stories that they believed were "important but dull."[90]

ONE REASON WHY MEDIA COVERAGE FALLS SHORT: MARKET FORCES

The deeper question about the American media's coverage of politics is *why* there is so much attack journalism, soft news, sensationalism, and scandal. If journalists are aware of the problem, why don't they take their role as political watchdogs for the public interest more seriously? One response is that journalists may feel the need to demonstrate their independence from politicians and government interests, and perhaps counter or prevent claims of media bias. The result can be overly aggressive questioning of elected officials and cynical stories about the political process.[91]

Journalism throughout the World

One of the central themes in this chapter is that much of the media's coverage of political events is driven by the demands of the people who consume this coverage. A significant amount of political coverage tends to be somewhat shallow, focusing on scandals, horse races, and lurid events at the expense of detailed, dispassionate analyses of political events and policy proposals. Yet, for all that Americans complain about this type of coverage, it is what the average American is drawn to when searching for something to read or watch.

One of the interesting questions about this aspect of the American news media is whether the same pattern is observed in media coverage in other countries. Do journalists in other countries provide dispassionate coverage, or are they driven to be as sensationalistic as their colleagues in the United States? This is not an easy question to answer, because events tend to be local to a particular country or region, and it is hard to compare coverage of the same event. However, a truly global story broke in the spring of 2009, as countries throughout the world faced the swine flu epidemic. The Pew Center for Excellence in Journalism looked at newspaper coverage of the epidemic across seven countries: the United States, Mexico, Canada, Spain, France, China, and New Zealand, comparing both the amount of coverage and the content.[a]

The table shows the number of swine flu cases reported in each country during April and May 2009, the number of front page stories about swine flu in the major newspapers, and the ratio of cases to stories. Looking across the numbers, it is clear that although the United States had the highest number of cases and the highest number of front page stories, it also had the lowest ratio of cases to stories. In other words, newspapers in other countries made more (in terms of front page coverage) of a relatively smaller number of cases. Thus, in terms of sheer numbers, newspaper coverage of the swine flu epidemic in the United States was less sensational than the coverage in other countries.

U.S. newspaper coverage also compared well in terms of its content. The Pew researchers found that U.S. reporting covered "every angle" of the epidemic, including the spread of the disease throughout the world, how governments were reacting, the role played by international organizations, and how people could lower their chances of getting the disease. In contrast, coverage by Mexican newspapers focused on the impact of the epidemic on business and the economy as well as work and school closings but said nothing about the government's response. The state-controlled Chinese media gave full coverage to the aid that their government sent to Mexico but did not mention the quarantine that the Chinese government imposed on foreign tourists in China. Coverage in all of the other countries had similar lapses.

Of course, swine flu is only one case, and in this portion of the study the Pew researchers did not compare the various countries' television, Internet, or other types of media coverage. Nor did the study claim that the U.S. newspapers' coverage of the epidemic was perfect. But it does appear that in this case, the American newspapers did a noticeably better job than their counterparts in other countries. ■

HOW NEWSPAPERS IN DIFFERENT COUNTRIES COVERED SWINE FLU

Country	Cases of Swine Flu	Front-Page Stories	Stories per Case
United States	2,254	31	1:225
Mexico	1,626	20	1:81
Canada	240	6	1:47
Spain	93	7	1:13
France	12	2	1:6
New Zealand	7	6	1:1
China	1	9	9:1

The more significant explanation for the soft, sensationalistic nature of much political coverage is that reporters and their editors recognize that they are in a competitive business where the aim is to attract a paying audience. Describing the media as an information source for citizens makes sense in terms of how American politics works, but this description does not capture the sometimes-contradictory incentives facing journalists. Most American media outlets are for-profit enterprises. Because they need to produce coverage that attracts an audience, their strategy is often to create stories that consumers want to read and watch and that are consistent with how members of their target audience think about politics.

For example, as we discussed in the context of public opinion (Chapter 5) and will return to in the next chapters, many Americans hold dismal evaluations of the Republican and Democratic parties, of Congress, and of the American political system in general. Given these perceptions, the prevalence of attack journalism is no surprise; journalists give the American people coverage of politics that fits their preconceptions. Americans are not changing what they think in response to attack stories and soft news. Rather, the way journalists cover politics reflects the tone of American public opinion.[92] Although journalists can and do shape public opinion—as the discussion of media effects showed—media coverage is also substantially shaped by the need to attract an audience. The shift in the tone and content of political coverage also reflects the expansion in the number of media sources and the competition among them for a finite audience. As longtime ABC reporter Sam Donaldson put it,

> We're trying desperately to hold onto an ever-shrinking audience, as far as the big commercial networks are concerned. . . . We're reaching out more and more for people who believe there are three-headed cows. . . . I'm part of the process of trying to find a larger audience of people who never really cared about news. . . . And to get them, we have to do things we didn't ever used to do before.[93]

The same factors can lead media sources to emphasize stories about Americans and America over coverage of important events in other countries. Coverage may also be shaped by a reporter's background—for example, someone who grew up in a middle-class neighborhood may have difficulty understanding or reporting accurately on the problems of the poor.[94]

Even if reporters tried to explain how government works, especially the need for compromise to get things done, it is unlikely that citizens would respond favorably. As researchers John Hibbing and Elizabeth Theiss-Morse discovered in their focus group studies, "Citizens . . . dislike being exposed to processes endemic to democratic government. People do not wish to see uncertainty, conflicting options, long debate, competing interests, confusion, bargaining, and compromised, imperfect solutions."[95] In other words, coverage that offered exclusively hard news, policy details, and sober analysis rather than at least some soft news, cynicism, scandals, and attack journalism, would probably not find much of an audience. Market forces also explain other aspects of the political media. The focus on campaigns as horse races, for example, reflects the kind of stories that the average voter finds interesting: who's ahead in the race, rather than the details of their campaign promises.[96] Similarly, the trend toward political coverage by soft news programs reflects the expectation that viewers want to see these stories covered by these programs to find out about the personalities rather than the facts.[97]

Conclusion

The news media are the primary source of public information about American politics and policy. The considerable controversy about how well the media fulfill this role reflects both the importance of the task and the interest many people have in shaping political coverage. The news media landscape is currently undergoing a massive transition, as the Internet supports an ever-growing variety of new information sources and fewer people rely on newspapers or television for news. Even so, these traditional sources remain the most popular for political information. Their coverage of politics is nowhere near perfect, but the media's imperfections are generally not the product of reporters and editors working to color coverage with biased views.

The topic of child abduction neatly illustrates the causes and consequences of media coverage of American politics. In running story after story on kidnappings, media sources are to a large extent responding to public demand for dramatic coverage. Americans might be better informed if the media ignored sensational stories and focused on the details of public policy, but lurid stories help attract and keep the audience that media companies need to stay in business.

The case of child abduction also illustrates that the average American consults only a tiny fraction of the information provided by the media. Americans tend to learn about politics as a by-product of other activities and focus on vivid, exciting stories regardless of their importance. Although this process makes sense given the many demands people face every day, it can lead them to some peculiar conclusions, even about well-reported events—for example, being highly worried about children being abducted when in fact this event is relatively rare. These shortcomings should not necessarily be read as an indictment of the news media or of the average American. Still, they do illustrate the fact that even though politics is everywhere, many Americans are not particularly interested in the political process and political outcomes.

Who are the media, and how do they cover politics?

- Since the Founding, politicians have understood that Americans learn about politics largely from the media.
- The Federal Communications Commission has regulated broadcast media since the 1930s. Recent decisions have removed many constraints from media companies, accelerating the process of concentration, and facilitating cross-ownership and the growth of media conglomerates.
- In the modern era, there are many different places to find political news, from daily newspapers to television, radio, magazines, and the Internet.
- Media sources differ in terms of their timeliness, breadth, and resources, which affects how each type of source covers politics.

How is the Internet affecting both the media business and what Americans know about politics?

- The growth of the Internet has vastly increased the amount of political information available to the average American, from official reports to expert analyses.

- The Internet has also lowered barriers to publication, making possible home-grown media sites where ordinary citizens post reports and videos of political events.
- The growth of the Internet has not led to a better-informed American public. Some explanations include the lack of Internet access for some Americans, the difficulty of finding information, the inconsistent reliability of information, and the lack of an incentive to seek out information in the first place.

How do reporters do their jobs?

- Media coverage of American politics reflects trade-offs between reporters who want complete, accurate information and sources who want favorable coverage.
- The government can stop publication of a press story only under extreme circumstances. However, if leakers are found, they often can be fired or prosecuted.
- People in government often try to stage events as a way of shaping press coverage.
- Reporters often promise to keep their sources anonymous, although this protection is not absolute because there is no federal shield law.

How do people use the media to learn about politics?

- Americans use a variety of sources to learn about politics, with newspapers and television news programs ranking as the most popular.
- There are clear generational differences in media usage patterns, with younger people relying more on the Internet and older people more likely to use newspapers.
- The amount of political knowledge that people have is related to the particular media sources they use. Surprisingly, people who get political information from late-night comedy shows and from talk radio programs are often very well informed about politics.

How does media coverage influence public opinion and policy?

- There is clear evidence of media effects; what citizens know or believe about politics often changes after they read or watch a political news story.

- The mechanisms of media influence include priming, filtering, slant, and framing. However, the evidence suggests that these phenomena are inherent to media coverage, rather than part of a conscious strategy to shape public opinion.
- There is no evidence of a general media bias toward either liberal or conservative views.

Why is media coverage of American politics the way it is?

- Media coverage of American politics often falls short of the ideal of providing a full and complete understanding of the issues facing the government and what elected officials have done (or not done) to address these concerns.
- Contemporary political coverage is marked by attack journalism and a focus on soft news and the horse race aspect of elections.
- Market forces that fuel media outlets' desire to attract the largest possible audience are the principal explanation for this lapse.

⑤ STUDENT STUDYSPACE

Find quizzes and other review material at wwnorton.com/studyspace.

CRITICAL THINKING

1. One argument against deregulating the media is that consolidation and the formation of media conglomerates would reduce the number of independent sources of information that are available to the average American. Based on the media sources that you and your friends use, do you agree or disagree with this argument? Why?

2. To what extent are journalists, editors, and the owners of media businesses to blame for the fact that the average American is often uninformed about and uninterested in politics?

3. What advice would you give to someone who wants to learn about American politics? What types of media sources should they seek, which ones should they avoid, and why?

KEY TERMS

attack journalism (p. 211)
broadcast media (p. 188)
by-product theory (p. 200)
concentration (p. 190)
cross-ownership (p. 190)
equal time provision (p. 189)
fairness doctrine (p. 189)
Federal Communications Commission (FCC) (p. 188)
filtering (p. 203)
framing (p. 203)

hard news (p. 211)
horse race (p. 211)
hostile media phenomenon (p. 211)
investigative journalists (p. 188)
leak (p. 197)
mainstream media (p. 192)
mass media (p. 187)
media conglomerates (p. 190)
media effects (p. 203)
news cycle (p. 192)
off the record (p. 197)

on background (p. 197)
penny press (p. 188)
press conference (p. 197)
prime time (p. 192)
priming (p. 203)
shield laws (p. 199)
slant (p. 203)
soft news (p. 211)
wire service (p. 188)
yellow journalism (p. 188)

SUGGESTED READING

Baum, Matthew A. *Soft News Goes to War: Public Opinion and American Foreign Policy in the New Media Age*. Princeton, NJ: Princeton University Press, 2003.

Braestrup, Peter. *How the American Press and Television Reported and Interpreted the Crisis of Tet 1968 in Vietnam*. New Haven, CT: Yale University Press, 1983.

Cappella, J. N., and K. H. Jamieson. *Spiral of Cynicism: The Press and the Public Good*. New York: Oxford University Press, 1997.

Davenport, Christian. *Media Bias, Perspective, and State Repression: The Black Panther Party*. New York: Cambridge University Press, 2010.

Iyengar, Shanto. *Is Anyone Responsible? How Television Frames Political Issues*. Chicago: University of Chicago Press, 1991.

Kuklinski, James H., and Lee Sigelman. "When Objectivity Is Not Objective." *The Journal of Politics* 54:3 (1992): 810–33.

Lippman, Walter. *Public Opinion*. 1922. Reprint, New York: Free Press, 1997.

Nelson, Thomas E., Rosalee A. Clawson, and Zoe M. Oxley. "Media Framing of a Civil Liberties Conflict and Its Effect on Tolerance." *American Political Science Review* 91 (1997): 567–83.

Norris, Pippa. *A Virtuous Circle? Political Communications in Post-Industrial Democracies*. New York: Cambridge University Press, 2000.

Patterson, Thomas. *Out of Order*. New York: Knopf, 1993.

Prior, Markus. *Post-Broadcast Democracy: How Media Choice Increases Inequality in Political Involvement and Polarizes Elections*. New York: Cambridge University Press, 2007.

Democratic senators meet with President Obama to discuss differences over health care reform. The health care debate clearly shows that conflict exists within as well as between political parties.

Political Parties

An important book on American political parties titled *Why Parties?* asks the question, What role do political parties play in a democracy?[1] The answer may seem obvious: by competing for control of the presidency, House, and Senate, and by offering different visions of what government should do, parties and their candidates embody some of the most fundamental conflicts that underlie American politics. Parties are everywhere in American politics—they help shape the way Americans think about candidates, policies, and vote decisions. Parties also impact American elections by recruiting candidates, paying for campaign ads, and mobilizing supporters. After the election, the winning party's candidates implement their vision, while the losers try to derail these efforts and develop an alternative vision that will attract support in the next election. In doing so, parties unify and mobilize disparate groups in society, simplify the choices facing voters, and bring efficiency and coherence to government policy making.

CONFLICT AND COMPROMISE
in American Politics

However, although political parties are a fundamental part of American politics, they often do not behave according to the job description given above. Consider the Democratic Party in 2009 and 2010: while the party appeared to be united during the 2008 campaign, things looked very different a year later. Even though the party held majorities in both houses of Congress, Democrats in Congress seemed to spend more time fighting with each other than with their Republican colleagues. Disagreements within the party over the details of health care reform, including whether insurance plans would pay for abortions and the existence of a government-operated health insurance plan, came close to destroying the reform effort—and required significant changes in the plan to build support among Democrats in Congress. Ultimately, health care reform was enacted, but only after herculean efforts to compromise differences among Democrats in Congress. Similarly, when President Obama announced plans to send additional troops to Afghanistan, at least as many Democrats complained as Republicans.

For example, Senator Russ Feingold, the Democrat from Wisconsin, voted for health care reform proposals early on but made it clear that his future support would depend on the details—he would not automatically support whatever the president or the party leaders proposed. And after President Obama submitted the Afghanistan proposal, Feingold responded, "Fundamentally I think increasing troops is not the answer, and I will be actively opposing it. I am confused why

BIG QUESTIONS

- ✪ How are parties organized in the United States? How has the American party system developed over time?

- ✪ What are the characteristics of modern American political parties?

- ✪ Why parties? What is the role of political parties in American politics?

- ✪ Why do minor parties exist? What influence do they have on American politics?

- ✪ Are political parties good for American democracy?

we would spend three years taking enormous loss and enormous cost in Afghanistan [while] we have other priorities that are greater." Many other Democratic senators and House members made similar statements throughout the congressional term about health care, Afghanistan, and other issues.

Clearly, then, conflict in American politics occurs within as well as between the Democratic and Republican parties—both in Congress and throughout the nation. Accordingly, one feature of our discussion of political parties will be to examine where these conflicts come from and how they shape what parties do and cannot do in modern American politics. As you will see, having a majority in the House and Senate—or even enough votes (sixty) to close off debate in the Senate—does not guarantee that the president, party leaders, or even the party's leaders in Congress can enact their legislative programs.

The conflict within the Democratic Party in 2009 and 2010 also illustrates that the question "Why parties?" does not have an obvious answer—even though political parties are everywhere in American politics. Most candidates for office run as major party nominees, and most Americans think of themselves as either Republicans or Democrats. Moreover, throughout American history, many of the major public policy conflicts have divided politicians and citizens according to party affiliation. However, though American political parties often have an obvious impact on elections and policy, the same organizations can look inept and irrelevant in many other situations. A good answer to "Why parties?" must explain this variation. Why are American political parties sometimes powerful and in other cases powerless? The answer developed in this chapter rests on the notion that political process matters: understanding what parties do (and cannot do) requires an appreciation of how they are organized, as well as the rules and regulations that shape the behavior of party leaders, politicians, and citizens.

What Are Political Parties?

Political parties are organizations that run candidates for political office and coordinate the actions of officials elected under the party banner. Looking around the world, we find many different kinds of parties. In many western European countries, the major political parties typically have millions of dues-paying members, and party leaders control what their elected officials do. In contrast, in many new democracies, candidates run as representatives of a party, but party leaders have no control over

▲ American political parties have three separate, independent parts; the party organization, represented by Tim Kaine, chair of the Democratic National Committee; the party in government, represented here by former Democratic House Speaker Nancy Pelosi and her leadership team; and the party in the electorate, exemplified by the crowd at a Barack Obama rally in May 2008.

what candidates say during the campaign or how they act in office. America's major political parties, the Republicans and the Democrats, lie somewhere between these extremes. Many Americans have a deep, enduring connection to one of these parties, and these organizations' actions affect both election returns and policy outcomes.

However, rather than being unified organizations with party leaders at the top, candidates and party workers in the middle, and citizen-members at the bottom, American political parties are best described as a collection of **nodes**—groups and individuals who share a party label but are under no obligation to work together.[2] For example, the Speaker of the House of Representatives is the leader of House members from her party, but she works independently from the party's national committee chair; neither one is in charge of the other. Similarly, while many Americans think of themselves as members of a political party, neither the Republicans nor the Democrats have formal membership. Someone who identifies with the Republican Party does not have to work for or give money to the party, or vote for its candidates.

In light of this defining characteristic of American political parties, scholars describe these organizations as comprising three separate and largely independent pieces:[3] The **party organization** involves the structure of national, state, and local parties, including party leaders and workers. The **party in government** is made up of the politicians who were elected as candidates of the party. And the **party in the electorate** includes all the citizens who identify with the party. As you will see, organization matters: the fact that American political parties are split into three parts has important implications for what they do and for their impact on American politics.

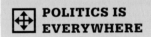 **POLITICS IS EVERYWHERE**

nodes Groups of people who belong to, are candidates of, or work for a political party but do not necessarily work together or hold similar policy preferences.

party organization A specific political party's leaders and workers at the national, state, and local levels.

party in government The group of officeholders who belong to a specific political party and were elected as candidates of that party.

party in the electorate The group of citizens who identify with a specific political party.

History of American Political Parties

The Republican and Democratic parties have existed for a long time—the Republicans since 1854 and the Democrats since even earlier in the 1800s. The nickname for the Republican Party is the G.O.P., or "Grand Old Party," a play on G.A.R.,

the Grand Army of the Republic, which refers to the Union Army in the Civil War. The symbol for the Republicans is an elephant; for the Democrats, a donkey. This section shows that at certain points in history both major American political parties have looked and acted very differently than they do today and that the contemporary parties do not resemble their historical counterparts.

Political scientists use the term **party system** to describe periods in which the major parties' names, their groups of supporters, and the issues dividing them are all constant. As shown in Table 7.1, there have been six party systems in America.[4] For each party system, the table gives the names of the two major parties, indicates which party dominated (won the most presidential elections or controlled Congress), and describes the principal issues dividing the parties.

▲ The symbols of the Republican and Democratic parties are an elephant and a donkey, respectively. They are often depicted feuding over government policy and refusing to compromise their differences.

THE FIRST PARTY SYSTEM, 1789–1828

Political parties formed soon after the Founding of the United States. The first American parties, the Federalists and the Democratic-Republicans, were primarily parties in government. As political scientist John Aldrich put it, members of Congress had ideas about what the new government should look like and what it should do, but they needed votes to translate these ideas into concrete policies.[5] The first parties were composed of like-minded legislators: Federalists wanted a strong central government and a national bank, and they favored assumption of state war debts by the national government; Democratic-Republicans took the opposite positions based on their preference for concentrating power at the state level. These political parties were quite different from their modern counterparts. In particular, there were no national party organizations, few citizens thought of themselves as party members, and candidates for office did not campaign as representatives of a political party.

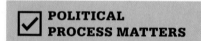

POLITICAL PROCESS MATTERS

party system A period in which the names of the major political parties, their supporters, and the issues dividing them remain relatively stable.

TABLE 7.1 AMERICAN PARTY SYSTEMS

Party System	Major Parties (dominant party in boldface)	Key Issues
First (1789–1828)	**Federalists**, Democratic-Republicans	Location of the capital, financial issues (e.g., national bank)
Second (1829–1856)	**Democrats**, Whigs	Tariffs (farmers vs. merchants), slavery
Third (1857–1892)	Democrats, **Republicans**	Slavery (pre–Civil War), Reconstruction (post–Civil War), industrialization
Fourth (1893–1932)	Democrats, **Republicans**	Industrialization, immigration
Fifth (1933–1968)	**Democrats**, Republicans	Size and scope of the federal government
Sixth (1969–present)	Democrats, Republicans (neither party is dominant)	Size and scope of the federal government (e.g., health care), civil rights, individual liberties (e.g., abortion), foreign policy

THE SECOND PARTY SYSTEM, 1829–1856

The second American party system began with the disintegration of the Federalist Party. Many Federalist legislators had opposed the War of 1812 and supported a politically unpopular pay raise for members of Congress.[6] Ultimately, Federalist politicians were either defeated for reelection or switched their party affiliation, eliminating the Federalist Party as a political force in American politics.

The demise of the Federalists gave way to the Era of Good Feelings, a decade-long period when there was only one political party, the Democratic-Republicans. Following the election of President Andrew Jackson in 1828, the organization that elected Jackson was transformed by him and by then-senator (later president) Martin Van Buren into the Democratic Party, the ancestor of the modern-day organization. At the same time, another new party, the Whigs, was formed, and the Democratic-Republican Party dissolved, with most of its politicians becoming Democrats.

The new Democratic Party embodied two important innovations. First, they cultivated electoral support as a way of strengthening the party's hold on power in Washington. The party built organizations at the state and local level to mobilize citizens to support the party's candidates. These efforts helped to bind citizens to the party, encouraging them to think of themselves as party members and creating the first American party in the electorate. The Democrats' second innovation was what Van Buren called the **party principle**, the idea that a party is not just a group of elected officials but an organization that exists apart from its candidates.[7] Jackson and Van Buren also created the **spoils system**, whereby individuals who worked for the party were rewarded with benefits such as federal government jobs.

THE THIRD PARTY SYSTEM, 1857–1892

The issue of slavery split the second party system. Most Democratic politicians and party officials either supported slavery outright or wanted to avoid debating the issue.[8] The Whig Party was split between politicians who agreed with the Democrats and abolitionists who wanted to end slavery. Ultimately, antislavery Whigs left the party and formed a new organization, the Republican Party, which also attracted antislavery Democrats. As the remaining Whig candidates began to have difficulty winning office against both Republican and Democratic opponents, Whig officeholders left the party and joined one of these two more powerful parties, dividing the country into a largely Republican Northeast, a largely Democratic South, and politically split midwestern and border states.[9]

The demise of the Whigs and the rise of the Republican Party illustrate that parties exist only because elites, politicians, party leaders, and activists want them to. The Republican Party was created by people such as Abraham Lincoln who wanted to abolish slavery, and many other politicians subsequently joined the party because of ambition: they believed their chances of winning political office were higher as a Republican than as a Whig or a Democrat.

THE FOURTH PARTY SYSTEM, 1893–1932

Although the Civil War settled the issue of slavery, it did not change the identity of the major American parties. In the postwar era, the Republicans and the Democrats remained the two prominent, national parties, and the same regional split persisted between these organizations. Slavery was no longer an issue, but the parties divided

party principle The idea that a political party exists as an organization distinct from its elected officials or party leaders.

spoils system The practice of rewarding party supporters with benefits like federal government positions.

▲ Although Democrat William Jennings Bryan's three presidential campaigns failed (in 1896, 1900, and 1908), his passionate fight for policies to aid farmers and working-class city dwellers helped to create the fourth party system.

on related concerns such as the withdrawal of the Union Army from southern states. At about the same time, the rapid growth of American cities and increased immigration raised new debate over the size and scope of the federal government: should it help farmers and rural residents, inhabitants of rapidly expanding cities, or neither group? A related concern was whether the federal government should regulate America's fast-growing industrial base.

The political parties took opposing positions on this issue, leading to a new party system. Democrats, led by three-time presidential candidate William Jennings Bryan, attempted to build a coalition of rural and urban voters by proposing a larger, more active federal government and other policies that would help these groups. Although Bryan was never elected president, the issues he stood for divided the major parties and defined the debate in Washington for more than a generation.

The move from the third to the fourth party system shows how American political parties reflect the basic divisions in society over what government should do. In the third party system, the parties were divided over slavery and, after the Civil War, the pace of Reconstruction. Once these issues were settled, politicians and party leaders found new issues to campaign on—partly because they cared about these issues and partly because taking these positions helped to attract votes and other forms of support to themselves and to their party.

THE FIFTH PARTY SYSTEM, 1933–1968

The fifth party system was born out of the Great Depression, a worldwide economic collapse. With millions unemployed, prices declining, and ever-growing soup lines of those unable to afford food becoming a common sight in major cities, the critical question was what the federal government should do to get things moving again.

▲ A key issue in the 1932 election between Republican Herbert Hoover (left) and Democrat Franklin Roosevelt (right) was how the federal government should respond to the Great Depression. Roosevelt proposed expanding programs to feed the poor and put people back to work, while Hoover favored letting the economy recover on its own and relying on state, local, and private charities to assist the poor. Roosevelt won and enacted his New Deal policies, which gave rise to the fifth party system.

Many Republican politicians, especially President Herbert Hoover, argued that conditions would improve given time and that government intervention would be costly and do little good. Democratic challenger Franklin Roosevelt proposed new government programs that would help people in need and spur economic growth. Roosevelt won the 1932 presidential election, and voters also elected many new Democrats to Congress. Together, the president and Congress enacted the New Deal, a series of federal programs designed to stimulate the national economy, help needy people, and impose a variety of new regulations.

The debate over the New Deal produced a lasting change in American politics: it brought together the **New Deal Coalition** of African Americans, Catholics, Jewish people, union members, and white southerners, who became strong supporters of Democratic candidates over the next generation.[10] This transformation also established the basic division between the Republican and Democratic parties that would persist for the rest of the twentieth century, with Democrats generally favoring a large federal government that takes an active role in managing the economy and regulating individual and corporate behavior, and Republicans believing that many of these programs should either be provided by state and local governments or kept entirely separate from government.

THE SIXTH PARTY SYSTEM, 1969–PRESENT

Changes in two areas drove the transition from the fifth to the sixth party system: political issues and technology. Beginning in the late 1940s, and more decisively during the 1960s, many Democratic candidates and party leaders, particularly outside the South, came out against the "separate but equal" system of racial discrimination in southern states and in favor of programs designed to ensure equal opportunity for minority citizens throughout the nation.

At the same time, Democratic politicians, particularly President Lyndon Johnson, argued for expanding the federal government into health care funding (in the form of the Medicare and Medicaid programs), antipoverty programs, education, and public works. Johnson called his plan the Great Society. Although some Republican politicians supported portions of the Great Society, particularly the civil rights reforms, there was considerable Republican opposition to expanding the role of government in society. This division, along with differences on new issues such as affirmative action, abortion rights, the war in Vietnam, and other foreign policy questions, produced a gradual but significant shift in the groups that identified with each party, with white southerners and some Catholics gradually moving to the Republican Party, and minorities, particularly African Americans, identifying more strongly as Democrats. Candidates (particularly those entering politics) either chose or changed their party affiliations to reflect the new party coalitions. By the late 1980s, all three elements of the Republican and Democratic parties (organization, government, and electorate) were much more like-minded than they had been a generation earlier.

The sixth party system also brought changes in the party organizations. Both the Republican and Democratic parties became **parties in service**, increasing their involvement in recruiting, training, fundraising, and campaigning for their party's congressional and presidential candidates.[11] This change was driven in part by the increased use of television (and later Internet-based) ads to mobilize supporters but also by increased competition in Congress over control of policy. Just as in the first party system, the parties in government became more involved in elections as a way of electing like-minded colleagues who would vote with them to enact their

New Deal Coalition The assemblage of groups who aligned with and supported the Democratic Party in support of New Deal policies during the fifth party system, including African Americans, Catholics, Jewish people, union members, and white southerners.

parties in service The role of the parties in recruiting, training, fundraising, and campaigning for congressional and presidential candidates. This aspect of party organization grew more prominent during the sixth party system.

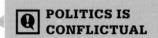

POLITICS IS CONFLICTUAL

realignment A change in the size or composition of the party coalitions or in the nature of the issues that divide the parties. Realignments typically occur within an election cycle or two, but they can also occur gradually over the course of a decade or longer.

crosscutting Issues that raise disagreements within a party coalition or between political parties about what government should do.

preferred policies. At the same time, the parties in government began to play a larger role in building policy compromises within and across the parties and working to shape legislative proceedings to enact these compromises into law.

REALIGNMENTS

Each party system is separated from the next by a **realignment**, a change in the issues that divide the people who identify with each party (the party in the electorate). These shifts may cause similar changes in the policy preferences of office-holders (the party in government) and among activists and party workers (the party organization). A realignment begins with the emergence of a new question or issue debate that captures the attention of large numbers of ordinary citizens, activists, and politicians.[12] In order to spur a realignment, the issue has to be **crosscutting**, meaning that within each party coalition, people disagree on what government should do.

In the case of the second party system (1829–1856), recall that the new issue was slavery.[13] Although most Democratic Party leaders and elected officials supported keeping slavery legal, the Whig Party was split between pro-slavery and abolitionist members. The result was the formation of a new political party, the Republicans, by antislavery Whigs and some Democrats. Within a few years, citizens and politicians moved to whichever party reflected their feelings about slavery, resulting in the realignment that yielded the third party system.

A realignment between the fifth party system (1933–1968) and the sixth (1969–present) produced the division between modern-day Republicans and Democrats.[14] The fifth party system was born during the Great Depression, when the parties were primarily divided by their positions on the appropriate size of the federal government and how much it should control the behavior of individuals and corporations, including issues such as the regulation of corporations, social welfare programs to help the poor and senior citizens, and public works. This conflict created the New Deal Coalition and gave the Democratic Party control of Congress and the presidency for most of the period between 1933 and 1969.

One of the new issues that drove the realignment between the fifth and sixth party systems was civil rights, and the question of whether the federal government should ensure that minority citizens were treated equally in all states, in terms of voting rights and access to public facilities.[15] Other new issues included the rights of people accused of crimes, the separation between church and state, freedom of speech, and abortion rights. Importantly, these volatile issues were crosscutting: within the Democratic and Republican parties, people disagreed about what government should do. Ultimately, the Democratic Party leaders and most of its politicians took a position generally favoring federal government intervention on these issues, whereas Republican Party officials and most Republican politicians generally favored a smaller, less active federal government.

In the electorate, these changes split the New Deal Coalition, with white southerners and evangelicals moving to the Republican Party, and African American voters becoming even stronger Democratic identifiers.[16] By the 1980s, the changes in the party coalitions and election outcomes were apparent, with control of Congress and the presidency divided between the two parties. Republicans gained House and Senate seats in southern states, and Democrats gained seats in the Northeast, West, and Southwest.[17] By early 2010, Republicans controlled only four Senate seats in the Northeast, with three of these held by the least conservative Republicans in the Senate, Olympia Snowe and Susan Collins of Maine and Scott Brown of Massachusetts.

Modern American Political Parties

In this section, we examine the contemporary Democratic and Republican parties in terms of their party organization, party in government, and party in the electorate. In doing so, we convey some basic information about the parties, show how each of their three distinct parts works, and consider some implications of this three-part structure.

THE PARTY ORGANIZATION

The principal body in each party organization is the **national committee**, which consists of representatives from state party organizations, usually one man and one woman per state. The state party organizations in turn are made up of some professional staff, plus thousands of party organizations at the county, city, and town levels. The job of these organizations is to run the day-to-day operations of the party, recruit candidates and supporters, raise money for future campaigns, and work to build a consensus on major issues of the day. (Of course, other groups in the party, as well as individual politicians, carry out similar tasks at the same time and not always in agreement with the national or state committees.)

Both parties also include a number of constituency groups (the Democrats' term) or teams (the Republicans' term), which are organizations within the party that work to attract the support of particular demographic groups considered likely to share the party's issue concerns—such as African Americans, Hispanics, people with strong religious beliefs, senior citizens, women, and many others—and assist in fund-raising.[18] In some cases, they also attempt to win over groups typically identified with the other party. For example, African Americans have long been strong supporters of Democratic candidates. Accordingly, the Democratic Party has a constituency group that informs African Americans about the party's candidates and works to convince these citizens to turn out and vote on Election Day. The Republican Party's corresponding constituency team works toward the opposite goal, trying to convince African Americans that Republican policies and candidates would better serve their interests.

Each party organization also includes a number of groups designed to gain support for or coordinate the efforts of particular individuals or politicians. These include the Democratic and the Republican Governors' Associations, the Young Democrats, the Young Republicans, and more specialized groups such as the Republican Lawyers' Organization or the Democratic Leadership Council (DLC), an organization of moderate Democratic politicians.[19] The parties use their college and youth organizations to help convince politically minded students to work for the party and its candidates. Karl Rove, former president George W. Bush's chief political adviser and a leading figure in organizing campaign activities among independent Republican organizations in 2010, got his start in politics as a leader of the Young Republicans.[20] Groups such as the Governors' Associations and the DLC hold meetings where elected officials discuss solutions to common problems and try to formulate joint strategies. People who work for a party organization carry out a wide range of tasks, from recruiting candidates and formulating political strategies to mobilizing citizens, fundraising, filling out campaign finance reports, researching opposing candidates and parties, and even developing Web sites for the party and its candidates.

While some of the national-level leadership positions in the major parties are paid, full-time jobs, national party committee slots and most state and local party positions are held by unpaid volunteers. Compared to the national party

POLITICS IS EVERYWHERE

national committee An American political party's principal organization, comprised of party representatives from each state.

organization, state and local party organizations are smaller, with proportionally more volunteers and fewer full-time staff. Local-level organizations, which are less common, are almost always staffed entirely by volunteers.

Many other groups, such as **political action committees (PACs)** or **527 organizations**, labor unions, and other interest groups and organizations, are loosely affiliated with one of the major parties. For example, the organization MoveOn.org typically supports Democratic candidates. Similar organizations on the Republican side include the Club for Growth, many evangelical groups, and Tea Party organizations that formed in 2009 and 2010. A number of blandly named organizations such as Americans for Job Security take advantage of a loophole in an obscure provision of the IRS code to legally solicit large, anonymous donations from corporate and individual contributors. Though these groups often favor one party over the other, they are not part of the party organization and do not always agree with the party's positions or support its candidates—in fact, many have to operate independently of the parties and their candidates in order to preserve their tax-exempt status. (For more details on campaign finance, see Chapters 8 [Elections] and 9 [Interest Groups].)

As this description suggests, the party organization has a fluid structure rather than a rigid hierarchy.[21] Individuals and groups work with a party's leaders and candidates when they share the same goals, but unless they are one of the relatively small number of paid party employees, they are under no obligation to do so (even paid party workers can, of course, quit rather than work for a candidate or a cause they oppose).

Party Brand Names The Republican and Democratic Party organizations have well-established **brand names**. Because the parties stand for different things, both in terms of their preferred government policies as well as their ideological leanings, the party names themselves become a shorthand way of providing information to voters about the parties' candidates.[22] Hearing the term "Democrat" or "Republican" calls to mind ideas about what kinds of positions the members of each party support, what kinds of candidates each party runs, and how these candidates will probably behave in office. Citizens can use these brand names as a voting cue to decide whom to vote for in an election. (See Chapter 8 for more information on voting cues.)

Figure 7.1 provides a general guide to the Democratic and Republican brand names. The figure reports voters' impressions of the two parties, measured on a liberal–conservative scale (1 = most liberal, 7 = most conservative). The average American sees significant differences between the parties, placing the Democratic Party toward the liberal end of the ideological spectrum and the Republican Party toward the conservative end. The specific positions vary over the years, but the parties are always far apart in the average American's mind. Moreover, as we show later, these differences in brand names reflect actual differences between Democratic and Republican politicians.

These data do not mean that the issue positions of American political parties are always distinct and easy to discern. Consider two of the biggest issues of President Barack Obama's first two years in office: health care reform and the war in Afghanistan. People in all three sections of the party—organization, government, and electorate—held a variety of positions on these matters. As a result, it would be difficult to say exactly where "the party" stood on these issues.

The Limits of the Party Organization The critical thing to understand about the Democratic and Republican Party organizations is that they are not hierarchies. No one person or group in charge determines what either organization does. Because the Republican National Committee (RNC) and Democratic National Committee (DNC) are organized in the same way, consider the example of Tim Kaine, chair

FIGURE 7.1   REPUBLICAN AND DEMOCRATIC BRAND NAMES

Over the last generation, Americans have consistently rated the Republican Party as more conservative than the Democratic Party. How might these perceptions shape candidates' decisions about which party to join and how to campaign?

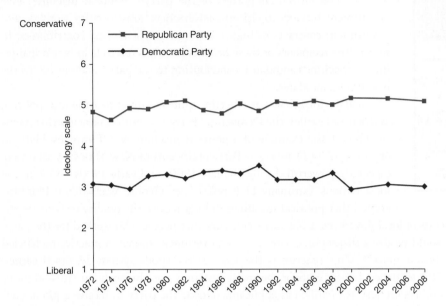

SOURCE: Calculated from the 1948–2004 American National Election Studies Cumulative Data File, available at www.electionstudies .org/studypages/cdf/cdf.htm.

of the DNC as of 2009. He has enormous influence over who works at the DNC. However, the party organization's issue positions are set not by Kaine's employees but by DNC members from all fifty states. Since individual committee members are appointed by their state party organizations, they do not owe their jobs to Kaine—and in fact, they can remove him from office if they like. If Kaine and the committee disagree, he can't force the committee members to do what he wants. In many cases, from civil rights proposals in the 1950s to health care reform in 2009, the Democratic Party has been internally divided, but party leaders have been unable to force a consensus.

The national party organization is also unable to force state and local parties to share its positions on issues or comply with other requests. State and local parties make their own decisions about state- and local-level candidates and issue positions. The national committee can cajole, it can threaten to withhold funds, and it can ask nicely. But if a state party organization, an independent group, or even an individual candidate disagrees with the national committee, there's little the national committee can do to force compliance.

An example of friction between the national committees and their respective state party organizations occurred during the spring and summer of 2007, as many state parties moved their states' presidential primaries and caucuses earlier in the primary season, such that one month into the five-month primary season, most states' delegates to the parties' presidential nominating conventions would already be committed to a candidate.[23] The Republican and Democratic national committees preferred a drawn-out process, in which many populous states with large numbers of delegates, such as New York and California, would not hold their primary or caucus until May or June. Both party organizations penalized states such as Florida and Michigan that held their primaries early without authorization by halving those

▲ The Tammany Hall political machine, depicted here as a rotund version of one of its leaders, William "Boss" Tweed, controlled New York City politics for most of the nineteenth and early twentieth centuries. Its strategy was "honest graft," rewarding party workers, contributors, and voters for their efforts to keep the machine's candidates in office.

states' convention delegations. But they were powerless to stop state party organizations from changing their primary dates in the first place.

Political Machines A political machine is a party organization built around the goal of gaining political power to enrich party leaders, party workers, and citizen supporters of the party.[24] Political machines give government services to citizens, government jobs to party workers, and government contracts to higher-level party officials and contributors. In return, the recipients of these benefits are expected to help by campaigning for machine candidates, contributing to the party, and voting for the machine's candidates.

Such patronage was at one time quite common in American politics; as discussed earlier, the Democratic Party was built on exactly this premise. One classic example of a political machine was Tammany Hall, an organization of Democratic Party politicians in New York City who were especially powerful during the late 1800s and early 1900s.[25] One of the most famous Tammany Hall politicians, George Washington Plunkitt, argued that political machines did not reduce the quality or increase the costs of local government but just made sure that people who worked for the party would receive a disproportionate share of government money, a practice he labeled "honest graft."[26] This practice is the same as the spoils system discussed earlier. At first glance, honest graft or the spoils system is not obviously hurtful—if party workers are just as qualified as applicants outside the party to receive a job or contract, then the spoils system looks a lot like giving a preference to former members of your college fraternity or sorority under the same conditions. Of course, there are numerous cases of political machines where the graft was not honest at all, where people who worked for the machine were incompetent or were given no-show jobs or contracts at inflated prices.

Although political machines were once common in cities and towns, they declined as a result of civil service legislation enacted in the 1890s, the expansion of government services to the poor and lower middle class, and an increase in the number of nonpartisan elections (in which candidates do not have party labels). American political parties at the national level have never operated as political machines. Major party leaders do not control anywhere near the amount of resources they would need if they wanted to use a machine-like system to attract large numbers of workers to their organizations or to win support for candidates by providing services to citizens.

THE PARTY IN GOVERNMENT

The party in government consists of elected officials holding national, state, and local offices who took office as candidates of a particular party. They are the public face of the party, somewhat like the players on a sports team. Though players are only one part of a sports franchise—along with owners, coaches, trainers, and support staff—their identities are what most people call to mind when they think of the team. Because the party in government is comprised of officeholders, it has a direct impact on government policy. Members of the party organization can recruit candidates, write platforms, and pay for campaign ads, but only those who win elections—the party in government—serve as members of Congress or as executive officials and actually propose, debate, vote on, and sign the legislation that determines what government does.

The party in government is largely independent of the party organization. Some elected officials or former elected officials serve as members of their party's national committee or hold a position in a state or local organization, but most American

political machine An unofficial patronage system within a political party that seeks to gain political power and government contracts, jobs, and other benefits for party leaders, workers, and supporters.

The "Dime's Worth of Difference" between Republicans and Democrats

George Wallace, a southern governor and independent candidate for president in 1968, coined a classic phrase when he said of his rivals, Democrat Hubert Humphrey and Republican Richard Nixon, that there was "not a dime's worth of difference" between them—meaning that Wallace was the only candidate offering something different to the electorate.[a]

Given all the data in this chapter that show disagreements between Republicans and Democrats, Wallace's claim may seem obsolete, something no one could conceivably argue in the modern era. Republicans and Democrats in Congress disagree on many issues, from raising the minimum wage to national defense policy. High levels of disagreement also exist among Republican and Democratic identifiers in the electorate. How could anyone say that the parties stand for the same things?

Oddly enough, people do. It is easy to find people and organizations who echo Wallace's claim. Ralph Nader, the Green Party presidential nominee in 2000 and an independent candidate in 2004 and 2008, argued that the major parties had "towering similarities," and that while some differences might exist, Nader believed that Democrats too often let the Republican view prevail.[b]

The Libertarian Party's Web site argues that Republican and Democratic politicians are united in their support for a large, expensive federal government and that any differences in their positions are in the details.[c] The Green Party's site contrasts its positions on a series of issues with those of the Republicans and the Democrats, which the Green Party views as nearly identical.[d] And an article on the Constitution Party's Web site refers to the major parties as "Demopublicans" and "Republicrats."[e] The

George Wallace ran for president in 1968 as an independent candidate. Wallace, whose platform included opposition to desegregation, claimed that there was "not a dime's worth of difference" between the major parties.

same article argued that George Wallace's "dime's worth of difference" had narrowed in recent years to a nickel or even a penny.

Are these individuals and organizations right about the similarities between Republicans and Democrats? And if they are, why do most Americans see real differences between the parties? Do minor parties have a keener sense of the American political system than other people? No, not in the main. As we argue in Chapter 8, Elections, the imperatives of attracting support and winning elections can lead candidates to campaign on similar issue positions, not because they want to sound alike but because they are trying to win support from the same voters—those who hold largely moderate preferences in their district or state. Even so, the Chapter 8 data on campaign platforms show that in many cases, there are clear differences between Republican and Democratic candidates.

Moreover, people who argue that the major parties in America are quite similar, if not the same, tend to hold relatively

extreme positions on most issues. The Constitution Party, for example, advocates an end to government civil service regulations; a ban on compulsory school attendance laws; withdrawal of the United States from the United Nations and all international trade agreements; abolishing foreign aid, the income tax, the Internal Revenue Service, and all federal welfare programs; and repealing all campaign finance legislation, the Endangered Species Act, and federal firearms regulations.[f]

These positions are extreme, not in the sense of being silly or dangerous, but in the sense that relatively few Americans share the Constitution Party's agenda. The Constitution Party's presidential candidate received very few votes in the 2008 election, and it has elected very few candidates to political office. Although the Greens, Libertarians, and Ralph Nader do not agree with the Constitution Party's positions, many aspects of their agendas are also extreme.

Even so, it makes sense that someone who supported one of these organizations would believe that Republicans and Democrats agree on most things. Given the large distance between the Constitution Party's positions and those espoused by its major party rivals, the distance between the two major parties may seem small indeed to Constitution Party members. (The same argument could be made about Wallace and his supporters a generation ago.) But for most Americans, whose preferences on most issues are relatively moderate and clustered around the Republican and Democratic brand names, the differences between the major parties are substantial. Put another way, the differences in platforms and brand names of the major American political parties are not as large as they could be—but from the perspective of the average American, there is much more than a dime's worth of difference. ∎

caucus (congressional) The organization of Democrats within the House and Senate that meets to discuss and debate the party's positions on various issues in order to reach a consensus and to assign leadership positions.

conference The organization of Republicans within the House and Senate that meets to discuss and debate the party's positions on various issues in order to reach a consensus and to assign leadership positions.

polarized The alignment of both parties' members with their own party's issues and priorities, with little crossover support for the other party's goals.

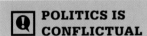

POLITICS IS CONFLICTUAL

politicians go through their entire political careers without holding a position in their party organization.

The Democratic and Republican parties in government in the House and Senate are organized around working groups—Democrats call theirs a **caucus**, and Republicans have a **conference**. The party caucus or conference serves as a forum for debate, compromise, and strategizing among a party's elected officials. For example, throughout 2009, members of the House Democratic Caucus held numerous meetings to decide their group's position on health care reform, including whether there would be a government-managed "public option" for coverage and, if so, how the new program would be paid for.[27] The Democrats' strategy for addressing these proposals reflected the consensus reached in the caucus. Each party's caucus or conference also meets to decide legislative committee assignments, leadership positions on committees, and leadership positions within the caucus or conference.[28] Caucus or conference leaders also serve as spokespeople for their respective parties, particularly when the president is from the other party. The party in government also contains elements of the party organization, such as groups that recruit and support candidates for political office. These are the Democratic Congressional Campaign Committee (DCCC), Democratic Senatorial Campaign Committee (DSCC), National Republican Senatorial Committee (NRSC), and the National Republican Congressional Committee (NRCC).

The modern Congress is **polarized**: in both the House and the Senate, Republicans and Democrats hold different views on government policy. Figure 7.2 compares legislators on the basis of their ideology, or their general feelings about government policy, as measured by a liberal–conservative scale, for two House sessions, the contemporary 110th House (served 2007–2009) and the 83rd House of almost sixty years ago (served 1953–1955). In the plots, a legislator's ideology is measured on the left–right scale using NOMINATE scores, which measure legislators' ideologies based on their roll call votes.[29]

These graphs tell us two things. First, over the last sixty years, the magnitude of ideological differences between the parties in Congress has increased. In the 83rd House, there was some overlap between the positions of Democrats and Republicans, but it had nearly disappeared by the 110th House.[30] These data confirm that disagreements between the parties reflect very real differences about what government should be doing. (For more details on why parties moved about during the years between the 83rd and 110th Congresses, see the What Do Political Scientists Do? box later in this chapter.)

Of course, the fact that Democrats and Republicans in Congress often disagree does not mean that compromise is impossible. In 2009, for example, even as the parties clashed over health care, the wars in Afghanistan and Iraq, and economic policy, they managed to find agreement on legislation that placed limits on fees and interest rates charged by credit card issuers and loosened rules on carrying concealed firearms in national parks.[31]

There are also a few questions on which Democrats and Republicans find themselves in outright agreement. In spring 2007, during the controversy surrounding the firing of several U.S. attorneys by the Justice Department, senators repealed the provision of the U.S. Code that allowed U.S. attorneys to be appointed without a Senate vote (this provision had been included in 2006 as part of the reauthorization of the Patriot Act).[32] The vote on this measure was 94 to 2; that is, virtually all senators, Republicans and Democrats alike, voted for repeal.

The second fact that Figure 7.2 reveals is that both parties in government include a heterogeneous mixture of ideologies, not a homogenous or uniform consensus opinion. In the 83rd House plot, for example, Democrats vary from the relatively liberal left end of the scale to the moderate (middle) and even somewhat conservative right side. Democrats in the 110th House were, on average, more

FIGURE 7.2 **IDEOLOGY OF THE PARTIES IN GOVERNMENT: HOUSE OF REPRESENTATIVES, 1952 AND 2006**

Over the last several decades, ideological differences between Democrats and Republicans in Congress have increased significantly. However, even in the 110th House, both parties still included a wide range of views. In light of these data, would you expect more or less partisan conflict in the modern Congress than there was in the early 1950s? According to these data, would you expect House members in each party to agree on what policies to pursue?

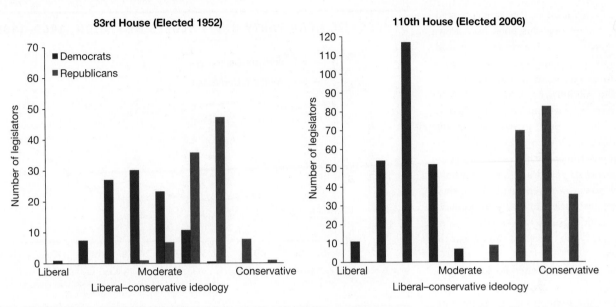

SOURCE: Calculated from Royce Carroll, Jeff Lewis, James Lo, Nolan McCarty, Keith Poole, and Howard Rosenthal, "DW-NOMINATE Scores with Bootstrapped Standard Errors," January 23, 2009, available at www.voteview.com/dwnomin.htm.

liberal than their colleagues were in the 83rd, but a wide range of ideologies were still represented in the Democratic caucus. The same is true for Republicans, who leaned in the conservative direction in both the 110th and the 83rd House.

The heterogeneity of the party in government can create situations where a caucus or conference is divided on a policy question. Compromise within a party caucus is not inevitable—even though legislators share a party label, they may not be able to find common ground. In the last few years, congressional Democrats have been divided on issues such as funding for the wars in Iraq and Afghanistan, health care reform, and plans for economic stimulus. These issues have also divided congressional Republicans, although they usually voted as a block against Democratic-sponsored proposals. On the Republican side, consider the debate over immigration reform. Before the 2006 midterm elections, Republicans held majorities in the House and the Senate, so if they could agree on a proposal, they had enough votes to enact it. Furthermore, since President Bush was a Republican, he would likely sign the proposal into law. However, some Republicans wanted to stiffen criminal penalties against illegal immigrants, but others, including President Bush, favored allowing illegal immigrants to eventually gain citizenship.[33] Ultimately, Republicans in the Senate enacted a reform proposal with some Democratic support, but House Republicans were unable to come to an agreement.[34]

THE PARTY IN THE ELECTORATE

The party in the electorate consists of citizens who identify with a particular political party. Most Americans say they are either Democrats or Republicans, although the percentage has declined over the last two generations. **Party identification**

party identification (party ID) A citizen's loyalty to a specific political party.

"Something's Happening Here"

Most college students reading this book have grown up in a partisan era, with Republicans and Democrats in Congress disagreeing on many issues and continuously battling each other to determine government policy. Accordingly, this chapter spends considerable time discussing the polarization of the parties in government, what party leaders do, how parties set agendas, and the significant role of parties in government. All of these concepts are critical to describing contemporary political parties and how they operate inside Washington and throughout the country.

You may be surprised to learn, then, that a generation ago most political scientists saw the Republican and Democratic parties as being almost irrelevant to congressional proceedings. As one put it in 1974, "No theoretical treatment of the United States Congress that posits parties as analytic units will go very far."[a] Most studies of Congress focused on individual members and their pursuit of reelection and whatever policy goals they happened to hold. The parties in government existed, but their influence was thought to be limited to relatively minor areas, and party

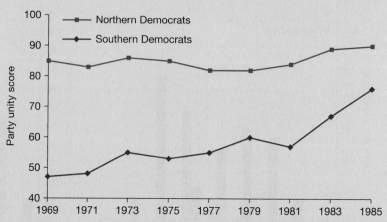

DEMOCRATIC MEAN PARTY UNITY SCORES BY REGION, 1969–1985

SOURCE: David W. Rohde, "'Something's Happening Here: What It Is Ain't Exactly Clear': Southern Democrats in the House of Representatives," in *Home Style and Washington Work*, Morris Fiorina and David W. Rohde, eds. (Ann Arbor, MI: University of Michigan Press, 1989).

leaders were relatively powerless servants of their caucus. One of the principal reasons for the irrelevancy of political parties was a split in the Democratic caucus between relatively liberal northern Democrats and conservative southern Democrats. Because these legislators could agree on little, neither group wanted to let the party have the power to encourage or even force a compromise.

Although this view was accurate for political parties as they existed in the 1950s and 1960s, we now know that somewhere in the late 1970s, things began to change. Members of Congress began to have new ideas about what they wanted their parties in government to do. The first person to provide evidence of the changing role of the party in government in the U.S. Congress was political scientist David Rohde, then

---

activists People who dedicate their time, effort, and money to supporting a political party or particular candidates.

running tally A frequently updated mental record that a person uses to incorporate new information, like the information that leads a citizen to identify with a particular political party.

(party ID) is a critical variable in understanding votes and other forms of political participation.

Party identification is different from formal membership in a political party. Although the Republicans and the Democrats have Web sites where people can sign up to receive e-mail alerts and to contribute to party causes, joining a party does not give a citizen any direct influence over what the party does. Day-to-day decisions are made by party leaders and the candidates themselves. Party leaders and candidates often heed citizens' demands, but there is no requirement that they do so. Real participation in party operations is open to citizens who become **activists** by working for a party organization or one of its candidates. Activists' contributions vary from stuffing envelopes to helping out with a phone bank, being a delegate to a party convention, attending campaign rallies, or campaigning door-to-door. Relatively few Americans are activists, perhaps 5 percent of the population.

a professor at Michigan State University and now at Duke University. He knew that his results would be surprising to many political scientists, so he chose the title of his 1986 paper carefully: "'Something's Happening Here, What It Is Ain't Exactly Clear': Southern Democrats in the House of Representatives."[b]

Rohde's paper uncovered two important changes in congressional voting. Looking at data from the early 1980s, he found a sharp increase in the percentage of votes on legislative proposals in the House that were party unity votes (a vote in which a majority of one party's legislators vote one way on a proposal while a majority of legislators from the other party votes the opposite way—that is, a majority of Democrats on one side and a majority of Republicans on the other). The percentage of party unity votes increased from 37 percent in 1981 to 55 percent in 1986. Moreover, Democrats (who were the majority party in the House at the time) were more and more likely to win on party unity votes. In other words, over this short period, the parties were increasingly likely to disagree on legislative proposals, and Democrats were more likely to win when these disagreements occurred. Why was this change happening?

Rohde's additional analysis of the data revealed an important change in the composition of the Democratic caucus: the long-standing divide between northern and southern Democrats in Congress was gradually disappearing. As the figure shows, northern Democrats always had high party unity scores—if party majorities disagreed, these legislators were likely to be voting with their fellow Democrats. For southern Democrats, the pattern was different. In 1969, the average southern Democrat voted with his or her party on a party unity vote only 47 percent of the time. The rest of the time, these legislators crossed party lines to vote with Republicans. By 1985, however, southern Democrats had a much higher average party unity score of 76, not much different than the average score for northern Democrats of 90.

To congressional scholars, these differences were a clear signal that the old descriptions of the parties in Congress were no longer accurate. Northern and southern Democrats were more likely to vote together on legislative proposals. And the higher percentage of party unity votes, along with more victories for Democrats on these votes, suggested that Democratic Party leaders were having an easier time finding legislative compromises that could unite their caucus, and using their agenda powers to make sure these proposals came to a vote and were successfully enacted.

In the twenty years since Rohde's paper was published, congressional scholars (including Rohde) have confirmed virtually all of the elements of his argument. We now know that the trends he identified were occurring because voters throughout the country (but especially in the South) were sorting themselves by party, so that liberals became Democrats and conservatives became Republicans. Politicians, in turn, sorted themselves by party in the same way. The result was that the party caucuses in Congress became more and more distinct from each other. Within each caucus, members were more likely to agree with each other on policy priorities and disagree with members of the other party. The result is a polarized Congress where lawmakers from the same party cooperate to shape policy outcomes. (See the What Do Political Scientists Do? box in Chapter 10 for more on current research into polarization in Congress.)

Rohde's work tells us that the disagreements between the parties in the modern Congress is not an accident or something invented by party leaders for political gain. Rather, these differences reflect sincere disagreements between Republican and Democratic legislators about what government should be doing—disagreements that arise from the policy concerns held by individual members and from differences in the demands expressed in the states and districts these legislators are elected to represent. Moreover, strong congressional parties are not inevitable. After all, a generation ago, these cross-party differences did not exist. But once Democrats and Republicans began to disagree, they naturally turned to the parties in government as the vehicles to achieve their policy goals. ■

Watch a video clip of David Rohde discussing this topic at wwnorton .com/studyspace.

Early theories of party identification described it as a deeply felt attachment to a party that was acquired early in life from parents, friends, and political events, and was generally unaffected by subsequent events.[35] Further work showed that party ID is a **running tally** or an evaluation that takes account of new information.[36] Thus, when someone says they identify with the Republican Party, they are saying that based on what they have seen in American politics, they like Republican candidates more than Democratic candidates—that they prefer the ideas and positions suggested by the Republicans' brand name or how Republicans behave in office. New information tends to reinforce existing loyalties, which is why Chapter 5, Public Opinion, described party identification as generally stable. However, citizens can revise their party identification when circumstances warrant.

Consider Figure 7.3, which shows the percentage of people who identified themselves as Republicans in Pew Research Center surveys taken during 2003 and 2004.

▼ Activist volunteers undertake most of the one-on-one efforts to mobilize support for a party and its candidates.

FIGURE 7.3 REPUBLICAN PARTY IDENTIFICATION, 2003–2004

Citizen party identification is sensitive to events: during 2003 and 2004, the percentage of Republican identifiers increased given positive events in the Iraq war and decreased given negative events. How would you expect party identification to be influenced by the state of the American economy in recent years?

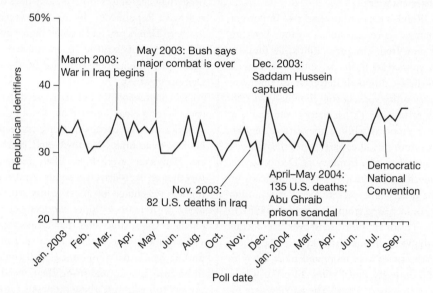

SOURCE: Pew Research Center, "Party Affiliation: What It Is and Is Not," September 23, 2004, available at http://people-press.org/commentary/pdf/97.pdf.

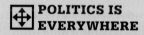

POLITICS IS EVERYWHERE

The figure also labels significant political events during that period, such as the 2004 Democratic National Convention, the beginning of the Iraq war, and the capture of former Iraqi president Saddam Hussein. The percentage of people surveyed who identified as Republicans varied from below 30 percent to nearly 40 percent. Good news in Iraq, such as the capture of Hussein, caused more people to identify with the Republican Party. Conversely, bad news about the war, such as the deaths of eighty-two American troops during a particularly violent month in Iraq, generated decreases. This pattern makes sense given that Republicans controlled Congress and the presidency during this time and so were seen as responsible for the conduct of the war. Some citizens used events in Iraq to update their running tally on the Republican Party, which in turn caused some of them to switch their party affiliation.

Figure 7.4 gives data on party identification in America over the last sixty years. The first plot shows that the Democratic Party had a considerable advantage in terms of the number of citizens identifying with the party from the 1930s until the late 1980s. During the 1970s, nearly half of adults identified with the Democratic Party, and only about 20 percent identified with the Republicans. During the 1990s, the percentage of Democratic identifiers decreased significantly and the percentage of Republican identifiers increased slightly, to the point that in 2002 the parties had roughly the same percentage of identifiers.[37] However, beginning in 2003 the Democrats again opened up a significant advantage in terms of identifiers although the difference has narrowed in recent years. The two lines in Figure 7.4 do not add up to 100 percent, and the difference represents the percentage of independent voters who do not identify with either party. Just like the percentages of Republican and Democratic identifiers, the percentage of independents fluctuates over time; not long ago, it climbed to nearly 40 percent.

FIGURE 7.4 **PARTY IDENTIFICATION TRENDS AMONG AMERICAN VOTERS**

In terms of party identification, the parties have moved from rough parity in the 1930s and 1940s, to a period of Democratic advantage that lasted from the 1950s to the 1980s. Recently, Democrats appear to have opened up another advantage. What events might have caused these changes in party identification?

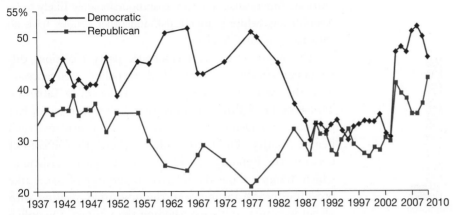

SOURCE: Pew Research Center, "With Growing Awareness of Census, Most Ready to Fill Out Forms," March 16, 2010, available at http://people-press.org/report/596/census-forms.

Some early analyses concluded that independents were unaffiliated with a party because they were in the process of shifting their identification from one party to the other.[38] Others saw independents as evidence of **dealignment**—a sign that more and more people regard the parties as irrelevant to their view of politics and their vote decisions.[39] The rise in the number of independents was also seen as an indication that Americans were becoming more politically savvy, learning more about candidates and not always blindly voting for the same party.[40]

More recent work has modified these findings. The percentage of independent voters has remained relatively constant over the last twenty years. Moreover, many people who identify as independents actually have some weak attachment to one of the major political parties.[41] And although some independents are angry about or alienated from politics, most of them simply do not find the parties attractive enough to identify with either of them.[42] In any case, independents are not necessarily better informed about candidates, parties, or government policy than party identifiers. One of the few identifiable differences is that independents' vote decisions are more sensitive to things that happen during political campaigns.[43]

Looking more closely at vote decisions, Figure 7.5 shows how Democrats, Republicans, and independents voted in the 2008 presidential election. As you can see, most Democrats voted for Barack Obama, the Democratic nominee, most Republicans voted for John McCain, the Republican nominee, and independent voters slightly favored Obama, but by a much smaller margin than Democrats did. Simply put, if you are trying to predict how someone will vote, the most important thing to know is their party identification.[44] Party ID shapes vote decisions even after we control for other factors. For example, economic issues dominated the 2008 election. Sixty percent of the people who were "very worried about economic conditions" voted for Barack Obama. However, among those who were concerned about the economy, the odds of voting for Obama increased if the voter was a Democrat.[45] Party ID also influences other kinds of political behavior. People whose identification is strong are

dealignment A decline in the percentage of citizens who identify with one of the major parties, usually over the course of a decade or longer.

FIGURE 7.5

THE IMPACT OF PARTY IDENTIFICATION ON VOTE DECISIONS IN THE 2008 PRESIDENTIAL ELECTION

Americans are much more likely to vote for candidates who share their party affiliation. What does this relationship tell us about the impact of campaign events (including speeches, debates, and gaffes) on vote decisions?

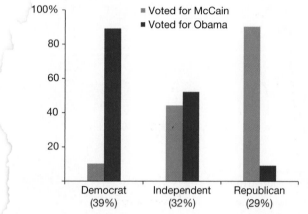

SOURCE: CNN Election Center, available at www.CNN.com/ELECTION/2008/results/polls/#val=USP00p1.

more likely to work for the party or to make a contribution compared to people with weak party identification.[46]

Party Coalitions Data on party ID allow scholars to identify the **party coalitions**, or groups of citizens who identify with each party. Table 7.2 shows the contemporary Democratic and Republican party coalitions. As you can see, some groups are disproportionately likely to identify as Democrats (African Americans), some are disproportionately likely to be Republicans (white evangelicals), and other groups have no clear favorite party (males).

The Republican and Democratic party coalitions differ systematically in terms of their policy preferences—what they want government to do—as shown in Table 7.3. The second and third columns give the percentages of Republican and Democratic identifiers who considered each item a priority. The fourth column shows the differences between the Republican and Democratic party coalitions, which disagree about the relative importance of issues like providing health insurance to the uninsured, dealing with global warming, and strengthening the military. On only a few issues are the percentages in both parties who consider the matter a priority nearly the same, such as reducing the

TABLE 7.2

THE PARTY COALITIONS

Many groups, such as African Americans and white evangelicals, are much more likely to affiliate with one party rather than the other. What are the implications of these differences for the positions taken by each party's candidates?

		Democratic/ Lean Democratic	Republican/ Lean Republican
Gender	Male	46%	43%
	Female	56	33
Age	18–29	58%	33%
	30+	50	39
Race	White	46%	43%
	African American	84	8
Region	Northeast	54%	34%
	Midwest	50	38
	South	49	40
	West	83	36
Education	No college	54%	34%
	Some college	50	39
	College graduate	50	46
Religion	White evangelical	30%	60%
	White mainline Protestant	46	42
	White Catholic	48	40
	Unaffiliated/agnostic	65	23

SOURCE: Pew Research Center, "Gen Dems: The Party's Advantage among Young Voters Widens," April 28, 2008, available at http://pewresearch.org/pubs/813/gen-dems.

party coalitions The groups that identify with a political party, usually described in demographic terms such as African American Democrats or evangelical Republicans.

TABLE 7.3 **ISSUE DIFFERENCES BETWEEN THE REPUBLICAN AND DEMOCRATIC PARTIES IN THE ELECTORATE**

The Republican and Democratic Party coalitions have different priorities on many issues, from health care reform to strengthening the military—and on a few issues their differences are small, such as trade and the budget deficit. Do these differences make sense in light of each party's "brand name"?

Percentage Considering Each as a "Top Priority"	Republicans	Democrats	Republican– Democratic Difference
Providing health insurance to uninsured	28%	66%	−38
Protecting the environment	20	54	−34
Dealing with global warming	16	45	−29
Dealing with problems of poverty	34	62	−28
Reducing health care costs	45	71	−26
Improving educational system	46	71	−25
Improving job situation	72	89	−17
Securing Medicare	48	65	−17
Reducing middle-class taxes	31	48	−17
Dealing with energy problems	51	66	−15
Securing Social Security	60	66	−6
Reducing crime	41	47	−6
Strengthening nation's economy	83	88	−5
Dealing with global trade	28	33	−5
Reducing budget deficit	51	52	−1
Dealing with moral breakdown	50	46	+4
Reducing influence of lobbyists	37	30	+7
Defending against terrorism	79	71	+8
Dealing with illegal immigration	46	34	+12
Strengthening the military	64	38	+26

SOURCE: Pew Research Center, "Economy, Jobs Trump All Other Policy Priorities in 2009," January 22, 2009, available at http://people-press.org/reports/pdf/485.pdf (accessed 12/16/09).

budget deficit. Though the structure of the questions (asking about priorities rather than specific proposals) overstates the level of disagreement between Republicans and Democrats, these data demonstrate that party labels are meaningful: if you know someone is a Republican (or a Democrat), this information tells you something about what she probably wants government to do, and how she will likely vote in the next election.

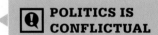
POLITICS IS CONFLICTUAL

The Role of Political Parties in American Politics

This section explains what political parties do in American politics, from contesting elections to building consensus across branches of government. It is important to remember, though, that these activities are not necessarily coordinated. Candidates

primary A ballot vote in which citizens select a party's nominee for the general election.

caucus (electoral) A local meeting in which party members select a party's nominee for the general election.

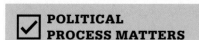
POLITICAL PROCESS MATTERS

and groups at different levels of a party organization may work together, refuse to cooperate, or even actively oppose each other's efforts.

CONTESTING ELECTIONS

In modern American politics, virtually everyone elected to a state or national political office is either a Republican or a Democrat. In the 111th Congress, elected in 2008, there were only two independent senators (Bernie Sanders of Vermont and Joe Lieberman of Connecticut) and no independent House members. In fall 2010, forty-nine of fifty states' governors were either Democrats or Republicans, and of more than 7,300 state legislators, very few were independents or minor-party candidates.

Recruiting and Nominating Candidates Actions taken inside party organizations shape citizens' choices on Election Day. Historically, the recruitment of candidates was left up to local party organizations. But the process has become much more systematic, with national party leaders playing a central role in finding and recruiting candidates—and often promising those candidates help assembling a staff, organizing a campaign, and raising money.[47]

After the 2004 election, for example, members of the Democratic House and Senate Campaign Committees believed that the party could win seats in the 2006 midterms by running candidates with military experience who supported changing the U.S. policy on Iraq.[48] They began a two-year process of finding retired military men and women, persuading them to run, and training them in the art of campaigning (none had ever run for political office). In all, Democrats recruited sixty-one military veterans to run for two Senate and fifty-nine House seats, including Vietnam War veteran James Webb, who had served as President Ronald Reagan's secretary of the Navy, and retired admiral Joe Sestak.[49] The Democrats' strategy proved very effective in the 2006 midterms.

For all of these efforts, parties do not control who runs in House or Senate races. In most states, candidates for these offices are selected in a **primary** election or a **caucus**, in which they compete for a particular party's spot on the ballot. (A few state parties use conventions to select candidates.) Nuts and Bolts 7.1 further explains these different ways that the parties select candidates.

Most party leaders remain neutral during the primaries and then support whoever wins the general election. An exception occurred during the 2010 Alaska Republican Senate primary, where incumbent Lisa Murkowski was defeated by Tea Party nominee Joe Miller. The outcome split national and state party officials—some stayed neutral, while others endorsed one of the two candidates. Ultimately, Murkowski won the election as a write-in candidate.

Running as a party's nominee is almost always the easiest way to get on the general election ballot. Some states give the Republican and Democratic nominees an automatic spot on the ballot; and even in states that don't automatically allocate ballot slots this way, the requirements for the major parties to get a candidate on the ballot are much less onerous than those for minor parties and independents. For example, in California, a party and its candidates automatically qualify for a position on the ballot if any of the party's candidates for statewide office received more than 2 percent of the vote in the previous election. Independent candidates need to file petitions with more than 150,000 signatures to get on the ballot without a major-party label—an expensive, time-consuming task.[50] These advantages help explain why virtually all prominent candidates for Congress and the presidency run

Types of Primaries and Caucuses

PRIMARY ELECTION	An election in which voters choose the major party nominees for political office, who subsequently compete in a general election.
Closed primary	A primary election system in which only registered party members can vote in their party's primary.
Nonpartisan primary	A primary election system in which candidates from both parties are listed on the same primary ballot. Following a nonpartisan primary, the two candidates who receive the most votes in the primary compete in the general election, even if they are from the same party.
Open ("crossover") primary	A primary election system in which any registered voter can participate in either party's primary, regardless of the voter's party affiliation.
CAUCUS ELECTION	A series of local meetings at which registered voters select a particular candidate's supporters as delegates who will vote for the candidate in a later, state-level convention. (In national elections, the state-convention delegates select delegates to the national convention.) Caucuses are used in some states to select delegates to the major parties' presidential nominating conventions. Some states' caucuses are open to members of any party, while others are closed.

as Democrats or Republicans. They may not agree with all that the party stands for, but the party label gives them access to the general election ballot.

National parties also manage the nomination process for presidential candidates, which involves a series of primaries and caucuses held over a six-month period beginning in January of a presidential election year. The type of election (primary or caucus) and its date are determined by each state's legislature, although national party committees can limit the allowable dates, using their control over seating delegates at the party conventions to motivate compliance. Voters in these primaries and caucuses don't directly select the parties' nominees for the presidential race. Instead, citizens' votes are used to determine how many of each candidate's supporters become delegates to the party's national **nominating convention**, where the delegates then vote to choose the party's presidential and vice-presidential nominees. The national party organizations determine how many delegates each state will send to the convention based on factors such as state population, the number of votes the party's candidate received in each state in the last presidential election, and the number of House members and senators from the party that each state elected.

Campaign Assistance Political scientist and party expert John Aldrich refers to America's contemporary political parties as parties in service, which reflects the idea that one of the parties' primary activities is helping candidates with their campaigns.[51] One of the most visible ways that the political parties support candidates is by contributing to and spending money on campaigns. Figure 7.6 shows the amount of money raised by the top groups within the Republican and Democratic parties for the 2008 election (through November 5). The final figures show that the parties raised more than $1.5 billion. The Democratic and Republican national committees (DNC and RNC) raised the most money, but the congressional campaign committees also raised significant sums. The RNC raised about $130 million more than the DNC because John McCain depended heavily on national party money,

nominating convention A meeting held by each party every four years at which states' delegates select the party's presidential and vice-presidential nominees and approve the party platform.

Should Parties Choose Their Candidates?

One of the facts of life for the leaders of the Democratic and Republican parties is that they cannot determine who runs as their party's candidate for Congress or for the presidency. They can encourage some candidates to run and attempt to discourage others by endorsing their favorites and funneling money, staff support, and other forms of assistance to the candidates they prefer. But in the end, candidates get on the ballot by winning a primary—or in the case of presidential candidates, a series of primaries and caucuses. The leaders of each party have to accept whoever emerges from the primary with the nomination.

As you have seen in this chapter, political parties don't always get the nominees that their leaders want. In the 2010 election cycle, for example, insurgent (and Tea Party–backed) candidates Christine O'Donnell in Delaware and Joe Miller in Alaska captured their party's nominations for U.S. Senate seats. In Alaska, Miller defeated incumbent Lisa Murkowski; in Delaware, O'Donnell won an open seat contest against a veteran House member, Mike Castle. After their primary victories, both candidates struggled to justify extreme positions they had taken in the past, and, in O'Donnell's case, to explain away an interview where she described her participation in a Wiccan ceremony. These problems came as no surprise to Delaware and Alaska Republican state party leaders, virtually all of whom had favored the losing candidates, based on the simple calculation that they were more likely to win in the general election. The expectations of the state party leaders proved correct, as Miller lost in the general election to a write-in campaign by Murkowski and O'Donnell was defeated by little-known Democratic opponent. However, because both state parties chose their nominees in primary elections, state party leaders had to accept whoever won the primary as their party's standard-bearer, even if they preferred another candidate on political or policy grounds.

Party leaders cannot force candidates out of a race—even in presidential nomination

Tea Party candidate Christine O'Donnell was the surprise winner of the 2010 Delaware Republican Senate primary, defeating veteran House member Mike Castle. Her victory was not celebrated by state party leaders, who believed—correctly, as it turned out—that she stood little chance of winning the general election.

contests. In spring 2008, many Democratic Party leaders wanted Hillary Clinton to end her presidential candidacy as it became increasingly clear that Barack Obama would win the nomination. Clinton stayed in the race until the primaries ended, forcing Obama to campaign aggressively, spend additional campaign funds, and respond to attacks from the Clinton campaign.

Why not let party leaders pick their candidates? Many scholars have argued that giving party leaders more control over the process would increase the chances of getting experienced, talented candidates on the ballot.[a] After all, party leaders probably know more than the average primary voter about who would make a good candidate or elected official. Plus, party leaders have a strong incentive to find good candidates and convince them to run—their party's influence over government policy increases with the number of people they can elect to political office.

Why, then, do voters in America get to pick party nominees in primaries? Direct

primaries were introduced in American politics during the late 1800s and early 1900s.[b] The goal was explicit: reform-mind party activists wanted to take the choice of nominees out of the hands of party leaders and give it to the electorate, with the assumption that voters should be able to influence the choice of candidates for the general election. Moreover, reformers believed that this goal outweighed the expertise held by party leaders.

Here is the trade-off: If party leaders select nominees, they would likely choose electable candidates who share the policy goals held by party leaders. If voters choose nominees, they can pick whoever they want, using whatever criteria they like—but there is no guarantee that these candidates will be skilled general-election campaigners or effective in office. How much do you value giving voters control over the nomination process versus ensuring an electable nominee? Do you think one of these systems is more likely to produce policies that reflect your concerns? ■

while Barack Obama raised more than $700 million on his own. (McCain accepted federal funding, which capped the amount that his campaign could spend directly.) Congressional Democratic committees, anticipating the vulnerability of Republican incumbents, substantially out-raised their Republican counterparts. State and local parties also raised nearly $400 million in the 2008 elections.[52]

The groups listed in Figure 7.6 clearly show the decentralized structure of American political parties. Though the national committees raise the most cash by far, state parties, individual candidates, and other groups raise an enormous amount by themselves—and decide independently how to spend the money. During the 2004 presidential campaign, Democratic Party leaders wanted John Kerry to donate money left over from his primary campaign to congressional candidates from his party to help the party win additional House and Senate seats.[53] And although Kerry surely wanted Democratic candidates to win their races, he refused; his surplus could be used for his own future campaigns, such as running for reelection to his Senate seat.

Such disagreements between candidates and party officials are not new. At the end of the 1996 presidential campaign, when incumbent Bill Clinton was a sure winner, Clinton's campaign managers decided against sending him to campaign with Democrats running for House and Senate seats.[54] They reasoned that although the strategy would not reduce Clinton's chances of winning, spending time on congressional campaigning and tying Clinton to an unpopular Congress might reduce

---

FIGURE 7.6 DEMOCRATIC AND REPUBLICAN FUND-RAISING IN THE 2007–2008 ELECTION CYCLE

In the 2007–2008 election cycle, party committees raised about $1.5 billion in campaign funds. Although most of this money was raised by the national committees, the state, local, and candidate committees also raised significant sums. To what extent might these funds allow the national committees to force candidates to run on the party platform?

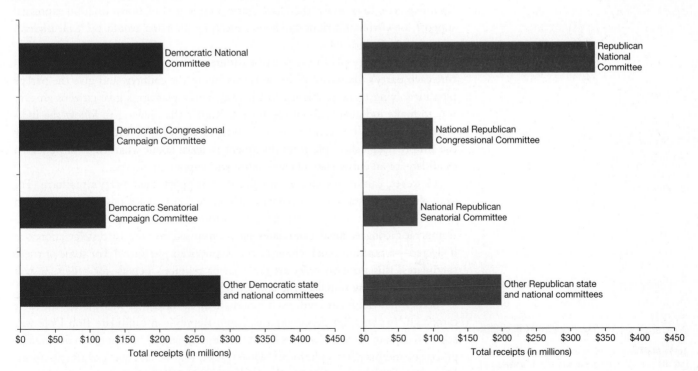

Note: Figures are based on Federal Election Commission data released on November 5, 2008.

SOURCE: Federal Election Commission data provided by the Center for Responsive Politics, available at www.opensecrets.org/parties/index.php.

▲ During the final days of a campaign, the volunteers who staff candidate and party phone banks contact potential supporters to encourage them to go to the polls and vote on Election Day.

his popular vote total and his margin of victory in the electoral college. Many other presidential candidates, such as Ronald Reagan in 1984, have made similar calculations.[55]

Along with supplying campaign funds, party organizations give candidates other kinds of assistance, ranging from offering campaign advice (on which issues to emphasize, how to deal with the press, and the like) to conducting polls. Party organizations at all levels also undertake GOTV or get-out-the-vote activities, encouraging supporters to get to the polls. During the last few elections, the Republican Party has organized a "72-Hour Task Force" of volunteers to spend the days just before the election staffing phone banks and going door-to-door campaigning for candidates in close races.

A more general example of party assistance comes from the Democratic Party's "Fifty State Strategy," which aims to recruit strong candidates and help fund their campaigns in all fifty states (and 435 congressional districts) regardless of whether their Republican opponents seem beatable.[56] As we discuss in more detail in Chapter 8, Elections, much of the Democrats' success in 2006 and 2008 stemmed from congressional scandals, a weak economy, an unpopular war in Iraq, and low approval ratings for then-president Bush. However, the Democrats' efforts to recruit and fund candidates helped them capitalize on these events by giving voters a plausible alternative to Republican candidates.

Party Platforms The **party platform** is a set of promises about what candidates from the party will do if elected. The most widely known party platform is the one approved at each party's presidential nominating convention, but the party organizations in the House and Senate also release platforms, as do other groups in the major parties. Party platforms generally reflect the brand name differences between the parties discussed earlier. For example, in the case of abortion rights, the 2008 Republican presidential platform favored abstinence, adoption, and enactment of the Human Life Amendment, which would outlaw abortion under most circumstances. In contrast, the Democratic presidential platform in 2008 expressed support for a woman's right to choose, meaning abortion would be legal under a wider range of conditions.

In theory, party platforms describe differences between the major parties, capture each party's diagnosis of the problems facing the country, and give the party's plan for solving those problems. In this way, party platforms give citizens an easy way to make judgments about candidates. Rather than having to follow the individual campaigns by reading news stories and tracking political Web sites, they can simply read a short platform document to learn about what kinds of policies a candidate, or an entire slate of candidates, will support if elected.

However, candidates are not obligated to support their party's platform. For example, notwithstanding the consistently strong pro-choice position on abortion in the Democratic Party's presidential platforms over the last generation, some Democratic congressional candidates have promised to vote to restrict abortions if elected—a position much closer to the Republican platform.[57] For some of these candidates, this position reflected personal or religious beliefs; for others, it was driven by the desire to reflect the opinion of voters in their district or state.

Sometimes candidates will even repudiate a platform that was written for their campaign. In the 1996 presidential election, Republican candidate Bob Dole was asked to explain some differences between the issue stands he had taken during the primaries and his party's platform.[58] Dole replied that he had not read the platform. Of course, Dole knew what was in the Republican platform, but since he did not agree with some of its positions, he tried to ignore it as much as possible.

party platform A set of objectives outlining the party's issue positions and priorities. Candidates are not required to support their party's platform.

COOPERATION IN GOVERNMENT

The theory of **conditional party government** states that as policy differences between the parties in government increase in number and intensity, the parties in government will become more and more active as a forum for like-minded legislators to develop policy plans and as a source for legislative strategies to enact these proposals. As discussed earlier, this theory is a good description of what has happened in Congress over the last fifty years. Although conditional party government has led to the enactment of many important proposals, there is no guarantee that party members will cooperate. Party leaders in the modern Congress work to find agreements that are attractive to their **backbenchers**, but in many recent instances these efforts have failed. And if the party in government can't reach agreement, it will stay on the sidelines.

Developing Agendas Throughout the year, the parties in government meet to devise strategies for legislative action. What proposals should they offer, and in what order should they be considered? Should they try to make a deal with the president or with legislators from the other party? For example, after the 2008 election, Democratic congressional leaders met with President-elect Barack Obama and his staff to discuss priorities for the 2009–2010 legislative term, including climate change legislation, health care reform, and an economic stimulus package.

Some of these efforts were highly successful. Less than a month after Obama took office, Congress passed a $787 billion stimulus plan, which Democrats passed with no Republican support in the House and only three Republican votes in the Senate. Moreover, particularly in the House, Democratic party leaders used their control over legislative proceedings, backed up by caucus support for the stimulus package, to thwart Republican attempts to delay, modify, or defeat the proposal.[59] Republican leaders in Congress did the same thing when they were in the majority.

However, the party in government can act collectively this way only when its members can agree on what they want. Such agreement is not always possible or may require extensive negotiation and compromise to achieve. For example, health care legislation was enacted only after protracted negotiations with Democratic senators, such as Ben Nelson of Nebraska, and the granting of significant concessions in return for their support. Similarly, in summer of 2006, the House Republicans, who were in the majority, split on immigration reform. Some members favored a proposal that created a path to citizenship for illegal immigrants, while others opposed amnesty and wanted to stiffen criminal penalties against them. Ultimately, they never reached an agreement, and no reform measure came to a vote.[60] This defeat on immigration reform is especially noteworthy because the Republicans held majorities in both houses of Congress. In other words, if Bush could have convinced Republican legislators to support his immigration proposals, he would have carried the day, because the Republicans in the House and Senate had enough votes to enact the proposals without support from Democrats. House Republicans now face similar problems: while they have a majority in the chamber, there are significant disagreements in their ranks about legislative priorities on issues such as budget cuts and immigration. Thus, leaving aside the problems of enacting their proposals through a Democrat-controlled Senate or persuading President Obama to sign them, efforts by House Republicans to change government policy may founder on their inability to find compromises within their own conference.

Coordination Political parties play an important role in coordinating the actions taken in different branches of government. Such coordination is extremely important for enacting new laws, because unless supporters in Congress can amass a

conditional party government The theory that lawmakers from the same party will cooperate to develop policy proposals.

backbenchers Legislators who do not hold leadership positions within their party caucus or conference.

▲ *Presidents seeking legislative backing for their proposals must persuade their party's representatives in Congress; they are unable to demand support. Even when the president's party holds majorities in both houses of Congress, he may have trouble getting policies approved. As part of the negotiations over the 2010 health care reform bill, President Obama agreed to sign a separate executive order reaffirming the ban on the use of federal funds to provide abortions. This agreement secured the vote of Michigan Democratic representative Bart Stupak, pictured here announcing his decision to back the bill.*

unified government A situation in which one party holds a majority of seats in the House and Senate and the president is a member of that same party.

party in power Under unified government, the party that controls the House, Senate, and the presidency. Under divided government, the president's party.

divided government A situation in which the House, Senate, and presidency are not controlled by the same party, such as if Democrats hold the majority of House and Senate seats, and the president is a Republican.

two-thirds majority to override a veto, they need the president's support. Similarly, the president needs congressional support to enact the proposals he favors. To these ends, the president routinely meets with congressional leaders from his party, and occasionally meets with the entire caucus or conference. The president also has staff in the Office of Legislative Liaison who meet with House and Senate members on a daily basis to present the president's proposals and hear what members of Congress from both parties want to enact.

During 2009, President Obama held many meetings with Democratic members of Congress to lobby them to support his proposals for health care reform. Although many congressional Democrats supported Obama's proposals, enactment was nearly derailed by several Democratic representatives and senators who demanded amendments to restrict government payment for abortions. Obama clearly opposed these efforts but was powerless to stop them. In fact, getting the last few votes needed for enactment required Obama to promise to issue an executive order that had essentially the same effect as the proposed amendments.

Coordination can also occur between caucuses or conferences in the House and Senate. At the same time President Obama and Democrats in Congress were negotiating over health care reform, congressional Republicans were devising strategies for delaying and defeating these proposals. Although their efforts did not prevent the enactment of reform legislation, their strong opposition required the president and congressional leaders to accept many changes favored by moderate and conservative Democrats in order to enact the legislation without Republican support.

Such coordination efforts require real work and compromise, as party leaders in the House and the Senate do not have authority over each other or over the elected members of their party. Nor can the president order a House member or senator to do anything, even if the legislator is from the president's own party. In 2010, for example, President Obama and congressional leaders needed the votes of several anti-abortion Democrats, including Congressman Bart Stupak, to pass health care legislation through the House of Representatives. The leaders and the president held repeated meetings with Stupak and his allies, and offered various promises and enticements to secure theses votes. Ultimately, these legislators voted for the proposal, but neither the president nor party leaders could have forced or ordered them to support it.

Accountability One of the most important roles of political parties in a democracy is giving citizens identifiable groups to reward or punish for government actions, thereby providing a means for voters to focus their desire for accountability. By rewarding and punishing elected officials, often based on their party affiliation and other party members' behavior in office, voters use the party system to hold officials accountable for outcomes such as the state of the economy or America's relations with other nations.

During periods of **unified government**, when one party holds majorities in both the House and the Senate and controls the presidency, that party is the **party in power**; they have enough votes to enact policies in Congress and a good chance of having them signed into law by a president who shares their party. During times of **divided government**, when one party controls Congress but not the presidency, or the House and Senate are controlled by different parties, the president's party is considered the party in power. Focusing on parties makes it easy for a citizen to issue rewards and punishments. Is the economy doing well? Then vote for the candidates from the party in power. But if the economy is doing poorly, or if a citizen feels that government is wasting tax money or enacting bad policies, he can vote for candidates from the party that is currently out of power. When citizens behave this way, they strengthen the incentive for elected officials from the party in power to work together to develop policies that address voters' concerns—on the premise that if they do, voters will reward them with another term in office.

In 2006, voters' disapproval of the Iraq war and President Bush's low approval ratings translated into Republican losses of thirty House seats and six Senate seats, giving control of the House and Senate to the Democrats. And in 2010, concerns over the economy led many Americans to support Republican candidates for the House and Senate, giving Republicans substantial seat gains in both chambers, returning the House to Republican control, and creating a new case of divided government.

▲ Focusing on parties can make it easier for voters to issue rewards and punishments. Here, Democratic senators Charles Schumer and Benjamin Cardin hold a press conference with an unemployed worker to publicize their party's proposals to increase job growth.

Some political scientists have argued that legislators from the same party should be forced to work as a team—to run on the same campaign platform, work together in Washington to enact their platform, and be collectively held accountable in elections for whether their proposals worked or not. Political organizations that function this way are called **responsible parties**,[61] and they have never existed in American politics. If American parties worked this way, it is likely that more people would hold the party in power and its officeholders directly accountable for the state of the economy and other national-level outcomes.

In contrast to the responsible party model, the three-part structure of contemporary American parties complicates decisions about accountability. Suppose, for example, a legislator from the party in power opposed the policies enacted by her party. If so, it may not make sense for a voter to reward this legislator for good outcomes of those policies or punish her for bad outcomes. Even though she is from the party in power, she did not cause the outcomes that the voter cares about. What should a voter do in this case?

Consider the 2010 election, when many Americans voted against Democratic candidates because of poor economic conditions. While Democrats lost seats in both the House and Senate, most Democratic incumbents were returned to office. Why? Some were elected from states or districts dominated by Democratic identifiers. But many others were reelected because they campaigned on a platform of changing policy or because of their efforts to help local businesses, saying in effect, "instead of punishing me for my party affiliation, reward me for working on your behalf."

Minor Parties

So far, this chapter has focused on the major American political parties, the Republicans and the Democrats, and paid less attention to other party organizations. The reason is that minor political parties in America are *so* minor that they are generally not significant players on the political stage. Many such parties exist, but few run candidates in more than a handful of races, and very few minor-party candidates win political office. Few Americans identify with minor parties, and most exist for only a short period, although the Republican Party began as a minor party in the 1840s.

responsible parties A system in which each political party's candidates campaign on the party platform, work together in office to implement the platform, and are judged by voters based on whether they achieved the platform's objectives.

▲ Minor party presidential candidates, such as Ralph Nader in 2000, sometimes attract considerable press attention because of their distinctive, often extreme policy preferences—but they rarely affect election outcomes.

Even so, you may think we're giving minor parties too little attention. Consider Ralph Nader, who ran as the Green Party nominee for president in 2000, winning almost 5 percent of the vote. In some states, the number of votes Nader received exceeded the margin separating Democrat Al Gore from Republican George Bush. In particular, in Florida, where Bush won by only a few hundred votes after a disputed recount, Nader received almost 100,000 votes—enough to swing the state, and the election, to Gore.

However, the outcome of Nader's 2000 presidential campaign doesn't so much highlight the importance of minor parties as it illustrates the closeness of the 2000 presidential election. If Nader had not run, Gore might have received enough additional support to win. But given that Bush's margin of victory in Florida was so small, any number of seemingly minor events (a polling station closing early, or rain in some areas and sunshine in others) could have changed the outcome.

Minor parties did not play a decisive role in the 2008 presidential election, but in several swing states such as North Carolina and Missouri, they received more votes than the margin of difference between Obama and McCain. The most successful were the Independent Party (661,000 votes) and the Libertarian Party (491,000), while others like the Boston Tea Party and the U.S. Pacifist Party received far fewer votes (2,305 and 97, respectively). Minor parties won about 1.5 million votes in the 2008 presidential race, whereas the two major parties received 121 million votes.

Even if you look at lower offices, minor-party candidates typically attract only meager support. The Libertarian Party claimed to have more than 600 officeholders as of 2006. However, many of these officials hold unelected positions such as seats on county planning boards or ran unopposed for relatively minor offices such as justice of the peace.[62]

Looking back in history, some minor-party candidates for president have attracted a substantial percentage of citizens' votes. George Wallace ran as the candidate of the American Independent Party in 1968, receiving about 13 percent of the popular vote nationwide (more than 9 million votes). Ross Perot, the Reform Party candidate for president in 1996, won 8.4 percent of the popular vote (about 8 million votes). Perot also ran as an independent in 1992, winning 18.2 percent of the popular vote (more than 19 million votes).

The differences between major and minor political parties in contemporary American politics grow even more substantial when considered in terms other than election outcomes. For most minor parties, the party in government does not exist, as few of their candidates win office. Many minor parties have virtually no organization beyond a small party headquarters and a Web site. Some minor parties, such as the Green Party, the Libertarian Party, and the Reform Party, have local chapters that meet on a regular basis. But these modest efforts pale in comparison to the nationwide network of offices, thousands of workers, and millions of dollars deployed by Republican and Democratic Party organizations.

Research by political scientists Steven Rosenstone, Roy Behr, and Edward Lazarus shows that people vote for minor-party candidates because they find these candidates' positions more attractive than those of the major parties and also because they believe that neither major party can govern effectively. That is, in general, a vote for a minor party first requires a citizen to reject both the Democratic and Republican organizations.[63] In 2008, for example, presidential candidate Ralph Nader advocated an immediate withdrawal of American troops from Iraq, as well as deep cuts in defense spending. To vote for Nader, a citizen would have had to like

Nader's issue stands and believe that neither of the major parties could effectively address these problems. However, precisely because minor parties appeal to the minority of Americans who want "something different" than what the major parties are offering, their platforms will not appeal to most Americans, whose goals and preferences are compatible with at least one major party platform. And when a minor party does find broad support in the electorate for a particular issue, such as the Progressive reforms in the late 1800s, one or both of the major parties respond by adopting this position as their own, preventing the minor party from attracting more support.

The basic structure of the American political system also works against minor political parties. This principle is summed up by **Duverger's law**, which states that in a democracy that has **single-member districts** and **plurality voting** (as America does), there will be only two political parties that elect a significant number of candidates to political office. Given these electoral institutions (discussed further in Chapter 8), many people consider a vote for a minor-party candidate to be a wasted vote, as there is no chance that the candidate will attract enough votes to win office. As a result, well-qualified candidates are driven to affiliate with one of the major political parties, because they know that running as a minor-party nominee will put them at a considerable disadvantage. These decisions reinforce citizens' expectations that minor-party candidates have no chance of winning elections and that a vote for them is a wasted vote. Although there is no evidence that the Founders wanted to choose electoral institutions that made it hard for minor parties and their candidates, there is no doubt that the rules of the American electoral game have these effects.

Moreover, as mentioned earlier, minor-party candidates face significantly higher legal hurdles to get on the ballot—in many cases these rules are deliberately chosen to discourage minor-party candidates. In 2007, when New York City mayor Michael Bloomberg considered running for president as an independent in the 2008 election, his staff estimated that he would need over 700,000 signatures to get on the ballot in all fifty states. And some states have additional hurdles: in Texas, for example, a candidate not affiliated with a major party needs signatures from registered voters who did not vote in either of the last Democratic or Republican presidential primaries.[64]

What Kind of Democracy Do American Political Parties Create?

Parties help political activists, party leaders, and citizens who identify with the party pursue their policy goals by focusing collective efforts on electing people to office who share their priorities. For politicians, parties provide ballot access, a brand name, campaign assistance, and a group of like-minded colleagues with whom they can coordinate, compromise, and strategize. For citizens, political parties provide information and a means of holding specific individuals accountable for what government does.

The question of whether political parties are good or bad for democracy depends on how the individual party members and officials carry out these tasks. Political parties can help democracy by filling the ballot with well-qualified candidates, helping them get elected, offering citizens clear choices about government policies, informing citizens about platforms and candidates, motivating citizens to vote, and, after the election, helping elected officials enact the party platform. The problem is

Duverger's law The principle that in a democracy with single-member districts and plurality voting, like the United States, only two parties' candidates will have a realistic chance of winning political office.

single-member districts An electoral system in which every elected official represents a geographically defined area, such as a state or congressional district, and each area elects one representative.

plurality voting A voting system in which the candidate who receives the most votes within a geographic area wins the election, regardless of whether that candidate wins a majority (more than half) of the votes.

that the people who make up American political parties are not primarily interested in democracy; they are interested in their own careers, policy goals, and winning political office. These goals often lead them away from actions that would improve American democracy.

RECRUITING CANDIDATES

One of the most important things the Republican and Democratic parties can do for democracy is to recruit candidates for national political offices who can run effective campaigns and responsibly uphold their elected positions. After all, your choices as a voter are limited to the people on the ballot. If good candidates decide against running or are prevented from doing so, citizens will be dissatisfied no matter who wins the election.

As we discussed, the Republican and Democratic parties work to find good candidates and persuade them to run. However, the potential candidates have to decide for themselves whether their chances of winning justify the enormous investment of time and money needed to run a campaign. When a party is popular with the American public, such as the Democrats in 2006 and 2008, party leaders can pick and choose among many well-qualified candidates. But when a party is unpopular, such as the Republicans in 2006 and 2008, the best potential candidates may decide to wait until the next election to run, leaving the already disadvantaged party with a relatively less competitive set of candidates.[65] And even when a party does not face economic or other headwinds, state- or district-level factors may deter good candidates from running under the party's banner. As a result, insofar as conditions favor one party's candidates over those from the other party, the disadvantaged party may find it difficult to offer citizens a compelling candidate to vote for on election day.

WORKING TOGETHER IN CAMPAIGNS

Parties can also work to simplify voters' choices by trying to get candidates to emphasize the same issues or take similar issue positions. That way, citizens know that when they vote for, say, a Democrat, they are getting someone whose policy positions differ in specific ways from those held by Republican candidates. The problem is that members of the party organization and the party in government do not always agree on what government should do. Sometimes the differences within the parties reflect the candidates' genuine differences of opinion. Other times, candidates are trying to match the preferences of citizens in their state or district. Either way, the simple fact is that political parties in America generally speak with many voices, not one.

Why don't party leaders simply order their candidates to support the party platform or to work together in campaigns? As we have discussed, party leaders actually have very little power over candidates.[66] They can't kick a candidate off the ballot, because candidates win the nomination in a primary election or at a convention. Even though parties have a lot of campaign money to dispense, their contributions typically make up only a fraction of what a candidate spends on a campaign. And incumbent candidates, who generally hold an advantage over their challengers when seeking reelection, are even less beholden to party leaders. Even if party leaders could somehow prevent an incumbent from running for reelection, they would have to find another candidate to take the incumbent's place, which would mean losing the incumbent's popularity and reputation and reducing the party's chances of holding the seat.

WORKING TOGETHER IN OFFICE

Because candidates are not required to support their party's platform, there is no guarantee that that they will be able to work together with other members of the party in office. Sometimes, as with the Democrats and the economic stimulus plan, the members of a party can compromise to resolve their differences. However, there are also many examples of issues that split a party wide open, such as Democrats and health care reform or Republicans and immigration reform. Sometimes party members can compromise their differences, as in the case of Democrats and health care reform, but at other times, such as the Republicans' immigration proposals, compromise may prove to be impossible.

The fact that American political parties are heterogeneous means that elected members of the party may not agree on spending, policy, or anything else. In that sense, voters can't expect that putting one party in power is going to result in specific policy changes. Instead, policy outcomes depend on how (and whether) individual officeholders from the party can resolve their differences. Institutions such as the party caucuses or conferences provide a forum in which elected officials can meet and seek common ground, but there is no guarantee that they will find acceptable compromises.

Moreover, concerted action by members of a party in government may be aimed at political rather than policy goals. For example, in 2009 and 2010, Republicans in the House and Senate uniformly opposed many Democratic initiatives. For many, opposition was based on their policy goals. But for others, their opposition reflected a political calculation—that this strategy was the party's best bet for gaining seats in the 2010 midterm elections. In this way, American political parties can work against the enactment of effective responses to public problems and increase rather than decrease the amount of conflict in American politics.

ACCOUNTABILITY

The final task for a party is to serve as an accountability mechanism that gives citizens an identifiable group to reward when policies work well and to punish when policies fail. However, individual legislators also work to build a reputation and standing with the voters that is independent of their party label. They are happy to emphasize their party affiliation when it brings them support but choose not to mention it when the party is associated with unpopular policies or outcomes. Republican legislators, for example, highlighted their party identification in the 2002 and 2004 elections, as the party was held in high regard by many voters.[67] However, by 2006, with voter evaluations of the party and President Bush at all-time lows, many Republican candidates deemphasized their connection to the party as much as possible.[68] The same was true for many Democratic candidates in 2010: given the unpopularity of many of President Obama's policies, their best bet for reelection was to emphasize their efforts to respond to district concerns and downplay their party affiliation or past support for the president.

When politicians work to secure their own political future in this way, they make it harder for voters to use party labels to decide who should be rewarded and who should be punished for government performance. The result is that legislators are held accountable for their own performance in office, such as how they voted—but no one in Congress is accountable for large-scale outcomes such as the state of the economy or for foreign policy. Of course, some voters hold legislators accountable based on whether they are members of the party in power, which is why Republicans lost House and Senate seats in 2006 and 2008 and Democrats lost seats

Party Organizations in Other Countries

Our description of American political parties highlights their lack of control over what their candidates say and do in elections and in government. Most American politicians—and nearly all officeholders—run as the candidate of a political party, but the major-party organizations have little power to determine who gets their nominations.

The situation is very different in many other democracies. In most western European countries, the leaders of political parties can force candidates from their party to run on the party platform and, if elected, to vote according to the wishes of party leaders.[a] Where do they get this power? For one thing, the party organizations can determine which politicians are nominated to run for office. In some countries, party organizations routinely move candidates from one district to another, a practice known as parachuting. The national party organizations may also control most of the campaign resources. Finally, after the election, the leaders of the party that won the election often get to decide which of the elected politicians from their party will serve in the winning candidate's cabinet and wield policy-making power. This combination of incentives and threats makes most politicians in western Europe highly loyal to their party organization.

In Germany, whose legislature is depicted here, candidates campaign as representatives of their party and must follow the dictates of their party leaders. Voters choose between party platforms rather than individual candidates, and they evaluate the winning party based on how successfully it has implemented its platform since the last election.

What are the consequences of these differences? Legislatures in western Europe show high levels of party discipline— elected officials generally vote according to party leaders' instructions. Elections in these countries focus on party platforms rather than the promises made by individual candidates; instead of comparing candidates, citizens compare parties and their platforms when deciding how to vote.

Which system is better? It depends on what you think is important. The organization of western European parties helps them devise meaningful platforms and coordinate the activities of their elected officials, and gives citizens a specific organization to hold accountable for government performance. However, precisely because candidates in these systems campaign as party members rather than as individuals, they cannot tailor their appeals to the specific demands of voters in their district or state. As a result, western European voters in some areas may find that none of the candidates they see in an election is addressing the issues that matter to them. ∎

in 2010. Even so, the fact that most Republicans and Democrats in Congress managed to survive these elections suggests that party-based accountability is rather weak in contemporary American politics.

CITIZENS' BEHAVIOR

As you have seen, most Americans identify as either a Republican or a Democrat, and many citizens use party labels to cue their vote decisions. However, citizens are under no obligation to give money or time to the party they identify with or to any of the party's candidates. They don't have to vote for their party's candidates or even to vote at all. All of these actions would strengthen party organizations, but citizens do not have to take them even if they strongly identify with a party.

Here again, citizens are free to choose how to participate in American politics, including the option of not participating at all. But many of the things citizens do—such as not contributing to campaigns or party organizations, voting for candidates from separate parties to hold different offices, or ignoring party affiliation in their retrospective evaluations—weaken party organizations and make it harder for them to operate as a team to enact policies and oversee the bureaucracy.

Conclusion

American political parties help organize elections, unify disparate social groups, simplify the choices facing voters, and build compromises around party members' shared policy concerns. However, in all of these activities their success depends on whether individual party members—candidates, citizens, and party leaders—are willing to take the actions necessary to achieve these goals. Sometimes they are, but other times they decide that their own interests, or those of their constituents, are best served by ignoring or even working against party priorities. And when party members refuse to cooperate, political parties may be unable to do the things that help American democracy to work well.

The case of the Democratic Party from 2006 to 2010 illustrates these limits. It was an easy choice for Democratic candidates to emphasize their party affiliation in the 2006 and 2008 elections, but the brand name was valuable during these contests only because of the unpopularity of then-president Bush and the Republicans in the House and Senate, who were seen as being responsible for the poor state of the economy and the unpopular wars in Iraq and Afghanistan.

After the 2008 election, however, divisions within the Democratic Party in government soon became apparent. Though Democrats were able to unite to enact an economic stimulus package, building consensus around health care reform legislation took considerable time and required jettisoning provisions that were supported by many Democratic legislators. Despite having strong majorities in both houses of Congress, Democratic leaders had to worry as much about keeping their own members in line as they did about thwarting Republican opposition.

And in the 2010 elections, with Democrats seen as the party responsible for poor economic conditions, many Democratic candidates tried to disassociate themselves from the party as much as possible and campaigned on their personal accomplishments.

Of course, these difficulties do not reflect a problem with Democrats per se—Republicans did little better when they controlled the House, Senate, and presidency, and may have similar problems given the additional seats their candidates won in 2010. Rather, they show that the individuals who make up American political parties often do not have an incentive to behave in the interests of their party or as theories of democracy would suggest they should.

How are parties organized in the United States? How has the American party system developed over time?

- American political parties include the party organization, the party in government, and the party in the electorate.
- American parties have looked and operated very differently over time. In some party systems, there was little or no party in the electorate; in others, the party organization did relatively little to help their candidates get elected.
- The variation in political parties across American history confirms that nothing about them is inevitable. Parties look and act as they do because many politicians, activists, and citizens support particular party features.
- Realignments define the issues that separate American political parties, determine the balance of power between the parties, and lead to changes in government policy.
- Realignments are rare because they occur only when a new crosscutting issue or set of issues captures the attention of large numbers of citizens and politicians.

What are the characteristics of modern American political parties?

- The Republican and Democratic Party organizations consist of thousands of groups at the national, state, and local levels, some of which are only informally connected to their party. Party organizations are not hierarchical, as neither party has one leader or group that all members have to obey.
- The party in government is the public face of a political party, consisting of officials (members of Congress and the president) who were elected as party-affiliated candidates. Decisions made inside the party in government influence legislative strategies and policy outcomes.
- The party in the electorate consists of voters who identify with a political party. Party identification has a strong influence on an individual's vote decisions and other aspects of political outlook and behavior. The Republican and Democratic Party coalitions differ in terms of the groups that tend to identify with each party and what they want government to do.

Why parties? What is the role of political parties in American politics?

- American political parties recruit and train candidates and provide ballot access, campaign cash, and a brand name.
- In government, party groups set the legislative agenda, coordinate action across the branches of the federal government, and give voters a way to reward and punish officeholders for government performance.
- The way party organizations operate is shaped by the way they are organized and particularly by the distinction between the party in government and the party organization.

Why do minor parties exist? What influence do they have on American politics?

- Minor political parties offer citizens additional candidates and platforms to vote for, but they only rarely elect candidates to national political office.
- Minor parties face significant legal hurdles to getting their candidates on the ballot. Moreover, would-be candidates often find that their chances of winning are better if they run for a major-party nomination.

Are political parties good for American democracy?

- The actions taken inside party organizations, parties in government, and parties in the electorate shape both election outcomes and policy outcomes in Washington, DC.
- American political parties are not organized as hierarchies; party leaders cannot control how their candidates campaign or what their elected officials do in office. The party also cannot force citizen members to support the party's candidates in elections.
- As a result, while many people expect political parties to work to simplify elections and streamline the policy process in government, the individuals inside these organizations often lack the means or the incentives to do so.

ⓢ STUDENT STUDYSPACE

Find quizzes and other review material at wwnorton.com/studyspace.

CRITICAL THINKING

1. Suppose you are the leader of your party's caucus or conference in the House of Representatives. Why would you want to convince your party's elected officials to support the party's position on an issue? Why might you want to let them vote as they think best?

2. Is the spoils system a good idea or a bad idea? Why?
3. How would we know that a realignment is taking place in American politics?

KEY TERMS

activists (p. 234)
backbenchers (p. 245)
brand names (p. 228)
caucus (congressional) (p. 232)
caucus (electoral) (p. 240)
conditional party government (p. 245)
conference (p. 232)
crosscutting (p. 226)
dealignment (p. 237)
divided government (p. 246)
Duverger's law (p. 249)
527 organization (p. 228)
national committee (p. 227)

New Deal Coalition (p. 225)
nodes (p. 221)
nominating convention (p. 241)
parties in service (p. 225)
party coalitions (p. 238)
party identification (party ID) (p. 233)
party in government (p. 221)
party in power (p. 246)
party in the electorate (p. 221)
party organization (p. 221)
party platform (p. 244)
party principle (p. 223)
party system (p. 222)

plurality voting (p. 249)
polarized (p. 232)
political action committee (PAC) (p. 228)
political machine (p. 230)
primary (p. 240)
realignment (p. 226)
responsible parties (p. 247)
running tally (p. 235)
single-member districts (p. 249)
spoils system (p. 223)
unified government (p. 246)

SUGGESTED READING

Aldrich, John. *Why Parties?* Chicago: University of Chicago Press, 1995.

Bartels, Larry M. "Partisanship and Voting Behavior, 1952–1996." *American Journal of Political Science* 44:1 (2000): 35–50.

Carmines, Edward G., and James A. Stimson. *Issue Evolution: Race and the Transformation of American Politics.* Princeton, NJ: Princeton University Press, 1989.

Cohen, Marty, David Karol, Hans Noel, and John Zaller. *The Party Decides: Presidential Nominations Before and After Reform.* Chicago: University of Chicago Press, 2008.

Cox, Gary. *Making Votes Count: Strategic Coordination in the World's Electoral Systems.* Cambridge, UK: Cambridge University Press, 1997.

Cox, Gary, and Mathew McCubbins. *Setting the Agenda: Party Government in the U.S. House of Representatives.* New York: Cambridge University Press, 2005.

Fiorina, Morris. *Retrospective Voting in American National Elections.* New Haven, CT: Yale University Press, 1981.

Green, Donald, Bradley Palmquist, and Eric Schickler. *Partisan Hearts and Minds.* New Haven, CT: Yale University Press, 2004.

Key, V. O. *Politics, Parties, and Pressure Groups.* New York: Crowell, 1956.

Polsby, Nelson. *Consequences of Party Reform.* New York: Oxford University Press, 1983.

Riordon, William L. *Plunkitt of Tammany Hall.* 1905. Reprint, New York: Dutton, 1963.

Rohde, David. *Parties and Leaders in the Post-Reform House.* Chicago: University of Chicago Press, 1991.

Schattschneider, E. E. *Party Government.* New York: McGraw-Hill, 1942.

Schlesinger, Joseph. *Political Parties and the Winning of Office.* Ann Arbor, MI: University of Michigan Press, 1994.

Stanley, Harold W., and Richard G. Niemi. "Partisanship, Party Coalitions, and Group Support, 1952–2004." *Presidential Studies Quarterly* 36:2 (2006): 172–88.

Sundquist, James L. *Dynamics of the Party System.* Rev. ed. Washington, DC: Brookings Institution, 1983.

Wattenberg, Martin P. *Where Have All the Voters Gone?* Cambridge, MA: Harvard University Press, 2002.

John McCain and Barack Obama participated
in their second presidential debate on
October 7, 2008, at Belmont University in
Nashville, Tennessee.

Elections

To appreciate why American elections are both fascinating and sometimes seemingly unexplainable, you need look no further than the 2008 presidential election. How did Barack Obama, a "tall skinny guy with big ears" (as he described himself), a man with little experience in government or running a national campaign, and a member of a minority group whose candidates were thought to have little chance of winning a national election, manage nevertheless to capture his party's nomination and win the presidency on November 4, 2008?

Obama's victory was even more startling when you consider his opposition. In the Democratic primaries, Obama bested Senator (and former First Lady) Hillary Clinton, who was well funded; received many endorsements from important politicians, civic leaders, and organizations; and had demonstrated her ability to win tough elections in two campaigns in New York State. In the general election, Obama defeated Senator John McCain, a former naval aviator and prisoner of war in Vietnam, and an experienced politician who had nearly won the Republican presidential nomination in 2000 and who had demonstrated a strong ability to gain support from Democratic and independent voters as well as from his Republican base.

CONFLICT AND COMPROMISE

in American Politics

Despite all of these advantages, neither candidate proved a match for Obama. Clinton stayed in the nomination race until the end (other candidates dropped out along the way), but after the first few primaries, many observers gave her little chance of winning. As for McCain, except for one brief period after the Republican National Convention, he consistently trailed Barack Obama in the polls. McCain was widely criticized for choosing Alaska governor Sarah Palin as his vice-presidential nominee (many saw her as ill-equipped for the job), and his attacks against Obama's inexperience, alleged ties to radicals, and plans to redistribute income went nowhere. When the financial crisis hit in September, McCain was seen as having no solutions to offer. By Election Day, there was little question that he would lose.

As illustrated by Obama's victory—and by the 2010 midterm battles discussed later in this chapter—American national elections often are extremely conflictual. The conflict is no surprise: Americans disagree about what government should do, and these differences play out among the candidates running for the House, Senate, and presidency. In the 2008 presidential primaries, Obama and Clinton sparred over foreign policy, health care, and economic policy—although

BIG QUESTIONS

- ✪ What role do elections play in a democracy?
- ✪ How do elections work in the United States?
- ✪ How do candidates win elections?
- ✪ How do voters decide?
- ✪ Do elections matter?

their differences were small enough that after the election Clinton became Obama's secretary of state. The differences on these issues between Obama and McCain in the general election were much sharper, reflecting the policy and ideological disagreements between Republicans and Democrats discussed in previous chapters.

On the other hand, compromise does exist in American elections. One important instance of compromise is debates over the electability of different candidates. On the Republican side in 2008, McCain was not the preferred candidate of many conservatives, but many compromised and supported him because they thought he had the best chance of winning the general election. Similar arguments were raised about Clinton over Obama in the Democratic contest, though clearly with less effect.

Elections illustrate that political process matters. Candidates in American elections compete for a wide variety of offices. They are elected for different periods of time to represent districts, states, or the entire nation—places that vary tremendously in terms of what constituents want from government. A variety of rules determine who can run, who can vote, and how candidates can campaign. Even ballot layouts and how votes are cast and counted vary across states. Elections also differ in the amount of media coverage they receive, the level of involvement of political parties and other organizations, and the amount of attention citizens pay to the contests. All these aspects of the election process—who runs, how they campaign, and how voters respond—shape outcomes.

Moreover, as we demonstrate in this chapter and throughout the book, it matters who wins Senate, House, and presidential elections, because government does different things depending on who controls the legislative and executive branches. There is little doubt, for example, that a hypothetical President McCain would have pushed for a vastly different health care proposal than President Obama, as well as different plans for economic stimulus, climate change, and other issues. On the other hand, in some areas, such as the wars in Iraq and Afghanistan, policy would likely have looked much the same regardless of who won the election. And in most areas, notably domestic policy and nominations to federal courts, outcomes reflect the need for compromise among the president and members of the House and Senate.

Elections, as prominent, public forums that give Americans the opportunity to debate policy preferences, provide further evidence that politics is everywhere. During election season, campaign coverage and ads for candidates become almost impossible to avoid. Even so, one of the most important tasks all campaigns face is getting citizens' attention and convincing them to listen to the candidate's appeals.

So, can we explain American elections, including the 2008 presidential contest? Our answer is yes. By making the election process more comprehensible, we aim to demonstrate how and why elections matter. We show that there are real differences between candidates running for national office and that these distinctions have profound implications for public policy. And we show that despite Americans' general detachment from politics, their votes reflect both their policy preferences and considerable insight into candidates' promises and performance.

American Elections: Basic Facts, Fundamental Questions

The first step in our analysis is to consider some basic information about recent American elections. Table 8.1 describes the outcomes of the last five presidential elections. Bolded candidates won their election; candidates followed by an asterisk were incumbent presidents running for reelection. In the 2008 election two candidates received more than 1 percent of the **popular vote**: Republican John McCain (45.7 percent), and Democrat Barack Obama (52.9 percent). However, McCain received 32 percent of the **electoral vote**, and Obama received 68 percent. In this election, 61 percent of people who were registered to vote actually voted, the highest turnout since 1968.

Table 8.1 raises a host of important questions: Where do candidates come from—how did McCain and Obama come to be the Republican and Democratic nominees? Why did Obama win—what issues did his campaign stress? How did people decide whether to vote and whom to support? Why was voter turnout so high? What is the difference between the popular vote and the electoral vote?

Table 8.2 reports the results of the last nine congressional elections, showing turnout; the **party ratios** for the newly elected House and Senate, or how many Democrats and how many Republicans hold office in each chamber; the **seat shift**, or the change in the party ratio since the last Congress; and the percentage of reelected incumbents in each chamber and party. To begin with, note that some (but not all) congressional elections are held in the same year as a presidential election. This regularity raises the question of whether the outcomes of the two elections are

popular vote The votes cast by citizens in an election.

electoral vote Votes cast by members of the electoral college; after a presidential candidate wins the popular vote in a given state, that candidate's slate of electors cast electoral votes for the candidate on behalf of that state.

party ratio The proportions of seats in the House and Senate that are controlled by each major party.

seat shift A change in the number of seats held by Republicans and Democrats in the House or Senate.

TABLE 8.1	PRESIDENTIAL ELECTION RESULTS, 1992–2008

Year	Turnout	Republican		Democratic		Independent/Minor Party	
		Popular	Electoral	Popular	Electoral	Popular	Electoral
1992	58.1%	George H. W. Bush*		**Bill Clinton**		Ross Perot (Reform)	
		37.4%	31% (168)	**43%**	**69% (370)**	18.9%	0
1996	51.7	Bob Dole		**Bill Clinton***		Ross Perot (Independent)	
		40.7%	30% (159)	**49.2%**	**70% (379)**	8.4%	0
2000	54.2	**George W. Bush**		Al Gore		Ralph Nader (Green)	
		47.9%	**51% (271)**	48.4%	49% (266)	2.4%	0
2004	60.3	**George W. Bush***		John Kerry		—	
		50.7%	**53% (286)**	48.3%	47% (251)		
2008	61.0	John McCain		**Barack Obama**		—	
		45.7%	32% (173)	**52.9%**	**68% (365)**		

*Denotes incumbent candidate. Election winner in boldface.

SOURCES: Calculated from statistics available from the Federal Election Commission at www.fec.gov, and the *Atlas of U.S. Presidential Elections* at www.uselectionatlas.org. Data for 2008 compiled from CNN at www.cnn.com/ELECTION and from Real Clear Politics at www.realclearpolitics.com.

TABLE 8.2 CONGRESSIONAL ELECTION RESULTS, 1994–2010

		House of Representatives				Senate			
Year	Turnout	Party Ratio	Seat Shift	Democrats Reelected	Republicans Reelected	Party Ratio	Seat Shift	Democrats Reelected	Republicans Reelected
1994	41.1%	204 D, 230 R	+54 R	83.9%	99.4%	47 D, 53 R	+10 R	87.5%	80.0%
1996	51.7	207 D, 227 R	+3 D	98.3	91.4	45 D, 55 R	–	100	85.7
1998	38.1	211 D, 223 R	+4 D	99.5	97.2	45 D, 55 R	–	92.3	87.5
2000	54.2	212 D, 222 R	+1 D	98.0	97.5	50 D, 50 R	+5 D	93.3	64.3
2002	39.5	205 D, 229 R	+8 R	97.4	97.5	48 D, 51 R	+ 1 R	83.3	93.3
2004	60.3	201 D, 232 R	+3 R	97.4	99.0	44 D, 55 R	+4 R	92.9	100
2006	40.2	233 D, 202 R	+30 D	100	89.6	50 D, 49 R	+6 D	100	57.1
2008	61.0	254 D, 173 R	+21 D	97.9	92.1	59 D, 41 R	+8 D	100	66.7
2010*	41.4	185 D, 239 R	+60 R	83.8	98.7	51 D, 47 R	+6 R	83.3	100

*2010 data omits two Senate races and eleven House races that were not decided as of November 3, 2010; turnout for 2010 is preliminary.

SOURCES: Calculated from Harold W. Stanley and Richard G. Niemi, *Vital Statistics on American Politics* (Washington, DC: CQ Press, 2007), Tables 1.1 and 1.10a, and from www.cnn.com/ELECTION.

normal election A typical congressional election in which the reelection rate is high and the influences on House and Senate contests are largely local.

nationalized election An atypical congressional election in which the reelection rate is relatively low for one party's House and Senate incumbents and national-level issues exert more influence than usual on House and Senate races.

▲ *American candidates, such as California House member Tom McClintock shown here, compete for different offices under a complex set of regulations. At the national level, their large campaign organizations often spend millions. Even so, elections are best understood in individual terms: one candidate trying to win one citizen's vote.*

linked. Do voters take account of the president or the presidential candidates when deciding how to vote for congressional candidates?

The congressional election data suggest some of the same questions raised about presidential elections: Why do particular individuals become candidates for the House and Senate? How do they campaign—and how do voters decide? Why are congressional incumbents so successful at getting reelected? Does low congressional turnover imply that most voters are apathetic and alienated, or that they are generally satisfied with the performance of their representatives?

The congressional election data also show a striking difference between two types of elections. Most congressional elections are **normal elections**, which result in a small number of seat shifts between the parties, elections turning largely on district- or state-level factors and high reelection rates for both parties.[1] Some congressional elections, such as 2006, 2008, and 2010 do not fit this description, however. In these cases, known as **nationalized elections**, turnover is much higher, and reelection rates are significantly lower for one party's incumbents. Results in these years also show a strong seat shift from one party to the other. In 2006, for example, Democrats won thirty House seats and six Senate seats, taking majority control of both chambers for the first time in twelve years. In 2008, Democrats gained twenty-one House seats and eight Senate seats, and reelected virtually all of their incumbents. In 2010, however, the pattern was reversed, with Republicans gaining at least sixty House seats (and majority control of the chamber) and at least six Senate seats (two were still being decided as this book went to press), and having significantly higher reelection rates compared to the Democrats.

These characteristics of congressional elections have important implications for what happens in government. Nationalized elections typically involve a change in party control of one or both houses of Congress or the presidency, and these changes can profoundly affect what government does. What determines whether an election will be normal or nationalized? Is it a change in how voters decide, or perhaps how candidates campaign? And what forces drive these changes? What factors have led to three nationalized elections in a row, and is this pattern likely to continue?

The most important thing you can bring to this discussion is an open mind, since many seemingly obvious intuitions about American elections are open to multiple interpretations. Recall the discussion in Chapter 1 of the "Purple America" map of the 2008 presidential election results (Figure 1.2, p. 23). This map offers a different perspective on the outcome than a red state–blue state map like the one at the back of this book, which shows state-level results. Both maps are valuable, and we're better off not relying on just one.

WHAT DO ELECTIONS DO?

Our working assumption for explaining the behavior of candidates and voters in an election is that their actions are tied directly to what elections do: select representatives and give citizens the opportunity to reward and punish officeholders seeking reelection.

Selecting Representatives The most visible function of American national elections is the selection of officeholders: members of the House and Senate and the president and vice president. Candidates can be **incumbents** or **challengers**. America has a representative democracy, which means that by voting in elections, Americans have an indirect effect on government policy. Though citizens do not make policy choices themselves, they determine which individuals get to make these choices. In this way, elections are supposed to connect citizen preferences and government actions.

Accountability The election process also creates a way to hold incumbents accountable. When a citizen faces a choice between voting for either an incumbent or a challenger, he makes a **retrospective evaluation**. The citizen considers the incumbent's performance and asks himself, "Has she done a good job on the issues I care about?"[2] Citizens who answer yes typically vote for the incumbent, and those who say no are more likely to vote for the challenger.

Retrospective evaluations are significant because they make incumbents responsive to constituent demands.[3] If an elected official wants to be reelected and anticipates that some constituents will make retrospective evaluations, he will try to take actions that these constituents will like. If an incumbent ignores the possibility of voters' retrospective evaluations, voters can make these judgments and opt to remove people from office whose performance they disapprove of. Retrospective evaluations can also form the basis for prospective judgments—voters' beliefs about how the country will fare if different candidates are elected—providing an additional reason for incumbents to be responsive to citizen demands.

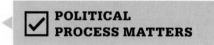

POLITICAL
PROCESS MATTERS

Many Americans use retrospective evaluations to judge members of Congress and the president. One of the important differences between normal and nationalized elections is that in nationalized elections, voters' overall evaluations of Congress and the president are much more negative, leading more voters to vote against incumbents from the party in power.

How Do American Elections Work?

This section describes the rules and procedures that define American national elections. We begin with congressional elections, then examine presidential contests. The first step in any election is to define who can vote. The Constitution limits voting rights to American citizens who are at least eighteen years old. There are also numerous restrictions on voter eligibility that vary across states, as shown in Nuts and Bolts 8.1.

incumbent A politician running for reelection to the office he or she currently holds.

challenger A politician running for an office that he or she does not hold at the time of the election. Challengers run against incumbents or in open-seat elections.

retrospective evaluation A citizen's judgment of an officeholder's job performance since the last election.

Voting Requirements across the States

REQUIREMENT	STATES WITH REQUIREMENT
Must be a U.S. citizen, at least eighteen years old on the day of the election, and residing in the state where registered	All states
Cannot have been convicted of a major crime and not pardoned	Alaska, Alabama, Arkansas, Connecticut, Delaware, Florida, Idaho, Iowa, Kentucky, Minnesota, Mississippi, Nebraska, Nevada, North Carolina, Rhode Island, Tennessee, Texas, Virginia, Washington, West Virginia, Wisconsin, and Wyoming
Cannot be in jail on Election Day	Alabama, California, Colorado, Georgia, Illinois, Indiana, Kansas, Louisiana, Maryland, Massachusetts, Michigan, Montana, New Jersey, New Mexico, New York, Ohio, Oklahoma, South Carolina, South Dakota, and Utah
Must have lived in the state where registered for at least a specified period before the election (usually thirty days)	Idaho, Indiana, Kentucky, Michigan, Mississippi, Montana, Nevada, New Jersey, New York, North Carolina, Pennsylvania, Rhode Island, Utah, and Wisconsin
Cannot have been ruled mentally incompetent by a court	**All states** *except* Alaska, Idaho, Illinois, Indiana, Maine, Michigan, New Hampshire, New Jersey, North Dakota, Oregon, Pennsylvania, Vermont, and Washington
Must swear an oath to the state and/or U.S. Constitution	Alabama, Florida, and Vermont
Cannot bet on the election outcome	Wisconsin

SOURCE: Compiled from the Eagleton Institute of Politics, Rutgers University, 2004, available at www-rci.rutgers.edu/~eagleton/News-Research/NewVoters/VoterRegRequire.html.

---

nomination The selection of a particular candidate to run for office in a general election as a representative of his or her political party.

open primary A primary election in which any registered voter can participate in the contest, regardless of party affiliation.

closed primary A primary election in which only registered members of a particular political party can vote.

general election The election in which voters cast ballots for House members, senators, and (every four years) a president and vice president.

TWO STAGES OF ELECTIONS

House and Senate candidates face a two-step procedure. First, if the prospective candidate wants to run on behalf of a political party, she must win the party's **nomination** in a primary election. If the would-be candidate wants to run as an independent, she needs to gather signatures on a petition to secure a spot on the ballot. Different states hold either **open primaries** or **closed primaries**, and the timing of these elections is set by state law. A few states, including California, Louisiana, and Washington, hold so-called single primaries, where there is one election involving candidates from both parties, with the top two finalists (regardless of party) receiving nominations to the general election. (California's use of this system is currently the subject of court proceedings and may be reversed.)

The second step in the election process, the **general election**, is held throughout the nation on the first Tuesday after the first Monday in November, which is designated by federal law as Election Day. General elections are the contests that determine who wins elected positions in government. The offices at stake vary depending on the year. Presidential elections are held every four years (2004, 2008 . . .). In a presidential election year, Americans elect the entire House of Representatives, one-third of the Senate, and a president and vice president. During midterm elections (2006, 2010 . . .), there is no presidential contest, but the entire House and a third of the Senate are up for election.

For both primaries and general elections, the location of polling places varies across the nation. In some areas, people cast their votes in schools, fire stations, or other public buildings. Some communities use private homes as polling stations—as of 2006, one-third of the polling stations in Los Angeles County were in private homes.[4]

A new development in American elections is an increase in the practice of early voting, casting a general election vote prior to Election Day.[5] Early voting has always been an option for voters who could show that they could not vote on Election Day because of travel, illness, religious obligations, or similar reasons. These voters could cast an **absentee ballot**, typically by mailing it to a designated location. In recent years, many states have established no-excuse-required absentee ballots or simply allowed voters to vote early by mail or at polling stations. Oregon votes entirely by mail, and over 98 percent of voters in Washington vote by mail. Though many Americans vote early (about 30 percent of voters in 2008, and about 33 percent in 2010) and studies show that early voters are more likely to have strong party identification (as well as high incomes and high commute times to work), it is not clear whether early voting has changed election outcomes.[6] If enough people vote early in future elections, it could have a significant impact on campaign tactics; for example, candidates would have to begin campaign advertising earlier to ensure that early voters see these appeals.

▲ *Americans vote in all sorts of places—even private homes. Here, people vote in a garage in Stockton, California, during the 2008 general elections.*

CONSTITUENCIES: WHO CHOOSES REPRESENTATIVES?

Another critical feature of American elections is that officeholders are elected in single-member districts in which only the winner of the most votes takes office. (Although each state's senators both represent the whole state, they are elected separately; they are not the first- and second-place election winners.) Candidates for the Senate compete at the state level; House candidates compete in congressional districts. In most states, congressional district lines are drawn by state legislatures, and in a few states, nonpartisan commissions or committees of judges perform this function. In the main, district lines are revised after each national census, to make sure the boundary lines reflect shifts in population across and within states, although redistricting can take place at any time. (For details on redistricting, including its impact on election outcomes, see Chapter 10.)

Because members of the House and Senate are elected from specific geographic areas, they often represent very different kinds of people, in terms of their age, race, income levels, and occupations, as well as their political leanings, including party affiliation and ideology. As a result, legislators elected from different areas of the country face very diverse demands from their constituents—leading them to pursue some very dissimilar kinds of policies.

For example, Democratic senator John Kerry, elected from Massachusetts, represents a fairly liberal state where gay marriage is legal, while Republican senator Orrin Hatch is from the conservative state of Utah. Suppose the Senate votes on a measure to ban gay marriage nationwide. Kerry would know that most of his constituents would probably want him to vote against the proposal, and Hatch would know that most of his constituents would probably want him to vote for it. This example illustrates that in many cases, congressional conflicts over policy reflect differences in constituents' demands. Kerry and Hatch may well hold different views on a gay marriage ban, but even if they agreed, their constituents' distinct demands would likely be enough to ensure that they voted differently.

DETERMINING WHO WINS

Most House and Senate contests involve **plurality voting**: the candidate who gets the most votes wins. However, some states use **majority voting**, meaning that a candidate needs a majority (more than 50 percent of the vote) to win. If no candidate

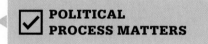

POLITICAL PROCESS MATTERS

absentee ballot A voting ballot submitted by mail before an election. Voters use absentee ballots if they will be unable to go to the polls on Election Day.

plurality voting A voting system in which the candidate who receives the most votes within a geographic area wins the election, regardless of whether that candidate wins a majority (more than half) of the votes.

majority voting A voting system in which a candidate must win more than 50 percent of votes to win the election. If no candidate wins enough votes to take office, a runoff election is held between the top two vote-getters.

Proportional Representation

The Congress and state legislatures in the United States are elected using single-member districts, but many other countries, particularly most West European countries, use proportional representation.[a] Under this system, there are no districts or other geographic units that elect their own representatives. Instead, there is a single nationwide campaign in which each party runs a list of as many candidates as there are seats in the legislature. On Election Day, citizens vote for a party, not a candidate. Votes are then counted nationwide for each party, and the parties receive the number of seats in the legislature proportional to the percentage of the nation's votes it received.

As an example, suppose America had used proportional representation in the 1996 presidential election and that people cast party votes in accordance with the votes they cast for presidential candidates. As shown in Table 8.1 (p. 259), in this election Republican Bob Dole received 40.7 percent of the popular vote, Democrat Bill Clinton received 49.2 percent, and Reform Party candidate Ross Perot received 8.4 percent. The 435 House seats would then be allocated proportionately to these results: the Republican Party would hold 177 seats (40.7 percent of 435), the Democrats would hold 214 seats, and the Reform Party would hold 39 seats.

This example illustrates the pros and cons of proportional representation. By counting votes nationwide rather than district by district, proportional representation enhances the political power of small interests that are organized into a political party. Under the system of single-member districts and the electoral college, the Reform Party was a failure; its congressional

In countries such as Germany, where there is no president and many legislative seats are allocated by proportional representation, elections sometimes produce coalition governments in which multiple parties share control. Here, leaders of Germany's Social Democratic Party and Christian Social Union are shown on either side of German chancellor and Christian Democratic Union leader Angela Merkel after the signing of their 2005 power-sharing agreement.

candidates never won a House or Senate seat, and its presidential candidates never won any electoral votes. Under proportional representation, the Reform Party would be a force to be reckoned with. Its candidates would hold nearly 10 percent of House seats. More important, under proportional representation in an election such as this one, the smaller party would hold the balance of power between the Republicans and the Democrats. Neither major party would hold enough seats to enact legislation on its own. Thus, to get anything done, they would both be forced to find common ground with Reform legislators.

Some scholars have proposed proportional representation in America as a way to increase the political power of minority groups or to give small ideological groups the opportunity to elect representatives to Congress.[b] However, because proportional representation enhances the power of small groups, countries that use this system tend to have many political parties, each of which elects some people to the legislature, with none of the parties even approaching holding a majority of seats. As a result, enacting new policies requires complex negotiations among many competing interests represented in the legislature. The implication is that enhancing representation for small groups through proportional representation comes at a price: the ability to get things done in the resulting legislature. ■

---

runoff election Under a majority voting system, a second election held only if no candidate wins a majority of the votes in the first general election. Only the top two vote-getters in the first election compete in the runoff.

has a majority, a **runoff election** takes place between the top two finishers. Some candidates have lost runoff elections even though they received the most votes in the first contest. In a 2007 special election for Georgia's 10th District, Republican Paul Broun lagged more than 20 percentage points behind state senator Paul Whitehead after the first round of voting (in the first round, Whitehead received 43.5 percent of the vote in a ten-candidate race.[7]) Broun went on to defeat Whitehead by a few hundred votes in the runoff.

The two-step process of primary and general elections can have a similar effect on the election's outcome. Sometimes the winner of a primary is not a party's best candidate for the general election. You may recall from Chapter 7, Political Parties, that in the 2010 Alaska Senate Republican primary, politically inexperienced challenger Joe Miller defeated incumbent Lisa Murkowski. Murkowski won the general election as a write-in candidate.[8]

Americans vote using a wide range of machines and ballots,[9] and the choice of voting technology can affect election outcomes.[10] Some counties use paper keypunch ballots, on which voters use a stylus to punch out holes in a ballot card next to the names of their preferred candidates. Other counties use mechanical voting machines that require voters to pull a lever next to the name of their preferred candidates. A few localities still use paper ballots on which voters mark their preferred candidate with an "X." Touch-screen voting machines are becoming increasingly popular, but the move to touch-screen voting is controversial because critics worry that the machines could be manipulated to change election outcomes.[11] Of course, earlier technologies aren't perfect either; vote totals in lever machines can also be manipulated, and paper ballots can be lost or altered. Moreover, the widespread use of touch screens in recent elections has occurred without major problems.[12] Still, many voting technology experts prefer optical scan voting in which voters indicate their preferences with a felt-tip pen on a paper ballot that is read by a scanner. This method is very accurate and inexpensive, and it leaves a paper trail.

Different voting methods show different rates of **undervotes**, which happen when a voter casts an unmarked ballot, votes in some races on the ballot but not others, or casts a ballot that cannot be counted for some reason. The various voting technologies are also associated with different rates of voter error, such as when a voter accidentally casts a ballot for someone other than his preferred candidate. (Of course, since votes are secret, it is impossible to be sure about these mistakes, but they have been observed in lab experiments involving hypothetical elections.) The confusion that surrounded the 2000 presidential election outcome in Palm Beach County, Florida, showed what a difference ballot structure can make. Palm Beach County residents voted on punch cards in combination with a device called a butterfly ballot. This ballot lists the candidates on both sides of a center column, and voters indicate their preference by pressing down on the circle in the center column that corresponds to the name of their preferred candidate using a stylus. A punch card inserted underneath the ballot records the stylus marks, and votes are counted by counting holes in the punch cards.

This ballot structure appears to have caused some supporters of Al Gore in Palm Beach County to mistakenly vote for Pat Buchanan. As the picture shows, Gore's name and Buchanan's were on facing pages at about the same level, so it would be easy for a voter to press down on the wrong circle, thereby voting for Buchanan when they intended to vote for Gore. Analyses suggested that the butterfly ballot cost Gore several thousand Palm Beach County votes—enough to change the results of the election in Florida, and thus the outcome of the 2000 presidential election.[13] Keep in mind, though, that the butterfly ballot in Palm Beach County is only one example of the influence of a voting method on the election results. We don't know whether ballots used in other counties and states favored Gore or some other candidates. But it is clear that choices about how ballots are structured can affect who wins elections.

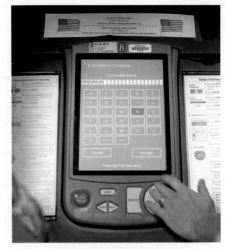

▲ Many different mechanisms are used to record votes in American elections, including paper keypunch ballots and computerized, electronic machines (above).

undervote Casting a ballot that is either incomplete or cannot be counted.

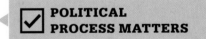

☑ **POLITICAL PROCESS MATTERS**

▼ The design of the infamous Palm Beach County, Florida, butterfly ballot, used in the 2000 presidential election, inadvertently led some people who intended to vote for Democrat Al Gore to select Reform Party candidate Patrick Buchanan.

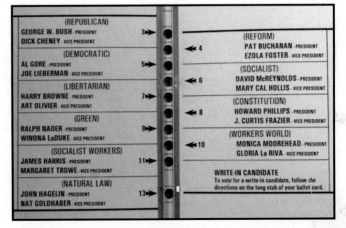

Constitutional Requirements for Candidates

The Constitution sets age limits and residency requirements for candidates who run for federal government positions. Presidential candidates must be thirty-five years or older at the time they take office and have been born in the United States. (Thus, Arnold Schwarzenegger, U.S. citizen, actor, and former governor of California, cannot be elected president: he was born in Austria.) A House candidate must be at least twenty-five when she takes office and needs to have been a U.S. citizen for at least seven years. A senator must be at least thirty and needs to have been a citizen for nine years. House and Senate candidates are also required to reside in the state that they seek to represent. In addition, members of the electoral college cannot vote for a president and vice president who reside in the same state.

The Constitution also sets the term of office (the number of years an officeholder serves before facing another election) for federal offices. The term of office for House members is two years, and senators serve six-year terms. The president and vice president are elected to a four-year term.

Ballot counting adds additional complexities. Most states have laws that allow vote recounts if a race is sufficiently close (within 1 percent or less). In the 2008 Minnesota Senate race, challenger Al Franken asked for a recount after an initial count showed he was within several hundred votes of unseating incumbent Norm Coleman. After a months-long process that included numerous court challenges over disputed ballots, Franken was declared the winner in July 2009. Even when a recount occurs, it may be impossible to definitively determine who won a particular election, as the statutes that determine which ballots are valid are often vague and open to interpretation. The deeper lesson of these examples is that when an election is close, the question of which candidate wins may depend on how ballots are structured and votes counted. The problem is not that election officials are dishonest; rather, close elections inherently tend to produce ambiguous outcomes.

Claims are often made that officials manipulate election rules to guarantee wins for their favored candidates. In the 2004 election, some Democrats charged that Republican local officials had changed registration laws, the location of polling stations, ballot-counting procedures, and other rules to help President Bush win Ohio.[14] It is difficult to definitively disprove these allegations, although investigations found no evidence of a conspiracy.[15] What is clear is that election rules can affect results. Particularly in close races, small changes in the rules governing elections can easily change outcomes. In the close 2008 Minnesota Senate race, press reports suggested that some voters were turned away because of a shortage of voting supplies. If polling stations were required to stock extra supplies, the election outcome might have been different.

PRESIDENTIAL ELECTIONS

Many of the rules governing elections, such as who is eligible to vote, are the same for both presidential and congressional elections. However, presidential contests have several unique rules regarding how nominees are determined and how votes are counted.

The Nomination: Primaries and Caucuses Presidential nominees from the Democratic and Republican parties are determined by a series of state-level **primaries** and **caucuses** over a five-month period beginning in January of an election year.[16] These elections select **delegates** to attend the nominating conventions that are held during the summer. At these conventions, the delegates cast the votes that determine their party's presidential and vice-presidential nominees. The format of these

primary A ballot vote in which citizens select a party's nominee for the general election.

caucus (electoral) A local meeting in which party members select a party's nominee for the general election.

delegates Individuals who attend their party's national convention and vote to select their party's nominee for the presidency. Delegates are elected in a series of primaries and caucuses that occur during winter and spring of an election year.

elections, including their timing and the number of delegates selected per state, is determined on a state-by-state basis by the state and national party organizations.[17] In some states, each candidate preselects a list of delegates who will go to the convention if the candidate wins sufficient votes in the primary or caucus. In other states, candidates select delegates off a list developed by party leaders. In both cases, a candidate's principal goal is to win as many delegates as possible—and also to select delegates who will be reliable supporters at the convention. Surprisingly, neither party requires delegates to support the candidate who selected them, but there is an expectation that they will do so.

The details of translating primary and caucus votes into convention delegates vary from state to state, but some general rules apply. All Democratic primaries and caucuses use **proportional allocation** to divide each state's delegate seats between the candidates, which means that if a candidate receives 40 percent of the votes in a state's primary, the candidate gets roughly 40 percent of the convention delegates from that state. Some Republican contests use proportional allocation, but others are **winner-take-all**, meaning that the candidate who receives the most votes gets all of the state's convention delegates. These rules matter: in the race for the 2008 Republican nomination, John McCain's early victories in winner-take-all primaries helped him build a large lead in delegates that caused some other candidates to drop out. Overall, McCain won only 47 percent of the primary and caucus vote but claimed 72 percent of the delegates. In contrast, senators Hillary Clinton and Barack Obama each won about 48 percent of the vote, and they also divided the pledged delegates almost evenly (Obama had 52 percent to Clinton's 48 percent). If Republicans used only proportional allocation, McCain would have faced tougher opposition through additional contests and might not have won the nomination.

The ordering of state primaries and caucuses is important because many candidacies do not survive beyond the early contests.[18] Most presidential candidates pour everything they have into the first few elections. Candidates who do well attract contributions, campaign workers, endorsements, and additional media coverage, enabling them to move on to subsequent primaries or caucuses. But for candidates who do poorly in the first contests, contributions and coverage dry up, and these candidates usually drop out. The result is that the candidate who leads after the first several primaries and caucuses generally wins the nomination, as John McCain did to become the 2008 Republican nominee.[19] However, when the first few contests do not yield a clear favorite, as in the race for the 2008 Democratic nomination when Hillary Clinton and Barack Obama split the early primaries and caucuses, the race can continue until the last states have voted, or even until the convention.

One candidate who downplayed the power of early momentum was 2008 Republican hopeful Rudy Giuliani, who devoted few resources to the early contests in Iowa, New Hampshire, and South Carolina, believing he would fare best by concentrating his efforts on the late-January Florida primary.[20] This strategy was partly driven by a calculation that most of the other candidates would devote their resources to the early contests, perform poorly, and then drop out, allowing Giuliani to dominate the remaining contests. It also reflected the fact that, as a moderate conservative, Giuliani was not expected to do well in the first few states' primaries and caucuses, as those states' Republican voters tend to be more conservative. Nonetheless, Giuliani's strategy backfired, as John McCain emerged from South Carolina as the clear frontrunner, then won the Florida primary by a significant margin. Giuliani dropped out of the race—and endorsed McCain—a few weeks later.

If a sitting president runs for reelection, as George Bush did in 2004, he typically faces little opposition for the party's general-election nomination—not because challengers defer to the president, but because most presidents are popular enough among their own party's faithful supporters that they can win the nomination

proportional allocation During the presidential primaries, the practice of determining the number of convention delegates allotted to each candidate based on the percentage of the popular vote cast for each candidate. All Democratic primaries and caucuses use this system, as do some states' Republican primaries and caucuses.

winner-take-all During the presidential primaries, the practice of assigning all of a given state's delegates to the candidate who receives the most popular votes. Some states' Republican primaries and caucuses use this system.

regional primaries A practice whereby several states in the same area of the country hold presidential primaries or caucuses on the same day.

frontloading The practice of states moving their presidential primaries or caucuses to take place earlier in the nomination process, often in the hopes of exerting more influence over the outcome.

superdelegates Democratic members of Congress and party officials selected by their colleagues to be delegates at the party's presidential nominating convention. (Republicans do not have superdelegates.) Unlike delegates selected in primaries or caucuses, superdelegates are not committed to a particular candidate and can exercise their judgment when deciding how to vote at the convention.

without too much trouble. Only presidents with particularly low approval ratings have faced serious opposition in their nomination bids, as did Gerald Ford in 1976 and Jimmy Carter in 1980. Both won renomination but lost the general election.

Among the states, the presidential nomination process is always changing.[21] There has been a trend toward **regional primaries**, when all of the states in a geographic area elect delegates on the same day, as well as **frontloading**, when states move their primaries to take place earlier in the process. For many years, the states of Iowa and New Hampshire have held the first presidential nomination contests in late January, with the Iowa caucus held a week before the New Hampshire primary. State party officials from other states often complained about the media attention given to these contests and the disproportionate influence of these states in winnowing the candidate pool. As a result, both parties' national committees decided that in 2008 Nevada would hold its caucus just after the Iowa caucus, and South Carolina would hold its primary a week after New Hampshire's vote.[22]

The national committees can issue rules and requirements about the timing of state presidential primaries, but the dates of these elections are set by state law, meaning that a committee's directives may not be followed. Indeed, the changes described above encouraged many state legislatures to frontload their states' primaries and caucuses. Twenty-one states held their presidential selections on "Super Tuesday," February 5, 2008, allotting more than 40 percent of Republican and Democratic convention delegates in a single day. In Michigan and Florida, the state legislatures moved their primaries to mid- and late January, respectively, prompting Iowa and New Hampshire to hold their contests even earlier than usual in an effort to hold on to their privileged position. (These schedule changes by Michigan and Florida occurred despite the major parties' threats to punish both states for the early votes by refusing to seat their delegations at the nominating conventions, meaning that these states' votes would not count toward selecting the parties' general-election nominees. Ultimately, both parties seated the wayward states' delegations and gave them full voting rights—but only because each party's presumptive nominee had enough votes to win the nomination regardless of how these delegates voted.) As a result of these broad changes, a large fraction of both parties' convention delegates were selected by early February, about one month into the nomination process. On the Republican side in 2008, these changes helped John McCain to become the presumptive nominee by the middle of February. However, on the Democratic side, both Hillary Clinton and Barack Obama emerged from Super Tuesday with roughly equal delegate counts and continued to fight for the nomination until the end of the primary process in early June.

Another recent change that distinguishes the candidate selection processes of the two parties is that about one-fifth of delegates to the Democratic Convention are not supporters of a particular candidate, chosen to attend the convention through primary and caucus results. Rather, they are elected officials and party officials who are selected by their colleagues to serve as **superdelegates**. Most of them are automatically seated at the convention regardless of primary and caucus results, and they are free to support any candidate for the nomination. By forcing candidates to court support from superdelegates, the party aims to ensure that the nominee is someone these officials believe can win the general election, and whom they can work with if he or she is elected.[23] In the 2008 Democratic nomination contest, many superdelegates waited until the end of the primaries in early June to announce their support, leaving the race open until then.

The National Convention Presidential nominating conventions are held late in the summer of an election year. The main task is the selection of the party's presidential election nominee.[24] To get the nomination, a candidate needs the support of a

◀ *One of the primary purposes for presidential nominating conventions is to showcase a party's nominee before a national audience. Here, Barack Obama accepts his party's nomination on August 28, 2008.*

majority of the delegates (before the 1930s, a two-thirds majority was required). If no candidate receives a majority after the first round of voting at the convention, the voting continues until someone does. Some conventions have required many ballots to select a nominee (the record is 103 ballots at the 1924 Democratic Convention).[25] However, all recent conventions have needed only one ballot to select a nominee.

After the convention delegates nominate a presidential candidate, they select a vice-presidential nominee. Typically the presidential nominee gets to choose whom to run with, and the convention delegates ratify this choice without much debate. Delegates also vote on the party platform that describes what the party stands for and what kinds of policies its candidates will supposedly seek to enact if they are elected.

The final purpose of a convention is to attract public attention to the party and its nominees. Public figures give speeches during the evening sessions when all of the major television networks have live convention coverage. Barack Obama gave a well-publicized speech at the 2004 Democratic Convention when he was the party's Senate nominee for Illinois. At some recent conventions, both parties have drawn press attention by recruiting speakers who support their political goals despite their association with the opposing party. Democratic senator Zell Miller spoke at the 2004 Republican Convention. The 2008 Republican Convention featured a speech by Connecticut senator Joe Lieberman, who had been Al Gore's running mate on the Democratic presidential ticket in 2000, while former Republican representative Jim Leech delivered a speech before the 2008 Democratic Convention.

Once presidential candidates are nominated, the general election campaign officially begins—though it often unofficially starts much earlier, as soon as the major parties' presumptive nominees are known. We say more about presidential campaigns in a later section.

Counting Presidential Votes Despite the set-up in the voting booth where you choose between the candidates by name, citizens don't vote directly for presidential candidates. Rather, when you select your preferred candidate's name, you are choosing that person's slate of pledged supporters from your state to serve as electors, who will then vote to elect the president. The number of electors for each state equals the state's number of House members (which varies based on state population) plus the number of senators (two per state). All together, the electors chosen by the citizens of each state constitute the **electoral college**, the body that formally selects the

electoral college The body that votes to select America's president and vice president based on the popular vote in each state. Each candidate nominates a slate of electors who are selected to attend the meeting of the college if their candidate wins the most votes in a state or district.

swing states In a presidential race, highly competitive states in which both major party candidates stand a good chance of winning the state's electoral votes.

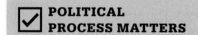

POLITICAL PROCESS MATTERS

president. Small-population states, therefore, have few electoral votes—Delaware and Montana each have only three—while the highest-population state, California, has fifty-five. In most states, electoral votes are allocated on a winner-take-all basis: the candidate who receives the most votes from a given state's citizens gets all of that state's electoral votes. Two states, Maine and Nebraska, allocate most of their electoral votes at the congressional district level, which means that in those states, the candidate who wins the most votes in each congressional district wins that district's single electoral vote. Then, the remaining two electoral votes are given to the candidate who gets the most votes statewide.[26]

The winner-take-all method of allocating most states' electoral votes focuses candidates' attention on two kinds of states: high-population states with lots of electoral votes to be gained and **swing states** where the contest is relatively close. It's better for a candidate to spend a day campaigning in California, with its fifty-five electoral votes, than in Montana, where only three electoral votes are at stake. However, if one candidate is sure to win a particular state, both candidates will direct their efforts elsewhere. In 2004, when polls indicated that Democrat John Kerry was very likely to win California, both Kerry and Bush pulled most of their staff and advertising out of California, and redeployed them to swing states like Ohio and Missouri.[27] As polls began to move against John McCain in October 2008, his campaign suspended advertising in Michigan and Wisconsin in favor of additional efforts in Ohio and Pennsylvania. Looking at the same polls, the Obama campaign redeployed advertising and volunteers to Ohio, Florida, Indiana, and even Arizona, McCain's home state. The result: Obama won all of these states except Arizona.

After citizens' votes are counted in each state, the chosen slates of electors meet in December in the state capitals. At their meetings, the electors almost always vote for the presidential candidate they have pledged to support. After the votes are certified by a special session of the Senate, the candidate who wins a majority of the nation's electoral votes (at least 270) is the new president. One peculiarity of the electoral college is that in a majority of states, it is legal for an elector to vote for a candidate they are not pledged to or to abstain from voting.[28] Some electors have done so, although never in large enough numbers to alter the outcome of an election.[29] Such events are uncommon for the simple reason that electors are selected by the presidential candidates. A candidate is unlikely to pick someone to serve as an elector if there seems to be any chance that the person will switch candidates or opt not to vote.

If no candidate receives a majority of the electoral college votes, the members of the House of Representatives choose the winner using a procedure in which the House members from each state decide which candidate to support, then cast one collective vote per state, with the winner needing a majority of these state-level votes to win. This procedure has not been used since 1824, although it might be required if a third-party candidate won a significant number of electoral votes or if a state's electors were unwilling to cast their votes.[30]

A presidential candidate can win the electoral college vote, and thus the election, without receiving a majority of the votes cast by citizens—particularly if the vote is divided between more than two candidates. When a third-party candidate for president receives a substantial number of votes, the election winner can easily end up receiving more votes than any other candidate without winning a majority of the popular vote. Bill Clinton, for example, won a substantial electoral college majority in 1992, while receiving only 43 percent of the popular vote, due to the fact that Ross Perot, running as a third-party candidate, received almost 19 percent of the national popular vote but not enough support in any one state to win electoral votes.

In addition, because of the way popular votes translate into electoral votes, a candidate can receive a majority of the electoral vote even though another candidate won more popular votes. Thus, George Bush, the winner of the 2000 election, received about 540,000 fewer votes than his main rival, Al Gore. The other presidents who won the electoral college vote but lost the popular vote were John Quincy Adams in 1824, Rutherford B. Hayes in 1876, and Benjamin Harrison in 1888—and this almost occurred in 1960, when John F. Kennedy was elected, and in 1976, when Jimmy Carter won the presidency.

election cycle The two-year period between general elections.

Electoral Campaigns

This section turns to the campaign process and what candidates do to convince people to go to the polls and vote for them on Election Day. Our emphasis is on things that candidates do regardless of the office they are running for, across the entire **election cycle**, the two-year period between general elections.

SETTING THE STAGE

On the day after an election, candidates, party officials, and interest groups all start thinking about the next election cycle: who won and who lost, which incumbents look like safe bets for reelection and which ones might be vulnerable, who might retire in the next couple of years or run for another office in the next election, and whether election returns reveal any new information about what kinds of campaigns or issues might increase turnout or support.

These calculations also reflect the costs of running for office. Challengers for House and Senate seats know that a campaign will take up a year or more of their time and deplete their financial resources, and presidential campaigns require even more money and effort. If a potential challenger for one of these offices already holds elected office, such as a state legislator running for the House or a House member running for the Senate, they may have to give up their current office in order to run for a new one.[31]

Party organizations and interest groups face similar constraints in recruiting candidates and keeping others from running. They do not have the funds to offer significant support to candidates in all 435 congressional districts, thirty-three or thirty-four Senate races, and a presidential contest.[32] Which races draw their attention? The answer depends on many factors, such as how well incumbents did in the last election and how much money those who were reelected have on hand for the next election, whether party affiliation in the state or district favors Republicans or Democrats (and by how much), and whether the newly elected officeholders are likely to run for reelection.

For example, in the year before the 2010 election, many reports noted the poor reelection prospects of Pennsylvania Republican senator Arlen Specter, who faced a well-funded challenger in the Republican primary, former representative Pat Toomey, who was likely to receive considerable support from the conservative Republican primary electorate over the more moderate Specter. Moreover, even if Specter won the primary, he would face a tough fight in the general election against Democratic representative Joe Sestak, particularly if Specter had taken conservative positions to win the nomination. Ultimately, Specter decided to switch his party affiliation to the Democratic Party, believing that party leaders would discourage Sestak from entering the race, and that his chances of beating the strongly conservative Toomey were higher in the general election, where the electorate was more moderate compared with the Republican primary.[33] However, Sestak continued his

▼ *Although nearly all serious candidates for federal offices campaign as the nominee of one of the major political parties, party leaders have relatively little control over how candidates campaign or what they do in office—or even whether they switch their party affiliations. Here, longtime Republican senator Arlen Specter, who switched to the Democratic Party in early 2009, tries to explain his decision at a town hall meeting in his home state of Pennsylvania.*

▲ House member Dennis Kucinich (D-OH) ran for the Democratic presidential nomination in 2004 and 2008. Though his efforts never attracted many supporters, he succeeded in drawing media attention to his principal campaign issues, an end to the war in Iraq and enactment of government-funded health care for all Americans.

campaign and defeated Specter in the Democratic primary, only to lose a close race to Toomey in the general election. However, state and national Democrats were probably not hurt by Sestak's insurgency; while it is impossible to be sure, it is likely that Specter would have lost the general election to Toomey by a significantly higher margin.

The Specter example illustrates the limits of the powers held by the party organization to determine who will run for office. From the viewpoint of winning the general election, party leaders would want to force either Specter or Sestak to drop out of the campaign, leaving the remaining candidate free to concentrate his attention and resources on the general election. But because party leaders do not have this power, they are forced to let costly primary fights play out to their conclusion, even when these contests lower the party's chances of holding the seat.

Party committees and candidates also consider the likelihood that incumbents might retire, creating an **open seat**. In the run-up to the 2010 election, many Democratic House members from moderate and conservative-leaning districts announced their retirements, believing that they would face a tough reelection fight in the next election. Open seats are of special interest to potential candidates and other political actors because incumbents generally hold an election advantage.[34] So, when a seat opens, candidates from the party that does not control the seat know that they may have a better chance to win because they will not have to run against an incumbent. Consequently, the incumbent's party leaders know that they have to recruit an especially strong candidate to hold the seat. Interest groups watch all of these decisions with an eye toward deciding whom they should endorse or support with campaign donations and advertisements.

Presidential campaigns work the same way. Virtually all first-term presidents run for reelection. So, potential challengers in the opposing party study the results of the last election to see how many votes the president received and how this support was distributed across the states, in order to figure out their own chances of winning a head-to-head contest against the president. Candidates in the president's party make the same calculations, although no sitting president in the twentieth century was denied renomination. Some presidents (Harry Truman in 1952, Lyndon Johnson in 1968) retired because their chances of being renominated were not good, while others (Gerald Ford in 1976, Jimmy Carter in 1980) faced tough primary contests, as previously mentioned.[35]

Some candidates run for office to gain publicity for causes they support. During the 2004 and 2008 presidential campaigns, Representative Dennis Kucinich of Ohio ran for the Democratic presidential nomination. Although Kucinich would have been happy to be the nominee, he knew that he had no realistic chance of winning the party's nomination. His goal was to focus the attention of other Democratic hopefuls on the war in Iraq, which he strongly opposed, and to pressure the eventual nominee to take a strong antiwar stance.[36] Similarly, Representative Ron Paul of Texas ran for the 2008 Republican nomination at least in part to draw attention to the conservative antiwar position and his libertarian ideology.

BEFORE THE CAMPAIGN

Most incumbent House members, senators, and presidents work throughout the election cycle to secure their reelection; political scientists label this activity the **permanent campaign**.[37] To stay in office, incumbents have to do two things: keep their constituents happy, and raise money for their campaign. As we see in Chapter 10, congressional incumbents try to keep their constituents happy by taking actions that ensure voters can identify something good that the incumbent has done, which boosts those voters' retrospective evaluations at election time.[38]

open seat An elected position for which there is no incumbent.

permanent campaign The actions officeholders take throughout the election cycle to build support for their reelection.

Incumbent presidents make the same kinds of calculations. During Barack Obama's first months in office, many of his advisers argued that he had to offer an economic stimulus plan in light of polls that showed the economy was an overriding concern to most Americans. Obama did so—a decision clearly driven by political as well as policy concerns. George W. Bush's advisers made a similar argument about the Medicare reform legislation in 2003.[39] Of course, many presidential actions are taken in response to events rather than initiated to gain voter support. Particularly in the case of wars and other conflicts, it is far-fetched to say that presidents initiate hostilities for political gain. Even so, presidents, just like other politicians, are keenly aware of the political consequences of their actions and the need to build a record they can run on in the next election.

Presidents can also use the federal bureaucracy to their own advantage and to help members of their party. During the 2006 congressional campaign, the Bush-appointed commissioner of the Internal Revenue Service ordered his staff to delay taxpayer audits, believing that people who received audit notices might take out their displeasure on Republican congressional candidates.[40] Some scholars have argued that presidents try to increase economic growth in the months prior to elections, with the aim of increasing support for themselves (if they are eligible to run for reelection) and for their party's candidates, a phenomenon called the **political business cycle**.[41] Given the size and complexity of the U.S. economy, and the fact that the independent Federal Reserve System controls monetary policy, it is unlikely that these kinds of efforts could have much success. Even so, out of a desire to stay in office and help their party's candidates, it seems clear that presidents would want to be seen as having a positive impact on the economy.

Candidates for all offices, incumbents and challengers alike, also devote considerable time before the campaign to raising campaign funds. Fund-raising helps an incumbent president or member of Congress in two ways.[42] First, it ensures that if the incumbent faces a strong opponent, she will have enough money to run an aggressive campaign. Successful fund-raising also deters opposition. Potential challengers are less likely to run against an incumbent if they see that he is well-funded with a sizable campaign war chest.[43]

The other thing candidates do before the campaign is build their campaign organization.[44] Just like fund-raising, the success or failure of these efforts is also read as a signal of a candidate's prospects: if experienced, well-respected people agree to work in a candidate's campaign, observers conclude that the candidate's prospects for being elected are probably good.

Skilled campaign consultants are among the most sought-after campaign staff. These consultants plan strategies, run public opinion polls, assemble ads and buy television time, and talk with members of the media on the candidate's behalf, to name just a few things required to run a successful campaign. For many consultants, electioneering is a full-time, year-round position. Many concentrate on electing candidates from one party, although some work for whomever will pay them.

Almost all campaigns have paid and volunteer staff, ranging from the dozen or so people who work for a typical House candidate to the thousands needed to run a major-party candidate's presidential campaign. Some campaign staff work full-time for an incumbent's campaign committee or are on the incumbent's congressional or presidential staff. With some exceptions for senior presidential staff, federal law prohibits government employees from engaging in campaign activities.[45] As a result, many congressional staffers take a leave of absence from their government jobs to work on their bosses' reelection campaigns during the last few months of the election cycle, then return to working for the government after the election—assuming the incumbent is reelected.

▲ Most officeholders are always campaigning—traveling around their states or districts, talking with constituents, and explaining their actions in office—all in the hope of winning and keeping support for the next election. Here, Republican representative Sam Graves greets constituents during a 2008 parade in Kearney, Missouri.

political business cycle Attempts by elected officials to manipulate the economy before elections by increasing economic growth and reducing unemployment and inflation, with the goal of improving evaluations of their performance in office.

Reelection Rates for Congressional Incumbents

As we have discussed throughout this chapter, in a typical congressional election, upwards of 90 percent of the sitting House members and senators who run for reelection win. Even in a nationalized election, most incumbents from both political parties return to Washington for a new term. As one analysis of a House election in 2000 put it, "[the incumbent] has as much chance of losing Tuesday as he does of getting hit by a blimp."[a] Similarly, in an opinion piece written just before the 2006 midterms, two political scientists wrote that congressional incumbents "enjoy reelection rates that would have been the envy of the Supreme Soviet."[b]

Why are congressional reelection rates so high? Aside from their extreme claims, both articles make the same point: members of Congress have insulated themselves from electoral challenges through a few specific tactics that draw on their power as officeholders. They raise large sums of campaign cash well in advance of upcoming elections, use redistricting to give themselves a safe district populated by supporters, and enact pork-barrel legislation that provides government benefits and programs to their constituents.

The result of these actions, goes the argument, is that House incumbents can get reelected without breaking a sweat, especially since they typically find themselves facing weak, poorly funded challengers. If so, the high reelection rates for congressional incumbents are not a sign that voters are satisfied with Congress at all. Rather, they reflect the poor choices that voters are offered at election time. A lack of real opposition also means legislators need not fear retribution at the polls even if they ignore their constituents. As political scientists Samuel Issacharoff and Jonathan Nagler put it, "The clear losers are the voters. An insulated Congress is one that becomes increasingly inattentive to the preferences of the electorate."[c]

Other political science research offers some important counters to these claims. First, if incumbents were so safe, they would not spend so much time in the permanent campaign, going home to their district or state nearly every weekend to meet with constituents, explain their behavior in Washington, and find out what they need to do to increase their chances of winning the next election.

Second, in nearly every congressional district, there are many state legislators, county executives, mayors, and other local elected officials who would love to serve in Congress. If they think an incumbent is unpopular or otherwise vulnerable, at least one of them would surely run against the incumbent in the next election.[d] Studies show that when such politically experienced candidates challenge a congressional incumbent, they are generally able to raise enough money to fund a credible campaign.[e]

Third, incumbents don't always win. In a nationalized election, incumbents from one party have significantly lower chances of reelection than their colleagues in the other party. And even in normal elections, a small number of incumbents lose a primary or a general election, and others retire because they know their chances of winning are problematic. Moreover, incumbent defeats don't happen at random: incumbents who lose have often cast votes that run counter to their constituents' demands or have become embroiled in a personal scandal.[f]

This evidence suggests that congressional incumbents are not necessarily safe from electoral defeat. Rather, their high reelection rates result from the actions they take every day, which are calculated to win favor with their constituents. As Congress scholar David Mayhew described it, "When we say, 'Congressman Smith is unbeatable,' we do not mean that there is nothing he could do that would lose him his seat. Rather we mean, 'Congressman Smith is unbeatable as long as he continues to do the things he is doing.'"[g] ∎

POLITICS IS EVERYWHERE

Clearly, it's hard to separate what candidates do at election time from what they do between elections—incumbents are *always* campaigning, which is part of the reason they are so likely to win reelection. In many cases, incumbent House members and senators also wind up running against poorly funded, inexperienced candidates. Stronger challengers see that the incumbent has been working hard to solidify a hold on the constituency, and they decide to wait until the incumbent retires, when they can run for an open seat. Thus, incumbents are not automatically favored for reelection, but they often win by large margins because of all the things they do while holding office in between elections.[46]

THE GENERAL ELECTION CAMPAIGN

General election campaigns begin in early September. By this point, both parties have their presidential nominees and their congressional candidates. Interest groups, candidates, and party committees have raised most of the funds they will use or donate in the campaign. The race is on.

Having made numerous trips to the first primary and caucus states, trying to build their organization and attract mass support, presidential campaigns largely shift their focus once primaries and caucuses start, putting more emphasis on **wholesale politics**, in which candidates contact voters indirectly, such as through media coverage and campaign advertising. At this point, presidential campaign events generally involve large numbers of citizens, or if they are smaller events or one-on-one encounters, they are designed to generate media coverage and thereby reach a larger audience. In contrast, some campaigns for the House and even a few Senate races are more likely to stress direct contact with voters, or **retail politics**. (Of course, people who work in a presidential campaign, particularly volunteers, also pursue direct contacts with citizens throughout the campaign.)

Basic Campaign Strategies One of the most fundamental campaign strategies, particularly in congressional campaigns, is to build name recognition. Simply put, a citizen needs to know a candidate's name before thinking about voting for him. And since many citizens tend not to be well-informed about congressional candidates, efforts to increase a candidate's name recognition in these races can deliver a few extra percentage points of support—enough to turn a close defeat into a victory. (Practically all voters can identify the major party presidential candidates, so name recognition efforts are not as central to these elections.)

A second basic strategy is **mobilization**. Turnout is not automatic: just because a citizen supports a candidate does not mean that he or she will actually vote. Candidates have to worry just as much about making sure that their supporters vote as they do about winning support in the first place. Moreover, focusing on getting supporters to the polls is often a relatively efficient use of candidates' resources. Given that most people don't pay much attention to politics, it's much easier to get a supporter to go to the polls than it is to convert an opponent into a supporter.

Campaign professionals refer to these voter mobilization efforts as **GOTV** ("get out the vote") or the **ground game**.[47] Most campaigns for Congress or the presidency use extensive door-to-door canvassing to contact citizens, as well as phone banks and e-mail. In 2008, Barack Obama's campaign launched a massive get-out-the-vote operation, staffing offices around the country with thousands of workers who identified potential supporters and helped to persuade them to vote for Obama on Election Day.[48] Both Republican and Democratic campaigns use sophisticated databases, combining voter registration, demographics, and even purchasing data to determine who their potential supporters are and how best to reach them.[49] Scholars have found clear evidence that these efforts boost a candidate's electoral support.[50]

Sometimes candidates also try to decrease support and turnout for their opponent. One tactic is **push polling**, in which a candidate or a group that supports a candidate conducts a voter "survey," typically by phone, that isn't actually designed to measure opinions so much as to influence them. Campaigns use these so-called polls to spread false or misleading information about another candidate by including this information in questions posed to large numbers of citizens.[51] Another strategy is to frighten people. In 2006, a staffer for a Republican House candidate in California sent letters to Latinos in their district, a group the campaign considered likely to support the opposing candidate, stating that it was illegal for immigrants

wholesale politics A mode of campaigning that involves indirect contact with citizens, such as running campaign ads.

retail politics A mode of campaigning in which a candidate or campaign staff contacts citizens directly, as would happen at a rally, a talk before a small group, or a one-on-one meeting between a candidate and a citizen.

mobilization Motivating supporters to vote in an election and, in some cases, helping them get to the polls on Election Day.

GOTV or the **ground game** A campaign's efforts to "get out the vote" or make sure their supporters vote on Election Day.

push polling A type of survey in which the questions are presented in a biased way in an attempt to influence the respondent.

▲ *American presidential campaigns depend on thousands of paid and volunteer staff. Here, workers for Republican candidate John McCain contact potential supporters.*

to vote.[52] (If immigrants are U.S. citizens and registered, it is completely legal for them to vote.) The staffer was fired when the use of this tactic was publicized, and the candidate lost the election.

Promises and Platforms The next set of campaign decisions have to do with the candidate's **campaign platform**, which includes stances on issues and promises about how the candidate will act in office. Given that few voters are well-informed about public policy or inclined to learn, candidates do not win elections by trying to educate the electorate or making complex promises. The average voter is not motivated to listen to or think through the details of long arguments. What works in a campaign is to make promises and take positions that are simple and consistent with what the average voter believes, even if these beliefs are inconsistent with reality.

For example, many people believe that interest groups have too much power in Washington, although as we see in Chapter 9, interest groups' influence is far less powerful than most Americans believe. Even so, many candidates accuse their opponent of being beholden to interest groups. These claims may be far-fetched, but they work well politically because they play to citizens' perceptions. One such ad that ran against Senator Harry Reid of Nevada claimed he had engineered a "giveaway to special interests" by providing federal funds to save the jobs of 1,400 teachers in Nevada—even though this funding was only a small fraction of a nearly $700 billion economic stimulus package that, among many other things, provided similar education funding to all fifty states.[53]

In writing their platform, candidates may be constrained by positions they have taken in the past or by their party affiliation. Chapter 7 showed that the parties have strong brand identities that lead many citizens to associate Democrats with liberal policies and Republicans with conservative ones. Candidates often find it difficult to make campaign promises that contradict these perceptions. In 2006, many Republican candidates tried to avoid talking about the increasingly unpopular war in Iraq, even though polls suggested that most voters were focused on this issue.[54] Why avoid the topic? Most Republican incumbents had previously supported the war, so voters might not see a newly adopted antiwar position as credible. Moreover, taking a strong stand against the war would place them at odds with Republican president George Bush. Democrats faced no such constraints: many had opposed the war from the start or offered only reluctant, qualified support. For them, it was easy and politically popular to take a strong antiwar stand. The war was much less important for platforms in the 2008 contest. With American casualties decreasing, voters were more concerned about candidates' positions on the economy, energy, and health care.

Another influence on a candidate's positions is where she is running for office. In a state or district with many conservative or Republican voters, opposition to health care reform legislation or to amnesty for illegal immigrants might be a winning electoral strategy (or, at a minimum, not a sure loser)—just as support for these proposals would generally be helpful for candidates running in states or districts where most voters are moderate to liberal or Democrats.

The two-step electoral process in American elections also influences candidate positions. To win office, candidates have to campaign twice, first in a primary and then in a general election. Voters in primary elections generally hold more extreme views than the average voter in a general election. As a result, in the typical congressional district, Republican candidates win primaries by taking conservative positions, while Democrats win their primaries by upholding liberal views. However, a position or promise that attracts votes in a primary election might not work so well in the general election, or vice versa. For example, in a 2006 Republican primary for the 8th District in Arizona, candidate Randy Graf won because of his strong anti-immigrant position.[55] Graf even opposed the immigration reform proposal

POLITICS IS CONFLICTUAL

POLITICAL PROCESS MATTERS

developed by House Republicans because its penalties for illegal immigrants were not severe enough. Although these positions helped Graf win the primary, they were a major factor in his defeat in the general election, because many voters strongly opposed his proposals.

For all these reasons, different parties' candidates for the same office often make some similar campaign promises even though they disagree on other matters. During the 2008 North Carolina Senate race, candidates Elizabeth Dole and Kay Hagan held roughly the same positions on issues such as immigration, the Iraq war, and the government's bailout of financial firms. As a result, the race turned on other issues, such as Dole's low effectiveness ranking in a survey of Senate staff.

Real Campaign Platforms Table 8.3 lists part of the campaign platforms of the 2008 presidential candidates and shows the similarities and differences in five issue areas that received considerable attention during the campaign: the economy, education, energy, immigration, and national security. In some areas, McCain and Obama offered sharply different ideas of what government should do. In the case of the war in Iraq, Obama pledged to withdraw American forces in sixteen months, whereas McCain opposed setting a firm timetable. And on the economic front, McCain favored making all of President Bush's temporary tax cuts permanent, while Obama proposed repealing them for households earning more than $250,000 per year.

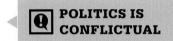

However, even on controversial issues, there were some similarities between the candidates' platforms. In the case of immigration policy, the candidates' positions were essentially identical, differing only in the details of their proposals. Both candidates supported merit pay for teachers, some amount of domestic offshore oil drilling, sending additional troops to Afghanistan, and many other policies.

Candidates from different parties agree on some things and disagree on many others. But no one watching the typical presidential or congressional contest would say the candidates were making the same promises about the future—or that they were taking diametrically opposed positions.

TABLE 8.3	PRESIDENTIAL CANDIDATES' ISSUE POSITIONS (SELECTED), 2008	
Issue	**John McCain**	**Barack Obama**
Economy	Make all Bush-era tax cuts permanent	Make Bush-era tax cuts permanent only for families earning under $250,000 per year
	Freeze most government spending	Increase regulation of financial firms
Education	Retain Bush-era No Child Left Behind program, but fund schools directly	Increase spending on teacher training and remedial and early childhood education
	Institute merit-based pay for teachers	Institute merit-based pay for teachers
Energy	Allow a large increase in domestic offshore oil drilling	Allow a small increase in domestic offshore oil drilling
	Offer tax credits for buying eco-friendly cars; offer prizes for developing new battery technologies	Increase spending on alternative and renewable energy technologies
Immigration	Increase border security	Increase border security
	Allow illegal immigrants to gain citizenship after paying a fine and back taxes	Allow illegal immigrants to gain citizenship after paying a fine and back taxes
National Security	Maintain open-ended commitment to keeping forces in Iraq	Set a timetable for withdrawing forces from Iraq
	Send additional troops to Afghanistan	Send additional troops to Afghanistan

SOURCE: Compiled from "Campaign Promises," *National Journal*, September 9, 2008, available at www.nationaljournal.com/campaigns/2008/wh08/promises.htm.

Issues matter in American elections. A candidate's issue positions help to mobilize supporters and attract volunteers, activists, interest-group endorsements, and contributions. Issue positions also define what's at stake in an election: what government will do differently depending on who gets elected. And as we see later in this chapter, some citizens vote based on candidates' issue positions. Even so, there is considerable evidence that many voters do not know very much about candidates' issue positions, particularly for House and Senate races. As a result, when a candidate wins a race, or a party wins seats across the country, it is risky to read the outcome as a sign that the winners had the most popular set of issue positions.

For example, in the 1994 congressional races, many Republican House candidates ran on a common platform called the Contract with America. The Contract promised a House vote on a series of proposals, from banning any new congressional pay raises from taking effect until after the next election (keeping a given Congress from raising its own salary) to imposing all federal workplace regulations on congressional offices. Many observers attributed the 1994 Republican landslide to the popularity of the Contract.[56] However, subsequent surveys found that only a minority of the electorate knew what the Contract was. Similarly, in the 2010 elections, Republican leaders released a series of proposals labeled the Pledge to America, which called for, among other things, repeal of President Obama's health care reforms, movement to a balanced budget, and deregulation. However, only a minority of Republican candidates used the Pledge as a part of their campaign, and the Pledge was short on crucial details. Thus, the Republican successes in 2010 had much more to do with voters punishing Democrats for economic hard times than with specific policy proposals.

Confronting Other Candidates This last set of campaign strategies involves a candidate's opponent. Candidates seek to contrast their own records or positions with those of the opposing candidates or make claims designed to lower citizens' opinions of their opponents. Sometimes these interactions occur during a formal debate. Most congressional campaigns involve one or more debates held in front of an audience of likely voters, a group of reporters, or the editorial board of a local newspaper. Typically candidates take questions from reporters, although in some cases candidates question each other or answer questions from citizens in the audience.

Presidential campaigns involve multiple debates during the primary and caucus season. During the months before the first primaries and caucuses, each party's candidates gather for many single-party debates using a variety of formats. During the general election, the Republican and Democratic nominees meet for several debates. (The exact number and the format are negotiated by the campaigns and the Commission on Presidential Debates, a nonpartisan organization that hosts the debates.)[57] The 2008 presidential campaign featured three debates between the presidential nominees and one between the vice presidential nominees. Though the debates did not generate sharp shifts in voter support, they gave Barack Obama, who had spent less time than John McCain on the national stage, a chance to show his readiness for the presidency. By responding in a calm, detailed manner to the questions and McCain's criticisms, Obama partly assuaged fears that he was too inexperienced or naïve to be president.

As this example illustrates, the debates give candidates a chance to present themselves to the electorate. They offer extremely valuable free exposure, which is particularly important for candidates who do not have the money to run an extensive paid ad campaign. In 2008, the audience for each of the presidential and vice-presidential debates was more than 50 million people.[58] In a sense, the entire campaign functions like an extended debate, as candidates try to court support from citizens. Candidates work to put their own qualifications and records before the electorate, emphasizing facts, stances, and achievements that they believe citizens will evaluate favorably. And each candidate works to publicize aspects of his opponent's record that citizens would be likely to view unfavorably.

Given a relatively uninterested electorate, candidates must figure out how to present themselves to voters in a way that captures their attention and gains their support. Thus, in the 2004 presidential debates, George Bush's first remarks emphasized the September 11 attacks, arguing that the overthrow of the Taliban in Afghanistan and the invasion of Iraq had reduced the chances of another terrorist attack in America.[59] This argument was politically advantageous given that many Americans saw preventing a terrorist attack as a top priority—and at the time, gave Bush high marks for his performance on September 11. During the 2008 campaign, John McCain tried to dramatize his criticisms of Barack Obama's tax policies by describing how they might affect "Joe the Plumber" (whose real name is Samuel J. Wurzelbacher), who had been taped asking Obama about his tax plan at an Ohio campaign stop.

Candidates also attempt to win support by emphasizing their understanding of citizens' concerns and their willingness to address these problems, and campaigns provide an opportunity for questioners to test a candidate's knowledge of everyday life. For example, candidates often find themselves quizzed about the prices of everyday items, such as loaf of bread, a pound of coffee, or a gallon of milk, or how much citizens pay in property taxes or at the gas pump.[60] Questions like these are such a part of American political lore that candidates are routinely briefed about local prices before a debate.

Many campaign events are designed to reinforce the impression that candidates share voters' concerns and values. Ideally, they have reporters watching in order to gain wide coverage. Just before the 2008 Democratic primaries in Indiana and Pennsylvania, Barack Obama visited a Pennsylvania bowling alley, where he bowled a game before a few startled patrons—and the reporters following his campaign.[61] A week later, rival Hillary Clinton visited a bar in Indiana, where she joined patrons in a round of beers and whiskey shots as reporters documented the event.[62] Although these efforts don't always work as intended, there is no doubt what candidates are trying to do: convince voters that they are "just like them." Sometimes these efforts combine presentation of personal characteristics and issues: in the 2010 West Virginia Senate campaign, Democrat Joe Manchin ran a campaign ad featuring him at a gun range, shooting at a target labeled "cap and trade legislation" (while West Virginia is a rural state where hunting and gun rights are popular, cap and trade legislation is strongly opposed because of the state's large coal mining industry).

Candidates also try to raise doubts about opponents by citing politically damaging statements or unpopular past behavior. In the first 2004 presidential debate, John Kerry criticized the conduct of the war in Afghanistan and the failure to capture the architect of the September 11 attacks, Osama bin Laden, by charging that Bush had "outsourced the job to Afghan warlords."[63] Other politicians use push polls to achieve the same goals, or rely on endorsements or ads funded by interest groups. During the 2006 campaign, one liberal interest group even tried to influence the results of Google searches about Republican candidates. The group constructed Web sites and links so that citizens who searched for information about Jon Kyl, a senator running for reelection in Arizona, would find an article criticizing Kyl as their first search result.[64]

Candidates and interest groups also do **opposition research**, digging into an opponent's past for embarrassing incidents or personal indiscretions, either by the candidate or a member of the candidate's family or staff. Campaigns may then leak this information to the media or release it on their own. Candidates, parties, and interest groups also routinely use trackers, staff who attend their opponents' events with video cameras in the hopes of recording embarrassing behavior or statements. The resulting videos may then be posted on the Internet, given to the press, or used in a campaign

opposition research Attempts by a candidate's campaign or other groups of supporters to uncover embarrassing or politically damaging information about the candidate's opponent.

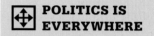

POLITICS IS EVERYWHERE

▼ *During campaigns, candidates often seek to strengthen the perception that they share (or at least are sympathetic to) average Americans' beliefs and interests. Here, Democratic candidate Hillary Clinton enjoys a beverage with patrons in an Indiana bar during the 2008 presidential primaries.*

ad. During the 2006 campaign, a tracker recorded Virginia senator George Allen referring to him as "macaca," a Tunisian term for monkey. (The tracker was of Indian descent; Allen's mother is Tunisian).[65] The video was posted on YouTube, and Allen's remarks remained a persistent story throughout the campaign. Allen lost the election by just over 9,000 votes. Although we can't be sure, this seemingly racist remark could easily have made the difference in such a close race.

The spread of trackers' sometimes unflattering videos shows just one effect of how much easier the Internet makes distributing information about candidates. Virtually all congressional nominees in 2010 had Web sites and Facebook pages.[66] Many candidates now routinely hold political events over the internet. Debates and campaign ads are available on YouTube; in 2008, CNN ran presidential debates in which citizens submitted questions for the candidates in the form of YouTube videos. Many candidates have also had to contend with Internet distribution of past interviews or public appearances, some made long before they decided to get into politics. Delaware Republican senatorial candidate Christine O'Donnell was never able to escape negative publicity from a several-years-old TV appearance in which she claimed to have attended several Wiccan events—even though she began one campaign ad by stating "I'm not a witch."

However, much of the information about candidates that was available over the Internet during recent elections would likely have found other outlets in previous elections. During the 1988 election, when the Internet was only a curiosity and Web browsers did not exist, voters learned through mainstream media sources that one of the Democratic presidential candidates, Joe Biden, had been accused of plagiarism while in law school—and that more recently Biden's speechwriter had lifted themes and text from a speech written by a party leader in Britain. If a candidate learns something that will help him win office or hurt an opponent's chances, he will find a way to get the information to the electorate. A more important use of the Internet in the 2008 campaign was Barack Obama's Web-based fund-raising operation. Obama raised more than $600 million, much of it through the Internet. This surplus enabled him to force the McCain campaign to abandon efforts in some states in order to remain competitive in others.

Candidates who are well ahead in the polls with victory virtually assured often try to avoid mentioning their opponent at all, assuming that to mention the opponent would only provide free publicity. Conversely, as we discuss in the next section, candidates who are behind in the polls sometimes resort to **attack ads**, campaign ads that focus on criticisms of their opponent. These candidates hope that attack ads will gain voters' attention and give them a reason for rethinking their support for the front-runner.

To achieve these goals, many attack ads often stretch the truth (or break it outright), trying to get voters to at least stop and think—or to get the opposing candidate to spend time and money denying the claims made in the ad. In the 2010 election, various candidates were accused of "wanting to gas house pets, inject young girls with dangerous drugs, let men beat their wives, and assist child molesters, whether by buying them Viagra or protecting their privacy."[67] Another ad run by Democrat Alan Grayson referred to his Republican opponent as "Taliban Dan," showing an excerpt from a video where he supposedly used biblical quotes to argue that wives should be subordinate to their husbands.

Do attack ads work? There are many stories of candidates who rode to victory on the back of some truly astounding claims about their opponents. However, assertions about candidates' virtues or their opponents' vices shape outcomes only when they are verifiable, or at least consistent with voters' preexisting evaluations or beliefs. In the case of Alan Grayson, the "Taliban Dan" ad backfired when his opponent released the full video, showing that he had been badly quoted out of context and was not making the argument the ad claimed he was. Grayson lost the election.

attack ads Campaign advertising that criticizes a candidate's opponent—typically by making potentially damaging claims about the opponent's background or record—rather than focusing on positive reasons to vote for the candidate.

CAMPAIGN ADVERTISING: GETTING THE WORD OUT

One of the realities of modern American electoral campaigns, particularly for the presidency, is that they are conducted largely through campaign advertising. Candidates for office, party committees, and interest groups spend more than several billion dollars during each election cycle on campaign-related activities by all candidates for federal office. Most of that money is spent on campaign advertising, usually in the form of thirty-second television spots. Campaign advertising is critical because candidates cannot assume citizens will take the time to learn from other sources about the candidates, their qualifications, and their issue positions.

Campaign advertising has evolved considerably over the last generation.[68] During the early years of television, many campaign ads consisted of speeches by candidates or endorsements from supporters, and they usually ran several minutes in length. In the 1964 presidential race, Lyndon Johnson's campaign ran a five-minute ad titled "Confessions of a Republican," featuring an actor talking about why he didn't want to vote for Republican Barry Goldwater.[69] The 1964 Johnson campaign also ran an ad that was a harbinger of political appeals yet to come: a one-minute ad, titled "Peace, Little Girl" and broadly nicknamed "Daisy," which featured a child counting the petals she is pulling from a daisy one by one, interspersed with a voice-over of a military countdown and images of the detonation of a nuclear bomb.[70] The implication was that electing Goldwater would increase the chances that nuclear weapons would be used in a future conflict. The ad ran only once, but it generated a great deal of controversy and remains one of the most iconic pieces of campaign advertising.

Much like the "Daisy" ad, modern campaign ads are typically short, with arresting images, and they often use photo montages and bold text in attempts to engage a distracted citizenry. A classic example of an ad designed to capture viewers' attention ran during the 2006 campaign and featured actor Michael J. Fox.[71] The ad showed Fox, a longtime sufferer of Parkinson's disease, weaving back and forth in his chair and jerking uncontrollably because of the neurological symptoms of the disease. Fox's message: elect Missouri Democrat Claire McCaskill to the Senate because she supports stem cell research that might cure Parkinson's and other diseases. During the 2008 presidential primaries, Republican Mike Huckabee ran an ad that featured actor Chuck Norris and Huckabee "endorsing" each other: Norris described Huckabee as a "lifelong hunter who will protect our 2nd Amendment rights"; Huckabee said that when Norris does a pushup, "he doesn't lift himself up, he pushes the earth down."[72]

As the main way that candidates reach the electorate, campaign ads abound in American elections.[73] A study of the 2002 midterm election found that the House and Senate races featured more than half a million TV ads run by candidates,

▲ The "Daisy" ad from the 1964 presidential campaign interspersed images of a child in a field of flowers and footage of a nuclear detonation. It was broadcast only once but caused much controversy—and helped to crystallize doubts about Republican candidate Barry Goldwater.

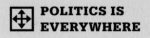

POLITICS IS EVERYWHERE

◀ During the 2006 Senate race, actor Michael J. Fox (left) appeared in a campaign ad for Missouri Democrat Claire McCaskill, highlighting her support for stem cell research. Early in the 2008 presidential primaries, actor Chuck Norris appeared with Republican candidate Mike Huckabee (far right) in an ad where they gave mutual endorsements. The Fox ad helped McCaskill to win election, while Huckabee was defeated.

political parties, and interest groups. The number of ads in congressional races was similar in the 2000 elections, but there were an additional 250,000 ads pertaining to the presidential contest. About 60 percent of these ads were run by candidates' campaigns, with the rest from political parties, political action committees, or 527 organizations (the next chapter looks closely at these latter two types of groups). These overall numbers translate into large numbers of ads in individual campaigns, particularly in close races. For example, a study by the Wisconsin Ad Project found that during the crucial Ohio Democratic presidential primary in 2008, Hillary

TABLE 8.4 CAMPAIGN ADVERTISING BY INTEREST GROUPS, 2004

Organization	Number of Ads Run
Liberal Groups, Total	**146,615**
Media Fund	74,915
MoveOn.org	43,143
New Democratic Network	10,609
Citizens for a Strong Senate	3,830
League of Conservation Voters	3,182
Municipal Employees	2,111
EMILY's List	2,399
Others	6,426
Conservative Groups, Total	**43,810**
Progress for America	23,354
Swift Vets and POWs for Truth	8,690
Club for Growth	8,151
Americans United to Preserve Marriage	705
National Rifle Association	1,083
Others	1,827
Labor Groups, Total	**24,502**
AFL-CIO	10,962
National Education Association	5,238
United Auto Workers	2,664
Service Employees International Union	2,213
Association of Federal, State, County, and Municipal Employees	2,111
Others	1,314
Business Groups, Total	**11,114**
Americans for Job Security	5,279
United Seniors Association	2,291
National Association of Realtors	1,701
American Medical Association	1,109
Others	734

SOURCE: Robert Boatright, Michael Malbin, Mark Rozell, and Clyde Wilcox, "Interest Groups and Advocacy Organizations after BCRA," in *The Election after Reform*, ed. Michael Malbin (Washington, DC: Rowman and Littlefield, 2006), pp. 112–82.

Clinton's campaign ran over 6,000 campaign ads in the month before the vote, while her opponent Barack Obama ran nearly 10,000.[74]

Virtually all kinds of political organizations run campaign ads. Table 8.4 shows the number of ads run by interest groups during the 2004 general election campaign for the presidency. Liberal groups ran the most ads in this particular election, although many ads came from all categories. (The proportion of ads from different sources varies; in the 2000 election, business groups ran more than half of the total.) The total number of ads is concentrated among a few organizations: in 2004, the Media Fund ran more than a quarter of the total.

The content of campaign ads varies depending on who is running the ads. Table 8.5 gives data from the 2000 and 2004 presidential elections showing that campaigns, parties, and interest groups run a mix of positive ads extolling a candidate's record, background, or campaign promises, and negative ads citing an opponent's shortcomings or failures. An interesting feature of Table 8.5 is that of all the groups that run campaign ads, candidates themselves run the highest percentage of positive ads. On the other hand, note that in the 2000 election, the authors of the study could not find a single positive ad run by an advocacy group. Analyses of the 2008 campaign showed little change: advocacy ads in the primaries and the general election were overwhelmingly negative.

One critical question about campaign advertising is whether ads work—whether they shape what people know or influence their vote decisions or other forms of participation. Some observers have complained that campaign ads depress turnout and reinforce citizens' negative perceptions of government.[75] Many of these arguments focus on attack ads or negative campaigning. During the 2010 campaign, candidates and independent organizations ran ads accusing their opponents of committing organ theft, being a "wolf in sheep's clothing" (complete with glowing red eyes), having "crazy ideas," committing "serious sin," and planning to "tax everything" if elected. One candidate's ad showed the opponent as an evil blimp hovering over Washington; another used video of a kindergarten while talking about the need to reduce conflict in Congress.[76] While probably only a few voters believed the ads' claims about glowing eyes or evil blimps, that's not the goal. These ads are designed to catch voters' attention, to get them to focus on a race long enough to consider the candidates and their real messages. For example, during the 2008 presidential race, the McCain campaign ran an ad claiming that Obama supported comprehensive sex education for kindergartners, while groups supporting Obama ran ads that argued McCain supported a thousand-year war in Iraq.[77]

TABLE 8.5   PERCENTAGE OF POSITIVE CAMPAIGN ADS IN RECENT PRESIDENTIAL ELECTIONS

Candidates are most likely to run positive ads, and parties and especially interest groups run mostly negative ads. Why would candidates want to avoid "going negative" against their opponents?

Ad Sponsor	2000	2004
Candidate	64.8%	43.6%
Party	37.2	8.6
Interest groups	0	7.5
Overall	46.2	31.5

SOURCE: Robert Boatright, Michael Malbin, Mark Rozell, and Clyde Wilcox, "Interest Groups and Advocacy Organizations after BCRA," in *The Election after Reform*, ed. Michael Malbin (Washington, DC: Rowman and Littlefield), pp. 112–82.

The question is, what do Americans learn from campaign ads? Do they simply believe what they are told, good and bad, or are they discerning about what they infer? Analyses suggest that Americans are reasonably thoughtful when assessing campaign ads. In 2008, an ad run by incumbent North Carolina senator Elizabeth Dole against her Democratic challenger, Kay Hagan, claimed that Hagan had taken "godless money" from the Godless Americans PAC. What, the ad asked, had she promised in return? The ad ended with a voice similar to Hagan's saying, "There is no God." In response, Hagan held a press conference with the minister of her church, who confirmed that she was a regular attendee and elder. Hagan also ran a counterattack ad accusing Dole of "bearing false witness against a fellow Christian." Exit polls suggested that Dole's initial ad backfired badly.

Perhaps surprisingly, the evidence suggests that campaign advertising has several beneficial effects. Scholars have found that people who are exposed to campaign ads tend to be more interested in the campaign and know more about the candidates.[78] Moreover, many campaign ads highlight real differences between the candidates and the parties.[79] Even so, average citizens are well aware that they cannot believe everything they see on television, so campaign advertising typically gets voters' attention without necessarily changing their minds.[80]

With regard to negative campaigning, early evidence suggested that attack ads depressed voter turnout, but later studies have shown that they do not have much of an effect.[81] However, negative ads run by a candidate's campaign can backfire, driving away supporters from the candidate who runs them. As a result, candidates often rely on party committees and interest groups to run negative ads, enabling them to run more positive ads (recall Table 8.5).

In the end, despite all of the money and effort poured into campaign advertising, these messages—like all other aspects of a campaign—must be designed to capture the attention of citizens whose interest in politics is relatively minimal, delivering a message that can be understood without too much interpretation. In this way, campaign advertising reflects an old political saying, that most things candidates do in campaigns are wasted efforts that have little impact on the election. The problem is that candidates don't know which of their actions will amount to wasted efforts and which will help them win, so they try them all.

CAMPAIGN FINANCE

Campaign finance refers to money collected for and spent on campaigns and elections by candidates, political parties, and other organizations and individuals. The **Federal Election Commission** is in charge of administering election laws, including the complex set of regulations pertaining to how campaigns can spend money. The most recent changes in campaign finance rules, which were passed as the Bipartisan Campaign Reform Act (BCRA), took effect after the 2002 elections and have been modified by subsequent Supreme Court decisions. (In particular, the recent Supreme Court decision in *Citizens United v. Federal Election Commission* effectively removes all restrictions on independent efforts funded by corporations and labor unions.) We will note the implications of this act throughout our discussion.

The limits on campaign contributions in the BCRA—also known as the McCain–Feingold Act after its chief sponsors, John McCain (R-AZ) and Russell Feingold (D-WI)—vary depending on whether contributions are made by an individual or a group, and by the type of group (see Nuts and Bolts 8.3). Political action committees (PACs) are groups that aim to elect or defeat particular candidates or political parties. A company or organization can form a PAC and solicit contributions from employees or group members. As Nuts and Bolts 8.3 shows, the amount PACs can give to each

Federal Election Commission The government agency that enforces and regulates election laws; made up of six presidential appointees, of whom no more than three can be members of the same party.

Contribution Limits in the 2010 Elections

The table below summarizes the Bipartisan Campaign Reform Act limitations on campaign contributions by individuals and political action committees (PACs). During the 2010 elections, individuals could contribute up to $2,300 to a candidate per election (donations to the primary and general elections count separately), $28,500 to a political party, $10,000 to a state party, and $5,000 to a PAC, with an overall limit of about $100,000. Individuals and corporations can also make unlimited contributions to 527 organizations, which can use the money for voter mobilization efforts or issue advocacy as long as they do not directly support or oppose a particular candidate, and can spend unlimited amounts on independent expenditures, which are efforts not connected to a particular candidate, party, or committee.

	INDIVIDUAL CANDIDATES	NATIONAL PARTY COMMITTEE	STATE PARTY	POLITICAL ACTION COMMITTEE	LIMIT ON TOTAL CONTRIBUTIONS
Individuals	$2,400	$30,400	—	—	$45,600 to candidates, $69,900 to organizations
Political action committees	$5,000	$15,000	$5,000	$5,000	—
National party committee	$5,000	—	Unlimited transfers	$5,000	—
State and local party committees	$5,000	Unlimited transfers	Unlimited transfers	$5,000	—

SOURCE: Federal Election Commission "Contribution Limits for 2009–2010," available at www.fec.gov/info/contriblimits0910.pdf (accessed 1/4/10).

candidate in an election is limited, but it's important to remember that these limits pertain to **hard money**, which means they restrict only the funds given directly to a candidate. PACs can also form 527 organizations, which can then accept unlimited amounts of **soft money**, which can be used to mobilize voters or advocate for a particular issue as long as these efforts are not tied to or controlled by a specific candidate or candidates.

As discussed in Chapter 7, political party committees are entities within the Republican and Democratic parties. Both of the major parties have a national committee and a campaign committee in each house of Congress. Party committees are limited in the amount of hard money they can give to a candidate's campaign, and in the amount they can spend on behalf of the candidate as a coordinated expenditure. However, a party committee (and, after the *Citizens United* decision, corporations and labor unions) can spend an unlimited amount in independent expenditures to elect a candidate or candidates. To be considered independent, expenditures must not be controlled, directed, or approved by any candidate's campaign. Independent expenditures can pay for campaign advertising, either to promote a party's candidate or to attack her opponent, but the candidate or candidates cannot be consulted on the specific messages.

The 527 organizations (named after the provision of the Internal Revenue Code that allows them) can raise unlimited soft money from individuals for voter mobilization and for issue advocacy, but these expenditures must not be coordinated with a candidate or party. Ads by 527s cannot advocate the election or defeat of a particular candidate or political party; any phrases in an ad that do so—and thereby change the ways the ad can be funded—are termed magic words.[82] Another type of organization, again described using the IRS code as a 501(c)(4), played a major role in the 2010 campaign—the principal difference between 527s and 501(c)(4)s is that

hard money Donations that are used to help elect or defeat a specific candidate.

soft money Contributions that can be used for voter mobilization or to promote a policy proposal or point of view as long as these efforts are not tied to supporting or opposing a particular candidate.

Campaign Finance in Presidential Elections

During the presidential primary process, the federal government provides matching funds to candidates who raise $5,000 in each of at least twenty states in contributions of $250 or less. Once a candidate passes this fund-raising threshold, the government matches the first $250 of each subsequent contribution. In order to receive these funds, candidates must agree to an overall cap on the amount they will spend during the nomination process ($42.05 million in 2008), and to spending caps for each primary or caucus of 67 cents per voting-age person in the state.[a] If candidates forgo the federal matching funds, they can ignore these spending caps—a strategy followed by Democratic candidates Hillary Clinton and Barack Obama as well as all the major Republican candidates for the 2008 presidential nomination.

During the general election, presidential candidates can receive federal funding for their campaigns: $84.1 million in 2008, along with an extra $16.4 million for the nominating convention. Candidates do not have to accept this funding, although every major party nominee did so between 1976, when the law took effect, and 2008, when Democrat Barack Obama became the first candidate to opt out. Funds are also given to minor political parties if their candidate received more than 5 percent of the vote in the previous election. Only one candidate has passed this threshold: John Anderson, who ran as an independent in 1980.

These federal funds are generated, in part, by money that taxpayers voluntarily allocate out of the taxes they pay to the federal government by checking off a particular box on their federal tax return form. In recent years, the amount of money an individual taxpayer can choose to put to this use is $3. (This donation does not reduce an individual's refund or increase their taxes.) When this voluntary check-off procedure has not allocated sufficient funds to pay for candidates' public funding, the rest has been taken from general government revenues.[b]

[a] The spending caps are adjusted in each election for inflation.

[b] Campaign Finance Institute Task Force on Financing Presidential Nominations, "So the Voters May Choose: Reviving the Presidential Matching Fund System," April 2005, available at www.cfinst.org/president/pdf/VotersChoose.pdf.

the latter organization does not have to disclose the names of its contributors. Nuts and Bolts 8.4 describes the additional financial regulations for presidential elections,[83] and Chapter 9 looks more closely at PACs, 527s, and 501(c)(4)s.

These complex campaign finance regulations reflect two simple truths. First, any limits on campaign activities involve balancing the right to free speech about candidates and issues with the idea that rich people or well-funded organizations should not be allowed to dominate what voters hear during the campaign. Striking this balance has created some arbitrary compromises: for example, BCRA originally prohibited unions and corporations from running ads within sixty days of an election but did not apply the same restriction to 527s. This provision was struck down by the Supreme Court in the *Citizens United* case. Second, an enormous amount of money is spent on American elections. Table 8.6 shows the amount raised by candidates, political parties, and others in 2004, 2006, 2008 and 2010. More than $4 billion was raised for the 2004 election, almost $2 billion in 2006, over $5 billion in 2008, and nearly $3 billion in 2010. The amount of midterm election independent expenditures (spending by other than candidates and party groups) sharply increased from just about $60 million in the 2006 to over $294 million in 2010. Moreover, campaign spending is concentrated among a relatively small number of organizations with sizable electioneering budgets. In each of the last several election cycles, the largest organizations have spent more than $50 million.

The principal concern about all this campaign cash is that the amount of money spent on a candidate's campaign might matter more than the candidate's

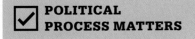

✓ POLITICAL
PROCESS MATTERS

TABLE 8.6 CANDIDATE, PARTY, AND INTEREST GROUP ELECTION FUND-RAISING, 2004–2010

Candidates and political parties raise and spend a great deal of money in their campaigns. Do these numbers help to explain the high reelection rates for members of Congress?

	2004	2006	2008	2010
Presidential Candidates*				
Republican	(Bush) $367,228,801	—	(McCain) $360,000,000	—
Democrat	(Kerry) $328,479,245	—	(Obama) $639,000,000	—
Congressional Candidates				
House incumbents	$456,994,049	$198,137,808	$539,879,135	$481,226,815
House challengers	$112,682,861	$27,680,023	$193,381,140	$256,639,703
House open seat candidates	$127,084,712	$16,453,309	$150,938,532	$141,773,031
Senate incumbents	$223,964,927	$190,492,258	$361,183,002	$186,563,786
Senate challengers	$79,852,042	$44,307,619	$100,188,001	$129,210,379
Senate open seat candidates	$239,197,856	$18,382,257	$59,328,470	$320,664,118
Political Parties				
Republicans	$875,704,006	$598,127,532	$1,228,025,068	$497,570,243
Democrats	$710,416,993	$493,311,599	$1,210,831,060	$559,585,362
Independent Expenditures	$190,884,688	$59,861,371	$286,459,718	$294,379,276
Totals	$4,121,051,315	$1,881,827,402	$5,268,316,289	$2,867,612,713

*Presidential spending includes federal matching funds for the general election.

SOURCE: Data compiled from the Center for Responsive Politics, November 1, 2010, www.opensecrets.org.

qualifications or issue positions. That is, a candidate could get elected regardless of how good a job he would do, simply because he has more money than competing candidates to pay for campaign ads, polls, a large staff, and mobilization efforts. A second concern is that individuals and organizations or corporations that can afford to make large contributions (or to fund their own electioneering efforts) might be able to dictate election outcomes or, by funding campaigns, garner a disproportionate amount of influence over the subsequent behavior of elected officials.

Making Sense of Campaign Finance Campaign finance records are amazingly transparent. It is easy to find out which individuals or organizations gave money to a candidate, political party, or other organization.[84] Thus, if you are worried that a particular organization is using campaign contributions to influence elected officials, it is easy to find out which officeholders have received the group's donations. In fact, campaign finance records are so readily available that it is often easy to identify fraudulent organizations. During the 2008 primary campaign, a group called Californians for Obama solicited contributions for Democratic candidate Barack Obama via a Web site complete with descriptions of endorsements and fundraising events. However, none of these endorsements or events actually happened, and Obama never received funds from the organization.[85] After the scam became public, the organization's Web site was taken down, but no one was prosecuted, as the relatively small amount of money raised made it difficult to prove that the operation had broken the law.

Campaign Finance Regulations

Campaign finance regulations are complex and place real restrictions on what Americans can do to influence election outcomes. Suppose you are a wealthy person or the head of a corporation with deep pockets. Under current law, you and your corporation can only donate about $15,000 to a candidate's campaign; corporations have to form a political action committee to do so and cannot pay for the contribution with business revenues. You can also form an organization called a 527 that can run campaign ads designed to help elect your preferred candidates or donate to an existing 527. You can also spend unlimited amounts on independent expenditures, efforts that help a particular candidate or campaign, as long as the candidate or committee has no control over these expenditures. But if your goal is to help your favorite candidate directly, whether by a cash contribution or an ad campaign that is somehow linked to the candidate's organization, you face serious limits.

These limits on campaign spending arguably conflict with fundamental tenets of American democracy. The Bill of Rights states that Congress cannot abridge "freedom of speech, or of the press; or the right of the people peaceably to assemble, and to petition the Government for a redress of grievances." One interpretation of the 1st Amendment is that people should be free to spend whatever they want on contesting elections—excluding bribes, threats, and other illegal actions, of course.

The principal argument for restricting campaign contributions is that money conveys political power. That is, if we let rich people spend as much as they want on electioneering, they could control election outcomes by giving their favored candidates enough money to

As this cartoon illustrates, many Americans believe there is too much money in politics and that a candidate can win only by raising more money than the opposition. The truth is more complicated: although a successful campaign requires substantial funds, particularly at the presidential level, many winning candidates have been significantly outspent.

win regardless of who ran against them. This argument implies that removing contribution restrictions would result in election outcomes driven purely by campaign spending rather than by voters' preferences. (Of course, the lack of limits on independent expenditures works against this logic.)

As discussed elsewhere in this chapter, it is easy to overstate the value of money as a political asset. Even with unlimited funds, it is hard to get voters' attention—and harder still to change their minds. There are many examples of candidates who lost despite outspending their opponents. And there is no evidence in the corporate world that a company that spends enough on advertising can dominate its market and put its competitors out of business. People watch ads, but their purchasing decisions appear to be driven by other factors, such as their own budgets and preferences.

Even so, because money for ads is a necessary component of a political campaign, the possibility remains that a rich donor could change election outcomes by

giving large sums to challengers in congressional elections. Many challengers never find out how voters would respond to their platforms because they lack the funds to prepare or air campaign ads. Though most poorly funded challengers would stand no chance of beating their incumbent opponents even with an unlimited advertising budget, some might.

Should unlimited contributions be allowed? In arriving at an opinion, consider these three questions:

1. Is the average underfunded candidate's problem simply a lack of money, or is their inability to attract campaign funds a symptom of a deeper problem, such as their lack of popularity with voters?

2. Should a candidate who faces a well-funded opponent be given public funds or some other advantage to counteract the opponent's spending?

3. If unlimited contributions are allowed, should candidates be made to disclose the identity of their contributors to ensure that voters can learn who is backing the candidates' ad campaigns? ∎

When you look at campaign finance data, the first thing you will see is that a lot of money is spent trying to win elections. However, the raw data do not always tell the whole story. For example, the huge amounts make more sense when you consider what is at stake during each election cycle: control of the federal government, with a budget of about $3 trillion a year, and the power to start wars and regulate many aspects of citizens' lives. It's not surprising that so many organizations and individual donors invest in getting their preferred candidates elected. It is also important to keep in mind that the total amount spent on electioneering represents the sum of all the funding for the 435 House contests, thirty-three or thirty-four Senate races, and a presidential election. Moreover, one of the reasons why American campaigns are so expensive is the cost of television advertising. Nearly 80 percent of campaign expenditures are for television time. In major media markets, a thirty-second ad on a major television network can cost a candidate tens or even hundreds of thousands of dollars.[86] Given that even House campaigns may run hundreds of ads, and presidential campaigns run tens of thousands, it is easy to see why campaign costs pile up so quickly.

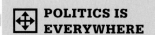

POLITICS IS EVERYWHERE

One way to put campaign expenses in context is to consider what major corporations pay in advertising expenses. A retail chain such as Walmart, Target, or Best Buy pays billions of dollars every year for newspaper, magazine, and television ads.[87] When you consider how much these companies spend in advertising, it's not surprising that American campaigns are so expensive. After all, retail chains want to contact average people and get their attention, just as candidates and other political organizations do. And corporations and candidates also use the same media, such as television ads, to deliver their messages to citizens.

More important, although money certainly matters in political campaigns, it cannot work miracles. Candidates for national political office need significant funding to have a realistic chance of winning, but money does not ensure success. In 2008, fifty-one House and Senate candidates each spent more than $500,000 of their own money on their campaigns. Only eleven of these candidates were elected; most didn't even win their party's primary.[88] In addition, many losing incumbents outspend their challengers. In the 2010 Connecticut Senate open-seat election, Republican challenger Linda McMahon (wife of World Wide Wrestling Federation CEO Vince McMahon) did not solicit campaign contributions, but spent over $46 million of her own money, only to lose decisively to her Democratic opponent, Richard Blumenthal, whose campaign spent less than a fifth of what McMahon did.[89]

For political actors, such as parties, PACs, and 527s, it is also important to distinguish between the amount of money an organization collects and the amount it actually spends on electioneering. Consider EMILY's List, a political action committee that supports pro-choice, Democratic female candidates, which collected more than $30 million during the 2004 election cycle.[90] Less than a third of this total was used for donations, advertising, phone banks, and other campaign activities. The rest was spent on the organization's payroll, office rent, and the direct mail operations that solicited the contributions.

Media coverage of campaign finance topics often takes an alarmist tone that is inconsistent with the actual content of the stories. One article reported on a 527 organization called Stop Her Now, whose main goal was to ensure the defeat of Senator Hillary Clinton in the 2008 presidential campaign—though she had not officially announced her candidacy at that time.[91] In any case, the article reported that a single wealthy donor, Richard Collins, was the principal contributor to the 527 and had also donated money to a PAC founded by a potential Republican presidential candidate, former New York City mayor Rudolph Giuliani. However, if you read through to the end of the article, you'd find that Collins had donated only $80,000 to the 527 and $10,000 to the PAC. This is real money, but only a tiny fraction of the money needed to influence the outcome of an election.

There is also little evidence that campaign contributions alter legislators' behavior, or that contributors are rewarded with votes supporting their causes or favorable policies. Research suggests that most contributions are intended to help elect politicians whom contributors already like, with no expectation that these officials will do anything differently because they received a contribution.[92] Contributions may help contributors gain access, getting the contributor an appointment to present arguments to a politician or her staff. But people and organizations who contribute are already friendly with the politicians they support, and the politicians would likely hear their arguments in any case.

In sum, although money helps shape elections, claims about the power of large contributors and big spenders are typically overstated. Much of the campaign spending in American elections is not funded by large corporations or rich people but by average Americans making small donations. Moreover, no candidate, political organization, or corporation has the ability to dominate the airwaves and crowd out other voices, although it will be important to reassess this conclusion as the long-term effects of the *Citizens United* decision become clearer. In the end, citizens are exposed to campaign advertising from a variety of sources, and they must decide which arguments to take seriously—just like they do with all the other information they receive during the campaign.

How Do Voters Decide?

All of the electoral activities we have considered so far are directed at citizens: making sure they are registered to vote, influencing their vote decisions, and getting them to the polls. In this section, we look more closely at how citizens respond to these influences. The first thing to understand is that the high level of attention, commitment, and energy exhibited by candidates and other campaign actors is not matched by ordinary citizens. We have seen throughout this chapter and others that politics is everywhere, and we have described elections as the primary mechanism citizens have to control the federal government. Even so, the average American citizen is far from being an expert, enthusiastic participant in elections. Only a minority of citizens report high levels of interest in campaigns, many people know little about the candidates or the issues, and many people do not vote.[93]

THE DECISION TO VOTE

Politics is everywhere, but getting involved is your choice; voting and other forms of political participation are optional. Surprisingly, even a strong preference between two candidates may not drive a citizen to the polls because each citizen's vote is just one of many.[94] The only time a vote "counts," in the sense that it changes the outcome, is when the other votes are split evenly so that one vote breaks the tie. Although this scenario was used in the 2008 movie *Swing Vote*, in which Kevin Costner's character had to cast the deciding vote in a presidential election, it is highly unlikely in any real election. Moreover, voting involves costs. Even if you don't attempt to learn about the candidates but decide to vote anyway, you still have to get to the polls on Election Day. Thus, the **paradox of voting** is, why does anyone vote, given that voting is costly and the chances of affecting the outcome are small?

Among Americans, the percentage of registered voters who actually voted has been, in recent presidential elections, between 65 and 70 percent, though the

paradox of voting The question of why citizens vote even though their individual votes stand little chance of changing the election outcome.

turnout is close to 50 percent (voter turnout is calculated based on the whole voting age population, including people who didn't vote because they opted not to register or were ineligible to register because of a felony conviction or other factors).[95] Turnout is significantly higher in presidential elections than in midterm elections and in primaries and caucuses. In the 2008 presidential primaries, some states reported turnout exceeding 30 percent, which were regarded as unusually high. For caucuses, which require individuals to spend several hours voting, turnout is generally only a few percentage points. (The turnout percentages reported in survey results are generally higher, as some people either misremember whether they voted or are unwilling to admit that they did not vote.)

Table 8.7 shows the considerable variation in turnout across different demographic groups. Turnout is higher for whites than nonwhites, and among older Americans compared to younger cohorts, and for college graduates relative to people with a high school education or less. Men and women, however, say they vote at roughly the same rate.

Table 8.8 shows how respondents explained their decisions about whether to go to the polls, and their reasons shed some light on these variations in turnout. People who vote regularly are more likely to see going to the polls as an obligation of citizenship, to feel guilty when they do not vote, and to believe that the election matters. These responses may help explain the paradox of voting. The first two reasons have to do with benefits an individual receives from the act of voting, rather than from the outcome of the election. The third reason suggests that if people believe that the election is important, this will be enough to drive them to the polls, even in the face of high odds that their vote will not change the outcome.

On the other hand, turnout is much lower among those who are angry with the government, believe that government actions do not affect them, or think that voting will have no impact on government policy. Citizens who hold these beliefs are unlikely to care about the outcome of the election and are unlikely to feel guilty for abstaining or to see voting as an obligation.

turnout The percentage of the voting age population who cast a ballot in a given election.

TABLE 8.7 TURNOUT IN THE 2004 ELECTION

	Regular Voter	Vote Sometimes	Rare Voter or Nonvoter
Total	35%	20%	45%
Men	36%	20%	44%
Women	34	21	45
White	37%	21%	42%
Black	31	23	45
Hispanic	24	16	60
18–29	22%	13%	65%
30–49	35	21	44
50–64	42	24	34
65+	41	22	37
College graduate	46%	22%	32%
Some college	38	20	43
High school or less	28	20	52

SOURCE: Pew Research Center, "Regular Voters, Intermittent Voters, and Those Who Don't," October 18, 2006, available at www.people-press.org/reports/pdf/292.pdf.

TABLE 8.8 — HOW AMERICANS EXPLAIN THEIR DECISION TO VOTE

	Regular Voter	Vote Sometimes	Rare Voter or Nonvoter
Percentage who agree . . .			
Duty as citizen to always vote	88%	80%	51%
This election matters more	83	74	67
Feel guilty when I don't vote	72	70	52
Angry with government	24	15	18
Issues in DC don't affect me	15	25	29
Voting doesn't change things	13	18	32
Difficult to get to polls	8	8	26
Lived in neighborhood less than one year	3	5	16

SOURCE: Pew Research Center, "Regular Voters, Intermittent Voters, and Those Who Don't," October 18, 2006, available at www.people-press.org/reports/pdf/292.pdf.

issue voters People who are well informed about their own policy preferences and knowledgeable about the candidates, and who use all of this information when they decide how to vote.

These data demonstrate the importance of mobilization in elections. As we discussed earlier, many candidates for political office spend at least as much time trying to convince their supporters to vote as they do attempting to persuade others to become supporters in the first place. Because many Americans either do not vote or vote only sporadically, mobilization is a vital strategy for winning elections.

The reasons nonvoters abstain can suggest what kinds of arguments might convince them to go to the polls. If a campaign can make nonvoters believe that the election matters and that it is their duty to vote, the chances that they will go to the polls on Election Day may increase. On the other hand, making people angry at Washington—perhaps with negative campaign ads—could lower turnout.

The turnout data provide another example of how the rules of the political process can shape outcomes. Among people who have moved within the last two years, turnout is extremely low, at least partly because moving often requires a citizen to re-register at his new address, and he must also locate his new polling place. Since passage of the Motor Voter Act in 1993, people have been able to register at the Department of Motor Vehicles at the same time that they renew their driver's license, which has increased turnout by a few percentage points.[96]

▼ In order to vote, citizens must be registered. Until recently, people who had either moved or turned eighteen just before an election often could not register in time to vote, but the 1993 Motor Voter Act lowered barriers to registration. The act required states to give citizens the opportunity to register to vote when applying for or renewing a driver's license.

HOW DO PEOPLE VOTE?

The image of the average citizen as distracted and uninterested in the details of politics still holds, even among those who decide to vote. Some **issue voters** are highly interested in politics, collect all the information they can about the candidates, and vote based on this information.[97] However, most citizens do not invest the time and effort to become an issue voter because they are not interested enough in politics to want to spend their time that way, and they aren't so concerned with voting for the candidates that come closest to their preferences. Reliable information about candidates is also often difficult to find. Although candidates, parties, and other organizations release a blizzard of endorsements, reports, and press releases throughout the campaign, much of this information may be difficult to interpret. It is a daunting task, even for the rare, highly motivated voter.

This combination of a lack of interest and a relatively complex task leads the majority of American voters to base their vote decision on easily interpretable pieces of information, or **voting cues**.[98] Voters in American national elections use many kinds of cues, including:

- *Incumbency*: Vote for the incumbent candidate.[99]
- *Partisanship*: Vote for the candidate whose party affiliation matches your own.[100]
- *Personal vote*: Vote for the incumbent if he or she has helped you get assistance from a government agency or has helped your community benefit from desirable government projects.[101]
- *Personal characteristics*: Vote for the candidate whose personal characteristics (age, race, gender, ethnicity, or religious beliefs) match your own or suggest you have common values, ideologies, or policy preferences.[102]
- *Retrospective evaluations*: Focus on a small set of votes the incumbent has cast while in office or other duties of the office that you care about, and vote for the incumbent if he or she has behaved the way you want in these circumstances.[103]
- *For (or against) the party in power*: Vote for a candidate based on a comparison of that candidate's party with an assessment of the party in power (the party that controls the presidency and has majorities in the House and Senate).[104]

Cues help voters shrink the complex question of whom they should support down to a more narrowly focused version that is easier to answer. They give people a low-cost way to cast what political scientist and campaign consultant Samuel Popkin called a **reasonable vote**—a vote that, more likely than not, is consistent with the voter's true preference among candidates.[105] Studies have found that citizens who use cues and are politically well-informed are more likely to cast a reasonable vote compared to those who use cues but are otherwise relatively politically ignorant. In essence, information helps people to select the right cue.[106]

Consider the partisanship cue. As discussed earlier, Republican and Democratic candidates usually hold different positions on many important issues. As a result, a candidate's party affiliation tells a voter something about how the candidate is likely to behave if elected. The signal is not foolproof: a Republican voter who is pro–gay rights might have used a partisan cue to vote for George Bush because he was the Republican nominee, even though more investigation would have revealed that Bush's position on gay rights is the opposite of her own. Even so, because partisan cues are so easy to employ, they are a favorite voting strategy in American elections; as noted in Chapter 7, many voters use these cues when voting for president. Partisan cues also play a strong role in congressional elections, and the importance of this cue seems to have increased in recent elections.[107]

A candidate's personal characteristics also play a crucial role in vote decisions. As we saw in Chapter 5, information about race, ethnicity, gender, religion, or age provides a fairly solid basis for predictions about some of a person's ideological beliefs. Thus, when voters choose a candidate who "looks like them," they are not necessarily behaving irrationally. Rather, they may be using a cue that suggests they share the candidate's priorities. Exit polls in the 2008 election suggested that Americans with strong religious beliefs were more likely to vote for the McCain–Palin ticket, partly because of Sarah Palin's membership in a charismatic Christian church.

Cues can also involve retrospective evaluations. A citizen can vote for or against a House member or senator based on how that person voted on a specific issue—even a single vote—or on judgments about an incumbent's honesty or qualifications, willingness to do casework to help constituents, or success at attracting government spending to the constituents' area. Although none of these factors tells the whole story about an incumbent's performance, each provides a rationale for deciding

voting cues Pieces of information about a candidate that are readily available, easy to interpret, and lead a citizen to decide to vote for a particular candidate.

reasonable vote A vote that is likely to be consistent with the voter's true preference for one candidate over the others.

POLITICS IS EVERYWHERE

whether an incumbent deserves another term.[108] Similarly, a voter might use the state of the economy to decide whether the president deserves another term in office or might focus on America's success or failure in recent foreign affairs to judge presidential performance. In fact, economic conditions such as rates of growth, inflation, and unemployment are very good predictors of how many people will vote for a president running for reelection.[109]

Conversely, it is also possible to vote prospectively, based an expectations of how any of these indicators will change over the next few years after the election.

Table 8.9, which is based on surveys of voters in congressional elections, shows how these incumbent-based cues shape vote decisions. People were more likely to vote for a House or a Senate incumbent if they believed that the incumbent had done a good job keeping in touch with constituents, had responded well to requests for casework, and had voted (or would vote) in line with the respondent's preferences.

Cues are an important determinant of vote decisions, but some Americans also look to the backgrounds and life experiences of the candidates. Table 8.10 offers some details on what these voters are looking for. Military service is an asset, particularly for Republicans, as is being a Christian. People from both parties like political experience and business experience. On the other hand, many Americans tend not to want a candidate who is an atheist, has never held an elected office, is older than seventy, is a Muslim, or has another feature perceived by some as problematic.

These data are a reminder that even though the average American spends little effort to learn about the candidates in congressional or even presidential elections, information about the candidates still matters to voters. If people happen to learn about a candidate's life experiences or beliefs from media coverage or an opponent's ads, this information can have an enormous impact on their willingness to support the candidate.

TABLE 8.9	VOTE DECISIONS IN CONGRESSIONAL ELECTIONS: CANDIDATE CUES

Americans are much more likely to vote for candidates who keep in touch, respond to contacts, vote as their constituents prefer, and do a good job on important problems. If you were a member of Congress who wanted to stay in office, what sorts of actions would you take to secure reelection?

Question	Response	Percentage Voting for Incumbent	
		House	Senate
How good a job does the incumbent do keeping in touch with people?	Very good	88%	87%
	Very poor	24	21
Level of satisfaction with incumbent's response to voter-initiated contact?	Very satisfied	90%	90%
	Not at all satisfied	13	26
Agreed or disagreed with incumbent's vote on particular bill?	Agreed	93%	—
	Disagreed	43	—
Which candidate would do a better job on the most important problem?	Incumbent	97%	—
	Challenger	11	—

Note: Latter questions were not asked in Senate survey.

SOURCE: Gary Jacobson, *The Politics of Congressional Elections*, 6th ed. (New York: Pearson Longman, 2004), Table 5.11.

TABLE 8.10   PREFERRED CANDIDATE TRAITS

When Americans evaluate candidates, they want military experience, Christian beliefs, and political experience. Many say they don't want atheists, Muslims, gays, or people who have had affairs or used drugs in the past. Do these preferences help to explain the success or failure of candidates in recent elections?

More likely to support a candidate who . . .

	Total	Republican	Democrat	Independent
Served in the military	48%	58%	38%	49%
Is Christian	39	61	32	31
Is a longtime DC politician	35	40	39	31
Is a former business executive	28	38	21	28
Attended prestigious university	22	24	28	15
Is in his or her forties	18	14	24	15
Has been a minister	15	21	14	14
Is a woman	13	8	21	9
Is black	7	4	13	5
Never held elective office	7	5	5	9

Less likely to support a candidate who . . .

	Total	Republican	Democrat	Independent
Does not believe in God	63%	86%	56%	57%
Never held elective office	56	64	59	50
Is in his or her seventies	48	42	60	43
Is Muslim	46	66	39	38
Is homosexual	46	64	37	42
Used drugs in the past	45	54	45	39
Had an extramarital affair	39	62	25	36
Has been a minister	25	22	28	28
Smokes cigarettes	18	29	14	13
Is a longtime elected official	15	18	10	19
Is Hispanic	14	16	17	12
Is a former business executive	13	10	16	13
Is a woman	11	21	5	7

Note: Traits with 5 percent or fewer of the public saying "more likely to support" are not shown. Traits with 10 percent or fewer of the public saying "less likely to support" are not shown.

SOURCE: Pew Research Center, "Republicans Lag in Engagement and Enthusiasm for Candidates," February 23, 2007, available at http://people-press.org/reports/pdf/307.pdf.

VOTING IN NORMAL AND NATIONALIZED ELECTIONS

All of these strategies for making vote decisions are used to some extent in every election. However, in normal elections, when congressional reelection rates are high and the seat shift between the parties is small, voters generally use cues that focus on the candidates themselves, such as incumbency, partisanship, a personal connection to a candidate, the candidate's personal characteristics, or retrospective evaluations. This behavior is consistent with what Tip O'Neill, Speaker of the House from 1977 to 1987, was talking about when he said that "all politics is local," meaning

Do Independents Really Vote Independently?

Many news stories about contemporary politics focus on independent voters—people who say they do not belong to a political party. We are told that independents are the largest political group in America (and getting larger), that independents evaluate candidates in terms of their qualifications and policy views rather than blindly voting on the basis of their party identification, and that understanding how independents think is necessary to make sense of American politics or predict future election outcomes.

For example, an increase in the number of independents might signal that Americans are rejecting the Republican and Democratic parties and might be attracted to a new political organization. Moreover, recall the data we presented in Chapter 7 about the relationship between party identification and voting in the 2008 presidential elections, which indicated the overwhelming majority of Democrats voted for Obama, just as the overwhelming majority of Republicans voted for McCain, with independents roughly split between the two candidates. If more and more people become independents, it seems that it will be much harder to predict how these individuals will vote in elections, making it more difficult to predict the outcomes of these elections.

One of the best responses to these assumptions was presented by John Sides, a professor at George Washington University who specializes in voting behavior and elections, on a blog called the Monkey Cage that he runs along with some other political

scientists.[a] His fundamental insight was to note that in studies showing a high and ever-increasing percentage of independents, pollsters generally ask one question about partisanship that usually looks like this: "Are you a Republican, Democrat, or Independent?" The problem with this question is that it gives people only three options and forces them to pick one. For example, someone who does not think of herself as a Democrat, but who usually votes for

Democratic candidates, would probably say she is an independent, just as someone who votes for Republicans but who does not identify as a Republican would give the same response. The result is that one-question surveys lump these Democratic or Republican leaners in the same category as "pure" independents, voters who have no connection with either party and who are just as likely to vote for Democrats as Republicans.

PERCENTAGE OF INDEPENDENTS AND PARTISANS

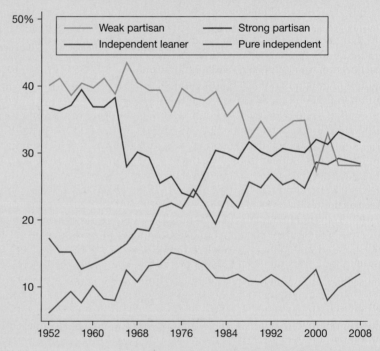

SOURCE: John Sides, "Three Myths about Political Independents," The Monkey Cage, December 17, 2009, http://www.themonkeycage.org/2009/12/three_myths_about_political_in.html.

coattails The idea that a popular president can generate additional support for candidates affiliated with his party. Coattails are weak or nonexistent in most American elections.

that congressional elections are independent, local contests in which a candidate's chances of winning depend on what voters think of the candidate in particular—not their evaluations of the president, Congress, or national issues. It also explains why electoral **coattails** are typically very weak in American elections, and why so many Americans cast **split tickets** rather than **straight tickets**. In the main,

PERCENTAGE VOTING FOR OWN OR PREFERRED PARTY'S PRESIDENTIAL CANDIDATE

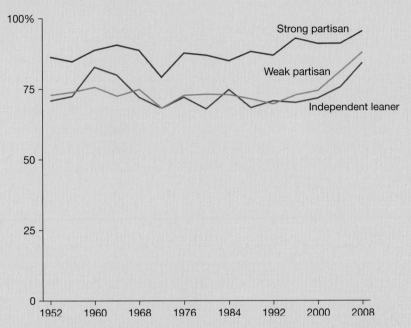

SOURCE: Data complied from the American National Election Study by John Sides, "Three Myths about Political Independents," The Monkey Cage, December 17, 2009, http://www.themonkeycage.org/2009/12/three_myths_about_political_in.html.

Most academic surveys, such as the American National Election Study (ANES), use a series of questions to measure the intensity of an individual's partisanship. In his blog post, Sides uses ANES data to show how the percentage of pure independents compares to the percentage of Republican and Democratic leaners, and how this percentage has varied over the last fifty years, as shown in the first figure. This graph makes it clear that the increase in the percentage of independent voters over the last generation consists entirely of partisan leaners; the percentage of pure independents has, if anything, declined a bit.

But even if the new independents are leaners, don't they behave more like independents than partisans? The answer, Sides shows, is that independent leaners vote a lot like partisans. The second figure shows that over the last two generations, the probability that an independent leaner votes for his party's presidential candidate is only a little lower than it is for strong partisans. (The figure also shows that weak partisans, the category in the middle between these extremes, vote like independent leaners.)

The take-away from Sides' analysis is that pundits who focus on the rise of independent voters in contemporary American politics may be focusing on the wrong kind of data. When we ask questions that get at the nuances of Americans' partisan evaluations, we find that the increase in the percentage of independent voters is almost completely comprised of people who have considerable partisan ties, despite their self-description as independents. And these seemingly weak partisan ties have a very strong influence on behavior. As Sides noted, "90% of the public is partisan and about 80–90% of those voters vote for their party's candidate. This is why the story of presidential elections is so often a story about partisans and not the fence-sitters who CNN recruits for debate dial groups." To put it another way, party identification remains an important influence on vote decisions and an important determinant of elections. However, getting accurate estimates of party identification requires careful construction of survey questions—in particular, asking questions that elicit the correct responses from weak partisans and partisan leaners.

It may seem exciting to talk about an America where partisan ties are weak and where people vote based on their assessments of the candidates. In such a world, campaigns would matter more than they do now, precisely because candidates could not count on support from a large number of partisans in their electorate. They would have to campaign with the goal of converting a large number of independents into supporters. For better or worse, American elections do not fit this description. Party identification plays a central role in modern elections, just as it has in elections for at least the last two generations. ■

Watch a video clip of John Sides discussing this topic further at wwnorton.com/studyspace.

vote decisions in presidential and congressional elections are made independently of each other.

Nationalized elections generally occur when a large number of voters switch to using the anti-party-in-power cue, which leads them to vote against candidates from the president's party. Typically this kind of shift happens when many voters

split ticket A ballot on which a voter selects candidates from more than one political party.

straight ticket A ballot on which a voter selects candidates from only one political party.

become highly concerned about a national issue such as the state of the economy or an international conflict. In the 1974 elections, voters focused on economic worries, and on the resignation of President Richard Nixon in connection with the Watergate scandal. In 1980, the crucial issue for many voters was the poor state of the economy. Economic concerns were salient again in 1994, along with disapproval of President Clinton and a recent tax increase. In 2006, surveys showed that many voters rated the war in Iraq as the most important issue, and they generally disapproved of how the war was being conducted.[110] And in 2010, economic concerns again returned to the fore, with many voters disapproving of economic conditions in general as well as corporate bailouts, economic stimulus legislation, and health care reform.

National-level concerns such as these cause citizens to lower their evaluations of the president and of Congress, and to use different cues to guide their voting decisions.[111] Specifically, many voters look for someone to blame, focusing on members of Congress from the party in power. They then vote against these members, either as a protest vote, because they disapprove of their performance, or because they want to put different individuals in charge in the hopes that conditions will improve. Whether viewed in terms of voting against one party's incumbents or for the other party's challengers, these motivations lead to the same voting behavior; the difference is a matter of voters' attitudes and emphases. Recent nationalized elections have generally brought losses for the party in power, such as the shift to Republican control of the House in 2010, but this is not always the case. In 1964, for example, Democratic president Lyndon Johnson won reelection in a landslide over Republican Barry Goldwater, and congressional Democrats in both houses substantially increased their majorities—the same kind of outcome occurred in 2008.

As we have seen throughout this chapter, nationalized elections like 2006 and 2010 can produce sharp shifts in Washington, and exit polls showed that all politics was *not* local in these elections. In 2006, the shift toward the Democratic Party was born out of national-level issues. Many voters strongly opposed the war in Iraq, believed that Congress was bedeviled by ethical lapses and corruption, and disapproved of President Bush's performance in office.[112] Similarly, in 2010, Democratic House members and Senators were blamed for the state of the economy and for

TABLE 8.11	ISSUES AND VOTING IN THE 2010 MIDTERM ELECTIONS

In the 2010 election, many Americans appeared to have based their vote on the state of the economy, evaluations of Congress and new health care legislation enacted in 2010, and economic concerns. Do these findings suggest that Republican candidates would be advantaged in the 2010 election? Was this expectation borne out?

Issue	Opinion	Vote in House Race	
		Democrat	Republican
How Congress Handling Job	Approve	81%	18%
	Disapprove	33	65
Worried about Economy	Approve	40%	57%
	Disapprove	80	19
Health Care Law	Expand	85%	14%
	No Change	67	30
	Repeal	11	86
President Barack Obama	Approve	85%	13%
	Disapprove	11	85

SOURCE: CNN Exit Poll data, available at http://www.cnn.com/ELECTION/2010/results/polls.main/#

enactment of unpopular health care legislation. As Table 8.11 shows, voters who had these concerns, or who disapproved of President Obama or of Congress in general, were much more likely to vote for Republican candidates in 2010.

Nationalized elections are rare because most of the time, relatively few citizens are highly concerned about national issues or hold strong opinions of the president, Congress, or the overall state of the nation. Congressional incumbents also work hard to focus attention on the good things they have done for their constituents. And it is important to remember that even in nationalized elections, some voters still use the incumbent-centered cues described earlier. In a nationalized election, voters don't suddenly become better informed about politics than they are the rest of the time. Rather, some of them just switch to a different set of voting cues depending on the circumstances of the election.

The 2008 and 2010 Elections

The 2008 elections were a substantial win for Democrats at all levels. Democrat Barack Obama won the presidency with 365 electoral votes (270 are needed to win) and more than 52 percent of the popular vote. Democrats gained eight seats in the Senate and twenty-one in the House.

Some characteristics of the 2008 contest distinguished it from all previous American elections. For the first time, an African American was elected president. The election also included the first female candidate to have a significant chance of winning a major party's nomination for the presidency, Democrat Hillary Clinton, and only the second female vice-presidential nominee, Alaska governor Sarah Palin. It was the first presidential race in half a century in which there was no incumbent president or vice president on the ballot. Obama was the first presidential candidate to decline federal funds for the general election campaign. For the first time since the 2000 election, the wars in Iraq and Afghanistan were not central issues. And, as the campaign unfolded, the American economy was faltering due to high energy prices, the failure of several large financial firms, the collapse of house prices, and banks' increasing unwillingness to lend money, even to well-established, secure firms.

As economic growth ground to a halt during the campaign, Americans began to evaluate candidates for the presidency and for Congress based on their proposals for handling this crisis. This focus favored Democratic candidates, because as we discuss throughout the text, most Americans view Democrats as relatively more likely to favor government intervention in the economy and see Republicans as more inclined to oppose such efforts. Democrats also benefited from the fact that unpopular Republican president George Bush was in charge during the economic meltdown, which led some voters to attribute responsibility for the crisis to Republican officeholders and candidates. As a result, many Democratic candidates, including Obama, were able to turn the election into a referendum on the economic policies of the Bush administration by arguing that electing John McCain and other Republicans would bring "more of the same."

The wars in Afghanistan and Iraq did not loom large in the campaign: during the month prior to the election, fewer than 10 percent of the population cited the wars as the most important issue facing the country. This shift in public opinion reflected the decline in American casualties and insurgent attacks that began in 2007 and continued into 2008. The War on Terror and the need to prevent future attacks had faded from the headlines. Thus, as the election neared, they were no longer top considerations for the average voter—but the economy was.

▲ The forty-fourth American president-elect, Barack Obama, with vice president-elect, Joe Biden, waves to a crowd of celebrating supporters on November 4, 2008.

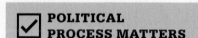
Republican candidates, including McCain and Palin, worked to shift public attention away from the economy to issues that they believed would help their candidacy. McCain and Palin argued that Obama was inexperienced, that he associated with a known terrorist (a reference to William Ayers, a former member of the 1960s-era radical Weather Underground Organization, now a professor, who served with Obama on a foundation board and held a fund-raiser for Obama's first campaign), and that Obama would redistribute wealth away from middle- and upper-class people to fund new government programs for the poor. These arguments might have worked in the absence of an economic crisis or if the Iraq war and terrorist attacks had remained central concerns. But the daily headlines about corporate bankruptcies, rising foreclosure rates, and a sagging stock market—coupled with Obama's steady performance during debates and his campaign's focus on the need for change—didn't allow McCain's and Palin's arguments to gain much traction. In addition, McCain's choice of Palin as his running mate became a liability after she committed several well-publicized gaffes that called into question her readiness for national office, whereas Barack Obama's choice of Delaware senator Joe Biden was generally considered a reasonable one.

The outcome of the 2008 contest was also shaped by the rules and procedures governing the process. One explanation for Republican losses in the House and Senate was that a disproportionate number of Republican officeholders retired rather than face two more years in the minority, which gave Democrats opportunities to pick up open seats. Republicans also had to defend more Senate seats than their Democratic counterparts: in 2008, twenty-three Senate seats held by Republicans were up for reelection, versus only twelve for Democrats. Of course, given the propensity for voters to blame President Bush and the Republicans for the poor state of the American economy in 2008, Republicans faced an uphill fight from the start. Nevertheless, these structural factors certainly increased their troubles.

In the presidential nomination contests, Barack Obama benefited from the large number of Democratic caucuses. Because turnout for caucuses is extremely low, they benefit candidates like Obama who have a strong get-out-the-vote operation and many enthusiastic volunteers. In fact, were it not for Obama's performance in the caucuses, Senator Hillary Clinton would have won the Democratic nomination, as she tended to outperform Obama in states that held primary elections. On the Republican side, many state primaries allocated delegates using a winner-take-all rule. Mitt Romney, who dropped out of the contest after John McCain amassed an insurmountable delegate lead, noted that if the delegates had been awarded proportionally, he would have had more delegates than McCain.

In the general election, Obama's get-out-the-vote operation was far more elaborate than McCain's, which helped Obama win swing states such as Ohio, Indiana, and Pennsylvania. The Obama campaign did all the usual things, from knocking on doors to organizing shuttle vans to drive voters to the polls, but their operation was one of the largest and most effective ever seen in a presidential race. The Obama campaign was also notable for its extensive use of the Internet for communication and fund-raising, and the McCain campaign was unable to match these efforts.

There were real differences between Republican and Democratic candidates in 2008 on issues such as how to address economic problems, how to reform health care, and what to do in Iraq. Exit poll data showed that a clear majority of voters cited the economy as the most important issue, and that Obama was the favorite among people who wanted government action to address economic problems. McCain, in contrast, won more support from citizens who believed that less government involvement would help solve economic woes, as well as those who ranked national security as their primary concern.

EXPLAINING CHANGE: THE 2010 MIDTERM ELECTIONS

The 2010 midterm elections were a sharp reversal of the patterns observed in 2006 and 2008, and a reminder that nothing in American politics is permanent. As we have discussed, in 2006, Democrats regained control of the House and the Senate. The 2008 elections consolidated Democratic gains, with the party capturing the presidency, increasing its majority in the House, and falling just short of a filibuster-proof majority in the Senate. Polls showed dramatic shifts toward the Democrats among independents and young voters. The stage seemed set for years of Democratic domination of Washington politics—and an expansion of the federal government in line with the party's priorities and the wishes of its supporters.

Two years later, this vision was upended. While significant portions of the party's policy agenda had been enacted, debate over these policies had exposed deep divisions within the House and Senate Democratic caucuses, as well as strong differences of opinion among voters who had elected Democrats to Congress and put Barack Obama in the White House. More important, Republicans seemed to have regained the initiative, offering proposals for sharp changes in government policy (although many changes were not spelled out), while most Democratic candidates seemed to avoid as much as possible talking about their party's policy accomplishments, even if they had formerly been strong supporters. And of course, a significant number of citizens who were strong supporters of the party in 2006 and 2008 switched to become equally strong supporters of Republican candidates. As a result, Republicans regained majority control of the House of Representatives, gaining more than sixty seats. Democrats held on to majority control of the Senate, but Republicans significantly narrowed the party split.

The easy explanations for the 2010 results do not stand up to investigation. One claim is that Democratic candidates lost because of Barack Obama's unpopularity. As we discuss in Chapter 11, Presidency, while Obama's popularity has declined since he took office in January 2009, it still remains significantly higher than for virtually all previous presidents at the middle of their first term.[113] While some citizens undoubtedly voted for Republicans because of their disapproval of Obama's performance in office, this cannot be the primary explanation for the election outcome.

Another argument is that Republicans benefited from the *Citizens United* Supreme Court decision, or from an estimated $100 million in campaign expenditures by organizations that took advantage of a loophole in the IRS code to run massive numbers of attack ads against Democrats without revealing the source of their contributions.[114] However, at least as of mid-October 2010, many Democrats in close races outspent their Republican opponents, even after accounting for spending by unaffiliated groups.[115] Moreover, as we have discussed in various chapters, campaign spending does not guarantee success: if all Republicans and their allies had was money to burn on their campaigns, that fact alone would not have produced their victories in 2010.

A third argument cites the Tea Party movement as a vital force that united Americans behind Republicans and their plans for reforming government. However, studies of the movement showed wide variation in these organizations—some were disciplined groups that ran extensive and sometimes successful campaign operations in 2010, but most were little more than Web sites or Facebook pages, with few members and virtually no activity.[116] And, by working to unseat several popular Republican incumbents and open-seat candidates, the Tea Party movement cost the party control of at least two Senate seats, in Delaware and Nevada. Moreover, even among the active Tea Party groups, there were few common issue positions, aside from economic concerns and a general distrust of government.

A better explanation for Republican successes in 2010 lies in two of our central themes. First, politics is conflictual. The last two years have been an education in what a president with united congressional majorities can accomplish. But they also

▲ The new Speaker of the House, Republican representative John Boehner of Ohio, won the support of his Republican colleagues by organizing their opposition to Democratic policy initiatives during the first two years of President Obama's term and by campaigning tirelessly for Republican candidates in the 2010 midterms.

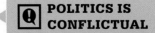

POLITICS IS CONFLICTUAL

reminded Americans of their policy disagreements, and, in doing so, gave Republicans a ready-made constituency of people who opposed some or all of Obama's achievements or who favored the party's overall goals but disagreed with their implementation.

In addition, Democratic candidates, representing the party in power in 2010, were saddled with a persistently weak economy, an issue that topped all polls of voter worries. In terms of the discussion introduced in Chapter 5, the state of the economy was at the "top of the head" for most Americans, which gave Republican candidates an additional advantage, as they could argue that their minority status meant they were not to blame for economic hardships. Exit polls show that of Americans who said that the economy was the most important problem, a strong majority voted for Republican candidates.

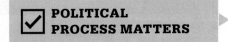

A second argument we have made throughout the book is that process matters. In 2010, all of the procedural advantages were on the Republican side. For example, Democratic gains in the 2006 and 2008 House elections gave them fifty or sixty incumbents in pro-Republican districts. These seats were winnable for Democrats as long as Republicans were saddled with an extremely unpopular war (2006) or an economy in freefall (2008). In 2010, Republican House candidates in these districts were free of these burdens for the first time in six years. Their victories in large part reflected the natural tendencies of these districts.

Republican gains in the Senate were also no surprise. While the parties had roughly equal numbers of seats to defend, Democrats had more vulnerable incumbents. For Republicans, the typical incumbent running for reelection was Mike Crapo of Idaho, whose opponent in 2010 barely cleared 30 percent of the vote. In contrast, the canonical Democrat was three-term liberal icon Russ Feingold of Wisconsin, whose low approval ratings showed he was in trouble a year before the elections, and who lost to a self-financed opponent, businessman Ron Johnson.

What happens next? The Republican takeover of the House means that President Obama will no longer be able to pass legislation using only Democratic votes—any new presidential proposals will require support from some House Republicans and the approval of House Republican leaders, who now control the chamber agenda.

However, the Republicans' newfound power is very limited. For one thing, it is hard to see how they can roll back any of President Obama's legislative accomplishments. Even in the House, they are far short of the two-thirds majority needed to override a presidential veto. Republican House leaders may force votes on repealing some programs, but they simply do not have the votes to be successful.

Moreover, if Republicans want to enact new proposals, they will have to solve two critical problems. For one thing, there is significant disagreement within Republican ranks on a wide range of issues, including cutting the budget deficit, changing the tax code, and immigration reform. Enacting new policies will require compromise within the Republican Party, along with making concessions to gain some Democratic support. And then, Republican leaders will need to make additional concessions to gain the president's support. All of this is not to say that no legislation of significance will be enacted in the next two years—but the era of large changes in the structure and function of the federal government is, at least for the moment, on hold.

Elections Matter

It is easy to complain about American elections. Citizens are not experts about public policy. They often know little about the candidates running for office. Candidates sensationalize, attack, and dissemble, rather than giving details about who they are and what they would do if elected. Billions of dollars are on elections. Even so, there are clear, systematic differences between Democratic and Republican candidates that translate into different government policies depending on who holds office. Moreover, the criteria that average Americans use to make vote decisions reflect these differences. People don't know everything about politics or about elections, but their votes are, by and large, reasonable.

Moreover, many examples of seemingly strange behavior in American elections make more sense once you examine them. It makes sense that so few Americans are issue voters and that many people decide to abstain. Both behaviors result from a lack of interest in politics and the almost nonexistent impact of each vote on the election outcome. For the same reasons, it makes sense that candidates trying to get the attention of distracted voters tend to emphasize sensationalism over sober discussion of policies. The outcome of the election, who wins and who loses, is the result of all these individual-level choices added together. In that sense, election outcomes reflect the preferences of the American people.

American elections are not perfect, but it is impossible to say that they are irrelevant. By determining who holds political office, elections determine what government does. The 2006 midterm election gave voters a clear choice: shift congressional power to the Democrats or leave it in the hands of Republicans. The 2008 elections presented a choice between continuing the shift toward the Democrats or returning the Republicans to power. The 2010 elections gave voters exactly the opposite choice as they were offered in 2006. You might prefer that voters were offered different choices, a detailed menu of policy options for dealing with economic crises and other questions. Even so, there is no ignoring the fact that voters face important choices and that the results of these elections had real policy consequences. The 2006 midterms brought Democrats back into power in the House and Senate, which pressured then-president Bush to reassess the nation's aims and strategy in Iraq, leading to the "troop surge" of 2007 and the subsequent withdrawal of American forces that continues to this day. The 2008 elections resulted in the election of the first African American president, Barack Obama, as well as additional Democrats to the House and Senate, making it possible to enact landmark health care reforms and many other significant policy proposals.

The 2010 midterms continue to illustrate this point. As a result of the switch in party control in the House of Representative, Republican representative John Boehner became the new Speaker of the House. A generation of veteran Democratic leaders, such as House Appropriations Chair David Obey, Armed Services Chair Ike Skelton, and veteran liberal icon Senator Russ Feingold of Wisconsin retired or were defeated. Facing a new Republican majority in the House and having a much smaller Democratic majority in the Senate, congressional Democrats and President Obama must scale back plans for new policy initiatives, as they now require substantial Republican support to enact legislation. Whether Republicans and Democrats will be able to find consensus on important issues such as deficit reduction in the coming two years remains an open question. But regardless of the outcome, it is clear that elections matter. The choices candidates offer, and how citizens assess those choices and make vote decisions, have important policy consequences.

Conclusion

Candidates in American national elections compete for different offices across the country using a variety of rules that determine who can run for office, who can vote, and how ballots are counted and winners determined. Election outcomes are shaped by who runs for office and how they campaign, who decides to vote and how they decide whom to support, but also by the rules that govern electoral competition.

These factors help to explain Barack Obama's victory in 2008. His strong organization, drawing on social networking tools, helped him to dominate a nomination process that emphasized caucuses. Obama's relative inexperience was also a benefit in a year when many voters had lost confidence in existing leaders and demanded policy change. And of course, Obama benefited from shifts in party identification that favored all Democratic candidates, as well as retrospective evaluations that had the same effect. Of course, none of these advantages is permanent—Republican candidates in 2010 had similar advantages, leading to their substantial gains in House and Senate elections.

The same factors disadvantaged Obama's main opponents. Senator Clinton attempted to match Obama's claims of being an agent of change, but her long-standing career in politics (including two terms as a First Lady involved in the policy process) hindered the success of this argument. Her strategy of emphasizing endorsements and building a large campaign organization for the general election hurt her in the hunt for the nomination, as she did not have the resources to mobilize support as Obama did. Finally, her initial support for the Iraq War cost her the support of many Democratic primary voters, especially when compared with Obama's consistent opposition.

In contrast, McCain moved from being advantaged by process and political factors in the nomination campaign to being disadvantaged by the same kinds of factors in the general election. McCain also benefited from rules in crucial states that allowed independents and registered Democrats to cross party lines and vote in the Republican primary, as well as the winner-take-all rules in some states that gave him a large majority of delegates despite winning less than 50 percent of the Republican primary vote. Moreover, although McCain had some obvious drawbacks as a candidate—his age and lack of connection to the evangelical community that makes up a large portion of Republican primary voters—other candidates had even greater liabilities, such as the perception that Mitt Romney had shifted positions on many issues to appeal to conservatives.

None of McCain's strengths helped him much in the general election. His steadfast support for the troop surge in Iraq was of little consequence given that the economy had displaced the war as most voters' top concern by the time of the election. Moreover, McCain's appeals to conservative Republicans during the primaries and the Republican Convention, symbolized by his selection of Alaska governor Sarah Palin for vice president, reduced his chances of winning support from independents and moderate Democrats—support he needed in order to win the general election given the downward trend in Republican registration.

Finally, McCain was the victim of bad luck. The economic crisis that began in September 2008 brought about the swift collapse of the stock market and several major financial firms. These events gave voters two reasons to vote Democratic: to punish Republicans for President Bush's economic policies and to demand government intervention to mitigate the impact of the economic crisis. This second reason was bolstered by the economic measures that Obama and many other Democrats were proposing. McCain might well have lost even if the American economy had remained strong, but the economic meltdown destroyed any chance he had of winning the election. In the same way, the continued economic weakness hurt many Democratic candidates in 2010.

What role do elections play in a democracy?

- American national elections allow voters to select members of Congress, the president, and the vice president, and they create a mechanism for holding these elected officials accountable for their behavior in office.
- The American political system is a representative democracy: Americans do not make policy choices themselves, but they vote for the individuals who get to make these choices.

How do elections work in the United States?

- American presidential elections are a two-step process: in primary elections and caucuses, candidates secure the party's nomination, and in the general election officeholders are chosen.
- Candidates for the House and Senate compete in single-member districts, with the winner decided using plurality (in some cases majority) voting. Presidential elections are decided by the electoral college vote.
- Many groups and individuals are active in elections, such as party organizations, interest groups, and activists. Their activities include working for candidates, making campaign contributions, and campaigning on behalf of candidates they favor.
- Election outcomes are shaped by who runs and how those people campaign—but also by the rules that govern electoral competition.

How do candidates win elections?

- Strategizing for the next election begins the day after the last election, as would-be candidates, party leaders, and interest group staff begin to interpret the election results and decide where to concentrate their efforts in the upcoming contests.
- Most incumbents work to secure their reelection throughout the entire election cycle. These efforts are known as the permanent campaign.
- During the campaign, candidates try to build name recognition, mobilize supporters, and publicize their campaign platform. Other important tactics include emphasizing their knowledge of and

sympathy to voters' concerns and going negative against their opponent.
- Campaigns feature thousands of ads commissioned by candidates, parties, and interest groups. There is considerable evidence that campaign advertising shapes citizens' beliefs about candidates, as well as their propensity to participate in the political process.
- Billions of dollars are spent on American elections. However, there is little evidence that money buys electoral success—or that the sum is excessive given the stakes and the cost of campaign advertising.

How do voters decide?

- The decision to vote is driven by a citizen's sense of obligation; the closeness of the election and a citizen's preferences between the candidates have relatively little to do with the decision.
- Very few people are issue voters who are well-informed about candidates, issues, and the election. The average voter uses a series of simple but powerful cues to make vote decisions.
- During normal elections, voters tend to use cues that focus attention on individual candidates and their performance in office.
- During nationalized elections, many voters focus on the party in power, leading them to vote against these candidates because of national-level issues such as a poor economy, a federal tax increase, or an international conflict.

Do elections matter?

- Elections matter because candidates from the Republican and Democratic parties stand for different things and behave differently in office.
- Most citizens are not policy experts, but they cast reasonable votes.
- Elections also create a way for citizens to hold elected officials accountable for their behavior in office.
- Many of the seemingly irrational features of American elections are the product of sensible behavior by candidates, citizens, and other political actors.

⊚ STUDENT STUDYSPACE

Find quizzes and other review material at wwnorton.com/studyspace.

CRITICAL THINKING

1. Can American elections be described as debates over government policy, given that the average voter knows so little about what government is doing or could do? Explain your answer.

2. Using cues to make vote decisions lowers the cost of voting, in terms of the time and effort involved in a voter's decision. Under what conditions will cues help a voter make the right choice in an election, defined as the same choice that would result from having complete information about the candidates? Under what conditions will cues lead a voter to make the wrong choice?

3. What kinds of candidates are helped by limits on campaign contributions by individuals and organizations such as PACs? What kinds of candidates do these restrictions hurt? Why do such limits affect these types of candidates differently?

KEY TERMS

absentee ballot (p. 263)
attack ads (p. 280)
campaign platform (p. 276)
caucus (electoral) (p. 266)
challenger (p. 261)
closed primary (p. 262)
coattails (p. 296)
delegates (p. 266)
election cycle (p. 271)
electoral college (p. 269)
electoral vote (p. 259)
Federal Election Commission (p. 284)
frontloading (p. 268)
general election (p. 262)
GOTV (p. 275)
ground game (p. 275)
hard money (p. 285)

incumbent (p. 261)
issue voters (p. 292)
majority voting (p. 263)
mobilization (p. 275)
nationalized election (p. 260)
nomination (p. 262)
normal election (p. 260)
open primary (p. 262)
open seat (p. 272)
opposition research (p. 279)
paradox of voting (p. 290)
party ratio (p. 259)
permanent campaign (p. 272)
plurality voting (p. 263)
political business cycle (p. 273)
popular vote (p. 259)
primary (p. 266)
proportional allocation (p. 267)

push polling (p. 275)
reasonable vote (p. 296)
regional primaries (p. 268)
retail politics (p. 275)
retrospective evaluation (p. 261)
runoff election (p. 264)
seat shift (p. 259)
soft money (p. 285)
split ticket (p. 296)
straight ticket (p. 296)
superdelegates (p. 268)
swing states (p. 270)
turnout (p. 291)
undervote (p. 265)
voting cues (p. 293)
wholesale politics (p. 275)
winner-take-all (p. 267)

SUGGESTED READING

Abramson, Paul, John Aldrich, and David Rohde. *Change and Continuity in the 2004 and 2006 Elections*. Washington, DC: CQ Press, 2007.

Bartels, Larry. *Presidential Primaries and the Dynamics of Public Choice*. Princeton, NJ: Princeton University Press, 1988.

Cramer, Richard Ben. *What It Takes: The Way to the White House*. New York: Vintage, 1993.

Donovan, Todd, and Shaun Bowler. *Reforming the Republic: Democratic Institutions for the New America*. New York: Pearson, 2007.

Fiorina, Morris P. *Retrospective Voting in American National Elections*. New Haven, CT: Yale University Press, 1981.

Hellemann, John, and Mark Halpern. *Game Change: Obama and the Clintons, McCain and Palin, and the Race of a Lifetime*. New York: Random House, 2009.

Jacobson, Gary. *The Politics of Congressional Elections,* 6th ed. New York: Pearson Longman, 2004.

Key, V. O. *The Responsible Electorate.* New York: Vintage, 1966.

Museum of the Moving Image, "The Living Room Candidate: Presidential Campaign Commercials, 1952–2004," online exhibit at http://livingroomcandidate.movingimage.us.

Niemi, Richard G., and Herbert F. Weisberg. *Controversies in Voting Behavior,* 4th ed. Washington, DC: CQ Press, 2001.

Popkin, Samuel. *The Reasoning Voter.* Chicago: University of Chicago Press, 1991.

Lobbyist Jack Abramoff (far left) on a golf outing in Scotland with his guests, including then-representative Bob Ney (far right). The crimes for which Abramoff and Ney were later convicted are relatively rare but nevertheless help shape citizens' negative perceptions of interest groups and their influence over politicians.

Interest Groups

Interest groups are one of the most visible manifestations of the idea that politics is conflictual. Given the pervasive influence of government on our lives, and given the many disagreements in society over what government should do, it makes sense that individuals, corporations, and other actors would organize groups to try to shape what government does, both by implementing their own views and by preventing opponents from doing so. For example, the National Rifle Association (NRA) fights to maintain and extend Americans' ability to own and carry firearms, while other groups, such as Handgun Control, work to impose restrictions on these rights. Government policy reflects, at least in part, the actions taken by these groups.

CONFLICT AND COMPROMISE
in American Politics

To many people, interest groups exemplify what's wrong with American politics. If interest groups are all about conflict, then it is clear why some Americans don't like them. Citizens who are on the losing side of important policy debates often attribute their defeat to actions taken by opposing interest groups. If you support restrictions on the ownership of assault weapons, for example, you're probably not happy about the NRA's success at defeating attempts to ban the sale of such weapons.

A more serious complaint has to do with the belief that many interest groups have an unfair advantage in the political process because of their resources, connections, or willingness to engage in unethical or illegal activities, allowing them to win regardless of who opposes them. A 2006 study found that three-quarters of Americans believed that interest groups and lobbyists had too much influence in Washington.[1] An even higher percentage (82 percent) believed that lobbyists often bribe members of Congress. And although the survey found broad support for tighter lobbying regulations, a majority of respondents believed that such regulations would have little or no effect.

It is easy to find headlines to support these views. In 2005, one major lobbyist, Jack Abramoff, was accused of using "golf junkets, meals at his restaurant, seats at sporting events, and, in some cases, old-fashioned cash"[2] to lobby members of Congress. Abramoff was convicted in 2006 of conspiracy, fraud, and tax evasion. Representative Bob Ney (R-OH) and several congressional aides and high-level bureaucrats were also convicted of accepting Abramoff's bribes or making false statements about their relationship with him.[3] The Abramoff scandal is not the

BIG QUESTIONS

✪ What are interest groups, what role do they play, what are their goals, and how are they organized?

✪ Why do interest groups form? How do interest groups solve their collective action problems?

✪ What strategies do interest groups use?

✪ How much power do interest groups have in the United States?

only recent example of lobbying misdeeds. In 2006, Representative Randy "Duke" Cunningham (R-CA) was convicted of taking $2.4 million in bribes from lobbyists in return for steering government contracts to their defense industry clients.[4]

The truth is that these criminal acts are relatively rare, but even if we leave them aside, it is easy to find interest groups that appear to have undue influence over government policy. One study found that the financial firms that received government funds from the Troubled Asset Relief Program (TARP) during the 2008 financial system bailout had spent more than $77 million on lobbying and an additional $39 million on campaign contributions and advertising, leading one member of Congress to claim that "Wall Street owns Washington."[5] Another study found that during the debate over health care reform in 2009, lobbying firms were spending more than $1.4 million a day to run ads, meet with members of Congress and bureaucrats, and organize citizens in favor of one option or another.[6] These firms also hired 350 ex-lawmakers and congressional staff to assist in their efforts. Such lobbying is not limited to health care, of course: during the first three months of 2009, energy company Exxon Mobil spent more than $9 million on lobbying; defense company Lockheed Martin and drug company Pfizer each spent more than $6 million.[7]

With examples like these, it is probably not surprising that Americans are suspicious of interest groups and worry about their ability to dominate the political process. What do these companies get from lobbying? How can average Americans change government policy when they are fighting against organizations that have millions of dollars and extensive connections on their side? Even if individuals try to form new groups to advance their policy goals, their battle against well-entrenched groups does not seem like a fair fight.

Moreover, despite the proliferation of interest groups and lobbyists in America, some large groups of like-minded Americans have no identifiable interest group fighting for their policy concerns. Where, for example, are the groups that lobby for what college students want? And how can debates over policy be considered a fair fight when some groups are unrepresented in the process?

This chapter surveys the wide range of interest groups in American politics, from large, powerful groups such as the NRA to small organizations that lobby on issues that concern only a few Americans. In part, our discussion will confirm the conventional wisdom: conflicts over government policy are the driving force behind interest group activities.

However, interest groups are not only the tool of the rich and powerful. Virtually all Americans belong to interest groups or have groups that lobby on their behalf. And many of the clubs, groups, and organizations to which Americans belong have little known yet extensive lobbying arms. Moreover, policy victories do not always go to the organization that spends the most money or has hired the most expensive talent. Groups can succeed by mobilizing their members, forming alliances with other groups, becoming sources of political or

▼ When the scandals surrounding Jack Abramoff came to light, many Americans considered him a typical lobbyist who used gifts, bribes, and favors to get advantageous policy decisions from elected officials and bureaucrats. Abramoff's actions were illegal, but the question remains: Are his tactics common in Washington, or was he a rare exception?

policy expertise, or using the courts to fight policy battles. Thus, although people are correct to understand interest groups in terms of conflict, they are wrong in thinking that these groups invariably work against the interests of average Americans.

The Interest Group Universe

Interest groups are organizations that seek to influence government policy by helping to elect candidates who support their policy goals and by **lobbying** elected officials and bureaucrats. In its most basic form, lobbying involves persuasion—using reports, protests, informal meetings, or other techniques to convince an elected official or bureaucrat to help enact a law, craft a regulation, or do something else that a group wants. The members of an interest group can be individual citizens, local governments, businesses, foundations or nonprofit organizations, churches, or virtually any other entity. An interest group's employees or members may lobby on the group's behalf, or a group may hire a lobbyist or lobbying firm to do the work for it.

Interest groups and political parties share the goal of changing what government does, but there are three critical differences between these organizations. First, political parties focus on running candidates for office and coordinating the activities of elected officials. Interest groups also electioneer, but they do not have an official position on electoral ballots to offer their candidates. Second, the major political parties hold certain legal advantages over even the largest interest groups when it comes to influencing policy, such as guaranteed positions on electoral ballots. Third, the elected members of political parties have a direct influence over government activity: they propose, debate, and vote on policies. Interest groups have, at best, an indirect influence: they must either persuade elected officials to support their point of view or help elect candidates who already share their goals.

Sometimes interest groups are primarily political organizations. One such group is Public Citizen, which carries out research projects, lobbies legislators and bureaucrats, and tries to rally public opinion on a wide range of environmental, health, and energy issues. More commonly, though, lobbying is only one part of what an organization does. The NRA, for example, endorses candidates, contributes to campaigns, and lobbies elected officials. But it also runs gun safety classes, holds competitions, and sells a variety of hardware to its members. In other cases, interest group activity is almost hidden within an organization. Consider the Automobile Association of America (AAA). Most drivers know AAA as a provider of emergency roadside service and maps, but AAA is also an interest group that lobbies for increased funding for highways and less for mass transit.

As these descriptions suggest, interest groups and lobbying are ubiquitous in American politics. Many organizations have lobbying operations or hire lobbyists to work on their behalf. You may think that you don't belong to a group that lobbies the federal government, but the odds are that you do.

In fact, one important view of American politics, pluralism, identifies interest groups as America's fundamental political actors.[8] Pluralists argue that most Americans participate in politics through their membership in interest groups like Public Citizen, the NRA, or even AAA. These groups lobby, electioneer, and negotiate among themselves to encourage legislators to

▼ More than 4 million individuals belong to the National Rifle Association, one of the most powerful interest groups in America. At their national convention shown here, members debate the group's goals and select leaders.

Interest Groups in Other Nations

Just as in America, people all over the world have ideas about what they would like government to do, and they organize to shape policies in line with their preferences, making interest groups a fundamental component of democracy.[a] Studies have even found that the longer a country has been a democracy, the more interest groups it has.[b] Interest groups in other countries are also structured similarly to those that operate in America. They are often either affiliated with or part of larger organizations, such as labor unions, ethnic associations, or religious groups. Citizens often belong to several interest groups—although, similar to Americans, they may not be aware of the groups' political activities.

Comparing countries reveals three important differences in how interest groups lobby. First, the targets of their lobbying vary. As discussed in Chapter 7, political parties are often much stronger in other countries than they are in America. Most European countries, such as Germany, France, Italy, and Great Britain, have highly influential party organizations. When parties are strong, individual politicians have to follow the orders of party leaders or risk being removed from office or prevented from running in the first place.[c] As a result, interest groups in these countries focus on lobbying party leaders rather than individual legislators, who ultimately have to do what party leaders demand.

Interest groups in other nations are also typically subject to stringent campaign finance restrictions.[d] In Great Britain, for example, interest groups cannot contribute to

Interest groups are active in almost every democracy. In Europe, these groups lobby both their national government and the European Union, whose legislators and bureaucrats determine policies that affect many local industries. Here, European farmers protest European Union plans to cut agricultural subsidies.

the campaigns of individual candidates for Parliament. In many other European countries, interest groups can run campaign ads but must cease doing so during the last days of the electoral campaign.

Differences in governmental institutions also change how interest groups lobby.[e] Consider parliamentary systems, in which the executive and legislative branches of government are linked. The party controlling the legislature selects not only the prime minister, who serves as the head of the government, but also the ministers who control specific organizations within the government. In the American system, the branches of government are often controlled by different political parties, so

interest groups face a choice. Should they lobby the executive branch to seek a regulation that suits their purposes, or should they lobby Congress for a budget request or new legislation? In a parliamentary system, this choice does not exist: interest groups can only lobby the party in power, which controls both branches of government.

A final difference in the way interest groups abroad lobby has to do with the influence of the European Union.[f] Interest groups in the member states who want a change in policy can lobby either their own government or the legislators and bureaucrats in the EU government for policies that would apply to all member states. ∎

pursue policies that benefit their members. Others describe America as an **interest group state**, meaning that these groups are involved whenever policy is made.[9]

THE BUSINESS OF LOBBYING

Interest group lobbying is heavily regulated.[10] Lobbying firms must file annual reports identifying their clients and specifying how much they were paid by each one. Similarly, interest groups and corporations must file reports listing staff members

interest group state A government in which most policy decisions are determined by the influence of interest groups.

who spent more than 20 percent of their time lobbying Congress, and detailing expenditures to lobbying firms. Existing laws also require most executive or legislative branch employees who take lobbying jobs to refrain from lobbying people in their former office or agency for one year—though elected officials who become lobbyists must wait two years.

One thing is for sure: lobbying involves billions of dollars a year. Figure 9.1 shows annual lobbying expenditures for 2000 through 2009, compiled from the official reports that interest groups and lobbyists are required to file with the federal government. As the figure shows, a total of $3.5 billion was spent on lobbying in 2009. The data in Figure 9.2 show that a multitude of groups and organizations lobby the federal government, and this number has increased significantly over the last decade, with more than $3 billion a year spent on lobbying in 2009.

The number of interest groups has also shot up in recent years. In a 1999 study, two scholars found that the number of interest groups in the United States had risen from about 5,000 in 1959 to more than 25,000 in 1995.[11] The current number is undoubtedly much higher: the 2008 *Encyclopedia of Associations* lists approximately 100,000 national and regional organized groups in America, though not all of these groups lobby the federal government.

POLITICS IS EVERYWHERE

Why are there so many interest groups and registered lobbyists, and why are their numbers increasing? Figure 9.2 suggests that this proliferation is related to the large size and widespread influence of the federal government. People get involved and lobby because they have a stake in what the government does. They want their company to get a government contract, or they want a new regulation to favor their business sector. They want the government to limit what citizens can do or relax restrictions on behavior. Simply put, the federal government does so many things and spends so much money that many individuals, organizations, and corporations have strong incentives for lobbying. Studies of Washington-based lobbying operations confirmed this idea: interest groups are more likely to form around issues or

---

FIGURE 9.1   **MONEY SPENT ON LOBBYING, 2000–2009**

These data show that in recent years, interest groups have spent several billion dollars lobbying the federal government—and their spending is steadily increasing. Does this amount seem surprisingly large or surprisingly small, given what lobbyists do?

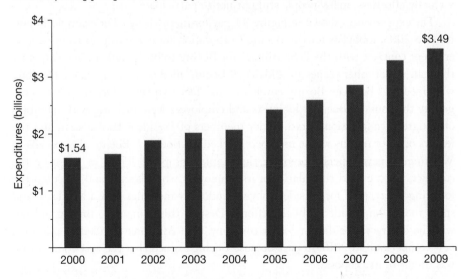

SOURCE: Center for Responsive Politics, "Total Lobbying Spending," available at www.opensecrets.org/lobby/index.php.

FIGURE 9.2   **GROWTH IN FEDERAL SPENDING AND IN LOBBYING**

In general, as the federal government has grown, so has the number of lobbyists. One explanation is that lobbyists get the government to spend money that it otherwise would not. Can you think of a different explanation that is consistent with the data?

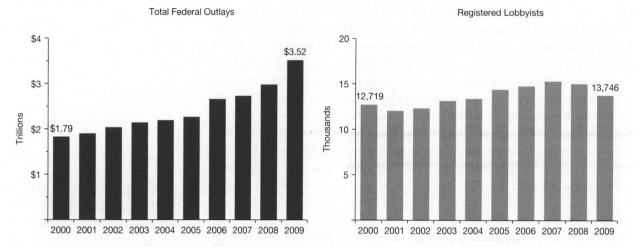

Total Federal Outlays

Registered Lobbyists

SOURCE: Center for Responsive Politics, "Lobbying Database," available at www.opensecrets.org/lobby/index.php; GPO Access, Budget of the United States Government, Historical Table 1.1 (FY 2009), available at http://www.gpoaccess.gov/usbudget/fy09/hist.html.

latent A group of politically like-minded people that is not represented by any interest group.

▼ *Throughout the early and mid-2000s, the Boeing Corporation mounted an extensive lobbying campaign as part of its efforts to win a contract to build air refueling planes for the U.S. Air Force. This campaign involved meetings with elected officials and bureaucrats, as well as advertising in many national publications.*

questions that have high levels of government involvement, or when new programs or changes in government policy are likely.[12] Moreover, as groups form on one side of a policy question and start to lobby, people who oppose what these groups are trying to do may form their own interest groups and commence lobbying as well.

Changes in communication technology may also contribute to the increasing numbers of interest groups and lobbyists.[13] Television and the Internet make it easier for people to realize that they have common interests, and cell phones, e-mail, social networking, and other forms of electronic communication make it easier for large, geographically dispersed groups to organize and implement lobbying strategies. Even so, many like-minded groups in America remain **latent** or unorganized, without a group to represent them, suggesting that even when participation can be virtually effortless, many people still opt not to participate.

The expenditures shown in Figure 9.1 pay for many things. For example, beginning in 2003, lobbyists for the Boeing Corporation were working to secure a government contract with the U.S. military for Boeing to build tanker aircraft (planes that can refuel other planes in midair). A Boeing memo detailed the effort: along with meetings between Boeing employees and Department of Defense staff to negotiate the contact, Boeing's lobbyists and employees were meeting with members of Congress, congressional staff, senior members of President Bush's staff, and the leaders of labor unions whose members worked for Boeing.[14] Boeing also ran ads in Washington newspapers promoting their tanker proposal. Thus, in pursuing the contract, Boeing paid the salaries of its employees who planned and executed the lobbying effort, paid for outside lobbyists and their meetings on Capitol Hill, and spent money on broader publicity efforts. Despite this campaign, Boeing did not win the contract, nor did any other company. The Air Force decided to initiate a new competition in 2010, in part because Boeing argued that the first competition was unfair to its proposal.

The disclosure data also reveal who the big spenders on lobbying are. As shown in Table 9.1, the list is dominated by corporations like General Electric and groups

Restrictions on Interest Group Lobbying

The case of Jack Abramoff and the congressmen and staff convicted of taking bribes from his organization suggest that some interest groups and lobbying firms are not playing by the rules. Rather than just making their case to officials, they are offering money and other inducements in return for policy change.

It seems that to solve this problem, interest groups and lobbying firms should be regulated to ensure that they cannot unfairly dominate the policy process, regardless of the public's opinion about their agendas, by buying support from members of Congress and bureaucrats. This proposal raises two questions. First, would new regulations prevent abuses of power? Second, are such abuses of power commonplace enough to justify a new regulation?

To place the argument for reform in context, consider the six-point lobbying reform proposal offered after the Abramoff scandal by a coalition of six groups: Public Citizen, Common Cause, Democracy 21, Public Campaign Legal Center, U.S. PIRG, and the League of Women Voters.[a]

1. Place low limits on interest groups' contributions to candidates.
2. Ban interest groups from providing subsidized travel to people in government.
3. Ban gifts from interest groups and their staff to members of Congress and congressional staff.
4. Establish an independent ethics review board to oversee interactions between lobbyists and both Congress and the bureaucracy, and increase penalties for ethics violations.
5. Ban former members of Congress, legislative staff, and bureaucrats from lobbying for two years after leaving office.
6. Require electronic filing of lobbying registration forms and congresspersons' financial disclosure forms.

Most of these proposals seem unobjectionable. For example, why should interest groups be allowed to give gifts to the officials they are lobbying?

This cartoon summarizes public assumptions about lobbying and its impact on members of Congress. In reality, Jack Abramoff's conduct is the exception rather than the rule among lobbyists.

Even so, there are three fundamental problems with these restrictions. First, some of them violate freedoms that many Americans value. The campaign finance restrictions in point one would make it harder for people to organize to influence elections. For example, the amount that groups such as the NRA or AARP contribute to political campaigns would be severely limited compared to the current rules. A second problem is that it is difficult to tell whether these regulations would work as intended. As discussed in this chapter, interest groups are already highly regulated in terms of who can lobby, how they can lobby, and what kinds of gifts and assistance they can offer to government officials. Giving legislators, staffers, or bureaucrats gifts in return for policy changes is already against the law, and if those laws aren't working, it is hard to see how new, similar laws will solve the problem.

Finally, this chapter shows that these reforms are, to some extent, based on a misunderstanding of how interest groups operate. The case of Jack Abramoff is interesting precisely *because* it is a glaring exception. Most interest groups are small and have such limited resources that they couldn't offer gifts or threaten to withhold large campaign donations even if they wanted to. Moreover, interest groups tend to focus on offering advice and information to people in government who already support their goals. None of the reforms described here would change anything about those practices, except to add some additional reporting requirements and further limit their (already restricted) ability to hire people who used to work in government. (Moreover, additional restrictions on electioneering might not be possible given the *Citizens United* decision discussed in Chapter 8.)

Is the case for reforming interest group regulations therefore weaker than it first appears? If existing laws do not deter violations, will new laws do so? Are these reforms aimed at exceptional cases or at average groups? And are they effective enough to warrant limiting Americans' ability to organize in support of candidates or to petition for policy changes? ■

TABLE 9.1 TOP TWENTY SPENDERS ON LOBBYING, 1998–2009

This table shows the corporations and associations that spent the most on lobbying between January 1998 and December 2009. Why do you think each organization spends so much on lobbying?

Lobbying Client	Expenditures
U.S. Chamber of Commerce	$606,758,180
American Medical Association	$220,832,500
General Electric	$196,410,000
AARP	$175,702,064
American Hospital Association	$174,850,431
Pharmaceutical Research and Manufacturers of America	$173,403,920
AT&T	$151,291,757
Northrop Grumman	$143,005,253
Exxon Mobil	$138,886,942
National Association of Realtors	$138,417,380
Blue Cross/Blue Shield	$136,317,077
Business Roundtable	$134,030,000
Edison Electric Institute	$133,995,999
Verizon Communications	$133,174,841
Lockheed Martin	$122,340,423
Boeing	$121,528,310
General Motors	$106,914,483
Southern Company	$104,620,694
Freddie Mac	$96,194,048
Altria Group	$93,650,000

SOURCE: Center for Responsive Politics, "Top Spenders," available at www.opensecrets.org/lobby/top.php?indexType=s.

of businesses such as the Chamber of Commerce. Two exceptions are the American Medical Association, which is a national organization of physicians, and AARP (formerly the American Association of Retired Persons). Of General Electric's $11.4 million spent on lobbying in 2006, more than $8 million was spent on GE employees, and the remaining $3 million paid for the services of a total of fourteen lobbying firms.[15]

Most interest groups or corporations spend much less on their lobbying efforts. The Sierra Club, for example, spent less than $100,000 on lobbying in 2006.[16] All of these funds helped pay the salaries of Sierra Club employees whose jobs include lobbying. Many other groups spend even less, barely scraping together enough cash to send someone to plead their case in Washington.

Other companies lobby through their membership in **trade associations** like the National Beer Wholesalers Association (NBWA), a nationwide group of local businesses that buy beer from brewers and resell it to stores and restaurants. The NBWA's principal lobbying goal is to ensure that laws remain in place requiring

trade association An interest group composed of companies in the same business or industry (the same "trade") that lobbies for policies that benefit members of the group.

middlemen between beer producers and the stores, bars, and restaurants that sell beer to consumers. If the rules change to allow beer producers to deal with the end-sellers directly, then the NBWA's members are out of a job.

Although the amount of money spent on lobbying by interest groups may seem like a lot, it is small compared to how much is at stake.[17] The federal government now spends more than $3 trillion every year. In recent years, spending by interest groups and by the lobbying arms of organizations and corporations amounts to $3 billion every year. That's a lot of money, but it's still only about 0.1 percent of total federal spending. This difference raises a critical question: if interest groups could control policy choices by spending money on lobbying, why aren't they spending more?

TYPES OF INTEREST GROUPS

Interest groups can be divided into three categories based on the type of concerns that drive their lobbying efforts: economic groups, citizen groups, and single-issue groups. Within each of these three broad categories there are several types of organizations with their own distinct policy goals.

The first type is the **economic groups**, such as corporations, trade associations, labor groups, and professional organizations. Economic interest groups aim to influence policy in ways that will help their members derive economic—that is, monetary—benefits. Trade associations, like the NBWA, are one kind of economic group. In rare cases, a group that seems to be a trade association is actually a front for a single corporation's own lobbying efforts. The Coalition for Luggage Security, for example, lobbies for laws that would force airline passengers to pre-ship their luggage to their destination. The supposed goal is to prevent terrorists from getting explosives on commercial airliners by not allowing anyone to check bags in the first place. However, the Coalition's Web site shows that its president is also the head of a company that offers pre-shipping services. Moreover, the Coalition has no other members—no individuals, no corporations.[18] It is simply a lobbying arm of a corporation.

Labor organizations are another kind of economic group. The American Federation of Labor and Congress of Industrial Organizations (AFL-CIO) is a federation of fifty-five labor unions with more than 10 million members. The AFL-CIO lobbies for several kinds of pro-union laws, including regulations that make it easy for workers to form labor unions, union shop laws that require workers at a company to join a union if one exists, and a wide range of other policies.[19] Professional organizations, a third type of economic group, also lobby for government policies that financially benefit their members. One such organization, the American Medical Association, is one of the top spenders on lobbying (see Table 9.1).

The second interest group category is **citizen groups** (also known as public interest groups). This category captures a wide range of organizations, from those with mass membership (such as the Sierra Club) to those that have no members but claim to speak for large segments of the population. One such group is the consumer advocacy organization Public Citizen, discussed earlier. Another is the Family Research Council, which describes itself as "promoting the Judeo-Christian worldview as the basis for a just, free, and stable society." This group lobbies for a wide range of policies, from legislation that defines marriage as between a man and a woman to the elimination of estate taxes.[20]

The third category of interest group is the **single-issue groups**. These groups focus their lobbying on a narrow range of topics or even a single government program or piece of legislation. Examples include the National Right to Life Committee,

▲ Many interest groups speak for large numbers of Americans, but some lobby for changes that would benefit only a few people or a single corporation. The Coalition for Luggage Security, for example, has only one member: a company that specializes in shipping travelers' baggage, which would gain considerable business if the Coalition's lobbying efforts succeeded.

economic group A type of interest group that seeks public policies that provide monetary benefits to its members.

citizen group A type of interest group that seeks changes in spending, regulations, or government programs concerning a wide range of policies (also known as a public interest group).

single-issue group A type of interest group that has a narrowly focused goal, seeking change on a single topic, government program, or piece of legislation.

which lobbies for restrictions on abortion rights, and NumbersUSA, which lobbies against guest worker programs for noncitizens.

Historically, economic interest groups outnumbered citizen groups and single-issue groups. However, although the number of all types of interest groups has increased in recent years, the increase in citizen groups has far outpaced the growth in economic groups.[21] This change might be due in part to the federal government's increased role in many aspects of citizens' everyday lives. The government has always regulated businesses to some degree, so businesses have always had a strong motivation to lobby. Since the 1960s, however, the government's increased role in regulating individual behavior may have given a similar boost to the number of citizen organizations.

Regardless of a group's goals, it is likely that some groups will be natural allies and others will oppose what the group is trying to do. During the debate over reforms to America's health care system, one large union, the Service Employees International Union (SEIU), was allied in support of the new legislation with other unions, such as the Communications Workers of America, and with several large corporations, such as Walmart, AT&T, and Intel. At the same time, these groups were opposed by a diverse group of corporations and lobbying groups, including the U.S. Chamber of Commerce and a coalition of health insurance providers. However, these alliances are often temporary; groups that work together on one issue may find themselves lobbying on opposite sides of another question.

ORGANIZATIONAL STRUCTURES

There are two main models of interest group structure. Most large, well-known organizations like AARP and the NRA are **centralized groups**. These national organizations typically have headquarters in Washington, DC, field offices in large state capitals, and members nationwide. The defining feature of a centralized group

▲ Centralized interest groups in America often have an office in Washington, DC, which helps them to stay in touch with members of Congress, bureaucrats, and the president and his staff. It also provides a venue for attracting press coverage of the group's concerns. This 2009 town hall meeting on health care held at the Washington headquarters of AARP was attended by President Obama.

is that the organization's leadership is concentrated in its headquarters. These leaders have the power and the responsibility to determine the group's lobbying goals and tactics. The other structural model is a **confederation**, which is made up of largely independent, local organizations. For example, the National Independent Automobile Dealers Association (NADA) is made up of fifty separate, state-level organizations that provide most of the membership benefits to car dealers who join the organization, and raise much of the money that NADA contributes to candidates running for political office (several million dollars in recent elections).

Both of these organizational structures have advantages and disadvantages. A centralized organization controls all of the group's resources and can deploy them efficiently, but it can be challenging for these groups to find out what members want. In the late 1980s, for example, AARP lobbied for a new federal insurance benefit for senior citizens, only to find that the overwhelming majority of its members opposed this program.[22]

Confederations have the advantage of maintaining independent chapters at the state and local levels, so it is easier for the national headquarters to learn what their members want—all they have to do is contact their local groups. But this strength of confederations is closely related to their main weakness. State and local chapters mostly function independently of the national headquarters, since they attract members and raise money largely on their own. The national headquarters depends on the local organizations for funds to pay its staff and make campaign contributions. Thus, the norm in most confederated organizations is that when local chapters send money to headquarters to be used for campaign contributions, they also specify which candidates they want to receive it.[23] As a result, confederated groups often are beset with conflict, as different local chapters have their own ideas about what to lobby for and which candidates to support.

One set of organizations that is hard to place into an interest group category is the Tea Party movement, which has become a vocal force in American politics in recent years. While there are little systematic data on the organizations that make up this movement, what we know suggests that they are very diverse. Some hold meetings or public protests, some collect money for candidates, and some are little more than a Web site run by one or two people. The set of issues that motivate each organization also varies widely, from opposition to President Obama to calls for radical changes in government. Virtually all lack formal dues-paying members, a headquarters, or a formal organizational structure, and few engage in the wide range of lobbying activities that we describe later in this chapter. Moreover, it is unclear whether many of these organizations will survive more than a few months or years. For all of these reasons, very few of the organizations that describe themselves as part of the Tea Party movement are interest groups as we describe them here, although some may evolve into formal interest groups in the future.

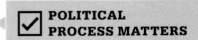

POLITICAL PROCESS MATTERS

STAFF

Interest group staff falls into two categories: experts on the group's main policy areas, and people with useful government connections and knowledge of procedures. The first group includes scientists, engineers, and others with advanced degrees; the second is dominated by people who have worked inside government as elected officials, bureaucrats, or legislative staff.[24] Sometimes these former members of the government are also policy experts, but their unique contribution is their knowledge of how government works and their relationships with officeholders and other former coworkers.

confederations Interest groups made up of several independent, local organizations that provide much of their funding and hold most of the power.

The practice of transitioning from government positions to working for interest groups or lobbying firms, or transitioning from lobbyist to offceholder, is often called the **revolving door**.[25] A 2005 study by Public Citizen found that from 1998 to 2005, more than 40 percent of members leaving the House or Senate joined a lobbying firm after their departure.[26] A separate study in June 2006 found that more than two-thirds of the Department of Homeland Security's original senior staff left their positions to work for corporations or lobbying firms.[27] Examples such as these were behind President Obama's policy to bar people who served in his administration from lobbying the government after they left their position, and preventing registered lobbyists who are appointed to government positions from administering policies or agencies that they once lobbied.[28]

The Obama policy highlights the dilemma of the revolving door. On one hand, people who have worked in industry or as lobbyists are likely to be familiar with a particular field and the relevant laws, making them well-qualified to work in this area for the executive branch. Similarly, former officeholders, congressional staff, and bureaucrats are attractive to lobbying firms, as they have first-hand knowledge of how policies are made and have established relationships with people in government. Thus, although Obama's policy was undoubtedly well-intentioned, it may lead to a shortage of experienced candidates for government positions. On the other hand, the problem with the revolving door is that people in government may try to help particular firms and interest groups in return for a well-paid position after they leave government service. Or, when the influence works in the opposite direction, lobbyists-turned-lawmakers may favor the firms and organizations that once employed them. It is very hard to craft restrictions that avoid these problems.

MEMBERSHIP

Interest groups can also be distinguished on the basis of the size of their membership and the members' role in the group's activities. Some interest groups are **mass associations** with large numbers of dues-paying members. One example is the Sierra Club, which advertises itself as the "oldest, largest and most influential grassroots environmental organization."[29] The Sierra Club has more than 750,000 members who each pay annual dues of about $30. Besides keeping its members informed about the making of environmental policy in Washington, DC, the Sierra Club endorses judicial nominees and candidates for elected positions, and works with members of Congress to develop legislative proposals. The group's members elect the organization's board of directors.

Not all mass associations give members a say in selecting a group's leaders or determining its mission. To join AARP, which has more than 35 million members, you don't have to be retired, but you have to be at least fifty years old and pay dues of up to $16 per year. Members get discounts on insurance, car rentals, and hotels, as well as driver safety courses and help doing their taxes. AARP claims to lobby for policies its members favor, but members actually have no control over which legislative causes the group chooses. Moreover, AARP does not poll members to determine its issue positions, nor do members pick AARP leadership.

Peak associations have a different type of membership,[30] exemplified by the Business-Industry Political Action Committee (BIPAC). This association of several hundred businesses and trade associations aims to elect "pro-business individuals" to Congress.[31] Individuals cannot join peak associations—they may work for the association's member companies or organizations, but they cannot become dues-paying members on their own.

RESOURCES

The resources interest groups use to support their lobbying efforts are people, money, and expertise. We examine interest group strategies in a later section; for now, the important thing to understand is that a group's resources influence its set of available lobbying strategies. Some groups have sufficient funding and staff to pursue a wide range of strategies, while smaller groups with fewer resources have only a few lobbying options.

People One of the most important resources for most interest groups is its members. Group members can write to or meet with elected officials, and even travel to Washington for demonstrations. A group's members may also offer its leaders expertise or advice. Even when the "members" of a group are corporations, as is the case with trade associations, CEOs and other corporate staff can help with the group's lobbying efforts.

Many mass organizations try to get their members involved in the lobbying process. MoveOn.org, for example, has a Web page that helps people send letters to the editors of various national and local newspapers. Many newspapers print selected letters from readers, so one way MoveOn hopes to bring public attention to its political priorities is by getting these Web-generated letters printed. Using their site, you provide your address, choose from a list of local and national papers to contact, and compose a message—using MoveOn's "talking points," which cover a wide range of issues—if you choose. The page automatically imports your message into correctly addressed e-mails to your selected newspapers.[32]

Similarly, the Web page of the Family Research Council alerts members to volunteer opportunities, announces where the organization's rallies will be held, and tells members how they can help local chapters by hosting dinners, stuffing envelopes, or similar activities.[33] And the National Paper Trade Association, which describes itself as "the Association for the paper, packaging, and supplies distribution

▲ Interest groups use a variety of tactics to draw attention to their concerns, including events designed to generate media coverage. Jon Davids, a Public Interest Research Group staffer, traveled nearly 20,000 miles across America with an eighteen-foot inflatable largemouth bass named Freddie to events that publicized the dangers of mercury pollution in lakes and streams.

channel," organized the CEOs of its member corporations to lobby senators about various pieces of legislation.[34]

Interest groups' ability to use people as a resource is limited by two major challenges. First, it requires members, but recruiting new members can be difficult and expensive. The second challenge is motivating members to participate, especially since those who don't participate will reap the same policy benefits as those who do if the group succeeds. As we discuss later, though there are instances where interest groups have changed government policy by persuading their members to write to and visit elected officials, the more common situation is that interest groups ask for members' help but receive little response.[35]

Money Virtually everything interest groups do, from meeting with elected officials to fighting for what they want in court, can be purchased as services by well-funded groups. Money can also be used to make campaign contributions or to develop and run campaign ads, and of course, money is necessary to fund interest groups' everyday operations.

Well-funded interest groups have a considerable advantage in the lobbying process. If they need an expert, a lobbyist, or a lawyer, they can hire one. They can pay for campaign ads and make campaign contributions, while groups with less cash are prevented from using these strategies. The importance of money for interest group operations can be seen in their funding appeals to members. If you look at the donations page from the Sierra Club's Web site, you'll see that supporters can give a membership as a gift, join as a life member, or pay dues monthly. They can make commemorative or memorial gifts, set up a planned giving scheme, or donate stock. The group even offers gift-giving plans for non-U.S. residents, specific parameters for Canadian residents, and a Spanish-language version of their donations page.

For many groups, spending on lobbying is sensitive to economic conditions. For example, many banking and financial firms slashed lobbying expenditures during early 2009, even though they faced new government proposals to limit the pay of top executives and to impose restrictions on everything from writing mortgages to creating exotic financial instruments. Because these firms were facing huge losses and declining revenues, they cut expenses across the board, including the amounts spent on lobbying.[36] (Their employees also gave far less in campaign contributions than they had at the same point in the previous election cycle.) As the balance sheets of these companies improved through the spring and summer of 2009, their spending on lobbying increased to previous levels.

Still, money isn't everything, and there are many ways for groups to be effective without spending much. Groups can rely on members to lobby for them, hire staff willing to work for low pay because they share the group's goals, or cite already-published research rather than funding their own studies to bolster their case for policy change. Moreover, the fact that a group has lots of money is no guarantee that their lobbying efforts will succeed (recall the Boeing example from earlier in this chapter).

Expertise Expertise takes many forms. Some interest group leaders know a lot about their members' preferences or about what people in a community, congressional district, or state want.[37] Other groups can offer information to elected officials and bureaucrats that ranges from detailed reports on policy questions to concrete legislative proposals. This information is an asset group leaders can use to negotiate with elected officials or bureaucrats as part of a trade to get what the group wants. Expertise can also involve knowledge of political factors, such as information about what kinds of policies party caucuses or individual legislators are willing to support, or information about the courts, such as the constitutionality of proposed laws and policies or the ideological leanings of different judges. Lobbying firms that employ ex-members of Congress and bureaucrats are a good source of such information.

Consider AARP, whose Web site offers a vast array of research and analyses, such as information about senior citizens' part-time employment, how people invest their 401(k) retirement accounts, and a comparison of long-term care policies in Europe and the United States.[38] AARP's lobbyists then use this research when they argue for policy changes in their public testimony and in private meetings with members of Congress and congressional staff. For example, in June 2009, AARP's executive vice president, John Rother, testified before a Senate committee on how health care reform proposals would affect medical treatment of senior citizens under the Medicare program.[39]

Not all interest groups have such expertise. Some groups focus on mobilizing people outside government, expecting that elected officials will respond to this pressure by developing policy solutions. However, particularly for groups headquartered in Washington or state capitals, expertise often comes naturally. In the course of their jobs, interest group staff often become well-versed in the details of current policies and the policy options that pertain to their interests. When they talk with members of Congress and bureaucrats on a daily basis, they learn who their friends are—and what they need to do to change enemies into friends.

Getting Organized

A new interest group's first priority is to get organized, which involves raising the money needed to hire staff, renting an office, setting up a Web site, and beginning to formulate policy goals and a lobbying strategy. Or, in some cases, a lobbying firm is hired to perform these jobs. Once organized, the group needs to continue to attract funds for ongoing operations. These tasks are not as easy as they might sound. Even if a group of people (or corporations) share the same goals, the challenge is to persuade them to donate time or money to a lobbying operation.

THE LOGIC OF COLLECTIVE ACTION

Research by political scientists has found that a fundamental problem arises when a group of individuals (or corporations) has an opportunity to make itself better off through the provision of public goods—for interest groups, the public good would be a change in government policy desired by members of the group. Scholars working in political science as well as in other social science disciplines refer to these situations as involving collective action. As Nuts and Bolts 9.1 explains, even when all members of a group agree on the desirability of public good and the costs of producing the good are negligible, cooperation is neither easy nor automatic. This problem is further illustrated with the classic example of a collective action problem, the **prisoners' dilemma**.

The logic of collective action provides important insights into how interest groups are organized and how they make lobbying decisions. To begin with, the logic of collective action tells us that group formation is not automatic. Even when a number of citizens want the same things from government, their common interest may not lead them to organize. Thus, some groups remain latent, which explains why some debates in Washington feature well-organized groups on one side of the issue but few if any on the other.

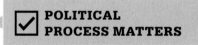

POLITICAL PROCESS MATTERS

prisoners' dilemma: A simple two-person game that illustrates how actions that are in a player's individual self-interest may lead to outcomes that all players consider inferior.

NUTS AND BOLTS

9.1

Collective Action Problems

Collective action refers to situations in which a group of individuals can work together to provide themselves with public goods. For example, changes in government policy (such as those lobbied for by interests groups) are public goods: if the government changes policy, such as increasing the size of college tuition grants, everyone who is eligible for the grants benefits from the increase. These circumstances make it hard to motivate people to contribute to collective efforts, because each would-be member can see that his contribution would be only a minuscule portion of what the group needs to succeed. Regardless of how many other people join, an individual is better off **free riding**—refusing to join but still being able to enjoy the benefits of any successes the group might have. But if everyone acts on this calculation, no one will join the group and the organization will be unable to lobby for tuition grants or anything else.

One class of real-world **collective action problems** involve situations where people can exploit a renewable natural resource, such as a forest or fishery. The problem is that each participant can maximize her profits by taking as much as she can from the resource area without worrying about whether it can sustain this activity. However, if everyone behaves this way, the common resource will be destroyed—all the fish will be caught or all the trees will be cut down.

The same kinds of problems arise in everyday life. As a college student, you may live in some sort of group housing situation, either a dormitory or an off-campus apartment or house. Anyone who has ever lived in such a situation knows that one constant problem is sharing the responsibility for common living spaces. Everyone typically agrees that these areas should be kept clean, but each resident sees an opportunity to free ride by leaving his mess for someone else to take care of. But if everyone follows this incentive, common living spaces will remain messy if not uninhabitable.

THE PRISONERS' DILEMMA

The prisoners' dilemma is a classic example of the collective action problem. In the example, two individuals are arrested on suspicion of having committed some serious crime. Upon arriving at the police station, they are questioned in separate rooms. Although the police are confident that the suspects are guilty, there is no concrete evidence. So the suspects are offered a deal. Confess and implicate your partner, each suspect is told, and you will be released outright. If you remain silent and your partner talks, you will be convicted for sure and

---

free riding The practice of relying on others to contribute to a collective effort while failing to participate on one's own behalf, yet still benefiting from the group's successes.

collective action problem A situation in which the members of a group would benefit by working together to produce some outcome, but each individual is better off refusing to cooperate and reaping benefits from those who do the work.

solidary benefits Satisfaction derived from the experience of working with like-minded people, even if the group's efforts do not achieve the desired impact.

purposive benefits Satisfaction derived from the experience of working toward a desired policy goal, even if the goal is not achieved.

coercion A method of eliminating nonparticipation or free riding by potential group members by requiring participation, as in many labor unions.

The logic of collective action offers important clues about how interest groups operate. Unless people can easily see benefits from participating, which does not happen often, group leaders must worry about finding the right strategies to get people to join. Put another way, given the logic of collective action, attracting members is just as important for a group's success as is the group's lobbying strategy.

Society is full of groups of like-minded people (like college students) who do not organize to lobby or choose to free ride and enjoy the benefits of organizations without participation. Most organizations develop mechanisms that engender cooperation in such situations. These solutions fall into three categories: benefits from participation, coercion, and selective incentives.

Studies of political parties and interest groups find that some individuals volunteer for these organizations out of a sense of obligation or duty—or simply because they enjoy working together with others toward a common goal. Scholars refer to these benefits of participation as either **solidary benefits**, which come from working with like-minded people, or **purposive benefits**, which come from working to achieve a desired policy goal.[40] If most people were spurred to political action because of participation benefits, the free rider problem wouldn't exist. However, in many cases these benefits are not enough, so groups must resort to other measures in order to become and remain organized.

A second way to solve the free rider problem is **coercion**, or requiring participation. Labor unions provide a good example of this strategy. Unions provide public

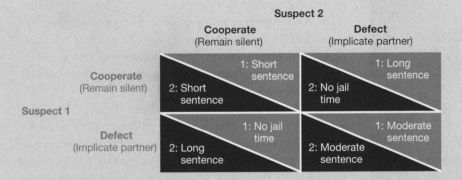

Suspect 2

	Cooperate (Remain silent)	Defect (Implicate partner)
Cooperate (Remain silent)	1: Short sentence / 2: Short sentence	1: Long sentence / 2: No jail time
Defect (Implicate partner)	1: No jail time / 2: Long sentence	1: Moderate sentence / 2: Moderate sentence

receive a long jail term. (If both suspects confess, they will both be convicted but receive a lesser sentence.) This police strategy creates the interaction described in the figure.

The choices available to the first suspect are arranged in rows, and the second suspect's choices are arranged in columns. Each cell shows the sentence the suspects would receive given a possible pair of choices. For example, the top left-hand cell shows that when both suspects cooperate and remain silent, they each receive a short sentence.

The figure shows that each suspect receives a shorter sentence when he defects or implicates his partner, regardless of what his partner does. Consider the second suspect. If the first suspect cooperates (top row), the second suspect receives a short sentence for cooperating (top left-hand cell) or no jail time if he defects (top right-hand cell). If the first suspect defects (bottom row), the second suspect receives a long sentence for cooperating (bottom left-hand cell) or a moderate sentence for defecting (bottom right-hand cell). Given these payoffs, each suspect avoids the worst if he defects and takes the police deal, regardless of what the other suspect does. However, when both suspects defect, producing the outcome in the bottom right-hand cell, they both receive moderate sentences—more jail time than they would have received if they had both cooperated (top left-hand cell, short sentence).

The prisoners' dilemma illustrates one kind of conflict that is endemic to politics—when participants agree on some things (the benefits of mutual cooperation) but disagree on others (each would rather defect than cooperate). When you see a political situation that looks like a dilemma, the critical thing to remember is that cooperation is not automatic, even if the stakes are high. The participants need to find a mechanism that removes the temptation to defect, and these solutions in turn influence political behavior and policy outcomes.

goods to workers in a particular factory or industry by negotiating with management on behalf of worker-members over pay and work requirements. Why don't union members free ride? In many cases, they are forced to join the union because of union shop laws mentioned earlier, which require people to pay union dues as a condition of their employment. These laws are critical to unions; states with right to work laws, which make union membership optional, typically have weak unions—if they have unions at all.

Finally, **selective incentives** (also called material incentives) are benefits given only to the members of an interest group. These incentives are not public goods: an individual can receive a selective incentive only by joining the group. Thus interest groups offer members selective incentives in the hope of providing a new reason to participate. Many people who join the Sierra Club, for example, receive a monthly magazine, a backpack, and opportunities for discounted vacations. One of the most interesting cases of selective incentives provided by an interest group is AAA. Members with car trouble can call AAA at any time, day or night, for emergency roadside car repair or towing service. AAA also provides annotated maps and travel guides to its members, a travel agency, a car-buying service, discounts at hotels and restaurants, and other benefits. These services mask the interest group role of AAA. For example, the organization's Foundation for Traffic Safety delivers research reports to legislators on topics ranging from lowering the blood alcohol level

selective incentives Benefits that can motivate participation in a group effort because they are available only to those who participate, such as member services offered by interest groups.

▲ The Automobile Association of America (AAA) is a well-known provider of emergency road service, yet few people are aware of its role as an interest group that lobbies for a wide range of policy changes.

POLITICS IS
EVERYWHERE

threshold that legally defines drunk driving to increasing the restrictions on driving by senior citizens.[41] It's unlikely that many AAA members—who join for the towing services, free maps, and other selective incentives—are aware of the organization's lobbying efforts. The inducements drive membership, which, through members' dues, funds the organization's lobbying operation.

The variety of recruitment strategies suggests that interest group members may have very different motivations for joining than their leaders do. Often members join because of coercion, selective incentives, or the enjoyment they get from being part of the group. In some cases, these members may not know or care about their group's lobbying efforts. Leaders, on the other hand, determine what their group lobbies for, so policy goals may more often drive their participation.

This theory of collective action also explains why economic groups, such as trade associations, have historically been easier to form than citizen groups. Because economic groups often involve a small number of corporations or individuals, the costs of free riding are relatively high: one actor's efforts or contributions can significantly boost the likelihood of success, and one member's failure to contribute can significantly compromise the group's efforts. (To put it another way, when groups are small, the logic of free riding is much less likely to apply—the benefits are smaller and costs higher.) Thus, economic groups can often form on the strength of their shared policy or monetary goals, without the need for coercion, selective incentives, or solidary benefits. In contrast, citizen groups, with many more potential members, typically need to use at least one of these three methods to solve their collective action problems.

The logic also explains why some interest groups have no members at all. Some interest groups, such as the Coalition for Luggage Security, are funded by a single wealthy company or individual. Other groups, such as Public Citizen, raise money from foundations or corporate donors.[42] Why not try to attract members? They can be surprisingly hard to find, and it takes even more time and money to convince them to participate.

Finally, the logic of collective action highlights the crucial role of leaders or interest group entrepreneurs in successful collective action. Of course, all groups have a leader in the sense that someone (or a committee) oversees the day-to-day activities of the group. But more importantly, interest groups need someone to make the case for the group, define its mission, identify goals, and develop a strategy for achieving them.[43]

Why would someone want this job? Studies show that many people who help to organize and run interest groups have strong policy goals—they sincerely believe in the group's mission. In effect, these individuals offer potential group members a trade: if the members join the group, the leaders will get the group organized, formulate its lobbying strategy, and manage its work to change government policy.[44] Moreover, leaders may have considerable freedom to determine what to lobby for: as noted earlier, in many mass interest groups, members do not have any influence over their group's lobbying efforts. And in organizations such as AAA, whose members join to get selective incentives and whose lobbying efforts are not well-known, lobby decisions may be completely unconstrained by member preferences.

For the leaders, organizing and operating the group is also a form of goal-directed political participation: by doing this work, they increase the chances that their policy preferences will become reality. Many interest group leaders, such as Ralph Nader of Public Citizen, fit this description. In some cases, however, the people who organize and operate interest groups have no strong policy goals and are driven instead by strictly financial considerations—members get the benefits of the group's lobbying efforts, and the leader gets a salary.[45]

Interest Group Strategies

Once a group has organized and determined its goals, the next step is to decide how to lobby. Interest groups have a number of possible tactics, which fall into two categories: **inside strategies**, which are actions taken in Washington, and **outside strategies**, which involve actions taken outside Washington.[46]

INSIDE STRATEGIES

Direct Lobbying When interest group staff meet with officeholders or bureaucrats, they plead their case through **direct lobbying**, asking government officials to change policy in line with the group's goals.[47] Such contacts are very common. If you visit a congressional office, you are likely to see someone from an interest group waiting to meet with the legislator or someone from their staff. A search of disclosure data maintained by Congress found that more than 47,000 groups and individuals lobbied members of Congress in 2007.[48]

Interest group representatives are not always middle-aged men in expensive suits. Some groups arrange visits from delegations of group members from a legislator's district to make the case that their issue matters to the legislator's constituents. Others use volunteers to represent the group. For example, the organization ProSpace, which encourages space exploration through tax credits and regulatory reform, sponsors an annual event called March Storm in which citizens who share the group's agenda travel to Washington (in March) to meet with members of Congress and their staff.

Direct lobbying is generally aimed at elected officials and bureaucrats who are sympathetic to the group's goals.[49] In these efforts, interest groups and their representatives do not try to convert opponents into supporters; rather, they help like-minded legislators secure policy changes that they both want. Their help can take many forms, such as sharing information about the proposed changes, providing lists of legislators who might be persuadable, or even drafting legislative proposals or regulations.

The important thing to understand is that these efforts usually are not part of a trade, in which the group expects certain legislative action in return for the group's help. Rather, the group's efforts function more like a subsidy, a way of helping a legislator to enact policies she prefers—and that the group prefers as well.[50] The legislator knows that a like-minded group has no reason to misrepresent its policy information. After all, the group and the legislator are on the same side and want to enact the same policies. In fact, the member and staff will be happy to meet with the group's representatives, as their information may be vital to the legislator's efforts to enact legislation, manage the bureaucracy, or keep the support of constituents back home in the district.[51]

Interest groups also contact legislators who disagree with their goals, as well as fence sitters (legislators who are not supporters or opponents), with the goal of converting them into supporters. These efforts are generally less extensive than the lobbying of supporters, because opponents are unlikely to change their minds unless a

inside strategies The tactics employed within Washington, DC, by interest groups seeking to achieve their policy goals.

outside strategies The tactics employed outside Washington, DC, by interest groups seeking to achieve their policy goals.

direct lobbying Attempts by interest group staff to influence policy by speaking with elected officials or bureaucrats.

group can provide some new information that causes them to rethink their position. However, lobbying opponents may be useful if it forces other interest groups with opposing views to use some of their limited resources lobbying their supporters to make sure that they do not change their position.[52]

Who do these groups contact for direct lobbying? Analysis of the annual disclosure forms that lobbyists are required to file shows that they contact people throughout the federal government, from elected officials to members of the president's staff as well as bureaucrats in the executive branch. They seek this wide range of contacts because different federal officials play distinct roles in the policy-making process, which means they have various types of influence to offer interest groups. Members of Congress shape legislation and budgets; presidential staff influence the formation of new policies and obtain presidential consent for new laws; and executive branch bureaucrats change the ways regulations are written and how policies are implemented.

Drafting Legislation and Regulations Another inside strategy involves writing draft versions of legislation or regulations. Interest groups sometimes draft legislative proposals and regulations, which they then deliver to legislators and bureaucrats as part of their lobbying efforts.[53] Surveys of interest groups found that more than three-quarters reported drafting proposals for members of Congress.[54] A 2006 *USA Today* story on relatives of members of Congress who work as lobbyists found that twenty-two out of thirty had succeeded in helping their clients by getting specific changes added to legislative proposals.[55]

Interest groups don't give proposals to just anyone. As with direct lobbying, they seek out legislators who already support their cause and who have significant influence within Congress, either by being on a powerful committee or by having their colleagues' respect. A lobbying effort aimed at cutting interest rates on student loans would target supporters of this change who are also members of the congressional committee that has jurisdiction over student loan programs—preferably someone who chairs the committee or one of its subcommittees, or who holds some other leadership position.[56] Interest groups also lobby bureaucrats to influence the details of new regulations.[57] If the type of regulations involved can go into effect without congressional approval, then lobbying can give groups what they want directly. But even if new regulations require approval by Congress or White House staff, interest groups can increase their chances of success by getting involved in the initial drafting of new regulations.

Research Interest groups often prepare research reports on topics of interest to the group. For example, Public Citizen recently featured on its Web site a series of research reports on a diverse set of topics, such as medical malpractice, the house building industry, toy safety, and international trade.[58] Such reports serve multiple purposes. They may sway public opinion or help persuade elected officials or bureaucrats. They also help interest group staff claim expertise on some aspect of public policy. Members of Congress are more likely to accept a group's legislative proposal if they believe that the group's staff have some research to back up their claims. Journalists are also more likely to respond to an interest group's requests for publicity if they believe that the group's staff has evidence supporting their claims.

Testimony Interest group staff often testify before congressional committees. In part, this activity is aimed at informing members of Congress about issues that matter to the group. For example the NRA's Web site shows that its staff testified in favor of "right to carry" laws as well as in support of laws that would grant immunity to gun manufacturers for harm committed with weapons they had produced.[59]

Litigation Another inside strategy involves taking the government to court. In bringing their case, groups can argue that the government's actions are not consistent with the Constitution or that the government has misinterpreted the provisions of existing law.[60] Groups can bring these actions using lawyers on their staff, by hiring a law firm to work for them, or by finding lawyers who are willing to work for free. Groups can also become involved in an existing case by filing *amicus curiae* or "friend of the court" briefs, documents that offer judges the group's rationale for how the case should be decided.

One famous example of interest group litigation was the legal battle waged by the National Association for the Advancement of Colored People (NAACP) during the 1950s to desegregate public facilities in southern states.[61] Realizing that southern legislatures would not repeal their discriminatory laws, and that Congress was unlikely to order the states to do so, NAACP staff focused their efforts on legal action, challenging the constitutionality of the laws that allowed separate schools for whites and blacks. This strategy was successful: in 1954, the Supreme Court's *Brown v. Board of Education* decision held that segregated schools were unconstitutional, the first step in the process of overturning the "separate but equal" system.

Modern interest groups continue to use litigation strategies. The American Civil Liberties Union (ACLU) went to court in 2002 in an attempt to overturn parts of the Patriot Act, such as the provisions that made it easier for federal law enforcement authorities to gather information about American citizens without first obtaining a warrant from a judge.[62] The ACLU's logic was the same as the NAACP's a generation earlier. However, after Congress reauthorized the Patriot Act in 2006, the ACLU abandoned its litigation strategy, focusing instead on direct lobbying and grassroots efforts.

Working Together To increase their chances for success, interest groups can work together in their lobbying efforts, formulating a common strategy and meeting, sometimes daily, to discuss progress and future plans. Generally these are short-term efforts focused on achieving a specific outcome, like when interest groups form coalitions to

▲ The American Civil Liberties Union is an interest group that often uses litigation strategies in its efforts to change government policy. Here, an ACLU attorney describes the group's efforts to limit the Department of Homeland Security's use of "no fly lists" to screen airline passengers.

grassroots lobbying A lobbying strategy that relies on participation by group members, such as a protest or a letter-writing campaign.

support or oppose confirmation of judicial and cabinet nominees.[63] Similarly, one of the larger groups active during the recent debate over health care reform was Better Health Care Together, a coalition of labor unions, large corporations, and Washington-based think tanks, including the SEIU, Walmart, and the Center for American Progress.

Why do groups work together? The most obvious reason is the power of large numbers; legislators are more likely to respond when many groups with large or diverse memberships are all asking for the same thing.[64] The groups involved may also have different kinds of resources to contribute to the effort. In the case of Better Health Care Together, the unions generated the grassroots support, while the think tanks provided research and contacts inside Congress and the government. Moreover, members of Congress are likely to at least listen to a labor union lobbyist if there are large numbers of union members in their district or to a corporation that employs many of their constituents.

The problem with working together is that groups may agree on general goals but disagree on specifics, requiring negotiation to arrive at a common position. If differences cannot be bridged, groups may undertake separate and possibly conflicting lobbying efforts or decide against lobbying entirely. For example, during the 2009 debate over climate change legislation, many environmental interest groups sat on the sidelines, despite having pressed for such legislation for more than a decade. The problem? The groups disagreed on which policies should be implemented, who should pay for them, and whether the government should aid companies forced to pay for new antipollution equipment. Lacking agreement and unwilling to act alone, many groups took no position at all on the legislation.[65]

OUTSIDE STRATEGIES

Grassroots Lobbying Directly involving interest group members in lobbying efforts is called **grassroots lobbying**. Members may send letters, make telephone calls, participate in a protest, or express their demands in other ways. Many groups encourage grassroots lobbying. For example, AARP's Web site has a page where members can find names and contact information for their representatives in Congress.[66] Other links allow members to e-mail or fax to their representatives letters that are pre-written by AARP to express the group's positions on various proposals, such as pension protection legislation and proposals to curb identity theft. AARP also organizes district meetings with elected officials and encourages their members to attend.

Mass protests are another form of grassroots lobbying. In addition to trying to capture the attention of government officials, mass protests have the secondary goal of gaining media attention, with the idea of publicizing the group's goals and perhaps gaining new members or financial support. Three months into President Obama's term, groups opposed to his economic stimulus proposals held "tea parties" on April 15 (the deadline for filing income tax returns) to mobilize public opinion against the proposals. Later, some of the same groups worked to get people to attend congressional town hall meetings to express their opposition to congressional health care reform proposals, while other groups worked to get supporters of the reform to the same meetings (as we discussed earlier in this chapter, the relatively new Tea Party movement is hard to classify as a defined interest group, but it has used some classic interest group strategies such as mass protests).[67]

Grassroots strategies are useful because elected officials are loath to act against a large group of citizens who care enough about an issue to express their position.[68] An experienced

▼ *Mass protests, such as this April 4, 2009, "tea party" rally in California, attract media attention and demonstrate the depth of public support for a group's goals.*

lobbyist once said that the biggest thing an interest group member has going for her is that she is "someone's constituent"—meaning that no matter what the group is asking for, there is at least one representative and two senators who have an interest in hearing what it has to say. These elected officials may not agree with the group's goals, but they are likely to at least arrange a meeting with its staff, so that they appear responsive and willing to learn more about their constituents' demands.[69] However, these member-based strategies work only for a small set of interest groups. To take advantage of them, groups first need a large number of members. Ten, twenty, or even a hundred letters are not necessarily going to spur a legislator to action. Legislators begin to pay attention to a letter-writing campaign only when they receive several thousand pieces of mail. (Remember, congressional districts contain roughly 700,000 citizens.)

In addition, for grassroots lobbying to be effective, the letters or other efforts have to come from a member's own constituents. For example, a representative who opposes increases in student aid is not going to worry about a letter-writing campaign if most of the letters come from people who don't live in his district. Put another way, the advantage of being "someone's constituent" doesn't help a group arrange meetings with legislators who do not represent group members.

The effectiveness of grassroots lobbying also depends on perceptions of how much a group has done to motivate participation. Suppose a representative gets 10,000 e-mails demanding an increase in student aid. However, virtually all the messages contain the same appeal because they were generated and sent from a group's Web site. People in Washington sometimes refer to these efforts as **astroturf lobbying**.[70] Given the similarity of the letters, the representative may discount the effort, believing that it says more about the group's ability to make participation in its campaign accessible and easy than it does about the number of people in the district who strongly support an increase in student aid. Even so, politicians are reluctant to completely dismiss astroturf efforts—the fact that so many people participated, even with facilitation by an interest group, means that their demands must at least be considered.

The evolution of the Internet has important implications for grassroots lobbying. As noted earlier, one argument is that technological developments such as blogs and e-mail make grassroots lobbying easier by lowering the costs of encouraging the members and would-be members of an interest group to get involved by writing a letter, sending an e-mail, making a phone call, or showing up for a protest. Certainly the Internet makes it easier to contact people and lowers the cost of getting involved in some kinds of lobbying efforts. However, if Internet-driven grassroots lobbying looks like astroturf lobbying, it may be less likely to achieve its goal of influencing the behavior of elected officials and bureaucrats.

Mobilizing Public Opinion One strategy related to grassroots lobbying involves trying to change what the public thinks about an issue. The goal is not to get citizens to do anything, but to influence public opinion in the hopes that elected officials will see this change and respond by enacting (or opposing) new laws or regulations in order to keep their constituents happy. Virtually all groups try to influence opinion. Most maintain a Web page that presents their message and write press releases to get media coverage of their demands, efforts, and successes. Any contact with citizens, whether to encourage them to join the group, contribute money, or engage in grassroots lobbying, also involves elements of persuasion—trying to transform citizens into supporters, and supporters into true believers.

A focused mobilization effort involves contacting large numbers of potential supporters through e-mail, phone calls, direct mail, television advertising, print media, and Web sites. In order to get legislators to respond, a group has to persuade large numbers of people to get involved; otherwise legislators will ignore the group's

astroturf lobbying Any lobbying method initiated by an interest group that is designed to look like the spontaneous, independent participation of many individuals.

501(c)(3) organization A tax code classification that applies to most interest groups; this designation makes donations to the group tax-deductible but limits the group's political activities.

political action committee (PAC) An interest group or a division of an interest group that can raise money to contribute to campaigns or to spend on ads in support of candidates. The amount a PAC can receive from each of its donors and the amount it can spend on federal campaigning are strictly limited.

527 organization A tax-exempt group formed primarily to influence elections through voter mobilization efforts and issue ads that do not directly endorse or oppose a candidate. Unlike political action committees, 527s are not subject to contribution limits and spending caps.

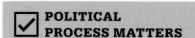

☑ **POLITICAL PROCESS MATTERS**

efforts. One example of mobilization occurs during congressional hearings on nominees to the Supreme Court or other federal judgeships. One study found that about one-third of the groups that lobbied for or against these nominees also deployed direct mail and leaflets, and ran phone banks to influence public opinion.[71] Similarly, a study of lobbying on health care policy found that interest groups and lobbyists from business, consumer groups, and other organizations routinely work to shape public opinion in order to build congressional support for their preferred outcomes.[72]

Electioneering Interest groups get involved in elections by making contributions to candidates, mobilizing people (including their staff) to help in a campaign, endorsing candidates, funding campaign ads, or mobilizing a candidate's or party's supporters. All of these efforts are aimed at trying to influence who gets elected, with the expectation that changing who gets elected will affect what government does.

Federal laws limit groups' electioneering and lobbying efforts. Most private organizations and associations in America are organized as **501(c)(3) organizations**, a designation based on their Internal Revenue Service classification, which means that donations to the group are tax-deductible. However, 501(c)(3)s are not allowed to engage in any political activities or lobbying (other than certain voter education programs or voter registration drives that are conducted in a nonpartisan manner). Groups that want to engage in lobbying or electioneering can incorporate under other IRS designations; in general, however, contributions to these organizations are not tax-deductible, which makes the 501(c)(3) designation attractive, as it helps in fund-raising efforts.

Interest groups that want to play a greater role in elections can form a separate **political action committee (PAC)** or a **527 organization** (another IRS designation; all PACs are 527s but not all 527s are PACs). A PAC can solicit funds from group members or others to spend on contributions to candidates or on ads in support of candidates, and 527s can spend unlimited amounts of money on voter mobilization and issue advocacy, as long as their efforts do not support or oppose a particular candidate.

In 2010, federally focused 527 organizations spent more than $150 million on electioneering, and PACs spent nearly $375 million.[73] Nuts and Bolts 9.2 reports campaign spending for the top ten 527 organizations. The top spending 527, American Solutions Winning the Future, spent almost $25 million in 2010, and even the tenth-ranked organization, the National Education Association, spent nearly $4 million, which was more than the largest PAC. The box also shows that most of the large 527 organizations are strongly tied to one of the major parties. The leaders of these organizations are people with strong ties to either the Republican or the Democratic Party, and the literature from these organizations leaves no doubt about their partisan leanings. The fairly even distribution of Republican- and Democratic-leaning groups helps to confirm the impression discussed elsewhere that well-funded groups are found on both sides of most issues. Though some 527s spend a lot on electioneering, the average is lower than you might think. In the 2008 election, the 292 active 527 organizations that participated in the campaign spent an average of about $685,000 each. In other words, although some 527s run substantial national ad campaigns, the average 527 only gets involved in a few races.

The data on the top ten PACs in 2010 are shown in Nuts and Bolts 9.3. The largest PAC contributed just over $3 million to candidates in the 2010 election, and the tenth largest slightly less than $2 million. Again, these organizations donating millions of dollars are the exception by a significant margin: in the 2008 election, the average PAC gave only $101,000 in contributions. Part of the reason for this lower spending is that PACs' direct contributions to candidates are capped at $5,000 per candidate, and their contributions to party committees are also strictly limited.

Two new options for electioneering for interest groups emerged in the 2010 election: "Super PACs" and 501(c)(4) organizations. The former was a consequence of the

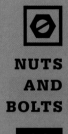

Big Spenders in the 2010 Election: 527 Organizations

ORGANIZATION	GENERALLY SUPPORTS	TOTAL EXPENDITURES
American Solutions Winning the Future	Republicans	$24,416,928
Service Employees International Union	Democrats	$9,387,001
Citizens United	Republicans	$8,376,968
America Votes	Democrats	$7,418,746
EMILY's List	Democrats	$7,325,185
College Republican National Committee	Republicans	$7,198,500
American Crossroads	Republicans	$6,700,312
International Brotherhood of Electrical Workers	Democrats	$4,449,117
ActBlue	Democrats	$3,881,064
National Education Association	Democrats	$3,664,670

SOURCE: Center for Responsive Politics, "527 Committees: Top Fifty Federally Focused Organizations," available at http://www.opensecrets.org/527s/527cmtes.php?level=C. Based on data released by the Federal Election Commission on October 18, 2010.

Citizens United Supreme Court decision that authorized unlimited independent spending by corporations and labor unions in federal elections. These Super PACs may raise unlimited amounts of money to spend for or against candidates, but they may not coordinate their spending with the candidates' campaigns and their contributors must be disclosed. President Bush's former political strategist Karl Rove set up the Super PAC American Crossroads to help elect Republicans in 2010. However, many businesses preferred that their contributions remain secret because they were afraid of angering shareholders and customers who may disagree with their political spending. Therefore, many chose to contribute money to nonprofits organized as 501(c)(4) groups, which can lobby and engage in electioneering as long as their "primary activity" (typically interpreted to mean that at least half of their overall activity) is not political. Rove established a 501(c)(4), Crossroads GPS, for businesses that did not want to have their contributions disclosed. Rove's two groups spent more than $50 million in the 2010 elections. 501(c)(4) groups existed before *Citizens United*, but they became an increasingly attractive vehicle for businesses to electioneer in the 2010 elections.

These data highlight a sharp difference in electioneering strategies between the very few large, well-funded interest groups and everyone else. A few 527s, Super PACs, 501(c)(4)s, and PACs have the money to deploy massive advertising and mobilizing efforts for a candidate or issue they like or against those they don't. There are also some mass associations, such as labor unions or ideological groups, that can persuade large numbers of members to work for and vote for candidates the group supports or against candidates the group wants to defeat. But these strategies are not available to the vast majority of interest groups, which simply don't have the resources needed to make a real difference in an election. For the most part, they hope to use their contributions to give modest help to candidates who are sympathetic to the group's goals, and to generate access. That is, they donate to a campaign in

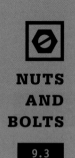

Big Spenders in the 2010 Election: Political Action Committees

ORGANIZATION	GENERALLY SUPPORTS	TOTAL CONTRIBUTIONS
Honeywell International	Mixed	$3,183,100
AT&T Inc	Mixed	$2,776,875
International Brotherhood of Electrical Workers	Democrats	$2,690,373
National Association of Realtors	Mixed	$2,685,054
National Beer Wholesalers Association	Mixed	$2,556,500
American Association for Justice	Democrats	$2,415,000
American Bankers Association	Republicans	$2,281,930
Operating Engineers Union	Democrats	$2,149,258
Carpenters & Joiners Union	Democrats	$2,004,875
American Crystal Sugar	Democrats	$1,962,500
American Federation of State, County, and Municipal Employees	Democrats	$1,962,000

Note: Support is mixed if fewer than 60 percent of contributions are given to one party.

SOURCE: Center for Responsive Politics, "Top PACs," available at http://www.opensecrets.org/pacs/toppacs.php?cycle=2010&party=A. Based on data released by the Federal Election Commission on October 25, 2010.

the hopes that, once elected, the officeholder will remember the contribution when the group asks for a meeting. Some groups give money to both candidates in a race (as long as neither candidate actively opposes the group's position), figuring that regardless of who wins, they will be able to meet with the winner.[74] A few groups use an extreme version of this strategy, waiting until after the election to make their contribution to the winning candidate, a strategy known as **taking the late train**.

Media Contacts Media coverage helps a group publicize its concerns without spending any money, so most interest group leaders talk often with journalists about the group's goals and activities in order to suggest news stories that pertain to the group's issues and pursue favorable coverage for the group. Such attention may lead people to join the group, contribute money, or demand that elected officials support the group's agenda. Favorable media coverage also helps a group's leaders assure members that they are actively working on member concerns.

Journalists listen when interest groups call if they believe that the group's story will catch their readers' attention or address their concerns. Smart interest group leaders make it easy for journalists to cover their cause, holding events that are designed to produce intriguing news stories. These stories may not change anyone's mind, but media coverage provides interest groups with free publicity for their policy agenda.

Bypassing Government: The Initiative Process A final outside strategy for interest groups bypasses government entirely: a group can work to get their proposed policy change voted on by the public in a general election through an **initiative** or

taking the late train An interest group strategy that involves donating money to the winning candidate after an election in hopes of securing a meeting with that person when he or she takes office.

initiative A direct vote by citizens on a policy change proposed by fellow citizens or organized groups outside government. Getting a question on the ballot typically requires collecting a set number of signatures from registered voters in support of the proposal. There is no mechanism for a national-level initiative.

a **referendum**. Referenda and initiatives allow citizens to vote on specific proposed changes in policy. The difference between these procedures lies in the source of the proposal. In a referendum, the legislature or another government body proposes the question that is put to a vote, whereas the initiative process allows citizens to put questions on the ballot, typically after gathering signatures of registered voters on a petition.

Initiatives can only occur in states and municipalities that have the appropriate procedures in place; there is no mechanism for a nationwide vote on an interest group's proposal. So, if a group wants to use this process to effect national change, it has to get its measure on the ballot in one state at a time. Moreover, only some states allow initiatives; others permit this kind of vote only on a narrow range of issues. The champion state for initiatives is California, whose citizens often vote on dozens of initiatives in each general election, ranging from funding for stem cell research to limits on taxation and spending.[75]

There are many examples of groups using the initiative process to change government policy. Most notably, advocates of term limits on state legislatures have used the initiative process to establish limits in twenty-one states, though some have since been overturned by legislative action or subsequent initiatives.[76]

One of the principal concerns about the initiative process is that it favors well-funded groups that can advertise heavily in support of their proposals and work to mobilize supporters to go to the polls on Election Day.[77] However, money often is not enough: even groups with substantial resources have sometimes been unable to reform policy through the initiative process.[78]

CHOOSING STRATEGIES

Most groups give testimony, do research, contact elected officials and bureaucrats, talk with journalists, and develop legislative and regulatory proposals.[79] In fact, as Table 9.2 shows, most groups use more than one of these strategies. Some groups do not contact legislators and bureaucrats at all, and only a bare majority of interest groups engage in grassroots lobbying. Relatively few groups organize protests, endorse candidates, or provide campaign workers.

A particular group's decisions about which strategies to use depend partly on its resources and partly on what approach the group believes will be most effective in promoting its particular issues. Some strategies that work well for one group's agenda might not be appropriate for another group. The Humane Society is an organization that lobbies to protect against abuse and neglect of animals. It has 10 million members and a $120 million annual budget but only a small Washington office.[80] This is because the group focuses on grassroots lobbying and electioneering. During 2009, the Humane Society organized grassroots efforts on behalf of legislation allowing wild horses to graze on government land, as well as to ban the importation of so-called exotic pets such as pythons.[81]

Other interest groups have expertise but few members and not much money. The Internet2 consortium is one such group comprised of universities, laboratories, and companies that are designing technical standards for a faster Internet. This organization has little money and few individual members, so strategies such as litigation and electioneering are impossible. What they have instead is expertise—knowledge of the demand for new kinds of Internet services, and the cost and feasibility of providing them—which representatives of Internet2 convey to members of Congress by giving testimony on these topics. In February 2006, the vice president of Internet2 testified against proposals to eliminate "net neutrality" (net neutrality prevents companies that control data transmission on the Internet from charging some users more than others).[82] The debate also involves major telecommunications companies such as Comcast and AT&T, which favor the elimination of net neutrality.

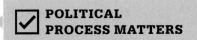

POLITICAL PROCESS MATTERS

referendum A direct vote by citizens on a policy change proposed by a legislature or another government body. Referenda are common in state and local elections, but there is no mechanism for a national-level referendum.

TABLE 9.2 INTEREST GROUP TACTICS

Most groups use both inside and outside strategies, and virtually all groups utilize a wide variety of inside strategies. Several outside strategies (advertising, endorsements, and protests) are used by relatively few groups. How might groups' resources drive these lobbying strategies?

Tactic	Percentage Using
Inside Strategies	
Contacting journalists	72%
Direct lobbying	84
Drafting new legislation	78
Drafting new regulations	85
Litigation	60
Research reports	81
Testimony	95
Outside Strategies	
Electioneering	
Campaign workers or advertising	24%
Candidate endorsements	22
Campaign contributions	58
Grassroots lobbying	
Organizing protests	20%
Soliciting letters or e-mails	68

SOURCE: After Table 8.1 in Frank Baumgartner and Beth Leech, *Basic Interests: The Importance of Groups in Politics and in Political Science* (Princeton, NJ: Princeton University Press, 1998), p. 152.

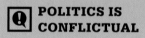

POLITICS IS CONFLICTUAL

These corporations deployed substantial funds for lobbying and electioneering as a way of achieving their policy goals.[83] However, as of this writing, no new legislation or regulations have addressed the issue.

How Much Power Do Interest Groups Have?

In April 2005, Jeffrey Birnbaum, a highly regarded reporter for the *Washington Post*, criticized elected officials for focusing on what he saw as minor issues, such as appointing federal judges, while ignoring problems such as the rise in Americans' health care costs and major international issues such as poverty and AIDS. The problem, Birnbaum argued, is that elected officials let interest groups define their agenda:

> Like it or not, we increasingly live in a stage-managed democracy where highly orchestrated interests filter our priorities for us. These groups don't have absolute power, of course. In the nation's capital, home to 30,000 registered lobbyists, hundreds of elected

politicians, thousands of journalists, and untold numbers of entrenched bureaucrats, no one's in charge. But long-established entities like the AARP, the Family Research Council, and the U.S. Chamber of Commerce mold our collective thinking and regularly dictate the language and tenor of our civil debates.[84]

Other critics echo Birnbaum's arguments. The Web site of the Alliance for Retired Americans includes detailed critiques of the Medicare Prescription Drug Benefit, arguing that key elements of the program, including the ban on importing cheaper prescription drugs from abroad, resulted from health care industry lobbying. As the Alliance sees it, drug companies got what they wanted; the rest of us did not. Interest groups are also thought to have enormous influence over the actions of unelected bureaucrats. The theory of bureaucratic capture posits that agencies are vulnerable to being "captured," or having their policy goals displaced by the aims of the individuals and corporations they are supposed to regulate. When this happens, bureaucrats become more interested in catering to interest groups than implementing policies that are good for the general population.[85] (See Chapter 12 for further discussion of bureaucratic capture.)

The scholarly evidence on interest group influence does not support these claims. Interest group scholars Frank Baumgartner and Beth Leech reviewed all the studies of interest group influence published in major political science journals and concluded that the literature was a "maze of contradictions."[86] Half of the studies they analyzed found that interest group lobbying had some impact on policy, while the other half found the influence marginal or nonexistent.[87] It seems that some interest groups get what they want from government some of the time, but that success can prove elusive even for groups with many members and large budgets.

This conclusion makes sense in light of five truths about interest group influence. First, interest groups lobby their friends in government rather than their enemies and tend to moderate their demands in the face of resistance. A high success rate for an interest group's efforts may reflect these kinds of calculations and compromises rather than supporting the case that they are extremely powerful. For example, the NRA leadership would probably favor a new federal law that made it legal to carry a concealed handgun throughout the nation, since the NRA has lobbied for these laws at the state level and sent their representatives to testify at congressional hearings.[88] Why doesn't the NRA demand federal legislation? There is no sign that Congress would enact this proposal. A proposal that would force states to honor concealed carry permits issued by other states has been introduced in Congress several times but never brought up for debate or a vote.[89] Thus, the NRA's decision to forgo lobbying for a federal concealed carry law shows the limits of the organization's power.

Second, some complaints about the power of interest groups come from the losing side in the political process. As Senator Mitch McConnell (R-KY) once said, "My favorite definition of 'special interest' is a group [that's] against what I am trying to do."[90] Consider the Alliance for Retired Americans and its claims about the Medicare Prescription Drug Benefit mentioned above. The Alliance lobbied against the Medicare legislation just as the drug companies lobbied for it. However, the Alliance was on the losing side of the debate, and many of the provisions they favored were not enacted, making them more prone to complain about the influence of "special interests."

Third, many interest groups claim responsibility for policies and election outcomes regardless of whether their lobbying made the difference. Consider former senator Elizabeth Dole (R-NC), who was defeated in her 2008 reelection bid. Many interest groups funded ads criticizing Dole or contributed to her opponent's campaign. But did they defeat Dole? They may have helped, but Dole was also hurt by strong Democratic Party support for her opponent, as well as by the popularity of President Obama, who carried Dole's home state of North Carolina in the 2008

▲ While many observers credit lobbying by the pharmaceutical industry for policies such as the Medicare Prescription Drug Benefit (and its ban on importing medicines), favorable public opinion, the efforts of AARP, and bureaucrats' independent judgments probably had greater influence on passing the Drug Benefit than the advertising, contributions, and direct contacts from industry representatives.

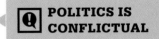

POLITICS IS CONFLICTUAL

The Economic Benefits of Lobbying

One of the pieces of evidence mentioned at the beginning of this chapter for the inordinate power of lobbying on government policy is the relationship between lobbying expenditures and the Troubled Assets Relief Program (TARP), the federal government's program to provide loans to troubled banks and corporations during the financial crisis of 2008–2009. An analysis conducted by the Center for Responsive Politics (CRP) argued that a firm's success in getting TARP funds hinged on their lobbying efforts. Twenty-five firms spent a total of $114 million on lobbying in 2008 and received a total of $295 billion from TARP. As the head of the CRP put it, "Even in the best economic times, you won't find an investment with a greater payoff than what these companies have been getting. Some of the companies and industries that have received payments may now consider their contributions and lobbying to be the smartest investments they've made in years."[a]

At first glance, data on lobbying and TARP money appears to support this claim about the benefits of lobbying. At the time

the CRP did its analysis (February 2009), 161 firms had received TARP funding; the 25 that lobbied received $295 billion, and the 138 that did not lobby received a total of about $28 billion.

However, the plot of lobbying expenditures and TARP funding (from data contained in the CRP press release) tells a very different story.

Each point in the figure shows how much a particular firm spent on lobbying in 2008 and the amount of money they received from TARP. Some of the larger TARP recipients are labeled—Bank of America, for example, spent more than $8 million on lobbying and received $45 billion in TARP money. This chart may appear to give support to the idea that firms bought access to TARP money through their lobbying efforts, as the firms that spent a lot on lobbying, such as AIG, Citigroup, and Bank of America, received some of the higher TARP allocations.

However, a closer look at the data paints a different picture, one that suggests that lobbying was not an automatic generator of TARP funding. For one thing, some firms received relatively little from TARP

even though they lobbied a lot—General Motors (GM), for example, spent the most on lobbying but received far less than the top TARP recipients. Wells Fargo spent only a tenth of what GM did on lobbying but received more than twice the TARP allocation.

Moreover, look at the cluster of points on the left-hand side of the figure—nearly 100 firms are plotted here, virtually all of which spent nothing on lobbying. Even so, many of them received billions from TARP, and some even received almost as much as GM.

Third, firms that had their TARP application rejected do not show up on this chart. E*TRADE, for example, spent nearly $700,000 on lobbying in 2008 but was denied TARP funding. If lobbying drives funding, why did E*TRADE do worse than firms that did not lobby?

Fourth, since the CRP did its analysis, nearly $300 billion of additional TARP funds have been distributed—$50 billion was allocated for mortgage refinancing programs for individuals, and about $150 billion funded purchases of corporate bonds by the government; the remainder, nearly

election. In particular, the leaders of interest groups have a considerable incentive to make strong claims about their group's influence and impact, as these claims help them attract members and keep their jobs.[91] But much of what groups do—issuing reports, testifying, sending out appeals, talking with journalists—has little direct impact on policy. Publicizing these activities may reflect a leader's desire to build support for themselves but say little about the group's influence.

Fourth, arguments about the impact of interest groups on election outcomes, such as Dole's defeat in 2008, ignore the fact that groups are almost always active on both sides of an election. Although Dole was the target of attack ads funded by interest groups, and though many groups gave contributions to her opponent, Kay Hagan, Dole also received considerable support from interest groups in the form of campaign contributions and independent ads. Thus, it doesn't make sense to attribute Dole's defeat to actions taken by one set of groups without asking why similar efforts on Dole's behalf had no effect. You can't conclude that interest groups are all-powerful without explaining why Dole's supporters were unable to save her seat.

TARP FUNDING AND LOBBYING: DID LOBBYING BUY GOVERNMENT HELP?

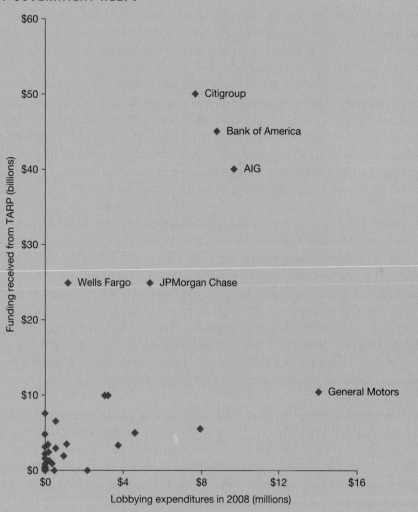

$100 billion, was given to several hundred smaller banks and other companies, most of which had never lobbied the federal government.[b]

Finally, a closer look at the TARP bailout suggests a less sinister interpretation of the amounts distributed as part of the program: government bureaucrats simply helped firms in proportion to their need. In other words, the correlation between lobbying expenditures and TARP funds was simply a coincidence—firms didn't lobby to get bailout funds, and bureaucrats were not influenced by lobbying efforts.

In sum, although it would be a mistake to say that lobbying doesn't matter, the claim that the existence of TARP or the allocations made by TARP bureaucrats were influenced by corporate lobbying efforts is clearly a stretch. Some large TARP recipients spent a lot of money on lobbying, but some did not, and others received relatively small allocations despite extensive lobbying efforts. Moreover, most TARP recipients did not do any lobbying at all. ■

Finally, the sizable amounts that groups spend to lobby Congress can easily overshadow the more important issue of what they get for their money. Lobbying elected officials and bureaucrats can be expensive, regardless of whether the efforts bring about legislative or regulatory success. As the Challenging Conventional Wisdom box suggests, lobbying efforts sometimes seem to have little effect on policy outcomes. This is not to say that legislators ignore interest groups; one study found that lobbying efforts on a particular issue increased the amount of time that legislators spent thinking about or working on the related policy proposals.[92] However, such efforts do not prompt legislators to drop everything else and do what the group wants.

WHAT DETERMINES WHEN INTEREST GROUPS SUCCEED?

Rather than asking why interest groups are so powerful, it makes more sense to ask when they are powerful.[93] Research points to two related factors that determine the success of lobbying efforts. The first is salience: How many Americans care about

what a group is trying to do? The second is conflict: To what extent do other groups or the public oppose the policy change?

Salience Interest groups are more likely to succeed when their request has low **salience**, or attracts little public attention.[94] When the average voter does not know or care about a group's request, legislators and bureaucrats do not have to worry about the political consequences of giving the group what it wants. The only question is whether the officials themselves favor the request or can be convinced that the group's desired change is worthwhile. In contrast, when salience is high, a legislator's response to lobbying will hinge on her judgment of constituent opinion: Do voters favor what the group wants? As discussed in Chapter 8, the average legislator has a strong interest in reelection and is unlikely to act against her constituents' wishes. As a result, lobbying may count for nothing in the face of public opposition or be superfluous when the group's position already has public support.[95]

Many of the policies that are the focus of lobbying efforts are not at all salient. Consider the National Turkey Federation, an association of turkey farmers and processors. The Federation sponsors the annual ritual of presenting the president with a live Thanksgiving turkey, which is officially "pardoned" by the president and sent to a local petting zoo. In 2002, the Federation was successful in getting federal bureaucrats to change federally funded school lunch program regulations in a way that increased the allowable amount of turkey in various entrees. The policy change resulting from the Federation's lobbying efforts may not sound like a big deal; in fact, it attracted no publicity, which is precisely the point. When few people know or care about a policy change, interest groups are able to dominate the policy-making process.

Low-salience issues are surprisingly common. The idea of interest group lobbying probably brings to mind titanic struggles on controversial issues, such as gun control, abortion rights, or judicial nominations, over which groups try to capture public attention as a way of pressuring people in government. And in fact, many groups are active on one side of these issues or the other. However, the typical issue attracts much less interest group activity. One analysis of lobbying disclosure forms found that 5 percent of issues attracted more than 50 percent of lobbying activity, and 50 percent of issues attracted less than 3 percent.[96] Thus, the typical issue debated by members of Congress may involve relatively little interest group activity, and a group's request may generate little or no opposition from other groups.

Conflict Lobbying is subject to two kinds of conflict. One involves disagreements between interest groups: some prefer spending more on a given program, some less. The other involves differences between what a particular interest group wants and the opinions or preferences of the general public. Both kinds of conflict can exist over the same issue, and both work against the success of a lobbying effort.[97]

In the case of the National Turkey Federation, for example, virtually no one in the general public knew about its proposal, and no interest group lobbied against it. In essence, bureaucrats heard one group asking for something, and, hearing no opposition to the request, decided the policy change was worth making. The situation might have been very different if another group—perhaps the American Pork Producers or the American Cattlemen—had lobbied against the Turkey Federation. If so, satisfying one group would have required displeasing at least one other group. Faced with this no-win situation, bureaucrats or legislators would be less likely to give the group what it wanted. At a minimum, they would have had to measure the Turkey Federation's arguments against those made by the other groups.

▼ *If you have ever heard of the National Turkey Federation, it's probably because of their participation in the annual presidential "pardoning" of a turkey before Thanksgiving. The Federation's relative anonymity has been beneficial: its effort to increase the amount of turkey served in federally funded school lunches was aided by most Americans' lack of awareness of the proposal.*

As the analysis mentioned earlier suggests, many cases of interest group influence look a lot like the Turkey Federation's request: a group asks for something, there is relatively little opposition, and Congress or the bureaucracy responds with appropriate policy changes. These cases are examples of true interest group influence, because a group asks for something and gets it. However, one of the primary reasons for the group's success is the fact that its efforts are essentially unopposed.

You may be wondering, if conflict is fundamental to politics, shouldn't there be at least one group opposing every lobbying effort? The answer is, not necessarily. Potential opponents may remain latent (unorganized) or decide against lobbying to concentrate their efforts on other matters. Many policy questions are just not that important to many people. Thus, the obstacles to a group's goals may not be the other groups that are directly opposed to its request; rather, the obstacles may be the groups that are asking for something completely different, because members of Congress and bureaucrats have time to make only so many policy changes in any year.

Interest group influence is much less apparent on conflictual issues—those over which public opinion is split and groups are typically active on both sides of the question. Consider a high-salience issue such as health care reform. As we have noted at several points in this chapter, the 2009–2010 debate over health care reform attracted many well-funded interest groups and coalitions, which supported different versions of reform or wanted no change at all. There was no consensus either among members of Congress, interest groups, or the American public about which policy changes were needed. Under these conditions, policy changes are likely to reflect a complex process of bargaining and compromise, with no groups getting exactly what they want, which is exactly what happened in the case of health care reform. In such cases, it is hard to say whether a particular group won or lost, or to attribute any aspect of the final bargain to a particular group's efforts.

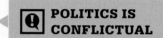

POLITICS IS CONFLICTUAL

The case of health care reform illustrates that being large or well-funded often does not help an interest group convince government officials to comply with its requests, which completely contradicts many Americans' view of interest groups. As mentioned earlier, many people worry that well-funded interest groups will use their financial resources to dominate the policy-making process, even if public opinion is against them, but these fears are largely unfounded. The conditions that are ripe for well-funded interest groups to become involved in a policy debate typically ensure that there will be well-funded groups on all sides of a question. Under these conditions, no group is likely to get everything it wants, and no group's lobbying efforts are likely to be decisive. Some groups may not get anything.

Does this mean that interest groups really have no influence on big-ticket, controversial issues? Hardly. Research and testimony may help members of Congress develop legislative proposals and give them arguments to use in the bargaining process. Grassroots and media efforts may mobilize public opinion, pressuring members to vote for options favored by their constituents. If a particular group decided against doing these things, and no other group took its place, then groups on the other side of the debate might be more likely to carry the day. But interest group leaders are well aware of the potentially dire consequences of not getting involved and are unlikely to be inactive on questions that matter to them and the members of their group—even if a full-fledged lobbying effort is unlikely to produce many identifiable benefits, given the opposition by other groups.

Even on high-salience issues, lobbying efforts may produce identifiable benefits when they are focused on relatively small details of a policy change. However, groups are successful in these efforts precisely because they are asking for relatively modest policy changes, which are nonetheless important to their members but generate relatively little opposition.

Does Money Buy Policy Outcomes?

As we note throughout this chapter, many Americans are deeply suspicious of the impact that money plays in congressional elections, believing that contributions are often made as an explicit trade—candidates get money to fund their campaigns, then pay their contributors back by voting as requested on legislative proposals. This claim that "money talks" strikes at the heart of the argument over whether democracy is a good form of government: If the small number of people who have the money to make campaign contributions can get the policy outcomes they want regardless of the preferences held by everyone else, does it matter if everyone has a vote?

At first glance, this claim about the role of money in elections should be easy to test. After all, groups are required to file reports detailing virtually all the contributions they make, and members of Congress generally cast recorded votes on significant proposals. The only task would be to tie contributions to votes in order to show how one is influenced by the other.

However, it turns out that linking campaign contributions to congressional voting behavior is an extraordinarily difficult task. The problem is that there are many other factors that might produce a link between contributions and votes, even when congressional members and their contributors make no deals of any kind. For example, suppose that contributors do not expect anything in return for their contributions but simply give money to legislators who happen to share their views on government policy, and further, that legislators ignore contributions when deciding how to vote, instead making their decision based on their personal evaluation of each proposal. Given these circumstances, if you looked at the data, you would see a positive link between contributions and votes, because

legislators who receive contributions from a like-minded group are more likely to support proposals favored by the group, even though contributions were made without expecting anything in return.

Three scholars, Stephen Ansolabehere, John de Figueiredo, and James Snyder, have published an analysis that provides insights into the relationship between campaign contributions and policy outcomes.[a] To begin with, the authors aggregated the results of all previous studies of this phenomenon that have appeared in scholarly journals—nearly forty in all. Of these, they found only a few that show any link between contributions and outcomes. Moreover, of those that do, three out of four found a negative relationship—in other words, receiving a contribution makes a legislator less likely to vote in line with the wishes of the group that made the contribution. All in all, there is simply no evidence of money buying policy outcomes.

The authors identified other evidence that is consistent with their aggregate analysis. Essentially, they asked the question, what if money really does buy policy outcomes in ways that previous analyses have not uncovered? If this is the case, what kinds of contribution patterns would we expect to see? Among other predictions, they argued that we would find that most campaign contributions had been made by political action committees, or PACs (which is the only way that corporations can make contributions to candidates), that most if not all major corporations would have a PAC, and that PACs would generally make the largest-possible contribution to a candidate in order to maximize their influence over the candidate's future voting behavior.

Their analysis of campaign finance data from the 1990s shows that none of this happened. The vast majority of campaign contributions are made by individuals, not PACs, and most of these contributions are

small (about $100 or so). In addition, although more than 3,000 PACs contributed to congressional candidates, the majority contributed to only a few. Thus, very few PACs contributed to enough candidates to influence policy outcomes. (Remember, there are 100 senators and 435 House members.) Moreover, only 60 percent of the Fortune 500 companies (the 500 largest companies in America) had a PAC; the rest do not make campaign contributions. Finally, only 4 percent of PAC contributions to candidates were the maximum amount allowed—the average is much, much lower. Thus, there is virtually no evidence that corporations are doing what we would expect to see if campaign contributions could be used to buy votes and policy outcomes.

Ultimately, Ansolabehere, de Figueiredo, and Snyder concluded that contributions may in some cases help interest groups or corporations gain access to members of Congress and their staff, but that they have little impact beyond this modest effect. After all, just about anyone can get an appointment with a member's staff, regardless of whether they give a campaign contribution or not. Ultimately, the authors concluded that rather than buying votes and outcomes, contributions fit the alternative explanation mentioned earlier: groups give money to legislators who share their policy views, with no expectation that the member will do anything different because of the contribution. Put another way, although there is a great deal of money in American politics, there is no evidence to support the alarmist view that contributions are eroding the foundation of democracy in America. ∎

Watch a video clip of Steve Ansolabehere discussing this topic at wwnorton.com/studyspace.

Another measure of the limits of lobbying on conflictual questions can be seen in groups' decisions about which issues to avoid lobbying on. Think about one of the most powerful interest groups, the NRA, and its advocacy of concealed carry laws (discussed earlier). There is little doubt that the NRA's leaders and most of its members favor the passage of such laws, but its efforts are unlikely to be successful given a well-funded opposition. As a result, the NRA chooses to focus its lobbying on other matters—policy questions where it might succeed or where its efforts are necessary to prevent other groups from succeeding in changing policies in ways that the NRA opposes.

Thus, being large or well-funded often does not help an interest group convince government officials to comply with its requests. It all depends on what the group is asking for, and in particular, whether there is significant opposition, either in the form of opposing groups or public opinion. As mentioned earlier, many Americans worry that well-funded interest groups will use their financial resources to dominate the policy-making process, even if public opinion is against them. It would be a considerable overstatement to say that interest groups have no power and lobbying makes no difference, because, if nothing else, groups may lobby to prevent the policy changes that would occur if they stayed inactive. And interest groups often succeed in efforts to change low-salience policies or small details of salient proposals. But when large, powerful groups ask for controversial changes, their resources are matched by the difficulty of the task. These groups can send staff to lobby officeholders, commission research reports, testify, bring lawsuits, and encourage grassroots activity, but these tactics are unlikely to prevail in the face of public opposition or counteractive lobbying by other groups. Fears of large groups dominating the policy-making process to the exclusion of public opinion are largely unfounded.

Conclusion

The number of American interest groups and the amount those groups spend on lobbying have increased rapidly in recent years, bringing a larger variety of organizations and lobbying tactics. The image of slick lobbyists representing rich corporations or well-to-do individuals fits only a small fraction of American interest groups. Not everyone who lobbies in Washington looks like Jack Abramoff or acts as he did.

Contrary to the image of interest groups as powerful manipulators, one of the biggest challenges for these organizations is getting their members to participate in their efforts. Interest groups are more likely to get what they want when their demands attract little public attention and no opposition from other groups. When a group asks for a large or controversial policy change, it stands little chance of success, even if the group has many members, a large lobbying budget—or an unprincipled leader like Jack Abramoff directing its operation.

Finally, data on how groups lobby show that representatives Randy Cunningham and Bob Ney, who were both sent to prison for taking bribes from lobbyists, are by far the exception rather than the rule. By and large, interest groups shape policy by providing information to like-minded officials in Congress and the bureaucracy, focusing media attention, or mobilizing public outcry about an issue.

What are interest groups, what role do they play, what are their goals, and how are they organized?

- The number of interest groups in America has increased dramatically over the last generation, largely due to the increasingly expansive role of government in American society.
- Interest groups and other organizations interested in influencing policy spend billions of dollars on lobbying each year. However, most individual groups have relatively modest lobbying efforts.
- Economic groups, citizen groups, and single-issue groups differ in terms of their goals. Groups can be divided into mass organizations and peak associations.
- The resources an interest group uses to lobby include people, money, and expertise.

Why do interest groups form? How do interest groups solve their collective action problems?

- The logic of collective action shows that common interests or goals are not enough to motivate people to join or contribute to an interest group. Before groups can cooperate, they must solve the free rider problem.
- Possible solutions to the free rider problem include benefits from participation, coercion, and selective incentives.
- The logic of collective action explains why some potential interest groups remain latent or unorganized. It also explains why some groups are more likely to form than others, and the important role that the leaders of interest groups play in organizing these groups and determining their lobbying strategies.

What strategies do interest groups employ?

- There are two kinds of interest group lobbying strategies. Inside strategies involve direct lobbying, drafting legislation and regulations, research, testimony, litigation, and working together. Outside strategies utilize grassroots lobbying, attempts to mobilize public opinion, electioneering, and contact with journalists.
- Most groups use multiple lobbying strategies and decide which strategies to use based on their available resources.

How much power do interest groups have in the United States?

- Many observers claim that lobbying allows interest groups to get what they want from Congress regardless of what they ask for and whether the public supports the request.
- Scholarly evidence suggests that these worries are unfounded: much of the time, lobbying by interest groups has little or no effect on policy.
- The success of a group's lobbying efforts depends in part on the salience of its request and the amount of conflict it engenders.

⊚ STUDENT STUDYSPACE

Find quizzes and other review material at wwnorton.com/studyspace.

CRITICAL THINKING

1. The chapter describes the last few decades' significant increases in the number of interest groups and lobbyists and in the amount spent on lobbying. What factors could cause this increase to level off or even reverse?
2. A friend complains to you about the enormous power of organized interests in American politics, citing a group's recent victory in getting members of Congress to approve its policy proposal. Present three other possible explanations for this victory that do not have anything to do with the political power of the interest group.
3. As described in this chapter, college students are a latent group in American politics. Based on the logic of collective action, what would an interest group entrepreneur have to do to organize this group?

KEY TERMS

astroturf lobbying (p. 331)

centralized groups (p. 318)

citizen group (p. 317)

coercion (p. 324)

collective action problem (p. 324)

confederations (p. 319)

direct lobbying (p. 327)

economic group (p. 317)

501(c)(3) organization (p. 332)

527 organization (p. 332)

free riding (p. 324)

grassroots lobbying (p. 330)

initiative (p. 334)

inside strategies (p. 327)

interest group (p. 311)

interest group state (p. 312)

latent (p. 314)

lobbying (p. 311)

mass association (p. 320)

outside strategies (p. 327)

peak association (p. 320)

political action committee (PAC) (p. 332)

prisoners' dilemma (p. 323)

purposive benefits (p. 324)

referendum (p. 335)

revolving door (p. 320)

salience (p. 340)

selective incentives (p. 325)

single-issue group (p. 317)

solidary benefits (p. 324)

taking the late train (p. 334)

trade association (p. 316)

SUGGESTED READING

Ainsworth, Scott. *Analyzing Interest Groups: Group Influence on People and Policies*. New York: W. W. Norton, 2002.

Baumgartner, Frank, and Beth Leech. *Basic Interests: The Importance of Interest Groups in Politics and in Political Science*. Princeton, NJ: Princeton University Press, 1999.

Carpenter, Daniel. *The Forging of Bureaucratic Autonomy: Reputations, Networks, and Policy Innovation in Executive Agencies, 1862–1928*. Princeton, NJ: Princeton University Press, 2002.

Kollman, Kenneth. *Outside Lobbying: Public Opinion and Interest Group Strategies*. Princeton, NJ: Princeton University Press, 1998.

Lowi, Theodore. *The End of Liberalism: The Second Republic of the United States*. New York: W. W. Norton, 1979.

Olson, Mancur. *The Logic of Collective Action*, 2nd ed. Cambridge, MA: Harvard University Press, 1971.

Schattschneider, E. E. *The Semi-Sovereign People*. New York: Harper and Row, 1959.

Schlozman, Kay Lehman, and John Tierney. *Organized Interests and American Democracy*. New York: HarperCollins, 1986.

Stigerwalt, Amy. *The Battle over the Bench: Senators, Interest Groups, and Lower Court Confirmations*. Blacksburg: University of Virginia Press, 2010.

Verba, Sidney, Kay Lehman Schlozman, and Henry Brady. *Voice and Equality: Civic Participation in America*. Cambridge, MA: Harvard University Press, 1995.

Walker, Jack. *Mobilizing Interest Groups in America*. Ann Arbor, MI: University of Michigan Press, 1991.

Democrats give a standing ovation while Republicans sit silently during a speech by President Obama to a joint session of Congress. Is Congress hopelessly divided, or is compromise still possible?

Congress

Nearly every major bill that Congress enacts into law involves conflict and compromise. For example, Congress passed health care reform early in 2010 after more than a year of intense partisan debate. Some controversial parts of the bill, such as the "public option" that would have provided a government-administered health insurance plan, were jettisoned to gain the support of moderate Democrats, while other parts of the bill that generated conflict, such as the requirement that all individuals purchase health insurance if it was not provided by their employer, were maintained as part of the final bill. The bill was passed along party lines and remained controversial in the 2010 midterm elections.

CONFLICT AND COMPROMISE
in American Politics

Another excellent recent example of conflict and compromise in Congress concerns legislation passed to address the financial meltdown of 2008–2009, an event that nearly ruined the U.S. and world economies. The first order of business in January 2009 for President Obama and Congress was to try to get the economy back on track. Congress had already passed the $700 billion Troubled Asset Relief Program (TARP) in October 2008 to give the Treasury and the Federal Reserve the assets they needed to avert a complete economic meltdown. Enacted with strong bipartisan majorities,[1] TARP had stabilized the banking system, but the economy was still in free fall when Obama took office with nearly 800,000 jobs lost in January alone. To restore economic health two things still needed to happen: the economy needed a short-term stimulus to get people back to work and spending money again, and then the financial sector needed to be reformed to make sure that the risky behavior that caused the collapse would be less likely to happen in the future. Normally, a stimulus bill should not produce as much conflict as health care reform. Members of Congress like passing stimulus bills because it means they get to cut taxes and spend money, which are popular with their constituents, whereas health care reform activates some of the central divides in politics. However, the bipartisan support for the TARP bill quickly disappeared, and partisan conflict prevailed. Republicans opposed the measures due to a mixture of political calculation (figuring they would gain in the midterm elections if the economy hadn't recovered) and sincere policy differences over the proper size of the bill and the balance among tax cuts, support for states, and spending on various health, education, and infrastructure policies. Moderate Democrats in the Senate were able to demand cuts of billions of dollars in spending in exchange for their support of the $787 billion bill (only three Republicans in the Senate voted for it).

BIG QUESTIONS

✪ What is Congress's place in the constitutional system? How are conflicts between competing interests built into the system?

✪ What is the nature of Congress's relationship with the public? Why do members of Congress act the way they do?

✪ What are the sources of incumbency advantage?

✪ How is Congress structured?

✪ How does a bill become a law?

✪ Can Congress be reformed?

Reforming the financial sector, one would think, also should have gained broad support in Congress because it required reining in Wall Street, the perceived villain of the meltdown. But here too, partisan differences generated conflict in Congress. Hailed as the most sweeping set of financial reforms since the New Deal, the comprehensive legislation (1) tackles the "too big to fail" problem in which the government had been forced to bail out large financial institutions that would have wrecked the economy if they had gone bankrupt, (2) creates a new Bureau of Consumer Financial Protection, (3) imposes new transparency and rules on a $600 trillion unregulated derivatives market (which are hedges on risk that were the source of the meltdown), and (4) limits risky in-house trading by financial institutions. Republicans agreed that something needed to be done to re-regulate the financial sector but argued that the bill was too aggressive.

Like the rest of the Democrats' domestic agenda in Obama's first two years, the politics of financial sector reform were dictated by the Senate filibuster. Needing sixty votes to break a filibuster, Democrats required the support of at least one Republican to go along with the fifty-seven Democrats and two independents who often supported Democratic legislation. After months of debate, the support of moderate Democrats and three Republicans was secured by (among other things) dropping a $19 billion tax on banks, weakening the limits on in-house trading, and exempting auto dealers from lending regulations issued by the new consumer protection agency. Without these compromises, the bill could not have been passed.

The essential nature of conflict and compromise in the legislative process is not very well understood by the general public. Americans often view the type of wheeling and dealing that is necessary to reach compromises as improper and wonder why there is so much conflict; a typical sentiment is, "Why does there have to be so much partisan bickering? Can't they just implement the best solutions to our problems?" Many don't even attempt to understand the legislative process and the nature of conflict and compromise because it seems hopelessly complex. Anyone who has watched congressional debates on C-SPAN knows that legislative maneuvers can make your head spin, and the discussions can seem mind-numbing. Certainly the legislative details of a 2,300-page financial sector reform bill are too complicated for more than a small handful of experts to comprehend.

In this chapter, we show that the basic characteristics of Congress are straightforward and that the motivations that guide members' behavior and the way that Congress works are transparent. This chapter argues that members' behavior is driven by their desire to respond to constituent interests (and the closely related goal of reelection) and constrained by the institutional structures within

▲ *Congress is often highly responsive to its constituents' needs, for example by providing funding for transportation projects such as new highways.*

which they operate (such as the committee system, parties, and leadership). At the same time, members try to be responsible for the broader national interests, which are often at odds with constituent interests and the goal of reelection.

This tension between being responsible and responsive is a source of conflict and requires members of Congress to make tough decisions, often involving political trade-offs and compromises. Should a House member vote for dairy price supports for her local farmers even if it means higher milk prices for families around the nation? Should a senator vote to subsidize the production of tobacco, the biggest cash crop in his state, despite the tremendous health costs it imposes on millions of Americans? Should a member vote to close a military base, as requested by the Pentagon, even if it means the loss of thousands of jobs back home? These are difficult questions. On a complex bill such as financial sector reform there is no obvious "responsible" solution: Republicans favored a more market-based approach while Democrats wanted more government regulation, which obviously leads to conflict. Even when a member may believe that a policy option would be the responsible thing to do, such as regulating auto loans, she may not favor that approach if the auto dealers in her district disagree.

The tension between responsibility and responsiveness illustrates the other two themes of this book as well. Members of Congress regularly make decisions that affect our everyday lives. Indeed, they spend much of their time trying to respond to our desires, which means that many laws are relevant for our interests, such as government support for education, transportation, tax laws, and energy policy. The idea that political process matters is probably more evident in this chapter than any other. By controlling the legislative agenda, determining which amendments will be allowed on a given bill, or stacking an important committee with sympathetic partisans, the legislative process affects political outcomes.

This chapter begins by examining the constitutional underpinnings of the representational tensions Congress must address. After exploring different ways of understanding representation, we describe Congress's image problem, the incumbency advantage, and Congress's central institutional features. We conclude by considering some potential reforms that might make Congress work better.

Congress's Place in Our Constitutional System

Congress was clearly the "first branch" in the early decades of our nation's history. The Constitution gave Congress the lead role in a vast array of enumerated powers, including regulating commerce, coining money, raising and supporting armies, creating the courts, establishing post offices and roads, declaring war, and levying taxes (see Article I, Section 8, of the Constitution in the Appendix). The president, in contrast, was given few explicit powers and played a much less prominent role in the early years of our history. Many of Congress's extensive powers come from its implicit powers rooted in the elastic clause of Article I, which gives Congress the power "to make all Laws which shall be necessary and proper for carrying into Execution the foregoing Powers."

A ROW IN CONGRESS.

▲ *The Founders viewed the House as more passionate than the Senate, or as the "hot coffee" that needed to be cooled in the "saucer" of the Senate. This perception probably did not include coming to blows over differences in policy (this specific instance was a fight between Congressmen Albert G. Brown and John A. Wilcox in 1851 about whether Mississippi should secede from the Union).*

As noted in Chapter 2, the compromises that gave rise to Congress's initial structure reflected an attempt to reconcile the competing interests of the day (large versus small states, northern versus southern interests, and proponents of strong national power versus state power). These compromises included establishing a **bicameral** (two-chambered) institution comprised of a popularly elected House and a Senate chosen by state legislatures, allowing slaves to count as three-fifths of a person for purposes of apportionment for the House, and setting longer terms for senators (six years) than for House members (two years). But these compromises also laid the foundation for the split loyalties that members of Congress have between their local constituencies and the nation's interests. Although the Founders hoped that Congress would pass legislation that emphasized the national good over local interests, they also recognized the importance of local constituencies. In *Federalist 56*, for example, Madison said that "it is a sound and important principle that the representative ought to be acquainted with the interests and circumstances of his constituents," and the two-year House term was intended to tie legislators to public sentiment.

At the same time, the *Federalist Papers* made it quite clear that the new government was by no means a direct democracy that would put all policy questions to the public. In *Federalist 57*, Madison pursued this line of thinking, asserting that "the aim of every political constitution is, or ought to be, first to obtain for rulers men who possess most wisdom to discern, and most virtue to pursue, the common good of society." This common good may often conflict with local concerns, as noted in the earlier examples. In these situations, members were expected to both "refine and enlarge the debate" to encompass the common good *and* represent their local constituents.

In general, the Founders viewed the Senate as the more likely institution to enlarge the debate and speak for the national interests; it was intended to check the more responsive and passionate House. Because senators were indirectly elected and served longer terms than House members, the Senate was more insulated from the people. A famous (though maybe fictional) story that points out the differences between the House and Senate involves an argument between George Washington and Thomas Jefferson. Jefferson did not think the Senate was necessary, while Washington supported having two chambers. During the argument, Jefferson poured some coffee he was drinking into his saucer. Washington asked him why he had done so. "To cool it," replied Jefferson. "Even so," said Washington, "we pour legislation into the senatorial saucer to cool it."

This idea of a more responsible Senate survived well into the twentieth century, even after ratification of the 17th Amendment in 1913, which began the direct, popular election of senators. Hubert H. Humphrey (D-MN), who served in the Senate from 1949 to 1965 and 1970 to 1978 (serving as Johnson's vice president in between) summarized this view: "The first four years are for God and country and the last two years are for the folks back home."[2] Today the Senate is still somewhat more insulated than the House. Because of the six-year term, only one-third of the 100 Senate seats are contested in each election, while all 435 House members are elected every two years. However, differences between the House and Senate's representational roles have become muted as senators seem to campaign for reelection 365 days a year, every year, just like House members.[3] This "permanent campaign" means that senators are less insulated from electoral forces than they once were.

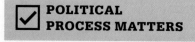

bicameralism The system of having two chambers within one legislative body, like the House and Senate in the U.S. Congress.

The relationship between the president and Congress has also evolved significantly since the Founding era. Congress's roots in geographic constituencies made it well-suited for the politics of the nineteenth century. In the first 125 years of U.S. history, several great presidents left their mark on national politics (George Washington, Andrew Jackson, and Abraham Lincoln, among others), but Congress dominated much of the day-to-day politics, which revolved around a relatively limited range of issues such as the tariff (taxes on imported or exported goods), slavery, and internal improvements such as building roads and canals. Given the tendency to address these issues with patronage and the **pork barrel** (that is, jobs and policies targeted to benefit specific constituents), Congress was better suited for the task than the president was.

Beginning around the turn of the twentieth century and accelerating with the New Deal of the 1930s that established modern social welfare and regulatory policies, the scope of national policy expanded and politics became more centered in Washington. With this nationalization of politics and the increasing importance of national security issues concerning World War II; the Cold War; wars in Korea, Vietnam, and Iraq; and the War on Terror, the president has assumed a more central policy-making role. However, the central tensions between representing local versus national interests remain a key factor in understanding the legislative process and the relationship between members of Congress and their constituents.

pork barrel Legislative appropriations that benefit specific constituents, created with the aim of helping local representatives win reelection.

descriptive representation When a member of Congress shares the characteristics (such as gender, race, religion, or ethnicity) of his or her constituents.

Congress and the People

Americans have a love-hate relationship with Congress; that is, we love our own member of Congress, but we hate the Congress as a whole. Well, "hate" is a strong word, but as we show later in this section, members of Congress routinely have approval ratings that are 30 to 40 points higher than the institution. Before explaining that puzzling pattern and exploring Congress's more general image problem, it is important to understand the nature of representation in Congress. What are the linkages between members of Congress and their constituents? How are congressional districts formed? And what do we really think about our members of Congress?

REPRESENTATION AND THE CONSTITUENCY

Styles of Representation To understand congressional behavior, we must first examine the two basic components of the relationship between a constituency and its member of Congress: descriptive and substantive representation. The former is rooted in the politician's side of the relationship. Does the member of Congress "look like" the constituents in demographic terms? Is the member African American, Latino, or white, male or female, Catholic, Protestant, or some other religion? Many people believe that such **descriptive representation** is a distinct value in itself. Having positive role models for various demographic groups helps create greater trust in the system, and there are benefits from being represented by someone who shares something as basic as skin color with constituents.

Descriptive representation is also related to the perceived responsiveness of a member of Congress. For example, African American members of Congress typically come from electorally safe majority-minority districts where they enjoy high levels of support and trust from their constituents.[4] In general, constituents report higher levels of satisfaction with representatives who are of their same race. This means that descriptively represented constituents are more likely to assume that their interests are being represented than those who are not.[5] If you doubt that descriptive representation makes a

FIGURE 10.1A WOMEN IN CONGRESS, 1933–2011

While Congress still does not have gender parity, there have been substantial gains in recent years (with the exception of 2011, when the number of women in the House dropped for the first time in thirty years). What difference does it make for policy to have more women in Congress?

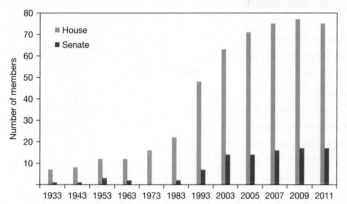

SOURCE: Jennifer E. Manning and Colleen J. Shogan, "Women in the United States Congress: 1917–2009," Congressional Research Service Report RL30261, December 23, 2009, www.senate.gov/CRSReports/crs-publish.cfm?pid=%270E%2C*PLS%3D%22%40%20%20%0A (accessed 1/4/10). Source for 2009 and 2011, *CQ Roll Call, Guide to the New Congress*, November 4, 2010, pp. 14–15, available at http://innovation.cq.com/newmember/2010elexnguide.pdf.

FIGURE 10.1B MINORITIES IN THE HOUSE, 1933–2011

Hispanics now comprise the largest ethnic minority in the United States, yet they still lag behind African Americans in terms of representation in the House. What do you think explains this difference? How might it affect policy?

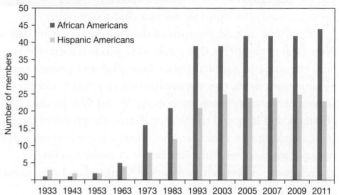

SOURCE: Compiled from Mildred L. Amer, "Black Members of the United States Congress: 1870–2005," Congressional Research Service Report RL30378, August 4, 2005; Government Printing Office, *Hispanic Americans in Congress, 1822–1995*. 1995, www.loc.gov/rr/hispanic/congress/ (accessed 1/4/10). Source for 2009 and 2011, *CQ Roll Call, Guide to the New Congress*, November 4, 2010, pp. 14–15, available at http://innovation.cq.com/newmember/2010elexnguide.pdf.

substantive representation When a member of Congress represents constituents' interests and policy concerns.

trustee A member of Congress who represents constituents' interests while also taking into account national, collective, and moral concerns that sometimes cause the member to vote against the preference of a majority of constituents.

delegate (congressional role) A member of Congress who loyally represents constituents' direct interests.

difference, ask yourself whether it would be fair if all 435 House members and 100 senators were white, male Protestants. Although the demographics of Congress are considerably more diverse than this, the legislature does not come close to "looking like us" on a nationwide scale. Figure 10.1 shows that, though we still have a long way to go, the nation is more descriptively represented now than at any point in history.

Although descriptive representation is important, it only goes so far. As one political observer pointed out, we do not expect lunatics to be represented by crazy people.[6] More important than a member's race, gender, or religion, many argue, is the *substance* of what the member of Congress does. Merely because a representative shares some characteristics with you does not necessarily mean that he or she will represent your interests (though, as noted above, the two tend to be linked, especially for racial representation). **Substantive representation** moves beyond appearances to specify how the member serves constituents' interests. Two models go back at least to the eighteenth century: (1) the **trustee**, who represents the interests of constituents from a distance, weighing a variety of national, collective, local, and moral concerns, and (2) the **delegate**, who has a simple mandate to carry out the direct desires of the voters. Another way to think about these roles is that trustees are more concerned with being responsible and delegates are more interested in responsiveness.

One of the most famous examples of a representative acting as a trustee was Marjorie Margolies-Mezvinsky (D-PA) in a crucial 1993 vote on President Clinton's budget, which included some controversial tax increases and spending cuts to balance the budget. Hours before the vote, she told reporters that she would vote against the budget, in accordance with the wishes of her constituents. But she had also promised President Clinton that she would support the bill if her vote was needed. As she walked down the aisle to cast the critical vote in the 218–216 cliffhanger (in which she fulfilled her promise to the president), Republican members chanted "Goodbye, Marjorie," accurately forecasting her defeat in the next election.[7] Representative Margolies-Mezvinsky did what she thought was in the best long-term interests of her constituents and the nation, even though it ended her career. Margolies (who has dropped the name Mezvinsky) revisited her iconic vote during the final days of the health care reform debate in March 2010. In an op-ed piece addressed "Dear wavering House Democrats," Margolies touted the virtues of doing what is right for the country, even if your constituents disagree, writing, "I urge you simply to cast the vote you can be proud of next week, next year and for years to come. Given the opportunity, I wouldn't change my vote."[8]

A delegate, on the other hand, does not have to worry about incurring the wrath of angry voters because he simply does what the voters want. Examples are so numerous it is pointless to single out one member for attention: when it comes to tax cuts, agricultural subsidies, increases in Medicare payments, or new highway projects, hundreds of representatives act as delegates for their districts' interests.

Truth be told, the trustee/delegate distinction is mostly important as a theoretical point of departure for talking about representation roles. Nearly all members act like trustees in some circumstances and like delegates in others. The third model of representation is the **politico**, who is more likely to act as a delegate on issues that are highly salient to the constituency, such as immigration reform, but is more likely to be a trustee on less salient or very complex issues, such as some foreign policies. Therefore, the crucial component of representation is the nature of the constituency and how the member of Congress attempts to balance and represent constituents' conflicting needs and desires.

The Role of the Constituency Our characterization of the representative–constituency relationship raises a host of questions. How much do voters monitor their representatives' behavior? Can representation work if voters are not paying attention? The most demanding theory of representation, known as policy responsiveness, requires that voters express basic policy preferences, representatives respond to those desires, and then voters monitor and assess the politician's behavior. However, those conditions are rarely met because most constituents do not follow congressional politics.

Despite this lack of attention, representational links remain strong through indirect mechanisms. Members of Congress behave as if voters were paying attention, even when constituents are inattentive. Incumbents know that at election time, challengers may raise issues that become salient after the public thinks about them, so they try to deter challengers by anticipating what the constituents would want *if they were fully informed*.[9] For example, the public didn't know much about stem cell research until it became a big issue in the 2006 midterm elections. Savvy incumbents would have tried to preempt any vulnerability on that issue *before* a strong challenger raised the issue in a campaign by staking out a position consistent with what the voters would want once they knew more about the issue. Richard Fenno points out that some segments of the constituency are more attentive and more important for the member's reelection than others. These constituents will have a different representational relationship than those who occupy one of the more distant concentric circles in Fenno's characterization (Figure 10.2).[10]

Another way to examine the representative–constituency relationship is to look at differences across districts. A representative from South Dakota will have to address different concerns than one from New York City. How do districts vary? First, and most obviously, they differ in size: Senate "districts" (that is, states) vary in terms of area from Alaska to Rhode Island, and in terms of population from California to Wyoming. House districts all have about 700,000 people, but they vary tremendously in geographic size (591,000 square miles for the at-large seat in Alaska to seven or eight square miles for several New York City districts). Districts also differ in terms of who lives there and what they want from government. Some districts are located in poor city neighborhoods, where voters often focus on economic

politico A member of Congress who acts as a delegate on issues that constituents care about (such as immigration reform) and as a trustee on more complex or less salient issues (some foreign policy or regulatory matters).

FIGURE 10.2 **FENNO'S CONCENTRIC CIRCLES**

The concentric circles of a congressional constituency illustrate the various parts of a district a member represents: personal (advisers, friends, and family), primary (strongest supporters), reelection (those who vote for the member), and geographic (the entire district). Can you think of an issue on which a House member would be more responsive to her reelection constituency than to her geographic constituency?

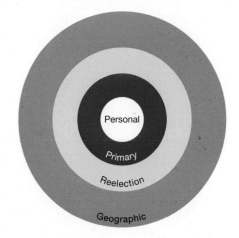

Personal
Primary
Reelection
Geographic

SOURCE: Based on Richard F. Fenno, *Home Style: House Members in Their Districts* (Boston: Little, Brown, 1978).

development, crime control, antipoverty programs, and looser immigration regulations. Some are wealthy and urban, where citizens are more supportive of foreign aid and support higher taxes to pay for domestic policy initiatives. Some are suburban, where funding for education and transportation are likely the critical issues. Some are conservative and rural, where agricultural policies typically dominate and support for tax cuts is strong. Districts vary from the religious to the secular, from domination by one industry to a diversified corporate base to no industry at all. Some consider government a force for good while others argue that government should get off the people's backs. And some districts are a mixture of all of these things.

Because districts have a variety of opinions, demands, and concerns, the legislators they elect differ from each other as well. Regardless of the office, most voters want to elect someone whose policy positions are as close to theirs as possible. As a result, legislators tend to reflect the central tendencies of their districts. At one level, electing a legislature that thinks like America sounds like a good thing. If legislators act and think like their districts, then the legislature will contain a good mixture of the demands and interests held across the country or state. The problem is that finding an acceptable compromise is not easy. We elect legislators to get things done, but they may be unable to agree on anything—not because they are stupid or unwilling to compromise, but because their disagreements are too fundamental to bridge. Consider abortion rights. The country is sharply divided on this issue, and the same divisions exist in the House and the Senate, and in most state legislatures. The fact that legislators have not arrived at a decision that puts this issue to rest is no surprise: just as citizens disagree, so do their elected representatives.

Despite the vast differences between congressional constituencies, voters want many of the same things: a healthy economy, a safe country (both in terms of national defense and local crime), good schools for their children, and effective health care. Figure 10.3 reports responses to a survey that asked citizens to rate the importance of three aspects of a legislator's job: dealing with national issues, making sure that

---

FIGURE 10.3 THE JOB OF A MEMBER OF CONGRESS

Congress is often criticized for passing pork-barrel policies that benefit specific districts. Yet this survey clearly shows that people want their "fair share" and are less concerned with whether their representative works on "national bills." Why do you think that is?

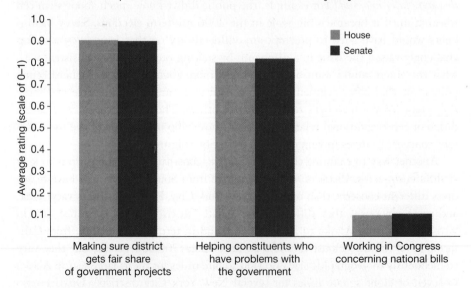

SOURCE: Adapted from Paul Gronke, *The Electorate, the Campaign, and the Office: A Unified Approach to Senate and House Elections* (Ann Arbor, MI: University of Michigan Press, 2001), Table 6.5.

their district received its fair share of federal support, and helping individual constituents deal with government. The survey showed strong support for the theme of this chapter concerning tensions between local and national concerns. Citizens clearly want their elected officials to get them a fair share of the federal pie and do **casework** for the district, the classic indicators of responsiveness. But the respondents in this poll showed little interest in having the representatives "work in Congress concerning national bills." Thus, responsibilities for national interests may be more difficult for members of Congress to explain to their constituents.

THE ELECTORAL CONNECTION

Members' relationship to their constituents also must be understood within the context of members' desire to be reelected. Political scientist David Mayhew argues in his classic book, *Congress: The Electoral Connection,* that reelection must come first.[11] Members certainly hold multiple goals, including making good policy, but if members cannot maintain their seats, they cannot attain other goals in office.

After assuming that reelection is central, Mayhew then asks the question "Members of Congress may be electorally motivated, but are they in a position to do anything about it?"[12] After all, if they were unable to work toward reelection, this goal would not be a very useful basis for understanding their behavior. Although individual members of Congress cannot do much to alter national economic or political forces, they can control their own activities in the House or Senate. The importance of the **electoral connection** in explaining the behavior of members of Congress seems especially clear for marginal incumbents constantly trying to shore up their electoral base. But for those from safe districts (which is a large and growing number), why should they worry? Objectively, it looks as though about 90 percent of House members (and a large proportion of senators) are absolutely safe, but incumbents realize that this security is not guaranteed. Even in elections with relatively low turnover, many incumbents are "running scared"; in every election, a few supposedly safe incumbents are unexpectedly defeated, and members tend to think that it could be them the next time around. Mayhew warns, "When we say 'Congressman Smith is unbeatable,' we do not mean that there is nothing he could do that would lose him his seat." As we noted in the Challenging the Conventional Wisdom box in Chapter 8, this means, "'Congressman Smith is unbeatable as long as he continues to do the things that he is doing.'"[13] Members recognize that becoming inattentive to the district, being on the wrong side of a key string of votes, or failing to bring home the district's share of pork could cost them their seat. A potential challenger is always waiting in the wings.

Mayhew outlines three ways that members promote their chances for reelection, each of which helps to shape how members relate to their constituents: advertising, credit claiming, and position taking. **Advertising** does not refer to the thirty-second spots on TV or radio during a campaign but to appeals or appearances without issue content that get the member's name before the public in a favorable way. Advertising includes activities associated with "working the district," such as attending town meetings, appearing on a float in a homecoming parade, going to a local Rotary Club lunch, or sending letters of congratulation for high school graduations, birthdays, or anniversaries. Members of Congress also spend a fair amount of time meeting with constituents in Washington: school groups, tourists, and interest groups flock to their members' offices expecting to see their representative.

The second activity, **credit claiming**, involves the member of Congress taking credit for something of value to the voter—most commonly pork-barrel policies targeted to specific constituents or the district. The goodies must be specific and small-scale enough that the member of Congress may believably claim credit. In

casework Assistance provided by members of Congress to their constituents in solving problems with the federal bureaucracy or addressing other specific concerns.

electoral connection The idea that congressional behavior is centrally motivated by members' desire for reelection.

advertising Actions taken by a member of Congress that are unrelated to government issues but have the primary goal of making a positive impression on the public, like sending holiday cards to constituents and appearing in parades.

credit claiming The acceptance of credit by a member of Congress for legislation that specifically benefits his or her constituents.

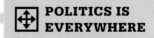

POLITICS IS
EVERYWHERE

position taking Any public statement in which a member of Congress makes his or her views on an issue known to his or her constituents.

other words, it is far less credible to take credit for a national drop in violent crime or an increase in SAT scores than for the renovations at a local veterans' hospital or a highway improvement grant. The other main source of credit claiming is casework for individual constituents who request help with tasks such as tracking down a lost Social Security check or expediting the processing of a passport. This activity, like advertising, has both district-based and Washington-based components.

Position taking refers to any public statement—such as a roll call vote, speech, editorial, or position paper—about a topic of interest to constituents or interest groups. This may be the toughest aspect of a member's job because, on many issues, the member alienates a certain segment of the population no matter what position she takes. Sometimes the congressional leadership tries to structure votes to help members duck some of the most controversial issues, but in many cases, members cannot avoid taking a definitive stance. In the pre-television era, members could present different positions to different audiences, but with a more vigilant press and video coverage of many events, this is no longer common. However, members still try to appeal to specific audiences within their district. For example, while speaking to the Veterans of Foreign Wars, a member might emphasize his support for a particular new weapons program, but in a meeting with college students, he might talk about his opposition to the war in Afghanistan.

The focus on reelection has some costs. One of the reasons Congress has come under such heavy fire in recent years is the perception that it has granted itself too many special privileges specifically aimed at securing reelection (such as funding for large staffs and the franking privilege of sending mail at no cost). Second, some evidence suggests that voters are starting to question the value of pork-barrel spending, even when it is targeted to their district. For example, conservative Republicans who try to bring home the pork while criticizing the government for its huge budget deficits are likely to suffer electoral consequences.[14] Third, members' desire to please means that Congress has a difficult time refusing any group's demands, which may create incoherent and contradictory policies. Fourth, given that most members are experts at getting reelected (typically about 95 to 97 percent of House incumbents are reelected), they achieve a certain level of independence from the party leadership; that is, they do not depend on party leaders for their reelection. This fact contributes to the fragmentation of Congress and creates difficulties for congressional leaders as they attempt to shepherd policies through the legislative maze. Finally, time spent actively campaigning takes time away from the responsibilities of enacting laws and overseeing their implementation. The fact that the average officeholder spends so much time away from formal responsibilities may strike you as a bad thing, and in some sense it is. But remember, incumbents work so hard at "meeting and greeting" because we, the voters, appreciate these activities enough to reward incumbents who do them. So constituents are also somewhat responsible for how incumbents allocate their time.

There is also another more subtle consequence of the electoral connection. Because congressional politics tends to be local, voters are not usually strongly influenced by the president or the national parties, although the president certainly can play a role in congressional elections, as Barack Obama's blitz of competitive House and Senate races demonstrated in 2010. Also, the national economy can have both direct and indirect influences on congressional races. However, the fact that most incumbents can insulate themselves from national forces makes it more difficult to hold the government accountable and may reduce the responsiveness of the political system. Many House and Senate candidates distance themselves from the national party. Recall Chapter 8's discussion of the 2010 West Virginia Senate race in which Democratic candidate Joe Manchin made his opposition to the Democratic Party's energy policy very clear with an ad in which he shoots a mock version of the bill with a rifle. However, as discussed in Chapter 8, in nationalized midterm elections, national issues can overwhelm the

▼ *Some Democrats who were successful in the 2010 elections had to distance themselves from the national party. One example is Joe Manchin, who won a Senate seat by emphasizing that he would fight for the people of West Virginia, even when it meant going against his party.*

incumbents' attempts to insulate themselves. In 2006, many House Republicans tried to distance themselves from President Bush and the unpopular war in Iraq, but more than twenty were defeated. In the 2010 midterms, the same thing happened to moderate Democrats who were ousted by voters who believed the government had gone too far in its response to the recession and health care. These national forces led to a loss of at least sixty House seats and six Senate seats for Democrats in 2010. More than half of the Blue Dog Democrats in the House, including most of those elected in 2006 and 2008, were defeated. National forces in congressional elections also may be evident in presidential years. In 2008, Republicans faced a backlash against Bush, whose approval ratings had hit record lows. Republican members of Congress avoided being seen with him, and Democrats highlighted their opponents' earlier support for the president. Despite the Democrats' efforts to nationalize the election, only fourteen House Republicans were defeated in what could have been a much worse year for their party. Overall, the localized nature of congressional elections and the incumbency advantage promotes congressional stability in the face of presidential change. This has profound implications for governance because it increases the likelihood that the presidency and Congress will be controlled by different parties. This kind of divided government complicates accountability because the president and Congress have become adept at blaming each other when things go wrong.

REDISTRICTING

To understand the context of legislative constituencies, we also must consider their physical boundaries. District boundaries determine who is eligible to vote in any given congressional race, and these boundaries are redrawn every ten years, after each national census. **Redistricting** is the task of state legislatures and its official purpose is to ensure that districts are roughly equal in population, which in turn ensures that every vote counts equally in determining the composition of the legislature. District populations vary over time as people move from state to state or from one part of a state to another. At the national level, states gain or lose legislative seats after each census through a process called **apportionment** as the fixed number of House seats (435) is divided among the states (that is, the states that are growing the fastest, like Arizona, Florida, and Texas, gain seats, and those that are not growing as fast, such as New York, Ohio, and Michigan, lose seats). The one legislature in America that is not redistricted is the U.S. Senate, which by design elects two legislators per state, giving voters in small states more influence than those in large states.

In theory, redistricting proceeds from a firm set of principles that define what districts should look like. One criterion has already been mentioned: districts should be roughly equal in population. Districts should also capture "communities of interest," meaning that they should group like-minded voters into the same district. There are also a variety of technical criteria such as compactness (districts should not have extremely bizarre shapes) and contiguity (one part of a district cannot be completely separated from the rest of the district). Mapmakers also try to respect traditional natural boundaries, avoid splitting municipalities, preserve existing districts, and avoid diluting the voting power of racial minorities.

Although these principles play an important role in redistricting, they are not the driving force in the redistricting process. Just as war is "diplomacy by other means," redistricting is electioneering by other means. Suppose a Democrat holds a state assembly seat from an urban district populated mainly by citizens with strong Democratic Party ties. After a census, the Republican-dominated state legislature develops a new plan that extends the representative's district into the suburbs, claiming that the change counteracts population declines within the city by adding suburban voters. However, these suburban voters will likely be Republicans, increasing the chance

redistricting Redrawing the geographic boundaries of legislative districts. This happens every ten years to ensure that districts remain roughly equal in population.

apportionment The process of assigning the 435 seats in the House to the states based on increases or decreases in state population.

gerrymandering Attempting to use the process of redrawing district boundaries to benefit a political party, protect incumbents, or change the proportion of minority voters in a district.

that the Democrat will face strong opposition in future elections and maybe lose her seat. Such changes have an important impact on voters as well. Voters moved to a new district by a change in boundaries may be unable to vote for the incumbent they have supported for years, instead getting a representative who doesn't share their views.

In congressional redistricting, a reduction in the number of seats allocated to a state can lead to districting plans that put two incumbents in the same district, forcing them to run against each other. Needless to say, incumbents from one party use these opportunities to defeat incumbents from the other party. For example, when Pennsylvania lost two congressional seats after the 2000 census, the Pennsylvania state legislature, with Republican majorities in both houses, created two districts in which Democratic incumbents faced each other in primary elections, thereby increasing the likelihood of a seat shift toward the Republicans. The most dramatic recent example of redistricting for partisan purposes was in Texas. Deviating from the standard practice of redrawing district lines only once every decade, Republicans decided to change the district boundaries that had only been in effect for one election. Democratic legislators were outraged by the partisan power grab and literally fled the state (they hid out in Oklahoma) to prevent the special session of the legislature from convening. Eventually Republicans were able to implement their plan and gain five House seats in the 2004 elections. The Supreme Court upheld the Texas plan, saying that even when partisan advantage is the only motivation for redistricting, this does not make the resulting plan unconstitutional (however, the Court left the door open for future challenges under the equal protection clause of the 14th Amendment).[15] These challenges are likely to emerge in 2012, after the first round of elections that reflect the population changes accounted for in the 2010 census.

These attempts to use the redistricting process for political advantage are called **gerrymandering**, after Elbridge Gerry, a Massachusetts House member and governor, vice president under James Madison, and author of one of the original partisan redistricting plans (including a district with a thin, winding shape resembling a salamander). In addition to the partisan gerrymanders discussed above, there are several other types outlined in Nuts and Bolts 10.1.

NUTS AND BOLTS

10.1

Types of Gerrymanders

Partisan gerrymanders: Elected officials from one party draw district lines that benefit candidates from their party and hurt candidates from other parties. This usually occurs when one party has majorities in both houses of the state legislature and occupies the governorship, and can therefore enact redistricting legislation without votes from the minority party.

Incumbent gerrymanders: Lines are drawn to benefit the current group of incumbents. This usually occurs when control of state government is divided between parties and support from both parties is required to enact a districting plan, or when plans must be approved by judges or bipartisan panels.

Racial gerrymanders: Redistricting is used to help or hurt the chances of minority legislative candidates. The Voting Rights Act (VRA) of 1965 mandated that districting plans for many parts of the South be approved by the U.S. Department of Justice or a Washington, DC, district court. Subsequent interpretation of the 1982 VRA amendments and Supreme Court decisions led to the creation of districts in which racial minorities are in the majority. The original aim of these majority-minority districts was to raise the percentage of African American and Latino elected officials. However, Republicans in some southern states have used this requirement to enact plans that elect minorities (who tend to be Democrats) in some districts but favor Republicans in adjoining districts.

Candidate gerrymanders: District plans that favor certain individuals, particularly state legislators planning to run for the U.S. House. For example, a Republican state legislator would want to construct a congressional district with a high percentage of Republican voters and as many of his current constituents as possible.

FIGURE 10.4 NORTH CAROLINA REDISTRICTING, 1992

This set of House districts was the subject of the landmark Supreme Court ruling *Shaw v. Reno* (1993), in which the Court said that "appearances matter" when drawing district lines. Do you agree? Should other factors such as race, party, and competitiveness play a greater role than district shape?

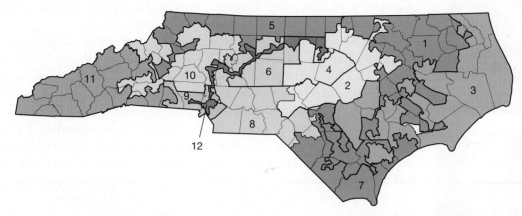

SOURCE: North Carolina General Assembly, 1992 Congressional Base Plan No. 10, available at www.ncga.state.nc.us/Redistricting/Archives/Defuncan10/92BP10_Map_ Detail.pdf.

Redistricting may yield boundaries that look highly unusual, even bizarre. Consider the 1992 redistricting in North Carolina, where the Justice Department told state legislators that they needed to create two districts with majority populations of minority voters (called majority-minority districts). Figure 10.4 shows the plan they enacted, in which the district boundaries look like a pattern of spider webs and ink blots. The most unusual was the 12th District, known as the "I-85 district," which began in Charlotte, proceeded up interstate I-85 to Greensboro, picked up some voters there, then followed the highway to Durham, where it gained additional voters. The strangest aspect of this plan was that in some areas the district was only as wide as I-85 itself, following the highway off an exit ramp, over a bridge, and down the entrance ramp on the other side. This unusual move prevented the I-85 district from bisecting the district through which it was traveling, which would have violated the state law requiring contiguous districts.

The North Carolina example shows how convoluted redistricting plans can become. Part of the complexity is due to the availability of census databases that allow line-drawers to divide voters as closely as they want, moving neighborhood by neighborhood, even house by house when developing their plans. Why bother with this level of detail? Redistricting influences who gets elected. Put another way, redistricting is not an academic exercise; it is active politicking in its most fundamental form. The North Carolina plan was ultimately declared unconstitutional by the Supreme Court—a ruling that opened the door for dozens of lawsuits about racial redistricting. The current legal standard after a decade-long series of cases is that race cannot be the predominant factor in drawing congressional district lines, but it may be a factor. However, there is still plenty of room to create districts that have profound political consequences.

The obvious political implications of redistricting often lead to demands that district plans be prepared or approved by nonpartisan committees or by panels of judges who are theoretically immune from political pressure. Some states such as Iowa have such requirements, but even districts drawn by unelected people have political consequences. For example, a plan that minimizes changes to district lines typically helps incumbents retain districts that they know they can win.

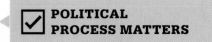

POLITICAL PROCESS MATTERS

▲ Unfortunately, members of Congress do include some of the "criminal class" noted by Mark Twain. Former representatives Randy "Duke" Cunningham (R-CA), shown with his wife Nancy (left), and William Jefferson (D-LA) are both serving time in federal prison.

CONGRESS'S IMAGE PROBLEM

Despite members' strong links to their constituents, efforts to secure reelection, and districts that are designed in their favor, public approval of Congress is generally very low. Bashing Congress has long been a favorite national pastime. Mark Twain said, "It could probably be shown by facts and figures that there is no distinctly native criminal class except Congress." He also said, "Assume you are a fool. Now assume you are a member of Congress . . . but I repeat myself."

Many Americans seem to agree with Twain. Approval of Congress rarely tops 50 percent (the most recent exception was following the terrorist attacks of September 11, 2001, as the public rallied behind all national institutions; support for Congress skyrocketed to 84 percent in one poll, with most polls in the 60 to 67 percent range). Through most of 2010, approval for Congress hovered in the low twenties and was only 19 percent before election day in November. The public's cynical view of Congress runs deep. Well over half of all Americans agree with statements such as "The government is pretty much run by a few big interests looking out for themselves." An NBC/*Wall Street Journal* poll found that 23 percent of respondents thought that "very few" members of Congress are "honest and trustworthy in their conduct," and another 18 percent thought that "fewer than half" of members were honest. An even more telling poll conducted by Fox News asked, "In general, which of the following do you think better describes most senators and representatives on Capitol Hill these days? (a) Statesmen doing service for their country; (b) Petty politicians fighting for personal gain." Only 17 percent answered "statesmen," and 63 percent said "petty politicians" (the rest said "mixed" or "unsure"). Another poll found that members of Congress landed fifth from the bottom in a ranking of twenty-six professions in terms of perceived honesty and ethical standards. Only 14 percent of the public said that members of Congress had "very high" or "high" standards, which placed them just ahead of stockbrokers, insurance salesmen, advertisers, and car salesmen.[16]

Why does Congress have such an image problem? Some of the abuse heaped on Congress is self-inflicted. Although political corruption for personal gain is rare in Congress (only four members have been indicted on bribery charges since 1981), there are periodic scandals such as the "check bouncing" incident involving members' accounts at the House bank and the misuse of House post office funds in the early 1990s, or public outrage over large pay increases for members of Congress.[17] More recently, Charles Rangel (D-NY) was accused of violating thirteen House rules, including failure to report rental income and going on corporate-sponsored trips. Rangel stepped down as Ways and Means committee chair in March 2010. Several members of Congress, Democrats and Republicans alike, were implicated in the scandal surrounding lobbyist Jack Abramoff (see Chapter 9). Mark Foley (R-FL) brought more shame on the House when his steamy e-mails to sixteen-year-old House pages were revealed. Foley quickly resigned when his inappropriate behavior was exposed, but the scandal had important implications for the 2006 midterm elections. Other sex scandals involved Senator Larry Craig (R-ID), who pled guilty to a "disorderly conduct" charge for an apparent attempt to solicit sex in a men's bathroom in the Minneapolis airport, and Senator John Ensign (R-NV), who had an affair with a campaign staffer who was the wife of Ensign's administrative assistant. The two most serious recent cases involved bribery. Randy "Duke" Cunningham (R-CA) was convicted of accepting $2.4 million in bribes and illegal gifts from a defense contractor, including a Rolls Royce, valuable rugs and antiques, and $700,000 in a fraudulent house deal, and is serving an eight-year jail term.[18] Representative William Jefferson (D-LA) was found guilty on eleven charges, including soliciting bribes, money laundering, and using his office as a racketeering enterprise, and was sentenced to the stiffest jail term ever imposed on a member of Congress (thirteen

WHAT WE DID THIS SUMMER
by
Congress

The end.

▲ *Poking fun at Congress's inability to get anything done is typical of the negative light in which the institution is often portrayed in political cartoons.*

years). Jefferson was infamous for being caught with $90,000 in marked bills hidden in his freezer that the FBI said were to be used to bribe Nigerian officials. Yet, despite all of these high-profile scandals, most members of Congress are dedicated public servants who work hard for their constituents.

Media Influences Although it is a time-worn tradition for politicians to blame the media for their poor standing in the polls, in this instance there is some basis for the complaints. One study examined stories on Congress in various national newspapers and magazines during ten important political periods between 1946 and 1992 and concluded that coverage of Congress has always been somewhat superficial and negative. The study concluded that "press coverage of Congress focuses on scandal, partisan rivalry, and interbranch conflict rather than the more complex subjects such as policy, process, and institutional concerns."[19] From this perspective, the professional context of journalism, with its short news cycle and the need to produce a salable product, creates pressure for superficial coverage that perpetuates Congress's image problem. Burdett Loomis, a congressional scholar, bets his students every year that they cannot find a post-1970 political cartoon that depicts Congress in an unambiguously positive light. In more than ten years, no student has been able to collect on the bet.[20] However, a more recent study that examined more than 8,000 newspaper stories on members of Congress over a two-year period found that 70 percent of news stories were neutral, and of the 30 percent that had some spin, positive stories outnumbered negative stories five to one. Letters to the editor and editorials or opinion pieces were evenly balanced between negative and positive viewpoints.[21]

The Responsibility–Responsiveness Dilemma Congress's image problem isn't simply a matter of negative media coverage or a cynical public. It is rooted in the basic representational conflicts that arise from Congress's dual roles discussed previously: responsibility for national policy making and responsiveness to local constituencies.[22] This duality may make members of Congress appear to be simultaneously small-minded seekers of meaningless symbolic legislation and great leaders who debate important issues. Indeed, the range of issues that

Party versus Principle

One source of the public's low regard for Congress is the widespread perception that Congress is dominated by partisan politics. The conventional wisdom generally maintains that Congress is ruled by party rather than principle (or other influences on members' behavior). As we discuss later in this chapter, there is some good evidence to support that view. Levels of party unity (a measure of how strongly the parties stay together on votes that divide the two parties) and party polarization (see the What Do Political Scientists Do? box on p. 374) are at their highest levels since the turn of the twentieth century.

This seemed especially true in the 111th Congress (2009–2010) as Republicans adopted a policy of stopping President Obama and the Democratic Congress's agenda. In 2008, Obama campaigned on a theme of "change," which included altering the tone of partisan politics in Washington.

Obviously, "right wingers" would not literally cheer at the prospect of the earth being vaporized. However, the cartoon captures the conventional wisdom that Republicans in Congress gain political advantage when President Obama (and the Democrats) fail.

▲ *Members of Congress try to keep the "folks back home" happy with projects like this groundbreaking ceremony in St. Louis for a $670 million Mississippi River bridge connecting Illinois and Missouri.*

gridlock An inability to enact legislation because of partisan conflict within Congress or between Congress and the president.

Congress must address is vast, from taxes and health care reform to overseeing the classification of black-eyed peas; from authorizing the war with Afghanistan and expanding free trade to declaring a National Cholesterol Education Month. (The latter is an example of commemorative legislation, which now comprises about half of the laws Congress enacts.) Part of the national frustration with Congress, then, arises because we want our representatives to be responsible *and* responsive; we want them to be great national leaders *and* take care of our local and even, at times, personal concerns. But often it is impossible to satisfy both of these demands at the same time—difficult choices have to be made between being responsive or responsible. Rather than understanding these issues as inherent in the legislative process, we often accuse members of **gridlock** and partisan bickering when our conflicting demands are not met (see the Challenging Conventional Wisdom box for an alternative view). For example, public opinion polls routinely show that the public wants lower taxes, more spending in many areas (such as education, the environment, and health care), and balanced budgets, but those three things cannot happen simultaneously. We often expect the impossible from Congress and then are frustrated when it doesn't happen.

The responsibility–responsiveness dilemma brings us back to the puzzle posed at the beginning of this section: Why is there a persistent 30 to 40 percent gap between approval ratings for individual members and for the institution? As one of the leading congressional scholars of the twentieth century, Richard Fenno, put it,

Despite Democratic efforts to reach out to Republicans on major legislation in 2009–2010, attempts at bipartisanship have largely failed. On the $787 billion stimulus package, Democrats included $288 billion of tax cuts, even though they would have preferred more spending to stimulate the economy. On health care reform, Democrats negotiated with key Republicans in the Senate for the better part of a year, dropping the "public option" (which was favored by a majority of Democrats) and focusing attention on rooting out fraud in Medicaid among other concessions to Republicans. In return, no Republicans in the House and only three senators voted for the stimulus package; no Republican senators and only one House member voted for health care reform. The low point may have come in October 2009, when many Republican leaders and media commentators cheered the failed bid by Chicago to host the 2016 Olympics. Obama had lobbied heavily for the bid, including a last-minute trip to Copenhagen to make an appeal to the Olympic committee. Republicans labeled this episode an Obama failure, inspiring the cartoon seen here.

However, the conventional wisdom oversimplifies a much more complicated picture. In a provocative article entitled "Where's the Party?," a leading congressional scholar, Keith Krehbiel, argues that congressional politics can be accurately explained without including parties at all.[a] Instead, what appears to be partisan behavior is actually members acting on the basis of their own preferences. This argument spawned a huge debate over the next fifteen years. Clearly, parties still matter in Congress, but it is equally clear that what is often mistaken for partisan behavior may actually be caused by other factors. Political scientist Gary Jacobson contributed to the debate by showing that the increased partisan polarization of Congress may be partly explained by increasingly polarized constituencies.[b] Therefore, members of Congress may be acting partisan not because of pressure from party leaders but because their constituents want them to behave in that manner.

Finally, members of Congress often disagree because of sincere differences in what they think would be best for the country, rather than partisan gain. When Obama sat down with Republican and Democratic congressional leaders for the day-long "health care summit" early in 2010, it was readily apparent that a gulf divided the parties in terms of what they viewed as the best approach to health care reform. Republicans wanted a much more incremental, market-based approach that would tackle relatively small parts of the problem, such as coverage for preexisting conditions and for children. Democrats pushed for a more comprehensive approach, arguing that the incremental strategy had failed. Both parties firmly believed that their view was correct, and each was rooted in basic philosophical, principled positions on the proper role of government.

Thus, rather than the conventional wisdom of partisan politics in Congress, the more complete and complex picture reveals a Congress that is driven by a mixture of partisan politics, constituency pressure, personal preferences, and differences in principles. ∎

"If Congress is the 'broken branch,' how come we love our congressman so much?"[23] The answer may simply be that members of Congress tend to respond more to their constituents' demands than take on the responsibility of solving national problems. And when Congress becomes embroiled in debates about constituencies' conflicting demands, the institution may appear ineffectual. But as long as members of Congress keep the "folks back home" happy, their individual popularity will remain high. The next section describes the ways in which members use this and other techniques to cultivate an incumbency advantage.

The Incumbency Advantage and Its Sources

The desire to be reelected influences House members' and senators' behavior both in the district and in Congress. Take, for example, the early career of Representative Tammy Baldwin (D-WI). In 1998 she became the first woman from Wisconsin and the first openly gay person ever elected to a freshman term in Congress.[24] In her first two elections, she won with the overwhelming support of liberal voters in Madison but lost the surrounding rural areas and suburbs, narrowly winning district-wide

▲ *Representative Tammy Baldwin (D-WI) meets with students at Edgewood High School in Madison, Wisconsin. This type of constituent meeting is an important way for incumbents to strengthen bonds to the district, or in this specific case to educate a group of future voters about the legislative process.*

with 52.5 percent and 51 percent of the vote. Baldwin recognized that she needed to shore up support outside Madison and spent considerable time over the next several years meeting with constituents in the rural and suburban parts of her district. She also spent a great deal of time on issues important to these voters, such as the dairy price support program and the problem of chronic wasting disease, which had infected Wisconsin deer. Having shored up her electoral base (and having benefited from favorable redistricting in 2002), she cruised to victories in her next two elections with 66 percent and 63 percent of the vote.

This story has been repeated hundreds of times across the country, and members' success at pleasing constituents has produced large rewards. As Figure 10.5 shows, very few members are defeated in their reelection races. One way that political scientists have documented the growth of **incumbency advantage** is to examine the electoral margins in House elections. If a member is elected with less than 55 percent of the vote, he or she is said to hold a marginal seat. Since the late 1960s, the number of marginal districts has been declining. Having fewer marginal districts does not necessarily translate into fewer incumbent defeats, but in the past two decades, incumbent reelection rates have been near record-high levels.[25] Even in 1992 and 1994, when there was a strong anti-incumbent mood in the nation, 93 percent of the incumbents who ran were reelected. In the 2004 general elections, only seven House incumbents were defeated—more than a 98 percent success rate—and four of them lost because of the partisan Texas redistricting. In 2006, the reelection rate was down a bit, but 94 percent of House incumbents (and all the Democratic incumbents) were reelected. In 2008, undoubtedly a historic election and one that many called "transformational," 95 percent of House incumbents were reelected. Although the Democrats picked up some seats in the Senate, reelection remained the norm there as well. Even in the "tsunami" election of 2010, in which Republicans made the largest gains in the House since 1948 in picking up at least sixty seats, 86 percent of incumbents were elected. Only two Senate incumbents were defeated in the November 2010 elections, but three others lost primary elections (one of those, Lisa Murkowski of Alaska, won back her seat as a write-in candidate, the first to do so since Strom Thurmond in 1954). Why are incumbents so successful? Scholars have offered several reasons for this increase in incumbency advantage.

incumbency advantage The relative infrequency with which members of Congress are defeated in their attempts for reelection.

FIGURE 10.5A HOUSE INCUMBENCY REELECTION RATES, 1948–2010

The rate of defeat for incumbent House members is very low, typically in the 5 to 10 percent range, while total turnover is quite a bit higher. Which data are more central for debates about the importance of term limits? Which data are more central to discussions of electoral accountability?

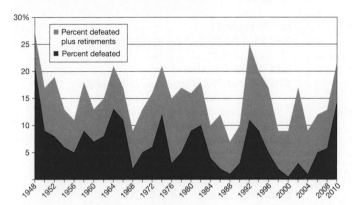

FIGURE 10.5B SENATE INCUMBENCY REELECTION RATES, 1948–2010*

Incumbency reelection rates are noticeably more volatile in the Senate than in the House. What implications does this have for the Founders' belief that the Senate should be more insulated from popular control than the House? Does the Senate's six-year term help provide that insulation?

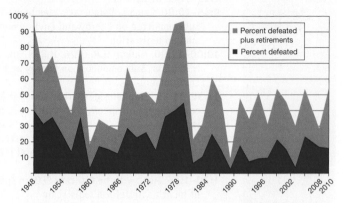

*Percentage for the Senate is of those up for reelection.

SOURCE: Compiled from Center for Responsive Politics, Reelection Rates over the Years, available at www.opensecrets.org/bigpicture/reelect.php; and Norman J. Ornstein, Thomas E. Mann, and Michael J. Malbin, *Vital Statistics on Congress: 1999–2000* (Washington, DC: CQ Press, 2000), pp. 60–63. 2010 percentages calculated from election results available at http://elections.nytimes.com/2010/results/house/big-board.

IN THE DISTRICT: HOME STYLE

One explanation for increasing incumbency advantage is directly rooted in the diversity of congressional districts and states. Members typically respond to the diversity in their districts by developing an appropriate home style: a way of relating to the district.[26] More specifically, a home style shapes the way members allocate resources, the way incumbents present themselves to others, and the way they explain their policy positions.

Given the variation among districts, it makes sense that members' home styles vary as well. In some rural districts it is important for representatives to have local roots, and voters expect extensive contact with members. Candidates who relocate from other areas rarely succeed in such districts. Urban districts expect a different kind of style. They have a more mobile population so it is not crucial to be home-grown. Voters tend to expect less direct contact and place more emphasis on how members explain their policy positions. Incumbency advantage may be explained in part by the skill with which members have cultivated their individual home styles in the last two decades. Members are spending more time at home and less time in Washington than was true a generation ago. This familiarity with the voters has certainly helped members remain in office, though a concrete measure of this variable is difficult to develop.

Nuts and Bolts 10.2 provides an example of how one member, Representative Tammy Baldwin, spends her time in Washington and in her district. In general, a legislator's workday in the Capitol is split between committee meetings, briefings, staff meetings, meetings with constituents, and various dinners and fund-raisers with interest groups and other organizations, punctuated by dashes to the floor of the House or Senate to vote. Days in the district are spent meeting with constituents to explain what is happening in Washington and listen to voters' concerns.

Typical Work Days for Representative Tammy Baldwin (D-WI)

IN WASHINGTON, DC
(Votes scheduled throughout the day)
9:15–9:45 Office time
9:45–10:00 Caucus, Democratic members, Subcommittee on Energy and Environment on markup legislation
10:00–12:00 Markup H.R. 3276, H.R. 3258, H.R. 2868, Subcommittee on Energy and Environment
11:30–11:45 Step outside markup to meet with constituents on specifics of health care reform legislation
12:00–12:15 Travel to Department of Justice
12:15–1:15 Lunch with Attorney General Eric Holder
1:30–1:45 Meet with health care CEO on specifics of health care reform legislation
2:00–3:00 Meet with members who support single-payer health care amendment
3:00–4:30 Markup H.R. 3792, Subcommittee on Health
4:30–5:30 Office time
5:30–6:00 Caucus, Democratic members, Energy and Commerce Committee on financial services bill
6:00–6:30 Meet with legislative staff
6:30–7:00 Meet with chief of staff

7:00–7:50 Office time
8:00–10:00 Dinner with chief of staff and political adviser

IN THE DISTRICT
7:00 ET–8:00 CT Fly from Washington, DC, to Madison, WI
8:15–10:30 Free time at home
10:30–10:40 Phone interview with area radio station on constituent survey, health care reform, and upcoming listening session
12:15–12:25 Travel to office
12:25–1:05 Office time, edit/sign correspondence
1:00–1:20 Travel to Madison West High School
1:30–1:55 Remarks at school plaza dedication ceremony
2:00–2:30 Travel to Stoughton, WI
2:45–5:00 Listening session (originally scheduled for one hour but continued until all present could speak)
5:00–5:40 Travel home
5:15–5:20 Phone interview with University of Wisconsin student radio station
6:15–6:45 Travel to Middleton, WI
7:00–8:00 Attend and give brief remarks at NAACP annual banquet
8:05–8:25 Travel home

Note: The authors would like to thank Representative Tammy Baldwin and her press secretary, Jerilyn Goodman, for sharing this information. Ms. Goodman emphasized that there really isn't a "typical day" for the member but said that these two days illustrate the work load.

CAMPAIGN FUND-RAISING

Raising money is also key to staying in office. Thomas "Tip" O'Neill, Speaker of the House in the 1970s and 1980s, used to say that "money is the mother's milk of politics." Incumbents need money to pay for campaign staff, travel, and advertising. It takes at least $1 million to make a credible challenge to an incumbent in most districts, and in many areas with expensive media markets the minimum price tag is $2 million or more (the average amount spent by a successful challenger in 2008 was nearly $2 million). Few challengers can raise that much money. The gap between incumbent and challenger spending has grown dramatically in the past decade, and incumbents now spend about 3 times as much, on average, as challengers. Incumbents have far greater potential to raise vast sums of money when it is needed, in part because political action committees (PACs) are typically unwilling to risk alienating an incumbent by donating to challengers. (For more details on campaign finance, including the changing role of PACs, see Chapters 8 and 9).

Money also functions as a deterrent to potential challengers. A sizeable reelection fund signals that an incumbent knows how to raise money (and could likely raise more) and will run a strong campaign. The aim is to convince would-be challengers that they have a slim chance of beating the incumbent—and to convince

contributors and party organizations that there's no point in trying to find or support a challenger.

This last point is crucial in explaining incumbency advantage because it is nearly impossible to beat an incumbent with a weak challenger. Political scientists Gary Jacobson and Samuel Kernell illustrate this point with a story about Representative Robert Leggett of California. Leggett was a principal target of the 1976 "Koreagate" investigation (a scandal involving several House members), but he was not considered vulnerable enough for any strong Republicans to challenge him. They note, "By the time it came out that he had fathered two children by an aide, had been supporting two households for years, and even forged his wife's name on a deed for the second house, the nominations had already been set. His Republican opponent was an obscure, retired state civil servant who thought that the outcome of the election 'was mostly up to God' and spent only $10,674 on the election."[27] Leggett managed to hang onto his seat for one more term. The moral of the story is that you cannot beat somebody with nobody. Only 10 to 15 percent of challengers in a typical election year have any previous elective experience; when such a high proportion of challengers are amateurs, it is not surprising so many incumbents win.

CONSTITUENCY SERVICE

In addition to cultivating a home style and raising money, another thing incumbents do to get reelected is to "work their districts," taking every opportunity to meet with their constituents, listen to their concerns, and perform casework, helping constituents interact with government programs or agencies. Most legislators travel around their districts or states with several staffers whose job is to follow in the incumbent's wake, talk to people who have met the incumbent, and write down contact information and what the incumbent has promised to do. High levels of constituency service may help explain why some incumbents have become electorally secure.

Members of Congress love doing constituency service because it is an easy way to make voters happy. If a member can help a constituent solve a problem, that person will be more likely to support the member in the future.[28] Many voters might give the incumbent some credit simply for being willing to listen, even if the member cannot help solve their problem. Therefore, most members devote a significant portion of their staff to constituency service, publish newsletters that tout their good deeds on behalf of constituents, and solicit citizens' requests for help through their newsletters and Web sites. Most House members have a link on their home page that says something like "How can I help?" with links to different categories such as government agencies, grants, internships, service academies, and visiting Washington, DC.

Most House members work their districts to an extreme; they are said to be in the "Tuesday to Thursday Club," meaning they are only in Washington during the middle of the week, spending the rest of their time at home in their districts. These members go from diner to diner on Saturday mornings to chat over coffee, spend the day at public events in their "Meet Your Representative" RV, then hit the bowling alleys at night to meet a few more people. One member has even joked that his wife has given up sending him out for groceries because he spends three hours talking with people while getting a loaf of bread.

This combination of factors means that incumbents have a lot of built-in advantages over candidates who might run against them. By virtue of their position, they can help constituents who have problems with an agency or program. They attract media attention because of their actions in office; small local newspapers will even

POLITICS IS
EVERYWHERE

reprint members' press releases verbatim because they do not have the resources to do their own reporting. Members can use the money and other resources associated with their position for casework and contact with voters (trips home to their district and the salaries of their staffers who do constituency service are taxpayer-funded). And they use their official position as a platform for raising campaign cash. A contributor who donates as a way to gain access to the policy-making process will be inclined to give to someone already in office. Finally, most incumbents represent states or districts whose partisan balance, the number of likely supporters of their party versus the number likely to prefer the other party, is skewed in their favor—if it wasn't, they probably wouldn't have won the seat in the first place.

The Structure of Congress

Much of the structure of Congress is set up to meet the electoral needs of its members. David Mayhew's key observation supporting this idea is that very little of what it takes to get reelected involves zero-sum processes, in which one person's gain is another's loss. If the institution were more zero-sum, then there would be more competition and rivalry. Instead, norms of universalism, reciprocity, and specialization, defined below, still dominate. There are several aspects of the structure of Congress that facilitate members' reelection, including informal structures (norms) and formal structures (staff, the committee system, parties, and the leadership).

Despite the importance of the electoral connection, the goal of being reelected cannot explain everything about members' behavior and the congressional structure. This section examines some other explanations for the way Congress is set up: the policy motivations of members, the partisan basis for congressional institutions, and the informational advantages of the committee system.

INFORMAL STRUCTURES

Various norms provide an informal structure for the way that Congress works. **Universalism** is a norm stating that when benefits are being divided up, as many districts and states as possible should benefit. Thus, when it comes to handing out federal highway dollars or expenditures for the Pentagon's weapons programs, the benefits are broadly distributed across the entire country, which means that votes in support of these bills tend to be very lopsided. For example, the $636.3 billion 2010 defense appropriations bill contained some spending in every part of the country and passed by an 88-to-10 vote in the Senate and a 395-to-34 margin in the House.[29]

Another norm, **reciprocity**, reinforces universalism with the idea that "if you scratch my back, I'll scratch yours." This norm (also called logrolling) leads members of Congress to support bills that they otherwise might not vote for in exchange for another member's vote on a bill that is very important to them. For example, a House member from a dairy state might vote for tobacco price supports even if there are no tobacco farmers in his state, and in return, he would expect a member from the tobacco state to vote for the dairy price support bill. This norm can produce the wasteful pork-barrel spending already discussed. For example, in 2010 a $447 billion omnibus appropriations bill contained more than 5,200 **earmarks** worth $3.9 billion, so nearly everyone gained something by passing it.[30] The You Decide box describes some of the fierce debates in Congress and among political commentators about the merit of this type of spending.[31]

universalism The informal congressional norm of distributing the benefits of legislation in a way that serves the interests of as many states and districts as possible.

reciprocity The informal congressional norm whereby a member votes for a bill that he or she might not otherwise support because a colleague strongly favors it, and in exchange, the colleague votes for a bill that the member feels strongly about (also known as logrolling).

earmarks Federally funded local projects attached to bills passed through Congress.

The Politics of Pork

The infamous "bridge to no-where" in Ketchikan, Alaska, discussed in Chapter 1 is one of the most famous examples of wasteful pork-barrel spending, but it is unusual only in its scale rather than its kind. It is also unusual because the outcry over the bridge prompted Alaska to pull the plug on the project, whereas most pork-barrel spending survives. Pork typically takes the form of earmarked funding for a specific project that is not subjected to standard, neutral spending formulas or a competitive process.

One tactic legislators often use to win approval for pork is to insert it into emergency spending bills that are expected to pass, such as disaster relief for flood and hurricane victims, spending for national security after the September 11 attacks, or funding for the wars in Iraq and Afghanistan. For example, the $636.3 billion 2010 defense appropriations bill included $128.3 billion for the wars in Iraq and Afghanistan and was stuffed with 1,719 earmarks worth $7.6 billion.[a] One controversial earmark was $2.5 billion for ten C-17 transport planes that had not been requested by the Pentagon. Senator John McCain (R-AZ) opposed the earmark, saying that the bill would "fund the purchase of new aircraft that we neither need nor can afford . . . That would have a significant impact on our ability to provide the day-to-day operational funding that our servicemen and women and their families deserve." Other earmarks in that bill included $23 million for the Hawaii Healthcare Network, $18.9 million for the Edward M. Kennedy Institute for the Senate, and $20 million for the National World War II museum in New Orleans.

Some broader definitions of pork include any benefit targeted to a particular political constituency (typically an important business in a member's district or a generous campaign contributor), even if the benefit is part of a stand-alone bill. Examples of this type of targeted federal largesse include the bill that provided federal support to the

Surrounded by members of Congress, President Obama signs the National Defense Authorization Act for 2010. The law included 1,719 earmarks worth $7.6 billion.

airlines after the September 11 attacks, which sailed through Congress without much debate, and the lucrative contracts to rebuild Iraq that were awarded to politically well-connected businesses.

Pork has plenty of critics. Citizens Against Government Waste, one of the most outspoken groups to tackle pork-barrel spending, compiles each year's federal pork-barrel projects into their annual *Pig Book* to draw attention to pork. Representative Dave Obey (D-WI) and Senator John McCain (R-AZ), among others, have been trying to get Congress to cut back on earmarks. The arguments against pork are especially urgent during a time of massive budget deficits. According to this view, the national interest in a balanced budget should take priority over localized projects.

However, some argue that pork is the "glue of legislating," because these small side-payments secure the passage of larger bills. If it takes a little pork for the home district or state in order to get important

legislation through Congress, so be it. The motives of budget reform groups that call for greater fiscal discipline in Congress may also be questioned, since many of these groups oppose government spending in general—not just on pork. In some cases, policies they identify as pork have significant national implications: military readiness, road improvements to support economic infrastructure, or the development of new agricultural and food products. National interests can be served, in other words, by allowing local interests to take a dip into the pork barrel. Put another way, "pork is in the eye of the beholder," or one person's pork is another person's essential spending. Finally, defenders of pork point out that even according to the critics' own definition, pork spending constitutes less than 1 percent of the total federal budget. If you were a member of Congress, would you work hard to deliver pork to your district or work to eliminate as much pork as you could from the budget? ■

The norm of **specialization** is also important, both for the efficient operation of Congress and for members' reelection. By specializing and becoming an expert on a given issue, members provide valuable information to the institution as a whole and also create a basis for credit claiming. This norm is stronger in the House where members often develop a few areas of expertise, whereas senators tend to be policy generalists. For example, Representative Henry Waxman (D-CA) has dedicated much of his decades-long House career to the issue of health care, while Senator John McCain (R-AZ) has had his hand in a wide variety of issues, including campaign finance and lobbying reform, tax policy, telecommunications and aviation issues, national defense, foreign policy, and immigration policy.

The **seniority** norm also serves individual and institutional purposes. This norm holds that the member with the longest service on a committee will chair the committee. Although there have been numerous violations of the seniority norm in the past thirty years, whereby the most senior member is passed over for someone favored by the party leaders, the norm benefits the institution by providing for orderly succession in committee leadership.[32] The norm also benefits members by providing a tangible reason why voters should return them to Congress year after year. Many members of Congress make this point when campaigning, and the issue is more than just posturing. Committee chairs *are* better able to "bring home the bacon" than a junior member who is still learning where the bathrooms are. For example, Don Young, the former Transportation Committee chair in the House, was able to secure funding for the infamous "bridge to nowhere" in Alaska described in Chapter 1 (they were even going to name the connecting highway Don Young Way).

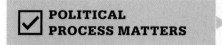

POLITICAL PROCESS MATTERS

FORMAL STRUCTURES

Parties and Party Leaders Political parties are important for allocating power in Congress. Party leaders are always elected on straight party-line votes, and committee leadership, the division of seats on committees, and the allocation of committee resources are all determined by the majority party. Parties in Congress also become more important when the two chambers are controlled by opposing parties, as was the case between 1981 and 1987 when Republicans controlled the Senate and Democrats controlled the House, and in part of 2001 and 2002 when the opposite was true.

A leading theory of congressional organization points to the importance of parties in solving collective action problems in Congress. Without parties the legislative process would be much more fractured and decentralized because members would be autonomous agents in battle with each other. Parties provide a team framework that allows members to work together for broadly beneficial goals. Just think how difficult it would be for a member of Congress to get a bill passed if she had to build a coalition from scratch every time. Instead, parties provide a solid base from which coalition building may begin. As discussed in Chapter 7, political parties provide the collective good of brand name recognition for members.

The top party leader in the House—and the only House leader mentioned in the Constitution—is the **Speaker of the House**, who influences the legislative agenda, committee assignments, scheduling, and overall party strategy. The Democratic Party made history in January 2007, when they elected Nancy Pelosi as the first woman to serve as Speaker. The Speaker is aided by the **majority leader**, the majority whip, and the caucus chair (in addition to many other lower-level party positions). The majority leader is one of the national spokespersons for the party and also helps with the day-to-day operation of the legislative process. The majority whip oversees the extensive **whip system**, which has three important functions: information

specialization The expertise of a member of Congress on a specific issue or area of policy. Specialization is more common in the House than the Senate, where members tend to be policy generalists.

seniority The informal congressional norm of choosing the member who has served the longest on a particular committee to be the committee chair.

Speaker of the House The elected leader of the House of Representatives.

majority leader The elected head of the party holding the majority of seats in the House or Senate.

whip system An organization of House leaders who work to disseminate information and promote party unity in voting on legislation.

▲ Party leadership is central in the legislative process. Following the overwhelming victory in the 2010 midterm elections that swept their party to power, Republicans John Boehner (R-OH) and Eric Cantor (R-VA) met to talk about strategy for the upcoming Congress. Boehner became the Speaker and Cantor the House Majority Leader in January 2011.

gathering, information dissemination, and coalition building. The whips meet regularly to discuss legislative strategy and scheduling. The whips then pass along this information to colleagues in their respective parties and indicate the party's position on a given bill. Whips also take a headcount of party members in the House on specific votes and communicate this information to the party leaders.

If a vote looks close, whips try to persuade members to support the party's position (the term "whip" comes from the term "whipper-in" from English fox hunts, the person responsible for making sure that the hounds did not wander too far from the pack; similarly, party whips try to ensure that members do not stray too far from the party position). The caucus chair (or the conference chair for the Republicans) runs the party meetings to elect floor leaders, make committee assignments, and set legislative agendas. The minority party in the House has a parallel structure: their leader is the **minority leader** and the second in command is the minority whip.

The Senate leadership does not have as much power as that of the House, mostly because individual senators have more power than House members because of the Senate's rule of unlimited debate. The majority leader and minority leader are the leaders of their respective parties, and those second in command are the assistant majority and minority leaders. The Senate also has a whip system, but it is not as developed as the House system. Republicans have a separate position for the conference chair, while the Democratic leader serves also as conference chair. The country's vice president is officially the president of the Senate, but he only appears in the chamber when needed to cast a tie-breaking vote. The Constitution also mentions the **president pro tempore** of the Senate, whose formal duties involve presiding over the Senate when the vice president is not there. This is typically the most senior member of the majority party, and the position does not have any real power (in fact, the actual president pro tempore rarely presides over the Senate, and the task is typically given to a more junior senator).

Political parties in Congress also reflect the individualism of the institution. Compared to parliamentary systems, U.S. congressional parties are very weak (see Comparing Ourselves to Others). They do not impose a party line or penalize members who vote against the party. Indeed, they have virtually no ability to impose electoral restrictions (such as denying the party's nomination) on renegade members. Thus, from the perspective of a member seeking reelection, parties are more useful for what they are not—they do not force members to vote with the party—than

minority leader The elected head of the party holding the minority of seats in the House or Senate.

president pro tempore A largely symbolic position usually held by the most senior member of the majority party in the Senate.

FIGURE 10.6A PARTY VOTES IN CONGRESS, 1962–2009

These graphs make two important points. First, partisanship has increased in the last two decades, both in terms of the proportion of party votes and the level of party unity. Second, despite these increased levels of partisanship, only about half of all votes in the House and Senate divide the two parties. Given these potentially conflicting observations, how would you assess the argument that partisanship in Congress is far too intense?

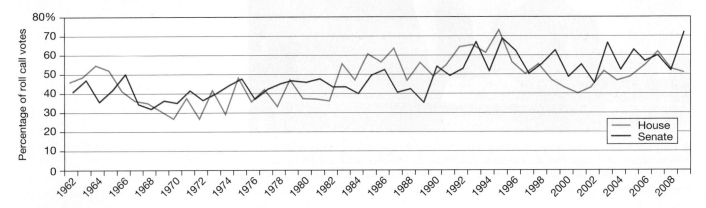

FIGURE 10.6B PARTY UNITY IN CONGRESS, 1962–2009

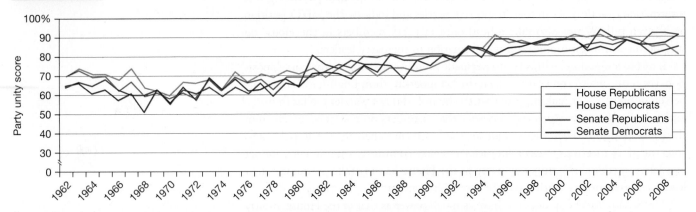

SOURCE: Data from Norman J. Ornstein, Thomas E. Mann, and Michael J. Malbin, *Vital Statistics on Congress: 1999–2000* (Washington, DC: CQ Press, 2000), pp. 201–3 and more recent editions of *Congressional Quarterly Almanac.*

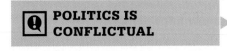

POLITICS IS CONFLICTUAL

roll call vote A recorded vote on legislation; members may vote yes, no, abstain, or present.

party votes A vote in which the majority of one party opposes the position of the majority of the other party.

party unity The extent to which members of Congress in the same party vote together on party votes.

what they are. Though there are significant party differences on many issues, on about half of all **roll call votes**, majorities of both parties are on the same side.

Although still weaker than their overseas counterparts, parties in Congress have greatly strengthened since the 1960s (Figure 10.6). Partisanship—when party members stick together in opposition to the other party—reached its highest levels in the post–World War II era in the mid-1990s. About 70 percent of all roll call votes were **party votes**, in which a majority of one party opposed a majority of the other party. The proportion of party votes has since fallen but remains between 50 and 60 percent; however in 2009 the Senate hit an all-time high since Congressional Quarterly created the measure in 1953 of 72 percent. **Party unity**, the percentage of party members voting together on party votes, soared during this period as well, especially in the House. The Democratic Party has become much more cohesive as southern Democrats have started to vote more like their northern counterparts, partly because of the increasing importance of African American voters in the South and because increasing Republican strength in the South means that remaining Democratic districts are more liberal. Similarly, there are fewer moderates within the Republican Party, as most regions of the country that used to elect them are now electing Democrats.[33] (See the What Do Political Scientists Do? box for an explanation of increasing partisan polarization.)

As discussed in Chapter 7, strong party leadership is referred to as conditional party government, which indicates that strong party government is possible, but conditional on the consent of party members.[34] Leaders' primary responsibility is to get their party's legislative agenda through Congress, but their negative powers are quite limited. The positive powers they have mostly take the form of agenda control and persuasion. Leaders' success largely depends on personal skills, communicative abilities, and trust. Some of the most successful leaders, such as Lyndon Johnson (D-TX), majority leader of the Senate from 1955 to 1961, and Sam Rayburn (D-TX), Speaker of the House for more than seventeen years, kept in touch with key members on a daily basis. Leaders also must have the ability to bargain and compromise. One observer noted, "To Senator Johnson, public policy evidently was an inexhaustibly bargainable product."[35] Such leaders find solutions where none appear possible. Leaders also do favors for members (such as making campaign appearances, helping with fund-raising, contributing to campaigns, helping them get desired committee assignments, or guiding pet projects through the legislative process) to engender a feeling of personal obligation to the leadership when it needs a key vote.

The party's most powerful positive incentives are in the area of campaign finance. In recent years the congressional campaign committees of both parties and the national party organizations have been supplying candidates with money and resources in an attempt to gain more influence in the electoral process. Party leaders may also help arrange a campaign stop or a fund-raiser for a candidate with party leaders or the president. For example, President Obama held dozens of fundraisers for Democrats in 2010, earning him the label of "Fundraiser-in-Chief" from CBS News.[36] Such events typically raise $500,000 to more than $1 million.

Despite these positive reinforcements, members' desire for reelection always comes before party concerns, and leadership rarely tries to force a member to vote against constituents' interests. For example, Democrats from rural areas, where most constituents support gun ownership and many are hunters, would not be expected to vote the party line favoring a gun-control bill. To be disciplined by the party, a member of Congress must do something much more extreme than not supporting them on roll call votes, such as supporting the opposing party's candidate for Speaker or passing strategic information to the opposition.

Two recent examples show that party leaders have limits in terms of how much they will tolerate. Former representative James Traficant of Ohio was a true maverick in the Democratic Party. He often took to the floor to give outrageous speeches, occasionally looking up to the ceiling, holding up his arms, and blurting out, "Beam me up Scottie." In April 2002, Traficant was convicted and eventually jailed for bribery, racketeering, and tax evasion. When the House Ethics Committee was investigating him, his closing statement was,

> I want you to disregard all the opposing counsel has said. I think they are delusionary. I think they've had something funny for lunch in their meal. I think they should be handcuffed to a chain-link fence, flogged, and all of their hearsay evidence should be thrown the hell out. And if they lie again, I am going to go over and kick them in the crotch. Thank you very much.[37]

While he was still fighting the investigation, he voted for the Republican candidate for Speaker, Dennis Hastert. The Democratic Party leadership promptly stripped him of his committee assignments and let him know that he was no

▼ President Barack Obama worked tirelessly as his party's chief fundraiser and campaigner in the 2010 midterm elections. He is shown here at a fundraiser for Senator Barbara Boxer (D-CA), in San Francisco.

Polarization in Congress

The evidence that parties in Congress have become increasingly polarized over the past forty years is not in dispute. Even political scientist Morris Fiorina, who wrote a book with the subtitle *The Myth of a Polarized America*, concedes that Congress is more polarized.[a] What *is* in dispute are the reasons *why* this is the case.

The debate over the causes of polarization in Congress is a good example of an important thing political scientists do: test rival explanations and offer alternatives that seem to explain things better. Testing alternative explanations is the cornerstone of any scientific inquiry and is especially revealing for long-standing questions such as the causes of polarization in Congress. In the What Do Political Scientists Do? box in Chapter 7, we discussed the first political scientist to notice this trend, David Rohde, and his work on parties in Congress. Rohde offered evidence of a shift in the behavior of southern Democrats that became the basis for electorally grounded explanations for

increased polarization in Congress. His initial insights are true, but subsequent work provided a more complete explanation.

The evolution of this topic shows the two distinct phases that most research questions go through: political scientists build on some original work (such as Rohde's) and then begin to offer challenges (often these two phases happen simultaneously rather than sequentially). Researchers have built on the electorally based explanations for polarization by offering three main reasons that Congress has become more polarized: ideological sorting, redistricting, and the nomination process. The first refers to the natural sorting of voters into purer partisan enclaves, which happens when people want to live with others who think like they do. For example, wealthy suburban communities tend to vote Republican; urban, racially diverse communities tend to vote Democratic. There is good evidence that this "big sort" has produced ideological polarization.[b] Redistricting initially seems to be another

Senate Minority Leader Mitch McConnell (R-KY) and Senate Majority Leader Harry Reid (D-NV) in a rare moment of comity. Why has polarization in Congress increased?

longer welcome in the party. Soon after that, Traficant became only the second representative since the Civil War (and only the fifth in U.S. history) to be expelled from the House.

Former senator Jim Jeffords (I-VT) also felt the pinch of party power. In 2001, when Jeffords left the Republican Party to become an independent, he became a hero to the Democratic Party, as his switch gave them control of the Senate. However, when Republicans retook control of the Senate in November 2002, they were in no mood to do any favors for Jeffords (such as allowing him to keep his committee chair). Many in the party viewed him as a traitor and were not interested in extending the olive branch.

Despite these occasional strong-arm tactics, party leaders have moved toward a service-oriented leadership in the last two decades, recognizing that their power is only as strong as the leeway granted by the rank-and-file membership. Within this context, however, leaders can gain a fair amount of power, as demonstrated by Newt Gingrich's reign as Speaker between 1995 and 1999 and Tom DeLay's service as whip and majority leader between 1995 and 2005. Gingrich largely engineered the Republican takeover of the House in 1994, placed his loyalists in top leadership positions, and then tried to push through his Contract with America (a set of promises made to the American people about what Republicans would do if they

appealing explanation for why Congress is more polarized. For example, it is clear that House districts have become far less competitive in the past forty years. Today it is more likely that one party dominates in a given district. Although redistricting would seem to be a plausible explanation (as parties try to make their incumbents more secure), evidence suggests this is not the case. Finally, increasing party influence over the nomination process may produce more polarizing candidates. The recent ouster of Republican senator Robert Bennett in the state party nominating convention is one example of parties implementing a "purity test" on their nominees (that is, any incumbent who works with the other party is vulnerable to a challenge from the more extreme flanks).

All of these strands of research provide some support for Rohde's initial claim, but recent work by University of Texas political scientist Sean Theriault suggests there may be more to the story. He argues that if increased polarization is caused only by electoral forces, polarization should be evident only in those districts that have become more homogenous in partisan and ideological terms. However, he finds that polarization is also evident in moderate, competitive districts. He says, "Democrats representing these moderate constituencies in the mid-2000s have roll call records that

are almost 25 percent more liberal than the Democrats who represented moderate constituencies in the mid-1970s; Republicans in these districts vote 50 percent more conservatively than their 1970s counterparts."[c]

So what explains the remaining variation? Why are House members in competitive districts more polarized now than they were forty years ago and why is the Senate, which is less affected by the "big sort" and completely unaffected by redistricting, also more polarized today? Theriault offers compelling evidence that much of the increased polarization in Congress is due to the larger proportion of procedural votes on legislative process (as opposed to final votes on legislation) in the past three decades. Procedural votes in the House include votes on motions to recommit and on the rules of debate; and in the Senate, on whether amendments will be allowed or on cloture. These votes tend to be much more polarized than votes on final passage because, as we have argued, process in Congress is a powerful force for determining winners and losers. For example, the motion to recommit gives the minority party their last shot at changing a bill. Those votes tend to break down along party lines. If that vote fails, then members of the minority party must either vote for or against the existing bill, and often there is enough they like about the bill that they vote for it,

even if they voted against it in the procedural vote. Thus, votes on final passage are often less polarized than procedural votes.

In subsequent work, Theriault examines the cosponsorship of legislation in the House on 968 bills. If the polarization of Congress is due to substantive differences between the parties, polarization should be evident in cosponsorship (Democrats cosponsor Democratic bills and Republicans cosponsor Republican bills). Indeed, the polarization of cosponsors has increased since the 1970s (thus about 80 percent of cosponsors are from the same party), but that increase is about 25 percent less than the increase in member polarization, which means that procedural polarization probably accounts for the difference.[d]

This important new work should be viewed as a complementary explanation to the previous electorally based arguments. As Theriault says, "Only when the changes within the constituency interact with the legislative process does the complete picture of party polarization in the U.S. Congress come into clearer focus." ∎

Watch a videoclip of Sean Theriault discussing this topic at wwnorton .com/studyspace.

---

became the majority party). DeLay, nicknamed "The Hammer," was a fund-raising and election-strategy genius who tried to make Republicans the majority party for the next generation. As whip, he was a strong legislative tactician and head-counter who excelled at pushing through his party's agenda. He was forced to step down as majority leader late in 2005 when he was indicted for his fund-raising activities in Texas. The Democratic Party's success in the 2006 midterm elections was attributable in part to voters' reaction against this "culture of corruption." Although House Minority Leader Pelosi and Majority Leader Reid do not have the same reputation for the strong-arm leadership of Gingrich and DeLay, in 2009 and 2010, they were quite effective in holding together Democratic majorities in the face of nearly unified Republican opposition on many important pieces of legislation.

The Committee System The committee system in the House and Senate is another crucial part of the legislative structure. There are four types of committees: standing, select, joint, and conference. **Standing committees**, which have ongoing membership and jurisdictions, are where most of the work of Congress gets done. These committees draft legislation and oversee the implementation of the laws they pass. **Select committees** are typically created to address a specific topic for one or two terms, such as the Select House Committee on Homeland Security (which later

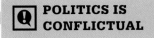

POLITICS IS CONFLICTUAL

standing committees Committees that are a permanent part of the House or Senate structure, holding more importance and authority than other committees.

select committees Committees in the House or Senate created to address a specific issue for one or two terms.

became a standing committee). These committees do not have the same legislative authority as standing committees. **Joint committees** are comprised of members of the House and Senate, and rarely have legislative authority (the last joint committee to have such authority was the Joint Committee on Atomic Energy, disbanded in 1977). The Joint Committee on Taxation, for example, does not have authority to send legislation concerning tax policy to the floor of the House or Senate. Instead, it gathers information and provides estimates of the consequences of proposed tax legislation. Some joint committees take care of common administrative housekeeping tasks: the Joint Committee on the Library oversees the Library of Congress and the Joint Committee on Printing oversees the Government Printing Office. **Conference committees** are formed to resolve specific differences between the House and Senate versions of legislation that passes each chamber. These committees are mostly comprised of standing committee members from each chamber who worked on the bill. Nuts and Bolts 10.3 shows the policy areas covered by each type of committee.

The committee system creates a division of labor that helps reelection by supporting members' specialization and credit claiming. For example, a chair of the Agriculture Committee or of an important agricultural subcommittee may reasonably take credit for passing an important bill for the farmers back home, such as the Cottonseed Payment Program that provides assistance to cottonseed farmers who lost crops due

NUTS AND BOLTS

10.3

Congressional Committees

Equivalent or similar committees in both chambers are listed across from each other.

HOUSE COMMITTEES
Agriculture
Appropriations
Armed Services
Budget
Education and Labor
Energy and Commerce
Financial Services
Foreign Affairs
Homeland Security

House Administration
Select Committee on Intelligence
Judiciary
Natural Resources
Small Business
Standards of Official Conduct
Transportation and Infrastructure
Veterans Affairs
Ways and Means

SENATE COMMITTEES
Agriculture, Nutrition, and Forestry
Appropriations
Armed Services
Budget
Health, Education, Labor, and Pensions
Commerce, Science, and Transportation
Banking, Housing, and Urban Affairs
Foreign Relations
Homeland Security and Governmental Affairs
Rules and Administration
Select Committee on Intelligence

Judiciary
Energy and Natural Resources
Small Business and Entrepreneurship
Select Committee on Ethics
Environment and Public Works

Veterans Affairs
Finance

JOINT COMMITTEES
Joint Economic Committee
Joint Committee on the Library
Joint Committee on Printing
Joint Committee on Taxation

The committees below are specific to one chamber.

Oversight and Government Reform
Rules
Science and Technology
Select Committee on Energy Independence and Global Warming

Special Committee on Aging
Select Committee on Indian Affairs

The Legislature in the Political Process

The U.S. Congress is quite different from many other legislatures around the world in terms of how its members are elected, its relations to the executive, and its internal operations. Congressional representation is based on geographically determined single-member districts that hold plurality, winner-take-all elections, whereas (as discussed in Chapter 8) most other legislatures are elected using party lists and some version of proportional representation. In an election with party lists, each party makes a list of people who would serve in the legislature. Using proportional representation with party lists means that the number of people from each party's list who actually serve as legislators depends on how much support the party receives in the election. For example, if there are 100 seats in the legislature and a party wins 40 percent of the vote, in a strictly proportional system the party would make the first 40 people from their list the legislators from that party. Legislatures that are elected from national party lists are much more likely to concern themselves with national rather than parochial interests. There are no incentives to "bring home the pork" to your district if you are not elected from a district.

Examining the 2010 parliamentary election in Iraq highlights the significance of these differences. Iraqi voters may select candidates or parties in an "open party list" system in which the nation's 325 legislators are chosen based on the proportion of

The Iraqi parliament in session.

votes each party receives. This means that even relatively small factions can elect a few people to the legislature as long as they muster a small percentage of the national vote. This has the virtue of creating more proportional representation, but it also fractures political power more broadly. Eighty-six parties competed and nine won representation. Party lists also allow more descriptive representation. Twenty-six percent of Iraqi legislators are women because the law mandates that every third person on the party lists has to be a woman (only about 17 percent of members of the U.S. Congress are women).

There are too many other differences among legislatures to describe them all in detail. Briefly, relations with the executive are much stronger in a parliamentary system than in a presidential system because the prime minister is elected from the legislature. Indeed, the lines between executive and legislative power are much more blurred in a parliamentary system. Parties tend to be highly unified in parliamentary systems and less so in presidential systems. Oversight powers, legislative capacity (ratifying treaties, amending constitutions, approving executive appointments, and impeachment power), the number of votes and how they are recorded, tenure and reelection rates, and the relative power of committees in the institution also vary tremendously.[a]

---

to hurricanes. The number of members who could make these credible claims expanded dramatically in the 1970s with the proliferation of subcommittees (there are ninety-seven in the House and sixty-eight in the Senate). One observer of Congress suggested, with some exaggeration, that if you ever forget a member's name, you can simply refer to him or her as "Mr. or Ms. Chairman" and you will be right about half the time. This view of congressional committees is based on the **distributive theory**, which is rooted in the norm of reciprocity and the incentive to provide benefits for the district. The theory holds that members will seek committee assignments to best serve their district's interests, the leadership will accommodate those requests, and

distributive theory The idea that members of Congress will join committees that best serve the interests of their district and that committee members will support each other's legislation.

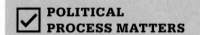

informational theory The idea that having committees in Congress made up of experts on specific policy areas helps to ensure well-informed policy decisions.

> **POLITICAL PROCESS MATTERS**

the floor will respect the views of the committees in a big institution-level logroll (that is, committee members will support each other's legislation).

However, the committee system does not exist simply to further members' electoral goals. It is also a *corrective* to individualism because the structure of committees creates more expertise than if the policy process were more ad hoc.[38] This expertise, according to the **informational theory**, provides collective benefits to the rest of the members because it helps reduce uncertainty about policy outcomes. By deferring to expert committees, members are able to achieve beneficial outcomes while using their time more efficiently. This informational theory is also consistent with the argument made by Richard Fenno more than thirty years ago that members will serve on committees for reasons other than simply trying to achieve reelection (which is implied by the distributive theory). Fenno argued that members also were interested in achieving power within the institution and making good policy.[39] Others argue that goals vary from bill to bill, and all members pursue reelection advantage, institutional power, and effective policy in different circumstances.[40] Thus, the committee system does not exist only to further members' electoral goals, but it often serves that purpose.

Committees also serve the policy needs of the majority party, especially the Rules Committee that structures the nature of debate in the House. The Rules Committee has become an arm of the majority party leadership, and in many instances it provides rules that support the party's policy agenda or protect its members from having to take controversial positions. For example, the Rules Committee prevented many amendments on the 2010 health care reform bill that, if they had come to a vote, would have divided the Democratic Party.

Congressional Staff The final component of the formal structure of Congress is congressional staff. The size of personal and committee staff exploded in the 1970s and 1980s and has since leveled off (Figure 10.7). The total number of congressional

---

FIGURE 10.7 **CONGRESSIONAL STAFF, 1935–2005**

The size of congressional staff increased substantially in the late 1960s and early 1970s. What are some possible explanations for this increase? What impact might it have on Congress's policy-making capacity and ability to meet constituents' needs?

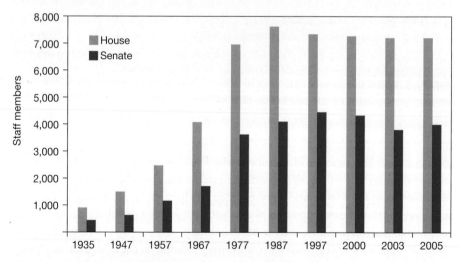

SOURCE: Data from Norman J. Ornstein, Thomas E. Mann, and Michael J. Malbin, *Vital Statistics on Congress: 2005–2006* (Washington, DC: CQ Press, 2008), available at http://library.cqpress.com/vsap/vsap07_figs5-2a.

staff is more than four times as large as it was fifty years ago. Part of the motivation for this growth was to reduce the gap between the policy-making capability of Congress and the president, especially with regard to fiscal policy. The larger committee staffs gave members of Congress independent sources of information and expertise with which to challenge the president. The other primary motivation was electoral. By increasing the size of their personal staff, members were able to open multiple district offices and expand the opportunities for casework. When the Republicans took control of Congress in 1994, they vowed to cut the waste in the internal operation of the institution, in part by cutting committee staff. However, although they reduced committee staff by nearly a third, they made no cuts in personal staff.

The structure of Congress generally serves its members' needs. The norms of the institution and its formal structure facilitate members' electoral and policy goals. If any aspect of this structure were to hinder Congress's goals, it is within members' power to change that aspect of the institution.

How a Bill Becomes a Law

Every introductory textbook on American politics has the obligatory section, including the neat little diagram, that describes how a bill becomes a law. This book is no exception; however, we provide an important truth-in-advertising disclosure: many important laws do not follow this orderly path. In fact, Barbara Sinclair's book *Unorthodox Lawmaking* argues that "the legislative process for major legislation is now less likely to conform to the textbook model than to unorthodox lawmaking."[41] After presenting the standard view, we describe the most important deviations from that path.

The details of the legislative process can be incredibly complex, but its basic aspects are fairly simple. The most important thing to understand about the process is that before a piece of legislation can become a law it must be passed *in identical form* by both the House and the Senate and signed by the president. If the president vetoes the bill, it can still be passed with a two-thirds vote in each chamber. The basic steps of the process are:

1. A member of Congress introduces the bill.
2. A subcommittee and committee craft the bill.
3. Floor action on the bill takes place in the first chamber (House or Senate).
4. Committee and floor action takes place in the second chamber.
5. The conference committee works out any differences between the House and Senate versions of the bill. (If the two chambers pass the same version, steps 5 and 6 are not necessary.)
6. Final approval of the conference committee version by the floor of each chamber.
7. The president either signs or vetoes the final version.
8. If the bill is vetoed, both chambers can attempt to override the veto.

The first part of the process, unchanged from the earliest Congresses, is the introduction of the bill. Only members of Congress can introduce the bill, either by dropping it into the "hopper," a wooden box at the front of the chamber in the House, or by presenting it to one of the clerks at the presiding officer's desk in the Senate. Even the president would need to have a House member or senator introduce his bill. Each bill has one or more sponsors and often many cosponsors.

FIGURE 10.8 HOW A BILL BECOMES A LAW

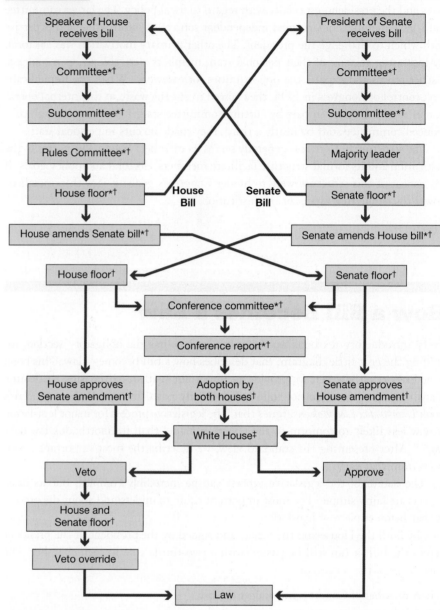

*Points at which a bill can be amended.
†Points at which a bill can die.
‡If the president neither signs nor vetoes a bill within ten days while Congress is in session, it automatically becomes law.

POLITICS IS EVERYWHERE

Members may introduce bills on any topic they choose, but often the bills are related to a specific constituency interest. For example, House Resolution 1079 was introduced by Representative Anh Cao of Louisiana to congratulate the New Orleans Saints on winning Super Bowl XLIV (Figure 10.9). Obviously, most legislation is more substantive, but members of Congress are always attentive to issues their constituents care about.

The next step is to send the bill to the relevant committee. House and Senate rules specify committee jurisdictions (there are more than 200 categories), and the bill is matched with the committee that best fits its subject matter. In the House, major legislation may be sent to more than one committee in a practice known as multiple referral, but one of them is designated the primary committee, and the

FIGURE 10.9 TAKING CARE OF THE FANS

H. Res. 1079

In the House of Representatives, U.S.,
March 4, 2010.

Whereas, on February 7, 2010, the New Orleans Saints defeated the Indianapolis Colts by a score of 31 to 17 to win the National Football League (NFL) Championship;

Whereas the Saints' victory is the first championship in the franchise's 43-year history;

Whereas the 2009 season was the best in Saints franchise history, including an unprecedented 13-game winning streak; [. . .]

Whereas during Super Bowl XLIV—

(1) the Saints accumulated a total of 332 yards;

(2) quarterback Drew Brees passed for 288 yards, threw 2 touchdowns, and tied a Super Bowl record with 32 pass completions; [. . .]

(5) Thomas Morstead's perfectly executed onside kick to start the second half and Tracy Porter's 74-yard interception for a touchdown late in the fourth quarter were integral in the Saints' victory and will forever be remembered by the 'Who Dat' faithful; [. . .]

Whereas the Saints repeatedly have been called a beacon of hope for the city of New Orleans and a catalyst for recovery throughout Louisiana and the Gulf Coast Region; [. . .]

Whereas the 2009 Saints are evidence of what can be accomplished when self is set aside and a teamwork mentality is adopted by all of the players: Now, therefore, be it

Resolved, That the House of Representatives—

(1) congratulates the New Orleans Saints, the team's coaches and players, and the loyal members of the 'Who Dat' Nation on winning Super Bowl XLIV; and

(2) recognizes—

(A) the New Orleans Saints as the soul of New Orleans; and

(B) the significant contributions made by the team in the recovery efforts of New Orleans, Louisiana, and the Gulf Coast Region.

SOURCE: Excerpted from H. Res. 1079, 111th Cong., 2nd sess. (March 4, 2010), available at http://thomas.loc.gov/cgi-bin/query/D?c11:2:./temp/~c111240v70::

bill is reviewed by different committees sequentially, or in parts. The practice is less common in the Senate, in part because senators have more opportunities to amend legislation on the floor.

Once the bill goes to a committee, the chair refers it to the relevant subcommittee where much of the legislative work is done. The subcommittee holds hearings, calls witnesses, and gathers the information necessary to rewrite, amend, and edit the bill. The final language of the bill is determined in a collaborative process known as the **markup**. During this meeting, members debate aspects of the issue and offer amendments to change the language or content of the bill. After all amendments have been considered, a final vote is taken on whether to send the bill to the full committee. The full committee then considers whether to pass along the bill to the floor. They, too, have the option of amending the bill, passing it as-is, or tabling it (which kills the bill). Every bill sent to the floor by a committee is accompanied by a report and full documentation of all the hearings. These documents constitute the bill's legislative history, which the courts, executive departments, and the public use to determine the purpose and meaning of the law.

When the bill makes it to the floor, it is placed on one of the various legislative calendars. Bills are removed from the calendar to be considered by the floor under

markup One of the steps through which a bill becomes a law, in which the final wording of the bill is determined.

ON AGREEING TO THE
RESOLUTION

H CON RES 104

	YEA	NAY	PRES	NV
REPUBLICAN	224		1	4
DEMOCRATIC	167	11	21	6
INDEPENDENT	1			
TOTALS	392	11	22	10

TIME REMAINING   0:00

▲ *This C-SPAN coverage of a House vote shows a relatively empty chamber. Few members are on the floor for most debates; they rush in to vote, then go back to other legislative work.*

a broad range of possible rules. (Some of the most important rules are discussed below, when we outline some of the differences between the House and Senate, but most of the technical details are not central to the basic story.) When the bill reaches the floor, the majority party and minority party each designate a bill manager who is responsible for guiding the debate on the floor. In the House, debate proceeds according to tight time limits and rules governing the nature of amendments. Senate debate is much more open and unlimited in most circumstances (unless all the senators agree to a limit). If you have ever watched C-SPAN, you know that often there are very few people on the floor during debates. Typically only the small number of people who are most interested in the bill (usually members of the committee that produced it) actively participate and offer amendments.

When debate is completed and all amendments have been considered, the presiding officer calls for a voice vote, with those in favor saying "aye," and those opposed "no." If it is unclear which side has won, any member may call for a "division vote," which requires members on each side to stand and be counted. At that point any member may call for a recorded vote (there is no way of recording members' positions on voice votes and division votes). If at least twenty-five members agree that a recorded vote is desired, an elaborate system of buzzers goes off in the office buildings and committee rooms, calling members to the floor for the vote. Once they reach the floor, members vote by an electronic system in which they insert ATM-like cards into slots and each vote is recorded on a big board at the front of the House or Senate chamber.

If the bill passes the House and the Senate in different forms, the discrepancies have to be resolved. On many minor bills, one chamber may simply accept the other chamber's version to solve the problem. On other minor bills and some major bills, differences are resolved through a process known as amendments between the chambers. In this case, one chamber modifies a bill passed by the other chamber and sends it back to them. These modifications can go back and forth several times before both houses agree on an identical bill. A complicated version of this approach was used to pass health care reform in 2010. The most common way to resolve differences on major legislation is through a conference committee comprised of the key players in the House and the Senate. About three-fourths of major bills go to a conference committee, but only 12 percent of all bills go this route.[42] Sometimes the conferees split the difference between the House and Senate versions, but other times the House and Senate approaches are so different that one must be chosen, an especially tricky prospect when different parties control the two chambers. Sometimes the conference cannot resolve differences and the bill dies. If the conference committee can agree on changes, each chamber must pass the final version, the conference report, by a majority vote and neither chamber is allowed to amend it.

The bill is then sent to the president. If he approves and signs the measure within ten days (not counting Sundays), it becomes law. If the president objects to the bill, he may **veto** it within ten days, sending it back to the chamber where it originated, along with a statement of objections. Unless both the House and the Senate vote to override the veto by a two-thirds majority, the bill dies. If the president does not act within ten days and Congress is in session, the bill becomes law without the president's approval. If Congress is not in session, the measure dies through what is known as a **pocket veto**. Each Congress is comprised of two one-year sessions, and there is some dispute whether pocket vetoes between sessions of Congress are legitimate, or whether they must happen at the end of the second session. Recent presidents have claimed that pocket vetoes between sessions are legitimate, but both Congress and the Washington, DC, Appeals Court disagreed. The Supreme Court has not offered a definitive ruling on this matter.[43]

veto The president's rejection of a bill that has been passed by Congress. A veto can be overridden by a two-thirds vote in both the House and Senate.

pocket veto The automatic death of a bill passed by the House and Senate when the president fails to sign the bill in the last ten days of a legislative session.

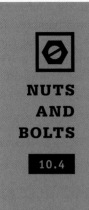
Types of Legislation

Bill: A legislative proposal that becomes law if it is passed by both the House and the Senate in identical form and approved by the president. Each is assigned a bill number, with "HR" indicating bills that originated in the House and "S" denoting bills that originated in the Senate. Private bills are concerned with a specific individual or organization and often address immigration or naturalization issues. Public bills affect the general public if enacted into law.

Simple resolution: Legislation used to express the sense of the House or Senate, designated by "H.Res." or "S.Res." Simple resolutions only affect the chamber passing the resolution, are not signed by the president, and cannot become public law. Resolutions are often used for symbolic legislation, such as congratulating sports teams (see Figure 10.9).

Concurrent resolution: Legislation used to express the position of both chambers on a nonlegislative matter to set the annual budget, or to fix adjournment dates, designated by "H.Con.Res" or "S.Con.Res." Concurrent resolutions are not signed by the president and therefore do not carry the weight of law.

Joint resolution: Legislation that has few practical differences from a bill unless it proposes a constitutional amendment. In that case, a two-thirds majority of those present and voting in both the House and the Senate, and ratification by three-fourths of the states, are required for the amendment to be adopted.

One final point on how a bill becomes a law is important: any bill that appropriates money must pass through the two-step process of authorization and appropriation. In the authorization process, members debate the merits of the bill, determine its language, and limit the amount that can be spent on the bill. The appropriations process involves both the Budget Committees in the House and the Senate, which set the overall guidelines for the national budget, and the Appropriations Committees in the two chambers, which determine the actual amounts of money that will be spent.

DEVIATIONS FROM THE TEXTBOOK PROCESS

There are many ways in which legislation may not follow the typical path. First, in some congresses as many as 20 percent of *major* bills bypass the committee system. This may be done by a discharge petition, in which a majority of the members force a bill out of its assigned committee, or by a special rule in the House. Second, about one-third of major bills are adjusted post-committee and before the legislation reaches the floor by supporters of the bill to increase the chances of passage. Sometimes the bill goes back to the committee after these changes, and sometimes it does not. Thus, although most of the legislative work is accomplished in committees, a significant amount of legislation bypasses committee review.

Third, summit meetings between the president and congressional leaders may bypass or jump-start the normal legislative process. For example, rather than going through the Budget Committees to set budgetary targets, the president may meet with top leaders from both parties and hammer out a compromise that is presented to Congress as a done deal. This technique is especially important on delicate budget negotiations or when the president is threatening to use the veto. Often the congressional rank-and-file go along with the end product of the summit meeting, but occasionally they revolt and reject it.

Fourth, **omnibus legislation**—massive bills that run hundreds of pages long and cover many different subjects and programs—often requires creative approaches by the leadership to guide the bill through the legislative maze. Leadership task

omnibus legislation Large bills that often cover several topics and may contain extraneous, or pork-barrel, projects.

suspension of the rules One way of moving a piece of legislation to the top of the agenda in the House: debate on the bill is limited to forty minutes, amendments are not allowed, and the bill must pass by a two-thirds vote.

forces may be used in the place of committees, and alternatives to the conference committee may be devised to resolve differences between the two chambers. In addition, the massive legislation is often accompanied by riders—extraneous legislation attached to the "must pass" bill to get pet projects approved that would otherwise fail. This is a form of pork-barrel legislation and another mechanism used in the quest for reelection.

DIFFERENCES IN THE HOUSE AND SENATE LEGISLATIVE PROCESSES

There are three central differences in the legislative processes of the House and the Senate: (1) the continuity of the membership and the impact this has on the rules, (2) how bills get to the floor, and (3) the structure of the floor process, including debate and amendments. First, as discussed earlier, the Senate is a continuing body, with two-thirds of its members returning to the next session without facing reelection (because of the six-year term), whereas all House members are up for reelection every two years. This has an important impact on the rules of the two chambers: there has been much greater stability in the rules of the Senate than the House. Whereas the House adopts its rules anew at the start of each new session (sometimes with major changes and other times with only minor modifications), the Senate has not had a general reaffirmation of its rules since 1789. However, the Senate rules can be changed at the beginning of a session to meet the needs of the new members.

The other two differences between the House and Senate are even more important. The process by which a bill gets to the floor is much more complicated in the House than the Senate. In the House, when a bill is reported from a committee it goes to the bottom of the legislative calendar. However, the leadership can move a bill to the top of the agenda in several ways. One mechanism is to have the bill considered under **suspension of the rules**, which is mostly used for noncontroversial legislation. Debate is limited to forty minutes, no amendments are allowed, and bills must pass by a two-thirds vote. Another mechanism used for major legislation is for the Rules Committee to make a special rule that, if approved by a majority vote of the House, moves the bill to the top of the list for immediate consideration.

The procedure is much easier in the Senate. As in the House, certain bills have privileged status over others, such as conference reports and vetoed bills on which Congress will attempt an override. Because they are in the final stages of the process, they are promoted to the top of the list so they don't have to wait in line with newer bills. Other than privileging these bills, the Senate does not use special rules or various calendars. If the majority leader wants action on a given bill, he simply puts it on the legislative agenda, either through a motion or unanimous consent.

The floor process is also much simpler and less structured in the Senate than in the House. In part, this is due to the relative size of the two chambers: the House with its 435 members needs to have more rules than the 100-person Senate. Ironically, however, the floor process is actually much easier to navigate in the House because of its structure. The House is a very majoritarian body (that is, a majority of House members can almost always have its way), while former majority leader Howard Baker compared leading the Senate to "herding cats." He said it was difficult "trying to make ninety-nine independent souls act in concert under rules that encourage polite anarchy and embolden people who find majority rule a dubious proposition at best."[44] Part of this difficulty is rooted in the fact that the Senate

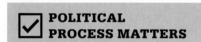

POLITICAL PROCESS MATTERS

has unlimited debate and a very open amendment process. Unless restricted by a unanimous consent agreement, senators can speak as long as they want and offer any amendment to a bill, even if it isn't germane (that is, directly related to the underlying bill). Debate may be cut off only if a supermajority of sixty senators agrees in a process known as invoking **cloture**. Therefore, one senator can stop any bill by threatening to talk the bill to death if forty of his or her colleagues agree. This practice is known as a **filibuster.**

The filibuster strengthens the hand of the minority party in the Senate, giving it veto power over legislation unless the majority party has sixty senators who unanimously support a bill. The filibuster has played a critical role in congressional policy making in recent years, especially after Republican Scott Brown won Ted Kennedy's seat in January 2010 (which gave the Republicans forty-one seats). Republicans filibustered the health care reform bill, which could have killed it if Democratic leaders had not managed to use the reconciliation process to pass the legislation (reconciliation is used in the budget process, typically as a budget-cutting device, and is not subject to the filibuster).

Before the 1960s, senators really did hold the floor for hours by reading from the phone book or reciting recipes. The late Strom Thurmond, the senator from South Carolina who was the longest serving and oldest senator until his retirement in January 2003 (at 100 years old and after 48 years in the Senate), holds the record of twenty-four hours and eighteen minutes of continuous talking. Today it is rare for a filibuster to tie up Senate business, since a senator's threat to filibuster a bill is often enough to take the bill off the legislative agenda. If the bill is actually filibustered, it goes on a separate legislative track so it does not bring the rest of the business of the Senate to a halt. Alternatively, if supporters of the bill think they have enough votes, they can invoke cloture before a filibuster starts.

Because of the practice of unlimited debate in the Senate, much of its business is conducted under unanimous consent agreements by which senators agree to adhere to time limits on debate and amendments. However, because these are literally *unanimous* agreements, a single senator can obstruct the business of the chamber by issuing a **hold** on the bill or presidential nomination. This practice is often a bargaining tool to extract concessions from the bill's supporters, but sometimes, especially late in a session when time gets tight, a hold can actually kill a bill by removing it from the active agenda.

In contrast the House is a more orderly, if complex, institution. The Rules Committee exerts great control over the legislative process, especially on major legislation, through special rules that govern the nature of debate on a bill. There are three general types of rules: **closed rules** do not allow any amendments to the bill, **open rules** allow any germane amendments and **modified rules** allow some specific amendments but not others. Once a special rule is adopted and the Committee of the Whole convenes, general debate is tightly controlled by the floor managers. All amendments are considered under a five-minute rule, but this rule is routinely bent as members offer phantom "pro forma" amendments to, for example, "strike the last word" or "strike the requisite number of words." This means that the member is not really offering an amendment but is simply going through the formal procedure of offering one in order to get an additional five minutes to talk about the amendment. So although the Senate is formally committed to unlimited debate, senators often voluntarily place limits on themselves through unanimous consent, which makes them operate much more like the House. Similarly, though the House has very strict rules concerning debate and amendments, there are ways of bending those rules to make the House operate a bit more like the potentially free-wheeling Senate.

▲ Scott Brown's (R-MA) victory in a special election in January 2010 gave Republicans the forty-one seats in the Senate needed to maintain a filibuster.

cloture A procedure through which the Senate can limit the amount of time spent debating a bill (cutting off a filibuster), if a supermajority of sixty senators agree.

filibuster A tactic used by senators to block a bill by continuing to hold the floor and speak—under the Senate rule of unlimited debate—until the bill's supporters back down.

hold An objection to considering a measure on the Senate floor.

closed rules Conditions placed on a legislative debate by the House Rules Committee prohibiting amendments to a bill.

open rules Conditions placed on a legislative debate by the House Rules Committee allowing relevant amendments to a bill.

modified rules Conditions placed on a legislative debate by the House Rules Committee allowing certain amendments to a bill while barring others.

Oversight

Once a bill becomes a law, Congress plays another crucial role by overseeing the implementation of the law to make sure the bureaucracy interprets it as Congress intended. Other motivations drive the oversight process as well, such as the desire to gain publicity that may help in the reelection quest or to embarrass the president if he is of the opposite party (for example, in President Bush's last two years, Democrats investigated fraud and cost-overruns in Defense Department contracts to rebuild Iraq that went to corporations with close Republican Party ties). However, the basic motivation for oversight is to ensure that laws are implemented properly.

There are several mechanisms that Congress may use to accomplish this goal; these will be addressed in more detail in Chapter 12, The Bureaucracy, but we will briefly describe them here. First, the bluntest instrument is the power of the purse. If members of Congress think an agency is not properly implementing their programs, they can simply cut off the funds. However, this approach to punishing agencies is rarely used because budget cuts often end up cutting good aspects of the agency along with the bad.

Second, Congress may hold hearings and investigations. By summoning administration officials and agency heads to a public hearing, Congress can use the media spotlight to focus attention on problems within the bureaucracy or on issues that have been overlooked. For example, the economic meltdown of 2008–2009 produced dozens of hearings on topics ranging from the bailout of the auto industry (and subsequent bankruptcy of General Motors) to the use of TARP money by financial institutions, executive pay in the financial sector, the housing market and subprime mortgage crises, and accountability of the Federal Reserve. National security issues continue to produce oversight hearings on a broad range of topics as well. The attempted bombing of a Northwest Airlines jet on Christmas Day 2009 prompted a new round of congressional hearings focusing on airport security and the sharing of intelligence across government agencies. This type of oversight is known as fire alarm oversight—that is, members wait until there is a crisis before they spring to action.[45] This is in contrast to police patrol oversight, which involves constant vigilance in overseeing the bureaucracy. For example, the Oversight and Government Reform Committee held several hearings to make sure that stimulus money from the Recovery Act was being spent as intended. Of the two, fire alarm oversight is far more common because Congress does not have the resources to constantly monitor the entire bureaucracy.

Third, Congress may use **legislative vetoes**, which resemble fire alarm oversight in being a reactive rather than proactive form of oversight. In writing laws, Congress often gives the bureaucracy broad discretion over how to implement policies, because it is impossible for Congress to foresee every scenario that might arise. However, Congress is reluctant to give full control to the implementing agencies. Legislative vetoes resolve this dilemma by allowing Congress to overturn bureaucratic decisions. There are one-house or two-house versions of legislative vetoes and some even allow committees to exercise a veto. In 1983, the Supreme Court ruled that many forms of legislative vetoes are unconstitutional.[46] Despite this ruling, however, Congress continues to use this form of oversight.

Finally, the Senate exercises specific control over other executive functions through its constitutional responsibilities to provide "advice and consent" on presidential appointments and approval of treaties. The Senate typically defers to the president

▼ The CEOs of General Motors, Ford, and Chrysler testify before the Senate Banking, Housing and Urban Affairs Committee about a proposed $34 billion federal bailout for the auto industry. When members of Congress took this extraordinary step in 2009, they wanted to make sure that taxpayers' money would be wisely spent.

on these matters, but it may assert its power, especially when constituent interests are involved. One current example would be the Senate's increasing skepticism about free trade agreements negotiated by the president's trade representatives and holds on presidential nominations.

The ultimate in congressional oversight is the process of removing the president, vice president, other civil officers, or federal judges through impeachment. The House and Senate share this power: the House issues articles of impeachment, which outline the charges against the official, and the Senate conducts the trial of the impeached officials. Two presidents have been impeached: Andrew Johnson in the controversy over Reconstruction after the Civil War, and Bill Clinton over the scandal involving White House intern Monica Lewinsky. However, neither president was convicted and removed by the Senate.

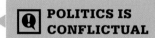

POLITICS IS CONFLICTUAL

Congressional Reform

The pork-laden 2010 defense appropriations bill is a good example of why many Americans are convinced that the entire political system is dysfunctional (see You Decide). This deep cynicism is rooted in the perception that government is not serving the public interest. Attempts to reform Congress address either Congress's external image or internal "quality of life" concerns. The former, which attempt to tackle the absence of institutional leadership and accountability, are difficult to address through congressional reforms. The only way to achieve complete accountability is through responsible party government (discussed in Chapter 7), though this is an elusive goal at best, even when the same party controls Congress and the presidency. However, in a decentralized, individualistic institution such as Congress, the only force for collective responsibility is the majority party. Specific reform proposals seeking to take advantage of this force include giving the Speaker more power over committee assignments (which Newt Gingrich briefly asserted in 1995), strengthening the role of the party caucus, reforming the filibuster in the Senate to give the majority party more control, and requiring the leadership to play a larger role in agenda setting. The latter could be accomplished through an annual "state of the Congress" address by congressional leaders, the creation of a specific agenda, and increased activism by the leadership in pushing the agenda. Unfortunately, providing the potential for stronger parties in Congress will not ensure that leaders use their new powers effectively. Some leaders may be reluctant to encroach on committees' turf. For example, Newt Gingrich, the strong Speaker during the mid-1990s, was much more willing to push committees to work with his agenda than was his successor to the speakership, Dennis Hastert. Nancy Pelosi's relationship with committee chairs fell somewhere between the style of these two extremes, while John Boehner has vowed to return more power to the chairs.

Proposals aimed at improving the quality of life in Congress attempt to expand the time available to members for legislative work and reduce some of the external pressures. Specific proposals that address quality of life concerns include revoking some of the "sunshine reforms" of the 1970s, which opened up committee hearings to the general public. By closing more of these meetings, members would be more insulated from interest group pressure. Other proposals include having fewer recorded votes, reducing the number of committee and subcommittee assignments, public financing of congressional elections, giving serious consideration to the minority party's grievances, and creating an ombudsman (a person who investigates complaints) office to handle most constituency requests rather than having the members' staff do it.

Unfortunately, the two reform agendas are at odds with one another. Most steps that would improve the quality of life in Congress, such as insulating members from outside pressure, would not enhance its image; most people would see this as a way of shielding Congress from public accountability. Strengthening parties in Congress could come at the expense of more partisan in-fighting. The minority party typically prefers weaker party leadership, while the majority party is willing to tolerate strong leadership while maintaining a solid base in committee power. Efforts to truly strengthen party leadership are often met with howls of protest from the minority party and sometimes from junior members of the majority party, thus exacerbating quality of life concerns.

The one exception to this trade-off is campaign finance reform, which would both free up time for members (if public financing is adopted) and enhance Congress's image if the public accepts it as true reform. After a decade-long battle, Congress passed the Bipartisan Campaign Reform Act, also called the McCain–Feingold Act after two of its primary sponsors, banning so-called soft money and limiting issue ads. However, in 2010, the Supreme Court struck down part of the law, allowing corporations and unions to spend directly on issue ads and other political ads without limitations. (See Chapter 8 for a discussion of this case and campaign finance more generally).

There have been some incremental congressional reforms, however. When Democrats regained majority control in 2007, they implemented several important reforms, including bans on gifts and meals paid for by lobbyists, restrictions on travel paid for by lobbyists, strong disclosure rules on earmarks, and a two-year "revolving door" ban on lawmakers becoming lobbyists after leaving Congress. The House established a new independent Office of Congressional Ethics (which fell short of the hopes of reformers because it does not have subpoena power). Some of the reforms have started to work; for example, earmarks are down by about 20 percent and are at their lowest levels since 2002.

One other topic that continues to receive attention from congressional critics and reformers is term limits. Critics complain that incumbents are too entrenched and there is not enough turnover. They point to the fact that more than 95 percent of the House incumbents who ran for reelection between 1984 and 2010 were returned to office (however, only 86 percent were reelected in 2010). This is much greater job security than most corporate presidents or blue-collar workers have.

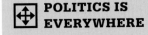

POLITICS IS EVERYWHERE

Most labor unions would readily accept a contract guaranteeing 95 percent of workers their jobs. As a reaction to incumbency advantage, a grassroots movement to limit terms started in 1990 and reached a fever pitch in 1992, as voters in ten states passed term limits for state legislators. Currently fifteen states limit terms for state legislators, but the movement appears to be losing steam. Twenty states had passed congressional term limits before the 5–4 Supreme Court decision in *U.S. Term Limits v. Thornton* (1995) ruled that terms limits on Congress could only be passed by constitutional amendment. Then in 1999, Mississippi voters rejected a state referendum that would have imposed term limits for their state legislature. Four state supreme courts have struck down term limits. In 2002, Idaho became the first state to have its legislature repeal term limits, and Utah followed suit in 2003.

There are two interesting ironies associated with the term limits movement. First, the Founders feared that the House would be an unstable body with excessive turnover and a lack of professionalism. Technically it *is* possible that 435 new members of Congress could be elected every two years, but obviously the opposite has happened. Second, as noted earlier, while the public is critical of Congress as an institution, most voters do not feel this way about their own individual representative. One bumper sticker opposing term limits succinctly captures this irony: "Stop me before I vote again." Thus, while many people claim to support term limits, they don't want to vote out their own members of Congress.

Conclusion

Though the details of the legislative process and the institutions of Congress can be complicated, the basic explanations for member behavior are quite straightforward when viewed in terms of the trade-off between responsiveness and responsibility. Members of Congress want to be reelected, so they are generally quite responsive to constituents' interests. They spend considerable time on casework, meeting with people in the district and delivering benefits for the district. At the same time, members are motivated to be responsible—to rise above local interests and attend to the nation's best interests. The conflict between these two impulses can create contradictory policies that contribute to Congress's image problem. For example, we subsidize tobacco farming at the same time that we spend billions of dollars to treat the health problems tobacco use creates. We have laws on water rights that encourage farmers to irrigate the desert at the same time we pay farmers to leave parts of their land unplanted in areas of the country that are well-suited for agriculture. These policies, and others, can be explained by the desire to serve local interests and by the norms of reciprocity and universalism.

Considering members' motivations is crucial to understanding how Congress functions, but their behavior is also constrained by the institutions in which they operate. The committee system is an important source of expertise and information, and it provides a platform from which members can take positions and claim credit. Parties in Congress provide coherence to the legislative agenda and help structure voting patterns on bills. Rules and norms constrain the nature of debate and the legislative process. Although these institutions shape members' behavior, it is important to keep in mind that members can also change those rules and institutions. Therefore, Congress has the ability to evolve with changing national conditions and demands from voters, groups, and the president.

In this context, much of what Congress does can be understood in terms of the conflicts inherent in politics. How can members act responsibly without sacrificing responsiveness? Can Congress be structured in a way that allows members to be responsive (and therefore have a better chance of getting reelected) without losing the ability to make tough, unpopular decisions when needed, like cutting budget deficits? The example of reforming the financial sector discussed in the chapter introduction demonstrates that comprehensive, important legislation can be passed despite partisan conflict in Congress. This chapter also shed light on some of the ways that political process matters. With a better understanding of how Congress operates, you are better able to assess the outputs of government. For example, this chapter provided a closer look at party leaders and pork-barrel spending: party leaders in Congress help members solve their collective action problems, rather than causing gridlock and policy failure, as is commonly assumed. Some pork may be wasteful, but in other cases it is important for the districts that receive the benefits and may serve broader collective interests as well. Congress does not always live up to the expectations of being the "first branch" of government, but it often does an admirable job of balancing the conflicting pressures it faces.

What is Congress's place in the constitutional system? How are conflicts between competing interests built into the system?

- The Founders created Congress as the first branch of government, giving it extensive enumerated powers and vast implied powers through the elastic clause.
- The debates at the Constitutional Convention over the nature of the legislative branch reflected the variety of regional and political interests of the day.
- The resulting compromises, bicameralism and the representation of national and state interests, reflect that politics necessarily involves conflictual trade-offs about what government does. The Founders' process of creating Congress involved many trade-offs and compromises, and the resulting institution is at the core of American policy making.

What is the nature of Congress's relationship with the public? Why do members of Congress act the way they do?

- Representing the interests of constituents always involves trade-offs, starting with the nature of the representation itself: Is descriptive representation important? Should a member act more like a delegate, trustee, or politico?
- Answering these questions depends on one's views of responsible versus responsive behavior from Congress. Should a member of Congress do what is right for the nation or for the district when those two constituencies want different things?
- Parts of the constituency from different regions, races, classes, and ethnicities require another set of trade-offs, as do Fenno's concentric circles. These trade-offs are illustrated most dramatically in redistricting, but they are inherent in the concept of representation.
- The electoral motivation influences how members of Congress relate to their constituents by encouraging advertising, credit claiming, and position taking.
- Congress is held in low regard by the public because of periodic scandals and conflicting expectations about Congress's role in policy making.

What are the sources of incumbency advantage?

- The goal of reelection is central to understanding congressional behavior.

- By developing an effective home style, building up a campaign war chest to deter challengers, working the district, and serving constituents, most members of Congress establish relatively secure districts.

How is Congress structured?

- The structure of Congress comprises informal norms and formal institutions, both of which have an important impact on how legislation is produced.
- Congress's informal norms include universalism, reciprocity, specialization, and seniority. The strength of these norms varies between the House and the Senate and changes over time.
- Congress's formal structures include political parties, leaders, committees, and staff.

How does a bill become a law?

- Bills may travel a number of different routes through Congress. The process by which a bill becomes a law is clearly more complicated than the basic textbook model that captures its essence.
- There are many important differences between the House and Senate, and both chambers often use alternative policy-making processes. However, in both chambers the rules governing political process shape outcomes. For example, the rules of the House mean that a majority can almost always have its way, whereas in the Senate, sixty votes are needed to pass most important legislation.

Can Congress be reformed?

- Most efforts to reform Congress address either Congress's external image or internal "quality of life" concerns.
- These two reform agendas tend to be at odds with one another: changes that would improve Congress's external image tend to worsen internal problems and vice versa.
- Campaign finance reform may be the one type of reform that could address both concerns.

⊚ STUDENT STUDYSPACE

Find quizzes and other review material at wwnorton.com/studyspace.

CRITICAL THINKING

1. If you had to choose between having a responsive or responsible member of Congress, which would you choose and why? Would your answer depend on how other members of Congress were behaving?

2. If you were in charge of the Commission on Congressional Reform, what proposals would you make to change how Congress operates? Would your proposals have a chance of being implemented?

3. What types of activities do members undertake to work toward reelection? How do they structure the institutions of Congress to help themselves achieve this goal? Do these behaviors and institutions serve broader public interests as well as the narrower goal of reelection?

KEY TERMS

advertising (p. 355)
apportionment (p. 357)
bicameralism (p. 350)
casework (p. 355)
closed rules (p. 385)
cloture (p. 385)
conference committees (p. 376)
credit claiming (p. 355)
delegate (congressional role) (p. 352)
descriptive representation (p. 351)
distributive theory (p. 377)
earmarks (p. 368)
electoral connection (p. 355)
filibuster (p. 385)
gerrymandering (p. 358)
gridlock (p. 362)

hold (p. 385)
incumbency advantage (p. 364)
informational theory (p. 378)
joint committees (p. 376)
legislative veto (p. 386)
majority leader (p. 370)
markup (p. 381)
minority leader (p. 371)
modified rules (p. 385)
omnibus legislation (p. 383)
open rules (p. 385)
party unity (p. 372)
party votes (p. 372)
pocket veto (p. 382)
politico (p. 353)
pork barrel (p. 351)

position taking (p. 356)
president pro tempore (p. 371)
reciprocity (p. 368)
redistricting (p. 357)
roll call vote (p. 372)
select committees (p. 375)
seniority (p. 370)
Speaker of the House (p. 370)
specialization (p. 370)
standing committees (p. 375)
substantive representation (p. 352)
suspension of the rules (p. 384)
trustee (p. 352)
universalism (p. 368)
veto (p. 382)
whip system (p. 370)

SUGGESTED READING

Bianco, William T. *Trust: Representatives and Constituents.* Ann Arbor, MI: University of Michigan Press, 1994.

Canon, David T. *Race, Redistricting and Representation: The Unintended Consequences of Black Majority Districts.* Chicago: University of Chicago Press, 1999.

Fenno, Richard F. *Congressmen in Committees.* Boston: Little, Brown, 1973.

Hall, Richard L. *Participation in Congress.* New Haven, CT: Yale University Press, 1996.

Jacobson, Gary C. *The Politics of Congressional Elections,* 5th ed. New York: Addison-Wesley, 2001.

Mayhew, David R. *Congress: The Electoral Connection.* New Haven, CT: Yale University Press, 1974.

Theriault, Sean. *Party Polarization in Congress.* New York: Cambridge University Press, 2008.

President Barack Obama and former president George W. Bush at the Capitol building on January 20, 2009, soon after Obama was sworn in as the forty-fourth president of the United States.

The Presidency

To appreciate the fundamental powers and responsibilities of America's presidents, consider Barack Obama's first 100 days in office. Among hundreds of actions taken by Obama and his appointees, he signed a $700 billion economic stimulus bill, ordered 17,000 more American troops to Afghanistan, ended the use of harsh interrogation tactics (what many called torture) by American military and intelligence personnel, ended the Bush-era ban on stem cell research, and reversed a Bush administration decision that prevented California from establishing strict standards for auto emissions. To put it in our terms, politics and government are everywhere—and in many cases, their influence is felt through presidential actions.

CONFLICT AND COMPROMISE
in American Politics

These successes do not make Obama an exception among American presidents. During his two terms in office, President George W. Bush saw many of his preferred policies enacted, including large tax cuts, the No Child Left Behind education reforms, the Medicare Prescription Drug Benefit, a ban on some types of late-term abortion, and the appointment of two conservative Supreme Court justices. In response to the September 11 attacks, Bush ordered American troops to invade and occupy Iraq and Afghanistan and restricted civil liberties by increasing government surveillance of American citizens and limiting the legal rights of suspected terrorists. These and similar examples are cited by many people as evidence that presidential power has grown out of control in recent years—or that presidents are virtual dictators, able to do whatever they want without congressional consent or judicial review.

This chapter offers a different interpretation of presidential power. U.S. presidents face decisions that are highly conflictual, with many people holding strong opinions on both sides of the question. Although some Americans approved of Obama's (or Bush's) accomplishments, many others were opposed. Success for these presidents was not automatic; they faced the problem of reaching their own policy goals while at the same time trying both to satisfy the demands of their supporters and their allies in Congress and to avoid alienating people who were on the losing side of these presidential decisions.

To put it another way, while presidents are powerful, they are not dictators: in virtually all cases, their actions either require congressional consent to take effect or can be undone by subsequent congressional action. Presidents must also cultivate public opinion in order to get reelected or to elect members of

BIG QUESTIONS

✪ Who are America's presidents? What effect have presidential actions had, and how has the presidency developed over time?

✪ What is the president's job description?

✪ What does the executive branch do? How is it organized?

✪ What do Americans want from the president? What determines whether presidential approval ratings are high or low?

✪ How much power do presidents really have, and under what circumstances do they exercise it?

Congress from their party, and must monitor the bureaucracy to make sure that their decisions are faithfully implemented. And sometimes, such as in the case of the 2009–2010 health care reform efforts for Obama or the failed 2005 Social Security reform initiative for Bush, presidents must decide whether to scale back their proposals in an effort to get them enacted or risk failing completely to accomplish their goals.

Accordingly, one of the fundamental questions we ask in this chapter is, what are the limits of presidential power? Are presidents always able to prevail in the face of conflict in the country, in Congress, or in the bureaucracy? Has presidential power grown over time? How does conflict affect the decisions they make and the ways they try to implement their policy goals?

The second fundamental question we ask is, what are the sources of presidential power? The answer lies in our political process theme. In some situations, the powers allocated in the Constitution enable the president to change government policy unilaterally. However, there are limits on this power. Congress and the Supreme Court can and do overturn presidential actions. Moreover, many policy changes require explicit congressional approval. This chapter shows that all presidents face these opportunities and constraints, and their success in office depends on the particular challenges that arise, their personal policy goals, and their skill at using the power of the presidency.

America's Presidents

This section introduces America's presidents using the book's three themes. Although presidents do not always achieve their political and policy-making goals, these presidential failures are just as significant as presidential successes because of what they reveal about the conflicts that divide American society, as well as the processes, rules, and procedures that grant power to the president and constrain its use. This section shows that successful presidents must be skilled politicians who can find ways to mitigate these inevitable conflicts. The president needs citizens' support to get reelected, to help elect legislators from his party, and get his policy priorities through Congress. The president must also work closely with Congress, bargaining with legislators over budgets, laws, and regulations. As a result, a president's success in implementing his vision for America depends not only on his knowledge of government and public policy but also on his ability to win the support of the public and other politicians. Thus, the impact of presidential actions is felt everywhere in American society.

PRESIDENTS, POWER, AND POLITICS

As discussed in previous chapters, presidential power has expanded over time, probably beyond what many of the framers intended. Concerns about presidential power were apparent even at the Constitutional Convention, as some delegates wanted to give the president a largely ceremonial role or to have executive power exercised by a small committee rather than a single individual. In the end, a combination of factors, such as the desirability of having a single individual represent the United States in dealings with other nations, the belief that the legislative branch would dominate the policy-making process in the new government, the reality that someone needed to be in charge of the government (particularly given that Congress would be adjourned for most of the year), and the expectation that George Washington would serve as the first president, convinced delegates to give the president control over the military, the executive branch, and the other powers discussed in this chapter.

Since the early years of the Republic, presidents' actions have had profound consequences for the nation. The first presidents, George Washington, John Adams, and Thomas Jefferson, helped forge compromises on issues such as choosing a permanent location for the nation's capital, setting up the federal courts, and deciding on a system for financing the government.[1] Presidents Andrew Jackson and Martin Van Buren were instrumental in forming the Democratic Party and its local party organizations.

Early presidents also made important foreign policy decisions, such as the Monroe Doctrine issued by President James Monroe in 1823, which stated that America would remain neutral in wars involving European nations and that these nations must cease attempts to colonize or occupy areas in North and South America.[2] Presidents John Tyler and James Polk oversaw the admission of Texas into the Union following the Mexican-American War, which ended with huge territorial concessions to the United States. Polk also negotiated the Oregon Treaty with Britain, which resulted in the acquisition of land that later became Oregon, Washington, Idaho, and parts of Montana and Wyoming.[3]

Several presidents were also active in the many attempts to devise a lasting compromise on slavery prior to the Civil War and to the prosecution of the war itself. President Millard Fillmore's support helped to enact the Compromise of 1850, which limited slavery in California. Democrat Franklin Pierce played a similar role when he supported the passage of the Kansas-Nebraska Act, which regulated slavery in these territories. Abraham Lincoln, who helped form the Republican Party in the 1850s, played a transformative role in setting policy as president during the Civil War. His orders raised the huge Union Army, and as commander in chief, he directed the conduct of the bloody war that kept the southern states from seceding permanently. Lincoln issued the Emancipation Proclamation, which freed the slaves in the South, and temporarily suspended the writ of habeas corpus, allowing the government to imprison people without filing charges against them.[4]

During the late 1800s and early 1900s, presidents were instrumental in the federal government's responses to the nation's rapid expansion and industrialization.[5] These changes in the country's size and its economy generated conflict over which services the federal government should provide to citizens, and how much the government should regulate individual and corporate behavior.[6] Republican president Theodore Roosevelt used the Sherman Antitrust Act to break up the Northern Securities Company, a nationwide railroad trust that was one of the largest companies of its day. He increased the power of the Interstate Commerce Commission to regulate businesses and expanded federal conservation programs. Democrat Woodrow Wilson further increased the government's role in managing the economy through his efforts to enact the Clayton Antitrust Act, the Federal Reserve Act, the first federal income tax, and legislation banning child labor.[7]

▲ *George Washington remains, for many Americans, the presidential ideal—a leader whose crucial domestic and foreign policy decisions shaped the growth of America's democracy.*

POLITICS IS EVERYWHERE

As these examples illustrate, presidential power has grown over time as the president and members of the executive branch have been given new regulatory powers over corporations and individual Americans, and as presidents have responded to shifts in public opinion by proposing new policies. To put it another way, because the president is the head of the bureaucracy, as the number of agencies and bureaucrats grows, so does presidential power.

At the same time, Wilson's foreign policy activities illustrate the limits of presidential power. While he campaigned in the 1916 election on a promise to keep America out of World War I, he ultimately changed his mind and ordered American troops to fight on the side of the Allies. After the war, Wilson offered a peace plan, the Fourteen Points, which proposed reshaping the borders of European countries in order to mitigate future conflicts; creating an international organization, the League of Nations, to prevent future conflicts; and taking other measures to encourage free trade and democracy.[8] However, America's allies rejected most of Wilson's proposals, and the Senate refused to allow American participation in the League of Nations, despite Wilson's intense lobbying efforts.

Presidential actions defined the government's response to the Great Depression, a worldwide economic collapse in the late 1920s and 1930s marked by high unemployment, huge stock market declines, and bank failures. Republican president Herbert Hoover favored only modest government actions in response, arguing that more substantial efforts would be of little use.[9] After Hoover lost the 1932 election, the new president, Democrat Franklin Roosevelt, and his staff began fundamentally reshaping American government. Roosevelt's New Deal reforms created many federal agencies that helped individual Americans and imposed many new corporate regulations, from financial industry reforms to tougher regulation of the drug industry.[10] This federal government expansion continued under Roosevelt's successors. Even Republican Dwight Eisenhower, whose party had initially opposed many New Deal reforms, presided over the creation of new agencies and the building of the interstate highway system.[11]

Presidents were instrumental in the civil rights reforms and expansion of the federal government in the 1960s. President John Kennedy established the Peace Corps and began the process of bargaining with members of Congress over legislation that would guarantee voting rights and civil rights for African Americans. Democrat Lyndon Johnson, who assumed the presidency after Kennedy was assassinated in November 1963, campaigned for reelection on his proposals for the Great Society and a War on Poverty. Together with a Democratic Congress, Johnson created a wide range of domestic programs, such as the Department of Housing and Urban Development, Medicare, Medicaid, and federal funding for schools, and finished the job of enacting voting rights and civil rights legislation. Here again, this expansion of the federal government added to presidential power.

Both Johnson and his successor, Richard Nixon, directed America's involvement in the Vietnam War, with the goal of forcing the North Vietnamese to abandon their plans to unify North and South Vietnam. Here again, presidential efforts did not meet with success: despite enormous deployments of American forces and more than 58,000 American soldiers killed, Nixon eventually signed an agreement that allowed American troops to leave but did not end the conflict, which concluded only after a North Vietnamese victory in 1975.

The two presidents after Nixon, Republican Gerald Ford and Democrat Jimmy Carter, faced the worst economic conditions since the Great Depression, largely due to increased energy prices. Both presidents offered plans to reduce unemployment and inflation, restore economic growth, and enhance domestic energy sources. In both cases, however, their efforts were largely unsuccessful, which became a critical factor in their failed reelection bids.

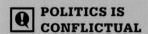

POLITICS IS CONFLICTUAL

▼ During the Great Depression, people who lost their homes built camps of ramshackle structures on vacant land. These "Hoovervilles" were nicknamed for President Herbert Hoover, whom many people blamed for the economic calamity.

In the last generation, the political and policy importance of presidential actions has only increased. The popularity of Republican Ronald Reagan's campaign platform of tax cuts, fewer regulations, smaller government, and a tougher stand against the Soviet Union helped Republicans gain majority control of the Senate in 1980 and attract many new voters to the party. Although Democratic opposition in the House and a lack of public support limited Reagan's success in reducing the size of government, he and his staff worked to negotiate important arms control agreements with the Soviet Union, efforts that accelerated under Reagan's former vice president and successor to the presidency, George H. W. Bush. Bush led American and international participation in the Persian Gulf War during 1990 and 1991, in which an American-led coalition removed invading Iraqi forces from Kuwait with minimal American casualties.

Democrat Bill Clinton's presidency was marked by passage of the North American Free Trade Agreement, welfare reform, arms control agreements, successful peacekeeping efforts by U.S. troops in Haiti and the Balkans, one of the longest periods of economic growth in U.S. history, and the first balanced budgets since the 1960s. However, despite considerable efforts to drum up public support for health care reform, congressional and public opposition doomed Clinton's proposals. The same factors delayed peacekeeping efforts in Bosnia and Kosovo, and deterred American efforts to stop the murders of hundreds of thousands of people because of civil war in Rwanda. And, as noted in the introduction, whether you approve or disapprove of Republican George W. Bush's many far-reaching actions in office, there is no doubt of their significance. Similarly, although President Obama has not yet completed his four-year term, his list of accomplishments noted earlier includes several notable changes in foreign and domestic policy, such as the enactment of health insurance reform. However, Obama was forced to compromise on many of these questions, and in some other cases, such as his efforts to enact comprehensive immigration reform, he was completely unsuccessful. In this chapter, we examine these and other instances of presidential successes and failures in order to understand the limits of presidential power.

The descriptions of presidential decisions that have shaped foreign policy illustrate another source of increasing presidential power. The evolution of the United States from a small colony on the Atlantic coast to the most powerful nation in the world has generated an increasing number of foreign policy questions, from the negotiation of trade deals to alliances, foreign conflicts, and international development. Given the Constitution's division of powers among the branches of government, many of these decisions fall to the president, either by himself or in concert with members of Congress.

constitutional authority (presidential) Powers derived from the provisions of the Constitution that outline the president's role in government.

statutory authority (presidential) Powers derived from laws enacted by Congress that add to the powers given to the president in the Constitution.

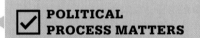

The President's Job Description

This section describes the presidency, focusing on both the president's **constitutional authority**, derived from the provisions of the Constitution that describe the president's governmental role, and on **statutory authority**, which comes from laws that give the president additional responsibilities. Throughout the section, our aim is to show how these provisions operate in modern-day American politics: what kinds of opportunities and constraints they create for the current president and future holders of the office.

▲ *In many cases, a president's policy-making authority is created by Congress. For example, the TARP bailout legislation gave bureaucrats in the Bush and Obama administrations the power to make loans to struggling banks and other firms. Treasury Secretary Timothy Geithner, shown here with the president, is one of the key members of the Obama administration responsible for implementing TARP.*

vesting clause Article II, Section 1, of the Constitution, which states that "executive Power shall be vested in a President of the United States of America," making the president both the head of government and the head of state.

head of government One role of the president, through which he or she has authority over the executive branch.

head of state One role of the president, through which he or she represents the country symbolically and politically.

HEAD OF THE EXECUTIVE BRANCH

The president's job description begins with the list of constitutional responsibilities of the office. The Constitution's **vesting clause,** "The executive Power shall be vested in a President of the United States of America," makes the president the **head of government,** granting authority over the executive branch, as well as **head of state,** or the symbolic and political representative of the country. The precise meaning of the vesting clause has been debated for more than 200 years. Presidents and their supporters argue for an expansive meaning; their opponents counter that the clause is so vague as to be meaningless. These debates are an important clue that a president's power is only partially due to the specific grants of power in the Constitution—some of it comes from less concrete statements such as the vesting clause.

The Constitution also places the president in charge of the implementation of laws, saying, "he shall take Care that the Laws be faithfully executed." Sometimes the implementation of a law is nearly automatic, as was the case in the 2005 transportation bill that allocated more than $280 billion to highway and mass transit construction nationwide—including, in its original form, funding for Alaska's "bridge to nowhere" discussed in Chapter 1. In that case, all the president needed to do to implement the law was to ensure that bureaucrats in the Department of Transportation used proper, lawful procedures to choose contractors to complete these projects.

More commonly, the president's authority to implement the law requires using judgment to translate legislative goals into programs, budgets, and regulations. For example, the bank bailout legislation enacted in late 2008 gave bureaucrats in the Bush (and later the Obama) administration funds to be used to help banks and other companies in financial distress but let the bureaucrats decide who would receive the money, how much, and under what terms.[12] Similarly, the Military Commissions Act of 2006 established the goal of using military tribunals to review evidence against terror suspects but allowed President Bush and his appointees to determine these tribunals' procedures, such as whether defendants could see classified information that was part of the evidence against them and whether evidence obtained through coercive interrogation could be used in the trials.[13] Presidents and their staff can also delay implementation of a law, either to avoid putting in place new policies they disapprove of or to give them time to lobby Congress to reverse the decision.

Finally, the president's control of the executive branch allows him to issue orders to government agencies that make significant policy changes. For example, in April 2010 President Obama directed the Department of Health and Human Services to prohibit discrimination against gay and lesbian couples in hospital visitation rules.[14] While this order could be overturned by Congress, the president's ability to act unilaterally in this way conveys significant power, as we discuss later in the chapter.

Appointments The president appoints ambassadors, senior bureaucrats, and members of the federal judiciary, including Supreme Court justices.[15] As the head of the executive branch, the president controls about 8,000 positions, ranging from high-profile jobs such as secretary of state to mundane administrative and secretarial positions. About 1,200 of these appointments—generally high-level positions such as cabinet secretaries—require Senate confirmation. Though this sounds like a large number of presidential appointees, remember that they are spread across the entire federal government. In the main, the Senate approves the vast majority of the president's nominees without much debate or controversy, with exceptions concentrated in defense, intelligence, and justice positions.

In addition, presidents make a substantial number of nominations to the federal courts; Presidents Bill Clinton and George W. Bush each appointed more than 400 judges. Because federal judgeships are lifetime appointments, they allow the president to put people into positions of power who will remain after he leaves office. For example, President George W. Bush appointed two conservative justices to the Supreme Court, John Roberts and Samuel Alito, whose impact was immediately apparent in a series of Court decisions released in 2007 on issues such as abortion rights, gun control, and affirmative action.[16] As of late 2010, Obama's two Supreme Court appointments, Sonia Sotomayor and Elena Kagan, have not had as dramatic an impact. Even so, the effects of lifetime appointments, along with the many other judicial appointments that Obama has made or will make, will not be fully apparent for years to come.

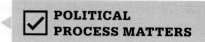

The Senate approves the vast majority of the president's nominees without much debate or controversy, but the need for Senate confirmation of the president's appointments fundamentally limits this presidential power. Rather than demanding that the Senate vote on every nomination, presidents have typically withdrawn the most controversial names and found other candidates who are more satisfactory to the Senate. For example, President Obama's nominee for secretary of health and human services, former senator Tom Daschle, withdrew his name from consideration after it was revealed that he had to pay more than $100,000 in back taxes for the use of a car and driver while he was a lobbyist.[17] President Bush took this same approach in 2005 when he allowed Bernard Kerik to withdraw his name from consideration for the position of secretary of homeland security following press reports that Kerik had, among other things, hired an illegal immigrant as a housekeeper.[18]

One way the president can temporarily dodge the need for Senate approval is to make a **recess appointment** during a period that Congress is not in session. These appointments, however, are temporary, lasting only for the rest of the legislative term. By making recess appointments, the president can fill vacant ambassadorships or designate heads of cabinet departments without waiting for a Senate vote. This provision was included in the Constitution because it was expected Congress would not be in session much of the year, but in the modern era, when Congress is in session almost continuously, recess appointments are sometimes used to bypass the confirmation process for controversial nominees. President Obama used this strategy in July 2010 to name Donald Berwick to head the Centers for Medicare and Medicaid Services.[19] Berwick had been nominated in April 2010 but faced significant Senate opposition. Obama's appointment was notable because at the time, the Senate was scheduled to be in recess for less than two weeks. Berwick can remain as a recess appointee until the end of the next session of Congress, in late 2011.

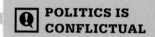

Executive Orders Presidents have the power to issue **executive orders**, proclamations that unilaterally change government policy without subsequent congressional consent.[20] (Presidents can also issue other kinds of orders that change policy, such as National Security Presidential Directives and Presidential Findings.)

One executive order issued by President Obama on December 17, 2009, gave federal employees a half-day off on Christmas Eve. Another order issued on December 29 changed the guidelines for classified information, declaring that "if there is significant doubt about the need to classify information, it should not be classified." A third executive order, issued on January 17, 2010, mobilized some reserve military personnel to participate in relief operations after the earthquake in Haiti.

Political scientists Kenneth Mayer and Kevin Price estimated that more than 1,000 executive orders issued between 1949 and 1999 were the subject of press coverage, congressional hearings, litigation, scholarly articles, or presidential public statements.[21] Most, like the Christmas Eve example noted above, dealt with relatively minor matters. However, some executive orders, such as the one about classifying information, make significant policy changes.

Executive orders may appear to give the president authority to do whatever he wants, even in the face of strong opposition from Congress. However, a president's

recess appointment When a person is chosen by the president to fill a position, such as an ambassadorship or the head of a department, while the Senate is not in session, thereby bypassing Senate approval. Unless approved by a subsequent Senate vote, recess appointees serve only to the end of the congressional term.

executive orders Proclamations made by the president that change government policy without congressional approval.

Executive Orders, Presidential Approval, and Presidential Power

One of the central arguments about presidential power in this chapter is that much of a president's ability to shape public policy comes from his ability to take unilateral actions—to implement policy changes that remain in place unless members of Congress can organize themselves to reverse them. It is easy to find examples of unilateral presidential power in action, from the creation of national parks to the limitation on harsh interrogation of terror suspects.

The problem with these examples is that they do not tell us the extent of a president's unilateral power: Is it something he does every day or only under rare circumstances? Moreover, it is not clear what factors might make the exercise of unilateral power more or less likely.

These questions were addressed in a paper co-authored by Professor Kenneth Mayer of the University of Wisconsin–Madison and one of his graduate students, Kevin Price.[a] Their study focused on identifying presidential executive orders that were "significant," meaning that they resulted in major policy changes or were controversial in some way. For example, President Obama's order in early 2009 to limit harsh interrogation of terror suspects would be categorized as significant, whereas another order issued in 2009 that allowed federal employees to leave work early on Christmas Eve was much less so. A high rate of significant executive orders means that a president frequently exercises unilateral powers in ways that matter, and a low rate suggests that, for whatever reasons, exercise of unilateral powers is a rare oc-

currence. However, a low rate of significant orders may not signal a lack of presidential power: for example, a president who has a loyal legislative majority may opt to pursue major policy changes through legislation rather than by executive order because he is confident of congressional support.

For their analysis, Mayer and Price first determined that about 7,500 executive orders had been issued between 1936 and 2000 (records before 1936 are incomplete). They analyzed a random sample of 1,028 orders and defined a significant order as one that satisfied one or more of the following criteria: there was some press coverage of the order, members of Congress held committee hearings to discuss the order, scholarly work referenced the order, the president who issued the order also issued subsequent statements that referred to the

power to issue executive orders is limited. In many cases (including several of those mentioned earlier), Congress enacts a law giving presidents the authority to issue an executive order on a particular question. Moreover, regardless of the authority used to issue an order, if members had objected to the policy changes, they could have passed a law overturning any executive orders or deny funding to implement them—although they would need support from two-thirds of both houses to override the expected presidential veto.

The president can, in theory, cite the Constitution as the sole source of his authority to issue an executive order, although this strategy is uncommon. If this happens, Congress can pass a law overturning the order, but the president could potentially refuse to abide by the new law, arguing that the constitutional grant of power can only be changed by amending the Constitution itself. Such a disagreement would likely end up before the Supreme Court, allowing the Court to decide whether the Constitution granted the president the authority he had claimed. If the Court disagreed with the president, their ruling would void the order.

Commander in Chief The Constitution makes the president the commander in chief of America's military forces but gives Congress the power to declare war. These provisions are potentially contradictory, and the Constitution leaves open the broader question of who controls the military.[22] In practice, however, the president controls day-to-day military operations through the Department of Defense and has

PRESIDENTIAL APPROVAL AND SIGNIFICANT EXECUTIVE ORDERS

Approval Rating	Probability of One or More Significant Orders
30%	.705
50	.503
70	.165

SOURCE: Adapted from Kenneth R. Mayer and Kevin Price, "Unilateral Presidential Powers: Significant Executive Orders, 1949–99," *Presidential Studies Quarterly* 32:2 (2002): 367–86.

order, there was litigation involving the order, or the order created a new governmental agency or institution that had real responsibility over public policy. Although these criteria are somewhat arbitrary—it may be that some insignificant orders received press coverage or were cited in a subsequent presidential statement—it makes sense to assume orders that satisfy none of these criteria are truly insignificant, meaning they do not reflect real presidential power.

Using their definitions, Mayer and Price found that 146 out of 1,028 (about 15 percent) of executive orders met their criteria for significance. On the one hand, this finding confirms that many executive orders deal with relatively trivial matters.

However, given that modern presidents issue hundreds of executive orders every year, a substantial number do involve important policy questions.

The authors also used their data to identify the conditions under which presidents issue significant executive orders. Mayer and Price hypothesized that popularity would influence whether a president would prefer to enact a policy change through the legislative process rather than with an executive order. As a president's popularity increases, he could be more confident that public pressure would lead members of Congress to acquiesce to his legislative proposals even if they don't like them, but as his popularity decreases, a president would be more likely to use an executive order to change policy rather than risk his proposal being rejected.

The results presented in the table confirm this expectation. For example, the probability that a president with a 30 percent approval rating issues at least one significant executive order in a year is .705; but the probability that a president with a (higher) 70 percent approval rating issues at least one significant order is only .165—in other words, popular presidents issue fewer significant executive orders, which is consistent with the study's hypothesis.

These findings show that American presidents exercise their unilateral powers on a regular basis. Moreover, they show how political factors, such as a president's approval rating, can influence the decision to make changes through executive order or by enacting legislation. Although unilateral power is not unlimited, it is clearly a significant asset for presidents. ∎

Ⓢ **Watch a video clip of Kenneth Mayer discussing this topic at wwnorton.com/studyspace.**

the power to order troops into action without explicit congressional approval. This happened in 2002, when President George W. Bush deployed more than 100,000 troops, hundreds of aircraft, and dozens of warships in anticipation of action against Iraq. Although Congress eventually passed a resolution authorizing combat operations against Iraq, this happened after the deployments had occurred. (Subsequent deployments of troops to Iraq and Afghanistan have also occurred without further congressional approval.)

Congress has the power to declare war, but this power by itself does not constrain the president. In fact, even though the United States has been involved in hundreds of military conflicts since the Founding, there have been only five declarations of war: the War of 1812, the Mexican-American War (1846), the Spanish-American War (1898), World War I (1917), and World War II (1941). However, especially in recent years, members of Congress have used other methods to try to constrain presidential war-making powers.

In particular, Congress enacted the War Powers Resolution in 1973; its provisions are described in Nuts and Bolts 11.1. However, a 2004 report by the Congressional Research Service found that between 1975 and 2003, despite dozens of U.S. military actions—ranging from embassy evacuations to large-scale operations, including the 1991 Persian Gulf War and the invasions of Iraq and Afghanistan—the War Powers Resolution has been invoked only once.[23] Moreover, despite being in effect for over thirty years, the War Powers Resolution has never faced Supreme

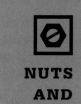

NUTS AND BOLTS

11.1

The War Powers Resolution of 1973

1. The President is required to report to Congress any introduction of U.S. forces into hostilities or imminent hostilities.
2. The use of force must be terminated within sixty days unless Congress approves of the deployment. The time limit can be extended to ninety days if the president certifies that additional time is needed to safely withdraw American forces.
3. The president is required whenever possible to consult with Congress before introducing American forces into hostilities or imminent hostilities.
4. Any congressional resolution authorizing the continued deployment of American forces will be considered under expedited procedures.

SOURCE: Richard F. Grimmett, "The War Powers Resolution: After Thirty Years," Congressional Research Service Report RL32267, March 11, 2004.

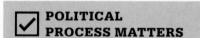

POLITICAL PROCESS MATTERS

Court review. Some scholars have even argued that the resolution actually expands presidential power because it gives the president essentially unlimited control for the first ninety days of a military operation.[24]

Despite its limitations, the War Powers Resolution has forced presidents to gain congressional approval, in the form of congressional resolutions, for large-scale military actions such as the invasion of Iraq, as well as for lesser operations, such as the deployments of peacekeeping forces in Bosnia during the 1990s. Members of Congress can also curb a president's war-making powers through budget restrictions, legislative prohibitions, and, ultimately, through impeachment.[25]

Treaty Making and Foreign Policy Treaty-making power is shared between Congress and the president: presidents and their staff negotiate treaties, which are typically then sent to the Senate for approval, which requires the support of a two-thirds majority. In the case of treaties negotiated under **fast-track authority**, both the House and Senate vote on the treaty, with majority support in each chamber required for approval. However, the president has a **first-mover advantage** in the treaty-making process. Congress considers treaties only after negotiations have ended; there is no way for members of Congress to force the president to negotiate a treaty.

Presidents have two strategies for avoiding a congressional treaty vote. One is to announce that the United States will voluntarily abide by a treaty without ratifying it. President Clinton used this tactic to implement the 1997 Kyoto Protocol, an agreement that set limits on carbon emissions by industrialized nations.[26] It is also possible to structure a deal as an **executive agreement** between the executive branch and a foreign government, which does not require Senate approval. Relative to a ratified treaty, which remains in force after the president who negotiated it leaves office, both voluntary compliance and executive agreements have the disadvantage that a subsequent president can simply undo the action, as President George W. Bush did in the case of compliance with the Kyoto Protocol.

The president also serves as the principal representative of the United States in foreign affairs other than treaty negotiations. These duties include communicating with foreign leaders, nongovernmental organizations, and even ordinary citizens to persuade them to do what the president believes is in the United States' interest. For example, in June 2009, President Obama gave a speech in Cairo, Egypt, aimed

fast-track authority An expedited system for passing treaties under which support from a simple majority, rather than a two-thirds majority, is needed in both the House and Senate, and no amendments are allowed.

first-mover advantage The president's power to initiate treaty negotiations. Congress cannot initiate treaties and can only consider them once they have been negotiated.

executive agreement An agreement between the executive branch and a foreign government, which acts as a treaty but does not require Senate approval.

at "convincing people throughout the Middle East of America's sympathy to their concerns, such as the creation of a Palestinian state."[27]

The amount of time the president devotes to foreign policy is subject to world events and therefore not entirely under his control. George W. Bush campaigned on the priorities of tax cuts and education reform[28] and against nation-building abroad. Nonetheless, in response to the September 11 attacks, he initiated efforts to build stable democracies in Afghanistan and Iraq.[29] Similarly, Barack Obama campaigned on a largely domestic agenda but spent considerable time reformulating American policy in Iraq and Afganistan, as well as on trips and speeches such as the trip to the Middle East mentioned above.

Looking at presidential actions since World War II, some scholars have argued that there are "**two presidencies**," with the high levels of citizen, interest group, and legislator interest in most domestic concerns, such as taxation, spending, or regulation of industries, and low levels of interest in many foreign policy questions, such as minor treaties or outcomes that only affect people in other countries.[30] As a result, these scholars argued, presidents may prefer to focus on foreign policy, because they can often act without congressional consent or public scrutiny. Although this thesis still makes some sense, the increasing connection between domestic and foreign policy in areas such as trade or environmental protection, as well as the increasing significance of international conflicts such as the wars in Iraq or Afghanistan, mean that more often, presidents face intense lobbying and close scrutiny of their actions regardless of whether these fall into the category of domestic policy, foreign policy, or something in between.

▲ *Particularly in the area of foreign policy, the president serves as the symbol and spokesman for the United States. President Obama, shown here during a 2009 visit to Egypt, has taken several trips to other countries and given numerous speeches in an attempt to improve foreign perceptions of America and its citizens.*

Legislative Power The Constitution establishes lawmaking as a shared power between the president and Congress.[31] The president can recommend policies to Congress, most notably in the annual **State of the Union** address. The president and his staff also work with members of Congress to develop legislative proposals, and although the president cannot formally introduce legislation, it is typically easy to find a member of Congress willing to sponsor a presidential proposal.[32] Presidents and their legislative staff also spend considerable time lobbying members of Congress to support their proposals and negotiating with legislative leaders over the details of policy. For example, compromises that led to Senate passage of Obama's economic stimulus package were reached in a meeting attended by Majority Leader Harry Reid, a group of Republican and Democratic senators, and then–White House Chief of Staff Rahm Emanuel.

The president's legislative power also stems from the ability to veto legislation, as discussed in Chapter 10. Under the two-step legislative process set by the Constitution, once both chambers of Congress have passed a bill by simple majority, the president must decide within two weeks of congressional action whether to sign it or issue a veto. Signed bills become law, but vetoed bills return to the House and Senate for a vote to override the veto. If both chambers enact the bill again with at least two-thirds majorities, the bill becomes law; otherwise it is defeated. If Congress adjourns before the president has made his decision, the president can pocket veto the proposal simply by not responding to it. Pocket vetoes cannot be overridden, but congressional leaders can avoid them by keeping Congress in session for two weeks after a bill is enacted, forcing the president to either sign the bill or veto it.

two presidencies The idea that presidents have more interest in and power over foreign policy issues compared to domestic policy issues. This asymmetry is created by the president's greater influence over the making of foreign policy and the generally lower salience of foreign policy issues.

State of the Union An annual speech in which the president addresses Congress to report on the condition of the country and recommend policies.

Presidential vetoes can have significant policy consequences. President Bill Clinton vetoed several bills that would have banned some types of late-term abortion. Supporters of these measures comprised a majority in both houses of Congress, but they could not amass the two-thirds majority required to override Clinton's veto.[33] After President Bush took office, however, the ban was approved by the House and Senate and signed into law.

Studies show that vetoes are most likely to occur under divided government, when a president from one party faces a House and Senate controlled by the other party.[34] Under these conditions, the veto allows the president to block proposals supported by legislators from the other party, producing gridlock.[35] Vetoes are much less likely under unified government, when one party controls Congress and the presidency, because the chances are much higher that the president and legislators from his party hold similar policy priorities.

Democratic president Bill Clinton faced divided government, working with a Republican-controlled Congress for all but the first two years of his eight years in office. Republican president George W. Bush, in contrast, had divided government with Democratic control of the Senate during most of his first two years, unified government for the middle four years, and divided government once again when the Democrats took control of Congress in the 2006 midterms. Clinton issued almost forty vetoes in his eight years in office, whereas Bush vetoed only eleven pieces of legislation in the same time. Bush's low number of vetoes was a consequence of the more unified government he enjoyed while in office. Two years into his term, President Obama has had unified control of Congress and, as of the end of 2010, had only issued one veto—although he is likely to issue more given Republican gains in the 2010 election.

Vetoes matter because they are not easily overridden—proponents must assemble a two-thirds majority of both houses of Congress for a successful override and do so in the face of a president's lobbying efforts to sustain the veto. Only four of Clinton's vetoes (and two of Bush's) were overridden. Thus, by vetoing legislation, presidents gain raw power over the legislative process, and they can stop a proposal dead in its tracks unless it has strong support in both houses of Congress.

A president's threats to veto legislation provide an additional source of power: they allow the president to specify what kinds of proposals he is willing or unwilling to accept from Congress. Legislators then know that they need to write a proposal that attracts two-thirds support in both houses or accede to a president's demands. For example, during the 2007 debate over funding for the war in Iraq, then-president Bush said he would veto any legislation that included a timetable for troop withdrawal. Whether Bush was willing to follow through with his threat is unclear, but the threat worked. The funding bill that ultimately passed Congress did not include any sort of timetable.

While the veto is useful to block legislation or issue a threat that encourages legislators to negotiate before casting their votes, it cannot force members of Congress to enact a proposal they oppose.[36] The president and his staff bargain with legislators, trying to craft proposals that a majority will support and sometimes offering inducements to individual lawmakers, such as presidential support for other favored policies. House members and senators from the president's party may feel obligated to help him, but it is very hard for a president to win over opponents in Congress, especially if helping the president will anger a legislator's constituents.

For example, one of President Obama's greatest domestic priorities in 2009 was enactment of health care legislation. Obama made many speeches on the subject, held numerous town hall meetings with the public, attended bargaining sessions with legislators from both parties, and dispatched many of his aides to lobby

▼ *When achieving policy goals requires legislation, presidents must negotiate with congressional leaders from both parties to assure that their proposals will be enacted into law. Here, negotiations are being conducted over the economic stimulus legislation enacted in 2009.*

Who Leads Other Countries?

The American president serves as both head of state and head of government, an arrangement that gives the president an enormous opportunity to shape what government does. However, these responsibilities create a huge workload for the president, even with the help of appointees to manage the federal government. How common is this arrangement among the world's democracies?

Scholars of comparative politics have identified three ways to structure a democracy. First, in a presidential system (or presidential republic), such as the United States, a single chief executive, who is elected separately from legislators, serves as both head of state and head of government.

Second, in a parliamentary system (or parliamentary monarchy), a member of the legislature—usually the leader of the majority party—serves as the head of government. Some of these countries do not have a head of state, and in those that do,

the position is usually held by a king or queen whose role is largely ceremonial. For example, David Cameron is Great Britain's prime minister, or head of government, and the country's head of state is Queen Elizabeth II. The queen delivers the annual message of the government to Parliament, which is the equivalent of the president's State of the Union address, but the speech is written by the prime minister and his staff; the queen simply reads the text.

The third type of democracy is a mixed republic (also called a semi-presidential system), which resembles a parliamentary system in that the head of government is chosen from the members of the legislature. Unlike a parliamentary system, however, a semi-presidential system also has a separately elected head of state or president. The powers of this chief executive vary widely between countries. In France the president largely focuses on foreign policy, while the prime minister generally handles domestic policy, but in some other

countries, such as Germany and Israel, the president's job is largely ceremonial.

The table below reports the distribution of these three systems and several other forms of government across the world. The most common form of government worldwide is a mixed republic with a separate head of government and head of state. There are also a substantial number of parliamentary monarchies. However, most of the semi-presidential systems listed in the table actually work much like parliamentary systems. In these countries, the chief executive has relatively little power, just like the monarch in a parliamentary monarchy.

Moreover, although America is not alone in having a presidential system, most other countries that use this system are new, relatively small democracies in Central or South America or in Africa, such as Nicaragua, Argentina, Nigeria, and South Africa. Among democracies in the developed world, America's presidential system is highly unusual. ■

SYSTEMS OF GOVERNMENT WORLDWIDE

	Presidential Republic	Parliamentary Monarchy	Mixed Republic	Monarchy	Military State	Other	Total
Sub-Saharan Africa	17	1	27	1	1	2	49
Asia-Pacific	8	10	14	4	1	0	37
Central and Eastern Europe	0	0	26	0	0	1	27
Middle East	1	0	8	7	1	2	19
North America	2	1	0	0	0	0	3
Central and South America	16	9	7	0	0	0	32
Scandinavia	0	3	2	0	0	0	5
Western Europe	1	7	8	1	0	2	19
Total	45	31	92	13	3	7	191

SOURCE: Based on Pippa Norris, *Driving Democracy* (New York: Cambridge University Press, 2008), Table 5.1.

members of Congress in favor of proposals that would reduce the number of uninsured individuals, end the ability of insurance companies to deny coverage for preexisting conditions, and, in theory, reduce the rate of increase in health care costs. However, although Obama's goals were popular, his proposals were not. As public opposition increased, congressional support even among Democrats began to waver, and Republicans were unified in their opposition. Although Obama ultimately prevailed and health care legislation was enacted in March 2010, the president was forced to make significant compromises to win support from reluctant Democrats. So although enactment of health care reform is rightly cited as an example of presidential power, it also illustrates the limits of this power.

In sum, by using a combination of their proposal power, lobbying, issuing vetoes and veto threats, and the other powers discussed in this section, presidents have considerable—but not unlimited—influence over legislative outcomes. One way to assess their influence is with a measure known as the presidential success score, a percentage that indicates how often a voting outcome in the House or Senate matches a president's stated position. During Obama's first year in office, for example, his success score was well over 90 percent, reflecting Democratic majorities in the House and Senate. However, Obama's percentages are not especially unusual; most presidents facing a unified Congress from their party have success scores in excess of 80 percent. Even in situations of divided government, such as Clinton after 1994 or Bush after 2006, success scores are generally no lower than 35 percent.[37] Thus, although it matters what a president asks for, and it matters how many legislators share the president's point of view, even presidents facing a hostile Congress enjoy considerable legislative success.

Other Duties and Powers The Constitution gives the president a number of additional powers, including the authority to pardon people convicted of federal crimes or commute their sentences. The only limit on this power is that a president cannot pardon anyone who has been impeached and convicted by Congress. (Thus, if a president is removed from office via impeachment, he can neither pardon himself nor be pardoned when his vice president assumes the presidency.)

Although most presidential pardons attract little attention, some have been extremely controversial. Presidents have pardoned their own appointees for crimes committed while serving in their administrations, as well as campaign contributors and personal friends. In July 2007, President Bush commuted a thirty-month jail term given to Lewis "Scooter" Libby, Vice President Dick Cheney's former aide.

▼ In July 2007, President Bush commuted the prison sentence of former vice-presidential chief of staff Lewis "Scooter" Libby, following Libby's conviction for lying to a grand jury about his role in the Valerie Plame affair.

Libby had been convicted of lying to a grand jury about his role in leaking the name of Valerie Plame, a covert CIA agent, to several journalists. As mentioned in Chapter 6, this information apparently was leaked to discredit a report written by Plame's husband, Joseph Wilson, that contradicted the administration's claims that Iraq was importing nuclear material for weapons development[38] and to punish Wilson for not endorsing the administration's claims.

The president's power to pardon raises the concern that pardons could become part of a tacit bargain between a president and his subordinates. That is, the possibility of a presidential pardon could allow executive branch employees to pursue the president's objectives with impunity, even if it meant breaking the law. Similarly, pardons granted to campaign contributors, such as President Clinton's pardon of contributor Marc Rich, who had been convicted of tax evasion, could become a way to trade money for leniency. (There is, however, no evidence that Clinton made such a bargain.) Nonetheless, even when a pardon is controversial, there is no way to reverse a president's decision.

The Constitution also gives the president a number of largely ceremonial powers, such as the power to convene Congress or to adjourn it if legislators cannot agree on an adjournment date. This provision gave the president real power during the early days of the Republic, when Congress was in session for only a few months every year. Now that Congress is in session for most of the year and party leaders set dates for the beginning and end of legislative sessions well in advance, this power is irrelevant. Similarly, the Constitution gives the president the responsibility for receiving ambassadors from other nations by officially recognizing that they speak on behalf of their countries' rulers. The president also signs commissions to formally appoint military officers.

Executive Privilege Finally, although it is not a formal power, all presidents have claimed to hold **executive privilege**, or the ability to shield themselves and their subordinates from revealing White House discussions, decisions, or documents (including e-mails) to members of the legislative or judicial branches of government.[39] The nature of executive privilege—exactly what it protects versus what Congress can force the president to release—is an unsettled question. Some constitutional scholars even argue that in legal terms, executive privilege doesn't exist.[40]

A late 2006 incident focused public attention on questions about the limits of executive privilege after senior political appointees in the Justice Department decided to remove several U.S. attorneys from office.[41] U.S. attorneys are presidential appointees who investigate and prosecute crimes under federal law. Senior Bush administration officials and spokesmen initially claimed that the attorneys were removed because of poor performance, but statements from the fired attorneys and lower-level Justice Department staff made it clear that the attorneys were dismissed because they were viewed as insufficiently loyal to President Bush. (The firings were not illegal, but they were embarrassing, as they suggested the Bush administration was more interested in political loyalty than job performance.) Several congressional committees subpoenaed Bush administration staff to testify about the matter, but Bush refused to allow the testimony to take place, arguing that conversations about the removal of the attorneys fell under executive privilege, meaning he had the right to keep these conversations confidential.[42] Ultimately, some political appointees in the Justice Department, including Attorney General Alberto Gonzalez, testified before Congress.

Even though claims of executive privilege have been made since the ratification of the Constitution in 1789, it is still not clear exactly what falls under the privilege and what does not. In the 1974 case *United States v. Nixon*, a special prosecutor appointed by the Justice Department to investigate the Watergate scandal challenged President Nixon's claims of executive privilege to force him to hand over tapes of potentially incriminating Oval Office conversations involving Nixon and his senior aides. The Supreme Court ruled unanimously that executive privilege does exist, but that the privilege is not absolute. Their decision required Nixon to release the tapes, which proved his involvement with attempts to cover up the scandal—but the ruling did not clearly state the conditions under which a future president could withhold such information.[43]

President Clinton invoked executive privilege thirteen times on matters such as an investigation of Secretary of Agriculture Mike Espy, the firing of employees in the White House Travel Office, and the investigation of his own conduct with White House intern Monica Lewinsky.[44] In all of these cases, however, federal courts ordered the documents to be released.

executive privilege The right of the president to keep executive branch conversations and correspondence confidential from the legislative and judicial branches.

The Limits of Executive Privilege

Deciding which information a president can be compelled to release to the public or to other branches of government and what he can keep confidential requires confronting fundamentally political questions. There are no right answers, and the limits of executive privilege remain unclear.

On the one hand, members of Congress need facts, predictions, and estimates from the executive branch to make good public policy. More importantly, members need to be able to weigh the pros and cons of a range of policy alternatives. Consider the controversy over the firing of eight U.S. attorneys in 2007 by senior Bush administration staff in the Justice Department. It is clear that the attorneys were fired for reasons other than poor performance, and while the precise motivations for the terminations may never be definitively proven, insufficient loyalty to the president and his policies appears to have played some role. Critics of the firing decisions noted that one of the dismissed attorneys had received complaints from a Republican senator for not bringing charges in a voting fraud case against Democrats. Another was replaced with a former aide to Bush's one-time campaign strategist and deputy chief of staff, Karl Rove.[a]

The U.S. attorney case may seem like a situation in which executive privilege does not apply. Shouldn't the American people know the reasons for hiring and firing senior government employees? If the Justice Department staff did nothing wrong, why wouldn't the Bush administration let them explain the reasons for the firings to Congress?

Congressional concerns over the firing of eight U.S. attorneys, some of whom are shown here at a House hearing, led to demands for documents and testimony from White House officials about the reasons for the firings—and claims by White House officials that this information was shielded by executive privilege.

First, testifying before Congress, or even releasing documents in response to a congressional request, is enormously time-consuming and can be surprisingly expensive. Presidential appointees who have testified before Congress have faced legal bills of $100,000 or more. If members of Congress could require information and testimony of executive branch employees whenever they wanted, it would be hard for the executive bureaucracy to get anything done—and hard to convince anyone to work there.[b]

The second argument for invoking executive privilege in the case of the U.S. attorneys is that under current law, U.S. attorneys can be removed by the president at any time, even for purely political reasons. Thus, part of the motivation for these congressional requests for information was to force Bush administration officials to publicly reveal that politics played a role in their decisions. That goal has to do with electoral politics—making Republicans look bad in the eyes of voters—as well as with members of Congress trying to acquire the information necessary to make sound decisions.

In sum, although being able to get information from a president can help members of Congress make better policy choices, there are situations in which confidentiality helps the president and his staff make good choices as well. However, executive privilege can also be used to hide crimes or questionable political tactics, or to prevent members of Congress from embarrassing the president by publicizing his mistakes or private comments. Should presidents have an executive privilege? What limits should apply to congressional requests for information and testimony? You decide. ■

Claims of executive privilege present a dilemma. On the one hand, members of Congress need to know what is happening in the executive branch. In the case of President Nixon and the Watergate scandal, claims of executive privilege allowed the Watergate cover-up to continue for more than a year and would have kept this information secret permanently if the Court had ruled in Nixon's favor.[45] Claims of executive privilege can also weaken accountability to the public, as restricting information may leave the average voter unaware of what an administration is doing. At the same time, the president and his staff need to be able to communicate freely, discussing alternative strategies and hypothetical situations or national security secrets without fearing that they will be forced to reveal conversations that could become politically embarrassing or costly. (Suppose the discussions included political strategies for the next election or a sarcastic remark about jailing their opponents.) Moreover, allowing aides to testify before Congress is enormously time-consuming and can be costly for the aides if they hire lawyers.

Even when executive privilege does not apply (because Congress has not issued a subpoena), presidents can and do refuse to provide information to the media, Congress, or the general public. For example, despite President Obama's promises to increase the transparency of government, his administration did not disclose the specifics of White House negotiations over health care reform, announcing the details of the deal only after it was carried out. However, this reluctance is no surprise given the conflict over heath care reform. Disclosure of what participants said in meetings and what they were willing to trade away would be politically embarrassing. In this sense, some confidentiality may be necessary for a president to arrive at the compromises needed to change government policy.

THE PRESIDENT AS POLITICIAN

As the head of the executive branch, the president has considerable influence over policy. However, much of what presidents do (or want to do) requires support from legislators, bureaucrats, and average citizens. As a result, the presidency is an inherently political office. The president has to take into account the political consequences of his decisions—both for his own reelection prospects and for the reelection of legislators from his party. He must also contend with the fact that achieving his policy goals often requires bargaining and compromising with others, both inside and outside of government.

Presidents try to deliver on their campaign promises not only because they believe in them but also because fulfilling them is politically advantageous. For example, one of President Obama's central campaign promises was to work to restore economic growth, a promise partly fulfilled by the enactment of economic stimulus legislation in February 2010. Whether this move turns out to be politically advantageous depends on the state of the U.S. economy in 2012, when Obama is up for reelection. If unemployment is down and growth restored, voters are likely to give Obama and his legislation at least some of the credit.

The president also typically keeps a close eye on **presidential approval**, a survey-based measurement of the percentage of the public who thinks he is doing a good job in office. Particularly during his first term, one of the president's primary concerns is to build a record that will get him reelected, and keeping approval levels as high as possible is a crucial part of this strategy. Figure 11.1, which shows the presidential approval ratings for the last six presidents who ran for reelection, reveals that first-term presidents with less than 50 percent approval are in real trouble. No recent president has been reelected with less than a 50 percent approval rating.

Various factors shape presidential popularity. In general, any issue that is at the top of the public's list of most important problems is likely to be reflected in presidential popularity. For example, the slow decline in public support for the war in Iraq, and the increase in the number of people who saw the war as the most important problem, was reflected in a systematic decline in then-president Bush's popularity in 2006 and 2007. By the time the war dropped from the top of the most

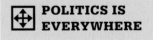
POLITICS IS EVERYWHERE

presidential approval The percentage of Americans who feel that the president is doing a good job in office.

FIGURE 11.1 PRESIDENTIAL POPULARITY AND REELECTION

This figure shows the pre-election year average approval ratings for recent presidents who ran for reelection. It shows that a president's chances of winning reelection are related to his popularity. At what level of approval would you say that an incumbent president is likely to be reelected?

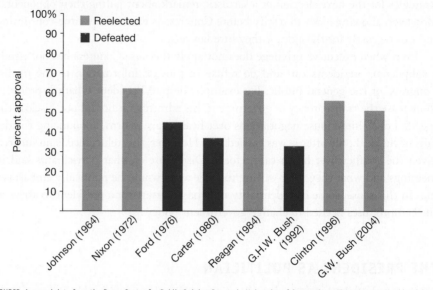

SOURCE: Approval data from the Roper Center for Public Opinion Research, University of Connecticut, "Data Access: Presidential Approval," available at http://webapps.ropercenter.uconn.edu/CFIDE/roper/presidential/ webroot/presidential_rating.cfm.

important problem list, it was replaced by the economy, which did not help Bush's approval ratings because most people were dissatisfied with economic conditions and blamed it on Bush's administration.

As this example indicates, presidential approval is mostly about outcomes, not a president's policies or actions. Approval doesn't arise from voters learning about a president's programs and voicing their support or opposition. Rather, most people look at the world around them, decide whether they like what they see, and express approval or disapproval accordingly. In this sense, presidential approval is to some extent out of a president's control. Bill Clinton enjoyed relatively high approval ratings during most of his eight years in office due to a strong domestic economy, but this economic strength probably had less to do with Clinton's policies and more to do with macroeconomic factors that were well out of Clinton's control. On the other hand, Presidents Carter and Ford had the misfortune to be in office at a time when macroeconomic conditions were relatively weak and largely out of their control. In this sense, presidential popularity is to some extent a matter of luck (see the Challenging Conventional Wisdom box for more on the president and the economy).

Conversely, the public is generally forgiving of scandal. President Clinton's affair with a White House intern had only a modest impact on his approval numbers. In fact, you have to go back to the 1970s and the Watergate scandal, which resulted in the resignation of President Nixon (and all-time low approval numbers), to find a scandal that significantly hurt a president's popularity.

All presidents have staff and consultants who regularly poll the public to discern its feelings about the president and find out what actions might increase approval. These findings influence but do not determine presidential actions. For example, poll results probably played no role in President Obama's decision to send additional

Is the President Responsible for America's Economic Conditions?

During the 2008 presidential campaign, Republican candidate John McCain and Democratic candidate Barack Obama disagreed on many things, from how to reform America's health care system to the withdrawal of troops from Iraq. Nonetheless, one point of agreement between the candidates was their willingness to blame their predecessor, President George W. Bush, for the poor state of the American economy in 2008. During a speech in June 2008, Obama charged, "We did not arrive at the doorstep of our current economic crisis by some accident of history. . . . This was not an inevitable part of the business cycle that was beyond our power to avoid. It was the logical conclusion of a tired and misguided philosophy that has dominated Washington for far too long."[a] A month later, in a speech in Denver, Colorado, McCain differed with Obama on some of the specifics but agreed that President Bush deserved some of the blame for economic conditions, saying, "This Congress and this administration have failed to meet their responsibilities to manage the government. Government has grown by 60 percent in the last eight years. That is simply inexcusable."[b]

Many Americans hold similar views. In a February 2008 survey by the Pew Research Center, almost half of the respondents assigned President Bush a "great deal" of responsibility for economic conditions—many more than blamed Congress (31 percent), multinational corporations (31 percent), or Ben Bernanke, the chairman of the Federal Reserve (6 percent).[c] These judgments fit a long-term pattern: as noted earlier, many incumbent presidents, such as Democrat Jimmy Carter (1980) and Republican George H. W. Bush (1992) have lost reelection bids because of poor economic conditions at the time they sought reelection.

For several reasons, it seems reasonable to hold the president accountable for the state of the economy. As discussed in this chapter,

Americans often blame the president for economic hardships, such as the mortgage crisis of 2007 and 2008, in which housing prices dropped significantly and many homeowners abandoned their mortgages.

the president is head of the government's executive branch, with the power to propose legislation and budgets, negotiate treaties, control the implementation of new policies, and implement a variety of changes using executive orders.

However, if you consider the president's powers in light of the overall structure of the federal government, the president has much less control over the economy than one might think. As described in Chapter 10, Congress, the president cannot influence the economy by increasing government spending, cutting taxes, or establishing major new programs without congressional consent. And even if he could, these efforts might not have much effect given that the federal budget ($3.1 trillion in 2008) is only about one-fifth of the total American economy (more than $14 trillion in 2008). Moreover, the president has no direct control over the Federal Reserve, which can influence economic growth and inflation by changing interest rates or the money supply. The Federal Reserve

operates as an independent agency, which means that its decisions are not subject to review by the president or Congress. And finally, even if the president could single-handedly manipulate legislation, government spending, interest rates, and the money supply, his impact on the American economy would still be subject to conditions in the much larger world economy (approximately $65 trillion in 2008) as well as the price of crucial inputs such as oil.

Though American citizens and candidates for office often blame the sitting president for the state of the economy, this attribution is based on a misperception of the president's powers. The president can do many things that help shape economic conditions in America, particularly if members of Congress or the Federal Reserve are willing to cooperate in these efforts. But the president cannot guarantee Americans high rates of economic growth or low inflation and unemployment. ■

troops to Afghanistan. Although the move received majority support, it is likely that Obama would have made the same decision even if he had faced much stronger public opposition. On the other hand, some legislators' tepid support for Obama's proposed health care reform proposals was driven, at least in part, by an absence of public enthusiasm for the proposal.

Political considerations matter somewhat less to a second-term president (since running for reelection is not an option), but politics still matters in the second term. Members of Congress are more likely to support policy initiatives proposed by a popular president, believing that this popularity reflects public support for the president's goals. Conversely, an unpopular president, such as President Bush in 2007 and 2008, finds it much harder to build support for new programs. For example, when Bush called on members of Congress to end the practice of earmarking federal funds for specific projects to benefit their own constituents, even members of Bush's party in the House and Senate ignored the proposal.[46]

The President as Party Leader The president is the unofficial head of his political party and generally picks the day-to-day leadership of the party, or at least has considerable influence over the selection. This process begins when a presidential candidate captures the party's nomination. For example, soon after Barack Obama became the presumptive Democratic Party nominee by amassing a majority of convention delegates, some of his senior aides and advisers took on leadership positions in the Democratic Party organization.[47]

The president's connection to the party reflects the fact that their interests are intertwined. The president needs support from his party members in Congress to enact legislation, and the party and its candidates need the president to compile a record of policy achievements that reflect well on the party and to help raise the funds needed for the next election. Therefore, party leaders generally defer to a presidential candidate's (or a president's) staffing requests, and most presidents and presidential candidates take time to meet with national party leaders and the congressional leadership from their party to plan legislative strategies, make joint campaign appearances, and raise funds for the party's candidates. For example, in 2009 alone, President Obama attended more than twenty-five fund-raising events for Democratic congressional candidates, with many more planned in advance of the 2010 midterm elections.[48]

On the other hand, when presidential approval ratings drop to low levels, most members of Congress see no political advantage to campaigning with the president or supporting his proposals, and they may become increasingly reluctant to comply with his requests. In the 2002 and 2004 elections, Republican legislators stressed their connection to President Bush and gladly accepted offers of joint campaign appearances. In 2006 and 2008, however, many Republican candidates tried to deemphasize their connection to the president and did not ask him to campaign with them.[49] A similar phenomenon arose in the 2010 midterms for Democratic candidates and President Obama: in many districts, incumbents believed that campaigning with Obama would reduce their chances of reelection, as it would remind voters of unpopular proposals championed by Obama, such as health care reform and the economic stimulus legislation, both enacted in 2009.

Going Public The president would appear to be in an excellent position to communicate with the American people because of his prominent role and the extensive media coverage devoted to anything he says to the nation. Broadcast and cable networks even give the president prime time slots for his State of the Union speech and other major addresses. The media attention that comes with the presidency provides the president with a unique strategy for shaping government policy: the ability to **go public**, or appeal directly to American citizens, in the hopes of getting the

go public A president's use of speeches and other public communications to appeal directly to citizens about issues the president would like the House and Senate to act on.

electorate to pressure members of the House and Senate to do what he wants.[50] By directly seeking the support of the electorate, the president can utilize what President Theodore Roosevelt called the bully pulpit—exploiting the fact that anything he says will receive a high level of media attention.[51]

The first American president to give a live nationwide address was Franklin Roosevelt, who used his 1936 State of the Union speech to argue against congressional attempts to undo his New Deal reforms.[52] Throughout his presidency, Roosevelt made thirty informal radio broadcasts, which he called fireside chats. Though it is hard to say for sure, as political scientists do not have good polling data from the 1930s, it appears that Roosevelt's efforts helped to restore public confidence and built support for his New Deal proposals. Such public appeals are partly designed to persuade, but they also serve to bring an issue that the president considers important to the attention of citizens who already share his views, in the hope that they will urge their elected representatives to support the president's requests.

▲ One way recent presidents have gone public is to hold "town hall meetings" with American citizens, such as this one from June 2009 that focused on health care reform. The goal of these meetings is not so much to persuade attendees to support the president, but to attract media attention and get the president's message out to a wider audience.

Of course, going public doesn't always bring success; the key to making it work is public opinion—whether people agree with what the president wants. In 1981 Ronald Reagan used televised speeches to build support for his tax cut proposals, which received a warm welcome from many Americans. In contrast, in 2006 and 2007, as public approval for the war in Iraq declined, President Bush gave several televised speeches in an attempt to regain support for the conflict, but these efforts had little effect.[53] Similarly, President Obama's speeches aimed at building support for health care reform had minimal effects on public opinion. More generally, studies suggest that most of the time, most Americans ignore or reject a president's attempts to go public. Thus, while presidents might want to shape public opinion by going public, in general, they will find it hard to be successful.[54] Going public may also have political consequences for the president. It can alienate members of Congress, as it represents an attempt to go over legislators' heads to reach the American people directly, thereby getting Congress to agree with the president without the benefit of the usual bargaining and negotiations.[55]

President Obama's experiences during the campaign and in office illustrate the limits and possibilities of going public. During the campaign, his organization made excellent use of social networking sites and e-mail to stay in contact with millions of supporters.[56] This network was a crucial mobilization tool that helped Obama win the nomination by dominating caucus elections where turnout is low and candidates need to get supporters to the polls. The network proved to be less useful as a way to lobby Congress in favor of Obama's proposals, such as health care, although some Democrats in Congress cited letters and e-mails from supporters as one reason for their vote in favor of Obama's proposals.

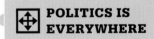

POLITICS IS EVERYWHERE

PRESIDENTIAL SUCCESSION

Under the Constitution, presidents are limited to two full terms in office. A vice president who becomes president in between elections can, if reelected, serve two more full terms even after taking over during the first half of his predecessor's term. Under the 25th Amendment, a vice president can also temporarily take over as president, a procedure used in 2007 when President George W. Bush had a medical procedure requiring anesthesia.[57]

If both the president and the vice president were to die or become incapacitated, the Speaker of the House of Representatives would become president. Next in line

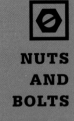

The Order of Presidential Succession

1. Vice President
2. Speaker of the House
3. President pro tempore of the Senate
4. Secretary of State
5. Secretary of the Treasury
6. Secretary of Defense
7. Attorney General
8. Secretary of the Interior
9. Secretary of Agriculture

10. Secretary of Commerce
11. Secretary of Labor
12. Secretary of Health and Human Services
13. Secretary of Housing and Urban Development
14. Secretary of Transportation
15. Secretary of Energy
16. Secretary of Education
17. Secretary of Veterans Affairs
18. Secretary of Homeland Security

is the president pro tempore of the Senate, and then a list of cabinet secretaries in the order shown in Nuts and Bolts 11.2. Whenever the entire cabinet and Congress gather in one place, such as at the annual State of the Union address, at least one member of the cabinet is assigned to be somewhere else, so that in the event of a catastrophe, someone in the line of succession would survive to assume the presidency.

In the event that the vice president must be replaced due to resignation, impeachment, or incapacity, the 25th Amendment allows the president to nominate a new vice president, who must be confirmed by majority votes in the House and the Senate. This procedure was used twice in the 1970s, first to make Gerald Ford vice president under Richard Nixon (replacing Spiro Agnew), then, after Nixon's resignation, to make Nelson Rockefeller vice president under Ford.[58]

The Executive Branch

As head of the executive branch, the president runs a huge, complex organization with hundreds of thousands of employees. This section describes the organizations and staff who help the president exercise his vast responsibilities, from managing disaster-response efforts to implementing policy changes.[59] Among these employees are appointees who hold senior positions in the government. These individuals serve as the president's eyes and ears in the bureaucracy, making sure that bureaucrats are following presidential directives.

Many other executive branch employees work within the Executive Office of the President, which has employed about 1,800 people in recent administrations. About one-third of these employees are concentrated in two offices, the Office of Management and Budget, which develops the president's budget proposals and monitors spending by government agencies, and the Office of the United States Trade Representative, which negotiates trade agreements with other nations.[60]

THE EXECUTIVE OFFICE OF THE PRESIDENT

Nuts and Bolts 11.3 lists the organizations that make up the **Executive Office of the President (EOP)** and one of its main components, the White House Office. Both include offices that have clear policy-related or political missions, such as the Office of Management and Budget mentioned above, or the Domestic Policy

Executive Office of the President (EOP) The group of policy-related offices that serves as support staff to the president.

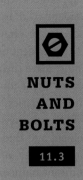

The Executive Office of the President

Council of Economic Advisors
Council on Environmental Quality
National Security Council
Office of Administration
Office of Management and Budget

Office of National Drug Control Policy
Office of Science and Technology Policy
Office of United States Trade Representative
President's Foreign Intelligence Advisory Board
White House Office

WHITE HOUSE OFFICE

Domestic Policy Council
Homeland Security Council
National Economic Council
Office of Faith-Based and Community Initiatives
Office of the First Lady

Office of National AIDS Policy
Privacy and Civil Liberties Oversight Board
USA Freedom Corps
White House Fellows Office
White House Military Office

Council, whose staff are involved in all aspects of policy making, from developing proposals to monitoring their implementation.

Regardless of their official job title and policy responsibilities, one of the most important duties of EOP staff is helping the president and candidates from his party achieve their policy goals and get reelected. Consider the Office of National Drug Control Policy (ONDCP). During 2006, representatives from the office traveled throughout the country to hold joint press conferences with Republican and Democratic members of Congress to announce federal grants for drug abuse prevention programs. However, three months before that year's midterm elections, with Republicans in danger of losing majority control of the House and Senate, ONDCP officials began holding press conferences exclusively with Republican legislators.[61] An e-mail from the head of the office, John Walters, revealed that this strategy was an attempt to help vulnerable Republican candidates. In other words, people in the ONDCP did not abandon their official duties, but they also did everything they could to help Republicans in the 2006 election.

Even the small, lower-level offices within the White House Office play political roles as they carry out their official responsibilities. One office that fulfils such a dual role is the Photo Office, whose official job is to "photographically document and maintain an archive of official events of the president, the first lady, the vice president, and his wife."[62] The office also photographs the president with political supporters, providing pictures that can be used to thank them for their contributions or other efforts.

The most influential EOP staff occupy the offices in the West Wing of the White House. The West Wing contains the president's office, known as the Oval Office, and space for the president's chief aide and personal secretary, as well as senior aides such as the vice president, the president's press secretary, and the chief of staff, who coordinates White House operations.

Many recent chiefs of staff, such as former congressman Rahm Emanuel, the first chief of staff to President Obama, are central figures in the development of policy proposals and negotiations with members of Congress. However, the chief of staff serves as the agent of the president—what matters is what the president wants, not a chief of staff's policy preferences.

▲ *Presidents rely on loyal staff members to develop and implement new policies, manage relations with Congress, oversee the bureaucracy, and inform the public. Many of these aides, such as President Obama's press secretary, Robert Gibbs, and senior adviser, David Axelrod, shown here, have worked for their president since the early days of his presidential campaign.*

Most EOP staff members are presidential appointees who retain their positions only as long as the president who appointed them remains in office. These individuals are often drawn to government service out of loyalty to the president or because they share his policy goals. However, most leave their positions after a year or two to escape the pressures of the job, the long hours, and the relatively low government salaries.[63] Despite the fairly frequent turnover in many EOP positions, some EOP offices, such as the Office of Management and Budget, the Office of the United States Trade Representative, and the National Security Council, also have a significant number of permanent staff analysts and experts.[64]

When the president appoints people to EOP positions, his primary expectation of them is loyalty, rather than a concern for the general public or policy expertise.[65] A look at the biographies of White House staffers shows that many had worked on the campaign of the president who appointed them, often from very early in the race for the party's general election nomination. The backgrounds of some of Barack Obama's prominent West Wing staffers underline this point. David Axelrod, who serves as a senior adviser, was a political strategist and campaign manager for Obama from the beginning of his presidential campaign. Obama's press secretary, Robert Gibbs, had held the same position during the presidential campaign and when Obama was a senator. Former chief of staff Rahm Emanuel was a longtime political ally of Obama's in Chicago—and Emanuel's replacement, Peter Rouse, had been Obama's Chief of Staff during Obama's two years as a Senator.

The exceptions to the loyalty rule for appointees are individuals who received their jobs because of their expertise, their connections to the president's political party (as opposed to the president himself), or links to an important group outside the government. For example, when he entered office, President Obama retained Robert Gates as secretary of defense. Gates had no direct connection to President Obama; in fact, Republican George W. Bush appointed Gates. However, he was an expert on defense policy who had held senior defense- and intelligence-related positions in previous administrations, and he had been a member of the Iraq Study Group, which produced a well-publicized report in late 2006 that led to significant changes in U.S. strategy in Iraq.

Why is loyalty so important? Put yourself in the position of a president whose packed day begins with an intelligence briefing and ends with a state dinner. All the while, crucial decisions about public policy are being made throughout the federal government. You have no time to make these decisions yourself or even to supervise those who make them, so you need staff who understand what you want the government to do and will dedicate themselves to implementing your vision.[66] The emphasis on loyalty in presidential appointments also has an obvious drawback: appointees may not know much about the jobs they are given and may not be very effective at managing the agencies they are supposed to control. As we discuss in Chapter 12, The Bureaucracy, many observers believe that delays in the provision of federal disaster relief after Hurricane Katrina stemmed in part from the fact that many of the senior positions in the Federal Emergency Management Agency were held by political appointees who knew little about such operations.[67]

THE VICE PRESIDENT

As set out in the Constitution, the vice president's job is to preside over Senate proceedings. This largely ceremonial job is usually delegated to the president pro tempore of the Senate, who in turn typically gives the duty to a more junior member.

The vice president also has the power to cast tie-breaking votes in the Senate.[68] For example, in 2005, Vice President Cheney cast the deciding vote to pass a package of budget cuts to various government programs, including Medicare, Medicaid, and federally funded student loans.[69] As mentioned earlier, the vice president's other formal responsibility is to become president if the current president dies, becomes incapacitated, resigns, or is impeached. Of the forty-four people who have become president, nine were vice presidents who became president in midterm.

These rather limited official duties of the vice president pale in comparison to the influential role played by recent vice presidents. Vice President Dick Cheney, who served with President George W. Bush, exerted a significant influence over many policy decisions, including the rights of terror suspects, tax and spending policy, environmental decisions, and the writing of new government regulations.[70] Many critics claimed that Cheney had too much power, and some even described him as a co-president.[71]

Cheney's influence stemmed from his expertise. He had served as President Gerald Ford's chief of staff, a long-time member of the Republican leadership in the House of Representatives, and as secretary of defense in President George H. W. Bush's administration. Moreover, Cheney and President George W. Bush held similar views on what government should do. In other words, Bush didn't blindly trust Cheney's judgment. Rather, he knew they usually agreed on what should be done.[72]

Although Dick Cheney's level of influence was unique, other recent vice presidents have also had real power. For example, Vice President Al Gore was an important adviser to President Bill Clinton. And Barack Obama's vice president, Joe Biden, also appears to play an important role, attending all significant meetings and serving as the last person the president talks to before making a decision.

The vice president's role as a senior adviser and trusted confidante is a recent development. Before this change, vice presidents were often chosen to provide political or regional balance to a presidential candidate's electoral appeal. Jack Garner, who was Franklin Roosevelt's first vice president, once said the office was "not worth a bucket of warm spit." Garner had been added to the ticket in an attempt to win southern votes in the 1932 election but had been ignored by Roosevelt and his aides after the election and given little to do. Similarly, Dwight Eisenhower chose then-senator Richard Nixon as his vice president in order to appeal to conservative groups in the Republican Party but excluded Nixon from many meetings once in office. However, the expansion of the federal government beginning in the 1960s appears to have led recent presidents to look beyond political or regional factors when choosing a vice president to find a like-minded individual who can help them manage the bureaucracy and achieve their policy goals. Barack Obama's choice of Joe Biden reflected these priorities, as Biden's foreign policy expertise was expected to offset Obama's relative inexperience in this area.

▲ George W. Bush's vice president, Dick Cheney, was one of the most influential vice presidents in American history.

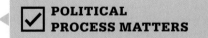

☑ **POLITICAL PROCESS MATTERS**

THE PRESIDENT'S CABINET

The president's **cabinet** is composed of the heads of the fifteen executive departments in the federal government, along with other appointees given cabinet rank by the president. Nuts and Bolts 11.4 lists the cabinet positions. The cabinet members' principal job is to be the front-line implementers of the president's agenda in their executive departments. As we discuss in more detail in Chapter 12, they monitor the actions of the lower-level bureaucrats who retain their jobs regardless of who is president and who are not necessarily sympathetic to the president's priorities.

Like other presidential appointees, cabinet members are chosen for a combination of loyalty to the president and expertise. Barack Obama's secretary of transportation,

cabinet The group of fifteen executive department heads who implement the president's agenda in their respective positions.

Cabinet Positions

Secretary of Agriculture

Secretary of Commerce

Secretary of Defense

Secretary of Education

Secretary of Energy

Secretary of Health and Human Services

Secretary of Homeland Security

Secretary of Housing and Urban Development

Secretary of the Interior

Secretary of Labor

Secretary of State

Secretary of the Treasury

Secretary of Transportation

Secretary of Veterans Affairs

Vice President

White House Chief of Staff

Attorney General

Head of the Environmental Protection Agency

Head of the Office of Management and Budget

Head of the Office of National Drug Control Policy

United States Trade Representative

Ray LaHood, a former moderate Republican congressman, had served on the Transportation and Infrastructure Committee while serving in the House of Representatives, so he had a good working knowledge of federal transportation programs. And Secretary of Energy Steven Chu was a Nobel Prize–winning physicist who had directed a major energy research laboratory.

The American Public and the President

As we have described, presidents need to cultivate public support to get reelected and to enact their policy proposals. Thus, to understand what kinds of policy goals presidents set and how they seek to come across to the public, it is important to consider what Americans want from their presidents and which characteristics they associate with a successful president.

Table 11.1 shows the results of several surveys about the qualities Americans want in a president. Large majorities want the president to have good judgment and to be ethical and compassionate, and smaller majorities want a president who says what he believes, holds consistent positions, and is forceful and decisive. A third or fewer want the president to be willing to compromise, to have political experience and savvy, to have Washington experience, or to be loyal to his party. Relatively few Americans consider military experience an important presidential asset.

The interesting part of this table lies in the comparison of items that received strong support (consistency, forcefulness, and decisiveness) with those that fewer people found appealing (compromise, political experience, political savvy, Washington experience, and party loyalty). We have seen that American politics is conflictual, which means that compromising and bargaining are fundamental parts of what successful politicians do. However, it seems that most Americans are not looking for a president who has the traits and experiences that facilitate negotiating and deal making. Moreover, presidents may face tough decisions between building a public reputation for firmness and making the compromises necessary to change or implement policies.

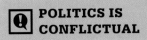

POLITICS IS CONFLICTUAL

TABLE 11.1 CITIZEN DEMANDS ON THE PRESIDENT

These data show that many Americans want the president to stick to his principles, say what he believes, and be forceful and decisive. Fewer consider political experience and willingness to compromise essential presidential qualities. How might the political necessity for bargaining and compromise affect a president's ability to satisfy citizens' expectations?

Essential Qualities	1995	1999	2003
Sound judgment	76%	78%	76%
High ethical standards	67	63	67
Compassion	64	63	63
Saying what one believes	59	57	56
Consistent positions	51	50	52
Forcefulness and decisiveness	50	46	49
Willingness to compromise	34	33	38
Experience in public office	30	38	37
Political savvy	31	–	36
Experience in Washington	21	27	32
Party loyalty	25	33	30
Military experience	–	–	16

SOURCE: Pew Research Center, "Bush Reelect Margin Narrows to 45%–43%," news release, September 25, 2003, available at http://people-press.org/reports/pdf/194.pdf.

Consider, for example, the welfare reforms enacted by President Clinton and Congress in 1996. The legislation was not Clinton's ideal; he opposed its five-year lifetime limit on benefits. However, Clinton supported other provisions in the bill that increased funding for job-training and day-care programs designed to help welfare recipients transition to gainful employment. Taken together, the package was probably the best Clinton could hope for from a Republican-controlled Congress. Moreover, the proposal attracted a high level of public support. Signing the bill did not help Clinton's reputation as a man of unwavering principle, but it did implement real changes to welfare programs and increased his support among fiscally conservative voters in the 1996 election.

EXPLAINING PRESIDENTIAL APPROVAL

Questions about the public's approval of the president have been asked in mass surveys since Franklin Roosevelt was president. Figure 11.2 reports presidential approval data for the three most recent presidents, Bill Clinton, George W. Bush, and Barack Obama. The data for Clinton show a relatively rare pattern of steady improvement throughout his time in office. In contrast, George W. Bush's popularity steadily declined following the sharp spike upward after the September 11 attacks. And halfway through his term, popularity figures for President Obama show gradual decline.

What explains this variation? Presidential approval generally spikes during national crises, such as the Iranian Hostage Crisis during Jimmy Carter's term, the Persian Gulf War during George H. W. Bush's term, or the September 11 attacks

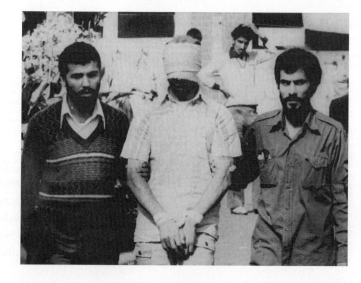

▼ Presidential approval is influenced by international events that concern Americans, such as the taking of American hostages by militant Iranian students in 1979. President Jimmy Carter initially saw his approval ratings increase, but they declined steadily as the crisis continued into 1980.

FIGURE 11.2 **PRESENTIAL APPROVAL RATINGS FOR RECENT PRESIDENTS**

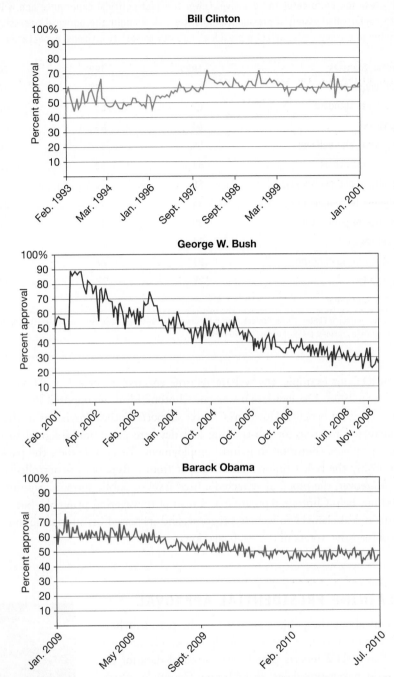

SOURCE: Approval data from the Roper Center for Public Opinion Research, University of Connecticut, "Data Access: Presidential Approval," available at http://webapps.ropercenter.uconn.edu/CFIDE/roper/presidential/webroot/presidential_rating.cfm.

during George W. Bush's first term. Recall from our discussion of public opinion that this phenomenon has been called the "rally 'round the flag" effect,[73] comparing the electorate to troops gathering around a flag during a battle.

There are no such spikes in the chart for Bill Clinton, reflecting the fact that there were no national crises during his time in office. In such relatively calm times, presidential approval reflects the overall state of the nation, including citizens' perceptions

of economic conditions and national security. In Clinton's case, economic conditions steadily improved throughout his presidency, generating the increase in his approval ratings. Even when Clinton was being impeached in 1998 and 1999, his popularity did not suffer. This finding may suggest that even if Americans want an ethical president, they forgive misdeeds given good performance on the issues they care about, such as the economy. In contrast, during George W. Bush's two terms in office, he presided over an increasingly unpopular war in Iraq, along with a deteriorating economy, particularly during his last two years in office. Both of these factors contributed to the steady decline in Bush's approval ratings.

Similarly, while President Obama's first two years in office have been largely free of scandal, and Obama has enacted a substantial portion of his campaign agenda, such as health care reform, withdrawal of American combat forces from Iraq, and financial stimulus legislation, his declining poll numbers suggest that most Americans are focused on the mediocre state of the economy—and that Obama's popularity will increase only if the economy improves.

◄ POLITICS IS EVERYWHERE

Assessing Presidential Power

Throughout American history, presidents have realized major achievements. They have expanded the United States, fought wars, and enacted large government programs. Yet, as discussed earlier, the Constitution grants the president only rather limited powers. Assessing presidential power requires examining this contradiction. Saying that the presidents gained power because of the expansion of the United States or the increased size of the federal budget or bureaucracy tells only part of the story. Why did this power go to the presidents rather than to Congress or to bureaucrats?

Debates over the source and extent of presidential powers have a long history. In the 1790s, Alexander Hamilton and James Madison, writing anonymously as Helvidius and Pacificus, argued about whether George Washington needed congressional approval to declare the United States neutral in the war between Britain and France.[74] Even after more than two centuries, many of the limits to presidential powers—including which executive actions require congressional approval and which ones can be reversed by Congress—are not well-defined.

These constitutional ambiguities are mirrored by the unwritten nature of many presidential powers. Recall our discussion of the president's ability to influence the legislative process. In the Constitution, the president's powers are limited to a vague reference to advising Congress on the state of the union and the power to veto legislation, subject to congressional override. But as we have noted, presidents often have very real influence at all points in the legislative process. One classic work in presidential studies argues that this influence comes from a president's **power to persuade** legislators to accept the president's point of view—presidents can offer a variety of small inducements like visits to the Oval Office and campaign assistance, and can draw on the natural respect that most people (including members of Congress) feel for the presidency regardless of who holds the office.[75] The relatively high presidential success scores noted earlier suggest that most presidents have considerable success in their persuasion efforts.

The very ambiguity of the Constitution also creates opportunities for the exercise of presidential power. Recall the case of the president's war-making powers: the

power to persuade The theory that a president's ability to shape government policy depends more on his ability to convince members of Congress, bureaucrats, and citizens to do what he wants than it does on the formal powers conveyed to him by the Constitution.

unilateral action (presidential) Any policy decision made and acted upon by the president and his staff without the explicit approval or consent of Congress.

unitary executive theory The idea that the vesting clause of the Constitution gives the president the authority to issue orders and policy directives that cannot be undone by Congress.

▼ *The president wields considerable power through the ability to take unilateral actions. Here, President Clinton signs an order establishing Utah's Grand Escalante National Monument on thousands of acres of federally owned land.*

Constitution makes the president military commander in chief but gives Congress the power to declare war and to raise and support armies, without specifying which branch of government is in charge of the military. Thus, at least part of presidential authority must be derived or assumed from what the Constitution *does not say*—ways in which it fails to define or delineate presidential power or grants inherent power to the president.[76]

Presidency scholars Terry Moe and William Howell argue that constitutional ambiguities about presidential power have allowed presidents to take **unilateral action**, changing policy on their own without consulting Congress or anyone else. Although Congress could, in theory, undo unilateral actions through legislation, court proceedings, or even impeachment, Moe and Howell argue that the costs of doing so, in terms of time, effort, and public perceptions, are often prohibitive. The result is that presidents can take unilateral action despite congressional opposition, knowing their actions stand little chance of being reversed. Of course, unilateral action may not lead to policy change—presidents and their staffs have to monitor subsequent actions by bureaucrats to make sure they are implementing the president's decision.

The 2007 debate over funding the war in Iraq provides a good example of how constitutional ambiguities create opportunities for unilateral actions. During the debate, many Democrats in Congress wanted to cut off war funding to force the withdrawal of American forces from Iraq, but supporters of the Bush administration responded with what they called the **unitary executive theory**. They argued that the Constitution's vesting clause allows the president to issue orders and policy directives that members of Congress cannot undo unless the Constitution explicitly gives them this power. In the case of funding the Iraq war, they maintained that the Constitution's description of the president as commander in chief of America's armed forces meant that even if Congress refused to appropriate funds for the war, the president could order American forces to stay in Iraq and order the Department of the Treasury to spend any funds necessary to continue operations. Ultimately, members of Congress approved a funding resolution—but if they hadn't and the president had refused to withdraw American forces, the disagreement likely would have required resolution by the Supreme Court.

Many unilateral actions occurred throughout the Bush presidency. President Bush acted unilaterally when he restricted the legal rights of terror suspects, made strategic decisions about the wars in Iraq and Afghanistan, froze the financial assets of members of Al Qaeda and other terror organizations, reorganized America's intelligence agencies to create the Department of Homeland Security, and relaxed environmental regulations. Bush unilaterally withdrew the United States from the Anti-Ballistic Missile Treaty that limited U.S. and Russian defensive missile installations, and he authorized wiretaps of Americans' international phone conversations without gaining warrants from the Foreign Intelligence Surveillance Court, a special federal court created to approve such requests.[77]

It is important to understand that Bush was not the only president to take (or threaten to take) broad, unilateral actions. President Obama, for example, unilaterally issued executive orders limiting how terror suspects could be interrogated and strengthening driver safety rules for federal employees and for commercial truck drivers.[78]

Moe and Howell cite many historical examples of unilateral presidential actions, such as the annexation of Texas, the freeing of slaves in the Emancipation Proclamation, the desegregation of the U.S. military, the initiation of affirmative action programs, and the creation of major agencies such as the Peace Corps.[79] Other studies found that the majority of federal administrative agencies had been created by unilateral presidential actions and that more than 90 percent of American agreements with other nations since the 1940s were concluded as executive agreements between the president and a foreign government, rather than as treaties requiring ratification by Congress.[80]

Most presidents have also tried to control the interpretation and implementation of laws by issuing a **signing statement** when signing a bill into law. These documents, which explain the president's interpretation of the new law, are issued most often when the president disagrees with the interpretation of members of Congress who supported the legislation but still wishes to approve the bill. Presidents issue signing statements so that if the courts have to resolve uncertainties about the bill's intent, judges can take into account not only the views expressed during congressional debates about the bill, but also the president's interpretation of it.[81] The president can also influence the implementation of a law through a signing statement, essentially telling the bureaucracy to follow his interpretation of the law rather than Congress's. (The same end can be achieved by giving bureaucrats internal instructions about how to implement a law.)

In some cases, presidents have found loopholes in laws designed to restrict their power. An analysis of several pieces of legislation designed to curb presidential power that were enacted in the 1970s (including the War Powers Resolution, the Ethics in Government Act, and measures dealing with budgets and intelligence agencies) found that subsequent presidents have actually used these laws to justify unilateral actions—the precise opposite of what was intended.[82] For example, current law requires the president to give congressional leaders "timely notification" of secret intelligence operations. During the Reagan administration, senior officials did not reveal the existence of ongoing operations for several months. When these operations were eventually discovered, officials claimed they were within the letter of the law because it did not specify a time limit for notification.[83]

Unilateral actions are especially likely in the last days of a presidency, especially if the next president is from the other party, as the outgoing president tries to influence as many important policies as possible before leaving office.[84] For example, in January 2001, President Clinton finalized regulations that would lower the amount of arsenic allowed in drinking water by 2006. When President George W. Bush took office, he and his staff debated whether to rescind the regulations, believing they imposed too many economic costs, but decided against it. They did not want to publicly oppose a regulation that made water safer to drink. However, President Obama issued an executive order in 2009 that reversed a Bush-era order that prevented California from implementing gas mileage standards that were higher than existing federal regulations.

In theory, members of Congress can undo a president's unilateral action by enacting a law to overturn it, but this is harder than it may sound.[85] Some members of Congress may approve of what the president has done or be indifferent to it, or may give a higher priority to other policies. Still, reversals do happen: after Obama announced plans to close the Guantánamo Bay detention center for terrorist suspects, the House and Senate added an amendment to a spending bill stating that the prison could not be closed until the administration released plans explaining where the prisoners would be sent.

Members of Congress can also write laws in a way that limits the president's authority over their implementation.[86] The problem with this approach is that members of Congress delegate authority to the president or the executive branch bureaucracy for good reasons—either because it is difficult for legislators to predict how a policy should be implemented or

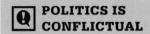

signing statement A document issued by the president when signing a bill into law explaining his interpretation of the law, which often differs from the interpretation of Congress, in an attempt to influence how the law will be implemented.

Q POLITICS IS CONFLICTUAL

▼ *The president's power to act unilaterally is constrained by many factors, including the ability of members of Congress to block most of these actions. For example, in 2009 President Obama ordered the closure of the detention center for terror suspects at Guantánamo Bay, Cuba, but Congress passed legislation preventing the closure until the Obama administration developed detailed plans for relocating the prisoners.*

▲ *Federal courts can undo unilateral presidential actions. A series of Supreme Court rulings forced the Bush administration to allow terror suspects such as Salim Hamdan, an Al Qaeda member captured in Afghanistan, to challenge their imprisonment. This courtroom sketch from the U.S. naval base in Guantánamo, Cuba, shows Hamdan (far left) and his legal team.*

because they cannot agree among themselves on an implementation plan.[87] Members of Congress from the president's party may also want him to have the authority because they hold similar policy goals and would therefore benefit from the exercise of unilateral power.

Even if members of Congress tried to use these strategies to limit the president's authority, the president could still argue—along the lines of the unitary executive theory—that Congress could not overturn his actions because the Constitution did not explicitly gave the legislature this power. The only option for members of Congress would be to take the president to court, probably all the way to the Supreme Court, to demonstrate that the president overstepped his constitutional authority, which is not a very practical or expedient option. Aside from the fact that the Court might not side with Congress, these legal proceedings could take years.

For example, in May 2010, executives from British Petroleum (BP) agreed to President Obama's request that they set up a $20 billion fund to compensate people whose homes or businesses were harmed by the oil spilled from BP's Deepwater Horizon oil well in the Gulf of Mexico. While several members of Congress opposed Obama's action, they could not muster enough votes to reverse the action; moreover, they could not mount a court challenge for the simple reason that BP had voluntarily agreed to set up the fund. Even so, opponents of some unilateral actions have used court decisions to limit presidential power. In 1952, when steel mill workers were planning to go on strike, President Truman argued that federal control of the steel mills was necessary to sustain the United States' efforts in the Korean War. Ninety minutes before the steelworkers were to go on strike, President Truman went on national television to announce that the U.S. government would seize the nation's steel mills to keep them operating. However, the Supreme Court's ruling in *Youngstown Sheet and Tube v. Sawyer* reversed President Truman's actions.[88] More recently, in the 2006 case *Hamdan v. Rumsfeld* and the 2008 case *Boumediene v. Bush,* the Supreme Court reversed the Bush administration's actions that had denied terror suspects access to federal courts.[89]

Congress also has the power to remove the president or vice president from office through the **impeachment** process. However, removing a president is much more difficult than passing a law to undo a unilateral action. First, House members must impeach (indict) the president by majority vote, which accuses him of a crime or breach of his sworn duties. Then senators hold a trial, followed by a vote—in which a two-thirds majority is required in order to remove the president from office.

These procedures are rarely used; only two presidents have faced an impeachment vote: Andrew Johnson in 1866 and Bill Clinton in 1999. Johnson was involved in a political dispute over administration of the southern states after the Civil War; Clinton was alleged to have lied under oath in a sexual harassment lawsuit. Though both of these presidents were impeached by the House, they were not convicted by the Senate, so they stayed in office. One reason impeachment is difficult is that members of Congress who are upset about certain presidential actions might nevertheless oppose removing the president from office. They might approve of his other initiatives, want to prevent the vice president from becoming president, or have concerns about the political backlash that impeachment could generate against them or their party.

In sum, ambiguities in the Constitution create opportunities for unilateral presidential action. These actions are subject to reversal through legislation, court decisions, and impeachment, but members of Congress face significant costs if they undertake any of these options. As long as the president is careful to limit exercise of unilateral power to actions that do not generate intense opposition in Congress, he can implement a wide range of policy goals without official congressional consent—provided, of course, that bureaucrats go along with the president's wishes, a question we take up in the next chapter. Thus, presidential power has important consequences for government policy—but it is not unlimited.

impeachment A negative or checking power over the other branches that allows Congress to remove the president, vice president, or other "officers of the United States" (including federal judges) for abuses of power.

Conclusion

A president's power over government policy is derived from constitutional authority, statutory authority, and ambiguities within these official grants of power that give the president a substantial ability to act unilaterally. Even so, presidential power is limited. The president shares many powers with Congress, including lawmaking, treaty-making, and war-making powers. Moreover, presidents are politicians who need public support, both to win reelection and to persuade members of Congress to approve their policy initiatives. The public evaluates the president based on how he handles issues that are a priority for many Americans, such as the economy, health care, and national security.

These factors suggest a very different explanation for the seemingly expansive power of Presidents Barack Obama and George W. Bush, which we discussed at the beginning of this chapter. For one thing, Bush's and Obama's policy successes are not unusual; many presidents have similar records of accomplishment. Moreover, although both presidents enjoyed notable successes, they were also forced to concede defeat in a number of cases, in the face of insufficient congressional or public support, or through reversal of their actions by the courts. Moreover, many of their successful unilateral actions concerned policy areas in which members of Congress and the public either favored their proposals or had no strong feelings about them. Thus, the president remains an important figure in American politics but is clearly not solely responsible for setting government policy.

Who are America's presidents? What effect have presidential actions had, and how has the presidency developed over time?

- Presidents have done important things, such as expanding U.S. territory, fighting wars, and creating new domestic programs. It matters who gets elected president.
- Many presidential accomplishments are made in the face of high levels of conflict between the president and Congress, the president and the courts, or between all three branches of government.
- The power of the presidency has expanded over time, in part because of the increased power and size of the United States.

What is the president's job description?

- The president's duties include overseeing the implementation of legislation; appointing senior government officials and federal judges; issuing executive orders; serving as military commander in chief; directing America's foreign policy; proposing, signing, and vetoing legislation; and carrying out other duties.
- The president is a politician who needs to cultivate citizens' support to get reelected, to pressure Congress to enact his proposals, and to help elect candidates from his party.
- Even after 220 years of American history, the limits of presidential power in such areas as national security and executive privilege remain unclear.

What does the executive branch do? How is it organized?

- Political appointees in the Executive Office of the President, along with the vice president and appointees in executive departments and agencies, help the president manage the federal government and provide political assistance to the president and to candidates from his political party.
- The primary mission of presidential appointees is to help the president achieve his or her policy goals. As

such, loyalty to the president is generally valued over policy expertise.

- Vice President Dick Cheney was the most powerful vice president in American history owing to his experience, expertise, and general agreement with President Bush.

What do Americans want from the president? What determines whether presidential approval ratings are high or low?

- Most Americans want the president to have good judgment and to be ethical and compassionate. Somewhat fewer Americans want a president who is politically experienced and willing to compromise.
- Issues such as the economy and health care are perennially important in presidential elections. In recent elections, national security issues such as preventing terrorist attacks and managing the wars in Iraq and Afghanistan have also come to the fore.
- Presidential approval ratings are driven by a president's performance on the major issues facing the country, such as the economy and national security.

How much power do presidents really have, and under what circumstances do they exercise it?

- Ambiguities in the Constitution and in statutory authority allow the president to act unilaterally—that is, to change policies without congressional approval. All recent presidents have taken unilateral actions, especially on foreign policy and at the end of their terms.
- Congress can try to undo unilateral presidential actions by passing legislation with a veto-proof, two-thirds majority. Even then, reversing the president's action may require a court challenge if the president claims he is using constitutional authority.
- Congress also has the power to remove the president from office through the impeachment procedure. Impeachment is a cumbersome and politically risky strategy, however, and it has never been successfully used to remove a president.

⊚ STUDENT STUDYSPACE

Find quizzes and other review material at wwnorton.com/studyspace.

CRITICAL THINKING

1. Why might bureaucrats who are not presidential appointees be more responsive to congressional mandates and demands than to the president's orders, even though the president heads the executive branch?

2. What can members of Congress do to stop a president from changing policy unilaterally? Which of these methods seems most effective, and why?

3. Why do you think Americans often hold the president more accountable than Congress for the state of the economy?

KEY TERMS

cabinet (p. 417)
constitutional authority (presidential) (p. 397)
executive agreement (p. 402)
Executive Office of the President (EOP) (p. 414)
executive orders (p. 399)
executive privilege (p. 407)

fast-track authority (p. 402)
first-mover advantage (p. 402)
go public (p. 412)
head of government (p. 398)
head of state (p. 398)
impeachment (p. 425)
power to persuade (p. 421)
presidential approval (p. 409)

recess appointment (p. 399)
signing statement (p. 423)
State of the Union (p. 403)
statutory authority (presidential) (p. 397)
two presidencies (p. 403)
unilateral action (presidential) (p. 422)
unitary executive theory (p. 422)
vesting clause (p. 398)

SUGGESTED READING

Alter, Jonathan. *The Promise: President Obama, Year One*. New York: Simon and Schuster, 2010.

Canes-Wrone, Brandice. *Who Leads Whom? Presidents, Policy, and the Public*. Chicago: University of Chicago Press, 2006.

Draper, Robert. *Dead Certain: The Presidency of George W. Bush*. New York: Free Press, 2007.

Howell, William G. *Power without Persuasion: The Politics of Direct Presidential Action*. Princeton, NJ: Princeton University Press, 2003.

Klein, Joe. *The Natural: The Misunderstood Presidency of Bill Clinton*. New York: Random House, 2002.

Krehbiel, Keith. *Pivotal Politics: A Theory of U.S. Lawmaking*. Chicago: University of Chicago Press, 1998.

Lewis, David E. *Presidents and the Politics of Agency Design*. Palo Alto, CA: Stanford University Press, 2003.

Mayer, Kenneth. *With the Stroke of a Pen: Executive Orders and Presidential Power*. Princeton, NJ: Princeton University Press, 2001.

Moe, Terry M., and William G. Howell. "The Presidential Power of Unilateral Action," *Journal of Law, Economics, and Organization* 15 (1999): 132–46.

Neustadt, Richard E. *Presidential Power and the Modern Presidents: The Politics of Leadership from Roosevelt to Reagan*. New York: Free Press, 1990.

Rudalevige, Andrew. *Managing the President's Program: Presidential Leadership and Legislative Policy Formation*. Princeton, NJ: Princeton University Press, 2002.

Schlesinger, Arthur M., Jr. *The Crisis of the Old Order, 1919–1933*. Boston: Houghton Mifflin, 1957.

Skowronek, Stephen. *The Politics Presidents Make: Leadership from John Adams to Bill Clinton*. Cambridge, MA: Harvard University Press, 1997.

Coast Guard vessels respond to the fire on BP's
Deepwater Horizon oil rig after it exploded in the Gulf
of Mexico. Some observers have accused regulators of
failing to properly oversee this and similar offshore oil
drilling operations. Are such failures the exception or
the rule in the federal bureaucracy?

The Bureaucracy

To many Americans, the bureaucracy signifies all the deficiencies of the federal government. In part, these beliefs are no surprise, as it is easy to find stories of bureaucratic inefficiency, fraud, and folly:

- The Minerals Management Service, which had jurisdiction over the BP oil rig that leaked over 5 million barrels of oil into the Gulf of Mexico in Spring 2010, apparently "shortened safety and environmental reviews; overlooked flaws in the spill response plan; and ignored warnings that crucial pieces of emergency equipment, blowout preventers, were prone to fail."[1]

CONFLICT AND COMPROMISE

in American Politics

- Government agencies have lost more than 1,000 laptop computers containing citizens' Social Security numbers and other personal information.[2]
- An audit of government credit cards at the Department of Agriculture found more than $5 million in employees' personal charges, including car payments, tattoos, and Ozzie Osborne concert tickets.[3]
- As part of its response to the devastation wreaked by Hurricane Katrina, the Federal Emergency Management Agency (FEMA) chartered three cruise ships to house relief and reconstruction workers in New Orleans, paying more than it would have cost to send the same number of people on a Caribbean cruise.[4]
- Employees of the Transportation Security Administration inadvertently posted a manual on a government procurement Web site that detailed how to evade airport security screening for weapons and explosives.[5]

On the other hand—and perhaps surprisingly—it is just as easy to find cases of bureaucratic accomplishment, effectiveness, and even heroism. Consider some of the government employees awarded a Service to America Medal in recent years by the Partnership for Public Service, a nonprofit, nonpartisan organization.[6]

- Janet Kemp of the Veterans Administration established a suicide-prevention hotline for veterans, a program that is credited with saving more than 5,000 lives.
- Doctors Douglas Lowy and John Schiller directed research at the National Institutes of Health that resulted in a new vaccine to prevent cervical cancer.
- Michael German of the Department of Housing and Urban Development developed new government–business partnerships that led to a 30 percent reduction in long-term homelessness in America.

BIG QUESTIONS

- ✪ What is the federal bureaucracy?
- ✪ How has the American bureaucracy developed over time?
- ✪ What are the characteristics of the modern American bureaucracy? What explains its current organization and size?

- ✪ Who are bureaucrats? What motivates them, and what constraints do they face?
- ✪ How do Americans see the bureaucracy?
- ✪ How can the bureaucracy be controlled?
- ✪ Why does the bureaucracy sometimes fail?

- Internal Revenue Service employee Terrence Lutes developed the eFile system for filing tax returns over the Internet, cutting processing costs by 90 percent and allowing citizens to receive their tax refunds in as little as ten days.

These examples—both the impressive and the confounding—illustrate the enormous range of the federal bureaucracy and its impact on life in America. The bureaucracy, it seems, is everywhere. Americans encounter the work of government employees every day: when they sort through mail delivered by the Postal Service, drive on highways funded by the Department of Transportation, or purchase food inspected by the Food and Drug Administration. The prices Americans pay to surf the Web, watch television, or use a cell phone are influenced by regulations issued by the Federal Communications Commission. When they go on vacation, their bags are inspected by the Transportation Security Administration, the aircraft and pilots are scrutinized by the Federal Aviation Administration, and the beaches may be maintained by the Army Corps of Engineers.

The paradox of the federal bureaucracy is that the same organization that accomplishes so many big tasks also does things that are inefficient, wasteful, and downright dumb. Do these shortcomings result from inevitable accidents—or are they the consequences of deliberate actions? And if so, why were agencies designed to fail or to do things that look a lot like failure?

▼ *Although many aspects of the federal government's response to Hurricane Katrina fit the stereotype of a bumbling, ineffectual bureaucracy, there were also many successes, such as the Coast Guard rescue operations after Katrina hit. Why do bureaucrats seem so competent in some cases but incompetent in others?*

These questions go well beyond the instances of success and failure noted above. Consider the recent financial meltdown in the American economy. What role was played by bureaucrats tasked with regulating and monitoring banks and other financial firms? Did they do the best job they could, or was their inability to prevent the meltdown the result of bureaucratic incompetence or malfeasance?

In this chapter, we show that many bureaucratic failures can be explained by the bureaucracy's procedures for making decisions, including the complexity of the tasks it undertakes and by the political conflicts that ensue when elected officials and interest groups attempt to control bureaucrats' actions. These conflicts are at the root of many seemingly inexplicable bureaucratic actions and outcomes. For example, the need to monitor bureaucrats to ensure that they carry out congressional mandates often leads to the use of rigid procedures that make it impossible for bureaucrats to shift policies in light of changing circumstances or local conditions. In many cases, these structures reflect compromises among lawmakers holding different ideas of what they would like bureaucrats to do. In this sense, the bureaucracy is just like Congress, multinational corporations, or other large enterprises that have many employees and undertake complex tasks. As the recent economic crisis suggests, managers in large corporations can be just as fallible as government bureaucrats.

This chapter also shows that the public's disdain for bureaucrats is not uniform. Most Americans award higher ratings to government agencies and offices with which they have personal experience. Similarly, most bureaucrats believe deeply in their agency's mission and work hard to achieve its goals.

bureaucracy The system of civil servants and political appointees who implement congressional or presidential decisions; also known as the administrative state.

civil servants Employees of bureaucratic agencies within the government.

political appointees People selected by an elected leader, such as the president, to hold a government position.

What Is the Federal Bureaucracy?

The American federal **bureaucracy** that makes up the government's executive branch is composed of millions of **civil servants**, who work for the government in permanent positions, and thousands of **political appointees** holding short-term, usually senior positions, who are appointed by and loyal to the president. Another name for the bureaucracy is the administrative state, which refers to the role bureaucrats play in administering government policies.[7] Most constitutional scholars agree that the president is nominally in charge of the bureaucracy—although, as we will see, in most cases he shares this power with members of Congress.

WHAT DO BUREAUCRATS DO?

The task of the bureaucracy is to implement policies established by congressional acts or presidential decisions. Sometimes the tasks associated with putting these laws and resolutions into effect are very specific. For example, in the appropriations bill for fiscal year 2010, which set federal spending levels for October 1, 2009 to September 30, 2010, Congress mandated a 3.4 percent pay increase for military personnel and funds for specific new military equipment.[8] These provisions require no discretion on the part of the bureaucrats who implement them. Their tasks were limited to making the administrative changes necessary to raise military pay and following through with the purchase of the specified equipment.

More commonly, however, legislation determines only the general guidelines for meeting governmental goals, allowing bureaucrats to develop specific policies and programs. In these cases, bureaucrats' actions determine the essence of government action, deciding "who gets what, when, and how."[9] For example, the 1938 Federal Food, Drug, and Cosmetic Act gave the Food and Drug Administration (FDA) the job of determining which drugs are safe and effective, but it allowed FDA bureaucrats to develop their own procedures for making these determinations.[10] Currently the FDA requires that drug manufacturers first test new drugs for safety, then conduct further trials to determine their effectiveness. An FDA advisory board of scientists and doctors reviews the results of these tests. Then FDA bureaucrats decide whether to allow the manufacturer to market the drug.

More generally, the job of the federal bureaucracy includes a wide range of activities, from regulating the behavior of individuals and corporations to buying everything from pencils to jet fighters. These activities are inherently political and often conflictual—ordinary citizens, elected officials, and bureaucrats themselves often disagree about how these decisions should be resolved and work to influence bureaucratic actions to suit their own goals.

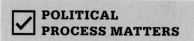 **POLITICAL PROCESS MATTERS**

Influences on Bureaucratic Rule Making

Rule making is one of the most important functions of the federal bureaucracy. By creating and revising regulations, bureaucrats influence the behavior of everyone, from individual Americans to large corporations. In theory, rule making is controlled by congressional mandates, with bureaucrats limited to translating legislative directives into law. But as we show in this chapter, there are many factors, from expertise to asymmetric information, that give bureaucrats a measure of discretion when drawing up rules. Rule making is generally carried out by unelected bureaucrats, often involving highly technical questions that attract little press attention. The question is, How do bureaucrats use their discretion, and whose interests are served and whose are ignored?

This issue is particularly important with regard to some aspects of the rule-making process, particularly the notice and comment procedure. These are designed to democratize the process, facilitate participation from small groups and even individuals, and give these actors some influence over rule making. Many observers have argued that even with these measures, rule making is often biased toward business interests, with little attempt to accommodate citizen preferences, regardless of whether they are expressed through the notice and comment procedure. Moreover, individuals may lack the technical resources to file a credible comment on a proposed regulation or may fall victim to the free rider problem and fail to organize a joint effort.

This empirical question about rule making is the subject of a collaboration between two political scientists, Susan Webb Yackee and Jason Webb Yackee, both of whom teach at the University of Wisconsin.[a] Their study focused on thirty rules issued by a range of government agencies from 1994 to 2001. These rules attracted almost 1,700 comments. The authors and their research assistants read each comment and noted the source (corporations, government agencies, individuals, public interest groups, etc.), what the comment asked for in the proposed regulation (for example, whether the authors of the comment wanted more or less government involvement), and the complexity and the salience of the proposed rules (complex rules were expected to attract fewer comments from individuals, whereas salient rules were expected to attract more comments).

The authors found, firstly, evidence of a high level of business participation in the rule-making process. Nearly 57 percent of the comments filed came from corporations or business groups. An additional 19 percent came from government agencies. Only 6 percent came from public interest groups and only a few from individuals. Thus, although the notice and comment procedure provides the opportunity for citizens to participate in the writing of regulations, either as individuals or as part of an organized group, it appears that most of the time, relatively few Americans take advantage of the opportunity.

The Yackees built on this finding by using statistical analysis to determine the relationship between what business groups are asking for in their comments (more or less government regulation on a particular activity) and the content of the rule ultimately issued by bureaucrats at the end of the rule-making process. Their analysis controlled for a variety of other factors, such as the kind of regulation being written, the number of comments received from business interests, and the complexity of the rule being written.

The results of the analysis are shown in the figure, which illustrates how the content

---

regulation A rule that allows the government to exercise control over individuals and corporations by restricting certain behaviors.

notice and comment procedure A step in the rule-making process in which proposed rules are published in the Federal Register and made available for debate by the general public.

Regulations A **regulation** is a government rule that affects the choices that individuals or corporations make, by either allowing or prohibiting behavior, setting out the conditions under which certain behaviors can occur, or assessing costs or granting benefits based on behavior. For example, in the case of deepwater offshore drilling, the Minerals Management Service developed regulations about every aspect of the drilling process—from how many lifeboats should be on a rig to what kinds of hardware should be used to drill and maintain the well site on the ocean floor, over six miles below the surface. Bureaucrats are given the authority to write regulations by the statute that sets up their agency or by a subsequent act of Congress. Regulations are developed in a process known as the **notice and comment procedure**.[11] Before a new regulation developed by a government agency or organization can take effect, it must be published in the Federal Register, an official, daily publication that includes rules, proposed rules, and several other types of government documents. Individuals and companies that will be affected by the regulation can then respond to the agency

of comments received from business interests affects the probability that bureaucrats will choose to write rules that result in more government involvement or less government involvement.[b] The horizontal axis measures the content of comments from business interests—on the left-hand side, all the comments ask for less government involvement, but moving rightward, the comments become increasingly pro-involvement. The vertical axis gives the predicted probability of different kinds of rules. As you can see, when business comments are uniformly anti-involvement, the probability that the rule will reduce government involvement is very high, but as the comments become more and more pro-involvement, the probability of reduced involvement becomes much smaller and the probability of more involvement increases substantially. When business interests are evenly divided (or nearly so), it is just as likely that no change will occur as move in the pro or anti direction.

These findings provide two important insights into the rule-making process. First, simply creating a way for citizens to participate in the writing of new regulations is not enough to motivate participation. Getting citizen opinions into the rule-making process will require additional measures to tap opinions directly through some sort of survey, help groups to organize, or motivate participation in other ways.

Second, the analysis shows that the notice and comment procedure is not just for show. The content of the regulations selected for analysis in this study appears to have been influenced by the content of the comments received from business interests. What we don't know is whether the things these groups were asking for were good only for business and harmful to everyone else or whether the rules served the interests of others in society. Even so, given the apparent lopsided influence of business interests on rule making, this study casts considerable doubt on the claim that the notice and comment procedure has democratized the rule-making process. ■

Watch a video clip of Susan Webb Yackee discussing this topic at wwnorton.com/studyspace.

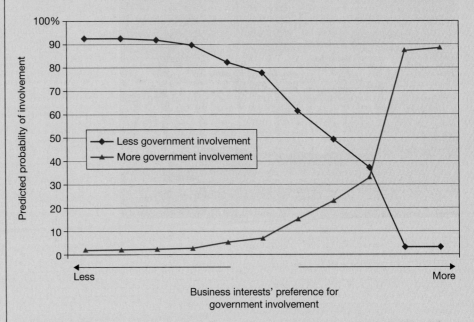

THE BUREAUCRACY'S RESPONSIVENESS TO COMMENTS FROM BUSINESS INTERESTS

Predicted probability of involvement

- ◆ Less government involvement
- ▲ More government involvement

Business interests' preference for government involvement

Less — More

SOURCE: Jason Webb Yackee and Susan Webb Yackee, *Journal of Politics* 68:1 (2006): 134.

that proposed it, either supporting the new regulation or opposing it, and offering different versions for consideration. Those potentially affected by the regulation can also appeal to members of Congress or to the president's staff for help in getting the proposed rule revised. The agency then issues a final regulation, incorporating, if deemed appropriate, changes based on the submitted comments. This final regulation is also published in the Federal Register and put into effect.

The process of devising or modifying regulations is often political. Members of Congress and the president often have strong opinions about how new regulations should look—and even when they don't, they may still get involved in the process on behalf of a constituent or interest group who would be affected by the proposed regulation. Bureaucrats take account of these pressures from elected officials for two reasons. First, the bureaucrats' policy-making power may have been created by a statute that members of Congress could overturn if they disapprove of how bureaucrats use their power. Second, bureaucrats need congressional support to get larger

▲ Federal regulations influence many aspects of everyday life that would not seem likely to be affected by government action. The increase in the number of women's intercollegiate athletic teams is partly due to regulations that require equal funding for men's and women's teams.

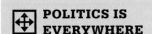

POLITICS IS EVERYWHERE

budgets and more important tasks for their agency, and to prevent budget cuts. Thus, despite bureaucrats' hands-on power to implement—and thereby often shape—policies, their agencies' budgets, appointed leaders, and overall missions are subject to elected officials' oversight. That said, regulations benefit from the expertise and information bureaucrats have gained from their education and work experience. Moreover, bureaucrats can take testimony from people and groups interested in a new regulation or government action, with the goal of becoming as well informed as possible about a proposed regulation's possible effects.[12]

Many regulations are issued each year. In recent years, the Federal Register has contained more than 22,000 pages and typically about 4,000 new regulations a year, of which about 150 are labeled "economically significant," meaning that they are estimated to have more than $100 million in economic impact.[13] Although nearly all government agencies issue regulations, most come from a few agencies, including the Federal Trade Commission, which regulates commerce; the Federal Communications Commission, which regulates the media companies that create content as well as the telecommunications companies that transmit information; and the FDA, which regulates drugs, medical products, food, and cosmetics.

Federal regulations affect every aspect of everyday life. Regulations influence the gas mileage of cars sold in the United States, the materials used to build roads, and the price of gasoline. Regulations determine the amounts that doctors charge senior citizens for medical procedures; the hours that medical residents can work; and the criteria used to determine who gets a heart, lung, or kidney transplant. Regulations set the eligibility criteria for student loans, limit how the military can recruit on college campuses, determine who can get a home mortgage and what their interest rate will be, and describe what constitutes equal funding for men's and women's college sports teams. Regulations also shape contribution limits and spending decisions in political campaigns.

Some regulations can have a life-or-death impact on individual Americans. In 2007 the Centers for Medicare and Medicaid Services established criteria that hospitals performing organ transplant operations must meet for their transplant procedures to qualify for Medicare reimbursement. In plain terms, these regulations determine which hospitals senior citizens on Medicare can use if they need a transplant. To qualify for reimbursement, a hospital needs to perform a set number of transplants per year, meet minimum success rates for those operations, manage their patient waiting lists according to certain criteria, and provide particular services to transplant recipients and their families—including advising transplant recipients on their diets.[14]

Regulations are often controversial because they involve trade-offs between incompatible goals, as well as decisions made under uncertain circumstances. For example, the FDA drug approval process prioritizes the goal of preventing harmful drugs from coming to market.[15] As a result, patients sometimes cannot get access to treatments that are still considered experimental because they have not received FDA approval, even when a yet-unapproved treatment is a patient's only remaining option.[16] Advocates for patients have argued that people with dire prognoses should be allowed to use an experimental treatment as a potentially life-saving last resort.[17] However, current FDA regulations prevent them from doing so except under very special circumstances, arguing that unapproved treatments may do more harm than good and that allowing wider access to these drugs may tempt manufacturers to market new drugs without adequate testing.

Procurement Bureaucrats also handle government purchases, buying everything from pencils to aircraft carriers. The General Services Administration (GSA) manages 8,600 buildings owned or leased by the government and a fleet of 208,000 vehicles, and provides government agencies with most of their supplies.[18]

Procurement seems a straightforward task: agencies determine what they need, find out who can supply it, and choose the lowest-cost provider. However, procurement for the federal government can be surprisingly complicated. Consider the purchase of a new model of fighter plane or an attack submarine. Bureaucrats must devise criteria for choosing between designs with very different strengths and weaknesses. Procurement decisions are also shaped by congressional and executive mandates. For example, when the GSA searches for suppliers of a particular product, it often has to give a preference to small businesses or firms owned by minorities or veterans. These guidelines are the result of the political process, as elected officials try to shape government actions to suit their own policy goals.

Finally, high-profile procurement decisions are often made in times of crisis, with little opportunity for evaluation. For example, it is not unreasonable to criticize FEMA for overpaying for the cruise ships it used as hotels—but it is important to keep in mind that FEMA needed housing in severely flooded areas for large numbers of relief workers and needed it right away. In the middle of the crisis, the cruise ships may well have been the best option, even at an inflated cost.

Just about every president has tried to reform the procurement process. President Obama, for example, has proposed an end to cost-plus and no-bid contracts (cost-plus refers to a system where contractors are paid whatever it costs to provide a service plus a percentage of costs as their profit; no-bid contracts are situations when contracts are awarded without a competitive bidding process). Although these practices may seem wasteful and inefficient, the government may be forced to use them because of the complex and unique goods and services it needs to buy.

Providing Services Street-level bureaucrats provide services to help ordinary Americans.[19] For example, many job-training programs are run by federal employees. The federal government provides disaster assistance, such as the benefits received by the residents of areas affected by Hurricane Katrina or the September 11 attacks. Federal employees manage tourist attractions from the National Zoo to the Statue of Liberty to Mount Rushmore. They inspect passenger baggage at airports, monitor aircraft maintenance, and direct aircraft in flight.

Research and Development Government scientists work in areas from medicine to astronomy to agriculture. Sometimes their work takes the form of basic research, such as discoveries by scientists working for the National Institutes of Health of some of the mechanisms that govern cell reproduction and death. Government scientists also do applied research, from developing new cancer drugs to improving crop management techniques. Federal funds also support research in many universities and corporations that examines similar questions.

Managing and Directing Some bureaucrats spend their time supervising actions taken by people outside government. For example, the Department of Defense uses civilian contractors to provide support services in Afghanistan, from cooking and laundry to some maintenance work on planes, trucks, and ships. Many workers at

street-level bureaucrats Agency employees who directly provide services to the public, such as those who provide job-training services.

POLITICS IS EVERYWHERE

state capacity The knowledge, personnel, and institutions that the government requires to effectively implement policies.

red tape Excessive or unnecessarily complex regulations imposed by the bureaucracy.

standard operating procedures Rules that lower-level bureaucrats must follow when implementing policies.

government facilities and public works projects are employees of private corporations working on government contracts.

BUREAUCRATIC EXPERTISE AND ITS CONSEQUENCES

This description of what bureaucrats do highlights the fact that in the main, bureaucrats are experts. Even compared to most members of Congress or presidential appointees, the average bureaucrat is a specialist in a certain policy area, with a better grasp of his agency's mission and rationale. For example, people who hold scientific or management positions in the FDA usually know more about the benefits and risks of new drugs than people outside the agency. Their decision to deny unapproved drugs to seriously ill patients may look cruel, but it may also reflect a thoughtful balancing of two incompatible goals: preventing harmful drugs from reaching the market, and allowing people who have exhausted all other treatments access to risky, experimental products. A bureaucracy of experts is an important part of what political scientists call **state capacity**—the knowledge, personnel, and institutions needed to implement policies that change society.[20]

Despite bureaucrats' policy expertise, their decisions may often appear to take too much time, be based on arbitrary judgments of what is important, and have unintended consequences—to the point that actions designed to solve one problem may create new and even larger ones. Many critics of the modern bureaucracy cite the abundance of **red tape**, which refers to unnecessarily complex procedures, or **standard operating procedures**, which are the rules that lower-level bureaucrats must follow when implementing policies regardless of whether they are applicable to the situation at hand. FEMA's performance after Hurricane Katrina, as well as some of the other bureaucratic blunders mentioned in the introduction to this chapter, are classic examples of these phenomena. Sometimes bureaucrats simply make mistakes. For example, the FDA has delayed helpful drugs from reaching the market or approved drugs that were later found to have harmful side effects. However, these decisions may have been justified based on the information available to bureaucrats at the time.

There have been many attempts to make the bureaucracy operate more smoothly and effectively by mandating that bureaucrats make decisions using specific procedures or criteria. These efforts have added many acronyms to the language of Washington bureaucrats: PPBS, MBO, ZBB, PBB, and REGO.[21] Though each of these efforts can claim some modest successes, none have fundamentally changed the way the government does business. The lesson seems to be that examples of poor performance by America's bureaucracy have little to do with the bureaucracy itself. Otherwise, one of these reform packages would have solved these problems, resulting in a well-functioning bureaucracy.

These cases of bureaucratic ineptitude and the failure of reform efforts raise a critical and perplexing question: How can an organization full of experts develop such dysfunctional ways of doing business? Bureaucrats are neither clueless nor malevolent. What, then, explains red tape and counterproductive standard operating procedures? The answer is the very strength of the American bureaucracy: its expertise.

Because bureaucrats know things that elected officials do not and because bureaucrats have their own policy goals, it is hard for elected officials to evaluate what bureaucrats are doing. For example, FEMA's use of a cruise ship to house

▼ *Despite their policy expertise, bureaucrats still sometimes make mistakes. When the Medicare program implemented the new Prescription Drug Benefit, information about the new coverage was available on an easy-to-read Web site, but the agency soon learned that many seniors who needed to access the information did not know how to use a Web browser.*

NUTS AND BOLTS

12.1

The Problem of Control: Principals and Agents

The principal–agent game describes one common interaction in politics that involves an individual or group (an "agent") acting on behalf of another (the "principal"). The problem of control captures the difficulty principals have when trying to ensure that their agent does things that are good for the principal, rather than pursuing the agent's own goals. In the federal government, for example, the president and Congress are principals, and bureaucrats are agents. An agent may not want to work, or may prefer outcomes that the principal does not like. Moreover, because the agent is an expert at the task he has been given, he has private information inaccessible to the principal. The problem for the principal, then, is this: giving the agent explicit orders prevents the agent from acting based on expertise; but if the principal gives the agent the freedom to make decisions based on expertise, the principal has no control over the agent's actions.

For example, suppose Congress and the president direct the FDA to shorten its drug approval process. FDA officials might have mandated a lengthy process based on their expert assessment of the best way to screen out harmful drugs. By giving orders that supersede the FDA officials' screening process, elected officials would be sacrificing the valuable bureaucratic expertise behind the policy and risking the hasty approval of unsafe drugs. On the other hand, if Congress and the president allow FDA bureaucrats to devise their own procedures and regulations, there is a chance that the FDA could use this freedom to pursue goals that have nothing to do with drug safety. For example, critics of the FDA's procedures have asserted that a drawn-out approval process is designed to favor large companies that already have drugs on the market over smaller companies trying to get approval for drugs that would compete with existing products.

The principal–agent game captures another aspect of conflict in politics—conflict that occurs within an organization between the people who make policy choices and the people who implement them. It shows that in a situation in which the implementers are experts, the people who give orders are not completely in charge, and may defer to the experts even if they suspect that their wishes are being ignored.

relief workers after Hurricane Katrina may have looked expensive, but, as we have suggested, the FEMA staffer who was on the scene and signed the contract may have found that all other options were either more expensive or simply impossible. Without knowing the specifics, it is impossible to judge the efficacy of the decision. Similarly, the Minerals Management Service's decision to skimp on routine safety inspections on oil rigs may have been the result of laziness—but it may also have reflected a decision to focus on what were at the time thought to be more serious concerns. Without looking deeper into the issue, it is impossible to be sure.

Political scientists refer to the difficulty that elected officials and their staff face when they try to interpret, understand, or influence bureaucratic actions as the **problem of control**,[22] a classic example of which is the **principal–agent game**. For more details, see Nuts and Bolts 12.1. The "problem" in a principal–agent game is that elected officials (the principals) face an unpleasant trade-off. They can allow bureaucrats (the agents) to make policy decisions on their own, which allows bureaucrats to take advantage of whatever expertise or knowledge they might have but also frees bureaucrats from scrutiny, allowing them to implement their own version of good public policy rather than the goals set by Congress. Or elected officials can force bureaucrats to do what members of Congress think is best, which means that policy decisions will not incorporate bureaucratic expertise.

There is no doubt that members of Congress are sometimes right to be suspicious of the motives held by members of the bureaucracy. Sometimes bureaucratic actions are the result of what scholars call **regulatory capture**, a situation in which bureaucrats cater to a small group of individuals or corporations regardless of the impact of these actions on public welfare. For example, in the case of the Minerals Management

problem of control A difficulty faced by elected officials in ensuring that when bureaucrats implement policies, they follow these officials' intentions but still have enough discretion to use their expertise.

principal–agent game The interaction between a principal (such as the president or Congress), who needs something done, and an agent (such as a bureaucrat), who is responsible for carrying out the principal's orders.

regulatory capture A situation in which bureaucrats favor the interests of the groups or corporations they are supposed to regulate at the expense of the general public.

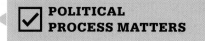

POLITICAL PROCESS MATTERS

▲ Hank Paulson, who served as CEO of Goldman Sachs before becoming secretary of the Treasury for President George W. Bush, is shown here ringing the opening bell at the New York Stock Exchange. Paulson exemplifies concerns about the "revolving door" of political appointees regulating the very industries that they served in before joining government—and which they may well return to after their service ends.

POLITICS IS CONFLICTUAL

neutral competence The idea, credited to theorist Max Weber, that suggests bureaucrats should provide expertise without the influence of elected officials, interest groups, or their own political agendas.

Service, press reports documented how agency employees accepted meals, gifts, and sporting trips from companies they were regulating. Several employees even used drugs and had sex with industry employees. But more significantly, the agency's mission changed from regulating with an eye on safety to encouraging as much drilling as possible—an ideal scenario for profit-minded energy companies.[23]

Similar complaints arose during the financial crisis of 2008–2009. Critics charged that large financial firms were being given favorable treatment (such as bailouts on attractive terms) by federal bureaucrats who were former employees, including the individual who was secretary of the Treasury at the time, Hank Paulson, former CEO of Goldman Sachs, one of the largest U.S. investment banks. In retrospect, the bailout terms appear to have been driven by the necessity of trying to prevent a crisis rather than a desire to help former colleagues. Even so, the controversy illustrates just how difficult it is to discern the motives behind bureaucratic decisions.

You might think that the problem of control isn't too difficult to solve as long as bureaucrats act as impartial experts and leave their own policy goals out of their decisions. Many studies of bureaucracies, beginning with the work of the early political theorist Max Weber, argue for **neutral competence**, the idea that bureaucrats should provide information and expertise, and avoid taking sides on policy questions or being swayed by elected officials, people outside government, or their own policy goals.[24] However, bureaucrats' behavior doesn't always fit Weber's vision. Many enter the bureaucracy with their own ideas about what government should do and work to make decisions in line with those goals. Bureaucrats may also be tempted to favor interest groups or corporations to secure a better-paying job after they leave government service. However, even if bureaucrats wanted to remain completely dispassionate, they would face a government in which many other people with their own policy goals and interests attempted to influence their behavior. Members of Congress or the president sometimes try to use the bureaucracy to implement policies that reflect their personal preferences or reward their political supporters.[25]

As you will see, the problem of control has existed throughout the history of the federal government. It affects both the kinds of policies that bureaucrats are given to implement and the structure of the federal bureaucracy, including the number of agencies and their missions, who is hired to staff the bureaucracy, and their everyday tasks. Moreover, elected officials use a variety of methods to solve the problem of control, including making it easier for people outside government to learn about agency actions before they take effect. However, all of these tactics are at best partial solutions to the problem of control. The trade-off between expertise and control remains.

History of the American Bureaucracy

The evolution of America's federal bureaucracy was not steady or smooth. Rather, most of its important developments occurred during three fairly short periods: during the late 1890s and early 1900s, in the 1930s, and in the 1960s.[26] In all three eras, the driving force was a combination of new demands from citizens for enhanced government services and the desire of people in government, including elected officials, to either respond to these demands or to increase the size and scope of the federal government in line with their own policy goals.

THE BEGINNING OF AMERICA'S BUREAUCRACY

From the beginning of the United States until the election of Andrew Jackson in 1828, the staff of the entire federal bureaucracy numbered no more than in the low thousands. There were only three executive departments (State, Treasury, and War), along with a Postmaster General.[27] The early federal government also performed a narrow range of tasks. It collected taxes on imports and exports and delivered the mail. The national army consisted of a small Corps of Engineers and a few frontier patrols. The attorney general was a private attorney who had the federal government as one of his clients. Members of Congress outnumbered civil servants in Washington; the president had very little staff at all.[28]

The small size of the federal government during these years reflected Americans' deep suspicion of government, especially unelected officials. In the Declaration of Independence, one of the charges against King George III was that he had "erected a multitude of new offices and sent hither swarms of officers to harass our people and eat out their substance."[29] Executive branch offices were formed only when absolutely necessary. Nonetheless, conflicts soon arose around control of the bureaucracy. The legislation that established the departments of State, Treasury, and War allowed the president to nominate the people in charge of these departments but made these appointments subject to Senate approval. (The same is true today for the heads of all executive departments and many other presidential appointments.)

The election of Andrew Jackson in 1828 brought the first large-scale use of the spoils system, in which people who had worked in Jackson's campaign were rewarded with new positions in the federal government, usually working as local postmasters.[30] The spoils system was extremely useful to party organizations, as it gave them a powerful incentive with which to convince people to work for the party—a particularly important tool for Jackson, as his campaign organization was at that time the largest ever organized.

The challenge facing the spoils system was ensuring that these government employees, who often lacked experience in their new fields, could actually carry out their jobs. The solution was to develop routines and procedures for these employees, so that they knew exactly what to do even if they had little or no experience or training.[31] These instructions became one of the earliest uses of standard operating procedures, and they ensured that the government could function even if large numbers of employees were hired only to reward them for political work rather than because of their qualifications.[32]

As America expanded in size, so did the federal government, which saw an almost eightfold increase in the size of the bureaucracy between 1816 and the beginning of the Civil War in 1861. This growth did not reflect a fundamental change in what the government did—in fact, much of the increase came in areas such as the Post Office, which needed to grow to serve a geographically larger nation—and, of course, to provide "spoils" for party workers in the form of government jobs.[33] Even by the end of the Civil War, the federal government still had very little involvement in the lives of ordinary Americans. Services such as education, public works, and welfare benefits were provided by state and local governments, if they were provided at all, with the federal government's role in daily life limited to mail delivery, collecting import and export taxes, and a few other areas.

▲ This cartoon of a monument to President Andrew Jackson riding a pig decries his involvement in the spoils system, which allowed politicians to dole out government service jobs in return for political support.

BUILDING A NEW AMERICAN STATE: THE PROGRESSIVE ERA

Changes in the second half of the nineteenth century transformed America's bureaucracy.[34] This transformation began after the Civil War, but the most significant changes took place during the Progressive Era, between 1890 and 1920. Many

federal civil service A system created by the 1883 Pendleton Civil Service Act in which bureaucrats are hired on the basis of merit rather than political connections.

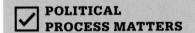

POLITICAL PROCESS MATTERS

different laws and executive actions increased the government's regulatory power during this period, including the Sherman Antitrust Act of 1890, the Pure Food and Drug Act of 1906, the Meat Inspection Act, expansion of the Interstate Commerce Commission, and various conservation measures.[35] With these changes, the federal government was no longer simply a deliverer of mail and defender of borders; rather, it had an indirect impact on several aspects of everyday life. When Americans bought food or other products, went to work, or traveled on vacation, the choices available to them were shaped by the actions of federal bureaucrats in Washington and elsewhere.

These developments were matched by a fundamental change in the federal bureaucracy following the passage of the 1883 Pendleton Civil Service Act. This measure created the **federal civil service**, in which the merit system (qualifications, not political connections) would be the basis for hiring and promoting bureaucrats.[36] In other words, when a new president took office, he could not replace members of the civil service with his own campaign workers. Initially, only about 13,000 federal jobs were given civil service protections, but over the next two decades, many additional positions were incorporated into the civil service, to the point that in the modern era, virtually all full-time, permanent government employees have civil service protection. In some cases, presidents gave civil service protections to people who had been hired under the spoils system to prevent the next president from replacing these bureaucrats with their own loyalists.

Over time, these reforms created a bureaucracy in which people were hired for their expertise and allowed to build a career in government without having to fear being fired when a new president or Congress took office.[37] These changes also attracted government employees who were motivated primarily by their interest in shaping government policy. Studies of this transformation have found that one of the driving forces behind the changes was a shift in citizens' demands. People wanted a greater role for government, both in regulating the behavior of large corporations and delivering more services to citizens.[38]

When civil service reforms were adopted, their impact on party organizations was well understood. As one New York City machine politician, George Washington Plunkitt, put it, "This civil service law is the biggest fraud of the age. It is the curse of the nation. . . . How are you going to interest our young men in their country if you have no offices to give them when they work for their party?"[39] What Plunkitt meant was that without the spoils system, organizations like his would be in serious danger of losing their hold on government, as they would be unable to use the promise of a government job to motivate people to help elect the machine's candidates. Members of Congress, some of whom were members of spoils-based organizations, enacted civil service legislation because of strong public pressure to reform the bureaucracy—and because the protections would apply to current federal workers, some of whom had received their position in return for partisan work.[40]

Increased bureaucratic activity during the Progressive Era also highlights another interesting feature of government regulation: under some conditions, the targets of new regulation actually welcome government intervention. For example, early efforts to regulate the food production industry were supported by some very large producers that wanted a level playing field against smaller competitors who skimped on sanitation and safety requirements. More recently, some auto companies have lobbied the federal government for more stringent gas mileage and pollution standards not because they are enthusiastic about the new rules but because they want to preempt even stiffer requirements from being imposed by states such as California.

THE NEW DEAL, THE GREAT SOCIETY, AND THE REAGAN REVOLUTION

The New Deal The New Deal refers to the government programs implemented during Franklin Roosevelt's first term as president in the 1930s. At one level, these programs were a response to the Great Depression and the inability of local governments and private charities to respond to this economic crisis. Many advocates of the New Deal also favored an expanded role for government in American society, regardless of the immediate need for intervention.[41] Roosevelt's programs included reforms to the financial industry as well as efforts to help people directly and to stimulate employment, economic growth, and the formation of labor unions. The Social Security Act, which was the first federally funded pension program for all Americans, was also passed as part of the New Deal.[42]

These reforms represented a vast increase in the size, responsibilities, and capacity of the bureaucracy, as well as a large transfer of power to bureaucrats and to the president.[43] While the Progressive Era reforms created an independent bureaucracy and increased its state capacity, the New Deal reforms increased the range of policy areas in which this capacity could be applied. Before the New Deal, the federal government influenced citizens' choices through activities such as regulating industries and workplace conditions. Afterwards, the federal government took on the role of delivering a wide range of benefits and services directly to individuals, from jobs to electricity, as well as increased regulation of many industries, including the banking and financial industries.

The expansion of the federal government and the subsequent delegation of power to bureaucrats and to the president were controversial changes, both at the time they were enacted and as they were implemented in subsequent years.[44] Many Republicans opposed New Deal reforms because they believed that the federal government could not deliver services efficiently and that an expanded federal bureaucracy would create a modern spoils system. Many southerners worried that the federal government's increased involvement in everyday life would endanger the system of racial segregation in southern states.[45] Even so, Democratic supporters of the New Deal, aided by public support, carried the day.

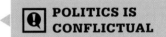 **POLITICS IS CONFLICTUAL**

The Great Society The Great Society was a further expansion in the size, capacity, and activities of the bureaucracy that occurred during the presidency of Lyndon Johnson (1963–1969). During these years, President Johnson proposed and Congress enacted programs that funded bilingual education, loans and grants for college students, special education, preschools, construction of elementary and secondary schools, mass transit programs in many cities, health care for seniors and poor people, job training and urban renewal, enhanced voting rights and civil rights for minorities, environmental protection, and funding for the arts and cultural activities.[46] Members of Congress frequently attempted to control these new programs, with the goal of delivering valuable benefits to their own constituents. In the case of the Model Cities Program, which was designed to fund efforts to revitalize decaying urban areas, members of Congress demanded expansion of the program from a small set of experimental projects to a nationwide, 150-city effort. In return for this congressional support of the agencies associated with the program, members of Congress forced bureaucrats to fund lucrative projects in their districts.[47]

The Great Society programs had mixed success. Voting rights and civil rights reforms ended the "separate but equal" system of social order in southern states and dramatically increased political participation by African Americans.[48] At the same

▲ Reducing the number and complexity of government regulations was one of President Ronald Reagan's priorities in office, but his efforts were largely unsuccessful, and subsequent presidents have had similarly little success.

time, many antipoverty programs were dismal failures. Poverty rates among most groups remained relatively constant, and other indicators, such as the rate of teen pregnancies, actually increased.[49] In retrospect, the people who designed and implemented these programs did not realize the complexities of the problems they were trying to address.[50] For example, many antipoverty programs were built on the assumption that most people receiving welfare needed job training programs in order to transition from welfare to permanent, paid employment. However, additional data that was available a decade later showed that most people receiving welfare do so for short periods because of divorce or medical hardship—problems that the Great Society programs did not touch.[51] Despite these shortcomings, the expansion of the federal government during the New Deal and Great Society has remained in place over the last generation.

The Reagan Revolution The election of Ronald Reagan to the presidency in 1980, along with a Republican takeover of the Senate and significant Republican gains in the House of Representatives, created an opportunity for conservatives to roll back the size and scope of the federal government. However, after eight years of Reagan in office followed by four years of his vice president, George H. W. Bush, and Republican control of Congress during most of Democrat Bill Clinton's presidency as well as during most of the presidency of Republican George W. Bush, the growth of the federal government did not slow. Few programs were eliminated, and the federal budget steadily increased.[52] Conservative presidents and members of Congress have enacted programs and regulations that increased the impact of government on society. For example, Republican President George W. Bush's administration added the No Child Left Behind education reforms, which imposed many new requirements on local schools; the Medicare Prescription Drug Benefit, which was the biggest new health care program since the 1960s; the Sarbanes–Oxley Act, which increased financial reporting requirements for corporations; and a host of other regulations, from specifications on backyard play sets to inspections of baggage on commercial aircraft.[53] The trend toward increased federal regulation is likely to continue in the Obama administration given the enactment of new health care and financial legislation, as well as the response to the Gulf oil spill.

The Modern Federal Bureaucracy

Figure 12.1 shows the structure of the executive branch of the federal government. As discussed in Chapter 11, the Executive Office of the President (EOP) contains organizations that support the president and implement presidential policy initiatives. Among its many offices, the EOP contains the **Office of Management and Budget**, which prepares the president's annual budget proposal and monitors government spending as well as the development of new regulations. Below the EOP are the fifteen executive departments, from the Department of Agriculture to the Department of Veterans Affairs, which comprise the major divisions within the executive branch. The heads of these fifteen organizations make up the president's cabinet.

Each executive department contains many smaller organizations. Figure 12.2 shows the organizational chart for the Department of Agriculture. As you can see, Agriculture includes offices that help farmers produce and sell their crops, as well as

Office of Management and Budget An office within the Executive Office of the President that is responsible for creating the president's annual budget proposal to Congress, reviewing proposed rules, and other budget-related tasks.

FIGURE 12.1
THE EXECUTIVE BRANCH OF THE FEDERAL GOVERNMENT

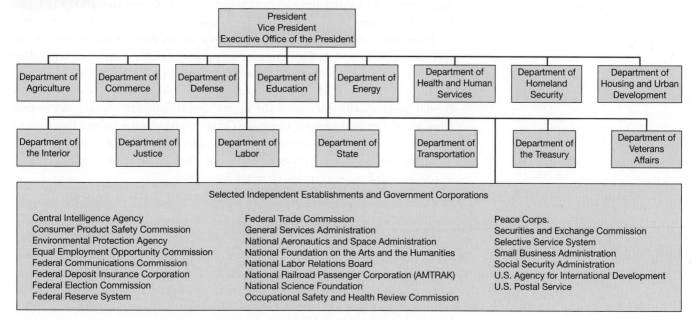

SOURCE: Based on GPO Access: Guide to the U.S. Government, available at http://bensguide.gpo.gov/files/gov_chart.pdf.

FIGURE 12.2
THE STRUCTURE OF THE DEPARTMENT OF AGRICULTURE

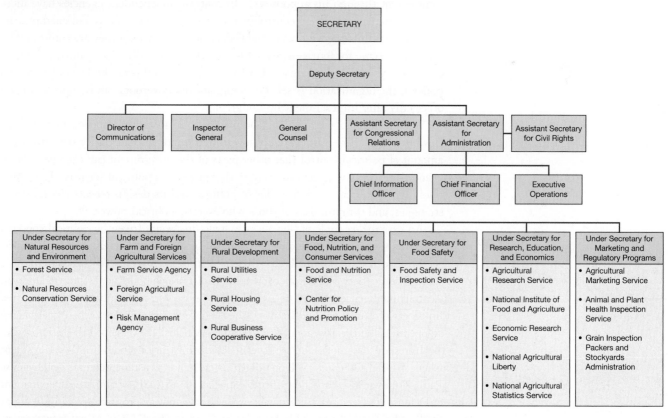

SOURCE: U.S. Department of Agriculture, USDA Organization Chart, available at www.usda.gov/documents/AgencyWorkflow.pdf (accessed 4/23/10).

independent agencies Government offices or organizations that provide government services and are not part of an executive department.

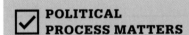

POLITICAL PROCESS MATTERS

offices that ensure food safety, but it also houses the Forest Service and offices that manage issues related to housing and utilities in rural areas. The Department of Agriculture also administers the food stamps program, even though the program has no direct connection to farming or food safety.

Below the executive departments, but not subordinate to them, are a set of agencies, commissions, and government corporations that are called **independent agencies**, or independent establishments, to highlight that they are not part of an executive department. Most of these carry out specialized functions, such as the Federal Reserve (which manages the money supply, banking system, and interest rates) and the Federal Deposit Insurance Corporation (which regulates the banking industry and during 2008–2010 closed or merged several hundred banks that had lost money as a result of increased foreclosures). The figure only includes some note-worthy or well-known agencies; there are many more.

There are two important lessons to draw from these charts. First, the federal government serves an enormous range of functions. Second, the division of activities among executive departments and independent agencies does not always have an obvious logic. Why, for example, does the Department of Agriculture administer rural utilities programs or food stamps? Similarly, it is not always clear why certain tasks are handled by an independent agency while others fall within the scope of an executive department.[54] Why is the Federal Reserve an independent agency rather than part of the Department of the Treasury?

Organizational decisions like these often reflect elected officials' attempts to shape agency behavior—and the extent to which political process matters. Part of the difference between independent agencies and the organizations contained within executive departments has to do with the president's ability to control these organizations' activities. Organizations that are housed within an executive department, such as the Internal Revenue Service, can be controlled by the president to some extent through his appointees.[55] In contrast, independent agencies have more freedom from oversight and control by the president and Congress. For example, the president nominates governors of the Federal Reserve, who, if they are confirmed by the Senate, serve for fourteen years. Outside the nomination and confirmation process, the president and Congress have very little control over the Federal Reserve's policies; the organization is self-financing, and its governors can be removed from office only after impeachment by Congress.

These details about the hiring and firing of bureaucrats and the location of agencies in the structure of the federal government matter because they determine the amount of political control that other parts of the government can exercise over an agency, as well as who gets to exercise this power. As political scientist Terry Moe puts it, "The bureaucracy rises out of politics, and its design reflects the interests, strategies, and compromises of those who exercise political power."[56]

An extreme example of bureaucratic structure being driven by political concerns rather than efficiency or effectiveness comes from the use of intelligence agencies by the Bush administration in the months before the Iraq War. At the time, there was a spirited debate between members of the administration about the justification for war. Central Intelligence Agency (CIA) reports expressed strong doubts about purported links between Al Qaeda and Iraq, and they believed that Iraq was nowhere near having an operational nuclear weapon.[57] Both of these conclusions weakened the case for war.

In response, senior leaders in the Bush administration, including Vice President Cheney, Defense Secretary Donald Rumsfeld, and Assistant Secretary of Defense Paul Wolfowitz, set up the Office of Special Plans (OSP) within the Department of Defense to develop an alternate view on Iraq's nuclear program, placing Douglas Feith, who favored war with Iraq, at its head.[58] The OSP used an information-gathering tactic known as stovepiping, relying on raw intelligence reports—including information from defectors—rather than summaries and interpretations of this information prepared by the CIA and other agencies. The resulting OSP reports made a strong case for invading Iraq, based on links between the country's leadership and terrorist organizations and the claim that the country had developed weapons of mass destruction—conclusions that later proved almost completely false. In retrospect, it is clear that the OSP was created and staffed to make the case for war that other agencies were unwilling to make based on the available evidence.

THE SIZE OF THE FEDERAL GOVERNMENT

The federal government employs millions of people. Table 12.1 reports the number of employees in each executive department and selected independent agencies. The Department of Defense is the largest cabinet department, with more than 600,000

TABLE 12.1 EMPLOYMENT IN SELECTED FEDERAL ORGANIZATIONS

Some federal agencies, such as the Department of Defense, have many employees, but many others are quite small. The Department of Education, for example, has only 4,000 employees. Does this variation in size make sense given the differences in the missions of these organizations?

Organization	Total Employees
Cabinet Departments	
Defense (civilian only)	652,000
Veterans Affairs	280,000
Homeland Security	171,000
Justice	108,000
Treasury	88,000
Agriculture	82,000
Interior	67,000
Health and Human Services	64,000
Transportation	55,000
Commerce	39,000
Labor	16,000
Energy	15,000
State	15,000
Housing and Urban Development	9,000
Education	4,000
Independent Agencies	
Social Security Administration	64,000
National Aeronautics and Space Administration	18,000
Environmental Protection Agency	18,000
General Services Administration	12,000
Federal Deposit Insurance Corporation	5,000
Smithsonian Institution	4,000

SOURCE: U.S. Bureau of Labor Statistics, Career Guide to Industries, "Federal Government, Excluding the Postal Service," Table 1, November 2008, available at http://www.bls.gov/oco/cg/cgs041.htm.

FIGURE 12.3   THE SIZE OF THE FEDERAL BUDGET

The graph on the left shows that federal spending has increased sharply since the 1940s. However, the one on the right shows that as a percentage of gross domestic product (GDP), which measures the size of the American economy, the increase is much smaller, except for the financial bailout and economic stimulus programs enacted in 2008 and 2009. What might these figures suggest about the increase in government spending?

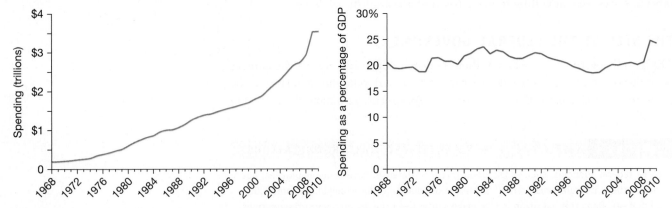

SOURCE: Congressional Budget Office, Historical Budget Data, "Revenues, Outlays, Deficits, Surpluses, and Debt Held by the Public," available at http://www.cbo.gov/budget/data/historical.shtml.

civilian personnel. The Department of Education is the smallest, with only 4,000. Many departments are on the small side: five cabinet departments have fewer than 20,000 employees. Many independent agencies also have relatively modest numbers of employees. The General Services Administration, for example, has only 12,000 employees. The remaining independent agencies generally have only a few thousand employees each. And the Minerals Management Service, which had jurisdiction over offshore drilling, had only about 1,500 employees. Millions of additional people work for the government as members of the armed forces, as employees of the Postal Service, for civilian companies that contract with the government, or as recipients of federal grant money.

Figure 12.3 shows the size of the federal budget since 1968. As you can see, the budget has steadily increased, to the point that annual spending in recent years is more than $3 trillion per year. The best explanation for the size of the federal government is the size of America itself—a diverse population of more than 300 million spread out over an area more than twice the size of the European Union—coupled with America's position as the most powerful nation in the world. However, some observers argue that the real explanation has to do with bureaucrats themselves. This view suggests that the government is so large because bureaucrats are **budget maximizers** who never pass up a chance to increase their own funding, regardless of whether the new spending is worthwhile.[59]

This argument misses some important points. First, the increase in total federal spending masks the fact that many agencies see their budgets shrink.[60] Particularly in recent administrations, one of the principal missions of presidential appointees, both in agencies and in the Executive Office of the President, has been to scrutinize budget requests with an eye to cutting spending as much as possible.[61] And every year, some government agencies are eliminated.[62]

Moreover, public opinion data provide an explanation for the overall growth in government: the American public's demand for services.[63] Despite complaints about the federal bureaucracy, polls find little evidence of demands for less government. When the Harris Poll asked people in 2007 to decide which two programs should have their spending cut as a way of reducing the budget deficit, a majority

budget maximizers Bureaucrats who seek to increase funding for their agency whether or not that additional spending is worthwhile.

The Size of America's Government

Many Americans believe that taxes are too high and that the federal government is wasteful and inefficient. These complaints raise the question of how U.S. government spending compares to spending by other countries. Although the extent of the services provided by different governments varies considerably, generally speaking the United States provides a much narrower range of benefits to its citizens compared to other developed nations, such as the industrialized democracies of western Europe. Many other countries offer benefits such as government-funded universal health care, a free or low-cost college education, and more generous old-age pensions. Thus, if the United States spends more than these countries, this would suggest that the federal government really is wasteful and inefficient—spending more and delivering less.

The Organization for Economic Cooperation and Development (OECD) collects a large variety of economic statistics about its thirty-three member nations, which include the United States and most western European democracies. The figure reports government spending in some of these countries, measured as a percentage of gross domestic product (GDP), which includes the value of all the goods and services produced in an economy over a set period—usually one year. (Note that much of recent U.S. spending on the wars in Iraq and Afghanistan is excluded from the figure.) We report government spending relative to the country's GDP because these countries differ greatly in terms of the overall size of their economies and populations. That is, a country that spends more than others in absolute terms might simply be richer or have a larger population than most. Considering spending as a percentage of GDP allows us to factor in the size of each country's population and economy to compare more accurately. (The data do not account for spending by state and local governments, which is significantly higher in America than elsewhere. On the other hand, the U.S. federal government spends more on defense, which offsets the difference in terms of social services.)

The data show that compared to other countries, the United States has one of the lowest levels of government spending. In fact, in some countries, such as Sweden, spending is almost double the level of spending in the United States. Of course, this doesn't imply that Swedish bureaucrats are doubly wasteful—rather, it reflects the fact that the Swedish government provides many services to its citizens, such as health care, child care, and unemployment compensation, that the U.S. government either does not provide or provides at lower levels.

No one likes to pay taxes. It is important to consider what Americans get from government for their contributions or whether additional spending on new programs is warranted. It is also important to explore other ways of delivering services, such as substituting private companies for government operations. However, the fact that many Americans believe the government is too large does not mean it is inherently wasteful or harmful to the nation's economy. Also, as these data show, the U.S. government is actually small relative to other Western democracies. ■

THE SIZE OF AMERICA'S GOVERNMENT COMPARED TO THOSE OF OTHER NATIONS

While the federal bureaucracy is very large and does many things, total federal spending as a percentage of the U.S. gross domestic product is one of the lowest for all industrialized countries. Based on these data, how would you respond to complaints about the magnitude of federal spending?

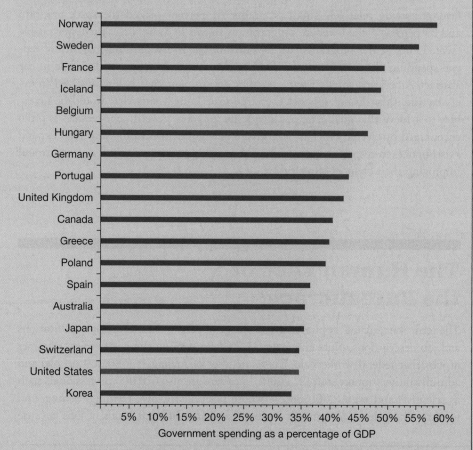

Government spending as a percentage of GDP

SOURCE: Organization for Economic Cooperation and Development. "OECD in Figures, 2009," available at www.oecd.org/infigures.

TABLE 12.2 PUBLIC PREFERENCES FOR SPENDING CUTS

Many Americans complain about the size of the federal government. However, their complaints do not translate into support for cuts in specific programs that could significantly reduce spending. Based on these data, are there any kinds of proposals for significantly reducing the size of the federal government that might attract widespread support?

Program	Percentage Favoring Cuts
Space program	51%
Welfare	28
Defense spending	28
Farm subsidies	24
Environmental programs	16
Homeland Security	12
Transportation	11
Medicaid	4
Education	3
Social Security	2
Medicare	1

SOURCE: Harris Poll, "Closing the Budget Deficit," April 30, 2007, available at http://www.harrisinteractive.com/harris_poll/index.asp?PID=746.

favored cutting relatively small programs: 51 percent picked the space program and 28 percent picked welfare programs, as shown in Table 12.2. Far fewer people favored cuts in the programs that account for the overwhelming majority of federal spending: defense, Medicare, and Social Security. In other words, while in the abstract Americans might want a smaller government that is less involved in everyday life, they do not support the large-scale budget cuts that would be necessary to achieve this goal. The public's desire for more government services is often encouraged by elected officials, who create new government programs (and expand existing ones in response to constituent demands), as a way of building support and improving their chances of reelection.

The Human Face of the Bureaucracy

The term "bureaucrat" applies to a wide range of people with different qualifications and job descriptions. Nuts and Bolts 12.2 shows data on the wide variety of types of jobs that federal workers do. There are a lot of managers (680,000 people) and administrative support staff (273,000), but there are also 670,000 professionals such as scientists and even 8,000 people whose positions involve farming, fishing, and forestry. The federal government includes so many different kinds of jobs because

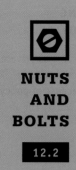

Types of Federal Workers

OCCUPATION	EMPLOYEES	PERCENTAGE OF FEDERAL WORK FORCE
Management, business, and financial jobs (e.g., purchasing agents, accountants, tax collectors)	680,000	34%
Professional and related jobs (e.g., scientists, engineers, computer specialists, lawyers, doctors, nurses)	670,000	33
Office and administrative support jobs (e.g., secretaries, record clerks)	273,000	14
Service jobs (e.g., jailers, police officers, detectives)	161,000	8
Installation, maintenance, and repair jobs (e.g., mechanics, electricians)	101,000	5
Transportation and moving jobs (e.g., air traffic controllers, transportation inspectors)	61,000	3
Farming, fishing, and forestry jobs (e.g., agricultural inspectors, farmworkers, loggers)	8,000	0.4

SOURCE: Based on the U.S. Bureau of Labor Statistics, "Career Guide to Industries, 2010–2011 Edition," Table 3, available at www.bls.gov/oco/cg/cgs041.htm (accessed 2/4/10).

of the vast array of services it provides. This section describes who these people are and the terms of their government employment.

MOTIVATIONS

Figure 12.4 describes a 2003 survey that asked bureaucrats and people working for private firms whether their primary interest was job security or the desire to help the public.[64] The bars on the left show that a large majority of federal employees mentioned their salary and benefits as prime motivations. Even so, about one-third reported that their main incentive was an interest in public service or in what government does. The right side of Figure 12.4 shows that federal employees' motivations closely parallel those expressed by people working outside government. Like everyone else, the average federal employee's work-related decisions are often driven by self-interest, including the desire to make money. However, just like people who work outside government, many federal employees have other motivations, including the desire to do a good job.[65]

CIVIL SERVICE REGULATIONS

One of the most important characteristics of most jobs in the federal bureaucracy is that they are subject to the civil service regulations mentioned earlier.[66] The current civil service system sets out a job description and pay ranges for virtually all federal jobs.[67] People with less than a college degree are generally eligible for clerical and

FIGURE 12.4 **MOTIVATIONS FOR EMPLOYMENT: COMPARING BUREAUCRATS AND PRIVATE SECTOR EMPLOYEES**

This chart shows that the motivations of federal employees are much the same as private sector workers' reasons for pursuing particular jobs. Some join the bureaucracy for the pay and benefits, but a substantial proportion work for the government because of policy goals—they want to help people or make a difference in how government works. For an elected official worried that bureaucrats will ignore congressional directives in favor of their own preferences, are these results good news or bad news?

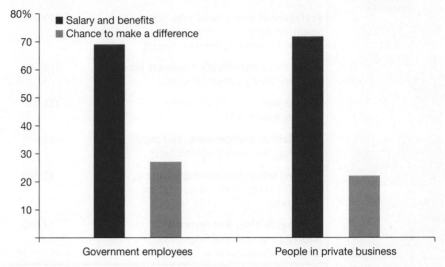

SOURCE: Data from Paul Light, "The Content of Their Character: The State of the Nonprofit Workforce," *The Nonprofit Quarterly* (Fall, 2002): 6–16.

low-level technical jobs. As in the private sector, a college degree or an advanced degree and work experience qualify an individual for higher-level positions. Federal salaries are supposed to be comparable to what people earn in similar, private sector positions, and salaries are increased somewhat for federal employees who work in areas with a high cost of living.

The civil service system also established a set of tests used to determine who is hired for low-level clerical and secretarial positions. These exams are given on set dates, and the people who receive the highest scores are hired as vacancies arise. A similar system is used for Postal Service employees and for federal air traffic controllers. Higher-level jobs are filled by comparing the qualifications and experience of candidates who meet the educational requirements for the position. Seniority, or the amount of time a person has worked for the government or at a particular type of position, is also used to determine which employees receive promotions.

Civil service regulations also provide job security. After three years of satisfactory performance, employees cannot be fired except "for cause," meaning the firing agency must cite a reason for the termination, such as poor performance. Civil service regulations set out a detailed, multistep procedure that has to be followed to fire someone, beginning with low performance evaluations, then moving to warning letters given to the employee, followed by a lengthy appeals process before a firing takes place. In simple terms, it is very hard to fire someone from the federal bureaucracy as long as they show up for work. One study calculated that fewer than 500 civil servants are fired in a given year.[68] A subpar performer may be given other duties, transferred to another office, or even given nothing to do in the hope that the person will leave voluntarily out of boredom.

Despite the difficulties associated with firing an individual underperforming bureaucrat, it is possible to reduce the size of the federal workforce through reductions in force (RIF), which are occasionally carried out when an entire office or program is terminated. Employees who have been laid off due to an RIF can apply for civil service positions in other parts of government. Another strategy for reducing the federal workforce is to simply not replace employees who decide to leave government service.

If you think civil service regulations look extraordinarily cumbersome, you're right.[69] The hiring criteria remove a manager's discretion to hire someone who would do an excellent job but lacks the education or work experience that the regulations specify as necessary for the position. The firing requirements make it extremely difficult to remove poor performers. The salary and promotion restrictions create problems with rewarding excellent performance or promoting the best employees rather than those with the most seniority.

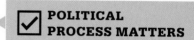

Why do civil service requirements exist? Recall that the aim of these regulations was to separate politics from policy. The mechanism for achieving this goal was a set of rules and requirements that made it hard for elected officials to control the hiring and firing of government employees to further their own political goals. In effect, even though civil service regulations have the obvious drawbacks just described, they also provide this less apparent but very important benefit.

Although loyalty to the president is a widely known and accepted criterion for hiring agency heads and other presidential appointees, professionals with permanent civil service positions are supposed to be hired on the basis of their qualifications, not their political beliefs. In fact, it is illegal to bring politics into these hiring decisions. However, there are well-documented cases in which administrations have made political beliefs a priority in hiring mid-level bureaucrats. For example, during the presidency of George W. Bush, Justice Department officials admitted to screening job applicants based on their ideological leanings. Membership in a liberal organization such as Greenpeace listed on a candidate's resume reduced the likelihood of being hired, while membership in conservative organizations such as the Federalist Society boosted an applicant's chances.[70] Though the Bush administration is the most severe known recent example of this practice, it is likely that other administrations have behaved similarly.

LIMITS ON POLITICAL ACTIVITY

Federal employees are also limited in their political activities. The Hatch Act, enacted in 1939 and amended in 1940, prohibited federal employees from engaging in organized political activities.[71] Under the act, employees could vote and contribute to candidates but could not work for candidates or for political parties. These restrictions were modified in the 1993 Federal Employees Political Activities Act, allowing federal employees to undertake a wider range of political activities, including fund-raising and serving as an officer of a political party.

Senior members of the president's White House staff and political appointees are exempt from most of these restrictions, though they cannot use government resources for political activities. This became an issue early in the 2006 election campaign when, at a NASA awards ceremony, NASA administrator Michael Griffin referred to Congressman Tom DeLay, whose district contained NASA's Johnson Space Center, by saying, "The space program has had no better friend in its entire existence than Tom DeLay. He's still with us and we need to keep him there."[72] The problem was not what Griffin said; he was a political appointee and could endorse DeLay if he wanted to. Rather, the problem was that Griffin had flown to Texas for the NASA ceremony on a government aircraft, which, because of the endorsement, could be construed as using government resources for political purposes.

▼ Federal law prohibits the use of government money, facilities, or services for political activities. Here, former Republican representative Tom DeLay (left), whose Texas district included NASA's Johnson Space Center, attends an awards ceremony with NASA administrator Michael Griffin. Although Griffin flew to Houston on a government plane primarily to present awards to NASA employees, his trip was cited as an illegal use of funds because his speech praised DeLay, who was running for reelection.

turkey farms Agencies where campaign workers and donors are often appointed to reward them for their service because it is unlikely that their lack of qualifications will lead to bad policy.

These regulations make life especially difficult for presidential appointees whose job duties often mix government service with politics, such as helping the president they work for get reelected. In order to comply with Hatch Act restrictions, these officials need to carry separate cell phones to make calls related to their political activities and maintain separate e-mail accounts—usually provided by the party or campaign committee—for their political communications. Inevitably, some messages are sent using the wrong system. During the Bush administration, various political appointees used the Republican Party e-mail system to send messages relating to the controversial dismissal of several U.S. attorneys.[73]

It is not completely clear which activities are allowed or prohibited by these laws. For example, in spring 2007, congressional Democrats complained that Karl Rove, deputy White House chief of staff and a close political adviser to President George W. Bush, had given a series of briefings to senior political appointees on Republican losses in the 2006 midterm elections and plans for the 2008 campaign. Although these meetings had been approved as legal by the White House counsel, their political content is obvious. During one briefing, the head of the General Services Administration asked how her agency could help elect Republican candidates in 2008.[74] As a senior member of the White House staff, Rove was exempt from the Hatch Act's prohibitions, but the more junior White House staff involved in the briefings probably were not. While ultimately no action was taken against Rove or his aides, this example illustrates the ambiguities inherent in separating the political and policy role of federal bureaucrats, especially those who work in the White House.

POLITICAL APPOINTEES AND THE SENIOR EXECUTIVE SERVICE

Not every federal employee is a member of the civil service. The president appoints over 7,000 individuals to senior positions in the executive branch that are not subject to civil service regulations, such as the leaders of executive departments and independent agencies, as well as members of the Executive Office of the President. (In some cases, these nominees need to be confirmed by a majority vote in the Senate.) Some of these presidential appointees get their jobs as a reward for service during the campaign. They may have worked on the campaign staff, contributed substantial funds, or raised money from other donors. These individuals may not be given positions with real decision-making power. Some government agencies have the reputation of being "turkey farms," places where campaign stalwarts can be appointed without the risk that their lack of experience will lead to bad policy.[75]

The majority of a president's appointees are intended to act as the president's eyes, ears, and hands throughout the executive branch. They hold positions of power within government agencies, serving as secretaries of executive departments, agency heads, or senior deputies. Their jobs involve finding out what the president wants from their agency and ordering, persuading, or cajoling their subordinates to implement presidential directives.

In many agencies, people who serve in the top positions are members of the Senior Executive Service (SES), who are also exempt from civil service restrictions.[76] As of 2010, there were a few thousand SES members, most of whom were career government employees who held relatively high-level agency positions before moving to the SES. This change of employment status costs them their civil service protections but allows them to apply for senior leadership positions in the bureaucracy.

Some political appointees are also given SES positions, although most do not have the experience or expertise held by career bureaucrats who typically move to the SES.

The president's ability to appoint bureaucrats in many different agencies helps him control the bureaucracy. By selecting people who are loyal or like-minded, a president can attempt to control the actions of lower-level bureaucrats and implement his policy agenda. The SES also gives civil servants an incentive to do their jobs well, as good performance in an agency position can help build a career that might allow them to transfer to the SES.

How Americans See the Bureaucracy

Americans have mixed feelings about the bureaucracy. Figure 12.5 shows that a majority of survey respondents agreed that the federal government is typically inefficient and wasteful—although the percentage agreeing with this assessment in 2009 had declined significantly from its peak in 1992. A survey conducted in 1999 found similar results. Only 8 percent of respondents believed that the federal government has had a large number of policy successes, whereas a near-majority could not name a single government success.[77]

FIGURE 12.5   HOW AMERICANS VIEW THE FEDERAL BUREAUCRACY

Many Americans believe the bureaucracy is wasteful and inefficient. Note, however, that the magnitude of negative feelings varies over time. Consider the time frame represented on the graph. What happened during these years that might explain the changes in citizens' opinions about the government?

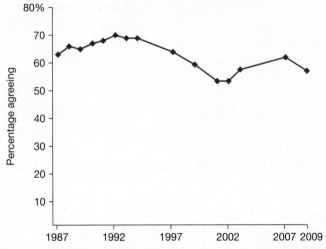

SOURCE: Pew Research Center, "Trends in Political Values and Core Attitudes," May 21, 2009, available at http://people-press.org/reports/pdf/517.pdf.

Bureaucratic Efficiency and the General Services Administration

The introduction to this chapter cited several examples of bureaucratic waste. Many researchers and political experts would see these instances as fitting into a broader pattern in which anything government does is sure to cost more than it should and deliver less of what people need. The public opinion data discussed earlier in this chapter show that many Americans agree. However, like most broad assertions about American politics, claims about bureaucratic waste need to be evaluated with data—and one agency in the federal bureaucracy is an ideal place to look: the General Services Administration (GSA).

The GSA provides management and purchasing services to the federal government. It manages and leases office space and other facilities for government agencies and procures everything from office supplies to liquid helium for resale to other government agencies. The GSA also has an airline ticketing service and a hotel reservation service for federal employees. GSA employees manage the federal government's real estate portfolio and its vehicle fleet, both of which are among the largest in the country. They even provided 520 SUVs to U.S. agencies working in Iraq after the invasion.

Because much of what the GSA does is similar to activities in private companies, it is possible to evaluate the GSA's operations by comparing what it pays for goods and services to the prices paid by private corporations. Specifically, do government agencies pay more

General Services Administration employees begin a renovation of the White House press briefing room.

by getting their goods and services through the GSA than they would by using local realtors to find office space, buying cars through dealers, and getting their pencils, computers, and furniture at the local office supply store?

By law, the GSA must complete an annual performance review that measures its efforts against a variety of indicators, and its 2008 report completely contradicts conventional views about government waste and inefficiency.[a]

- The GSA pays 9 percent less rent for office space than private companies pay for comparable space.
- Service costs (heating, lighting, etc.) for GSA-managed buildings are 1 percent less than they are for comparable,

privately managed space. During 2008 the GSA reduced energy consumption in the buildings it managed by 9.7 percent.

- The vacancy rate in buildings operated by the GSA is only 1.5 percent, which is quite low compared to major corporations.
- The GSA buys cars at 29 percent below the invoice price, whereas most private citizens are doing well if they pay no *more* than the invoice price.

Contrary to the notion that the federal bureaucracy is necessarily wasteful, GSA bureaucrats appear to be working efficiently—at a low cost to taxpayers. ■

Why do Americans dislike bureaucrats? Many of these negative assessments result from low levels of trust in government, economic conditions, and media coverage that highlights examples of bureaucratic incompetence.[78] However, Americans tend to have more positive impressions of the government agencies with which they have personal experience.[79] A survey that targeted groups of people who had first-hand contact with a set of government agencies, such as professional tax preparers who often interact with bureaucrats from the Internal Revenue Service, found that a majority of the people who were familiar with an agency reported favorable impressions of its operations.

These studies have an important implication: if you want to know what Americans think about the bureaucracy, it depends on how you ask the question and whom you ask. Asked about government in general, most Americans will complain. However, if you ask about parts of the bureaucracy that people know something about, their impressions are much more likely to be favorable.

Controlling the Bureaucracy

As the expert implementers of legislation and presidential directives, bureaucrats hold significant power to influence government policy. This situation creates the problem of political control illustrated by the principal–agent game: elected officials must figure out how to reap the benefits of bureaucratic expertise without simply giving bureaucrats free reign do whatever they want. One strategy is to take away discretion entirely and give bureaucrats simple, direct orders. One such case came to light in summer 2007 when outgoing surgeon general Richard Carmona revealed in a congressional hearing that he had been ordered to mention President Bush's name at least three times on every page of his speeches and to refrain from criticizing administration policies in the controversial areas of stem cell research, abstinence-only sex education programs, and the "morning-after pill" method of birth control called Plan B.[80]

Similarly, after NASA scientist James Hansen gave a speech in 2006 calling for policies to combat global warming that did not reflect the Bush administration's preferences, he was told to submit all future papers, lectures, and interview requests to NASA political appointees for review.[81] In this case, NASA reversed the order after it received press attention, and Michael Griffin, then-head of NASA, released a statement supporting scientific openness.[82] Soon after this episode, however, NASA's official mission statement was modified to exclude studies of Earth, thereby choking off its studies of climate change entirely.[83]

Attempts such as these to control the bureaucracy are fairly common. At the same hearing that featured Bush's outgoing surgeon general, David Satcher, who was surgeon general during the Clinton administration, testified that he had been ordered to not release a report on sexuality and public health in order to avoid embarrassing President Clinton, who was then being accused of having an extramarital affair with White House intern Monica Lewinsky.

The problem with eliminating bureaucrats' discretion is that this also limits the positive influence of their expertise. Particularly when new policies are being developed, taking away bureaucratic discretion is costly for legislators or presidential appointees, as it forces them to take the time to work out the policy details themselves—and may still produce less effective policies than those constructed by bureaucrats with specialized knowledge.[84] Moreover, preventing bureaucrats from using their judgment makes it impossible for them to craft policies that take into account new developments or unforeseen circumstances.[85]

▲ The transfer of the Coast Guard from the Department of Transportation to the Department of Homeland Security, and its subsequent shift in emphasis from search and rescue to port security, illustrates how changes in political institutions can be used to minimize bureaucratic drift.

bureaucratic drift Bureaucrats' tendency to implement policies in a way that favors their own political objectives rather than following the original intentions of the legislation.

For all of these reasons, elected officials must find ways to reduce or eliminate **bureaucratic drift**—that is, bureaucrats pursuing their own goals rather than their assignments from officeholders or appointees—while still reaping the benefits of bureaucratic expertise. This section describes two common strategies: changing the way agencies are organized and staffed, and using standardized procedures for monitoring agency actions. In both cases, the aim is to set up the agency so that bureaucrats can use their expertise, while making sure their actions are consistent with elected officials' wishes.[86] These measures mitigate—but do not eliminate—the problem of control discussed earlier.

AGENCY ORGANIZATION

Over the last twenty years, political scientists have shown how agencies can be organized to minimize bureaucratic drift.[87] Specifically, when an agency is set up or given new responsibilities, the officials who initiated the change don't simply tell the agency what to do. To make sure that they get the policies they want, they also determine where the agency is located within the federal government structure and who runs it. These efforts may occur solely within Congress, involve both Congress and the president, or be arranged by presidential actions.[88]

For example, when legislation was written to form the Department of Homeland Security in 2002, the Bush administration pushed to have the Coast Guard transferred out of the Department of Transportation and into the new department. This move was designed to change the Coast Guard's priorities from search and rescue operations and routine patrol to a focus on port security, without increasing its budget. The shift worked: over the next few years, the amount of effort expended by Coast Guard personnel on port security increased from only a few percent of total effort to nearly 50 percent, with a corresponding decrease in other activities.[89] A similar agreement can be made about the Minerals Management Service's placement in the Department of the Interior: this placement could pressure Minerals Management Service bureaucrats to emphasize production over safety.

Another strategy is to impose limits on who is allowed to run the agency. In the case of the Federal Communications Commission, for example, one of elected officials' principal concerns about the organization is that it will adopt regulations on political advertising that favor one political party over the other. To prevent this, the legislation that created the agency mandates that it will be run by five commissioners, all of whom are nominated by the president and confirmed by the Senate.[90] However, no more than three of the commissioners can be from the same political party. As a result, if a partisan majority on the commission tries to enact laws that favor one party, opponents only need to convince one supporter to switch positions in order to block the measure. The same rule is used to select commissioners for other agencies. The Federal Election Commission has six commissioners, three Democrats and three Republicans, to guard against one party gaining control of the agency and making biased decisions.[91] In many cases, commissioners are also prohibited from having a business relationship (as a consultant, stockholder, or otherwise) with any company that is subject to their agency's rulings.

Delegation of rule-making power to an agency can also allow federal courts to review agency action.[92] One study of rule making by the Federal Communications Commission, which regulates television, radio, and other broadcasting firms, found that relying on the courts reduced the uncertainties faced by members of Congress, because they have more faith in the impartiality of federal judges than of bureaucrats or other members of Congress.

MONITORING

One of the most important ways elected officials prevent bureaucratic drift is to know what bureaucrats are doing or planning to do. Information gathering by members of Congress about bureaucratic actions is termed **oversight**. Congressional committees often hold hearings to question members of the bureaucracy, typically agency heads, secretaries of executive departments, or senior agency staff. Similarly, one of the primary responsibilities of presidential appointees is to monitor how bureaucrats are responding to presidential directives. The problem, as we discuss in previous chapters, is that presidential appointees may often be unable to fulfill this role. Because they are chosen for their loyalty to the president, they may lack the experience needed to fully understand what bureaucrats in their agency are doing. Moreover, given that appointees typically hold their position for only a year or two, they have little time to learn the details of agency operations.

Advance Warning Members of Congress, the president, and his staff gain advance knowledge of bureaucratic actions through the notice and comment procedure described earlier in the chapter, which requires bureaucrats to disclose their proposed changes before they take effect.[93] This delay gives people who oppose a change the opportunity to register complaints with their congressional representatives, and it allows these legislators time either to pressure the agency to revise the regulation or even to enact another law undoing or modifying the agency action.

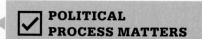

POLITICAL PROCESS MATTERS

Investigations: Police Patrols and Fire Alarms Investigations involve Congress, legislative staff, or presidential appointees selecting some government program or office and scrutinizing the organization, its expenditures, and its activities. Ideally, every agency would be investigated as often as possible, with agencies that had large budgets or carried out important functions being investigated more frequently. These investigations may involve fact-finding trips to local offices, interviews with senior personnel, audits of agency accounts, and even calls to the agency to see how they respond to citizens' requests. This method of investigation is called **police patrol oversight**.[94] Think of a police officer walking her beat, rattling doors to see if they are locked, checking out broken windows, and looking down alleys for suspicious behavior.

The disadvantage of police patrol oversight is that it is costly, both in terms of money and staff time. Moreover, these investigations often find that agencies are doing what they should. Because of these drawbacks, Congress and the president also look outside government for information on what bureaucrats are doing. Rather than undertaking a series of investigations, they wait until they receive a complaint about bureaucratic actions, then focus investigative efforts on those cases, a practice labeled **fire alarm oversight**.[95]

The so-called fire alarm can take many different forms. Representatives and their staff meet frequently with constituents, who may let them know of a problem with the bureaucracy. Similarly, the president and his staff are often contacted by lobbyists, corporate executives, or even ordinary citizens with complaints about bureaucratic actions. Newspaper reporters and Internet bloggers also provide information on what bureaucrats are doing. Some agencies have advisory committees that not only help make agency decisions but also serve to keep Congress and the president informed about them.[96]

The case of NASA climate change scientist James Hansen described earlier provides a clear example of fire alarm oversight. The order requiring that Hansen submit all his public statements and work for review became known when it was reported by the *New York Times* and other newspapers. The resulting firestorm of protest from members of Congress forced NASA head Michael Griffin to rescind the order.

These fire alarms provide exactly the sort of information that Congress and the president often lack about how bureaucrats are implementing laws and directives,

oversight Congressional efforts to make sure that laws are implemented correctly by the bureaucracy after they have been passed.

police patrol oversight A method of oversight in which members of Congress constantly monitor the bureaucracy to make sure that laws are implemented correctly.

fire alarm oversight A method of oversight in which members of Congress respond to complaints about the bureaucracy or problems of implementation only as they arise rather than exercising constant vigilance.

Is Political Control of the Bureaucracy Beneficial?

When working with bureaucrats, elected officials face the problem of political control: Should they allow bureaucrats to exercise judgment when implementing policies or give them specific, narrow directives? Letting bureaucrats set policy allows them to base decisions on their expertise or private information, but it also gives them the freedom to ignore elected officials' policy goals and preferences in favor of their own.

Discretion also allows bureaucrats to say things that contradict the public statements of members of Congress or the president. Statements by NASA scientist James Hansen about the need to actively combat global warming, for example, contradicted then-president Bush's view that global warming deserved further study but nothing more. Such cases seem clear cut, suggesting that Americans should support bureaucrats, who often know more about the details of policy problems and solutions than members of Congress. Likewise, it seems obvious that government scientists such as Hansen should be allowed to conduct research without political

Attempts by NASA bureaucrats to suppress public comments about global warming by James Hansen, director of NASA's Goddard Institute for Space Studies, were abandoned after they attracted media coverage.

intervention. Indeed, NASA's policy on scientific freedom notes the agency's commitment to "a culture of scientific and technical openness which values the free exchange of ideas, data and information, [and in which] scientific and technical information concerning

agency programs and projects will be accurate and unfiltered."[a]

The problem with bureaucratic discretion is that it cuts both ways. Allowing bureaucrats to act as they think best means that they can disregard the stated goals of legislation or the preferences of elected officials and simply implement the policies they favor. Even bureaucrats' public statements can have policy consequences—they may influence public opinion and in turn shape government policy. When a scientist such as Hansen sounds the alarm, many people listen.

Another down side that comes with bureaucratic discretion is that bureaucrats are unelected and most are very difficult to fire because of their civil service protections. A misbehaving elected official can be removed from office via an election or impeachment; bureaucrats have more staying power. Moreover, if bureaucrats are given a great deal of leeway to use their judgment in policy making, it becomes very difficult to determine the criteria for judging whether their removal is warranted or not. How much discretion should elected officials allow bureaucrats to use? You decide. ■

including cases when bureaucrats are doing (or planning to do) something that contradicts their mandate. These communications tell Congress and the president where to focus their efforts to monitor the bureaucracy, drawing their attention to agencies or programs where problems have been reported, rather than trying to oversee the entire government at once.

CORRECTING VIOLATIONS

When members of Congress or the president find a case of bureaucratic drift, they can take steps to influence the bureaucrats' actions. Many tactics can be used to bring a wayward agency into line. Legislation or an executive order can send a clear

directive to an agency or remove its discretion, tasks and programs can be moved to an agency more closely aligned with elected officials' goals, political appointees at an agency can be replaced, and agencies can be reorganized. For example, in the wake of the BP oil spill, there were numerous congressional hearings about proposals to reorganize the Minerals Management Service, expand its staff and budget, and refocus its mission on safety and preventing spills. In extreme situations, members of Congress can even fail to renew an agency's statutory authority, in effect putting the agency out of business.

One of the most significant difficulties in dealing with bureaucratic drift is disagreement between members of Congress and the president about whether an agency is doing the right thing—regardless of whether the agency is following its original orders. Most of the tactics listed above require joint action by the president and congressional majorities. Without presidential support, members of Congress need a two-thirds majority to impose corrections. Without congressional support, the president can only threaten to cut an agency's proposed budget, change its home within the federal bureaucracy, or set up a new agency to do what the errant agency refuses to do—actually carrying out these threats requires congressional approval. As a result, disagreements between the president and Congress can give an agency significant freedom, as long as it retains the support of at least one branch of government. For example, a study of Federal Reserve policy making found that the Fed has been able to quash attempts to end its independence from political control by choosing monetary policies that are always considered acceptable by at least one branch of government, either Congress or the president.[97]

An agency may also be able to fend off elected officials' attempts to take political control if it has a reputation for expertise. For example, one reason that attempts to pass legislation forcing the FDA to alter its drug approval process have met with little success is that the FDA's process is thought to have worked mostly as intended, approving new drugs that are safe and effective and keeping ineffective or unsafe drugs off the market. At the same time, the FDA has also responded to pressure from Congress and the president to revise some rules on its own.[98]

Finally, agencies can sometimes combat attempts to control their behavior by appealing to groups in society who benefit from agency actions.[99] For example, since the 1980s, the Occupational Safety and Health Administration (OSHA) has resisted attempts by Republican presidents and Republican members of Congress to eliminate the agency.[100] One element of their strategy has been to build strong ties to labor unions; as a result, OSHA is much more likely to receive complaints about workplace safety from companies with strong unions. The second prong of the strategy has involved building cooperative arrangements with large companies to prevent workplace accidents, an approach that not only protects workers but can save companies a lot of money over the long term. Moreover, when OSHA levies fines against companies that violate safety regulations, they are generally much less than would be allowed by law. As a result, when proposals to limit or eliminate OSHA are debated in Congress, members hear from unions as well as many large corporations in support of keeping the agency in place. Over time, this strategy has generated support for the agency from Democrats and Republicans in the House and Senate.

Many other agencies have followed similar strategies, even when the bureaucracy was much smaller. For example, during the early 1900s, bureaucrats in the Department of Agriculture and in the Forest Service won congressional approval to move the Forest Service out of the Department of the Interior and into their own department. Republicans in Congress opposed the move, believing (correctly) that it would allow the Forest Service to impose user fees and limit grazing rights, which the Republican members opposed. The move happened because leaders in

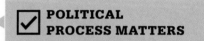

POLITICAL PROCESS MATTERS

the Forest Service and the Department of Agriculture had cultivated the support of interest groups such as the Audubon Society, the Sierra Club, and organizations representing ranchers, all of whom lobbied Congress in favor of the change.[101]

Explaining the Anomalies

This chapter began with two lists: one describing bureaucratic failures and embarrassments and another highlighting significant bureaucratic accomplishments. In light of the vast capabilities of the federal government, the accomplishments need little explaining, so this section focuses on explaining the failures. Put another way, how can a government that functions so well in some areas be a dismal failure in others?

The first reason for bureaucratic shortfalls is the complexity of the tasks that bureaucrats undertake. Even when members of Congress and the president agree on which problems deserve attention, bureaucrats are often given the much harder task of translating these officials' lofty problem-solving goals into concrete policies. Given the magnitude of this job, it is no surprise that even the best efforts of government agencies do not always succeed. Consider the Great Society's goal of eliminating poverty in America.[102] When these antipoverty programs were implemented in the 1960s, the causes of poverty were not well understood. Years later, it became clear that without a better understanding of the problem, it would be impossible to develop effective policies to help the poor.[103] Similarly, while it's clear that officials at the Minerals Management Service could have been more aggressive about inspecting the Deepwater Horizon oil platform, it is not clear whether any of these steps would have prevented the explosion and oil spill.

Second, the use of standard operating procedures is rooted partly in the complexity of bureaucrats' tasks—but also in the desire of agency heads and elected officials to control the actions of lower-level staff. Some of FEMA's failures after Hurricane Katrina were the product of preset plans and procedures that did not anticipate a disaster of the magnitude faced in New Orleans. Giving laptops to government employees so they can work while out of the office sounds like a good idea, but it also puts sensitive data at risk because laptops are more easily lost or stolen. And while the FDA's drug approval process succeeds for the most part at preventing harmful drugs from coming to market, the delays imposed by the process do prevent some patients from receiving life-saving treatments. However, in all of these cases, the decisions do not reflect incompetence or malice. Rules and procedures are needed in any organization to ensure that decisions are made fairly and that they reflect the goals of the organization. However, it is impossible to find procedures that will work well in all cases, particularly for the kinds of policy decisions made by bureaucrats.

It's also important to remember that many government regulations, even those that are the product of standard operating procedures, work as intended and provide socially beneficial results. For example, regulations restricting pollution have led to dramatic increases in air and water quality throughout the United States.

▼ Many government regulations work as intended. An increase in regulatory attention to environmental protection and cleanup of polluted sites has dramatically improved water quality nationwide, including that of the Hudson River in New York, shown here.

Dysfunctional bureaucratic behavior can also arise from the problem of political control. Requiring the surgeon general to mention the president's name three times on each page of his speeches sounds absurd, and perhaps it is—but it is also true that the president and his appointees are genuinely worried about being undercut by unelected bureaucrats who may disagree with their plans. Similarly, government reorganizations such as the formation of the Department of Homeland Security may be designed to bring about some bureaucratic "failures" as priorities shift and agencies' goals are redefined. That is, no one expects agencies like the Coast Guard to take on new responsibilities without shifting resources away from the jobs they are already doing. In a sense, the Guard has fallen short in its routine patrol mission since it became part of Homeland Security. But the reason for moving the Guard into the new department was to refocus its efforts on port security rather than its traditional missions. From the viewpoint of political control, the reorganization worked exactly as planned.

In sum, when government agencies do things that look bizarre or counter-productive, it would be wrong to immediately conclude that the organizations involved are inept or willfully shirking their responsibilities. Rather, they may be doing the best they can to achieve formidable goals, carrying out procedures that are often—but not always—productive, or responding to directives from elected officials.

Conclusion

Bureaucrats implement government policy—often in situations where the problems as well as potential solutions are vast and poorly understood, and in the face of sharp disagreements about what government should do. On the government's behalf, they spend money on everything from pencils to aircraft carriers. They formulate regulations that determine what can be created, produced, transported, bought, sold, consumed, and disposed of in America. Elected officials, from members of Congress to the president, want to control what bureaucrats do while also tapping into their expertise on policy matters. In this way, conflict over public policy often translates into conflicting ideas about what bureaucrats should do, resulting in complex, often contradictory mandates and directions imposed on bureacrats.

These characteristics of the bureaucracy and the fundamentally political na-ture of bureaucrats' jobs explain many cases of bureaucratic ineptitude and red tape. Sometimes bureaucrats simply make mistakes, choosing the wrong policy because they—and, in some cases, everyone else—lack full information about the tasks they were given. Bureaucrats may drag their feet when they oppose their tasks on policy grounds. Policies may reflect direct orders given by elected offi-cials or political appointees. Attempts at political control also shape the structure of the bureaucracy, from influencing which agencies function independently and which are housed within executive departments to determining the qualifications for commissioners and agency heads and the rules they must follow when making decisions.

What is the federal bureaucracy?

- The bureaucracy, or administrative state, comprises the civil service employees, political appointees, and organizations that make up the executive branch of the federal government.
- Bureaucrats develop regulations, procure goods and services for government agencies, provide services to citizens, carry out research and development, and manage government contractors.
- Most bureaucrats are experts who know more about the policies administered by their agency than the average citizen or member of Congress.
- Bureaucratic expertise creates a problem of political control. Thus, bureaucrats are not above or apart from politics but in the middle of the political process.

How has the American bureaucracy developed over time?

- For several decades after the Founding, America's bureaucracy was small, with many employees hired because of their political activity.
- The Progressive Era saw a vast increase in the state capacity of the federal government—the creation of a bureaucracy that was separate from Congress and the president, with the resources to implement policies to change society.
- Other significant increases in the size of the bureaucracy and the scope of its activities occurred during the New Deal of the 1930s and the Great Society of the late 1960s.
- Despite efforts over the last generation to reduce the size and mission of the federal bureaucracy, such as the Reagan Revolution, only marginal reductions have been made.

What are the characteristics of the modern American bureaucracy? What explains its current organization and size?

- The federal bureaucracy is organized into fifteen executive departments, each containing a number of agencies, and many independent agencies that operate outside the executive departments' control.
- Decisions about where an agency is located within the federal government structure have important implications for political control.
- Public demand for government services provides the best explanation for the size of the federal government.

Who are bureaucrats? What motivates them, and what constraints do they face?

- Like employees in the private sector, bureaucrats are motivated by financial concerns, but many also take a strong interest in enacting good public policy.
- Civil service regulations protect bureaucrats against being fired for political reasons but also make it hard for supervisors to remove incompetent employees or reward top performers.
- Federal employees face significant restrictions on their political activity.
- The Senior Executive Service allows high-level bureaucrats to take leadership positions in government agencies, at the cost of removing their civil service protections.

How do Americans see the bureaucracy?

- Very few Americans believe the federal government can claim a large number of policy successes. However, Americans tend to have a more positive impression of government agencies with which they have personal experience.

How can the bureaucracy be controlled?

- Elected officials can exercise political control over bureaucrats by giving them simple directives and little discretion. However, this strategy eliminates the benefits of allowing bureaucrats to act on their expertise.
- To solve this problem, elected officials use agency organization, restrictions on agency leaders and staff, and oversight mechanisms such as police patrols and fire alarms.
- In response, agencies work to build public and interest group support for their policies.
- Agencies have more discretion when the president and members of Congress disagree on what the agency should be doing.

Why does the bureaucracy sometimes fail?

- Bureaucrats undertake highly complex tasks given to them by Congress and the president. Even when members of Congress and the president agree on what should be done, it can still be very difficult to translate legislative goals into concrete policies.
- Bureaucrats must follow standard operating procedures because of the complexity of the tasks they are given and to help solve the problem of control. However, no standard procedure works in all cases.
- Efforts to control the bureaucracy also mean that politicians and agency heads sometimes override the judgment of bureaucrats or change an agency's mission, resulting in some "failures" that are not caused by the bureaucrats themselves.

STUDENT STUDYSPACE

Find quizzes and other review material at wwnorton.com/studyspace.

CRITICAL THINKING

1. Suppose you are a member of Congress who must decide whether to give bureaucrats in a particular agency direct orders that allow them little or no input, or to allow them to exercise their own discretion. What factors should you consider when making this decision?

2. What are the advantages and disadvantages of the fact that bureaucrats often have their own preferences about how to implement the policies they administer?

3. Why might bureaucrats pay more attention to orders and directives from members of Congress than those from the president or his political appointees?

KEY TERMS

budget maximizers (p. 446)
bureaucracy (p. 431)
bureaucratic drift (p. 456)
civil servants (p. 431)
federal civil service (p. 440)
fire alarm oversight (p. 457)
independent agencies (p. 444)
neutral competence (p. 438)

notice and comment procedure (p. 432)
Office of Management and Budget (p. 442)
oversight (p. 457)
police patrol oversight (p. 457)
political appointees (p. 431)
principal–agent game (p. 437)
problem of control (p. 437)

red tape (p. 436)
regulation (p. 432)
regulatory capture (p. 437)
standard operating procedures (p. 436)
state capacity (p. 436)
street-level bureaucrats (p. 435)
turkey farms (p. 452)

SUGGESTED READING

Aaron, Henry J. *Politics and the Professors: The Great Society in Perspective.* Washington, DC: Brookings Institution Press, 1978.

Brehm, John, and Scott Gates. *Working, Shirking and Sabotage.* Ann Arbor, MI: University of Michigan Press, 1998.

Carpenter, Daniel P. *The Forging of Bureaucratic Autonomy: Reputations, Networks, and Policy Innovation in Executive Agencies, 1862–1928.* Princeton, NJ: Princeton University Press, 2001.

Epstein, David, and Sharyn O'Halloran. *Delegating Powers: A Transaction Cost Politics Approach to Policy Making under Separate Powers.* New York: Cambridge University Press, 1999.

Huber, John D., and Charles R. Shipan. *Deliberate Discretion? The Institutional Foundations of Bureaucratic Autonomy.* New York: Cambridge University Press, 2002.

Lewis, David E. *The Politics of Presidential Appointments: Political Control and Bureaucratic Performance.* Princeton, NJ: Princeton University Press, 2010.

Light, Paul. *A Government Well-Executed: Public Service and Public Performance.* Washington, DC: Brookings Institution Press, 2003.

McCubbins, Mathew D., Roger G. Noll, and Barry R. Weingast. "Structure and Process as Solutions to the Politicians' Principal–Agency Problem," *Virginia Law Review* 74 (1989): 431–82.

Miller, Gary. *Managerial Dilemmas: The Political Economy of Hierarchy.* New York: Cambridge University Press, 1987.

Moe, Terry M. "Political Control and the Power of the Agent," *Journal of Law, Economics, and Organization* 22 (2006): 1–21.

Nelson, Michael. "A Short, Ironic History of American National Bureaucracy," *Journal of Politics* 44 (1982): 747–78.

Skowronek, Stephen. *Building a New American State: The Expansion of National Administrative Capacities, 1877–1920.* New York: Cambridge University Press, 1982.

Wilson, James Q. *Bureaucracy: What Government Agencies Do and Why They Do It,* 2nd ed. New York: Basic Books, 2000.

The sun sets over the Guantánamo Bay detention facility's Camp Justice, site of controversial military tribunals for suspected terrorists.

13

The Courts

How do the courts fit our theme of "conflict and compromise"? The conflict part makes sense: our legal system is based on the premise that conflict between competing sides of a case will produce the correct and just outcome. But compromise? Don't the courts objectively apply the law and interpret the Constitution for each given case? This chapter argues that as one of the three political branches, the courts are an equal partner in our system of separated powers. The courts respond to and shape politics in ways that often involve compromise, both within the courts themselves (yes, judges take politics into account) and in the broader political system. An example from the War on Terror illustrates this argument.

Fighting terrorism involves a trade-off: giving the government more power to hunt and catch terrorists probably means sacrificing some civil liberties. Congress, the president, and the Supreme Court have at various times held very different ideas about the proper balance in that trade-off, which produces conflict between the branches. Following the September 11 attacks and the invasion of Afghanistan, President Bush broadly interpreted his war powers to give him the right to declare terrorism suspects "unlawful enemy combatants" who could be held indefinitely without access to lawyers or to the courts. If the government brought charges against the suspects, they could be tried in military tribunals with different rules of procedure and fewer rights for the defendants. The Republican-controlled Congress agreed with the president, but in a series of cases, the Supreme Court struck down those assertions of presidential power.

In the first two cases, the Court ruled that detainees had been improperly deprived of their due process rights and were entitled to challenge their detention in federal court.[1] Two more recent cases were more far-reaching. The first case involved Salim Ahmed Hamdan, the former driver for Osama bin Laden; the central issues were whether military tribunals were legal and whether Congress had the power to remove pending cases from the jurisdiction of the courts. On both issues, the Court ruled against the administration, saying, "The executive is bound to comply with the rule of law that prevails in this jurisdiction." The Court ruled that military tribunals violate military law and the Geneva Conventions on the treatment of prisoners of war. Mr. Hamdan's lawyer said that Hamdan was "awe-struck that the court would rule for him and give a little man like him an equal chance. Where he's from, that is not true."[2] Congress responded

CONFLICT AND COMPROMISE

in American Politics

465

BIG QUESTIONS

✪ How did the federal judiciary become independent and powerful?

✪ What is the nature of the American legal and judicial system?

✪ How do cases reach the Supreme Court?

✪ What is the Court's process for hearing cases?

✪ How does the Supreme Court make decisions?

✪ Can the Court be a policy maker?

to the decision by passing the Military Commissions Act of 2006, which restored the military's ability to prosecute unlawful enemy combatants in military tribunals and stripped from federal courts their jurisdiction over appeals from prisoners being held at the Guantánamo Bay detention facility. Two years later, however, the Supreme Court struck down parts of the law, restoring prisoners' right to challenge their indefinite detention, saying, "The practice of arbitrary imprisonments has been, in all ages, the favorite and most formidable instrument of tyranny."[3] In August 2008, a military commission found Hamdan guilty of providing material support for terrorism. He was acquitted of the more serious conspiracy charge and given a prison sentence of five and a half years, of which he was given credit for his sixty-one months in detention at Guantánamo.

President Obama had to address some of these unresolved issues when he took office in 2009. In some instances he was responsive to the Court's call for stronger civil liberties for suspected terrorists. He promised to close the Guantánamo facility, and several high-profile terror suspects were tried in civilian court, rather than military tribunals, including Umar Farouk Abdulmutallab, the Nigerian accused of trying to detonate a bomb on board a U.S. airplane on Christmas Day 2009, and Faisal Shahzad, who tried to blow up a bomb-laden SUV in New York's Times Square. However, closing Guantánamo has been delayed as the federal government seeks a permanent facility for the remaining prisoners. President Obama also clashed with the courts over the detention of suspected terrorists.

When the Supreme Court rules that military tribunals are unconstitutional, the president and Congress must scramble back to the drawing board and figure out what to do: they have to compromise based on the Court's different view of the trade-off between security and civil liberties. At the same time, the Court's decision of which path to take in a given case is often very political, involving conflict, trade-offs, and compromise much like decision making in Congress. That the Supreme Court is a policy-making and political institution may seem inappropriate. After all, the guiding principles of the "rule of law" in the American political system—embodied in the words carved above the entrance to the Supreme Court ("equal justice under the law") and the statue of Justice represented as a blindfolded woman holding a set of scales—seem to contradict the view of a political Court.

The reality is more complicated. Politics is an inherent part of the judiciary and a single set of objective standards is not always available for a given case. Although we certainly expect them to be fair and objective, judges have their own political views and opinions, and these often shape their views of cases in part *because* there are usually multiple legal justifications for any case. For example, there is no simple or clear-cut way to determine objectively the relative legal merits of Justice Clarence Thomas's dissenting view that the *Hamdan* decision was "untenable" and "dangerous" or the majority's view that "Congress

has not issued the executive a blank check" to pursue the War on Terror without oversight. To a large extent, this depends on the justices' views of the trade-offs between a broad view of presidential powers, civil liberties, and legal due process, and our commitments under international treaties.

For those who resist the view that the courts are a policy-making institution, at least in the same way that Congress is, the theme "political process matters" may not seem to apply in this chapter. However, the courts often *do* make policy, and the manner in which they make decisions has an impact on outcomes. To see how political process matters for the courts, it is important to answer the following questions: What are the different roles of the courts? What is the structure of the judicial system? How do court decisions shape policy? In a nutshell, what is the nature of judicial decision making?

The role of the Court as a policy-making and political institution also illustrates the third theme of this book. On the one hand, the courts seem to resist our characterization that politics is everywhere. There is an aura of mystery and prestige to the courts that seems to isolate them from the rest of the political process. However, most Americans will come into contact with the court system at some point in their lives, whether it is to contest a traffic ticket, fight a local zoning change, or serve on a jury (we assume that you will not be on the "wrong side" of the law). The relevance of the courts in national politics is similarly self-evident. Dramatic moments, such as the *Bush v. Gore* decision that determined the 2000 presidential election, are the most obvious examples of the relevance (and political nature!) of the courts. Less visible decisions that are handed down every day in the federal courts affect the lives of millions of Americans across a broad range of areas, including environmental policy, employment law, tax policy, civil rights, and civil liberties. In fact, some critics of the courts complain about an "imperial judiciary" that has become *too* powerful in the political system. This chapter examines the issues centered on the proper place of the courts within our political system. How much power should unelected judges have? Are they a necessary check on the other branches of government or a source of unaccountable power that contradicts core principles of democracy? How do the courts interact with the other branches? Before addressing these questions we discuss how the Founders viewed the judicial system.

▲ *The most widely recognized symbol of justice, a blindfolded woman holding a set of scales in one hand and a sword in the other, is seen at hundreds of courthouses around the world.*

The Development of an Independent and Powerful Federal Judiciary

THE FOUNDERS' VIEWS OF THE COURTS: THE WEAKEST BRANCH?

The Federalists and Antifederalists did not see eye-to-eye on much, and the judiciary was no exception. Alexander Hamilton, writing in *Federalist 78*, said that the Supreme Court would be "beyond comparison the weakest of the three departments

of power." On the other hand, the author of what came to be known as the *Anti-federalist Papers* wrote, "The supreme court under this constitution would be exalted above all other power in the government and subjected to no control."[4] Hmmm, which is it, weakest or strongest? While the framers could not agree on their predictions of the relative power of the Court, there was surprisingly little debate at the Constitutional Convention about the judiciary, at least when compared to the more extended battles over Congress and the executive. Article III of the Constitution, which lays out the power of the Court, is much shorter than Article I or II. Article III created one Supreme Court and gave the courts independence by providing federal judges with lifetime terms (that is, they can serve during "good behavior") and stipulating that judges' salaries cannot be reduced during their terms in office.

The main disagreements at the Constitutional Convention about the judiciary had to do with how independent the courts should be vis-à-vis the other branches and how much power to give the courts. Some of the framers feared a tyrannical Congress and wanted to create a judicial and executive branch that could check this power. Some argued for making the executive and judicial branches much more closely related so they would be better able to balance Congress. A central debate on this topic was whether to give the judiciary some "revisionary power" over Congress, similar to the president's veto power. This idea of judicial review (as we call it today), which we discuss more fully below, would have given the Supreme Court the power to strike down laws passed by Congress that violated the Constitution. The framers could not agree on the more general issue of judicial review, so the Constitution remained silent on the matter. As the power of judicial review has evolved, it has become a central part of the system of checks and balances discussed in Chapter 2.

Many details about the Supreme Court were left up to Congress, including its size, the time and place it would meet, and its internal organization. These details, and the system of lower federal courts, were outlined in the **Judiciary Act of 1789**. This law set the number of justices at six (one chief justice and five associates) who were to meet twice a year, in February and August. The number of justices gradually increased to ten by the end of the Civil War and was then restricted to seven (a target that would be reached through retirements) as part of the Reconstruction policies imposed on President Andrew Johnson. However, the number did not ever get below eight and was set at nine in 1869, where it has remained since.[5] The act also created a system of federal courts, which included thirteen **district courts** and three circuit courts, which were the intermediate-level courts that heard appeals from the district courts. The district courts each had one judge, and the circuits were made up of two Supreme Court justices and one district judge. This odd arrangement for staffing the circuit courts remained in place for more than 100 years, over the objections of the justices who resented having to "ride circuit" in difficult traveling conditions.[6] Today, separate judges are appointed to fill the circuit courts (what we call "appeals courts" today). The other most important part of the act refined and clarified the jurisdiction of the federal courts. One controversial provision along these lines was Section 25 of the act, which expanded the Court's **appellate jurisdiction**, cases that are heard on appeal from lower courts, to include state supreme court cases involving conflicts between state law and federal law or treaties or the U.S. Constitution.

The Supreme Court had a rough start. Indeed, it seemed determined to prove Alexander Hamilton right that it was the weakest branch. Of the six original justices appointed by George Washington, one declined to serve and another accepted the appointment but never showed up for a formal session. The first sessions of

Judiciary Act of 1789 The law in which Congress laid out the organization of the federal judiciary. The law refined and clarified federal court jurisdiction and set the original number of justices at six. It also created the Office of the Attorney General and established the lower federal courts.

district courts Lower-level trial courts of the federal judicial system that handle most U.S. federal cases.

appellate jurisdiction The authority of a court to hear appeals from lower courts and change or uphold the decision.

the Court lasted only a few days because it did not have much business. In fact, the Court did not decide a single case in 1791 or 1792. When Justice Rutledge resigned in 1791 to take a state court position, two potential appointees turned down the job to keep their positions in their state legislatures! Such career decisions would be unimaginable today, as the Supreme Court is seen as the pinnacle of a legal career.[7]

JUDICIAL REVIEW AND *MARBURY V. MADISON*

The Court started to gain more power and stature when John Marshall was appointed chief justice by outgoing President John Adams in 1801. Marshall served in that position for thirty-four years and single-handedly transformed the Court into an equal partner in the system of checks and balances. The most important step toward that equal partnership was the decision *Marbury v. Madison* (1803), which gave the Supreme Court the power of judicial review. As noted above, the framers were split on the wisdom of giving the Court the power to strike down laws passed by Congress and therefore ducked the issue. However, historians have established

NUTS AND BOLTS

13.1

Jurisdiction of the Federal Courts as Defined in Article III of the Constitution

JURISDICTION OF LOWER FEDERAL COURTS

- Cases involving the U.S. Constitution, federal laws, and treaties.
- Controversies between two or more states. (Congress passed a law giving the Supreme Court exclusive jurisdiction over these cases.)
- Controversies between citizens of different states.
- Controversies between a state and citizens of another state. (The 11th Amendment removed federal jurisdiction in these cases.)
- Controversies between a state or its citizens and any foreign states, citizens, or subjects.
- Cases affecting ambassadors, public ministers, and consuls.
- Cases of admiralty and maritime jurisdictions.
- Controversies between citizens of the same state claiming lands under grants of different states.

JURISDICTION OF THE SUPREME COURT

Original Jurisdiction[a]

- Cases involving ambassadors, public ministers, and consuls.
- Cases to which a state is a party.

Appellate Jurisdiction

- Cases falling under the jurisdiction of the lower federal courts, "with such exceptions, and under such Regulations as the Congress shall make."

[a] This does not imply exclusive jurisdiction. For example, the Supreme Court may refer to a district court a case involving an ambassador (the more likely outcome).

SOURCE: Lee Epstein and Thomas G. Walker, *Constitutional Law for a Changing America: Institutional Powers and Constraints*, 5th ed. (Washington, DC: CQ Press, 2004), 65.

judicial review The Supreme Court's power to strike down a law or executive branch action that it finds unconstitutional.

writs of mandamus Orders issued by a higher court to a lower court, government official, or government agency to perform acts required by law.

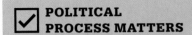

POLITICAL PROCESS MATTERS

▼ *William Marbury was the plaintiff in* Marbury v. Madison *(1803), the case that established the principle of judicial review. Although Marbury never got the job he was seeking from his lawsuit, his case established the Supreme Court as an equal partner in the system of checks and balances.*

that a majority of the framers, including the most influential ones, favored **judicial review**. Given the silence of the Constitution, Marshall simply asserted that the Supreme Court had the power to determine when a law was unconstitutional.

The facts of *Marbury* and the legal reasoning through which the Court claimed the power of judicial review are fairly complicated, but they are worth explaining in some detail because this is one of the most important court cases in American history. The Federalists had just lost the election of 1800 to Thomas Jefferson and the Democratic-Republicans. In a last-minute power grab, the Federalist-controlled lame-duck Congress gave President Adams an opportunity to appoint forty-two new justices of the peace for the District of Columbia (the nation's capital moved to the District of Columbia in 1801) and Alexandria, Virginia. Adams made the appointments, and they were confirmed by the Senate, but time ran out before the new administration took over, and the secretary of state, John Marshall, did not ensure that all of the legal documents concerning the appointments were delivered by midnight (the same Marshall who had just been confirmed as chief justice; as they say in mystery novels, "The plot thickens"). When President Jefferson assumed office, his secretary of state, James Madison, ordered that at least five of them not be delivered because of partisan differences with the outgoing administration (the historical record is mixed on the exact number of appointments affected). William Marbury was one of the people who did not receive his commission, so he asked the Supreme Court to issue an order giving him the position.

As leading figures in opposing parties, Chief Justice Marshall and President Jefferson did not really like each other. This put Marshall in an especially difficult position because he was very concerned that if he issued the order that Marbury wanted (giving Marbury his job), Jefferson probably would ignore it (technically, Secretary of State Madison was the other party in the lawsuit, but President Jefferson was calling the shots). Given the weakness of the Court, having such an order disregarded by the president could have been a final blow to its position in the national government. However, if the Court did not issue the order, it would be giving in to Jefferson, despite the merits of Marbury's case—he really had been cheated out of his job. It appeared that the Court would lose whether it issued the order or not.

To get out of the mess, Marshall established the idea of judicial review. Although the idea was not original to Marshall (as noted above, the framers debated the issue and Hamilton endorsed it in some detail in *Federalist 78*), the Court had never exercised its authority to rule on the constitutionality of a federal law. Marshall's reasoning was quite clever: the Court's opinion said that Marbury was due his commission, but the Court did not have the power to give him his job because the part of the Judiciary Act of 1789 that gave it that power was unconstitutional! The core issue was Section 13 of the 1789 act, which gave the Court the power to issue orders (**writs of mandamus**) to anyone holding federal office. This section of the act expanded the "original jurisdiction" of the Supreme Court, and that was where Congress overstepped its bounds, according to Marshall. The original jurisdiction of the Court is clearly specified in the Constitution, so any attempt by Congress to change that jurisdiction through legislation would be unconstitutional; the only way original jurisdiction could be changed was through a constitutional amendment.[8] Marshall writes, "The question, whether an act, repugnant to the constitution, can become the law of the land, is a question deeply interesting to the United States." He goes on to assert that the Court must answer that question: "It is emphatically the province and duty of the judicial department to say what the law is. . . . If two laws conflict with each other, the courts must decide on the operation of each. So if a law be in opposition to the Constitution . . . the courts must determine which of these conflicting rules governs the case. This is of the very essence of judicial duty."[9]

The Irrepressible Myth of *Marbury*

Apparently nothing in the conventional wisdom is sacred: even the origins of judicial review in the landmark decision *Marbury v. Madison* are challenged by revisionist historians, legal scholars, and political scientists. One of the strongest challenges comes from Michael Stokes Paulsen, whose *Michigan Law Review* article is excerpted here:

Nearly all of American constitutional law today rests on a myth. The myth, presented as standard history both in junior high civics texts and in advanced law school courses on constitutional law, runs something like this: A long, long time ago—1803, if the storyteller is trying to be precise—in the famous case of *Marbury v. Madison,* the Supreme Court of the United States created the doctrine of "judicial review." Judicial review is the power of the Supreme Court to decide the meaning of the Constitution and to strike down laws that the Court finds unconstitutional. . . . Judicial review (the myth continues) thus serves as the ultimate check on the powers of the other branches of government, and is one of the unique, crowning features of our constitutional democracy. . . . Indeed, the Court's authority over constitutional interpretation by now must be regarded, rightly, as one of the pillars of our constitutional order, on par with the Constitution itself.

So the myth goes. But nearly every feature of the myth is wrong. For openers, *Marbury v. Madison* did not create the concept of judicial review, but (in this respect) applied well-established principles. . . . Moreover, and also contrary to the mythology that has come to surround *Marbury*, the power of judicial review was never understood by proponents and defenders of the Constitution as a power of judicial supremacy over the other branches, much less one of judicial exclusivity in constitutional interpretation. Nothing in the text of the Constitution supports a claim of judicial supremacy. . . . Nothing in Chief Justice Marshall's opinion in *Marbury* makes such a claim of judicial supremacy either. The standard civics-book (and law school casebook) myth misrepresents and distorts what John Marshall and the Framers understood to be the power of judicial review: a coordinate, coequal power of courts to judge for themselves the conformity of acts of the other two branches with the fundamental law of the Constitution, and to refuse to give acts contradicting the Constitution any force or effect insofar as application of the judicial power is concerned. [. . .]

Alas, that is not the constitutional world we inhabit today. Instead, we live in a constitutional world in which the Supreme Court is sultan and a perversion of *Marbury v. Madison* is our governing constitutional myth. The myth is, by now, an ingrained one. The Supreme Court lives by the myth. The political branches by and large have accepted it. And it has been taught as Holy Writ to several generations of elementary school and law school students. Disentangling our political culture from the Myth of *Marbury* is not a mere day's work. On this, the occasion of *Marbury*'s 200th anniversary, however, it is worth reflecting on the fact that The Myth is a betrayal of everything that *Marbury* stands for, and a betrayal of the written Constitution that *Marbury* identifies as the appropriate object of veneration.[a]

Pretty strong stuff! Once the hyperbole is stripped away (for example, it is unlikely that many elementary school students examine the intricacies of *Marbury*), Paulsen and the other revisionists make several important points.[b] Two of these are already incorporated into this book's account of judicial review and therefore are probably not as "revisionist" as the revisionists would like to think: (1) John Marshall did not invent judicial review. As we note, Hamilton developed the idea in *Federalist 78*, and it was discussed at the Constitutional Convention. (2) The Supreme Court does not have a monopoly on constitutional interpretation, and Marshall himself did not make the claim of judicial supremacy (a point that is broadly accepted by constitutional scholars even if it is not well understood by the general public).

Three other points made by the revisionists are not as widely cited. (3) *Marbury* was not cited in subsequent Supreme Court cases as a precedent for judicial review until the late nineteenth century. Legal scholars in the early twentieth century were the first to promote the idea that *Marbury* was a landmark decision. (4) When the opinion was delivered in 1803, it was not controversial. Even the Jeffersonian Democrats, who were at odds with Marshall's Federalists, thought that it was a reasonable decision and not the institutional power-grab that is described in modern accounts. (5) Marshall made a very narrow case for judicial review, arguing that the Supreme Court could declare legislation that was contrary to the Court's interpretation of the Constitution null and void only if it concerned judicial powers. Revisionists argue that what appear to be broad claims of judicial power in *Marbury* (e.g., the Court has the power "to say what the law is") are taken out of the context of a much more narrow claim of power.

One reason the revisionist accounts have not received broader acceptance is that they often have a conservative, anti-court agenda. For example, in developing the argument that *Marbury* is significant for establishing the idea that the Constitution should be supreme and be interpreted by all three branches rather than having the courts at the center of this process, Paulsen goes on to say, "constitutional supremacy implies strict textualism as a controlling method of constitutional interpretation, not free wheeling judicial discretion."[c]

While these disputes cannot be resolved here, one key point of agreement between the revisionist and standard accounts of *Marbury* is that the decision established judicial independence by Marshall's assertion of the autonomy of the courts from the other branches. ■

JUDICIAL REVIEW IN PRACTICE

Chief Justice Marshall lost the battle—poor Mr. Marbury never did get his job and Jefferson was able to appoint the people he wanted to be justices of the peace—but the Supreme Court clearly won the war. By asserting the power of the Court to review the constitutionality of laws passed by Congress, the Court became an equal partner in the institutional balance of power. Although it would be more than fifty years until the Court would use judicial review again to strike down a law passed by Congress (in the unfortunate 1857 *Dred Scott* case concerning slavery that basically led to the Civil War), the reasoning of *Marbury* has never been challenged by subsequent presidents or Congresses (but see Challenging Conventional Wisdom for an alternative view of *Marbury*).

Interpreting federal laws may be viewed as a logical responsibility for the Supreme Court, even if judicial review is not mentioned in the Constitution. But what about state laws? Should their constitutionality be a matter for state courts to decide, or should the Supreme Court have final say over state laws as well? As with its silence on the broader issue, the Constitution does not directly answer this question. However, the supremacy clause requires that the U.S. Constitution and national laws take precedence over state constitutions and state laws when they conflict. As noted above, the Judiciary Act of 1789 made it clear that the Supreme Court would rule on these matters.

It didn't take long for the Court to assert its power in this area. In 1796 the Court heard a case concerning a British creditor who was trying to collect a debt from the state of Virginia. The state had passed a law canceling all debts owed by Virginians (or the state) to British subjects. However, the Treaty of Paris, which ended the Revolutionary War and achieved American independence, ensured the collection of such debts. This conflict was resolved when the Court struck down the state law and upheld Americans' commitments under the treaty.[10] Advocates of states' rights were not happy with this development, but it was crucial for the national government that the Constitution be applied uniformly rather than be subject to different interpretations by every state. The precise contours of the relationship between the national government and the states were defined in large part by how active the Supreme Court was in asserting its power of judicial review and how willing it was to intervene in matters of state law. As outlined in Chapter 3, for much of the nineteenth century the Court embraced dual federalism, in which the national government and the states operated on two separate levels. Later, the Court became more willing to involve itself in state law as it moved toward a more active role for the national government in regulating interstate commerce and selectively incorporating the amendments that comprise the Bill of Rights under the 14th Amendment (discussed in Chapter 4).

All in all, the Court has struck down more than 170 acts of Congress and about 1,400 state acts. This sounds like a lot, but Congress passed more than 60,000 laws in its first 220 years, so only about one-quarter of 1 percent have been struck down by the Court. The number of state laws passed throughout history is more difficult to measure, but the percentage of state laws that have been struck down is also quite small. The Court has ruled on state laws in many important areas, including civil liberties, desegregation and civil rights, abortion, privacy, redistricting, labor laws, employment and discrimination, and business and environmental regulation.

When the Supreme Court strikes down a congressional or state law, it is engaging in **constitutional interpretation**—that is, it determines that the law is unconstitutional. But the Supreme Court also engages in **statutory interpretation** on a regular basis: applying national and state laws to particular cases. Often the language of a statute may be unclear, and the Court must interpret how the law

constitutional interpretation The process of determining whether a piece of legislation or governmental action is supported by the Constitution.

statutory interpretation The various methods and tests used by the courts for determining the meaning of a law and applying it to specific situations. Congress may overturn the courts' interpretation by writing a new law; thus it also engages in statutory interpretation.

The Use of Judicial Review

Scholars and philosophers have described and categorized judicial systems from the time the ancient Greek philosopher Plato examined the various rules of Greek city-states to come up with his ideal legal institutions. However, the practice of judicial review is a much more recent development. The early precursor to judicial review goes as far back as 1180 in the old German Reich, where judicial bodies dealt with disputes between individual rulers. However, the modern practice of judicial review, in which a high court strikes down a law of the national government, started with *Marbury v. Madison* in 1803.

The practice was slow to take hold in the rest of the democratic world. A recent study of judicial review explains why with this summary of British thinking on the subject: "Parliament had the 'right to make or unmake any law whatever; and further, that no person or body is recognized by the law of England as having a right to override or set aside the legislation of Parliament.' "[a] This thinking dominated Europe through the nineteenth and early twentieth centuries, as legislatures were seen as the truest expression of the will of the people. Norway had the first European

Pakistani lawyers and party activists hold portraits of the deposed chief justice of the Supreme Court in May 2008. Then-president Pervez Musharraf sacked forty-one judges because of challenges to his controversial reelection, sparking a nationwide protest and demands for an independent judiciary. The controversy contributed to Musharraf's decision to resign in August 2008.

court to establish judicial review in 1866, but several Scandinavian countries did not adopt the practice until a few years ago.[b] Today Great Britain remains one of the few democracies in which courts do not have judicial review of national legislation (though the House of Lords and the European Court of Justice can review the laws of Parliament).

Judicial review has spread dramatically during the "third wave" of democracy. Unlike our hybrid system of checks and balances and separation of powers, which has been largely shunned by established and emerging democracies in favor of the parliamentary form of government, judicial review has become an important American export. Of the seventy nations that became democratic between 1986 and 2000, twenty-nine have some form of judicial review by the courts (in eight of those nations, judicial review is shared with another special body), twenty-four have judicial review by a special body, and only seventeen have limitations on judicial review.[c] Of course, many of these nations have judicial review in name only, as the courts are largely compliant with the dominant regime. Nonetheless, the idea of a court that can check the power of the elected branches of government, especially to protect the political rights of the minority, has become an increasingly important component of democratic governance. ■

should be applied. For example, should the protection of endangered species prevent economic development that may destroy the species' habitat? How does one determine if an employer is responsible for sexual harassment in the workplace? How should the voting rights of minorities be protected? In each of these cases, the Court must interpret the words of the relevant statutes and try to figure out what Congress really meant. In addition, the Court is sometimes required to assess the appropriateness of statutory interpretation by federal agencies that are responsible for implementing laws passed by Congress. Often, this involves the controversial practice of consulting legislative histories—floor debates, congressional hearings, and so on—to determine legislative intent. Justice Antonin Scalia argues that such searches are inherently subjective and that justices should confine themselves to interpreting the actual statutory text.

Although judicial review is universally accepted by politicians and other political actors as a central part of the political system, critics of the practice are concerned about its antidemocratic nature. Why do we give nine unelected justices

plaintiff The person or party who brings a case to court.

defendant The person or party against whom a case is brought.

verdict The final decision in a court case.

plea bargain An agreement between a plaintiff and defendant to settle a case before it goes to trial or the verdict is decided. In a civil case this usually involves an admission of guilt and an agreement on monetary damages; in a criminal case it often involves an admission of guilt in return for a reduced charge or sentence.

standard of proof The amount of evidence needed to determine the outcome of a case. The standard is higher in a criminal case than in a civil one.

burden of proof The responsibility of having to prove guilt; it rests with the plaintiff in criminal cases but could be with either party in a civil trial.

▼ *O. J. Simpson dons a pair of gloves during testimony in his double-murder trial in Los Angeles in June 1995. The jury was not convinced of his guilt "beyond all reasonable doubt" and thus acquitted Simpson in this criminal trial. However, a subsequent civil trial found that a "preponderance of evidence" was against him.*

such awesome power over our elected representatives? Debates about the proper role for the Court will continue as long as it is involved in controversial decisions. We take up this question later in the chapter when we address the concepts of judicial activism and judicial restraint.

The American Legal and Judicial System

Two sets of considerations are necessary to understand the overall nature of our judicial system: the fundamentals of the legal system that apply to all courts in the United States and the structure of the court system within our system of federalism.

COURT FUNDAMENTALS

The general characteristics of the court system begin with the people who are in the courtroom. The **plaintiff** brings the case and the **defendant** is the person or party who is being sued or charged with a crime. If the case is appealed, the petitioner is the person bringing the appeal and the respondent is on the other side of the case. In a civil case, the plaintiff is suing to determine who is right or wrong and to gain something of value, such as monetary damages, the right to vote, or admission to a university. For example, imagine that your neighbor accidentally backs his car into the fence that divides your property, destroying a large section of it. The neighbor does not have adequate insurance to cover the damages and refuses to pay for the repairs out of his own pocket. You do not want to pay the $1,000 deductible on your insurance policy, so you (the plaintiff) sue your neighbor (the defendant) to see who is right and whether your neighbor has to pay for the repairs. In a criminal case, the plaintiff is the government, and the prosecutor attempts to prove the guilt of the defendant (the person accused of the crime). Many, but not all, civil and criminal cases are heard before a jury that decides the outcome in the case, which is called the **verdict**. Often cases get settled before they go to a trial (or even in the middle of the trial) in a process known as **plea bargaining**. In a civil case, this would mean that the plaintiff and defendant agree on a monetary settlement and admission of guilt (or not; in some cases the defendant may agree to pay a fine or damages but not to admit guilt). In a criminal case, the defendant may agree to plead guilty in exchange for a shorter sentence or being charged with a lesser crime. Plea bargaining is an excellent example of how legal conflict between two parties can be resolved through a compromise that is satisfactory to both sides.

There are some important differences between civil and criminal cases, such as the **standard of proof** that is used to determine the outcome of the case. In civil cases the jury has to determine whether the "preponderance of evidence"—that is, a majority of the evidence—proves that the plaintiff wins. In a criminal case, a much stiffer burden must be met—"beyond all reasonable doubt." Thus, when O. J. Simpson, the former star NFL running back, was accused of murdering his wife and her friend, he was not found guilty in criminal court but lost a civil case and had to pay significant monetary damages. Another difference is where the **burden of proof** lies. In criminal cases there is a presumption of "innocent until proven guilty." That is, the state must prove the guilt of the defendant. However, in civil cases the burden of proof may be on the plaintiff or the defendant depending on the underlying law that governs the case. To make matters even more complicated, in civil cases the plaintiff may have to prove certain points and the defendant other points. For example, in certain race-based voting rights cases, the plaintiff would have to prove that race was the predominant motivation for creating a black-majority congressional district. If that point is demonstrated, then the burden of proof shifts to the defendant to show that there was some "compelling state interest" to justify the use of race as a predominant factor.

One special type of civil suit is the **class action lawsuit**, a case brought by a group of individuals on behalf of themselves and others in the general public who are in similar circumstances. The target of these suits may be a corporation that produced hazardous or defective products, or that engaged in illegal behavior that harmed a particular group. For example, more than 1 million current and former female Walmart employees have sued the retailing giant for sex discrimination, claiming that the store had a pattern of paying women less than men for the same work and promoting fewer women than men. Any woman who worked at Walmart since December 26, 1998, can be part of the suit if she joins the "class." Walmart will be liable for billions of dollars in damages if it loses the case. Suits are often filed on behalf of shareholders of companies that have lost value because of fraud committed by corporate leaders. Enron, Tyco, WorldCom, Health South, and many other corporations have cost their shareholders billions of dollars through their illegal actions. Class action suits attempt to help shareholders recover some of those losses. Although there are many frivolous class action suits (such as the suit against several makers of guacamole dip because the dips had "little, if any, avocado"), these cases are a very important mechanism for providing accountability and justice in our economic system. Federal regulators do not have the ability to ensure the complete safety of food, drugs, and consumer products. Therefore, consumers rely on the legal system and class action lawsuits to provide businesses with the incentive to produce safe products.

There are several other characteristics of the judicial system that apply to all cases. First, ours is an **adversarial system** in which lawyers on both sides have an opportunity to present their case, challenge the testimony of the opposing side, and try to convince the court that their version of the events is true. The process of "discovery," in which both sides share the information that will be presented in court, ensures a fair process and few last-minute surprises (contrary to the "Perry Mason moments" that Hollywood loves so much, in which the star of the show comes up with some new evidence or a star witness just minutes before the closing arguments). Second, forty-nine of the fifty states and the federal courts operate under a system of **common law**, which means that legal decisions build from precedent established in previous cases and apply commonly throughout the jurisdiction of the court. The alternative, which is practiced only in Louisiana, is the civil law tradition that is based on a detailed codification of the law that is applied to each specific case.

The notion of **precedent** (or *stare decisis*—"let the decision stand") deserves special attention. Precedent is a previously decided case or set of decisions that serves as a guide for future cases on the same topic. Lower courts are bound by Supreme Court decisions when there is a clear precedent that is relevant for a given case. In many cases, following precedent is not clear-cut because several precedents may seem relevant. The lower courts have a fair amount of discretion in sorting out which precedents are the most important. The Supreme Court tries to follow its own precedents, but in the past fifty years justices have been much more willing to deviate from earlier decisions when they think that the precedent is flawed. As shown in Table 13.1, more than twice as many decisions have been overruled by the Court since 1953 than in the previous 164 years. Part of this can be explained by

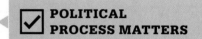

POLITICAL PROCESS MATTERS

class action lawsuit A case brought by a group of individuals on behalf of themselves and others in the general public who are in similar circumstances.

adversarial system A two-sided court structure in which lawyers on both sides of a case attempt to prove their argument over their opponent's version of the case.

common law Law based on the precedent of previous court rulings rather than on legislation. It is used in all federal courts and forty-nine of the fifty state courts.

precedent A legal norm established in court cases that is then applied to future cases dealing with the same legal questions.

The Supreme Court has overruled precedent in a far higher proportion of cases in the past 50 years than it did during the first 160 years of U.S. history. More acts of Congress have also been struck down in recent years—but even in some earlier periods, the Court has played an activist role. What do these data say about the role of the Supreme Court within our constitutional system?

Court (Chief Justice)	Years	Cases Overruling Precedent	Precedents Overruled	Cases Overruling Acts of Congress	Acts Overruled per Year
Jay Court	1789–1795	0	0	0	0
Rutledge Court	1795	0	0	0	0
Ellsworth Court	1796–1800	0	0	0	0
Marshall Court	1801–1836	1	1	1	0.03
Taney Court	1836–1864	2	3	1	0.03
Chase Court	1864–1874	1	1	8	0.8
Waite Court	1874–1888	9	11	7	0.5
Fuller Court	1888–1910	3	4	13	0.52
White Court	1910–1921	4	4	10	1.1
Taft Court	1921–1930	5	6	13	1.44
Hughes Court	1930–1941	15	22	15	1.36
Stone Court	1941–1946	8	11	1	0.20
Vinson Court	1946–1953	6	11	2	0.28
Warren Court	1953–1969	37	53	23	1.44
Burger Court	1969–1986	46	62	31	1.82
Rehnquist Court	1986–2005	38	44	35	1.84
Roberts Court	2005–present	8	n.a.	6	1.2

Note: This table only includes cases in which the reversal of precedent is clearly stated in the Court decision. A single case can overrule more than one precedent.

SOURCE: For 1789–2003, David G. Savage, *Guide to the Supreme Court,* 4th ed. (Washington, DC: CQ Press, 2004), pp. 320, 1192–1204. For 2004–2009, The Supreme Court Database, Washington University, http://scdb.wustl.edu.

the relatively small number of precedents that *could* have been overturned in the first few decades of our history. Indeed, no precedents were overturned in the first three Courts and only a total of four in the first eighty-five years of the nation's history. But even accounting for this natural accumulation of more precedents to potentially overturn, recent courts have been much more willing to deviate from precedent than previous courts. As this record indicates, precedent is not a rule the Court must follow but a norm that constrains its behavior.

Two more points must be considered before a case is filed. First, the person bringing the case must have **standing** to sue in a civil case, which means that there is a legitimate basis for bringing the case. This usually means that the individual must have suffered some direct and personal harm from the action that is being addressed in the court case. Standing is easy to establish for private parties—if your neighbor destroys your fence, you have been harmed. However, it gets more interesting when the government is a party. For example, when an environmental group challenged the Interior Department's interpretation of the Endangered Species Act, the Court ruled that it did not have standing because it did not demonstrate that the government's policy would cause "imminent" injury to the group.[11] Similarly the

standing Legitimate justification for bringing a civil case to court.

Court has ruled that thirty-one members of Congress did not have standing to challenge American bombing in Kosovo and taxpayers do not have standing to sue the government if they disagree with a specific policy.[12] Depending on your politics, you may not want your hard-earned cash going to buy school lunches for poor children or to fund the war in Afghanistan. However, your status as a taxpayer does not give you enough of a personal stake in these policies to challenge them in court. You would not have standing.

The final general characteristic of the legal system is the **jurisdiction** of the court—when bringing a case before the court, you have to make sure you have chosen a court that actually has the power to hear your case. A simple example: if you want to contest a speeding ticket, you would not file your case in the state supreme court or the federal district court, but in your local traffic court. What if you believed you were the victim of discrimination in the workplace? Would you sue in state or federal court? You probably could do either, but the decision would be based on which set of laws would provide you more protection from discrimination. This obviously varies by state, so the proper jurisdiction for a given case is often a judgment call based on specific legal questions (this practice of seeking the best court for your case is called "venue shopping").

jurisdiction The sphere of a court's legal authority to hear and decide cases.

appeals courts The intermediate level of federal courts that hear appeals from district courts. More generally, an appeals court is any court with appellate jurisdiction.

STRUCTURE OF THE COURT AND FEDERALISM

The structure of the court system is just like the rest of the political system: it is divided within and across levels of government. Across the levels of government, the court system operates on two parallel tracks within the state and local courts and the national courts. Within each level of government, both tracks are comprised of courts of original jurisdiction, appeals courts, and courts of special jurisdiction (see Figure 13.1). There is much variation in the structure of state courts in terms of their names and the number of levels of courts. However, they all follow the same general pattern of trial courts with limited and general original jurisdiction and appeals courts (either one or two levels, depending on the state).

District Courts As we briefly outlined earlier, the lower federal courts were created by the Judiciary Act of 1789. The district courts are the workhorses of the federal system. District courts handle more than a quarter of a million filings a year, and their workload has steadily increased over the past half-century. There are eighty-nine districts in the fifty states, with at least one district court for each state. There are also district courts in Puerto Rico, the Virgin Islands, the District of Columbia, Guam, and the Northern Mariana Islands to bring the total to ninety-four districts with 678 judges.[13] There are two limited jurisdiction district courts: the Court of International Trade, which addresses cases involving international trade and customs issues, and the U.S. Court of Federal Claims, which handles most claims for money damages against the United States, disputes over federal contracts, unlawful "takings" of private property by the federal government (a rapidly growing area of federal law), and other claims against the United States.

Appeals Courts The **appeals courts** (or "circuit courts," as they were called until 1948) are the intermediate courts of appeals, but in practice they are the final court for most federal cases that are appealed from the lower courts. The losing side in a federal case can appeal to the Supreme Court, but given that the highest court in the land hears so few cases, the appeals courts usually get the final word. Appeals courts did not always have this much power; in fact, through much of

POLITICS IS EVERYWHERE

FIGURE 13.1 THE STRUCTURE OF THE COURT SYSTEM

The system of federalism means that we have a two-track court system at the national level and at the state and local levels. What advantages and disadvantages of this two-track system can you think of?

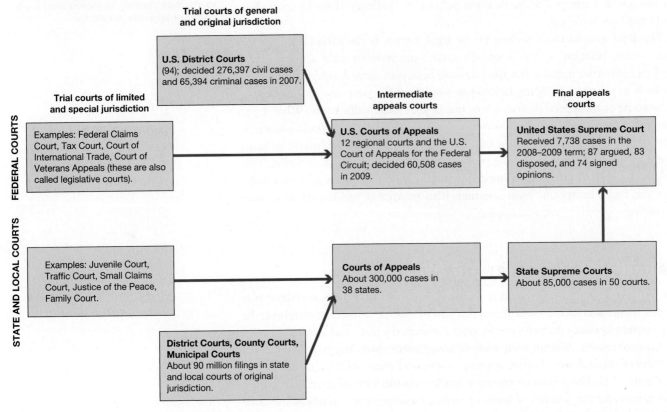

SOURCE: Caseload data from U.S. Courts, Federal Court Management Statistics, available at www.uscourts.gov/fcmstat/index.html; and U.S. Supreme Court, Chief Justice's Year-End Report on the Federal Judiciary, 2009, available at www.supremecourtus.gov/publicinfo/year-end/2009year-endreport.pdf.

the nineteenth century they were "judicial stepchildren."[14] They had very limited appellate jurisdiction and did not hear many significant cases. The only real effort to create an independent set of federal appellate courts in the first 100 years of our nation's history was the aborted effort by the outgoing Adams administration in 1800. As part of the Federalists' plan to stack the federal courts (recall the maneuver with the justice of peace positions that led to *Marbury v. Madison*), the Federalists created eighteen appeals court judgeships that were filled at the last minute by President Adams and a sympathetic Senate. Rather than allow the Federalists to have that much power over the federal courts, the incoming Jefferson administration and the Democratic-Republican Congress simply abolished these courts the next year (possibly in violation of the constitutional mandate of life tenure for federal judges, but that was a fight that Chief Justice John Marshall did not want to take on).

In 1869 the circuit courts finally were given some of their own judges rather than being staffed entirely by district court judges and Supreme Court justices, which meant the Supreme Court justices had to "ride circuit" only once every two years.[15] The Judiciary Act of 1891 created nine regional circuit courts and expanded their appellate jurisdiction to include most cases from the district courts. This process of expanding the power of the appeals courts was largely completed in the 1925

FIGURE 13.2 MAP OF THE FEDERAL APPEALS COURTS

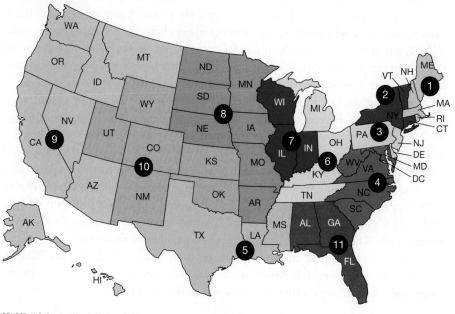

SOURCE: U.S. Courts, Circuit Map, available at www.uscourts.gov/courtlinks.

Judiciary Act.[16] Today the only appeals of district court cases that go directly to the Supreme Court and bypass the appeals court are cases that concern legislative reapportionment and redistricting, voting rights, and some issues related to the 1964 Civil Rights Act.[17] The number of appeals courts slowly expanded as the workload grew, to the current twelve regional courts (the eleven numbered districts shown in Figure 13.2, plus the appeals court for the District of Columbia) and the Court of Appeals for the Federal Circuit, which handles specialized cases from all over the country. The smallest of the regional appeals courts is the First Circuit, which has nine judges, and the largest is the Ninth Circuit with twenty-eight judges.[18] In 2009, there were 179 appeals court judges and 91 "senior judges" (these numbers include the twelve judges and five senior judges of the appeals court for the federal circuit).[19] Senior judges are retired judges who hear certain cases to help out with the overall workload; they typically handle about 15 percent of the workload for the federal court system.

The Supreme Court The Supreme Court sits at the top of the federal court system. The rest of this chapter outlines many of the important aspects of the Court, including how cases get to the Court, nominations, decision making, and relations to the other branches. The immediate discussion concerns the Court's place within the judicial system and its relationship to the other courts. The Supreme Court is the "court of last resort" for cases coming from both the state and federal courts. One of the important functions of the Court is to resolve conflicts between lower courts, or between a state law and federal law, or between the states, to ensure that the application and interpretation of the Constitution is consistent across the United States. For example, before the Court took up the issue of affirmative action in higher education, there were several conflicting lower court decisions, which meant that affirmative action was legal in certain parts of the country and unconstitutional in other parts. A district court or appeals court ruling is applicable only for the specific region of that court, whereas Supreme Court rulings apply to the entire country.

Although the Supreme Court is the most important interpreter of the Constitution, the president and Congress also interpret the Constitution on a regular basis. This means that the Supreme Court does not always have the final say. For example, if the Court strikes down a federal law for being overly vague, Congress can rewrite the law to clarify the offending passage. When this happens, Congress may have the final word. Even on matters of constitutional interpretation rather than statutory interpretation, Congress can fight back by passing a constitutional amendment. However, this is a difficult and time-consuming process; as we discussed in Chapter 2, hundreds of amendments are proposed every year, but very few even get a hearing or come to a vote in Congress, and even fewer are passed by Congress and submitted to the states for ratification. Nevertheless, that option is available as a way of overturning an unpopular Court decision. Perhaps the best example of this is the very first major case ever decided by the Supreme Court—*Chisholm v. Georgia* (1793). This case upheld the right of a citizen of one state to sue another state in federal court. The states were shocked by this challenge to their sovereignty, and a constitutional amendment to overturn the decision quickly made its way through Congress. By 1798 the 11th Amendment had been ratified and citizens could no longer sue a state in which they did not live in federal court.

HOW JUDGES ARE SELECTED

There are many different mechanisms for placing judges in courts. At the national level, which we discuss in more detail below, the president makes the appointments with the advice and consent of the Senate, and at the state level, many different methods are in use.

State-Level Judges At the state level there are five different means for selecting judges for trial courts: appointment by the governor (two states), appointment by the state legislature (two states), partisan elections (nine states), nonpartisan elections (seventeen states), and the system called the Missouri Plan in which the governor makes appointments from a list that has been compiled by a nonpartisan screening committee (seventeen states; four more states use the Missouri Plan for some courts and another means for other courts).[20] With this last method, the appointed judge usually has to run in a retention election within several years of the appointment, making this system a hybrid of the political nomination and popular election routes to the court.

There is some controversy over the wisdom of electing judges. Elections certainly mean that courts will be more responsive to public opinion, but they may undermine the courts' role as the protector of unpopular minority rights. Also, even in states where judicial elections are officially nonpartisan, it is quite clear who the liberal and conservative candidates are, so judicial elections can be very partisan. Interest groups often are involved in the process by making endorsements or running their own advertisements for or against the judicial candidates. Electing judges also raises the potential for conflicts of interest if campaign contributors have cases before the court. For example, West Virginia state supreme court justice Brent Benjamin refused to recuse himself from a case involving a coal company, A. T. Massey, that was appealing a $50 million verdict. Benjamin had benefited from $3 million in campaign spending by the CEO of the coal company, which was more than his opponent's total spending on his campaign. The losing party in the case,

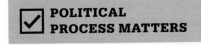

POLITICAL PROCESS MATTERS

Hugh Caperton, appealed to the U.S. Supreme Court, which ruled that his due process rights under the 14th Amendment had been violated. Given the disproportionate and significant spending by Massey and the timing of the spending (while the case was pending), the majority ruled, "On these extreme facts the probability of actual bias rises to an unconstitutional level."[21] The case received extensive national attention and was the basis for the 2008 best-selling novel by John Grisham, *The Appeal.*

Federal Judges The Constitution does not specify requirements for serving on the federal courts, unlike the detailed stipulations for Congress and the president. Federal judges don't even have to have a law degree! (This is probably due to the limited number of law schools at the time of the Founding; it was far more common for someone who wanted to be a lawyer to serve as an apprentice to learn the trade rather than to go to a law school.) The president appoints federal judges with the "advice and consent" of the Senate (the Senate must approve the appointees with a majority vote).

The nomination battles for federal judges can be intense because the stakes are high. As the discussion of judicial review made clear, the Supreme Court plays a central role in the policy process, and because a justice has life tenure, a justice's impact can outlive the president and Senate who put him or her on the Court. Although the average tenure for presidents is only four years and the average tenure for a House member or senator is around ten years, the justices serve for decades, much longer than the people who appoint them.

The Role of the President Given the Constitution's silence on the qualification of federal judges, presidents have broad discretion over whom to nominate. Presidents have always tried to influence the direction of the Court by picking people who share their views on important issues. Because the Senate often has different ideas about the proper direction for the Court, nomination disputes end up being a combination of debates over the merit and qualifications of a nominee and of bare-fisted partisan battles about the ideological composition of the Court.

Although presidents would *like* to influence the direction of the Court, it is not always possible to predict how judges will behave once they are on the Court. Earl Warren is probably the best example. He was appointed by Republican president Dwight Eisenhower and had been the Republican governor of California, yet he turned out to be one of the most liberal chief justices in the last century. Eisenhower called Warren's nomination the biggest mistake he ever made.[22] Former justices Brennan, Souter, and Stevens were nominated by Republican presidents but regularly voted with the liberal bloc.

The president can make a good guess about how a justice is likely to vote based on the nominee's party affiliation and the nature of his or her legal writings and decisions (if he or she has prior judicial experience). Not surprisingly, 98 of 108 justices who have served on the Court have shared the president's party (just over 90 percent). Overall, more than 90 percent of the lower court judges appointed by presidents in the twentieth century have also belonged to the same party as the president. The lowest percentage of same-party appointments for any president in the twentieth century was 81 percent by Gerald Ford, who faced a strongly Democratic Senate when he became president after Richard Nixon resigned because of the Watergate scandal. Ford hoped that giving nearly a fifth of his judicial appointments to Democrats would help bring the country together.[23]

At the other extreme, the most partisan move to influence the Court was President Franklin Delano Roosevelt's infamous plan to pack the Court. FDR was

▲ West Virginia Supreme Court Chief Justice Brent Benjamin listens to arguments in a rehearing of a $76 million judgment against Massey Energy Company. The U.S. Supreme Court ruled that Benjamin should have recused himself because a wealthy coal executive who had an interest in the case financially supported Benjamin's 2004 election.

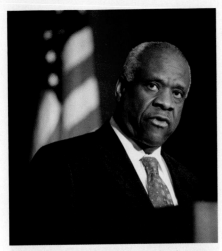

▲ *Since the late 1960s the Senate has become more assertive in providing "advice and consent" on Supreme Court nominations. The confirmation hearings for Justice Clarence Thomas in 1991 were among the most contentious in recent decades. Thomas was confirmed by the second narrowest margin in U.S. history for a Supreme Court justice (52 to 48).*

frustrated because the Court had struck down several pieces of important New Deal legislation, so to get a more sympathetic Court, he proposed nominating a new justice for every justice who was over seventy years old. Six justices were older than seventy, so this would have increased the size of the Court to fifteen. This effort to disguise the partisan power play as a humanitarian gesture (to help the old-timers with their workload) didn't fool anyone. The plan to pack the Court ran into opposition, but in what has been dubbed the "switch in time that saved nine," the Court started ruling in favor of the New Deal legislation, so the plan was dropped. In addition to the ideological considerations about whom to nominate, the president also considers the reputation of the potential nominee as a legal scholar and his personal relationship to the candidate, as well as the candidate's ethical standards, gender, and race (see Table 13.2 for data on the latter two points).

The other half of the equation to determine the composition of the federal courts is the Senate. The Senate has shifted from a very active role in providing its "advice and consent" on court appointments to a passive role and then back to an active role. One constant in the role of the Senate is that nominees are rarely rejected because of their qualifications, but rather for political reasons. Of twenty-eight nominees rejected by the Senate in the history of the United States (twelve by a roll call vote in the Senate and sixteen that were withdrawn or not acted upon), only two were turned down because they were seen as unqualified: George Williams in 1873 and G. Harold Carswell in 1970. Serious questions were also raised about a third, current justice Clarence Thomas, who had served for only eighteen months as a federal judge before being nominated to the Court. Thomas also was accused in a highly charged Senate Judiciary Committee hearing of sexual harassment by a former colleague. Thomas won confirmation by a 52-to-48 vote, the second narrowest successful margin in history. The other twenty-six nominees were rejected for political reasons. Most commonly, when a "lame duck" president makes a nomination and the Senate is controlled by the opposing party, the Senate often kills the nomination, hoping that its party will win the presidency and nominate a justice more to its liking. John Tyler holds the record for having *five* nominations killed in the last fifteen months of his presidency (from January 1844 through March 1845) by a Senate controlled by the opposing party.

Throughout the nineteenth century the Senate was very willing to turn down Court nominations for political reasons. In fact, twenty-one nominees were not confirmed by the Senate from 1793 through 1894 (about a third of the total number of nominees). Then in the first half of the twentieth century the Senate allowed presidents to appoint whom they wanted. Between 1894 and 1968 only one nominee, Judge John Parker, nominated by Herbert Hoover in 1930, was defeated. The Senate did not even require nominees to testify throughout this period.

A rethinking of this passive role emerged in the late 1960s. President Nixon vowed to move the Court back from the "liberal excesses" of the Warren Court, but the Senate stiffened its spine and rejected two nominees in a row in 1969 (Clement Haynsworth) and 1970 (Harold Carswell). For Haynsworth there were some ethical problems having to do with his participation in cases in which he had a financial interest. As noted above, Carswell had a mediocre judicial record and civil rights groups raised questions about his commitment to enforcing antidiscrimination laws. Nixon must have thought that the Senate wouldn't reject his choice twice in a row! The most recent Senate rejection was of Judge Robert Bork, a brilliant, very conservative, and controversial figure. Liberal interest groups mobilized against him, and the Senate rejected him by the widest margin of any nominee since 1846 (the vote was 42 to 58), giving the English language a new verb: to get "borked" means to have your character and record challenged in a very public way.

TABLE 13.2 **THE DEMOGRAPHICS OF THE FEDERAL BENCH**

All presidents try to appoint qualified candidates to the federal courts; however, there is variation in the types of people they nominate. Identify some characteristics common to most judges and some that vary across presidents. Which traits vary by the president's party?

	Obama		W. Bush		Clinton		Bush		Reagan	
Experience										
Judicial	58%	(22)	52%	(136)	52%	(159)	47%	(69)	46%	(134)
Prosecutorial	32	(12)	47	(123)	41	(126)	39	(58)	44	(128)
Neither	32	(12)	25	(65)	29	(88)	32	(47)	29	(83)
Average age at nomination	50.4		49.1		49.5		48.2		48.6	
Law school education										
Public	50%	(19)	49%	(128)	40%	(121)	53%	(78)	45%	(130)
Private	29	(11)	39	(102)	41	(124)	33	(49)	43	(126)
Ivy League	21	(8)	12	(31)	20	(60)	14	(21)	12	(34)
Gender										
Male	47%	(18)	79%	(207)	72%	(218)	80%	(119)	92%	(226)
Female	53	(20)	21	(54)	29	(87)	20	(29)	8	(24)
Ethnicity/race										
White	58%	(22)	82%	(213)	75%	(229)	89%	(132)	92%	(268)
African American	24	(9)	7	(18)	17	(53)	7	(10)	2	(6)
Hispanic	8	(3)	10	(26)	6	(18)	4	(6)	5	(14)
Asian	11	(4)	1	4	1.3	(4)	–	–	0.7	(2)
Native American	–		–	–	0.3	(1)	–	–	–	–
Percentage white male	29	(11)	67	(176)	52	(160)	73	(108)	85	(246)
Political identification										
Democrat	76%	(29)	8%	(21)	88%	(267)	6%	(9)	5%	(14)
Republican	–		83	(217)	6	(19)	89	(131)	92	(266)
Other	–		–	–	0.3	(1)	–	–	–	–
None	24%	(9)	9	(23)	6	(18)	5	(8)	3	(10)
Net worth										
Under $200,000	3%	(1)	5%	(13)	13%	(41)	10%	(15)	18%	(52)
$200–499,999	11	(4)	18	(47)	22	(66)	31	(46)	38	(109)
$500–999,999	21	(8)	22	(57)	27	(82)	26	(39)	22	(63)
$1+ million	67	(25)	55	(144)	38	(116)	32	(48)	23	(66)
Total number of appointees	38		261		305		148		290	

SOURCE: Sheldon Goldman, Sara Schiavoni, and Elliot Stotnick, "W. Bush's Judicial Legacy: Mission Accomplished," *Judicature* 92:6 (2009): 279. Data on Obama appointees provided to the authors by Sheldon Goldman.

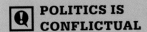

senatorial courtesy A norm in the nomination of district court judges in which the president consults with his party's senators from the relevant state in choosing the nominee.

However, not all recent Supreme Court nominations have been controversial. President Bill Clinton's two Supreme Court picks were judicial moderates who were overwhelmingly confirmed—Ruth Bader Ginsburg by a 96-to-3 vote and Stephen Breyer by a 87-to-9 margin. George W. Bush's nominees, John Roberts and Samuel Alito, were confirmed by comfortable margins; the former by a 78-to-22 vote, with half of the Democrats supporting him, and the latter by a 58-to-42 margin. President Obama appointed the first Hispanic to serve on the Supreme Court, Sonia Sotomayor, who was confirmed by a 68-to-31 vote. Elena Kagan's confirmation by a 63-to-37 vote in 2010 meant that three women were serving on the Court for the first time.

The contentious battles between the president and the Senate over nominees to the federal bench and the Supreme Court have recently expanded to include nominees to the district and appeals courts as well. For much of the nation's history the president did not play a very active role in the nomination process for district courts, instead deferring to the home-state senator of the president's party to suggest candidates—a norm called **senatorial courtesy**. If there was no senator of the president's party from the relevant state, the president would consult House members and other high-ranking party members from the state. The president typically has shown more interest in appeals court nominations. The Justice Department plays a key role in screening candidates, but the local senators of the president's party remain active as well.

Recently, the process has become much more contentious. As Figure 13.3a shows, the confirmation rate for federal judges has gone from between about 80 and 100 percent to less than 50 percent in recent years. When Republicans took control of the Senate in 1995, they stopped more than sixty of President Clinton's nominees to the lower federal courts through a process of holds (when a single senator can stop a nomination) and committee action known as "pocket filibusters." The average length of delay from nomination to confirmation has increased from less than 50 days in the mid-1960s through the mid-1980s to 150 days or more in recent years (see Figure 13.3b). The situation has become even more tense in the last few years (see You Decide).

Q POLITICS IS CONFLICTUAL

| **FIGURE 13.3A** CONFIRMATION RATE FOR JUDICIAL NOMINEES, 1947–2006 | **FIGURE 13.3B** AVERAGE CONFIRMATION DELAY FOR JUDICIAL NOMINEES, 1947–2006 |

Presidential nominations to the federal courts have had a tougher time in recent years, in terms of both the rejection rate and the time it takes to get nominees confirmed by the Senate. What accounts for these changes?

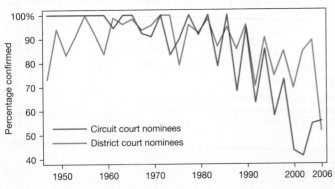

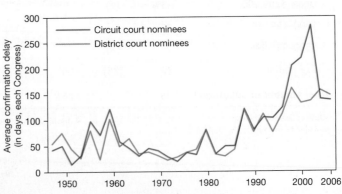

SOURCE: Sarah A. Binder and Forest Maltzman, *Advice and Dissent: The Struggle to Shape the Federal Judiciary* (Washington, DC: Brookings Institution Press, 2009).

Advice and Consent: Principled Opposition or Obstructionism?

The use of the filibuster to stop presidential nominations to the federal courts has been the source of intense partisan battles in the past fifteen years (recall that forty-one senators can stop action on any bill or nomination through a filibuster). However, the positions in those battles are determined by which party controls the Senate and the presidency. Democrats who railed against Republican obstruction when Clinton was president used the same tactics when they were in the minority party and Bush was president. Now the tables are turned again and some of the strongest Republican critics of Democratic filibusters, such as Jeff Sessions, led the first filibuster against an Obama appeals court nominee (which failed).

The partisan struggles have led to serious discussion about limiting the use of the filibuster for court nominations. In Bush's first term, Senate Democrats stopped lower court nominees through the filibuster. After winning reelection in 2004, President Bush resubmitted seven nominees who had been rejected in the previous Senate (and thirteen more who were nominated in the previous term but did not come up for a vote). After Democrats indicated that they were not going to abandon the filibusters, the Republican leadership in the Senate considered implementing the "nuclear option," which would have prevented filibusters on judicial nominations (this plan gets its name because Democrats threatened to essentially shut down the Senate if they lost the filibuster). This crisis was defused when the "Gang of 14"—seven moderate Republicans and seven moderate Democrats—agreed to a compromise that preserved the Democrats' right to filibuster but only in the most

When they are the minority party in the Senate, both Democrats and Republicans have been willing to use the filibuster to block judicial nominees that they oppose.

extreme cases. The compromise was not put to a critical test (both of Bush's Supreme Court nominees were confirmed without filibusters), and it is not clear if Democrats will tolerate many filibusters of Obama's nominees.

Let's do a thought experiment to try to strip partisanship from this issue and figure out if you support the principle of filibustering judicial nominations. Put yourself in the place of a Democratic senator on the Judiciary Committee during the Bush years. President Bush has nominated a candidate for an appeals court position who you believe is wholly unqualified. Should you support a filibuster to stop the nomination even if it means that the Republican leadership might take away the filibuster? Now put yourself in the place of a Republican senator. You strongly favor President Bush's right to nominate whom he wants to the federal courts, and you support his policy positions, especially on abortion and the regula-

tion of the free market. However, the Democrats are opposed and threatening to filibuster. You have to decide whether to support the "nuclear option" to take away the Democrats' right to filibuster the nomination. There are at least fifty-six votes in favor of the nominee but not the sixty needed to cut off the filibuster. On the one hand, you don't think it is fair that Democrats are obstructing the vote. On the other hand, you were in the Senate back when the Republicans were in the minority, and you remember how important the filibuster was to protect the views of the minority party. You are worried that supporting the "nuclear option" would seriously damage the institution that you value and respect as the world's greatest deliberative body. What do you do? Now to complete the thought experiment, flip the positions of the senators for an Obama nominee to the appeals court. Is your position still the same? ■

Although there is no definitive answer as to how active the Senate should be in giving its "advice and consent"—especially how much power a minority of forty-one senators should have—it is clear that the Founders intended the Senate to play an active role. The first draft of the Constitution gave the Senate the sole power to appoint Supreme Court justices. However, the final version of the Constitution made the appointment power a shared power with the goal of promoting responsibility through the president's role and "security" through the Senate's role. It was not expected that the Senate would compete with the president over whom to nominate, but it *was* assumed that the Senate would exercise independent judgment as to the suitability of the president's nominees. Furthermore, the Founders did not expect the process to be free of politics or that the Senate would be an essentially passive and subordinate player in a nominally joint enterprise. Even George Washington had two of his nominations turned down by the Senate for political reasons! Therefore, politics will continue to play an important role in deciding who serves on the federal bench.

Access to the Supreme Court

It is extremely difficult to have a case heard by the Supreme Court. Currently the Court hears about 1 percent of the cases submitted (85 of about 8,000 cases). This section explains how the Court decides which cases to hear. When a case is submitted to the Court, the clerk of the Court assigns it a number and places it on the **docket**, which is simply the schedule of cases.

THE SUPREME COURT WORKLOAD

Statistics on the Supreme Court's workload initially suggest that the size of the docket has increased dramatically, from fewer than 5,000 cases a year in the 1970s to nearly 9,000 cases a year in some recent sessions (see Figure 13.4). However, a majority of cases are frivolous and are dismissed after limited review. One law clerk described these frivolous petitions as "sometimes handwritten, occasionally illegible, and often inscrutable."[24] The Court has become increasingly impatient with these frivolous petitions and has moved to prevent "frequent filers" from harassing the Court. One often-cited case involved Michael Sindram, who asked the Court to order the Maryland courts to remove a $35 traffic ticket from his record. Our favorite example concerned a wealthy drug dealer, Frederick W. Bauer, who was convicted on ten counts of dealing drugs (seven counts involved a total of 4,100 pounds of marijuana, two counts for nearly 250 pounds of cocaine, and one count for six gallons of hashish oil and a package of black gum hashish) and repeatedly petitioned the Court. In his initial trial he applied for a court-appointed attorney (which is supplied for people who cannot afford their own legal counsel) but was turned down because a court hearing revealed that he had "unencumbered assets [that] totaled almost $500,000." The court found the petitioner's testimony that he was poor "ambiguous, evasive and in many respects completely incredible."[25] Bauer petitioned the Court twelve times on various issues and finally the justices had had enough. They ruled that "Bauer has repeatedly abused this Court's certiorari and extraordinary writ processes" and directed "the Clerk not to accept any further petitions for certiorari or petitions for extraordinary writs from Bauer in noncriminal matters" unless he paid his docketing fees. They concluded that the order will

The Supreme Court's workload appears to be headed in two directions: the Court is receiving more cases but hearing fewer of them. What are the implications of having the Supreme Court hear fewer cases? Should something be done to try to get the Court to hear more cases?

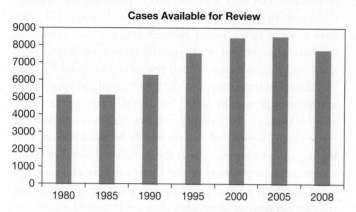

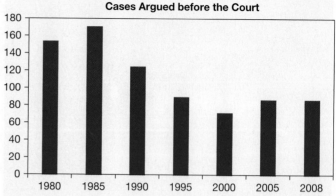

SOURCE: Data compiled from "Chief Justice's Year-End Reports on the Federal Judiciary," available at http://www.supremecourtus.gov/publicinfo/year-end/2009year-endreport.html.

"allow this Court to devote its limited resources to the claims of petitioners who have not abused our processes."[26]

Though the increase in workload is not as significant as it appears due to the high number of frivolous cases, another change in how cases are handled by the Court is more important: the number of opinions issued by the Court has fallen by more than half in the past twenty years. The Court heard about 150 cases a year through the 1980s, but this number has fallen to only 75 to 85 in recent years (see Figure 13.4).[27] The change is even more dramatic when one considers that the Court has reduced the number of "summary decisions" it issues (cases that do not receive a full hearing, but the Court rules on the merits of the case) from 150 a year in the 1970s to a handful today. The number of summary judgments declined when Congress gave the Court more control over its docket and dramatically reduced the number of cases that it was *required* to hear on appeal. However, there is no good explanation for why the Court issues half as many opinions as it used to, other than that the chief justices have decided that the Court shouldn't issue so many opinions.[28]

RULES OF ACCESS

With the smaller number of cases being heard, it is even more important to understand how the Court decides which cases to hear. There are four paths that a case may take to get to the Supreme Court. First, Article III of the Constitution specifies that the Court has **original jurisdiction** in cases involving foreign ambassadors, foreign countries, or cases in which a state is a party. As a practical matter, the Court shares jurisdiction with the lower courts on these issues. In recent years, the Court has invoked original jurisdiction only in cases involving disputes between two or more states over territorial or natural resource issues. For example, New Jersey and New York had a disagreement about which state should control about twenty-five acres of filled land that the federal government had added around Ellis Island. Another case involved a dispute between Kansas and Colorado over who should have access to water from the Arkansas River (recent disputes often concern water rights).[29] If original jurisdiction is granted and there are factual issues to be resolved, the Court will appoint a "special master" (usually a retired federal judge) to hold a hearing, gather evidence, and make a recommendation to the Court. This process is

original jurisdiction The authority of a court to handle a case first, as in the Supreme Court's authority to initially hear disputes between two states. However, original jurisdiction for the Supreme Court is not exclusive; it may assign such a case to a lower court.

▲ On rare occasions the Supreme Court serves as a court of original jurisdiction. One of those unusual times is when there is a dispute between two states, such as when the Court had to settle a disagreement between New York and New Jersey over Ellis Island.

necessary because the Supreme Court is not set up to be a trial court. The "special master" arrangement allows the Court to function in its normal capacity as an appeals court by treating the master's recommendation as a lower court decision, even if technically the Court is a trial court in these original jurisdiction cases. In the history of our nation, only about 175 cases have made it to the Court through this path, an average of less than one per year, and typically these cases do not have any broader significance beyond the parties involved.[30]

The other three routes to the Court are all on appeal: as a matter of right (usually called "on appeal"), through certification, or through the writ of certiorari. **Cases on appeal** are those that Congress has determined to be so important that the Supreme Court must hear them. Before 1988 these cases comprised a larger share of the Court's docket and included cases in which a lower court declared a state or federal law unconstitutional or in which a state court upheld a state law that had been challenged as unconstitutional under the U.S. Constitution. As noted above, since 1988, Congress has given the Court much more discretion on these cases; the only ones that the Court is still compelled to take on appeal are some voting rights and redistricting cases. A **writ of certification** is when an appeals court asks the Court to clarify a new point of federal law in a specific case. The Court can agree to hear the case, but given that appeals court and state supreme court judges are the only people who can make these requests, this path to the Court is very rare (in fact, since 1982 the Court has not taken up a certified question from one of the appeals courts and has certified only five cases from state supreme courts).[31]

The third path is the most common: in fact, at least 95 percent of the cases in most sessions arrive through a **writ of certiorari** (from the Latin "to be informed"). In these cases, a litigant who lost in lower court can file a petition to the Supreme Court explaining why it should hear the case. If four justices agree, the case will get a full hearing (this is called, reasonably enough, the "Rule of Four"). This process may sound simple, but sifting through the 8,000 or so cases that the Court receives every year and deciding which 85 of them will be heard is daunting. Former justice William O. Douglas said that this winnowing process is "in many respects the most important and interesting of all our functions."[32]

THE COURT'S CRITERIA

How does the Court decide which cases to hear? Several factors come into play, including the specific characteristics of the case and the broader politics surrounding it. Although several criteria generally must be met before the Court will hear the case, justices still have leeway in defining the boundaries of these conditions.

Collusion, Mootness, and Ripeness First, there are the constitutional guidelines, which are sparse. The Constitution limits the Court to hearing actual "cases and controversies," which has been interpreted to mean that the Court cannot offer advisory opinions about hypothetical situations, but must be dealing with an actual case. The term "actual controversy" also includes several other concepts that limit whether a case will be heard: collusion, mootness, and ripeness. **Collusion** simply means that the litigants in the case cannot want the same outcome and cannot be testing the law without an actual dispute between the two parties.[33]

cases on appeal Cases brought before the Supreme Court because Congress has determined that they require the Court's attention.

writ of certification An uncommon way in which a case is brought before the Supreme Court, whereby an appeals court asks the Court for instructions on a point of law never before decided.

writ of certiorari The most common way for a case to reach the Supreme Court, in which at least four of the nine justices agree to hear a case that has reached them via an appeal from the losing party in a lower court's ruling.

collusion Agreement between the litigants on the desired outcome of a case, causing a federal court to decline to hear the case. More generally, collusion can refer to any kind of conspiracy or complicity.

Mootness means that the controversy must still be relevant when the Court hears the case. For example, a student sued a law school for reverse discrimination, saying that he had not been admitted because of the university's affirmative action policy. A lower court agreed and ordered that the student be admitted. The appeals court reversed the decision, but the student was allowed to remain enrolled while the case was appealed to the Supreme Court. By the time the Court received the case, the student was in his last semester of law school and the university said that he would graduate no matter the outcome of the case. Therefore, the Court refused to hear the case because it was moot.[34] However, there have to be exceptions to this principle because some types of cases would always be moot by the time they got to the Supreme Court. For example, exceptions have been made for abortion cases because a pregnancy lasts only nine months and the time that it takes to get a case from district court, to the appeals court, to the Supreme Court always takes longer than that.

Ripeness can be considered the opposite of mootness. With mootness the controversy is already over; with ripeness the controversy has not started yet. Just as you wouldn't want to eat a piece of fruit before it is ripe, the Court doesn't want to hear a case until it is ripe. Sometimes ripeness can affect standing. One example is the line item veto, which Congress gave to President Clinton at the start of his second term. Almost immediately some members of Congress challenged the constitutionality of the law because they believed that the president should not be able to veto part of a bill. A district court agreed with the members of Congress and ruled that the law was unconstitutional. The case was appealed to the Supreme Court, but it refused to hear the case: because the issue was not ripe, the members of Congress did not have standing. That is, President Clinton had not yet used the line item veto, so there was no controversy and the members had not been harmed. Two months later, Clinton used the veto, another case was filed, and the Court eventually struck down the law.[35] One other type of case will generally not be heard by the Court—those involving "political questions." We will return to this important topic later in the chapter.

Thousands of cases every year meet these basic criteria. One very simple guideline eliminates the largest number of cases: if a case does not involve a "substantial federal question," it will not be heard. This is clearly the vaguest criterion; it means that the Court does not have to hear a case if it does not think the case is important enough. As discussed earlier in the chapter, standing is also a key criterion for whether a case gets heard (recall that standing means the plaintiff bringing the case has sustained "an injury in fact"). Standing, as with the other criteria mentioned in this section, can be grounds for dismissing any civil suit. However, the Supreme Court has a bit more leeway than lower courts in using this criterion. If the Court does not want to decide a case on the merits (for example, if it is a politically sensitive case), it may be able to argue that the plaintiff does not have standing. The "political question doctrine," which we discuss below, is another basis upon which the Court may decide not to hear a case. This still leaves about 20 to 30 percent of the cases that are winnowed to the final list with the more specific guidance of Rule 10 in the Supreme Court rules (see Nuts and Bolts 13.2). Of the criteria listed in Rule 10, conflict between appeals court decisions is most likely to produce a Supreme Court hearing.

Internal Politics Not much is known about the actual discussions that determine which cases will be heard. The justices meet in conference with no staff or clerk. Leaks are rare, but a few insider accounts and the papers of retired justices have provided some insights into the process. First, since the late 1970s most justices have used a **cert pool**, whereby their law clerks take a first cut at the cases (the law clerks to the justices are top graduates of elite law schools who help justices with

mootness The irrelevance of a case by the time it is received by a federal court, causing the court to decline to hear the case.

ripeness A criterion that federal courts use to decide whether a case is ready to be heard. A case's ripeness is based on whether its central issue or controversy has actually taken place.

cert pool A system initiated in the Supreme Court in the 1970s in which law clerks screen cases that come to the Supreme Court and recommend to the justices which cases should be heard.

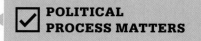

☑ **POLITICAL PROCESS MATTERS**

Rule 10 and Writs of Certiorari

A case is more likely to be heard by the Supreme Court when:

- there is conflict between appeals court opinions,
- there is conflict between a federal appeals court and a state supreme court on a substantial federal question,
- a lower court decision has "departed from the accepted and usual course of judicial proceedings,"
- a state court or appeals court has ruled on a substantial federal question that has not yet been addressed by the Court, or
- a state supreme court or appeals court ruling conflicts with Supreme Court precedent.

Rule 10 also states that certiorari is unlikely to be granted when "the asserted error consists of erroneous factual findings or the misapplication of a properly stated rule of law."

SOURCE: U.S. Supreme Court, *Rules of the U.S. Supreme Court,* adopted January 27, 2003, effective May 1, 2003, available at www.supremecourtus.gov/ctrules/rulesofthecourt.pdf.

background research at several stages of the process). Clerks write joint memos about groups of cases, providing their recommendations about which cases should be heard. The ultimate decisions are made by the justices, but clerks have significant power to help shape the agenda. Most justices take advantage of the cert pool, but John Paul Stevens never used it and Justice Alito withdrew from the pool in late 2008 (their poor clerks had to sift through all of the cases!). Second, the chief justice has an important agenda-setting power: he decides the "discuss list" for a given day. Any justice can add a case to the list, but there is no systematic evidence on how often this happens. As noted above, only 20 to 30 percent of the cases are discussed in conference, which means that about three-quarters of the cases that are submitted to the Supreme Court are never even discussed by the Court. Of course, in most cases this is completely justified because of the high proportion of frivolous suits submitted to the Court.[36]

Many factors outside the legal requirements or internal processes of the Court influence access to the Court and which cases will be heard. Cases that have generated a lot of activity from interest groups or other governmental parties, such as the solicitor general, are more likely to be heard. The **solicitor general** is a presidential appointee who works in the Justice Department and supervises the litigation of the executive branch. In cases in which the federal government is a party, the solicitor general or someone from that office will represent the government in court. The Court accepts about 70 to 80 percent of cases in which the U.S. government is a party compared to fewer than 1 percent overall.[37]

Even with these influences, the Court has a great deal of discretion on which cases it hears. Well-established practices such as standing, ripeness, and mootness may be ignored (or at least modified) if the Court wants to hear a specific case. As legal scholar H. W. Perry points out, "What makes a case important enough to be certworthy is a case [the justices] consider important enough to be certworthy."[38] However, one final and very important point must be noted on this topic: although the justices may pick and choose their cases, they cannot set their own agenda. They can only select from the cases that come to them. If, for example, they thought that the Endangered Species Act was an unfair burden on the expansion of logging in old-growth forests, the justices could not make their opinions known on that issue until someone filed a lawsuit and there was an actual "case or controversy."

solicitor general A presidential appointee in the Department of Justice who conducts all litigation on behalf of the federal government before the Supreme Court and supervises litigation in the federal appellate courts.

Hearing Cases before the Supreme Court

A surprisingly small proportion of the Court's time is actually spent hearing cases—only thirty-nine days in the 2009–2010 term. The Court is in session from the first Monday in October through the end of June or early July. It hears cases on Mondays through Wednesdays in alternating two-week cycles in which it is in session from 10 A.M. to 3 P.M. with a one-hour break for lunch. In the other two weeks of the cycle when it is not in session, justices review briefs, write opinions, and sift through the next batch of petitions. On most Fridays when the Court is in session the justices meet in conference to discuss cases that have been argued and decide which cases they will hear. Opinions are released throughout the term, but the bulk of them come in May and June.[39]

The Court is in recess from July through September. Justices may take some vacation, but they mostly use the time for study, reading, writing, and preparing for the next term. During the summer the Court will also consider emergency petitions (such as stays of execution) and occasionally will hear important cases. For example, during the Watergate scandal of Richard Nixon's presidency, the Court was asked to decide whether the president had to hand over tapes of conversations that had been secretly recorded in the White House. In a unanimous ruling on July 24, 1974, the Court said that Nixon had to release the tapes. Two weeks later Nixon resigned.[40] More recently, on September 9, 2009 (nearly a month before the fall session started), the Court heard a challenge to the Bipartisan Campaign Reform Act, more commonly known as the McCain–Feingold Act after its two principal sponsors. Congress urged the Court to give the law a speedy review given its importance for the upcoming 2010 elections. In the blockbuster case *Citizens United v. Federal Election Commission*, the Supreme Court decided that independent spending in campaigns by corporations and labor unions is protected by the 1st Amendment (see Chapter 8).

BRIEFS

During the regular sessions, the Court follows rigidly set routines. The justices prepare for a case by reading the **briefs** that are submitted by both parties. Because the Supreme Court hears only appeals, it does not call witnesses or gather new evidence (recall that the relatively few cases that come to the Court by original jurisdiction are heard by "special masters"). Instead, in tightly structured briefs of no more than fifty pages, the parties present their arguments about why they either support the lower court decision or believe the case was improperly decided. Interest groups often submit *amicus curiae* ("friend of the court") briefs that convey their opinions to the Court; in fact, 85 percent of cases before the Supreme Court have at least one *amicus* brief. In a typical term in the 1990s, about 400 *amici curiae* were submitted, with an average of 5 groups cosigning each brief for a total of about 1,800 organizational participants.[41] The federal government also files *amici curiae* on important issues such as school busing, school prayer, abortion, reapportionment of legislative districts, job discrimination against women, and affirmative action in higher education. It is difficult to determine the impact *amici curiae* have on the outcome of a case, but *amici curiae* that are filed early in the process increase the chances that the case will be heard. Interestingly, even *amici curiae* that are filed *against* a case increase the chances that the case will be heard.[42] Given the limited information

briefs Written documents prepared by both parties in a case, and sometimes by outside groups, presenting their arguments in court.

amicus curiae Latin for "friend of the court," referring to an interested group or person who shares relevant information about a case to help the Court reach a decision.

oral arguments Spoken presentations made in person by the lawyers of each party to a judge or appellate court outlining the legal reasons why their side should prevail.

that justices have about any given case, interest group involvement can be a strong signal about the importance of a case.

ORAL ARGUMENT

Once the briefs are filed and have been reviewed by the justices, cases are scheduled for **oral arguments**. Except in unusual circumstances, each case gets one hour, which is divided evenly between the two parties. In especially important cases, extra time may be granted. Usually there is only one lawyer for each side who presents the case, but parties that have filed *amicus* briefs may participate if their arguments "would provide assistance to the Court not otherwise available." Given the tight time pressures, the Court is usually unwilling to extend the allotted time to allow "friends of the court" to testify (Court rules say that "such a motion will be granted in only the most extraordinary circumstances").[43] The relevant party can share part of its thirty minutes if it wants, but that doesn't happen often. Therefore, the participation of friends of the court is usually limited to written briefs rather than oral arguments.

The Court is strict about its time limits and uses a system of three lights to show the lawyers how much time is left. A green light goes on when the speaker's time begins, a white light provides a five-minute warning, and a red light means to stop. Most textbooks cite a few well-known examples of justices cutting people off in midsentence or walking out of the courtroom as the hapless lawyer drones on. One leading source on the Court implies that these anecdotes are generally revealing of Court procedure, saying, "Anecdotes probably tell as much about the proceeding of the Court during oral argument as does any careful study of the rules and procedures."[44] However, having a preference for "careful study" over anecdotes, we were curious about how common it was for justices to strictly impose the time limits. We examined forty-two cases from the 2004–2005 term, using the online transcripts on the Court's Web site.[45] We found that most lawyers did not use all their allotted time, with 62 percent of the cases coming in under sixty minutes, 17 percent exactly an hour, and 21 percent over an hour. One-sixth of the lawyers still

▲ *Cameras are not allowed in the Supreme Court, so artists' sketches are the only images of oral arguments. This sketch shows Solicitor General Elena Kagan (now the newest Supreme Court justice), addressing the Court.*

had at least five minutes left on the clock, which means they probably should have practiced their presentation a few more times in front of the mirror or the family dog. We found only two instances in which a justice cut someone off in midsentence after the person had gone over the half-hour limit. In one case an attorney asked, "May I finish this?" and then went on to speak another several sentences. We updated the analysis for the Roberts Court, examining all seventy-four cases argued in the 2009 calendar year. Roberts was not much of a stickler for adhering to the time limits: nearly 60 percent of oral arguments went past their allotted time (most by only a minute or two), 13.5 percent were exactly an hour, and 27 percent were under an hour. Again, only two of the seventy-four oral arguments ended with an attorney being cut off in midsentence by the chief justice. Thus, while the Court tries to stay within its time limits, it is not quite as draconian as some anecdotes may have us believe.

Some lawyers may not use all of their time because their train of thought is interrupted by aggressive questioning. Transcripts reveal that justices jump in with questions almost immediately, and some attorneys never regain their footing. The frequency and pointedness of the questions vary by justice, with Justices Scalia, Breyer, and Ginsburg being the most aggressive on the current Court (Sotomayor also was a frequent participant in oral arguments in her first year), while Justice Thomas often goes months at a time without asking a single question. Cameras are not allowed in the courtroom, so most Americans have never seen the Court in action—though a small live audience is admitted every morning the Court is in session. However, if you are curious about oral arguments, audio recordings have been made of every case since 1995 and are available at www.oyez.org.

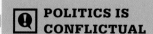
POLITICS IS CONFLICTUAL

CONFERENCE

After oral arguments, the justices meet in conference to discuss and then vote on the cases. As with the initial conferences, these meetings are conducted in secret. We know, based on notes in the personal papers of retired justices, that the conferences are orderly and structured but can become quite heated. The justices take turns discussing the cases and outlining the reasons for their positions. Justice Thurgood Marshall described the decision-making process in conference and the need for secrecy as

> a continuing conversation among nine distinct individuals on dozens of issues simultaneously. The exchanges are serious, sometimes scholarly, occasionally brash and personalized, but generally well-reasoned and most often cast in understated, genteel language. . . . The months-long internal debate on a case often focuses on how much law to change or make. Sometimes, cases come right down to the wire. . . . In other cases, a majority of justices start down one path, only to reverse direction. . . . This is the kind of internal debate that the justices have argued should remain confidential, taking the position that only their final opinions have legal authority. They have expressed concern that premature disclosure of their private debates and doubts may undermine the court's credibility and inhibit their exchange of ideas.[46]

OPINION WRITING

After justices indicate how they are likely to vote on a case, the most senior justice in the majority decides who will write the majority opinion. Usually this is the chief justice; for example, Warren Burger assigned 1,891 of the 2,201 opinions (about 86 percent) when he was chief justice in the 1970s and 1980s.[47] Many considerations

▲ Harlan Fiske Stone served on the Supreme Court from 1925 until his death in 1946 (serving as chief justice from 1941 to 1946). One important role of the chief justice is to assign opinion writing. In some cases, such as those involving civil rights, Stone made these assignments in a strategic manner that was sensitive to public opinion.

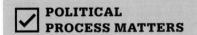

POLITICAL PROCESS MATTERS

come into play in deciding how a case will be assigned. First, the chief justice will try to ensure the smooth operation of the Court. Along these lines, in 1989, Chief Justice Rehnquist announced a change in how he assigned opinions. In his first three terms, he simply tried to give each justice the same number of cases, but he recognized that "this policy does not take into consideration the difficulty of the opinion assigned or the amount of work that the 'assignee' may currently have backed up in his chambers. . . . It only makes sense in the assignment of additional work to give some preference to those who are 'current' with respect to past work."[48] A second factor is the justices' individual areas of expertise. For example, Justice Blackmun had developed expertise in medical law when he was in private practice, including extensive work at the famous Mayo Clinic. This experience played a role in Chief Justice Burger's decision to assign Blackmun the majority opinion in the landmark abortion decision, *Roe v. Wade*. Likewise, Justice O'Connor developed expertise in racial redistricting cases and authored most of those decisions in the 1990s.

The final set of factors is more strategic and includes the Court's external relations, internal relations, and the personal policy goals of the opinion assigner. The Court must be sensitive to how others might respond to its decisions because it must rely on the other branches of government to enforce its decisions. One famous example of this consideration in an opinion assignment came in a case from the 1940s that struck down a practice that had prevented African Americans from voting in Democratic primaries.[49] Originally, the opinion was assigned to Justice Felix Frankfurter, but Justice Robert Jackson wrote a memo suggesting that it might be unwise to have a liberal, politically independent Jew from the Northeast write an opinion that was sure to be controversial in the South. Chief Justice Harlan Fiske Stone agreed and reassigned the opinion to Justice Stanley Reed, a Protestant and Democrat from Kentucky.[50] It may not seem that the Court is sensitive to public opinion, but these kinds of considerations happen fairly frequently in important cases. Internal considerations occasionally cause justices to vote strategically— different from the justice's sincere preference—in order to be in the majority so the justice can assign the opinion (often to himself or herself).

Justices may also assign opinions to help achieve their personal policy goals. The most obvious way to do this is for the chief justice to assign opinions to justices who are closest to his position. Obviously, this practice is constrained by the first point—ensuring the smooth operation of the Court. If the chief justice assigned all the opinions to the justices who are closest to him ideologically, then justices with other ideological leanings would get a chance to write opinions only in the 15 to 20 percent of cases in which the chief is in the minority. Clearly that wouldn't work. Charles Hughes, who was chief justice from 1930 to 1941, sometimes assigned opinions on liberal decisions to conservative justices and conservative opinions to liberal justices to downplay the importance of ideology on the Court.[51]

Although these constraining factors prevent the assigning justice from using opinion assignments to further his policy goals in most cases, there is evidence of this type of behavior on the most important Court cases. One study found that on cases with a large number of *amicus* briefs (a good measure of importance), the justice who is closest to the chief is 61 percent more likely to get the assignment than the justice who is most distant from the chief.[52] This same study also found that the chief justice was more likely to assign the opinion to justices who were ideologically distant from the chief when it was necessary to hold together fragile coalitions. For example, a case decided by a 5–4 vote was more than twice as likely to go to a justice who was distant from the chief than a case that was decided by at least a 7–2 margin.[53] This shows that the chief justice is willing to set aside his own policy views when it is important to hold together a coalition. These same patterns tended to hold when associate justices made the assignments rather than the chief

Types of Supreme Court Decisions

Majority opinion: The core decision of the Court that must be agreed upon by at least five justices. The majority opinion presents the legal reasoning for the Court's decision.

Concurring opinion: Written by a justice who agrees with the outcome of the case but not with the legal reasoning. Concurring opinions may be joined by other justices. A justice may sign on to the majority opinion and write a separate concurring opinion.

Plurality opinion: Occurs when a majority cannot agree on the legal reasoning in a case. The plurality opinion is the one that has the most agreement (usually three or four justices). Because of the fractured nature of these opinions, they typically are not viewed as having as much clout as majority opinions.

Dissent: Submitted by a justice who disagrees with the outcome of the case. Other justices can sign on to a dissent or write their own, so there can be as many as four dissents. Justices can also sign on to part of a dissent but not the entire opinion.

Per curiam opinion: (Latin for "by the court") An unsigned opinion of the Court or a decision written by the entire Court. However, this is not the same as a unanimous decision that is signed by the entire Court. Per curiam opinions are usually very short opinions on noncontroversial issues, but not always. For example, *Bush v. Gore*, which decided the outcome of the 2000 presidential election, was a per curiam opinion. Per curiam decisions may also have dissents.

justice. The most significant difference was that associate justices were not quite as constrained by the desire to balance the workload.

After the opinions are assigned, the justices work on writing a draft opinion. Law clerks typically help with this process. Some justices still insist on writing all of their opinions, while others allow a clerk to write the first draft. The drafts are circulated to the other justices for comment and reactions. Some bargaining may occur, in which a justice says he or she will withdraw support unless a provision is changed. Justices may join the majority opinion, they may write a separate concurring opinion, or they may dissent (see Nuts and Bolts 13.3 for details on the types of opinions).

Two final points should be made about the process of writing and issuing opinions. First, until the 1940s there was a premium placed on unanimous decisions. This practice was started by John Marshall, who was chief justice from 1800 to 1835. Through the 1930s, about 80 to 90 percent of decisions were unanimous. This changed dramatically in the 1940s, when most cases had at least one dissent. In recent decades, about two-thirds of cases have a dissent. Dissents serve an important purpose. Not only do they allow the minority view to be expressed, but they also often provide the basis for reversing a poorly reasoned case. When justices strongly oppose the majority opinion, they may take the unusual step of reading a portion of the dissent from the bench.

Supreme Court Decision Making

There are many different influences on judicial decision making. The two main categories are legal and political. The legal factors include the precedent of earlier cases and norms that justices must follow the language of the Constitution. Political

influences include the justices' preferences or ideologies, their stances on whether the Court should take a restrained or activist role with respect to the elected branches, and external factors such as public opinion and interest group involvement. Some scholars dispute these basic categories, arguing that all court behavior is political and that the use of legal factors is just a smoke screen for hiding personal preferences.

LEGAL FACTORS

Those who put forward the legal view usually present their position in normative terms; that is, justices *should* be led by precedent and the words of the Constitution. Advocates of this view recognize that justices often stray from these legal norms, but they criticize the interjection of personal preferences as a harmful politicization of the courts. Our view is that legal factors are often used as justification for political positions on the Court, but they also independently influence judicial decision making on a broad range of cases.

Precedent The most basic legal factor is *stare decisis* or precedent, which we discussed above. Precedent does not determine the outcome of any given case, because every case has a range of precedent that can be drawn upon to justify a justice's decision. The "easy" cases, in which settled law makes the outcome obvious, are less likely to be heard by the Court because of its desire to focus on the more controversial areas of unsettled law. However, there are areas of the law, such as free speech, the death penalty, and search and seizure, in which precedent is an important explanation for how justices decide a case.

The Language of the Constitution The various perspectives that emphasize the language of the Constitution all fall under the heading of **strict construction**. The most basic of these is the literalist view of the Constitution. Sometimes this view is also referred to as a textualist position because it sees the text of the document as determining the outcome of any given case. Literalists argue that justices need to look no farther than the actual words of the Constitution. Justice Hugo Black was one of the most famous advocates of this position. When the 1st Amendment says that "Congress shall make no law . . . abridging the freedom of speech," that literally means *no* law. Justice Black said, "My view is, without deviation, without exception, without any ifs, buts, or whereases, that freedom of speech means that government shall not do anything to people . . . either for the views they have or the views they express or the words they speak or write."[54] While that may be clear enough with regard to political speech, how about pornography, Internet speech, or symbolic speech, such as burning an American flag or wearing an armband to protest the Vietnam War? A literal interpretation of the Constitution does not necessarily help determine whether these forms of speech should be restricted. Indeed, Hugo Black was one of the two dissenters in a case that upheld students' right to wear armbands as a form of symbolic speech. Black believed that school officials should be allowed to decide whether a symbolic protest would be too disruptive in the classroom. So much for "without deviation, without exception"!

Critics of strict construction also point out that the Constitution is silent on many important points (such as a right to privacy) and could not have anticipated the changes in technology in the twentieth and twenty-first centuries that have many legal implications, such as eavesdropping devices, cloning, and the Internet. Also, though the language of the 1st Amendment is relatively clear, other equally important words of the Constitution such as "necessary and proper," "executive power," "equal protection," and "due process" are open-ended and vague. Some

▼ Mary Beth Tinker and two other students in the Des Moines, Iowa, public schools were suspended for wearing armbands to protest the Vietnam War. The Supreme Court ruled that the 1st Amendment protected symbolic political speech, even in public schools. Mary Beth is shown here with her mother at the trial. (Photo by Dave Penney, Copyright 1965, The Des Moines Register and Tribune Company. Reprinted with permission.)

strict constructionists respond by arguing that if the words of the Constitution are not clear, the justices should be guided by what the Founders *intended*, a perspective called the **original intent** or originalist perspective. Clarence Thomas is the current justice who is most influenced by this view, especially on issues of federalism. Justice Antonin Scalia has a similar view, arguing that the text of the Constitution should be closely followed and if the text is ambiguous, justices should figure out what the words generally meant to people at the time they were written. This view leads Scalia to some unpopular positions, such as his view that the 6th Amendment provision that "in all criminal prosecutions the accused shall enjoy the right . . . to be confronted with the witnesses against him" applies even in the case of an accused child molester. The majority of the Court disagreed and held that it was acceptable to have the child testify in front of the prosecutor and defense attorney, with the judge, jury, and the accused viewing from another room over closed-circuit television because of the potential trauma the child would experience by having to confront the defendant face-to-face.[55]

Critics of the strict constructionist view are often described as supporting a **living Constitution** perspective on the document (see Chapter 2). They argue that originalism or other versions of strict construction can "make a nation the prisoner of its past, and reject any constitutional development save constitutional amendment."[56] If the justices are bound to follow the literal words of the Constitution, *with the meaning they had when the document was written*, we certainly could be legally frozen in time. The option of amending the Constitution is a long and difficult process, so that is not always a viable way for the Constitution to reflect changing norms and values.

POLITICAL FACTORS

The living Constitution perspective points to the second set of influences on Supreme Court decision making: political factors. As we noted in the introduction to this chapter, many people are uncomfortable thinking about the Court in political terms and prefer to think of the image of "blind justice," in which constitutional principles are fairly applied. However, political influences are clearly evident in the Court—maybe less than in Congress or the presidency, but they are certainly present.

Political Ideology and Attitudes The most important political factor is the justice's ideology or attitudes about various issues (this is often called the **attitudinalist approach** to understanding Supreme Court decision making). Liberal judges are strong defenders of individual civil liberties, including defendants' rights, tend to be pro-choice on abortion, support regulatory policy to protect the environment and workers, support national intervention in the states, and favor race-conscious policies such as affirmative action. Conservative judges favor state regulation of private conduct (especially on moral issues), support prosecutors over defendants, tend to be pro-life on abortion, and support the free market and property rights over the environment and workers, states' rights over national intervention, and a color-blind policy on race. These are, of course, just general tendencies. However, they do provide a strong basis for explaining patterns of decisions, especially on some types of cases. For example, there were dramatic differences in the chief justices' rulings on civil liberties cases from 1953 to 2001: Earl Warren took the liberal position on 79 percent of the 771 cases he participated in, Warren Burger took the liberal position on 30 percent of 1,429 cases, and William

original intent The theory that justices should surmise the intentions of the Founders when the language of the Constitution is unclear.

living Constitution A way of interpreting the Constitution that takes into account evolving national attitudes and circumstances rather than the text alone.

attitudinalist approach A way of understanding decisions of the Supreme Court based on the political ideologies of the justices.

▼ *Chapter 5 cited a survey in which most respondents were unable to name any Supreme Court justices. Just so you are not in danger of falling into that category, as of fall 2010 the justices are (front row, left to right) Clarence Thomas, Antonin Scalia, John G. Roberts Jr. (chief justice), Anthony M. Kennedy, Ruth Bader Ginsburg, (standing, left to right) Sonia Sotomayor, Stephen Breyer, Samuel Alito Jr., and Elena Kagan.*

FIGURE 13.5 | IDEOLOGY OF SUPREME COURT JUSTICES

Notice that the estimates of the justices' ideology vary in their precision. What might explain the relatively tight distribution for Breyer or Kennedy, compared to the broad distribution for Sotomayor?

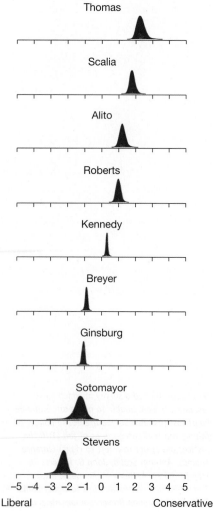

Thomas

Scalia

Alito

Roberts

Kennedy

Breyer

Ginsburg

Sotomayor

Stevens

–5 –4 –3 –2 –1 0 1 2 3 4 5

Liberal   Conservative

SOURCE: Alexander Tahk and Stephen Jesse, Supreme Court Ideology Project, http://sct.tahk.us/current.html.

Rehnquist took the liberal position on only 22 percent of his 2,127 cases.[57] If justices were neutrally applying the law, there would not be such dramatic differences.

Proponents of the attitudinalist view also argue that justices who *claim* to be strict constructionists or originalists are really driven by ideology because they selectively use the text of the Constitution. For example, in a recent case Justice Thomas voted against the University of Michigan's affirmative action program without considering whether the authors of the 14th Amendment supported the practice (a brief review of the historical record would have shown that they did). Therefore, if Justice Thomas had been true to his originalist perspective, he would have supported affirmative action, but his ideology led him to oppose the policy. The example of Hugo Black's contradictory position on free speech rights cited above demonstrates that a liberal textualist view may also be inconsistently applied.

The Strategic Model A strategic approach to understanding Supreme Court decision making focuses on justices' calculations about the preferences of the other justices, the president, and Congress, the choices that other justices are likely to make, and the institutional context within which they operate. After all, justices do not operate alone: at a minimum they need the votes of four of their colleagues if they want their position to prevail. Therefore, it makes sense to focus on the strategic interactions that take place to build coalitions. The median voter on the Court—the one in the middle when the justices are arrayed from the most liberal to the most conservative—has an especially influential role in the strategic model. For many years the median justice was Sandra Day O'Connor; when Samuel Alito replaced her, Anthony Kennedy became the new median (see Figure 13.5). The four conservatives to his right (Thomas, Scalia, Roberts, and Alito) and the four liberals to his left (Breyer, Ginsberg, Souter, and Stevens) all wanted to attract his vote. When Justice Sotomayor replaced Justice Souter and when Justice Kagan replaced Justice Stevens, Kennedy remained the median voter on the Court (because Souter, Sotomayor, Stevens, and Kagan are all to his left). Research shows that at least one justice switches his or her vote at some stage in the process (from the initial conference to oral arguments to the final vote) on at least half of the cases, so strategic bargaining appears to be fairly common.[58] Our earlier discussion of opinion assignment and writing opinions to attract the support of a specific justice is more evidence in support of the strategic model.

Separation of Powers Another political influence on justices' decision making is their view of the place of the Court with respect to the democratically elected institutions (Congress and the president). Specifically, do they favor an activist or a restrained role for the Court? Advocates of **judicial restraint** argue that judges should defer to the elected branches and not strike down their laws or other actions. On the other hand, advocates of **judicial activism** argue that the Court must play an active role in interpreting the Constitution to protect minority rights even if it means overturning the actions of the elected branches. Yet another approach says that these normative arguments about how restraint or activism ought to work are fine and good, but they don't really matter because the Court usually follows public opinion and rarely plays a lead role in promoting policy change. One scholar found that three-fifths to two-thirds of Supreme Court decisions are consistent with public opinion when the public has a clear preference on an issue.[59] However, there are plenty of examples of when the Court has stood up for unpopular views, such as banning prayer in schools, allowing flag burning, and protecting criminal defendants' rights.

Often, assessments of the Court's role vary with the views of a specific line of cases. A political conservative may favor "activist" decisions striking down environmental laws or workplace regulations but oppose activist decisions that defend flag burning or defendants' rights. Political liberals may be the opposite—calling for judicial restraint on the first set of cases but activism when it comes to protecting civil liberties. Sometimes, the popular media mistakenly assert that liberal justices are more activist than conservative justices. In fact, that is not always the case. The current Court is quite conservative, but it is also activist.[60] The 1930s Court that struck down much of the New Deal legislation was also conservative and activist, but the Warren Court of the late 1950s and early 1960s was liberal and activist (see Table 13.1). Two conservatives, Justice Kennedy and Justice Thomas, have voted to overturn laws passed by Congress 93 percent and 81 percent of the time, respectively, whereas two of the most liberal justices, Breyer and Ginsburg, have taken the activist position in only 42 percent and 48 percent of the cases.[61]

A prominent legal journalist observed that the way the popular media describe activism and restraint typically boils down to ideology: if you like a decision, it is restrained; if you do not like a decision, it is activist. For example, *Bush v. Gore*, the decision that decided the outcome of the 2000 presidential election, shows that "most conservatives tie themselves in knots to defend judicial activism when they like the results and to denounce it when they do not. As the reaction to *Lawrence* [the recent gay sex case] and, earlier, *Roe* [the landmark abortion case] has shown, liberals have been no less selective in their outrage at judicial adventurousness."[62] There are instances in which restraint is more than ideology and preferences. Justice O'Connor, for example, took restrained positions on abortion and affirmative action, despite her personal views against these policies. However, it is important to define activism and restraint in terms of the Court's role in our system of separated powers: Does it check the elected branches by overturning their decisions through judicial review? This is the only objective way to define activism and restraint.

Outside Influences: Interest Groups and Public Opinion Finally, there are external influences on the Court, such as public opinion and interest groups. We have already talked about the role of interest groups in filing *amicus* briefs. This is the only avenue of influence open to interest groups; other tactics such as lobbying or fund-raising are either inappropriate or irrelevant (because justices are not elected). The role of public opinion is more complex. Obviously, justices do not consult public opinion polls the way elected officials do. However, there are several indirect ways that the Court expresses the public's preferences. The first was most colorfully expressed by Mr. Dooley, a fictional Irish American bartender who was created at the turn of the nineteenth century by a newspaper satirist named Finley Peter Dunne. Mr. Dooley offered keen insights on politics and general social criticism, including this gem on the relationship between the Supreme Court and the public, "th' supreme coort always follows th' iliction returns."[63] That is, the public elects the president and the Senate, who appoint and confirm the justices. Therefore, sooner or later, the Court should reflect the views of the public. Subsequent work by political scientists has confirmed this to be largely the case,[64] especially in recent years when Supreme Court nominations have become more political and more important to the public.[65]

The second mechanism through which public opinion may influence the Court is more direct: when the public has a clear position on an issue that is before the Court, the Court tends to agree with the public. One study found that the "public mood" and Court opinions correlated very highly between 1956 and 1981, but their association was weaker through the rest of the 1980s.[66] Several high-profile examples support the idea that the Court is sensitive to public opinion: the Court's switch during the New Deal in the 1930s to support Roosevelt's policy agenda after standing in the way for four years, giving in to wartime opinion to support the internment of Japanese Americans during World War II, limiting an accused child molester's right to confront his accuser in a court room, declaring that the execution

judicial restraint The idea that the Supreme Court should defer to the democratically elected executive and legislative branches of government rather than contradicting existing laws.

judicial activism The idea that the Supreme Court should assert its interpretation of the law even if it overrules the elected executive and legislative branches of government.

of mentally retarded defendants was "cruel and unusual punishment," and declaring that laws limiting sex between consenting gay adults were unconstitutional. In each of these cases the justices reflected the current public opinion of the nation rather than a strict reading of the Constitution or the Founders' intent.

Sometimes the Court may shift its views to reflect *international* opinion. The most recent example struck down the death penalty for minors in twelve states. Ruling by a 5–4 margin that the execution of sixteen- or seventeen-year-olds violated the 8th Amendment's prohibition against "cruel and unusual punishments," the majority opinion overturned a 1989 case and said the new decision was necessary to reflect the "evolving standards of decency" concerning the definition of "cruel and unusual punishments." Justice Kennedy, who voted on the other side of this issue sixteen years earlier, wrote, "It is fair to say that the United States now stands alone in a world that has turned its face against the juvenile death penalty." Since 1990, he noted, only seven other countries have executed people for crimes they committed as juveniles, and all seven—Iran, Pakistan, Saudi Arabia, Yemen, Nigeria, China, and Congo—no longer execute minors. Justice Kennedy said that although the Court was not obligated to follow foreign developments, "it is proper that we acknowledge the overwhelming weight of international opinion" for its "respected and significant confirmation for our own conclusions." This explicit recognition of the role of public opinion firmly placed a majority of the Court on the side of the "living Constitution" perspective on this issue, while rejecting the strict constructionist view of the dissenters. Justice Ginsburg explicitly made this point in a concurring opinion in which she wrote, "Perhaps even more important than our specific holding today is our reaffirmation of the basic principle that informs the court's interpretation of the Eighth Amendment"—that the amendment's meaning has evolved rather than being fixed with an eighteenth-century understanding of the term.[67]

Another way that the Court may consider the public mood is to shift the timing of a decision. The best example here is the landmark school desegregation case, *Brown v. Board of Education*, that the Court sat on for more than two years—until after the 1952 presidential election—because it didn't think the public was ready for its bombshell ruling.[68] Others have argued that the Court rarely *changes* its views to reflect public opinion,[69] but at a minimum the evidence supports the notion that the Court is usually in step with the public.

The Role of the Court as a Policy Maker

We conclude with the topic addressed at the beginning of the chapter—the place of the Court within the political system. Is the Court the "weakest branch"? As Alexander Hamilton pointed out, the Court has "neither the power of the purse nor the sword." Therefore, it is not clear how it can enforce decisions. In some instances the Court can force its views on the other branches; in other cases it needs their support to enforce its decisions (see What Do Political Scientists Do?).

COMPLIANCE AND IMPLEMENTATION

To gain compliance with its decisions, the Court can rely only on its reputation and on the actions of Congress and the president to back them up. If the other branches don't support the Court, there isn't much it can do. The extreme example was

Can the Supreme Court Be an Agent of Change?

Ever since Chief Justice Earl Warren led the liberal Supreme Court in the 1950s and 1960s, many political observers have assumed that the Supreme Court can bring about social change. On a range of topics that include school desegregation, criminal defendants' rights, school prayer, one-person-one-vote requirements in legislative redistricting, the right to privacy and family planning, and the freedom of speech, the Supreme Court has been ahead of public opinion and seemed to lead the elected branches.

However, in his book *The Hollow Hope*, political scientist Gerald Rosenberg argues that courts can almost never produce significant social reform. He says, "At best, they can second the social reform acts of the other branches of government."[a] In his conclusion, entitled "The Fly Paper Court," Rosenberg warns that social reformers may be seduced by the "lure of litigation," wasting their time in the courts when they could be using their resources more effectively elsewhere. He argues that the American political system inherently limits the effectiveness of the courts through three structural constraints: (1) the limited nature of constitutional rights (for example, there is no constitutional right to "housing, adequate levels of welfare, a job, or a clean environment," all goals of social reformers), (2) Congress's constraints on judicial independence through the nomination process and statutory interpretation, and (3) the judiciary's limited enforcement powers. These constraints can only be overcome when there is adequate legal precedent for change, when there is support for legal change from Congress and the president, when there is either strong support from some citizens or weak opposition from all citizens, and when conditions otherwise support compliance with the judicial decision.

Rosenberg then looked at the evidence of whether these constraints can be overcome and the Court can be an agent for social change. Rosenberg tackled the instances

Earl Warren served as chief justice of the Supreme Court from 1953 to 1969. Decisions during his tenure on racial segregation, civil rights, and criminal defendants' rights raised expectations that the Court be an agent of social change.

in which most people have assumed that the Court *did* produce change: civil rights, abortion and women's rights, the environment, legislative reapportionment, criminal law, and gay marriage. But in each instance, Rosenberg argues, this was not the case. For example, although the *Brown v. Board of Education* (1954) decision officially desegregated schools in the South, no real progress was made until after the 1964 Civil Rights Act was passed. In the 1964–1965 school year, the last year before the Civil Rights Act would have had any impact, only 2.3 percent of black children in the South attended elementary or secondary school with white children. By 1972–1973, that figure was 91.3 percent. Similarly, the 1965 Voting Rights Act had a much bigger impact on black voter registration in the South than the series of court cases on voting rights in the 1950s and 1960s.

Legislative apportionment appears to be one of the strongest examples of the impact of the courts. *Baker v. Carr* (1962) and subsequent cases mandated that legislative

districts be of equal population ("one person, one vote"). Indeed, by the end of the 1960s, nearly every state legislative district and U.S. House district was in compliance with the Court decisions. However, as Rosenberg points out, for the social reformers, getting legislative districts to be equal in size was only a means to an end, and that end was not achieved: reformers were concerned that rural interests were over-represented in legislatures, which skewed policy away from the interests of urban residents; however, most studies of the impact of population equalization in legislative districts show little to no impact on policy.

The responses to Rosenberg's argument range from, "What's the big deal? Since Alexander Hamilton pointed it out in *Federalist 78*, we have known that the Court depends on the other branches to enforce its decisions" to those who argue that Rosenberg is using an improper causal model for determining the impact of Supreme Court decisions—rather than a unitary actor that influences the behavior of other institutions through its decisions, the Court must be viewed within our system of separated and shared powers. That is, the Court cannot produce change by itself, but this is not a realistic expectation, given our system of government. Furthermore, the Court may be a catalyst for change by helping create the climate in which it is possible for the other branches of government to act.[b]

The Hollow Hope is an excellent example of how empirical evidence can be brought to bear on an important question and produce novel and provocative arguments. The twenty years of debate produced by the book is strong testimony to the continued disagreements over the role of the Court within our political system. ■

◎ **Watch a video clip of political scientist Michael McCann discussing this topic at wwnorton.com/studyspace.**

▲ High school students in Maize, Kansas, join hands around a flagpole at the annual nationwide event calling Christian youth to pre-class schoolyard prayer at the start of the new school year. Enforcing the prohibition of school prayer and drawing the line between permissible and impermissible prayer have both been difficult for the Court.

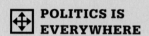 **POLITICS IS EVERYWHERE**

the result of an ongoing feud between Chief Justice John Marshall and President Andrew Jackson in the 1830s. The case concerned a missionary, Samuel Worcester, who was arrested on Cherokee land in Georgia because he did not have the proper license to be there. Worcester claimed that the U.S. government, not the state of Georgia, should have control over the Cherokee Nation, and that therefore Georgia had no right to arrest him under its laws. Marshall agreed, writing, "The Cherokee Nation, then, is a distinct community, occupying its own territory, with boundaries accurately described, in which the laws of Georgia can have no force, and which the citizens of Georgia have no right to enter but with the assent of the Cherokees themselves or in conformity with treaties and with the acts of Congress."[70] After the decision, Jackson remarked, "John Marshall has made his decision. Now let him enforce it if he can." Georgia instead enforced its laws and ignored the Court—Worcester remained in jail for another year.

At the other extreme, some decisions of the Court are nearly self-enforcing because of their visibility and narrow application. If the decision primarily affects one party, the attention and focus on the case compels compliance. For example, Richard Nixon knew that he had to go along with the Court ruling forcing him to give up his secret tapes for the Watergate investigation or he would have been immediately impeached. But even cases that seem to have relatively narrow application, such as *Bush v. Gore*, which the Court tried to define narrowly, often are applied broadly by lower courts and future litigants. If the Court knows it is likely to face resistance, one thing it can do is attempt to get a unanimous vote, since even one dissent can provide a rationale for resisting a Court ruling.

The Court's lack of enforcement power is especially evident when a ruling applies broadly to millions of people who care deeply about the issue. One of the best examples is school prayer, which still exists in hundreds of public schools around the country despite having been ruled unconstitutional more than forty years ago. It is impossible to enforce the ban unless someone in the school complains and is willing to bring a lawsuit.

In most cases that involve a broad policy, the Court depends on the president for enforcement. After *Brown v. Board of Education*, the landmark school desegregation case, presidents Eisenhower and Kennedy had to send in the National Guard to desegregate public schools and universities. On the other hand, if presidents drag their feet, they can have a big impact on how the law is enforced. President Nixon attempted to lessen the impact of a school busing decision in 1971 that forced the integration of public schools by interpreting it very narrowly. Republican presidents who are opposed to abortion have limited the scope of *Roe v. Wade*, which legalized abortion in 1973, by denying federal support for abortions for people on Medicaid, banning abortions on military bases, and implementing a "gag rule," which prevented medical doctors from mentioning abortion as an option during pregnancy counseling. The Court must rely on its reputation and prestige to compel the president and Congress not to stray too far from its decisions.

RELATIONS WITH THE OTHER BRANCHES

The Court's relations with other branches may be strained as it has to rule on fundamental questions about institutional power. The Court has limited the power of the president in several high-profile cases, including Lincoln's suspension of the writ of habeas corpus during the Civil War, Truman's use of the National Guard to open steel mills that had been shut down by a labor dispute during the Korean War, Nixon's attempt to suppress information about the Vietnam War, and George W. Bush's suspension of civil liberties for "enemy combatants" during the War on Terror.[71] On the other hand, the Court has consistently upheld the president's broader war-making power, including Lincoln's blockade of southern ports when Congress was out of session in 1861 and unilateral military action in Vietnam, El Salvador, Grenada, Panama, the Persian Gulf, and Iraq.

The president and Congress often fight back when they think the Court is exerting too much influence, which can limit the Court's power as a policy-making institution. For the president this can escalate to open conflict, as in the battle between Jackson and Marshall over jurisdiction within the Cherokee Nation; the conflict between Jefferson and Marshall, which included the impeachment of a Supreme Court justice for political reasons (although the Senate acquitted the justice on all charges), and the repeal of the 1801 Judiciary Act; FDR's court-packing scheme, which was his response to the obstructionist New Deal Court; and President Obama's calling out the Supreme Court in his 2010 State of the Union message for a decision he disagreed with. In the latter case, when Obama said that the Supreme Court's ruling in *Citizens United v. Federal Election Commission* had opened the floodgates for corporate spending—including foreign corporations—in elections, Justice Alito was caught on camera mouthing the words "not true." Washington was abuzz for the next few days about whether the president's comment or Alito's response was out of line. Chief Justice Roberts added fuel to the fire a few weeks later when he said he found the president's comment and the partisan atmosphere of the speech "very troubling," and he indicated that justices may not attend State of the Union addresses in the future.

The president can also counter the Court's influence in a more restrained way by failing to enforce a decision as vigorously as he might otherwise, as we noted above. Congress can try to control the Court by blocking appointments it disagrees with (however, this often involves a disagreement with the president more than the Court), limiting the jurisdiction of the federal courts, or in the most extreme case, impeaching a judge. These latter two options are rarely used, but Congress often threatens to take these drastic steps. The most common way for Congress to respond to a Court decision that it disagrees with is simply to pass legislation that overturns the decision (if the case concerns the interpretation of a law). Sometimes these disputes can go on for a while, as with the recent flap over sentencing guidelines. Congress wanted the federal courts to get tougher on criminals, so it passed a law telling federal judges the range of sentences that they had to give for specific crimes. Chief Justice Rehnquist was upset when Congress passed the law without any input from the judiciary and said, "It seems that the traditional interchange between Congress and the judiciary broke down."[72] The Court struck back when it invalidated the federal sentencing guidelines as an unfair imposition on the judiciary. The Roberts Court is deeply involved in this issue as well, with at least seven rulings that are directly related to sentencing guidelines and ten more that are indirectly related. The Roberts Court has defined the specific boundaries of the general position articulated by the Rehnquist Court that sentencing guidelines should be viewed by the lower courts as advisory rather than mandatory. To this point, Congress has not responded to the latest salvos in this inter-branch contest.[73]

In general, the Court is careful not to step on the toes of the other branches unless it is absolutely necessary. The Court often exercises self-imposed restraint and refuses to act on "political questions"—issues that are outside the judicial domain and should be decided by elected officials. One of the earliest applications was an 1804 dispute over whether a piece of land by the Mississippi River belonged to Spain or the United States. The Court observed, "A question like this, respecting the boundaries of nations, is, as has been truly said, more a political than a legal question, and in its discussion, the courts of every country must respect the pronounced will of the legislature."[74] A more recent application of the doctrine was a 1948 case in which the Court refused to review orders of the Civil Aeronautics

Board granting or denying applications by citizen carriers to engage in overseas and foreign air transportation. The Court's reasons to avoid this issue show its deference to the elected branches on foreign policy:

> The very nature of executive decisions as to foreign policy is political, not judicial. Such decisions are wholly confided by our Constitution on the political departments of government, executive and legislative. They are delicate, complex, and involve large elements of prophecy. They are and should be undertaken only by those directly responsible to the people whose welfare they advance or imperil. They are decisions of a kind for which the Judiciary has neither aptitude, facilities, nor responsibility and which has long been held to belong in the domain of political power not subject to judicial instrument or inquiry.[75]

Though this self-imposed limitation on judicial power is important, one must also recognize that the Court reserves the right to decide what a political question is. Therefore, one could argue that this is not much of a limit on judicial power after all. For example, for many decades the Court avoided the topic of legislative redistricting, saying that it did not want to enter that "political thicket." However, it changed its position in the 1960s in a series of cases that imposed the idea of "one person, one vote" on the redistricting process. The Court's ability to define the boundaries of political questions is an important source of its policy-making power.

This "big picture" question about the relationship of the Court to the other branches ultimately boils down to this: Does the judiciary constrain the other branches, or does it defer to their wishes? Given the responsiveness of the elected branches to the will of the people, this question can alternatively be stated: Does the Court operate in a countermajoritarian way as protector of minority interests, or does it defer to the popular will? The evidence on this is mixed.

Clearly the Court is activist on many issues, exercising judicial review, but on many other issues it defers to the elected institution. Sometimes an activist Court defends minority interests on issues like criminal defendants' rights, school prayer, gay rights, and flag burning, but that is certainly not always the case. Is the Court acting undemocratically when it exercises its power of judicial review (or as critics would say, "legislates from the bench")? Or is it playing its vital role in our constitutional system as a check on the other branches?

The answers depend to some extent on one's political views. Conservatives would generally applaud the activism of the Rehnquist and Roberts Courts, while liberals would see it as an unwarranted check on the elected branches. Second, the role of the Court has varied throughout history: in some instances it defended unpopular views and strongly protected minority rights; in other cases it followed majority opinion and declined to play that important role. Clearly the Court has the *potential* to play an important policy-making role in our system of checks and balances; whether or not it actually plays that role depends on the political, personal, and legal factors outlined in this chapter.

Conclusion

The courts demonstrate that politics is conflictual. Although plenty of unanimous Supreme Court decisions do not involve much conflict between the justices, many landmark cases deeply divide the Court on constitutional interpretation and how to balance those competing interpretations against other values and interests. These conflicts in the Court often reveal deeper fault lines in the broader political system.

It shouldn't be surprising that political process matters in the courts. The rules of courtroom procedures, including discovery and how evidence is presented, can have an important impact on outcomes. Political process is also important for selecting judges and determining which cases get heard by the Supreme Court.

Politics is indeed everywhere, even in the courts, where you would least expect to see it. Despite the idealized image of Justice as a blindfolded woman holding a set of scales, politics affects everything from the selection of judges to the decisions they make. Some characteristics of the federal courts, most importantly judges' lifetime tenure, insulate the system from politics. However, courts are influenced by judges' ideologies, interest groups, and the president and Senate, who try to shape their composition through the nomination process.

Returning to the example that opened this chapter—the role of the courts in defining the government's role in the War on Terror—demonstrates the important role that the courts play in the political system. The federal courts may serve as a referee between the other branches, defining the boundaries of permissible conduct. In this case, they have limited the president's ability to unilaterally hold or try suspected terrorists without following established legal procedures. They also have forced Congress to clarify its laws to state more clearly what the executive branch can and cannot do in military tribunals. These cases illustrate another important role of the courts: standing up for the rights of individuals who would not be protected elsewhere in the political system. Protecting the rights of suspected terrorists may not strike you as an important role for the courts, but procedural fairness and the rule of law are the cornerstone of political freedom for all Americans.

How did the federal judiciary become independent and powerful?

- The Founders had mixed views about the role of the Supreme Court. They knew they wanted an independent judicial institution but were not sure how much power it should have.
- Judicial review made the Supreme Court an equal partner in the system of checks and balances and separation of powers. With the power to strike down the decisions of the other branches, the Court clearly plays a central role in deciding how the government exercises power.
- Somewhat counter to the popular view of the Court, it is a very *political* institution. Rather than neutrally handing down decisions according to an objective standard, it regularly must resolve conflicts over alternative interpretations of the law. Politics truly is everywhere, even in the judicial system.

What is the nature of the American legal and judicial system?

- There are fundamental characteristics of the court system that distinguish the different types of cases: who can bring a case, which court has jurisdiction over the case, and what the burdens of proof are.

- The federalist nature of the U.S. government defines another important characteristic of the court system: the parallel state and federal systems.
- Within each system there is great variation in how judges are selected, but in all instances the contests over nominations reveal the political nature of the judicial branch of government.

How do cases reach the Supreme Court?

- About 1 percent of all appeals to the Supreme Court are actually heard by the Court.
- Cases may reach the Supreme Court by original jurisdiction, on appeal, or a writ of certification, but by far the most common route to the Court is through a writ of certiorari.
- Cases that are heard by the Court must be "cases and controversies" and must qualify under the rules of standing, collusion, ripeness, and mootness.
- Even after considering all of these factors, justices still have a great deal of discretion over which cases they hear.

What is the Court's process for hearing cases?

- There are several steps in the process of hearing a case before the Supreme Court. First, interested parties submit briefs to the Court outlining their arguments about how they think the case should be decided.

- Next, the Court hears oral arguments, usually thirty minutes for each side.
- After hearing the case, the justices meet in conference to discuss the case.
- Finally, the opinions are assigned and written, outlining the reasons for the Court's decision. This part of the process involves a great deal of political maneuvering and bargaining among the justices.

How does the Supreme Court make decisions?

- Supreme Court decision making is influenced by a variety of legal and political factors.
- The power of precedent and the language of the Constitution explain many decisions, especially those involving areas of settled law.

- Political factors such as justices' ideology, the strategic interactions among justices, and their views about judicial activism and restraint also come into play.
- Outside considerations, such as involvement from interest groups and the views of the public, may also influence how justices decide a specific case.

Can the Court be a policy maker?

- In some senses, the judiciary is the "weakest branch" in that it must rely on the other branches to enforce its decisions.
- Although the Court does not often check the other branches, deciding to not get involved in political questions, it may strike down actions by Congress or the president.
- Defining the proper role of the Court within our system usually depends on one's political views concerning a specific case.

Ⓢ STUDENT STUDYSPACE

Find quizzes and other review material at wwnorton.com/studyspace.

CRITICAL THINKING

1. Should suspected terrorists receive the full protections of our legal system, or should the president have more leeway to identify "enemy combatants" and prosecute them under a different set of rules?
2. Should unelected judges have the ability to overturn laws passed by the elected branches? If so, should there be any mechanism for *political* accountability?

3. What is the proper role for the Senate in providing "advice and consent" on the selection of federal judges? Should the Senate play the role of an equal partner to the president or simply approve most of the president's choices?

KEY TERMS

adversarial system (p. 475)
amicus curiae (p. 491)
appeals courts (p. 477)
appellate jurisdiction (p. 468)
attitudinalist approach (p. 497)
briefs (p. 491)
burden of proof (p. 474)
cases on appeal (p. 488)
cert pool (p. 489)
class action lawsuit (p. 475)
collusion (p. 488)
common law (p. 475)
constitutional interpretation (p. 472)
defendant (p. 474)

district courts (p. 468)
docket (p. 486)
judicial activism (p. 498)
judicial restraint (p. 498)
judicial review (p. 470)
Judiciary Act of 1789 (p. 468)
jurisdiction (p. 477)
living Constitution (p. 497)
mootness (p. 489)
oral arguments (p. 492)
original intent (p. 497)
original jurisdiction (p. 487)
plaintiff (p. 474)
plea bargain (p. 474)

precedent (p. 475)
ripeness (p. 489)
senatorial courtesy (p. 484)
solicitor general (p. 490)
standard of proof (p. 474)
standing (p. 476)
statutory interpretation (p. 472)
strict construction (p. 496)
verdict (p. 474)
writ of certification (p. 488)
writ of certiorari (p. 488)
writs of mandamus (p. 470)

SUGGESTED READING

Baum, Lawrence. *Judges and Their Audiences: A Perspective on Judicial Behavior.* Princeton, NJ: Princeton University Press, 2006.

Cornell University Law School, Supreme Court Collection, available at http://supct/law.cornell.edu/supct.

Eisgruber, Christopher L. *Constitutional Self-Government.* Cambridge, MA: Harvard University Press, 2001.

Hansford, Thomas G., and James F. Spriggs II. *The Politics of Precedent on the U.S. Supreme Court.* Princeton, NJ: Princeton University Press, 2006.

Northwestern University, Oyez: Supreme Court Multimedia, available at www.oyez.org.

O'Brien, David M. *Storm Center: The Supreme Court in American Politics,* 9th ed. New York: W. W. Norton, 2011.

Rosen, Jeffrey. *The Most Democratic Branch: How the Courts Serve America.* New York: Oxford University Press, 2006.

Sunstein, Cass R., David Schkade, Lisa M. Ellman, and Andres Sawicki. *Are Judges Political? An Empirical Analysis of the Federal Judiciary.* Washington, DC: Brookings Institution Press, 2006.

Tushnet, Mark. *A Court Divided: The Rehnquist Court and the Future of Constitutional Law.* New York: W. W. Norton, 2006.

U.S. Supreme Court Web site, available at www.supremecourt .gov.

A group of teenagers is detained and questioned by police. When is a police stop legitimate? How do we know if it might be a violation of civil rights?

Civil Rights

You are driving home one night with a few of your friends after a party. It is late at night, but you have not had anything to drink and you are following all traffic laws. Your heart sinks as you see the red flashing lights of a squad car signaling you to pull over. As the police officer approaches your car, you wonder if you have been pulled over because you and your friends are African Americans driving in an all-white neighborhood. Have your civil rights been violated?

Change the scene to a car full of white teenagers with all the other facts the same. Can an officer pull you over just because he thinks that teenagers are more likely to be engaging in criminal activity than older people? Scenario two: you are a twenty-one-year-old Asian American woman applying for your first job out of college. After being turned down for the job at an engineering firm, you suspect that you didn't get the job because you are a woman and would not fit in with the "good ol' boy" atmosphere of the firm. Have your civil rights been violated?

Scenario three: you and your gay partner are told that "your kind" are not welcome in the apartment complex that you wanted to live in. Should you call a lawyer? Scenario four: you are a white male graduating from high school. You have just received a letter of rejection from the college that was first on your list. You are very disappointed, but then you get angry when a friend tells you that one of your classmates got into the same school even though he had virtually the same grades as you and his SAT scores were a bit lower. Your friend says that it is probably because of the school's affirmative action policy—the classmate who was accepted is Latino. Are you a victim of "reverse discrimination"? Have your civil rights been violated? How about if you are a white contractor who lost a bid on a city contract to a minority-owned business because of a "set-aside" program put in place partly to reverse years of discrimination against minority-owned firms? Can you sue the city?

To answer these questions we must start with a definition of the term "civil rights." In general it means the right to be free from discrimination, but a more specific understanding of the term comes from the mission statement of the U.S. Commission on Civil Rights, a bipartisan, independent, federal commission that was established by the 1957 Civil Rights Act.[1] Its mission is to "appraise federal laws and policies," investigate complaints, and collect information with regard to citizens who are "being deprived of their right to vote," discriminated against, or

509

BIG QUESTIONS

- ✪ What are civil rights?
- ✪ What is the nature of the racial divide today?
- ✪ How has civil rights policy been made?
- ✪ What civil rights issues do we confront today, and which will be important in the future?

being denied the "equal protection of the laws under the Constitution because of race, color, religion, sex, age, disability, or national origin." It investigates government actions, such as allegations of racial discrimination in the 2000 presidential election in Florida, and the actions of individuals in the workplace, commerce, housing, and education.

Given this definition and scope of coverage, all of the scenarios above would seem to be civil rights violations. However, some of them are, some are not, and two of them depend on additional considerations. Applying civil rights law can be very complex, but consistent with our argument that American politics makes sense, one of the central goals of this chapter is to highlight and summarize the central debates concerning civil rights policy today. A second goal of the chapter is to provide a better understanding of the origins of specific civil rights by examining the policy-making process.

This chapter also illuminates the three themes of the book. As the opening scenarios illustrate, civil rights issues are very conflictual. This is evident on both a personal level (those who are affected by discrimination) and in the policy-making process. Race, gender, religion, age, and sexual orientation are often at the heart of political conflict, and the political debates over how to resolve or address those conflicts are intense. It would seem that something as fundamental as a civil right, such as freedom from discrimination in the workplace, would not be very amenable to compromise. However, Congress, the president, and the courts have to balance a variety of considerations when making civil rights policy, and this process often involves compromise. And the role that the three branches of government have in creating and enforcing these policies shows that political process matters. Finally, the opening scenarios are a good reminder that politics is everywhere: policies concerning discrimination in the workplace and in housing, and against women, minorities, gays, and the disabled, affect millions of Americans every day.

The Context of Civil Rights

Civil rights and civil liberties are often used interchangeably, but there are some important differences. Civil liberties refer to the freedoms guaranteed in the Bill of Rights, such as the freedom of speech, religious expression, and the press, and the "due process" protection of the 14th Amendment, whereas **civil rights** protect all persons from discrimination and are rooted in laws and the equal protection clause of the 14th Amendment. Another difference is that civil liberties primarily limit what the government can do to you ("*Congress* shall make no law . . . abridging the freedom of speech"), whereas civil rights protect you from discrimination both by the government and by individuals. To oversimplify a bit, civil liberties are about freedom, and civil rights are about equality.

civil rights Rights that guarantee individuals freedom from discrimination. These rights are generally grounded in the equal protection clause of the 14th Amendment and more specifically laid out in laws passed by Congress, such as the 1964 Civil Rights Act.

It is somewhat surprising that neither civil liberties nor civil rights figured very prominently at the Constitutional Convention. Equality is not even mentioned in the Constitution or the Bill of Rights. The Bill of Rights is centrally concerned with freedom, but it was not added to the Constitution until the Antifederalists made it a condition for ratification, as discussed in Chapter 2. However, equality was very much on the Founders' minds, as is made clear in this ringing passage from the Declaration of Independence: "We hold these truths to be self evident, that all men are created equal, that they are endowed by the Creator with certain unalienable rights, that among these are life, liberty, and the pursuit of happiness." Despite the broad language, this was a limited conception of equality. Jefferson's reference to "men" was an intentional oversight of the other half of the population: women had virtually no political or economic rights in the late eighteenth century. Similarly, equality did not apply to the slaves or to Native Americans. Even propertyless white men did not have full political rights until several decades after the Constitution was ratified. Therefore, equality and civil rights in the United States have been a continually evolving work in progress.

One way to gauge the awareness of different racial and ethnic groups (if not their acceptance) is to track the changes in the U.S. Census categories. The census is taken every ten years, as required by the Constitution, to gather information about the size and characteristics of the U.S. population. In 1860 Native Americans became the second ethnic minority group to be acknowledged on the census (after African Americans); however, those living on reservations or in the Indian Territories were not counted in the U.S. population for purposes of congressional apportionment until 1890. The Chinese were first listed as a separate group in 1860 only in California and then more generally in 1870; the Japanese were added in 1890; and Asian and Pacific Islander categories were included in 1910 (including Hindu, Korean, and Filipino). Although "Mexican" was designated as a race in the 1930 census and data had been collected previously on mother tongue and Spanish surnames, the first attempt to identify Hispanics comprehensively was in 1970.

The method for collecting information about race has also changed over the years. Before 1960, the census taker identified a person's race according to Census Bureau guidelines. In 1960 and 1970 a combination of direct interview and self-identification was used, and since 1980 people have identified their own race on census forms. In 2000, for the first time, people were allowed to check more than one racial category to reflect the growing reality of a multiracial United States. This evolution of census practices is significant because it shows that even though different racial groups have always been present in the United States, the way they are classified and counted varies significantly depending on the policies of a bureaucratic agency.

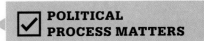

POLITICAL PROCESS MATTERS

AFRICAN AMERICANS

From the early nineteenth century, with the concerted efforts of the abolitionists, until the mid-twentieth century and the civil rights movement, the central focus of civil rights had been on the experiences of African Americans. Other groups received attention more gradually. Starting in the mid-nineteenth century, women began their fight for equal rights, and over the next century the civil rights movement expanded to include other racial and ethnic groups such as Native Americans, Latinos, and Asian Americans. Most recently, attention has turned to the elderly, the disabled, and gays and lesbians. The most divisive civil rights issue with the greatest long-term impact, however, has clearly been slavery and its legacy.

Slavery was part of the American economy and culture from nearly the beginning of our history. Dutch traders brought twenty slaves to Jamestown, Virginia,

THE COTTON GIN.

▲ Eli Whitney's cotton gin greatly increased the efficiency of cotton production by automating the process of separating the cottonseed from the raw cotton fibers, which increased the need for slaves to pick and grow the cotton.

in 1619, a year before the Puritans came to Plymouth Rock. The number of slaves remained fairly small until the late seventeenth century, when three developments greatly increased the demand for slaves from Africa. First, the growth of the southern plantation system and the increased importance of tobacco as a cash crop created a need for labor. Second, the ready supply of indentured servants decreased rapidly.[2] Then, just as the demand for slaves started to wane, Eli Whitney patented the cotton gin in 1794, which created an even greater demand for slaves. Between 1619 and 1808, when the importation of slaves was banned, about 600,000 to 650,000 slaves were imported from Africa to the United States.

It is impossible to overstate the importance of slaves to the southern economy. Slavery was everywhere in the South. The 1860 census shows that there were 2.3 million slaves in the Deep South, comprising 47 percent of the population of those states, and there were nearly 4 million slaves overall. Most slaves worked on plantations, but others worked in almost every part of the economy, as shipyard workers, carpenters, bakers, stone masons, millers, spinners, weavers, and domestic servants. In the states that would secede from the Union, 30.8 percent of households owned slaves. Nearly a majority of households owned slaves in Mississippi and South Carolina. The economic benefits of slavery for the owners were clear. By 1860, the per capita income for whites in the South was $3,978; in the North it was $2,040. The South had only 30 percent of the nation's free population, but it had 60 percent of the wealthiest men.[3]

Abolitionists worked to rid the nation of slavery as its importance to the South grew, setting the nation on the collision course that would not be resolved until the Civil War. The Founders largely ducked the issue, as was discussed in Chapter 2, and subsequent legislatures and courts did not fare much better. The **Missouri Compromise** of 1820, which limited the expansion of slavery and kept the overall balance between slave states and free states, eased tensions for a while, but the issue would not go away. Slave owners became increasingly frustrated with the success of the Underground Railroad, which helped slaves escape to the North. The debate over admitting California as a free state or a slave state (or making it half free and half slave) threatened to split the nation once again. Southern states agreed to admit California as a free state, but only if Congress passed the Fugitive Slave Act, which required northern states to treat escaped slaves as property and return them to their owners. Soon after, Congress enacted the Compromise of 1850, which overturned the Missouri Compromise and allowed each new state to decide for itself whether to be a slave state or a free state. Northern states were not pleased with the possibility of expansion of slavery in newly admitted states. All possibility of further compromise on the issue was killed by the misguided *Dred Scott v. Sandford* decision in 1857. The Supreme Court ruled that states could not be prevented from allowing slavery. It also held that slaves were property rather than citizens and had no legal rights. With Abraham Lincoln's victory in the 1860 presidential election, the southern states believed that slavery was in jeopardy, so they seceded from the Union and created the Confederacy.

The outcome of the Civil War restored national unity and ended slavery, but the price was very high. About 528,000 Americans died in the war, and the casualty rate of 25 percent among combatants is nearly four times as high as that of any other war in which American soldiers participated.[4] Republicans moved quickly to ensure that the changes accomplished by the Civil War could not be easily undone by passing and adopting the Civil War Amendments to the Constitution: the 13th banned slavery, the 14th guaranteed that states could not deny the newly freed slaves the

Missouri Compromise An agreement between pro- and antislavery groups passed by Congress in 1820 in an attempt to ease tensions by limiting the expansion of slavery while also maintaining a balance between slave states and free states.

equal protection of the laws and provided citizenship to anyone born in the United States, and the 15th gave African American men the right to vote. These amendments were ratified in the five years following the war, though southern states resisted giving the newly freed slaves anything approaching the "equal protection of the laws" over the next 100 years.

In the Reconstruction Era (1866–1877) blacks in the South gained considerable political power through institutions such as the Freedmen's Bureau and the Union League, with substantial help (some would argue manipulation and exploitation) from the Radical Republicans. When federal troops withdrew and the Republican Party abandoned the South, blacks were almost completely **disenfranchised** through the imposition of residency requirements, poll taxes, literacy tests, the **grandfather clause**, physical intimidation, and other forms of disqualification. Later the practice known as the "white primary" allowed only whites to vote in Democratic primary elections; given that the Republican Party did not exist in most southern states, blacks were effectively disenfranchised. Although most of these provisions claimed to be race neutral, their impact fell disproportionately on black voters. The most obvious of these was the grandfather clause, which was the way that illiterate whites were able to get around the literacy test.[5] Many states also had "understanding" or "good character" exceptions to the literacy tests, which gave election officials substantial discretion over who would be allowed to vote. The collective impact of these obstacles virtually eliminated black voting; for example, only 6 percent of blacks were registered to vote in Mississippi in 1890, and only 2 percent were registered in Alabama in 1906. After the last post-Reconstruction black congressman left the House in 1901, it was seventy-two years until another black represented a southern district in Congress. In Mississippi, one county in 1947 had 13,000 blacks who were eligible to vote, but only six were actually registered. Despite the constitutional guarantees of the 14th and 15th Amendments, blacks had been effectively removed from the political system in the South, and they did not have much success in winning office at any level in the rest of the nation either.[6]

The social and economic position of blacks in the South followed a path similar to their political fortunes. In the years right after the Civil War, sympathetic Republicans passed the Civil Rights Acts of 1866 and 1875, which were supposed to outlaw segregation and provide equal opportunity for blacks. However, there were no enforcement provisions, and when Reconstruction ended in 1877, southern states swiftly moved to enact "black codes" or **Jim Crow laws** that led to the complete segregation of the races. The final blow came in 1883 when the Supreme Court ruled that the 1875 Civil Rights Act was unconstitutional because Congress did not have the power to forbid racial discrimination in private business. The Court argued that the 14th Amendment addresses the actions of state governments but not private citizens. This decision was interpreted by the South as a signal that the national government was unconcerned about protecting the rights of blacks. Jim Crow laws forbid interracial marriage and mandated the complete separation of the races in neighborhoods, hotels, apartments, hospitals, schools, restrooms, drinking fountains, restaurants, elevators, and cemeteries (even dead people were not allowed to mix across racial lines). In cases where it would have been too inconvenient to completely separate the races, as in public transportation, blacks had to sit in the back of the bus or in separate cars on the train and give up their seats to whites if asked. The Supreme Court validated these practices in *Plessy v. Ferguson* (1896) in establishing the **"separate but equal"** doctrine, officially permitting segregation as long as blacks had equal facilities.

In the first several decades after Reconstruction the rest of the nation mostly ignored the plight of blacks, because at the turn of the century 90 percent of all African Americans lived in the South. But the northward migration of blacks to

disenfranchised To have been denied the ability to exercise a right, such as the right to vote.

grandfather clause A type of law enacted in several southern states to allow those who were permitted to vote before the Civil War, and their descendants, to bypass literacy tests and other obstacles to voting, thereby exempting whites from these tests while continuing to disenfranchise African Americans and other people of color.

Jim Crow laws State and local laws that mandated racial segregation in all public facilities in the South, many border states, and some northern communities between 1876 and 1964.

"separate but equal" The idea that racial segregation was acceptable as long as the separate facilities were of equal quality; supported by *Plessy v. Ferguson* and struck down by *Brown v. Board of Education*.

▲ *Jackie Robinson became the first player in the modern era to break the color barrier in major league baseball. Robinson played his first season on an all-white team in 1946 for the Brooklyn Dodgers minor-league affiliate, the Montreal Royals. He moved up to the Dodgers in 1947 and was named Rookie of the Year. He won many other honors and titles in his ten years with the Dodgers as one of the best players of his era.*

urban areas throughout the first half of the twentieth century dramatically transformed the demographic profile of the United States and changed racial politics. America's "race problem" was no longer a southern problem. Although conditions for blacks were generally better outside the South, blacks still faced discrimination and lived largely segregated lives throughout the United States. In World Wars I and II, black soldiers fought and died for their country in segregated units. Professional sports teams were segregated, and black musicians and artists could not perform in many of the leading theaters across the nation, including in northern states. Blacks were largely relegated to the lowest-paying, menial jobs.

Progress was slow, but it began in the 1940s. The Supreme Court struck down the white primary in 1944, Jackie Robinson broke the color line in major league baseball in 1947, and the U.S. armed services were integrated in 1948 by Harry Truman's executive order. The most important civil rights development of the 1940s and 1950s was the landmark decision *Brown v. Board of Education* (1954), which rejected the "separate but equal" doctrine and then in *Brown II* (1955) ordered that public schools be desegregated "with all deliberate speed." This set the stage for the growing success of the civil rights movement discussed later in this chapter.

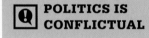

POLITICS IS CONFLICTUAL

NATIVE AMERICANS, ASIANS, AND LATINOS

The legacy of slavery and racial segregation in the South has been the dominant focus of civil rights policies in the United States, but many other groups have fought for equal rights over the past two centuries. Each racial and ethnic group in the United States has a different history of interactions with the majority white population. In general, the history is not pretty: the majority population has done some awful things to minorities in addition to the civil rights abuses of African Americans outlined above, from the systematic eradication and removal of Native Americans from huge parts of the East and Midwest, to battles with and discrimination against Mexicans in the Southwest, to the poor treatment of Asian Americans on the West Coast and then their internment during World War II. This historical review is necessary to understand today's civil rights policies, which were not created in a vacuum but, at least in part, in response to historical events and current conditions.

The Native Americans were the first group to confront the European immigrants. Though initial relations between the native population and the new arrivals were good in many places, the Europeans' appetite for more land and their insensitivity to Native American culture and traditions soon led to continual conflict. The Native Americans were systematically pushed from their land and placed on reservations. They had no political rights within the American system; indeed, through much of the nineteenth century they were considered "savages" who should be eliminated. They did not gain the universal right to vote until 1924, just after women and well after black men. However, the U.S. government signed many treaties with them that treated the tribes as sovereign nations. (The Constitution does not consider Native American tribes to be foreign nations; as one Supreme Court case put it, they were "domestic dependent nations.")[7] Most of these treaties were routinely ignored by the U.S. government, and only in recent decades has the government started to uphold its obligations—though compliance has remained spotty. Native

From the beginning of European settlement until the early twentieth century, Native Americans were continually forced from their land onto reservations. Today, many Native Americans still live on those reservations, such as the San Carlos Apache Indian Reservation in Arizona.

Americans have struggled to maintain their cultural history and autonomy in the face of widespread poverty and unemployment.

In addition to the internment of Japanese Americans during World War II (discussed more fully later in this chapter), Asian Americans have experienced various forms of discrimination since their arrival in the United States in the nineteenth century. The first wave of Chinese immigrants came with the 1848 California gold rush. In the early years, foreign miners, including the Chinese, were able to stake out their claims along with Americans. However, by 1850, when the easy-to-find gold was gone, Americans tried to drive out the Chinese through violence and the Foreign Miners Tax, which was applied in a discriminatory fashion against the Chinese. Chinese immigrants played a crucial role in building the intercontinental railroad between 1865 and 1869. Given the more difficult and dangerous jobs, as many as a thousand Chinese lost their lives. After the railroad was completed, Chinese workers returned to cities on the West Coast, where they were subjected to increasing discrimination and violence. Following several race riots, Congress passed the Chinese Exclusion Act of 1882, which prevented Chinese already in the United States from becoming U.S. citizens, but the Supreme Court later ruled that their American-born children were automatically citizens under the 14th Amendment.[8] The law also barred virtually all immigration from China—the first time in U.S. history that a specific ethnic group was singled out in this way.

Latinos have had their own long fight for political and economic equality. The early history is rooted in the Mexican-American War (1846–1848) and the conquest by the United States of much of the territory that today makes up most of the southwestern states. Since that time, Mexicans have resided in large numbers in that part of the country. While many Mexican Americans have roots that go back hundreds of years, a majority of Latinos have been in the United States for less than two generations. Consequently, Latinos have started to become a political force only recently, despite the fact that they now are the largest minority in the United States. Their relative lack of political clout when compared

Chinese immigrants played an important role in building the intercontinental railroad between 1865 and 1869. After their work on the project, they were discriminated against as they tried to assimilate into American life.

to African Americans can be explained by two factors. First, Latinos vote at a much lower rate than African Americans because of continued language barriers and the fact that about one-third of Latinos are not citizens (which is a requirement for voting in national elections). Second, unlike African Americans, Latinos are a relatively diverse group politically. Latinos include Mexican Americans, Cuban Americans, Puerto Ricans, Dominicans, and people from many other Latin American nations. Most Latino voters tend to be loyal to the Democratic Party, but a majority of Cuban Americans are strong Republicans. Although this diversity means that Latino voters do not speak with one voice, it brings opportunity for increased political clout in the future. The diversity of partisan attachments among Latinos and their relatively low levels of political involvement mean that both parties are eager to attract them as new voters.

WOMEN AND CIVIL RIGHTS

When John Adams was at the Constitutional Convention in 1787, his wife Abigail advised him not to "put such unlimited power in the hands of the husbands. Remember, all men would be tyrants if they could. . . . If particular care and attention is not paid to the ladies, we are determined to foment a rebellion, and will not hold ourselves bound by any laws in which we have no voice or representation."[9] John Adams did not listen to his wife. The Constitution did not give women the right to vote, and they were not guaranteed that basic civil right until the 19th Amendment was ratified in 1920—though sixteen states, most of them western, allowed women to vote before then. Until the early twentieth century, women in most parts of the country could not hold office, serve on juries, bring lawsuits in their own name, own property, or serve as legal guardians for their children. A woman's identity was so closely tied to her husband that if she married a noncitizen, she automatically gave up her citizenship!

The rationale for these policies was called **protectionism**, which was similar to the offensive claims made by slave owners that the slaves were actually better off on the plantations than they would be as free people. For women the argument was that they were too frail to compete in the business world and that they needed to be protected by men. This rationale was used in many court cases to deny women equal rights. For example, in 1869 Myra Bradwell requested admission to the Illinois bar to practice law. She was the first woman to graduate from law school in Illinois, the editor of *Chicago Legal News*, and held all the qualifications to be a lawyer in the state except for one—she was a woman. Her request was denied, and she sued all the way to the Supreme Court, which ruled in 1873 that the prohibition against women lawyers did not violate the 14th Amendment's privileges and immunities clause because there was no specific constitutional right to be an attorney. If the Court had stopped there, the decision would have been unremarkable for its time. But Justice Joseph Bradley went on to provide a classic example of "protectionism":

The civil law as well as nature itself has always recognized a wide difference in the respective spheres and destinies to man and woman. Man is, or should be, women's protector and defender. The natural and proper timidity and delicacy which belongs to the female sex evidently unfits it for many of the occupations of civil life. The constitution of the family organization which is founded in the divine ordinance, as well as the nature of things, indicates the domestic sphere as that which properly belongs to the domains and functions of womanhood.[10]

protectionism The idea under which some people have tried to rationalize discriminatory policies by claiming that some groups, like women or African Americans, should be denied certain rights for their own safety or well-being.

Ismail White examined another subtle influence of race on behavior: Do political ads prime racial attitudes during campaigns? Subjects watched different versions of the same presidential campaign ad for George W. Bush featuring a discussion of government spending, tax cuts, and health care reform. The ads had the same narrative, but the visual cues changed: some were neutral; some compared whites and blacks; some depicted "undeserving blacks." The neutral version showed images of the Statue of Liberty, George Bush sitting on a couch, a neighborhood with no people on the street, and hospital workers in surgical garb (so their race could not be determined). The race comparison ad showed many of those same images but also an African American counting money at the point the narrator says, "Democrats want to spend your tax dollars on wasteful government programs." As the narrator noted that Bush supports tax cuts "because you know best how to spend the money you earn," positive white images appeared. The "undeserving black" version was the same as the comparison version but without the images of white people.

After seeing the "undeserving" ad, viewers were more likely to express negative attitudes toward African Americans and toward government policies they believed

Research on campaign commercials has shown that images of African Americans counting money can prime negative racial attitudes.

would benefit African Americans than they were after seeing the "neutral" ad. Viewers of the "comparison" ad were also more likely to express negative attitudes toward African Americans. The authors concluded, "Far from being a spent force, the impact of race and racism in America can emerge from some of the most common political messages that mainstream candidates rely upon as their stock-in-trade."[b] However, they also found that when ads present blacks in a favorable light, the impact of racial attitudes declines.

These two studies suggest that the influence of race on behavior may be subtle and not readily detected if one is only looking for obviously racist behavior. However, even if one accepts the findings of these studies (and there are alternative views),[c] the policy implications of more subtle forms of racially motivated behavior are still open to debate. ■

Ⓢ **Watch a video clip of Vincent Hutchings discussing this topic at wwnorton.com/studyspace.**

midwestern city that prides itself on being tolerant and progressive. The first example represents unintentional stereotyping, while the second is clear racial discrimination. One Saturday morning one of the authors was at the checkout line at a local grocery store, and the lady ahead of him was being given a hard time by the cashier. The woman had a large basket of groceries, and the bill was well over $100. She wanted to pay for some of the groceries with food stamps and then the rest of them with a personal check. The cashier wanted to see a driver's license or two other forms of photo ID, and the lady did not have them. The author wasn't close enough to see exactly what was going on, but she had some type of ID that was not adequate. After calling over the store manager and a lot of hemming and hawing, the cashier finally accepted her check. The author unloaded his similarly sized cart of groceries and paid by check, and the cashier never hesitated. In fact, he has never been asked for identification when paying by check in that store. The author would like to reach a different conclusion, but it seemed clear that the woman and he were treated so differently because she was black and using food stamps and he is white.

The second example involved a former graduate student in our department who is white and is married to an African American woman. They wanted to rent a bigger apartment, so they searched the want ads and made appointments to see the apartments. One landlord told them to meet him in front of the apartment at a specific time the next day. They waited where they were told, but the landlord didn't show up. After thinking about it, they remembered seeing a car that slowed down and almost stopped in front of the apartment but then sped away. They realized they had been victimized by a "drive-by landlord"—that is, a landlord who checks out the race of the potential tenants from a distance; if they are not white, he or she skips the appointment and tells them it is rented if they ask. Indeed, this is exactly what happened. They called the landlord and asked what had happened and were told the apartment was rented. To check their suspicions, they had some friends call and ask about the apartment and they were told it was available. Their friends (who were both white) made an appointment to meet the landlord, and this time the same car slowed down but pulled up and stopped. The landlord showed them around the apartment and was very friendly. The next day the graduate student slapped him with a racial discrimination lawsuit (he ended up winning a small settlement).

These kinds of stories, ranging from irritating and demeaning to a serious violation of the law, could be repeated by nearly every racial minority, woman, and gay person in the United States: the well-dressed businessman who cannot get a cab in a major city because he is black, the woman who is sexually harassed by her boss but is afraid to say anything because she doesn't want to lose her job, the teenage Latino who is followed around the music store by a clerk, the Arab American who must endure taunts about the head covering she wears, or the gay couple that has trouble finding an apartment. Discrimination is far too common in the United States and clearly indicates that we have not reached the color-blind (or gender and sexual orientation neutral) society desired by advocates of civil rights.

The election of Barack Obama as the first African American president may indicate the beginning of a new era in which race is a less significant factor in elections. Obama won 43 percent of the white vote, which is more than the percentages won by the last two Democratic presidential nominees, John Kerry in 2004 and Al Gore in 2000. Nine percent of voters said that race was an important factor in their vote, but of these, 53 percent voted for Obama. Although race did not seem to have a big impact on the outcome of the election, this should not be seen as sufficient evidence that we have entered a period in which race doesn't matter.

Race did not dominate Obama's first year in office, but several incidents arose in which race became an issue. As Obama said at the end of his first year in office, "[O]n the heels of that victory over a year ago, there were some who suggested that somehow we had entered into a post-racial America. There were those who argued that because I had spoken of a need for unity in this country, that our nation was somehow entering into a period of post-partisanship. That didn't work out so well."[13]

The Racial Divide Today

In addition to the unequal treatment of racial minorities, women, and gays, a gulf remains between the objective condition of minorities and that of whites and the political views that they hold. Although substantial progress has been made in bridging that divide, the political, social, and economic condition of racial minorities is not as good as it is for whites. The political divide is mostly evident in lower levels of voter turnout among racial minorities relative to whites (however, as noted above, the gap is largest between Latinos and whites). Different rates of voter turnout can mostly be accounted for by education and income—especially between blacks and whites—but there are many examples of practices and institutions that are designed to depress minority turnout. The tactics include moving and reducing the number of polling places in minority-majority areas, changing from district-based to at-large elections, redistricting that dilutes minority voting power, withholding information about registration and voting procedures from blacks, and "causing or taking advantage of election day irregularities."[14]

The most well-known example comes from the 2000 presidential election in Florida, where the U.S. Commission on Civil Rights investigated dozens of complaints from minorities who were not allowed to vote. One target of the investigation was the "voter purge list" that the state had created to remove voters from the registration list who should not be allowed to vote. Most people on the list were supposed to be felons, who are not allowed to vote under Florida state law. The problem was that the list was created without cross-checking to make sure that the people on the list were felons. Thousands of people ended up on the list who had not committed any crime, including a disproportionate number of minorities, and they had to clear their name before they were allowed to vote. Many people did not realize the problem until Election Day, and attempts to clear up the confusion usually failed. In addition, the commission described the use of police roadblocks close to voting places in predominantly minority neighborhoods as another practice that depressed minority voter turnout. Finally, the high incidence in minority areas of "spoiled ballots" that could not be counted was not accounted for by differences in the income or education levels of voters.[15] Given that the outcome of the 2000 presidential election was decided by a few hundred votes in Florida, these efforts to depress minority turnout had an important impact on the election outcome (large majorities of African American voters supported Al Gore). Florida was not the only state in which such allegations were made. New Jersey, Missouri, Arkansas, and Louisiana also were accused of various tactics to depress minority turnout in recent elections.

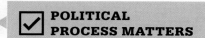

POLITICAL PROCESS MATTERS

In the 2008 elections, the Brennan Center for Justice at the New York University School of Law identified a variety of practices that could lead to voter suppression and intimidation, some of which were based on race. Three states removed voters from the voting rolls if there wasn't an identical match between the name the voter used when he or she registered to vote and the name as it appeared in another state database (often the database of driver's license information). States also used voter purges (seven states), voter challenges targeted at minority voters (five states), technical barriers to voter registration and voting (six states), student voting barriers (seven states), voter registration access (a number of states were not complying with the law that requires voter registration services at social services offices), voter intimidation and deceptive practices (fourteen states), and poor ballot design (three states).[16]

The racial divide is also evident in social and economic terms. Nearly three times as many black families are below the poverty line as white families: 25.8 percent compared to 9.4 percent in 2009. The poverty rate of 25.3 percent for Hispanic families in 2009 was similar to that of black families.[17] Furthermore, while black median household income in 2009 was $32,584, only 59.8 percent of white family income, the gap in overall wealth is much more dramatic. The average white household has nearly six times the assets of the typical nonwhite family. In 2007 the median household net worth was $170,400 for whites and $27,800 for nonwhites. Figures for Hispanics are somewhat better, but the gaps are still large. Hispanic household income was 68.3 percent of white income, $37,913 compared to $55,530.[18] Poverty is not distributed equally throughout the United States, but rather is concentrated in areas where the minority population is the highest (see Figures 14.1a and 14.1b).

FIGURE 14.1A **PERCENTAGE OF PEOPLE IN POVERTY, 2009**

Together, these maps show that the poverty rate in the United States is closely related to the minority population. How do you think these patterns might affect the politics of civil rights policies that are aimed at reducing discrimination in the workplace or housing?

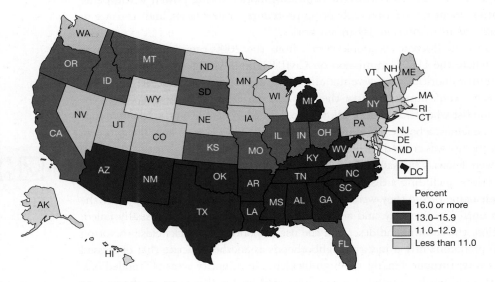

Percent
- 16.0 or more
- 13.0–15.9
- 11.0–12.9
- Less than 11.0

FIGURE 14.1B **PERCENTAGE OF THE POPULATION THAT IS WHITE, 2008**

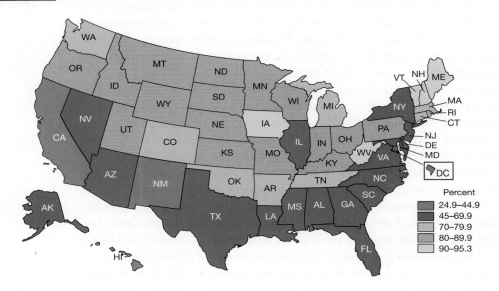

Percent
- 24.9–44.9
- 45–69.9
- 70–79.9
- 80–89.9
- 90–95.3

SOURCE: Poverty data from U.S. Census Bureau, "Poverty: 2008 and 2009 American Community Surveys," September 2010, www.census.gov/acs; race data from U.S. Census Bureau, "Annual State Resident Population Estimates for 6 Race Groups (5 Race Alone Groups and One Group with Two or More Race Groups) by Age, Sex, and Hispanic Origin: April 1, 2000 to July 1, 2008," May 14, 2009, www.census.gov/compendia/statab/2010/tables/10s0019.pdf.

Other indicators show similar patterns. The rate of black, adult male unemployment has been about twice as high as that of white adult males for the past forty-five years (which is substantially higher than the nearly equal ratio of 1.26 in 1940). In July 2010, the unemployment rate among blacks was 15.6 percent compared to 8.6 percent for whites and 12.1 percent for Latinos.[19] The other most depressing statistic on the objective position of blacks is that a little more than one-third of black children (38.1 percent) lived in two-parent households in 2009, compared to

78.1 percent of white children and 68.7 percent of Latino children. (In 1940, two-thirds of black children and 91 percent of white children lived with two parents.)[20] Blacks are more likely than whites to be victimized by crime, and some of the figures are stunning. A black male between the ages of eighteen and twenty-four is 10.5 times as likely to be murdered as a white male in that same age range.[21] On every measure of health—life expectancy, infectious diseases, infant mortality, cancer rates, heart disease, and strokes—the gaps between whites and blacks are large, and in many cases, they are growing. For example, the life expectancy for blacks is about five years shorter than for whites (73.6 years compared to 78.4), the infant mortality rate is more than double for blacks (13.69 deaths per 100,000 births compared to 5.76 for whites), and maternal mortality is more than quadruple (24.9 deaths per 100,000 births for blacks compared to 5.6 for whites). Similar gaps exist for incidence of cancer, diabetes, strokes, and heart attacks.[22]

The greatest disparity between racial minorities and whites may be in the criminal justice system. Racial profiling subjects many innocent blacks to intrusive searches. Studies have shown that blacks are not only more likely than whites to be convicted for the same crimes but that blacks also serve longer sentences.[23] In many large American cities, tensions between police departments and minority communities periodically boil over. The largest race riots since 1990 were in Los Angeles in 1992 following the acquittal of four white police officers who had been videotaped brutally beating a black man, Rodney King. The riots left 54 people dead and more than 2,000 injured and caused more than $1 billion in damage. In 1999 New York police killed Amadou Diallo, a law-abiding African immigrant, in a hail of forty-one bullets as he was standing in his own doorway. The four officers were looking for a black suspect, and when Diallo reached for his wallet, they assumed it was a gun. The African American community was outraged when the officers were acquitted. A similar killing of an unarmed black man, nineteen-year-old Timothy Thomas, by police in Cincinnati in 2001 led to three days of rioting in which dozens of people were injured and more than 800 were arrested. The officer in this case was also acquitted. More recent cases include James Dennis, who was killed by Norfolk police in October 2007, and Sean Bell, who was shot dead in November 2006 in New York City hours before his wedding. In July 2010, residents of Oakland rioted after a white transit officer was convicted only of voluntary manslaughter (rather than second-degree murder) for shooting Oscar Grant in the back as he lay facedown and unarmed on a subway platform. Civil rights advocates point out that such incidents are far too common.

African Americans and other minorities are also subjected to hate crimes much more frequently than whites. One especially gruesome murder that received national attention in 1998 involved a black man, James Byrd Jr., who was chained to the back of a pickup truck by three white men and dragged to his death. Two of the murderers were sentenced to death, and the other received life in prison. According to the FBI's hate crime statistics, of the 7,780 hate crimes in 2008, 51 percent were race related. Of these, nearly three-fourths were "anti-black," and only 17 percent were "anti-white," which means that the rate of anti-black hate crimes is more than five times what would be expected based on the percentage of African Americans in the United States, while the rate of anti-white hate crimes is about one-fourth as high as would be expected.[24]

This backdrop of racial inequality, discrimination, and violence provides continued motivation for civil rights activists to push their agenda in the three branches of government: legislative, executive, and judicial. In some instances, issues are pursued in several arenas simultaneously; in others, redress is sought in one arena after exhausting alternatives. The civil rights movement, which was crucial in the early policy successes, also continues to mobilize the grassroots. These various paths through the policy process are explored in the next section.

▲ James Byrd Jr. was murdered in Jasper, Texas, by three white supremacists who chained him to a pickup truck and dragged him down a road until he was decapitated. According to FBI statistics, in 2008 nearly three-quarters of race-related hate crimes in the United States were "anti-black."

The Policy-Making Process and Civil Rights

Our system of separated and shared powers almost ensures that each of the three branches has some say in making policy. Each branch has played a central role at different points in history, depending on the political context. For example, in the 1940s and the 1950s the courts were seen as the most sympathetic branch for advancing the civil rights agenda because segregationist southern Democrats controlled key committees in Congress and none of the presidents of this era made civil rights a top priority (though some positive steps were taken, as we discuss below). Then in the mid-1960s Congress took the lead role in civil rights policy by passing landmark legislation.

The policy-making process in the area of civil rights also provides insight into the importance of federalism. For African Americans' civil rights, the national government forced the southern states to desegregate the schools, allow blacks to vote, and generally dismantle the system of segregation, thus demonstrating the importance of nation-centered federalism. However, for gay rights—the most recent civil rights issue—state and local governments have taken the lead role while Congress has taken steps to restrict gay rights, especially on the question of gay marriage. For women's rights, both the national and state governments have taken important actions at various times.

SOCIAL MOVEMENTS

Much of our discussion of civil rights focuses on the *governmental* policy-making process, but no discussion of this topic would be complete without first noting the importance of social movements. From the early women's rights movement and abolitionists of the nineteenth century to the gay rights and civil rights movement of the mid-twentieth century, activists pressured the political system to change its civil rights policies. Through collective action, social movements put issues on the policy agenda that otherwise would have been ignored by politicians. In some cases, as with the women's movement, politicians continued to ignore demands for many years. Women started to push for the right to vote at a convention in 1848 at Seneca Falls, New York. A constitutional amendment to give women the right to vote was regularly introduced in Congress between 1878 and 1913 but never was passed, despite the efforts of women such as Susan B. Anthony and Elizabeth Cady Stanton. After a parallel movement at the state level had some success, the conditions were finally right for passing the constitutional amendment in 1919 (it was ratified in 1920). The critical moment that spurred the gay rights movement came in the early morning hours of June 28, 1969, during a routine police raid on the Stonewall Inn in New York City (police often raided gay bars to harass the patrons and selectively enforce liquor laws).[25] Rather than submitting to the arrests, the customers fought back, throwing stones and beer bottles, breaking windows, and starting small fires. A crowd of several hundred people gathered outside the bar, and the fighting raged for three nights. The Stonewall Rebellion was a galvanizing event for the gay community by demonstrating the power of collective action.

The civil rights movement of the 1950s and 1960s, aimed at ending segregation and gaining equal political and social rights for blacks, is the most famous example of a successful social movement (see Figure 14.2). The *Brown v. Board of Education* decision, which struck down the practice of segregation in public schools, gave the movement a boost, but nothing really changed in the daily lives of most blacks living in the South. White school boards and local governments resisted integration at all costs; change was not going to come easily. Black leaders became convinced that the courts could not be counted on to bring about change because of resistance to their decisions. The only way to change the laws was to get the public, both black and white, to demand change.

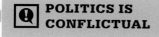
The spark that civil rights leaders had been waiting for came on December 1, 1955, in Montgomery, Alabama, when a woman named Rosa Parks refused to give up her seat on a bus to a white person, as she was required to do by law. Parks is often described as a seamstress who was tired after a long day's work and simply did not want to give up her seat. While that is true, there is a lot more to the story. Local civil rights leaders had been waiting for years for an opportunity to call a boycott of the local bus company because of its segregation policy. They needed a perfect test case—someone who would help draw attention to the cause.

Rosa Parks was just that person. She was a well-educated, law-abiding citizen who had been active in local civil rights organizations. In her book, *My Story*, Parks says, "I was not tired physically, or no more tired than I usually was at the end of a working day. . . . No, the only tired I was, was tired of giving in."[26] When she was arrested for refusing to give up her seat, local civil rights leaders organized a boycott of the bus company that lasted more than a year. Whites in Montgomery tried everything to stop the boycott, including arresting and fining blacks who arranged a complex car pooling system to get to work: people waiting for a car to pick them up were arrested for loitering, and car pool drivers were arrested for not having the right kind of insurance or having too many people in their car. Martin Luther King Jr. was elected leader of the group, and he was subjected to harassment and violence—his house was firebombed and he was arrested several times. Finally a federal district court ruled that the segregation policy was unconstitutional, and the Supreme Court upheld that ruling.

Nonviolent Protest On February 1, 1960, four black students in Greensboro, North Carolina, went to a segregated lunch counter at a local Woolworth's and asked to be served. They sat there for an hour without being served and were forced to leave when the store closed. Twenty students returned the next day, and the story

◀ Four African American college students protest at a whites-only lunch counter in Greensboro, North Carolina. These sit-ins spread throughout the South in 1960 as civil rights activists were able to put pressure on businesses to integrate through their nonviolent protests.

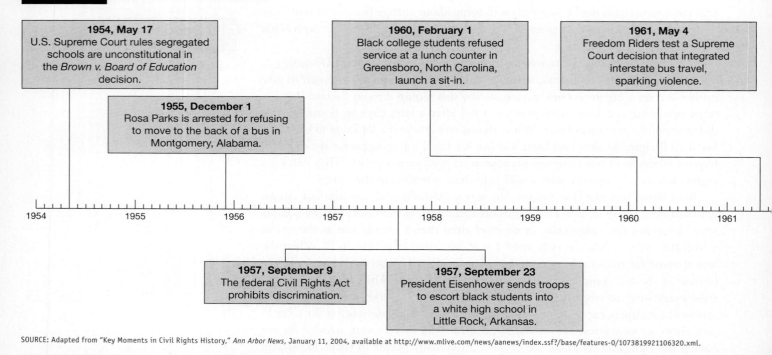

FIGURE 14.2 CIVIL RIGHTS TIMELINE

1954, May 17
U.S. Supreme Court rules segregated schools are unconstitutional in the *Brown v. Board of Education* decision.

1955, December 1
Rosa Parks is arrested for refusing to move to the back of a bus in Montgomery, Alabama.

1960, February 1
Black college students refused service at a lunch counter in Greensboro, North Carolina, launch a sit-in.

1961, May 4
Freedom Riders test a Supreme Court decision that integrated interstate bus travel, sparking violence.

1957, September 9
The federal Civil Rights Act prohibits discrimination.

1957, September 23
President Eisenhower sends troops to escort black students into a white high school in Little Rock, Arkansas.

1954   1955   1956   1957   1958   1959   1960   1961

SOURCE: Adapted from "Key Moments in Civil Rights History," *Ann Arbor News*, January 11, 2004, available at http://www.mlive.com/news/aanews/index.ssf?/base/features-0/1073819921106320.xml.

was picked up by the national wire services. Within two weeks the sit-ins spread to eleven cities. In some cases the students were met with violence; in others they were simply arrested. However, the students continued to respond to the violence with passive resistance, and there was always another wave of protesters to replace those who were arrested. The Student Nonviolent Coordinating Committee (SNCC) was created to coordinate the protests. The Greensboro Woolworth's was integrated on July 26, 1961, but the protests continued in other cities. By August 1961, the sit-ins had 70,000 participants and 3,000 arrests.[27] The sit-ins marked an important shift in the tactics of the civil rights movement away from the court-based approach and toward the nonviolent civil disobedience that had been successful in Montgomery on a smaller scale.

Another important event during this period was the effort by the Freedom Riders to get President Kennedy to enforce two Supreme Court decisions that banned segregation in interstate travel, including bus terminals, waiting rooms, restaurants, and other public facilities related to interstate travel.[28] On May 4, 1961, a group of whites and blacks boarded two buses in Washington, DC, headed for New Orleans. The whites and blacks sat together and went into segregated areas of bus stations. The trip was uneventful until Rock Hill, South Carolina, where several of the Riders were beaten. Then in Anniston, Alabama, one bus had its tires slashed and was fire-bombed. The Riders were beaten as they fled the burning bus. The second group was confronted by an angry mob at the bus station in Birmingham and severely beaten with baseball bats and iron pipes. When it became clear that police protection would not be provided, the Riders abandoned the trip and regrouped in Nashville. After much internal debate, they decided to continue the rides. After more violence in Montgomery, President Kennedy intervened, and his brother, Robert Kennedy, the attorney general, worked out a deal in which the Riders would be provided

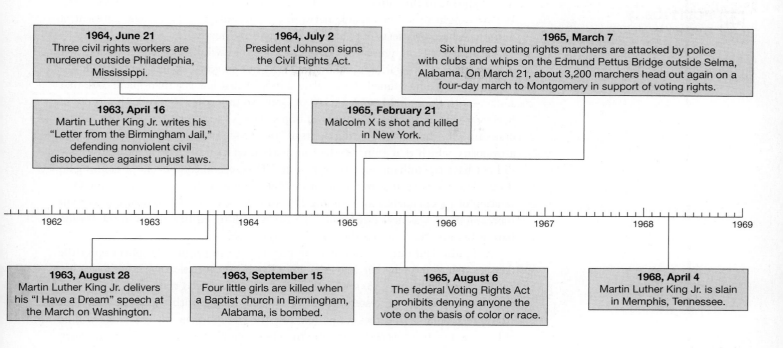

1964, June 21
Three civil rights workers are murdered outside Philadelphia, Mississippi.

1964, July 2
President Johnson signs the Civil Rights Act.

1965, March 7
Six hundred voting rights marchers are attacked by police with clubs and whips on the Edmund Pettus Bridge outside Selma, Alabama. On March 21, about 3,200 marchers head out again on a four-day march to Montgomery in support of voting rights.

1963, April 16
Martin Luther King Jr. writes his "Letter from the Birmingham Jail," defending nonviolent civil disobedience against unjust laws.

1965, February 21
Malcolm X is shot and killed in New York.

1962   1963   1964   1965   1966   1967   1968   1969

1963, August 28
Martin Luther King Jr. delivers his "I Have a Dream" speech at the March on Washington.

1963, September 15
Four little girls are killed when a Baptist church in Birmingham, Alabama, is bombed.

1965, August 6
The federal Voting Rights Act prohibits denying anyone the vote on the basis of color or race.

1968, April 4
Martin Luther King Jr. is slain in Memphis, Tennessee.

police protection, federal troops would not intervene, and the Riders would have to face the local courts upon their arrest for "disturbing the peace." The Freedom Rides continued throughout the summer. More than 350 Riders were jailed and fined, and many others sustained permanent injuries from the beatings. The Freedom Rides successfully drew national attention to the continuing resistance in the South to desegregation rulings, forced the Kennedy administration to take a stand on this issue, and led to a stronger Interstate Commerce Commission ruling banning segregation in interstate travel.[29]

The Letter from the Birmingham Jail The next significant set of events was in Birmingham, Alabama, in 1963. Birmingham had more racial violence than any southern city, with eighteen unsolved bombings of black churches and homes in a six-year period (its nickname was "Bombingham" during this period). The city had closed its parks and golf courses rather than integrate them, and there was no progress on integrating the local schools. One of the leading supporters of integration had been castrated to intimidate other blacks who might advocate the policy. The city was run by the police chief, "Bull" Connor, a strong segregationist who had allowed the attacks on the Freedom Riders. During a peaceful protest in early April 1963, Martin Luther King Jr. and many others were arrested. While in solitary confinement, King wrote his famous "Letter from the Birmingham Jail," an eloquent statement of the principles of nonviolent civil disobedience. The letter was a response to white religious leaders who had told King in a newspaper ad that his actions were "unwise and untimely" and that "when rights are consistently denied, a cause should be pressed in the courts and in negotiations among local leaders, and not in the streets." King responded, "History is the long and tragic story of the fact that privileged groups seldom give up their privileges voluntarily." In arguing for direct action, he wrote, "I cannot sit idly by in Atlanta and not be concerned about what happens in Birmingham. Injustice anywhere is a threat to justice everywhere. We are caught in an inescapable network of mutuality tied in a single garment of destiny. Whatever affects one directly affects all indirectly."

In his letter King presented the justification for civil disobedience, writing that everyone had an obligation to follow just laws but an equal obligation to break unjust laws, which he defined in two ways. First, "A just law is a man-made code that squares with the moral law of the law of God. An unjust law is a code that is out of harmony with moral law." Second, an unjust law is "a code that a majority inflicts on a minority that is not binding on itself" or "a code that a majority inflicted upon a minority which that minority had no part in enacting or creating because they did not have the unhampered right to vote." This second component of defining an unjust law is very similar to the rationale that Thomas Jefferson laid out in the Declaration of Independence for resisting British rule. The cry of "no taxation without representation" was heard from the colonists who dumped British tea in the Boston harbor because they viewed the tax on tea as unjust.

King also laid out the four steps of nonviolent campaigns: (1) collection of the facts to determine whether injustices are alive; (2) negotiation with white leaders to change the injustices; (3) self-purification, which involved training to make sure that the civil rights protesters would be able to put up with the abuse that they would receive; and (4) direct action to create the environment where change will be able to happen (such as the sit-ins and marches), but always in a nonviolent manner. By following these four steps, civil rights protesters ensured that their social movement would draw attention to their cause while turning public opinion against the violent tactics of their opponents.

King was released from jail shortly after writing his letter, but the situation escalated dramatically. The protest leaders decided to use children in the next round of demonstrations. After more than 1,000 children between the ages of six and eighteen were arrested and the jails were overflowing, the police turned powerful fire hoses and police dogs on the children who were trying to continue their march. Media coverage of the incident turned the tide of public opinion in favor of the civil rights marchers as the country expressed outrage over the violence in Birmingham. Similar protests occurred throughout the South, with more than 1,000 actions in over 100 different southern cities with more than 20,000 people arrested throughout the summer.

On June 11, 1963, President Kennedy gave a historic speech on civil rights, calling on Congress to take action. The next day Medgar Evers, a civil rights leader in Mississippi, was shot and killed in his driveway. A week later Kennedy sent his comprehensive civil rights bill to Congress that would guarantee equal social and political rights to blacks. On August 28, King delivered his "I Have a Dream" speech to a crowd of 250,000 people who had participated in the March on Washington (estimates of the crowd ranged from 200,000 to 500,000; it was clearly the largest political protest in the country's history up to that point). Two weeks later four African American girls were killed when a Birmingham church was bombed. President Kennedy was assassinated before his legislation could be passed, but the civil rights activists' courageous actions and concerted efforts over two decades played a key role in putting pressure on Congress to pass meaningful legislation. The details of this legislation are discussed later in the chapter, in the section on the legislative arena.

▼ *A fifteen-year-old civil rights demonstrator, defying an anti-parade ordinance, is attacked by a police dog in Birmingham, Alabama, on May 3, 1963. The next day, during a meeting at the White House, President Kennedy discussed this photo, which had appeared on the front page of the* New York Times. *Reaction against this police brutality helped spur Congress and the president to enact civil rights legislation.*

With the passage of this landmark legislation, large-scale activity for civil rights for African Americans started to decline. However, mass protest became the preferred tool of many social movements. Vietnam War protesters marched on Washington by the hundreds of thousands in the late 1960s and early 1970s. The women's rights, gay rights, and environmental movements have staged many mass demonstrations in Washington and other major cities. Even groups outside the traditional civil rights movement, such as the Nation of Islam, have used the tactics of mass protest. The Million Man March in October 1995 was organized by Louis Farrakhan and attracted about 400,000 to Washington, DC. Traditional civil rights leaders had distanced themselves from Farrakhan in the past because of his racist and anti-Semitic views. However, the Million Man March helped establish Farrakhan as a political force that was difficult to ignore. Most recently, large-scale demonstrations against international organizations, such as the International Monetary Fund and the World Trade Organization, and against the war in Iraq have swept the nation. Conservative activists, such as those in the pro-life movement, have also used the tactics of nonviolent protest, sit-ins, and mass demonstrations. Protests against President Obama's policies early in 2009 evolved into the "Tea Party" movement (evoking the Boston Tea Party of the American Revolution). Rooted in their opposition to high taxes and activist government, the Tea Party movement organized protests on Tax Day (April 15) that drew more than 300,000 people in 346 cities, according to the most reliable estimates. The largest protest, with 15,000 people, was in Atlanta.[30] The legacy of the civil rights movement was not only to help change unjust laws but also to provide a new tool for political action.

THE JUDICIAL ARENA

In the early years of the civil rights movement in the 1930s and 1940s, the Supreme Court provided most of the successes, especially in voting rights and desegregation. Later the attention of the Court would turn to discrimination cases in employment (in addition to cases in voting rights), and here its record was more mixed from the perspective of civil rights supporters. In two of the early voting rights cases the Court struck down the grandfather clause in 1915 and the white primary in 1944.[31] Both of these devices had prevented blacks from voting.

Challenging "Separate but Equal" in Education The National Association for the Advancement of Colored People (NAACP), which was formed in 1909 to fight for equal rights for blacks, started a concerted effort to nibble away at the "separate but equal" doctrine. Rather than tackle segregation head-on, the NAACP decided to challenge an aspect of segregation that would be familiar to the Supreme Court justices: the various ways in which states kept blacks out of all-white law schools. Another important part of the NAACP's strategy was to challenge admission practices in law schools outside the Deep South to demonstrate that segregation was not just a "southern problem" and to raise the chances for compliance with favorable Court decisions. A young attorney named Thurgood Marshall, who would later become the first African American Supreme Court justice, argued the NAACP's first successful case in 1936. This suit challenged the University of Maryland's practice of sending black students to an out-of-state law school rather than admitting them to the university's all-white law school. (The state gave black students a $200 scholarship, which was not adequate to cover the costs of tuition and travel and not available to all black students who wanted to attend law school.) The Maryland appeals court rejected this arrangement and ordered that black students be admitted to the University of Maryland law school.[32]

The Supreme Court's first ruling on these cases came two years later in a similar case from Missouri. Here, rather than providing a scholarship, the state paid the black students' tuition to attend an out-of-state school, while white students attended the in-state school tuition-free. The state defended the practice under the separate but equal doctrine, pointing out that the law schools in the adjacent states were as good as the Missouri law school and had essentially the same curriculum. The state also distinguished their case from Maryland's by arguing that Missouri had a provision for creating a law school at Lincoln University, the state school for African Americans. The Court rejected both arguments in very strong terms, saying, "We think that these matters are beside the point." They expressed skepticism that the state would ever create a black law school that was equal in quality to the white school. The bottom line was that white students could go to law school in the state and similarly qualified black students could not, which violated the 14th Amendment's equal protection of the laws.[33]

In 1948 the Court ruled that a black student had to be admitted to the state law school in Oklahoma rather than being required to wait until a "separate but equal" black law school was constructed, or alternatively no white students could be admitted to law school until the equal school was available.[34] Another case from Oklahoma ruled that black students had to be fully integrated into a graduate program rather than being required to sit in a separate row in the classroom and at separate tables in the library and cafeteria.[35] Although these cases were incremental steps toward eliminating segregation, the basic doctrine of "separate but equal" remained intact.

The next case chipped away at the principle itself. In 1950 Texas had a separate law school for black students, but it clearly was not equal to the law school for whites. When the lawsuit was brought, the law school for black students had only four part-time faculty, none of whom had offices at the school; no librarian in the law library; and a library with few of the promised books. The situation started to improve after the case was underway; the Court observed, "[The black law school] is apparently on the road to full accreditation. It has a faculty of five full-time professors; a student body of 23; a library of some 16,500 volumes serviced by a full-time staff; a practice court and legal aid association; and one alumnus who has become a member of the Texas Bar." However, and this is the crucial part of this case, the Court ruled that *this was not good enough*. There were more intangible aspects of the quality of law school that could not be measured by the number of books or faculty, such as the reputation of the school, the "position and influence of the alumni," and "traditions and prestige." This came very close to saying that "separate but equal" was a contradiction in terms, but the Court stopped just short of reaching that conclusion.[36]

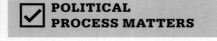

POLITICAL PROCESS MATTERS

After these victories there was a debate within the NAACP whether to continue the case-by-case approach against the separate but equal doctrine, striking down segregation where it clearly was unequal, or to directly challenge the principle itself. The latter approach was risky because it was not clear if the Court was ready to take this bold step and because defeat in the Court could set back the movement for many years. However, the signals increasingly indicated that the Supreme Court was ready to strike down the separate but equal doctrine. In addition to the law school cases, in 1948 the Court said that "restrictive covenants," clauses in real estate contracts that prevented the owner of a property from selling to an African American, could not be enforced by state or local courts because of the 14th Amendment's prohibition against a state denying blacks the "equal protection of the laws."

This application of the 14th Amendment was expanded in the landmark ruling *Brown v. Board of Education.* The case arrived on the Court's docket in 1951, was postponed for argument until after the 1952 elections, and then was reargued in

December 1953. The ruling was postponed for so long (almost three years from when it first arrived) because the Court was keenly aware of the firestorm that would ensue. In its unanimous decision the Court ruled, "In the field of public education, the doctrine of separate but equal has no place. Separate educational facilities are inherently unequal, depriving the plaintiffs of the equal protection of the laws. Segregated facilities may generate in black children a feeling of inferiority that may affect their hearts and minds in a way unlikely ever to be undone."[37] The case was significant not only because it required all public schools in the United States to desegregate but also because it used the equal protection clause of the 14th Amendment in a way that had potentially far-reaching consequences.

However, the decision was limited in its scope by focusing on segregation in schools rather than segregation more generally and by focusing on the psychological damage done to the black school children because of segregation rather than on the broader claim that racial classification itself was not allowed by the Constitution. Chief Justice Earl Warren wanted a unanimous vote and knew that two justices would not support a broader ruling that would overturn *Plessy v. Ferguson* and rule segregation unconstitutional in all contexts. Even if segregation in other public places still was legal, the Court's *Brown* ruling provided an important boost to the civil rights movement (however, see the Chapter 13 What Do Political Scientists Do? box for an argument that the courts cannot be agents of social change).

The Push to Desegregate Schools In 1955, *Brown v. Board of Education II* addressed the implementation of desegregation and required the states to "desegregate with all deliberate speed."[38] The odd choice of words, "all deliberate speed," was taken as a signal by southerners that they could take their time with desegregation. The phrase does seem to be contradictory: being deliberate does not usually involve being speedy. Southern states engaged in a concerted effort of "massive resistance" to the desegregation order, as articulated by segregationist Virginia senator Harry F. Byrd, in some cases even closing public schools rather than integrating them—and then reopening the schools as "private," segregated schools for which the white students received government vouchers. However, the ruling did have some immediate impact: Maryland, Kentucky, Tennessee, Missouri, and the District of Columbia desegregated their schools within two years.

Eight years after *Brown I*, little had changed in the Deep South: fewer than 1 percent of black children attended school with white children.[39] The Supreme Court became frustrated with the lack of progress in desegregating the schools, saying that there was "too much deliberation and not enough speed."[40] Through the 1960s the courts had to battle against the continued resistance to integration. In 1971 the Court shifted its focus from **de jure** segregation—that is, segregation that was mandated by law—to **de facto** segregation—that is, segregation that existed because of segregated housing patterns—and approved school busing as a tool to integrate schools.[41] This approach was extremely controversial in many cities. The Court almost immediately limited the application of busing by ruling in a Detroit case that busing could not go beyond the boundaries of a city's school district; that is, students did not have to be bused from suburbs to cities unless it could be shown that the school district's lines were drawn in an intentionally discriminatory way.[42] This rule encouraged "white flight" from the cities to the suburbs in response to court-ordered busing. The Supreme Court retreated further from enforcing desegregation in 1991 when it said that a school district could be released from a court-ordered desegregation plan if the district had taken "all practicable steps" to desegregate. Furthermore, districts do not have to address segregation in public schools that is caused by segregated housing.[43] The Supreme Court ruled in 1995 that low minority achievement scores are not evidence of a district's failure to

de jure Relating to actions or circumstances that occur "by law," such as the legally enforced segregation of schools in the American South before the 1960s.

de facto Relating to actions or circumstances that occur outside the law or "by fact," such as the segregation of schools that resulted from housing patterns and other factors rather than from laws.

▼ *Some of the strongest reactions against court-ordered busing as a means of public school integration were outside the South. Black students being bused to a predominantly white and Irish part of South Boston required a heavy police escort in September 1974.*

desegregate, and said that school districts cannot be forced by the courts to spend money to establish magnet schools with special programs that could attract white students from the suburbs.[44]

In what observers have called the most important decision on race in education since *Brown*, in 2007 the Court invalidated voluntary desegregation plans implemented by public school districts in Seattle and Louisville. Both districts set goals for racial diversity and denied assignment requests if they tipped the racial balance above or below certain thresholds. In a ringing endorsement of the color-blind approach, the majority opinion said, "The way to stop discrimination on the basis of race is to stop discriminating on the basis of race." In this case, the discrimination was against white students who wanted to be in schools with few minority students rather than black students who wanted to be in integrated schools. However, it was not immediately clear exactly how race could factor into school desegregation plans in the future, because only four justices signed on to the strict color-blind view. Justice Anthony Kennedy, who provided the fifth vote for some of the majority opinion, did not agree to substantial parts of it and articulated a position between the conservatives' position, that race may not be used to classify students, and the liberals' view, that racial considerations are necessary to achieve integrated schools.[45]

Expanding Civil Rights The other significant Court rulings of this period in the area of civil rights struck down state laws that forbid interracial marriages (sixteen states had such laws), upheld all significant parts of the Civil Rights Act, and upheld and expanded the scope of the Voting Rights Act. The central cases ruled Congress had the power to eliminate segregation in public places, such as restaurants and hotels, under the commerce clause of the Constitution. The first case involved a 216-room hotel in Atlanta that was close to an interstate highway, advertised extensively on the highway, and had about 75 percent of its customers from out of state. The Court ruled that this establishment was clearly engaging in interstate commerce, so Congress had the right to regulate it.[46] One aspect of this decision usually goes unnoticed: the white hotel owner claimed that his 13th Amendment rights were being violated by his being forced by Congress to serve black people. That is, he was claiming to have been forced into "involuntary servitude." The irony is pretty amazing—a white person who is discriminating against black people claiming that he was forced into slavery. The Court rejected that argument. The second case was a little more difficult. Unlike the Atlanta hotel, "almost all, if not all" of the patrons of Ollie's Barbeque in Birmingham, Alabama, were local. However, the Court pointed out that meat purchased for the restaurant came from out of state, and this comprised 46 percent of the total amount spent on supplies. Therefore, the practice of segregation would place significant burdens on "the interstate flow of food and upon the movement on products generally."[47]

The next important area of cases came in employment law. In 1971 the Court ruled that employment tests, such as written exams or general aptitude tests, that are not related to job performance and that discriminate against blacks violate the 1964 Civil Rights Act.[48] The burden of proof was placed on the employer to show that the test is a "reasonable measure of job performance" and was not simply an excuse to exclude African Americans from certain jobs. Another important aspect of this **disparate impact standard** of discrimination is that the *intent* of the company or person who is discriminating does not matter, but whether the practice has an adverse *effect* on a racial group. This decision had a tremendous impact on integrating the workplace. In 1989, however, the Supreme Court reversed itself and placed the burden of proof on the employee to show that the discriminatory practice did not result from some business necessity.[49] This obviously made it much more difficult

disparate impact standard The idea that discrimination exists if a practice has a negative effect on a specific group, whether or not this effect was intentional.

Race-Related Discrimination as Defined by the Equal Employment Opportunity Commission

Below are excerpts from the U.S. Equal Employment Opportunity Commission's publication defining race/color discrimination.

RACE/COLOR DISCRIMINATION

Race discrimination involves treating someone (an applicant or employee) unfavorably because he/she is of a certain race or because of personal characteristics associated with race (such as hair texture, skin color, or certain facial features). Color discrimination involves treating someone unfavorably because of skin color complexion. . . . Discrimination can occur when the victim and the person who inflicted the discrimination are the same race or color.

RACE/COLOR DISCRIMINATION & WORK SITUATIONS

The law forbids discrimination when it comes to any aspect of employment, including hiring, firing, pay, job assignments, promotions, layoff, training, fringe benefits, and any other term or condition of employment.

RACE/COLOR DISCRIMINATION & HARASSMENT

It is unlawful to harass a person because of that person's race or color. Harassment can include, for example, racial slurs, offensive or derogatory remarks about a person's race or color, or the display of racially-offensive symbols. Although the law doesn't prohibit simple teasing, offhand comments, or isolated incidents that are not very serious, harassment is illegal when it is so frequent or severe that it creates a hostile or offensive work environment or when it results in an adverse employment decision (such as the victim being fired or demoted). The harasser can be the victim's supervisor, a supervisor in another area, a co-worker, or someone who is not an employee of the employer, such as a client or customer.

RACE/COLOR DISCRIMINATION & EMPLOYMENT POLICIES/PRACTICES

An employment policy or practice that applies to everyone, regardless of race or color, can be illegal if it has a negative impact on the employment of people of a particular race or color and is not job-related and necessary to the operation of the business.

SOURCE: U.S. Equal Employment Opportunity Commission, "Race/Color Discrimination," www.eeoc.gov/laws/types/race_color.cfm (accessed 5/25/10).

to prove workplace discrimination, and Congress subsequently overruled the Court on this issue, as discussed below (see Nuts and Bolts 14.1 for the legal definition of race-based workplace discrimination).

The Color-Blind Court and Judicial Activism The Roberts and Rehnquist Courts of the past two decades have been gradually imposing a "color-blind jurisprudence" over a broad range of issues. One area in which the color-blind approach had a big impact was in the racial redistricting that occurred in 1992 in which fifteen new U.S. House districts were specifically drawn to help elect African Americans and ten districts were drawn to provide an opportunity to elect Latino members. This dramatic change in the number of minorities in Congress (the increase was greater than 50 percent) was rooted in the 1982 amendments to the Voting Rights Act. Instead of mandating a fair *process*, this law and subsequent interpretation by the Supreme Court in the 1980s mandated that minorities be able to "elect representatives of

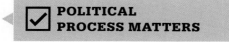

POLITICAL PROCESS MATTERS

their choice" when their numbers and configuration permitted. This shift meant that the legislative redistricting process now had to avoid discriminatory *results* rather than being concerned only with discriminatory *intent*. However, in a series of decisions starting with the 1993 landmark case *Shaw v. Reno*, the Supreme Court's adherence to a color-blind jurisprudence has thrown the constitutionality of black-majority districts into doubt. The Court has ruled that black-majority districts are legal as long as they are "done right,"[50] but it has consistently held that if race is the predominant factor in drawing district lines, the districts are unconstitutional because they violate the equal protection clause of the 14th Amendment. This line of cases struck down black-majority districts in North Carolina, Georgia, Louisiana, Virginia, Texas, and Florida. The most recent case, in 2001, upheld the redrawn 12th District in North Carolina, which no longer was black majority, arguing that when race and partisanship are so intertwined—as they are when 90 percent of African Americans vote for the Democratic candidate—plaintiffs cannot simply assume that African Americans were placed together for racial reasons. This opens the door for a greater consideration of race than had been allowed in the previous cases. However, racial redistricting is an unsettled area of the law, and many other countries have used more aggressive policies such as quotas to ensure more equal representation for minorities and women (see Comparing Ourselves to Others).[51]

The racial redistricting cases illustrate a central concern in the institutional balance of power in the policy-making process that is also of great importance to civil rights advocates: the Supreme Court is increasingly activist in civil rights. The Court is unwilling to defer to any other part of government if that branch disagrees with its view of discrimination and equal protection. Thus, as we discussed in Chapter 3, the Court was willing to overturn state laws in racial redistricting, congressional legislation with the Violence Against Women Act and the Americans with Disabilities Act (though the ruling only limited the scope of the law rather than striking it down entirely), U.S. executive branch contracting policies in cases that subjected racial "set-aside" programs to the "strict scrutiny" standard, the Florida State Supreme Court ruling on the 2000 presidential election, and California state law in a 2001 employment discrimination case.[52] This string of cases indicates that the Court's central tendency is not one of preferring state power to national power, as some have argued. Rather, it is a consistently activist assertion of judicial power over the elected institutions and a desire to have *its* interpretation of the law and of the Constitution rule rather than that of either of the other two branches. This trend illustrates that the Court's activism may be used either to further civil rights, as with the desegregation cases from the 1950s, or to limit civil rights.

Women's Rights The Supreme Court has also played a central role in determining women's civil rights. As mentioned earlier in this chapter, until relatively recently the Court did not apply the Constitution to women, despite the 14th Amendment's language that states may not deny any *person* the equal protection of the laws. Clearly women were not regarded as people when it came to political and economic rights in the nineteenth and early twentieth centuries. These protectionist notions were finally rejected in three cases between 1971 and 1976, when the Supreme Court made it much more difficult for states to treat men and women differently.

The first case involved an Idaho state law that said that a man was given priority over a woman when they were otherwise equally entitled to be the executor of a person's estate. This was justified on the "reasonable" grounds that it reduced the workload of the state courts by having an automatic rule that would limit challenges. However, the Court unanimously ruled that the law was arbitrary, did not meet the "reasonableness" test, and therefore violated the woman's equal protection

Representation of Women and Minorities

A central problem for representative democracy is to provide a voice for minority interests in a system that is dominated by the votes of the majority. The legitimacy and stability of any democracy depends, in part, on its ability to accomplish that difficult aim. The recent experiences in nation building in Iraq, Afghanistan, and Sudan provide dramatic evidence for this point: if minorities are excluded from the political process, they often resort to violence and terrorism to gain a seat at the table. The American experiment in nation building in Philadelphia in 1787 faced similar, if less severe, divisions. The Founders' institutional solution of the separation of powers within and across levels of government provided multiple points of access for various interests and some assurance that no single interest would dominate government for extended periods. Majority tyranny was prevented by a pluralist politics in which "minorities rule," to use Robert Dahl's famous phrase. However, for at least forty years, scholars and politicians have recognized that our system did not provide adequate representation for certain groups in society, especially racial minorities and women (even if women are a numerical majority in most countries, they do not control the majority of political power).[a] Our pluralist system does not deal very well with specific racial, ethnic, or gender-based interests because our electoral system is based on single-member, winner-take-all (WTA) districts where the majority (or at least the plurality) clearly rule. Some U.S. communities are experimenting with different electoral mechanisms to enhance minority representation, but many other countries have better formal representation of racial minorities and women than the United States.

Nations that have proportional representation are more likely to represent

Many nations officially require proportional representation for party lists or reserved seats (a form of quotas) to ensure more equal representation of women in electoral office. Iraq, for example, requires that 25 percent of the members of parliament are women, a policy that Iraqi politician Nisreen Barwari strongly advocated.

minority interests than those with WTA systems. Usually there is a threshold that a party must meet (often 5 percent) before it is represented in a national legislature. Therefore, any racial or ethnic group with a strong common identity could conceivably gain representation in the national legislature with as little as 5 percent of the population. Some nations, such as Germany, Denmark, and Poland, even waive the threshold if the party is representing an ethnic minority. The strongest provision for the representation of racial, ethnic, and gender-based interests in legislatures is known as "reserved communal seats." For example, Jordan reserves 18 of its 80 seats for Christians, Circassians, and Bedouins, while Taiwan reserves 8 of its 225 seats for Aboriginals. Overall, at least seventeen countries use this mechanism to promote equal representation of racial and ethnic minori-

ties and twelve use it for gender equity.[b] This system of reserved seats, which is a form of quotas, was explicitly rejected in the 1982 Voting Rights Act amendments that provided minority voters in the United States an equal opportunity to elect candidates of their choice but said that the new law should not be seen as endorsing proportional representation or quotas.

Another mechanism that is commonly used to enhance representation for women but less so for racial and ethnic minorities is requiring that a certain percentage of candidates on the party list are women. In Iraq, for example, where women did not serve in public office under the previous regime, the Iraqi constitution requires that at least 25 percent of the seats in parliament are held by women. As it turned out, in the March 2010 elections, 25.5 percent of the seats in the new parliament went to women. Twenty-three nations have party list requirements for women ranging from 50 percent to 5 percent. Ensuring representation of different racial and ethnic groups can also be an important mechanism for bringing peace to war-torn areas: Bosnia, Cyprus, Rwanda, Fiji, Sri Lanka, Zimbabwe, Kosovo, Macedonia, Afghanistan, and Iraq have all produced power-sharing settlements that require a certain number of seats for the various factions within their nations.

Finally, it is important to note that WTA systems can incorporate reserved seats into their system of district elections. India, Pakistan, and Samoa, among others, provide representation for minority interests through reserved seats even if they have single-member-district WTA elections. As the United States continues to struggle with issues of how to best represent its increasingly diverse electorate, it may learn some valuable lessons from other nations that have used a variety of techniques for many decades. ■

reasonable basis test The use of evidence to suggest that differences in the behavior of two groups can rationalize unequal treatment of these groups, such as charging sixteen- to twenty-one-year-olds higher prices for auto insurance than people over twenty-one because younger people have higher accident rates.

intermediate scrutiny test The middle level of scrutiny the courts use when determining whether unequal treatment is justified by the effect of a law; this is the standard used for gender-based discrimination cases and for many cases based on sexual orientation.

strict scrutiny test The highest level of scrutiny the courts use when determining whether unequal treatment is justified by the effect of a law. It is applied in all cases involving race. Laws rarely pass the strict scrutiny standard; a law that discriminates based on race must be shown to serve some "compelling state interest" in order to be upheld.

▼ In 2008 Army PFC Monica Brown was awarded the Silver Star for courage under fire while serving in Afghanistan. The number of women in the armed forces has increased in recent decades, but a 1981 Supreme Court ruling still allows the military to maintain male-only draft registration.

rights under the 14th Amendment.[53] The second case involved a female Air Force officer who wanted to count her husband as a dependent for purposes of health and housing benefits. Under the current law a military man could automatically count his wife as a dependent, but a woman could claim her husband only if she brought in more than half the family income. The Court struck down this practice, saying protectionist laws "in practical effect, put women not on a pedestal, but in a cage."[54]

These two cases still relied on the **reasonable basis test** for the discrimination between men and women. It wasn't until 1976 that the Court established the new **intermediate scrutiny test** in a case involving the drinking age. In the early 1970s some states had a lower drinking age for women than for men on the "reasonable basis" that eighteen- to twenty-year-old women are more mature than men of that age (states argued that women were less likely to be drunk drivers and less likely to abuse alcohol than men). The new intermediate scrutiny standard meant that the government's policy must be "substantially related" to an "important government objective" to justify the unequal treatment of men and women, so the law was struck down.[55]

Before this case only two standards were used to apply the 14th Amendment to different categories of people: the reasonable basis test and the strict scrutiny test. Racial minorities received the strongest protection as the "suspect classification" where the **strict scrutiny test** is applied. Under this test there must be a "compelling state interest" to discriminate among people if race is involved. The suspect classification was first used in a case involving the internment of Japanese Americans during World War II. It is one of the few instances in which racial classification has survived strict scrutiny. In a controversial ruling, the Court said that the internment camps were justified on national security grounds.[56] The only other test before the new intermediate one said that it was acceptable to discriminate against a group of people as long as there was a "reasonable basis" for that state law (such as the efficiency argument made by the state of Idaho in the case involving control of an estate). Today, for example, states can pass a twenty-one-year-old drinking law on the grounds that traffic fatalities will be lower with a twenty-one-year-old drinking age rather than allowing eighteen-year-olds to drink.

The intermediate scrutiny test gives women stronger protections than the reasonable basis test, but it is not quite as strong as strict scrutiny. To use the legal jargon, the gender distinction would have to serve an "important government objective," but not a "compelling state interest," in order to withstand intermediate scrutiny. Some distinctions between men and women are still allowed. For example, in 1981 the Supreme Court said that gender differences influence combat roles and military needs and therefore justify male-only draft registration. This issue has not been relevant in recent years because of the all-volunteer armed services, but it would become relevant again if the draft were reinstated.[57]

In many instances, as with the Idaho case, the rights of women were strengthened by the new standard of equal protection. However, in other instances the rights of women and men were equalized by making things worse for women. For example, in the drinking age case, instead of dropping the drinking age for men to eighteen, states raised the age for women to twenty-one. Similarly, the Court struck down an Alabama divorce law in which husbands but not wives could be ordered to pay alimony.[58] Arguably women would have been better off in these two specific instances under the old discriminatory laws (because they could drink at eighteen instead of twenty-one and did not have to pay alimony in some states). However, the more aggressive application of the 14th Amendment for women was an important step in providing them the equal protection of the laws, as clearly shown in a Court decision that struck down the Virginia Military Institute's male-only admission policy. The majority opinion stated that VMI violated the 14th Amendment's equal protection clause because it failed to show an "exceedingly persuasive justification" for its sex-biased admissions policy.[59]

Two other areas where the Supreme Court helped advance women's rights were affirmative action and protection against sexual harassment. In 1987 the Court approved affirmative action in a case involving a woman who was promoted over a man despite the fact that he scored slightly higher than she did on a test. The Court ruled that this was acceptable to make up for past discrimination.[60] The Court made it easier to sue employers for sexual harassment in 1993, saying that a woman did not have to reach the point of a nervous breakdown before being able to claim that she was harassed; it was enough to demonstrate a pattern of "repeated and unwanted" behavior that created a "hostile workplace environment."[61] Later rulings stated that if a single act is flagrant the conduct did not have to be repeated to create a hostile environment. This was the standard used by Paula Jones to bring a lawsuit against President Clinton. She alleged that as governor of Arkansas, Clinton invited her to his hotel room and then exposed himself to her and asked her to perform oral sex (Jones was a state employee at the time, which is why she could argue that this incident was related to workplace harassment). The case was eventually settled out of court, but not before testimony in the case dredged up the Monica Lewinsky affair, which nearly brought down the Clinton presidency.

As with civil rights for minorities, the Court has also restricted the rights of women in some instances. In 1984 the Court ruled that Title IX of the Education Amendments of 1972, which prohibits sex discrimination in "any education program or activity receiving Federal financial assistance," applied to private colleges and universities in which students received federal financial aid. However, in a blow to equal treatment for women, the Court said that only the specific program that received federal funds could not discriminate, rather than the institution as a whole. This ruling released many athletic programs from their obligation to provide equal opportunity for women athletes.[62] Congress overturned this ruling with the Civil Rights Restoration Act, which was passed in 1988 over a veto by Ronald Reagan. More recently, Lilly Ledbetter sued Goodyear Tire and Rubber Company for receiving lower pay than men for the same work over a twenty-year period, which she claimed was gender discrimination. However, the Court rejected her claim, saying that she did not meet the time limit required by the law, as the discrimination must have occurred within 180 days of the claim. Dissenters in the case pointed out pay discrimination usually occurs in small increments over long periods of time, so it would be impossible to recognize the discrimination within 180 days (in this instance, there was a 40 percent difference between Ledbetter's pay and that of her male colleagues after twenty years). Furthermore, workers do not have access to information about their fellow workers' pay, so it would be almost impossible to meet the standard set by the Court. The long-standing policy of the Equal Employment Opportunity Commission (EEOC) was that each new paycheck restarted the 180-day clock as a new act of discrimination, but the Court overturned that policy, making it almost impossible to sue for discriminatory pay based on gender or race under the Civil Rights Act.[63] Congress overturned this decision and restored the old standard in January 2009 by passing the Lilly Ledbetter Fair Pay Act. It was the first act signed by President Obama. As shown in Figure 14.3, significant pay disparities between men and women remain throughout much of the United States.

Recent verdicts won by the EEOC include a $19 million settlement that Outback Steakhouse agreed to pay in a sex discrimination and "glass ceiling" lawsuit. Thousands of female employees at hundreds of restaurants alleged they were denied equal opportunities for advancement. The EEOC has also won large settlements for

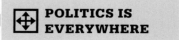

POLITICS IS EVERYWHERE

FIGURE 14.3 WOMEN'S EARNINGS AS A PERCENTAGE OF MEN'S EARNINGS, 2007

There is a substantial difference between women's and men's earnings in the United States. What could account for this variation? How much do you think it has to do with levels of discrimination and how much with differences in the nature of the jobs that men and women hold?

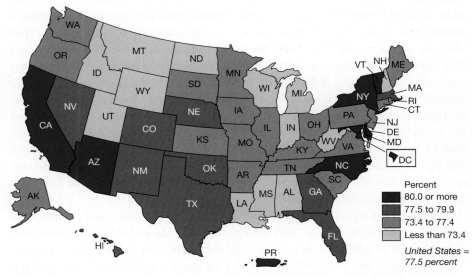

Percent
- 80.0 or more
- 77.5 to 79.9
- 73.4 to 77.4
- Less than 73.4

United States = 77.5 percent

SOURCE: Alemayehu Bishaw and Jessica Semega, "Income, Earnings, and Poverty Data from the 2007 American Community Survey," U.S. Census Bureau, August 2008, available at www.census.gov/prod/2008pubs/acs-09.pdf.

▼ *Betty Dukes, a plaintiff in a sexual discrimination lawsuit—the largest in the nation's history—filed against Walmart, leaves a San Francisco courthouse with her attorney. Walmart lost its appeal to remove the class-action status for plaintiffs and will face billions of dollars in damages if it loses the case.*

sexual harassment and pay discrimination in recent years against FedEx, Jack in the Box, Dunkin' Donuts, Ruby Tuesday, IHOP, and dozens of other corporations.[64]

The largest sexual discrimination lawsuit in the nation's history was filed in 2001 against Walmart, and as of 2010 it is still in the federal courts. The suit gained class-action status in 2004 on behalf of the 2 million women who have worked at Walmart since 1998. In April 2010, the Ninth Circuit Court of Appeals denied Walmart's argument that there are too many differences across the 2 million women to comprise a coherent class, so the case is moving forward. Among other things, the plaintiffs in the case allege the following:

- Over objections from a female executive, senior management regularly referred to female store employees as "little Janie Qs" and "girls."
- Female managers were required to go to Hooters sports bars as well as strip clubs for meetings and office outings.
- A Sam's Club [Walmart's warehouse retail chain] manager in California told another woman that she should "doll-up" to get promoted.
- Managers have repeatedly told female employees that men "need to be paid more than women because they have families to support."
- A male manager in South Carolina told a female employee that "God made Adam first, so women would always be second to men."
- A female manager in Arizona was told she got paid less than a less qualified male because she "didn't have the right equipment."

- A female personnel manager in Florida was told by her manager that men were paid more than women because "men are here to make a career and women aren't. Retail is for housewives who just need to earn extra money."[65]

Walmart's liabilities could be in the billions of dollars if it were to lose the case.

Gay Rights The Supreme Court has a similarly mixed record on gay rights. The early cases were not supportive of gay rights. One of the first concerned Georgia's law banning sodomy. The Supreme Court ruled in *Bowers v. Hardwick* that homosexual behavior was not protected by the Constitution, and state laws banning it could be justified under the most lenient "reasonable basis" test.[66] In other recent cases the Supreme Court sidestepped the controversial issue of gay rights, choosing alternative constitutional grounds to reach its decisions. For example, in 1995 the Court ruled that the South Boston Allied War Veterans Council did not have to let the Irish-American Gay, Lesbian, and Bisexual Group of Boston march in its St. Patrick's Day parade because of the veterans' 1st Amendment rights of free expression, thus ignoring the alternative "equal protection" claim made by the gay group.[67] A similar ruling held that the Boy Scouts of America did not have to admit an "avowed homosexual" as an assistant scoutmaster and ruled that New Jersey's public accommodations law did not require them to do so because of the Boy Scouts' 1st Amendment right of expressive association.[68]

In the first endorsement of civil rights for gays, the Supreme Court struck down an amendment to the Colorado state constitution that would have prevented gays from suing for discrimination in employment or housing. The Court said that gays' equal protection rights were violated by the state amendment because it "withdrew from homosexuals, but no others, specific legal protection from the injuries caused by discrimination."[69] The Court explicitly rejected the "reasonable basis" arguments made by the state and came close to putting gays in the "suspect classification" that has been restricted to racial and ethnic minorities.

An even more important ruling came seven years later in a case involving two Houston men. John Geddes Lawrence and Tyron Garner were prosecuted for same-sex sodomy after police entered Lawrence's apartment—upon receiving a false tip about an armed man in an apartment complex—and found the two having sex. Under Texas law, sodomy was illegal for gays but not for heterosexuals. In a landmark 6–3 ruling, the Supreme Court said that the liberty guaranteed by the 14th Amendment's due process clause allows homosexuals to have sexual relations. "Freedom presumes an autonomy of self that includes freedom of thought, belief, expression, and certain intimate conduct."[70] This reasoning is rooted in the **substantive due process doctrine** that serves as the basis for the constitutional protections for birth control, abortion, and decisions about how to raise one's children. The decision explicitly overturned *Bowers v. Hardwick*, and the majority opinion had harsh words for that decision, saying it "was not correct when it was decided, and it is not correct today." Five members of the majority signed onto the broad "due process" reasoning of the decision, while Justice O'Connor wrote a concurring opinion in which she agreed that the Texas law was unconstitutional but on narrower grounds. With the broader due process logic, a total of thirteen state laws that banned sodomy were struck down. Justice Scalia wrote a strong dissent and took the unusual step of reading part of his dissent from the bench when the decision was announced. He said the decision was "the product of a court that has largely signed on to the so-called homosexual agenda" and warned that the ruling "will have far-reaching implications beyond this case." He predicted that the ruling will serve as the basis for constitutional protections for gay marriage.

substantive due process doctrine One interpretation of the due process clause of the 14th Amendment; in this view the Supreme Court has the power to overturn laws that infringe on individual liberties.

The Supreme Court has yet to rule on gay marriage, but California may provide the test case. In November 2008, California voters narrowly passed Proposition 8, striking down the state's gay marriage law. In August 2010, a federal district court struck down Proposition 8, but gay marriage in California is still on hold until appeals to that ruling are decided.

This summary of cases demonstrates that the courts can be a strong advocate of and impediment to civil rights. In general, however, the courts have a limited *independent* impact on policy. As Alexander Hamilton pointed out in *Federalist 78*, the Supreme Court has "neither the power of the purse nor the sword." That is, it must rely on the other branches of government to carry out its policy decisions, as the school desegregation cases so clearly demonstrate.

THE LEGISLATIVE ARENA

The bedrock of equal protection that exists today stems from landmark legislation passed by Congress in the 1960s—namely, the 1964 Civil Rights Act, the 1965 Voting Rights Act, and the 1968 Fair Housing Act. President Kennedy was slow to work actively for civil rights legislation for fear of alienating southern Democrats. The events in Birmingham prompted him to act, but he was assassinated before the legislation was passed. President Lyndon Johnson, a native Texan and former segregationist, helped push through the Civil Rights Act when he became president. The Civil Rights Act barred discrimination in employment based on race, sex, religion, or national origin, banned segregation in public places, and set up the EEOC as the enforcement agency for the legislation. One of the southern opponents of the legislation inserted the language referring to sex, thinking that it would defeat the bill (figuring, perhaps, that there would be a majority coalition of male chauvinists and segregationists), but it became law anyway.

The Voting Rights Act of 1965 (VRA) eliminated direct obstacles to minority voting in the South such as discriminatory literacy tests and other voter registration tests and also provided the means to enforce the law: federal marshals were charged with overseeing elections in the South, something that had not happened since Reconstruction. The VRA is often cited as one of the most significant pieces of civil rights legislation passed in our nation's history.[71] President Johnson compared the critical events at Selma, Alabama, in which voting rights marchers were brutally attacked by police with clubs and whips on the Edmund Pettus Bridge, and which helped provide impetus for passage of the VRA, to the American Revolution and the Civil War. He cited all three as moments when "history and fate meet at a single time in a single place to shape a turning point in man's unending search for freedom."[72] After its passage, President Johnson hailed the VRA as a "triumph for freedom as huge as any ever won on any battlefield."[73] The VRA precipitated an explosion in black political participation in the South. The most dramatic gains came in Mississippi, where black registration increased from 6.7 percent before the VRA to 59.8 percent in 1967. As one political scientist noted, "The act simply overwhelmed the major bulwarks of the disenfranchising system. In the seven states originally covered, black registration increased from 29.3 percent in March, 1965, to 56.6 percent in 1971–72; the gap between black and white registration rates narrowed from 44.1 percentage points to 11.2."[74] The last piece of landmark legislation, the Fair Housing Act of 1968, barred discrimination in the rental or sale of a home.

There have been many amendments to these laws since the 1960s. The most important changes were the 1975 amendments to the VRA that extended coverage of many of the provisions of the law to language minorities; the 1982 VRA amendments, which extended important provisions of the law for twenty-five years and made it easier to bring a lawsuit under the act; the 1991 Civil Rights Act; and the 2006 extension of the VRA for another twenty-five years. The 1991 law overruled or altered parts of twelve Supreme Court decisions that had eroded the intent of Congress when it passed the civil rights legislation. It expanded earlier legislation and increased the costs to employers for intentional, illegal discrimination. Two of the central debates were over the standard that had to be met in discrimination cases and where the burden of proof should lie: on the employer or on the employee. After vetoing an earlier version of the bill, President George H. W. Bush ultimately agreed that the burden of proof should be on the employer. Thus, the central question was how to define the discriminatory standard. Democrats in Congress pushed for a relatively tough standard that discrimination be "essential to business practice" in order to be permitted. For example, if a university required all assistant professors to have a Ph.D., and it could be shown that more white applicants had Ph.D.s than minority applicants, the university would have the burden of proof to demonstrate that the Ph.D. was essential for doing the job. President Bush wanted a less stringent standard of "legitimate business objectives." Congress ended up adopting language that was somewhere in between: the employer must show that the practice is "job related for the position in question and consistent with business necessity."

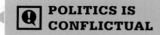

POLITICS IS CONFLICTUAL

Women have also received extensive protection through legislation. As noted above, Title VII of the Civil Rights Act, which barred discrimination based on gender, was almost an accidental part of the bill (given that it was included by an opponent to the legislation). Indeed, the first executive director of the EEOC would not enforce the gender part of the law because it was a "fluke." In 1966 the National Organization for Women (NOW) was formed to push for enforcement of the law. Its members convinced President Johnson to sign an executive order that eliminated sex discrimination in federal agencies and among federal contractors, but it was difficult to enforce. Finally in 1970 the EEOC started enforcing the law. Before long, one-third of civil rights cases involved sex discrimination, and those numbers have remained quite high in recent years (see Figure 14.4). In a breakthrough case in 1970, AT&T had to give its female workers $38 million in back pay because they had received lower wages than men for doing the same work.

Congress passed the next piece of important legislation for women in 1972: Title IX of the Higher Education Act. This law prohibits sex discrimination in institutions that receive federal funds and has had the greatest impact in women's sports. In the 1960s and 1970s the opportunities for women to play sports in college or high school were extremely limited. Very few scholarships were set aside for women at the college level, and budgets for women's sports were tiny when compared to the budgets for men. Though it took nearly thirty years to reach its goal of parity between men and women, most universities are now in compliance with Title IX. Though the law has clearly been a great benefit for women athletes, it has its critics. Many men's sports, such as baseball, tennis, wrestling, and gymnastics, were cut at universities that had to bring the number of student athletes into rough parity (partly because the football program at most schools is so large). Critics argued that such cuts were not fair, especially given that the interest in women's sports was not as high. Defenders of the law argue that the gap in interest in women's and men's sports will not change until there is equal opportunity. There is some evidence to support that claim, as the interest is increasing in women's soccer and professional basketball with the WNBA, as well as continued interest in well-established women's professional sports such as golf and tennis.

The other significant effort on behalf of women's rights during this period was the failed Equal Rights Amendment to the Constitution. The amendment passed

▼ In November 2006, students from James Madison University rallied outside the Department of Education in Washington, DC, to protest the university's plan to cut ten of its men's athletic teams. The cuts were made to bring the school into compliance with the federal law requiring equity in men's and women's sports.

FIGURE 14.4 **DISCRIMINATION CASES IN THE EQUAL EMPLOYMENT OPPORTUNITY COMMISSION, 2009**

Discrimination based on race and on sex are the two types that are most frequently reported, but there is a significant amount of discrimination based on age and disability as well. What types of discrimination do you think would be most likely to go unreported?

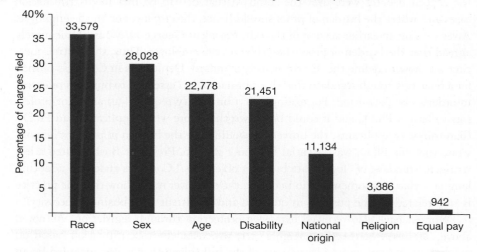

Note: Percentages do not sum to 100 because complaints may be filed in more than one category.

SOURCE: U.S. Equal Employment Opportunity Commission, Charge Statistics, available at www.eeoc.gov/eeoc/statistics/enforcement/charges.cfm.

in 1972 (it was first introduced in Congress in 1923!) and was sent to the states for ratification. The wording of the amendment was very simple: "Equality of rights under the law shall not be denied or abridged by the United States or any state on the account of sex." Many states passed it within months, but the process lost momentum, and the amendment fell three states short of the required thirty-eight states after the required seven years. The amendment received a three-year extension from Congress but still did not get the additional three states.

In 1994 Congress passed the Violence Against Women Act, which allowed women who were the victims of physical abuse and violence to sue in federal court. As mentioned above, this law was overturned by the Supreme Court, which ruled that Congress had exceeded its powers under the commerce clause.[75]

The other most important piece of civil rights legislation in recent years was the 1990 Americans with Disabilities Act, which provided strong federal protections for the 45 million disabled Americans. The law included tough language on workplace discrimination and access to public facilities. This law produced the curb-cuts in sidewalks, access for wheelchairs to public buses and trains, special seating in sports stadiums, and many other changes that have made the daily lives of the disabled a little easier and that provide them an equal opportunity to participate more fully in society. The scope of the law was narrowed by the Supreme Court when it ruled that it did not apply to state employees.[76]

Congress's track record in protecting gay rights is not quite as strong. In fact, most of the steps taken by Congress have been to restrict rather than expand gay rights. In 1996 Congress reacted to the possibility that some liberal states such as Hawaii would allow gay marriage by passing the Defense of Marriage Act. Its concern was rooted in the "full faith and credit clause" of the Constitution, which says that all states have to respect the laws of other states. So if gay marriages were allowed in one state, all other states would have to recognize that marriage as legal if the couple were to move to another state. President Clinton signed the bill even though he considered it unnecessary.

More recently Congress has proposed an amendment to the Constitution that would ban gay marriage. Acting on the fears expressed by Justice Scalia, members of Congress were concerned that the Supreme Court may strike down the Defense of Marriage Act. President George W. Bush endorsed the amendment, and Democrats have criticized it as a divisive gimmick to appeal to the conservative base of the Republican Party. President Obama opposes the amendment, and while the Democrats are in control of Congress, any action on the amendment is unlikely.

In what may represent a change of course, in October 2009 Congress passed the Matthew Shepard and James Byrd, Jr. Hate Crimes Prevention Act, which expanded the previous hate crime laws based on race, color, religion, or national origin to include attacks based on a victim's sexual orientation, gender identity, or mental or physical disability. The law also lifted a requirement that a victim had to be attacked while engaged in a federally protected activity, such as attending school, for it to be a federal hate crime. In signing the bill, President Obama said, "After more than a decade of opposition and delay, we've passed inclusive hate crimes legislation to help protect our citizens from violence based on what they look like, who they love, how they pray or who they are."[77] The law commemorates the horrific murders of James Byrd Jr. (mentioned earlier) and Matthew Shepard, a gay teenager who in 1998 was beaten by two men, tied to a fence, and left to die.

THE EXECUTIVE ARENA

The civil rights movement has also benefited greatly from presidential action, such as President Truman's integration of the armed services in 1948, and President Eisenhower's use of the National Guard to enforce a court order to integrate Central High School in Little Rock, Arkansas, in 1957. Executive orders by presidents Kennedy and Johnson in 1961 and 1965, respectively, established affirmative action; and in 1969 Richard Nixon expanded the "goals and numerical ranges" for hiring minorities. The most significant unilateral action taken by a president in the area of civil rights for gays was President Clinton's effort to follow through on his campaign promise to end the ban on gays in the military. Clinton was surprised by the strength of the opposition to his plan, so he ended up crafting a compromise policy of "don't ask, don't tell," which pleased no one. Under this policy the military would stop actively searching for and discharging gays from the military ranks, and recruits would not need to reveal their sexual orientation. However, if without an investigation the military somehow found out a person was gay, he or she still could be disciplined or discharged.

During the 2008 campaign, President Obama promised to repeal "don't ask, don't tell." In May 2010, the House voted to end the policy, 234 to 194, but the Senate fell four votes short of ending a Republican filibuster (56 to 43), so the effort to repeal the policy failed.

The low priority that recent presidential candidates have given to civil rights policy more generally means that it is less likely that significant and dramatic change will come from unilateral action by the president. Instead, attention to civil rights concerns in the executive branch has primarily been in two areas since 1993: racial diversity in presidential appointments and use of the bully pulpit to promote racial concerns and interests.

President Clinton excelled on both of these dimensions. In 1992, as a presidential candidate, Clinton promised a government that "looks like America." Clinton's cabinet, subcabinet, and judicial appointments achieved the greatest gender and racial balance of any in history. Fourteen percent of Clinton's first-year presidential appointments were African American (compared to 12 percent of the population in 1992), 6 percent were Hispanic (compared to 9.5 percent of the population), and the percentage of Asian American and Native American appointees was identical to their proportions in the population. Clinton truly delivered an administration that "looked like us" (the proportion of women appointees—27 percent—is well short of their proportion in the population, but it still was a record high). President Clinton also used the bully pulpit to advocate a civil rights agenda. For example, when affirmative action came under attack from the courts, he advocated an approach of "mend it, don't end it." More significant was Clinton's sustained effort to promote a "National Conversation on Race." Many critics dismissed the effort as empty symbolism, but Clinton's Race Initiative did help focus national attention on many of the problems faced by minorities.

President George W. Bush did not achieve the same level of diversity in his appointments as Clinton, but his administration was more diverse than that of other Republican presidents. His initial nineteen cabinet and cabinet-rank appointments included fifteen men, four women, and six racial minorities. The rhetoric that surrounded these appointments, however, was not couched in terms of affirmative action, but rather merit. Critics argued that gender and race played a central role in these decisions, just as they did with Clinton, even if the rhetoric had a different tone. Despite the different approach, President Bush made serious overtures to minorities, especially Latinos, in his effort to expand the base of the Republican Party.

Although it is too early to know the impact of the Obama presidency on the civil rights movement, the historical significance of his successful campaign is clear. At the 2008 Democratic National Convention, some African American delegates openly wept as Obama accepted the party's nomination. Many delegates had not expected that they would live to see an African American become a strong contender for the presidency. Like his predecessors, Obama nominated a diverse cabinet with fourteen men, seven women, and seven racial minorities. But in general, Obama tried to downplay race and not make it central to his governing style. In a few instances race asserted itself onto the agenda, as when Obama publicly rebuked a

▲ President Obama's cabinet is one of the most demographically diverse in our nation's history. Having political leaders who "look like us" as a nation is an important part of descriptive representation.

police officer for arresting one of the most eminent African American scholars in the nation, Henry Louis Gates Jr. of Harvard University, as he was trying to get his front door unstuck (the police officer thought he was breaking into the house). That flap died away after Obama hosted a "beer summit" with the officer and Professor Gates at the White House. Racially insensitive comments by Senate Majority Leader Harry Reid caused another brief firestorm that quickly subsided after Obama accepted Reid's apology. Some argue that Obama's victory signals the beginning of a new "post-racial politics" that places less emphasis on race and devotes more attention to issues that concern all Americans, such as the economy, education, and heath care. However, as noted above, Obama himself rejects this view.

Continuing and Future Civil Rights Issues

There is vigorous debate over the future direction of the civil rights movement as it moves into the new century. There are three main perspectives. The first group, whose views are articulated by such scholars as Stephan Thernstrom of Harvard University and Abigail Thernstrom of the Manhattan Institute, has suggested that our nation must "move beyond race." This group argues that on many social and economic indicators, the gap between blacks and whites has narrowed and that public opposition to race-based policies indicates that a new approach is needed. The Supreme Court has largely endorsed this view by implementing a "color-blind jurisprudence" over a broad range of issues. The second group is represented by traditional civil rights activists and groups such as the Congressional Black Caucus and the NAACP; it argues that the civil rights movement must continue to fight for the equality of opportunity by enforcing existing law and pushing for equality of outcomes by protecting and expanding racially targeted affirmative action programs and other policies that address racial inequality. These first two groups share the goal of racial equality and integration but differ on how much progress we have made in achieving those goals and how to make further progress. A final group does not support the goal of integration; instead, activists in this group, such as Louis Farrakhan and the Nation of Islam, argue for African American self-sufficiency and separation. They believe that African Americans can never gain equality within what they see as the repressive, white-dominated economic and political system.

A large majority of civil rights advocates endorse the second view. They argue that it would be a mistake to conclude that racial politics has become inconsequential at the turn of the new century in the United States or that the work of the civil rights movement is complete. They point to the resegregation of public schools, persistent gaps between whites and racial minorities in health and economic status, racial profiling, hate crimes, a backlash against immigrant groups, and continuing discrimination in employment and housing as ample evidence that our nation is not ready to "move beyond race." At the same time, this group rejects calls for racial separation as ultimately short-sighted and self-defeating.

The other two groups would respond by arguing that although the traditional civil rights agenda made important contributions to racial equality, further progress will require a different approach. Advocates of the color-blind approach argue that the only way toward progress on racial issues is to stop making distinctions between people based on race: use government policies to make sure there is no overt discrimination and provide equal opportunity for all, and then let merit decide outcomes. The segregationists, who comprise a relatively small group, have basically given up on the civil rights agenda and believe that minorities can achieve success only on their own. Debates between advocates of these three views play out over a broad range of issues. Three of these issues are outlined in this last section of the chapter.

AFFIRMATIVE ACTION

The Civil Rights Act of 1964 ensured that, at least on paper, all Americans would enjoy equality of opportunity. But even after the act was passed, blacks continued to lag behind whites in socioeconomic status; that is, there was still a substantial gap between the equality of opportunity and the equality of outcomes (see Nuts and Bolts 14.2, President Johnson's speech on this topic). Beginning in 1965, President Johnson tried to address these inequalities with a policy of affirmative action. By executive order, Johnson required all federal agencies and government contractors to submit written proposals to provide an equal opportunity for employment of blacks, women, Asian Americans, and Native Americans within various job categories and to outline specific programs to achieve those goals. The policy was expanded and strengthened under President Nixon, and throughout the 1970s and 1980s affirmative action programs grew in the private sector, higher education, and government contracting. Through such programs, employers and universities gave special opportunities to minorities and women, either to make up for past patterns of discrimination or to pursue the general goals of diversity.

Affirmative action takes many forms. The most passive type is extra effort to recruit women and minorities for employment or college admission by taking out ads in newspapers and magazines, visiting inner-city schools, or sending out targeted mailings. A more active form is to include race or gender as a "plus factor" in the admissions or hiring decision. That is, from a pool of qualified candidates, a minority applicant may be given an advantage over white applicants. (Women generally do not receive special consideration in admissions decisions, but gender may be a "plus factor" in some employment decisions; in fact, many selective schools have been quietly applying affirmative action for men because more highly qualified women apply than men.) The strongest form of affirmative action is the use of quotas—strict numerical targets to hire or admit a specific number of applicants from underrepresented groups.

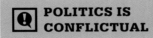

POLITICS IS CONFLICTUAL

Affirmative action has been a controversial policy, almost from its inception. Many whites view the policy as "preferential treatment" and "reverse discrimination." Polls indicate that minorities are much more supportive of the practice than whites. A majority of whites support more passive forms of affirmative action, such as "education programs to assist minorities in competing for college admissions," but draw the line at preferences, even when they are intended to make up for past discrimination.[78] This backlash against affirmative action has spilled over into state politics. California passed Proposition 209 in 1996, which banned the use of "race, sex, color, ethnicity or national origin as a criterion for either discriminating against, or granting preferential treatment to, any individual or group in the operation of the State's system of public employment, public education, or public contracting." Voters in Washington passed a similar resolution in 1999, Florida banned the use of race in college admission decisions in that year as well, and Michigan passed a broad ban on affirmative action in 2006. Several other state legislatures have considered taking up the issue, but the state and local decisions have been mixed. Voters in Houston, Texas, voted to continue affirmative action in their city in November

President Johnson's Commencement Address at Howard University

WASHINGTON, DC, JUNE 4, 1965

"To Fulfill These Rights"

[After outlining the legal protections for African Americans that had recently been provided by Congress, President Johnson presents his famous argument that true equality must be based on outcomes, not just opportunity.]

But freedom is not enough. You do not wipe away the scars of centuries by saying: Now you are free to go where you want, and do as you desire, and choose the leaders you please.

You do not take a person who, for years, has been hobbled by chains and liberate him, bring him up to the starting line of a race and then say, "you are free to compete with all the others," and still justly believe that you have been completely fair. Thus it is not enough just to open the gates of opportunity. All our citizens must have the ability to walk through those gates.

This is the next and the more profound stage of the battle for civil rights. We seek not just freedom but opportunity. We seek not just legal equity but human ability, not just equality as a right and a theory but equality as a fact and equality as a result.

For the task is to give 20 million Negroes the same chance as every other American to learn and grow, to work and share in society, to develop their abilities—physical, mental and spiritual, and to pursue their individual happiness.

To this end equal opportunity is essential, but not enough, not enough. Men and women of all races are born with the same range of abilities. But ability is not just the product of birth. Ability is stretched or stunted by the family that you live with, and the neighborhood you live in—by the school you go to and the poverty or the richness of your surroundings. It is the product of a hundred unseen forces playing upon the little infant, the child, and finally the man.

[President Johnson describes the persistent gulf between the socioeconomic status of blacks and whites, the causes of poverty, and some of the solutions to inequalities between whites and blacks.]

For what is justice? It is to fulfill the fair expectations of man. Thus, American justice is a very special thing. For, from the first, this has been a land of towering expectations. It was to be a nation where each man could be ruled by the common consent of all—enshrined in law, given life by institutions, guided by men themselves subject to its rule. And all—all of every station and origin—would be touched equally in obligation and in liberty. . . . This is American justice. We have pursued it faithfully to the edge of our imperfections, and we have failed to find it for the American Negro.

So, it is the glorious opportunity of this generation to end the one huge wrong of the American Nation and, in so doing, to find America for ourselves, with the same immense thrill of discovery which gripped those who first began to realize that here, at last, was a home for freedom.

All it will take is for all of us to understand what this country is and what this country must become. The Scripture promises: "I shall light a candle of understanding in thine heart, which shall not be put out." Together, and with millions more, we can light that candle of understanding in the heart of all America. And, once lit, it will never again go out.

SOURCE: *Public Papers of the Presidents of the United States: Lyndon B. Johnson, 1965,* vol. II, entry 301 (Washington, DC: Government Printing Office, 1966), pp. 635–40.

1997, perhaps illustrating the importance of the question wording on the resolution. In California the wording of Proposition 209 mentioned the hot-button term "preferential treatment," whereas the Houston resolution simply asked voters if they wanted to retain the city's affirmative action program.[79] Fifty-five percent of voters in California and 58 percent in Michigan voted to get rid of "preferential treatment," while 55 percent of Houston's voters supported keeping the city's affirmative action program.

The Supreme Court has helped define the boundaries of this policy debate. The earliest cases concerning affirmative action in employment upheld preferential treatment and even rigid quotas when the policies were needed to make up for past discrimination. The cases involved a worker training program that set aside 50 percent of the positions for blacks (which meant that some less-qualified blacks were admitted into the program ahead of more-qualified whites), a labor union that was required to hire enough minorities to get its nonwhite membership to 29.23 percent, and the Alabama state police force, which was required to promote one black officer for every white even if there was a smaller pool of blacks who were eligible for promotion.[80] In each instance there had been a pattern of discrimination and exclusion that was the target of the affirmative action program.

The Supreme Court started moving in a "color-blind" direction in 1989 concerning "set-aside" programs in government contracting. In 1983 Richmond, Virginia, adopted a policy requiring contractors who had won city construction contracts to subcontract at least 30 percent of the work to minority-owned businesses. The city council noted that 50 percent of Richmond's population was black but only 0.67 percent of the city's prime construction contracts had gone to minority-owned businesses. A white business owner, J. A. Croson, had bid for a city contract and lost to a minority-owned business. Croson sued, saying that his 14th Amendment equal protection rights had been violated. The Court agreed, ruling that set-asides were unconstitutional without specific evidence of patterns of discrimination against minorities and that any such programs had to be "narrowly tailored to meet a compelling state interest." "Generalized assertions" of past discrimination were not adequate to justify such rigid quotas.[81] This same reasoning was applied to federal contracting set-aside programs in 1995.[82]

The Court applied a similar line of analysis to an important reverse-discrimination employment case in 2009. In that case, seventeen white firefighters and one Hispanic firefighter sued the city of New Haven, Connecticut, for throwing out the results of a test that would have been used to promote them. The city tried to ignore the results of the test because no African American firefighters would have qualified for promotion and the city feared a "disparate impact" lawsuit. However, the Court ruled that the exam did appear to be "job related and consistent with business necessity" (as required by Section VII of the Civil Rights Act) and that unless the city could provide a "strong basis in evidence" that they would have been sued, they had to consider the results of the exam.[83]

The landmark decision for affirmative action in higher education is *University of California Regents v. Bakke* (1978).[84] Allan Bakke, a white student, sued when he was denied admission to medical school at the University of California, Davis, in successive years. Bakke showed that his test scores and GPA were significantly higher than those of some of the minority students who were admitted under the school's affirmative action program. Under that program, 16 of the 100 slots in the entering class were reserved for minority or disadvantaged students. The Supreme Court agreed with Bakke that rigid racial quotas were unconstitutional but allowed race to be used in admissions decisions as a "plus factor" to promote diversity in the student body. This standard was widely followed and largely unquestioned until 1996 when the Fifth Circuit Court of Appeals held that it was unconstitutional to consider race in law school admissions at the University of Texas. An appeals court in Washington reached the opposite conclusion in a different case.

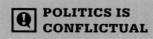

POLITICS IS CONFLICTUAL

Even more puzzling were two conflicting cases from the University of Michigan. A district court held that race-conscious undergraduate admissions were acceptable, but a decision a few months later in the same district court held that considering race in law school admissions was not constitutional. An appeals court reversed the law school decision, leaving the Supreme Court to sort out the mess. The Court's rulings were consistent with *Bakke*, saying that the law school's "holistic approach" that considered race as one of the factors in the admission decision was acceptable

Affirmative Action at the University of Michigan

If you were serving on the Supreme Court, how would you have decided the University of Michigan affirmative action cases? In the undergraduate case, Jennifer Gratz had a high school GPA of 3.76 and an ACT score of 25 (eighty-third percentile), and Patrick Hamacher had a GPA of 3.37 and an ACT of 28 (eighty-ninth percentile), but they were denied admission to Michigan. The student in the law school case, Barbara Grutter, was a forty-three-year-old returning student who had an undergraduate GPA of 3.81 at Michigan State University and a 161 on the LSAT. All three students showed that they had higher scores than some of the minority students who were admitted under the university's affirmative action program. The legal question that the Court had to decide was whether the university's affirmative action program violated the equal protection clause of the 14th Amendment and civil rights laws barring discrimination on the basis of race, or if the program could be justified as serving a "compelling state interest" under the strict scrutiny standard.

The crucial point of contention in the debate over the use of race in college admissions decisions is "viewpoint diversity"; the claimed advantage of affirmative action is the diversity that it brings to classroom discussions. Advocates of affirmative action argue that viewpoint diversity is essential to learning and that having racial diversity in the student body is likely to produce more viewpoint diversity than having an all-white student body. Furthermore, proponents argue, the courts are not the proper place to decide these issues. Instead, as with the complex and highly charged topic of racial redistricting, the political branches of government are

University of Michigan students are shown hanging out on campus. Debates over the importance of racial diversity in the classroom have played a central role in court cases concerning affirmative action in higher education.

where these decisions should be made. Advocates also make a very pragmatic argument that getting rid of affirmative action would almost certainly lead to a system that is *less* rooted in merit-based admissions than the current system. This is because states that get rid of race as a factor in admissions often adopt a "10 percent solution," which says that the top 10 percent of any graduating high school class can be admitted to the state university. This means that a student who may be in the top 20 percent of an excellent school might not be admitted even if she had better test scores and grades than a student who was in the top 10 percent of a high school that was not as good.

Opponents reply that supporters of affirmative action have not provided convincing evidence that racial diversity in colleges has any beneficial effects. They also argue that "viewpoint diversity" arguments assume that members of all racial minorities think alike, drawing a comparison to racial profiling in law enforcement. It is just as offensive, they say, that an admissions committee thinks that one black student has the same views as another black student as it is that a police officer may pull over a black teenage male just because he fits a certain criminal profile. Opponents also argue that affirmative action amounts to "reverse discrimination" and that any racial classification is harmful.

How would you decide these cases? To what extent should race be used as a "plus factor" to promote racial diversity and viewpoint diversity, if at all? How would you justify your decision? Is viewpoint diversity an important goal? Think of your own experiences from high school and college. Has racial diversity contributed to viewpoint diversity? ∎

Immigration

The long-standing conventional wisdom in the United States concerning immigration points to its central role in building our nation: we are a country of immigrants. America's ability to assimilate and integrate a broad range of people and cultures produced an image of a melting pot in which these diverse groups become something uniquely American. Others point to an image of a patchwork quilt in which different cultures are stitched together into the same American blanket while maintaining parts of their unique identity. Whatever the image, the Statue of Liberty in New York Harbor serves as the central symbol of this long-standing conventional wisdom, and the noble words at the base of the statue are a warm welcome to generations of immigrants: "Give me your tired, your poor, your huddled masses yearning to breathe free, the wretched refuse of your teeming shore. Send these, the homeless, tempest tossed, to me: I lift my lamp beside the golden door."

Like most conventional wisdom, this viewpoint has always had its dissenters. Immigrants have always been discriminated against as they try to make their new home, whether it was Italians, Germans, Irish, or Poles in the first wave of immigration in the nineteenth and early twentieth centuries or Asians, Mexicans, and other Latin Americans in the next wave. A recent expression of this nativist tradition in American politics has been evident in the debate over reforming immigration policy. Politicians such as James Sensenbrenner (R-WI), former chair of the House Judiciary Committee; media figures such as Lou Dobbs; and academics such as Harvard professor Samuel Huntington weighed in against the attempt to fashion a compromise between those who want to close the border with Mexico and deport all illegal immigrants and those who take a more forgiving line. The compromise includes a proposal to beef up border security while offering amnesty to illegal immigrants willing to pay fines and meet other conditions.

Opponents say that we need to focus our efforts on keeping out illegal immigrants and making it a felony to assist anyone who is in the country illegally. That provision drew howls of protest from churches and charitable organizations that run homeless shelters and food banks, saying that many of their volunteers could be in violation of the law. The intensity of the debate increased in 2010 when Arizona enacted a tough anti-immigration law that requires local law enforcement officials to check the immigration status of a person in a "lawful stop, detention, or arrest" if there is a "reasonable suspicion" that the person is an illegal alien. Opponents of the law argue that this is racial profiling, while supporters say the state is just enforcing federal law (the law being challenged in federal court). The most sustained critique of the

but that the University of Michigan's more rigid approach to undergraduate admissions, which automatically gave minority students 20 of the 100 points needed to guarantee admission, was not acceptable.[85] Though these two decisions affirmed *Bakke*, it was the first time that a majority of the Court clearly stated that "student body diversity is a compelling state interest that can justify the use of race in university admissions."[86]

MULTICULTURAL ISSUES

There are a host of issues involving the multicultural, multiracial nature of American society that will become more important as white people in the United States stop constituting the majority of the population by the middle of this century. Two of these issues are English as the official language and immigration.

The decision by many states to adopt laws establishing English as the official language has had practical consequences. For example, the Supreme Court upheld an Alabama state law that required that the state driver's license test be conducted only in English. A Mexican immigrant, Martha Sandoval, sued under Title VI of the 1964 Civil Rights Act, saying that the state law had a disparate impact on

conventional wisdom on immigration came from Huntington, who wrote in *Who Are We: The Challenges to America's National Identity,*

> Americans like to boast of their past success in assimilating millions of immigrants into their society, culture, and politics. But . . . they have overlooked the unique characteristics and problems posed by contemporary Hispanic immigration. The extent and nature of this immigration differ fundamentally from those of previous immigration, and the assimilation successes of the past are unlikely to be duplicated with the contemporary flood of immigrants from Latin America.

He suggested that this development posed "a major potential threat to the cultural and possibly political integrity of the United States." Therefore, Huntington (who died in 2008) would have argued that he wasn't challenging the conventional wisdom on immigration as much as trying to uphold the traditional view of an assimilationist America that embraces new groups but expects them to adopt an American identity.

Huntington's critics point out that much of his evidence was pretty thin and that Mexican Americans and immigrants from other parts of Latin America appear to be assimilating at about the same rate as other immigrants. On some critical characteristics such as work ethic, family values, and religion, Mexican Americans already embrace many aspects of American culture. While only 5 percent of first-generation Mexican American immigrants speak English at home, by the third generation that figure is 60 percent.[a] There is some evidence that first-generation immigrants depress wages for native low-income workers, but that effect is gone by the second generation (there are some difficult issues here, however, concerning the replacement of each generation with new immigrants, which continues to depress the wages of low-income workers). Overall, the evidence appears to support the conventional wisdom more than Huntington's view.

The American public is divided on this issue, in some cases sharing Huntington's pessimism and in other cases embracing a more optimistic view of immigration. A 2008 Gallup poll found that 39 percent of respondents wanted to keep the present level of immigration, 18 percent wanted more immigration, and 39 percent wanted less. An AP poll found that 52 percent of Americans thought that immigrants had a "good influence on the way things are going in the United States," and 46 percent thought they had a bad influence. The same poll found that slightly more thought that immigrants helped improve their community (22 percent) than created problems (18 percent), but most (58 percent) thought they did not have much effect either way. The most negative view of immigrants tied them to crime: 19 percent said that immigrants were more likely than the native-born to be involved in crime, 12 percent thought they were less likely, and 68 percent said no difference. The most positive view was that by huge margins (51 percent to 5 percent), Americans think that "immigrants work harder than people born here."[b] Given these mixed views, it is not surprising that a significant majority of Americans favor a compromise policy on this issue that combines stronger border controls with a "path to citizenship" for current illegal aliens. However, such a compromise was rejected by conservatives in Congress when President Bush proposed it, and action on a similar proposal favored by President Obama and the Democratic leadership in Congress was postponed until after the 2010 midterm elections. ■

---

non–English-speaking residents. However, the Court held in *Alexander v. Sandoval* (2001) that individuals may not sue federally funded state agencies over policies that have a discriminatory effect on minorities under Title VI. This decision could have far-reaching consequences for the use of the Civil Rights Act to fight patterns of discrimination. Two areas that could be affected are education policy (for example, civil rights advocates have challenged the use of standardized testing because of its disparate impact on minorities) and environmental policy (lawsuits brought under Title VI have alleged "environmental racism" in decisions to site hazardous waste dumps in predominantly minority areas).

The second increasingly prominent multicultural issue, immigration, was thrust back into center stage in the wake of the September 11 terrorist attacks. In light of these attacks, some people came to see immigration as a threat that must be curtailed. The government made it clear that it would not engage in racial profiling of Arab Americans—for example, subjecting them to stricter screening at airports—but many commentators argued that such profiling would be justified, and there was at least anecdotal evidence of an increase in discrimination against people of Middle Eastern descent.

Over the past two decades, immigration has been central in many political debates. Some of these debates are nominally about social welfare benefits, but

▲ Border Patrol agents detain undocumented immigrants apprehended near the Mexican border outside McAllen, Texas. Illegal immigration continues to be a "hot-button" issue in national electoral and legislative politics. Attempts at major immigration policy reform were postponed until after the 2010 midterm elections.

deeper racial issues often are just below the surface (see Challenging Conventional Wisdom). For example, in 1994 voters in California adopted Proposition 187, which denied most public benefits to illegal immigrants but was viewed by critics as discriminatory to Mexican Americans. Debates over immigration have important political implications. Republicans were strongly in favor of Proposition 187, while Democrats opposed it. When the measure was struck down by the courts and Democrats won the 1998 gubernatorial race in California with the strong support of the newly galvanized and growing Hispanic population, Republicans softened their position on immigration. President George W. Bush was instrumental in trying to move the Republican Party in this direction. He actively cultivated the Hispanic vote, often presenting part of his speeches in Spanish, and won a record (for Republican presidential candidates) 44 percent of the Latino vote in 2004. Bush pushed for comprehensive immigration reform in 2006, making an alliance with Democratic senator Ted Kennedy. However, anti-immigration Republicans in Congress rejected this effort and passed a strong measure aimed at enforcing existing immigration laws and building a barrier along the border with Mexico. Strong Latino turnout in 2006 is credited, at least in part, with a return of control of Congress to the Democrats, and Obama won 67 percent of the Latino vote in 2008. How to deal with immigration deeply divides the country and is likely to become even more controversial in the next decade.

Conclusion

We now can answer the questions about possible civil rights violations that introduced this chapter. The African American teenagers who were pulled over by the police may or may not have had their civil rights violated, depending on the laws in their state. In Massachusetts, for example, it is prohibited to consider the "race, gender, national or ethnic origin of members of the public in deciding to detain a person or stop a motor vehicle" except in "suspect specific incidents." That is, if the police officer was in pursuit of a specific African American suspect, it would have been legitimate to use racial profiling.[87] Pulling over the car full of white teenagers would have been acceptable as long as there was some "probable cause" to justify the stop. The Asian American woman who did not get the job could certainly talk to a lawyer about filing a "disparate impact" discrimination suit. Under the 1991 Civil Rights Act, the employer would have the burden of proof to show that she was not victimized by the "good ol' boy" network. The gay couple who could not get the apartment because of their sexual orientation may have a basis for a civil rights lawsuit based on the 14th Amendment; however, this would depend on where they live, given that there is no federal protection against discrimination against gays and lesbians. The Court decisions concerning affirmative action at the University of Michigan show that the white student who was not admitted to the university of his choice would just have to take his lumps, as long as the affirmative action program considered race as a general "plus factor" rather than assigning more or fewer points for it. Finally, the white contractor definitely could claim that he was a victim of reverse discrimination and sue the city. The burden of proof would be on the city to demonstrate a specific pattern of discrimination against minority-owned businesses to justify a "narrowly tailored" set-aside program.

This review of civil rights policy has only highlighted some of the most important issues, but it is clear that a broad and significant agenda remains. The civil rights movement will continue to use the multiple avenues of the legislative, executive, and judicial branches to secure equal rights for all Americans. Civil rights in the United States is an evolving work in progress.

What are civil rights?

- Civil rights protect all persons from discrimination by the government and individuals. They are rooted in laws and the equal protection clause of the 14th Amendment.
- The legacy of slavery and racial segregation in the South has been the dominant focus of civil rights policies in the United States.
- Starting in the mid-nineteenth century, women began their fight for equal rights, and over the next century the civil rights movement expanded to include gays and other racial and ethnic groups such as Native Americans, Asian Americans, and Latinos.

What is the nature of the racial divide today?

- The dream of a color-blind society is shared by most Americans, but there is strong disagreement over how much progress we have made toward that goal.

- Though there are differences about *perceptions* of progress on racial differences, there are also large gaps between whites and racial minorities on objective measures of political participation and social and economic well-being.

How has civil rights policy been made?

- The civil rights movement put pressure on the political system through nonviolent protest and civil disobedience to enact far-reaching legislation to end segregation, prohibit discrimination, and guarantee equal voting rights.
- The *Brown v. Board of Education* decision to end segregation in public schools was an important step toward ending legal segregation and discrimination in other parts of social life.
- Starting in the 1980s the Supreme Court moved toward a "color-blind" jurisprudence that tried to

minimize the impact of race in various social and political contexts. The Court has also played a central role in determining women's civil rights and gay rights.

- The bedrock of equal protection for racial minorities that exists today stems from landmark legislation passed by Congress in the 1960s—namely, the 1964 Civil Rights Act, the 1965 Voting Rights Act, and the 1968 Fair Housing Act. Women have also received extensive protection through legislation, most importantly, Title VII of the Civil Rights Act and Title IX of the Higher Education Act.
- Presidents have been very important in promoting civil rights, both through executive orders and through

the "bully pulpit" of the presidency and symbolic politics.

What civil rights issues do we confront today, and which will be important in the future?

- Affirmative action and multicultural issues, including proposals to make English the country's official language and conflicts over immigration, are among the civil rights issues that Americans will confront now and for the foreseeable future.

⊚ STUDENT STUDYSPACE

Find quizzes and other review material at wwnorton.com/studyspace.

CRITICAL THINKING

1. Have you ever faced discrimination based on your race, gender, or sexual orientation? If so, what did you learn in this chapter about whether your civil rights were violated?
2. Should government attempt to provide a level playing field by making sure that there is no discrimination, or should it go

beyond providing equality of opportunity to also be concerned with the equality of outcomes?
3. Which policy-making institution has historically played the most important role in protecting the civil rights of Americans? Does that institution still play that role today?

KEY TERMS

civil rights (p. 510)
de facto (p. 531)
de jure (p. 531)
disenfranchised (p. 513)
disparate impact standard (p. 532)

grandfather clause (p. 513)
intermediate scrutiny test (p. 536)
Jim Crow laws (p. 513)
Missouri Compromise (p. 512)
protectionism (p. 516)

reasonable basis test (p. 536)
"separate but equal" (p. 513)
strict scrutiny test (p. 536)
substantive due process doctrine (p. 539)

SUGGESTED READING

Canon, David T. *Race, Redistricting, and Representation: The Unintended Consequences of Black-Majority Districts.* Chicago: University of Chicago Press, 1999.

Dawson, Michael C. *Behind the Mule: Race and Class in African-American Politics.* Princeton, NJ: Princeton University Press, 1994.

Gross, Ariela J. *What Blood Won't Tell: A History of Race on Trial in America.* Cambridge, MA: Harvard University Press, 2008.

Hochschild, Jennifer L. *Facing Up to the American Dream: Race, Class, and the Soul of the Nation.* Princeton, NJ: Princeton University Press, 1995.

Katznelson, Ira. *When Affirmative Action Was White: An Untold History of Racial Inequality in Twentieth-Century America.* New York: W. W. Norton, 2005.

Kluger, Richard. *Simple Justice: The History of* Brown v. Board of Education *and Black America's Struggle for Equality.* New York: Vintage, 2004.

Kousser, J. Morgan. *Colorblind Injustice: Minority Voting Rights and the Undoing of the Second Reconstruction.* Chapel Hill, NC: University of North Carolina Press, 1999.

Lublin, David. *The Paradox of Representation: Racial Gerrymandering and Minority Interests in Congress.* Princeton, NJ: Princeton University Press, 1997.

Tate, Katherine. *Black Faces in the Mirror: African Americans and Their Representatives in Congress.* Princeton, NJ: Princeton University Press, 2003.

Thernstrom, Stephan, and Abigail Thernstrom. *America in Black and White: One Nation, Indivisible: Race in Modern America.* New York: Simon and Schuster, 1997.

Globalization makes it more complicated to "buy American," as foreign firms establish operations in the United States and American firms expand abroad.

Economic Policy

It is difficult to pick up a newspaper today without seeing a discussion of the globalization of the world economy. Some articles are distraught accounts of the "outsourcing" of American jobs as firms seek cheaper labor. Others report the benefits of cheap, high-quality imported consumer goods that are so readily available. Globalization creates an economic system that increasingly operates at an international rather than national level, which makes national boundaries less meaningful. Columnist Thomas Friedman argues that the telecommunication revolution, international travel, and multinational corporations have created a "flat world."[1] By this he means that globalization has shortened the distances between people and leveled the playing field so that a computer technician in India can answer a call to the help-line of an American computer company or the customer service center for an American credit card company can actually be based in China.

CONFLICT AND COMPROMISE in American Politics

Friedman is on to something. Just look around you. There is a good chance the clothes and shoes you are wearing came from China, Singapore, or the Philippines; your MP3 player and television probably came from Japan; almost half of the cars sold in the United States are foreign; many paper products are from Canada; the fruit you eat may come from Mexico or Chile; your cell phone may be from Norway or Germany; and so on. Nokia, Siemens, Phillips, Honda, Canon, Sony, and Nintendo are as familiar in the United States as Dell, Motorola, Ford, Procter & Gamble, Pfizer, and Microsoft.

Globalization complicates some common perceptions about the role of the United States in the world economy. Those who are concerned about the loss of American jobs urge people to "buy American." But what does that mean in a global economy? If you buy a Ford Focus that was made in Saarlouis, Germany, is that an American car or a German car? (The 10 millionth Ford recently rolled out of that German plant.)[2] How about if you buy a Honda Civic that was made in East Liberty, Ohio? Is that a Japanese car or an American car? A Dodge Grand Caravan is American and a Volkswagen Routan is German, right? Nope, they are actually twins that are made in the same Canadian plant in a joint Chrysler-Volkswagen venture. Most auto manufacturers are truly global corporations. General Motors has manufacturing operations in thirty-four countries, and its vehicles are sold in 140 countries. Ford assembles cars in Argentina, Germany, Ireland, Malaysia, Mexico, New Zealand, the Philippines, Spain, South Africa, Taiwan, Uruguay, and Venezuela, among other countries.

So, the economic world is "flatter" and more global, but why is this central to our discussion of economic policy making? The political implications of economic globalization illustrate the central theme of the book that politics is conflictual. Most economists examining increasing international trade and even the outsourcing of jobs are likely to look at the data and say, "Good. Markets are becoming more efficient, and society is better off." Politicians looking at the same information see angry constituents who wonder if they will lose their jobs (see Challenging Conventional Wisdom). Therefore, globalization and related issues, such as free trade agreements, are the sources of great political conflict. Economic interests that are harmed by free trade, outsourcing, and the power of international corporations will fight to protect those interests. Sometimes this conflict can be resolved through compromise, such as a free trade treaty that makes exceptions for specific industries or protects workers' interests in the United States in other ways.

But in some instances, the effects of economic globalization cannot be resolved through political compromise. In these instances, the international economic system and its multinational corporations, capital markets, and currency traders drive economic outcomes more than government economic policy making. Indeed, if this argument is taken to its logical extreme, we could end this chapter right now and skip to Chapter 16, Social Policy. Why even talk about economic policy making in the context of the American political system if globalization makes national boundaries increasingly meaningless? If this is true, then multinational corporations and not governments make economic policy. Although this is increasingly the case for smaller and even medium-size nations, the United States is the largest economy in the world. So while globalization is a reality and the economic world is increasingly flat, political leaders can still influence the state of the economy—in both positive and negative ways.

The conflictual nature of politics generally extends to economic policy rather than simply the politics of economic globalization. Policies aimed at helping one segment of the economy usually come at the expense of another part. For example, if tax policy is used to help the poor, the wealthy will obviously pay a larger share of their income in taxes than the poor. The policy responses to the economic meltdown of 2008–2009 caused a great deal of conflict. The stimulus bill in early 2009, for example, pitted those who favored tax cuts against those who wanted more government spending to stimulate the economy. On the spending side, policy makers had to decide between supporting the states, rebuilding the nation's infrastructure, and promoting alternative energy (among many other options). The bailouts of Wall Street and the auto industry also were conflictual, as constituents questioned the use of taxpayers' money to support private businesses.

Many of America's central political debates concern economic policy: Should we run deficits or have balanced budgets? Have a progressive income tax or a flatter tax? Have a largely unregulated, free market or regulations for things like

▼ Workers on an automobile assembly line for General Motors in Shandong Province, China. Gaining access to foreign markets is increasingly important for American corporations in a globalized economy.

pollution and health care? Democrats tend to favor a more activist government that supports a broader range of programs to help the poor and disadvantaged and regulates the economy to ensure a range of public goods. Republicans tend to favor a more limited approach to government that promotes lower taxes and less regulation and allows the free market to determine more social and economic decisions.

The idea that political process matters also is demonstrated through a discussion of the economic policy-making process. We show how Congress, the president, and the bureaucracy all have a hand in attempting to promote a healthy economy. The ways in which politics is everywhere may be less obvious in the area of economic policy, which, one might think, should be determined more by rational economic theories than by rough-and-tumble, partisan politics. We explicitly address this theme in the chapter's conclusion, but the discussion throughout will make it clear that politics is central to the making of economic policy.

This chapter has three main parts. First, we discuss the goals of economic policy making and the trade-offs among those goals. Next, we review the main players in economic policy making—Congress, the president, bureaucratic agencies, and to some extent, the courts. Finally, we talk about the tools and theories of economic policy making, including fiscal policy, monetary policy, regulatory policy, and trade policy. Although we can only scratch the surface of the theories behind these tools, this chapter will give you a basic understanding of how economic theory and politics shape economic policy making.

full employment The theoretical point at which all citizens who want to be employed have a job.

economic depression A deep, widespread downturn in the economy, like the Great Depression of the 1930s.

Council of Economic Advisers A group of economic advisers, created by the Employment Act of 1946, which provides objective data on the state of the economy and makes economic policy recommendations to the president.

Goals of Economic Policy

Policy makers have a set of goals in mind when they try to influence the economy. Many of these goals seem obvious, such as full employment (it is better to have more people working than not working), but others may be less clear. Also, it is difficult to pursue all the goals simultaneously because there are trade-offs, at least in the short run, between some of them.

FULL EMPLOYMENT

Employment seems like a good starting point for a healthy economy. If people have jobs, they are paying taxes and are not dependent on the government for support. Despite this, **full employment** was not an explicit goal of economic policy until 1946, when Congress passed the Employment Act. Leaders were concerned that with millions of veterans returning from World War II and the wartime economy gearing down, there was a good chance that the nation could slide back into the **economic depression** that had created so much hardship in the 1930s. Although the act was largely symbolic (there was no guaranteed right to employment), it did create the **Council of Economic Advisers**, which provides the president with economic information and advice. A more concrete effort to make sure that returning veterans could find jobs was the Servicemen's Readjustment Act (commonly known as the GI Bill). Enacted in 1944, it provided higher education assistance to 7.8 million veterans by the time the law expired in 1956 and low-interest home

▼ American soldiers wave and cheer as their ship docks in New York in July 1945. When soldiers returned from World War II, political leaders feared that a lack of jobs for veterans could cause the economy to fall back into a recession. They passed the Employment Act of 1946 in an effort to make sure that didn't happen.

The Outsourcing of Jobs

The debate over the outsourcing of jobs—that is, American companies laying off people in the United States and hiring people in other nations for lower wages—is an instance of conventional wisdom in economics challenging conventional thinking in politics. Economists have long touted the virtues of exploiting "comparative advantage" through free trade. In 1817 David Ricardo was the first to develop this notion with the example of the production of wine and cloth in Portugal and Britain.[a] According to the argument, Portugal should produce excess wine and export it to Britain because that is where their greatest *relative* advantage lay. Even if it seems counterintuitive, Britain should produce excess cloth and export it, even if Portugal could produce cloth more cheaply than Britain. By focusing on this comparative advantage, free trade maximizes wealth in both countries.[b]

This argument makes perfect economic sense, but it is bad politics. Many Americans are very concerned about the loss of jobs, especially in high-tech areas such as computer programming. When IBM announced that it was laying off 13,000 U.S. workers and hiring 14,000 new employees

A worker on strike at the Goodyear Tire and Rubber plant in Akron, Ohio.

in India, it only added fuel to the fire. Current estimates are that the United States could lose 3 million jobs overseas between 2000 and 2015. When programmers or computer customer support staff in India earn about one-tenth of what they make in the United States, it is difficult for American firms to compete in international markets unless they employ cheaper labor.[c] The same pressures have led to the virtual extinction of some U.S. industries, such as the manufacturing of consumer electronics, textiles, shoes, and, increasingly, clothing. Politicians who are not sensitive to the loss

of jobs usually are told the error of their ways by the voters.

Although generally supporting free trade, President Obama has criticized the outsourcing of jobs since the 2008 campaign. In 2009 he proposed to end tax incentives for outsourced jobs but met with resistance from members of Congress who thought the proposal was too broad. Obama reintroduced the idea in his 2010 State of the Union address, saying, "To encourage . . . businesses to stay within our borders, it is time to finally slash the tax breaks for companies that ship our jobs overseas, and give those tax breaks to companies that create jobs right here in the United States of America."[d] Obama included in his 2011 budget a proposal to stop the practice of allowing American corporations to take immediate tax deductions for jobs created in their foreign subsidiaries but then defer paying taxes on the profits they make from those investments (something American corporations cannot do for their U.S. businesses). Such policies may be smart politics in an economy that shed 8.4 million jobs in two years (2008–2009), but economists still worry about their impact on the free flow of capital. ■

mortgages for 2.4 million veterans. Today the government has the goal of supporting the creation of as many jobs as possible through a strong economy. With the unemployment rate hovering around 10 percent since late 2009 (its highest level since the early 1980s), President Obama and Congress tried to make sure that the recession wouldn't turn into a "jobless recovery" by passing a $17.5 billion jobs bill in March 2010.

One other, more technical point is that full employment does not literally mean that everyone is working. There is always a substantial portion of the potential workforce that is not looking for a job. It does not even mean that everyone who is looking for work can get a job, because there is always a certain amount of "frictional unemployment" as people are between jobs. Instead, economists consider a 5 to 5.5 percent unemployment rate to be the level of full employment, or the "natural rate of unemployment."

STABLE PRICES

The importance of having stable prices is not as obvious as the need for jobs. Why are rising prices—**inflation**—a problem? This is a more common question now, during a period of low inflation. Especially for workers who have automatic raises (cost of living adjustments, or COLAs) as part of their basic pay package, moderate inflation isn't much of a problem. For example, if your rent goes up 4 percent, the price of groceries goes up 3 percent, and the cost of entertainment goes up 3 percent, and you get a 4 percent raise, you are probably going to be at least as well off as you were in the previous year. However, from 1979 to 1980 inflation was running at 12 to 14 percent rather than the 2 to 3 percent that has been typical in recent years (Figure 15.1). Double-digit inflation can have serious effects on the economy. First, the entire economy is not indexed to inflation, so some people see an erosion of their purchasing power. So if your rent goes up 10 percent and groceries are up 15 percent, but your pay only goes up by 4 percent, you are substantially worse off. Second, high inflation penalizes savers and rewards debtors as savings interest rates may be outstripped by inflation (so savings are actually worth less over time), but people who go into debt can repay those debts with cheaper dollars in the future. Finally, long-term economic planning by businesses becomes more difficult when inflation is high. With high inflation, investors demand high interest rates to compensate for the added risk of future inflation. In 1979 and 1980, short-term interest rates spiked as high as 18 percent. Very few businesses were willing to take on additional debt at that rate of interest as opposed to the more typical 6 to 8 percent, so the economy headed into a recession.

The period of relatively high unemployment and inflation generated two new economic terms: stagflation (a stagnant economy with inflation) and the Misery Index (the sum of the inflation rate and the unemployment rate). Typically unemployment

inflation The increase in the price of consumer goods over time.

FIGURE 15.1 **INFLATION AND UNEMPLOYMENT, 1960–2010**

The Misery Index is the sum of the unemployment rate and the inflation rate. Which periods had the highest misery rate since 1960? Were there any external explanations for the high misery rate? How did the government respond to the high levels of unemployment and inflation?

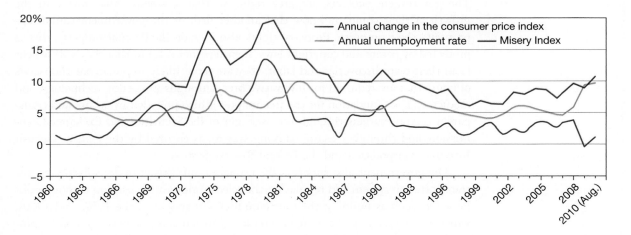

SOURCE: Data from the U.S. Department of Labor, Bureau of Labor Statistics. Inflation data from "Consumer Price Index," available at www.bls.gov/CPI, and unemployment data from "Labor Force Statistics from the Current Population Survey," available at www.bls.gov/cps.

▲ The 1970s witnessed economic stagnation along with high inflation, yielding the new term "stagflation." As the economy started to recover after the 2008–2009 financial crisis, rising prices remained a concern and the possibility of stagflation returned.

and inflation are not high at the same time, so policy makers were desperate to do something about them. The Misery Index first started to creep up in 1970–1971 and President Nixon wanted to halt inflation in its tracks, in part to help his reelection chances in 1972. He announced a ninety-day wage freeze in 1971, which was followed up with wage and price controls after his reelection. The experiment was abandoned in 1974 when it became obvious that interfering with market forces was not working.[3] From that point on, fighting inflation has largely been left to the Federal Reserve, which raises interest rates to cool down the economy. This process is discussed in detail below.

Nixon's concern about inflation reveals one other important point about inflation and unemployment. There tend to be basic partisan differences on the goals of full employment and stable prices, with Democrats being more concerned about employment and Republicans more concerned about inflation. This shouldn't be too much of a surprise given the Democratic Party's base of support within labor unions and blue-collar workers and the Republicans' stronger support on Wall Street and with investors who are likely to have their income eroded by high inflation.

PROMOTE THE FREE MARKET AND GROWTH

The American economy is a capitalist system, which means that most economic decisions are voluntarily made between individuals and firms for their mutual benefit. The government generally stays out of most economic activity, except to regulate the market when it produces too much of something that is not in the public's interest, such as pollution or unsafe products. Economists tout the central advantage of the free market as promoting the most efficient use of resources. Economic growth is also a central goal. A growing economy provides a better standard of living for each generation.

The government does not get directly involved in most economic transactions, but it can provide the foundation for a strong free market and economic growth. The government protects property rights so that businesses that invest in the growth of their company know that another firm or the government cannot appropriate their property. Property rights also include intellectual property that is protected by patent and copyright laws. If entrepreneurs know that they will benefit from their own discoveries and labor, they are more likely to put in the thousands of hours that are required for innovative breakthroughs in science, technology, and medicine. The foundation for the free market is also provided by secure and transparent capital markets through the oversight of the Securities and Exchange Commission, and through a secure banking system, as ensured by the Federal Deposit Insurance Corporation and the Federal Reserve System.

The government also supports the economic infrastructure by subsidizing the transportation system and regulating the telecommunication system; through public works such as building the interstate highway system in the 1950s and 1960s, which provided a huge boost to economic expansion and productivity; and by promoting economic growth with support of basic research in the sciences and medicine through agencies such as the National Science Foundation and the National Institutes of Health.

Critics of the government's focus on the market and growth point out that the free market often produces inequality, and growth doesn't measure well-being. In addition to environmentalists who advocate a "small is beautiful"[4] approach and point out the environmental costs of economic growth, a small group of economists have questioned the traditional interpretations of economic growth measurements, in particular the increase in **gross domestic product (GDP)**, which is a measure of the overall economic output and activity of the country. They point out that a significant part of GDP actually captures a decline in well-being. For example, if we have to spend billions of dollars putting alarms in our homes and cars to warn against intruders, this is not an improvement in the standard of living from the time when such alarms were not needed. Yet the purchase of such crime-fighting tools adds to GDP. An ideal measure of economic growth would distinguish between positive and negative forms of economic activity.[5]

The economic meltdown of 2008–2009 raised basic questions about the efficiency of economic markets and the need for more regulation of the financial sector. We discuss this in more detail later in the chapter, but briefly, Alan Greenspan, chair of the Federal Reserve from August 1987 to January 2006, testified before a House committee that there had been a "flaw" in his market ideology and that a "once-in-a-century credit tsunami" forced him to rethink some of his free-market policies. Greenspan conceded that the financial industry had not served its shareholders and that more regulation of complex derivatives and the subprime mortgage market may have helped to prevent the economic crisis.[6]

▲ *One important way that the government supports the free market and economic growth is by promoting the stability of the banking system. The Federal Deposit Insurance Corporation (FDIC) bolsters confidence in banks by insuring each account holder's deposits in its member banks up to $250,000.*

BALANCED BUDGETS

Maintaining a **balanced budget** has been a central economic goal since the 1980s when **budget deficits** skyrocketed (see Figure 15.2a for this trend and Nuts and Bolts 15.1 for an explanation of deficits and debt). Large deficits are a concern for several reasons. First, they take a big bite out of current spending. About $247 billion or 6.8 percent of the 2011 fiscal year budget went to financing the federal debt. These dollars went to people who own federal bonds and securities; they did not buy a single uniform for a soldier, highway exit ramp, or student loan. Second, the total federal debt is a burden on future generations. Each man, woman, and child in the United States in effect carries more than $42,000 of debt (total debt has grown steadily; see Figure 15.2b). Third, public borrowing "crowds out" private borrowing, because there is a finite pool of dollars that people are able to invest. Let's say you

gross domestic product (GDP) The value of a country's economic output taken as a whole.

balanced budget A spending plan in which the government's expenditures are equal to its revenue.

budget deficit The amount by which a government's spending in a given fiscal year exceeds its revenue.

NUTS AND BOLTS

15.1

Deficits and Debt

Budget deficits and the federal debt are related concepts that are easily confused. A *budget deficit* occurs when tax revenue is not sufficient to cover government spending in a given year. If tax revenue is higher than spending, then there is a budget surplus. The *federal debt* is the total accumulation of all outstanding borrowing by the government. The concepts of deficit and debt are related because when the government runs a deficit, it must borrow money to cover the gap. This borrowing then builds up the federal debt.

You can think of this in terms of your own spending habits. Any time you spend more money in a given month than you earn, you are running a deficit. You must borrow money to make up that deficit from a bank, from your parents, or by running up the balance on your credit card. The accumulated sum of your monthly deficits is the total debt that you owe.

FIGURE 15.2A FEDERAL BUDGET DEFICITS AND SURPLUSES

The federal deficit is the amount by which the government's spending exceeds its revenue in a given year; the federal debt is the accumulation of these annual deficits. Why do the federal deficits and debt matter? Does the answer depend on the state of the economy?

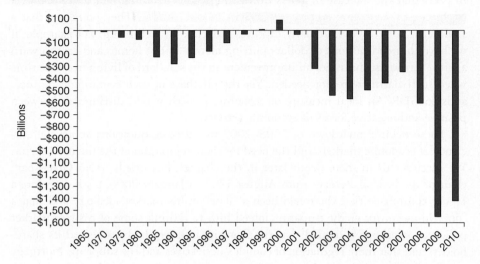

FIGURE 15.2B FEDERAL DEBT

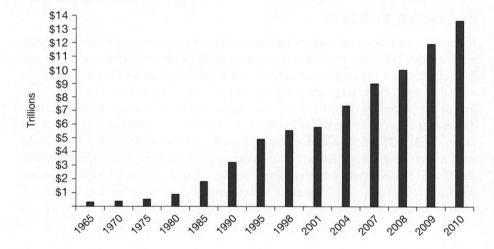

Note: Totals in Figure 15.2a exclude the Social Security Trust Fund.

SOURCE: Data on budget deficits from the Congressional Budget Office, Historical Budget Data, available at www.cbo.gov/budget/historical.shtml for budget deficits. Data on federal debt from the U.S. Department of the Treasury, TreasuryDirect, available at www.treasurydirect.gov/govt/govt.htm.

have $1,000 to invest. You could choose to invest it in the stock market or buy corporate bonds that provide businesses the capital they need to expand, or you could buy government bonds to fund the national debt. In the aggregate, this means that if $250 billion is going to fund the federal deficits every year, then that $250 billion is not available for private borrowing that could go directly to creating more jobs and generating economic growth.

BALANCE OF PAYMENTS, OR THE CURRENT ACCOUNT

The broadest measure of a nation's balance of payments with the rest of the world is the **current account**: the difference between a nation's receipts (exports and money that Americans earn on foreign investments) and its payments (imports and money that foreigners earn on American investments). The aspect of the current account that gets the most political attention is the **trade deficit**, the difference between imports and exports, which recently hit record levels of more than $1 trillion a year before falling back to $541 billion in 2009 (due to the recession, which cut demand for imports). The American appetite for foreign goods is huge, and even a weaker dollar, which makes foreign goods more expensive, has not corrected the imbalance. The overall current account has also received more attention in recent years as the United States has gone from the world's largest creditor nation to the world's largest debtor nation.

There are differences of opinion over whether the United States' debtor status is a problem. Most economists agree that if the current account deficit is driven by a surplus in investments (more foreign investment in America than America has invested overseas), that is not a great cause for concern. Though some are worried about having an increasing share of U.S. businesses and real estate owned by foreign investors, overall this is simply evidence of the strength of the U.S. economy—that is, investors think they can get a greater return on their investments in America than in other countries. However, when the current account deficit is driven by the trade deficit, which is based on consumption rather than investment, this creates longer-term potential problems for the economy that are not sustainable. We go into this topic in more detail in the section on trade policy.[7]

current account The balance of a country's receipts and its payments in international trade and investment.

trade deficit A measure of how much more a nation imports than it exports.

TRADE-OFFS BETWEEN ECONOMIC GOALS

One challenge facing economic policy makers is that it is difficult to "have it all." The period of economic growth, low unemployment, and low inflation with falling budget deficits (and even a surplus by the end of the decade) and a healthy current account that the United States enjoyed through much of the 1990s was relatively unusual. Typically at least part of the economy is not performing well and some goals are not being met. For example, if inflation starts to increase, the Federal Reserve will attempt to bring it down by increasing interest rates. When this happens, the economy slows down because businesses are less willing to expand when the cost of borrowing increases, so unemployment increases. Therefore, there is a trade-off, at least in the short run, between stable prices and full employment and economic growth. But the strength of this relationship has been challenged by various economic schools of thought (more on these below). Indeed, the stagflation of the 1970s that had both high inflation and unemployment was a real-life event that powerfully called the trade-off into question.

Steps to address the trade deficit also conflict with other goals. Politicians are often under pressure to protect American jobs and prevent them from going overseas. But if policy makers impose tariffs or other barriers to free trade to protect domestic products and jobs, this violates the goal of promoting an efficient free market. Tackling trade imbalances through a weaker dollar can undermine the goal of keeping inflation low. When the dollar weakens, imports become more expensive, which can increase the inflation rate. Policy makers must tread carefully when addressing economic problems to make sure that they are not making some other problem worse. The next section explores who these policy makers are.

fiscal policy Government decisions about how to influence the economy by taxing and spending.

monetary policy Government decisions about how to influence the economy using control of the money supply and interest rates.

budget making The processes carried out in Congress to determine how government money will be spent and revenue will be raised.

budget reconciliation The process by which congressional committees are held to the spending targets specified in the budget resolution. During this process, the House and Senate Budget Committees combine the budgetary changes from all the legislative committees into an omnibus reconciliation bill to be approved by Congress.

The Key Players in Economic Policy Making

CONGRESS

The Constitution places Congress at the center of economic policy making by giving legislators the "power of the purse"—that is, power over the nation's fiscal policy of taxing and spending. In a way, everything Congress does has an impact on the economy, whether it is providing money for an interstate highway or a student loan, regulating the level of air pollutants, or funding the Social Security system. Some committees are more directly related to economic policy: budget, appropriations, and tax committees (the Ways and Means Committee in the House and the Finance Committee in the Senate) direct Congress's **fiscal policy**—taxing and spending— whereas the banking committees have a hand in overseeing aspects of the nation's **monetary policy**—controlling the money supply and interest rates. (However, as we discuss below, monetary policy is primarily the domain of the Federal Reserve System, or the Fed.) The commerce committees, especially in the House, also have their hand in a broad range of economic policies. Because it is the most important of Congress's economic policy-making responsibilities, we focus our discussion on the budget process and how it has evolved in the past fifty years.

Budget making in Congress was quite decentralized through much of its history, with various committees and subcommittees serving as the center of the legislative process and no real way to coordinate activity among them. The appropriations committees, especially in the House, tried their best to be the "guardians of the Treasury," but it was difficult to keep the spending requests from other committees in line with overall budgetary expectations.[8] As a result, budgetary power shifted from Congress to the president, starting with the Budget and Accounting Act of 1921. From that point on, presidents have played a central role in the budget process by submitting their budgets to Congress. The president's budget often serves as the starting point for the congressional budget.

The decline in Congress's budgetary power came to a head in the early 1970s during the presidency of Richard Nixon.[9] President Nixon stepped on many congressional toes by exerting unprecedented power over the budget (this was in addition to the dramatic wage and prices controls that we already mentioned). The most serious action was his impoundment of appropriated money; that is, he simply refused to spend money on congressionally authorized programs. Congress finally responded by passing the Budget and Impoundment Control Act of 1974, which stipulated that unless Congress passed a bill agreeing with the president's impoundment within forty-five days, the impoundment was canceled.[10] More important, the act also restored the *institutional* balance between the president and Congress on the budget by creating the Budget Committees in the House and Senate, setting up the budget process outlined in Nuts and Bolts 15.2, and establishing the Congressional Budget Office that gave Congress independent expertise and advice on budgetary matters so it did not have to rely on the president's numbers. For the first time, Congress had the institutional capacity on budgetary matters to deal with the president on an equal footing.

However, the new process and institutions didn't guarantee smooth sailing. In fact, Congress had a difficult time meeting the various deadlines, and the new process didn't help eliminate the budget deficits. There was a powerful tool in the Budget Act that was basically ignored for the first five years that the law was in effect: **budget reconciliation** was first used in 1980 to bring spending levels into line with the budget resolution. This process forces committees to meet specific

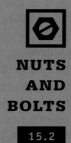

NUTS AND BOLTS

15.2

Budget Timetable

DATE	ACTION
First Monday in February	President submits budget
February 15	Congressional Budget Office issues budget and economic outlook report
Within six weeks of the president's budget submission	Committees submit views and estimates to the Budget Committees
April 1	Budget Committees report resolution
April 15	Congress completes budget resolution
May 15	Appropriations bills may be considered in the House
June 10	House Appropriations Committee reports last bill
June 30	House completes action on annual appropriation bills
July 15	President submits midsession review
October 1	Fiscal year begins

SOURCE: Senate Budget Committee, "About the Committee," available at http://budget.senate.gov/democratic/timetable.html.

spending targets, and then all of these changes are combined into one huge omnibus reconciliation bill. This process has two main advantages in terms of adopting budget cuts, which are always difficult because most programs have strong advocates who will fight the cuts. First, having everything in a single huge bill makes it much more difficult for members to vote against it because that would mean turning down the entire package, including elements of the bill that individual members of Congress like as well as those that they oppose. Depending on the timing, failure to pass an omnibus spending bill may mean shutting down the government. Second, the Senate treats reconciliation bills differently than other bills or amendments. They cannot be filibustered, and debate is limited to twenty hours, amendments must be germane, which means they must relate to the bill, and other extraneous provisions unrelated to deficit reduction can be struck down. This last point is known as the Byrd Rule, named after Senator Robert C. Byrd. It was adopted in 1985 and has been an important tool in deficit reduction.[11] Overall, reconciliation has been used in about two-thirds of the budgets since 1980 and has been responsible for cutting hundreds of billions of dollars of spending. As we discuss in the next chapter, reconciliation was crucial in passing health care reform in 2010 because it allowed Democrats to avoid a Republican filibuster.

Even the powerful tool of reconciliation was not enough to come to grips with the exploding budget deficits of the early to mid-1980s. In 1985 Congress tried to get control of the deficits by passing the Balanced Budget and Emergency Control Act, informally known as Gramm–Rudman–Hollings after its primary sponsors,

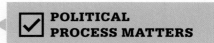

POLITICAL PROCESS MATTERS

but it didn't work. When the law was adopted, the budget deficit for the next fiscal year was $221 billion, or 5.4 percent of GDP. The law was supposed to eliminate the deficit within five years, but in 1991 the budget deficit was $269 billion, or 5.5 percent of GDP. Congress was just spinning its wheels.

The budget process was changed once again with the Budget Enforcement Act of 1990. There were several important changes, but the one that seemed to give Congress the most traction in getting a handle on the deficits was a zero-sum, pay-as-you-go (PAYGO) process whereby any new tax cut or spending increase had to be paid for by raising another tax or cutting spending in some other program. The PAYGO procedure, along with the tax increases in Clinton's 1993 budget, put the nation on the path for the first budget surpluses since the 1960s. There were a few more bumps in the road, including a major budget showdown between Clinton and the Republican Congress in 1995 and 1996 which led to two government shut-downs: one for six days in November 1995, and another for almost a month, from December 1995 to January 1996. Opinion polls suggested Republican leaders were blamed for the shutdown, so Clinton was able to win support for most of his budget priorities. Tensions between Clinton and Congress eased when strong economic growth led to higher revenue than had been forecast, which meant that reducing the deficit became a less contentious process. By 1999, the budget was balanced, and in 2000 there was a substantial surplus ($86.3 billion) for the first time in nearly fifty years.[12]

The surpluses evaporated and massive budget deficits returned in 2002 (the deficit hit $317 billion in 2002 and averaged $475 billion over the next five years). One major contribution to this explosion in the deficits is that PAYGO was allowed to lapse for the 2002 budget—in part to make it easier to fund the war in Iraq and the War on Terror, but also to make it politically easier to pass additional tax cuts. Without the need to pay for tax cuts or spending increases, it is simply too tempting to let the deficits increase to unsustainable levels. When Democrats regained control of Congress in January 2007, they reinstated the PAYGO rule. However, Congress waived the rule to create a short-term fix for the alternative minimum tax, which was raising taxes for millions of upper-middle-class Amercians,[13] and then again for the Economic Stimulus Act of 2008, which cut taxes for millions of Americans without offsetting the drop in revenue with savings elsewhere in the budget.[14] The PAYGO rule was strengthened further in February 2010, when Congress passed a statute giving it the force of law. There was one significant exception built into the law—Congress would not have to make up for extending the Bush-era tax cuts for the middle class—and three smaller exceptions for the alternative minimum tax, estate tax, and Medicare reimbursement, which would all be phased out in two to five years.[15]

THE PRESIDENT

"It's the economy, stupid" read the sign in Bill Clinton's 1992 campaign head-quarters. James Carville, the campaign's top political strategist, put up the sign to keep everyone focused and "on message." Once they are in office, presidents rarely need this reminder; they quickly realize that the public expects them to promote a healthy economy. President Obama focused on the economy in his first months in office, pushing through a massive stimulus bill; later, in the face of major unemployment, Obama also signed legislation aimed at creating more jobs.

As mentioned in Chapter 11, on the economic front the president is unable to accomplish much single-handedly: Congress, the Fed, and broader domestic and international economic forces all exert an equal or greater influence on the health of

POLITICS IS CONFLICTUAL

POLITICS IS EVERYWHERE

the U.S. economy. However, the president has a large advising structure to help formulate economic policy. The Office of Management and Budget (OMB), the Council of Economic Advisers (CEA), the Office of the **United States Trade Representative (USTR)**, and the most recent addition, the **National Economic Council (NEC)**, all provide important economic advice to the president. The responsibilities of each of these groups of advisers is described below.

The department with the longest track record of this group is the OMB. Its direct predecessor, the Bureau of the Budget, was created by the 1921 Budget and Accounting Act and was renamed the OMB in 1970. The OMB plays a central role in creating the budget by soliciting spending requests from all federal agencies, suggesting additional cuts, and then coordinating these requests with presidential priorities. It is ultimately responsible for putting together the president's budget, which is then submitted to Congress. The printed budget is four or five volumes and more than 2,000 pages, but the 2009 budget was the first one submitted to Congress in electronic form, saving 20 tons of paper and 480 trees. Though the Government Printing Office still printed 29,491 copies of the 2009 budget, this was more than 4,000 fewer than in the previous year.[16] The OMB also oversees government reorganization plans and recommends improvements in departmental operations.

▲ The reminder that hung on the wall of Bill Clinton's campaign headquarters in 1992 was just as relevant for President Obama in 2009 when he took office during the deepest economic recession since the 1930s.

Created by the Employment Act of 1946, the CEA's central function is to provide the president with objective data on the state of the economy and expert advice on economic policy. The CEA is responsible for creating the *Annual Economic Report of the President*, which has a wealth of data on various aspects of the economy and an overview of the president's policies. Presidents have varied in how closely they work with the CEA or with other parts of their economic team. Some prominent CEA members, such as Walter Heller under John F. Kennedy, were extremely influential in shaping and promoting the administration's tax policy and jobs program. Others have been relegated to a more secondary role.

The USTR is responsible for developing and coordinating U.S. international trade, commodity, and direct investment policy and overseeing negotiations on trade policy with other countries.[17] With the increasing importance of globalization, international trade, and Congress's deference to the executive branch on trade issues through the "fast track" procedure, the USTR is an important player in economic policy making.

The NEC was established in 1993 to fulfill a campaign promise by President Clinton to elevate economic policy to the level of national security and foreign policy (after all, we have a National Security Council, so if it really *is* "the economy, stupid," we should have an NEC as well). The NEC has four principal functions: "to coordinate policy-making for domestic and international economic issues, to coordinate economic policy advice for the President, to ensure that policy decisions and programs are consistent with the President's economic goals, and to monitor implementation of the President's economic policy agenda."[18] The NEC coordinates policy by bringing together cabinet secretaries who work on economic issues, such as the Treasury secretary, budget director, Commerce secretary, CEA chairman, and Labor secretary. As Gene Sperling, head of the NEC in the late 1990s, explained:

> We drive things, but the policy decisions are made through a team effort. Instead of Treasury just deciding tax policy, or OMB just deciding budget policy, they are instead the lead presenters in an NEC process where the decisions are made as a team, with differences being fairly taken up for decision by the President. . . . The NEC is not a set group of people; it is a fair-process commitment.[19]

United States Trade Representative (USTR) An agency founded in 1962 to negotiate with foreign governments to create trade agreements, resolve disputes, and participate in global trade policy organizations. Treaties negotiated by the USTR must be ratified by the Senate.

National Economic Council (NEC) A group of economic advisers created in 1993 to work with the president to coordinate economic policy.

Federal Reserve System An independent agency that serves as the central bank of the United States to bring stability to the nation's banking system.

Treasury Department A cabinet-level agency that is responsible for managing the federal government's revenue. It prints currency, collects taxes, and sells government bonds.

The NEC initially appeared to challenge the CEA's turf, but a division of labor has preserved an important role for each: the NEC is the political arm that coordinates economic policy, and the CEA is the technical arm that provides information about the economy. However, there is also some evidence that the NEC *has* replaced the CEA in the White House pecking order: for example, people tend to move from CEA to the NEC but not the other way, and the NEC has its office in the West Wing of the White House while the CEA is across the street in the Old Executive Office Building.

These last two sections described the roles of Congress and the president separately, but obviously their interactions are central to understanding economic policy. If the president's party controls Congress, then the president's budget becomes the starting point for congressional negotiations over the budget. If the opposing party controls Congress, then the president's budget is usually considered "dead on arrival" and Congress creates its own document. Of course the president can use the veto threat to try to move Congress closer to his position, but when the budget is contained in one large package that must be signed or vetoed in its entirety, it is difficult to carry out such threats.[20]

THE BUREAUCRACY

All of the departments explained in the previous section could be considered part of the larger bureaucracy, but they are included within the Executive Office of the President and therefore are usually considered along with the president. Two other bureaucratic agencies are very important in creating economic policy: the first, the **Federal Reserve System**, is an independent agency, and the second, the **Treasury Department**, is a cabinet-level department.

The Federal Reserve Act of 1913 established the Federal Reserve System to bring stability and continuity to the nation's banking system. The chair and six other governors serve on the Board of Governors of the Federal Reserve System. The chair has a four-year term and the others have fourteen-year overlapping terms. All governors are appointed by the president and approved by the Senate. The board is responsible for establishing monetary policy for the nation, which includes influencing interest rates and the money supply and regulating the lending activity of member banks (this is discussed in more detail later in the chapter). There are twelve regional Federal Reserve banks and more than 2,900 member banks out of the approximately 7,800 banks in the nation.[21] We discuss the operations of the Fed in more detail in the section on monetary policy, but briefly, the regional banks loan money to banks, hold reserves for them, supply currency and coins, buy and sell government securities, and report on the state of the economy in their regions. The other important part of the Federal Reserve is the Open Market Committee, which comprises the seven members of the Board of Governors and the twelve regional bank presidents. However, the bank presidents have only five votes at any given time; therefore, the board controls a majority of the votes.[22]

One crucial characteristic of the Fed is its political independence, which has three primary sources. First, the Fed is an independent agency, which means that its decisions are not subject to review by the president or Congress. Second are the lengthy fourteen-year terms for the six governors and the four-year term for the chair and vice chair, which by design do not overlap with the federal election calendar. One strong indication of the Fed's independence is that presidents typically reappoint chairs who were initially appointed by presidents of the other party: William McChesney Martin was appointed by Harry Truman, served through the presidencies of Eisenhower, Kennedy, and Johnson, and retired in 1970 when

Richard Nixon was president. Paul Volcker was appointed by Carter and reappointed by Reagan. Alan Greenspan's tenure spanned the presidencies of Reagan, Bush, Clinton, and the second Bush.[23] Ben Bernanke was nominated by Bush and renominated by Obama. Unlike other presidential appointees in the bureaucracy, members of the **Federal Reserve Board** can be removed only "for cause," the precise definition of which has never been tested. This provides the Fed with a certain amount of insulation from the political process.

Third, the Fed does not depend on Congress for its operating budget because it can literally create its own money (we discuss how this happens later in the chapter). As discussed in Chapter 12, Congress's control of the bureaucracy is rooted in the power of the purse. Because Congress does not provide the Fed's budget, it has much less leverage over it. The Fed's primary source of income is interest on the Treasury securities it owns. After paying for all of its expenses, the Fed returned about $47.4 billion to the Treasury in 2009. Overall, in 2009 the Fed employed 17,398 people with total expenditures of $4.98 billion.[24] The employees are not subject to civil service rules or pay grades; thus the Fed can offer top salaries and hire some of the best people in finance and economics.

Is the Fed's independence a good thing or bad thing? Supporters of the Fed point out that the Fed's central goal is shared by nearly all politicians and Americans: a stable economy and slow, steady growth (the Federal Reserve Reform Act of 1977 gives the Fed a dual mandate of pursuing stable prices and maximum employment). Therefore, the argument goes, we should just leave them alone, let them do their job, and keep politics out of monetary policy. However, critics of the Fed argue that its lack of accountability means that it can do things that hurt the economy and voters have no recourse. For example, during Ben Bernanke's confirmation hearings for his second term late in 2009, senators grilled the chair on the Fed's regulatory failures that helped precipitate the financial crisis, its decisions during the bailout of American International Group (AIG), and its inability to spur job growth by encouraging more bank lending.[25] If these failures were indeed the Fed's fault—and that point can be debated—there isn't anything that voters can do about it.

But the Fed is not immune to political influence. In fact, one line of research argues that the Fed tries to help presidents during reelection years by encouraging a pro-growth economy.[26] Evidence on this point is mixed, but at a minimum, presidents do have the ability to make it clear when they disagree with the Fed's policies. Presidents also have the opportunity to appoint the chair and vice chair of the Fed, but as noted above, presidents rarely fire them because they do not want to upset the financial markets (which hate uncertainty more than anything else). Other research has shown that the Fed is at least somewhat sensitive to the preferences of the president and Congress.[27]

The Fed's ultimate accountability is to Congress, because if things really got out of hand—say, for example, the Fed decided to increase interest rates to 20 percent without a good reason—Congress could amend the Federal Reserve Act and take away the Fed's responsibility or autonomy in specific areas. The Fed must report to Congress annually on its activities and to the banking committees of Congress twice a year on its plans for monetary policy. The Fed's annual report is subject to an outside audit. Fed officials also frequently testify before Congress on a broad range of issues. Congress may also publicly criticize the Fed when it disagrees with its policies. For example, during Bernanke's confirmation hearings, Senator Jim Bunning (R-KY) blasted him as "the definition of moral hazard" and said, "I will do everything I can to stop your nomination and drag out the process as long as possible. We must put an end to your and the Fed's failures, and there is no better time than now. The AIG bailout alone is reason enough to send you back to Princeton."[28] It is not clear that such broadsides have much of an effect, but it probably made Bunning feel better.

▲ *Federal Reserve Chairman Ben Bernanke makes his case during his Senate confirmation hearing for a second term. The Fed played a key role in supporting the economic recovery in 2009–2010 by keeping interest rates low.*

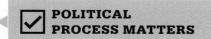

Federal Reserve Board The group of seven presidential appointees who govern the Federal Reserve System.

The Treasury Department is another part of the bureaucracy that plays an important role in economic policy making. According to its Web site, the mission of the Treasury "is to promote the conditions for prosperity and stability in the United States and encourage prosperity and stability in the rest of the world." Specifically, the range of its responsibilities that are relevant for economic policy making include:

- Managing federal finances
- Collecting taxes, duties, and monies paid to and due to the United States and paying all bills of the United States
- Producing currency and coinage
- Managing government accounts and the public debt
- Supervising national banks and thrift institutions
- Advising on domestic and international financial, monetary, economic, trade, and tax policy
- Enforcing federal finance and tax laws
- Investigating and prosecuting tax evaders, counterfeiters, and forgers[29]

Some of these responsibilities overlap with the Fed's, especially supervising banks and managing the public debt. In most instances the responsibilities are complementary rather than competing, such as the management of currency and coins: the Treasury produces currency at the Bureau of Engraving and Printing (about 37 million bills are printed every day, 95 percent of which go to replace worn out currency) and coins at the United States Mint (which makes between 5 and 14 *billion* coins a year, depending on demand), and the Fed distributes them to member banks.[30] Financing federal debt is another matter. The Treasury generally prefers to have lower interest rates to keep down the cost of financing the debt and to promote economic growth, while the Fed is more worried about keeping rates high enough to avoid inflation. Therefore, the Fed and Treasury must often coordinate their policies to make sure they are not working at cross-purposes.

The most dramatic example of cooperation between the Fed and Treasury came in a dizzying period that began in mid-September 2008. Problems in the subprime, or high-risk, mortgage market, the collapse of housing prices, and the tightening of credit markets had been putting pressure on the economy through the spring and summer. The first sign of serious trouble came on September 7, when the federal government took over the Federal National Mortgage Association and the Federal Home Mortgage Corporation because they were about to go under. These two government-sponsored enterprises, nicknamed "Fannie Mae" and "Freddie Mac," fund most of the home loans in the nation. This federal acquisition, involving a commitment of $200 billion to back up Fannie and Freddie's assets, was "one of the most sweeping government interventions in private financial markets in decades."[31] The takeover calmed the credit markets for a few days, until it became evident that two Wall Street giants, the investment banks Lehman Brothers and Merrill Lynch, were becoming financially unstable because of subprime mortgage exposure and other bad debt. Lehman Brothers went bankrupt, Merrill Lynch was bought by Bank of America, and the markets panicked.

The next day brought more bad news: the world's largest insurance company, AIG, was also up to its ears in the subprime mess and teetering on the edge of bankruptcy, so the Fed stepped in with an $85 billion loan to save it. Despite these dramatic moves, credit markets seized up, and investors started pulling money out of anything that looked like it could be related to the financial crisis. A few days later,

▼ Fed Chairman Ben Bernanke tries to convince American taxpayers that the federal takeover of the home mortgage institutions Fannie Mae and Freddie Mac is a good idea. With the multibillion-dollar bailout of AIG, the world's largest insurance company, and the broad commitment to buy bad mortgage debt from financial institutions, the Fed and Treasury tried mightily to curb the financial meltdown in fall 2008.

Washington Mutual, the nation's sixth-largest bank, failed. This series of disasters and near-disasters led to around-the-clock meetings of Fed and Treasury leaders who produced a plan for the government to buy mortgage-related assets from banks and other financial institutions. The three-page proposal was a sweeping request for Congress to grant the Treasury secretary unprecedented, unilateral powers to spend taxpayers' money. Congressional leaders embraced the idea of helping financial institutions deal with their bad debt but questioned the lack of oversight and accountability in the proposal.

Congressional leaders hammered out a compromise bailout bill over the weekend, and on Monday, September 29, they put it up for a vote, assuming that they had enough votes to pass it. In a stunning rebuke to party leaders and President Bush, the House defeated the $700 billion bailout bill by a vote of 205 to 228, with 133 Republicans and 95 Democrats opposing it. The stock market plummeted by 7 percent in the hours after the bill failed. Analysis of the House vote showed that two factors were central: ideology and electoral vulnerability. It was a coalition of the "ends against the middle," with extreme liberals and conservatives voting against it and moderates voting for it. Politically vulnerable members also voted against the unpopular bill, believing their constituents viewed it as an unfair bailout of Wall Street.

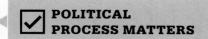

POLITICAL PROCESS MATTERS

Throughout the crisis, which was the worst since the Great Depression, Fed Chair Ben Bernanke and Treasury Secretary Henry Paulson worked together to restore confidence in financial institutions.[32] Secretary Paulson said, "The financial security of all Americans—their retirement savings, their home values, their ability to borrow for college and the opportunities for more and higher-paying jobs—depends on our ability to restore our financial institutions to a sound footing."[33] Congressional leaders picked up this theme, emphasizing the benefits of the plan for "Main Street" rather than just for Wall Street. They emphasized that small businesses were having a hard time getting short-term loans to meet payroll and individuals were getting turned down for loans to buy cars or pay college tuition. They even started calling the plan a "rescue" rather than a "bailout."

POLITICS IS EVERYWHERE

The Senate took the lead on retooling the bill, given the House's earlier inability to act. Wanting to ensure a solid majority behind the bill, leaders added sweeteners, such as increasing the amount of savings insured by the federal government from $100,000 to $250,000 per account to help restore confidence in regular savings accounts, and imposed more accountability by limiting to $350 billion the amount of mortgage-related assets the Treasury secretary could buy (he was required to seek permission from Congress for an additional $350 billion if he needed more). The Senate passed the bill by a 75-to-24 margin, with support from 39 Democrats, 35 Republicans, and 1 Independent.[34] Two days later the House voted for the bill by a 263-to-171 margin, with 91 Republicans joining 172 Democrats.[35] President Bush signed the Emergency Economic Stabilization Act into law on October 3, 2008.

Despite this significant rescue plan, the crisis spiraled out of control in the following weeks. Stock markets plunged worldwide, with the U.S. stock market shedding 35 percent of its value in the two months after the crisis began in mid-September. Credit markets remained frozen, and it became clear that an alternative approach was needed. The government's purchase of "toxic debt" posed many technical obstacles, and financial markets had no confidence that the plan would work. European leaders swiftly agreed to an approach in which governments would directly invest in banks, providing them with desperately needed capital in return for equity stakes in the banks. The United States followed suit with an initial allocation of $250 billion to directly invest in banks, followed by an announcement that the Treasury would abandon its plan to buy toxic debt and use all the funds to directly invest in banks. By mid-November, the economic panic had eased, but the situation remained fragile.

► Protesters at a rally against government bailouts for Wall Street called for the resignation of the chief executive of Goldman Sachs and cancellation of bonuses for all Goldman employees. Huge profits and bonuses on Wall Street in 2009–2010 were very controversial, as the unemployment rate remained at nearly 10 percent.

When President Obama took office in 2009, things were still very grim. Stocks finally bottomed in March 2009 (down 56 percent from their October 2007 high), shortly after Treasury Secretary Timothy Geithner announced the administration's Financial Stability Plan. The plan focused on four problems: frozen credit markets, weakened bank capital, a backlog of troubled mortgage assets on bank balance sheets, and falling home prices. Working with the Fed to stabilize the financial markets, the Treasury had largely resolved three of those four problems one year later. Credit markets were operating, and banks were in much better shape, having raised more than $140 billion in capital and $60 billion in unsecured debt. Banks used these funds to repay the Treasury, which as of July 2010 had recovered three-fourths of its investments in banks, earning $25 billion in income. The Treasury expects to eventually recover all of the TARP expenditures. The housing market, though not fully recovered, has also stabilized, with sales up and prices steady in most markets. Troubled mortgage assets remained on the balance sheets of many banks, but with their stronger base of capital and the strengthened housing market, they were not as great a concern as they had been a year earlier.[36] Banks earned $21.6 billion in profits in the second quarter of 2010—their best showing since 2007.

Despite the broad success of the financial rescue, it remained a political liability. The rescue was widely perceived as a bailout of Wall Street. Many citizens were outraged over corporate salaries and bonuses (especially the $16.2 billion given to Goldman Sachs employees in 2009), the bailout of the auto industry, and the perception that not enough was being done to help average Americans. The economy lost 8.4 million jobs in 2008–2009, millions of Americans were losing their homes, and unemployment remained stuck around 9.5 percent. Discontent with the bailout contributed to the crushing defeat for Democrats in the 2010 midterm elections, despite the fact that it was a bipartisan plan that was passed at the end of the Bush administration. Exit polls showed that the 47 percent of voters in 2010 incorrectly thought that the bailout was passed under Obama, while only 34 percent knew it was under Bush and 19 percent said they didn't know.[37]

POLITICS IS CONFLICTUAL

THE COURTS

The courts are not directly involved in creating economic policy the way that Congress, the president, and the Fed are. However, the U.S. court system influences economic policy in a way that is often taken for granted but becomes readily apparent

The Independence of the Federal Reserve

After the economic meltdown of 2008–2009 and the Federal Reserve's extraordinary intervention to stabilize the banking system and ease credit markets, critics of the Fed had new ammunition to go after their favorite target. Critics questioned why the Fed bailed out some financial institutions, including foreign banks, so they did not have to take losses on billions of dollars of investments guaranteed by the American International Group (AIG) while many other investors and institutions were forced to take a financial haircut. Many members of Congress, most prominently Representative Ron Paul (R-TX) and Senator Bernie Sanders (I-VT), challenged the independence of the Fed by calling for more transparency in its operations and additional congressional oversight. Paul pushed for regular audits of the Fed, saying, "This claim that the Fed should have 'independence' is a canard. They very much enjoy their comfortable pattern of bailing out friends and devaluing the currency with no oversight and no accountability. . . . The Fed should be accountable to Congress because it is a creature of Congress."[a] But after Fed chairman Ben Bernanke warned that giving Congress the power to audit the Fed at any time "would seriously threaten monetary-policy independence, increase inflation fears and market interest rates, and damage economic stability and job creation," the Senate opted for a more modest one-time audit of the central bank's emergency lending program and disclosure of the financial institutions it assisted. Congress also maintained Fed oversight of banks with less than $50 billion in assets.

The question of the independence of the Fed is related to a more general question that is the focus of political science research: When does Congress delegate policy responsibility to an independent agency (such as the Fed), and how does Congress decide how much control to give the president over the agency? One could

Protesters hold signs in the background as Federal Reserve Chairman Ben Bernanke testifies at a congressional hearing about AIG.

imagine that Congress and the president would both want to have control over monetary policy and interest rates because they are so important to the functioning of the economy. So why was the Fed given so much independence?

Political scientist David Lewis has studied the conditions under which Congress will delegate power to an agency and insulate it from outside control or allow for more presidential control. Based on a theoretical approach called the New Economics of Organization, Lewis argues that if we can understand the "incentives of the actors, their policy preferences, and the degree of uncertainty, we can predict what the decisions will be."[b] In general, Congress prefers a larger degree of insulation in an agency than the president. This preference for insulation is strong when Congress is controlled by a majority of the party in opposition to the president and when those majorities are relatively large. But under unified government, when the president and Congress are controlled by the same party, larger majorities for the president's party in Congress mean a lower probability of creating insulated agencies (because Congress wants to give the president more control). Lewis tested these hypotheses by examining every agency created between 1946 and 1997, determining

whether these agencies are relatively insulated or more open to presidential control. He found strong support for his theory.

It is somewhat surprising then that the creation of the Federal Reserve in 1913 is not consistent with the hypothesis that unified government with large majorities is more likely to create agencies that are subject to presidential control (Democrat Woodrow Wilson was president and the Democrats had a 290-to-127 margin in the House and a 51-to-44 majority in the Senate). This anomaly and the nearly complete independence of the Fed may be explained by the need for a consistent monetary policy: if the Fed were not insulated, Congress and the president would be tempted to influence monetary policy for short-term political gain.

The example of the Fed also runs against Lewis's general preference for a hierarchically structured, functionally organized bureaucracy that is subject to presidential influence in its design. He recognizes that there are some instances in which insulation and independence may be necessary. He says, "Delegating control over interest rates and monetary policy to the Federal Reserve, for example, is probably a case where the loss of efficiency in coordination are outweighed by the potential policy losses from flip-flopping presidential economic policy."[c] Recent efforts by Congress to impose more accountability on the Fed reflect public outrage over the bailouts for Wall Street. But the measured response of a limited audit while preserving the Fed's regulatory power over banks demonstrates that Congress continues to recognize the need for an independent Fed. ■

Watch a video clip of David Lewis discussing this topic at wwnorton .com/studyspace.

when comparing America's political system to the developing world. One key difficulty poor nations face in promoting economic development is the lack of an independent, honest legal system. Contract law, patent law, banking and finance law, and property rights are all necessary elements of a legal system that provides the foundation for economic development. If international corporations cannot count on having their contracts honored or their technological secrets protected, or if they must bribe legal officials at every turn, they are far less likely to consider doing business in that country.[38] The courts provide this necessary legal foundation. They issue rulings on the regulation of the telecommunications, banking, and energy industries and decisions on environmental law and eminent domain that affect property rights. All of these policies have an impact on economic policy.

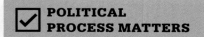

Tools and Theories of Economic Policy

FISCAL POLICY

Fiscal policy is the use of the government's taxing and spending power to influence the direction of the economy. In the 1930s, economist John Maynard Keynes developed the idea of fine-tuning the economy through "countercyclical" taxing and spending policy, which is usually referred to as **Keynesian economics**. Keynes argued that policy makers can soften the effects of a recession by stimulating the economy when overall demand is low—during a recession, when people aren't spending as much—through tax cuts or increased government spending. Tax cuts put more money in people's pockets, allowing them to spend more than they otherwise would, while government spending stimulates the economy through the purchase of various goods, such as highways or military equipment, or direct payments to individuals, such as Social Security checks. From this perspective, it is acceptable to run budget deficits in order to increase employment and national income to give a short-term boost to the economy. Keynes also pointed out that if overall demand is too high, which might result in inflation, policy makers should cool off the economy by cutting spending or raising taxes.[39]

The best example of a Keynesian tax cut used to stimulate the economy was the Revenue Act of 1964. The politics of getting the bill passed were tricky: in a reversal of today's partisan politics, liberal Democrats favored the tax cuts to stimulate the economy and conservative Republicans opposed them because they were afraid of ballooning deficits. The debates between them delayed the bill for ten months, but extensive lobbying by President Johnson eventually led to strong bipartisan support.[40] The tax cut was one of the largest in the twentieth century and helped lay the foundation for a period of unprecedented economic expansion in the 1960s.[41]

A more recent version of fiscal policy was the basis for Ronald Reagan's tax cuts in 1981 and has been the centerpiece of economic policy for many Republicans since then. **Supply-side economics**, as the label suggests, focuses on the ways that tax policy and regulations affect the labor supply rather than on the impact of these policies on overall demand. The primary focus was on how tax rates affect how much people work rather than how they spend. The idea is based on the relationship between the top marginal tax rate and total tax revenue as shown in the Laffer curve, named for economist Arthur Laffer. If tax rates are too high, people will

Keynesian economics The theory that governments should use economic policy, like taxing and spending, to maintain stability in the economy.

supply-side economics The theory that lower tax rates will stimulate the economy by encouraging people to save, invest, and produce more goods and services.

work less because a large percentage of their income is going to the government. The basic shape of the curve is intuitive and the endpoints of the curve are noncontroversial: if the tax rate is zero, there will be no tax revenue, and if the tax rate is 100 percent, nobody will work because they won't get to keep any of their money, so total tax revenue at that end of the curve is also zero. Laffer argued that if tax rates are too high (to the right of the peak in the graph; see Figure 15.3), the government should cut taxes in order to raise total government revenue, which is counterintuitive.[42]

It should have seemed too good to be true, and it was. When taxes were cut, with the top marginal rate going from 70 to 50 percent, revenue fell and the budget deficits exploded. Supporters of the supply-side theory argue that the problem was on the spending side of the equation rather than on tax revenue. That is, deficits went up because the Democratic Congress spent too much, not because of Reagan's tax cuts. However, taxes and spending as a share of the overall economy both fell during the Reagan presidency: tax revenue fell from 19.6 percent of GDP in 1981, the last year before the tax cuts went into effect, to 18.1 percent of GDP in 1988, the last year of the Reagan presidency. Individual income tax revenue fell from 9.3 percent to 8 percent of GDP over this same period, so most of the decrease in revenue was due to lower individual income taxes. While overall government spending did increase during the 1982–83 recession, spending from the beginning of Reagan's term to the end dropped slightly from 22.2 percent to 21.2 percent of GDP.[43] This suggests that spending was not the source of the budget deficits in the 1980s.

Economists continue to debate the extent to which fiscal policy can influence the economy. Two factors have limited the effectiveness of fiscal policy. First, fiscal policies often cannot be implemented quickly enough to have the intended impact on the **business cycle**—the normal expansion and contraction of the economy. This is especially true during divided government, when one party controls Congress and the other controls the presidency, but it happens even during unified government.

The $787 billion American Recovery and Reinvestment Act of 2009, which was designed to stimulate the economy and create jobs, ran into some problems along these lines. Although the legislation clearly had some immediate impact on the economy, it is impossible to spend that much money (or implement tax cuts) without some time lag. The Web site that tracks the spending of the stimulus money, Recovery.gov, reports that, of the $787 billion, tax cuts comprise $288 billion; contracts, grants, and loans are $275 billion; and entitlements are $224 billion. One year after the recovery bill was enacted, the government reported that nearly 600,000 jobs had been saved but only 34.6 percent of the money had been spent ($272.2 billion). Republicans criticized the Democrats for spending too much money and not enacting policies that would have had a more immediate effect (such as payroll tax cuts), and critics on the left argued that the stimulus wasn't big enough.

Second, on the other side of the Keynesian coin, increasing taxes or cutting spending during good economic times is much more difficult to implement than the more politically popular tax cuts or spending increases. Although the latter is limited by the difficulty of timing the fiscal policy to have a maximum economic impact, the former is limited by politics: politicians do not like to raise taxes or cut spending. Furthermore, even if politicians *wanted* to cut spending, this aspect of fiscal policy is becoming increasingly difficult to use because a growing portion of the federal budget is devoted to **mandatory spending**—that is, entitlements such as Social Security, which must be spent by law, and interest on the federal debt, which must be paid (if the United States defaulted on its debt there would be an international economic meltdown). So reducing the federal deficit by cutting spending is increasingly difficult. With the 2011 deficit running close to $1.4 trillion, Congress

FIGURE 15.3 | **THE LAFFER CURVE**

The Laffer curve shows the theoretical relationship between the tax rate and total tax revenue. How did this curve help contribute to the budget deficits of the 1980s?

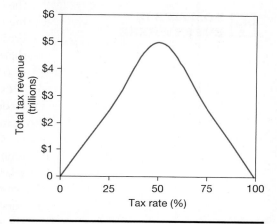

business cycle The normal pattern of expansion and contraction of the economy.

mandatory spending Expenditures that are required by law, such as the funding for Social Security.

POLITICS IS EVERYWHERE

would have to eliminate nearly all **discretionary spending**—spending that can be cut from the budget without changing the underlying law—including defense spending ($895 billion) and everything else the government does ($520 billion), to balance the budget.[44] This would literally mean shutting down the Pentagon; the State Department; Homeland Security; the Justice Department, which includes the FBI and all federal law enforcement; and the Interior Department, which includes the national park and forest systems; and eliminate all spending on science, including the National Science Foundation and NASA; transportation; the arts and public broadcasting; student loans; and the food stamps and child nutrition programs. The share of the budget comprised by discretionary spending is projected to fall from 67.6 percent of the budget in 1962 to only 29.9 percent by 2015 (see Figure 15.4). This has clear implications for efforts to balance the budget in the future: it cannot be done through cutting discretionary spending alone but will have to include cuts in mandatory spending (such as Social Security and Medicare) and tax increases.

Given this tenuous relationship between fiscal policy and the state of the economy, critics have suggested an alternative rationale for large budget deficits in relatively good economic times (recall that a Keynesian account says that the government should run surpluses during good times and supply-siders argue that tax cuts should produce surpluses rather than deficits). Instead of an effort to stimulate the economy, the large tax cuts and budget deficits of the 1980s and early 2000s were, as Reagan's budget director David Stockman called it, an attempt to "starve the beast."[45] That is, large deficits are the only way to cut down the size of government. If there is no money available, liberals will not be able to propose new programs and conservatives will be more likely to cut existing programs. The only alternative is raising taxes, which is usually politically unpopular, even though in comparison to other countries, our tax bite is still relatively small (see Comparing Ourselves to Others).

Fiscal policy may have a relatively modest impact on the economy, but it determines how the tax burden is distributed and which parts of the economy and policy areas benefit from federal spending—in other words, fiscal policy has *redistributive* implications. There are two ways of thinking about the characteristics of federal taxes: (1) the different types of taxes and (2) the redistributive nature of those taxes—that is, whether a specific tax is regressive, neutral, or progressive (defined

---

FIGURE 15.4 **MANDATORY AND DISCRETIONARY SPENDING, 1962–2015**

The percentage of the budget allocated for discretionary spending has been shrinking since the 1960s. What implications does this have for members of Congress and the president as they try to reduce the federal deficits?

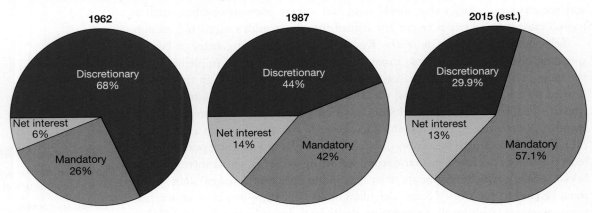

SOURCE: U.S. Government Printing Office, Budget of the United States Government: Historical Tables, available at http://www.gpoaccess.gov/usbudget/fy11/hist.html.

Tax Rates around the World

As we established in our discussion of the size of America's government (Chapter 12), Americans love to complain about their taxes. Ask typical Americans what they think about paying taxes and nobody would rate it high on their list of favorite activities; few would say that they wouldn't mind paying higher taxes. Nonetheless, the United States has one of the lowest overall tax burdens of any developed nation in the world. It is important to examine the overall tax burden because the federal income tax is a relatively small proportion of total taxation for most Americans. In our country, poor to lower-middle-class people pay more in sales taxes and payroll tax than they do in federal income tax. Property taxes and state income taxes also figure in heavily for many people in figuring out the total tax burden. Overall, the total tax burden in the United States was 34.5 percent of GDP in 2007. Of all the nations listed here, only five countries have a lower tax burden. Most European nations have total tax burdens between 40 and 50 percent, and taxes in Scandinavian countries are more than 50 percent of the size of the economy.

This means that Americans have more disposable income than their counterparts in other countries, but it also means that Americans must pay more for health care and save more for their retirement. The smaller public sector, most significantly in health care and for pensions, also places American companies at a competitive disadvantage with foreign firms that do not have to pay for health care for their employees.

For example, General Motors has pointed out for years that they spend more on health care than on steel for the average car they produce. Japanese and German car companies have taken advantage of this situation by grabbing an increasing share of the American market, in part because their national health care plans cover their employees. Health care reform enacted in the United States in 2010 did not alter the basic nature of employer-funded health care, so large corporations such as General Motors are still at a comparative disadvantage.

Therefore, although tax policy is normally considered one of the cornerstones of fiscal policy, it also can play a significant role in helping shape trade policy and trade imbalances between the United States and its trading partners. ■

COMPARING GLOBAL TAX RATES

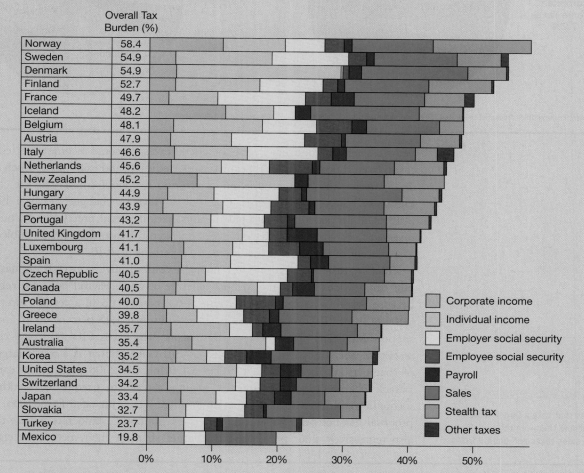

	Overall Tax Burden (%)
Norway	58.4
Sweden	54.9
Denmark	54.9
Finland	52.7
France	49.7
Iceland	48.2
Belgium	48.1
Austria	47.9
Italy	46.6
Netherlands	45.6
New Zealand	45.2
Hungary	44.9
Germany	43.9
Portugal	43.2
United Kingdom	41.7
Luxembourg	41.1
Spain	41.0
Czech Republic	40.5
Canada	40.5
Poland	40.0
Greece	39.8
Ireland	35.7
Australia	35.4
Korea	35.2
United States	34.5
Switzerland	34.2
Japan	33.4
Slovakia	32.7
Turkey	23.7
Mexico	19.8

Legend:
- Corporate income
- Individual income
- Employer social security
- Employee social security
- Payroll
- Sales
- Stealth tax
- Other taxes

0%   10%   20%   30%   40%   50%

SOURCE: Jack Anderson, "Tax Burden & Spending," *Forbes Magazine*, April 13, 2009, available at www.forbes.com/global/2009/0413/034-tax-burden-spending.html.

FIGURE 15.5 FEDERAL REVENUES AND SPENDING, 1962 AND 2010

A much larger share of tax revenue comes from payroll taxes than was true in the 1960s. What implications does this have for the redistributive nature of federal taxes? What have been the biggest changes since the 1960s in the way the federal tax dollar is spent? Are these trends likely to reverse or continue in the next thirty years?

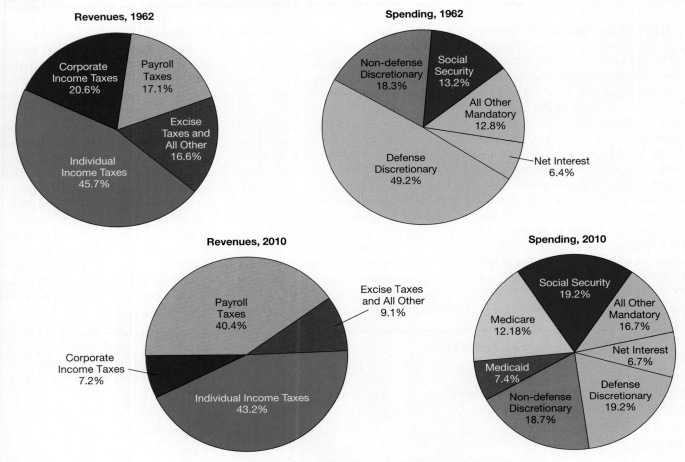

SOURCE: U.S. Government Printing Office, Budget of the United States Government: Historical Tables, available at www.gpoaccess.gov/usbudget/fy11/hist.html.

below). There are four major types of federal taxes: personal income taxes, corporate taxes, payroll taxes (for Social Security and Medicare), and excise taxes (such as taxes on cigarettes, alcohol, gasoline, air travel, and telephone lines). The pie charts in Figure 15.5 show how the distribution of tax revenue changed between 1962 and 2010. The proportion of personal income taxes has held pretty steady, but excise taxes and corporate taxes have fallen, and payroll taxes more than doubled, from 17.1 percent of tax revenue in 1962 to 40.4 percent in 2010.

The increasing share of tax revenue that comes from the payroll tax has important implications for the redistributive nature of taxes. Payroll taxes are **regressive** because everybody pays the same rate of 6.2 percent up to a certain income level ($106,800 in 2010; everyone also pays an additional 1.45 percent on all income to support Medicare). This means that someone who earns $106,800 pays the same *amount* of Social Security tax ($6,622) as Bill Gates, but it is a much larger share of that person's income than for Gates. During the 2008 presidential campaign, Barack Obama proposed lifting the earnings cap on the payroll tax to address this inequality and place Social Security on a more secure financial foundation, but the proposal has not been widely supported, even among Democrats. Excise taxes are also regressive—poor people spend a larger share of their income on cigarettes,

regressive Taxes that take a larger share of poor people's income than wealthy people's income, such as sales taxes and payroll taxes.

FIGURE 15.6 **TOP MARGINAL TAX RATES, 1913–2010**

The top marginal tax rate, which is the tax rate paid by the richest Americans, has plummeted in the past fifty years from more than 90 percent to 35 percent. What are the arguments for and against increasing the top marginal tax rate?

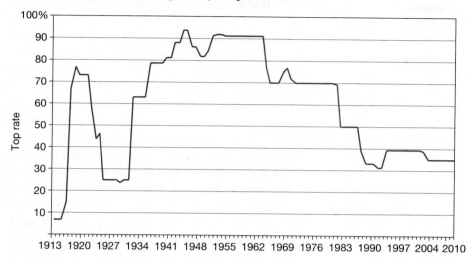

SOURCE: Data from the Internal Revenue Service, "Internal Revenue Bulletin: 2007-45," November 5, 2007, Rev. Proc. 2007-66, available at www.irs.gov/irb/2007-45_IRB/ar19.html.

alcohol, and gas than wealthier people. Income taxes, on the other hand, are **progressive**: upper-income people pay a larger share of their income in taxes than poorer people. In 2005, the last year for which complete data are available, the top fifth of the income distribution had an effective personal income tax rate of 14.1 percent, whereas the bottom two-fifths paid no income taxes—and actually got money back from the federal government because of the earned income tax credit.[46]

One criticism of President Bush's tax cuts in 2001 and 2002 was that a disproportionate share of the cuts went to the wealthiest people in the country. On the one hand, one could argue that this makes sense, given that the bottom 40 percent of taxpayers do not pay any personal income tax. Still, poor and lower-middle-income people do pay a large share of the total payroll tax; thus, that burden could have been reduced by either cutting the payroll tax or increasing the earned income tax credit, which is a way of redistributing tax revenue to poorer people. The effective tax rate—that is, the total tax a person pays divided by the person's income—for the top fifth of the income distribution dropped from 17.5 percent in 2000 to 14.1 percent in 2005, but their overall share of the income tax revenue collected increased from 81.2 percent to 86.3 percent, because their incomes were rising faster than those of middle-income people.[47] At the same time, the top marginal tax rate is close to the lowest it has been since the 1920s (Figure 15.6).

progressive Taxes that require upper-income people to pay a higher tax rate than lower-income people, such as income taxes.

MONETARY POLICY

The starting point of this discussion is to define money. You are probably thinking that you know what the green stuff in your wallet is. You may wish there were more of it, but you know what it is. But if you think about it, money is much more than bills and coins. You probably pay for more things with plastic (debit and credit cards) than coins and currency. Is that money as well? Economists include debit cards in defining money because they simply allow you to spend the money that you already have in your checking account, which is basically the same as cash, but credit cards are not considered money because they are a way of getting a short-term loan. Broader definitions of money also include savings accounts and certificates of deposit. So far, so good. The trickier part comes in understanding where money comes from. Again, the answer may seem simple: the government prints it. But what about the banking part of it? If you haven't ever thought this through, it can be confusing or even unsettling.

Consider this example: you have just graduated from college and you decide that you want to start your own business as a political consultant. You have worked on several campaigns as a volunteer and have even run a few state-wide campaigns. You have two candidates who want to hire you for the next election cycle, but you need to rent an office and buy some computers, phones, and other things for the office. This will obviously take some money. So you go to a bank with your business proposal and show them your contracts for the coming election and your plan for repaying the $100,000 loan that you are requesting. Somewhat to your surprise, the loan officer says yes, and you leave the bank with a checkbook and debit card that suddenly have $100,000 behind them! The bank just created $100,000 seemingly out of thin air.[48] How can that be? Doesn't money have to be something more tangible, based on gold or other real assets rather than simply a promise to repay the money? Nope—at least not in this country since 1933 when the United States abandoned the gold standard. Why doesn't the whole system fall apart? Because it is based on trust and confidence in the banking system. After you get your loan, you could walk down the street to the computer store and buy $10,000 worth of computers with your new debit card and the sales staff wouldn't ask where the money came from. They would just give you the computers.

The banking system did not always work so smoothly. In fact, it nearly collapsed in the Great Depression in the 1930s. Between 1929 and 1934 nearly 40 percent of banks failed or were closed by the government (the number of banks shrank from 24,663 to 15,015), and thousands of people lost their life savings because the banks did not have the money to honor all of their deposits when everyone wanted to withdraw their money at once. On March 6, 1933, two days after taking the oath of office, Franklin Roosevelt closed all of the nation's banks for a full week and only allowed those that were fiscally sound to reopen. In 1933, 4,000 banks were suspended; some of these reopened, but many did not.[49] In order to restore confidence in the banking system, Congress passed the Glass–Steagall Act in 1933, which separated commercial and investment banking and created the Federal Deposit Insurance Corporation, which insured all deposits up to $5,000 (today it is $250,000). Separate legislation also tightened control of the stock market by creating the Securities and Exchange Commission. In 1934, only sixty-one banks were suspended, and almost overnight, confidence in the system was restored.

Today most people rarely think about how the banking system works and simply take for granted that their money is safe. But now that we have gotten you thinking about where money comes from, we will provide more details about the banking system by examining the targets and tools of monetary policy. The Fed monitors levels of bank lending, the money supply, and interest rates and tries to meet specific targets set at its monthly meetings. Bank lending is important to monitor and regulate because, as explained above, it is the source of most new money in the economy. This is crucial for economic growth because businesses borrow money to expand, and as they grow, they add jobs. If credit is tight and businesses cannot borrow money,

▼ *About 40 percent of banks failed in the United States between 1929 and 1934 as people lost confidence in the banking system. "Runs on the bank," like the one shown here in New York in 1931, still happen today when banks or financial institutions are rumored to be in trouble. But government policies to insure deposits and provide liquidity to the banking system make these panic-induced mass withdrawals relatively rare.*

economic growth will suffer, as became painfully evident in late 2008 and 2009. Large public corporations can raise money by selling shares of their company in the stock market, but small businesses do not have this option.

The second target of monetary policy, the money supply, is also central to economic growth and is directly related to levels of lending activity. The Fed can influence the amount of money in the system by making it easier or harder for banks to lend money. According to the **monetarist theory** of macroeconomic policy, as pioneered by Milton Friedman, the amount of money in circulation is the most important determinant of economic activity and inflation. If there is too much money chasing too few goods, there could be inflationary pressure on the economy and prices might rise too quickly.[50] On the flip side, if there isn't enough money available, there could be a recession.

Perhaps the most obvious targets of monetary policy are interest rates. Changing interest rates affect the economy by making borrowing money either cheaper or more expensive. Businesses and consumers are more likely to borrow if the interest rate is 6 percent than if it is 12 percent. Consumer purchases of big-ticket items, things that are financed by borrowing rather than purchased with cash, also increase when interest rates are low and dry up when interest rates are high. That is why so many appliance stores and car dealers try to get you to buy their products with ads that blare out, "Zero dollars down, and zero percent interest until next January!" Entire sectors of the economy, such as housing, construction, consumer durables, and cars, are very sensitive to interest rates.

What can the Fed do to meet targets it sets on credit availability, the money supply, and interest rates? There are three central tools of monetary policy. The **reserve requirement** is the most obvious and potentially powerful tool for affecting the availability of credit, but it isn't used as often as the other two tools. Banks are required to have a certain amount of money in reserve to make sure they have cash on hand to cover withdrawals. The banking crisis of the early 1930s was created by "runs on the banks" when people lost faith in banks, panicked, and all wanted to withdraw their money at the same time. Even today, if everyone decided they wanted to take all their money out at once, the banking system could collapse, because banks are only required to have 10 percent of all deposits on reserve.

By simply changing the amount of money that banks are required to hold for every deposit, the Fed can have a big impact on the amount of money that banks can lend. For example, if banks were required to hold 15 percent of all deposits in reserve instead of 10 percent, that would contract the amount of money they could lend, whereas if the requirement were dropped to 5 percent, it would have the opposite effect. However, because changing the reserve requirement has such a powerful impact on the economy, the Fed has used this tool only four times since 1980.[51]

Interest rates are more difficult to manage than the reserve requirement. With the reserve requirement, the Fed simply announces the change in the rate and that's all there is to it. With interest rates, there is only one rate—the **discount rate**—that the Fed directly sets. The discount rate is the rate that the Fed charges to member banks for short-term loans. However, this is far less important as a policy tool than the **federal funds rate (FFR)**, the rate that member banks charge each other on overnight loans, which are the short-term loans that banks use to meet their reserve requirements. Beginning in 1995, the FFR has been the central interest rate target for the Fed.[52] The FFR is set by the demand for overnight loans that are necessary to settle accounts, but the Fed greatly affects those rates.

To make this process clearer, let's go back to our example of the enterprising campaign consultant who got the $100,000 loan. If the bank that gave that loan also had some unexpected withdrawals over the course of that business day, its "vault cash" at the end of the day may have been short of the 10 percent reserve

monetarist theory The idea that the amount of money in circulation (the money supply) is the primary influence on economic activity and inflation.

reserve requirement The minimum amount of money that a bank is required to have on hand to back up its assets.

discount rate The interest rate that a bank must pay on a short-term loan from the Federal Reserve Bank.

federal funds rate (FFR) The interest rate that a bank must pay on an overnight loan from another bank.

▼ *Hyperinflation in Germany, Hungary, and other parts of Europe between the World Wars was so high that some countries' currency became essentially worthless. As shocking as it may seem, it was cheaper to burn money than to buy wood, as this German woman in 1923 demonstrates—using several million deutsche marks as kindling.*

requirement. The bank would be required to go to the federal funds market and borrow money from a bank that had excess reserves on that given day. This process of borrowing and lending allows money to flow smoothly throughout the banking system. If reserves are tight all around the country, the price of the short-term loans will be bid up and the FFR will rise. If this happens, the Fed can inject more reserves into the system to keep the FFR at its target (we will explain how that happens in the next section). The FFR has a broader impact on the economy because many short-term interest rates track the FFR quite closely.

Despite the Fed's ability to influence short-term interest rates, it has only indirect impact on long-term interest rates, including consumer rates such as mortgages and home equity loans. These rates are set by the market—specifically by the expectations of the bond market for inflation. If an investor thinks that inflation will increase from 3 percent to 6 percent over the next five years, the investor will demand a higher interest rate for loaning their money to the government or a corporation than if they think inflation will hold steady at about 3 percent. For example, starting in June 2004, the Fed raised the target FFR ten times in quarter-point increments from 1 percent to 3.5 percent by August 2005. Short-term consumer rates, such as the prime interest rate, which is the loan rate given to banks' best customers, followed by rising from 4 percent to 6.5 percent over that period. However, long-term rates, such at the ten-year Treasury note, actually *fell* in the first six months of 2005 by nearly a full percentage point, much to the surprise of many financial experts, including former Fed Chair Alan Greenspan, who called it a "conundrum" and "clearly without precedent in our recent experience."[53] Clearly the bond market felt pretty confident that long-term inflation was being held in check, because it did not demand higher interest rates for long-term loans.

The last tool that the Fed uses to meet its monetary targets is **open market operations**—the buying and selling of securities. This is the most important tool because it is used to influence the FFR and the level of bank reserves, and thus the money supply. If the Fed wants to increase the money supply and put downward pressure on the FFR, it will purchase securities such as government bonds from a bank. The bank gives the Fed its bond, and the Fed deposits the appropriate amount of money into the bank's account at the Fed. This money can be used by the bank to support new loans. You may be wondering where the Fed gets its money to buy the bond from the bank. Well, the Fed simply creates the money. You probably have heard the claim that if the government wants to, it could just "print money" to pay for its programs and policies. That claim is literally true, but it would be completely irresponsible. Any government that would run the printing presses to pay for its programs, rather than raising the money through taxes, fees, and borrowing would soon find itself with hyperinflation as experienced in Germany, Poland, Austria, and Hungary after World War I. (The worst inflation ever recorded was in Hungary after World War II: between July 1945 and August 1946, prices rose by a factor of 30,000,000,000,000,000,000,000,000,000!)[54] Our government prints money only to meet the demand for currency from its member banks. However, the Fed's purchase of a government security is like "printing money," and it has the same potential inflationary impact, so this powerful tool must be used with care and only when new money is needed in the system. The tool may also be used to contract the money supply or raise interest rates; if this is the desired outcome, the Fed will sell government securities. The member bank will give the Fed money to cover the cost of the bond and therefore take money out of circulation.

The FFR has not always been the target of Fed policy. In the early 1980s, the money supply was seen as the most important target. The focus on the money supply lasted for only a few years, and by 1983 the Fed shifted back to targeting the FFR and the availability of credit more generally. Monetarist theory had fallen out of favor because the money supply became more difficult to measure and control as the banking industry offered an increasing array of types of bank deposits, such as interest-bearing checking accounts. Also, the velocity of money, the number of times money changes hands in a certain period, became much more volatile, which made it more difficult to predict the economic impact of a change in the money supply.[55] Alan Greenspan made this point when he said, "We don't know what money is anymore." The comment was picked up by Jay Leno on *The Tonight Show*, who quipped, "I don't know who should be running this country's central bank, but surely it should be someone who does know what money is."[56]

In the late 1920s, the Fed took an accommodationist approach of using the discount window (its loans to member banks) to provide additional credit to banks when the economy was expanding and to reduce credit when businesses were not expanding and didn't need loans. At first, this seems to make perfect sense to support the general direction of the economy. But on further reflection it is like pouring gasoline on a fire that is already burning at the level you like, or like pouring water on a fire that is just getting started. This accommodationist policy contributed to the onset of the Great Depression and the increase in the Depression's severity in the early 1930s by choking off the supply of money just when it was most needed. Critics of this approach pointed out that the Fed should have acted proactively, in a countercyclical way. Rather than passively sitting back and simply saying, "Well, there aren't any banks that want to borrow money from us, so there isn't much we can do to stimulate the economy," the Fed should have "flooded the street with money," as the famous banker Benjamin Strong argued shortly before his death in 1928.[57] Starting in 1935, the Fed adopted this countercyclical approach, attempting to stimulate the economy when it started to shrink and cool it down when it grew too fast.

Fed Chair Ben Bernanke used this approach to help stop the "credit crunch" that emerged with the meltdown of the subprime mortgage market and related problems in the bond markets in 2008. The Fed increased its balance sheet (its statement of assets and liabilities) from $927 billion on September 10, 2008, to an eye-popping $2.26 trillion by November 11, 2008 (where it has remained through 2010). About $1.6 trillion of the money injected into the economy came through efforts to stabilize short-term lending, money market funds, and the bailout of AIG (among other things). By February 2010, those loans had shrunk to $224 billion as credit markets stabilized. However, overall Fed assets remained at $2.26 trillion, as the securities held by the Fed climbed from $514 billion to $2 trillion from February 2009 to September 2010 (including $1.1 trillion in mortgage-backed securities that the Fed purchased from stressed financial institutions).[58] This unprecedented intervention in the financial sector clearly prevented a serious crisis, but as we noted above, critics argue that the Fed has become too powerful and unaccountable a player in economic policy making.

REGULATORY POLICY

Government regulation has a huge impact on the economy. For example, the federal government regulates the quality of food and water, the safety of workplaces and airspaces, and the integrity of the banking and finance system. In general, regulations address various market failures such as monopolies, imperfect information, and negative externalities (these are explained below). There are two main types of regulation: economic and social. Economic regulation sets prices or conditions on entry of firms into an industry, whereas social regulation deals with issues of quality and safety.[59]

A common type of economic regulation concerns price regulation of monopolies. A monopoly occurs when a single firm controls the entire market for a product so it is not subject to competition. When this happens, the monopoly could charge extremely high prices if the government did not regulate it. Sometimes a "natural monopoly" occurs because it is so costly to get into a specific business that it only makes sense to have one company. For example, it wouldn't make sense to have more than one water company or sewer system in a given town or city because it costs so much to install water and sewage pipes. In these instances, there is only one company, but the prices it can charge are regulated by the government; alternatively, the water system may be owned by the local government (about 85 percent of water systems are publicly owned and 15 percent are privately owned in the United States).

When the competitive situation is not a natural monopoly, a large firm may act in a monopolistic way to restrict competition—for example, by slashing prices to drive the competition out of business. As soon as all competitors go out of business, the monopoly is free to raise prices again. Concern about this type of behavior led to the first two significant laws aimed at economic regulation: the Interstate Commerce Act (1887), which created the Interstate Commerce Commission to regulate railroad rates, and the Sherman Antitrust Act (1890), which was used to break up Standard Oil in 1910, among other monopolies.

More common than a true monopoly are firms that control most of a market rather than all of it and start acting like a monopoly. For example, Microsoft was sued by the Justice Department and nineteen states in 1998 for trying to quash its competition in the rapidly growing area of Internet browsers. Microsoft claimed that Internet Explorer was an integral part of its Windows operating system, while the government prosecutors argued that it was a separate piece of software that was being given away for free, putting competitors like Netscape at a huge disadvantage. The district court judge agreed with the Justice Department and ordered that Microsoft be broken up into a Windows-based company and another company that would sell Internet Explorer and other programs. This ruling was overturned on appeal. In the meantime, George W. Bush was elected to his first term as president, and his Justice Department announced that it would not challenge the appeals court ruling. Instead, it proposed a settlement that required Microsoft to share its application programming interfaces with third-party companies.[60] This settlement was challenged by several states but upheld by an appeals court in 2004.

The Microsoft example offers two broad lessons. First, regulation affects our daily lives in ways that may not be obvious. The extent to which Microsoft dominates the software industry is determined, at least in part, by the extent to which the government regulates its behavior. Second, politics plays a key role in this process. An important event in the Microsoft case was the election of a president who took a less aggressive stance on regulating potential monopolies than his predecessor had. Recall that Republicans tend to favor a strong role for the free market and a pro-business perspective, which requires a smaller role for government regulation, whereas Democrats generally favor more government regulation to protect the interests of consumers—in the Microsoft case, this meant a broader range of options for Internet browsers—the environment, and workers.

The most common market failures that lead to social regulation are negative externalities: when the costs of a firm's behavior are not entirely borne by the firm but are passed on to other people. When this happens, the firm produces more of an unwanted good than is socially desirable. The classic example is pollution. In a free market, the owners of a coal-fired power

▼ The corporate leadership of Microsoft, including co-founder and former chairman Bill Gates on the left, are shown here defending their company's position against the U.S. Justice Department's lawsuit concerning unfair trade practices with their Internet browser. One important regulatory responsibility of the national government is to limit monopolistic behavior in the economy.

plant do not bear the cost of the pollution spewing out of its smokestacks. The people who live downwind from the plant bear the cost. Therefore, the power plant owners have little incentive to curb pollution unless it is regulated by the government. Other examples of agencies that set social regulations are those that were set up to promote safety, such as the National Highway Traffic Safety Administration, Consumer Product Safety Commission, and Occupational Safety and Health Administration.

Other than the creation of the Interstate Commerce Commission (ICC) and Federal Trade Commission to regulate monopolies, the federal government has experienced two big spurts of regulation: the mid-1930s and the mid-1960s through the mid-1970s. Most of the regulation in the first period was economic. In addition to the creation of the Federal Communications Commission (FCC), Securities and Exchange Commission, Federal Deposit Insurance Corporation, and Federal Power Commission, the ICC expanded its regulatory reach into trucking, water barges, oil pipelines, and buses in the 1930s. Other agencies have also expanded the scope of their activities, such as the FCC, which was created to regulate radio but now is also involved in television, cable, and other forms of communication. One type of economic regulation that came to the fore in 2009 and 2010 concerned the financial sector. As noted above, Alan Greenspan, among many others, attributed the economic meltdown to various market failures, which implies a need for new regulations. Congress followed through in 2010, passing a massive financial sector reform bill that focused on such topics as the "too big to fail" problem, greater protections for consumers in the financial services sector, derivatives trading, and the securitization of subprime mortgages. Others claim that new action was not needed because it was regulators, not regulations, that failed.

Most social regulation came in the 1960s and 1970s as citizens became more concerned about public safety and air and water quality. Public interest groups such as the Sierra Club, Common Cause, the Environmental Defense Fund, Friends of the Earth, Greenpeace, and Public Citizen (the group led by consumer activist Ralph Nader) all pushed for environmental and public safety legislation.[61] Some high-profile reports and events also had an impact on the push for more social regulation. Ralph Nader's 1965 exposé *Unsafe at Any Speed* about the Chevrolet Corvair, and Cleveland's polluted Cuyahoga River catching fire in 1969 increased the pressure on politicians to address these concerns. Congress responded by creating the

▲ Public pressure for stronger environmental regulations increased after the Cuyahoga River, near downtown Cleveland, Ohio, caught fire in 1969. The running joke at the time was that anyone unlucky enough to fall into the polluted river would dissolve rather than drown.

Environmental Protection Agency and passing the Clean Air Act and Clean Water Act. The range of dangerous chemicals that have been regulated since this time is extensive: the pesticide DDT, asbestos, lead (in both paint and gasoline), chlorofluorocarbons, phosphates, and arsenic, to name just a few examples.[62]

Social regulation has continued to expand and enjoy strong political support, but Congress has pared back economic regulation in the past thirty years, with the one exception being the financial sector, for which regulations were strengthened in 2010. The trend toward deregulation started with the airline industry in the mid-1970s. For years economists had argued that the government was keeping the price of airline tickets artificially high by limiting the number of airlines and restricting competition. In 1978 Congress passed the Airline Deregulation Act, which got the federal government out of the business of regulating entry and pricing in the airline industry. The impact of deregulation is a mixed bag. Overall, consumers have benefited from lower ticket prices (10 to 18 percent lower, for savings of about $20 billion a year),[63] more airlines flying more routes to bigger cities, and a rapid expansion in air travel since 1978, which means that flying is now much more common for middle-class Americans. However, many small cities lost air service in the 1980s, despite Congress's promise that this would not happen, and people who live in cities like Minneapolis, Minnesota, or Charlotte, North Carolina, pay more for their tickets on comparable flights than people who live in Chicago, Atlanta, New York, or other cities that have more competition. Over the past thirty years, Congress passed laws that deregulated many other major industries, including banking, trucking, telephone service, radio, and public utilities. In each instance there have been many advantages for consumers but also some costs.

Even in the area of social regulation, economists have long argued for introducing more market forces and reducing government regulation. Politicians are starting to listen. In the 2008 presidential campaign, both John McCain and Barack Obama endorsed the idea of "cap and trade" policies as a market approach to reducing carbon emissions. Environmentalists have learned that using market principles can work to their advantage, as the example of grazing rights in the West discussed in the You Decide box shows.

The Politics of Regulation Economists and political scientists have developed many theories to explain the politics of regulation. The approach one would like to believe is true is called the public interest theory of regulation, in which politicians regulate the economy when there are market failures in order to serve the public interest. For example, the government breaks up monopolies to prevent unfair pricing, prevents companies from polluting as much as they otherwise would, and requires companies to provide equal information for all stockholders so "insiders" cannot benefit unfairly. However, this view ignores the fact that political parties have very different ideas about the public interest. Furthermore, even when members of Congress agree on some aspect of the public interest that should be served—for example, limiting air pollution—they often cannot agree on the precise mechanisms for achieving that goal, so they delegate authority to a regulatory agency to make the difficult decisions.

One explanation of the implications of this bureaucratic delegation is regulatory capture theory, which you may recall from Chapter 12. This theory argues that although Congress may create regulations to serve the public interest, regulatory agencies quickly become controlled by the industries that they are supposed to be regulating.[64] The Food and Drug Administration, Federal Aviation Administration, and U.S. Department of Agriculture (USDA), among others, have been accused of serving the industries they are supposed to regulate rather than protecting consumers.

A modification of this view called the economic theory of regulation takes an even more bleak view of the process in asserting that Congress doesn't even *intend*

Grazing Rights and Free Market Environmentalism

You are a Republican U.S. House member who represents a western state. You are a firm believer in the free market, capitalism, and limited government. In other words, whenever possible you would like people to make choices in the free market without government interference or regulation. By the way, this conveniently is a view that is held by a large majority of your constituents. You also are a strong supporter of grazing rights for ranchers in your state. You have often done battle with environmentalists who want to reserve more public lands for recreational uses and conservation rather than for grazing cattle. On this issue, your constituents are more divided: there is strong support for ranchers, but an increasing proportion of the residents in your district are dependent on tourism.

The scenario that you have to consider here is an actual case that was first publicized in a *New York Times* op-ed piece.[a] The case involves a fifth-generation rancher in southern Utah named Dell LeFevre. He is no friend of environmentalism, saying, "We've got Easterners who don't know the land telling us what to do with it. I am a bitter old cowboy." His bitterness was deepened back in 1991 when he found two dozen of his cows shot to death. He thinks the deed was done by an environmentalist who was trying to get ranchers to leave a scenic part of the Escalante River canyon. So he seems to be a very unlikely candidate to have sat down with an environmentalist named Bill Hedden to accomplish that very goal of ending ranching in the area. Hedden works for a group called the Grand Canyon Trust (GCT) that, as the *Times* article explained, "doesn't use lobbyists or lawsuits (or guns) to drive out ranchers. These environmentalists get land the old-fashioned way. They buy it." Hedden spent about $100,000 to buy and retire the grazing rights from LeFevre for this scenic canyon area. The environmentalists are happy because the vegetation is coming back, and LeFevre is happy because he doesn't have to

Using free-market forces is an increasingly common way to address a variety of environmental issues, from grazing and water rights to air pollution and global warming.

battle the environmentalists anymore and was able to buy grazing rights in a different area that is better for his cattle. Supporters of "free market environmentalism" say this is a perfect example of allowing the market to determine the best use of the land. If an environmentalist is willing to buy a rancher's grazing rights, this means that the market has determined that hiking and conservation have a greater value than grazing for that piece of land.

If the story ended here, there would be no controversy for you to consider. But as you probably guessed, the story does not end here. Local groups, such as the Canyon Country Rural Alliance, which opposed all limitations on ranchers' grazing rights, lobbied Congress and the Interior Department to disallow such arrangements that remove grazing rights from some public lands. Bowing to pressure, the Interior Department decided that "only Congress may permanently exclude lands from grazing use," so GCT had no guarantee that the Bureau of Land Management wouldn't change its mind and allow grazing. The process of resolving this conflict bounced around the Interior Department and the federal courts for nearly ten years.

In the meantime, GCT went to Plan B from the "if you can't lick 'em, join 'em" school of thought: they decided to become ranchers. If the Interior Department

wouldn't grant permanent conservation use permits on land designated for grazing, they would buy some cattle. GCT is now one of the largest ranchers in the Colorado Plateau with 1,000 acres of private land and grazing permits that cover 860,000 acres of federal and state lands, including a large part of the Kaibab National Forest adjacent to the North Rim of the Grand Canyon. They are managing the land in an eco-friendly manner with only 800 head of cattle. Though it may seem odd that an environmental group had to take up ranching to get the policy outcome they wanted, it was a compromise that made all sides of the dispute relatively happy. As one opponent of GCT put it, "We turned them from environmentalists into cowboys. I guess what they can do is get their cows and start losing money like the rest of us."[b]

If you were the member of Congress representing this district, what would you decide to do? Would you support the limitations on permanently removing grazing rights because they are consistent with the desires of many of your constituents? If so, how would you reconcile this with your free market views, and how would you justify the decision to your constituents who support free market environmentalism? Does the compromise position of GCT taking up ranching strike you as a reasonable middle ground? ■

to serve the public interest when it sets up regulatory agencies.[65] As federal judge Richard Posner sees it, "Regulation is not about the public interest at all, but is a process by which interest groups seek to promote their private interest."[66] From this perspective, regulation redistributes resources, and interest groups fight to benefit from that redistribution. So when the USDA sets standards on what types of food can be described as "organic," a broad range of farmers and corporations in the food industry have an interest in how "organic" is defined. Given that members of Congress want to get reelected, the interest groups will compete against each other to gain the most favorable treatment from the legislators, seeking influence partly through campaign contributions. In this view, regulation is not an effort to solve market failures but rather to redistribute income toward certain industries in exchange for political support.

There is some truth in each of these relatively simple theories. If you combine elements from these various approaches, you come up with a fairly accurate picture of the situation. Regulation is usually a response to a legitimate problem, but sometimes regulatory agencies end up serving the interests of the businesses they are supposed to be regulating. Politicians do indeed gain from having groups compete over regulatory policy, but the public interest is often served by regulations that protect the environment, ensure the safety of the food supply, and regulate the dumping of hazardous chemicals. In each instance, *politics* end up defining the public interest that is served through regulation.

TRADE POLICY AND THE BALANCE OF PAYMENTS

In many ways, policy aimed at influencing trade is the most difficult area of economic policy making because many factors that shape trade policy are beyond the control of policy makers. The strength of the dollar relative to other currencies, consumer tastes, the low cost of labor in developing nations (especially China and India), and economic conditions around the world all influence the trade balance but are extremely difficult to control.

When the dollar is strong, imports are relatively cheap in the United States and U.S. exports are expensive. Therefore, if the United States is running a trade deficit, it would like the value of the dollar to fall. However, there isn't much it can do about the value of the dollar because it is determined by international currency markets. How does the value of the dollar affect the trade deficit? Consider the following example. As of this writing, a euro is worth about $1.25. Therefore, a BMW 135i that would sell for 29,000 euros in Germany would go for about $36,250 in the United States, while a Cadillac CTS that would retail in America for $36,250 would sell for about 29,000 euros in Europe—though this example obviously doesn't factor in shipping costs, dealer incentives, higher taxes in Europe, and so on.

Now see what happens if the dollar falls in value so a euro is worth $1.50. It may seem backward to say that the value of the dollar falls when the value of a euro goes from $1.25 to $1.50, but think of it this way: at the new exchange rate, it takes more dollars to buy the same number of euros, so the dollar is worth less. Now that Cadillac could be purchased in Germany for 24,167 euros and the BMW would still cost 29,000 euros, while the BMW would cost an American consumer $43,500 and the Cadillac is still $36,250. Nothing has changed except the value of the dollar, but suddenly the car buyer's choices have changed dramatically. In both countries the Cadillac has become a much better bargain, and therefore, at least theoretically, Cadillac sales (and sales of other GM models, as well as those of Chrysler and Ford) should increase and BMW (and Mercedes, Volkswagen, MINI Cooper, etc.) sales should fall.

We say "at least theoretically" because of the second factor—consumer tastes. If consumers are willing to pay an increasing premium for foreign goods, then a weaker dollar may not help the trade deficit. There isn't much policy makers can do about consumer tastes, despite the ongoing campaign urging citizens to "buy American." The low cost of labor is another factor that policy makers cannot do much to influence. If a foreign firm pays its workers a weekly wage that is equal to what American workers make in an hour for the same job, the foreign firm has a huge competitive advantage. Consequently, the United States has been flooded with cheap consumer goods from nations where labor is very cheap. Low prices are good for American consumers, but they come at the price of large trade deficits and lost American jobs. Furthermore, foreign firms sometimes absorb some currency fluctuations and do not raise the price of their goods in the United States as the dollar falls in value relative to their currency. The final factor—the strength of foreign economies—is also outside the control of American policy makers. If foreign economies are weak, consumers abroad do not have the income to purchase U.S. exports.

Though it is difficult to control trade outcomes, Congress and the president still try by altering trade policies. The main target of trade policy is the trade balance: the difference between the total value of our exports and imports. In recent years the balances have reached record deficits exceeding $1 trillion a year in 2008 before falling back to $519 billion in 2009 during the recession. (Figure 15.7). The current account deficit, the broadest measure of the balance of payments including investments, has also been running at record levels. Economists have warned that deficits of this level are not sustainable. One observer noted that these warnings have been like the annoying car alarms that go off in the middle of the night when

---

FIGURE 15.7 **TRADE DEFICITS, 1974–2009**

The trade deficit remains high. Which groups are most likely to support policies aimed at reducing the trade deficit, and which groups would oppose these policies?

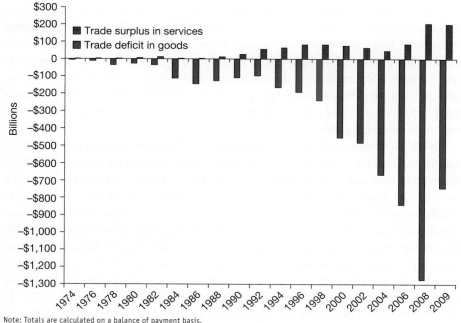

Note: Totals are calculated on a balance of payment basis.

SOURCE: Data from the U.S. Department of Commerce, Bureau of Economic Analysis, International Economic Accounts: Trade in Goods and Services, available at www.bea.gov/international/index.htm#trade.

WELL, I THOUGHT I WAS BUYING AMERICAN, BUT WHEN IT WOULDN'T START I FOUND OUT IT WAS AN AMERICAN CAR BUILT IN MEXICO BY A COMPANY OWNED BY A EUROPEAN COMPANY FULL OF PARTS FROM CHINA.

DID YOU COMPLAIN?

YEAH. THEY TRANSFERRED ME TO A CALL CENTER IN INDIA.

▲ Many American consumer products, including cars, clothing, and electronics, are made overseas because labor is so much cheaper in developing countries. Even people who want to "buy American" have a difficult time, given the increasing globalization of multinational corporations.

nothing is really wrong.[67] However, there is increasing consensus that something must change—either we need to stop buying as many imports and sell more exports, or the value of the dollar must fall to help make this happen.

The trade deficits have to be financed with borrowing from overseas. In the past, these loans came largely from foreign investment by private individuals who saw greater returns on their investments in the United States than in other countries. The net international investment position at the end of 2009 was –$2.7 trillion (that is, the value of foreign investments in the United States exceeded the value of U.S. investments abroad).[68] Foreign governments now own about 46 percent of publicly owned foreign debt (57 percent including all foreign-owned debt), with China buying more than any other country in the past ten years. Why does this matter? If these foreign governments decide to stop investing in American assets or even to start selling them, interest rates will have to rise to attract buyers for our debt, perhaps dramatically.

The types of policies that can be used to reduce the trade deficit are protectionist policies such as trade sanctions, tariffs, and quotas, or attempts to reduce the value of the dollar. Advocates for protectionist policies argue that "free trade" is a myth and we are being taken advantage of by nations that engage in unfair trade practices while selling goods in our open markets. Former senator Ernest F. Hollings once said, "We hear those in the national Congress running around saying, 'Free trade, free trade, I am for free trade,' when they know free trade is like dry water. There is no such thing."[69] It is only fair, they argue, that we set up trade barriers or impose quotas to support our own goods and protect American jobs.

Although broadly based protectionist policies have been rare in the past couple of decades, U.S. policy makers have applied protection in selected markets. For example, in 1983 Harley Davidson won special trade protection from the Reagan administration that raised tariffs on imported Japanese motorcycles from 4 percent to 49 percent. In September 2009, President Obama imposed a 35 percent tariff on Chinese tires. In general, Congress and the president have supported free trade much more than protectionism. The North American Free Trade Agreement in 1993, the Uruguay round of the General Agreement on Trade and Tariffs in 1994, fast-track authorization for the U.S. trade representative to negotiate trade agreements with minimal congressional interference (2002), most-favored-nation trading status for China (2000), and the Central American Free Trade Agreement, which passed by a 217-to-215 margin in the House in 2005, are major trade agreements that expanded free trade by reducing barriers and opening markets. Critics of the laws say that they do not provide adequate protections for workers and the environment, promoting a "race to the bottom" to cut costs while putting additional pressure on American jobs and wages.

With the stakes this high, it is not surprising that politics often plays a central role in trade policy. There are two main explanations for the nature of political influence on trade policy: constituency and ideology.[70] The constituency explanation sees the two major parties representing different groups—Democrats and labor, Republicans and capital—which tends to make the Democrats more protectionist and the Republicans more supportive of free trade. Elaborations of this view agree with the central tendency but note divisions within each constituency. For example, auto and steel workers' unions are much more protectionist than dock-workers' unions because any industry with strong exports will support free trade, whereas those that have relatively few exports but are vulnerable to cheap imports are more likely to be protectionist. The ideological explanation focuses on the bipartisan consensus on trade that emerged after the Great Depression, which was seen as having been caused in part by the protective tariffs of the 1930 Smoot-Hawley Act.[71] As with the theories of regulation, both perspectives explain part of the truth. Our political leaders largely support a free trade ideology, but there are divisions along constituency lines on some legislation.

Conclusion

There is a common perception that economic policies would work better if we could just take politics out of the economic policy-making process. But that would be like saying "football would be better if we could eliminate the contact," or "poker would be better if we could take out the element of chance." Economic policy making is inherently political. It isn't possible or desirable to have economic policy produced by economists who would deftly push and pull the levers of growth, productivity, and efficiency, implementing their economic theories without interference from politicians. Politics must enter into this process. Economic policy determines who wins and who loses, and elected leaders must be involved in this process if representative democracy is to have any meaning. This is especially true of the budget process because the redistributive implications of taxing and spending are so clear, but as we have discussed in this chapter, even monetary policy is not insulated from politics. This role for politics is guaranteed by our system of checks and balances: Congress, the president, and to some extent the courts all have a hand in shaping economic policy. The clash between politics and economic theory and the conflicted nature of economic policy making can be illustrated with a few examples.

We discussed earlier the limitation of implementing Keynesian economic theories in fiscal policy. Often, political considerations make it impossible to implement the swift, targeted action called for in the theory. That is because the budget inherently involves debates over some central political questions: How large should the government be? How progressive should the income tax be? Should budget deficits be allowed to expand to put pressure on government spending (the "starve the beast" argument), rather than to stimulate the economy? These are not purely economic questions but also political ones that must be answered through debate and conflict between the opposing parties and branches of government. Sometimes the debate is intense enough to shut down the government, as with the showdown between President Clinton and the Republican congressional leadership in 1995–1996.

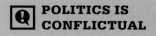
POLITICS IS CONFLICTUAL

Monetary policy is supposed to be more insulated from politics, but even here political pressures are evident. One important example is how fiscal policy—taxing and spending decisions by Congress and the president—can put pressure on monetary policy—the Fed's decisions concerning interest rates and the money supply. With the large budget deficits that the government is currently running, it can become difficult to finance $1.4 trillion a year in new debt. If the demand from private investors, banks, and foreign governments is not sufficient, interest rates may have to rise to attract enough money. This could run counter to Fed policy, which may be concerned that a large increase in long-term interest rates could lead to a recession. However, the alternative would be for the Fed to step in to buy the additional debt, which can create inflationary pressures on the economy. This can put the Fed in a difficult position. The chair of the Fed routinely warns Congress and the president that our budget deficits, debt, and current accounts deficit are not sustainable, but there isn't anything that the chair of the Fed can do to make them change their political decisions about what they think are the best economic policies for the country.

Another useful example of the clash between politics and economic theory is the debate over the proper role for the U.S. government in addressing the late 2008 financial meltdown. Many Republicans resisted the active involvement of the government in credit and financial markets because of their belief in the corrective power of markets. Even as the Bush administration jumped in with both feet by bailing out Freddie Mac and Fannie Mae, AIG, and money market funds; buying up bad debt; and directly investing in banks, there was political resistance to telling banks how to use the federal assistance. European leaders, on the other hand, insisted that banks use the infusion of government capital to begin making more loans. But in the United States, the Fed and Treasury did not require anything of the banks that were provided with desperately needed funds.

Democrats in Congress fumed that taxpayers' money should not be used for paying stock dividends or bonuses for management. They also argued that banks that took federal money should be required to lend more money to businesses (thus helping solve the central problem of the credit freeze), rather than just holding the cash or using it to acquire other banks. This reveals the fundamental difference between Democrats' and Republicans' approaches to the problem: many Democrats advocated more intervention and government regulation, and Republicans tended to favor less regulation and more reliance on market forces to sort things out.

The consequences of figuring out the right approach are higher than at any time since the 1930s. The globalization of financial markets means that problems in the United States spread like wildfire through the rest of the world. Within a month of the start of the crisis, emerging capitalist economies such as Hungary, Iceland, Belarus, Poland, Ukraine, and Pakistan teetered on the brink of financial collapse. Early in 2010, Greece and Portugal put pressure on the entire euro zone with their financial weakness. If entire countries start to fail, rather than specific financial institutions, it would be increasingly difficult to contain the damage.[72]

These examples of the budget, financing the debt, and the financial rescue plan are not intended to suggest that politics shouldn't enter into the economic policy-making process. Indeed, just the opposite. They are excellent illustrations of the themes that politics is everywhere and politics is conflictual. However, it shouldn't be surprising when politics enters the policy debate. Even in a period of globalization in which international trade and the free market are playing increasingly important roles, decisions made by American political leaders still play a central role in shaping economic policy and outcomes.

What are the goals of economic policy?

- Policy makers have a set of goals when they try to influence the direction of the economy: full employment, stable prices, promoting the free market and growth, balanced budgets, and a balance of payments.
- It is difficult to pursue all of the goals simultaneously because there are trade-offs, at least in the short run, between some of the goals. For example, imposing tariffs on trade to address the balance of payments would restrain the free market.

Who are the key players in economic policy making?

- Congress is at the center of economic policy making through its control over the nation's fiscal policy of taxing and spending (the "power of the purse").

- Despite not having direct control over the economy, the president is expected to keep the economy running smoothly. A large advising system helps the president in this task, including the CEA, USTR, NEC, and OMB (the OMB helps create the president's budget).
- The Federal Reserve System and the Treasury Department control monetary policy, and the courts provide the necessary legal basis for the U.S. economic system.

What are the tools and theories of economic policy?

- Fiscal policy is the use of the government's taxing and spending power to influence the direction of the economy.

- The Fed controls monetary policy by monitoring levels of bank lending, the money supply, and interest rates and by trying to meet related targets by using a variety of policy tools.
- Policy makers engage in both economic and social regulation to achieve broader policy goals.

- Many factors that shape trade policy are beyond the control of policy makers, but trade policy remains a potent political issue given the impact the trade deficit can have on domestic labor markets.

⊚ STUDENT STUDYSPACE

Find quizzes and other review material at wwnorton.com/studyspace.

CRITICAL THINKING

1. Assuming it was politically possible, do you think economic policy should be made by economists and other experts rather than politicians? Why, or why not?
2. If you were a member of Congress, what would your position be on international trade? Would you support free trade or more protectionist policies? Why?
3. Do you support an active role for the government in regulating the economy, or would you prefer the free market to be largely unregulated?

KEY TERMS

balanced budget (p. 563)
budget deficit (p. 563)
budget making (p. 566)
budget reconciliation (p. 566)
business cycle (p. 577)
Council of Economic Advisers (p. 559)
current account (p. 565)
discount rate (p. 583)
discretionary spending (p. 578)
economic depression (p. 559)
federal funds rate (FFR) (p. 583)

Federal Reserve Board (p. 571)
Federal Reserve System (p. 570)
fiscal policy (p. 566)
full employment (p. 559)
gross domestic product (GDP) (p. 563)
inflation (p. 561)
Keynesian economics (p. 576)
mandatory spending (p. 577)
monetarist theory (p. 583)
monetary policy (p. 566)
National Economic Council (NEC) (p. 569)

open market operations (p. 584)
progressive (p. 580)
regressive (p. 580)
reserve requirement (p. 583)
supply-side economics (p. 576)
trade deficit (p. 565)
Treasury Department (p. 570)
United States Trade Representative (USTR) (p. 569)

SUGGESTED READING

Friedman, Milton. *Capitalism and Freedom*, 40th Anniversary Ed. Chicago: University of Chicago Press, 2002.

Friedman, Thomas L. *The World Is Flat: A Brief History of the Twenty-First Century*. New York: Farrar, Straus and Giroux, 2005.

Keynes, John Maynard. *General Theory of Employment, Interest and Money*. New York: Macmillan, 2007, originally published in 1936.

Krugman, Paul. *The Great Unraveling: Losing Our Way in the New Century*. New York: W. W. Norton, 2003.

Lewis, Michael. *The Big Short: Inside the Doomsday Machine*. New York: W. W. Norton, 2010.

Phillips, Kevin. *Bad Money: Reckless Finance, Failed Politics, and the Global Crisis of American Capitalism*. New York: Viking, 2008.

Soros, George. *The New Paradigm for Financial Markets: The Credit Crash of 2008 and What It Means*. New York: PublicAffairs Books, 2008.

Stiglitz, Joseph E. *Globalization and Its Discontents*. New York: W. W. Norton, 2003.

In 2010 the Patient Protection and Affordable Care Act was signed into law, a victory for supporters, including then–House Speaker Nancy Pelosi.

Social Policy

President Obama signed the Patient Protection and Affordable Care Act into law on March 30, 2010. This comprehensive and historic health care reform legislation was the culmination of a fifteen-month-long partisan struggle in Congress. The $1 trillion bill (over ten years) will make health insurance available to an additional 32 million Americans while preventing health insurance companies from dropping sick policyholders or refusing to cover people with preexisting conditions.

Many of the lasting images of this political process are related to the deep conflict over the controversial law. Representative Joe Wilson (R-SC), for example, shouted "You lie" when President Obama told a joint session of Congress that his health care plan would not cover illegal immigrants. This breech of decorum was roundly criticized by leaders of both parties, and Wilson later apologized to the president. The broader policy debate often was quite substantive, but it also degenerated into charges of government-run "death panels." House Minority Leader John Boehner (R-OH), for example, said the bill "may start us down a treacherous path toward government-encouraged euthanasia."[1] There was nothing in the bill to support the charge, but by the time this and similar comments filtered through conservative talk radio, angry demonstrators around the country were blasting the legislation as socialized medicine and comparing it to Hitler's atrocities during the Holocaust.

CONFLICT AND COMPROMISE
in American Politics

Inside Congress, the negotiations were intense. For the first six months of the process, the Senate Finance Committee chair, Max Baucus (D-MT), tried to reach out to moderate Republicans to create a bipartisan bill. Early in the fall, as public opposition grew, it became clear that the votes for health care reform would have to come from within the Democratic Party. Needing sixty votes to stop a filibuster, this meant that Democratic leaders would have to hang onto every Democratic vote, plus the two Independents. This gave great power to conservatives in the party, such as Ben Nelson (D-NE), and to Independent Joe Lieberman (I-CT). Significant conflict also emerged between House and Senate versions of the bill on issues such as federal funding of abortion, how illegal immigrants would be excluded from the policy, and how the programs would be funded. Toward the end of the process, conflict over abortion policy almost killed the bill when pro-life Democrats, led by Bart Stupak (D-MI), insisted on strong language in the bill prohibiting health insurance companies from paying

BIG QUESTIONS

✪ What is social policy, and how has American social policy developed over time?

✪ How are poverty and income inequality related to social policy?

✪ Who are the key players in making social policy?

✪ How does the social policy-making process work?

✪ What is the state of American social policy today, and what issues will be faced in the future?

for abortions if they participated in the insurance exchanges. Pro-choice Democrats threatened to vote against the bill if the Stupak amendment remained in the final version. A last-minute compromise brokered by President Obama defused the conflict by assuring the pro-life Democrats that he would issue an executive order maintaining the current prohibition against federally funded abortions.

The House passed its version of the bill in November, and the Senate finally passed its bill on Christmas Eve after an all-night session. Some congressional leaders wanted to push ahead with negotiations between the House and Senate to get the bill done before the end of the year, but Obama convinced them to wait until the new year because everyone was too exhausted.[2] Then came the bombshell of January 19, 2010, when Republican Scott Brown won the Massachusetts Senate seat that had been held by Ted Kennedy for half a century, denying Democrats their filibuster-proof majority. Most pundits and many Democratic leaders thought this would be the end of comprehensive health care reform, but ironically, it provided the impetus to get it passed. Knowing that they no longer had the sixty votes to pass a new bill in the Senate, the House decided to pass the Senate version and amend it with a third bill, the Health Care and Education Reconciliation Act of 2010. The Senate then passed an amended version of the third bill by a 56-to-43 vote (it only required a simple majority because it was passed under a reconciliation process that is typically used to reduce deficits). The amended third bill was then sent back to the House, where it passed 220 to 207, and the president signed it into law.[3]

Republicans cried foul, saying that Democrats had circumvented the normal legislative process and used reconciliation in an unorthodox manner. Representative John Boehner (R-OH) called the legislation "a sloppy mess that the majority of the American people believe should be repealed and replaced."[4] Some opponents turned violent in the week following the passage of health care reform; President Obama and at least ten members of Congress, including Speaker Pelosi, received death threats, and windows were smashed at Democratic offices in four states.[5]

Although this level of anger is unusual in American politics, trade-offs between social policy and other government priorities often produce political conflict. More money for health insurance subsidies, Social Security, Medicare, food stamps, and welfare means less money for building highways, supporting the war in Afghanistan, or developing alternative energy. These trade-offs become especially acute as an aging population requires that an increasing share of federal spending goes to Social Security and Medicare. Resolving these trade-offs must be done through a political process filled with conflict and compromise.

That the political process matters is clearly shown by the importance of the filibuster in the Senate and the reconciliation process that allowed passage of the bill with a majority vote; also, process matters in that decisions made by individual presidents and members of Congress shape social policy. In each instance, policies and their effect on Americans' daily lives could have been very different if alternative procedures had been used or different proposals had passed.

The politics of social policy is everywhere in two ways. First, social policy directly affects all Americans at some point in their lives—possibly from the very beginning of life (with programs such as Women, Infants, and Children [WIC] and Head Start), through the middle of life (income support, job training, housing, food stamps, Medicaid, and need-based scholarships), to the end of life (Social Security and Medicare). Second, the same impetus for social policy at the national level also drives millions of Americans to help take care of the less fortunate through community organizations, churches, and other charities. You have probably participated at some point in a community service program that assists the poor or disadvantaged.

This chapter discusses the evolution of social policy in the United States, outlines the conditions that create the need for social policies, describes the key players in the social policy-making process, and explains the status of key social policies today and the efforts to reform them. We begin with the historical background of social policy.

History and Background of Social Policy

Social policy is generally defined in terms of the "social safety net," or **welfare**, which the *American Heritage Dictionary* defines as "receiving regular assistance from the government or a private agency because of need." A broader conception of social policy includes government programs aimed at achieving some general social goal, such as support for public education, the income tax deduction for interest paid on home mortgages (to encourage home ownership), or even policies aimed at helping job creation and growth (sometimes called "corporate welfare" by critics of these programs). In this chapter we focus primarily on the narrower conception but also include a brief discussion of more general social policies. We also discuss how some traditional social welfare programs such as Social Security are not based on need. This section outlines the evolution of social policy in the United States and describes the various types of social policy.

POLITICS IS EVERYWHERE

In the early years of our nation's history, the federal government took little responsibility for social welfare. Private charities, churches, and families largely took care of the poor and disadvantaged. The first significant social policy appeared in the nineteenth century in the form of federal financial support for Civil War veterans and their families. Between 1880 and 1910, the national government spent more than a quarter of its budget on Civil War pensions and support for veterans' widows. This was a larger share of the budget than any other single item other than interest on the debt and was a greater percentage of federal spending than today's expenditure on Social Security (today we spend about one-fifth of our budget on Social Security, but of course the overall size of the budget was much smaller then).[6] During the recession of the mid-1890s, populist and progressive reformers pushed for a national system of unemployment compensation, but such broad-scale policies were still several decades ahead of their time.

social policy An area of public policy related to maintaining or enhancing the well-being of individuals.

welfare Financial or other assistance provided to individuals by the government, usually based on need.

Types of Social Policy

There are two main types of social policy: contributory and noncontributory. The former includes programs such as Social Security, Medicare, disability insurance, and unemployment compensation. These are similar to insurance programs in that people pay a specified amount of money to cover some future benefit (either expected, as with the programs related to retirement, or unexpected, as with disability and unemployment). These contributory programs are not means-tested; that is, all people may participate in the program regardless of their income. For noncontributory programs, recipients are not expected to pay for the programs, and they are means-tested, which means that they are aimed at helping poor people. These programs include Medicaid, food stamps, housing assistance, welfare, and school lunches. The new health care law has elements of both a contributory and noncontributory program. People who are required to buy health insurance are "contributing" to their own insurance. However, those who cannot afford to pay for their insurance receive government subsidies (and thus are participating in a noncontributory program).

The crash of the stock market in 1929 and the Great Depression that followed created a desperate economic situation for millions of Americans. The value of the stock market shrank by 80 percent, the gross national product decreased by 25 percent, and unemployment climbed to at least 25 percent in the depth of the Depression in 1933. Yet, during the presidential campaign of 1932, the Republican incumbent Herbert Hoover upheld the administration's policy of limited government intervention in the economy and in social welfare policies. The Democratic candidate, Franklin D. Roosevelt, pledged in his speech before the nominating convention "a new deal for the American people." FDR won a sweeping victory in the 1932 elections. Democrats also gained control of both houses of Congress, which provided the platform for enacting FDR's policies. An immediate concern was to alleviate the suffering caused by unemployment. As FDR argued in his second fireside chat, "No country, however rich, can afford the waste of its human resources. Demoralization caused by vast unemployment is our greatest extravagance. Morally, it is the greatest menace to our social order."[7] But FDR also wanted to implement a broader "preventative social policy" as outlined by the "Wisconsin School" social scientists at the University of Wisconsin, including John R. Commons, who was a significant force in the creation of unemployment compensation policies, and Edwin Witte, the architect of Social Security.[8] The **New Deal** policies that were enacted between 1933 and 1935 included:

- The Agricultural Adjustment Administration, which provided farmers with much-needed assistance (farmers were among the hardest hit in the Great Depression when commodity prices dropped to levels that forced many family farms into bankruptcy)
- The National Recovery Administration and Public Works Administration, which reinvigorated the business sector
- The Federal Emergency Relief Administration, which provided $500 million in emergency aid for the poor (about $7 billion in today's dollars)
- Jobs programs such as the Civil Works Administration and Civilian Conservation Corps, which put more than 2 million people to work, and later the Works Progress Administration, which was a much broader program that employed at least one-third of the nation's unemployed
- Social Security, which included the familiar retirement policy and supported the states for spending on unemployment compensation, disability programs, and support for dependent children of single mothers—the precursor of the

New Deal The set of policies proposed by President Franklin Roosevelt and enacted by Congress between 1933 and 1935 to promote economic recovery and social welfare during the Great Depression.

central welfare program, Aid to Families with Dependent Children (AFDC), which existed until 1996

- The National Labor Relations Act, which guaranteed the right to organize a union and set regulations for collective bargaining between management and labor[9]

The role of the federal government in social policy was forever changed. Although some aspects of the New Deal were never repeated on such a broad scale, such as the jobs programs, most of its other programs became the cornerstone of social policy for subsequent generations.

The next major expansion of social policy came during the **Great Society** of President Lyndon Johnson in the mid-1960s. One central part of this social agenda was discussed in Chapter 14: the civil rights movement, which culminated with the passage of the Civil Rights Act in 1964 and the Voting Rights Act in 1965. The other important aspect of Johnson's Great Society included the War on Poverty and other programs concerning health, education, and housing. Johnson's "unconditional" War on Poverty brought economic development and jobs to depressed areas, especially the inner cities, by creating the Office of Economic Opportunity, the Jobs Corps, the Neighborhood Youth Corps, Volunteers in Service to America (VISTA, a domestic counterpart to the Peace Corps), and the Model Cities program. Other programs focused on helping children, including Head Start, which provided preschool education and enrichment for poor children, the Child Nutrition Act of 1966, and an expanded school lunch program. The Food Stamp program was also greatly expanded; urban renewal expanded public housing; a new cabinet-level department, Housing and Urban Development, was created; and the federal government got more involved in an area that typically had been left to the states in the Elementary and Secondary Education Act of 1965. Perhaps the most significant legislation of the period was in health care, with the creation of Medicare, the national program that funds medical care for the elderly, and Medicaid, which funds health care for the poor.[10]

The mounting costs of the Vietnam War created a trade-off: it wasn't possible to continue to fund ambitious social programs and the war without creating inflation. Over the next couple of decades there was some conservative backlash against the "welfare state," especially during the Reagan years from 1981 to 1989, as spending on social programs was cut and some programs were even eliminated. However, with some exceptions, the Great Society programs remain core components of today's social safety net.

President George W. Bush continued this general direction for social policy, maintaining most existing programs with some specific cuts and one major expansion, the addition of a prescription benefit to Medicare. Bush attempted to place his stamp on social policy as a "compassionate conservative" with his idea of an "**ownership society**," in which people take more responsibility for their own social welfare. Bush proposed privatizing part of Social Security and creating private savings accounts to cover more out-of-pocket medical expenses, in combination with more free market forces and a bigger role for private charity. President Obama has favored an approach that emphasizes the market and community, while preserving an important role for government. As the recent recession and natural disasters such as Hurricane Katrina have demonstrated, crises may overwhelm even the most aggressive and sustained community responses. Market forces cannot adequately address the needs of the unemployed and very poor, especially in times of economic recession. Obama's social policies in his first term have focused on enacting comprehensive health care reform, while maintaining and expanding the social safety net for those devastated by the recession.

▲ *A VISTA volunteer works with a patient in a Hardeeville, South Carolina, health clinic in 1976. VISTA was a Great Society antipoverty program created in 1964 as a domestic version of the Peace Corps. In 1993 it was incorporated into President Clinton's AmeriCorps program. There are currently more than 6,500 volunteers in 1,200 AmeriCorps VISTA programs and another 70,000 in other AmeriCorps programs.*

Q POLITICS IS CONFLICTUAL

Great Society The wide-ranging social agenda promoted by President Lyndon Johnson in the mid-1960s that aimed to improve Americans' quality of life through governmental social programs.

ownership society The term used to describe the social policy vision of President George W. Bush, in which citizens take responsibility for their own social welfare and the free market plays a greater role in social policy.

Poverty and Income Inequality

In the previous section we noted that the economic dislocation and poverty of the Great Depression and the desire to eliminate poverty in the 1960s were the two central stimuli for social policy. Although these policies had some success in reducing poverty, the persistence of poverty remains the primary motivator for most social policy. In 2010, the poverty line for a family of four was an annual income of $22,050; for a single person it was $10,830. In 2009, 43.6 million Americans were in poverty—14.3 percent of the nation's population. Even the social programs that are not directly tied to helping the poor and disadvantaged, such as Social Security and Medicare, have an important impact on poverty. As shown in Figure 16.1, the percentage of the elderly population living in poverty has plummeted from more than 35 percent in 1959 to 8.9 percent in 2009. Official statistics on poverty were not collected before 1959, but the rate was certainly much higher in the 1930s before Social Security was established.[11] Given that more than half of the elderly rely on Social Security as their primary income—for the bottom quintile, nearly 80 percent of their income in retirement comes from Social Security—the poverty rate for the elderly would be much higher if Social Security and Medicare did not exist.

Another source of concern for some policy advocates is the growing income and wealth inequality in the United States. It may be true that "a rising tide lifts all boats," but the top income levels in the nation are benefiting disproportionately from income increases. Since 1980, 80 percent of the net income gains have gone to the top 1 percent of the income distribution.[12] In 2009, the top 5 percent of households—those households earning more than $180,001 a year—earned 21.7 percent of the income, and in 2006, the top quintile earned just over half of the nation's income.[13] From 1979 to 2005, the average income of the top 1 percent grew by nearly

---

FIGURE 16.1 **POVERTY RATES BY AGE**

Children today are in poverty at nearly twice the rate of the elderly, whereas forty years ago the poverty rate among the elderly was three times that of children. What changes in social policies in the past seventy-five years could help explain this change?

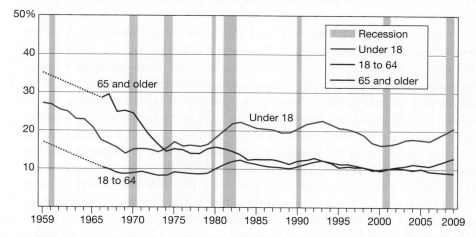

Note: The data points are placed at the midpoints of the respective years. Data for people age eighteen and older are not available from 1960 to 1965.

SOURCE: U.S. Census Bureau, Current Population Survey, 1960 to 2010 Annual Social and Economic Supplements, Figure 5, available at www .census.gov/prod/2010pubs/p260-238.pdf.

$1 million to $1,558,500 (a 273 percent gain), compared to a $200 gain to $15,900 (1.3 percent) for the bottom fifth of the income levels.[14] The wealth gap is far greater. The median (meaning that half are above this level and half are below) net worth of U.S. households in 2007 was $120,300, but the median wealth for the top 10 percent was $1.89 million, and this group held 73 percent of the nation's wealth. Even within the top 10 percent, the wealth is very concentrated at the top. *Forbes* magazine publishes a list of the wealthiest Americans every year. Bill Gates topped the 2010 list for the seventeenth year in a row, with a net worth of $54 billion, and the person at the bottom of the "*Forbes* 400" was worth $1 billion. The collective net worth of the nation's wealthiest 400 people grew $130 billion in the past year to reach $1.4 trillion.[15] In contrast, the bottom *half* of the American public (58 *million* households in 2007) was worth about the same as the wealthiest 400 people at $1.61 trillion.[16]

According to a study by the nonpartisan Congressional Budget Office (CBO), despite these patterns of inequality, people who earn more than $100,000 receive more benefits from the federal government ($5,690 on average) than people who earn less than $10,000 ($5,560). The study concludes, "Quite simply, if the federal government wanted to flatten the nation's income distribution, it would do better to mail all its checks to random addresses."[17]

How can that be? Take one big social welfare program: housing. Poor people receive about $35 billion a year from the federal government in direct subsidies for their rent and for public housing. However, this number is dwarfed by the $261 billion spent on tax expenditures for housing in 2011, most of which went to relatively wealthy people through the mortgage interest deduction and capital gains tax exclusions.[18] For example, 68 percent of the tax savings from deducting mortgage interest goes to people in the top fifth of the income ladder.[19] Other government policies that help the wealthy include patent and copyright law, bankruptcy law, bailouts of the financial sector, immigration policy, enforcement of tax law, and monetary policy.[20]

Government programs that help the wealthy are not only aimed at individuals, but also benefit corporations. These policies are often called "corporate welfare" and are defined by the Cato Institute, a libertarian think tank, as "any government spending program that provides unique benefits or advantages to specific companies or industries. That includes programs that provide direct grants to businesses, programs that provide research and other services for industries, and programs that provide subsidized loans or insurance to companies." By this definition the Cato Institute estimates that there are more than 100 corporate welfare programs in the federal budget, including crop subsidies to large corporate farmers and tax deductions for oil companies to encourage exploration and drilling, with annual expenditures of about $92 billion.[21] Liberal groups like Citizens for Tax Justice estimate levels of corporate welfare at nearly 3 times that amount. Clearly there is much more to welfare than programs for the poor.

These statistics generate different reactions among politicians and are a good reminder that politics is conflictual. Republicans look at the statistics on poverty and inequality and policies that help the wealthy and argue that the best way to address poverty is to create jobs and have a healthy economy. As we discussed in Chapter 15, Economic Policy, many Republicans believe that the best way toward this goal is supply-side tax cuts that promote the creation of capital, investment, and jobs. From this perspective, income inequality is not necessarily a bad thing—in fact, it may be a necessary

▼ *The bailouts of Wall Street and the auto industry, and other "corporate welfare" policies, give the impression that many government programs serve powerful interests while average people are left to sink or swim on their own.*

Income Inequality and Policy

Growing income inequality in the United States has received much attention and debate over the past ten years. Income inequality is relevant for the subject of social policy because it reveals a continued need for social programs to help the poor. But Larry Bartels, a political scientist at Princeton University, has a different set of questions that drive his research on the topic. After reviewing the economic data showing the dramatic increase in income inequality in the past two generations, Bartels wants to discover whether public policies have created a "New Gilded Age." He concludes that "economic inequality is, in substantial part, a political phenomenon."[a]

Before presenting evidence to support this point, Bartels establishes his credentials as an objective social scientist. Acknowledging that his research could be seen as very partisan (because he concludes that most people fare much better economically under Democratic presidents

than under Republican presidents), he says that was not his intention when he started his research. He points out that he is "an unusually apolitical political scientist" and that the last time he voted was in 1984 (for Ronald Reagan). He says that he was surprised by some of his results and that "I have done my best to follow my evidence where it led me."[b]

Evidence of the partisan basis for income inequality is strong. Using economic data from the post–World War II period, Bartels shows that income inequality increased under Presidents Eisenhower, Nixon, Ford, Reagan, and both Bushes, while it declined during the presidencies of four of the five Democrats during this period (Jimmy Carter was the exception). These differences can be explained by the fact that Democratic presidents tend to pursue policies aimed at creating jobs and economic growth, whereas Republicans are more concerned about keeping inflation low, which has little impact on the income

Democratic president Lyndon Johnson immediately after signing the landmark "War on Poverty" bill in August 1964. Political science research shows that, since World War II, economic inequality has tended to decrease under Democratic presidents and increase under Republican ones.

condition for bringing people out of poverty because wealthy people are the only ones who have enough money to invest to create jobs. Democrats look at the figures on poverty and inequality and argue that making the wealthy pay a larger share of their income in taxes could fund programs to help the poor directly rather than waiting for the trickle-down effect of tax cuts for the wealthy. From this perspective, a direct trade-off exists between inequality and reducing poverty, and progressive taxes are needed to help the poor.

Figure 16.2 shows a significant difference between the performance of Democrats and Republicans in reducing poverty. Between 1960 and 2009, Democrats controlled the White House during twenty-one years and Republicans during twenty-nine years. During Democratic presidencies the poverty rate fell from the previous year in seventeen of those twenty-one years, and one year remained the same as the previous year. The poverty rate fell during Republican presidencies in only fourteen of the twenty-nine years they were in power and remained the same in three years. Overall, the mean change in the poverty rate was −0.48 percent in Democratic years, and it went up by 0.07 percent in Republican years. These differences may not sound like much, but given that each percentage point change in the poverty rate represents more than 3 million people today, these differences are significant. Political scientist Larry Bartels finds that in the past six decades, the real

of middle-income and poor Americans but helps those at the top. Tax policies are also consistent with this pattern, with Republican tax cuts that have disproportionately helped the wealthiest Americans. Bartels also concludes that the Republican supply-side theory (or "trickle-down economics," as it has been called by its critics) as a justification for inequality is not valid, concluding that there is "little evidence that large disparities in income and wealth promote growth."[c]

If this is true, why do voters put up with it? That is, if Republican policies are primarily helping people in the top 20 percent income bracket, why don't the other 80 percent consistently vote for Democrats? One theory is that Republican politicians appeal to middle- and low-income voters on social issues, emphasizing the "values divide" on issues such as abortion, stem cell research, and gay marriage. The argument that the poorer classes vote against their own economic interests is advanced by Thomas Frank in a popular book entitled *What's the Matter with Kansas? How Conservatives Won the Heart of America*. However, through the statistical analysis of economic and voting data, Bartels convincingly demonstrates that this is not the case. The working class, especially those without a college education, still vote strongly for the Democratic Party.

Instead, part of the answer appears to be that Republican presidents have had more fortunate timing, being up for election during periods of economic growth. Although Republican presidents have an overall pattern of increasing the gap between rich and poor by primarily helping wealthier Americans, they often have presided over faster economic growth rates in presidential election years, whereas growth rates during Democratic administrations have been spread more evenly over the four-year political cycle. "Myopic voters"—those who consider the recent past more heavily than the full four-year term—rewarded Republican presidents for their relative success during election years. Bartels concludes, "Whether through political skill or pure good luck, Republican presidents have been remarkably successful in targeting income growth to coincide with presidential elections."

One source of growing income inequality is that the real value of the minimum wage has declined by more than 40 percent since the late 1960s, despite strong support for a higher minimum wage in public opinion surveys. Republican presidents are more likely than Democrats to listen to business owners who argue that a higher minimum wage will cut into their profits and undermine their ability to hire more workers. Although Democratic presidents are more sensitive to public opinion on this issue, the public's views are not always consistent with their economic self-interest. Bartels cites surveys showing that two-thirds of people say the wealthier should pay more taxes, yet similar percentages favor repealing the estate tax, which is only paid by the heirs of the wealthiest 1 or 2 percent. These two views are inconsistent: there is no better way to tax the wealthy than the estate tax, yet most people want to see it abolished.

Larry Bartels' work on income inequality is an excellent example of political science research that is politically relevant and rigorous, and that addresses questions of central importance to understanding the politics of the policy-making process. ■

Watch a video clip of Larry Bartels discussing this topic at wwnorton.com/studyspace.

incomes of working poor families (at the twentieth percentile of income) increased 6 times faster under Democratic presidents than under Republican presidents.[22] This makes some sense given the political base of the two parties: Democrats win large percentages of the votes of poor people, and Republicans usually do much better among wealthier voters. An exception was the 2008 election, in which President Obama won the support of 52 percent of voters earning more than $200,000 a year, compared to John McCain's 46 percent.

With all of the statistics on income inequality and poverty, it is sometimes easy to lose sight of the human face of poverty. Hurricane Katrina, one of the worst natural disasters in the history of our nation, serves as a reminder of that human face. The hurricane killed more than 1,800 people, displaced 1.5 million people, and caused more than $100 billion in damage. Middle-class and wealthier people were able to leave the city as the hurricane approached, but 100,000 New Orleans residents did not own cars, and there weren't enough buses to handle all the people. David Brooks, a conservative columnist for the *New York Times*, delivered a bitter assessment of the government's response: "The first rule of the social fabric—that in times of crisis you protect the vulnerable—was trampled. Leaving the poor in New Orleans was the moral equivalent of leaving the injured on the battlefield. No wonder confidence in civic institutions is plummeting."[23] The media coverage of

FIGURE 16.2 | CHANGES IN POVERTY RATES BY PARTY

The poverty rate tends to decrease under Democratic presidents and to go up by about the same margin under Republican presidents. What could explain this difference between the two parties?

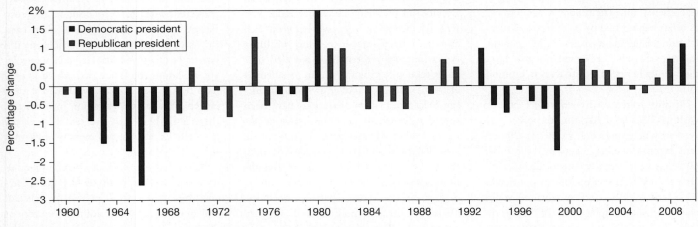

SOURCE: Data from the U.S. Census Bureau, Poverty: Historical Tables, available at www.census.gov/hhes/www/poverty/poverty.html.

Hurricane Katrina was shocking to millions of Americans. The images of bodies floating in the water and people standing outside the Louisiana Superdome with their arms stretched out to passing helicopters served as a stark reminder of the costs of poverty. Many Americans believe that such a thing should not be allowed to happen in our country, and national leaders vowed to address the problems exposed by the hurricane.

The Key Players in Social Policy Making

CONGRESS AND THE PRESIDENT

The argument about the differences between Democratic and Republican administrations' performance in lowering the poverty rate ignored one important point: Democratic presidents were more likely than Republican presidents to have a Congress controlled by their party. In fifteen of the twenty-one years of Democratic presidents, Democrats also controlled Congress, while Republican presidents enjoyed unified control in only four of the twenty-nine years from 1960 to 2009. (Ronald Reagan also had six years in which Republicans controlled the Senate, but not the House.) This means that Democratic presidents had more of an opportunity to implement their agendas, while Republican presidents had to do more negotiating with the other party. You might argue that this divided control only prevented Republican presidents from making even deeper cuts in social programs that could have driven the poverty rate even higher, because Democrats in Congress would have been supporting those policies. Although this is certainly a possibility, especially during the Reagan years, divided control may also have prevented Republican

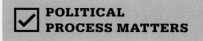

POLITICAL
PROCESS MATTERS

The Social Welfare State

On many "quality of life" measures, the United States does not stack up very well when compared to the other developed nations. The Organization for Economic Co-operation and Development (OECD) is an organization of thirty of the world's most developed nations, including all of the big European countries, Japan, Canada, Mexico, South Korea, New Zealand, and Australia. OECD data show that among all the OECD's members the United States is tied for seventh from the bottom in terms of life expectancy (78.1 years compared to 82.6 years for the top country—Japan—and a median of 79.7 years), third from the bottom in infant mortality (6.7 deaths per 1,000 live births compared to a median of 3.8), and dead last in obesity (34.3 percent of Americans are obese compared to a median of 14.9 percent).

How could this be, given that the United States is one of the wealthiest nations in the world? Part of the reason is that our government spends a great deal less on social welfare than other OECD countries: we are fourth from the bottom, at 15.9 percent of gross domestic product (GDP), which leads only Mexico, South Korea, and Turkey, and is only about three-fourths of the OECD median of 20.6 percent. The OECD defines social spending as direct spending and tax expenditures in support of pensions, disability payments, health care, child care, unemployment compensation, housing, cash payments to the poor (welfare),

job training, and "other benefits that address one or more social purposes" (education is not included in this definition).[a] Most other OECD countries have publicly funded national health care systems, paid maternity leave (up to two years in some countries), extensive job training programs, and generous retirement benefits. This social welfare state is the product of a long-standing commitment in many European countries to take care of those who are less fortunate. The earliest European health care plan, for example, goes back to 1883 in the Bismarck Republic in Germany. In the last half of the twentieth century, many left-leaning and socialist governments in Europe dramatically increased the size of the social welfare state.

While the *public* social welfare state is definitely much smaller in the United States than in most developed countries, the United States ranks much higher if total social spending—public and private—is measured: we are just above the OECD median of 23.3 percent (at 27.2 percent of GDP). The United States ranks first in the OECD in private spending (10.1 percent of GDP compared to the median of 2.9 percent). The main category driving this difference is health care. The United States spends far more on health care than any other nation in the world: $7,290 per person compared to the second highest spender, Norway, at $4,763; the OECD median is $3,323. Given this average level of overall spending on social welfare and the tremendously high

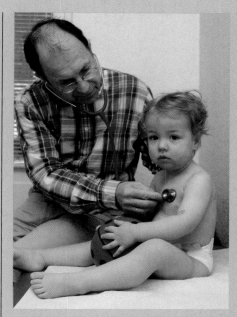

Americans spend far more on health care than any other nation in the world, yet overall health outcomes in the United States are in the bottom third of developed nations. This German doctor is caring for a child as part of a national health care system in which all basic costs are covered by the government.

total spending on health care, it is even more puzzling why the United States has such a low ranking on health statistics such as life expectancy, infant mortality, and obesity. The relative performance of the United States to its peers may change after health care reform is fully implemented in 2018. ■

presidents from implementing their alternative vision of the best way to address poverty.

This discussion underlies the more basic point: Congress and the president both play central roles in shaping social policy. In some instances the president may take the lead, as with FDR and the New Deal or Lyndon Johnson and the Great Society. In other instances, Congress plays a central role, as with health care reform in 2009–2010. In all cases the president and Congress must hammer out their differences and find some common ground. This may be especially difficult under divided government, but even when the president and Congress are of the same party, Congress may be obstructionist: in 1993–1994 the Democratic Congress shot down President Clinton's health care proposal, and in 2005 a Republican-controlled Congress ignored President Bush's effort to partially privatize Social Security.

THE BUREAUCRACY

It may seem safe to assume that the bureaucracy makes little difference in social policy and simply implements the policies that are determined by Congress and the president. For some policies, that is fairly close to what happens. For policies such as Social Security that have levels of benefits determined by law, implementing policy is largely a matter of determining that the proper amount of money is going to the right people and mailing out the checks. However, as discussed in Chapter 12, with many social policies, the "on-the-ground" public employees have a great deal of discretion. One study found that welfare agencies that handed out AFDC benefits had a more "hostile and punitive" attitude toward their clients than those who administered the disability program under Social Security. Welfare offices in general tend not to be very welcoming places. People often have to wait for hours without knowing how much longer they will have to wait. Welfare office workers can sometimes be rude and dismissive and ask personal questions that are not required by the law. Some potential welfare recipients are so alienated by the process of seeking benefits that they give up.[24] This obviously is not true of all welfare offices, but there are general differences in how recipients are treated in different types of social welfare programs.

Bureaucratic discretion may also be used for more positive ends. Political scientist Daniel Carpenter reported that many bureaucratic agencies in the late nineteenth and early twentieth centuries developed political autonomy and strong reputations that allowed them to analyze and solve problems, create new programs, and plan and

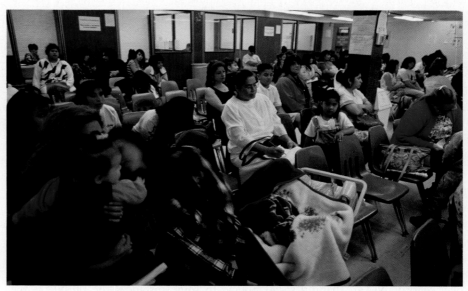

▲ Welfare offices can often be alienating places in which it is very difficult to navigate through the bureaucracy. Dozens of women and children wait to speak to counselors in this East Los Angeles welfare office.

administer programs efficiently.[25] Many of these same insights apply to agencies that deliver social policies today, such as the Social Security Administration, which has a very strong base of popular and political support.

THE STATES

Social policy has always been strongly influenced by our system of federalism. As long as welfare has existed in the United States, it has been administered at the state and local level, with varying degrees of national control. The 1996 welfare reform bill, Temporary Assistance to Needy Families, gave more power to the states and eliminated all national guarantees. Medicaid is administered at the state level (with federal assistance), and education is almost completely controlled by local and state governments. One big sticking point with health care reform in 2009–2010 was the extent to which policy would be centered in the states or have a stronger national component. Many Democrats argued for a national "public option," while Republicans favored a more limited approach that would create insurance exchanges in which insurance companies would be allowed to compete across state lines. (The stronger national approach failed, as Democrats were not able to include the public option in the final version of the bill, but the new law clearly signaled a shift to a more national role in health care.) Education policy is another area of social policy where the trend has been toward more involvement of the national government, rather than returning more power to the states. But even with the national accountability mechanisms and testing requirements put into place by President Bush's No Child Left Behind Act, and the incentives provided by President Obama's "Race to the Top" program, education policy remains largely a state and local affair.

INTEREST GROUPS

In general, interest groups advocating for social policy are not as strong and influential as groups in other areas, such as business, labor, many other professional associations, or even other public interest groups such as environmental groups or those that focus on specific issues such as gun ownership. The one major exception is AARP, which you may recall from Chapter 9 as one of the most powerful lobbies in the United States. AARP has had a strong voice on behalf of Social Security and Medicare. For example, when President Bush proposed "personal savings accounts" to replace part of the Social Security system, AARP mobilized its significant political muscle to crush the idea before it could receive much serious debate in Congress. Similarly, as politicians discussed how to pay for relief efforts following Hurricane Katrina, one proposal was to delay or eliminate the new Medicare prescription drug benefit. Given the political climate, AARP was not as vocal on this issue (it is difficult to argue against "everyone chipping in" to pay for the hurricane relief), but it worked behind the scenes to make sure that the drug benefit was implemented.

Many interest groups and think tanks work on behalf of the poor, homeless, and other disadvantaged people, but decision makers in Washington tend not to be as responsive to their concerns because these groups are not politically powerful. The poor tend not to vote, and they certainly do not donate money to political campaigns. Many politicians in Washington care deeply about issues concerning poverty, homelessness, and other social policy problems, but the interest groups and think tanks that try to focus politicians' attention on these issues face a particularly difficult task *because of* the relatively disadvantaged position of the people they represent.

School Vouchers

One of the most controversial areas of education policy over the past fifteen years has been school vouchers—the practice of providing taxpayers' money directly to families to allow them to send their children to private schools rather than public schools. The vouchers are similar to a scholarship and range from $4,250 for elementary school students and $5,000 for high school students in Ohio to $6,601 in Milwaukee (figures are for the 2009–2010 school year).[a] In the 2009–2010 school year, spending on the Milwaukee voucher program was $129 million and reached 25 percent of Milwaukee students. Several other states, including Florida, Ohio, Pennsylvania, and Utah, also have extensive voucher programs.[b]

Supporters of the program say that it introduces competition into public education, which suffers from the inefficiencies that are typical of monopolies. They argue that many urban school systems have failed to educate their children and that poor, minority students deserve a better education than they can get in public schools. They say that students who are given the opportunity to leave public schools often improve their academic performance in private schools. Opponents make several arguments. They say that private schools engage in "cherry picking," choosing the more motivated students and leaving the more difficult to educate in the public schools, contributing to a downward spiral. Opponents also argue that standardized test scores do not improve for students who participate in voucher programs. Finally, they also say that voucher programs are an unconstitutional violation of the separation between church and state because an overwhelming proportion of

School vouchers are controversial. Supporters see them as a way to allow poor, inner-city students to escape failing public schools. Critics are concerned that vouchers compound the problems facing public schools, while potentially violating the separation of church and state: most school vouchers go to private, Catholic schools, like the one shown here.

the students in these programs attend Catholic parochial schools.

Evidence on opponents' first two points is mixed, but the bulk of the evidence supports their views. The most studied voucher program is the first in the nation, which was established in Milwaukee, Wisconsin, in 1990 using state funding. In the most systematic analysis of that program, John Witte argues that vouchers should be evaluated on a basic question of values, the clash between freedom of choice and equality of opportunity, rather than specific programmatic outcomes, because the effects are small to nonexistent.[c]

The politics of school vouchers has created an unusual alliance between free market conservatives, who are typically Republicans, and inner-city minorities, who normally are strong Democrats. The former believe that school systems can benefit from introducing competitive

market forces, and the latter are desperate for anything that will rescue their children from failing public schools. These supporters of vouchers are opposed by teachers' unions, most Democratic politicians, and those who favor strengthening the public schools by investing more money in them and trying new approaches, such as public magnet schools, charter schools, and public school choice. This issue divided the presidential candidates in 2008, with John McCain supporting vouchers and Barack Obama generally opposing them.

The Supreme Court has upheld voucher programs while asserting that they did not violate the separation of church and state. However, in a case upholding Cleveland's voucher program, the Court did not give vouchers a green light beyond the narrow facts of the case. Indeed, that 5–4 decision required a voucher program to, among other things,

- be a part of a much wider program of multiple educational options, such as magnet schools and after-school tutorial assistance;
- offer parents a real choice between religious and nonreligious education, perhaps even providing incentives for nonreligious education; and
- not only address private schools, but ensure that benefits go to schools regardless of whether they are public or private, religious or not.[d]

Meanwhile, the Arizona state supreme court struck down school voucher programs as a violation of the separation of church and state.

What do you see as the advantages and disadvantages of providing vouchers to allow students to attend any school they want? Should these programs be expanded, or would they undermine the quality of public schools? ■

The Policy-Making Process

Another way to understand the role of key players in making policy is to examine the various stages of the process (Figure 16.3). All policies go through similar steps throughout their life cycle. The first stage is to define a problem as an issue that requires attention from the federal government. There are thousands of issues, but a relatively small number are ever acted on by Congress. It is a problem when kids fight over who got the biggest piece of pie for dessert or over space in the back seat of the car, but obviously these are not concerns that even the most paternalistic government would get involved with. A more serious example would be a social policy like food stamps. Poor and hungry people have been part of American society since the arrival of the first settlers, but as we discussed at the beginning of the chapter, this was not seen as a problem requiring government intervention until the twentieth century. What causes a society to change its assumptions about whether and how government should address social problems?

Sometimes there is a triggering event: the assassination of President John F. Kennedy led to the passage of gun control legislation, the energy crisis of the early 1970s led to the first comprehensive discussions of energy policy, and Hurricane Katrina led to a reexamination of our readiness for emergencies and our social safety net. Sometimes redefining an issue can move the policy to the next step of the process. The estate tax has been part of our tax system continuously since 1917 (and three previous times for brief periods to fund wars) but when Republican leaders in Congress redefined it as the "death tax" in the late 1990s, it transformed the politics of the debate and made it a problem that needed a solution. After all, who could support a tax on dead people? (Of course, dead people don't pay taxes—the heirs of the estate pay taxes—but that nuance was lost in the redefinition of the problem.)

Recognizing and defining a problem is just the first step; it still needs to come to the attention of political leaders and get on the **policy agenda**. Political scientists have come up with many colorful terms to describe the process through which this happens, including models based on "garbage cans" or a "policy primeval soup."[26] Whatever the image, the basic idea is that when the conditions are right, with the appropriate national political mood and participation from key interest groups

▲ The flag-draped casket of President John F. Kennedy passes in front of the U.S. Capitol on November 25, 1963. External events may prompt the government to address a social issue, as was the case with Kennedy's assassination and gun control legislation.

FIGURE 16.3 **STAGES OF THE POLICY-MAKING PROCESS**

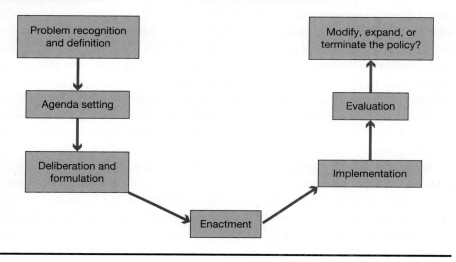

policy agenda The set of desired policies that political leaders view as their top priorities.

and government actors, an issue can reach the agenda. Political scientists Frank Baumgartner and Bryan Jones describe a process of more abrupt change in the policy agenda as issues appear suddenly and then disappear almost as quickly after they are addressed, in a process they call "punctuated equilibrium."[27]

Once the issue is on the active agenda, alternatives are proposed and debated, and the final version of the policy is formulated in Congress (if it is a bill) or the executive branch (if it is an administrative action). Enactment involves a roll call vote in the House and the Senate and then a signature by the president, or a regulatory decision or administrative action by the bureaucracy, or unilateral action by the president (such as an executive order or agreement). Many factors affect whether or not the policy is implemented successfully. First, the problem has to be solvable and the policy must be clear and consistent in its objectives. It wouldn't make sense for Congress to pass a law telling the Department of Health and Human Services to "eliminate poverty." Poverty can never be eliminated, so such a law could not indicate how this should be done. Second, the policy must be funded adequately and administered by competent bureaucrats who have the required expertise. Finally, external support from the public and relevant interest groups may be critical to the success of the policy. For example, AARP's support is critical for the success of any social policy that affects older people. Its support helped pass the prescription drug benefit that was added to Medicare in 2003 and comprehensive health care reform in 2010, and its opposition to the Catastrophic Coverage Act forced Congress to repeal the program one year after it was passed.[28]

Implementation of a policy is an ongoing process. To make sure that the desires of Congress and the president are being followed, policy evaluation is a critical stage of the process (see Chapter 12, The Bureaucracy, for a discussion of Congress and the president's attempts to control the bureaucracy). Policy evaluation has become an increasingly visible part of the policy-making process in the past decade, following the passage of the Government Performance and Results Act of 1993. During George W. Bush's presidency, his administration increasingly used this law, which was largely ignored throughout much of the 1990s, to impose accountability. Under the law, agencies are required to publish strategic plans and performance measures. Though these efforts sound very impressive, it is incredibly difficult to assess whether or not a government program is achieving its aims.

Political scientist James Q. Wilson's famous book on bureaucracy explains the difference between measuring success in the private sector and the public sector—specifically, he compares McDonald's to the Department of Motor Vehicles (DMV).[29] It is relatively easy to know whether McDonald's is doing a good job: simply look at the profits that are being generated and compare them to those of the previous period. If profits are going up at a reasonable pace, the burger flippers and fry cooks are doing their jobs. The DMV's performance is much more difficult to assess because there is no simple measure, such as profit, to look at. Maybe you could look at the number of people served per hour or the average length of time that people have to wait to get their driver's license. But just doing that would ignore many other considerations, such as how well the DMV serves disadvantaged populations such as the elderly or people for whom English is a second language. We wouldn't expect a DMV office where 50 percent of its applicants don't speak English to be as efficient as one at which all applicants speak English.

Evaluating a public agency such as the State Department is even more difficult. How do we know if diplomacy is being conducted in a manner that is consistent with congressional and presidential preferences? Would success be defined as staying out of war? Increasing economic activity or cultural exchanges between countries? Strengthening democratic institutions in emerging democracies? Getting

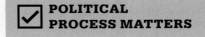

POLITICAL PROCESS MATTERS

cooperation in the War on Terror? The possibilities are endless, and measuring the objectives achieved is very difficult even if those goals can be clearly defined.

Despite these limitations, extensive efforts to evaluate policy do provide decision makers with some basis for deciding whether to modify, expand, or terminate a policy. Programs are notoriously difficult to cut or eliminate. Examples abound, such as wool and mohair subsidies that were implemented after World War II and the Korean War. More than half of the wool needed to make uniforms during these wars was imported, so the Pentagon wanted to increase domestic production of wool. The National Wool Act in 1954 provided direct subsidies to farmers. By 1994 the program was spending nearly $240 million a year (about one-third going to mohair producers and two-thirds to wool), despite the fact that the Pentagon removed wool from its "strategic materials" list in 1960! The subsidies were finally killed in 1994, but the 2002 Farm Act added wool and mohair to the list of commodities eligible for marketing assistance loans.[30] Some policies are like the zombies in old horror movies—they just keep coming back after you kill them.

Social Policy Today

SOCIAL SECURITY

Social Security is the most popular social program in the United States. Consequently it has developed a reputation as the "third rail" of politics—like the dangerous, power-conducting rail on electrified train tracks—because a politician who dares to touch Social Security policy risks political death. Despite serious problems concerning its long-term solvency, Social Security has proven remarkably immune to any steps that could be taken to shore up its financial health, such as cutting benefits or raising taxes. The "third rail" quality of the program has been especially evident to those who would like to privatize part of Social Security. As mentioned earlier, President George W. Bush made a serious push for "personal savings accounts" that would replace some Social Security benefits, but he was rebuffed by Congress when his appeals fell flat with the American public. Why is Social Security so popular, what are the long-term challenges it faces, and what are the possible solutions to ensure its long-term viability?

One reason that Social Security is so popular is its universal quality—that is, nearly every working American participates in the program, from Bill Gates to the teenager flipping burgers at McDonald's. Once people retire, everyone is entitled to their Social Security checks without regard to how much income they have from other sources, such as dividends, interest, or other pensions. So unlike many social programs that develop an "us against them" mentality ("Why should we have to support other people?"), Social Security does not pit people from different classes or races against each other. Social Security is also popular because it works. It is more efficient than most privately managed pensions, with about 0.8 percent going to administrative expenses, compared with the average mutual fund that spends more than 1 percent. More important, Social Security has accomplished its central goal of helping most Americans have an adequate retirement income: fewer than 10 percent of the elderly are in poverty today, which is a lower rate than the general public (see Figure 16.1) and significantly lower than the 35 percent of the elderly who were in poverty in 1960. Census data also show that nearly half of the elderly (46.2 percent) would be in poverty today without their Social Security payments.[31]

Social Security A federal social insurance program that provides cash benefits to retirees based on payroll taxes they have paid over the course of their careers. It is a "pay as you go" program in which working Americans pay taxes to support today's retirees, with a promise that when today's workers retire, their benefits will be paid by the next generation.

Social Security

NUMBER OF RECIPIENTS FOR OLD-AGE, SURVIVORS, AND DISABILITY INSURANCE

- Old-Age Insurance (the basic retirement program)   37,123,000
- Survivors Insurance (retirement program for widows, widowers, and the children of deceased primary wage earners)   6,325,000
- Disability Insurance (payments for people and their families who cannot work because of a disability and are not yet retired)   9,942,000

MONTHLY RETIREMENT BENEFITS

- Individual: Average = $1,171, maximum = $2,346
- Couple: Average = $1,902, maximum = $3,539 (if one spouse does not work and the other earns the maximum)

SOURCE: All figures are from the U.S. Social Security Administration Office of Policy, "Monthly Statistical Snapshot, July 2010," available at www.ssa.gov/policy/docs/quickfacts/stat_snapshot/.

However, Social Security faces long-term problems. President Bush tried to convince the American public that Social Security was in crisis, but they didn't want to hear it. Maybe "crisis" is too strong a word, but there are fundamental issues that must be addressed, or the program will be unable to cover its obligations. The longer we wait to address the shortfall, the more difficult solving the problem will be.

The source of the problem is basic changes in the demographic profile of the nation. To put it more bluntly, the **Baby Boom generation** born between 1946 and 1964 is just starting to retire, and between 2000 and 2030, the number of Americans over the age of sixty-five will more than double, while the number under sixty-five will grow by only 18 percent.[32] When this happens, there won't be as many workers to support the retirees. In fact, the number of workers per Social Security recipient has fallen from 15 in 1950 to about 3.3 today; by 2034 it will only be 2.[33] See Figure 16.4 for evidence of the aging population.

"Wait a minute," you may be saying, "Why does it matter how many workers there are for each retiree? I thought that Social Security was a pension program that you pay into while you are working and then get the benefits when you retire." Well, not exactly. Social Security is not a self-funded pension, but a "pay-as-you-go" system in which today's workers support today's retirees. Therefore, the huge increase in the number of retirees will strain the system because each worker will have to pay higher taxes to maintain the same level of Social Security benefits for retirees. Of course, benefits could be cut, but the "third rail" status of the program has prevented that, at least up to now. This problem was exacerbated by the deep recession and prolonged unemployment starting in 2008, which reduced revenue from the payroll tax. To address the mounting structural deficits, President Obama appointed a bipartisan commission to make recommendations to Congress.

Another problem with the pay-as-you-go nature of Social Security is the intergenerational transfer of wealth. The flip side of Social Security's success in reducing the poverty rate for seniors is that more children and working poor are in poverty today. Therefore, some critics have wondered if it makes sense, for example, to have a single mother who is working for the minimum wage pay 6.2 percent of her income in taxes to support the benefits of some people who are living quite comfortably in retirement. This critique also points out that current retirees will receive far more in benefits than they paid in Social Security taxes, while many current

Baby Boom generation Americans born between 1946 and 1964 who will be retiring in large numbers over the next twenty years.

FIGURE 16.4
PEOPLE SIXTY-FIVE AND OLDER AS A SHARE OF THE U.S. POPULATION

Elderly people will comprise a much larger share of the population in 2030 than they do today. How might the aging population affect social policy—both in terms of the politics of policy making and the fiscal implications of this trend?

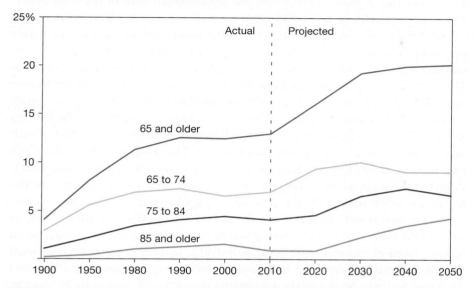

SOURCE: Grayson K. Vincent and Victoria A. Velkoff, "The Next Four Decades, the Older Population in the United States: 2010 to 2050," U.S. Census Bureau, May 2010, p. 10, available at www.census.gov/prod/2010pubs/p25-1138.pdf (accessed 6/17/10).

workers won't get back as much as they paid in (if interest on the taxes paid is considered). For example, an average worker who retired in 1990 got back all of his Social Security taxes, plus interest, by 1999. It is difficult to project the rate of return for current workers because we don't know what future benefits or taxes will be.[34] However, it is safe to bet that taxes will be higher and benefits will not keep up the same rate of increase that they have had for the past several decades. Therefore, today's retirees are reaping a windfall that strikes some critics as unfair, especially given that they are better off, on average, than the workers who are currently paying taxes.

▲ The "pay-as-you-go" nature of Social Security creates intergenerational inequities. Relatively poor young people working for minimum wage help to fund the Social Security benefits for retired people who are usually better off.

You probably are beginning to see why reforming Social Security is so controversial. Debate over Social Security reform exposes highly charged class-based and intergenerational tensions. Before we get into more details about the various proposals to change Social Security, it is important to have a better understanding of how the program works and of previous reform efforts. Social Security is funded by a payroll tax of 6.2 percent on income up to $106,800 (in 2010) with an equal 6.2 percent that is paid by employers; the self-employed have to pay both halves. The payroll tax also includes 1.45 percent on all income for Medicare (discussed below). This is a regressive tax because poor and middle-income people pay a higher percentage of their income for the Social Security tax than wealthy people pay. The maximum Social Security tax you can pay is $6,622 a year, which is 6.2 percent of $106,800. So a millionaire would pay a little more than 0.5 percent of her income in payroll tax (0.66 percent, to be exact) compared to the 6.2 percent that everyone earning less than $106,800 pays. Although the taxes are regressive, the benefits are progressive; that is, poorer people receive back in benefits a larger share of their lifetime payroll taxes than wealthy people receive. One solution to Social Security's long-term fiscal problem is to increase, or even eliminate, the cap on income that is subjected to the payroll tax. This solution is opposed, however, by some people who fear that it would undermine Social Security's popularity among wealthier people.

Policy makers have known about the Baby Boomers since the early 1960s, so why haven't they remedied the Boomers' effect on Social Security? Actually, Social Security faced its first real crisis in the early 1980s, well before the Boomers started retiring. Benefits had increased faster than payroll taxes throughout the 1970s, and the Social Security Administration estimated that it would not be able to meet its obligations as early as August 1983. President Reagan and Congress appointed the National Commission on Social Security Reform (informally known as the **Greenspan Commission**, after its chair, Alan Greenspan) to make recommendations regarding the program's short-term crisis and long-term problems. The commission issued its report in January 1983, which served as the basis for the 1983 Social Security Amendments. This law solved Social Security's short-term problems and made many other significant changes in the program.

The 1983 law's most significant changes were the gradual increase in the retirement age from sixty-five to sixty-seven and increases in the payroll tax that generated surpluses for a trust fund to take care of the Boomers' retirement. The first of these changes was relatively straightforward: people who were born in 1937 or earlier could retire in 2002 at age sixty-five and receive full benefits. Between 2003 and 2027 the retirement age increases gradually to sixty-seven for full benefits. Early retirement at sixty-two is an option, if the retiree is willing to accept a permanently reduced benefit level.

The second change, concerning the trust fund, is the source of great confusion and controversy. The idea behind the trust fund was sound: build up a surplus while the Boomers are working and use that money to pay for their retirement. The problem is that the money wasn't really saved but spent on current government programs. The best way to understand this is to examine the numbers from the Trustees Report on Social Security. In 2009, Old-Age, Survivors, and Disability Insurance had $698 billion in income (mostly from payroll taxes, but also $108 billion from interest on the trust fund and $20 billion from taxation of Social Security benefits) and $564 billion in expenditures, which meant that there was a surplus of $134 billion for that year. That money was used for general government spending (for example, for the war in Afghanistan, food stamps, school loans, and funding the FBI) and in turn the government gave the Social Security trust fund an IOU in the form of "special public-debt obligation." This means that the government will pay off these IOUs, but the only way it can do so is through increasing taxes,

Greenspan Commission The informal name of the National Commission on Social Security Reform created by President Ronald Reagan in 1981 to address short-term and long-term problems facing the Social Security program.

FIGURE 16.5 | THE SOCIAL SECURITY TRUST FUND

In 2014 the cost of the Social Security program will exceed Social Security payroll taxes, at which point taxes will need to be raised to cover the trust fund's obligations and the program's ongoing expenses. What do you think are the best solutions to address the long-term future of Social Security? What are the politically viable solutions?

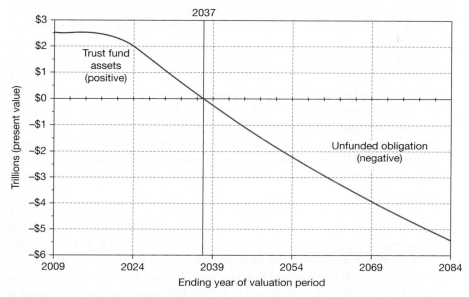

SOURCE: Social Security Administration, 2010 OASDI Trustees Report, Figure II D4, available at www.ssa.gov/OACT/TR/2010/trLOF.html.

cutting spending in other areas, or additional borrowing. As shown in Figure 16.5, the present value of the trust fund peaks at $2.7 trillion in 2014, and then turns downward when promised benefits start to exceed payroll tax revenue. (Payroll taxes did not cover expenditures in 2010 but were expected to rebound and remain higher than expenditures until 2014.) The trust fund runs out in 2037, at which point the Social Security system will be able to fund only about 75 percent of its obligations.[35]

Democrats and Republicans alike have misused this issue for political purposes. Democrats criticize Republicans any time they try to reform Social Security, claiming that it is on strong fiscal ground while ignoring that the need for $2.4 trillion from general taxes over a twenty-four-year period will further strain the system and that a huge shortfall remains even after coming up with that additional money. Republicans note that 2014 is the year in which Social Security starts to be in trouble (which is correct) but then use this to argue that the system is in crisis and that privatization is the only way out. President Bush suggested that Social Security would be "bankrupt" in 2037, which is incorrect given that it would still be able to pay about 75 percent of its obligations. Although both sides have used the issue as demagoguery, both sides make important points as well. Republicans are correct that the sooner we act, the better. The system may not be in crisis today, but it *will* be if we don't do anything about it soon. Democrats are correct that the problems can be solved with relatively small changes to benefits and taxes, but the required changes won't be small if we wait much longer.

SOCIAL SECURITY REFORM

So what is to be done? Dozens of plans to reform Social Security and make it fiscally sound for coming generations have been suggested. There is a surprising amount

privatization The process of transferring the management of a government program (like Social Security) from the public sector to the private sector.

of agreement among all of the serious plans that saving Social Security requires a mixture of benefit cuts and tax increases. The calculations get very complicated in terms of the projected fiscal impact of various reforms, but a mixture of these options (which have all been presented in various plans) would take care of the long-term fiscal problems of Social Security:[36]

- Raise payroll taxes by 1 percent and increase the income ceiling that is taxable.
- Lower benefits for nonworking spouses. Currently nonworking spouses receive 50 percent of the benefit of their working spouse. Some proposals would cut that benefit to 33 percent.
- Index current and future benefits to inflation instead of wages. Currently benefit increases are linked to national average wage increases. Because inflation does not increase as fast as wages, linking benefit increases to inflation would generate significant savings. Because this would mean a large reduction of benefits over the long run, a less extreme version has been proposed called progressive price indexing. This would reduce benefits only for those in the top 50 percent or 70 percent of the income distribution by indexing them to inflation (those in the bottom half of the income distribution would still have benefits indexed to wage increases).
- Gradually raise the retirement age to 70 (by 2030). This change in the policy is viewed by many as fair because it simply adjusts for the fact that people are living longer now than they did in the early years of Social Security. Life expectancy of people who turned 65 in 1940 was 78.7 years. Therefore, the average Social Security recipient would receive about 14 years of benefits. For those who turned 65 in 2005, they could expect to live 18.7 years, and life expectancy is expected to grow about six months per decade. Therefore, by 2030, the average life expectancy for those who reach 65 will be 85. To bring the expected stream of benefits back in line with where it was in 1940, the retirement age would have to be increased to 71.5.[37] Changing the retirement age to 70 would save $620 billion by 2040.

A more controversial proposal is:

- Lower benefits for wealthier recipients—that is, means-test Social Security benefits. The strongest argument in favor of this approach is that Bill Gates doesn't need the measly couple of thousand dollars he will receive each month from Social Security. In fact, he wouldn't even notice if that money was used to reduce Social Security's deficit. More broadly, if benefits are phased out for those who are in the top third of income levels, it will save billions of dollars a year. The main argument against this proposal is that it would end the universal nature of Social Security and possibly turn it into another welfare program.

The most controversial plans concern partial or full **privatization** of Social Security. This is the main issue that divides Democrats and Republicans: Democrats favor maintaining the basic structure of Social Security's public social insurance system, and Republicans favor moving part or all of the "pay-as-you-go" system to private accounts. The central argument in favor of private accounts is that over the long term, investing in the stock market has historically provided higher returns than the expected returns from Social Security. Also, with private

▼ One proposal to help address Social Security's long-term funding shortfall is to allow the government to invest the trust fund surplus in stocks (the trading floor of the New York Stock Exchange is shown here). Supporters say that this would provide tangible assets for the trust fund to draw on when Baby Boomers retire, but critics are concerned that government policies could be compromised if it owns a large share of companies.

accounts, all of the assets in the account are owned by the individual and that person's heirs, whereas with Social Security, when you die, your heirs do not receive any additional benefits from your lifetime contributions to Social Security. Advocates argue that if everyone were able to take their 6.2 percent payroll tax and put that in a retirement account, they would have a nice little nest egg by the time they retired that would almost certainly provide a stream of benefits larger than the Social Security check that they would receive under the current system.

The Democrats point out the problems with this approach, most importantly the transition costs. Because the current system is "pay-as-you-go," if we stopped taking payroll taxes and allowed people to put the money into private accounts, there wouldn't be any money to pay for today's retirees. These transition costs—basically having to cover the retirement of all current retirees and everyone else who has paid into the system for a substantial number of years—are estimated to be $7 to 8 *trillion*! Some plans, such as President Bush's partial privatization plan, would borrow all of the money to pay the transition costs, but this simply shifts the accounting entries and doesn't address long-term financial problems.

A second criticism of these plans is that Social Security should be a part of everyone's retirement plan that they can count on. Investing in the stock market is fine as a supplement to Social Security, but everyone needs that dependable check, and investing in the stock market is too risky as the collapse of the stock market in 2008–2009 reminded us. Although it is true that the stock market outperforms other investments over the long haul, there have been periods as long as twenty years when stock market returns have been flat. So if you happened to retire at the end of one of those slumps, you could find yourself with a much smaller nest egg than you had counted on. Finally, critics point out that the administrative overhead costs of these private accounts would eat up any additional returns that they may earn. Jack Bogle, the founder of Vanguard Investments and one of the leading proponents of low-fee index funds, points out that $1,000 invested in 1950 in a mutual fund that mirrored the returns of the S&P 500 stocks (with reinvesting dividends) would be worth about $500,000 today. However, if the mutual fund charged a relatively modest administrative fee of 2 percent a year, the nest egg would be reduced to $230,000![38]

These issues are not likely to be resolved anytime soon, which clearly illustrates that politics is conflictual. Social Security reform can pit one generation against another or wealthy people against poor people. The stakes in Social Security are extremely high because it is the most popular and visible social program, which, of course, makes it all the more difficult to handle.

HEALTH CARE

Health care policy appeared to be as difficult to reform as Social Security. Every president since Theodore Roosevelt who attempted comprehensive reform failed until President Obama's success in 2010. In order to understand the new law, it is important to understand how health care is provided in the United States and that the underlying health care problems being addressed were that we have an aging population, the costs of health care are rising faster than inflation, and more than 46 million Americans do not have health insurance.[39] Yet we spend more on health care than any other nation in the world—more than $2.5 trillion, or more than 16 percent of GDP, compared to about 10 or 11 percent of GDP in many other Western countries (Switzerland spends 10.8 percent of its GDP on health care, Germany 10.4 percent, Canada 10.1 percent, and France 11 percent).[40] All of these countries have universal health care; thus we spend about 50 percent more than these other countries (in relative terms) but—at least until the new health care law is implemented—leave more than 46 million people without coverage. This set up a two-tier system in which those who had access to health care got some of the best care in the world and those who did not have access were much less likely to get the health care they needed.

How is health care provided in this country, and how will it be changed by the new law? As Figure 16.6 shows, our current system is a mixture of government spending (Medicare and Medicaid), private insurance, charity (donated care), and out-of-pocket payments. **Medicare** is the federal health care program for retired people, and Medicaid is the program that covers poor people. Both programs were created in 1965 as part of the Social Security Administration but currently are administered by the Department of Health and Human Services.

Medicare has three main parts. Part A automatically applies to retirees when they qualify for Social Security and covers inpatient care in hospitals and skilled nursing facilities, hospice care, and some home health care. Medicare Part B helps cover doctors' services, outpatient hospital care, and some other medical services that Part A does not cover, such as some physical and occupational therapy, and other types of home health care. In 2003, an important new benefit was added when Congress passed the Medicare Prescription Drug Improvement and Modernization Act (Part D). Fully implemented on January 1, 2006, the plan covers about 75 percent of the cost of prescription drugs for anyone who is enrolled in Part A or Part B of Medicare, up to a certain level of expenses (see Nuts and Bolts 16.3 for details). The price tag for the plan was originally estimated at $400 billion over its first ten years, but two years after it was passed, that estimate went up to $593 billion and it is now about $750 billion for 2010–2019.[41]

FIGURE 16.6 **THE HEALTH CARE DOLLAR: WHERE IT CAME FROM AND WHERE IT WENT**

Funding for our current health care system comes from a great variety of sources and is spent on many types of care. In trying to slow the increases in health care costs, which areas should receive the most attention?

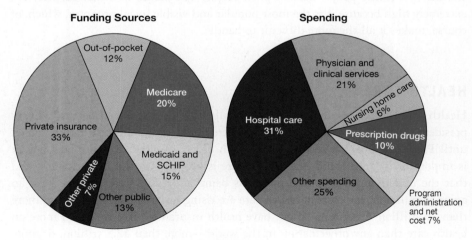

Note: Percentages shown may not add up to 100% because of rounding.

SOURCE: Centers for Medicare and Medicaid Services, Office of the Actuary, National Health Statistics Group, available at www.cms.hhs.gov/NationalHealthExpendData/downloads/PieChartSourcesExpenditures2008.pdf.

The other government health care program is **Medicaid**, which serves poor people who otherwise would have no health care. Medicaid is administered through the states with substantial funding from the federal government. Although Medicaid is an **entitlement**, states have a great deal of discretion over the program. As the government's Web site on Medicaid explains, each state

> (1) establishes its own eligibility standards; (2) determines the type, amount, duration, and scope of services; (3) sets the rate of payment for services; and (4) administers its own program. Medicaid policies for eligibility, services, and payment are complex and vary considerably, even among states of similar size or geographic proximity. Thus, a person who is eligible for Medicaid in one state may not be eligible in another state, and the services provided may differ considerably in amount, duration, or scope.[42]

This variation in state coverage means that some states cover virtually all poor people, and others cover as few as one-third of those in need. Overall nearly 40 million Americans receive health care through Medicaid at a cost of $305 billion. The federal government reimburses the states for about 60 percent of the costs ($265 billion in 2011), but this percentage varies by the income level of the state. The federal government paid 75 percent of the Medicaid costs for the poorest state in 2011, Mississippi, and 50 percent of the costs for the twelve wealthiest states, which is the minimum level set by law (in 2011, states also received up to an additional 15 percent in reimbursements).[43] Like Medicare, Medicaid faces growing budgetary pressures in the coming years. An increasing share of Medicaid's costs, about 40 percent in 2008,

Medicaid An entitlement program funded by the federal and state governments that provides health care coverage for low-income Americans who would otherwise be unable to afford heath care.

entitlement Any federal government program that provides benefits to Americans who meet requirements specified by law.

NUTS AND BOLTS

16.3

Medicare Coverage

MEDICARE PREMIUMS FOR 2010

Part A (hospital insurance): Most people do not pay Part A premiums because they or a spouse has forty or more quarters of Medicare-covered employment.

Part B (medical insurance): $110.50 per month.

Part D (prescription drugs): $32.34 per month.

MEDICARE DEDUCTIBLE AND COINSURANCE AMOUNTS FOR 2010

Part A: Medicare pays all covered costs except a deductible of $1,100 during the first 60 days and coinsurance amounts of $275 per day for days 61 through 90 of a hospital stay and $550 per day for up to 60 "lifetime reserve days" that can be used at any time during one's lifetime. No costs beyond 150 days are covered.

Part B: $155.00 per year and then a 20 percent co-pay after meeting the $155.00 deductible.

Part D: $310 per year and then a 25 percent co-pay for the first $2,840 of drugs. The beneficiary then pays 50 percent of the next $2,840 of drug costs. After a $4,550 out-of-pocket annual limit is reached, Medicare pays 95 percent of the costs of drugs.

Note: You may have noticed the discrepancy between the "three main parts" of Medicare and the appearance of "Part D" as the third part. "What happened to Part C?" the inquiring mind wants to know. There is a Part C, known as Medicare Advantage, which was enacted as part of the 1997 Balanced Budget Act. This part of Medicare allows a broader range of health care options for Medicare recipients, including HMO-style managed care plans, preferred provider organization plans (PPOs), and medical savings accounts. However, this option has not been used nearly as widely as Part A or Part B. Also, the provisions of this part of Medicare get quite complicated, so you don't need to worry about this part until you are ready to retire!

SOURCE: Health and Human Services, "Advancing the Health, Safety, and Well-Being of Our People: FY 2011 President's Budget for HHS," pp. 54–55, available at www.hhs.gov/asfr/ob/docbudget/2011budgetinbrief.pdf.

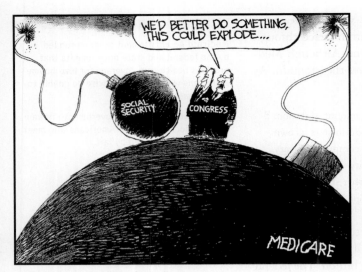

▲ The unfunded liabilities for Medicare are estimated to be about 6 times as large as the Social Security shortfall. Yet Congress has a very difficult time acting, because any solution involves the politically unpopular combination of tax increases and benefit cuts.

Q POLITICS IS CONFLICTUAL

are for long-term nursing home care for the indigent elderly, which continues to grow as the population ages.

The long-term fiscal problems of Medicare and Medicaid are severe. In fact, they dwarf Social Security's problems. The 2010 Medicare Trustees report estimates that Social Security's unfunded liabilities through 2085, or the amount of additional money (beyond the current payroll tax) required to fund all the program's commitments, is $7.8 trillion, while Medicare has unfunded liabilities of $20 trillion (plus another $2.9 trillion to pay for trust fund redemptions). The unfunded liability of Medicare's new prescription drug benefit alone ($7.2 trillion) is about the same as Social Security's liability.[44] Even though such projections depend on assumptions about future economic performance, demographic trends, and other uncertain variables, the *relative* difference between the two programs is significant. Medicare's troubles are more than two and a half times as serious as Social Security's! While the long-term Medicare deficit is huge, it is less than half the size of the projected unfunded liabilities before health care reform was passed. However, the Trustees noted that their projections assume that cuts in Medicare reimbursements mandated in new health care law will stick. The report expressed skepticism that this would happen, saying "there is a significant likelihood that the projected [Medicare] expenditures are substantially understated as a result of potentially impracticable elements of current law."[45] Another long-term study by the nonpartisan Congressional Budget Office showed that federal spending on health care (including Medicare, Medicaid, and subsidies for the new health insurance exchanges) will continue to grow through 2080 (see Figure 16.7). The CBO estimated that by 2080 federal health care spending would reach about 19 percent of GDP. That is, if the size of the federal government stayed around its historic average of 20 percent of GDP, health care spending would comprise nearly all of noninterest federal spending by 2080. The choices are clear: either everything else must be cut from budget (defense, education, transportation), health

FIGURE 16.7 PROJECTED NATIONAL SPENDING ON HEALTH CARE

If current spending patterns hold, an increasing percentage of federal spending will be devoted to health care, crowding out other programs. Clearly such trends are not sustainable. What changes do you support to reduce health care spending in the long run?

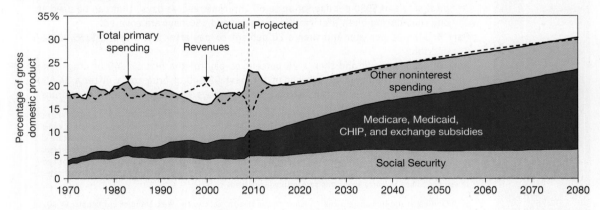

SOURCE: Congressional Budget Office, "The Long-Term Budget Outlook," June 2010 (revised August 2010), Figure A-1, p.68, available at www.cbo.gov/ftpdocs/115xx/doc11579/06-30-LTBO.pdf.

care costs must be reined in, or the size of government will grow. There wouldn't be any money for anything else—defense, Social Security, education…nothing. Clearly the current trends are not sustainable.

HEALTH CARE REFORM

Although comprehensive health care reform had been shot down repeatedly before 2010, several incremental reforms added up to substantial change. In 1996 Congress passed the Health Insurance Portability and Accountability Act, which guaranteed that people could not be denied health care coverage when they switched jobs. The new law also protected the privacy of a patient's health information, though some health experts argue that this area needs additional reform. Medicaid was expanded in 1997 to provide health care for children in families that make too much to qualify for Medicaid but not enough to buy private insurance for their children (incomes that are no more than double the poverty level). By 2009, about 5 million children were enrolled in the program. The Bush administration pushed for, and Congress passed, limited tax-free health savings accounts that may be used for paying routine out-of-pocket health care expenses or saving for more substantial, unexpected health care costs. Also, as noted above, Medicare Part D, the prescription drug plan, went into effect in January 2006. Despite this set of incremental reforms, discontent with the system continued to build.

President Obama's primary focus when he took office in January 2009 was to get the economy going. However, he also campaigned on reforming our health care system, and he remained committed to that goal. Yet through his first eight months in office, Obama stayed out of the legislative fray in an effort to avoid the centralized micromanaging that had doomed President Clinton's attempt at comprehensive reform in 1993–1994. After poll numbers showed the public turning against health care reform, and a series of angry town-hall meetings in August in which members of Congress faced questions about "death panels" and a government takeover of health care, Obama decided he needed to regain control of the debate. In a nationally televised speech before a joint session of Congress, Obama outlined his priorities, answered his critics, and linked the two top priorities of a revitalized economy and health care reform. He vowed to create a health care system

> that eases up the pressure on businesses and unleashes the promise of our economy, creating hundreds of thousands of jobs, making take-home wages thousands of dollars higher, and growing our economy by tens of billions more every year. That's how we will stop spending tax dollars to prop up an unsustainable system, and start investing those dollars in innovations and advances that will make our health care system and our economy stronger.[46]

In the speech, Obama presented several goals that he wanted to achieve: controlling health care costs, providing as close to universal coverage as possible, and paying for the program without adding to the deficit. He then urged Congress to get to work and hammer out the details.

In formulating the legislation, Congress sifted through hundreds of options that can be distilled down to three main types: national single-payer plans, state-regulated health insurance networks combined with public subsidies to help pay for insurance for those who cannot afford it, and **market-based solutions** based on tax credits and flexible spending accounts. The first of these was quickly rejected by Congress (despite having some support among liberal Democrats) and is never likely to be implemented in the United States, despite being the program of choice

market-based solutions Reform options for social policies that are based on tax credits, flexible spending accounts, and other approaches that rely on competition in the free market.

for nearly all other Western developed nations. Critics dismiss single-payer plans as "socialized medicine" and point to the rationing of care that often occurs under such programs. Similarly, market-based solutions, which were supported by most Republicans, were rejected by Democratic leaders who believed that the approach would leave too many Americans uninsured. This approach has the greatest potential for addressing the inflation of health care costs, but some health care professionals argued that many people would not have the knowledge base necessary to make the appropriate decisions concerning their own health care, because buying health care is much more difficult than shopping for food, clothing, or other consumer goods.

This left the middle ground between a single-payer plan and market-based approaches. The politics of how reform passed was discussed in the introduction to this chapter. Here we summarize the main provisions, as it is impossible to discuss all the details of a law that one reporter described as "twice as long, and half as intelligible, as Tolstoy's masterwork *War and Peace*" (that is, more than 2,000 pages).[47]

The president's first goal—comprehensive coverage—was essential. The problem had to be tackled as a whole. If insurance companies were forced to cover people with preexisting conditions without a mandate that everyone have insurance, people would wait until they were seriously ill to get coverage. Healthy people had to be pooled with sick people to spread the costs of expensive care. This was achieved by requiring businesses with more than fifty employees to provide coverage, and individuals not covered by employers to purchase insurance through new state-regulated private health insurance exchanges that must be in place by 2014. Businesses and individuals who do not comply with the mandate will face government fines. However, individuals who cannot afford insurance will receive federal subsidies on a sliding scale (a complicated formula that provides the biggest subsidies to the poorest people and some support all the way up to 4 times the federal poverty rate). The individual mandate was one of the most controversial parts of the bill, but supporters point out that states already require people to purchase auto insurance if they have a car. People who already have health insurance provided by their employer and are happy with their current policy do not have to change anything.

Other features of the law include incentives to computerize medical records, which would improve the quality of care, reduce the number of mistakes, and provide the basis for evaluating quality of care. This is related to one of the law's central cost-control mechanisms: a new nonprofit organization, the Patient-Centered Outcomes Research Institute, will engage in "comparative effectiveness research" to identify the best practices in health care. Which health care procedures work to make people healthier, and which are a waste of money? Why do some parts of the country spend more than twice as much on treating the same conditions? Health care providers will be encouraged to adopt these best practices. The law also focuses more resources on preventive care to keep people healthy rather than spend money on them once they get sick.

One other goal was that health care had to pay for itself. Obama vowed that the bill would not "add one dime to the deficit." With a price tag of just under $1 trillion over the first ten years, paying for the bill was a challenge. However, a combination of higher Medicare taxes, a new investment tax on the wealthy, an excise tax on insurers for expensive health care plans, new fees for drug companies and health insurers, and cuts in Medicare reimbursement (especially the Medicare Advantage program) meant that the law would actually reduce the federal deficit by $143 billion over the first decade.[48]

Yet the battle over health care reform was not over when Obama signed the bill into law. Opponents of the bill promised to repeal the law and used this pledge as a central part of their campaign strategy in the 2010 midterm elections. Despite Republican leaders' interpretation of their decisive midterm victory as a mandate to repeal health care reform, and their vow to do so, it is unlikely they will be successful: Democrats still control the Senate, and Obama would veto any attempt to completely repeal the law. Furthermore, many popular parts of the law already went into effect in September 2010. These include a temporary high-risk insurance pool for adults with preexisting conditions, since the permanent requirement that insurance companies cover people with preexisting conditions does not go into effect until 2014 (in addition, children under 19 with preexisting conditions could not be dropped from their parents' policies); a fix for the Medicare prescription drug plan "donut hole" (under previous law, people who spent above a minimal level on drugs but below a high amount were not covered by the law); and coverage for young adults (up to age 26) on their parents' plan. Other popular parts of the law that are already in effect prohibit insurers from charging co-payments or deductibles for preventative care on all new insurance plans, and prevent insurers from dropping policyholders when they get sick.

Legal challenges from the states also mean that health care reform is far from settled. Attorneys general from twenty states have filed suit in federal court to challenge Congress's ability to compel individuals to buy health insurance and require states to pick up the tab for expanding Medicaid coverage and administer the health insurance exchanges. One of the lead attorneys in the lawsuit, David Rivkin, calls it "the most important constitutional challenge in our generation, and one of the two or three most important in our history."[49] At least thirty-nine states have initiated legislation to overturn parts of the law, including three states that have passed legislation voiding the individual mandate and four more that put the issue to voters in a referendum on a constitutional amendment.[50] Most constitutional experts give the state challenges little chance of success because of broad congressional powers recognized by the Court under the commerce clause, the necessary and proper clause, and Congress's taxing and spending powers. However, the lawsuits and legislation raise many important constitutional questions, and it is not entirely clear how the Court would rule.

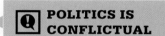 **POLITICS IS CONFLICTUAL**

Despite the uncertainty about the legal challenges and efforts by Republicans in Congress to repeal the legislation, chances are quite good that the law will survive and be strengthened over the years. The legislation is far from perfect: about 10 to 15 million Americans will remain without health insurance when it is fully implemented in 2018, the funding for the policy is a bit shaky, and enforcement of the individual mandate is essentially voluntary (through the federal tax code). But if experience with other examples of important social legislation is any guide, the law is likely to be amended and improved as problems become evident. As Senator Tom Harkin put it, health care reform is not a mansion, but a "starter home with a solid foundation, a strong roof, and plenty of room for additions and improvements."[51]

There are many other issues related to health care that will come up in the next decade, including assisted suicide and the "right to die." Voters in Oregon approved a law that went into effect in 1997 allowing the terminally ill to take a fatal dose of medication, which was upheld by the Supreme Court in 2006.[52] Other issues are raised by the increasingly high-tech nature of health care: DNA research provides great promise for curing many diseases, while basic moral and ethical questions arise about cloning, surrogate parenthood, and stem cell research. The next several years will be a very interesting period for health care policy!

income support Government programs that provide support to low-income Americans, such as welfare, food stamps, unemployment compensation, and the Earned Income Tax Credit.

When most people think of social policy aimed at helping the poor, they think of welfare. The earlier section on the history of social policy outlined the evolution of welfare from a relatively limited policy aimed at helping dependent children of single mothers to a much broader policy that was directed to single-headed households more generally. Welfare is usually thought of as cash support for people who cannot support themselves. However, **income support** can take many forms other than traditional welfare, including food stamps, unemployment insurance, Supplemental Security Income, and the Earned Income Tax Credit. We will briefly discuss each of these and then describe the major reform of welfare in 1996.

The Supplemental Nutrition Assistance Program provides food stamps, which are government-issued coupons that may be used as cash to buy groceries. Anyone who has an income that is less than 130 percent of the poverty level and has resources that do not exceed specific levels may qualify for food stamps. In 2010, the maximum monthly gross income to qualify for food stamps for a family of four was $2,389. As the economic crisis deepened late in 2009, the number of people using food stamps hit an all-time record of nearly 38.2 million, with an average monthly benefit of $133.75 per person.[53]

The Federal-State Unemployment Compensation Program was established in 1935 as part of the Social Security Act. The U.S. Department of Labor oversees the program, but it is administered by the states. The program is designed to provide temporary and partial wage replacement for people who have been laid off (the legal term is "involuntarily unemployed") and to help stabilize the economy during recessions. States set a broad range in benefit levels, minimum amount of income that must have been earned, and hours that must have been worked during the period leading up to unemployment. That is, you couldn't have worked five hours a week in a minimum wage job and qualify for unemployment insurance. Also, laid-off workers have to make themselves "available for work." About 97 percent of all workers are covered by unemployment insurance, but only about half of the unemployed who are eligible currently make use of the benefit. The regular state programs provide up to twenty-six weeks of income support and the Federal-State Extended Benefits Program temporarily provides up to twenty additional weeks in states that have relatively high unemployment rates. In January 2010, the average weekly benefit check was $310, which replaced 35.9 percent of the average worker's previous salary. Workers received benefits for an average of 17.4 weeks in 2009.[54]

The Earned Income Tax Credit (EITC) is one of the most successful programs for providing income support for the working poor. Established in 1975, the program is aimed at helping poor people move from welfare to work by providing tax credits to people who do not earn enough to pay taxes and are relatively poor. In 2010, you could qualify for an EITC if you had two children and earned less than $40,363, one child and earned less than $35,535, or no children and earned less than $13,460; the figures are slightly higher if you are married and filing jointly.[55] The federal government provided $49.3 billion in EITCs in 2008 to 23.7 million recipients, with an average monthly benefit of $173 per recipient; Figure 16.8 shows average monthly figures for other means-tested programs.[56] Clearly nobody is getting rich from this program, but it provides added assistance for the working poor.

Another important source of income support for poor people is Supplemental Security Income (SSI), a program for aged,

▼ *The food stamp program gives poor people coupons that can be used as cash to buy groceries. Though the benefits are modest, the program helps put food on the table for more than 38 million Americans.*

FIGURE 16.8

AVERAGE MONTHLY BENEFITS IN MEANS-TESTED PROGRAMS

Some types of social welfare benefits have increased in the past few decades, while others have decreased, and others have remained the same. Identify examples from each category and try to provide a political explanation for why those benefits have been increased, decreased, or funded at about the same level.

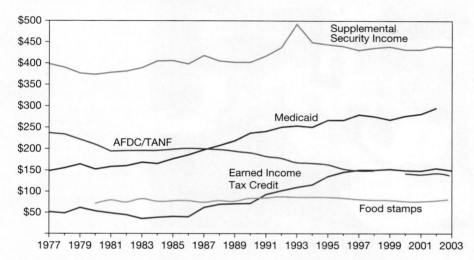

Note: AFCD is Aid to Families with Dependent Children; TANF is Temporary Assistance for Needy Families. Data from AFDC/TANF and the Earned Income Tax Credit cover people of all ages, including the elderly. Data are not available for some programs for certain years, such as TANF in 1999.

SOURCE: Congressional Budget Office, Economic and Budget Issue Brief, "Changes in Participation in Means-Tested Programs," April 20, 2005, p. 5, available at www.cbo.gov/ftpdocs/63xx/doc6302/04-20-Means-Tested.pdf.

blind, and disabled people who have limited income. The Social Security Administration runs the SSI program, but it is financed through general tax revenues, not Social Security taxes, and it is a means-tested program rather than a contributory program. Many states supplement the maximum monthly federal benefit of $674 for an individual and $1,011 for a couple (in 2010). More than 7.6 million people received SSI benefits in 2009, 85 percent of whom were disabled or blind.[57]

Welfare is straight cash assistance for people who are not working and do not qualify for unemployment compensation. The primary welfare program for the latter half of the twentieth century was **Aid to Families with Dependent Children (AFDC)**. This program became increasingly unpopular through the 1980s, and in 1992 Bill Clinton was the first Democratic presidential nominee to campaign against welfare, promising to "end welfare as we know it."[58] President Clinton did not make this the top priority of his first year in office and instead focused on health care reform and balancing the budget. However, Clinton got the ball rolling on welfare reform in June 1993, by appointing a twenty-seven-member task force on the issue. Republican leaders offered their own alternatives in the House and Senate late in 1993 and early in 1994. Clinton's commission released its bipartisan plan in January 1994, and the president's plan was submitted to Congress in June. At least a dozen other welfare reform alternatives were proposed in Congress, and some hearings were held, but no action was taken as the midterm elections loomed (it is difficult to get bipartisan compromise on major legislation in the partisan context of election battles).

Aid to Families with Dependent Children (AFDC) The federal welfare program in place from 1935 until 1996, when it was replaced by Temporary Assistance for Needy Families (TANF) under President Clinton.

The Politics of Welfare Reform

The welfare reforms enacted in 1996 have been widely hailed as a huge success. The number of people on welfare has plummeted from 13.2 million in 1996 (the last year of the old AFDC program) to a low of 3.8 million in 2008, spending on welfare is down, and many people who used to be on welfare are now working. Although the number of welfare recipients went back up a bit during the recession (to just over 4 million in late 2009),[a] the worst case scenarios of a "race to the bottom" have not come true. However, this conventional wisdom must be tempered with some of the negative aspects of welfare reform. Most of the women who left welfare have low-paying, unskilled jobs. Given that the minimum wage was not increased between 1997 and 2007, and in January 2007 it was at its lowest level in real terms since 1950, most former welfare recipients are not earning a "living wage" and are below the poverty level. The situation improved a bit with three minimum wage increases from 2007 to 2009 that brought the federal minimum wage to $7.25 (and it is higher in fourteen states, with Washington's the highest at $8.55), but the minimum wage is still much lower than its 1967 peak (in real wages) of $9.47 and is still at about the level of the real minimum wage of the mid-1950s. In addition, the high unemployment rate has made it very difficult for people with limited job skills to find work.

The proportion of children in poverty increased steadily in the 2000s. States generally have not been willing to spend the money on job training, education, and child care that would be necessary to help former welfare recipients move into better-paying jobs. Finally, the complexity of the system means that more than half of those eligible for welfare payments do not even apply. One critic of the current system, Mark Greenberg of the liberal Center for American Progress, says, "We now simply

The welfare reforms implemented in 1996 moved millions of Americans from welfare to work. States vary in the amount of worker training they provide to people on welfare. The Center for Employment Training in Alexandria, Virginia, teaches welfare recipients valuable computer skills that will help them find jobs.

have a system that provides less help in times when people are without work."[b]

Supporters of welfare reform might dismiss all of these concerns by saying, "Well, of course welfare reform cannot eliminate poverty. Nobody claimed that getting people to work would solve all of the problems of the poor." But another challenge to the conventional wisdom on welfare reform takes this discussion in a different direction. Rather than focusing on the anticipated and actual *economic* impact of welfare reform, this study looks at the anticipated and actual *political* impact. When President Clinton promised to "end welfare as we know it," most liberals were strongly opposed to the proposed policy. However, some supported it (especially over the more restrictive and tougher version proposed by Republicans in Congress) because they believed welfare reform would produce three positive political consequences. First, it would get the monkey off the back of the Democratic Party of always being tied to welfare policies. A substantial portion of the public have always had negative views of welfare, and they tend to associate the Democratic Party with those negative views. By reforming welfare, the thought was, those negative views could be neutralized. Second,

negative stereotypes of racial minorities (in terms of being associated with welfare) could also be neutralized. Third, welfare reform would allow Democrats to attack poverty more effectively because people would no longer associate spending for the poor with welfare, but rather with work. Clinton pollster Dick Morris articulated this view: "By ending welfare, Clinton wasn't rejecting liberalism; he was clearing the way for its rejuvenated influence over one of its central concerns, ghetto poverty."[c]

An interesting study by political scientists Joe Soss and Sanford Schram shows that none of these anticipated political effects turned out as expected. Public opinion polls taken before and after the period of intense political debate over welfare (1992–1996) showed relatively little change in public attitudes about welfare, welfare recipients, or the impact of attitudes toward welfare on racial stereotypes and views of the parties. That is, the negative perceived connection between welfare, racial minorities, and the Democratic Party did not change. Therefore, although the conventional wisdom of the economic impact of welfare reform is largely true—with the qualifications noted above—the political effects did not work out as progressive reformers had hoped. ∎

When the Republicans took over Congress in 1994, the momentum for reform grew. House leaders submitted the Personal Responsibility Act as part of the Republican Contract with America. This bill promised to end welfare as an entitlement, allowing states more flexibility in setting benefit levels and work requirements, creating lifetime limits for the amount of time that people could receive welfare, and attempting to curb out-of-wedlock births by denying benefits. Clinton and Congress went back and forth on the issue several times over the next two years, with the president vetoing three versions of the bill that he believed were too harsh. Finally, in 1996 they agreed on a major reform called **Temporary Assistance for Needy Families (TANF)**. The new law set a five-year lifetime limit on welfare benefits, required single mothers with children above the age of five to find work after two years of receiving benefits, required unmarried mothers who were less than eighteen years old to live with an adult and attend school to get full benefits, denied benefits to drug users who were convicted of a felony, and limited people who were not raising children and were between the ages of eighteen and fifty to three months of food stamps in any three-year period in which they were not working. Perhaps most important, welfare lost its status as an entitlement and would be administered by the states with the assistance of federal block grants. In February 2006, Congress reauthorized TANF and required that half of a state's caseload participate in work activities for at least thirty hours per week. Welfare reform had a huge impact on reducing the number of people on welfare, as shown in Figure 16.9, but it has been criticized for being too hard on the people who need government assistance the most.[59]

EDUCATION POLICY

As noted above, education policy is largely the domain of state and local governments. For the first century of our nation's history, the national government played virtually no role in education. One important exception was the Morrill Act in

Temporary Assistance for Needy Families (TANF) The welfare program that replaced Aid to Families with Dependent Children (AFDC) in 1996, eliminating the entitlement status of welfare, shifting implementation of the policy to the states, and introducing several new restrictions on receiving aid. These changes led to a significant decrease in the number of welfare recipients.

FIGURE 16.9 PARTICIPATION IN MEANS-TESTED PROGRAMS

The social policy "safety net" is supposed to protect poor Americans during periods of economic recession. A deep recession happened in the early 1980s, and the other recession during the time frame depicted here was in the early 1990s. To what extent did the safety net play its intended role?

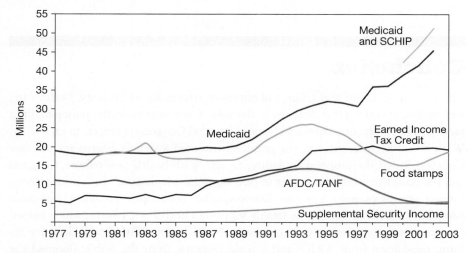

SOURCE: Congressional Budget Office, Economic and Budget Issue Brief, "Changes in Participation in Means-Tested Programs," April 20, 2005, p. 3, available at www.cbo.gov/ftpdocs/63xx/doc6302/04-20-Means-Tested.pdf.

1862, also known as the Land Grant College Act. This law gave land to eligible states to establish colleges that would promote education in the practical professions such as agriculture and mechanical arts. More than seventy-five colleges and universities today are land grant institutions.

The next major forays by the federal government into education policy came nearly a century later with the GI Bill of Rights in 1944 that provided access to higher education for the veterans returning from World War II, and the previously mentioned Elementary and Secondary Education Act of 1965 that was part of President Johnson's War on Poverty. The Department of Education was created in 1980, signaling the national government's interest in playing an important role in education policy by:

- establishing and monitoring policies on federal financial aid for education,
- collecting data on America's schools and disseminating research,
- focusing national attention on key educational issues, and
- prohibiting discrimination and ensuring equal access to education.[60]

A more recent debate concerning the national government's role in education policy has focused on standards-based education reform: Should the national government establish standards and impose accountability as a way to improve public schools? Supporters of this approach enacted the No Child Left Behind Act of 2001, which requires yearly statewide standardized testing in math and reading. If the test results show that a school is not meeting annual academic benchmarks, it is labeled a "failing school," which means that it loses some federal funding and its students are allowed to transfer to another public school. Critics argue that standardized test results are a poor measurement of progress, as schools "teach to the test" and manipulate other aspects of the evaluation system. Even with these efforts at imposing a national approach, there is substantial room for variations in state and local implementation of the national law.

President Obama's "Race to the Top" program dedicated $4 billion to competitive grants in 2010 and a proposed $1.35 billion in 2011 to encourage schools to adopt more challenging standards and better tools of assessment, promote better leadership and methods for assessing and rewarding excellent teaching, create better data systems for tracking students' progress, and obtain stronger commitments for improving the worst-performing schools. These grants were aimed at improving the quality of public education while improving accountability.[61]

Conclusion

The varying successes and failures of efforts to reform Social Security, health care, and welfare reveal a great deal about the role of key players in the policy-making process. The interaction between the president and Congress is central to each story. With Social Security reform, the president initiated a serious reform agenda, but Congress killed the proposal by failing to act. With health care reform, Congress and the president worked together to pass significant legislation. In both instances, interest groups played a key role. Doctors, other health care providers, insurance companies, and drug companies largely supported health care reform, which helped Congress pass the historic but controversial legislation. With Social Security reform, opposition from AARP and a tepid response from the public doomed the idea of private savings accounts, at least for now. As our discussion of the long-term problems faced by Social Security and Medicare should make clear, the last chapter on reform is yet to be written. Sooner or later policy makers will have to confront the massive long-term deficits in these programs.

Welfare reform also illustrates the roles of the various players in policy making. As with health care reform, the president and Congress were the most important players in shaping the massive overhaul of the welfare system. However, there were some key differences. First, although the policy-making process in Congress for health care reform was almost entirely partisan, with the Democratic Party dictating the final shape of the bill, welfare reform was shaped by a more bipartisan process between the Republicans in Congress and Democratic President Clinton. Second, those who benefited from welfare were much weaker politically than those who stood to be directly affected by the reform of health care. As a component of the public, the poor simply do not have very much clout because they do not vote, participate in campaigns, or contribute to campaigns as much as the rest of the public. Therefore, they could do little to stop welfare reform. Third, the organized groups opposed to welfare reform and representing the poor do not have the same political power as the health care groups supporting reform. Thus, reform was enacted into law in both instances but with a different mix of players.

The experiences with social policy reform also illustrate the themes of the book. First, as discussed in the chapter opener, health care reform is a perfect example of the conflictual nature of politics. From fictitious "death panels" to health coverage for illegal immigrants and abortion, health care reform ignited many contentious debates. Substantive disagreements about the scope of coverage and how to pay for it also revealed deep fault lines across and within the parties. Despite this conflict, congressional leaders pieced together a set of compromises that created an imperfect but historic law. However, conflict over social policy is far from resolved. The reform of Social Security and Medicare provide fertile ground for intergenerational struggle and class warfare. It is impossible to discuss these issues for more than five minutes and not see that resolving the long-term problems facing social policy in the United States will involve many intense debates.

Social policy, especially the legislative struggles over health care reform, demonstrates that political process matters. The filibuster in the Senate played an important role in the first stages of shaping health care reform, and the decision to use the reconciliation process late in the game ensured passage of the law. Politicians' decisions have a key impact on policy outcomes, and the timing and politics of the policy-making process clearly drive the results. Had congressional leaders made different decisions, it is quite possible that health care reform would have failed. Finally, politics is everywhere. Social policies touch every American at some point in their lives, and the struggles over reforming these policies are at the core of contemporary American politics.

What is social policy, and how has American social policy developed over time?

- Social policies provide a "safety net" to help the poor and disadvantaged.
- In the early years of our nation's history, the federal government took little responsibility for social welfare.
- The New Deal in the 1930s and the Great Society in the 1960s were the two main periods of social policy creation.

How are poverty and income inequality related to social policy?

- Poverty and income inequality create greater need for many social programs aimed at helping the poor.
- There are partisan differences in the growth in income inequality during presidential administrations.

Who are the key players in making social policy?

- Congress and the president both play central roles in shaping social policy; either the legislative or executive branch may take the lead on a given policy, but both branches are needed to enact significant policy.
- The bureaucracy and state governments have the biggest impact on the way social policy is implemented.
- Social policy interest groups tend to be weaker than other interest groups, but they can help mobilize the public for or against a given social policy.

How does the policy-making process work?

- Policies go through a normal progression, from problem recognition and definition, to getting on the agenda, to deliberation and formulation.
- After a policy is enacted into law, it must be implemented by the national or state and local bureaucracies.
- The last stages of the policy-making process are evaluation and deciding whether to modify, expand, or terminate the program.

What is the state of American social policy today, and what issues will be faced in the future?

- Social Security is the most popular social program in the United States, as it provides (or will provide) income for virtually every retired American.
- The United States spends 50 percent more on health care than all other Western nations, yet there are 47 million Americans without health insurance.
- Social Security and Medicare face serious long-term funding issues because of the retirement of the Baby Boom generation.
- Income support programs include welfare, food stamps, unemployment compensation, and the Earned Income Tax Credit (EITC).
- Education policy is controlled by state and local governments, but the national government has played an increasingly important role in recent decades.

ⓢ STUDENT STUDYSPACE

Find quizzes and other review material at wwnorton.com/studyspace.

CRITICAL THINKING

1. What differences may be expected in the shaping of social policy with Barack Obama having been elected president in 2008 rather than John McCain? Does it matter which party controls Congress?
2. What do you think should be the government's responsibilities in the area of social policy? Do you favor more of an "ownership society" or more of a direct role for the government?
3. Do you support the health care reform law that was enacted in 2010? Or do you think the law was not ambitious enough, or alternatively, an over-reach by the national government?

KEY TERMS

SUGGESTED READING

Altman, Nancy J. *The Battle for Social Security: From FDR's Vision to Bush's Gamble*. New York: Wiley, 2005.

Bartels, Larry M. *Unequal Democracy: The Political Economy of the New Gilded Age*. Princeton, NJ: Princeton University Press, 2008.

King, Ronald F. *Budgeting Entitlements: The Politics of Food Stamps*. Washington, DC: Georgetown University Press, 2000.

Oberlander, Jonathan. *The Political Life of Medicare*. Chicago: University of Chicago Press, 2003.

Skocpol, Theda. *Social Policy in the United States: Future Possibilities in Historical Perspective*. Princeton, NJ: Princeton University Press, 1995.

Soss, Joe. *Unwanted Claims: The Politics of Participation in the U.S. Welfare System*. Ann Arbor, MI: University of Michigan Press, 2000.

Weaver, R. Kent. *Ending Welfare as We Know It*. Washington, DC: Brookings Institution Press, 2000.

American foreign policies, such as the invasions of Iraq and Afghanistan, are closely interwined with American domestic policies. Here, a solidier with the U.S. Army's 82nd Airborne Division keeps watch over a street in Tal Afar, Iraq.

Foreign Policy

For anyone who came of age after September 11, 2001, it is obvious that foreign policy matters. The September 11 attacks leveled the World Trade Center towers, damaged the Pentagon, killed more than 3,000 people, and aimed to destroy the U.S. Capitol Building. Since then, America has spent hundreds of billions of dollars on the invasion and occupation of Afghanistan and Iraq and lost thousands of lives, captured or killed terrorists and suspected terrorists in many countries, and granted generous aid packages to nations that supported these policies. Some of these actions have been controversial in the United States and extremely unpopular throughout the rest of the world, damaging America's reputation as a benign superpower and a bastion of democracy and freedom.

CONFLICT AND COMPROMISE
in American Politics

Besides the tragic loss of life, the events of September 11 changed the lives of Americans in many other ways. Routine video surveillance and monitoring of international phone calls and e-mails have increased, passports are required to enter the United States regardless of the point of entry, and airline passengers face a variety of new security checks and restrictions. Increased military spending has crowded out other governmental programs, and extended military deployments have caused financial hardship and emotional distress for many families.

These events and their aftermath illustrate a general point about foreign policy: it is hard to find a domestic issue that does not have a foreign policy component. Take the state of America's economy. As discussed in Chapter 15, over the last generation American politicians have approved a series of treaties that reduced tariffs on imports and exports, generating enormous profits for some American companies. American aircraft manufacturers, for example, prospered under trade liberalization, selling passenger and cargo jets to airlines throughout the world. However, trade liberalization has hurt companies that could not respond to increased foreign competition, such as the financially troubled American auto producers that have required substantial federal aid just to stay in business. Many of their workers have been laid off or have taken buyouts to quit their jobs or retire early, rather than face an uncertain future of layoffs and wage cuts.[1] A study of displaced workers across a number of industries found that two years after losing their jobs, only one-third had jobs that paid as well as their old positions.

More recent events reinforce the idea that foreign and domestic policies are intertwined. The American stock market declined significantly in the spring

✪ What is foreign policy?

✪ Who makes American foreign policy?

✪ What are the tools of foreign policy?

✪ What characterizes the politics of American foreign policy?

✪ What key foreign policy issues do we face now and in the future?

of 2010 because of concerns about the willingness of Greece and some other European countries to implement financial austerity plans needed to repay their national debt. Similarly, attempts by the Obama administration to force BP to pay cleanup and compensation costs for its oil spill in the Gulf of Mexico created tensions between the United States and one of its closest allies, as BP is headquartered in Great Britain and is one of the largest payers of stock dividends to British citizens.

These examples, even the September 11 attacks and their aftermath, also illustrate the fundamentally conflictual nature of American foreign policy. The initial surge of unity and common purpose seen after the attacks soon dissolved into debate over the specifics of America's response—from the initial decisions to invade Afghanistan and Iraq to contemporary debates over how best to fight the ongoing threat of terrorist attacks. Again, this conflict is nothing new. Throughout American history there have been many disagreements over foreign policy issues, from whether and how to use military force or form alliances, to questions about foreign trade agreements and human rights policies. Although these debates often have political consequences, with positions sometimes taken for political gain, in the main they reflect sincere differences of opinion; in this sense, foreign policy closely resembles domestic policy.

Finally, political process matters in foreign policy. The president's central role in the making of foreign policy stems in part from constitutional allocations of executive power, such as the president's leadership of the executive branch and his role as commander in chief of the U.S. armed forces. The president also benefits from his ability to act unilaterally, as discussed in Chapter 11. Even so, presidents do not have complete authority to determine America's foreign policy. Factors such as congressional control over federal spending, as well as judicial review exercised by federal judges, impose significant limits on presidential power in this area.

What Is Foreign Policy?

Foreign policy refers to government actions involving countries, groups, and corporations that lie outside America's borders. Foreign policy includes military operations, economic interactions, human rights policies, environmental agreements, foreign aid, democracy assistance, interventions in civil wars and other conflicts, and international efforts to limit weapons of mass destruction, including nuclear weapons.

The goals behind many foreign policy actions are varied and complex. For example, some observers argued that America's invasion of Iraq was aimed at securing inexpensive oil for American businesses and consumers. Although this goal may

foreign policy Government actions that affect countries, corporations, groups, or individuals outside America's borders.

have motivated some politicians to support the war, others favored invasion for different reasons. They might have believed Iraq possessed weapons of mass destruction or viewed the country as a supporter of terrorist groups. On the other hand, they might have thought that establishing a democratic government in Iraq would serve as a model for other countries in the Middle East or wanted to end human rights abuses by the Iraqi government.

Because foreign policy is often complex, debates over what the United States should do in a particular situation are often framed in terms of general principles or rules. These principles are a way of summarizing the arguments on each side of a foreign policy question, or in some cases, showing how seemingly different foreign policy issues are actually quite similar. This section outlines three pairs of important concepts: unilateral versus multilateral action, isolationism versus internationalism, and idealism versus realism. These concepts are more than theoretical guides for decision making; many scholars of international relations see these principles as descriptions of how states actually act.

Unilateral action occurs when one country does something on its own, without coordinating with other countries. For example, some U.S. antiterror operations under both Presidents Bush and Obama, particularly in Pakistan, have been undertaken without any consultation or notice to U.S. allies—not even to the Pakistanis.[2]

American foreign policy more commonly involves **multilateral action** by the United States alongside other countries or international organizations such as the United Nations. Since early 2008, more than twenty nations, including the United States, have conducted naval patrols off the Gulf of Aden in an attempt to deter pirate attacks against civilian shipping. The United States, in cooperation with the United Nations and several other nations, has been working to improve security in Afghanistan and rebuild its government and civilian infrastructure. Along these same lines, the Quartet on the Middle East is a group composed of the United States, Russia, the European Union, and the United Nations, which is working to facilitate peace negotiations between Israel and the Palestinians. Similarly, the United Nations, the African Union, several relief groups, and various nations, including the United States, have cooperated to try to broker a deal to end armed conflict in the Darfur region of Sudan and to aid and protect Darfur's civilian population. And the United States participated in the six-nation talks that attempted to end North Korea's nuclear weapons program.

A second important distinction in foreign policy is between **isolationism** and **internationalism**. Isolationists believe that the United States should avoid making alliances and agreements with other nations, concentrate on defending America's borders, and let the people in other countries work out their problems for themselves. In the case of Darfur, for example, an isolationist might argue that U.S. intervention would be futile or potentially counterproductive, too costly, or simply inappropriate.[3]

An internationalist, on the other hand, would argue that the United States should establish many agreements with other nations and intervene in international crises whenever it may be able to help, both because of possible economic and security gains and because intervening in civil wars and helping to solve humanitarian crises is morally right. In the case of Darfur, internationalists would support U.S. efforts to help and protect the local population, either in concert with other nations or even alone if other nations are unwilling to intervene.[4]

The third major distinction in foreign policy making is between **realism** and **idealism**.[5] Realists believe that countries pursue their own interests, seeking to increase their economic and military power and their international influence. In approaching a policy decision, a realist would choose the policy that maximized American military and economic power relative to other states. Idealists, on the

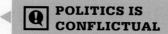

POLITICS IS CONFLICTUAL

unilateral action (national) Independent acts of foreign policy undertaken by a nation without the assistance or coordination of other nations.

multilateral action Foreign policy carried out by a nation in coordination with other nations or international organizations.

isolationism The idea that the United States should refrain from involvement in international affairs.

internationalism The idea that the United States should be involved in the affairs of other nations, out of both self-interest and moral obligation.

realism The idea that a country's foreign policy decisions are motivated by self-interest and the goal of gaining more power.

idealism The idea that a country's foreign policy decisions are based on factors beyond self-interest, including upholding important principles or values.

Should America Act Unilaterally or Multilaterally? The Case of the International Criminal Court

Foreign policy presents Americans with a fundamental choice: Should America act alone or cooperate with other nations? Unilateral action means that American policy makers can act to further America's self-interest—as these individuals define it, of course. The advantage of multilateral action is that working with other nations may allow the United States to achieve goals that would be unattainable by acting alone, such as devising and implementing solutions to global warming. However, multilateral action may sometimes produce policies that are not ideal, or even acceptable, to the United States.

As an example of this problem, consider the International Criminal Court (ICC), an agency within the United Nations that was set up in 2002 to prosecute cases of genocide, war crimes, and crimes against humanity.[a] Before the ICC was established, new courts had to be created every time someone was tried for such crimes, such as the International Criminal Tribunal for the Former Yugoslavia, which prosecuted more than 100 political leaders, military leaders, and soldiers from Yugoslavia and Serbia, including the former president of Serbia, Slobodan Milosevic. The ICC was created as a permanent international body that would adjudicate these high-profile, international cases. The ICC began its prosecution efforts with the 2006 arrest of Thomas Lubanga Dyilo, a militia leader in a civil war in the Democratic Republic of Congo. The Court has more recently arrested Radovan Karadzic, the leader of Serbia during the mid-1990s civil war in the Balkans, and issued arrest warrants for the prime minister of Sudan and the leader of local militias in Darfur.[b]

As of July 2010, 110 nations have ratified the ICC treaty, which essentially gives the ICC jurisdiction over their citizens.[c] These nations include U.S. allies Great Britain, France, and Germany. However, the United States has not ratified the treaty, nor have allies Israel and Japan. Others who have not ratified include China, Russia, Iran, and North Korea.

The United States signed the ICC treaty during President Clinton's administration, but, as noted in Chapter 11, the treaty was never sent to the Senate for a ratification vote. (Clinton expressed some doubts about the treaty but also faced a Senate where support for the treaty was weak.) Clinton's successor, George W. Bush, nullified the signature and declared that the United

other hand, believe that states' concerns extend beyond simply increasing their power, including principles such as freedom, liberty, or democracy. For an idealist, upholding these principles should be a primary goal of U.S. foreign policy.

To illustrate the debate between realists and idealists, consider the cases made by each side regarding the invasion of Iraq. Realists John Mearsheimer and Steven Walt argued in February 2003, one month before the U.S. invasion, that there was no need to invade.[6] In their view, the threat of retaliation by America and other countries would deter Saddam Hussein from invading neighboring countries, using weapons of mass destruction, or giving these weapons to terrorists. According to Mearsheimer and Walt, invading Iraq and deposing Hussein was a bad idea because it would not improve America's national security and might harm America's relations with other countries in the Middle East. In contrast, the idea that America is morally obligated to establish a democratic Iraq is a clear example of idealism.

These terms are used often in debates over foreign policy because they offer convenient ways to summarize the motivations behind policy decisions. That is how we use these terms in this chapter, but it is important to keep in mind that none of

States would not allow its citizens to be prosecuted by the ICC. Bush administration officials even threatened to withhold U.S. forces from UN peacekeeping missions unless they were granted full immunity from ICC prosecution.[d] As of late 2010, this policy remains in place under President Obama, although the United States has agreed to send observers to monitor ICC proceedings.[e]

U.S. criticism of the ICC centers on whether defendants are given full due process rights as they are in American courts, such as the right to see the evidence against them and protection against self-incrimination.[f] However, an analysis by the group Human Rights Watch, which supports the ICC, argued that ICC procedures are similar to those in U.S. courts.[g]

These debates miss a deeper concern. By joining the ICC, the United States would lose the ability to protect its citizens from prosecution by this court. In theory, the ICC could prosecute American forces and military leaders for such actions as the invasion and occupation of Iraq or the interrogation techniques used against terror suspects in the detention facility at Guantánamo

The International Criminal Court, shown here during one of its meetings, was set up to allow the prosecution of terrorists and international war criminals, such as individuals involved in genocide. The United States, whose empty seat at the Court is shown here, has refused to join the organization, partly due to concerns that American troops might be tried for their actions during armed conflicts.

Bay. These concerns are not merely abstract. British soldiers have been prosecuted and convicted by the ICC for abuse of prisoners in Iraq.[h] And American military lawyers expressed concerns that interrogation methods that were commonly used by American forces would put these individuals at risk of ICC prosecution.[i]

The stakes are high on both sides of the question. If the United States joins the ICC, it will pressure other holdout nations to do so, thus increasing the Court's value as a potential deterrent to future cases of genocide, crimes against humanity, and war crimes. But joining the ICC would also put American soldiers and statesmen at risk of prosecution by a court outside U.S. control. What would you decide? ■

---

these terms provides a fully accurate, one-word definition of what motivates nations or individuals. No one is a realist or an idealist all the time.

Even President George W. Bush, whom many people have described as an idealist,[7] criticized his opponent, Al Gore, during the 2000 presidential campaign for supporting what Bush called **nation building**—the idea that the United States should intervene to end civil wars in countries such as Bosnia and Kosovo. This criticism is a realist argument; it suggests that because these conflicts did not directly affect the United States, there was no reason to get involved. Yet several years later, when discussing his reasons for going to war in Iraq, Bush said, "I believe we have a duty to free people, to liberate people."[8] Was President Bush a realist or an idealist? It depends on the circumstances. His goals and preferences motivated him to advocate a realist position in some cases and take an idealist view of other situations. The same is true for President Obama. His campaign promise to meet with hostile foreign leaders suggested an idealist perspective, but his deployment of additional troops to Afghanistan and increased use of drone aircraft against Al Qaeda in Pakistan and other countries is more consistent with realism. Ultimately,

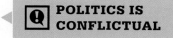

POLITICS IS CONFLICTUAL

nation building The use of American resources, including the military, to help create democratic institutions abroad and prevent violence in other countries.

Obama's actions will likely reflect a combination of both philosophies. For any leader, the realist and idealist labels summarize the motivations behind individual foreign policy decisions and may or may not suggest what kinds of foreign policies he would be expected to prefer in the future.

HISTORY OF AMERICAN FOREIGN POLICY

This section gives a brief overview of the evolution of American foreign policy. Its aim is to illustrate what foreign policy is all about, including the types of choices American politicians face, how these policy options have changed over the country's history, and the lack of agreement among American politicians about how these issues should be resolved.

The Founding to World War I Until America's entry into World War I in 1917, American foreign policy was primarily but not completely isolationist. Most presidents and other elected officials tended to behave in accordance with George Washington's assertion in his farewell address that the United States should "avoid entangling alliances" with other nations.[9] Isolationism made sense during this period for several reasons. America's distance from Europe reduced the potential for international economic interactions, lowered the level of military threat, and gave early America room to expand without coming into conflict with European nations.[10] The **Monroe Doctrine**, established by President James Monroe in 1823, stated that America would remain neutral in wars involving European nations, and that the United States expected these nations to stop trying to colonize or occupy areas in North and South America.[11] During this time, America expanded by purchasing land from other countries—adding much of the Midwest through the Louisiana Purchase—and by annexing land after military conflicts, such as the large section of the Southwest acquired from Mexico following the Mexican-American War. America also controlled some territories such as the Philippines as colonies.

America's foreign policy was never completely isolationist, however, even in the early years. The American navy was deployed on many occasions to protect U.S. ships and citizens, and, as noted above, America had several colonies far beyond its borders. America also built the Panama Canal, leasing land from Panama in the

▶ The Treaty of Versailles, which officially ended World War I, was also intended to create institutions that would make future wars less likely. However, America's refusal to join the League of Nations proposed by the treaty, along with limits on the League's power, made that goal unattainable.

process, and sent troops into conflicts in Nicaragua and other Central American countries. America also maintained significant trading relationships with nations in Europe and elsewhere.

Still, America's involvement in World War I marked a sharp departure in foreign policy, both in America's enthusiastic participation in an international alliance, and in the willingness of the president (but not others in government) to continue these activities after the conflict.[12] With the war almost over, President Woodrow Wilson offered a peace plan, the Fourteen Points, which proposed reshaping the borders of European countries in order to mitigate future conflict, measures to encourage free trade and democracy, and an international organization that would prevent future conflicts.[13] American diplomats participated in the negotiations that culminated in the Treaty of Versailles, which officially ended the war, though most of Wilson's proposals were not part of the final document.[14] The treaty did create the League of Nations, an organization similar to the modern United Nations, but the U.S. Senate rejected the Treaty of Versailles, which meant that the United States never joined the League of Nations.[15]

◄ **POLITICS IS CONFLICTUAL**

The Rise of Internationalism A great transition in American foreign policy occurred during World War II (1939–1945). The war started in September 1939, but the United States only became directly involved in the conflict on December 8, 1941, declaring war on Japan the day after Japanese air attacks on Pearl Harbor in Hawaii and various American bases in the Philippines. Germany subsequently declared war on the United States on December 11. However, prior to the United States' official involvement, the U.S. military had been supplying Great Britain and its allies with arms, ships, and other supplies, in return for payments and long-term leases on British military bases throughout the world.

During World War II, the Allied Powers—the United States, Great Britain, the Soviet Union, and other countries—fought as a formal alliance, forming joint plans, allowing troops from one country to be led by a commander from another, and sharing military hardware and intelligence. After World War II, the consensus among American politicians and scholars was that the United States should be a central actor in world affairs. This new policy was justified by realist arguments, such as the need to deter future conflicts and the desire for economic benefits from trading with other nations.[16] Idealists argued for the same policies on grounds that America had a moral obligation to preserve world peace.[17]

The Cold War Soon after World War II ended, the **Cold War** (1945–1991) began as the victorious Allies disagreed over the reconstruction of Germany and the reformation of Eastern European countries that Germany had occupied during the war. In a 1946 speech in Fulton, Missouri, former British prime minister Winston Churchill referred to an "iron curtain" that had split Eastern and Western Europe, leaving the East under Soviet domination with few political freedoms.[18] Influential American diplomat George Kennan argued for **containment**, the idea that America should use diplomatic, economic, and military means to prevent the Soviet Union from expanding the set of countries that it controlled or was allied with.[19] This policy was summarized in the Truman Doctrine, which served as a guiding principle for American foreign policy over the next generation.[20]

During this period the United States implemented several measures to build and strengthen alliances against the Soviet threat. The first of these was the Marshall Plan, a series of aid and development programs enacted in the late 1940s to restore the economies of Western European countries devastated during World War II.[21] The United States was also instrumental in the formation of the World Bank and the International Monetary Fund, as well as international trade agreements such

Cold War The period of tension and arms competition between the United States and the Soviet Union that lasted from 1945 until 1991.

containment An important feature of American Cold War policy in which the United States used diplomatic, economic, and military strategies in an effort to prevent the Soviet Union from expanding its influence.

as the General Agreement on Tariffs and Trade. (These are discussed later in the chapter.)

The United States also formed a series of alliances with other countries, including the North Atlantic Treaty Organization (NATO) in 1949. The goal of these organizations was collective security, based on the principle that "an attack against one is an attack against all."[22] The aim was to deter Soviet attacks throughout the world by formalizing America's commitment to defend its allies. The Soviets formed their own alliances, most notably the Warsaw Pact with nations in Eastern Europe.[23]

The United States was also a prime mover behind the 1945 creation of the United Nations (UN), an international organization with the aim of preventing wars by facilitating negotiations between combatants, and, if necessary, sending military forces from member states to stop conflicts. Other aspects of the UN's role have included administering relief efforts for refugees, running development efforts, codifying international law, and publicizing and condemning human rights violations.

As this discussion illustrates, the goal of containment influenced virtually every aspect of American foreign policy after World War II.[24] The Korean War, in which America sent troops to defend South Korea against invasion by North Korea, was motivated largely by containment—North Korea's efforts had the strong support of the Soviet Union and China.[25] America also supported brutal dictators in other countries, such as the Shah of Iran during the 1970s, and overlooked these governments' dismal human rights records on the grounds that their leaders would be valuable allies against the Soviets.[26]

America also maintained large military forces, beginning its first peacetime draft in the 1950s and building a large store of nuclear weapons. These weapons were intended to deter war with the Soviet Union through the threat of **mutually assured destruction**, the idea that even if the Soviet Union unleashed an all-out nuclear assault on U.S. forces, enough American weapons would remain intact to deliver a similarly devastating counterattack. The United States stationed hundreds of thousands of troops in Western Europe and elsewhere to deter the Soviet threat.

War nearly broke out between the United States and the Soviet Union during the Cuban Missile Crisis, when the Soviets attempted to station nuclear missiles in Cuba—within striking range of the United States. However, the issue was defused by a Soviet withdrawal in the face of an American naval blockade of Cuba and a secret American promise to withdraw similar missiles from Turkey in return.

In the early 1960s America became militarily involved in the conflict in Vietnam—which later escalated into the Vietnam War—based on the belief that North Vietnam's drive to take over South Vietnam was part of the Soviet Union's plan for world domination.[27] The **domino theory** posited that if the United States did not prevent the fall of South Vietnam, the next step would be a Soviet-backed conflict in the Philippines, Australia, or some other American ally. The Vietnam War demonstrated that the domino theory was fundamentally inaccurate; the initial conflict between North and South Vietnam was a civil war rather than an international event.[28] Though the North Vietnamese were happy to have Soviet support, especially given America's support of the South, they did not take orders from the Soviets.

Beginning in the early 1970s, President Richard Nixon and his national security adviser, Henry Kissinger, began a process of **détente** with the Soviet Union, a series of negotiations and cultural exchanges designed to reduce tensions and find issues on which the two superpowers could cooperate.[29] These efforts culminated in the 1972 Strategic Arms Limitation Treaty (SALT I), which limited the growth of U.S. and Soviet missile forces.[30]

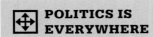

POLITICS IS EVERYWHERE

mutually assured destruction The idea that two nations that possess large stores of nuclear weapons—like the United States and the Soviet Union during the Cold War—would both be annihilated in any nuclear exchange, thus making it unlikely that either country would launch a first attack.

domino theory An idea held by American foreign policy makers during the Cold War that the creation of one Soviet-backed communist nation would lead to the spread of communism in that nation's region.

détente An approach to foreign policy in which cultural exchanges and negotiations are used to reduce tensions between rival nations, such as between the United States and the Soviet Union during the 1970s.

At the same time, the embargo prohibiting oil shipments to Western nations that was implemented by Arab nations after the 1973 Arab–Israeli war was a sharp reminder that containment of the Soviet Union could not be America's only foreign policy priority. Tensions over oil increased again when the Organization of the Petroleum Exporting Countries (OPEC) raised prices in 1979. Both events contributed to a recession in America and the electoral defeats of two incumbent presidents, Gerald Ford in 1976 and Jimmy Carter in 1980. Carter's defeat was also, in part, the result of the Iran hostage crisis, in which Iranian students, with government backing, held American embassy staff hostage for more than fourteen months.[31]

Tension with the Soviet Union increased again with the Soviets' support for the Sandinista rebellion in Nicaragua in the late 1970s and their invasion of Afghanistan in 1980.[32] In response to Soviet military actions in Afghanistan, President Carter withdrew the U.S. Olympic team from the 1980 games in Moscow, suspended sales of wheat to the Soviets, and began to increase defense spending. These increases steepened under Carter's successor, Ronald Reagan, who vowed to put communism "on the ash heap of history." Notwithstanding this rhetoric, Reagan also worked to negotiate arms control agreements with the Soviet Union.[33]

The real change in U.S.–Soviet relations began with the selection of Mikhail Gorbachev as leader of the Soviet Union in 1985, and his policies of *glasnost* ("openness") and *perestroika* ("restructuring"). The Warsaw Pact was dissolved in 1991, with most of its former members becoming democracies—some have even joined NATO. The Soviet Union splintered into fifteen countries in December 1991, effectively ending the Cold War. Scholars are still debating the reasons for these changes. Some argue that the costs of responding to America's military buildup bankrupted the Soviet state, while others point to disaffection with the communist ideology and the inability of the Soviet economy to provide goods and services.[34]

Since the end of the Cold War, the United States and Russia have continued to disagree over many policies, including the enlargement of NATO to include some Warsaw Pact countries, the proposed installation of anti-missile batteries in Poland, the international response to ethnic cleansing in Bosnia and Kosovo, the U.S. invasion of Iraq in 2003, and the Russian invasion of Georgia in 2008.[35] However, it is important to remember that only twenty years ago, both countries had enough weapons aimed at each other to destroy the entire world. Although differences remain, the two countries have significantly increased commercial and diplomatic ties, to the point that military conflict seems highly unlikely for the foreseeable future.

After the Cold War: Human Rights, Trade, and Terrorism The end of the Cold War, along with the increase in the number of democracies worldwide and the development of democratic peace theories (which argue that democracies will not fight other democracies), suggested to some observers that military conflicts would become much rarer, so that other concerns would become more influential in America's foreign policy.[36] Events in the first few years of the post–Cold War era seemed to support this thesis. Human rights became a more important foreign policy topic.[37] The United States became involved in humanitarian relief and nation-building efforts in Somalia, Bosnia, and Kosovo. A series of agreements, including the North American Free Trade Agreement (NAFTA) in 1994 and the formation of the World Trade Organization (WTO) in 1995, lowered tariffs throughout the world. Technological advances in transportation also lowered the cost of shipping goods worldwide, and the industrialization of many third world countries made them low-cost suppliers of manufactured goods to the United States, resulting in the closing of many domestic factories.

However, new security threats emerged in the form of terrorist groups, most notably Al Qaeda, led by Osama bin Laden. Al Qaeda organized several attacks

▲ In a 1987 speech given in Berlin, President Reagan famously demanded that Soviet leader Mikhail Gorbachev "tear down down this wall," referring to the Berlin Wall that separated the democratic and the communist sections of the city. However, the fall of communism in the 1990s had more to do with the failure of communist governments to sustain economic growth and to provide for their citizens than with presidential rhetoric.

▲ *The Al Qaeda terrorist organization headed by Osama bin Laden has been the driving force behind many terrorist attacks on Americans, including the October 2000 bombing of the USS Cole and the September 11, 2001, attacks on the World Trade Center and the Pentagon.*

Bush Doctrine The foreign policy of President George W. Bush, under which the United States would use military force preemptively against threats to its national security.

on Americans, including the bombing of U.S. embassies in Tanzania and Kenya in 1998 and an attack on an American warship, the USS *Cole*, in 2000. Then came the Al Qaeda attacks of September 11, 2001. Some analysts and politicians, including President George W. Bush, described these attacks as part of a worldwide "clash of civilizations" or a global War on Terror, pitting the secular, open West against radical Islam.[38] In the wake of the attacks, President George W. Bush announced a new U.S. policy, the **Bush Doctrine**, or the doctrine of preemption, whereby the United States would not wait until after an attack to respond but would use military force to eliminate potential threats before they could be put in motion. This policy was behind the decision to invade Iraq in 2003.

In several important respects, the presidency of Barack Obama represents a sharp reversal of many Bush-era policies, with the emphasis now on improving foreign perceptions of America and Americans, and avoiding unilateral action in favor of multilateral coalitions. Obama's 2009 speech in Cairo, in which he acknowledged past American mistakes and called for cooperation around shared interests, is typical of this new approach.[39] However, as we describe throughout this chapter, many of Obama's policies in regards to the War on Terror and other areas are quite similar to those established by the Bush administration.

We discuss these and other current areas of concern, including global warming, human rights, the War on Terror, and the impact of the 2008 global financial crisis, in the Contemporary Foreign Policy Issues section later in this chapter.

Foreign Policy Makers

This section focuses on the makers of American foreign policy. Simply put, Who shapes the United States' relations with other nations, and what is the source of their influence? We begin with the president and the executive branch, then consider Congress, the courts, and finally, other groups and individuals outside the government. Our discussion is framed in terms of the book's three themes and our assertion that politics is explainable. Foreign policy often deals with complex global issues, but it can still be analyzed.

This discussion focuses on people and organizations in government whose primary job is foreign policy making, but virtually all executive branch departments and agencies have some responsibility for issues with international reach. For example, the Department of Education administers programs that fund undergraduate, graduate, and scholarly study of the politics, history, and culture of other nations, as well as educational exchanges with universities abroad.[40] Similarly, the Department of Agriculture oversees programs that encourage food exports to other nations and that protect Americans against unsafe imports.[41]

THE PRESIDENT AND THE EXECUTIVE BRANCH

The president is the dominant actor in American foreign policy.[42] As discussed in Chapter 11, the president and his staff can negotiate treaties or executive agreements with other nations, change policy through executive orders or findings, mobilize public opinion to prompt action by Congress, and shape foreign policy by appointing people to agencies and departments that administer these policies. The president also serves as the commander in chief of America's armed forces.

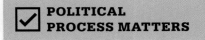

☑ **POLITICAL PROCESS MATTERS** ▶

Within the Executive Office of the President (EOP), the principal foreign policy agency is the **National Security Council (NSC)**, which focuses on developing foreign policy options and presenting them to the president. The EOP also includes the Office of the U.S. Trade Representative, which focuses on tariffs and trade disputes; the president's Foreign Intelligence Advisory Board, a group of academics, politicians, and former government officials who advise the president; the Homeland Security Council, which coordinates antiterrorism policies; and the Office of Management and Budget, which prepares the president's annual budget proposals for federal agencies and departments, including those with foreign policy responsibilities.

The Department of State The principal foreign policy department in the executive branch is the Department of State, and its head, the secretary of state, acts as the official spokesperson for the United States in foreign relations and is an important adviser to the president. State Department officials operate U.S. embassies abroad and represent the United States in everyday interactions with the leaders of other countries; they also offer expertise on the politics, economics, and cultures of other nations. Aside from senior staff like the secretary of state, who is nominated by the president and confirmed by the Senate, State Department personnel are generally career civil servants who remain in their positions even after a new president takes office. There are many different offices and working groups in the State Department, from people who deal with treaties to coordinators of international aid to others who focus on arms control or assistance for refugees. This wide variation highlights the broad range of issues that are considered foreign policy.

The Department of Defense The job of the Department of Defense is to carry out military actions as ordered by civilian authorities, ranging from waging full-scale wars such as those in Iraq and Afghanistan, to conducting smaller operations such as the peacekeeping missions in Bosnia and Kosovo that began in the late 1990s, and carrying out other uses of force such as the bombing of suspected terrorist-related targets in Sudan in 1998.

The military's role in foreign policy is not limited to uses of force. Military personnel also deliver humanitarian aid or help American citizens evacuate from areas where conflict has broken out. For example, U.S. Navy ships and helicopters delivered food and other relief aid to Haiti after the 2010 earthquake, and wounded Haitians were airlifted to military ships and facilities in the United States for medical treatment. The American military advises and trains armed forces in other countries. And military personnel may also play a role in foreign policy making. The president, his advisers, and members of Congress regularly consult senior military officials during policy debates. Finally, mid-level officers serve in the NSC and on the staff of some congressional committees.

Department of Homeland Security The Department of Homeland Security was formed after the September 11 attacks by combining the Coast Guard, the Transportation Security Administration, the Border Patrol, and several other agencies. Its responsibilities are to secure America's borders, prevent future terrorist attacks, and coordinate intelligence gathering. Homeland Security's record is mixed. Although there has not been a major terrorist attack on American soil since September 11, 2001, the department has to some extent failed in its mission to facilitate information-sharing and cooperation among various intelligence agencies in government. Department of Homeland Security inaction was

National Security Council (NSC) Within the Executive Office of the President, a committee that advises the president on matters of foreign policy.

▼ *Umar Farouk Abdulmutallab, the so-called Underwear Bomber who tried to blow up an American passenger airliner on Christmas Day 2009 using a bomb hidden in his pants, demonstrated the extreme difficulty of the task faced by the U.S. Department of Homeland Security, which must defend the nation against a vast range of potential threats.*

cited as one factor in the failure to prevent the so-called Underwear Bomber, Umar Farouk Abdulmutallab, from attempting to blow up a Detroit-bound airliner on Christmas Day 2009. (The attack was foiled by a passenger on the plane.)[43]

Intelligence Agencies Agencies such as the Central Intelligence Agency (CIA) and National Security Agency (NSA) are primarily responsible for government intelligence-gathering. You may think of these organizations as filled with daring spies, but most of their work is more mundane, consisting of gathering information from public or semipublic sources, such as data on industrial outputs. The director of national intelligence in the EOP leads and coordinates the activities of the various intelligence agencies.

How Much Foreign Policy Power Does the President Have? Some people argue that the broad powers of the modern presidency have allowed for "imperial presidents" who can implement their preferred policies without the consent of Congress, the American people, or anyone else.[44] Many of the foreign policy actions of President George W. Bush, which we discussed in detail in Chapter 11, are cited as examples in making this argument.

Nonetheless, President Bush was typical of recent presidents. As we have discussed, presidents dominate the making of American foreign policy. During Ronald Reagan's administration, his staff carried out a plan to sell arms to Iran in return for help freeing seven American hostages in Lebanon. The proceeds from the weapons sales were then used to fund opponents of the Sandinista regime controlling Nicaragua, despite a congressional ban on such aid. Reagan also ordered the invasion of Grenada and the bombing of Libya, both without congressional consent.[45] His successor, George H. W. Bush, ordered the invasion of Panama and sent half a million American troops to the Middle East in 1990, asking for congressional authorization only on the eve of battle.[46] During the 1990s President Clinton ordered humanitarian aid for Bosnia and Kosovo and sent troops on peacekeeping missions, all despite considerable opposition from Congress.[47] And during the first two years of his presidency, Barack Obama ordered additional American troops to Afghanistan and expanded drone strikes on terror groups in Pakistan, Yemen, and other countries without explicit congressional approval.

The explanation for presidents' dominance of foreign policy lies in the theory of unilateral presidential power discussed in Chapter 11.[48] Though the Constitution grants the president several foreign policy powers, including naming him military commander in chief, the document does not set explicit limits on exactly what the president can and cannot do. This ambiguity has given presidents the latitude to make foreign policy as they see fit, calculating that members of Congress will either approve of the actions or be unable to prevent or counteract them. Members of Congress who disagree with the president must build veto-proof, two-thirds majorities in the House and Senate to overturn presidential foreign policy actions—an especially daunting task when the president's party holds the majority of seats in one or both chambers.

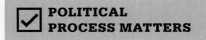

POLITICAL
PROCESS MATTERS

Nonetheless, presidents sometimes pull back from a new foreign policy if they believe congressional support will not be forthcoming. For example, President Clinton never submitted the Kyoto Protocol, an international treaty on combating climate change, for ratification by the Senate, believing that if the treaty were put to a vote, it would fail.[49] Similarly, no president has ever submitted the 1996 Nuclear Test Ban Treaty for Senate ratification, although Presidents Clinton, Bush, and Obama have implemented a voluntary moratorium on tests.

Clearly, the president dominates foreign policy—but as discussed in the next section, Congress can reverse or thwart presidential initiatives. Thus, in most cases when presidents appear to have acted without constraints, either members of Congress actually approved of the president's action, were unaware of the action, or were either unwilling or unable to organize to overturn the president's policy.

CONGRESS

Several groups within Congress participate in the making of foreign policy. Two standing committees, the Committee on Foreign Affairs in the House and the Foreign Relations Committee in the Senate, are responsible for writing legislation that deals with foreign policy, including setting the annual budget for agencies within the State Department and elsewhere that carry out those policies. These committees also hold hearings in which they pose questions to foreign policy experts from inside and outside government. These hearings help to educate committee members on foreign policy matters, as well as draw media and public attention to issues important to the committee.

The House and Senate each have an Intelligence Committee that oversees covert operations and the actions of the CIA, NSA, and similar agencies. Under current law, the president is supposed to give Congress "timely notification" of covert intelligence operations.[50] The intent is to ensure that someone outside the executive branch knows about secret operations and can organize congressional opposition if these actions are deemed illegal, immoral, or unwise.

Congress holds three types of influence over foreign policy. The first is Congress's constitutional power of the purse. Since members of Congress write annual budgets for every government department and agency, one way for members to shape foreign policy is to forbid expenditures on activities that members want to prevent.

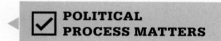

POLITICAL PROCESS MATTERS

The second area of congressional influence on foreign policy is the Senate's power to approve treaties and confirm the appointments of senior members of the president's foreign policy team, including the secretaries of state and defense, the director of national intelligence, and America's ambassador to the UN. It is rare for senators to reject a treaty or nominee. Sometimes senators issue preemptive warnings about what kinds of treaties they are willing to accept—in 2009, for example, ten moderate Senate Democrats warned President Obama that their support for a treaty to reduce global warming hinged on whether the treaty would protect American manufacturers from undue foreign competition.[51] More commonly, treaties in danger of being voted down are never put to a vote, as was the case with the Kyoto Protocol and the Nuclear Test Ban Treaty.

The final congressional power over foreign policy also comes from the Constitution, which grants Congress the power to declare war on other nations. However, the Constitution does not say that this declaration must occur before hostilities can begin or whether the declaration is necessary at all. In fact, although the United States has been involved in hundreds of military conflicts since the Founding, there have been only five U.S. declarations of war: the War of 1812, the Mexican-American War (declared in 1846), the Spanish-American War (in 1898), and both World Wars (declared in 1917 and 1941, respectively).

In an attempt to codify war-making powers, in 1973 members of Congress adopted the War Powers Resolution. You may recall from Chapter 11 that this legislation was designed to limit the president's war-making powers and to give members of Congress a way to reverse a president's decision to deploy American forces. Although the resolution has been in effect for over thirty years, the question of which branch of the government controls America's armed forces remains controversial. There is even some question over the constitutionality of the resolution, although it has never faced a test in the Supreme Court.

Of course, members of Congress always have the power to block a president's foreign policy initiatives, but doing so requires enacting a law with enough votes to override a presidential veto. In the case of debate over funding for the Iraq war, in 2007 the House and Senate passed a funding resolution that included a withdrawal timeline for U.S. troops, but it was approved by a margin of only a few votes in each chamber. After President Bush vetoed the resolution, the two Houses passed a new funding resolution that dropped these restrictions. Thus, without broad-based opposition to a president's initiatives with enough votes to override a veto, Congress often remains the subordinate player in the making of foreign policy.

THE FEDERAL COURTS

The federal courts, including the Supreme Court, weigh in on foreign policy questions through their exercise of judicial review, determining whether laws, regulations, and presidential actions are consistent with the Constitution. For example, as discussed in Chapter 11, a series of lower court and Supreme Court decisions forced the Bush administration to revise its policies of holding terror suspects indefinitely without charges; the rulings required that these suspects be charged with crimes and tried on those charges. Although this example shows how the courts can reverse presidential actions, two points must be remembered. First, the trials did not give the defendants the same rights as those afforded to American citizens in criminal cases, allowing the presentation of evidence gained through coercion. Moreover, these trials occurred only after several cases had worked their way through the judicial system in a process that took years to complete. During that time, the administration's policy remained in place, and the defendants were imprisoned without trial or any way to contest their imprisonment.[52]

GROUPS OUTSIDE THE FEDERAL GOVERNMENT

Foreign policy choices are also influenced by a variety of individuals and groups outside government, from corporate, citizen, and single-interest groups to the media, public opinion, and international and nongovernmental organizations. In this section, we focus on the ways that these groups participate in the making of foreign policy.

Interest Groups Recall from Chapter 9 that interest groups are organizations that work to convince elected officials and bureaucrats to implement policy changes in line with the group's goals. A diverse set of groups and organizations lobby government over foreign policy, including some foreign corporations and even foreign governments.[53]

One of the most prominent interest groups in the area of foreign policy is the American Israel Public Affairs Committee (AIPAC), which describes itself as working "to help make Israel more secure by ensuring that American support remains strong."[54] In real terms, AIPAC lobbies for increased military aid to Israel and American sanctions against Iran, among other matters, and the group contributes to the campaigns of congressional candidates who share its goals.[55]

Lobbying efforts can even involve foreign governments. A search of the lobbying database maintained by the Center for Responsive Politics found nearly fifty countries listed as clients of lobbying firms during 1998–2009. (The list excludes countries that used a foundation or other organization as a front for their lobbying.) These lobbying efforts center on economic and military aid, trade deals, and more general efforts to improve a country's image among members of Congress and the bureaucracy.

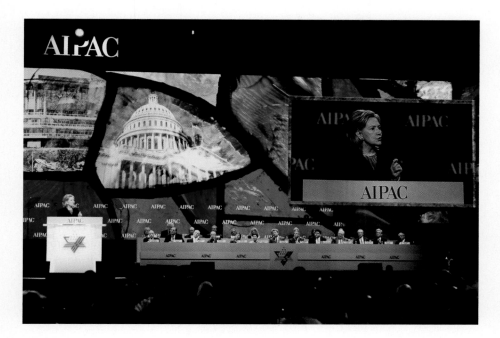

◀ Politicians and government officials such as Secretary of State Hillary Clinton regularly speak before the American Israel Public Affairs Committee at events such as their annual convention shown here. However, it would be a mistake to conclude that the attention paid to AIPAC or other interest groups automatically translates into support for the groups' policy proposals.

Sometimes interest group lobbying pits business interests against moral concerns. During the debate over granting China more favorable trade terms with U.S. companies in 2007, some groups argued that the legislation should be shelved until the Chinese government guaranteed religious freedoms to its citizens.[56] Other groups favored imposing tariffs on Chinese goods as retaliation for the Chinese government's refusal to revalue its currency—a move that would make Chinese goods more expensive and help U.S. manufacturers. Ultimately, members of Congress sympathetic to both groups blocked the trade proposals, although the U.S. government did implement some small trade agreements with China that did not require congressional approval.[57] Clearly the political process matters in foreign policy making: the inability to get legislation through Congress meant that the Bush administration had to settle for small steps in liberalizing trade with China.

Finally, some groups focus on publicizing international events in the hope of prompting citizens to demand that their government take action. The Save Darfur Coalition, an association of more than 150 local groups across America, used newspaper and television ads in 2008 to highlight the plight of people living in Darfur, Sudan, and to propose a no-fly zone in the region and deployment of a multilateral military force to protect civilians.[58] The coalition's proposal, which was met with resistance from a number of aid organizations, shows how political conflicts can arise even among groups that share the same goals. The other humanitarian groups objected to the suggestions, in part, because declaring a no-fly zone would prohibit their use of helicopters to distribute relief aid and also because they feared that sending multinational forces would provoke retaliation from the Sudanese government.[59]

As you will recall from Chapter 9, the impact of these lobbying efforts is hard to determine. Although AIPAC is considered a powerful interest group, it is likely that America's foreign policy would largely favor Israel regardless of AIPAC's actions, given the continuing strong support for Israel among the American public and elected officials.[60] Interest groups' influence over foreign policy depends mainly on the same two factors as their influence over domestic policy. They hold the most sway when the salience of the issue is low (few citizens know or care about the matter) and the issue is noncontroversial (so that few citizens or groups oppose the group's objective).

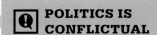
◀ **Q POLITICS IS CONFLICTUAL**

The Media Television, radio, print media, and the Internet all inform the public about events in America and elsewhere. Recall Figure 5.1 (p. 144), which showed several years' worth of data on citizens' opinions of the wars in Iraq and Afghanistan. When the news was good, such as when Saddam Hussein was captured or the number of insurgent attacks fell, the percentage of citizens who thought the war was going well increased; when the news was bad, such as when there were spikes in American casualties, that percentage dropped.

As we discussed in Chapter 6, although media coverage is a prime source of information about domestic and foreign policy for most Americans, it is inaccurate to say that opinions or evaluations of America's foreign policy are driven solely by the news media's decisions about what to cover and how to report it. In the case of Iraq, for example, there is no doubt that media coverage during 2005 and 2006 was generally negative and that public opinion on the war declined during this period. However, both trends reflected the facts on the ground during that time: a growing insurgency, limited reconstruction, political stalemate, and steadily rising American casualties. Similarly, in 2008–2009, as casualties decreased and the number of American troops stationed in Iraq began to decline, more and more Americans reported that the war effort was going well.

Public Opinion Foreign policy decisions are also sensitive to public opinion. Congressional attempts in 2007 to make funding for the Iraq conflict conditional on setting troop withdrawal deadlines were driven in part by the shift in public opinion against the war—and by the influence of that shift on the 2006 elections, in which many Republicans who had supported the war were defeated or came close to defeat.[61]

Though elected officials generally consider public opinion when making foreign policy decisions, their judgments about what the public supports and opposes must take into account the problems of measuring opinions discussed in Chapter 5. Recall that public opinion is sensitive to context, including both how and when survey questions are asked. For example, fears of another terrorist attack on the United States increase sharply every time there is an attack elsewhere in the world. Approval of the war in Iraq varies with recent events. And judgments about whether to withdraw American forces from Iraq depend on whether the question is posed as a choice between either staying or withdrawing, or whether more options are available, including a gradual withdrawal.

The fact that public opinion is sensitive to context means that Americans may sometimes ignore foreign policy questions (or their representative's positions on these issues) in favor of other concerns. For example, as economic conditions worsened in 2008 and 2009, mentions in mass surveys of the economy as the most important issue facing the country rose sharply, while mentions of Iraq, Afghanistan, and other foreign policy issues declined. As long as this decline persists, elected officials can place a low priority on responding to public opinion on foreign policy questions.

A second reason that foreign policy does not always mirror public opinion was discussed in Chapter 10. Most politicians have political goals other than winning reelection, including affecting some aspect of American relations with other nations. During the 2008 presidential primaries, for example, Republican John McCain at times voiced support for a continued American military presence in Iraq, despite opinion polls that showed that a majority of Americans opposed the war.

The final reason why American public opinion is not decisive is that many Americans know little about other countries. Table 17.1 provides some sense of what eighteen- to twenty-four-year-old Americans know about the rest of the world. Aside from the questions on the United States, Canada, and Mexico, a majority of young adults surveyed could not locate the other countries on a map. (Older Americans do somewhat better but not by much.)

TABLE 17.1 YOUNG AMERICANS' GLOBAL KNOWLEDGE

These data reveal a marked lack of geographic knowledge among 18- to 24-year-old Americans. Most can find the United States, Canada, and Mexico on a world map, but only slightly more than a third can locate Iraq on a map of the Middle East, despite the fact that when the survey was taken, America had been fighting a major war there for nearly three years. Identification rates for the other countries are similarly dismal. What might explain this lack of geographical knowledge?

Percent Who Can Locate on a World Map	
United States	94%
Canada	92
Mexico	88
Great Britain	36
On a Map of the Middle East	
Saudi Arabia	37%
Israel	25
Iraq	37
Iran	26

SOURCE: National Geographic–Roper Global Geographic Literacy Survey, 2006, available at www.national geographic.com/roper2006/findings.html (accessed 8/20/08).

Americans are more likely to pay attention to foreign policy news or concerns following an important or significant event. Thus, six months after the September 11 attacks, a Pew Trust poll found that Americans rated preventing future attacks as a higher priority than any particular domestic policy, even though domestic policy as a general category took priority over foreign policy by a margin of almost two to one.[62] However, as the September 11 attacks receded into the past, the intensity of public concern about preventing future attacks declined somewhat as well.

Nongovernmental Organizations and International Organizations America's relationship with the rest of the world is not just about government action. The members of **nongovernmental organizations (NGOs)** provide information and humanitarian assistance, and carry out other activities that the U.S. government is unable or unwilling to undertake. Thousands of American NGOs operate throughout the world.[63]

A primary goal of NGOs is promoting global economic development and growth. The **World Bank** funds economic development projects throughout the world, and the **International Monetary Fund** helps countries manage budget deficits and control the value of their currencies. Many smaller organizations, such as the Asia Foundation, focus on development in a particular region or on certain activities, such as microlending, in which banks or other institutions provide small loans to citizens in developing nations as a way of stimulating business growth and reducing poverty.

A second role of NGOs is providing humanitarian relief. In the wake of a disaster such as an earthquake or a flood, or during a famine or a war, organizations such as Oxfam International supply populations in crisis with basic necessities. Other

nongovernmental organizations (NGOs) Groups operated by private institutions (rather than governments) to promote growth, economic development, and other agendas throughout the world.

World Bank A nongovernmental organization established in 1944 that provides financial support for economic development projects in developing nations.

International Monetary Fund A nongovernmental organization established in 1944 to help stabilize the international monetary system, improve economic growth, and aid developing nations.

groups such as Doctors without Borders provide medical care to populations threatened by violence, epidemics, or natural disasters. Some NGOs also promote human rights. Amnesty International works to draw international attention to cases of people jailed for their political beliefs or held without trial, or to the use of cruel punishments such as stoning. Amnesty's campaigns, as well as those of other NGOs, are not always supportive of U.S. policy. For example, Amnesty has taken a strong stand against rendition of terror suspects by the United States, in the hope of stimulating domestic and foreign pressure against these policies.[64]

Finally, NGOs help to build democracies. The Open Society Institute, founded by investor George Soros, funds efforts to increase mass political participation, strengthen political organizations, and verify the fairness of elections in new democracies throughout the world. The National Democratic Institute and the International Republican Institute carry out similar activities.[65]

The United States is also a member of many international organizations. The best-known of these is the **United Nations (UN)**, an assembly of ambassadors representing almost all of the world's nations that works to address issues of worldwide concern. The UN is involved in economic development, environmental protection, humanitarian relief, and peacekeeping efforts. The United Nations has deployed peacekeeping forces to separate warring parties in Africa, the Middle East, and the former Yugoslavia. As of spring 2010, more than 116,000 UN peacekeeping troops, police, and other personnel were deployed in twenty-two different areas.

Inside the UN, the Security Council, a group of fifteen nations (permanent members Britain, China, France, Russia, and the United States, plus ten rotating nations) makes the most important UN decisions, particularly those involving its military missions. The UN General Assembly, in which each nation has one vote, debates and votes on other concerns.

The Tools of Foreign Policy

This section describes the tools or methods used to implement American foreign policy—most obviously the use of military force, but also less visible methods such as changes in trade policy or the provisions of foreign or military aid. Although these strategies differ in their costs, and some, such as military force, are considered morally questionable by many Americans, all nations use these strategies in pursuit of desired policy outcomes.

▼ The American troops stationed at the Demilitarized Zone between North and South Korea are a visible reminder of America's promise to help defend South Korea against an attack by the North.

MILITARY FORCE

Military force is a fundamental tool of foreign policy. America's military forces are used throughout the world as a deterrent to conflict. For example, the United States stations more than 28,000 troops in South Korea. Many of these forces are deployed right at the demilitarized zone that separates North Korea from South Korea. Similarly, until the fall of the Soviet Union in 1991, hundreds of thousands of American troops were stationed in Western Europe (as of 2010, only about 40,000 remained). Military exercises by U.S. troops, aircraft, and ships are used to remind potential adversaries of America's military power. In early 2007, for example,

Military Forces around the World

The U.S. armed forces are considerably more powerful than those of any other nation, but history has shown that American military might is not the universal solution to international problems, even those involving the use of force. Sometimes, in fact, military force is all but useless as a tool of foreign policy.

The table compares the United States' armed forces to those of its major allies and potential adversaries. As the table indicates, America spends vastly more on its military than any of its potential adversaries and deploys far more troops to all corners of the globe. America's navy and air force are also much larger than those of any other nation. America's military superiority is also reflected in an extensive network of satellites that are used to photograph foreign sites, eavesdrop on communications, and provide early warning of attacks. America also has the best communications and computer technology, as well as cutting-edge weapons technology such as radar-evading stealth aircraft.

The question is, what advantages does overwhelming military force convey? The American experience in Iraq demonstrates that even a large military force cannot always achieve easy or quick victories. American and coalition forces were able to overrun Iraq quickly in the spring of 2003 and depose its government with minimal casualties, but the same forces, even augmented with additional troops, were unable to prevent subsequent attacks by insurgent groups and violence between different ethnic groups in the country. American and Iraqi forces gradually regained control of the country, but this outcome occurred

MILITARY FORCES OF U.S. ALLIES AND POTENTIAL ADVERSARIES

	Military Budget (Billions)	Active Troops	Deployed Troops	Nuclear Weapons
United States	$466	1,625,000	393,000	6,390
China	$65	2,250,000	0	325
Russia	$50	960,000	17,000	3,242
France	$45	259,000	28,500	350
United Kingdom	$43	206,000	36,000	200
Israel	$9.5	125,000	0	200
North Korea	$5	1,075,000	0	13
Iran	$4.3	540,000	150	0

SOURCE: Data from Global Security, "World Military Guide," available at www.globalsecurity.org/military/world/index.html.

only after several years of intense violence and thousands of casualties.

In part, the issue in Iraq was that the American military was designed to fight other armies—not to deal with a multi-pronged insurgency scattered across an entire country. Tanks, artillery, smart bombs, and aircraft carriers are simply useless for the kind of small-scale, urban fighting that took place in Iraq after the initial invasion. As time went on, American forces learned how to respond more effectively to the insurgency, using new technologies such as unmanned aircraft, and working with increasing numbers of Iraqi government forces. However, these real successes should not obscure the fact that America's military superiority did not produce an easy or quick victory.

More important, the economic, political, and human costs of military force make this strategy useless in many foreign policy situations. Consider the problem of negotiating trade agreements with other nations: there is no chance that the United

States will make military threats against its allies in order to extract favorable tariffs or quotas—carrying out these threats would end trade entirely, as well as disrupt diplomatic and other connections. Threats are also unlikely to work against adversaries when the costs of carrying them out exceed the potential benefits to the United States. For example, although the U.S. government might prefer that Iran end its nuclear research, the cost of sustained military action against Iran may exceed the benefits of ending this threat.

For all of these reasons, claims about the value of America's military power need to be kept in perspective. Smaller countries and groups have means at their disposal to significantly complicate U.S. military efforts and sometimes even negate our vast military superiority. Thus, while America has the most powerful military in the world, this status does not mean that America can always achieve its foreign policy goals. ■

during negotiations between the government of Iran and the International Atomic Energy Association (IAEA) over Iran's attempts to enrich uranium, which had the potential to be used in nuclear weapons, the United States sent two carrier battle groups to the Persian Gulf near Iran, where they spent a week practicing naval air operations.

The United States has also fought numerous wars and lesser conflicts to further its foreign policy goals. Some of these are all-out military operations, such as the invasion of Iraq. More commonly, these deployments are small, short-lived operations ranging from the evacuation of American civilians from areas of unrest to the delivery of humanitarian assistance or the use of ship-launched cruise missiles to attack terrorist camps and similar targets.[66]

The size and power of America's military provides numerous options for policy makers. For example, after the September 11 attacks, in an attempt to prevent future terror attacks by Al Qaeda, U.S. forces invaded Afghanistan, which had been used as a base of operations for the organization.[67] It is highly unlikely that any other country could carry out such a large-scale operation so far from home. Nonetheless, military force is not all-powerful. At the end of 2010, American troops were still fighting in Afghanistan, with their mission a long way from being accomplished. We discuss the Afghanistan war in more detail later in the chapter.

TRADE AND ECONOMIC POLICIES

Foreign policy is also aimed at sustaining economic growth in the United States and elsewhere, as well as creating foreign markets for the goods produced by America's domestic industries. Figure 17.1 shows total American trade (imports and exports) with other countries over the last thirty years, expressed as a percentage of U.S. gross domestic product (GDP), which measures the size of the U.S. economy. These data come from an annual report prepared by the Office of the U.S. Trade Representative. In recent years, imports and exports have made up more than 40 percent of GDP. Investment returns (profits from American-owned companies located abroad)

FIGURE 17.1   **U.S. IMPORTS AND EXPORTS AS A PERCENTAGE OF GROSS DOMESTIC PRODUCT (GDP)**

This figure illustrates the importance of trade to the U.S. economy. In recent years, imports and exports have made up more than 40 percent of U.S. economic activity, and the percentage is steadily increasing. Based on these data, what arguments would you make for lowering or increasing barriers to trade?

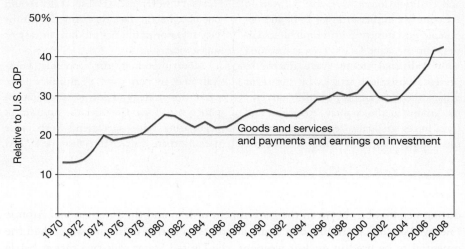

SOURCE: Office of the U.S. Trade Representative, "2010 Trade Policy Agenda and 2009 Annual Report," February 2010, available at www.ustr.gov/2010-trade-policy-agenda.

are also becoming an ever-larger component of total trade. In dollar terms, the same report estimated that the total value of U.S. trade with other nations was more than $6 trillion per year. Clearly, foreign trade is a critical component of the American economy.

The main tools of trade policy are tariffs and trade agreements. A **tariff** is a tax collected by the government for the import or export of certain commodities, and a **trade agreement** sets tariff levels or limits the quantities of particular items that can be imported or exported. The United States International Trade Commission maintains a list of all tariffs in effect; in mid-2010, the document was more than 3,000 pages long.[68] By adjusting tariff rates, the government can help or hurt domestic industries. High tariffs on imports help American producers to charge lower prices than foreign competitors, and low tariffs on exports help American producers sell to overseas markets.

Over the last two generations, the United States and most other nations have been lowering tariffs and establishing **free trade zones**, agreements to eliminate tariffs on all imports and exports between specific nations. Examples include the North American Free Trade Agreement (NAFTA), involving the United States, Canada, and Mexico, and the Central American Free Trade Agreement (CAFTA) between the United States, five Central American nations, and the Dominican Republic. Other organizations, such as the **World Trade Organization (WTO)** facilitate negotiations over tariffs and provide a mechanism for adjudicating cases where one nation believes that another is using tariffs unfairly. Finally, the United States has granted many other countries **most-favored-nation status**, meaning that the tariffs placed on imports to the United States from these nations are set at the lowest rate placed on any other nation.

Trade is an important part of foreign policy. The United States can use free trade agreements and tariffs to bargain with countries for concessions in other areas. For example, in the 1990s the administration of President Clinton used tariffs, most-favored-nation status, and other inducements to force China to moderate its human rights policies and crack down on illegal copying of software and videos.[69] Similarly, among the incentives given to Jordan during peace negotiations with Israel in the 1990s were the promises to eliminate tariffs on textile exports to America and to write off $213 million of the $488 million Jordanian debt to the United States.[70]

Economic policies, which may involve the United States acting alone or with other nations, are also used to threaten or **sanction** countries as a way of inducing them to change their behavior. As noted earlier, in 2007, the UN Security Council authorized a package of sanctions against Iran aimed at forcing the nation to stop enriching uranium, a first step in the production of nuclear weapons.[71] These sanctions included freezing bank accounts held by members of Iran's nuclear team and banning arms sales to the country. If Iran agreed to stop its program, it would receive incentives such as civilian nuclear reactor technology and direct talks with the United States over various issues. However, these sanctions did not prove sufficient to lead Iran to abandon its enrichment program, and stronger sanctions were vetoed by China in the UN Security Council. Thus, although sanctions and the threat of sanctions are important diplomatic tools, they are often insufficient to generate policy change.

DIPLOMACY

The process of **diplomacy** involves using personal contact and negotiations with national leaders and representatives to work out international agreements or persuade other nations to change their behavior. Sometimes these efforts involve the

tariff A tax levied on imported and exported goods.

trade agreement A contract between nations that specifies tariff levels and sets terms on which goods can be imported and exported.

free trade zones Designated areas where tariffs on imports and exports between specific countries do not apply.

World Trade Organization (WTO) An international organization created in 1995 to oversee trade agreements between nations by facilitating negotiations and handling disputes.

most-favored-nation status A standing awarded to countries with which the United States has good trade relations, providing the lowest possible tariff rate. World Trade Organization members must give one another this preferred status.

sanction A trade penalty that one nation places on another to encourage the penalized nation to change its actions or policies.

diplomacy The process of negotiation on international issues between national leaders.

shuttle diplomacy Negotiations carried out by a third party mediator who travels between two nations to relay information when those two nations' negotiators refuse to meet face-to-face.

treaty A formal written agreement between nations involving security, trade or economic development, human rights, or other important policies.

alliance An agreement between two or more countries pledging support if one of those countries is attacked.

threat of military action or economic sanctions, or incentives such as economic assistance or other forms of aid. The United States may act as a direct participant in such efforts or as a mediator between the parties in a dispute, helping them to resolve their differences. When two countries refuse to meet face-to-face, U.S. diplomats may take part in **shuttle diplomacy**, in which they facilitate negotiations by meeting separately with each country's representatives to convey the other country's proposals and counterproposals.

Diplomacy has often been a useful but limited foreign policy tool. For example, the efforts of American diplomats were instrumental in establishing an international aid fund to help Haiti rebuild after the 2010 earthquake. Similarly, American and Mexican diplomats signed an agreement in 2010 to deter the transportation of illegal drugs across the U.S.–Mexican border. And American diplomats are involved in many behind-the-scenes efforts to help resolve international disputes, such as the disagreement between Argentina and Great Britain over ownership of the Falkland Islands.

Of course, diplomacy doesn't always work. In the case of North Korea and Iran, international efforts to deter production of nuclear weapons have met with resistance and refusals to negotiate. Even so, diplomacy remains a valuable tool for American foreign policy.

FOREIGN AID

Foreign aid is money, products, or services given to other countries or the citizens of these countries. Sometimes aid is driven by the desire to provide basic assistance to satisfy fundamental human needs. As discussed earlier, the American military was used to deliver food and medical supplies to Haiti after the devastating 2010 earthquake. Foreign aid is also used to stimulate economic growth in other nations. Funding from the United States is used to build factories; to advise locals on how to construct and operate water, power, or sewage treatment plants; or to buy hardware to support infrastructure such as Internet access or telephone networks. Foreign aid is also used to facilitate international agreements. For example, the peace treaty between Egypt and Israel in 1979 was facilitated by America's agreement to provide substantial military and economic assistance to both countries.[72]

▼ American humanitarian aid efforts often involve military personnel, as in the case of relief operations after the 2010 Haiti earthquake. These operations highlight the varied roles that can be played by America's armed forces in support of foreign policy.

Figure 17.2 shows the level of American nonmilitary foreign aid in 2010, measured as a percentage of gross national income (GNI, which includes GDP as well as accounting for investment income from other countries), compared to other members of the Organization for Economic Cooperation and Development. Considering the amount of U.S. foreign aid as a percentage of GNI suggests that the United States gives relatively little to other countries. Part of the reason for this perception lies in the size of the U.S. economy: America's foreign aid contributions are the largest of any country when measured in total dollars ($21.8 billion in 2007), but it also has the largest GNI of any country.

ALLIANCES AND TREATIES

A **treaty** is an agreement between nations to work together on economic or security issues. An **alliance** is an agreement that commits nations to some form of security guarantees, which are assurances that one country will help another if it is

FIGURE 17.2 U.S. FOREIGN AID IN COMPARATIVE PERSPECTIVE

This figure shows foreign aid contributions expressed as a percentage of gross domestic income. Do these data imply that America is less generous than other nations in its willingness to donate aid?

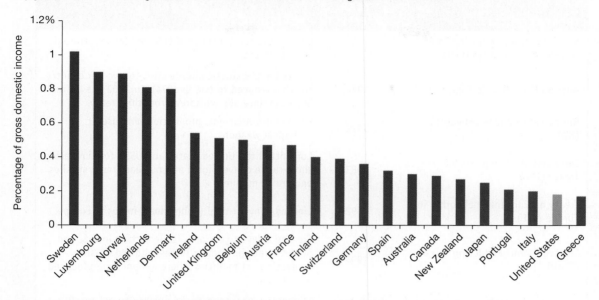

SOURCE: Organization for Economic Co-operation and Development, "Development Co-operation Report 2010," April 23, 2010, available at www.oecd.org/dac/dcr.

attacked. America is a member of many international alliances, most notably the **North Atlantic Treaty Organization (NATO)**; as mentioned earlier, the name reflects the fact that the alliance was formed by the North Atlantic Treaty after World War II to provide collective security against the Soviet Union and Warsaw Pact countries. The organization's mission shifted after the Cold War to focus on coordinating military force toward common goals.[73] For example, the missions in the 1990s to end Serbian conquest of Bosnia and Kosovo were NATO operations.[74] Troops from NATO nations are also involved in providing security in Afghanistan.

The United States is a party to many treaties: the State Department's current list of America's treaties with other countries runs to 471 pages. These include both **bilateral agreements** between the United States and one other country, and **multilateral agreements** involving the United States and several countries.[75] Nuts and Bolts 17.1 lists some major national security treaties involving the United States, the Soviet Union, and other countries. These treaties implemented major changes in both U.S. and other military forces, from capping the size of nuclear forces, to implementing restrictions in the numbers of these forces, to banning some kinds of weapons.

Treaties and alliances allow the United States to commit itself to a course of action or signal its intentions to other nations.[76] By joining NATO and stationing troops in Europe, the United States guaranteed that if Warsaw Pact troops invaded the West, U.S. forces would be a part of the resistance. Moreover, if the United States failed to honor its treaty obligations, it would be difficult for the country to convince other nations to enter into future agreements.

North Atlantic Treaty Organization (NATO) An international alliance between the United States, Canada, and several European nations, originally created to provide security against the Soviet Union during the Cold War.

bilateral agreements Treaties between two nations.

multilateral agreements Treaties among multiple nations.

Selected Major National Security Treaties

TREATY	YEAR IN EFFECT	PROVISIONS
Strategic Arms Limitation Talks Interim Agreement (SALT I)	1972	Capped the total number of U.S. and Soviet strategic nuclear forces.
Anti-Ballistic Missile Treaty (ABM)	1972	Limited anti-ballistic missile sites to two per country (further reduced to one in 1974). In 2002 the United States unilaterally withdrew from this treaty.
Biological Weapons Convention (BWC)	1972	Banned development, production, and use of biological weapons.
Intermediate-Range Nuclear Forces Treaty (INF)	1987	Committed the United States and USSR to eliminating short-range conventional and nuclear-armed missiles and cruise missiles.
Treaty on Conventional Forces in Europe (CFE)	1992	Limited conventional (nonnuclear) forces in Europe.
Strategic Arms Reduction Talks (START I)	1994	Created a seven-year plan for reduction in U.S. and Soviet strategic nuclear forces; allowed on-site inspections of facilities where weapons are produced and stored.
Strategic Arms Reduction Talks (START II)	1996	Eliminated most land-based nuclear-armed missiles; committed the United States and Russia to further reductions of nuclear forces beyond START I levels.
Comprehensive Test Ban Treaty (CBT)	1996	Banned all nuclear explosions, including weapons tests. (The United States has not ratified the treaty, although it has voluntarily abided by its provisions.)
Chemical Weapons Convention (CWC)	1997	Banned production, acquisition, and use of chemical weapons.
New START Treaty	Not yet ratified	Further reductions in U.S. and Russian nuclear arsenals

SOURCE: Federation of American Scientists, "Arms Control Agreements," available at www.fas.org/nuke/control/index.html.

The Politics of Foreign Policy

The making of foreign policy, like everything else that happens in the federal government, is a political act—a contest involving elected officials, bureaucrats, interest groups, and other interested actors, all of whom have their own goals pertaining to what the government should do. Politics does not "stop at the water's edge," as some have argued, meaning it should be reserved for domestic issues—it just keeps going. And, of course, as with domestic issues, the amount of attention paid to foreign policy matters varies over time.

Conflict over foreign policy comes from several sources, including Americans' different ideas of what foreign policy should look like. Consider Iraq. Table 17.2 shows that in January 2003, American public opinion was divided in important ways. Although respondents favored multilateral military action by well over two to one, more than half of these people opposed the conflict unless America's allies

TABLE 17.2 AMERICAN PUBLIC OPINION ON THE INVASION OF IRAQ

These data illustrate the conflict in American public opinion over the decision to go to war in Iraq. A majority supported the decision to invade when this question was asked by itself, but many individuals supported the war only with certain qualifications, such as if America received support from its allies or if casualties were low. Based on these data, to what extent did the decision to invade Iraq reflect public opinion just before the invasion?

Favor or Oppose Military Action in Iraq	January 2003
Favor	68%
Even if allies won't join	26
Only if allies agree	37
Don't know	5
Oppose	25
Don't know	7
Even If U.S. Suffered Thousands of Casualties	
Favor	43%
Even if allies won't join	21
Only if allies agree	20
Don't know	2
Oppose	48
Don't know	9

SOURCE: Pew Research Center, "Public Wants Proof of Iraqi Weapons Programs," January 16, 2003, available at http://people-press.org/reports/display.php3?ReportID=170.

agreed to participate. Moreover, support for the use of force declined by about a third when respondents were asked to consider the impending conflict as one in which U.S. forces would suffer thousands of casualties. These data demonstrate the significant divisions in American public opinion at the time of the invasion.[77]

Where do differences of opinion on foreign policy come from? One source is the realist–idealist distinction discussed earlier: recall that professors Mearschimer and Walt offered a realist argument for staying out of the conflict, and President Bush gave, in part, an idealist argument for invasion. Self-interest is another powerful motive. Several studies found that as National Guard units were mobilized for service in Iraq, support for the war declined in the communities where these units were based.[78]

Disagreements over foreign policy may also reflect citizens' exposure to different information or their disparate ways of understanding the world at large. As we discussed in Chapter 5, Public Opinion, there are sharp disagreements among citizens over the existence of global warming and its cause—whether it is due to some natural phenomenon or human activity.[79] The same study also found that an individual's support for policies designed to combat global warming depends on his diagnosis of the problem. Most people who see humans as the cause favor policies that would alleviate the problem, and most who believe global warming is a natural phenomenon favor the status quo.

Similarly, one of the Bush administration's primary justifications for invading Iraq in 2003 was the belief that Iraq had or would soon have weapons of mass destruction (WMDs).[80] At the time of the invasion, these beliefs were not unreasonable. Though some experts said that Iraq's weapons programs were defunct or far from posing a threat, others claimed that Iraq already had WMDs, and still others said Iraqi scientists were hard at work developing these technologies.[81] Investigations after the war had begun showed that Iraq's WMD programs were years away from producing usable weapons. As one of the leaders of the UN's prewar inspection effort put it, "We were all wrong."[82] But as the comment indicates, at the time of the invasion, many people working for arms control or intelligence agencies throughout the world were sincerely concerned about Iraq's WMDs.

Disagreements may also be rooted in differing expectations about whether policies will work as intended. During the House debate in 2000 over granting China permanent most-favored-nation status, supporters and opponents disagreed on whether increased trade between the two countries would cause an influx of cheap foreign imports into the United States, forcing closures of domestic factories and causing Americans to lose their jobs.[83] It is hard to tell whether such concerns are warranted—the answer depends on which goods are imported at lower prices and whether the changes in trade rules would help American manufacturers increase exports to China as well as increasing American imports of Chinese goods.

As these examples illustrate, foreign policies are beset by conflicting values and by conflicting sources of information. For example, in the months before Umar Farouk Abdulmutallab, a passenger on a Delta Airlines flight bound for Detroit, attempted to detonate a bomb hidden in his underwear, various government agencies had received numerous relevant warnings, both about this type of attack and about the individual himself.[84] Did individuals in these agencies make a mistake in failing to follow up on these warnings, perhaps by increasing the use of armed air marshals on international flights or by banning Abdulmutallab from flights to the United States? The problem is that intelligence agencies receive thousands of such warnings every week and cannot respond to all of them—not without shutting down air travel or taking other extreme steps. In retrospect, it is easy to say that they should have realized that the threat from Abdulmutallab was real. At the time the warnings were received, however, they probably looked no more serious than the many others that turned out to be false alarms.

Although disagreements over America's foreign policy often occur between members of the Republican and Democratic parties—conflict over the war in Iraq being a prime example—officials from the same party may hold different views about how foreign policy decisions should be resolved. For example, in late 2009 many Democratic senators and House members opposed President Obama's plan to expand American combat operations in Afghanistan—not enough to block the plans, especially given widespread support from Republicans, but enough to suggest that future expansions might be met with organized opposition.

Moreover, despite the expectation that senior presidential appointees will be loyal to the president, disagreements are not uncommon even among a president's senior appointees. In both the Bush and Obama administrations, for example, there has been considerable conflict among the senior advisers to both presidents as to whether to arrest foreign terror suspects, where to hold them, whether to treat them according to the Geneva Conventions, and whether to allow them access to U.S. civilian or military courts.

In sum, disagreements about foreign policy are unavoidable, both in government and among the general public. In the case of the War on Terror and the invasions of Iraq and Afghanistan, differences between Republican and Democratic officeholders are evident in debates over war funding, timetables for withdrawal, and the treatment of terror suspects.[85] The inevitability of conflicts over American foreign policy means that there is no reason to expect politics to "stop at the water's edge." For a variety of reasons, citizens and elected officials will disagree on what America's foreign policy should look like and work in elections and in the government to influence these choices.

Contemporary Foreign Policy Issues

This section describes some of the major foreign policy issues facing American citizens and elected officials. From economic crises to weapons of mass destruction, these issues illustrate that foreign policy is everywhere, and the decisions made by people in government will affect the lives of ordinary Americans. They demonstrate the power of the political process in foreign policy making: decisions reflect the people who make them and the rules that structure the debates. And they highlight conflicts over foreign policy, both in government and among the American people.

In addition, this section argues against claims about the decline of American influence throughout the world. Although it is true that other countries such as China and India are increasing their economic and military power and that America faces many new and complex issues, the fact is that America continues to be an international power, and in many respects the strongest nation, with enormous influence over economic, social, and military events throughout the world. How the issues described in this section will be resolved remains in question, but there is no doubt that America's foreign policy choices will play a decisive role in their resolution.

GLOBAL WARMING

Decades of scientific research has shown that the Earth is getting warmer, as illustrated in Figure 17.3. Available evidence points to human activity—specifically the burning of fossil fuels, which increases the amount of carbon dioxide in the atmosphere—as a significant cause of global warming.[86]

In some ways, the solution to global warming seems straightforward: the nations of the world must reduce carbon dioxide emissions by taxing and otherwise limiting carbon-producing activities and by developing cheaper and more efficient energy sources that produce less carbon. This solution may be clear, but it is not easy; research is expensive, and new technologies may carry their own environmental and economic impacts.

Another complication is that efforts to combat global warming require spending money in the present to prevent effects that will only be felt over the next century. In effect, one generation must pay the price so that future generations benefit from the investment. As a result, legislation to reduce carbon emissions may not be very popular with the average American, who is expected to pay for these measures in the form of taxes, higher prices, or lifestyle changes, without necessarily receiving direct benefits.

Addressing global warming also requires a multilateral effort. Even if the United States cuts its carbon emissions, this reduction will have little effect if other nations

FIGURE 17.3   **THE GLOBAL WARMING TREND**

These data show that global temperature levels have increased steadily since the early 1900s. How would a believer in human-caused global warming interpret this data? What would a skeptic say?

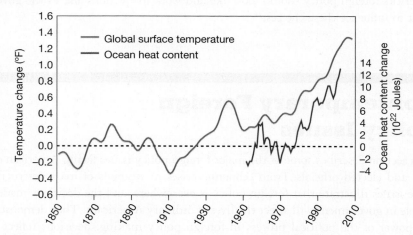

SOURCE: Pew Center on Global Climate Change, *Climate Change 101*, January 2009, available at www.pewclimate.org/docUploads /Climate101-Overview-Jan09.pdf (accessed 2/17/10).

simultaneously increase emissions. The problem is particularly acute for developing nations such as China, India, and Brazil. These nations are reluctant to agree to limit their carbon emissions because doing so will make it much harder for them to industrialize and raise their citizens' standard of living.[87] The **Kyoto Protocol** discussed earlier, which set limits on carbon emissions, was signed by developing nations only because the agreement did not significantly limit their future carbon emissions.[88] Subsequent efforts, such as the 2009 Copenhagen climate conference, were unable to devise an international agreement that bridged this gap between developed and developing nations.

HUMAN RIGHTS

In many countries, the freedoms set out in the Bill of Rights, such as freedom of religion, freedom of speech, freedom of association, freedom of the press, and the rights of the accused simply do not exist. Many governments routinely use arrests and other forms of repression to silence political opponents or condone violence and ethnic cleansing against minority ethnic or religious groups.

Organizations such as Freedom House and Amnesty International publicize human rights violations, with the goal of alerting citizens worldwide and thereby pressuring governments to end these violations. In 2009, Freedom House's annual survey of political and civil rights in 193 countries found that in many nations, press freedoms, due process rights, and freedom from torture were on the decline.[89] The United States' status as the most powerful nation in the world, coupled with the logic of idealism discussed earlier, suggests to some that America should protect human rights throughout the world. In this view, an individual's rights shouldn't depend on where they live or on their leaders' or neighbors' willingness to respect these rights. As the world's most powerful nation, the argument goes, the United

Kyoto Protocol An international agreement signed in 1997 that set limits on carbon emissions in an effort to slow global warming.

TABLE 17.3 AMERICANS' FOREIGN POLICY PRIORITIES

Politicians often cite protecting human rights and promoting democracy as U.S. foreign policy priorities, but these goals find relatively little support among the American public. How might this difference affect America's foreign policy choices?

Protecting against terror attacks	85%
Protecting jobs of American workers	85
Preventing the spread of WMDs	74
Reducing dependence on foreign oil	64
Fighting international drug trafficking	56
Reducing illegal immigration	46
Dealing with global climate change	40
Strengthening the United Nations	37
Defending human rights around the world	29
Improving living standards in the third world	26
Promoting democracy in other nations	21

SOURCE: Pew Research Center, *U.S. Seen as Less Important, China More Powerful,* December 3, 2009, available at http://people-press.org/report/569/americas-place-in-the-world.

States has a responsibility to secure basic human rights for everyone, regardless of where they live.

A realist would counter with three arguments. First, there is relatively little support among the American people for protecting human rights in other countries. As Table 17.3 shows, defending human rights falls near the bottom of the list of Americans' foreign policy priorities, with only 29 percent of those surveyed identifying it as a priority.

Second, attempts to protect human rights around the world may make it harder for the United States to achieve other goals. For example, the government of Pakistan is routinely cited for human rights abuses, but Pakistani officials have also provided America with valuable intelligence in the War on Terror and have aided in the capture of Taliban fighters in Afghanistan. If America pressures the Pakistani government to safeguard its citizens' human rights, Pakistan might respond by cutting off U.S. access to its intelligence, disrupting American efforts to stabilize Afghanistan and fight Al Qaeda in other areas.

Third, protecting human rights may strain American military forces. In the case of the mass killings in Darfur, the leaders of Sudan have allowed local militias to attack civilians despite other countries' attempts to encourage Sudanese intervention with offers of economic aid, threats of economic sanctions, and promises to send peacekeeping forces to the region. If the Sudanese leaders continue to ignore these threats and incentives, the only remaining way to stop their abuses is to launch a potentially large-scale military operation. At a minimum, America would provide transportation and logistical support, and such an operation could easily expand to involve American ground forces, which are in short supply given ongoing operations in Afghanistan and Iraq and commitments elsewhere in the world.

INTERNATIONAL TRADE

For the United States, trade is a necessity. America imports an increasing percentage of its oil and natural gas, as well as significant quantities of other resources and manufactured goods. Many economic analyses describe trade in terms of the theory of comparative advantage, which says that nations export items they can produce cheaply, in return for imports that can be produced more efficiently elsewhere. Similarly, outsourcing jobs to foreign countries with lower labor costs makes American companies more efficient. Microsoft, for one, has several large offices throughout the world, and in some of them software developers are paid much less than they are in the United States.[90] Even high-level professional jobs can be outsourced: the NightHawk Corporation uses Australian and Swiss radiologists to read X-rays and CAT scans of American patients.[91]

These practices are examples of globalization, the trend toward increasing interaction and connections between individuals, corporations, and nations discussed at length in Chapter 15. Recall our discussion of journalist Thomas Friedman's book on globalization, titled *The World Is Flat*, meaning that new technologies have leveled the global playing field, allowing the cheapest suppliers of goods and services to sell their products throughout the world. Many American companies and their employees profit from this process. More than half the cars that General Motors sells are purchased abroad, and in recent years more Kentucky Fried Chicken restaurants have opened in China than in the United States.

Reflecting all of these factors, the last generation of American politics has been marked by international agreements such as NAFTA to reduce or eliminate tariffs between nations, the growth of international organizations such as the WTO to regulate trade and adjudicate trade disputes, and increases in outsourcing of manufacturing jobs and services from developed countries to developing countries.[92] Although these moves toward increased trade and globalization generate significant benefits for many people, it is important to remember that these changes do not make everyone better off. Many American manufacturing jobs have been lost as factories that could not compete with cheaper foreign suppliers have either closed or moved to another country.[93]

Nonetheless, globalization, with all its benefits and challenges, is a reality. This raises two broad questions for American citizens and elected officials. First, how should America respond to nations that close off their markets? As noted in the Challenging Conventional Wisdom box, in recent years the Chinese government has done many things to restrict imports and expand exports. Though these requirements seem arbitrary and unfair to many American exporters, the American government also imposes its own restrictions. In 2007 the U.S. Food and Drug Administration blocked American imports of fish farmed in China on the grounds that it contained unapproved drugs and additives, even though these drugs and additives are not illegal in China.[94]

The second question concerns how to help people who are hurt by globalization. The U.S. Department of Labor's Trade Adjustment Assistance Program provides American workers who lose their jobs because of new trade agreements with extended unemployment benefits, tax credits for health insurance, and money for retraining programs. However, many workers who have lost their jobs due to globalization (for example, because of outsourcing) are not eligible for these programs, and others are unaware that these programs exist.[95] Moreover, it is often extremely difficult to retrain people to compete for new jobs that will provide pay and benefits comparable to their old positions.[96] What should government do to help these victims of globalization? That question will continue to influence debates over exports, imports, and trade agreements for years to come.

⬥ **POLITICS IS EVERYWHERE**

▼ *U.S. dependence on foreign sources of oil and other resources is not just a trade or economic issue—the potential for oil-producing nations to wreak havoc on the American economy by withholding oil or increasing its price is a fundamental security issue. Nevertheless, international trade is a necessity for the United States because it brings significant benefits as well as risks.*

Is China America's Greatest Adversary?

Many press accounts, politicians, and pundits identify China as America's greatest adversary in the world. According to one account,

> We now have a "strong and united" China which supports tyranny, nuclear proliferation, and lawless mercantilism. This undemocratic China is a greater challenge than a weak, disunited China. Because the vast majority of Chinese now acquiesce in the regime's domestic repression at the price of economic prosperity and national power, there is no possibility that China can democratize by itself. American leaders therefore must not legitimize the regime.[a]

The comment about tyranny refers to the lack of political rights in China. Although the government has loosened restrictions on economic activity, the Chinese Communist Party remains in full control of the government. With regard to nuclear proliferation, China initially opposed the use of sanctions or military force to stop nuclear proliferation in Iran and North Korea, although its government has since given tacit or outright approval to economic sanctions. The "lawless mercantilism" argument concerns the Chinese government's unwillingness or inability to stop firms from producing and selling illegal copies of DVDs and software created by companies in other countries.[b]

Moreover, China has an enormous trade surplus with America and holds hundreds of billions of dollars in American government bonds. Some observers believe these assets give the Chinese the ability to severely damage the American economy, either by withholding exports or by selling large amounts of American government bonds on international markets, raising the interest rate the United States would have to offer to finance its budget deficit. (Because prospective purchasers of U.S. government bonds could buy them from the Chinese government instead, the U.S. government would have to agree to

One of the most conflictual issues involving international trade is the enforcement of copyrights on movies, music, and computer software. The Chinese government's refusal to enforce American copyrights has been a source of tension between the two nations.

pay a higher interest rate on the bonds in order to lure these buyers away from the Chinese.) China has also resisted efforts by the United States and other nations to cap carbon dioxide emissions in order to combat global warming, and it has limited imports and increased exports by keeping the value of its currency artificially low. Finally, as noted earlier, China has one of the largest armies in the world and has modernized its forces, expanding its air force and navy.

Military powerhouse, economic titan, supporter of "tyranny"—this certainly sounds like an American adversary, but the reality is more complex. For one thing, much of America's trade deficit with China is the result of factories built in China by companies headquartered in other Asian countries such as Japan and Korea. Thus, as America's trade deficit with China increases because of new factories, the closure of factories in these other countries causes a corresponding decline in the overall trade deficit. Moreover, though China has a

large military, it lacks the air transports and ships needed to move these troops throughout the world. Without air and sea lift, China is at best a regional power.

As for threats to cut off trade with America or sell off U.S. bonds, doing so would substantially harm the Chinese economy. Eliminating the U.S. market for exports would leave Chinese factories without one of their major buyers. And selling bonds at below-market prices to increase American interest rates would likely damage the Chinese economy even more than the American economy.

Moreover, the Chinese government has major challenges to deal with inside its own country: reducing pollution caused by industrialization, providing public services for its increasingly urban population, and fostering capitalism without democracy. Worrying about the potential for China to dominate the United States or the rest of the world overlooks the greatest struggle for Chinese political leaders—staying in power, given the demands of their citizens.

All these factors limit China's international power, but there is an even more important and simpler response to the theory that China is a major adversary to America: there is little significant conflict between the two countries. Aside from the trade deficit, illegal sales of pirated media and software, and admittedly serious human rights disputes such as the status of Tibet as a province of China, the only major issue that the two countries disagree on is the status of Taiwan, which China considers a renegade province.[c] Moreover, both America and China in practice seem to prefer the status quo, in which Taiwan is treated as an independent state but does not formally declare its independence from China. In other areas, such as curbing nuclear weapons programs in Iran and North Korea, China and America have cooperated despite their disagreements over sanctions and military actions. China is probably not about to become America's close ally, but it would be hard to support the claim that it is America's main adversary. ■

AMERICA'S ECONOMY AND THE WORLD

Trade is an example of a more general phenomenon: the state of the American economy is increasingly linked to economic conditions throughout the world. In part, these linkages result from increased imports and exports, giving American companies both new markets and new competitors. But more fundamentally, over the last generation, global financial markets have become increasingly interconnected and overlapping. Many investors and hedge funds, for example, buy and sell stocks, bonds, and other financial instruments on a twenty-four-hour basis, trading in American, Asian, and European stock markets whenever they are open. As a result, the impact of gains or declines in one market can be magnified enormously, as traders react in whatever stock market happens to be open. For example, when American markets were roiled in 2008 by the collapse of two financial firms, Bear Sterns and Lehman Brothers, traders worldwide responded by selling holdings in other financial firms, leading to much larger declines in American stock prices than would have occurred without these global connections.

Along the same lines, the interconnectedness of financial markets means that it is hard to insulate one country from another's hard times. Many Americans lost wealth due to sharp decreases in home prices in 2008 and 2009, but foreigners who had invested in American banks, financial firms, and real estate also suffered. The same is true for Americans whose overseas holdings lost value as world stock markets declined during this period.

America also faces a situation in which a significant fraction of its government debt is held by foreign banks, governments, and individuals, most notably by the Chinese, but in other countries as well. As discussed in the Challenging Conventional Wisdom box, it is hard to see how the debt could be used to threaten U.S. interests. Even so, in an era of significant U.S. budget deficits, the ability to sustain American economic growth is to some extent contingent on the willingness of others to continue purchasing this debt.

IRAQ AND AFGHANISTAN

Much of the conflict over American foreign policy stems from its military operations in Iraq, Afghanistan, and neighboring countries. Though American involvement in Iraq appears to be on the decline, the recent troop increase in Afghanistan, as well as ongoing operations against Al Qaeda forces operating out of Pakistan, mean that these conflicts—and debate over American policy—will remain central to American politics.

Since the invasion of Iraq in March 2003, American military personnel and civilians have attempted to quell a violent insurgency, rebuild the country's economic and social infrastructure, and encourage the development of a stable democracy. This effort has cost hundreds of billions of dollars and more than 4,000 American lives. Recent years have seen marked improvement in the situation in Iraq. After the "troop surge" of 30,000 additional American forces into the country in 2007, along with promises of contracts and employment to insurgent sympathizers and the expansion of Iraqi security forces, the number of insurgent attacks on American and Iraqi forces and Iraqi civilians has declined sharply, oil production is up, and American forces have transitioned to a largely supporting role. Combat forces have been withdrawn as of August 2010, although the United States will likely have bases and training operations in Iraq for some time to come. Moreover, although fighting between rival religious groups (Sunni and Shiite Muslim) and ethnic cleansing of neighborhoods and cities by both groups have gradually abated, it remains unclear whether this trend reflects a permanent change in behavior.

The situation in Afghanistan is much more fluid. American-led forces invaded the country soon after the September 11 attacks and after initial successes have struggled to defeat Taliban and Al Qaeda forces and to rebuild both the Afghani government and its civilian infrastructure. In late 2009, President Obama ordered a significant increase in American combat forces in Afghanistan, along with a new strategy of engagement similar to what was used in Iraq. This strategy has resulted in some military victories, but the success of American efforts to convert insurgents into supporters of the civilian government is very much in doubt. In the meantime, American forces, along with help from some NATO allies, will continue combat operations. And attacks by unmanned aircraft on Al Qaeda and Taliban sanctuaries in Pakistan's tribal areas will also continue.

American forces have succeeded in stabilizing Iraq, at least for the moment, and may succeed in doing so in Afghanistan, but it is important to remember that these gains have been achieved at high cost. Although the United States managed to sustain and even increase troop levels in Iraq and Afghanistan in the years since the invasion, it has done so by requiring that soldiers serve multiple tours of duty, lengthening deployments, and mobilizing reserves and the National Guard (though these policies have been relaxed in recent years). Moreover, the invasion and occupation of Iraq has severely damaged the United States' image throughout the world, although President Obama's engagement strategy appears to have reversed this situation somewhat.

The final question that remains for U.S. policy makers is to determine America's exit strategy from these conflicts. Before the invasion of Iraq, Secretary of State Colin Powell referred to the risks involved in overthrowing the Iraqi government, citing the so-called Pottery Barn rule—"If you break it, you buy it"—meaning that once the United States invaded, it could not leave until stability was restored.[97] American troops no longer patrol Iraqi streets, but the plans are for them to continue to provide important logistical and training support to Iraqi forces for the indefinite future. In many ways, these efforts are just as important as direct combat operations, as they help to build a professional military in Iraq that can secure its borders and protect the population. An early American exit could jeopardize all of the gains made in recent years.

▲ As American operations in Iraq began to wind down in 2009 and 2010, additional forces were sent to Afghanistan in the hopes that the "surge" tactic used to good effect in Iraq would be similarly successful in Afghanistan. Here, a group of U.S. Marines participating in the surge listens to a briefing at Camp Dwyer in Helmand Province, Afghanistan.

These concerns apply equally to Afghanistan. A rapid withdrawal would curb the financial and human costs to America, but it could trigger a full-fledged Afghani civil war, and result in a government that might give terrorist groups safe haven—the prevention of which was precisely the reason for invading Afghanistan in the first place. However, in comparison to Iraq, Afghanistan has fewer natural resources, little civilian infrastructure, and equally deep ethnic divisions. Though near-term success may lead to some withdrawals of American combat forces, Afghanistan will remain a central foreign policy question for at least the next decade.

TERRORISM

There have been no major terrorist attacks on America since September 11, 2001, but terrorist organizations have carried out bombings in London, Madrid, Bali, and Kenya, and in the wake of the September 11 attacks, anthrax spores were mailed to several news organizations and to some members of Congress, although the anthrax attacks appear to have been organized by a disgruntled employee of an Army weapons lab working alone. Many other terror plots have been stopped before they caused harm, such as the attempt to detonate a car bomb in New York's Times Square in May 2010.

Much like the solutions to global warming, the proper response to terrorism may seem clear. The United States should deploy its armed forces, law enforcement, intelligence teams, and diplomatic assets, both at home and abroad, to discern what terrorists are planning and disrupt their attacks, as well as discourage would-be terrorists from joining radical groups. However, what exactly should be done depends on a number of factors, including the reasons behind the attacks.

One hypothesis mentioned earlier in the chapter is that terrorism results from a "**clash of civilizations**."[98] In this view, most terrorists are motivated by hatred of Western religions, culture, ideology, or the West itself—and most of their country-men agree with their motives, even if many do not condone their methods. If this is the case, then America faces a long war, with no room to negotiate or form alliances with Islamic nations—but public opinion data from Islamic countries contradicts this argument. One study found that strong anti-American sentiments are held by a narrow range of organizations and individuals, not an entire region, race, or religion.[99] This finding suggests that in some of these countries, leaders and citizens may be willing to work with the United States to end terror attacks and would respond with friendship and support to positive gestures by the United States, such as offers of development aid.[100]

The second big question in the War on Terror has to do with the rights of ter-ror suspects. The Bush administration, while disavowing torture of suspects and prisoners, authorized aggressive interrogation methods that many believe amount to torture and curtailed suspects' access to lawyers and international observers.[101] (These policies were reversed to some extent by congressional legislation and by Supreme Court decisions.) The Obama administration has prohibited aggressive interrogation, pledged to close the Guantánamo prison for terror suspects, and announced plans to hold civilian trials for most of those still being held. However, the latter two plans have met with considerable opposition from local govern-ments and members of Congress, and it is not clear when (or whether) they will be implemented.

A final question involves the practicalities of predicting and preventing terror-ism. Given the fact of limited resources, does it really make sense to say "we'll do everything we can"? (See the What Do Political Scientists Do? box.)

clash of civilizations The theory that terror-ism is motivated by a hatred of Western culture and religion.

WEAPONS OF MASS DESTRUCTION

The term **weapons of mass destruction (WMDs)** refers to nuclear bombs, chemical weapons such as nerve gas, and biological weapons such as anthrax. Given the potential for these weapons to inflict mass casualties, the United States and many other nations have placed a high priority on limiting the number of nations that have these weapons and preventing terrorist organizations from obtaining or developing them.

Until recent years, very few countries possessed WMDs. Only five countries admitted to having nuclear weapons: the United States, Russia, China, Great Britain, and France—though a sixth nation, Israel, was generally thought to have them as well. Most nations had signed the Nuclear Non-Proliferation Treaty, which prohibited the development of nuclear weapons and mandated inspection of civilian nuclear installations by the IAEA. All signatories were supposed to have destroyed their stockpiles of biological and chemical weapons after the enactment of the Biological Weapons Convention in 1975 and the Chemical Weapons Convention in 1992.

Two developments put WMDs on the foreign policy agenda. The first was new efforts to develop nuclear weapons. Neither Pakistan nor India signed the nonproliferation treaty; both countries developed and tested nuclear weapons in the 1990s.[102] North Korea withdrew from the treaty in 2003, banned IAEA inspectors, began reprocessing nuclear reactor fuel into bomb-grade material, and detonated nuclear devices in 2006 and 2009. It has subsequently reneged on several agreements to dismantle its nuclear weapons program. Iraq had nuclear, chemical, and biological weapons programs in the late 1980s, although these facilities were damaged in the Gulf War (1990–1991) and apparently never rebuilt.[103] And, as noted earlier, Iran has begun to reprocess reactor fuel, although Iranian leaders insist that these efforts are not aimed at producing nuclear weapons.

The other development was the disintegration of the Soviet Union in 1991. Many former Soviet states had bases or depots containing nuclear weapons, bomb-grade plutonium or uranium, and missiles and aircraft capable of delivering these weapons. Moreover, when the USSR collapsed, many Soviet scientists and engineers who had built the Soviet arsenal lost their jobs and needed to find new employment. These developments raised two concerns for American decision makers. The first is that an increase in the number of nations with nuclear weapons elevates the chances that such weapons will be used—particularly between nuclear-armed adversaries such as India and Pakistan, or Iran and Israel. The second concern is that the proliferation of nuclear weapons, coupled with the availability of nuclear materials and Soviet scientists, might enable terrorist organizations to buy or steal bomb-grade material or a weapon, or hire people to build one. Chemical and biological weapons have also been used by nonstate groups. Besides the anthrax attacks mentioned earlier, the Aum Shinrikyo group released sarin nerve gas into the Tokyo subway system in 1995, killing twelve people and injuring hundreds more.[104]

As noted earlier, through multilateral efforts the United States and other nations have worked to discourage some countries, such as North Korea and Iran, from building nuclear weapons. The approach has emphasized incentives as well as threats—economic and military sanctions are used to pressure nations that continue to develop weapons, while economic aid and even civilian nuclear reactors are promised to nations for giving up their weapons programs.[105]

The critical question for American citizens and elected officials is what should be done if a nation refuses to give up WMDs or if they fall into the hands of a terror organization. The problem is that responding with force may not eliminate the threat and may even provoke the very attacks it is intended to prevent. Moreover, how should America respond to a WMD attack against its citizens or its allies, particularly if it is not clear which nation or group is responsible for the attack?

weapons of mass destruction (WMDs) Weapons that have the potential to cause large-scale loss of life, such as nuclear bombs and chemical or biological weapons.

Predicting Future Terror Attacks

In the wake of the September 11 attacks, federal, state, and local authorities implemented many new policies and restrictions in an attempt to prevent future attacks—from placing cameras in public places, to developing lists of possible terror targets, to requiring X-ray scans of shoes at airport security checkpoints. Although these measures have had significant costs in terms of money, lost freedoms, and inconvenience, many would argue that they have worked, in that there have been no major terrorist incidents within the continental United States since 2001.

This conclusion—that restrictions on civil liberties and efforts to predict the sites of future attacks are effective ways to prevent such terror attacks—has been strongly challenged by the work of John Mueller, a political scientist at The Ohio State University and author of several notable works on American politics and foreign policy. In a series of books and papers,[a] Mueller begins by articulating a series of simple

Since September 11, 2001, armed security forces have become more common at train stations, malls, and other public places. Is this additional security likely to prevent terrorist attacks?

propositions about who terrorists are and how they pursue their goals, and draws from these propositions a new set of ideas about how to protect America from terrorism. In contrast to much of the research discussed in this chapter, Mueller's work does not involve large data sets or statistical analysis. Rather, it is an exercise in deduction. He begins with the question, What are terrorists trying to do?, and then moves from his answer to predicting what kinds of targets they will look for and how best to respond to these attacks.

Mueller begins by noting that the question of what should be done to prevent future attacks is not simple. Saying "We'll do everything we can" is probably not the right answer, as it ignores the costs and trade-offs that all measures inevitably involve. In other words, the right strategy probably involves taking some risks, just as we do in all other aspects of our everyday lives. Moreover, thinking in absolutes is an invitation to making bad policies, such as eliminating all air travel in order to prevent

OTHER FOREIGN POLICY ISSUES

These seven major issues are just a few of America's most prominent foreign policy questions. Resource availability is another pressing problem. The United States increasingly imports natural resources that are essential to the U.S. economy. Oil and natural gas imports heat homes, generate electricity, and power factories, while other imports such as chromium are essential for manufacturing high-tech equipment, from computers to commercial aircraft. The question is, How can American consumers secure these materials without paying an exorbitant cost or making the U.S. economy overly dependent on foreign suppliers?

An additional resource-related concern is that American consumers and corporations compete more intensely for resources than in past decades. Developing countries such as China, India, and Brazil require increasing amounts of energy and other imports to build factories, improve public services, construct housing, and increase citizens' standard of living. Faced with these growing demands, U.S. policy makers must ensure that American consumers and businesses can obtain the resources they need and decide when and how to encourage Americans to use

airliners from being used as weapons as they were on September 11.

Mueller's central proposition is that because terrorists are interested in frightening people, the number of possible targets in America is very large. We normally think of terrorists attacking big, visible targets such as the World Trade Center, the Pentagon, or the U.S. Capitol, but the fact is that there are many, many public places, from malls to urban centers, where an attack could cause high casualties, and there is an equally large number of bridges, buildings, and dams whose destruction could cause significant loss of life or large monetary damages. Put another way, if terrorist attacks are aimed at causing terror for Americans, there is a nearly infinite number of places where terrorists can achieve this goal. Even a modest shopping mall in a small town could be a notable target under the right circumstances.

The large number of potential targets, Mueller argues, makes the job of preventing future attacks virtually impossible. Attempts to make one target safer and less vulnerable to an attack simply makes other targets less safe, for if authorities take steps to secure a target or targets, would-be terrorists can simply switch to another less-guarded one that would be equally attractive given their goals. There are simply too many potential terror targets scattered throughout America to guard all of them. And given that the number of actual terrorists is quite small, they are extremely difficult to find, regardless of whether they are in other countries or in America.

Mueller's argument has an implication that is chilling at first glance: although we would like to think that American know-how and effort can eliminate the danger of terror attacks, the fact is that this goal is essentially impossible. As long as people seek to create terror, there exists the risk of future attacks. But Mueller notes that living with risk is nothing new: virtually all of us live with risk in our everyday lives, from driving cars to dealing with the possibility of earthquakes, tornados, or hurricanes. For the average American, the chances of being involved in a terrorist incident is far lower than these everyday risks. Thus, Mueller argues, though we should think about how to prevent future attacks, we need to place these risks in context and not let fear shape our policy choices.

Most important, Mueller says, our anti-terrorism policies should de-emphasize efforts to construct lists of possible terror targets. Even if we identify the 200 most important bridges in the country, or the 100 largest malls, the likelihood of an attack on any of these sites is very small. And more important, any efforts we might make to protect these targets will be very obvious to potential attackers, who can respond by switching their efforts to the 201st bridge, the 101st largest mall, or an entirely different target.

The one exception to this logic, Mueller notes, are targets where the potential damage from an attack is inordinately high, such as civilian nuclear reactors or chemical plants, symbolic targets like the Statue of Liberty or the U.S. Capitol, or truly critical pieces of infrastructure such as major ports or bridges.

Mueller's final inference is that it may be possible to loosen precautions against terror attacks that were implemented out of the "do everything you can" instinct mentioned earlier. Since all security measures have a cost, and if their benefits are minimal to nonexistent, there is no reason for them to continue. For example, he notes that British authorities have eliminated the requirement that passengers have their shoes x-rayed at airport security checkpoints. Given that this change has not produced any new shoe bombers on flights originating in Britain, Mueller argues, it makes sense for American authorities to consider eliminating this requirement as well. ▪

Watch a video clip of political scientist Navin Bapat discussing this topic at wwnorton.com/studyspace.

alternative resources, such as solar or nuclear power, that would reduce dependence on imported sources of energy.

A third question for the makers of American foreign policy is whether and how to mediate between Israel and the Palestinians. Since Israel became a state in 1948, it has fought four major wars and countless minor conflicts with Syria, Jordan, Egypt, Lebanon, and various groups of Palestinians. America has been Israel's strongest ally and a major supplier of military hardware and economic aid.[106] However, America has also encouraged the parties in these conflicts to negotiate a peaceful settlement through diplomacy and offers of military and economic aid to both sides. These efforts produced a peace treaty between Egypt and Israel in 1979, and almost yielded a deal between Israel and the Palestinians in 2000.[107] The United States has also worked to limit Israeli settlements in the West Bank and Gaza Strip, as these areas are largely populated by Palestinians and might become part of a new Palestinian state in the event of a peace agreement. (In 2005 Israel removed its settlements from Gaza and turned it over to the Palestinians.) In recent years, the European Union and other nations have also participated in the negotiation process, although no one has been able to broker a comprehensive agreement or persuade the

▲ The United States has been involved in trying to help the Palestinians and Israelis end their generations-old conflict, including efforts to limit Israeli settlements in the West Bank and Gaza (shown here under construction). Despite major efforts by many American presidents and diplomats, the unresolved conflict remains on the president's agenda.

Israelis to abandon the building of new settlements. The Obama administration has initiated efforts toward both goals, with few signs of success so far.

Over the course of the negotiations, several major issues have persisted, including how to devise an acceptable deal that would establish Israel's borders, force all parties to abandon hostilities, and address the Palestinians' desire for a state of their own. The task is especially difficult because the Palestinians are not a single, uniform group; they are represented by many groups, most notably Fatah and Hamas, each with their own leaders and set of demands.[108] Negotiations have been ongoing for a generation and show no signs of yielding an agreement.

Finally, American citizens and elected officials must decide when America should defer to the judgments of international organizations. It is easy for Americans to support these organizations when their decisions are consistent with American policy, such as when the UN coordinates sanctions against Iran, when the WTO enforces American copyrights abroad, or when the International Criminal Court tries deposed leaders for crimes committed while in office. The challenge for America is deciding what to do when these organizations act against the interests of individual Americans, American businesses, or the country as a whole. For example, the UN withdrew most of its staff from coordinating the reconstruction of Iraq after a series of attacks on UN staff in 2003 (until expanding its presence in the country again in 2007), and the WTO has forced America to lower trade barriers.

International organizations present a trade-off for American policy makers. These organizations' decisions may be harmful to American interests, but if America accepts them—especially when compliance imposes costs—this behavior may increase the chances that other nations will also comply in international efforts that would serve U.S. goals. In this way, international organizations may reduce the extent to which America acts as the world's policeman, protector of human rights, and enforcer of economic policies. The task for U.S. policy makers is to balance these long-term benefits against the real, short-term costs of compliance.

Conclusion

Foreign policy matters. National security is a top priority for many Americans. The state of the American economy, from home prices to the unemployment rate, is affected by economic conditions elsewhere. Trade agreements with other nations determine how much American companies are allowed to export and what taxes and fees they must pay for imports of raw materials and other goods. Solutions to pressing environmental problems such as global warming are inherently international. It is hard to find a domestic issue that does not have a foreign policy component.

Foreign policy is also conflictual. Disagreements between elected officials over what to do in Afghanistan, or over trade agreements or any other question of foreign policy, are not just attempts to attract political support or get media attention. Rather, these differences of opinion reflect real dilemmas over what government should do.

In all of these respects, the September 11 attacks, the invasions of Iraq and Afghanistan, and the worldwide economic crisis of 2008–2009 are not exceptions to the rule—rather, they epitomize just how close to home foreign policy is. The lives of ordinary Americans are increasingly affected by actions taken outside America's borders. This trend has been underway for over a generation and shows no signs of stopping.

What is foreign policy?

- America's foreign policy was largely isolationist until World War I and internationalist thereafter. The Cold War dominated foreign policy from the end of World War II in the mid 1940s until the demise of the Soviet Union in 1991. In recent years, human rights, trade, and terrorism have become important concerns.

- Foreign policy involves controversial choices—and throughout American history, politicians have disagreed about whether, when, and how America should interact with other nations. America did not have to be isolationist before World War I nor internationalist afterward. The Marshall Plan was not inevitable, nor were the policy of containment or the interventions in Vietnam or Iraq.

- The effects of foreign policy are everywhere. America's foreign policy, including decisions to use military force in Iraq and elsewhere, affect everything from energy prices to economic growth.

Who makes American foreign policy?

- The president is the dominant figure in American foreign policy, owing to provisions of the Constitution that make the president military commander in chief and the leader of the executive branch of government.

- Members of Congress have a significant role in foreign policy, owing to their control of agency budgets, their power to approve some presidential appointments to senior foreign policy positions, and the War Powers Resolution of 1973.

- The federal courts use the process of judicial review to determine whether laws, regulations, and presidential actions pertaining to foreign policy are constitutional.

- Implementation of America's foreign policy also sometimes involves international organizations such as the United Nations or the International Monetary Fund. Other participants, such as the media, interest groups, and the general public, rarely have a decisive influence on foreign policy.

What are the tools of foreign policy?

- The tools of foreign policy include military force, trade and economic policies, diplomacy, foreign aid, and alliances and treaties.

- America's foreign policy uses all of these tools. The United States stations military forces throughout the world, is a party to many trade agreements, undertakes frequent diplomatic efforts, gives foreign aid to many countries and groups, and has negotiated many treaties and alliances.

- None of these tools work all of the time. The case of the war in Iraq, for example, illustrates the limits of military power.

What characterizes the politics of American foreign policy?

- Debates over particular foreign policies often reflect sincere, sharp differences of opinion about what America's relations with other countries should look like.

- Despite the best efforts of information-gathering agencies, incomplete or contradictory sources of information can also drive disagreements about the world at large or about the significance of particular pieces of information, which gives rise to differences of opinion about foreign policy.

- Disagreements over foreign policy occur between the political parties, within each party, and even among senior advisers to the president.

What key foreign policy issues do we face now and in the future?

- Solutions to global warming will require complex negotiations between developed and developing nations. Moreover, implementing these agreements will require costly changes in the behavior of individuals, companies, and nations throughout the world.

- Many other nations do not uphold the same freedoms and rights experienced by American citizens. However, American efforts to protect human rights worldwide, especially by using military force, are expensive, controversial, and may conflict with other policy goals.

- Trade agreements and globalization can enhance economic growth and create jobs, yet some people in America and elsewhere are hurt by these policies. Policy makers must weigh the gains from policies like liberalized trade or outsourcing against the costs and decide whether the government should try to mitigate the costs.

- The wars in Iraq and Afghanistan, the War on Terror, and global attempts to discourage WMDs illustrate the limits of American military force and economic power. Even with the largest economy and the most military power in the world, the United States cannot simply impose its preferences.

⊚ STUDENT STUDYSPACE

Find quizzes and other review material at wwnorton.com/studyspace.

CRITICAL THINKING

1. The American president has much more influence over foreign policy than members of Congress do. What are the pros and cons of this allocation of power?

2. Pick one of the foreign policy problems described in this chapter. What policy choices would a realist make? What choices would an idealist make?

3. Using evidence such as international public opinion data from the Pew Research Center or some other source, argue for or against the theory of a contemporary "clash of civilizations."

KEY TERMS

alliance (p. 656)
bilateral agreements (p. 657)
Bush Doctrine (p. 644)
clash of civilizations (p. 668)
Cold War (p. 641)
containment (p. 641)
détente (p. 642)
diplomacy (p. 655)
domino theory (p. 642)
foreign policy (p. 636)
free trade zones (p. 655)
idealism (p. 637)
International Monetary Fund (p. 651)
internationalism (p. 637)

isolationism (p. 637)
Kyoto Protocol (p. 662)
Monroe Doctrine (p. 640)
most-favored-nation status (p. 655)
multilateral action (p. 637)
multilateral agreements (p. 657)
mutually assured destruction (p. 642)
nation building (p. 639)
National Security Council (NSC) (p. 645)
nongovernmental organizations (NGOs) (p. 651)
North Atlantic Treaty Organization (NATO) (p. 657)

realism (p. 637)
sanction (p. 655)
shuttle diplomacy (p. 656)
tariff (p. 655)
trade agreement (p. 655)
treaty (p. 656)
unilateral action (national) (p. 637)
United Nations (UN) (p. 652)
weapons of mass destruction (WMDs) (p. 669)
World Bank (p. 651)
World Trade Organization (WTO) (p. 655)

SUGGESTED READING

Bueno de Mesquita, Bruce. *Principles of International Politics*. Washington, DC: CQ Press, 2005.

Fisher, Louis. *Presidential War Power*. Lawrence, KS: University Press of Kansas, 2004.

Friedman, Thomas L. *The World Is Flat 3.0: A Brief History of the Twenty-first Century*. New York: Farrar, Straus and Giroux, 2007.

Huntington, Samuel P. *The Clash of Civilizations and the Remaking of World Order*. New York: Free Press, 2002.

Keohane, Robert O. *After Hegemony: Cooperation and Discord in the International System*. Princeton, NJ: Princeton University Press, 2005 (originally published 1984).

Mearsheimer, John J. *The Tragedy of Great Power Politics*. New York: Norton, 2001.

National Commission on Terrorist Attacks upon the United States. *The 9/11 Commission Report: Final Report of the National Commission on Terrorist Attacks upon the United States*. New York: W. W. Norton, 2004. Full text also available from the U.S. Government Printing Office at www.gpoaccess.gov/911/index .html.

Ricks, Thomas. *The Gamble: General David Petraeus and the American Military Adventure in Iraq, 2006–2008*. New York: Penguin Press, 2009.

Roach, Stephen. *The Next Asia: Opportunities and Challenges for a New Globalization*. New York: Wiley, 2009.

Sen, Amartya. *Identity and Violence: The Illusion of Destiny*. New York: Norton, 2007.

Simmons, Beth, Frank Dobbin, and Geoffrey Garrett. *The Global Diffusion of Markets and Democracy*. New York: Cambridge University Press, 2008.

Stiglitz, Joseph E. *Making Globalization Work*. New York: W. W. Norton, 2007.

Appendix

The Declaration of Independence

In Congress, July 4, 1776

The unanimous Declaration of the thirteen united States of America,

When in the Course of human events, it becomes necessary for one people to dissolve the political bands which have connected them with another, and to assume among the powers of the earth, the separate and equal station to which the Laws of Nature and of Nature's God entitle them, a decent respect to the opinions of mankind requires that they should declare the causes which impel them to the separation.

We hold these truths to be self-evident, that all men are created equal, that they are endowed by their Creator with certain unalienable Rights, that among these are Life, Liberty and the pursuit of Happiness.—That to secure these rights, Governments are instituted among Men, deriving their just powers from the consent of the governed. —That whenever any Form of Government becomes destructive of these ends, it is the Right of the People to alter or to abolish it, and to institute new Government, laying its foundation on such principles and organizing its powers in such form, as to them shall seem most likely to effect their Safety and Happiness. Prudence, indeed, will dictate that Governments long established should not be changed for light and transient causes; and accordingly all experience hath shewn, that mankind are more disposed to suffer, while evils are sufferable, than to right themselves by abolishing the forms to which they are accustomed. But when a long train of abuses and usurpations, pursuing invariably the same Object evinces a design to reduce them under absolute Despotism, it is their right, it is their duty, to throw off such Government, and to provide new Guards for their future security.—Such has been the patient sufferance of these Colonies; and such is now the necessity which constrains them to alter their former Systems of Government. The history of the present King of Great Britain is a history of repeated injuries and usurpations, all having in direct object the establishment of an absolute Tyranny over these States. To prove this, let Facts be submitted to a candid world.

He has refused his Assent to Laws, the most wholesome and necessary for the public good.

He has forbidden his Governors to pass Laws of immediate and pressing importance, unless suspended in their operation till his Assent should be obtained; and when so suspended, he has utterly neglected to attend to them.

He has refused to pass other Laws for the accommodation of large districts of people, unless those people would relinquish the right of Representation in the Legislature, a right inestimable to them and formidable to tyrants only.

He has called together legislative bodies at places unusual, uncomfortable, and distant from the depository of their public Records, for the sole purpose of fatiguing them into compliance with his measures.

He has dissolved Representative Houses repeatedly, for opposing with manly firmness his invasions on the rights of the people.

He has refused for a long time, after such dissolutions, to cause others to be elected; whereby the Legislative powers, incapable of Annihilation, have returned to the People at large for their exercise; the State remaining in the mean time exposed to all the dangers of invasion from without, and convulsions within.

He has endeavoured to prevent the population of these States; for that purpose obstructing the Laws for Naturalization of Foreigners; refusing to pass others to encourage their migrations hither, and raising the conditions of new Appropriations of Lands.

He has obstructed the Administration of Justice, by refusing his Assent to Laws for establishing Judiciary powers.

He has made Judges dependent on his Will alone, for the tenure of their offices, and the amount and payment of their salaries.

He has erected a multitude of New Offices, and sent hither swarms of Officers to harrass our people, and eat out their substance.

He has kept among us, in times of peace, Standing Armies without the Consent of our legislatures.

He has affected to render the Military independent of and superior to the Civil power.

He has combined with others to subject us to a jurisdiction foreign to our constitution, and unacknowledged by our laws; giving his Assent to their Acts of pretended Legislation:

For Quartering large bodies of armed troops among us:

For protecting them, by a mock Trial, from punishment for any Murders which they should commit on the Inhabitants of these States:

For cutting off our Trade with all parts of the world:

For imposing Taxes on us without our Consent:

For depriving us in many cases, of the benefits of Trial by Jury:

For transporting us beyond Seas to be tried for pretended offences:

For abolishing the free System of English Laws in a neighboring Province, establishing therein an Arbitrary government, and enlarging its Boundaries so as to render it at once an example and fit instrument for introducing the same absolute rule into these Colonies:

For taking away our Charters, abolishing our most valuable Laws, and altering fundamentally the Forms of our Governments:

For suspending our own Legislatures, and declaring themselves invested with power to legislate for us in all cases whatsoever.

He has abdicated Government here, by declaring us out of his Protection and waging War against us.

He has plundered our seas, ravaged our Coasts, burnt our towns, and destroyed the lives of our people.

He is at this time transporting large Armies of foreign Mercenaries to compleat the works of death, desolation and tyranny, already begun with circumstances of Cruelty & perfidy scarcely paralleled in the most barbarous ages, and totally unworthy the Head of a civilized nation.

He has constrained our fellow Citizens taken Captive on the high Seas to bear Arms against their Country, to become the executioners of their friends and Brethren, or to fall themselves by their Hands.

He has excited domestic insurrections amongst us, and has endeavoured to bring on the inhabitants of our frontiers, the merciless Indian Savages, whose known rule of warfare, is an undistinguished destruction of all ages, sexes and conditions.

In every stage of these Oppressions We have Petitioned for Redress in the most humble terms: Our repeated Petitions have been answered only by repeated injury. A Prince whose character is thus marked by every act which may define a Tyrant, is unfit to be the ruler of a free people.

Nor have We been wanting in attentions to our Brittish brethren. We have warned them from time to time of attempts by their legislature to extend an unwarrantable jurisdiction over us. We have reminded them of the circumstances of our emigration and settlement here. We have appealed to their native justice and magnanimity, and we have conjured them by the ties of our common kindred to disavow these usurpations, which, would inevitably interrupt our connections and correspondence. They too have been deaf to the voice of justice and of consanguinity. We must, therefore, acquiesce in the necessity, which denounces our Separation, and hold them, as we hold the rest of mankind, Enemies in War, in Peace Friends.

We, Therefore, the Representatives of the United States of America, in General Congress, Assembled, appealing to the Supreme Judge of the world for the rectitude of our intentions, do, in the Name, and by Authority of the good People of these Colonies, solemnly publish and declare, That these United Colonies are, and of Right ought to be Free and Independent States; that they are Absolved from all Allegiance to the British Crown, and that all political connection between them and the State of Great Britain, is and ought to be totally dissolved; and that as Free and Independent States, they have full Power to levy War, conclude Peace, contract Alliances, establish Commerce, and to do all other Acts and Things which Independent States may of right do. And for the support of this Declaration, with a firm reliance on the protection of divine Providence, we mutually pledge to each other our Lives, our Fortunes and our sacred Honor.

The foregoing Declaration was, by order of Congress, engrossed, and signed by the following members:

John Hancock

NEW HAMPSHIRE
Josiah Bartlett
William Whipple
Matthew Thornton

MASSACHUSETTS BAY
Samuel Adams
John Adams
Robert Treat Paine
Elbridge Gerry

RHODE ISLAND
Stephen Hopkins
William Ellery

CONNECTICUT
Roger Sherman
Samuel Huntington
William Williams
Oliver Wolcott

NEW YORK
William Floyd
Philip Livingston
Francis Lewis
Lewis Morris

NEW JERSEY
Richard Stockton
John Witherspoon
Francis Hopkinson
John Hart
Abraham Clark

PENNSYLVANIA
Robert Morris
Benjamin Rush
Benjamin Franklin
John Morton
George Clymer
James Smith
George Taylor
James Wilson
George Ross

DELAWARE
Caesar Rodney
George Read
Thomas M'Kean

MARYLAND
Samuel Chase
William Paca
Thomas Stone
Charles Carroll,
of Carrollton

VIRGINIA
George Wythe
Richard Henry Lee
Thomas Jefferson
Benjamin Harrison
Thomas Nelson, Jr.
Francis Lightfoot Lee
Carter Braxton

NORTH CAROLINA
William Hooper
Joseph Hewes
John Penn

SOUTH CAROLINA
Edward Rutledge
Thomas Heyward, Jr.
Thomas Lynch, Jr.
Arthur Middleton

GEORGIA
Button Gwinnett
Lyman Hall
George Walton

Resolved, That copies of the Declaration be sent to the several assemblies, conventions, and committees, or councils of safety, and to the several commanding officers of the continental troops; that it be proclaimed in each of the United States, at the head of the army.

The Articles of Confederation

Agreed to by Congress November 15, 1777;
ratified and in force March 1, 1781

To all whom these Presents shall come, we the undersigned Delegates of the States affixed to our Names, send greeting. Whereas the Delegates of the United States of America, in Congress assembled, did, on the fifteenth day of November, in the Year of Our Lord One thousand Seven Hundred and Seventy seven, and in the Second Year of the Independence of America, agree to certain articles of Confederation and perpetual Union between the States of Newhampshire, Massachusetts-bay, Rhodeisland and Providence Plantations, Connecticut, New-York, New-Jersey, Pennsylvania, Delaware, Maryland, Virginia, North-Carolina, South-Carolina and Georgia in the words following, viz. "Articles of Confederation and perpetual Union between the states of Newhampshire, Massachusettsbay, Rhodeisland and Providence Plantations, Connecticut, New-York, New-Jersey, Pennsylvania, Delaware, Maryland, Virginia, North-Carolina, South-Carolina and Georgia.

Art. I. The Stile of this confederacy shall be "The United States of America."

Art. II. Each state retains its sovereignty, freedom and independence, and every Power, Jurisdiction and right, which is not by this confederation expressly delegated to the United States, in Congress assembled.

Art. III. The said states hereby severally enter into a firm league of friendship with each other, for their common defence, the security of their Liberties, and their mutual and general welfare, binding themselves to assist each other, against all force offered to, or attacks made upon them, or any of them, on account of religion, sovereignty, trade, or any other pretence whatever.

Art. IV. The better to secure and perpetuate mutual friendship and intercourse among the people of the different states in this union, the free inhabitants of each of these states, paupers, vagabonds and fugitives from Justice excepted, shall be entitled to all privileges and immunities of free citizens in the several states; and the people of each state shall have free ingress and regress to and from any other state, and shall enjoy therein all the privileges of trade and commerce, subject to the same duties, impositions and restrictions as the inhabitants thereof respectively, provided that such restriction shall not extend so far as to prevent the removal of property imported into any state, to any other state, of which the Owner is an inhabitant; provided also that no imposition, duties or restriction shall be laid by any state, on the property of the united states, or either of them.

If any Person guilty of, or charged with treason, felony, or other high misdemeanor in any state, shall flee from Justice, and be found in any of the united states, he shall, upon demand of the Governor or executive power, of the state from which he fled, be delivered up and removed to the state having jurisdiction of his offence.

Full faith and credit shall be given in each of these states to the records, acts and judicial proceedings of the courts and magistrates of every other state.

Art. V. For the more convenient management of the general interests of the united states, delegates shall be annually appointed in such manner as the legislature of each state shall direct, to meet in Congress on the first Monday in November, in every year, with a power reserved to each state, to recall its delegates, or any of them, at any time within the year, and to send others in their stead, for the remainder of the Year.

No state shall be represented in Congress by less than two, nor by more than seven Members; and no person shall be capable of being a delegate for more than three years in any term of six years; nor shall any person, being a delegate, be capable of holding any office under the united states, for which he, or another for his benefit receives any salary, fees or emolument of any kind.

Each state shall maintain its own delegates in a meeting of the states, and while they act as members of the committee of the states.

In determining questions in the united states, in Congress assembled, each state shall have one vote.

Freedom of speech and debate in Congress shall not be impeached or questioned in any Court, or place out of Congress, and the members of congress shall be protected in their persons from arrests and imprisonments, during the time of their going to and from, and attendance on congress, except for treason, felony, or breach of the peace.

Art. VI. No state without the Consent of the united states in congress assembled, shall send any embassy to, or receive any embassy from, or enter into any conference, agreement, or alliance or treaty with any King, prince or state; nor shall any person holding any office or profit or trust under the united states, or any of them, accept of any present, emolument, office or title of any kind whatever from any king, prince or foreign state; nor shall the united states in congress assembled, or any of them, grant any title of nobility.

No two or more states shall enter into any treaty, confederation or alliance whatever between them, without the consent of the united states in congress assembled, specifying accurately the purposes for which the same is to be entered into, and how long it shall continue.

No state shall lay any imposts or duties, which may interfere with any stipulations in treaties, entered into by the united states in congress assembled, with any king, prince or state, in pursuance of any treaties already proposed by congress, to the courts of France and Spain.

No vessels of war shall be kept up in time of peace by any state, except such number only, as shall be deemed necessary by the united states in congress assembled, for the defence of such state, or its trade; nor shall any body of forces be kept up by any state, in time of peace, except such number only, as in the judgment of the united states, in congress assembled, shall be deemed requisite to garrison the forts necessary for the defence of such state; but every state shall always keep up a well regulated and disciplined militia, sufficiently armed and accoutred, and shall provide and constantly have ready for use, in public stores, a due number of field pieces and tents, and a proper quantity of arms, ammunition and camp equipage.

No state shall engage in any war without the consent of the united states in congress assembled, unless such state be actually invaded by enemies, or shall have received certain advice of a resolution being formed by some nation of Indians to invade such state, and the danger is so imminent as not to admit of a delay, till the united states in congress asssembled can be consulted; nor shall any state grant commissions to any ships or vessels of war, nor letters of marque or reprisal, except it be after a declaration of war by the united states in congress assembled, and then only against the kingdom or state and the subjects thereof, against which war has been so declared, and under such regulations as shall be established by the united states in congress assembled, unless such state be infested by pirates; in which case vessels of war may be fitted out for that occasion, and kept so long as the danger shall continue, or until the united states in congress assembled shall determine otherwise.

Art. VII. When land-forces are raised by any state for the common defence, all officers of or under the rank of colonel, shall be appointed by the legislature of each state respectively, by whom such forces shall be raised, or in such manner as such state shall direct, and all vacancies shall be filled up by the state which first made the appointment.

Art. VIII. All charges of war, and all other expences that shall be incurred for the common defence or general welfare, and allowed by the united states in congress assembled, shall be defrayed out of a common treasury, which shall be supplied by the several states in proportion to the value of all land within each state, granted to or surveyed for any Person, as such land and the buildings and improvements thereon shall be estimated according to such mode as the united states in congress assembled, shall from time to time direct and appoint.

The taxes for paying that proportion shall be laid and levied by the authority and direction of the legislatures of the several states within the time agreed upon by the united states in congress assembled.

Art. IX. The united states in congress assembled, shall have the sole and exclusive right and power of determining on peace and war, except in the cases mentioned in the sixth article—of sending and receiving ambassadors—entering into treaties and alliances, provided that no treaty of commerce shall be made whereby the legislative power of the respective states shall be restrained from imposing such imposts and duties on foreigners, as their own people are subjected to, or from prohibiting the exportation of any species of goods or commodities whatsoever—of establishing rules for deciding in all cases, what captures on land or water shall be legal, and in what manner prizes taken by land or naval forces in the service of the united states shall be divided or appropriated—of granting letters of marque and reprisal in times of peace—appointing courts for the trial of piracies and felonies committed on the high seas and establishing courts for receiving and determining finally appeals in all cases of captures, provided that no member of congress shall be appointed a judge of any of the said courts.

The united states in congress assembled shall also be the last resort on appeal in all disputes and differences now subsisting or that hereafter may arise between two or more states concerning boundary, jurisdiction or any other cause whatever; which authority shall always be exercised in the manner following. Whenever the legislative or executive authority or lawful agent of any state in controversy with another shall present a petition to congress stating the matter in question and praying for a hearing, notice thereof shall be given by order of congress to the legislative or executive authority of the other state in controversy, and a day assigned for the appearance of the parties by their lawful agents, who shall then be directed to appoint by joint consent, commissioners or judges to constitute a court for hearing and determining the matter in question: but if they cannot agree, congress shall name three persons out of each of the united states, and from the list of such persons each party shall alternately strike out one, the petitioners beginning, until the number shall be reduced to thirteen; and from that number not less than seven, nor more than nine names as congress shall direct, shall in the presence of congress be drawn out by lot, and the persons whose names shall be so drawn or any five of them, shall be commissioners or judges, to hear and finally determine the controversy, so always as a major part of the judges who shall hear the cause shall agree in the determination: and if either party shall neglect to attend at the day appointed, without shewing reasons, which congress shall judge sufficient, or being present shall refuse to strike, the congress shall proceed to nominate three persons out of each state, and the secretary of congress shall strike in behalf of such party absent or refusing; and the judgment and sentence of the court to be appointed, in the manner before prescribed, shall be final and conclusive; and if any of the parties shall refuse to submit to the authority of such court, or to appear to defend their claim or cause, the court shall nevertheless proceed to pronounce sentence, or judgment, which shall in like manner be final and decisive, the judgment or sentence and other proceedings being in either case transmitted to congress, and

lodged among the acts of congress for the security of the parties concerned: provided that every commissioner, before he sits in judgment, shall take an oath to be administered by one of the judges of the supreme or superior court of the state, where the cause shall be tried, "well and truly to hear and determine the matter in question, according to the best of his judgment, without favour, affection or hope of reward:" provided also, that no state shall be deprived of territory for the benefit of the united states.

All controversies concerning the private right of soil claimed under different grants of two or more states, whose jurisdictions as they may respect such lands, and the states which passed such grants are adjusted, the said grants or either of them being at the same time claimed to have originated antecedent to such settlement of jurisdiction, shall on the petition of either party to the congress of the united states, be finally determined as near as may be in the same manner as is before prescribed for deciding disputes respecting territorial jurisdiction between different states.

The united states in congress assembled shall also have the sole and exclusive right and power of regulating the alloy and value of coin struck by their own authority, or by that of the respective states—fixing the standard of weights and measures throughout the united states—regulating the trade and managing all affairs with the Indians, not members of any of the states, provided that the legislative right of any state within its own limits be not infringed or violated—establishing and regulating post-offices from one state to another, throughout all the united states, and exacting such postage on the papers passing thro' the same as may be requisite to defray the expences of the said office—appointing all officers of the land forces, in the service of the united states, excepting regimental officers—appointing all the officers of the naval forces, and commissioning all officers whatever in the service of the united states—making rules for the government and regulation of the said land and naval forces, and directing their operations.

The united states in congress assembled shall have authority to appoint a committee, to sit in the recess of congress, to be denominated "A Committee of the States," and to consist of one delegate from each state; and to appoint such other committees and civil officers as may be necessary for managing the general affairs of the united states under their direction—to appoint one of their number to preside, provided that no person be allowed to serve in the office of president more than one year in any term of three years; to ascertain the necessary sums of Money to be raised for the service of the united states, and to appropriate and apply the same for defraying the public expenses—to borrow money, or emit bills on the credit of the united states, transmitting every half year to the respective states an account of the sums of money so borrowed or emitted,—to build and equip a navy—to agree upon the number of land forces, and to make requisitions from each state for its quota, in proportion to the number of white inhabitants in such state; which requisition shall be binding, and thereupon the legislature of each state shall appoint the regimental officers, raise the men and cloath, arm and equip them in a soldier like manner, at the expense of the united states; and the officers and men so cloathed, armed and equipped shall march to the place appointed, and within the time agreed on by the united states in congress assembled: But if the united states in congress assembled shall, on consideration of circumstances judge proper that any state should not raise men, or should raise a smaller number than its quota, and that any other state should raise a greater number of men than the quota thereof, such extra number shall be raised, officered, cloathed, armed and equipped in the same manner as the quota of such state, unless the legislature of such state shall judge that such extra number cannot be safely spared out of the same, in which case they shall raise officer, cloath, arm and equip as many of such extra number as they judge can be safely spared. And the officers and men so cloathed, armed and equipped, shall march to the place appointed, and within the time agreed on by the united states in congress assembled.

The united states in congress assembled shall never engage in a war, nor grant letters of marque and reprisal in time of peace, nor enter into any treaties or alliances, nor coin money, nor regulate the value thereof, nor ascertain the sums and expenses necessary for the defence and welfare of the united states, or any of them, nor emit bills, nor borrow money on the credit of the united states, nor appropriate money, nor agree upon the number of vessels of war, to be built or purchased, or the number of land or sea forces to be raised, nor appoint a commander in chief of the army or navy, unless nine states assent to the same: nor shall a question on any other point, except for adjourning from day to day be determined, unless by the votes of a majority of the united states in congress assembled.

The congress of the united states shall have power to adjourn to any time within the year, and to any place within the united states, so that no period of adjournment be for a longer duration than the space of six Months, and shall publish the Journal of their proceedings monthly, except such parts thereof relating to treaties, alliances or military operations, as in their judgment require secrecy; and the yeas and nays of the delegates of each state on any question shall be entered on the Journal, when it is desired by any delegate; and the delegates of a state, or any of them, at his or their request shall be furnished with a transcript of the said Journal, except such parts as are above excepted, to lay before the legislatures of the several states.

Art. X. The committee of the states, or any nine of them, shall be authorised to execute, in the recess of congress, such of the powers of congress as the united states in congress assembled, by the consent of nine states, shall from time to time think expedient to vest them with; provided that no power be delegated to the said committee, for the exercise of which, by the articles of confederation, the voice of nine states in the congress of the united states assembled is requisite.

Art. XI. Canada acceding to this confederation, and joining in the measures of the united states, shall be admitted into, and entitled to all the advantages of this union: but no other colony shall be admitted into the same, unless such admission be agreed to by nine states.

Art. XII. All bills of credit emitted, monies borrowed and debts contracted by, or under the authority of congress, before the assembling of the united states, in pursuance of the present confederation, shall be deemed and considered as a charge against the united states, for payment and satisfaction whereof the said united states and the public faith are hereby solemnly pledged.

Art. XIII. Every state shall abide by the determinations of the united states in congress assembled, on all questions which by this confederation are submitted to them. And the Articles of this confederation shall be inviolably observed by every state, and the union shall be perpetual; nor shall any alteration at any time hereafter be made in any of them; unless such alteration be agreed to in a congress of the united states, and be afterwards confirmed by the legislatures of every state.

And Whereas it hath pleased the Great Governor of the World to incline the hearts of the legislatures we respectively represent in congress, to approve of, and to authorize us to ratify the said articles of confederation and perpetual union. Know Ye that we the undersigned delegates, by virtue of the power and authority to us given for that purpose, do by these presents, in the name and in behalf of our respective constituents, fully and entirely ratify and confirm each and every of the said articles of confederation and perpetual union, and all and singular the matters and things therein contained: And we do further solemnly plight and engage the faith of our respective constituents, that they shall abide by the determinations of the united states in congress assembled, on all questions, which by the said confederation are submitted to them. And that the articles thereof shall be inviolably observed by the states we respectively represent, and that the union shall be perpetual. In Witness whereof we have hereunto set our hands in Congress. Done at Philadelphia in the state of Pennsylvania the ninth day of July, in the Year of our Lord one Thousand seven Hundred and Seventy-eight, and in the third year of the independence of America.

The Constitution of the United States of America

We the People of the United States, in Order to form a more perfect Union, establish Justice, insure domestic Tranquility, provide for the common defence, promote the general Welfare, and secure the Blessings of Liberty to ourselves and our Posterity, do ordain and establish this Constitution for the United States of America.

Article I

SECTION 1

[LEGISLATIVE POWERS]

All legislative Powers herein granted shall be vested in a Congress of the United States, which shall consist of a Senate and House of Representatives.

SECTION 2

[HOUSE OF REPRESENTATIVES, HOW CONSTITUTED, POWER OF IMPEACHMENT]

The House of Representatives shall be composed of Members chosen every second Year by the People of the several States, and the Electors in each State shall have the Qualifications requisite for Electors of the most numerous Branch of the State Legislature.

No Person shall be a Representative who shall not have attained to the Age of twenty five Years, and been seven Years a Citizen of the United States, and who shall not, when elected, be an Inhabitant of that State in which he shall be chosen.

Representatives and *direct Taxes*[1] shall be apportioned among the several States which may be included within this Union, according to their respective Numbers, *which shall be determined by adding to the whole Number of free Persons, including those bound to Service for a Term of Years, and excluding Indians not taxed, three fifths of all other Persons.*[2] The actual Enumeration shall be made within three Years after the first Meeting of the Congress of the United States, and within every subsequent Term of ten Years, in such Manner as they shall by Law direct. The Number of Representatives shall not exceed one for every thirty Thousand, but each State shall have at Least one Representative; *and until such enumeration shall be made, the State of New Hampshire shall be entitled to chuse three, Massachusetts eight, Rhode-Island and Providence Plantations one, Connecticut five, New-York six, New Jersey four, Pennsylvania eight, Delaware one, Maryland six, Virginia ten, North Carolina five, South Carolina five, and Georgia three.*[3]

When vacancies happen in the Representation from any State, the Executive Authority thereof shall issue Writs of Election to fill such Vacancies.

The House of Representatives shall chuse their Speaker and other Officers; and shall have the sole Power of Impeachment.

SECTION 3

[THE SENATE, HOW CONSTITUTED, IMPEACHMENT TRIALS]

The Senate of the United States shall be composed of two Senators from each State, *chosen by the Legislature thereof,*[4] for six Years; and each Senator shall have one Vote.

Immediately after they shall be assembled in Consequence of the first Election, they shall be divided as equally as may be into three Classes. The Seats of the Senators of the first Class shall be vacated at the Expiration of the second Year, of the second Class at the Expiration of the fourth Year, and of the third Class at the Expiration of the sixth Year, so that one third may be chosen every second Year; *and if Vacancies happen by Resignation, or otherwise, during the Recess of the Legislature of any State, the Executive thereof may make temporary Appointments until the next Meeting of the Legislature, which shall then fill such Vacancies.*[5]

No Person shall be a Senator who shall not have attained to the Age of thirty Years, and been nine Years a Citizen of the United States, and who shall not, when elected, be an Inhabitant of that State for which he shall be chosen.

The Vice President of the United States shall be President of the Senate, but shall have no Vote, unless they be equally divided.

The Senate shall chuse their other Officers, and also a President pro tempore, in the Absence of the Vice President, or when he shall exercise the Office of President of the United States.

The Senate shall have the sole Power to try all Impeachments. When sitting for that Purpose, they shall be on Oath or Affirmation. When the President of the United States is tried, the Chief Justice shall preside: And no Person shall be convicted without the Concurrence of two thirds of the Members present.

Judgment in Cases of Impeachment shall not extend further than to removal from Office, and disqualification to hold and enjoy any Office of honor, Trust or Profit under the United States: but the Party convicted shall nevertheless be liable and subject to Indictment, Trial, Judgment and Punishment, according to Law.

SECTION 4

[ELECTION OF SENATORS AND REPRESENTATIVES]

The Times, Places and Manner of holding Elections for Senators and Representatives, shall be prescribed in each State by the Legislature thereof; but the Congress may at any time by Law make or alter such Regulations, except as to the Places of chusing Senators.

The Congress shall assemble at least once in every Year, and such Meeting shall be on the first Monday in December, unless they shall by Law appoint a different Day.[6]

SECTION 5

[QUORUM, JOURNALS, MEETINGS, ADJOURNMENTS]

Each House shall be the Judge of the Elections, Returns and Qualifications of its own Members, and a Majority of each shall constitute a Quorum to do Business; but a smaller Number may adjourn from day to day, and may be authorized to compel the Attendance of absent Members, in such Manner, and under such Penalties as each House may provide.

---

[1]Modified by Sixteenth Amendment.
[2]Modified by Fourteenth Amendment.
[3]Temporary provision.
[4]Modified by Seventeenth Amendment.
[5]Modified by Seventeenth Amendment.
[6]Modified by Twentieth Amendment.

Each House may determine the Rules of its Proceedings, punish its Members for disorderly Behaviour, and, with the Concurrence of two thirds, expel a Member.

Each House shall keep a Journal of its Proceedings, and from time to time publish the same, excepting such Parts as may in their Judgment require Secrecy; and the Yeas and Nays of the Members of either House on any questions shall, at the Desire of one fifth of those Present, be entered on the Journal.

Neither House, during the Session of Congress, shall, without the Consent of the other, adjourn for more than three days, nor to any other Place than that in which the two Houses shall be sitting.

SECTION 6
[COMPENSATION, PRIVILEGES, DISABILITIES]

The Senators and Representatives shall receive a Compensation for their Services, to be ascertained by Law, and paid out of the Treasury of the United States. They shall in all Cases, except Treason, Felony and Breach of the Peace, be privileged from Arrest during their Attendance at the Session of their respective Houses, and in going to and returning from the same; and for any Speech or Debate in either House, they shall not be questioned in any other Place.

No Senator or Representative shall, during the Time for which he was elected, be appointed to any civil Office under the Authority of the United States, which shall have been created, or the Emoluments whereof shall have been encreased during such time; and no Person holding any Office under the United States, shall be a Member of either House during his Continuance in Office.

SECTION 7
[PROCEDURE IN PASSING BILLS AND RESOLUTIONS]

All Bills for raising Revenue shall originate in the House of Representatives; but the Senate may propose or concur with Amendments as on other Bills.

Every Bill which shall have passed the House of Representatives and the Senate, shall, before it become a Law, be presented to the President of the United States: If he approve he shall sign it, but if not he shall return it, with his Objections to that House in which it shall have originated, who shall enter the Objections at large on their Journal, and proceed to reconsider it. If after such Reconsideration two thirds of that House shall agree to pass the Bill, it shall be sent, together with the Objections, to the other House, by which it shall likewise be reconsidered, and if approved by two thirds of that House, it shall become a Law. But in all such Cases the Votes of both Houses shall be determined by yeas and Nays, and the Names of the Persons voting for and against the Bill shall be entered on the Journal of each House respectively. If any Bill shall not be returned by the President within ten Days (Sundays excepted) after it shall have been presented to him, the Same shall be a Law, in like Manner as if he had signed it, unless the Congress by their Adjournment prevent its Return, in which Case it shall not be a Law.

Every Order, Resolution, or Vote to which the Concurrence of the Senate and House of Representatives may be necessary (except on a question of Adjournment) shall be presented to the President of the United States; and before the Same shall take Effect, shall be approved by him, or being disapproved by him, shall be repassed by two thirds of the Senate and House of Representatives, according to the Rules and Limitations prescribed in the Case of a Bill.

SECTION 8
[POWERS OF CONGRESS]

The Congress shall have Power

To lay and collect Taxes, Duties, Imposts and Excises, to pay the Debts and provide for the common Defence and general Welfare of the United States; but all Duties, Imposts and Excises shall be uniform throughout the United States;

To borrow Money on the credit of the United States;

To regulate Commerce with foreign Nations, and among the several States, and with the Indian Tribes;

To establish an uniform Rule of Naturalization, and uniform Laws on the subject of Bankruptcies throughout the United States;

To coin Money, regulate the Value thereof, and of foreign Coin, and fix the Standard of Weights and Measures;

To provide for the Punishment of counterfeiting the Securities and current Coin of the United States;

To establish Post Offices and post Roads;

To promote the Progress of Science and useful Arts, by securing for limited Times to Authors and Inventors the exclusive Right to their respective Writings and Discoveries;

To constitute Tribunals inferior to the supreme Court;

To define and punish Piracies and Felonies committed on the high Seas, and Offences against the Law of Nations;

To declare War, grant Letters of Marque and Reprisal, and make Rules concerning Captures on Land and Water;

To raise and support Armies, but no Appropriation of Money to that Use shall be for a longer Term than two Years;

To provide and maintain a Navy;

To make Rules for the Government and Regulation of the land and naval Forces;

To provide for calling forth the Militia to execute the Laws of the Union, suppress Insurrections and repel Invasions;

To provide for organizing, arming, and disciplining, the Militia, and for governing such Part of them as may be employed in the Service of the United States, reserving to the States respectively, the Appointment of the Officers, and the Authority of training the Militia according to the discipline prescribed by Congress;

To exercise exclusive Legislation in all Cases whatsoever, over such District (not exceeding ten Miles square) as may, by Cession of particular States, and the Acceptance of Congress, become the Seat of the Government of the United States, and to exercise like Authority over all Places purchased by the Consent of the Legislature of the State in which the Same shall be, for the Erection of Forts, Magazines, Arsenals, dock-Yards, and other needful Buildings;—And

To make all Laws which shall be necessary and proper for carrying into Execution the foregoing Powers, and all other Powers vested by this Constitution in the Government of the United States, or in any Department or Officer thereof.

SECTION 9
[SOME RESTRICTIONS ON FEDERAL POWER]

The Migration or Importation of such Persons as any of the States now existing shall think proper to admit, shall not be prohibited by the Congress prior to the Year one thousand eight hundred and eight, but a Tax or duty may be imposed on such Importation, not exceeding ten dollars for each Person.[7]

The Privilege of the Writ of Habeas Corpus shall not be suspended, unless when in Cases of Rebellion or Invasion the public Safety may require it.

No Bill of Attainder or ex post facto Law shall be passed.

No Capitation, or other direct, Tax shall be laid, unless in Proportion to the Census or Enumeration herein before directed to be taken.[8]

No Tax or Duty shall be laid on Articles exported from any State.

---

[7]Temporary provision.
[8]Modified by Sixteenth Amendment.

No Preference shall be given by any Regulation of Commerce or Revenue to the Ports of one State over those of another; nor shall Vessels bound to, or from, one State, be obliged to enter, clear, or pay Duties in another.

No Money shall be drawn from the Treasury, but in Consequence of Appropriations made by Law; and a regular Statement and Account of the Receipts and Expenditures of all public Money shall be published from time to time.

No Title of Nobility shall be granted by the United States: And no Person holding any Office of Profit or Trust under them, shall, without the Consent of the Congress, accept of any present, Emolument, Office, or Title, of any kind whatever, from any King, Prince, or foreign State.

SECTION 10
[RESTRICTIONS UPON POWERS OF STATES]

No State shall enter into any Treaty, Alliance, or Confederation; grant Letters of Marque and Reprisal; coin Money; emit Bills of Credit; make any Thing but gold and silver Coin a Tender in Payment of Debts; pass any Bill of Attainder, ex post facto Law, or Law impairing the Obligation of Contracts, or grant any Title of Nobility.

No State shall, without the Consent of the Congress, lay any Imposts or Duties on Imports or Exports, except what may be absolutely necessary for executing its inspection Laws: and the net Produce of all Duties and Imposts, laid by any State on Imports or Exports, shall be for the Use of the Treasury of the United States; and all such Laws shall be subject to the Revision and Control of the Congress.

No State shall, without the Consent of Congress, lay any Duty of Tonnage, keep Troops, or Ships of War in time of Peace, enter into any Agreement or Compact with another State, or with a foreign Power, or engage in War, unless actually invaded, or in such imminent Danger as will not admit of delay.

Article II

SECTION 1
[EXECUTIVE POWER, ELECTION, QUALIFICATIONS OF THE PRESIDENT]

The executive Power shall be vested in a President of the United States of America. *He shall hold his Office during the Term of four Years, and, together with the Vice President, chosen for the same Term, be elected, as follows*[9]

Each State shall appoint, in such Manner as the Legislature thereof may direct, a Number of Electors, equal to the whole Number of Senators and Representatives to which the State may be entitled in the Congress: but no Senator or Representative, or Person holding an Office of Trust or Profit under the United States, shall be appointed an Elector.

The electors shall meet in their respective States, and vote by ballot for two Persons, of whom one at least shall not be an Inhabitant of the same State with themselves. And they shall make a List of all the Persons voted for, and of the Number of Votes for each; which List they shall sign and certify, and transmit sealed to the Seat of the Government of the United States, directed to the President of the Senate. The President of the Senate shall, in the Presence of the Senate and House of Representatives, open all the Certificates, and the Votes shall then be counted. The Person having the greatest Number of Votes shall be the President, if such Number be a Majority of the whole Number of Electors appointed; and if there be more than one who have such Majority, and have an equal Number of Votes, then the House of Representatives shall immediately chuse by Ballot one of them for President; and if no Person have a Majority, then from the five highest on the List the said House shall in like Manner chuse the President. But in chusing the President, the Votes shall be taken by States, the Representation from each State having one Vote; A quorum for this Purpose shall consist of a Member or Members from two thirds of the States, and a Majority of all the States shall be necessary to a Choice. In every Case, after the Choice of the President, the person having the greatest Number of Votes of the Electors shall be the Vice President. But if there should remain two or more who have equal Votes, the Senate shall chuse from them by Ballot the Vice President.[10]

The Congress may determine the Time of chusing the Electors, and the Day on which they shall give their Votes; which Day shall be the same throughout the United States.

No Person except a natural born Citizen, or a Citizen of the United States, at the time of the Adoption of this Constitution, shall be eligible to the Office of President; neither shall any Person be eligible to that Office who shall not have attained to the Age of thirty five Years, and been fourteen Years a Resident within the United States.

In Case of the Removal of the President from Office, or his Death, Resignation, or Inability to discharge the Powers and Duties of the said Office, the Same shall devolve on the Vice President, and the Congress may by Law provide for the Case of Removal, Death, Resignation or Inability, both of the President and Vice President, declaring what Officer shall then act as President, and such Officer shall act accordingly, until the Disability be removed, or a President shall be elected.

The President shall, at stated Times, receive for his Services, a Compensation, which shall neither be increased nor diminished during the Period for which he shall have been elected, and he shall not receive within that Period any other Emolument from the United States, or any of them.

Before he enter on the Execution of his Office, he shall take the following Oath or Affirmation:—"I do solemnly swear (or affirm) that I will faithfully execute the Office of President of the United States, and will to the best of my Ability, preserve, protect and defend the Constitution of the United States."

SECTION 2
[POWERS OF THE PRESIDENT]

The President shall be Commander in Chief of the Army and Navy of the United States, and of the Militia of the several States, when called into the actual Service of the United States; he may require the Opinion, in writing, of the principal Officer in each of the executive Departments, upon any Subject relating to the Duties of their respective Offices, and he shall have Power to grant Reprieves and Pardons for Offences against the United States, except in Cases of Impeachment.

He shall have Power, by and with the Advice and Consent of the Senate, to make Treaties, provided two thirds of the Senators present concur; and he shall nominate, and by and with the Advice and Consent of the Senate, shall appoint Ambassadors, other public Ministers and Consuls, Judges of the supreme Court, and all other Officers of the United States, whose Appointments are not herein otherwise provided for, and which shall be established by Law: but the Congress may by Law vest the Appointment of such inferior Officers, as they think proper, in the President alone, in the Courts of Law, or in the Heads of Departments.

The President shall have Power to fill up all Vacancies that may happen during the Recess of the Senate, by granting Commissions which shall expire at the End of their next Session.

SECTION 3
[POWERS AND DUTIES OF THE PRESIDENT]

He shall from time to time give to the Congress Information of the State of the Union, and recommend to their Consideration such Measures as he shall judge necessary and expedient; he may, on extraordinary Occasions, convene both Houses, or either of them, and in Case of Disagreement between them, with Respect to the Time of Adjournment, he may adjourn them to such Time as he shall think proper; he shall receive Ambassadors and other public Ministers; he shall take Care that the Laws be

---

[9]Number of terms limited to two by Twenty-second Amendment.
[10]Modified by the Twelfth and Twentieth Amendments.

faithfully executed, and shall Commission all the Officers of the United States.

SECTION 4
[IMPEACHMENT]

The President, Vice President and all civil Officers of the United States, shall be removed from Office on Impeachment for, and Conviction of, Treason, Bribery, or other high Crimes and Misdemeanors.

Article III

SECTION 1
[JUDICIAL POWER, TENURE OF OFFICE]

The judicial Power of the United States, shall be vested in one supreme Court, and in such inferior Courts as the Congress may from time to time ordain and establish. The Judges, both of the supreme and inferior Courts, shall hold their Offices during good Behaviour, and shall, at stated Times, receive for their Services, a Compensation, which shall not be diminished during their Continuance in Office.

SECTION 2
[JURISDICTION]

The judicial Power shall extend to all Cases, in Law and Equity, arising under this Constitution, the Laws of the United States, and Treaties made, or which shall be made, under their Authority;—to all Cases affecting Ambassadors, other public Ministers and Consuls;—to all Cases of admiralty and maritime Jurisdiction;—to Controversies to which the United States shall be a Party;—to Controversies between two or more States;—*between a State and Citizens of another State;*—between Citizens of different States,—between Citizens of the same State claiming Lands under Grants of different States, *and between a State,* or the Citizens thereof, *and foreign States, Citizens or Subjects.*[11]

In all Cases affecting Ambassadors, other public Ministers and Consuls, and those in which a State shall be Party, the supreme Court shall have original Jurisdiction. In all the other Cases before mentioned, the supreme Court shall have appellate Jurisdiction, both as to Law and Fact, with such Exceptions, and under such Regulations as the Congress shall make.

The Trial of all Crimes, except in Cases of Impeachment, shall be by Jury; and such Trial shall be held in the State where the said Crimes shall have been committed; but when not committed within any State, the Trial shall be at such Place or Places as the Congress may by Law have directed.

SECTION 3
[TREASON, PROOF, AND PUNISHMENT]

Treason against the United States, shall consist only in levying War against them, or in adhering to their Enemies, giving them Aid and Comfort. No Person shall be convicted of Treason unless on the Testimony of two Witnesses to the same overt Act, or on Confession in open Court.

The Congress shall have Power to declare the Punishment of Treason, but no Attainder of Treason shall work Corruption of Blood, or Forfeiture except during the Life of the Person attainted.

Article IV

SECTION 1
[FAITH AND CREDIT AMONG STATES]

Full Faith and Credit shall be given in each State to the public Acts, Records, and judicial Proceedings of every other State. And the Congress may by general Laws prescribe the Manner in which such Acts, Records and Proceedings shall be proved, and the Effect thereof.

SECTION 2
[PRIVILEGES AND IMMUNITIES, FUGITIVES]

The Citizens of each State shall be entitled to all Privileges and Immunities of Citizens in the several States.

A Person charged in any State with Treason, Felony or other Crime, who shall flee from Justice, and be found in another State, shall on Demand of the executive Authority of the State from which he fled, be delivered up, to be removed to the State having Jurisdiction of the Crime.

No person held to Service or Labour in one State, under the Laws thereof, escaping into another, shall, in Consequence of any Law or Regulation therein, be discharged from such Service or Labour, but shall be delivered up on Claim of the Party to whom such Service or Labour may be due.[12]

SECTION 3
[ADMISSION OF NEW STATES]

New States may be admitted by the Congress into this Union; but no new State shall be formed or erected within the Jurisdiction of any other State; nor any State be formed by the Junction of two or more States, or Parts of States, without the Consent of the Legislatures of the States concerned as well as of the Congress.

The Congress shall have Power to dispose of and make all needful Rules and Regulations respecting the Territory or other Property belonging to the United States; and nothing in this Constitution shall be so construed as to Prejudice any Claims of the United States, or of any particular State.

SECTION 4
[GUARANTEE OF REPUBLICAN GOVERNMENT]

The United States shall guarantee to every State in this Union a Republican Form of Government, and shall protect each of them against Invasion; and on Application of the Legislature, or of the Executive (when the Legislature cannot be convened), against domestic Violence.

Article V
[AMENDMENT OF THE CONSTITUTION]

The Congress, whenever two thirds of both Houses shall deem it necessary, shall propose Amendments to this Constitution, or, on the Application of the Legislatures of two thirds of the several States, shall call a Convention for proposing Amendments, which, in either Case, shall be valid to all Intents and Purposes, as Part of this Constitution, when ratified by the Legislatures of three fourths of the several States, or by Conventions in three fourths thereof, as the one or the other Mode of Ratification may be proposed by the Congress; *Provided that no Amendment which may be made prior to the Year One thousand eight hundred and eight shall in any Manner affect the first and fourth Clauses in the Ninth Section of the first Article;*[13] and that no State, without its Consent, shall be deprived of its equal Suffrage in the Senate.

Article VI
[DEBTS, SUPREMACY, OATH]

All Debts contracted and Engagements entered into, before the Adoption of this Constitution, shall be as valid against the United States under this Constitution, as under the Confederation.

---

[11]Modified by the Eleventh Amendment.
[12]Repealed by the Thirteenth Amendment.

This Constitution, and the Laws of the United States which shall be made in Pursuance thereof; and all Treaties made, or which shall be made, under the Authority of the United States, shall be the supreme Law of the Land; and the Judges in every State shall be bound thereby, any Thing in the Constitution or Laws of any State to the Contrary notwithstanding.

The Senators and Representatives before mentioned, and the Members of the several State Legislatures, and all executive and judicial Officers, both of the United States and of the several States, shall be bound by Oath or Affirmation, to support this Constitution; but no religious Test shall be required as a Qualification to any Office or public Trust under the United States.

Article VII
[RATIFICATION AND ESTABLISHMENT]

The Ratification of the Conventions of nine States, shall be sufficient for the Establishment of this Constitution between the States so ratifying the Same.[14]

Done in Convention by the Unanimous Consent of the States present the Seventeenth Day of September in the Year of our Lord one thousand seven hundred and Eighty seven and of the Independence of the United States of America the Twelfth. *In Witness* whereof We have hereunto subscribed our Names,

G:⁰ WASHINGTON—
Presidt. and deputy from Virginia

NEW HAMPSHIRE
John Langdon
Nicholas Gilman

MASSACHUSETTS
Nathaniel Gorham
Rufus King

CONNECTICUT
Wm. Saml. Johnson
Roger Sherman

NEW YORK
Alexander Hamilton

NEW JERSEY
Wil: Livingston
David Brearley
Wm. Paterson
Jona: Dayton

PENNSYLVANIA
B Franklin
Thomas Mifflin
Robt. Morris
Geo. Clymer
Thos. FitzSimons
Jared Ingersoll
James Wilson
Gouv Morris

DELAWARE
Geo: Read
Gunning Bedford jun
John Dickinson
Richard Bassett
Jaco: Broom

MARYLAND
James McHenry
Dan of St Thos. Jenifer
Danl. Carroll

VIRGINIA
John Blair—
James Madison Jr.

NORTH CAROLINA
Wm. Blount
Richd. Dobbs Spaight
Hu Williamson

SOUTH CAROLINA
J. Rutledge
Charles Cotesworth Pinckney
Charles Pinckney
Pierce Butler

GEORGIA
William Few
Abr Baldwin

Amendments to the Constitution

*Proposed by Congress and Ratified by the Legislatures of the
Several States, Pursuant to Article V of the Original Constitution.*

Amendments I–X, known as the Bill of Rights, were proposed by Congress on September 25, 1789, and ratified on December 15, 1791.

Amendment I
[FREEDOM OF RELIGION, OF SPEECH, AND OF THE PRESS]

Congress shall make no law respecting an establishment of religion, or prohibiting the free exercise thereof; or abridging the freedom of speech, or of the press; or the right of the people peaceably to assemble, and to petition the Government for a redress of grievances.

Amendment II
[RIGHT TO KEEP AND BEAR ARMS]

A well regulated Militia, being necessary to the security of a free State, the right of the people to keep and bear Arms, shall not be infringed.

Amendment III
[QUARTERING OF SOLDIERS]

No Soldier shall, in time of peace be quartered in any house, without the consent of the Owner, nor in time of war, but in a manner to be prescribed by law.

Amendment IV
[SECURITY FROM UNWARRANTABLE SEARCH AND SEIZURE]

The right of the people to be secure in their persons, houses, papers, and effects, against unreasonable searches and seizures, shall not be violated, and no Warrants shall issue, but upon probable cause, supported by Oath or affirmation, and particularly describing the place to be searched, and the persons or things to be seized.

Amendment V
[RIGHTS OF ACCUSED PERSONS IN CRIMINAL PROCEEDINGS]

No person shall be held to answer for a capital, or otherwise infamous crime, unless on a presentment or indictment of a Grand Jury, except in cases arising in the land or naval forces, or in the Militia, when in actual service in time of War or in public danger; nor shall any person be subject for the same offence to be twice put in jeopardy of life or limb; nor shall be compelled in any criminal case to be a witness against himself, nor be deprived of life, liberty, or property, without due process of law; nor shall private property be taken for public use, without just compensation.

Amendment VI
[RIGHT TO SPEEDY TRIAL, WITNESSES, ETC.]

In all criminal prosecutions, the accused shall enjoy the right to a speedy and public trial, by an impartial jury of the State and district wherein the crime shall have been committed, which district shall have been previously ascertained by law, and to be informed of the nature and cause of the accusation; to be confronted with the witnesses against him; to have compulsory process for obtaining witnesses in his favor, and to have the Assistance of Counsel for his defence.

Amendment VII
[TRIAL BY JURY IN CIVIL CASES]

In suits at common law, where the value in controversy shall exceed twenty dollars, the right of trial by jury shall be preserved, and no fact tried by a jury, shall be otherwise reexamined in any Court of the United States, than according to the rules of the common law.

Amendment VIII
[BAILS, FINES, PUNISHMENTS]

Excessive bail shall not be required, nor excessive fines imposed, nor cruel and unusual punishments inflicted.

Amendment IX
[RESERVATION OF RIGHTS OF PEOPLE]

The enumeration in the Constitution, of certain rights, shall not be construed to deny or disparage others retained by the people.

Amendment X
[POWERS RESERVED TO STATES OR PEOPLE]

The powers not delegated to the United States by the Constitution, nor prohibited by it to the States, are reserved to the States respectively, or to the people.

Amendment XI
[*Proposed by Congress on March 4, 1794; declared ratified on January 8, 1798.*]
[RESTRICTION OF JUDICIAL POWER]

The Judicial power of the United States shall not be construed to extend to any suit in law or equity, commenced or prosecuted against one of the United States by Citizens of another State, or by Citizens or Subjects of any Foreign State.

Amendment XII
[*Proposed by Congress on December 9, 1803; declared ratified on September 25, 1804.*]
[ELECTION OF PRESIDENT AND VICE PRESIDENT]

The Electors shall meet in their respective states and vote by ballot for President and Vice-President, one of whom, at least, shall not be an inhabitant of the same state with themselves; they shall name in their ballots the person voted for as President, and in distinct ballots the person voted for as Vice-President, and they shall make distinct lists of all persons voted for as President, and of all persons voted for as Vice-President, and of the number of votes for each, which lists they shall sign and certify, and transmit sealed to the seat of the government of the United States, directed to the President of the Senate;—the President of the Senate shall, in presence of the Senate and House of Representatives, open all the certificates and the votes shall then be counted;—The person having the greatest number of votes for President, shall be the President, if such number be a majority of the whole number of Electors appointed; and if no person have such majority, then from the persons having the highest numbers not exceeding three on the list of those voted for as President, the House of Representatives shall choose immediately, by ballot, the President. But in choosing the President, the votes shall be taken by states, the representation from each state having one vote; a quorum for this purpose shall consist of a member or members from two-thirds of the states, and a majority of all the states shall be necessary to a choice. And if the House of Representatives shall not choose a President whenever the right of choice shall devolve upon them, before the fourth day of March next following, then the Vice-President shall act as President, as in the case of the death or other constitutional disability of the President.—The person having the greatest number of votes as Vice-President, shall be the Vice-President, if such number be a majority of the whole number of Electors appointed, and if no person have a majority, then from the two highest numbers on the list, the Senate shall choose the Vice-President; a quorum for the purpose shall consist of two-thirds of the whole number of Senators, and a majority of the whole number shall be necessary to a choice. But no person constitutionally ineligible to the office of President shall be eligible to that of Vice-President of the United States.

Amendment XIII

[Proposed by Congress on January 31, 1865; declared ratified on December 18, 1865.]

SECTION 1

[ABOLITION OF SLAVERY]

Neither slavery nor involuntary servitude, except as a punishment for crime whereof the party shall have been duly convicted, shall exist within the United States, or any place subject to their jurisdiction.

SECTION 2

[POWER TO ENFORCE THIS ARTICLE]

Congress shall have power to enforce this article by appropriate legislation.

Amendment XIV

[Proposed by Congress on June 13, 1866; declared ratified on July 28, 1868.]

SECTION 1

[CITIZENSHIP RIGHTS NOT TO BE ABRIDGED BY STATES]

All persons born or naturalized in the United States, and subject to the jurisdiction thereof, are citizens of the United States and of the State wherein they reside. No State shall make or enforce any law which shall abridge the privileges or immunities of citizens of the United States; nor shall any State deprive any person of life, liberty, or property, without due process of law; nor deny to any person within its jurisdiction the equal protection of the laws.

SECTION 2

[APPORTIONMENT OF REPRESENTATIVES IN CONGRESS]

Representatives shall be apportioned among the several States according to their respective numbers, counting the whole number of persons in each State, excluding Indians not taxed. But when the right to vote at any election for the choice of electors for President and Vice-President of the United States, Representatives in Congress, the Executive and Judicial officers of a State, or the members of the Legislature thereof, is denied to any of the male inhabitants of such State, being twenty-one years of age, and citizens of the United States, or in any way abridged, except for participation in rebellion, or other crime, the basis of representation therein shall be reduced in the proportion which the number of such male citizens shall bear to the whole number of male citizens twenty-one years of age in such State.

SECTION 3

[PERSONS DISQUALIFIED FROM HOLDING OFFICE]

No person shall be a Senator or Representative in Congress, or elector of President and Vice-President, or hold any office, civil or military, under the United States, or under any State, who, having previously taken an oath, as a member of Congress, or as an officer of the United States, or as a member of any State legislature, or as an executive or judicial officer of any State, to support the Constitution of the United States, shall have engaged in insurrection or rebellion against the same, or given aid or comfort to the enemies thereof. But Congress may by a vote of two-thirds of each House, remove such disability.

SECTION 4

[WHAT PUBLIC DEBTS ARE VALID]

The validity of the public debt of the United States, authorized by law, including debts incurred for payment of pensions and bounties for services in suppressing insurrection or rebellion, shall not be questioned. But neither the United States nor any State shall assume or pay any debt or obligation incurred in aid of insurrection or rebellion against the United States, or any claim for the loss or emancipation of any slave; but all such debts, obligations and claims shall be held illegal and void.

SECTION 5

[POWER TO ENFORCE THIS ARTICLE]

The Congress shall have power to enforce, by appropriate legislation, the provisions of this article.

Amendment XV

[Proposed by Congress on February 26, 1869; declared ratified on March 30, 1870.]

SECTION 1

[NEGRO SUFFRAGE]

The right of citizens of the United States to vote shall not be denied or abridged by the United States or by any State on account of race, color, or previous condition of servitude.

SECTION 2

[POWER TO ENFORCE THIS ARTICLE]

The Congress shall have power to enforce this article by appropriate legislation.

Amendment XVI

[Proposed by Congress on July 2, 1909; declared ratified on February 25, 1913.]
[AUTHORIZING INCOME TAXES]

The Congress shall have power to lay and collect taxes on incomes, from whatever source derived, without apportionment among the several States, and without regard to any census or enumeration.

Amendment XVII

[Proposed by Congress on May 13, 1912; declared ratified on May 31, 1913.]
[POPULAR ELECTION OF SENATORS]

The Senate of the United States shall be composed of two Senators from each State, elected by the people thereof, for six years; and each Senator shall have one vote. The electors in each State shall have the qualifications requisite for electors of the most numerous branch of the State legislatures.

When vacancies happen in the representation of any State in the Senate, the executive authority of such State shall issue writs of election to fill such vacancies: *Provided,* That the legislature of any State may empower the executive thereof to make temporary appointments until the people fill the vacancies by election as the legislature may direct.

This amendment shall not be so construed as to affect the election or term of any Senator chosen before it becomes valid as part of the Constitution.

Amendment XVIII

[*Proposed by Congress December 18, 1917; declared ratified on January 29, 1919.*]

SECTION 1

[NATIONAL LIQUOR PROHIBITION]

After one year from the ratification of this article the manufacture, sale, or transportation of intoxicating liquors within, the importation thereof into, or the exportation thereof from the United States and all territory subject to the jurisdiction thereof for beverage purposes is hereby prohibited.

SECTION 2

[POWER TO ENFORCE THIS ARTICLE]

The Congress and the several States shall have concurrent power to enforce this article by appropriate legislation.

SECTION 3

[RATIFICATION WITHIN SEVEN YEARS]

This article shall be inoperative unless it shall have been ratified as an amendment to the Constitution by the legislatures of the several States, as provided in the Constitution, within seven years from the date of the submission hereof to the States by the Congress.[1]

Amendment XIX

[*Proposed by Congress on June 4, 1919; declared ratified on August 26, 1920.*]
[WOMAN SUFFRAGE]

The right of citizens of the United States to vote shall not be denied or abridged by the United States or by any State on account of sex.

Congress shall have power to enforce this article by appropriate legislation.

Amendment XX

[*Proposed by Congress on March 2, 1932; declared ratified on February 6, 1933.*]

SECTION 1

[TERMS OF OFFICE]

The terms of the President and Vice President shall end at noon on the 20th day of January, and the terms of Senators and Representatives at noon on the 3d day of January, of the years in which such terms would have ended if this article had not been ratified; and the terms of their successors shall then begin.

SECTION 2

[TIME OF CONVENING CONGRESS]

The Congress shall assemble at least once in every year, and such meeting shall begin at noon on the 3d day of January, unless they shall by law appoint a different day.

SECTION 3

[DEATH OF PRESIDENT-ELECT]

If, at the time fixed for the beginning of the term of the President, the President elect shall have died, the Vice President elect shall become President. If a President shall not have been chosen before the time fixed for the beginning of his term, or if the President elect shall have failed to qualify, then the Vice President elect shall act as President until a President shall have qualified; and the Congress may by law provide for the case wherein neither a President elect nor a Vice President elect shall have qualified, declaring who shall then act as President, or the manner in which one who is to act shall be selected, and such person shall act accordingly until a President or Vice President shall have qualified.

SECTION 4

[ELECTION OF THE PRESIDENT]

The Congress may by law provide for the case of the death of any of the persons from whom the House of Representatives may choose a President whenever the right of choice shall have devolved upon them, and for the case of the death of any of the persons from whom the Senate may choose a Vice President whenever the right of choice shall have devolved upon them.

SECTION 5

[AMENDMENT TAKES EFFECT]

Sections 1 and 2 shall take effect on the 15th day of October following the ratification of this article.

SECTION 6

[RATIFICATION WITHIN SEVEN YEARS]

This article shall be inoperative unless it shall have been ratified as an amendment to the Constitution by the legislatures of three-fourths of the several States within seven years from the date of its submission.

Amendment XXI

[*Proposed by Congress on February 20, 1933; declared ratified on December 5, 1933.*]

SECTION 1

[NATIONAL LIQUOR PROHIBITION REPEALED]

The eighteenth article of amendment to the Constitution of the United States is hereby repealed.

SECTION 2

[TRANSPORTATION OF LIQUOR INTO "DRY" STATES]

The transportation or importation into any State, Territory, or Possession of the United States for delivery or use therein of intoxicating liquors, in violation of the laws thereof, is hereby prohibited.

SECTION 3

[RATIFICATION WITHIN SEVEN YEARS]

This article shall be inoperative unless it shall have been ratified as an amendment to the Constitution by conventions in the several States, as provided in the Constitution, within seven years from the date of the submission hereof to the States by the Congress.

---

[1]Repealed by the Twenty-first Amendment.

Amendment XXII

[*Proposed by Congress on March 21, 1947; declared ratified on February 27, 1951.*]

SECTION 1

[TENURE OF PRESIDENT LIMITED]

No person shall be elected to the office of President more than twice, and no person who has held the office of President or acted as President, for more than two years of a term to which some other person was elected President shall be elected to the office of the President more than once. But this Article shall not apply to any person holding the office of President when this Article was proposed by the Congress, and shall not prevent any person who may be holding the office of President, or acting as President, during the term within which this Article becomes operative from holding the office of President or acting as President during the remainder of such term.

SECTION 2

[RATIFICATION WITHIN SEVEN YEARS]

This article shall be inoperative unless it shall have been ratified as an amendment to the Constitution by the legislatures of three-fourths of the several States within seven years from the date of its submission to the States by the Congress.

Amendment XXIII

[*Proposed by Congress on June 16, 1960; declared ratified on March 29, 1961.*]

SECTION 1

[ELECTORAL COLLEGE VOTES FOR THE DISTRICT OF COLUMBIA]

The District constituting the seat of Government of the United States shall appoint in such manner as the Congress may direct:

A number of electors of President and Vice President equal to the whole number of Senators and Representatives in Congress to which the District would be entitled if it were a State, but in no event more than the least populous State; they shall be in addition to those appointed by the States, but they shall be considered, for the purposes of the election of President and Vice President, to be electors appointed by a State; and they shall meet in the District and perform such duties as provided by the twelfth article of amendment.

SECTION 2

[POWER TO ENFORCE THIS ARTICLE]

The Congress shall have power to enforce this article by appropriate legislation.

Amendment XXIV

[*Proposed by Congress on August 27, 1962; declared ratified on January 23, 1964.*]

SECTION 1

[ANTI-POLL TAX]

The right of citizens of the United States to vote in any primary or other election for President or Vice President, for electors for President or Vice President, or for Senator or Representative of Congress, shall not be denied or abridged by the United States or any State by reason of failure to pay any poll tax or other tax.

SECTION 2

[POWER TO ENFORCE THIS ARTICLE]

The Congress shall have power to enforce this article by appropriate legislation.

Amendment XXV

[*Proposed by Congress on July 6, 1965; declared ratified on February 10, 1967.*]

SECTION 1

[VICE PRESIDENT TO BECOME PRESIDENT]

In case of the removal of the President from office or his death or resignation, the Vice President shall become President.

SECTION 2

[CHOICE OF A NEW VICE PRESIDENT]

Whenever there is a vacancy in the office of the Vice President, the President shall nominate a Vice President who shall take the office upon confirmation by a majority vote of both houses of Congress.

SECTION 3

[PRESIDENT MAY DECLARE OWN DISABILITY]

Whenever the President transmits to the President pro tempore of the Senate and the Speaker of the House of Representatives his written declaration that he is unable to discharge the powers and duties of his office, and until he transmits to them a written declaration to the contrary, such powers and duties shall be discharged by the Vice President as Acting President.

SECTION 4

[ALTERNATE PROCEDURES TO DECLARE AND TO END PRESIDENTIAL DISABILITY]

Whenever the Vice President and a majority of either the principal officers of the executive departments, or of such other body as Congress may by law provide, transmit to the President pro tempore of the Senate and the Speaker of the House of Representatives their written declaration that the President is unable to discharge the powers and duties of his office, the Vice President shall immediately assume the powers and duties of the office as Acting President.

Thereafter, when the President transmits to the President pro tempore of the Senate and the Speaker of the House of Representatives his written declaration that no inability exists, he shall resume the powers and duties of his office unless the Vice President and a majority of either the principal officers of the executive department, or of such other body as Congress may by law provide, transmit within four days to the President pro tempore of the Senate and the Speaker of the House of Representatives their written declaration that the President is unable to discharge the powers and duties of his office. Thereupon Congress shall decide the issue, assembling within forty eight hours for that purpose if not in session. If the Congress, within twenty one days after receipt of the latter written declaration, or, if Congress is not in session, within twenty one days after Congress is required to assemble, determines by two-thirds vote of both Houses that the President is unable to discharge the powers and duties of his office, the Vice President shall continue to discharge the same as Acting President; otherwise, the President shall resume the powers and duties of his office.

Amendment XXVI

[*Proposed by Congress on March 23, 1971; declared ratified on July 1, 1971.*]

SECTION 1

[EIGHTEEN-YEAR-OLD VOTE]

The right of citizens of the United States, who are eighteen years of age or older, to vote shall not be denied or abridged by the United States or by any State on account of age.

SECTION 2

[POWER TO ENFORCE THIS ARTICLE]

The Congress shall have power to enforce this article by appropriate legislation.

Amendment XXVII

[*Proposed by Congress on September 25, 1789; declared ratified on May 8, 1992.*]

[CONGRESS CANNOT RAISE ITS OWN PAY]

No law varying the compensation for the services of the Senators and Representatives, shall take effect, until an election of representatives shall have intervened.

The Federalist Papers

No. 10: Madison

Among the numerous advantages promised by a well constructed Union, none deserves to be more accurately developed than its tendency to break and control the violence of faction. The friend of popular governments never finds himself so much alarmed for their character and fate, as when he contemplates their propensity to this dangerous vice. He will not fail therefore to set a due value on any plan which, without violating the principles to which he is attached, provides a proper cure for it. The instability, injustice, and confusion introduced into the public councils have, in truth, been the mortal diseases under which popular governments have everywhere perished, as they continue to be the favorite and fruitful topics from which the adversaries to liberty derive their most specious declamations. The valuable improvements made by the American constitutions on the popular models, both ancient and modern, cannot certainly be too much admired; but it would be an unwarrantable partiality to contend that they have as effectually obviated the danger on this side, as was wished and expected. Complaints are everywhere heard from our most considerate and virtuous citizens, equally the friends of public and private faith and of public and personal liberty, that our governments are too unstable, that the public good is disregarded in the conflicts of rival parties, and that measures are too often decided, not according to the rules of justice and the rights of the minor party, but by the superior force of an interested and overbearing majority. However anxiously we may wish that these complaints had no foundation, the evidence of known facts will not permit us to deny that they are in some degree true. It will be found, indeed, on a candid review of our situation, that some of the distresses under which we labor have been erroneously charged on the operation of our governments; but it will be found, at the same time, that other causes will not alone account for many of our heaviest misfortunes; and, particularly, for that prevailing and increasing distrust of public engagements and alarm for private rights which are echoed from one end of the continent to the other. These must be chiefly, if not wholly, effects of the unsteadiness and injustice with which a factious spirit has tainted our public administration.

By a faction I understand a number of citizens, whether amounting to a majority or minority of the whole, who are united and actuated by some common impulse of passion, or of interest, adverse to the rights of other citizens, or to the permanent and aggregate interests of the community.

There are two methods of curing the mischiefs of faction: the one, by removing its causes; the other, by controlling its effects.

There are again two methods of removing the causes of faction: the one, by destroying the liberty which is essential to its existence; the other, by giving to every citizen the same opinions, the same passions, and the same interests.

It could never be more truly said than of the first remedy, that it is worse than the disease. Liberty is to faction what air is to fire, an aliment without which it instantly expires. But it could not be a less folly to abolish liberty, which is essential to political life, because it nourishes faction, than it would be to wish the annihilation of air, which is essential to animal life, because it imparts to fire its destructive agency.

The second expedient is as impracticable, as the first would be unwise. As long as the reason of man continues fallible, and he is at liberty to exercise it, different opinions will be formed. As long as the connection subsists between his reason and his self-love, his opinions and his passions will have a reciprocal influence on each other; and the former will be objects to which the latter will attach themselves. The diversity in the faculties of men, from which the rights of property originate, is not less an insuperable obstacle to a uniformity of interests. The protection of these faculties is the first object of Government. From the protection of different and unequal faculties of acquiring property, the possession of different degrees and kinds of property immediately results; and from the influence of these on the sentiments and views of the respective proprietors, ensues a division of the society into different interests and parties.

The latent causes of faction are thus sown in the nature of man; and we see them everywhere brought into different degrees of activity, according to the different circumstances of civil society. A zeal for different opinions concerning religion, concerning Government, and many other points, as well of speculation as of practice; an attachment to different leaders ambitiously contending for pre-eminence and power; or to persons of other descriptions whose fortunes have been interesting to the human passions, have in turn divided mankind into parties, inflamed them with mutual animosity, and rendered them much more disposed to vex and oppress each other, than to co-operate for their common good. So strong is this propensity of mankind to fall into mutual animosities, that where no substantial occasion presents itself, the most frivolous and fanciful distinctions have been sufficient to kindle their unfriendly passions, and excite their most violent conflicts. But the most common and durable source of factions has been the various and unequal distribution of property. Those who hold and those who are without property have ever formed distinct interests in society. Those who are creditors, and those who are debtors, fall under a like discrimination. A landed interest, a manufacturing interest, a mercantile interest, a moneyed interest, with many lesser interests, grow up of necessity in civilized nations, and divide them into different classes, actuated by different sentiments and views. The regulation of these various and interfering interests forms the principal task of modern Legislation, and involves the spirit of party and faction in the necessary and ordinary operations of Government.

No man is allowed to be judge in his own cause, because his interest would certainly bias his judgment and, not improbably, corrupt his integrity. With equal, nay with greater reason, a body of men are unfit to be both judges and parties at the same time; yet what are many of the most important acts of legislation but so many judicial determinations, not indeed concerning the rights of single persons, but concerning the rights of large bodies of citizens; and what are the different classes of legislators but advocates and parties to the causes which they determine? Is a law proposed concerning private debts? It is a question to which the creditors are parties on one side and the debtors on the other. Justice ought to hold the balance between them. Yet the parties are, and must be, themselves the judges; and the most numerous party, or in other words, the most powerful faction must be expected to prevail. Shall domestic manufacturers be encouraged, and in what degree, by restrictions on foreign manufacturers? are questions which would be differently decided by the landed and the manufacturing classes, and probably by neither with a sole regard to justice and the public good. The apportionment of taxes on the various descriptions of property is an act which seems to require the most exact impartiality; yet there is, perhaps, no legislative act in which greater opportunity and temptation are given to a predominant party to trample on the rules of justice. Every shilling with which they overburden the inferior number is a shilling saved to their own pockets.

It is in vain to say that enlightened statesmen will be able to adjust these clashing interests and render them all subservient to the public good. Enlightened statesmen will not always be at the helm. Nor, in many cases, can such an adjustment be made at all without taking into view indirect and remote considerations, which will rarely prevail over the immediate interest which one party may find in disregarding the rights of another or the good of the whole.

The inference to which we are brought is that the *causes* of faction cannot be removed and that relief is only to be sought in the means of controlling its *effects*.

If a faction consists of less than a majority, relief is supplied by the republican principle, which enables the majority to defeat its sinister views by regular vote. It may clog the administration, it may convulse the society; but it will be unable to execute and mask its violence under the forms of the Constitution. When a majority is included in a faction, the form of popular government, on the other hand, enables it to sacrifice to its ruling passion or interest both the public good and the rights of other citizens. To secure the public good and private rights against the danger of such a faction, and at the same time to preserve the spirit and the form of popular government, is then the great object to which our enquiries are directed. Let me add that it is the great desideratum by which alone this form of government can be rescued from the opprobrium under which it has so long labored and be recommended to the esteem and adoption of mankind.

By what means is this object attainable? Evidently by one of two only. Either the existence of the same passion or interest in a majority at the same time must be prevented, or the majority, having such co-existent passion or interest, must be rendered, by their number and local situation, unable to concert and carry into effect schemes of oppression. If the impulse and the opportunity be suffered to coincide, we well know that neither moral nor religious motives can be relied on as an adequate control. They are not found to be such on the injustice and violence of individuals, and lose their efficacy in proportion to the number combined together, that is, in proportion as their efficacy becomes needful.

From this view of the subject it may be concluded that a pure Democracy, by which I mean a Society consisting of a small number of citizens, who assemble and administer the Government in person, can admit of no cure for the mischiefs of faction. A common passion or interest will, in almost every case, be felt by a majority of the whole; a communication and concert results from the form of Government itself; and there is nothing to check the inducements to sacrifice the weaker party or an obnoxious individual. Hence it is that such Democracies have ever been spectacles of turbulence and contention; have ever been found incompatible with personal security or the rights of property; and have in general been as short in their lives as they have been violent in their deaths. Theoretic politicians, who have patronized this species of Government, have erroneously supposed that by reducing mankind to a perfect equality in their political rights, they would at the same time be perfectly equalized and assimilated in their possessions, their opinions, and their passions.

A Republic, by which I mean a Government in which the scheme of representation takes place, opens a different prospect and promises the cure for which we are seeking. Let us examine the points in which it varies from pure Democracy, and we shall comprehend both the nature of the cure and the efficacy which it must derive from the Union.

The two great points of difference between a Democracy and a Republic are: first, the delegation of the Government, in the latter, to a small number of citizens elected by the rest; secondly, the greater number of citizens and greater sphere of country over which the latter may be extended.

The effect of the first difference is, on the one hand, to refine and enlarge the public views by passing them through the medium of a chosen body of citizens, whose wisdom may best discern the true interest of their country and whose patriotism and love of justice will be least likely to sacrifice it to temporary or partial considerations. Under such a regulation it may well happen that the public voice, pronounced by the representatives of the people, will be more consonant to the public good than if pronounced by the people themselves, convened for the purpose. On the other hand, the effect may be inverted. Men of factious tempers, of local prejudices, or of sinister designs, may, by intrigue, by corruption, or by other means, first obtain the suffrages, and then betray the interests of the people. The question resulting is, whether small or extensive Republics are most favorable to the election of proper guardians of the public weal; and it is clearly decided in favor of the latter by two obvious considerations.

In the first place it is to be remarked that however small the Republic may be, the Representatives must be raised to a certain number in order to guard against the cabals of a few; and that however large it may be they must be limited to a certain number in order to guard against the confusion of a multitude. Hence, the number of Representatives in the two cases not being in proportion to that of the Constituents, and being proportionally greatest in the small Republic, it follows that if the proportion of fit characters be not less in the large than in the small Republic, the former will present a greater option, and consequently a greater probability of a fit choice.

In the next place, as each Representative will be chosen by a greater number of citizens in the large than in the small Republic, it will be more difficult for unworthy candidates to practise with success the vicious arts by which elections are too often carried; and the suffrages of the people being more free, will be more likely to centre on men who possess the most attractive merit and the most diffusive and established characters.

It must be confessed that in this, as in most other cases, there is a mean, on both sides of which inconveniencies will be found to lie. By enlarging too much the number of electors, you render the representative too little acquainted with all their local circumstances and lesser interests; as by reducing it too much, you render him unduly attached to these, and too little fit to comprehend and pursue great and national objects. The Federal Constitution forms a happy combination in this respect; the great and aggregate interests being referred to the national, the local and particular to the State legislatures.

The other point of difference is the greater number of citizens and extent of territory which may be brought within the compass of Republican than of Democratic Government; and it is this circumstance principally which renders factious combinations less to be dreaded in the former than in the latter. The smaller the society, the fewer probably will be the distinct parties and interests composing it; the fewer the distinct parties and interests, the more frequently will a majority be found of the same party; and the smaller the number of individuals composing a majority, and the smaller the compass within which they are placed, the more easily will they concert and execute their plans of oppression. Extend the sphere and you take in a greater variety of parties and interests; you make it less probable that a majority of the whole will have a common motive to invade the rights of other citizens; or if such a common motive exists, it will be more difficult for all who feel it to discover their own strength and to act in unison with each other. Besides other impediments, it may be remarked, that where there is a consciousness of unjust or dishonorable purposes, communication is always checked by distrust in proportion to the number whose concurrence is necessary.

Hence, it clearly appears that the same advantage which a Republic has over a Democracy in controlling the effects of faction is enjoyed by a large over a small republic—is enjoyed by the Union over the States composing it. Does this advantage consist in the substitution of representatives whose enlightened views and virtuous sentiments render them superior to local prejudices and to schemes of injustice? It will not be denied that the representation of the Union will be most likely to possess these requisite endowments. Does it consist in the greater security afforded by a greater variety of parties, against the event of any one party being able to outnumber and oppress the rest? In an equal degree does the increased variety of parties comprised within the Union increase this security? Does it, in fine, consist in the greater obstacles opposed to the concert and accomplishment of the secret wishes of an unjust and interested majority? Here again the extent of the Union gives it the most palpable advantage.

The influence of factious leaders may kindle a flame within their particular States but will be unable to spread a general conflagration through the other States: a religious sect may degenerate into a political faction in a part of the Confederacy; but the variety of sects dispersed over the entire face of it must secure the national Councils against any danger from that source: a rage for paper money, for an abolition of debts, for an equal division of property, or for any other improper or wicked project, will be less apt to pervade the whole body of the Union than a particular member of it; in the same proportion as such a malady is more likely to taint a particular county or district than an entire State.

In the extent and proper structure of the Union, therefore, we behold a republican remedy for the diseases most incident to Republican Government. And according to the degree of pleasure and pride we feel in being republicans ought to be our zeal in cherishing the spirit and supporting the character of federalist.

PUBLIUS

No. 51: Madison

To what expedient, then, shall we finally resort, for maintaining in practice the necessary partition of power among the several departments as laid down in the constitution? The only answer that can be given is that as all these exterior provisions are found to be inadequate the defect must be supplied, by so contriving the interior structure of the government as that its several constituent parts may, by their mutual relations, be the means of keeping each other in their proper places. Without presuming to undertake a full development of this important idea I will hazard a few general observations which may perhaps place it in a clearer light, and enable us to form a more correct judgment of the principles and structure of the government planned by the convention.

In order to lay a due foundation for that separate and distinct exercise of the different powers of government, which to a certain extent is admitted on all hands to be essential to the preservation of liberty, it is evident that each department should have a will of its own; and consequently should be so constituted that the members of each should have as little agency as possible in the appointment of the members of the others. Were this principle rigorously adhered to, it would require that all the appointments for the supreme executive, legislative, and judiciary magistracies should be drawn from the same fountain of authority, the people, through channels having no communication whatever with one another. Perhaps such a plan of constructing the several departments would be less difficult in practice than it may in contemplation appear. Some difficulties, however, and some additional expense would attend the execution of it. Some deviations, therefore, from the principle must be admitted. In the constitution of the judiciary department in particular, it might be inexpedient to insist rigorously on the principle: first, because peculiar qualifications being essential in the members, the primary consideration ought to be to select that mode of choice which best secures these qualifications; second, because the permanent tenure by which the appointments are held in that department must soon destroy all sense of dependence on the authority conferring them.

It is equally evident that the members of each department should be as little dependent as possible on those of the others for the emoluments annexed to their offices. Were the executive magistrate, or the judges, not independent of the legislature in this particular, their independence in every other would be merely nominal.

But the great security against a gradual concentration of the several powers in the same department consists in giving to those who administer each department the necessary constitutional means and personal motives to resist encroachments of the others. The provision for defence must in this, as in all other cases, be made commensurate to the danger of attack. Ambition must be made to counteract ambition. The interest of the man must be connected with the constitutional rights of the place. It may be a reflection on human nature that such devices should be necessary to control the abuses of government. But what is government itself but the greatest of all reflections on human nature? If men were angels, no government would be necessary. If angels were to govern men, neither external nor internal controls on government would be necessary. In framing a government which is to be administered by men over men, the great difficulty lies in this: You must first enable the government to control the governed; and in the next place oblige it to control itself. A dependence on the people is, no doubt, the primary control on the government; but experience has taught mankind the necessity of auxiliary precautions.

This policy of supplying, by opposite and rival interests, the defect of better motives, might be traced through the whole system of human affairs, private as well as public. We see it particularly displayed in all the subordinate distributions of power, where the constant aim is to divide and arrange the several offices in such a manner as that each may be a check on the other; that the private interest of every individual may be a sentinel over the public rights. These inventions of prudence cannot be less requisite in the distribution of the supreme powers of the State.

But it is not possible to give to each department an equal power of self-defense. In republican government, the legislative authority necessarily predominates. The remedy for this inconveniency is to divide the legislature into different branches; and to render them, by different modes of election and different principles of action, as little connected with each other as the nature of their common functions and their common dependence on the society will admit. It may even be necessary to guard against dangerous encroachments by still further precautions. As the weight of the legislative authority requires that it should be thus divided, the weakness of the executive may require, on the other hand, that it should be fortified. An absolute negative on the legislature appears, at first view, to be the natural defense with which the executive magistrate should be armed. But perhaps it would be neither altogether safe nor alone sufficient. On ordinary occasions it might not be exerted with the requisite firmness, and on extraordinary occasions it might be perfidiously abused. May not this defect of an absolute negative be supplied by some qualified connection between this weaker branch of the stronger department, by which the latter may be led to support the constitutional rights of the former, without being too much detached from the rights of its own department?

If the principles on which these observations are founded be just, as I persuade myself they are, and they be applied as a criterion to the several State constitutions, and to the federal Constitution, it will be found that if the latter does not perfectly correspond with them, the former are infinitely less able to bear such a test.

There are, moreover, two considerations particularly applicable to the federal system of America, which place that system in a very interesting point of view.

First. In a single republic, all the power surrendered by the people is submitted to the administration of a single government; and usurpations are guarded against by a division of the government into distinct and separate departments. In the compound republic of America, the power surrendered by the people is first divided between two distinct governments, and then the portion allotted to each subdivided among distinct and separate departments. Hence a double security arises to the rights of the people. The different governments will control each other, at the same time that each will be controlled by itself.

Second. It is of great importance in a republic not only to guard the society against the oppression of its rulers, but to guard one part of the society against the injustice of the other part. Different interests necessarily exist in different classes of citizens. If a majority be united by a common interest, the rights of the minority will be insecure. There are but two methods of providing against this evil: The one by creating a will in the community independent of the majority—that is, of the society itself; the other, by comprehending in the society so many separate descriptions of citizens as will render an unjust combination of a majority of the whole very improbable, if not impracticable. The first method prevails in all governments possessing an hereditary or self-appointed authority. This, at best, is but a precarious security; because a power independent of the society may as well espouse the unjust views of the major as the rightful interests of the minor party, and may possibly be turned against both parties. The second method will be exemplified in the federal republic of the United States. Whilst all authority in it will be derived from and dependent on the society, the society itself will be broken into so many parts, interests and classes of citizens, that the rights of individuals, or of the minority, will be in little danger from interested combinations of the majority. In a free government the security for civil rights must be the same as that for religious rights. It consists in the one case in the multiplicity of interests, and in the other in the multiplicity of sects. The degree of security in both cases will depend on the number of interests and sects; and this may be presumed to depend on the extent of country and number of people comprehended under the same government. This view of the subject must particularly recommend a proper federal system to all the sincere and considerate friends of republican government: Since it shows that in exact proportion as the territory of the Union may be formed into more circumscribed Confederacies, or States, oppressive combinations of a majority will be facilitated; the best security, under the republican form, for the rights of every class of citizens, will be diminished; and consequently the stability and independence of some member of the government, the only other security, must be proportionally increased. Justice is the end of government. It is the end of civil society. It ever has been and ever will be pursued until it be obtained, or until liberty be lost in the pursuit. In a society under the forms of which the stronger faction can readily unite and oppress the weaker, anarchy may as truly be said to reign as in a state of nature, where the weaker individual is not secured against the violence of the stronger: And as, in the latter state, even the stronger individuals are prompted, by the uncertainty of their condition, to submit to a government which may protect the weak as well as themselves: So, in the former state, will the more powerful factions or parties be gradually induced, by a like motive, to wish for a government which will protect all parties, the weaker as well as the more powerful. It can be little doubted that if the State of Rhode Island was separated from the Confederacy and left to itself, the insecurity of rights under the popular form of government within such narrow limits would be displayed by such reiterated oppressions of factious majorities that some power altogether independent of the people would soon be called for by the voice of the very factions whose misrule had proved the necessity of it. In the extended republic of the United States, and among the great variety of interests, parties, and sects which it embraces, a coalition of a majority of the whole society could seldom take place on any other principles than those of justice and the general good; and there being thus less danger to a minor from the will of the major party, there must be less pretext, also, to provide for the security of the former, by introducing into the government a will not dependent on the latter, or, in other words, a will independent of the society itself. It is no less certain than it is important, notwithstanding the contrary opinions which have been entertained, that the larger the society, provided it lie within a practicable sphere, the more duly capable it will be of self-government. And happily for the *republican cause,* practicable

sphere may be carried to a very great extent by a judicious modification and mixture of the *federal principle.*

PUBLIUS

No. 78: Hamiton

To the People of the State of New York:

WE PROCEED now to an examination of the judiciary department of the proposed government.

In unfolding the defects of the existing Confederation, the utility and necessity of a federal judicature have been clearly pointed out. It is the less necessary to recapitulate the considerations there urged, as the propriety of the institution in the abstract is not disputed; the only questions which have been raised being relative to the manner of constituting it, and to its extent. To these points, therefore, our observations shall be confined.

The manner of constituting it seems to embrace these several objects: 1st. The mode of appointing the judges. 2d. The tenure by which they are to hold their places. 3d. The partition of the judiciary authority between different courts, and their relations to each other.

First. As to the mode of appointing the judges; this is the same with that of appointing the officers of the Union in general, and has been so fully discussed in the two last numbers, that nothing can be said here which would not be useless repetition.

Second. As to the tenure by which the judges are to hold their places; this chiefly concerns their duration in office; the provisions for their support; the precautions for their responsibility.

According to the plan of the convention, all judges who may be appointed by the United States are to hold their offices DURING GOOD BEHAVIOR; which is conformable to the most approved of the State constitutions and among the rest, to that of this State. Its propriety having been drawn into question by the adversaries of that plan, is no light symptom of the rage for objection, which disorders their imaginations and judgments. The standard of good behavior for the continuance in office of the judicial magistracy, is certainly one of the most valuable of the modern improvements in the practice of government. In a monarchy it is an excellent barrier to the despotism of the prince; in a republic it is a no less excellent barrier to the encroachments and oppressions of the representative body. And it is the best expedient which can be devised in any government, to secure a steady, upright, and impartial administration of the laws.

Whoever attentively considers the different departments of power must perceive, that, in a government in which they are separated from each other, the judiciary, from the nature of its functions, will always be the least dangerous to the political rights of the Constitution; because it will be least in a capacity to annoy or injure them. The Executive not only dispenses the honors, but holds the sword of the community. The legislature not only commands the purse, but prescribes the rules by which the duties and rights of every citizen are to be regulated. The judiciary, on the contrary, has no influence over either the sword or the purse; no direction either of the strength or of the wealth of the society; and can take no active resolution whatever. It may truly be said to have neither FORCE nor WILL, but merely judgment; and must ultimately depend upon the aid of the executive arm even for the efficacy of its judgments.

This simple view of the matter suggests several important consequences. It proves incontestably, that the judiciary is beyond comparison the weakest of the three departments of power; that it can never attack with success either of the other two; and that all possible care is requisite to enable it to defend itself against their attacks. It equally proves, that though individual oppression may now and then proceed from the courts of justice, the general liberty of the people can never be endangered from that quarter; I mean so long as the judiciary remains truly distinct from both the legislature and the Executive. For I agree, that "there is no liberty, if the power of judging be not separated from the legislative and executive powers." And it proves, in the last place, that as liberty can have nothing to fear from the judiciary alone, but would have every thing to fear from its union with either of the other departments; that as all the effects of such a union must ensue from a dependence of the former on the latter, notwithstanding a nominal and apparent separation; that as, from the natural feebleness of the judiciary, it is in continual jeopardy of being overpowered, awed, or influenced by its co-ordinate branches; and that as nothing can contribute so much to its firmness and independence as permanency in office, this quality may therefore be justly regarded as an indispensable ingredient in its constitution, and, in a great measure, as the citadel of the public justice and the public security.

The complete independence of the courts of justice is peculiarly essential in a limited Constitution. By a limited Constitution, I understand one which contains certain specified exceptions to the legislative authority; such, for instance, as that it shall pass no bills of attainder, no ex-post-facto laws, and the like. Limitations of this kind can be preserved in practice no other way than through the medium of courts of justice, whose duty it must be to declare all acts contrary to the manifest tenor of the Constitution void. Without this, all the reservations of particular rights or privileges would amount to nothing.

Some perplexity respecting the rights of the courts to pronounce legislative acts void, because contrary to the Constitution, has arisen from an imagination that the doctrine would imply a superiority of the judiciary to the legislative power. It is urged that the authority which can declare the acts of another void, must necessarily be superior to the one whose acts may be declared void. As this doctrine is of great importance in all the American constitutions, a brief discussion of the ground on which it rests cannot be unacceptable.

There is no position which depends on clearer principles, than that every act of a delegated authority, contrary to the tenor of the commission under which it is exercised, is void. No legislative act, therefore, contrary to the Constitution, can be valid. To deny this, would be to affirm, that the deputy is greater than his principal; that the servant is above his master; that the representatives of the people are superior to the people themselves; that men acting by virtue of powers, may do not only what their powers do not authorize, but what they forbid.

If it be said that the legislative body are themselves the constitutional judges of their own powers, and that the construction they put upon them is conclusive upon the other departments, it may be answered, that this cannot be the natural presumption, where it is not to be collected from any particular provisions in the Constitution. It is not otherwise to be supposed, that the Constitution could intend to enable the representatives of the people to substitute their WILL to that of their constituents. It is far more rational to suppose, that the courts were designed to be an intermediate body between the people and the legislature, in order, among other things, to keep the latter within the limits assigned to their authority. The interpretation of the laws is the proper and peculiar province of the courts. A constitution is, in fact, and must be regarded by the judges, as a fundamental law. It therefore belongs to them to ascertain its meaning, as well as the meaning of any particular act proceeding from the legislative body. If there should happen to be an irreconcilable variance between the two, that which has the superior obligation and validity ought, of course, to be preferred; or, in other words, the Constitution ought to be preferred to the statute, the intention of the people to the intention of their agents.

Nor does this conclusion by any means suppose a superiority of the judicial to the legislative power. It only supposes that the power of the people is superior to both; and that where the will of the legislature, declared in its statutes, stands in opposition to that of the people, declared in the Constitution, the judges ought to be governed by the latter rather than the former. They ought to regulate their decisions by the fundamental laws, rather than by those which are not fundamental.

This exercise of judicial discretion, in determining between two contradictory laws, is exemplified in a familiar instance. It not uncommonly happens, that there are two statutes existing at one time, clashing in whole or in part with each other, and neither of them containing any repealing clause or expression. In such a case, it is the province of the courts to liquidate and fix their meaning and operation. So far as they can, by any fair construction, be reconciled to each other, reason and law conspire to dictate that this should be done; where this is impracticable, it becomes a matter of necessity to give effect to one, in exclusion of the other. The rule which has obtained in the courts for determining their relative validity is, that the last in order of time shall be preferred to the first. But this is a mere rule of construction, not derived from any positive law, but from the nature and reason of the thing. It is a rule not enjoined upon the courts by legislative provision, but adopted by themselves, as consonant to truth and propriety, for the direction of their conduct as interpreters of the law. They thought it reasonable, that between the interfering acts of an EQUAL authority, that which was the last indication of its will should have the preference.

But in regard to the interfering acts of a superior and subordinate authority, of an original and derivative power, the nature and reason of the thing indicate the converse of that rule as proper to be followed. They teach us that the prior act of a superior ought to be preferred to the subsequent act of an inferior and subordinate authority; and that accordingly, whenever a particular statute contravenes the Constitution, it will be the duty of the judicial tribunals to adhere to the latter and disregard the former.

It can be of no weight to say that the courts, on the pretense of a repugnancy, may substitute their own pleasure to the constitutional intentions of the legislature. This might as well happen in the case of two contradictory statutes; or it might as well happen in every adjudication upon any single statute. The courts must declare the sense of the law; and if they should be disposed to exercise WILL instead of JUDGMENT, the consequence would equally be the substitution of their pleasure to that of the legislative body. The observation, if it prove any thing, would prove that there ought to be no judges distinct from that body.

If, then, the courts of justice are to be considered as the bulwarks of a limited Constitution against legislative encroachments, this consideration will afford a strong argument for the permanent tenure of judicial offices, since nothing will contribute so much as this to that independent spirit in the judges which must be essential to the faithful performance of so arduous a duty.

This independence of the judges is equally requisite to guard the Constitution and the rights of individuals from the effects of those ill humors, which the arts of designing men, or the influence of particular conjunctures, sometimes disseminate among the people themselves, and which, though they speedily give place to better information, and more deliberate reflection, have a tendency, in the meantime, to occasion dangerous innovations in the government, and serious oppressions of the minor party in the community. Though I trust the friends of the proposed Constitution will never concur with its enemies, in questioning that fundamental principle of republican government, which admits the right of the people to alter or abolish the established Constitution, whenever they find it inconsistent with their happiness, yet it is not to be inferred from this principle, that the representatives of the people, whenever a momentary inclination happens to lay hold of a majority of their constituents, incompatible with the provisions in the existing Constitution, would, on that account, be justifiable in a violation of those provisions; or that the courts would be under a greater obligation to connive at infractions in this shape, than when they had proceeded wholly from the cabals of the representative body. Until the people have, by some solemn and authoritative act, annulled or changed the established form, it is binding upon themselves collectively, as well as individually; and no presumption, or even knowledge, of their sentiments, can warrant their representatives in a departure from it, prior to such an act. But it is easy to see, that it would require an uncommon portion of fortitude in the judges to do their duty as faithful guardians of the Constitution, where legislative invasions of it had been instigated by the major voice of the community.

But it is not with a view to infractions of the Constitution only, that the independence of the judges may be an essential safeguard against the effects of occasional ill humors in the society. These sometimes extend no farther than to the injury of the private rights of particular classes of citizens, by unjust and partial laws. Here also the firmness of the judicial magistracy is of vast importance in mitigating the severity and confining the operation of such laws. It not only serves to moderate the immediate mischiefs of those which may have been passed, but it operates as a check upon the legislative body in passing them; who, perceiving that obstacles to the success of iniquitous intention are to be expected from the scruples of the courts, are in a manner compelled, by the very motives of the injustice they meditate, to qualify their attempts. This is a circumstance calculated to have more influence upon the character of our governments, than but few may be aware of. The benefits of the integrity and moderation of the judiciary have already been felt in more States than one; and though they may have displeased those whose sinister expectations they may have disappointed, they must have commanded the esteem and applause of all the virtuous and disinterested. Considerate men, of every description, ought to prize whatever will tend to beget or fortify that temper in the courts: as no man can be sure that he may not be to-morrow the victim of a spirit of injustice, by which he may be a gainer to-day. And every man must now feel, that the inevitable tendency of such a spirit is to sap the foundations of public and private confidence, and to introduce in its stead universal distrust and distress.

That inflexible and uniform adherence to the rights of the Constitution, and of individuals, which we perceive to be indispensable in the courts of justice, can certainly not be expected from judges who hold their offices by a temporary commission. Periodical appointments, however regulated, or by whomsoever made, would, in some way or other, be fatal to their necessary independence. If the power of making them was committed either to the Executive or legislature, there would be danger of an improper complaisance to the branch which possessed it; if to both, there would be an unwillingness to hazard the displeasure of either; if to the people, or to persons chosen by them for the special purpose, there would

be too great a disposition to consult popularity, to justify a reliance that nothing would be consulted but the Constitution and the laws.

There is yet a further and a weightier reason for the permanency of the judicial offices, which is deducible from the nature of the qualifications they require. It has been frequently remarked, with great propriety, that a voluminous code of laws is one of the inconveniences necessarily connected with the advantages of a free government. To avoid an arbitrary discretion in the courts, it is indispensable that they should be bound down by strict rules and precedents, which serve to define and point out their duty in every particular case that comes before them; and it will readily be conceived from the variety of controversies which grow out of the folly and wickedness of mankind, that the records of those precedents must unavoidably swell to a very considerable bulk, and must demand long and laborious study to acquire a competent knowledge of them. Hence it is, that there can be but few men in the society who will have sufficient skill in the laws to qualify them for the stations of judges. And making the proper deductions for the ordinary depravity of human nature, the number must be still smaller of those who unite the requisite integrity with the requisite knowledge. These considerations apprise us, that the government can have no great option between fit character; and that a temporary duration in office, which would naturally discourage such characters from quitting a lucrative line of practice to accept a seat on the bench, would have a tendency to throw the administration of justice into hands less able, and less well qualified, to conduct it with utility and dignity. In the present circumstances of this country, and in those in which it is likely to be for a long time to come, the disadvantages on this score would be greater than they may at first sight appear; but it must be confessed, that they are far inferior to those which present themselves under the other aspects of the subject.

Upon the whole, there can be no room to doubt that the convention acted wisely in copying from the models of those constitutions which have established GOOD BEHAVIOR as the tenure of their judicial offices, in point of duration; and that so far from being blamable on this account, their plan would have been inexcusably defective, if it had wanted this important feature of good government. The experience of Great Britain affords an illustrious comment on the excellence of the institution.

PUBLIUS

Presidents and Vice Presidents

	PRESIDENT	VICE PRESIDENT		PRESIDENT	VICE PRESIDENT
1	George Washington *(Federalist 1789)*	John Adams *(Federalist 1789)*	15	James Buchanan *(Democratic 1857)*	John C. Breckinridge *(Democratic 1857)*
2	John Adams *(Federalist 1797)*	Thomas Jefferson *(Dem.-Rep. 1797)*	16	Abraham Lincoln *(Republican 1861)*	Hannibal Hamlin *(Republican 1861)*
3	Thomas Jefferson *(Dem.-Rep. 1801)*	Aaron Burr *(Dem.-Rep. 1801)*			Andrew Johnson *(Unionist 1865)*
		George Clinton *(Dem.-Rep. 1805)*	17	Andrew Johnson *(Unionist 1865)*	
4	James Madison *(Dem.-Rep. 1809)*	George Clinton *(Dem.-Rep. 1809)*	18	Ulysses S. Grant *(Republican 1869)*	Schuyler Colfax *(Republican 1869)*
		Elbridge Gerry *(Dem.-Rep. 1813)*			Henry Wilson *(Republican 1873)*
5	James Monroe *(Dem.-Rep. 1817)*	Daniel D. Tompkins *(Dem.-Rep. 1817)*	19	Rutherford B. Hayes *(Republican 1877)*	William A. Wheeler *(Republican 1877)*
6	John Quincy Adams *(Dem.-Rep. 1825)*	John C. Calhoun *(Dem.-Rep. 1825)*	20	James A. Garfield *(Republican 1881)*	Chester A. Arthur *(Republican 1881)*
7	Andrew Jackson *(Democratic 1829)*	John C. Calhoun *(Democratic 1829)*	21	Chester A. Arthur *(Republican 1881)*	
		Martin Van Buren *(Democratic 1833)*	22	Grover Cleveland *(Democratic 1885)*	Thomas A. Hendricks *(Democratic 1885)*
8	Martin Van Buren *(Democratic 1837)*	Richard M. Johnson *(Democratic 1837)*	23	Benjamin Harrison *(Republican 1889)*	Levi P. Morton *(Republican 1889)*
9	William H. Harrison *(Whig 1841)*	John Tyler *(Whig 1841)*	24	Grover Cleveland *(Democratic 1893)*	Adlai E. Stevenson *(Democratic 1893)*
10	John Tyler *(Whig and Democratic 1841)*		25	William McKinley *(Republican 1897)*	Garret A. Hobart *(Republican 1897)*
11	James K. Polk *(Democratic 1845)*	George M. Dallas *(Democratic 1845)*			Theodore Roosevelt *(Republican 1901)*
12	Zachary Taylor *(Whig 1849)*	Millard Fillmore *(Whig 1849)*	26	Theodore Roosevelt *(Republican 1901)*	Charles W. Fairbanks *(Republican 1905)*
13	Millard Fillmore *(Whig 1850)*		27	William H. Taft *(Republican 1909)*	James S. Sherman *(Republican 1909)*
14	Franklin Pierce *(Democratic 1853)*	William R. D. King *(Democratic 1853)*	28	Woodrow Wilson *(Democratic 1913)*	Thomas R. Marshall *(Democratic 1913)*

PRESIDENT	VICE PRESIDENT	PRESIDENT	VICE PRESIDENT
29 Warren G. Harding *(Republican 1921)*	Calvin Coolidge *(Republican 1921)*	37 Richard M. Nixon *(Republican 1969)*	Spiro T. Agnew *(Republican 1969)*
			Gerald R. Ford *(Republican 1973)*
30 Calvin Coolidge *(Republican 1923)*	Charles G. Dawes *(Republican 1925)*	38 Gerald R. Ford *(Republican 1974)*	Nelson Rockefeller *(Republican 1974)*
31 Herbert Hoover *(Republican 1929)*	Charles Curtis *(Republican 1929)*	39 James E. Carter *(Democratic 1977)*	Walter Mondale *(Democratic 1977)*
32 Franklin D. Roosevelt *(Democratic 1933)*	John Nance Garner *(Democratic 1933)*	40 Ronald Reagan *(Republican 1981)*	George H. W. Bush *(Republican 1981)*
	Henry A. Wallace *(Democratic 1941)*	41 George H. W. Bush *(Republican 1989)*	J. Danforth Quayle *(Republican 1989)*
	Harry S. Truman *(Democratic 1945)*	42 William J. Clinton *(Democratic 1993)*	Albert Gore Jr. *(Democratic 1993)*
33 Harry S. Truman *(Democratic 1945)*	Alben W. Barkley *(Democratic 1949)*	43 George W. Bush *(Republican 2001)*	Richard Cheney *(Republican 2001)*
34 Dwight D. Eisenhower *(Republican 1953)*	Richard M. Nixon *(Republican 1953)*	44 Barack Obama *(Democratic 2009)*	Joseph R. Biden Jr. *(Democratic 2009)*
35 John F. Kennedy *(Democratic 1961)*	Lyndon B. Johnson *(Democratic 1961)*		
36 Lyndon B. Johnson *(Democratic 1963)*	Hubert H. Humphrey *(Democratic 1965)*		

Glossary

absentee ballot A voting ballot submitted by mail before an election. Voters use absentee ballots if they will be unable to go to the polls on Election Day.

activists People who dedicate their time, effort, and money to supporting a political party or particular candidates.

adversarial system A two-sided court structure in which lawyers on both sides of a case attempt to prove their argument over their opponent's version of the case.

advertising Actions taken by a member of Congress that are unrelated to government issues but have the primary goal of making a positive impression on the public, like sending holiday cards to constituents and appearing in parades.

Aid to Families with Dependent Children (AFDC) The federal welfare program in place from 1935 until 1996, when it was replaced by Temporary Assistance for Needy Families (TANF) under President Clinton.

alliance An agreement between two or more countries pledging support if one of those countries is attacked.

amicus curiae Latin for "friend of the court," referring to an interested group or person who shares relevant information about a case to help the Court reach a decision.

Antifederalists Those at the Constitutional Convention who favored strong state governments and feared that a strong national government would be a threat to individual rights.

appeals courts The intermediate level of federal courts that hear appeals from district courts. More generally, an appeals court is any court with appellate jurisdiction.

appellate jurisdiction The authority of a court to hear appeals from lower courts and change or uphold the decision.

apportionment The process of assigning the 435 seats in the House to the states based on increases or decreases in state population.

Articles of Confederation Sent to the states for ratification in 1777, these were the first attempt at a new American government. It was later decided that the Articles restricted national government too much, and they were replaced by the Constitution.

astroturf lobbying Any lobbying method initiated by an interest group that is designed to look like the spontaneous, independent participation of many individuals.

attack ads Campaign advertising that criticizes a candidate's opponent—typically by making potentially damaging claims about the opponent's background or record—rather than focusing on positive reasons to vote for the candidate.

attack journalism A type of increasingly popular media coverage focused on political scandals and controversies, which causes a negative public opinion of political figures.

attitudinalist approach A way of understanding decisions of the Supreme Court based on the political ideologies of the justices.

Baby Boom generation Americans born between 1946 and 1964 who will be retiring in large numbers over the next twenty years.

backbenchers Legislators who do not hold leadership positions within their party caucus or conference.

balanced budget A spending plan in which the government's expenditures are equal to its revenue.

bicameralism The system of having two chambers within one legislative body, like the House and Senate in the U.S. Congress.

bilateral agreements Treaties between two nations.

Bill of Rights The first ten amendments to the Constitution; they protect individual rights and liberties.

block grants Federal aid provided to a state government to be spent within a certain policy area, but the state can decide how to spend the money within that area.

brand names The use of party names to evoke certain positions or issues. For instance, "Adidas" might immediately call to mind athletics in the same way that "Democrat" might remind you of environmental policies or universal health care.

briefs Written documents prepared by both parties in a case, and sometimes by outside groups, presenting their arguments in court.

broadcast media Communications technologies, such as television and radio, that transmit information over airwaves.

budget deficit The amount by which a government's spending in a given fiscal year exceeds its revenue.

budget making The processes carried out in Congress to determine how government money will be spent and revenue will be raised.

budget maximizers Bureaucrats who seek to increase funding for their agency whether or not that additional spending is worthwhile.

budget reconciliation The process by which congressional committees are held to the spending targets specified in the budget resolution. During this process, the House and Senate Budget Committees combine the budgetary changes from all the legislative committees into an omnibus reconciliation bill to be approved by Congress.

burden of proof The responsibility of having to prove guilt; it rests with the plaintiff in criminal cases but could be with either party in a civil trial.

bureaucracy The system of civil servants and political appointees who implement congressional or presidential decisions; also known as the administrative state.

bureaucratic drift Bureaucrats' tendency to implement policies in a way that favors their own political objectives rather than following the original intentions of the legislation.

Bush Doctrine The foreign policy of President George W. Bush, under which the United States would use military force preemptively against threats to its national security.

business cycle The normal pattern of expansion and contraction of the economy.

by-product theory The idea that many Americans acquire political information unintentionally rather than by seeking it out.

cabinet The group of fifteen executive department heads who implement the president's agenda in their respective positions.

campaign platform A candidate's description of his or her issue positions and the kinds of policies he or she will seek to enact while in office.

cases on appeal Cases brought before the Supreme Court because Congress has determined that they require the Court's attention.

casework Assistance provided by members of Congress to their constituents in solving problems with the federal bureaucracy or addressing other specific concerns.

categorical grants Federal aid to state or local governments that is provided for a specific purpose, such as a mass transit program within the transportation budget or a school lunch program within the education budget.

caucus (congressional) The organization of Democrats within the House and Senate that meets to discuss and debate the party's positions on various issues in order to reach a consensus and to assign leadership positions.

caucus (electoral) A local meeting in which party members select a party's nominee for the general election.

centralized groups Interest groups that have a headquarters, usually in Washington, DC, as well as members and field offices throughout the country. In general, these groups' lobbying decisions are made at headquarters by the group leaders.

cert pool A system initiated in the Supreme Court in the 1970s in which law clerks screen cases that come to the Supreme Court and recommend to the justices which cases should be heard.

challenger A politician running for an office that he or she does not hold at the time of the election. Challengers run against incumbents or in open-seat elections.

checks and balances A system in which each branch of government has some power over the others.

citizen group A type of interest group that seeks changes in spending, regulations, or government programs concerning a wide range of policies (also known as a public interest group).

civil liberties Basic political freedoms that protect citizens from governmental abuses of power.

civil rights Rights that guarantee individuals freedom from discrimination. These rights are generally grounded in the equal protection clause of the 14th Amendment and more specifically laid out in laws passed by Congress, such as the 1964 Civil Rights Act.

civil servants Employees of bureaucratic agencies within the government.

Civil War Amendments The 13th, 14th, and 15th Amendments to the Constitution, which abolished slavery and granted civil liberties and voting rights to freed slaves after the Civil War.

clash of civilizations The theory that terrorism is motivated by a hatred of Western culture and religion.

class action lawsuit A case brought by a group of individuals on behalf of themselves and others in the general public who are in similar circumstances.

clear and present danger test Established in *Schenk v. United States*, this test allows the government to restrict certain types of speech deemed dangerous.

closed primary A primary election in which only registered members of a particular political party can vote.

closed rules Conditions placed on a legislative debate by the House Rules Committee prohibiting amendments to a bill.

cloture A procedure through which the Senate can limit the amount of time spent debating a bill (cutting off a filibuster), if a supermajority of sixty senators agree.

coattails The idea that a popular president can generate additional support for candidates affiliated with his party. Coattails are weak or nonexistent in most American elections.

coercion A method of eliminating nonparticipation or free riding by potential group members by requiring participation, as in many labor unions.

coercive federalism A form of federalism in which the federal government pressures the states to change their policies by using regulations, mandates, and conditions (often involving threats to withdraw federal funding).

Cold War The period of tension and arms competition between the United States and the Soviet Union that lasted from 1945 until 1991.

collective action problem A situation in which the members of a group would benefit by working together to produce some outcome, but each individual is better off refusing to cooperate and reaping benefits from those who do the work.

collusion Agreement between the litigants on the desired outcome of a case, causing a federal court to decline to hear the case. More generally, collusion can refer to any kind of conspiracy or complicity.

commerce clause Part of Article I, Section 8, of the Constitution that gives Congress "the power to regulate Commerce . . . among the several States." The Supreme Court's interpretation of this clause has varied, but today it serves as the basis for much of Congress's legislation.

commerce clause powers The powers of Congress to regulate the economy granted in Article I, Section 8, of the Constitution.

commercial speech Public expression with the aim of making a profit. It has received greater protection under the 1st Amendment in recent years but remains less protected than political speech.

common law Law based on the precedent of previous court rulings rather than on legislation. It is used in all federal courts and forty-nine of the fifty state courts.

competitive federalism A form of federalism in which states compete to attract businesses and jobs through the policies they adopt.

concentration The trend toward single-company ownership of several media sources in one area.

concurrent powers Responsibilities for particular policy areas, such as transportation, that are shared by federal, state, and local governments.

conditional party government The theory that lawmakers from the same party will cooperate to develop policy proposals.

confederal government A form of government in which states hold power over a limited national government.

confederations Interest groups made up of several independent, local organizations that provide much of their funding and hold most of the power.

conference The organization of Republicans within the House and Senate that meets to discuss and debate the party's positions on various issues in order to reach a consensus and to assign leadership positions.

conference committees Temporary committees created to negotiate differences between the House and Senate versions of a piece of legislation that has passed through both chambers.

"consent of the governed" The idea that government gains its legitimacy through regular elections in which the people living under that government participate to elect their leaders.

conservative One side of the ideological spectrum defined by support for lower taxes, a free market, and a more limited government; generally associated with Republicans.

considerations The many pieces of information a person uses to form an opinion.

constitutional authority (presidential) Powers derived from the provisions of the Constitution that outline the president's role in government.

constitutional interpretation The process of determining whether a piece of legislation or governmental action is supported by the Constitution.

constitutional revolution A significant change in the Constitution that may be accomplished either through amendments (as after the Civil War) or shifts in the Supreme Court's interpretation of the Constitution (as in the New Deal era).

containment An important feature of American Cold War policy in which the United States used diplomatic, economic, and military strategies in an effort to prevent the Soviet Union from expanding its influence.

cooperative federalism A form of federalism in which national and state governments work together to provide services efficiently. This form emerged in the late 1930s, representing a profound shift toward less concrete boundaries of responsibility in national–state relations.

Council of Economic Advisers A group of economic advisers, created by the Employment Act of 1946, which provides objective data on the state of the economy and makes economic policy recommendations to the president.

credit claiming The acceptance of credit by a member of Congress for legislation that specifically benefits his or her constituents.

crosscutting Issues that raise disagreements within a party coalition or between political parties about what government should do.

cross-ownership The trend toward single-company ownership of several kinds of media outlets.

culture wars Political conflict in the United States between "red-state" Americans, who tend to have strong religious beliefs, and "blue-state" Americans, who tend to be more secular.

current account The balance of a country's receipts and its payments in international trade and investment.

de facto Relating to actions or circumstances that occur outside the law or "by fact," such as the segregation of schools that resulted from housing patterns and other factors rather than from laws.

de jure Relating to actions or circumstances that occur "by law," such as the legally enforced segregation of schools in the American South before the 1960s.

dealignment A decline in the percentage of citizens who identify with one of the major parties, usually over the course of a decade or longer.

defendant The person or party against whom a case is brought.

delegate (congressional role) A member of Congress who loyally represents constituents' direct interests.

delegates Individuals who attend their party's national convention and vote to select their party's nominee for the presidency. Delegates are elected in a series of primaries and caucuses that occur during winter and spring of an election year.

descriptive representation When a member of Congress shares the characteristics (such as gender, race, religion, or ethnicity) of his or her constituents.

détente An approach to foreign policy in which cultural exchanges and negotiations are used to reduce tensions between rival nations, such as between the United States and the Soviet Union during the 1970s.

diplomacy The process of negotiation on international issues between national leaders.

direct incitement test Established in *Brandenberg v. Ohio*, this test protects threatening speech under the 1st Amendment unless that speech aims to and is likely to cause imminent "lawless action."

direct lobbying Attempts by interest group staff to influence policy by speaking with elected officials or bureaucrats.

discount rate The interest rate that a bank must pay on a short-term loan from the Federal Reserve Bank.

discretionary spending Expenditures that can be cut from the budget without changing the underlying law.

disenfranchised To have been denied the ability to exercise a right, such as the right to vote.

disparate impact standard The idea that discrimination exists if a practice has a negative effect on a specific group, whether or not this effect was intentional.

distributive theory The idea that members of Congress will join committees that best serve the interests of their district and that committee members will support each other's legislation.

district courts Lower level trial courts of the federal judicial system that handle most U.S. federal cases.

divided government A situation in which the House, Senate, and presidency are not controlled by the same party, such as if Democrats hold the majority of House and Senate seats, and the president is a Republican.

docket The official schedule of cases in a court of law.

doctrine of interposition The idea that if the national government passes an unconstitutional law, the people of the states (through their state legislatures) can declare the law void. This idea provided the basis for southern secession and the Civil War.

domino theory An idea held by American foreign policy makers during the Cold War that the creation of one Soviet-backed communist nation would lead to the spread of communism in that nation's region.

double jeopardy Being tried twice for the same crime. This is prevented by the 5th Amendment.

dual federalism The form of federalism favored by Chief Justice Roger Taney in which national and state governments are seen as distinct entities providing separate services. This model limits the power of the national government.

due process clause Part of the 14th Amendment that forbids states from denying "life, liberty, or property" to any person without due process of law. (A nearly identical clause in the 5th Amendment applies only to the national government.)

due process rights The idea that laws and legal proceedings must be fair. The Constitution guarantees that the government cannot take away a person's "life, liberty, or property, without due process of law." Other specific due process rights are found in the 4th, 5th, 6th, and 8th Amendments, such as protection from self-incrimination and freedom from illegal searches.

Duverger's law The principle that in a democracy with single-member districts and plurality voting, like the United States, only two parties' candidates will have a realistic chance of winning political office.

earmarks Federally funded local projects attached to bills passed through Congress.

economic depression A deep, widespread downturn in the economy, like the Great Depression of the 1930s.

economic group A type of interest group that seeks public policies that provide monetary benefits to its members.

economic individualism The autonomy of individuals to manage their own financial decisions without government interference.

election cycle The two-year period between general elections.

electoral college The body that votes to select America's president and vice president based on the popular vote in each state. Each candidate nominates a slate of electors who are selected to attend the meeting of the college if their candidate wins the most votes in a state or district.

electoral connection The idea that congressional behavior is centrally motivated by members' desire for reelection.

electoral vote Votes cast by members of the electoral college; after a presidential candidate wins the popular vote in a given state, that candidate's slate of electors cast electoral votes for the candidate on behalf of that state.

entitlement Any federal government program that provides benefits to Americans who meet requirements specified by law.

enumerated powers Powers explicitly granted to Congress, the president, or the Supreme Court in the first three articles of the Constitution. Examples include Congress's power to "raise and support armies" and the president's power as commander in chief.

equal time provision An FCC regulation requiring broadcast media to provide equal airtime on any non-news programming to all candidates running for an office.

establishment clause Part of the 1st Amendment that states "Congress shall make no law respecting an establishment of religion," which has been interpreted to mean that Congress cannot sponsor or favor any religion.

exclusionary rule The principle that illegally or unconstitutionally acquired evidence cannot be used in a criminal trial.

executive agreement An agreement between the executive branch and a foreign government, which acts as a treaty but does not require Senate approval.

Executive Office of the President (EOP) The group of policy-related offices that serves as support staff to the president.

executive orders Proclamations made by the president that change government policy without congressional approval.

executive powers clause Part of Article II, Section 1, of the Constitution that states, "The executive Power shall be vested in a President of the United States of America." This broad statement has been used to justify many assertions of presidential power.

executive privilege The right of the president to keep executive branch conversations and correspondence confidential from the legislative and judicial branches.

factions Groups of like-minded people who try to influence the government. American government is set up to avoid domination by any one of these groups.

fairness doctrine An FCC regulation requiring broadcast media to present several points of view to ensure balanced coverage. It was created in the late 1940s and eliminated in 1987.

fast-track authority An expedited system for passing treaties under which support from a simple majority, rather than a two-thirds majority, is needed in both the House and Senate, and no amendments are allowed.

federal civil service A system created by the 1883 Pendleton Civil Service Act in which bureaucrats are hired on the basis of merit rather than political connections.

Federal Communications Commission (FCC) A government agency created in 1934 to regulate American radio stations and later expanded to regulate television, wireless communications technologies, and other broadcast media.

Federal Election Commission The government agency that enforces and regulates election laws; made up of six presidential appointees, of whom no more than three can be members of the same party.

federal funds rate (FFR) The interest rate that a bank must pay on an overnight loan from another bank.

federal preemptions Impositions of national priorities on the states through national legislation that is based on the Constitution's supremacy clause.

Federal Reserve Board The group of seven presidential appointees who govern the Federal Reserve System.

Federal Reserve System An independent agency that serves as the central bank of the United States to bring stability to the nation's banking system.

federalism The division of power across the local, state, and national levels of government.

Federalist Papers A series of eighty-five articles written by Alexander Hamilton, James Madison, and John Jay that sought to sway public opinion toward the Federalists' position.

Federalists Those at the Constitutional Convention who favored a strong national government and a system of separated powers.

fighting words Forms of expression that "by their very utterance" can incite violence. These can be regulated by the government but are often difficult to define.

filibuster A tactic used by senators to block a bill by continuing to hold the floor and speak—under the Senate rule of unlimited debate—until the bill's supporters back down.

filtering The influence on public opinion that results from journalists' and editors' decisions about which of many potential news stories to report.

fire alarm oversight A method of oversight in which members of Congress respond to complaints about the bureaucracy or problems of implementation only as they arise rather than exercising constant vigilance.

first-mover advantage The president's power to initiate treaty negotiations. Congress cannot initiate treaties and can only consider them once they have been negotiated.

fiscal federalism A form of federalism in which federal funds are allocated to the lower levels of government through transfer payments or grants.

fiscal policy Government decisions about how to influence the economy by taxing and spending.

501(c)(3) organization A tax code classification that applies to most interest groups; this designation makes donations to the group tax-deductible but limits the group's political activities.

527 organization A tax-exempt group formed primarily to influence elections through voter mobilization efforts and issue ads that do not directly endorse or oppose a candidate. Unlike political action committees, 527s are not subject to contribution limits and spending caps.

foreign policy Government actions that affect countries, corporations, groups, or individuals outside America's borders.

framing The influence on public opinion caused by the way a story is presented or covered, including the details, explanations, and context offered in the report.

free exercise clause Part of the 1st Amendment that states Congress cannot prohibit or interfere with the practice of religion.

free market An economic system based on competition among businesses without government interference.

free rider problem The incentive to benefit from others' work without making a contribution, which leads individuals in a collective action situation to refuse to work together.

free riding The practice of relying on others to contribute to a collective effort while failing to participate on one's own behalf yet still benefiting from the group's successes.

free trade zones Designated areas where tariffs on imports and exports between specific countries do not apply.

frontloading The practice of states moving their presidential primaries or caucuses to take place earlier in the nomination process, often in the hopes of exerting more influence over the outcome.

full employment The theoretical point at which all citizens who want to be employed have a job.

full faith and credit clause Part of Article IV of the Constitution requiring that each state's laws be honored by the other states. For example, a legal marriage in one state must be recognized across state lines.

gag order An aspect of prior restraint that allows the government to prohibit the media from publishing anything related to an ongoing trial.

general election The election in which voters cast ballots for House members, senators, and (every four years) a president and vice president.

general revenue sharing (GRS) A type of grant used in the 1970s and 1980s in which the federal government provided state governments with funds to be spent at each state's discretion. These grants provided states with more control over programs.

gerrymandering Attempting to use the process of redrawing district boundaries to benefit a political party, protect incumbents, or change the proportion of minority voters in a district.

go public A president's use of speeches and other public communications to appeal directly to citizens about issues the president would like the House and Senate to act on.

GOTV A campaign's efforts to "get out the vote" or make sure their supporters vote on Election Day (also known as the ground game).

government The system for implementing decisions made through the political process.

grandfather clause A type of law enacted in several southern states to allow those who were permitted to vote before the Civil War, and their descendants, to bypass literacy tests and other obstacles to voting, thereby exempting whites from these tests while continuing to disenfranchise African Americans and other people of color.

grassroots lobbying A lobbying strategy that relies on participation by group members, such as a protest or a letter-writing campaign.

Great Compromise A compromise between the large and small states, proposed by Connecticut, in which Congress would have two houses:

a Senate with two legislators per state and a House of Representatives in which each state's representation would be based on population (also known as the Connecticut Compromise).

Great Society The wide-ranging social agenda promoted by President Lyndon Johnson in the mid-1960s that aimed to improve Americans' quality of life through governmental social programs.

Greenspan Commission The informal name of the National Commission on Social Security Reform created by President Ronald Reagan in 1981 to address short-term and long-term problems facing the Social Security program.

gridlock An inability to enact legislation because of partisan conflict within Congress or between Congress and the president.

gross domestic product (GDP) The value of a country's economic output taken as a whole.

ground game A campaign's efforts to "get out the vote" or make sure their supporters vote on Election Day (also known as GOTV).

hard money Donations that are used to help elect or defeat a specific candidate.

hard news Media coverage focused on facts and important issues surrounding a campaign.

hate speech Expression that is offensive or abusive, particularly in terms of race, gender, or sexual orientation. It is currently protected under the 1st Amendment.

head of government One role of the president, through which he or she has authority over the executive branch.

head of state One role of the president, through which he or she represents the country symbolically and politically.

hold An objection to considering a measure on the Senate floor.

horse race A description of the type of election coverage that focuses more on poll results and speculation about a likely winner than on substantive differences between the candidates.

hostile media phenomenon The idea that supporters of a candidate or issue tend to feel that media coverage is biased against their position, regardless of whether coverage is actually unfair.

idealism The idea that a country's foreign policy decisions are based on factors beyond self-interest, including upholding important principles or values.

ideological polarization The effect on public opinion when many citizens move away from moderate positions and toward either end of the political spectrum, identifying themselves as either liberals or conservatives.

ideology A cohesive set of ideas and beliefs used to organize and evaluate the political world.

impeachment A negative or checking power over the other branches that allows Congress to remove the president, vice president, or other "officers of the United States" (including federal judges) for abuses of power.

implied powers Powers supported by the Constitution that are not expressly stated in it.

income support Government programs that provide support to low-income Americans, such as welfare, food stamps, unemployment insurance, and the Earned Income Tax Credit.

incumbency advantage The relative infrequency with which members of Congress are defeated in their attempts for reelection.

incumbent A politician running for reelection to the office he or she currently holds.

independent agencies Government offices or organizations that provide government services and are not part of an executive department.

inflation The increase in the price of consumer goods over time.

informational theory The idea that having committees in Congress made up of experts on specific policy areas helps to ensure well-informed policy decisions.

initiative A direct vote by citizens on a policy change proposed by fellow citizens or organized groups outside government. Getting a question on the ballot typically requires collecting a set number of signatures from registered voters in support of the proposal. There is no mechanism for a national-level initiative.

inside strategies The tactics employed within Washington, DC, by interest groups seeking to achieve their policy goals.

interest group An organization of people who share common political interests and aim to influence public policy by electioneering and lobbying.

interest group state A government in which most policy decisions are determined by the influence of interest groups.

intermediate scrutiny test The middle level of scrutiny the courts use when determining whether unequal treatment is justified by the effect of a law; this is the standard used for gender-based discrimination cases and for many cases based on sexual orientation.

International Monetary Fund A nongovernmental organization established in 1944 to help stabilize the international monetary system, improve economic growth, and aid developing nations.

internationalism The idea that the United States should be involved in the affairs of other nations, out of both self-interest and moral obligation.

investigative journalists Reporters who dig deeply into a particular topic of public concern, often targeting government failures and inefficiencies.

isolationism The idea that the United States should refrain from involvement in international affairs.

issue scale A survey response format in which respondents select their answers from a range of positions between two extremes.

issue voters People who are well informed about their own policy preferences and knowledgeable about the candidates, and who use all of this information when they decide how to vote.

Jim Crow laws State and local laws that mandated racial segregation in all public facilities in the South, many border states, and some northern communities between 1876 and 1964.

joint committees Committees that contain members of both the House and Senate but have limited authority.

judicial activism The idea that the Supreme Court should assert its interpretation of the law even if it overrules the elected executive and legislative branches of government.

judicial restraint The idea that the Supreme Court should defer to the democratically elected executive and legislative branches of government rather than contradicting existing laws.

judicial review The Supreme Court's power to strike down a law or executive branch action that it finds unconstitutional.

Judiciary Act of 1789 The law in which Congress laid out the organization of the federal judiciary. The law refined and clarified federal court jurisdiction and set the original number of justices at six. It also created the Office of the Attorney General and established the lower federal courts.

jurisdiction The sphere of a court's legal authority to hear and decide cases.

Keynesian economics The theory that governments should use economic policy, like taxing and spending, to maintain stability in the economy.

Kyoto Protocol An international agreement signed in 1997 that set limits on carbon emissions in an effort to slow global warming.

latent A group of politically like-minded people that is not represented by any interest group.

latent opinion An opinion formed on the spot, when it is needed (as distinct from a deeply held opinion that is stable over time).

leak The release of either classified or politically embarrassing information by a government employee to a member of the press.

legislative veto A form of oversight in which Congress overturns bureaucratic decisions.

Lemon test Established in *Lemon v. Kurtzman*, the Supreme Court uses this test to determine whether a practice violates the 1st Amendment's establishment clause.

level of conceptualization The amount of complexity in an individual's beliefs about government and policy, and the extent to which those beliefs are consistent with each other and remain consistent over time.

libel Written false statements that damage a person's reputation. Such statements can be regulated by the government but are often difficult to distinguish from permissible speech.

liberal One side of the ideological spectrum defined by support for stronger government programs and more market regulation; generally associated with Democrats.

liberal–conservative ideology A way of describing political beliefs in terms of a position on the spectrum running from liberal to moderate to conservative.

libertarians Those who prefer very limited government and therefore tend to be conservative on issues such as welfare policy, environmental policy, and public support for education, but liberal on issues of personal liberty such as free speech, abortion, and the legalization of drugs.

limited government A system in which the powers of the government are restricted to protect against tyranny.

living Constitution A way of interpreting the Constitution that takes into account evolving national attitudes and circumstances rather than the text alone.

lobbying Efforts to influence public policy through contact with public officials on behalf of an interest group.

mainstream media Media sources that predate the Internet, such as newspapers, magazines, televisions, and radio.

majority leader The elected head of the party holding the majority of seats in the House or Senate.

majority voting A voting system in which a candidate must win more than 50 percent of votes to win the election. If no candidate wins enough votes to take office, a runoff election is held between the top two vote-getters.

mandatory spending Expenditures that are required by law, such as the funding for Social Security.

market-based solutions Reform options for social policies that are based on tax credits, flexible spending accounts, and other approaches that rely on competition in the free market.

markup One of the steps through which a bill becomes a law, in which the final wording of the bill is determined.

mass associations Interest groups that have a large number of dues-paying individuals as members.

mass media Sources that provide information to the average citizen, such as newspapers, television networks, radio stations, and Web sites.

mass survey A way to measure public opinion by interviewing a large sample of the population.

media conglomerates Companies that control a large number of media sources across several types of media outlets.

media effects The influence of media coverage on average citizens' opinions and actions.

Medicaid An entitlement program funded by the federal and state governments that provides health care coverage for low-income Americans who would otherwise be unable to afford heath care.

Medicare The federal heath care plan created in 1965 that provides coverage for retired Americans for hospital care (Part A), medical care (Part B), and prescription drugs (Part D).

melting pot The idea that as different racial and ethnic groups come to America, they should assimilate into American culture, leaving their native languages, customs, and traditions behind.

Miller test Established in *Miller v. California*, the Supreme Court uses this three-part test to determine whether speech meets the criteria for obscenity. If so, it can be restricted by the government.

minority leader The elected head of the party holding the minority of seats in the House or Senate.

Miranda rights The list of civil liberties described in the 5th Amendment that must be read to a suspect before anything the suspect says can be used in a trial.

Missouri Compromise An agreement between pro- and antislavery groups passed by Congress in 1820 in an attempt to ease tensions by limiting the expansion of slavery while also maintaining a balance between slave states and free states.

mobilization Motivating supporters to vote in an election and, in some cases, helping them get to the polls on Election Day.

modified rules Conditions placed on a legislative debate by the House Rules Committee allowing certain amendments to a bill while barring others.

monarchy A form of government in which power is held by a single person, or monarch, who comes to power through inheritance rather than election.

monetarist theory The idea that the amount of money in circulation (the money supply) is the primary influence on economic activity and inflation.

monetary policy Government decisions about how to influence the economy using control of the money supply and interest rates.

Monroe Doctrine The American policy initiated under President James Monroe in 1823 stating that the United States would remain neutral in conflicts between European nations and that these nations should stop colonizing or occupying areas of North and South America.

mootness The irrelevance of a case by the time it is received by a federal court, causing the court to decline to hear the case.

most-favored-nation status A standing awarded to countries with which the United States has good trade relations, providing the lowest possible tariff rate. World Trade Organization members must give one another this preferred status.

multilateral action Foreign policy carried out by a nation in coordination with other nations or international organizations.

multilateral agreements Treaties among multiple nations.

mutually assured destruction The idea that two nations that possess large stores of nuclear weapons—like the United States and the Soviet Union during the Cold War—would both be annihilated in any nuclear exchange, thus making it unlikely that either country would launch a first attack.

nation building The use of American resources, including the military, to help create democratic institutions abroad and prevent violence in other countries.

national committee An American political party's principal organization, comprised of party representatives from each state.

National Economic Council (NEC) A group of economic advisers created in 1993 to work with the president to coordinate economic policy.

National Security Council (NSC) Within the Executive Office of the President, a committee that advises the president on matters of foreign policy.

national supremacy clause Part of Article VI, Section 2, of the Constitution stating that the Constitution and the laws and treaties of the United States are the "supreme Law of the Land," meaning national laws take precedent over state laws if the two conflict.

nationalized election An atypical congressional election in which the reelection rate is relatively low for one party's House and Senate incumbents and national-level issues exert more influence than usual on House and Senate races.

natural rights Also known as "unalienable rights," the Declaration of Independence defines them as "Life, Liberty, and the pursuit of Happiness." The Founders believed that upholding these rights should be the government's central purpose.

necessary and proper clause Part of Article I, Section 8, of the Constitution that grants Congress the power to pass all laws related to one of its expressed powers; also known as the elastic clause.

neutral competence The idea, credited to theorist Max Weber, that suggests bureaucrats should provide expertise without the influence of elected officials, interest groups, or their own political agendas.

New Deal The set of policies proposed by President Franklin Roosevelt and enacted by Congress between 1933 and 1935 to promote economic recovery and social welfare during the Great Depression.

New Deal Coalition The assemblage of groups who aligned with and supported the Democratic Party in support of New Deal policies during the fifth party system, including African Americans, Catholics, Jewish people, union members, and white southerners.

New Jersey Plan In response to the Virginia Plan, smaller states at the Constitutional Convention proposed that each state should receive equal representation in the national legislature, regardless of size.

news cycle The time between the release of information and its publication, like the twenty-four hours between issues of a daily newspaper.

nodes Groups of people who belong to, are candidates of, or work for a political party, but do not necessarily work together or hold similar policy preferences.

nominating convention A meeting held by each party every four years at which states' delegates select the party's presidential and vice-presidential nominees and approve the party platform.

nomination The selection of a particular candidate to run for office in a general election as a representative of his or her political party.

nongovernmental organizations (NGOs) Groups operated by private institutions (rather than governments) to promote growth, economic development, and other agendas throughout the world.

normal election A typical congressional election in which the reelection rate is high, and the influences on House and Senate contests are largely local.

North Atlantic Treaty Organization (NATO) An international alliance between the United States, Canada, and several European nations, originally created to provide security against the Soviet Union during the Cold War.

notice and comment procedure A step in the rule-making process in which proposed rules are published in the Federal Register and made available for debate by the general public.

off the record Comments a politician makes to the press on the condition that they can be reported only if they are not attributed to that politician (also known as "on background").

Office of Management and Budget An office within the Executive Office of the President that is responsible for creating the president's annual budget proposal to Congress, reviewing proposed rules, and other budget-related tasks.

omnibus legislation Large bills that often cover several topics and may contain extraneous, or pork-barrel, projects.

on background Comments a politician makes to the press on the condition that they can be reported only if they are not attributed to that politician (also known as "off the record").

open market operations The process by which the Federal Reserve System buys and sells securities to influence the money supply.

open primary A primary election in which any registered voter can participate in the contest, regardless of party affiliation.

open rules Conditions placed on a legislative debate by the House Rules Committee allowing relevant amendments to a bill.

open seat An elected position for which there is no incumbent.

opposition research Attempts by a candidate's campaign or other groups of supporters to uncover embarrassing or politically damaging information about the candidate's opponent.

oral arguments Spoken presentations made in person by the lawyers of each party to a judge or appellate court outlining the legal reasons why their side should prevail.

original intent The theory that justices should surmise the intentions of the Founders when the language of the Constitution is unclear.

original jurisdiction The authority of a court to handle a case first, as in the Supreme Court's authority to initially hear disputes between two states. However, original jurisdiction for the Supreme Court is not exclusive; it may assign such a case to a lower court.

outside strategies The tactics employed outside Washington, DC, by interest groups seeking to achieve their policy goals.

oversight Congressional efforts to make sure that laws are implemented correctly by the bureaucracy after they have been passed.

ownership society The term used to describe the social policy vision of President George W. Bush, in which citizens take responsibility for their own social welfare and the free market plays a greater role in social policy.

paradox of voting The question of why citizens vote even though their individual votes stand little chance of changing the election outcome.

parliamentary system A system of government in which legislative and executive power are closely joined. The legislature (parliament) selects the chief executive (prime minister) who forms the cabinet from members of the parliament.

parties in service The role of the parties in recruiting, training, fundraising, and campaigning for congressional and presidential candidates. This aspect of party organization grew more prominent during the sixth party system.

party coalitions The groups that identify with a political party, usually described in demographic terms such as African American Democrats or evangelical Republicans.

party identification (party ID) A citizen's loyalty to a specific political party.

party in government The group of officeholders who belong to a specific political party and were elected as candidates of that party.

party in power Under unified government, the party that controls the House, Senate, and the presidency. Under divided government, the president's party.

party in the electorate The group of citizens who identify with a specific political party.

party organization A specific political party's leaders and workers at the national, state, and local levels.

party platform A set of objectives outlining the party's issue positions and priorities. Candidates are not required to support their party's platform.

party principle The idea that a political party exists as an organization distinct from its elected officials or party leaders.

party ratio The proportions of seats in the House and Senate that are controlled by each major party.

party system A period in which the names of the major political parties, their supporters, and the issues dividing them remain relatively stable.

party unity The extent to which members of Congress in the same party vote together on party votes.

party votes A vote in which the majority of one party opposes the position of the majority of the other party.

peak associations Interest groups whose members are businesses or other organizations rather than individuals.

penny press Newspapers sold for one cent in the 1830s, when more efficient printing presses made reduced-price newspapers available to a larger segment of the population.

permanent campaign The actions officeholders take throughout the election cycle to build support for their reelection.

picket fence federalism A more refined and realistic form of cooperative federalism in which policy makers within a particular policy area work together across the levels of government.

plaintiff The person or party who brings a case to court.

plea bargain An agreement between a plaintiff and defendant to settle a case before it goes to trial or the verdict is decided. In a civil case this usually involves an admission of guilt and an agreement on monetary damages; in a criminal case it often involves an admission of guilt in return for a reduced charge or sentence.

pluralism The idea that having a variety of parties and interests within a government will strengthen the system, ensuring that no group possesses total control.

plurality voting A voting system in which the candidate who receives the most votes within a geographic area wins the election, regardless of whether that candidate wins a majority (more than half) of the votes.

pocket veto The automatic death of a bill passed by the House and Senate when the president fails to sign the bill in the last ten days of a legislative session.

polarized The alignment of both parties' members with their own party's issues and priorities, with little crossover support for the other party's goals.

police patrol oversight A method of oversight in which members of Congress constantly monitor the bureaucracy to make sure that laws are implemented correctly.

policy agenda The set of desired policies that political leaders view as their top priorities.

policy mood The level of public support for expanding the government's role in society; whether the public wants government action on a specific issue.

political action committee (PAC) An interest group or a division of an interest group that can raise money to contribute to campaigns or to spend on ads in support of candidates. The amount a PAC can receive from each of its donors and the amount it can spend on federal campaigning are strictly limited.

political appointees People selected by an elected leader, such as the president, to hold a government position.

political business cycle Attempts by elected officials to manipulate the economy before elections by increasing economic growth and reducing unemployment and inflation, with the goal of improving evaluations of their performance in office.

political machine An unofficial patronage system within a political party that seeks to gain political power and government contracts, jobs, and other benefits for party leaders, workers, and supporters.

political socialization The process by which an individual's political opinions are shaped by other people and the surrounding culture.

politico A member of Congress who acts as a delegate on issues that constituents care about (such as immigration reform) and as a trustee on more complex or less salient issues (some foreign policy or regulatory matters).

politics The process that determines what government does.

popular vote The votes cast by citizens in an election.

population The group of people that a researcher or pollster wants to study, such as evangelicals, senior citizens, or Americans.

pork barrel Legislative appropriations that benefit specific constituents, created with the aim of helping local representatives win reelection.

position taking Any public statement in which a member of Congress makes his or her views on an issue known to his or her constituents.

positive externalities Benefits created by a public good that are shared by the primary consumer of the good and by society more generally.

power of the purse The constitutional power of Congress to raise and spend money. Congress can use this as a negative or checking power over the other branches by freezing or cutting their funding.

power to persuade The theory that a president's ability to shape government policy depends more on his ability to convince members of Congress, bureaucrats, and citizens to do what he wants than it does on the formal powers conveyed to him by the Constitution.

precedent A legal norm established in court cases that is then applied to future cases dealing with the same legal questions.

president pro tempore A largely symbolic position usually held by the most senior member of the majority party in the Senate.

presidential approval The percentage of Americans who feel that the president is doing a good job in office.

press conference An event at which a politician speaks to journalists and, in most cases, answers their questions afterward.

primary A ballot vote in which citizens select a party's nominee for the general election.

prime time Evening hours when television viewership is at its highest and networks often schedule news programs.

priming The influence on the public's general impressions caused by positive or negative coverage of a candidate or issue.

principal–agent game The interaction between a principal (such as the president or Congress), who needs something done, and an agent (such as a bureaucrat), who is responsible for carrying out the principal's orders.

prior restraint A limit on freedom of the press that allows the government to prohibit the media from publishing certain materials.

prisoners' dilemma A simple two-person game that illustrates how actions that are in a player's individual self-interest may lead to outcomes that all players consider inferior.

privacy rights Liberties protected by several amendments in the Bill of Rights that shield certain personal aspects of citizens' lives from governmental interference, such as the 4th Amendment's protection against unreasonable searches and seizures.

privatization The process of transferring the management of a government program (like Social Security) from the public sector to the private sector.

privileges and immunities clause Part of Article IV of the Constitution requiring that states must treat nonstate residents within their borders as they would treat their own residents. This was meant to promote commerce and travel between states.

problem of control A difficulty faced by elected officials in ensuring that when bureaucrats implement policies, they follow these officials' intentions but still have enough discretion to use their expertise.

progressive Taxes that require upper-income people to pay a higher tax rate than lower-income people, such as income taxes.

proportional allocation During the presidential primaries, the practice of determining the number of convention delegates allotted to each candidate based on the percentage of the popular vote cast for each candidate. All Democratic primaries and caucuses use this system, as do some states' Republican primaries and caucuses.

protectionism The idea under which some people have tried to rationalize discriminatory policies by claiming that some groups, like women or African Americans, should be denied certain rights for their own safety or well-being.

public goods Services or actions (such as protecting the environment) that, once provided to one person, become available to everyone. Government is typically needed to provide public goods because they will be under-produced by the free market.

public opinion Citizens' views on politics and government actions.

purposive benefits Satisfaction derived from the experience of working toward a desired policy goal, even if the goal is not achieved.

push polling A type of survey in which the questions are presented in a biased way in an attempt to influence the respondent.

random sample A subsection of a population chosen to participate in a survey through a selection process in which every member of the population has an equal chance of being chosen. This kind of sampling improves the accuracy of public opinion data.

realignment A change in the size or composition of the party coalitions or in the nature of the issues that divide the parties. Realignments typically occur within an election cycle or two, but they can also occur gradually over the course of a decade or longer.

realism The idea that a country's foreign policy decisions are motivated by self-interest and the goal of gaining more power.

reasonable basis test The use of evidence to suggest that differences in the behavior of two groups can rationalize unequal treatment of these groups, such as charging sixteen- to twenty-one-year-olds higher prices for auto insurance than people over twenty-one because younger people have higher accident rates.

reasonable vote A vote that is likely to be consistent with the voter's true preference for one candidate over the others.

recess appointment When a person is chosen by the president to fill a position, such as an ambassadorship or the head of a department, while the Senate is not in session, thereby bypassing Senate approval. Unless approved by a subsequent Senate vote, recess appointees serve only to the end of the congressional term.

reciprocity The informal congressional norm whereby a member votes for a bill that he or she might not otherwise support because a colleague strongly favors it, and in exchange, the colleague votes for a bill that the member feels strongly about (also known as logrolling).

red tape Excessive or unnecessarily complex regulations imposed by the bureaucracy.

redistributive tax policies Policies, generally favored by Democratic politicians, that use taxation to attempt to create greater social equality (i.e., higher taxation of the rich to provide programs for the poor).

redistricting Redrawing the geographic boundaries of legislative districts. This happens every ten years to ensure that districts remain roughly equal in population.

referendum A direct vote by citizens on a policy change proposed by a legislature or another government body. Referenda are common in state and local elections, but there is no mechanism for a national-level referendum.

regional primaries A practice whereby several states in the same area of the country hold presidential primaries or caucuses on the same day.

regressive Taxes that take a larger share of poor people's income than wealthy people's income, such as sales taxes and payroll taxes.

regulation A rule that allows the government to exercise control over individuals and corporations by restricting certain behaviors.

regulatory capture A situation in which bureaucrats favor the interests of the groups or corporations they are supposed to regulate at the expense of the general public.

remedial legislation National laws that address discriminatory state laws. Authority for such legislation comes from Section 5 of the 14th Amendment.

republican democracy A form of government in which the interests of the people are represented through elected leaders.

republicanism As understood by James Madison and the framers, the belief that a form of government in which the interests of the people are represented through elected leaders is the best form of government.

reserved powers As defined in the 10th Amendment, powers that are not given to the national government by the Constitution, or not prohibited to the states, are reserved by the states or the people.

reserve requirement The minimum amount of money that a bank is required to have on hand to back up its assets.

responsible parties A system in which each political party's candidates campaign on the party platform, work together in office to implement the platform, and are judged by voters based on whether they achieved the platform's objectives.

retail politics A mode of campaigning in which a candidate or campaign staff contacts citizens directly, as would happen at a rally, a talk before a small group, or a one-on-one meeting between a candidate and a citizen.

retrospective evaluation A citizen's judgment of an officeholder's job performance since the last election.

revolving door The movement of individuals from government positions to jobs with interest groups or lobbying firms, and vice versa.

ripeness A criterion that federal courts use to decide whether a case is ready to be heard. A case's ripeness is based on whether its central issue or controversy has actually taken place.

roll call vote A recorded vote on legislation; members may vote yes, no, abstain, or present.

running tally A frequently updated mental record that a person uses to incorporate new information, like the information that leads a citizen to identify with a particular political party.

runoff election Under a majority voting system, a second election held only if no candidate wins a majority of the votes in the first general election. Only the top two vote-getters in the first election compete in the runoff.

salience The level of familiarity with an interest group's goals among the general population.

sample Within a population, the group of people surveyed in order to gauge the whole population's opinion. Researchers use samples because it would be impossible to interview the entire population.

sampling error A calculation that describes what percentage of the people surveyed may not accurately represent the population being studied. Increasing the number of respondents lowers the sampling error.

sanction A trade penalty that one nation places on another to encourage the penalized nation to change its actions or policies.

seat shift A change in the number of seats held by Republicans and Democrats in the House or Senate.

select committees Committees in the House or Senate created to address a specific issue for one or two terms.

selective incentives Benefits that can motivate participation in a group effort because they are available only to those who participate, such as member services offered by interest groups.

selective incorporation The process through which the civil liberties granted in the Bill of Rights were applied to the states on a case-by-case basis through the 14th Amendment.

senatorial courtesy A norm in the nomination of district court judges in which the president consults with his party's senators from the relevant state in choosing the nominee.

seniority The informal congressional norm of choosing the member who has served the longest on a particular committee to be the committee chair.

"separate but equal" The idea that racial segregation was acceptable as long as the separate facilities were of equal quality; supported by *Plessy v. Ferguson* and struck down by *Brown v. Board of Education.*

separation of powers The division of government power across the judicial, executive, and legislative branches.

shield laws Legislation, which exists in some states but not at the federal level, that gives reporters the right to refuse to name the sources of their information.

shuttle diplomacy Negotiations carried out by a third party mediator who travels between two nations to relay information when those two nations' negotiators refuse to meet face-to-face.

signing statement A document issued by the president when signing a bill into law explaining his interpretation of the law, which often differs from the interpretation of Congress, in an attempt to influence how the law will be implemented.

single-issue group A type of interest group that has a narrowly focused goal, seeking change on a single topic, government program, or piece of legislation.

single-member districts An electoral system in which every elected official represents a geographically defined area, such as a state or congressional district, and each area elects one representative.

slander Spoken false statements that damage a person's reputation. Such statements can be regulated by the government but are often difficult to distinguish from permissible speech.

slant The imbalance in a story that covers one candidate or policy favorably without providing similar coverage of the other side.

social policy An area of public policy related to maintaining or enhancing the well-being of individuals.

Social Security A federal social insurance program that provides cash benefits to retirees based on payroll taxes they have paid over the course of their careers. It is a "pay as you go" program in which working Americans pay taxes to support today's retirees, with a promise that when today's workers retire, their benefits will be paid by the next generation.

soft money Contributions that can be used for voter mobilization or to promote a policy proposal or point of view as long as these efforts are not tied to supporting or opposing a particular candidate.

soft news Media coverage that aims to entertain or shock, often through sensationalized reporting or by focusing on a candidate or politician's personality.

solicitor general A presidential appointee in the Department of Justice who conducts all litigation on behalf of the federal government before the Supreme Court and supervises litigation in the federal appellate courts.

solidary benefits Satisfaction derived from the experience of working with like-minded people, even if the group's efforts do not achieve the desired impact.

Speaker of the House The elected leader of the House of Representatives.

specialization The expertise of a member of Congress on a specific issue or area of policy. Specialization is more common in the House than the Senate, where members tend to be policy generalists.

split ticket A ballot on which a voter selects candidates from more than one political party.

spoils system The practice of rewarding party supporters with benefits like federal government positions.

standard of proof The amount of evidence needed to determine the outcome of a case. The standard is higher in a criminal case than in a civil one.

standard operating procedures Rules that lower-level bureaucrats must follow when implementing policies.

standing Legitimate justification for bringing a civil case to court.

standing committees Committees that are a permanent part of the House or Senate structure, holding more importance and authority than other committees.

state capacity The knowledge, personnel, and institutions that the government requires to effectively implement policies.

State of the Union An annual speech in which the president addresses Congress to report on the condition of the country and recommend policies.

states' rights The idea that states are entitled to a certain amount of self-government, free of federal government intervention. This became a central issue in the period leading up to the Civil War.

states' sovereign immunity Based on the 11th Amendment, immunity that prevents state governments from being sued by private parties in federal court unless the state consents to the suit.

statutory authority (presidential) Powers derived from laws enacted by Congress that add to the powers given to the president in the Constitution.

statutory interpretation The various methods and tests used by the courts for determining the meaning of a law and applying it to specific situations. Congress may overturn the courts' interpretation by writing a new law; thus it also engages in statutory interpretation.

straight ticket A ballot on which a voter selects candidates from only one political party.

street-level bureaucrats Agency employees who directly provide services to the public, such as those who provide job-training services.

strict construction A way of interpreting the Constitution based on its language alone.

strict scrutiny test The highest level of scrutiny the courts use when determining whether unequal treatment is justified by the effect of a law. It is applied in all cases involving race. Laws rarely pass the strict scrutiny standard; a law that discriminates based on race must be shown to serve some "compelling state interest" in order to be upheld.

substantive due process doctrine One interpretation of the due process clause of the 14th Amendment; in this view the Supreme Court has the power to overturn laws that infringe on individual liberties.

substantive representation When a member of Congress represents constituents' interests and policy concerns.

superdelegates Democratic members of Congress and party officials selected by their colleagues to be delegates at the party's presidential nominating convention. (Republicans do not have superdelegates.) Unlike delegates selected in primaries or caucuses, superdelegates are not committed to a particular candidate and can exercise their judgment when deciding how to vote at the convention.

supply-side economics The theory that lower tax rates will stimulate the economy by encouraging people to save, invest, and produce more goods and services.

suspension of the rules One way of moving a piece of legislation to the top of the agenda in the House: debate on the bill is limited to forty minutes, amendments are not allowed, and the bill must pass by a two-thirds vote.

swing states In a presidential race, highly competitive states in which both major party candidates stand a good chance of winning the state's electoral votes.

symbolic speech Nonverbal expression, such as the use of signs or symbols. It benefits from many of the same constitutional protections of verbal speech.

taking the late train An interest group strategy that involves donating money to the winning candidate after an election in hopes of securing a meeting with that person when he or she takes office.

tariff A tax levied on imported and exported goods.

Temporary Assistance for Needy Families (TANF) The welfare program that replaced Aid to Families with Dependent Children (AFDC) in 1996, eliminating the entitlement status of welfare, shifting implementation of the policy to the states, and introducing several new restrictions on receiving aid. These changes led to a significant decrease in the number of welfare recipients.

Three-fifths Compromise The states' decision during the Constitutional Convention to count each slave as three-fifths of a person in a state's population for the purposes of determining the number of House members and the distribution of taxes.

trade agreement A contract between nations that specifies tariff levels and sets terms on which goods can be imported and exported.

trade association An interest group composed of companies in the same business or industry (the same "trade") that lobbies for policies that benefit members of the group.

trade deficit A measure of how much more a nation imports than it exports.

Treasury Department A cabinet-level agency that is responsible for managing the federal government's revenue. It prints currency, collects taxes, and sells government bonds.

treaty A formal written agreement between nations involving security, trade or economic development, human rights, or other important policies.

trustee A member of Congress who represents constituents' interests while also taking into account national, collective, and moral concerns that sometimes cause the member to vote against the preference of a majority of constituents.

turkey farms Agencies where campaign workers and donors are often appointed to reward them for their service because it is unlikely that their lack of qualifications will lead to bad policy.

turnout The percentage of the voting age population who cast a ballot in a given election.

two presidencies The idea that presidents have more interest in and power over foreign policy issues compared to domestic policy issues. This asymmetry is created by the president's greater influence over the making of foreign policy and the generally lower salience of foreign policy issues.

undervote Casting a ballot that is either incomplete or cannot be counted.

unfunded mandates Federal laws that require the states to do certain things but do not provide state governments with funding to implement these policies.

unified government A situation in which one party holds a majority of seats in the House and Senate and the president is a member of that same party.

unilateral action (national) Independent acts of foreign policy undertaken by a nation without the assistance or coordination of other nations.

unilateral action (presidential) Any policy decision made and acted upon by the president and his staff without the explicit approval or consent of Congress.

unitary executive theory The idea that the vesting clause of the Constitution gives the president the authority to issue orders and policy directives that cannot be undone by Congress.

unitary government A system in which the national, centralized government holds ultimate authority. It is the most common form of government in the world.

United Nations (UN) An international organization made up of representatives from nearly every nation, with a mission to promote peace and cooperation, uphold international law, and provide humanitarian aid.

United States Trade Representative (USTR) An agency founded in 1962 to negotiate with foreign governments to create trade agreements, resolve disputes, and participate in global trade policy organizations. Treaties negotiated by the USTR must be ratified by the Senate.

universalism The informal congressional norm of distributing the benefits of legislation in a way that serves the interests of as many states and districts as possible.

verdict The final decision in a court case.

vesting clause Article II, Section 1, of the Constitution, which states that "executive Power shall be vested in a President of the United States of America," making the president both the head of government and the head of state.

veto The president's rejection of a bill that has been passed by Congress. A veto can be overridden by a two-thirds vote in both the House and Senate.

Virginia Plan A plan proposed by the larger states during the Constitutional Convention that based representation in the national legislature on population. The plan also included a variety of other proposals to strengthen the national government.

voting cues Pieces of information about a candidate that are readily available, easy to interpret, and lead a citizen to decide to vote for a particular candidate.

weapons of mass destruction (WMDs) Weapons that have the potential to cause large-scale loss of life, such as nuclear bombs and chemical or biological weapons.

welfare Financial or other assistance provided to individuals by the government, usually based on need.

whip system An organization of House leaders who work to disseminate information and promote party unity in voting on legislation.

wholesale politics A mode of campaigning that involves indirect contact with citizens, such as running campaign ads.

winner-take-all During the presidential primaries, the practice of assigning all of a given state's delegates to the candidate who receives the most popular votes. Some states' Republican primaries and caucuses use this system.

wire service An organization that gathers news and sells it to other media outlets. The invention of the telegraph in the early 1800s made this type of service possible.

World Bank A nongovernmental organization established in 1944 that provides financial support for economic development projects in developing nations.

World Trade Organization (WTO) An international organization created in 1995 to oversee trade agreements between nations by facilitating negotiations and handling disputes.

writ of certification An uncommon way in which a case is brought before the Supreme Court, whereby an appeals court asks the Court for instructions on a point of law never before decided.

writ of certiorari The most common way for a case to reach the Supreme Court, in which at least four of the nine justices agree to hear a case that has reached them via an appeal from the losing party in a lower court's ruling.

writs of mandamus Orders issued by a higher court to a lower court, government official, or government agency to perform acts required by law.

yellow journalism A style of newspaper popular in the late 1800s that featured sensationalized stories, bold headlines, and illustrations to increase readership.

Endnotes

CHAPTER 1

1. Ronald D. Utt, "The Bridge to Nowhere: A National Embarrassment," (Washington, DC: The Heritage Foundation, October 20, 2005), www.heritage.org/Research/Budget/wm889.cfm (accessed 11/15/07).

2. Jonathan Weisman and Jim VandeHei, "Road Bill Reflects the Power of Pork," *Washington Post*, August 11, 2005, p. A1.

3. "Federal Spending on Collision Course," *Washington Post*, October 23, 2005, p. F2.

4. Carl Hulse, "Two 'Bridges to Nowhere' Tumble Down in Congress," *New York Times*, November 17, 2005, p. A18.

5. Governor Sarah Palin, "Gravina Access Project Redirected," press release, September 21, 2007, www.gov.state.ak.us/archive.php?id= 623&type=1 (accessed 11/12/07).

6. www.thedailyshow.com/watch/wed-march-11-2009/pet-projects.

7. Philip Rucker, "One of Those Earmarks That Bug People; But Utahans Consider Cricket Measure Vital," *Washington Post*, March 17, 2009, p. A1.

8. See the Alaska Department of Transportation Web site at http://dot .alaska.gov/stwdplng/projectinfo/ser/Gravina/index1.shtml.

9. Governor Sarah Palin, "Gravina Access Project Redirected."

10. "Mr. Stevens's Tirade," *Washington Post*, October 23, 2005, p. B6.

11. For example, see the Federal Aviation Administration's report on funding the aviation infrastructure at www.gao.gov/new.items/ d071104t.pdf; see the Government Accountability Office's report on the highway and bridge infrastructure at www.gao.gov/new.items/ d02702t.pdf.

12. Thomas Hobbes, *Leviathan* (1651; repr. Indianapolis, IN: Bobbs, Merrill, 1958).

13. Alexander Hamilton, James Madison, and John Jay, *The Federalist Papers*, ed. Roy P. Fairfield, 2nd ed., (1788; repr. Baltimore, MD: Johns Hopkins University Press, 1981), p. 160.

14. Hamilton, Madison, and Jay, *The Federalist Papers*, p. 18.

15. David Hume, *A Treatise of Human Nature*, ed. T. H. Green and T. H. Grose (New York: Longmans, Green, and Co., 1898), p. 301.

16. Morris Rosenberg, "Some Determinants of Political Apathy," *Public Opinion Quarterly* 18 (Winter, 1954–55): 349–66; Jane Mansbridge, *Beyond Adversary Democracy* (New York: Basic Books, 1980); Nina Eliasoph, *Avoiding Politics: How Americans Produce Apathy in Everyday Life* (New York: Cambridge University Press, 1998); Melanie C. Green, Penny S. Visser, and Philip E. Tetlock, "Coping with Accountability Cross-pressures: Low-Effort Evasive Tactics and High Effort Quests for Complex Compromises," *Personality and Social Psychology Bulletin* 26:11 (2000): 1380–91.

17. Diana C. Mutz, *Hearing the Other Side: Deliberative versus Participatory Democracy* (New York: Cambridge University Press, 2006); Diana C. Mutz, "The Consequences of Cross-Cutting Networks for Political Participation," *American Journal of Political Science* 46:4 (October, 2002): 838–55.

18. John R. Hibbing and Elizabeth Theiss-Morse, *Stealth Democracy: Americans' Beliefs about How Government Should Work* (New York: Cambridge University Press, 2002), p. 147. See Diana E. Hess, *Controversy in the Classroom: The Democratic Power of Discussion* (New York: Routledge, 2009) for evidence that diverse viewpoints in the classroom have important effects on discussion.

19. Associated Press, "Ozone Layer Should Keep Healing, UN Says," September 15, 2005, http://msnbc.msn.com/id/9369129.

20. Sen. Jim Jeffords (VT) left the Republican Party and became an Independent on May 24, 2001, giving control of the Senate to the Democrats until January 2003. Republicans controlled the House for Bush's first six years and the Senate for the first five months of his presidency and then from January 2003 to January 2007.

21. Donald Green, Bradley Palmquist, and Eric Schickler, *Partisan Hearts and Minds* (New Haven, CT: Yale University Press, 2004); Christopher Achen, "Political Socialization and Rational Party Identification," *Political Behavior* 24:2 (2002): 151–70.

22. Robert S. Erikson, Michael B. Mackuen, and James A. Stimson, *The Macro Polity* (New York: Cambridge University Press, 2002).

23. Pew Research Center, "Two-in-Three Critical of Bush's Relief Efforts," September 8, 2005, http://people-press.org/reports/display. php3?ReportID=255 (accessed 1/13/08).

24. The origin of this quote is unknown; *Bartlett's Familiar Quotations* lists the author as "anonymous."

25. Here again, the author is unknown. Some people attribute the quote to the sociologist C. Wright Mills. Others give authorship to the feminist theorist Carol Hanisch. See http://research.umbc.edu/~korenman/ wmst/pisp.html.

26. Linda Feldmann, "How Lines of the Culture War Have Been Redrawn," *Christian Science Monitor*, November 15, 2004, www .csmonitor.com/2004/1115/p01s04=ussc.html (accessed 10/10/07).

27. Edward G. Carmines and James A. Stimson, *Issue Evolution: Race and the Transformation of American Politics* (Princeton, NJ: Princeton University Press, 1989).

28. Samuel Huntington, *Who Are We? The Challenges to America's National Identity* (New York: Simon and Schuster, 2004); Arthur M. Schlesinger Jr., *The Disuniting of America: Reflections on a Multicultural Society* (New York: Whittle Direct Books, 1991).

29. Charles Taylor, *Multiculturalism: Examining the Politics of Recognition*, ed. Amy Gutmann, with commentary by K. Anthony Appiah, Jürgen Habermas, Steven C. Rockefeller, Michael Walzer, and Susan Wolf (Princeton, NJ: Princeton University Press, 1994); Will Kymlicka, *Multicultural Citizenship: A Liberal Theory of Minority Rights* (New York: Oxford University Press, 1995).

30. Morris P. Fiorina, with Samuel J. Abrams and Jeremy C. Pope, *Culture War: The Myth of a Polarized America*, 2nd ed. (New York: Pearson Longman, 2006), pp. 46–47.

31. Fiorina, *Culture War*.

CHAPTER 2

1. See the section of the Starr Report entitled "There Is Substantial and Credible Information that President Clinton Committed Acts that May Constitute Grounds for an Impeachment," http://icreport.loc. gov/icreport/7grounds.htm#L1 (accessed 11/10/07).

2. A classic text on the Founding period is Gordon S. Wood, *The Creation of the American Republic* (New York: Norton, 1969).

3. J. W. Peltason, *Corwin and Peltason's Understanding the Constitution*, 7th ed. (Hinsdale, IL: Dryden Press, 1976), p. 12.

4. The pamphlet sold 120,000 copies within a few months of publication, a figure that would leave the Harry Potter books in the dust in terms of the proportion of the literate public that purchased the book.

5. Thomas Hobbes, *Leviathan* (1651; repr. Indianapolis, IN: Bobbs, Merrill, 1958); John Locke, *Second Treatise of Government* (1690; repr. Indianapolis, IN: Bobbs, Merrill, 1952).

6. Charles A. Beard, *An Economic Interpretation of the Constitution of the United States* (New York: MacMillan, 1913).

7. David Brian Robertson, *The Constitution and America's Destiny* (New York: Cambridge University Press, 2005), p. 4.

8. Robert A. Dahl, *How Democratic Is the American Constitution?* (New Haven, CT: Yale University Press, 2001), p. 12.

9. Alexander Hamilton, John Jay, and James Madison, *The Federalist Papers*, ed. Roy P. Fairfield, 2nd ed. (1788; repr. Baltimore, MD: Johns Hopkins University Press, 1981), p. 22.

10. Quoted in Dahl, *How Democratic Is the American Constitution?*, p. 64.

11. Locke, *Second Treatise of Government*.

12. Quoted in Dahl, *How Democratic Is the American Constitution?*, p. 74.

13. Many delegates probably assumed that the electors would reflect the wishes of the voters in their states, but there is no clear indication of this in Madison's notes. (Hamilton makes this argument in *The Federalist Papers*.) Until the 1820s, many electors were directly chosen by state legislatures rather than by the people. In the first presidential election, George Washington won the unanimous support of the electors, but in only five states were the electors chosen by the people.

14. Dahl, *How Democratic Is the American Constitution?*, p. 67.

15. The actual language of the section avoids the term "slavery." Instead it says, "The Migration or Importation of such Persons as any of the States now existing shall think proper to admit, shall not be prohibited by Congress prior to the Year one thousand eight hundred and eight." The ban on the importation of slaves was implemented on the earliest possible date, January 1, 1808.

16. The Avalon Project, Madison's notes to the convention, July 12, 1787, www.yale.edu/lawweb/avalon/debates/712.htm (accessed 11/15/07).

17. Patrick Henry, "Shall Liberty or Empire Be Sought?" in *America, 1761–1837*, vol. VIII of *The World's Famous Orations*, ed. William Jennings Bryan (New York: Funk and Wagnalls, 1906), pp. 73, 76.

18. Thomas Jefferson to John Adams, 1787, in *The Writings of Thomas Jefferson*, Memorial Edition, ed. Andrew A. Lipscomb and Albert Ellery Bergh (Washington, DC: Thomas Jefferson Memorial Association of the United States, 1903), vol. 6, p. 370.

19. Louis Fisher, *Constitutional Conflicts between Congress and the President* (Lawrence, KS: University Press of Kansas, 1997), p. 244.

20. This ban prompted the White House to seek covert channels through which to support the Contras, which led to the ill-conceived secret arms deal with Iran (a nation that was under a complete U.S. trade embargo at the time) in which the money from the arms sales was funneled to the Contras.

21. Linda Greenhouse, "Chief Justice Attacks a Law as Infringing on Judges," *New York Times*, January 1, 2004.

22. Charlie Savage, "Obama's War on Terror May Resemble Bush's in Some Areas," *New York Times*, February 17, 2009, p. A1.

23. William E. Gladstone, "Kin beyond Sea," *The North American Review*, September/October 1878, p. 185.

24. Dahl, *How Democratic Is the American Constitution?*, p. 2.

25. Thomas Jefferson to James Madison, in *Thomas Jefferson on Democracy*, ed. Saul Padover (New York: Mentor Books, 1953), p. 153.

26. Cass R. Sunstein, "Making Amends," *The New Republic*, March 3, 1997, p. 42.

27. *Furman v. Georgia*, 408 U.S. 238 (1972).

28. Deroy Murdock, "Ignorance and American Liberty," *National Review Online*, July 3, 2000, www.nationalreview.com (accessed 11/15/07).

Comparing Ourselves to Others

a. "EU Voting Row Explained," BBC News, December 13, 2003, http://news.bbc.co.uk/1/hi/world/europe/3309773.stm; "From Jefferson's Brevity to Convolutions of Bureaucrats," *The Observer*, December 14, 2003, www.guardian.co.uk/eu/story/ 0,7369,1106851,00.html.

What Do Political Scientists Do?

a. *Gompers v. United States*, 233 U.S. 604 (1914).

b. Edward S. Corwin, "Some Probable Repercussions of 'Nira' on Our Constitutional System," *Annals of the American Academy of Political and Social Science*, 172 (March, 1934): 139–44. See also Bruce Ackerman, "The Living Constitution," *Harvard Law Review* 120:7 (2007): 1737, for a discussion of how policy changes that are ratified in "triggering elections" have become part of the broader Constitution over the past seventy-five years.

c. Thurgood Marshall, speech given at the annual seminar of the San Francisco Patent and Trademark Law Aassociation, Maui, Hawaii, May 6, 1987, www.thurgoodmarshall.com/speeches/constitutional_speech.htm.

d. Philip B. Kurland and Ralph Lerner, eds., *The Founders' Constitution*, vol. 2, *Preamble*, Document 7 (Chicago: University of Chicago Press, 1987), http://press-pubs.uchicago.edu/founders/documents/preambles7.html.

e. Bruce Ackerman, "The Living Constitution," p. 1752.

f. Keith E. Whittington, "Originalism within the Living Constitution," American Constitution Society for Law and Policy, July 2007, www.acslaw.org/files/Keith%20E. %20Whittington %20Vanderbilt%20 Paper%207-2007.pdf.

g. Akhil Reed Amar, *The Bill of Rights* (New Haven, CT: Yale University Press, 1998).

Challenging Conventional Wisdom

a. Albert P. Blaustein, "The U.S. Constitution: America's Most Important Export," http://usinfo.state.gov/journals/itdhr/0304/ijde/blaustein.htm.

b. Graham K. Wilson, *Only in America? The Politics of the United States in Comparative Perspective* (Chatham, NJ: Chatham House Publishers, 1998), p. 7.

You Decide

a. Douglas Linder, "What in the Constitution Cannot Be Amended?" *Arizona Law Review* 23 (1981): 717–33.

b. Kathleen M. Sullivan, "What's Wrong with Constitutional Amendments?" in *New Federalist Papers*, ed. Alan Brinkley, Nelson W. Polsby, and Kathleen M. Sullivan (New York: Norton, 1997), p. 63.

c. Jamin B. Raskin, "A Right to Vote," *The American Prospect*, August 27, 2001, pp. 10–12.

CHAPTER 3

1. *South Dakota v. Dole*, 483 U.S. 203 (1987).

2. See www.cisstat.com/eng/cis.htm for more information on the Commonwealth of Independent States.

3. Arthur S. Banks and Thomas Muller, eds., *Political Handbook of the World* (Binghamton, NY: CSA Publications, 1998), p. 1083.

4. Pam Belluck, "Massachusetts Gay Marriage to Remain Legal," *New York Times*, June 14, 2007, www.nytimes.com/2007/06/15/us/15gay.html (accessed 10/18/07). The state supreme court decision that required the state legislature to recognize gay marriage was *Goodridge v. Dept. of Public Health*, 798 N.E.2d 941 (Mass. 2003).

5. *Nancy Wilson and Paula Schoenwether v. Richard Lake and John Ashcroft* (2005) No. 8:04-cv-1680-T-30TBM.

6. "The Supreme Court; Excerpts from Court's Welfare Ruling and Rehnquist's Dissent," *New York Times*, May 18, 1999, p. A20.

7. The Sedition Act was passed within a month of three other laws—the Naturalization Act, the Alien Friends Act, and the Alien Enemies Act—that were all aimed at strengthening the hand of the national government in its naval war against France. Collectively, these four laws are often referred to as the Alien and Sedition Acts. But for our purposes here, the relevant law is the Sedition Act.

8. Stanley Elkins and Eric McKitrick, *The Age of Federalism* (New York: Oxford University Press, 1993).

9. John W. Wright, ed., *New York Times 2000 Almanac* (New York: Penguin Reference, 1999), p. 165. Estimates from various online sources are quite a bit higher, averaging about 620,000 deaths.

10. *Mayor of City of New York v. Miln*, 36 U.S. (11 Pet.) 102 (1837).

11. *Cooley v. Board of Wardens of the Port of Philadelphia*, 53 U.S. 229 (1851).

12. *Slaugterhouse Cases*, 83 U.S. 36 (1873). See Ronald M. Labbe and Jonathan Lurie, *The Slaughterhouse Cases: Regulation, Reconstruction, and the Fourteenth Amendment* (Lawrence, KS: University Press of Kansas, 2003).

13. *Civil Rights Cases*, 109 U.S. 3 (1883).

14. *United States v. E.C. Knight Co.*, 156 U.S. 1 (1895).

15. *Hammer v. Dagenhart*, 247 U.S. 251 (1918).

16. *Lochner v. New York*, 198 U.S. 45 (1905).

17. *Schechter Poultry Corporation v. United States* (1935).

18. Four key cases are *West Coast Hotel Company v. Parrish* (1937), *Wright v. Vinton Branch* (1937), *Virginia Railway Company v. System Federation* (1937), and *National Labor Relations Board v. Jones & Laughlin Steel Corporation* (1937).

19. *Wickard v. Filburn*, 317 U.S. 111 (1942).

20. Martin Grodzins, *The American System* (New York: Rand McNally, 1966).

21. John Shannon, "Middle Class Votes Bring a New Balance to Federalism," February 1, 1997, policy paper 10 from the Urban Institute series "The Future of the Public Sector," www.urban.org/url.cfm?ID=307051 (accessed 1/3/08).

22. Max Sawicky, "An Idea Whose Time Has Returned: Anti-recession Fiscal Assistance for State and Local Governments," briefing paper (Washington, DC: Economic Policy Institute, October, 2001).

23. This number varies depending on which grants are counted. Tim Conlan finds fifteen block grants in this period. See his *From New Federalism to Devolution* (Washington, DC: Brookings Institution, 1998).

24. *Brown v. Board of Education*, 347 U.S. 483 (1954); *Swann v. Charlotte-Mecklenburg Board of Education*, 402 U.S. 1 (1971).

25. *Baker v. Carr*, 369 U.S. 186 (1962); *Reynolds v. Sims*, 377 U.S. 533 (1964); and *Wesberry v. Sanders*, 376 U.S. 1 (1964). Martha Derthick, *Keeping the Compound Republic: Essays in American Federalism* (Washington, DC: Brookings Institution, 2001).

26. *Miranda v. Arizona*, 384 U.S. 436 (1966); *Mapp v. Ohio*, 367 U.S. 643 (1961).

27. John Kincaid, "Governing the American States," in *Developments in American Politics*, ed. Gillian Peele, Christopher J. Bailey, Bruce Cain, and Guy Peters (Chatham, NJ: Chatham House Publishers, 1995), pp. 208–16.

28. Paul Posner, "The Politics of Coercive Federalism in the Bush Era," *Publius* 37:3 (May, 2007): 390–412.

29. Barry Rabe, "Environmental Policy and the Bush Era: The Collision between the Administrative Presidency and State Experimentation," *Publius* 37:3 (May, 2007): 413–31.

30. From a review of Michael S. Greve, *Real Federalism: Why It Matters, How It Could Happen* (Washington, DC: American Enterprise Institute Press, 1999), www.federalismproject.org/publications/books (accessed 10/10/07).

31. Cass Sunstein, *Designing Democracy: What Constitutions Do* (New York: Oxford University Press, 2001), p. 107.

32. Linda Greenhouse, "The Nation: 5-to-4, Now and Forever; At the Court, Dissent over States' Rights Is Now War," *New York Times*, June 9, 2002, sec. 4, p. 3.

33. Michael S. Greve, "Federalism on the Bench," *The Weekly Standard*, December 3, 2001, p. 34.

34. J. W. Peltason, *Corwin and Peltason's Understanding the Constitution*, 7th ed. (Hinsdale, IL: Dryden Press, 1976), p. 177.

35. *Garcia v. San Antonio Metropolitan Transit Authority*, 469 U.S. 528 (1985).

36. *Gregory v. Ashcroft*, 501 U.S. 452 (1991).

37. *New York v. United States* (1992) 112 S. Ct. at 2431–32. For a detailed discussion of these issues, see "Constitution of the United States: Analysis and Interpretation" (Washington, DC: Government Printing Office, 2006), www.access.gpo.gov/congress/senate/constitution/con021.pdf.

38. *Printz v. United States*, 521 U.S. 898 (1997).

39. *City of Boerne v. Flores*, 521 U.S. 507 (1997), 520.

40. *Kimel et al. v. Florida Board of Regents*, 528 U.S. 62 (2000).

41. *Alabama v. Garrett*, 531 U.S. 356 (2001).

42. *Tennessee v. Lane*, 541 U.S. 509 (2004).

43. *Nevada Department of Human Resources v. Hibbs*, 538 U.S. 721 (2003).

44. *United States v. Lopez*, 514 U.S. 549 (1995).

45. *United States v. Morrison*, 529 U.S. 598 (2000).

46. *U.S. Term Limits, Inc. v. Thornton*, 514 U.S. 779 (1995).

47. *Romer v. Evans*, 517 U.S. 620 (1996).

48. *Atkins v. Virginia*, 536 U.S. 304 (2002); *Roper v. Simmons*, 543 U.S. 551 (2005).

49. Jonathan Turley, "It's Not the Cannabis, It's the Constitution," *Los Angeles Times*, August 5, 2002, Metro section, part 2, p. 11.

50. *Gonzales v. Raich*, 545 U.S. 1 (2005).

51. From a review of Greve, *Real Federalism*.

52. Martha Derthick, *Keeping the Compound Republic: Essays in American Federalism* (Washington, DC: Brookings Institution, 2001), pp. 9–32.

Comparing Ourselves to Others

a. Jonathan Rodden, "The Dilemma of Fiscal Federalism: Grants and Fiscal Performance around the World," *American Journal of Political Science* 46:3 (July, 2002): 670–87.

b. Alfred Stepan, "Federalism and Democracy: Beyond the U.S. Model," *Journal of Democracy* 10:4 (1999): 19–34.

c. Spain has a unitary government, but it is often referred to as a "de facto federation" because it would be politically impossible for the central government to revoke the autonomy of Galicia, Catalonia, or the Basque Country.

What Do Political Scientists Do?

a. *New State Ice Co. v. Liebmann*, 285 U.S. 262 (1932).

b. Charles R. Shipan and Craig Volden, "The Mechanisms of Policy Diffusion," *American Journal of Political Science* 52:4 (October 2008): 840–57.

Challenging Conventional Wisdom

a. Dale A. Krane, "The State of American Federalism, 2001–2002: Resilience in Response to Crisis," *Publius* 32:4 (Fall, 2002): 1–27.

b. Kiki Caruson, Susan A. MacManus, Matthew Kohen, and Thomas A. Watson, "Homeland Security Preparedness: The Rebirth of Regionalism," *Publius* 35:1 (Winter, 2005): 143–71.

c. Gallup Poll, August 31–September 2, 2009, www.pollingreport.com/institut.htm#Federal (accessed 10/5/09).

d. The data for the national government are from Gallup Poll, August 31–September 2, 2009, www.pollingreport.com/institut.htm#Federal

(accessed 10/13/09). The data for the "get the least for the money" question and the "too much power" question for state and local government are from John Kincaid and Richard L. Cole, "Public Opinion on Issues of U.S. Federalism in 2005: End of the Post-2001 Pro-Federal Surge?" *Publius* 35:1 (Winter, 2005): 169–88.

CHAPTER 4

1. Darren W. Davis and Brian D. Silver, "Civil Liberties vs. Security: Public Opinion in the Context of the Terrorist Attacks on America," *American Journal of Political Science* 48:1 (January, 2004): 33, 44.

2. Richard Morin and Claudia Deane, "Belief Erodes in the First Amendment," *Washington Post*, September 2, 2002.

3. Jane Mayer, "Outsourcing Torture: The Secret History of America's 'Extraordinary Rendition' Program," *The New Yorker*, February 14, 2005, www.newyorker.com/archive/2005/02/14/050214fa_fact6 (accessed 11/15/07).

4. Quoted in Linda Greenhouse, "O'Connor Foresees Limits on Freedom," *New York Times*, September 29, 2001.

5. *Arar v. Ashcroft et al.*, 2006 WL 346439 (E.D.N.Y.). The case was also dismissed because Arar, a Canadian citizen, did not have standing to sue the U.S. government. Supporters of this decision (and the practice more generally) say that it is an essential part of the War on Terror and that the enemy combatants who are arrested have no legal rights. Opponents say that the practice violates international law and our own standards of decency; furthermore, torture almost never produces useful information because people will say anything to get the torture to stop.

6. Pew Research Center, "Trends in Political Values and Core Attitudes: 1987–2007," March 22, 2007, http://people-press.org/reports/display.php3?ReportID=312 (accessed 2/8/08).

7. *State v. Massey et al.*, Supreme Court of North Carolina, 51 S.E.2d 179 (1949). The case was appealed to the Supreme Court, but the Court declined to hear the case, which means that the state decision stands (*Bunn v. North Carolina*, 336 U.S. 942 [1949]).

8. *Pennsylvania v. Miller*, Pennsylvania Court of Common Pleas, WL 31426193 (2002). However, supreme courts in Minnesota, Wisconsin, and several other states have decided that requiring the Amish to use orange SMV triangles violates their free exercise of religion.

9. *Wisconsin v. Yoder*, 403 U.S. 205 (1972).

10. Jeffrey Rosen, "Lemon Law," *The New Republic*, March 29, 1993, p. 17.

11. Max Farrand, ed., *The Records of the Federal Convention of 1787*, rev. ed. (New Haven, CT: Yale University Press, 1937), pp. 587–88, 617–18.

12. *The Papers of Thomas Jefferson*, ed. J. Boyd (Princeton, NJ: Princeton University Press, 1958), pp. 557–83, cited in Lester S. Jayson., ed., *The Constitution of the United States of America: Analysis and Interpretation* (Washington, DC: U.S. Government Printing Office, 1973), p. 900.

13. Ralph Ketcham, *The Anti-Federalist Papers and the Constitutional Convention Debates* (New York: Penguin Putnam, 2003), p. 237.

14. Ketcham, *The Anti-Federalist Papers and the Constitutional Convention Debates*, p. 247.

15. The two that were not ratified by the states were a complicated amendment on congressional apportionment and the pay raise amendment discussed in note 29.

16. 1 *Annals of Congress* 755 (August 17, 1789), cited in Jayson, *The Constitution of the United States of America*, p. 898.

17. Henry J. Abraham and Barbara A. Perry, *Freedom and the Court: Civil Rights and Civil Liberties in the United States*, 8th ed. (Lawrence, KS: University Press of Kansas, 2003), p. 34.

18. *Barron v. Baltimore*, 32 U.S. 243 (1833), 250.

19. Akhil Reed Amar, *The Bill of Rights* (New Haven, CT: Yale University Press, 1998), p. 290.

20. There is an intense scholarly debate on the topic, but we believe the evidence indicates that the authors of the 14th Amendment intended for it to apply the Bill of Rights to the states. The strongest argument against this position is Raoul Berger's *The Fourteenth Amendment and the Bill of Rights* (1989) and a good book in support is Amar's *The Bill of Rights* (1998).

21. *The Slaughterhouse Cases*, 83 U.S. 36 (1873). The plaintiffs also made a 13th Amendment claim (that the monopoly forced them to work in "involuntary servitude") and a "due process" claim, but both of those were rejected by the Court as well. The Court focused on the "privileges and immunities" argument and the idea of dual citizenship.

22. Abraham and Perry, *Freedom and the Court*, p. 51.

23. *Chicago, Burlington, and Quincy Railroad v. Chicago*, 166 U.S. 226 (1897).

24. *Twining v. New Jersey*, 211 U.S. 78, 98 (1908).

25. *Gitlow v. New York*, 268 U.S. 652, 666 (1925).

26. The exceptions are the establishment clause of the 1st Amendment and the 6th Amendment right to a public trial. *Wolf v. Colorado* also came between the two periods of increased activity, but it only partially applied the 4th Amendment's prohibition against unreasonable searches and seizures. The Court said that states may not engage in such searches, but then allowed the state to use evidence gathered in an "unreasonable" search. It wasn't until *Mapp v. Ohio* in 1961 that the Court ruled that illegally obtained evidence could not be used in a trial, thus giving the incorporation of the 4th Amendment some teeth.

27. *Palko v. Connecticut*, 302 U.S. 319 (1937).

28. Abraham and Perry, *Freedom and the Court*, p. 65.

29. One of them, which said that Congress could not raise its pay until an election had been held, was ratified more than 200 years later in 1992 as the 27th Amendment! Usually time limits are set for the ratification of constitutional amendments, but the original Bill of Rights did not have a time limit. Only six of the original thirteen states ratified the pay raise amendment. By 1982 only eight states had ratified it, but Gregory Watson, a student at the University of Texas, rediscovered the amendment when writing a term paper. He pushed the amendment through a letter-writing campaign, and his timing was perfect given the controversy over congressional pay raises in the 1980s and the generally low public opinion of Congress. See William T. Bianco, *Trust Representatives and Constituents* (Ann Arbor, MI: University of Michigan Press, 1994).

30. *Schenk v. United States*, 249 U.S. 47 (1919), 52.

31. Alan Dershowitz, *Shouting Fire: Civil Liberties in a Turbulent Age* (New York: Little, Brown, 2002).

32. *Debs v. United States*, 249 U.S. 211 (1919); *Frohwerk v. United States*, 249 U.S. 204 (1919).

33. *Abrams v. United States*, 250 U.S. 616 (1919), 630–31.

34. *Dennis v. United States*, 341 U.S. 494 (1951).

35. *Brandenburg v. Ohio*, 395 U.S. 444 (1969).

36. *Smith v. Goguen*, 415 U.S. 566 (1974).

37. *Tinker v. Des Moines School District*, 393 U.S. 503 (1969).

38. *Spence v. Washington*, 418 U.S. 405 (1974).

39. *Spence v. Washington*, 409–410.

40. *Texas v. Johnson*, 491 U.S. 397 (1989).

41. *United States v. Eichman*, 496 U.S. 310 (1990).

42. *United States v. O'Brien*, 391 U.S. 367, 376 (1968).

43. *Morse v. Frederick*, 127 S. Ct. 2618 (2007).

44. *Davis v. Federal Election Commission*, 128 S. Ct. 2749 (2008).

45. *Buckley v. Valeo*, 424 U.S. 1 (1976); *McConnell v. Federal Election Commission*, 540 U.S. 93 (2003).

46. *Board of Regents of the University of Wisconsin System et al., Petitioners v. Scott Harold Southworth et al.*, 529 U.S. 217 (2000).

47. Kermit L. Hall, "Free Speech on Public College Campuses: Overview," www.firstamendmentcenter.org/speech/pubcollege/overview.aspx (accessed 2/10/08).

48. Carolyn J. Palmer, Sophie W. Penney, Donald D. Gehring, and Jan A. Neiger, "Hate Speech and Hate Crimes: Campus Conduct Codes and Supreme Court Rulings," *National Association of Student Personnel Administrators Journal* 34:2 (1997), http://publications.naspa.org/naspajournal/vol34/iss2/art4 (accessed 12/18/07).

49. *City of St. Paul v. RAV*, 505 U.S. 377 (1992).

50. *Virginia v. Black*, 538 U.S. 343 (2003).

51. *De Jonge v. State of Oregon*, 299 U.S. 353 (1937).

52. *Edwards v. South Carolina*, 372 U.S. 229 (1963).

53. The Supreme Court declined to review the case in *Smith v. Collin*, 439 U.S. 916 (1978), which meant that the lower court rulings stood (447 F.Supp. 676 (1978), 578 F.2d 1197 (1978)). See Donald A. Downs, *Nazis in Skokie: Freedom, Community and the First Amendment* (Notre Dame, IN: University of Notre Dame Press, 1985), for an excellent analysis of this important case.

54. *Forsyth County v. Nationalist Movement*, 505 U.S. 123 (1992).

55. *Frisby et al. v. Schultz et al.*, 487 U.S. 474 (1988).

56. *Near v. Minnesota*, 283 U.S. 697 (1931), 719–20.

57. *New York Times v. United States*, 403 U.S. 713 (1971).

58. *Nebraska Press Assn. v. Stuart*, 427 U.S. 539 (1976), 556–62. See Abraham and Perry, *Freedom and the Court*, pp. 209–10, for a discussion of the two cases that reversed and then reinstated the standard of allowing press coverage of trials except in exceptional cases.

59. Douglas Lee, "Gag Orders," www.firstamendmentcenter.org/Press/topic.aspx?topic=gag_orders (accessed 2/10/08).

60. *Chaplinsky v. State of New Hampshire*, 315 U.S. 568 (1942).

61. *Chaplinsky v. State of New Hampshire.*

62. *New York Times v. Sullivan*, 376 U.S. 254 (1964), cited in Abraham and Perry, *Freedom and the Court*, p. 193.

63. *Hustler v. Falwell*, 485 U.S. 46 (1988).

64. *Hutchinson v. Proxmire*, 443 U.S. 111 (1979); *Wolston v. Reader's Digest Association*, 443 U.S. 157 (1979).

65. *Valentine v. Chrestensen*, 316 U.S. 52 (1942).

66. *Virginia State Board of Pharmacy v. Virginia Citizens Consumer Council, Inc.*, 425 U.S. 748 (1976); *City of Cincinnati v. Discovery Network, Inc. et al.*, 507 U.S. 410 (1993).

67. *Central Hudson Gas & Electric v. Public Service Commission*, 447 U.S. 557 (1980).

68. In 1996, Congress passed the Child Pornography Prevention Act. This law makes the possession, production, or distribution of child pornography a criminal offense punishable with up to fifteen years in jail and a fine. However, two parts of the law were struck down by the Court for being "overbroad and unconstitutional." *Ashcroft v. Free Speech Coalition*, 353 U.S. 234 (2002).

69. BBC News, "Curtains for Semi-nude Justice Statue," January 29, 2002, http://news.bbc.co.uk/2/hi/americas/1788845.stm (accessed 3/3/08).

70. *Jacobellis v. Ohio*, 378 U.S. 184, 197 (1964).

71. *Miller v. California*, 413 U.S. 15 (1973).

72. Kathleen Sullivan, "The First Amendment Wars," *The New Republic*, September 28, 1992, pp. 14, 35–40.

73. Quoted in Walter Kendrick, *The Secret Museum: Pornography in Modern Culture* (Berkeley, CA: University of California Press, 1996), p. 219.

74. *Reno et al. v. American Civil Liberties Union et al.*, 521 U.S. 844 (1997).

75. *Ashcroft v. American Civil Liberties Union*, 535 U.S. 564 (2004).

76. *Federal Communications Commission v. Pacifica Foundation*, 438 U.S. 726 (1978).

77. *Federal Communications Commission et al. v. Fox Television Stations*, 556 U.S. __ (2009).

78. *Federal Communications Commission and United States v. CBS Corporation*, 556 U.S. __ (2009).

79. James Hudson, "'A Wall of Separation,'" *Library of Congress Information Bulletin* 57:6 (June, 1998), www.loc.gov/loc/lcib/9806/danbury.html (accessed 3/3/08).

80. Abraham and Perry, *Freedom and the Court*, p. 300.

81. *Engle v. Vitale*, 370 U.S. 421 (1962).

82. *Wallace v. Jaffree*, 482 U.S. 38 (1985).

83. *Lee v. Weisman*, 505 U.S. 577 (1992); *Sante Fe Independent School District v. Doe*, 530 U.S. 290 (2000).

84. *Marsh v. Chambers*, 463 U.S. 783 (1983); *Jones v. Clear Creek Independent School*, 61 LW 3819 (1993).

85. *Lemon v. Kurtzman*, 403 U.S. 602 (1971).

86. *Lynch v. Donnelly*, 465 U.S. 668 (1984), 672–73.

87. Jeffrey Rosen, "Big Ten," *The New Republic*, March 14, 2004, p. 11.

88. *Van Orden v. Perry*, 03-1500 (2005); *McCreary County et al. v. American Civil Liberties Union of Kentucky*, 03-1693 (2005).

89. *Zelman v. Simmons-Harris*, 536 U.S. 639 (2002).

90. *Zobrest v. Catalina School District*, 509 U.S. 1 (1993). A similar decision in 1997 allowed a public school teacher to teach in a special program in a parochial school, *Agostini v. Felton*, 521 U.S. 203 (1997).

91. *Mitchell v. Helms*, 530 U.S. 793 (2000).

92. *Rosenberger v. University of Virginia*, 515 U.S. 819 (1995).

93. *Minersville School District v. Gobitis*, 310 U.S. 586 (1940).

94. *West Virginia Board of Education v. Barnette*, 319 U.S. 624 (1943), 642.

95. We will not cite all of the cases here. See Abraham and Perry, *Freedom and the Court*, Chap. 6, for a summary of cases on this topic, especially Tables 6.1 and 6.2.

96. *Employment Division, Department of Human Resources of Oregon v. Smith*, 494 U.S. 872 (1990), 878–80. This case is often erroneously reported as having banned the religious use of peyote. In fact, the Court said, "Although it is constitutionally permissible to exempt sacramental peyote use from the operation of drug laws, it is not constitutionally required."

97. *City of Boerne v. Flores*, 521 U.S. 527 (1997).

98. The court case was *Cutter v. Wilkinson*, No. 03-9877 (2005). See Linda Greenhouse, "Supreme Court Rules in Ohio Prison Case," *New York Times*, June 1, 2005, for a discussion of the broader debate.

99. *Gonzales v. O Centro Espirita Beneficente Uniao Do Vegetal (UDV) et al.*, 546 U.S. 418 (2006). The *Sherbert* test comes from *Sherbert v. Verner*, 374 U.S. 398 (1963).

100. *United States v. Miller*, 307 U.S. 174 (1939).

101. Robert J. Spitzer, *The Politics of Gun Control* (Chatham, NJ: Chatham House, 1995). Also see www.gunlawsuits.org/downloads/militiav.pdf for a complete list of the cases. The two cases recognizing the individual right to bear arms were *United States v. Timothy Joe Emerson*, 46 F. Supp. 2d 598 (1999), and the DC Circuit Court case that was appealed in the landmark ruling *Parker v. District of Columbia*, 478 F.3d 370 (DC Cir. 2007).

102. *District of Columbia v. Heller*, 554 U.S. 290 (2008).

103. *McDonald v. Chicago* 08-1521 (2010).

104. Edward Walsh, "U.S. Argues for Wider Gun Rights; Supreme Court Filing Reverses Past Policy," *Washington Post*, May 8, 2002, p. A1. For a lengthy memo from the attorney general that explores the individual rights argument, see www.usdoj.gov/olc/secondamendment2.htm#N_33_.

105. *Safford United School District No. 1 et al. v. Redding*, 557 U.S. __ (2009).

106. See Abraham and Perry, *Freedom and the Court*, Chap. 4, for a discussion of these cases.

107. *Mapp v. Ohio*, 367 U.S. 643 (1961).

108. *United States v. Calandra*, 414 U.S. 338 (1974).

109. *Illinois v. Gates*, 462 U.S. 213 (1983).

110. *United States v. Leon*, 468 U.S. 897 (1984).

111. *Herring v. United States*, 555 U.S. __ (2009).

112. *Murray v. United States*, 487 U.S. 533 (1988).

113. *Vernonia School District v. Acton*, 515 U.S. 646 (1995); *Board of Education of Pottawatomie County v. Earls*, 536 U.S. 832 (2002).

114. Sharon L. Larson, Joe Eyerman, Misty S. Foster, and Joseph C. Gfroer, "Worker Substance Use and Workplace Policies and Programs," June 2007, Substance Abuse and Mental Health Services Administration, www.oas.samhsa.gov/work2k7/work.pdf (accessed 3/3/08).

115. *Chandler v. Miller*, 520 U.S. 305 (1997).

116. Leslie Cauley, "NSA Has Massive Database of Americans' Phone Calls," *USA Today*, May 11, 2006, p. 1.

117. Lorraine Woellert and Dawn Kopecki, "The Snooping Goes Beyond Phone Calls," *Business Week*, May 29, 2006, p. 38; "Data Mining: Federal Efforts Cover a Wide Range of Uses," GAO Report 04-548, May 2004, www.gao.gov/new.items/dO4548.pdf.

118. Eric Lichtblau and James Risen, "Officials Say U.S. Wiretaps Exceeded Law," *New York Times*, April 16, 2009.

119. *Miranda v. Arizona*, 384 U.S. 436 (1966).

120. *New York v. Quarles*, 467 U.S. 649 (1984).

121. *Nix v. Williams*, 467 U.S. 431 (1984).

122. *Maryland v. Shatzer*, No. 08-680 (2010).

123. *Dickerson v. United States*, 530 U.S. 428 (2000).

124. *Benton v. Maryland*, 395 U.S. 784 (1969).

125. *Powell v. Alabama*, 287 U.S. 45 (1932).

126. *Gideon v. Wainwright*, 372 U.S. 335 (1963).

127. *Evitts v. Lucy*, 469 U.S. 387 (1985); *Wiggins v. Smith*, 539 U.S. 510 (2003). See Elizabeth Gable and Tyler Green, "*Wiggins v. Smith*: The Ineffective Assistance of Counsel Standard Applied Twenty Years after *Strickland*," *Georgetown Journal of Legal Ethics* (Summer, 2004), for a discussion of many of these issues.

128. *Klopfer v. North Carolina*, 386 U.S. 213 (1967).

129. The law is 18 U.S.C. § 3161(c)(1) and the ruling is *Zedner v. United States*, 05-5992 (2006).

130. The case concerning African Americans is *Batson v. Kentucky*, 106 S. Ct. 1712 (1986); the case about Latinos is *Hernandez v. New York*, 500 U.S. 352 (1991); and the gender case is *J.E.B. v. Alabama ex rel. T.B.*, 511 U.S. 127 (1994). Two recent cases affirming that peremptory challenges could not be used in a racially discriminatory fashion were *Miller-El v. Dretke*, 545 U.S. 231 (2005), and *Snyder v. Louisiana*, 552 U.S. 472 (2008).

131. *Furman v. Georgia*, 408 U.S. 238 (1972); *Gregg v. Georgia*, 428 U.S. 513 (1976).

132. See Abraham and Perry, *Freedom and the Court*, pp. 72–73, for a discussion of the earlier cases, and Charles Lane, "5–4 Supreme Court Abolishes Juvenile Executions," *Washington Post*, March 2, 2005, p. A1, for a discussion of the 2002 and 2005 cases. The 2008 case was *Kennedy v. Louisiana*, 554 U.S. __ (2008).

133. Lane, "5–4 Supreme Court Abolishes Juvenile Executions." Both sets of numbers on the increase in the number of states banning the death penalty include the twelve states that prohibit capital punishment in all instances.

134. *Baze and Bowling v. Rees*, 533 U.S. 35 (2008).

135. *Weems v. United States*, 217 U.S. 349 (1910).

136. *Trop v. Dulles*, 356 U.S. 86 (1958).

137. *Robinson v. California*, 370 U.S. 660 (1962).

138. *Hudson v. McMillian*, 503 U.S. 1 (1992); *Helling v. McKinney*, 509 U.S. 25 (1993).

139. *Solem v. Helm*, 463 U.S. 277 (1983).

140. *Harmelin v. Michigan*, 501 U.S. 957 (1991).

141. *Ewing v. California*, 538 U.S. 11 (2003); *Lockyer v. Andrade*, 538 U.S. 63 (2003). For a general discussion of these issues, see Editors' Note, "The Eighth Amendment, Proportionality, and the Changing Meaning of 'Punishments.'" *Harvard Law Review* 122:3 (January, 2009): 960–81.

142. *Griswold v. Connecticut*, 381 U.S. 479 (1965), 482–86.

143. *Griswold v. Connecticut*, 512–13.

144. *Roe v. Wade*, 410 U.S. 113 (1973), 129.

145. *Planned Parenthood of Southeastern Pennsylvania v. Casey*, 505 U.S. 833 (1992).

146. Adam Liptak, "The New 5-to-4 Supreme Court," *New York Times*, April 27, 2007.

147. Department of Human Services, Office of Disease Prevention and Epidemiology, "Seventh Annual Report on Oregon's Death with Dignity Act," March 10, 2005, www.oregon.gov/DHS/ph/pas/docs/year7.pdf (accessed 2/10/08).

148. *Gonzales v. Oregon*, 546 U.S. 23 (2006).

You Decide

a. Linda Greenhouse, "Justices Decline to Rule on Limits for Drug-Sniffing Dogs," *New York Times*, April 5, 2005, p. A19.

What Do Political Scientists Do?

a. Bruce Ackerman, *Before the Next Attack: Preserving Civil Liberties in an Age of Terrorism* (New Haven, CT: Yale University Press, 2006); Richard A. Posner, *Not a Suicide Pact: The Constitution in a Time of National Emergency* (New York: Oxford University Press, 2006).

b. Ackerman, *Before the Next Attack*, p. 2.

c. Ackerman, *Before the Next Attack*, p. 4.

d. Posner, *Not a Suicide Pact*, p. 84.

Challenging Conventional Wisdom

a. *Lucas v. South Carolina Coastal Council*, 505 U.S. 1003 (1992).

b. The dissenters' argument was that when the plaintiff became the owner, the law was already in effect so the market value of the land would already be lower because the wetlands could not be developed. Therefore, having paid the lower price, the owner should not be able to claim that the land was devalued by the regulation (see the dissent in *Palazzolo v. Rhode Island*, 533 U.S. 606 [2001]). This case gets a little more complicated because Palazzolo indirectly owned the land through shares he bought in a corporation in 1961 before the wetlands regulations had been passed. He became sole owner of the land after the regulation was enacted in the 1970s. Also, the Court ruled that he was not entitled to compensation because a portion of the land still could be developed and was worth at least $200,000, so he had not been denied "all beneficial use of his property."

c. *Kelo v. City of New London*, 545 U.S. 469 (2005).

d. Jeffrey Rosen, "The Unregulated Offensive," *New York Times Magazine*, April 17, 2005, pp. 42–49, 66, 128, 130.

Comparing Ourselves to Others

a. *Roper v. Simmons*, 543 U.S. 551 (2005).

b. Charles Lane, "5–4 Supreme Court Abolishes Juvenile Executions," *Washington Post*, March 2, 2005, p. A1.

c. *Roper v. Simmons*.

d. *Roper v. Simmons*.

e. Charles Lane, "Scalia Tells Congress to Mind Its Own Business," *Washington Post*, May 19, 2006, p. A19.

CHAPTER 5

1. Adam Nagourney and Megan Thee, "With Election Driven by Iraq, Voters Want New Approach," *New York Times*, November 2, 2006, p. A1.

2. For examples, see www.pollingreport.com, which collects poll results from many sources.

3. For examples of these claims, see Larry J. Sabato, *Feeding Frenzy: Attack Journalism and American Politics* (New York: Lanahan, 2000) and W. Lance Bennett and Robert M. Entman, *Mediated Politics: Communication in the Future of Democracy* (New York: Cambridge University Press, 2001).

4. For a review, see Arthur Lupia and Mathew D. McCubbins, *The Democratic Dilemma* (New York: Cambridge University Press, 1998).

5. Larry Bartels, "Partisanship and Voting Behavior, 1952–1996," *American Journal of Political Science* 44 (2000): 35–50.

6. Robert S. Erikson, Michael B. Mackuen, and James A. Stimson, *The Macro Polity* (New York: Cambridge University Press, 2002).

7. Angus Campbell, Phillip Converse, Warren Miller, and Donald Stokes, *The American Voter* (New York: Wiley, 1960); Phillip E. Converse, "The Nature of Belief Systems in Mass Publics," in *Ideology and Discontent*, ed. David E. Aptor (Glencoe, IL: The Free Press of Glencoe, 1964), pp. 209–61. For more modern versions of these arguments, see Eric R. A. N. Smith, *The Unchanging American Voter* (Berkeley, CA: University of California Press, 1989); Phillip E. Converse and Gregory Markus, "Plus ça Change . . .: The New CPS Election Study Panel," *American Political Science Review* 73:1 (March, 1979): 32–49.

8. Converse, "The Nature of Belief Systems in Mass Publics," p. 259.

9. Associated Press, "D'oh! More Know Simpsons Than Constitution," March 1, 2006, www.msnbc.msn.com/id/11611015/ (accessed 2/20/08).

10. Ipsos News Center, "Most Americans Can't Name Any Supreme Court Justices, Says FindLaw.com Survey," press release, January 10, 2006, www.ipsos-na.com/news/pressrelease.cfm?id=2933 (accessed 2/20/08).

11. Valerie Strauss, "Despite Lessons on King, Some Unaware of His Dream," *Washington Post*, January 15, 2007, p. B1.

12. Samuel Popkin, *The Reasoning Voter* (Chicago: University of Chicago Press, 1991).

13. John E. Sullivan, James E. Pierson, and Gregory E. Marcus, "Ideological Constraint in the Mass Public: A Methodological Critique and Some New Findings," *American Journal of Political Science* 23 (1978): 244–49.

14. Norman Nie, Sidney Verba, and John Petrocik, *The Changing American Voter* (Cambridge, MA: Harvard University Press, 1976).

15. Michael X. Delli Carpini and Scott Keeter, *What Americans Know about Politics and Why It Matters* (New Haven, CT: Yale University Press, 1997).

16. For an example focusing on foreign policy opinions, see John Aldrich, John Sullivan, and Eugene Borgida, "Foreign Affairs and Issue Voting: Do Presidential Candidates Waltz before a Blind Audience?," *American Political Science Review* 83 (1989): 125–41.

17. Donald Green, Bradley Palmquist, and Eric Schickler, "Macropartisanship: A Replication and Critique," *American Political Science Review* 92 (1998): 883–99; Robert S. Erikson, Michael B. Mackuen, and James A. Stimson, "What Moves Macropartisanship? A Response to Green, Palmquist, and Schickler," *American Political Science Review* 92 (1998): 901–12.

18. John Zaller, "Coming to Grips with V. O. Key's Concept of Latent Opinion," unpublished paper (Los Angeles: University of California, Los Angeles, 1998).

19. Morris Fiorina, *Retrospective Voting in American National Elections* (Cambridge, MA: Harvard University Press, 1981).

20. John Zaller, *The Nature and Origins of Mass Opinion* (New York: Cambridge University Press, 1992).

21. R. Michael Alvarez and John Brehm, *Hard Choices, Easy Answers* (Princeton, NJ: Princeton University Press, 2002).

22. John Zaller and Stanley Feldman, "A Theory of the Survey Response: Revealing Preferences Versus Answering Questions," *American Journal of Political Science* 36 (1992): 579–616.

23. Janet M. Box-Steffensmeier and Susan DeBoef, "Macropartisanship and Macroideology in the Sophisticated Electorate," *Journal of Politics* 63:1 (2001): 232–48.

24. Jack Citrin, Donald P. Green, Christopher Muste, and Cara Wong, "Public Opinion toward Immigration Reform: The Role of Economic Motivations," *American Journal of Political Science* 59:3 (1997): 858–82.

25. William G. Jacoby, "Issue Framing and Public Opinion on Government Spending," *American Journal of Political Science* 44:4 (2000): 750–67; L. M. Bartels, "Beyond the Running Tally: Partisan Bias in Political Perceptions," *Political Behavior* 24:2 (2002): 117–50.

26. Donald R. Kinder, "Exploring the Racial Divide: Blacks, Whites, and Opinion on National Policy," *American Journal of Political Science* 45:2 (2001): 439–49; Paul M. Sniderman and Thomas Piazza, *The Scar of Race* (Cambridge, MA: Harvard University Press, 1993).

27. Robert Huckfeldt, Jeffery Levine, William Morgan, and John Sprague, "Accessibility and the Political Utility of Partisan and Ideological Orientations," *American Journal of Political Science* 43:3 (July, 1999): 888–911.

28. George E. Marcus, John L. Sullivan, Elizabeth Theiss-Morse, and Sandra L. Wood, *With Malice toward Some: How People Make Civil Liberties Judgments* (New York: Cambridge University Press, 1995).

29. Stanley Feldman and Marco R. Steenbergen, "The Humanitarian Foundation of Public Support for Social Welfare," *American Journal of Political Science* 45:3 (2001): 658–77.

30. R. Michael Alvarez and John Brehm, "American Ambivalence towards Abortion Policy: Development of a Heteroskedastic Probit Model of Competing Values," *American Journal of Political Science* 39:4 (1995): 1055–82.

31. R. Michael Alvarez and John Brehm, "Are Americans Ambivalent towards Racial Policies?" *American Journal of Political Science* 41 (1997): 345–74.

32. Virginia Sapiro, "Not Your Parents' Political Socialization: Introduction for a New Generation," *Annual Review of Political Science* 7 (2004): 1–23.

33. Christopher Achen, "Parental Socialization and Rational Party Identification," *Political Behavior* 24 (2002): 151–70.

34. M. Kent Jennings and Richard G. Niemi, *Generations and Politics: A Panel Study of Young Adults and Their Parents* (Princeton, NJ: Princeton University Press, 1981).

35. Robert Putnam, *Bowling Alone: The Collapse and Revival of American Community* (New York: Simon and Schuster, 2000).

36. Richard G. Niemi and Mary Hepburn, "The Rebirth of Political Socialization," *Perspectives on Politics* 24 (1995): 7–16.

37. David Campbell, *Why We Vote: How Schools and Communities Shape Our Civic Life* (Princeton, NJ: Princeton University Press, 2006).

38. Sidney Verba, Kay Schlozman, and Henry Brady, *Voice and Equality: Civic Volunteerism in American Politics* (Cambridge, MA: Harvard University Press, 1995).

39. Paul Allen Beck and M. Kent Jennings, "Pathways to Participation," *American Political Science Review* 76 (1982): 94–108.

40. Fiorina, *Retrospective Voting in American National Elections*.

41. Edward G. Carmines and James A. Stimson, *Issue Evolution: Race and the Transformation of American Politics* (Princeton, NJ: Princeton University Press, 1990).

42. Stephen Ambrose, *Citizen Soldiers* (New York: Touchstone Books, 1997); Tom Brokaw, *The Greatest Generation* (New York: Random House, 1998).

43. Suzanne Mettler and Eric Welch, "Civic Generation: Policy Feedback Effects of the BI Bill in Political Involvement over the Life Course," *British Journal of Political Science* 34 (2004): 497–518.

44. Darren W. Davis and Brian D. Silver, "Civil Liberties vs. Security: Public Opinion in the Context of the Terrorist Attacks on America,"

American Journal of Political Science 48:1 (2004): 28–46; Leonie Huddy, Nadia Khatib, and Theresa Capelos, "The Polls: Trends," *Public Opinion Quarterly* 66 (2002): 418–50.

45. Pew Research Center, "Public More Optimistic About the Economy, But Still Reluctant to Spend," June 19, 2009, available at http://people-press.org/report/523/economy-spending (accessed 11/4/09).

46. Robert S. Erikson, Michael B. Mackuen, and James A. Stimson, "Macropartisanship," *American Political Science Review* 83 (1989): 1125–42.

47. John Zaller, *The Nature and Origins of Mass Opinion* (New York: Cambridge University Press, 1992).

48. Richard Nadwau et al., "Class, Party, and South-Nonsouth Differences," *American Politics Research* 32 (2004): 52–67.

49. James H. Kuklinski et al., "Racial Prejudice and Attitudes toward Affirmative Action," *American Journal of Political Science* 41 (1997): 402–19.

50. Donald P. Green, Bradley Palmquist, and Eric Schickler, *Partisan Hearts and Minds* (New Haven, CT: Yale University Press, 2002).

51. Don Balz, "Contests Serve as Warning to Democrats: It's Not 2008 Anymore," *Washington Post*, November 4, 2009, p. A1.

52. For elaboration on this point, see William T. Bianco, Richard G. Niemi, and Harold W. Stanley, "Partisanship and Group Support over Time: A Multivariate Analysis," *American Political Science Review* 80 (September, 1986): 969–76.

53. Arthur Lupia and Mathew D. McCubbins, *The Democratic Dilemma* (New York: Cambridge University Press, 1998).

54. Lawrence R. Jacobs and Robert Y. Shapiro, *Politicians Don't Pander: Political Manipulation and the Loss of Democratic Responsiveness* (Chicago: University of Chicago Press, 2000).

55. Pollster.com, "IVR and Internet: How Reliable?" September 28, 2006, www.pollster.com/mystery_pollster/ivr_internet_how_reliable.php (accessed 2/21/08).

56. Alvarez and Brehm, "American Ambivalence towards Abortion Policy."

57. For data on reported and actual turnout, see Chapter 8.

58. Gary Langer, "Two Years from Election, Looking at Early Polls," *ABC News*, January 18, 2007, http://abcnews.go.com/Politics/story?id=2802742&page=1 (accessed 2/21/08).

59. James H. Kuklinski et al., "Misinformation and the Currency of Democratic Citizenship," *Journal of Politics* 62:3 (2000): 790–816.

60. Pew Research Center, "Health Care Reform Closely Followed, Much Discussed," available at http://people-press.org/reports/pdf/537.pdf (accessed 11/5/09).

61. George H. Bishop, *The Illusion of Public Opinion: Fact and Artifact in Public Opinion Polls* (Washington, DC: Roman and Littlefield, 2004).

62. Delli Carpini and Keeter, *What Americans Know about Politics and Why It Matters*.

63. Delli Carpini and Keeter, *What Americans Know about Politics and Why It Matters*.

64. Morris P. Fiorina, Samuel J. Abrams, and Jeremy C. Pope, *Culture War? The Myth of a Polarized America* (New York: Longman, 2002).

65. For data on how responses to these questions changed over time, see "Quick Tables for the GSS 1972–2004 Cumulative Datafile," http://sda.berkeley.edu:8080/quicktables/quickconfig.do?gss04 (accessed 2/13/08).

66. For a review of the literature on trust in government, see Karen Cook, Russell Hardin, and Margaret Levi, *Cooperation without Trust* (New York: Russell Sage Foundation, 2005), as well as Marc J. Hetherington, *Why Trust Matters: Declining Political Trust and the Demise of American Liberalism* (Princeton, NJ: Princeton University Press, 2004).

67. William T. Bianco, *Trust: Representatives and Constituents* (Ann Arbor, MI: University of Michigan Press, 1994).

68. Sean M. Theriault, *The Power of the People: Congressional Competition, Public Attention, and Voter Retribution* (Columbus, OH: Ohio State University Press, 2005).

69. John R. Hibbing and Elizabeth Theiss-Morse, *Congress as Public Enemy: Public Attitudes toward American Political Institutions* (New York: Cambridge University Press, 1995).

70. Thomas Rudolph and Jillian Evans, "Political Trust, Ideology, and Public Support for Government Spending," *American Journal of Political Science* 49 (2005): 660–71.

71. Patricia Moy and Michael Pfau, *With Malice toward All? The Media and Public Confidence in Democratic Institutions* (Boulder, CO: Praeger, 2000).

72. Richard Fenno, *Home Style: U.S. House Members in Their Districts* (Boston: Little, Brown, 1978).

73. William T. Bianco, Daniel Lipinski, and Ryan W. Work, "What Happens when House Members 'Run with Congress'? The Electoral Consequences of Institutional Loyalty," *Legislative Studies Quarterly* 26 (2003): 413–27.

74. Robert S. Erikson, Michael B. Mackuen, and James A. Stimson, *The Macro Polity* (New York: Cambridge University Press, 2002).

75. James A. Stimson, *Public Opinion in America: Moods, Swings, and Cycles* (Boulder, CO: Westview Press, 1999).

76. Robert S. Erikson, Michael B. Mackuen, and James A. Stimson, "American Politics: The Model" (unpublished paper, Columbia University, 2000).

77. See, for example, Pew Research Center, "Iraq Looms Large in Nationalized Election," October 5, 2006, http://people-press.org/reports/display.php3?ReportID=290, as well as data at www.pollingreport.com.

78. Pew Research Center, "Nation's Real Estate Slump Hits Wealthy Areas," October 11, 2007, http://people-press.org/reports/display.php3?ReportID=361 (accessed 5/5/08).

79. Robert Kuttner, "The American Health Care System," *New England Journal of Medicine* 340 (1999): 163–68.

80. Hope Yen, "Frist Wants Immigration Vote This Week," ABC News, September 24, 2006, http://abcnews.go.com/Politics/wireStory?id=2484862 (accessed 2/22/08).

81. Quinnipiac University Poll, "Let Illegal Immigrants Become Citizens, U.S. Voters Tell Quinnipiac Poll," November 21, 2006, www.quinnipiac.edu/x1284.xml?ReleaseID=988&What=700%20mile%20fence&strArea=;&strTime=120 (accessed 2/25/08).

82. Data aggregated from various polls; see Pollingreport.com, "Law and Civil Rights," www.pollingreport.com/civil.htm (accessed 2/25/08).

83. Thom Shanker and David S. Cloud, "The Reach of War: Bush's Plan for Iraq Runs into Opposition in Congress," *New York Times*, January 12, 2007, p. A1.

84. Andrew Revkin, "A New Middle Stance Emerges in Debate over Climate," *New York Times*, January 1, 2007, p. 16.

What Do Political Scientists Do?

a. James Stimson, *Tides of Consent: How Public Opinion Shapes American Politics* (New York: Cambridge University Press, 2004).

CHAPTER 6

1. James Hirsen, "Shaniya Davis's Death Can Bring Attention to Trafficking of Children," *LA Legal Examiner*, November 17, 2009, available at www.examiner.com/x-19663-LA-Legal-Examiner~y2009m11d17-Shaniya-Daviss-death-can-bring-attention-to-trafficking-of-children (accessed 11/19/09).

2. Christopher Beam, "800,000 Missing Kids? Really?" January 17, 2007, available at www.slate.com/id/2157738/ (accessed 11/20/09).

3. Monica Davey, "Case Shows Limits of Sex Offender Alert Programs," *New York Times*, September 1, 2009.

4. Glenn Muschert, Melissa Young-Spillers, and Dawn Carr, "Childhood Abduction Policy: Influenced by Media Coverage or Empirical Data?," unpublished paper, 2005, www.drc.ohio.gov/web/reports/Muschert PaperRevised.pdf.

5. Jason Barabas, and Jennifer Jerit, "Estimating the Causal Effects of Media Coverage on Policy-Specific Knowledge," *American Journal of Political Science* 53 (2008): 73–89.

6. Thomas E. Patterson, *Out of Order* (New York: Alfred A. Knopf, 1993); Robert D. Putnam, *Bowling Alone* (New York: Basic Books, 2000).

7. Thomas Patterson, "Bad News, Period," *Political Science and Politics* 29 (1996): 17–20.

8. Charles E. Clark, *The Public Prints: The Newspaper in Anglo-American Culture, 1665–1740* (New York: Oxford University Press, 1994).

9. William H. Riker, *The Strategy of Rhetoric: Campaigning for the American Constitution* (New Haven, CT: Yale University Press, 1996).

10. Geoffrey R. Stone, *Perilous Times: Free Speech in Wartime from the Sedition Act of 1798 to the War on Terrorism* (New York: Norton, 2004).

11. John D. Stevens, *Sensationalism and the New York Press* (New York: Columbia University Press, 1991).

12. Michael Schudson, *Discovering the News: A Social History of American Newspapers* (New York: Basic Books, 1978).

13. Robert C. Williams, *Horace Greeley: Champion of American Freedom* (New York: New York University Press, 2006).

14. W. Joseph Campbell, *Yellow Journalism: Puncturing the Myths, Defining the Legacies* (Boulder, CO: Praeger, 2003).

15. Lincoln Steffens, *The Shame of the Cities* (New York: McClure, Phillips & Co., 1904); Upton Sinclair, *The Jungle* (New York: Doubleday, Page, 1906).

16. Gay Talese, *The Kingdom and the Power* (New York: Calder and Boyars, 1983).

17. For a detailed history, see United States Early Radio History, www.earlyradiohistory.us.

18. This discussion draws on the summary "Merging Media: How Relaxing FCC Ownership Rules Has Affected the Media Business," available at www.pbs.org/newshour/media/conglomeration/fcc2.html (accessed 2/26/08).

19. Peter Braestrup, *Big Story: How the American Press and Television Reported and Interpreted the Crisis of Tet 1968 in Vietnam* (New Haven, CT: Yale University Press, 1983).

20. For an extended discussion of the fairness doctrine and related issues, see "Fairness Doctrine: U.S. Broadcasting Policy," http://www.museum.tv/archives/etv/F/htmlF/fairnessdoct/fairnessdoct.htm.

21. Chris Cillizza and Shailagh Murray, "Contemplating a Run for Office Can Complicate Television Reruns," *Washington Post*, July 15, 2007, p. A2.

22. The Project for Excellence in Journalism, "The State of the News Media, 2007: Ownership" (2007), www.stateofthenewsmedia.org/2007/narrative_overview_ownership.asp?cat=5&media=1 (accessed 2/26/08).

23. The FCC Web site has a detailed discussion of the regulatory changes and the logic behind these revisions. See "Strategic Goals: Media," www.fcc.gov/mediagoals.

24. The *Columbia Journalism Review* maintains a list of holdings for major media companies at Who Owns What, www.cjr.org/tools/owners.

25. Joanna Glasner, "Tech a Key in Media Rule Change," *Wired*, June 3, 2003, www.wired.com/techbiz/media/news/2003/06/59079 (accessed 2/26/08).

26. Glasner, "Tech a Key in Media Rule Change."

27. For details, see the FCC's Research Studies on Media Ownership, July 31, 2007, www.fcc.gov/ownership/studies.html.

28. Jacques Steinberg, "Howard Stern Prepares for Life without Limits," *New York Times*, October 20, 2005; Stephen Labaton, "Decency Ruling Thwarts FCC on Vulgarities," *New York Times*, June 5, 2007.

29. Bryan Curtis, "The Shock Jock in Winter," *Slate*, March 2, 2004, www.slate.com/id/2096493 (accessed 2/26/08).

30. Adam Cohen, "Editorial Observer; Fighting for Free Speech Means Fighting for . . . Howard Stern," *New York Times*, May 3, 2004.

31. Cohen, "Editorial Observer; Fighting for Free Speech Means Fighting for . . . Howard Stern."

32. Jacques Steinberg, "Stern Likes His New Censor: Himself," *New York Times*, January 8, 2007.

33. See, for example, James J. Cramer, "Newspapers Still Stumble Online," RealMoney.com, May 2, 2005, www.thestreet.com/p/_rms/rmoney/jamesjcramer/10221101.html (accessed 2/26/08).

34. Magazine Publishers of America, "Average Circulation for Top 100 Magazines," www.magazine.org/Circulation/circulation_trends_and_magazine_handbook/1353.cfm (accessed 2/26/08).

35. Paul Starr, "Reclaiming the Air," *The American Prospect*, March 2004, pp. 57–61.

36. The president's current budget is available at www.whitehouse.gov/omb/budget, the Federal Register can be found at www.gpoaccess.gov/fr, and Government Accountability Office reports are available at www.gao.gov.

37. The Iraq Index is available at www.brookings.edu/iraqindex.

38. The Center for Responsive Politics, www.opensecrets.org.

39. Pollster, www.pollster.com.

40. Larry Craig Mug Shot, The Smoking Gun, www.thesmokinggun.com/mugshots/larrycraigmug1.html (accessed 11/20/09).

41. Hardblogger, http://hardblogger.msnbc.msn.com.

42. National Review Online, www.nationalreview.com.

43. The Note, http://abcnews.go.com/Politics/TheNote.

44. SCOTUSblog, www.scotusblog.com/movabletype.

45. Politico, www.politico.com; Slate, www.slate.com.

46. Salon, www.salon.com; The Huffington Post, www.huffingtonpost.com; Power Line, www.powerlineblog.com; Town Hall, www.townhall.com.

47. A. J. Liebling, "Do You Belong in Journalism?" *The New Yorker*, May 14, 1960, p. 105.

48. John Hockenberry, "The Blogs of War," *Wired*, August 2005, www.wired.com/wired/archive/13.08/milblogs.html (accessed 2/26/08).

49. The video "Allen's Listening Tour" is available at http://youtube.com/watch?v=9G7gq7GQ71c (accessed 2/26/08).

50. The *Washington Post* has an archive of previous online discussions at "Post Politics Hour," www.washingtonpost.com/wp-dyn/content/linkset/2005/09/30/LI2005093000746.html.

51. For a skeptical introduction to this argument, see the proceedings of "MeetUp, Craigslist, eBay: Has the Web Changed Politics?," a conference at the Harvard School of Law, December 9–11, 2004, http://cyber.law.harvard.edu/is2k4/home.

52. Bruce Bimber, "Information and Political Engagement in America: The Search for Effects of Information Technology at the Individual Level," *Political Research Quarterly* 54 (2001): 53–67; Caroline J. Tolbert and Ramona S. McNeal, "Unraveling the Effects of the Internet on Political Participation," *Political Research Quarterly* 56 (2003): 175–85.

53. Pew Research Center, "Public Knowledge of Current Affairs Little Changed by News and Information Revolutions," April 15, 2007, http://people-press.org/reports/display.php3?ReportID = 319 (accessed 2/28/08).

54. "Pew Internet & American Life Project surveys 2000–2009," available at www.pewinternet.org/static-pages/trend-data/online-activities-20002009.aspx (accessed 12/1/09).

55. Markus Prior, *Post-Broadcast Democracy: How Media Choice Increases Inequality in Political Involvement and Polarizes Elections* (New York: Cambridge University Press, 2007).

56. Dana Priest, "CIA Holds Terror Suspects in Secret Prisons," *Washington Post*, November 2, 2005, p. A1. Various Bush administration staffers and Republicans in Congress demanded an investigation that would identify and prosecute the people who leaked information about the prison network.

57. James Risen and Eric Lichtblau, "Spying Program Snared U.S. Calls," *New York Times*, December 21, 2005, p. A1.

58. Scott Shane and David E. Sanger, "Criminal Inquiry Opened into Leak in Eavesdropping," *New York Times*, December 31, 2005, p. A1.

59. Federation of American Scientists, Secrecy and Government Bulletin, issue 64, January 1997, www.fas.org/sgp/bulletin/sec64.html (accessed 2/26/08).

60. David Folkenflik, "'Times' Held Story on U.S. Surveillance for a Year," *All Things Considered*, December 16, 2005, www.npr.org/templates/story/story.php?storyId=5058710 (accessed 2/26/08).

61. Michael Calderone, "Obama Calls on HuffPost for Iran Question," June 23, 2009, www.politico.com/michaelcalderone/0609/Obama_calls_on_HuffPost_for_Iran_question.html (accessed 11/20/09).

62. Bob Woodward, "How Mark Felt Became Deep Throat," *Washington Post*, June 2, 2005, p. A1.

63. Matthew A. Baum, *Soft News Goes to War: Public Opinion and American Foreign Policy in the New Media Age* (Princeton, NJ: Princeton University Press, 2003).

64. John Zaller, *The Nature and Origins of Mass Opinion* (New York: Cambridge University Press, 1992).

65. S. H. Chaffee, X. Zhao, and G. Leshner, "Political Knowledge and the Campaign Media of 1992," *Communication Research* 21 (1994): 305–24; Jeffrey J. Mondak, *Nothing to Read: Newspapers and Elections in a Social Experiment* (Ann Arbor, MI: University of Michigan Press, 1995).

66. For a discussion of these concepts, see Paul M. Sniderman and Sean M. Theriault, "The Structure of Political Argument and the Logic of Issue Framing," in *Studies in Public Opinion*, ed. William E. Saris and Paul M. Sniderman (Princeton, NJ: Princeton University Press, 2004); Shanto Iyengar and Donald Kinder, *News That Matters* (Chicago: University of Chicago Press, 1987). See also Maxwell McCombs and Donald L. Shaw, "The Agenda-Setting Functions of Mass Media," *Public Opinion Quarterly* 36 (1972): 176–87; and Amos Tversky and Daniel Kahnemann, "The Framing of Decisions and the Psychology of Choice," *Science* 211 (1981): 453–58.

67. Walter Lippman, *Public Opinion* (1922; repr. New York: Free Press, 1997).

68. J. T. Klapper, *The Effects of Mass Communication* (New York: Free Press, 1960); see also Paul F. Lazarsfeld, Bernard Berelson, and Hazel Gaudet, *The People's Choice* (New York: Columbia University Press, 1944).

69. Stephen Ansolabehere, Roy Behr, and Shanto Iyengar, "The Evolution of Media Effects Research," in *The Media Game: American Politics in the Television Age*, ed. Stephen Ansolabehere, Roy Behr, and Shanto Iyengar (New York: MacMillan, 1993), 129–38. Steven E. Finkel, "Reexamining the 'Minimal Effects' Model in Recent Presidential Campaigns," *Journal of Politics* 55 (1993): 1–21. Kathleen H. Jamieson, *Everything You Think You Know about Politics . . . And Why You're Wrong* (New York: Basic Books, 2000). Shanto Iyengar and Adam Simon, "New Perspectives and Evidence on Political Communication and Campaign Effects," *Annual Review of Psychology* 51 (2000): 149–69.

70. James N. Druckman and Michael Parkin, "The Impact of Media Bias: How Editorial Slant Affects Voters," *Journal of Politics* 67 (2005): 4, 1030–49; for similar results, see Kim Fridkin Kahn and Patrick J.

Kenney, "The Slant of the News," *American Political Science Review* 96 (2002): 381–94.

71. Jon A. Krosnick and Laura Brannon, "The Impact of the Gulf War on the Ingredients of Presidential Evaluations: Multidimensional Effects of Political Involvement," *American Political Science Review* 87 (1993): 963–75.

72. Jon A. Krosnick and Joanne Miller, "News Media Impact on the Ingredients of Presidential Evaluations: Politically Knowledgeable Citizens Are Guided by a Trusted Source," *American Journal of Political Science* 44 (2000): 295–309.

73. The entire list can be found at www.projectcensored.org/top-stories/category/two-thousand-and-ten-book.

74. Pew Research Center, "Cable and Internet Loom Large in a Fragmented Political Universe," January 11, 2004, http://people-press.org/reports/display.php3?ReportID=200 (accessed 2/26/08).

75. Mark Silva, "Fox Rolls Wrong Video, Heads May Roll," November 18, 2009, http://www.swamppolitics.com/news/politics/blog/2009/11/fox_rolls_wrong_tape_heads_may.html (accessed 12/1/09).

76. Media Research Center, "Media Refusing to Report Positive News from Iraq," press release, January 16, 2006, www.mediaresearch.org/press/2006/press20060117.asp (accessed 2/29/08).

77. Richard Noyes, "TV's Bad News Brigade: ABC, CBS and NBC's Defeatist Coverage of the War in Iraq," Media Research Center Special Report, October 13, 2005, www.mrc.org/SpecialReports/2005/report101405_p1.asp (accessed 2/29/08).

78. Noyes, "TV's Bad News Brigade," p. 2.

79. See "Rumsfeld on Iraq," *Washington Times*, December 6, 2005, www.washingtontimes.com/op-ed/20051205-094913-3994r.htm (accessed 2/29/08); and "On Balance," *Washington Times*, December 7, 2005, www.washingtontimes.com/op-ed/20051206-091140-1752r.htm (accessed 2/29/08).

80. This description runs on the editorial masthead of every issue of *The Nation*.

81. For these and other data, see the Brookings Iraq Index, www.brookings.edu/iraqindex.

82. Matthew Gentzkow and Jessie M. Shapiro, "Media Bias and Reputation," *Journal of Political Economy* 114 (2006): 280–316.

83. Paul Allen Beck, Russell J. Dalton, Steven Greene, and Robert Huckfeldt, "The Social Calculus of Voting: Interpersonal, Media, and Organizational Influences on Presidential Choices," *American Political Science Review* 96 (2002): 57–73.

84. Patterson, "Bad News, Period."

85. Iyengar, *Is Anyone Responsible?*

86. Thomas Patterson, "Doing Well and Doing Good: How Soft News and Critical Journalism Are Shrinking the News Audience and Weakening Democracy—and What News Outlets Can Do about It," (Cambridge, MA: Joan Shorenstein Center on the Press, Politics, and Public Policy, Harvard University, 2000), www.ksg.harvard.edu/presspol/research_publications/reports/softnews.pdf (accessed 2/29/08).

87. Baum, *Soft News Goes to War.*

88. Frank D. Gilliam Jr. and Shanto Iyengar, "Prime Suspects: The Influence of Local Television News on the Viewing Public," *American Journal of Political Science* 44:3 (2000): 560–73.

89. Patterson, *Out of Order.*

90. Pew Research Center, "Self Censorship: How Often and Why: Journalists Avoiding the News," April 30, 2000, http://people-press.org/reports/display.php3?ReportID=39 (accessed 2/29/08).

91. T. E. Patterson, *The Vanishing Voter* (New York: Knopf, 2002); J. N. Cappella and K. H. Jamieson, *Spiral of Cynicism: The Press and the Public Good* (New York: Oxford University Press, 1997).

92. Pippa Norria, *A Virtuous Cycle* (New York: Cambridge University Press, 2003).

93. Quoted in Baum, *Soft News Goes to War*, p. 57.

94. Brent Cunningham, "Across the Great Divide: Class," *Columbia Journalism Review* 3 (May/June, 2004), http://cjrarchives.org/issues/2004/3/cunningham-class.asp (accessed 2/29/08).

95. John R. Hibbing and Elizabeth Theiss-Morse, *Congress as Public Enemy* (New York: Cambridge University Press, 1995); see also, John R. Hibbing and Elizabeth Theiss-Morse, "The Media's Role in Public Negativity toward Congress: Distinguishing Emotional Reactions and Cognitive Evaluations," *American Journal of Political Science* 42 (April, 1998): 475–98.

96. Shanto Iyengar, Helmut Norpoth, and Kyu S. Hahn, "Consumer Demand for Election News: The Horserace Sells," *Journal of Politics* 66:1 (2004): 157–75.

97. Baum, *Soft News Goes to War*, p. 57.

You Decide

a. Porter Goss, "Loose Lips Sink Spies," *New York Times*, February 10, 2006, p. 25.

What Do Political Scientists Do?

a. Stefano Della Vigna and Ethan Kaplan, "The FOX News Effect: Media Bias and Voting," *Quarterly Journal of Economics* 122 (2007): 1187–1234.

b. Thomas E. Nelson, Rosalee A. Clawson, and Zoe M. Oxley, "Media Framing of a Civil Liberties Conflict and Its Effect on Tolerance," *American Political Science Review* 91 (1997): 567–83.

c. Dennis Chong and James N. Druckman, "A Theory of Framing and Opinion Formation in Competitive Elite Environments," *Journal of Communication* 57 (2007): 99–118.

d. Shanto Iyengar, *Is Anyone Responsible? How Television Frames Political Issues* (Chicago: University of Chicago Press, 1991).

Challenging Conventional Wisdom

a. Michael Kelly, "Left Everlasting (Cont'd)," *Washington Post*, December 18, 2002, p. A35.

b. For details on the survey, see American Society of Newspaper Editors, Survey Report Page 19, July 7, 1997, www.asne.org/kiosk/reports/97reports/journalists90s/survey19.html, and Fairness and Accuracy in Reporting, "Examining the 'Liberal Media' Claim," June 1, 1998, www.fair.org/reports/journalist-survey.html.

Comparing Ourselves to Others

a. Pew Center for Excellence in Journalism, "Swine Flu Coverage around the World," May 28, 2009, available at www.journalism.org/analysis_report/Swine_Flu_Coverage_around_the_World (accessed 11/18/09).

CHAPTER 7

1. John Aldrich, *Why Parties?* (Chicago: University of Chicago Press, 1995).

2. Joseph Schlesinger, *Political Parties and the Winning of Office* (Ann Arbor, MI: University of Michigan Press, 1994).

3. The three-part description first appeared in V. O. Key, *Politics, Parties, and Pressure Groups* (New York: Crowell, 1956). For a more recent description, see Paul Allen Beck and Marjorie Hershey, *Party Politics in America* (New York: Longman, 2004).

4. William Nesbit Chambers and Walter Dean Burnham, *The American Party Systems: Stages of Political Development* (Oxford, UK: Oxford University Press, 1966).

5. Aldrich, *Why Parties?*

6. Donald H. Hickey, "Federalist Party Unity and the War of 1812," *Journal of American Studies* 12 (April, 1978): 23–39; William T. Bianco, David B. Spence, and John D. Wilkerson, "The Electoral Connection in the Early Congress: The Case of the Compensation Act of 1816," *American Journal of Political Science* 40 (February, 1996): 145–71.

7. Aldrich, *Why Parties?*

8. James MacPherson, *Battle Cry of Freedom: The Civil War Era* (New York: Oxford University Press, 1988).

9. Michael F. Holt, *The Rise and Fall of the Whig Party: Jacksonian Politics and the Onset of the Civil War* (New York: Oxford University Press, 1999).

10. Harold W. Stanley, William T. Bianco, and Richard G. Niemi, "Partisanship and Group Support over Time: A Multivariate Analysis," *American Political Science Review* 80 (1986): 969–76.

11. John Aldrich, *Why Parties?* re ed. notes 15–20.

12. James L. Sundquist, *Dynamics of the Party System*, rev. ed. (Washington, DC: Brookings Institution, 1983).

13. Aldrich, *Why Parties?*

14. John H. Aldrich and Richard G. Niemi, "The Sixth American Party System: Electoral Change, 1952–1992," in *Broken Contract: Changing Relationships between Americans and Their Governments*, ed. Steven Craig, (Boulder, CO: Westview Press, 1993).

15. Edward G. Carmines and James A. Stimson, *Issue Evolution: Race and the Transformation of American Politics* (Princeton, NJ: Princeton University Press, 1989).

16. Harold W. Stanley and Richard G. Niemi, "Partisanship, Party Coalitions, and Group Support, 1952–2004," *Presidential Studies Quarterly* 36:2 (2006): 172–88.

17. Charles S. Bullock III, Donna R. Hoffman, and Ronald Keith Gaddie, "Regional Variations in the Realignment of American Politics, 1944–2004," *Social Science Quarterly* 87:3 (2006): 494–518.

18. The full list of Democratic constituency groups is available at www.democrats.org/communities.html. A list of Republican teams is available at www.gop.com/Teams/default.aspx.

19. Jon F. Hale, "The Making of the New Democrats," *Political Science Quarterly* 110:2 (1995): 207–32.

20. James C. Moore and Wayne Slater, *Bush's Brain: How Karl Rove Made George W. Bush Presidential* (New York: Wiley, 2003).

21. James Monroe, *The Political Party Matrix* (Albany, NY: SUNY Press, 2001).

22. Gary Cox and Mathew McCubbins, *Legislative Leviathan* (Berkeley, CA: University of California Press, 1993); James M. Snyder and Michael M. Ting, "An Informational Rationale for Political Parties," *American Journal of Political Science* 46 (2002): 90–110.

23. Adam Nagourney and Cassi Feldman, "Early Primary Rush Upends '08 Campaign Plans," *New York Times*, March 12, 2007, p. A1; Linda Feldmann, "An Uproar Over '08 Primary Calendar," May 25, 2007, *Christian Science Monitor*, p. 2; Christopher Cooper, "Early Voting May Clip Iowa's Role," *Wall Street Journal*, May 22, 2007, p. A4.

24. Raymond Wolfinger, "Why Political Machines Have Not Withered Away and Other Revisionist Thoughts," *Journal of Politics* 34:2 (1972): 365–98.

25. For details on Tammany Hall, see William L. Riordon, *Plunkitt of Tammany Hall* (1905; repr. New York: Dutton, 1963) also available at www.marxists.org/reference/archive/plunkett-george/tammany-hall.

26. Riordan, *Plunkitt of Tammany Hall*.

27. David Kirkpatrick, "Pelosi Faces Competing Pressures on Health Care," *New York Times*, November 9, 2009, p. A1.

28. Jason Roberts and Steven Smith, "Procedural Contexts, Party Strategy, and Conditional Party Government," *American Journal of Political Science* 47:2 (2003): 205–317.

29. For details on NOMINATE scores, see Keith Poole and Howard Rosenthal, *Congress: A Political-Economic History of Roll Call Voting* (New York: Oxford University Press, 1997).

30. David Rohde, *Parties and Leaders in the Post-Reform House* (Chicago: University of Chicago Press, 1991).

31. Carl Hulse, 2009, "Advocates of Gun Rights Are Poised for a Victory," *New York Times*, May 20, 2009, p. A16.

32. Carl Hulse and Sheryl Gay Stolberg, "Changes Sought in Naming of Prosecutors," *New York Times*, March 20, 2007, p. A15.

33. John Holusha, "Senate Continues Debate over Immigration Reform," *New York Times*, April 4, 2006, p. A1.

34. Rachel Swarns, "Bill to Broaden Immigration Law Gains in Senate," *New York Times*, March 28, 2006, p. A1.

35. Donald Green, Bradley Palmquist, and Eric Schickler, *Partisan Hearts and Minds* (New Haven, CT: Yale University Press, 2004); Christopher Achen, "Political Socialization and Rational Party Identification," *Political Behavior* 24:2 (2002): 151–70.

36. Morris Fiorina, *Retrospective Voting in American National Elections* (New Haven, CT: Yale University Press, 1981).

37. Michael Meffert, Helmut Norpoth, and Anirudh V. S. Ruhil, "Realignment and Macropartisanship," *American Political Science Review* 95:4 (2001): 953–62.

38. Walter Dean Burnham, "The Reagan Heritage," in *The Election of 1988: Reports and Interpretations*, ed. Gerald M. Pomper et al. (Chatham, NJ: Chatham House, 1989).

39. Martin P. Wattenberg, *The Decline of American Political Parties: 1952–1994* (Cambridge, MA: Harvard University Press, 1996).

40. David S. Broder, *The Party's Over: The Failure of Partisan Politics in America* (New York: Harper and Row, 1971).

41. Donald P. Green and Bradley Palmquist, "Of Artifacts and Partisan Instability," *American Journal of Political Science* 34:3 (August, 1990): 872–902.

42. Warren E. Miller and J. Merrill Shanks, *The New American Voter* (Cambridge, MA: Harvard University Press, 1996); Steven J. Rosenstone and John Mark Hansen, *Mobilization, Participation, and Democracy in America* (New York: Macmillan, 1993).

43. D. Sunshine Hillygus and Simon Jackman, "Voter Decision Making in Election 2000: Campaign Effects, Partisan Activation, and the Clinton Legacy," *American Journal of Political Science* 47 (2003): 583–96.

44. Larry M. Bartels, "Partisanship and Voting Behavior, 1952–1996," *American Journal of Political Science* 44:1 (2000): 35–50.

45. Data from CNN 2008 Election Center, www.cnn.com/ELECTION/2008/results/polls/#val=USP00p5 (accessed 11/5/08).

46. Martin P. Wattenberg, *Where Have All the Voters Gone?* (Cambridge, MA: Harvard University Press, 2002).

47. Jill Lawrence, "Party Recruiters Lead Charge for '06 Vote; Choice of Candidates to Run in Fall May Decide Who Controls the House," *USA Today*, May 25, 2006, p. A5.

48. James Dao and Adam Nagourney, "Soldier-Candidates: They Served, and Now They're Running," *New York Times*, February 19, 2006.

49. Jackie Calmes and Greg Hitt, "Can the Class of 2006 Save the Democrats?" *Wall Street Journal*, November 4, 2006, p. A1. For a full list of veteran Democratic candidates, see Fighting Dems for America, www.fighting-dems.com/node/25 (accessed 6/2/07).

50. Compiled from information available at www.ballot-access.org. (accessed 12/17/09).

51. Aldrich, *Why Parties?*

52. Data compiled from the Center for Responsive Politics, "Political Parties Overview: Election Cycle 2008," www.opensecrets.org/parties/index.php (accessed 11/5/08).

53. Rick Klein and Charlie Savage, "Some Democrats Decry Kerry's Unspent $16m," *Boston Globe*, November 19, 2004, www.boston.com/news/nation/articles/2004/11/19/some_democrats_decry_kerrys_unspent_16m (accessed 3/10/08).

54. Michael Duffy and Nancy Gibbs, "Our Journey Is Not Done: The Voters Hand Clinton a Historic Victory, but Send a Message: Work with the Republicans," *Time*, November 18, 1996.

55. Paul M. Weyrich, "Give President Bush Credit for Putting His Popularity to Work," *Enter Stage Right*, November 4, 2002, www.enterstageright.com/archive/articles/1102/1102politicalcapital.htm (accessed 3/27/08).

56. See Democratic Party, "A 50 State Strategy," www.democrats.org/a/party/a_50_state_strategy, (accessed 3/27/08).

57. Patricia Zapor, "Pro-life Democrats Describe Lonely Role, but See Improvements," *Catholic News Service*, July 28, 2004, www.catholicnews.com/data/stories/cns/0404122.htm (accessed 3/27/08).

58. Jim Yardley, "Campaign Tests Bush's Balancing Skills," *New York Times*, April 16, 2000, p. 22.

59. For details, see http://topics.nytimes.com/reference/timestopics/subjects/v/unitedstateseconomy/economic_stimulus/index.html (accessed 12/15/09).

60. John Holusha, "Senate Continues Debate over Immigration Reform," *New York Times*, April 4, 2006, p. A1.

61. E. E. Schattschneider, *Party Government* (New York: McGraw Hill, 1942); Nelson Polsby, *Consequences of Party Reform* (New York: Oxford University Press, 1983).

62. See Libertarian National Committee, "Frequently Asked Questions about the Libertarian Party," www.lp.org/article_85.shtml (accessed 3/27/08).

63. Steven J. Rosenstone, Roy L. Behr, and Edward Lazarus, *Third Parties in America: Citizen Response to Major Party Failure* (Princeton, NJ: Princeton University Press, 1984).

64. Alan Nagourney and Jin Rutenberg, "For Two Years, Bloomberg Aides Prepared for Bid," *New York Times*, June 21, 2007.

65. Janet Hook and Peter Wallsten, "GOP Feels Sting of Candidates' Rejection," *Los Angeles Times*, October 10, 2005, p. A1.

66. Gary Cox, *Making Votes Count: Strategic Coordination in the World's Electoral Systems* (Cambridge, UK: Cambridge University Press, 1997).

67. Thomas B. Edsall, "GOP Gains Advantage on Key Issues, Polls Say," *Washington Post*, January 27, 2002, p. A4.

68. John D. McKinnon, "Backing Away from Bush; Some Republican Candidates Avoid Ties with Unpopular President," *Wall Street Journal*, May 23, 2006, p. A4.

Challenging Conventional Wisdom

a. Richard C. Pearson, "Former Alabama Governor George C. Wallace Dies," *Washington Post*, September 14, 1998, p. A1.

b. Nader made this claim throughout the campaign; for an example, see the transcript of his comments during a February 22, 2004, appearance on the television program *Meet the Press*, www.msnbc.msn.com/id/4304155.

c. Libertarian National Committee, "The Libertarian Party on Today's Issues," www.lp.org/issues/issues.shtml.

d. Green Party, "The Real Difference: Issue Comparison," www.therealdifference.org/issues.html.

e. Gary Benoit, "Demopublicans vs. Republicrats," Constitution Party News Articles, November 3, 2006, www.constitutionparty.com/news.php?aid=357.

f. Constitution Party, "The Constitution Party National Platform," www.constitutionparty.org/party_platform.php.

What Do Political Scientists Do?

a. David Mayhew, *Congress: The Electoral Connection* (New Haven, CT: Yale University Press, 1974).

b. David W. Rohde, "Something's Happening Here: What It Is Ain't Exactly Clear: Southern Democrats in the House of Representatives," in *Home Style and Washington Work*, Morris Fiorina and David W. Rhode, eds. (Ann Arbor, MI: University of Michigan Press, 1989).

You Decide

a. Nelson Polsby, *Consequences of Party Reform* (New York: Oxford University Press, 1983).

b. Daniel A. Smith and Caroline J. Tolbert, *Educated by Initiative: The Effects of Direct Democracy on Citizens and Political Organizations in the American States* (Ann Arbor, MI: University of Michigan Press, 2004).

Comparing Ourselves to Others

a. Michael Gallagher, Michael Laver, and Peter Mair, *Representative Government in Western Europe* (New York: McGraw Hill, 2000).

CHAPTER 8

1. James Campbell, "The 2002 Midterm Election: A Typical or Atypical Midterm?" *Political Science and Politics* 36 (2003): 203–06.

2. Morris P. Fiorina, *Retrospective Voting in American National Elections* (New Haven, CT: Yale University Press, 1981); V. O. Key, *The Responsible Electorate* (New York: Vintage, 1966).

3. David Mayhew, *Congress: The Electoral Connection* (New Haven, CT: Yale University Press, 1973).

4. Melonyce McAfee, "Can I Vote without Going Outside?" *Slate*, November 6, 2006, www.slate.com/id/2153111 (accessed 3/31/08).

5. For details on early voting, see the Early Voting Information Center site at http://earlyvoting.net/states.php.

6. Paul Gronke, "Early Voting Reforms and American Elections" (paper presented at the 2004 American Political Science Association Annual Meeting, Chicago, IL). For 2006 data, see Pew Research Center, "Public Cheers Democratic Victory," November 16, 2006, http://people-press.org/reports/display.php3?ReportID=296 (accessed 3/30/08).

7. "Major Campaign Upset Brewing in Georgia's 10th District," *Politico*, July 18, 2007, www.politico.com/blogs/thecrypt/0707/Major_campaign_upset_brewing_in_Georgias_10th_District.html (accessed 3/31/08).

8. www.cnn.com/ELECTIONS.

9. For details, see the Caltech/MIT Voting Technology Project site at www.vote.caltech.edu.

10. Steven Ansolabehere and Charles Stewart, "Residual Votes Attributable to Technology," *Journal of Politics* 67 (2005): 365–80.

11. Randall Stross, "The Big Gamble on Electronic Voting," *New York Times*, September 24, 2006, p. 3.

12. An invaluable source for information on election technology, including reports on the use of touch screens in 2006, is the blog Election Updates written by California Institute of Technology professor Michael Alvarez and others at http://electionupdates.caltech.edu/blog.html.

13. Jonathan N. Wand, Kenneth W. Shotts, Jasjeet S. Sekhon, Walter R. Mebane, Michael C. Herron, and Henry E. Brady, "The Butterfly Ballot Did It: The Aberrant Vote for Buchanan in Palm Beach County, Florida," *American Political Science Review* 95 (2001): 793–809.

14. Robert F. Kennedy Jr., "Was the 2004 Election Stolen?" *Rolling Stone*, June 1, 2006, www.rollingstone.com/news/story/10432334/was_the_2004_election_stolen (accessed 3/29/08).

15. Frhad Manjoo, "Was the 2004 Election Stolen? No," *Salon*, June 3, 2006, www.salon.com/news/feature/2006/06/03/kennedy (accessed 3/31/08).

16. Minor party candidates are typically selected during party conventions.

17. Barbara Norrander, "Presidential Nomination Politics in the Post-Reform Era," *Political Research Quarterly* 49 (1996): 875–90.

18. Larry Bartels, *Presidential Primaries and the Dynamics of Public Choice* (Princeton, NJ: Princeton University Press, 1988).

19. William G. Mayer, "Forecasting Presidential Nominations or, My Model Worked Just Fine, Thank You," *Political Science and Politics* 36 (2003): 153–59.

20. Elisabeth Bumiller, "Edwards Is Out; Guiliani Quits and Backs McCain," *New York Times*, January 31, 2008.

21. Marty Cohen, David Karol, Hans Noel, and John Zaller, "Beating Reform: The Resurgence of Parties in Presidential Nominations, 1980 to 2000" (paper presented at the 2001 American Political Science Association Annual Meeting, San Francisco, CA).

22. Adam Nagourney, "Democrats Propose Moving Up Nevada in Presidential Caucuses," *New York Times*, July 23, 2006, p. 18.

23. Richard Herrera, "Are 'Superdelegates' Super?" *Political Behavior* 16 (1994): 79–93.

24. For a discussion of the 2004 conventions, see Kennedy School of Government, *Campaigning for President: The Managers Look at 2004* (New York: Rowman and Littlefield, 2005).

25. Robert K. Murray, *The 103rd Ballot: The Incredible Story of the Disastrous Democratic Convention in 1924* (New York: Harper and Row, 1976).

26. FairVote, "Maine and Nebraska," www.fairvote.org/e_college/me_ne.htm (accessed 3/31/08).

27. Adam Nagourney, "The 2004 Campaign: Strategy; Bush and Kerry Focus Campaigns in 11 Key States," *New York Times*, October 24, 2004, p. 1.

28. Robert Bennett, "The Problem of the Faithless Elector," *Northwestern University Law Review* 100 (2004): 121–30.

29. Timothy Noah, "Faithless Elector Watch: Ask Doctor Faithless," *Slate*, December 7, 2000, www.slate.com/id/1006644 (accessed 3/30/08).

30. James Q. Wilson, "Is the Electoral College Worth Saving?" *Slate*, November 3, 2000, www.slate.com/id/92663 (accessed 3/31/08).

31. Linda Fowler and Robert McClure, *Political Ambition: Who Decides to Run for Congress* (Ann Arbor, MI: University of Michigan Press, 1989).

32. Robin Kolodny, *Pursuing Majorities: Congressional Campaign Committees in American Politics* (Norman, OK: University of Oklahoma Press, 1999).

33. Paul Kane, Chris Cillizza, and Shailagh Murphy, "Specter Leaves GOP, Shifting Senate Balance," *Washington Post*, April 29, 2009, p. A1.

34. Steven Ansolabehere and Allan Gerber, "Incumbency Advantage and the Persistence of Legislative Majorities," *Legislative Studies Quarterly* 22 (1997): 161–80.

35. For a discussion of Johnson's decision, see Robert A. Caro, *The Path to Power* (New York: Knopf, 1983).

36. Rick Lyman, "Down but Not Out, Kucinich Keeps on Fighting," *New York Times*, May 17, 2004, p. 18.

37. Thomas Mann and Norman Ornstein, *The Permanent Campaign and Its Future* (Washington, DC: American Enterprise Institute, 2000).

38. David Mayhew, *Congress: The Electoral Connection* (New Haven, CT: Yale University Press, 1973).

39. Jacob Weisberg, "Drug Addled: Why Bush's Prescription Drug Plan Is Such a Fiasco," *Slate*, January 16, 2006, www.slate.com/id/2134456 (accessed 3/31/08).

40. David Johnston, "IRS Going Slow before Election," *New York Times*, October 27, 2006, p. A1.

41. Henry Chappell and William Keech, "A New Model of Political Accountability for Economic Performance," *American Political Science Review* 79 (1985): 10–19.

42. Jonathan Krasno and Donald P. Green, "The Dynamics of Campaign Fundraising in House Elections," *Journal of Politics* 56 (1991): 459–74.

43. Michael J. Goff, *The Money Primary: The New Politics of the Early Presidential Nomination Process* (New York: Rowman and Littlefield, 2007).

44. Chris Cillizza, "Consulting Firms Face Conflict in 2008," *Roll Call*, June 20, 2005, p. 1.

45. For details, see Committee on Standards of Official Conduct, "Rules and Standards of Conduct Relating to Campaign Activity," memorandum, March 2, 2000, www.house.gov/ethics/m_CampaignActivity2000 .htm (accessed 3/29/08).

46. Cherie Maestas, Walter Stone, and L. Sandy Maisel, "Quality Counts: Extending the Strategic Politician Model of Incumbent Deterrence," *American Journal of Political Science* 48 (2004): 479–90.

47. Matt Bai, "Turnout Wins Elections," *New York Times Magazine*, December 14, 2003, p. 100.

48. Bob Drogin and Robin Abcarian, "In Ohio, Obama's Ground Game Outguns McCain's," *Los Angeles Times*, November 3, 2008, p. A1.

49. Christopher Drew, "New Telemarketing Ploy Steers Voters on Republican Path," *New York Times*, November 6, 2006.

50. Donald Green and Alan Gerber, "The Effects of Canvassing, Phone Calls, and Direct Mail on Voter Turnout: A Field Experiment," *American Political Science Review* 94 (2000): 653–69; Lynn Vavreck, Constantine J. Spiliotes, and Linda L. Fowler, "The Effect of Retail Politics in the New Hampshire Primary," *American Journal of Political Science* 46 (2002): 595–610.

51. John Dickerson, "Weak Poll," *Slate*, October 30, 2006, http://www .slate.com/id/2152529 (accessed 3/31/08).

52. Sonya Geis, "California Campaign in Turmoil over Letters," *Washington Post*, October 20, 2006, p. 4.

53. Ed Pearce, "Adwatch: Reid vs. Angle on Education," August 23, 2010, www.kolotv.com/home/headlines/101343584.html (accessed 11/5/10).

54. Adam Nagourney and Megan Thee, "With Election Driven by Iraq, Voters Want New Approach," *New York Times*, November 2, 2006, p. A1.

55. Jake Tapper and Avery Miller, "Border Politics on the Campaign Trail," *ABC News*, September 21, 2006, http://i.abcnews.com/WNT/ story?id=2475262&page=1 (accessed 3/31/08).

56. For a detailed discussion of the debate over the Contract's effects in the 1994 election, see "Ignoring Evidence to the Contrary, *USA Today* Editorial Asserted 1994 'Contract with America' Was 'Effective . . . in Bringing Republicans to Power,'" October 20, 2006, http:// mediamatters.org/items/200610210001?show=1 (accessed 3/30/08).

57. For a history of presidential debates, see the Commission on Presidential Debates site at www.debates.org.

58. Compiled from Eric M. Appleman/Democracy in Action, "Debates: 2008 Presidential Campaign," www.gwu.edu/~action/2008/ chrndebs08.html#1 (accessed 11/5/08).

59. See the transcript of the first debate: Commission on Presidential Debates, Debate Transcript, September 30, 2004, www.debates.org/ pages/trans2004a.html (accessed 3/31/08).

60. For an example in the 2006 New Jersey Senate campaign, see Jonathan Tamari, "Senate Rivals Spar over Iraq War," *Home News Tribune Online*, October 18, 2006, www.thnt.com/apps/pbcs.dll/ article?AID=/20061018/NEWS/610180376/1001 (accessed 3/29/08).

61. Michael Powell, "Barack Bowl," *New York Times*, March 30, 2008, http://thecaucus.blogs.nytimes.com/2008/03/30/barack-bowl (accessed 4/15/08).

62. Maureen Dowd, "Eggheads and Cheese Balls," *New York Times*, April 16, 2008.

63. Kerry made this charge in many speeches, most notably in the first presidential debate. See Commission on Presidential Debates, Debate Transcript, September 30, 2004: The First Bush-Kerry Presidential Debate, www.debates.org/pages/trans2004a_p.html (accessed 4/16/08).

64. Tom Zaller, "The 2006 Campaign: A New Campaign Tactic: Manipulating Google Data," *New York Times*, October 26, 2006, p. 20.

65. Peter J. Boyer, "The Strangest Senate Race of the Year," *New Yorker*, September 30, 2006, pp. 23–45.

66. Helen A. S. Popkin and Ree Hines, "MySpace: A Place for Candidates," MSNBC, June 20, 2007, www.msnbc.msn.com/id/19337775 (accessed 3/31/08).

67. Molly Ball, "This Year's Attack Ads Cut Deeper," Politico, October 17, 2010, www.politico.com/news/stories/1010/43698.html (accessed 10/29/10).

68. For a video library of presidential campaign ads, see Museum of the Moving Image, "The Living Room Candidate: Presidential Campaign Commercials 1952–2004," available at http://livingroomcandidate .movingimage.us/index.php (accessed 3/31/08).

69. Museum of the Moving Image, "The Living Room Candidate: 1964: Johnson vs. Goldwater," available at http://livingroomcandidate .movingimage.us/election/index.php?ad_id=1014 (accessed 3/31/08).

70. Museum of the Moving Image, "The Living Room Candidate: 1964: Johnson vs. Goldwater."

71. Katherine Shaver, "A Star Says He Finds Validation in Public Interest in Stem Cells," *Washington Post*, November 3, 2006, p. B4.

72. See "Mike Huckabee Ad: 'Chuck Norris Approved,'" available at www.youtube.com/watch?v=MDUQW8LUMs8 (accessed 3/31/08).

73. Kenneth Goldstein and Joel Rivlin, "Advertising in the 2000 and 2004 Elections: Findings from the 2000 Election," unpublished presentation, University of Wisconsin, www.polisci.wisc.edu/tvadvertising/ Analysis_Of_2000_Elections/cfi%20presentation.ppt (accessed 3/31/08). For 2002 data, see Kenneth Goldstein and Joel Rivlin, *Political Advertising in the 2002 Elections*, unpublished manuscript, University of Wisconsin, www.polisci.wisc.edu/tvadvertising/Analysis% 20of%20the%202000%20elections.htm (accessed 3/31/08).

74. "Obama Dominated Television Advertising in Ohio," Wisconsin Ad Project, March 12, 2008, http://wiscadproject.wisc.edu/wiscads_ pressrelease_031208.pdf (accessed 10/29/10).

75. For examples of this argument, see Thomas Patterson, *The Vanishing Voter* (New York: Knopf, 2002), and Jules Witcover, *No Way to Pick a President: How Money and Hired Guns Have Debased American Politics* (London, UK: Routledge, 2001).

76. For examples of these and other campaign ads, see "Most Intriguing Campaign Ads of 2010," ABC News, http://abcnews.go.com/politics/ slideshow/intriguing-political-ads-2010-10887147 (accessed 11/1/10).

77. Darrell W. West, "2008 Campaign Attack Ads Hit an All-Time Low," CNN Politics.com, September 15, 2008, www.cnn.com/2008/ politics/09/15/west.negative/index.html.

78. Paul Freeman, Michael Franz, and Kenneth Goldstein, "Campaign Advertising and Democratic Citizenship," *American Journal of Political Science* 48 (2004): 723–41.

79. Constantine J. Spilotes and Lynn Vavreck, "Campaign Advertising: Partisan Convergence or Divergence," Journal of Politics 64 (2002): 249–61.

80. Kathleen Hall Jameson, Packaging the Presidency: A History and Criticism of Presidential Campaign Advertising (New York: Oxford University Press, 1996).

81. Steven Ansolabehere and Shanto Iyengar, Going Negative: How Political Advertisements Shrink and Polarize the Electorate (New York: Free Press, 1997); Richard Lau, Lee Sigelman, Caroline Heldman, and Paul Babbitt, "The Effects of Negative Political Advertisements: A Meta-Analytic Analysis," American Political Science Review 93 (1999): 851–70.

82. Jonathan Krasno and Frank J. Sorauf, "For the Defense," *Political Science and Politics* 37 (2004): 777–80.

83. For the details on these rules, see Federal Election Commission, "Public Funding of Presidential Elections," February 2008, www.fec.gov/pages/brochures/pubfund.shtml (accessed 3/31/08).

84. Contribution and spending data are available from the Center for Responsive Politics at www.opensecrets.org.

85. Newser.com, "Fake Obama Group Keeps Donations," July 25, 2007, www.newser.com/story/4766.html (accessed 3/21/08).

86. Brian Stelter, "The Price of 30 Seconds," *New York Times*, October 1, 2007, http://tvdecoder.blogs.nytimes.com/2007/10/01/the-price-of-30-seconds, accessed (4/17/08).

87. Wal-Mart Stores, Inc., "Annual Report to Shareholders, 2006," March 29, 2006, www.sec.gov/Archives/edgar/data/104169/000119312506066792/dex13.htm (accessed 3/31/08).

88. Center for Responsive Politics, "Millionaire Candidates," www.opensecrets.org/bigpicture/millionaires/php?cycle=2008 (accessed 1/10/10).

89. Data compiled from Federal Election Commission reports as of November 1, 2010, www.fec.gov.

90. For the details on EMILY's List receipts and expenditures during the 2004 election cycle, see Center for Responsive Politics, "EMILY's List 2004 PAC Summary Data," www.opensecrets.org/pacs/lookup2.asp?strid=C00193433&cycle=2004 (accessed 3/31/08).

91. Raymond Hernandez, "Anti-Clinton Donor Reported as Donor to Giuliani," *New York Times*, November 29, 2006.

92. For a review of this literature, see Michael Malbin, *The Election after Reform: Money, Politics, and the Bipartisan Campaign Reform Act* (Washington, DC: Roman and Littlefield, 2006).

93. For a discussion, see Patterson, *The Vanishing Voter*, especially Chapter 1, "The Incredible Shrinking Electorate," pp. 3–22.

94. William H. Riker and Peter Ordeshook, "A Theory of the Calculus of Voting," *American Political Science Review* 62 (1968): 25–39.

95. Michael McDonald, The United States Elections Project, available at http://elections.gmu.edu (accessed 3/30/08).

96. Raymond Wolfinger and Jonathan Hoffman, "Registering and Voting with Motor Voter," *Political Science and Politics* 34 (2001): 85–92.

97. For a review of the literature on issue voters, see Jon K. Dalager, "Voters, Issues, and Elections: Are Candidates' Messages Getting Through?" *Journal of Politics* 58 (1996): 486–515.

98. Richard P. Lau and David P. Reslawsk, *How Voters Decide: Information Processing during Electoral Campaigns* (New York: Cambridge University Press, 2006).

99. Gary Cox and Jonathan Katz, "Why Did the Incumbency Advantage in U.S. House Elections Grow?" *American Journal of Political Science* 40 (1996): 478–96.

100. Charles Franklin, "Eschewing Obfuscation: Campaigns and the Perceptions of U.S. Senate Incumbents," *American Political Science Review* 85 (December, 1991): 1193–1214; Wendy M. Rahn, "The Role of Partisan Stereotypes in Information Processing about Political Candidates," *American Journal of Political Science* 37 (May, 1993): 472–96.

101. Bruce Cain, John Ferejohn, and Morris Fiorina, *The Personal Vote* (Cambridge, MA: Harvard University Press, 1985).

102. Jeffrey Koch, "Gender Stereotypes and Citizens' Impressions of House Candidates' Ideological Orientations," *American Journal of Political Science* 46 (2002): 453–62; Monica McDermott, "Candidate Occupations and Voter Information," *Journal of Politics* 67 (2005): 201–18; Carol Sigelman, Lee Sigelman, Barbara Walkosz, and Michael Nitz, "Black Candidates, White Voters: Understanding Racial Bias in Political Perceptions," *American Journal of Political Science* 39 (February, 1995): 243–65.

103. Fiorina, *Retrospective Voting in American National Elections*; Key, *The Responsible Electorate*.

104. Alfred J. Tuchfarber, Stephen E. Bennett, Andrew E. Smith, and Eric W. Rademacher, "The Republican Tidal Wave of 1994: Testing Hypotheses about Realignment, Restructuring, and Rebellion," *Political Science and Politics* 28 (1995): 689–93.

105. Samuel Popkin, *The Reasoning Voter* (Chicago: University of Chicago Press, 1991).

106. Richard R. Lau and David P. Redlawsk, "Advantages and Disadvantages of Cognitive Heuristics in Political Decision Making," *American Journal of Political Science* 45 (2001): 951–71.

107. Larry M. Bartels, "Partisanship and Voting Behavior, 1952–1996," *American Journal of Political Science* 44 (2000): 35–50.

108. Morris P. Fiorina, "Keystone Reconsidered," in *Congress Reconsidered*, 8th ed., ed. Lawrence Dodd and Bruce Oppenheimer (Washington, DC: CQ Press, 2004), pp. 159–77.

109. James Campbell and James Garrand, *Forecasting Presidential Elections* (Beverley Hills, CA: Sage Publications, 2000).

110. For 2006 exit poll data, see Pew Research Center, "Public Cheers Democratic Victory," November 16, 2006, http://people-press.org/reports/display.php3?ReportID=296 (accessed 3/31/08).

111. For data on presidential approval and evaluations of Congress in normal and nationalized elections, see Pew Research Center, "Democrats Hold Double-Digit Lead in Competitive Districts," October 6, 2006, http://people-press.org/reports/display.php3?ReportID=293 (accessed 3/31/08).

112. For 2006 exit poll data, see Pew Research Center, "Public Cheers Democratic Victory," November 16, 2006, http://people-press.org/reports/display.php3?ReportID=296 (accessed 3/31/08).

113. "Midterm Snapshot: Enthusiasm for Obama Reelection Bid Greater Than for Reagan in 1982," Pew Research Center, October 25, 2010. http://pewresearch.org/pubs/1778/public-split-on-obama-run-in-2012-but-better-than-reagan-outlook-in-1982?src=prc-latest&proj=forum (accessed 10/27/10).

114. Amanda Terkel, "The One-Person Funded Super-PAC: How Wealthy Donors Can Skirt Campaign Finance Restrictions." Huffington Post, October 22, 2010, www.huffingtonpost.com/2010/10/21/super-pac-taxpayers-earmarks-concerned-citizens-campaign-finance_n_772214.html (accessed 10/27/10).

115. Michael Luo and Griff Palmer, "Democrats Retain Edge in Campaign Spending," *New York Times*, October 27, 2010, p. A1.

116. Amy Gardner, "Gauging the Scope of the Tea Party Movement in America," *Washington Post*, October 24, 2010, p. A1.

Comparing Ourselves to Others

a. For details on proportional representation in these countries, see Michael Gallagher, Michael Laver, and Peter Mair, *Representation of Government in Modern Europe* (London, UK: McGraw-Hill Europe, 2000).

b. Lani Guinier, "No Two Seats: The Elusive Quest for Political Equality," *Virginia Law Review* 77 (1991): 1414–28.

Challenging Conventional Wisdom

a. David Plotz, "The House Incumbent: He Can't Lose," *Slate*, November 3, 2000, www.slate.com/id/92692 (accessed 4/1/08).

b. Samuel Issacharoff and Jonathan Nagler, "Our Insulated Congress," *Pittsburgh Post-Gazette*, October 27, 2006, www.post-gazette.com/pg/06300/733341-109.stm (accessed 4/1/08).

c. Isscharoff and Nagler, "Our Insulated Congress."

d. Cherie Maestas, Sarah Fulton, Walter Stone, and L. Sandy Maisel, "When to Risk It: Institutions, Ambition and the Decision to Run for the U.S. House," *American Political Science Review* 100 (2006): 195–208.

e. Jonathan S. Krasno, Donald P. Green, and Jonathan A. Cowden, "The Dynamics of Campaign Fundraising in House Elections," *Journal of Politics* 56 (1994): 459–74.

f. Brandice Canes-Wrone, David W. Brady, and John F. Cogan, "Out of Step, Out of Office: Electoral Accountability and House Members'

Voting," *American Political Science Review* 96 (2002): 127–40; Gary C. Jacobson and Michael A. Dimock, "Checking Out: The Effects of Bank Overdrafts on the 1992 House Elections," *American Journal of Political Science* 38 (1994): 601–24.

g. David Mayhew, *Congress: The Electoral Connection* (New Haven, CT: Yale University Press, 1973), p. 36.

What Do Political Scientists Do?

a. Sides' post about independent votes, "Three Myths about Political Independents," available at www.themonkeycage.org/2009/12/three_myths_about_political_in.html (accessed 2/25/10).

CHAPTER 9

1. Massie Ritsch and Courtney Mabeus, "Casting Off Abramoff," *Capital Eye*, April 6, 2006, Center for Responsive Politics, www.capitaleye.org/inside.asp?ID=210 (accessed 4/3/08).

2. Jacob Weisberg, "Three Cities, Three Scandals: What Jack Abramoff, Anthony Pellicano, and Jared Paul Stern Have in Common," *Slate*, April 9, 2006, www.slate.com/id/2140238 (accessed 4/4/08).

3. Associated Press, "Others Caught Up in Abramoff Scandal," *New York Times*, March 23, 2007, www.nytimes.com/aponline/us/AP-Griles-Abramoff-Glance.htm (accessed 4/5/07). Associated Press, "Former Deputy Interior Secretary to Plead Guilty in Lobbyist Case," *New York Times*, March 23, 2007, www.nytimes.com/aponline/washington/AP-Griles-Abramoff.html (accessed 4/5/07).

4. Timothy Noah, "Duke Cunningham's Little Helpers," *Slate*, October 18, 2006, www.slate.com/id/2151748 (accessed 4/5/08).

5. Capital Eye Blog, "TARP Recipients Paid Out $114 Million for Politicking Last Year," February 4, 2009, www.opensecrets.org/news/2009/02/tarp-recipients-paid-out-114-m.html; see also Joe Weisenthal, "Congressmen: Yep, Wall Street Owns Washington," June 4, 2009, www.businessinsider.com/congressman-yep-wall-street-owns-washington-2009-6, (accessed 8/28/09).

6. Dan Eggen, and Kimberly Kindy, "Familiar Players in Health Bill Lobbying," *Washington Post*, July 6, 2009, p. A1.

7. Timothy P. Carnet, "Lobbying Kings: Exxon, Chevron, Lockheed, Pfizer," *Washington Examiner*, April 22, 2009, www.washingtonexaminer.com/politics/Lobbying-kings-Exxon-Chevron-Lockheed-Pfizer_04_22-43393937.html (accessed 8/28/09).

8. Robert A. Dahl, *A Preface to Democratic Theory* (Chicago: University of Chicago Press, 1951); and David Truman, *The Governmental Process* (New York: Harper and Row, 1951).

9. Theodore Lowi, *The End of Liberalism: The Second Republic of the United States* (New York: Norton, 1979).

10. Lobbying regulations are often changed; the discussion here is just a general guide. Regular reports on past, current, and proposed lobbying regulations can be found on the Web site of the Congressional Research Service at www.opencrs.com.

11. Frank Baumgartner and Beth Leech, *Basic Interests: The Importance of Interest Groups in Politics and in Political Science* (Princeton, NJ: Princeton University Press, 1999), p. 109.

12. Beth L. Leech, Frank R. Baumgartner, Timothy La Pira, and Nicholas A. Semanko, "Drawing Lobbyists to Washington: Government Activity and Interest-Group Mobilization," *Political Research Quarterly* 58 (2005): 19–30.

13. Frances Cairncross, *The Death of Distance: How the Communication Revolution Is Changing Our Lives* (Cambridge, MA: Harvard Business School Press, 2001).

14. Leslie Wayne, "Documents Show Extent of Lobbying by Boeing," *New York Times*, September 3, 2003.

15. Center for Responsive Politics, Lobbying Spending Database, "General Electric Summary, 2006," www.opensecrets.org/lobbyists/clientsum.asp?txtname=General+Electric&year=2006 (accessed 4/7/08).

16. Center for Responsive Politics, Lobbying Spending Database, "Sierra Club Summary, 2006," www.opensecrets.org/lobbyists/clientsum.asp?txtname=Sierra+Club&year=2006 (accessed 4/7/08).

17. For more on this argument, see Tim Harford, "There's Not Enough Money in Politics," *Slate*, April 1, 2006, www.slate.com/id/2138874 (accessed 4/8/08); and Stephen Ansolabehere, John M. de Figueiredo, and James M. Snyder, "Why Is There So Little Money in American Politics?" *Journal of Economic Perspectives* 17 (2003): 105–30.

18. See Coalition for Luggage Security, "About the Coalition for Luggage Security," www.luggagesecuritycoalition.com/about.asp (accessed 4/9/08).

19. For details on the AFL-CIO's lobbying operations, see AFL-CIO, "Issues: Main Topics," www.aflcio.org/issues (accessed 4/8/08).

20. Family Research Council, "About Family Research Council," www.frc.org/get.cfm?c=ABOUT_FRC (accessed 4/8/08).

21. Baumgartner and Leech, *Basic Interests*, Chapter 6, pp. 100–19.

22. For a discussion of these events, see William Bianco, *Trust: Representatives and Constituents*, Chapter 6 (Ann Arbor, MI: University of Michigan Press, 1994), pp. 123–46.

23. John R. Wright, *Interest Groups and Congress: Lobbying, Contributions, and Influence* (New York: Longman, 1995).

24. Scott Ainsworth, *Analyzing Interest Groups: Group Influence on People and Policies* (New York: Norton, 2002).

25. Timothy Egan, "For Thirsty Farmers, Old Friends at Interior," *New York Times*, March 3, 2006, p. A1.

26. Public Citizen Congress Watch, "Congressional Revolving Doors: The Journey from Congress to K Street," July 2005, www.lobbyinginfo.org/documents/RevolveDoor.pdf (accessed 4/9/08).

27. Eric Lipton, "Former Antiterror Officials Find Industry Pays Better," *New York Times*, June 18, 2006, p. A1.

28. Jacob Weisberg, "A Tale of Two Lobbyists," April 19, 2009, www.slate.com/id/2216433/.

29. Sierra Club, www.sierraclub.org (accessed 5/22/08).

30. Robert H. Salisbury, John P. Heinz, Edward O. Laumann, and Robert L. Nelson, "Who Works with Whom? Interest Group Alliances and Opposition," *American Political Science Review* 81 (1987): 1217–34.

31. Business-Industry Political Action Committee, "About BIPAC," www.bipac.org/about/about.asp (accessed 4/8/08).

32. One example campaign is MoveOn.org Political Action Committee, "Letter to the Editor: Tell the Media: We Want to End the War. The President Wants Endless War," http://pol.moveon.org/lte/?lte_campaign_id=72 (accessed 4/8/08).

33. Family Research Council, "Volunteer," www.frc.org/volunteer (accessed 8/11/10).

34. National Paper Trade Association Alliance, "Senate Debate on EFCA to Begin," www.gonpta.com/report/articles/article.cfm?ArticleID=1491 (accessed 4/8/08).

35. Thomas Holyoke, "Choosing Battlegrounds: Interest Group Lobbying across Multiple Venues," *Political Science Quarterly* 56 (2003): 325–36.

36. John Carney, "Wall Street Shuts Off Money Supply to Capitol Hill," August 26, 2009, www.businessinsider.com/bankers-shut-off-money-supply-to-capitol-hill-2009-4 (accessed 8/27/09).

37. Scott Ainsworth, "Regulating Lobbyists and Interest Group Influence," *Journal of Politics* 55 (1993): 41–55.

38. AARP, "Policy and Research for Professionals in Aging," www.aarp.org/research/ppi (accessed 4/8/08).

39. John Rother, "Health Care Reform Legislative Options," testimony before the Senate Education and Labor Committee, June 11, 2009,

www.aarp.org/aarp/presscenter/testimony/articles/Health_Reform_
Testimony.html.

40. James Q. Wilson, *Political Organizations* (New York: Basic Books, 1974).

41. American Automobile Association, Foundation for Traffic Safety, www.aaafoundation.org/home (accessed 4/8/08).

42. Jack Walker, *Mobilizing Interest Groups in America* (Ann Arbor, MI: University of Michigan Press, 1991).

43. Kenneth Kollman, *Outside Lobbying: Public Opinion and Interest Group Strategies* (Princeton, NJ: Princeton University Press, 1998).

44. Robert Salisbury, "An Exchange Theory of Interest Groups," *Midwest Journal of Political Science* 13 (1969): 1–32.

45. Walker, *Mobilizing Interest Groups in America.*

46. Kollman, *Outside Lobbying.*

47. Walker, *Mobilizing Interest Groups in America.*

48. Derived from a search of the congressional lobbying disclosure database at http://idsearch.house.gov/idsearch.aspx (accessed 7/4/08).

49. John P. Heinz, Edward O. Laumann, and Robert Salisbury, *The Hollow Core: Private Interests in National Policymaking* (Cambridge, MA: Harvard University Press, 1993).

50. Richard L. Hall and Alan V. Deardorff, "Lobbying as Legislative Subsidy," *American Political Science Review* 100 (2006): 69–84.

51. Hall and Deardorff, "Lobbying as Legislative Subsidy."

52. David Austen-Smith and John R. Wright, "Counteractive Lobbying," *American Journal of Political Science* 38:1 (1994): 25–44.

53. Schlozman and Tierney, *Organized Interests and American Democracy.*

54. Baumgartner and Leech, *Basic Interests*, p. 152.

55. Matt Kelly and Peter Eisler, "Relatives Have 'Inside Track' on Lobbying for Tax Dollars," *USA Today*, October 17, 2006.

56. Christine A. DeGregorio, *Networks of Champions: Leadership, Access, and Advocacy in the U.S. House of Representatives* (Ann Arbor, MI: University of Michigan Press, 1992).

57. Daniel Carpenter, *The Forging of Bureaucratic Autonomy: Reputations, Networks, and Policy Innovation in Executive Agencies, 1862–1928* (Princeton, NJ: Princeton University Press, 2002).

58. Public Citizen Publications, www.citizen.org/publications, (accessed 7/25/09).

59. Derived from a search of the NRA Institute for Legislative Action site, www.nraila.org.

60. Kim Scheppele and Jack L. Walker, "The Litigation Strategies of Interest Groups," in *Mobilizing Interest Groups in America*, ed. Jack Walker (Ann Arbor, MI: University of Michigan Press, 1991).

61. Juan Williams and Julian Bond, *Eyes on the Prize: America's Civil Rights Years, 1954–1965* (New York: Penguin, 1988).

62. See American Civil Liberties Union, "USA PATRIOT Act," http://action.aclu.org/reformthepatriotact (accessed 4/8/08).

63. Lauren Cohen Bell, *Warring Factions: Interest Groups, Money, and the New Politics of Senate Confirmation* (Columbus, OH: Ohio State University Press, 2002).

64. Kevin W. Hula, *Lobbying Together: Interest Group Coalitions in Legislative Politics* (Washington, DC: Georgetown University Press, 1999).

65. Jeanne Cummings, "Word Games Could Threaten Climate Bill," June 9, 2009, www.politico.com/news/stories/0609/24059.html.

66. AARP, "Elected Officials," http://capwiz.com/aarp/dbq/officials (accessed 4/8/08).

67. Dana Milbank, "Obama Is Just Not Their Cup of Tea," *Washington Post*, April 16, 2009; David Espo, "'Special Interests' on Both Sides in Health Fight," Associated Press, August 19, 2009, http://abcnews.go.com/Politics/wireStory?id=8366819.

68. Richard Fenno, *Home Style: U.S. House Members in Their Districts* (Boston: Little, Brown, 1978). See also Brandice Caines-Wrone, David W.

69. Brady, and John F. Cogan, "Out of Step, Out of Office: Electoral Accountability and House Members' Voting," *American Political Science Review* 96 (2002): 127–40.

69. Emily Yoffe, "Am I the Next Jack Abramoff?" April 1, 2006, www.slate.com/id/2137886/ (accessed 8/28/09).

70. Kollman, *Outside Lobbying.*

71. Gregory Calderia, Marie Hojnacki, and John R. Wright, "The Lobbying Activities of Organized Interests in Federal Judicial Nominations," *Journal of Politics* 62 (2000): 51–69.

72. Robert Pear, "Medicare Law Prompts a Rush for Lobbyists," *New York Times*, August 23, 2005.

73. For these and other campaign finance data, see the Federal Election Commission Web site at www.fec.gov, or the Center for Responsive Politics site at www.opensecrets.org.

74. John R. Wright, "PAC Contributions, Lobbying, and Representation," *Journal of Politics* 51:3 (August, 1989): 713–29.

75. John G. Matsusaka, "Direct Democracy and Fiscal Gridlock: Have Voter Initiatives Paralyzed the California Budget?" *State Politics and Policy* 5 (2005): 346–62.

76. Thad Kousser, *Term Limits and the Dismantling of State Legislative Professionalism* (New York: Cambridge University Press, 2004).

77. John G. Matsusaka, *For the Many or the Few: The Initiative, Public Policy, and American Democracy* (Chicago: University of Chicago Press, 2004).

78. Elizabeth R. Gerber, *The Populist Paradox: Interest Group Influence and the Promise of Direct Legislation* (Princeton, NJ: Princeton University Press, 1999).

79. Baumgartner and Leech, *Basic Interests*, Chapter 8, pp. 147–67.

80. Jeffrey Birnbaum, "The Humane Society Becomes a Political Animal," *Washington Post*, January 30, 2007, p. A15.

81. For details, see the blog of the Humane Society's president, Wayne Pacelle, at http://hsus.typepad.com/wayne (accessed 7/25/09).

82. For this testimony, see "Testimony of Gary R. Bachula, Vice President, Internet2 before the Senate Committee on Commerce, Science and Transportation," Hearing on Net Neutrality, February 7, 2006, www.educause.edu/ir/library/pdf/EPO0611.pdf (accessed 4/9/08). For details on the net neutrality debate, see Tim Wu, "Network Neutrality FAQ," www.timwu.org/network_neutrality.html (accessed 4/9/08).

83. Tim Wu, "Does YouTube Really Have Legal Problems?" *Slate*, October 26, 2006, www.slate.com/id/2152264 (accessed 4/9/08); and Tim Wu, "Ma Bell Is Back: Should You Be Afraid?" *Slate*, January 4, 2007, www.slate.com/id/2156918 (accessed 4/9/08).

84. Jeffrey H. Birnbaum, "The Forces That Set the Agenda," *Washington Post*, April 24, 2005, p. B1.

85. For a review, see Carpenter, *The Forging of Bureaucratic Autonomy.*

86. Baumgartner and Leech, *Basic Interests*, Chapter 7, especially Table 7.1 and Table 7.2, pp. 130 and 132.

87. Baumgartner and Leech, *Basic Interests*, p. 133.

88. National Rifle Association Institute for Legislative Action, "Fact Sheet: Right-to-Carry 2007," www.nraila.org/Issues/FactSheets/Read.aspx?ID=18 (accessed 4/9/08).

89. National Rifle Association Institute for Legislative Action, "Fact Sheet: Right-to-Carry: The Stearns/Boucher Right-to-Carry Reciprocity Bill," www.nraila.org/Issues/FactSheets/Read.aspx?id=189&issue=003 (accessed 4/9/08).

90. Quoted in William Saletan, "The Money Jungle," *Slate*, March 22, 2001, http://slate.msn.com/id/102994 (accessed 4/9/08).

91. David Lowery, "Why Do Organized Interests Lobby? A Multi-Goal, Multi-Context Theory of Lobbying," *Polity* 39 (2007): 29–54.

92. Richard L. Hall and Frank W. Wayman, "Buying Time: Moneyed Interests and the Mobilization of Ideas in Congressional Committees," *American Political Science Review* 84 (1990): 797–820.

93. Baumgartner and Leech, *Basic Interests*, Chapter 7, pp. 120–46.

94. John M. Berry, *The Interest Group Society* (New York: Harper Collins, 1997); Raymond A. Bauer, Ithiel de Sola Pool, and Lewis Dexter, *American Business and Public Policy* (New York: Atherton Press, 1963).

95. Ken Kollman, *Outside Lobbying* (Princeton, NJ: Princeton University Press, 1998).

96. Frank Baumgartner and Beth Leech, "Interest Niches and Policy Bandwagons: Patterns of Interest Group Involvement in National Politics," *Journal of Politics* 63 (2001): 1191–1213.

97. Austen-Smith and Wright, "Counteractive Lobbying"; Frank R. Baumgartner and Beth L. Leech, "The Multiple Ambiguities of 'Counteractive Lobbying,'" *American Journal of Political Science* 40 (1996): 521–42.

Comparing Ourselves to Others

a. Mancur Olson, *The Rise and Decline of Nations* (Cambridge, MA: Harvard University Press, 1984).

b. James E. Curtis, Douglas E. Baer, and Edward G. Grubb, "Nations of Joiners: Explaining Voluntary Association Membership in Democratic Societies," *American Sociological Review* 66 (2001): 783–805.

c. Michael Gallagher, Peter Mair, and Michael Laver, *Representative Government in Modern Europe* (New York: McGraw-Hill, 2005).

d. Fritz Plasser and Gunda Plasser, *Global Political Campaigning: A Worldwide Analysis of Campaign Professionals and Their Practices* (New York: Praeger, 2002).

e. Daniel Nelson, "Supplying Trade Reform: Political Institutions and Liberalization in Middle-Income Presidential Democracies," *American Journal of Political Science* 47 (2003): 470–93; Nina Rudra, "Globalization and the Decline of the Welfare State in Less-Developed Countries," *International Organization* 56 (2002): 411–45.

f. Justin Greenwood, *Interest Representation in the European Parliament* (London: Palgrave Macmillan, 2003).

You Decide

a. For the full text of this proposal, see League of Women Voters et al., "Ethics and Lobbying Reform: Six Benchmarks for Lobbying Reform," January 23, 2006, www.lwv.org.

Challenging Conventional Wisdom

a. Capital Eye Blog, "TARP Recipients Paid Out $114 Million for Politicking Last Year," February 4, 2009, www.opensecrets.org/news/2009/02/tarp-recipients-paid-out-114-m.html.

b. For details, see Matthew Ericson, Elaine He, and Amy Schoenfeld, "Tracking the $700 Billion Bailout," *New York Times*, June 24, 2009, http://projects.nytimes.com/creditcrisis/recipients/table (accessed 8/27/09).

What Do Political Scientists Do?

a. Stephen Ansolabehere, John de Figueiredo, and James Snyder, "Why Is There So Little Money in American Politics?" *Journal of Economic Perspectives* 17 (2003): 105–30.

CHAPTER 10

1. The margins were 263–171 in the House, with 172 Democrats and 91 Republicans voting yes, and 74–25 in the Senate, with 45 Democrats and 29 Republicans voting yes.

2. Quoted in Alan I. Abramowitz and Jeffrey A. Segal, *Senate Elections* (Ann Arbor, MI: University of Michigan Press, 1992), p. 231.

3. See Paul Gronke, *The Electorate, the Campaign, and the Office: A Unified Approach to Senate and House Elections* (Ann Arbor, MI: University of Michigan Press, 2000), for research showing the House and Senate elections share many similar characteristics. See Richard F. Fenno, *Senators on the Campaign Trail: The Politics of Representation* (Norman, OK: University of Oklahoma Press, 1996), for a good general discussion of Senate elections.

4. David T. Canon, *Race, Redistricting, and Representation: The Unintended Consequences of Black Majority Districts in the U.S. House* (Chicago: University of Chicago Press, 1999); Katherine Tate, *Black Faces in the Mirror: African Americans and Their Representatives in the U.S. Congress* (Princeton, NJ: Princeton University Press, 2003).

5. Claudine Gay, "Spirals of Trust? The Effect of Descriptive Representation on the Relationship between Citizens and Their Government," *American Journal of Political Science* 46:4 (October, 2002): 717–32; Tate, *Black Faces in the Mirror*, Chapter 7. However, Tate shows that African Americans who are represented by African Americans in Congress are not any more likely to vote, be involved in politics, or have higher overall approval rates of Congress than African Americans who are not descriptively represented.

6. A. Phillips Griffiths, quoted in Anne Phillips, *The Politics of Presence* (New York: Clarendon Press/Oxford University Press, 1995), p. 39. However, Senator Roman Hruska of Nebraska challenged Griffiths's argument, at least in the context of the Supreme Court. In defending President Nixon's appointee to the Supreme Court, G. Harrold Carswell, Hruska said, "Even if he were mediocre, there are a lot of mediocre judges and people and lawyers. They are entitled to a little representation, aren't they, and a little chance? We can't have all Brandeises and Frankfurters and Cardozos and stuff like that." Michael Barone, Grant Ujifusa, and Douglas Matthews, *The Almanac of American Politics* (New York: Dutton, 1975), p. 494. Note that "stuff like that" refers to three of the country's greatest justices.

7. Richard E. Cohen, *Changing Course in Washington: Clinton and the New Congress* (New York: Macmillian, 1994), pp. 210–11.

8. Marjorie Margolies, "Democrats: Vote Your Conscience on Health Care," *Washington Post*, March 18, 2010.

9. R. Douglas Arnold, *The Logic of Congressional Action* (New Haven, CT: Yale University Press, 1990), pp. 60–71.

10. Richard F. Fenno, *Home Style: House Members in Their Districts* (Boston: Little, Brown, 1978).

11. David R. Mayhew, *Congress: The Electoral Connection* (New Haven, CT: Yale University Press, 1974).

12. Mayhew, *Congress*, p. 17.

13. Mayhew, *Congress*, p. 37.

14. Patrick J. Sellers, "Fiscal Consistency and Federal District Spending in Congressional Elections," *American Journal of Political Science* 41:3 (July, 1997): 1024–41.

15. Dan Eggen, "Justice Staff Saw Texas Districting as Illegal: Voting Rights Finding on Map Pushed by DeLay Was Overruled," *Washington Post*, December 2, 2005, p. A1. The court case is *League of United Latin American Citizens v. Perry*, 547 U.S. (2006).

16. All poll data except the poll comparing Congress to other occupations are from PollingReport.com (www.pollingreport.com). The occupations poll was cited in Karlyn Bowman and Everett Carll Ladd, "Public Opinion toward Congress: A Historical Look," in *Congress, the Press, and the Public*, ed. Thomas E. Mann and Norman J. Ornstein (Washington, DC: Brookings Institution Press, 1994), p. 50.

17. "Check bouncing" is in quotes because the checks did not actually bounce. The scandal involved penalty-free overdrafts permitted in members' accounts in the House bank (which allowed some members to abuse the privilege by using the overdrafts as short-term, interest-free loans). Many voters saw this as another unfair benefit to members of Congress, but others considered it a nonscandal because no taxpayers' money was at stake.

18. Charles R. Babcock and Jonathan Weisman, "Congressman Admits Taking Bribes, Resigns: GOP's Cunningham Faces Jail Term," *Washington Post*, November 29, 2005, p. A1.

19. Mark J. Rozell, "Press Coverage of Congress, 1946–1992," in *Congress, the Press, and the Public*, ed. Thomas E. Mann and Norman J. Ornstein (Washington, DC: Brookings Institution Press, 1994), p. 110.

20. Burdett A. Loomis, *The Contemporary Congress* (Belmont, CA: Wadsworth, 2000), p. 47.

21. R. Douglas Arnold, *Congress, the Press, and Political Accountability* (Princeton, NJ: Princeton University Press, 2004), p. 80.

22. See Kenneth R. Mayer and David T. Canon, *The Dysfunctional Congress: The Individual Roots of an Institutional Dilemma*, 2nd ed. (New York: Columbia University Press, 2011) for an extended discussion of this argument.

23. Richard F. Fenno, "If as Ralph Nader Says, Congress Is the 'Broken Branch,' How Come We Love Our Congressman So Much?" in *Congress in Change: Evolution and Reform*, ed. Norman J. Ornstein (New York: Praeger, 1975), pp. 277–87.

24. David T. Canon, "History in the Making: The 2nd District in Wisconsin," in *The Battle for Congress: Candidates, Consultants, and Voters*, ed. James A. Thurber (Washington, DC: Brookings Institution Press, 2001), pp. 199–238.

25. Gary C. Jacobson, *The Politics of Congressional Elections*, 5th ed. (New York: Longman, 2001), pp. 24–30.

26. Fenno, *Home Style*.

27. Gary C. Jacobson and Samuel Kernell, *Strategy and Choice in Congressional Elections* (New Haven, CT: Yale University Press, 1983).

28. Morris Fiorina, *Congress: Keystone of the Washington Establishment*, rev. ed. (New Haven: Yale University Press, 1989).

29. John D. McKinnon and Brody Mullins, "Defense Bill Earmarks Total $4 Billion," *Wall Street Journal*, December 23, 2009, p. A1.

30. Ben Pershing, "Democrats Clear Spending Bill in Senate," *Washington Post*, December 14, 2009 p. A1.

31. Jonathan Weisman and Jim VandeHei, "Road Bill Reflects the Power of Pork; White House Drops Effort to Rein in Hill," *Washington Post*, August 11, 2005, p. A1.

32. An important qualification to the norm was imposed by Republicans in 1995 when they set a six-year term limit for committee and subcommittee chairs.

33. David W. Rohde, *Parties and Leaders in the Postreform House* (Chicago: University of Chicago Press, 1991).

34. David Rohde and John Aldrich, "The Transition to Republican Rule in the House: Implications for Theories of Congressional Politics," *Political Science Quarterly* 112:4 (Winter, 1997–1998): 541–67.

35. Nelson W. Polsby, *Congress and the Presidency*, 4th ed. (Englewood Cliffs, NJ: Prentice Hall, 1986), p. 111.

36. CBS News, "Obama: Fundraiser-in-chief," August 5, 2010, www.cbsnews.com/video/watch/?id-6747632n (accessed 8/18/10).

37. "James Traficant Hearing; Kick Them in the Crotch," www.youtube.com/watch?v=tQ5Os1400uc&feature=related (accessed 5/7/08).

38. David E. Price, "Congressional Committees in the Policy Process," in *Congress Reconsidered*, 3rd ed., ed. Lawrence C. Dodd and Bruce I. Oppenheimer (Washington, DC: CQ Press, 1985), pp. 161–88.

39. Richard F. Fenno, *Congressmen in Committees* (Boston: Little, Brown, 1973).

40. Richard L. Hall, *Participation in Congress* (New Haven, CT: Yale University Press, 1996).

41. Barbara Sinclair, *Unorthodox Lawmaking* (Washington, DC: CQ Press, 2000), p. xiv.

42. Sinclair, *Unorthodox Lawmaking*, p. 59.

43. Louis Fisher, "The Pocket Veto: Its Current Status," Congressional Research Service Report RL30909, March 30, 2001. The appeals court case was *Barnes v. Kline*, 759 F.2d 21 (D.C. Cir., 1985).

44. Howard H. Baker Jr., Leaders Lecture Series Address to the Senate (Washington, DC, July 14, 1998) www.senate.gov/artandhistory/history/common/generic/Leaders_Lecture_Series_Baker.htm (accessed 5/7/08).

45. Mathew McCubbins and Thomas Schwartz, "Congressional Oversight Overlooked: Police Patrol versus Fire Alarm," *American Journal of Political Science* 28:1 (February, 1984): 165–77.

46. *Immigration and Naturalization Service v. Chadha*, 462 U.S. 919 (1983).

Challenging Conventional Wisdom

a. Keith Krehbiel, "Where's the Party?" *British Journal of Political Science* 23 (1993): 235–66.

b. Gary Jacobson, "Party Polarization in National Politics: The Electoral Connection," in *Polarized Politics: Congress and the President in a Partisan Era*, ed. Richard Fleisher and Jon Bond (Washington, DC: CQ Press, 2000).

You Decide

a. This figure comes from a report by the Citizens Against Government Waste, "Pork Alert: Defense Conference Report Loaded with Earmarks," www.cagw.org/newroom/releases/2009/pork-alert-defense.html (accessed 1/6/10). A lower figure of $4 billion in earmarks was reported in John D. McKinnon and Brody Mullins, "Defense Bill Earmarks Total $4 Billion," *Wall Street Journal*, December 23, 2009, p. A1.

What Do Political Scientists Do?

a. Morris P. Fiorina (with Samuel J. Abrams and Jeremy C. Pope), *Culture War? The Myth of a Polarized America* (New York: Pearson/Longman, 2006), p. 19.

b. Bill Bishop, *The Big Sort: Why the Clustering of Like-Minded America Is Tearing Us Apart* (Boston: Houghton Mifflin Harcourt, 2008).

c. Sean M. Theriault, *Party Polarization in Congress* (New York: Cambridge University Press, 2008).

d. Sean M. Theriault, "The Procedurally Polarized Congress," unpublished paper, April 6, 2009, http://harrisschool.uchicago.edu/programs/beyond/workshops/ampolpapers/spring09-theriault.pdf.

Comparing Ourselves to Others

a. Information was drawn from John M. Carey, "Legislative Organization," in *Oxford Handbook of Political Institutions*, ed. Sarah Binder, Rod Rhodes, and Bert Rockman (New York: Oxford University Press, 2005); Gerhard Lowenberg, Peverill Squire, and D. Roderick Kiewiet, ed., *Legislatures: Comparative Perspectives on Representative Assemblies* (Ann Arbor, MI: University of Michigan Press, 2002); and Gary W. Cox, "The Organization of Democratic Legislatures," in *Oxford Handbook of Political Economy*, ed. Barry Weingast and Donald Wittman (New York: Oxford University Press, 2005).

CHAPTER 11

1. John Aldrich, *Why Parties?* (Chicago: University of Chicago Press, 1995).

2. Ernest R. May, *The Making of the Monroe Doctrine* (Cambridge, MA: Harvard University Press, 1975).

3. Arthur M. Schlesinger Jr., *The Age of Jackson* (Boston: Little, Brown, 1945).

4. David Greenberg, "Lincoln's Crackdown," *Slate*, November 30, 2001, www.slate.com/id/2059132 (accessed 4/29/08).

5. Steven Skowronek, *Building a New American State: The Expansion of National Administrative Capacities* (New York: Cambridge University Press, 1982).

6. Theda Skocpol, *Protecting Soldiers and Mothers: The Political Origins of Social Policy in the United States* (Cambridge, MA: Harvard University Press, 1995).

7. Kendrick Clements, *The Presidency of Woodrow Wilson* (Lawrence, KS: University Press of Kansas, 1992).

8. Thomas J. Knock, *To End All Wars: Woodrow Wilson and the Quest for a New World Order* (New York: Oxford University Press, 1992).

9. Arthur M. Schlesinger Jr., *The Crisis of the Old Order, 1919–1933* (Boston: Houghton Mifflin, 1957).

10. William E. Leuchtenburg, *FDR Years: On Roosevelt and His Legacy* (New York: Columbia University Press, 1995).

11. Chester Pach and Elmo Richardson, *The Presidency of Dwight D. Eisenhower* (Lawrence, KS: University Press of Kansas, 1991).

12. Jackie Calmes, "Audit Finds TARP Program Effective," *New York Times*, December 9, 2009, p. D1.

13. Executive Order no. 13425, "Trial of Alien Unlawful Enemy Combatants by Military Commission," February 14, 2007, www.fas.org/irp/offdocs/eo/eo-13425.htm (accessed 4/29/08).

14. Michael D. Shear, "Obama Extends Hospital Visitation Rights to Same-Sex Partners of Gays," *Washington Post*, April 16, 2010, p. A1.

15. Thomas J. Weko, *The Politicizing Presidency: The White House Personnel Office, 1948–1994* (Lawrence, KS: University Press of Kansas, 1995).

16. Walter Dellinger and Dahlia Lithwick, "A Supreme Court Conversation," *Slate*, June 22, 2007, www.slate.com/id/2168856/entry/2168959 (accessed 4/29/08).

17. Jeff Zeleny, "Daschle Ends Bid for Post; Obama Concedes Mistake," *New York Times*, February 3, 2009, p. A1.

18. Kevin Flynn and William K. Rashbaum, "An Aborted Nomination: The Nominee's Past; Beyond the Disclosure about Kerik's Nanny, More Questions Were Lurking," *New York Times*, December 13, 2004.

19. "Obama Appoints Berwick to Head Medicare and Medicaid during Congressional Recess," *Boston Globe*, July 6, 2010, www.boston.com/news/politics/politicalintelligence/2010/07/obama_appoints_1.html (accessed 11/2/10).

20. Kenneth Mayer, *With the Stroke of a Pen: Executive Orders and Presidential Power* (Princeton, NJ: Princeton University Press, 2001).

21. Kenneth Mayer and Kevin Price, "Unilateral Presidential Powers: Significant Executive Orders, 1949–1999," *Presidential Studies Quarterly* 32 (2002): 367–85.

22. David G. Adler, "The Constitution and Presidential Warmaking: An Enduring Debate," *Political Science Quarterly* 103 (1988): 1–36.

23. Richard F. Grimmett, "The War Powers Resolution: After Thirty Years," Congressional Research Service Report RL32267, March 11, 2004.

24. Lewis Fisher and David G. Adler, "The War Powers Resolution: Time to Say Goodbye," *Political Science Quarterly* 113:1 (1998): 1–20.

25. William G. Howell and Jon C. Pevehouse, *While Dangers Gather: Congressional Checks on Presidential War Powers* (Princeton, NJ: Princeton University Press, 2007).

26. John M. Broder, "The Climate Accord: The Overview; Clinton Adamant on Third World Role in Climate Accord," *New York Times*, December 12, 1997, pp. A1, A16.

27. Jeff Zeleny and Alan Cowell, "Addressing Muslims, Obama Pushes Mideast Peace," *New York Times*, June 4, 2009, p. A1.

28. Richard M. Stevenson, "The Nation; The High-Stakes Politics of Spending the Surplus," *New York Times*, January 7, 2001.

29. Ivo H. Daalder and James M. Lindsay, *America Unbound: The Bush Revolution in American Foreign Policy* (Washington, DC: Brookings Institution Press, 2003).

30. Aaron Wildavsky, "The Two Presidencies," *Trans-Action* 4 (1966): 7–35.

31. Mark A. Peterson, *Legislating Together: The White House and Capitol Hill from Eisenhower to Reagan* (Cambridge, MA: Harvard University Press, 1990).

32. Andrew Rudalevige, *Managing the President's Program: Presidential Leadership and Legislative Policy Formation* (Princeton, NJ: Princeton University Press, 2002).

33. "Campaign 2000: Today—Abortion; The Enduring Battle over Choice," *New York Times*, October 11, 2000.

34. Charles Cameron and Nolan M. McCarty, "Models of Vetoes and Veto Bargaining," *Annual Review of Political Science* 7 (2004): 409–35.

35. Keith Krehbiel, *Pivotal Politics: A Theory of U.S. Lawmaking* (Chicago: University of Chicago Press, 1998).

36. Charles Jones, *The Presidency in a Separated System* (Washington, DC: Brookings Institution Press, 1994).

37. Don Gonyea, "CQ: Obama's Winning Streak on Hill Unprecedented," *National Public Radio*, January 11, 2010, www.npr.org/templates/story/story.php?storyId=122436116 (accessed 1/20/10).

38. Michael Abramowitz, "Commuting Libby's Sentence 'Fair' Bush Says," *Washington Post*, July 13, 2007, p. A5.

39. Mark J. Rozell, "The Law: Executive Privilege: Definition and Standards of Application," *Presidential Studies Quarterly* 29:4 (1999): 918–30.

40. Raoul Berger, *Executive Privilege: A Constitutional Myth* (Cambridge, MA: Harvard University Press, 1974). For commentary, see Saikrisha Prakash, "A Comment on the Constitutionality of Executive Privilege," *Minnesota Law Review* 83:5 (May, 1999): 1143–89.

41. Bruce Fein, "Executive Nonsense," *Slate*, July 11, 2007, www.slate.com/id/2170247 (accessed 4/29/08).

42. Peter Baker and Dan Eggen, "New Privilege Claim by Bush Escalates Clash over Firings," *Washington Post*, July 10, 2007, p. A3.

43. See Oyez, *United States v. Nixon*, 418 U.S. 683 (1974), www.oyez.org/cases/1970-1979/1974/1974_73_1766 for a summary of the case.

44. Mark J. Rozell, "Something to Hide: Clinton's Misuse of Executive Privilege," *Political Science and Politics* 32 (1999): 550–53.

45. Mark J. Rozell, *Executive Privilege: The Dilemma of Secrecy and Democratic Accountability* (Baltimore, MD: Johns Hopkins University Press, 1994).

46. David Kirkpatrick, "Question of Timing on Bush's Push on Earmarks," *New York Times*, January 29, 2008.

47. Ben Smith and David Paul Kuhn, "Obama Moves Quickly to Reshape DNC," Politico, June 13, 2008, www.politico.com/news/stories/0608/11045.html (accessed 7/2/08).

48. Associated Press, "Obama Trying to Boost Party Money, Morale," October 21, 2009, www.msnbc.msn.com/id/33393436 (accessed 1/26/10).

49. John D. McKinnon, "Backing Away from Bush; Some Republican Candidates Avoid Ties with Unpopular President," *Wall Street Journal*, May 23, 2006, p. A4; Carrie Budoff, "Is Bush's Support Worse Than No Support?" Politico, July 16, 2007, www.politico.com/news/stories/0707/4960.html (accessed 4/29/08).

50. George C. Edwards III, *The Public Presidency* (New York: St Martin's Press, 1983); George C. Edwards III, *On Deaf Ears* (New Haven, CT: Yale University Press, 2003).

51. Edmund Morris, *The Rise of Theodore Roosevelt* (New York: Collins, 1987).

52. Brandice Canes-Wrone, *Who Leads Whom: Presidents, Policy, and the Public* (Chicago: University of Chicago Press, 2006).

53. For the text of the January 2007 speech, see "Bush: 'We Need to Change Our Strategy in Iraq,'" January 11, 2007, www.cnn.com/2007/POLITICS/01/10/bush.transcript/index.html (accessed 4/29/08).

54. Edwards, *On Deaf Ears*.

55. Samuel Kernell, *Going Public: New Strategies of Presidential Leadership*, 2nd ed. (Washington, DC: Congressional Quarterly Press, 1993).

56. David Carr, "Obama's Social Networking Was the Real Revolution," *New York Times*, November 9, 2008, www.nytimes.com/2008/11/09/technology/09iht-carr.1.17652000.html (accessed 11/2/10).

57. Associated Press, "Bush Regains Power after Colonoscopy," *New York Times*, July 21, 2007, www.nytimes.com/aponline/us/AP-Bush-Colonoscopy.html?hp (accessed 4/29/08).

58. Richard Cohen and Jules Witcover, *A Heartbeat Away: The Investigation and Resignation of Spiro T. Agnew* (New York: Viking, 1974).

59. John Hart, *The Presidential Branch: From Washington to Clinton* (Chatham, NY: Chatham House Publishers, 1987).

60. John Hart, "President Clinton and the Politics of Symbolism: Cutting the White House Staff," *Political Science Quarterly* 110 (1995): 385–403.

61. Michael Fletcher, "White House Had Drug Officials Appear with GOP Candidates," *Washington Post*, July 18, 2007, p. A8.

62. See White House, "White House Offices," www.whitehouse.gov/government/off-descrp.html (accessed 4/29/08).

63. Kelly Chang, David Lewis, and Nolan McCarthy, "The Tenure of Political Appointees" (paper presented at the 2003 Midwest Political Science Association Annual Meeting, Chicago, April 4).

64. David E. Lewis, "Staffing Alone: Unilateral Action and the Politicization of the Executive Office of the President, 1988–2004," *Presidential Studies Quarterly* 35 (2005): 496–514.

65. Charles E. Walcott and Karen M. Hult, "White House Staff Size: Explanations and Implications," *Presidential Studies Quarterly* 29 (1999): 638–56.

66. Karen M. Hult and Charles E. Walcott, *Empowering the White House: Governance under Nixon, Ford, and Carter* (Lawrence, KS: University Press of Kansas, 2004).

67. David E. Lewis, *The Politics of Presidential Appointments: Political Control and Bureaucratic Performance* (Princeton, NJ: Princeton University Press, 2008).

68. For a complete listing of votes, see Office of the Secretary of the Senate, "Occasions when Vice Presidents Have Voted to Break Tie Votes in the Senate," www.senate.gov/artandhistory/history/resources/pdf/VPTies.pdf (accessed 4/29/08).

69. Andrew Taylor, "Cheney Breaks Senate Tie on Spending Cuts," Associated Press, December 21, 2005.

70. For a series of articles detailing Cheney's role, see "Angler: The Cheney Vice Presidency," *Washington Post*, June 24–27, 2007, www.washingtonpost.com/cheney (accessed 4/29/08).

71. For example, see David Talbot, "Creepier Than Nixon," *Salon*, March 31, 2004, http://dir.salon.com/story/news/feature/2004/03/31/dean/index.html (accessed 4/29/08).

72. Barton Gellman and Jo Baker, "A Different Understanding with the President," *Washington Post*, June 24, 2007, p. A1.

73. John Mueller, *War, Presidents, and Public Opinion* (New York: John Wiley and Sons, 1973).

74. Alexander Hamilton and James Madison, *The Pacificus-Helvidius Debates of 1793–1794: Toward the Completion of the American Founding*, ed. Martin J. Frisch (1793; repr. Indianapolis, IN: The Liberty Fund, 2007).

75. Richard E. Neustart, *Presidential Power and the Modern Presidents* (New York: Simon and Schuster, 1991).

76. Terry M. Moe and William G. Howell, "The Presidential Power of Unilateral Action," *Journal of Law, Economics, and Organization* 15 (1999): 132–46.

77. James Risen and Eric Lichtblau, "Spying Program Snared U.S. Calls," *New York Times*, December 21, 2005, p. A1; David E. Sanger, "After ABM Treaty: New Freedom for U.S. in Different Kind of Arms Control," *New York Times*, December 15, 2001.

78. For details, see the text of various executive orders at www.whitehouse.gov/briefing-room/presidential-actions/ (accessed 1/27/10).

79. These examples appear throughout Moe and Howell, "The Presidential Power of Unilateral Action"; see also William G. Howell, "Unilateral Powers: A Brief Overview," *Presidential Studies Quarterly* 35:3 (2005): 417–39.

80. David E. Lewis, *Presidents and the Politics of Agency Design* (Palo Alto, CA: Stanford University Press, 2003); William Howell and David Lewis, "Agencies by Presidential Design," *Journal of Politics* 64:4 (2002): 1095–114.

81. Louis Fisher, *Presidential War Power*, 2nd ed. (Lawrence, KS: University Press of Kansas, 2004); James M. Lindsay, "Deference and Defiance: The Shifting Rhythms of Executive–Legislative Relations in Foreign Policy," *Presidential Studies Quarterly* 33:3 (2003): 530–46; Lawrence Margolis, *Executive Agreements and Presidential Power in Foreign Policy* (New York: Praeger, 1985), 209–32.

82. Phillip Cooper, "George W. Bush, Edgar Allan Poe, and the Use and Abuse of Presidential Signing Statements," *Presidential Studies Quarterly* 35:3 (2005): 515–32.

83. Andrew Rudalevige, *The New Imperial Presidency: Renewing Presidential Power after Watergate* (Ann Arbor, MI: University of Michigan Press, 2005).

84. William G. Howell and Kenneth R. Mayer, "The Last One Hundred Days," *Presidential Studies Quarterly* 35:3 (2005): 533–53.

85. Christopher Deering and Forrest Maltzman, "The Politics of Executive Orders: Legislative Constraints on Presidential Power," *Political Research Quarterly* 52:4 (1999): 767–83.

86. David E. Lewis, *Presidents and the Politics of Agency Design: Political Insulation in the United States Government Bureaucracy, 1946–1997* (Palo Alto, CA: Stanford University Press, 2003).

87. David Epstein and Sharyn O'Halloran, *Delegating Powers* (Cambridge, UK: Cambridge University Press, 1999).

88. David G. Adler, "The Steel Seizure Case and Inherent Presidential Power," *Constitutional Commentary* 19 (2002): 155–208.

89. For a discussion of these and related cases, see Dahlia Lithwick and Walter Dellinger, "A Supreme Court Conversation," *Slate*, June 22, 2007, www.slate.com/id/2168856/entry/2168959 (accessed 7/4/08); and James Risen, "The Executive Power Awaiting the Next President," *New York Times*, June 22, 2008.

What Do Political Scientists Do?

a. Kenneth R. Mayer and Kevin Price, "Unilateral Presidential Powers: Significant Executive Orders, 1949–99," *Presidential Studies Quarterly* 32:2 (2002): 367–86.

You Decide

a. For a summary of the charges and counter-charges, see Paul Gottsching and Dahlia Lithwick, "Who's Blaming Whom," *Slate*, March 27, 2007, www.slate.com/id/2162775.

b. Sam Coates, "Stress, Fees Mount for Bush Aides Called to Testify," *Washington Post*, September 18, 2005; Adam Nagourney, "Working for Clintons Can Mean Big Legal Bills," *New York Times*, February 20, 1998.

Challenging Conventional Wisdom

a. John M. Broder, "Obama, Adopting Economic Theme, Criticizes McCain," *New York Times*, June 10, 2008.

b. For excerpts of the speech, see Mark Halperin's The Page, "Excerpts of McCain's Speech in Denver, Colorado," *Time*, July 14, 2007, http://thepage.time.com/excerpts-of-mccains-speech-in-denver-colorado.

c. Pew Research Center, "Economic Discontent Deepens as Inflation Concerns Rise," February 14, 2008, http://people-press.org/report/395/economic-discontent-deepens-as-inflation-concerns-rise.

CHAPTER 12

1. Jason DeParle, "Minerals Service Had a Mandate to Produce Results," *New York Times*, August 7, 2010, p. A1.

2. Douglass K. Daniel, "Commerce Dept. Lost 1,100 Laptops in Five Years," Associated Press, September 22, 2006, www.msnbc.msn.com/id/14946353 (accessed 7/15/08).

3. Brian M. Riedl, "Top 10 Examples of Government Waste," Heritage Foundation Backgrounder, www.heritage.org/Research/Budget/bg1840.cfm (accessed 7/15/08).

4. These examples can be found in Spencer S. Hsu, "Order Shows FEMA Aid Shortcomings," *Washington Post*, December 3, 2006, p. A16; Eric Lipton, "'Breathtaking' Waste and Fraud in Hurricane Aid," *New York Times*, June 27, 2006; Daniel Engber, "Who Unlocked My Trailer?" *Slate*, August 15, 2006, www.slate.com/id/2147790 (accessed 7/15/08); Shannon McCaffrey, Alison Young, and Seth Borenstein, "As New Orleans Flooded, Chertoff Discussed Avian Flu in Atlanta," Knight Ridder, September 15, 2005; Aaron C. Davis, "U.S. Paying a Premium to Cover Storm-Damaged Roofs," Knight Ridder, September 30, 2005; and Jonathan Weisman, "$236 Million Cruise Ship Deal Criticized," *Washington Post*, September 28, 2005, p. A1.

5. Spencer S. Hsu, "TSA Manual Misstep Leads to Discipline," *Washington Post*, December 10, 2009, p. A10.

6. For information on the Service to America Medals, see http://servicetoamericamedals.org/SAM/index.shtml.

7. Dwight Waldo, *The Administrative State: A Study of the Political Theory of American Public Administration* (1948; repr. Piscataway, NJ: Transaction Publishers, 2006).

8. Perry Bacon Jr., "House Passes Defense Spending Bill," *Washington Post*, December 16, 2009, http://voices.washingtonpost.com/44/2009/12/house-passes-defense-spending.html (accessed 2/8/10).

9. The original quote is from Robert Dahl and was used in this context in David E. Lewis, *Presidents and the Politics of Agency Design: Political Insulation in the United States Government* (Palo Alto, CA: Stanford University Press, 2003).

10. For a history of the Food and Drug Administration, see John P. Swann, FDA History Office, "History of the FDA," www.fda.gov/oc/history/historyoffda/section2.html (accessed 7/15/08).

11. For details, see Cornelius Kerwin, *Rulemaking: How Government Agencies Write Law and Make Policy* (Washington, DC: CQ Press, 1999).

12. John Bohte and B. Dan Wood, "Political Transaction Costs and the Politics of Agency Design," *Journal of Politics* 66 (2004): 176–202.

13. Enterprise Risk Management Initiative, "Costs Associated with Regulatory Risks," www.mgt.ncsu.edu/erm/index.php/articles/entry/regulatory-risk-cost/ (accessed 2/3/10).

14. The full text of the regulations and the rationale for them can be found at Centers for Medicare and Medicaid Services, "Transplants," www.cms.hhs.gov/certificationandcomplianc/20_transplant.asp (accessed 7/20/08).

15. Andrew Pollack, "New Sense of Caution at FDA," *New York Times*, September 29, 2006.

16. There are two exceptions. A patient can enroll in a clinical trial for a new drug during the approval process, but there is a good chance that the patient will get a placebo or a previously approved treatment rather than the drug being tested. The FDA does allow companies to provide some experimental drugs to patients who cannot participate in a trial but only those drugs that have passed early screening trials.

17. Susan Okie, "Access before Approval—A Right to Take Experimental Drugs?" *New England Journal of Medicine* 355 (2004): 437–40.

18. For details, see the U.S. General Services Administration site at www.gsa.gov.

19. Michael Lipsky, *Street Level Bureaucracy* (New York: Russell Sage Foundation, 1983).

20. Stephen Skowronek, *Building a New American State: The Expansion of National Administrative Capacities, 1877–1920* (New York: Cambridge University Press, 1982).

21. PPBS was Program Planning Budget System (Johnson administration), MBO was Management by Objectives (Nixon administration), ZBB was Zero-Based Budgeting (Carter administration), REGO was short for Reinventing Government (Clinton administration), and PBB (Performance Based Budgeting) was President George W. Bush's effort at bureaucratic reorganization. For details, see Cedilia Ferradino, "New Name, Old Challenges: Performance Budgeting's Continuing Struggle to Succeed in Washington," *Rockefeller College Review* 1:2 (2002): 6–23.

22. Terry Moe, "An Assessment of the Positive Theory of Congressional Dominance," *Legislative Studies Quarterly* 4 (1987): 475–98.

23. DeParle, "Minerals Service Had a Mandate to Produce Results."

24. Frances E. Rourke, "Responsiveness and Neutral Competence in American Bureaucracy," *Public Administration Review* 52 (1992): 539–46; Max Weber, *Essays on Sociology* (New York: Oxford University Press, 1958).

25. Terry M. Moe, "Power and Political Institutions," *Perspectives on Politics* 3 (2005): 215–33.

26. Karen Orren and Steven Skorownek, "Regimes and Regime Building in American Government: A Review of the Literature on the 1940s," *Political Science Quarterly* 113 (1998): 689–702.

27. Michael Nelson, "A Short, Ironic History of American National Bureaucracy," *Journal of Politics* 44 (1982): 747–78.

28. Nelson, "A Short, Ironic History of American National Bureaucracy."

29. Nelson, "A Short, Ironic History of American National Bureaucracy."

30. John Aldrich, *Why Parties?* (Chicago: University of Chicago Press, 1995).

31. Nelson, "A Short, Ironic History of American National Bureaucracy."

32. Matthew A. Crenson, *The Federal Machine: Beginnings of Bureaucracy in Jacksonian America* (Baltimore, MD: Johns Hopkins University Press, 1975).

33. James Q. Wilson, "The Rise of the Bureaucratic State," in *The American Commonwealth*, ed. Nathan Glazer and Irving Kristol (New York: Basic Books, 1976).

34. Skowronek, *Building a New American State.*

35. Robert Harrison, *Congress, Progressive Reform, and the New American State* (New York: Cambridge University Press, 2004).

36. The U.S. State Department has an excellent summary of the Pendleton Act at http://usinfo.state.gov/usa/infousa/facts/democrac/28.htm.

37. Lawrence C. Dodd and Richard L. Schott, *Congress and the Administrative State* (New York: John Wiley & Sons, 1979).

38. Richard F. Bensel, *The Political Economy of American Industrialization, 1877–1900* (New York: Cambridge University Press, 2000).

39. William Riordan, *Plunkitt of Tammany Hall: A Series of Very Plain Talks on Very Practical Politics* (1924; repr. New York: Signet Classics, 1995).

40. Sean Theriault, "Patronage, the Pendleton Act, and the Power of the People," *Journal of Politics* 65 (2003): 50–68.

41. Ira Katznelson and Bruce Pietrykowski, "Rebuilding the American State: Evidence from the 1940s," *Studies in American Political Development* 5:2 (1991) 301–39.

42. David Plotke, *Building a Democratic Political Order: Reshaping American Liberalism in the 1930s and 1940s* (New York: Cambridge University Press, 1996).

43. Theda Skocpol and Kenneth Finegold, "State Capacity and Economic Intervention in the Early New Deal," *Political Science Quarterly* 97 (1999): 255–70.

44. Michael Brown, "State Capacity and Political Choice: Interpreting the Failure of the Third New Deal," *Studies in American Political Development* 9 (1995): 187–212.

45. Ira Katznelson, Kim Geiger, and Daniel Kryder, "Limiting Liberalism: The Southern Veto in Congress, 1933–1950," *Political Science Quarterly* 108 (1993): 283–306.

46. Joseph Califano, "What Was Really Great about the Great Society," *Washington Monthly*, October 1999, www.washingtonmonthly.com/features/1999/9910.califano.html (accessed 7/16/08).

47. Douglas Arnold, *Congress and the Bureaucracy* (New Haven, CT: Yale University Press, 1978).

48. David T. Canon, *Race, Redistricting, and Representation: The Unintended Consequences of Black Majority Districts* (Chicago: University of Chicago Press, 1999).

49. Charles Murray, *Losing Ground: American Social Policy, 1950–1980* (New York: Basic Books, 1984).

50. Henry J. Aaron, *Politics and the Professors: The Great Society in Perspective* (Washington, DC: Brookings Institution Press, 1978).

51. Michael B. Katz, *In the Shadow of the Poorhouse: A Social History of Welfare in America* (New York: Basic Books, 1996).

52. Stephen Moore, "How the Budget Revolution Was Lost," Cato Policy Analysis no. 281, September 2, 1997, Cato Institute, www.cato.org/pubs/pas/pa-281.html (accessed 7/21/08).

53. Clyde Wayne Crews Jr., "Ten Thousand Commandments," An Annual Snapshot of the Federal Regulatory State," 2003 ed. (Washington, DC: Cato Institute, 2003), www.cato.org/tech/pubs/10kc_2003.pdf (accessed 7/15/08).

54. Andrew Rudalevige, "The Structure of Leadership: Presidents, Hierarchies, and Information Flow," *Presidential Studies Quarterly* 35 (2005): 333–60.

55. David E. Lewis, *Presidents and the Policy of Agency Design* (Palo Alto, CA: Stanford University Press, 2003).

56. Terry Moe, "An Assessment of the Positive Theory of Congressional Dominance," *Legislative Studies Quarterly* 4 (1987): 475–98.

57. Mark Hosenball, Michael Isikoff, and Evan Thomas, "Cheney's Long Path to War," *Newsweek*, November 17, 2003, pp. 34–40.

58. Eric Schmitt and Thom Shanker, "A CIA Rival: Pentagon Sets Up Intelligence Unit," *New York Times*, October 24, 2002, p. A1.

59. William A. Niskanen, *Bureaucracy and Public Economics* (Washington, DC: Edward Elgar Publishing, 1976); Robert Waples and Jac C. Heckelman, "Public Choice Economics: Where Is There Consensus?" *American Economist* 49 (2005): 66–79.

60. Alan Schick and Felix LoStracco, *The Federal Budget: Politics, Process, Policy* (Washington, DC: Brookings Institution Press, 2000).

61. Joel D. Aberbach, "The Political Significance of the George W. Bush Administration," *Social Policy and Administration* 39:2 (2005): 130–49.

62. David E. Lewis, "The Politics of Agency Termination: Confronting the Myth of Agency Immortality," *Journal of Politics* 64 (2002): 89–107.

63. Ronald A. Wirtz, "Put It on My . . . Er, His Tab: Opinion Polls Show a Big Gap between the Public's Desire for Services and Its Willingness to Pay for These Services," *Fedgazette*, January 2004, www.minneapolisfed.org/pubs/fedgaz/04-01/tab.cfm (accessed 7/16/08).

64. Paul Light, "Measuring the Health of the Public Service," in *Workways of Governance*, ed. Roger Davidson (Washington, DC: Brookings Institution Press, 2003).

65. John J. Brehm and Scott Gates, *Working, Shirking, and Sabotage* (Ann Arbor, MI: University of Michigan Press, 1998).

66. Paul Light, *A Government Well-Executed: Public Service and Public Performance* (Washington, DC: Brookings Institution Press, 2003).

67. This discussion of the details of the civil service system is based on Bureau of Labor Statistics, "Career Guide to Industries," March 12, 2008, www.bls.gov/oco/cg/cgs041.htm (accessed 7/16/08).

68. Chris Edwards and Tad DeHaven, "Federal Government Should Increase Firing Rate," *Tax and Budget Bulletin* 10, November 2002, Cato Institute, www.cato.org/pubs/tbb/tbb-0211-10.pdf (accessed 7/16/08).

69. Ronald N. Johnson and Gary D. Liebcap, *The Federal Civil Service System and the Problem of Bureaucracy* (Chicago: University of Chicago Press, 1993).

70. Eric Lichtblau, "Report Sees Illegal Hiring Practices at Justice Department," *New York Times*, June 25, 2008.

71. For the details of the Hatch Act, see Daniel Engber, "Can Karl Rove Plot Campaign Strategy on the Government's Dime?" *Slate*, April 21, 2006, www.slate.com/id/2140418 (accessed 7/16/08).

72. Samantha Levine, "NASA Denies Chief Made Formal DeLay Endorsement," *Houston Chronicle*, April 1, 2006.

73. Sheryl Gay Stolberg, "Advisers' E-Mail Accounts May Have Mixed Politics and Business, White House Says," *New York Times*, April 12, 2007.

74. Stephen Labaton and Edmund Andrews, "White House Calls Political Briefings Legal," *New York Times*, April 27, 2007.

75. Timothy Noah, "Low Morale at Homeland Security," *Slate*, September 14, 2005, www.slate.com/id/2126313 (accessed 7/17/08).

76. For details on the Senior Executive Service, see the Office of Personnel Management site at www.opm.gov/ses.

77. The survey was conducted by the Council for Excellence in Government. For the full survey results and interpretation, see Council for Excellence in Government, "Attitudes toward Government" www.excelgov.org/index.php?keyword=a432949724f861 (accessed 7/20/08).

78. Susan Webb Yackee and David Lowery, "Understanding Public Support for the U.S. Federal Bureaucracy," *Public Administration Review* 7:4 (2005): 515–30.

79. C. T. Goodsell, *The Case for Bureaucracy* (Chatham, NJ: Chatham House Press, 1994).

80. Christopher Lee, "Ex-Surgeon General Says White House Hushed Him," *Washington Post*, July 11, 2007, p. A1.

81. Andrew C. Revkin, "Climate Expert Says NASA Tried to Silence Him," *New York Times*, January 29, 2006.

82. Andrew C. Revkin, "A Young Bush Appointee Resigns His Post at NASA," *New York Times*, February 8, 2006.

83. Andrew C. Revkin, "NASA's Goals Delete Mention of Home Planet," *New York Times*, July 22, 2006.

84. John D. Huber and Charles R. Shipan, *Deliberate Discretion? The Institutional Foundations of Bureaucratic Autonomy* (New York: Cambridge University Press, 2002).

85. David Epstein and Sharyn O'Halloran, *Delegating Powers: A Transaction Cost Politics Approach to Policy Making under Separate Powers* (New York: Cambridge University Press, 1999).

86. Mathew D. McCubbins, Roger G. Noll, and Barry R. Weingast, "Structure and Process as Solutions to the Politician's Principal–Agency Problem," *Virginia Law Review* 74 (1989): 431–82.

87. Barry R. Weingast, "Caught in the Middle: The President, Congress, and the Political-Bureaucratic System," in *Institutions of American Democracy: The Executive Branch*, ed. Joel D. Aberbach and Mark A. Peterson (New York: Oxford University Press, 2006).

88. Keith Whittington and Daniel P. Carpenter, "Executive Power in American Institutional Development," *Perspectives on Politics* 1 (2003): 495–513.

89. Dara Cohen, Mariano-Florentino Cuéllar, and Barry R. Weingast, "Crisis Bureaucracy: Homeland Security and the Political Design of Legal Mandates," *Stanford Law Review* 59:3 (2006): 673–760.

90. Federal Communications Commission, "FCC Commissioners," April 1, 2008, www.fcc.gov/commissioners (accessed 7/17/08).

91. Federal Election Commission, "About the FEC: Commissioners," www.fec.gov/members/members.shtml (accessed 7/17/08); Federal Trade Commission, "Commissioners," www.ftc.gov/commissioners/index.shtml (accessed 7/17/08).

92. Charles Shipan, *Designing Judicial Review: Interest Groups, Congress, and Communication Policy* (Ann Arbor, MI Univeristy of Michigan Press, 2000).

93. Roger Noll, Mathew McCubins, and Barry Weingast, "Administrative Procedures as Instruments of Political Control," *Journal of Law, Economics and Organization* 3 (1987): 243–77.

94. Mathew McCubbins and Thomas Schwartz, "Congressional Oversight Overlooked: Fire Alarms vs. Police Patrols," *American Journal of Political Science* 28 (1984): 165–79.

95. McCubbins and Schwartz, "Congressional Oversight Overlooked."

96. Steven J. Balla and John R. Wright, "Interest Groups, Advisory Committees, and Congressional Control of the Bureaucracy," *American Journal of Political Science* 45 (2001): 799–812.

97. Irwin Morris, *Congress, the President, and the Federal Reserve: The Politics of American Monetary Policy-Making* (Ann Arbor, MI: University of Michigan Press, 2000).

98. Daniel P. Carpenter, "The Gatekeeper: Organizational Reputation and Pharmaceutical Regulation at the FDA" (unpublished paper, Harvard University, 2006).

99. Terry M. Moe, "Political Control and the Power of the Agent," *Journal of Law, Economics, and Organization* 22 (2006): 1–29.

100. See David Weil, "OSHA: Beyond the Politics," *Frontline*, January 9, 2003, www.pbs.org/wgbh/pages/frontline/shows/workplace/osha/weil.html (accessed 7/17/08).

101. Daniel P. Carpenter, *The Forging of Bureaucratic Autonomy: Reputations, Networks, and Policy Innovation in Executive Agencies, 1862–1928* (Princeton, NJ: Princeton University Press, 2001).

102. Katz, *In the Shadow of the Poorhouse.*

103. Henry J. Aaron, *Why Is Welfare So Hard to Reform?* (Washington, DC: Brookings Institution Press, 1973).

What Do Political Scientists Do?

a. The Yackees' analysis also considers the outcome in which rules lead to no change in government involvement, but we exclude this possibility to simplify the discussion.

Challenging Conventional Wisdom

a. These figures come from the General Services Administration, GSA Reports, www.gsa.gov/Portal/gsa/ep/contentView.do?contentId=9967&contentType=GSA_OVERVIEW.

You Decide

a. National Aeronautics and Space Administration, "NASA Public Affairs Policy FAQ," www.nasa.gov/pdf/145756main_comm_policy_faq.pdf.

CHAPTER 13

1. *Hamdi v. Rumsfeld*, 542 U.S. 507 (2004); *Rasul v. Bush*, 542 U.S. 466 (2004).

2. Linda Greenhouse, "The Ruling on Tribunals: The Overview; Justices, 5–3, Broadly Reject Bush Plan to Try Detainees," *New York Times*, June 30, 2006, p. A18. *Hamdan v. Rumsfeld*, 126 S. Ct. 2749 (2006).

3. *Boumediene v. Bush*, 553 U.S. (2008).

4. Ralph Ketcham, *The Anti-Federalist Papers and the Constitutional Convention Debates* (New York: Penguin Putnam, 2003), p. 304.

5. Lester S. Jayson, ed., *The Constitution of the United States of America: Analysis and Interpretation* (Washington, DC: U.S. Government Printing Office, 1973), p. 585.

6. David G. Savage, *Guide to the U.S. Supreme Court*, 4th ed. (Washington, DC: CQ Press, 2004), p. 7.

7. Savage, *Guide to the U.S. Supreme Court*, pp. 5–7.

8. Winfield H. Rose, "*Marbury v. Madison*: How John Marshall Changed History by Misquoting the Constitution," *Political Science and Politics* 36:2 (April, 2003): 209–14. Rose argues that in a key quotation in the case, Marshall intentionally left out a clause of the Constitution that suggests that Congress *did* have the power to expand the original jurisdiction of the Court. Other constitutional scholars reject this argument.

9. *Marbury v. Madison*, 1 CR. (5 U.S.) 137 (1803).

10. *Ware v. Hylton*, 3 U.S. 199 (1796).

11. *Lujan v. Defenders of Wildlife*, 504 U.S. 555 (1992).

12. *Campbell v. Clinton*, 99-1843 (this was a District of Columbia appeals court decision; the Supreme Court refused to hear the appeal of the decision), and *Raines v. Byrd*, 956 F. Supp. 25 (1997).

13. U.S. Courts, Federal Court Management Statistics, 2007: District Courts, www.uscourts.gov/cgi-bin/cmsd2007.pl (accessed 3/18/08).

14. The "stepchildren" label and the rest of the information in this paragraph are drawn from J. Woodford Howard Jr., *Courts of Appeals in the Federal Judicial System* (Princeton, NJ: Princeton University Press, 1981), pp. 1–15.

15. Federal Judicial Center, "The Judiciary Act of 1869: An Act to Amend the Judicial System of the United States," www.fjc.gov/history/home.nsf/page/10a_bdy (accessed 7/18/08).

16. Federal Judicial Center, "The U.S. Courts of Appeals and the Federal Judiciary," www.fjc.gov/history/home.nsf/page/ca_bdy?OpenDocument (accessed 7/18/08).

17. Howard, *Courts of Appeals*, p. 5.

18. U.S. Courts, Federal Judiciary: Frequently Asked Questions, "Federal Judges," www.uscourts.gov/faq.html (accessed 3/18/08).

19. U.S. Courts, Federal Court Management Statistics, 2007: Courts of Appeals, www.uscourts.gov/cgi-bin/cmsa2007.pl (accessed 3/18/08).

20. American Judicature Society, "Judicial Selection in the States: Appellate and General Jurisdiction Courts," 2004, www.ajs.org/js/JudicialSelectionCharts_old.pdf (accessed 9/14/06).

21. *Caperton v. A.T. Massey Coal Co.*, 556 U.S. __ (2009).

22. Savage, *Guide to the U.S. Supreme Court*, p. 1003.

23. Sheldon Goldman, "Reagan's Second Term Judicial Appointments: The Battle at Midway," *Judicature* 70 (1986–87): 328, 331; 78.8 percent of Ford's district court nominees and 91.7 percent of his appeals court nominees were Republicans. See also Michael J. Gerhardt, *The Federal Appointment Process: A Constitutional and Historical Analysis* (Durham, NC: Duke University Press, 2000), especially Chapter 4.

24. Edward Lazarus, *Closed Chambers: The Rise and Fall of the Modern Supreme Court* (New York: Penguin, Putnam, 1998), p. 30.

25. Supreme Court of the United States *In Re Frederick W. Bauer*, On Petition for a Writ of Mandamus to the United States Court of Appeals for the Seventh Circuit, Brief for the United States in Opposition, No. 90-6351, March 4, 1991, www.usdoj.gov/osg/briefs/1990/sg900418.txt (accessed 7/18/08).

26. Supreme Court of the United States *In Re Frederick W. Bauer*, On Motion for Leave to Proceed in forma pauperis, No. 99-5440, Decided October 18, 1999, per curiam, http://supreme.lp.findlaw.com/supreme_court/decisions/99-5440.html (accessed 7/18/08).

27. John Roberts, U.S. Supreme Court, "2007 Year-End Report on the Federal Judiciary," January 1, 2008, www.supremecourtus.gov/publicinfo/year-end/2007year-endreport.pdf (accessed 3/17/08).

28. For a critical account of the Supreme Court's reduced case load, which dates back to the Rehnquist Court, see Philip Allen Lacovara, "The

Incredible Shrinking Court," *American Lawyer*, December 1, 2003, www.judicialaccountability.org/download/shrinkinusgcourt.htm (accessed 7/18/08).

29. *New Jersey v. New York*, No. 120 Orig., 118 S. Ct. 1726 (1998), and *Kansas v. Colorado*, No. 105 Orig., 125 S. Ct. 526 (2004).

30. Abraham, *The Judiciary*, p. 25, says that original jurisdiction has been invoked "about 150 times." A Lexis search revealed an additional twenty-seven original jurisdiction cases between 1987 and December 2004. See U.S. Department of Justice, Help/Glossary, www.usdoj.gov/osg/briefs/help.html for a basic discussion of the Supreme Court's original jurisdiction.

31. Amanda L. Tyler, "Setting the Supreme Court's Agenda: Is There a Place for Certification?" *The George Washington Law Review Arguendo* 78 (May, 2010): 101–18.

32. Savage, *Guide to the U.S. Supreme Court*, p. 848.

33. See Thomas G. Walker and Lee Epstein, *The Supreme Court of the United States: An Introduction* (New York: St. Martin's Press, 1993), pp. 80–85, for a more detailed discussion of these concepts and citations to the relevant court cases.

34. *DeFunis v. Odegaard*, 416 U.S. 312 (1974).

35. The appeals court case is *Byrd v. Raines*, and the case that was finally heard by the Court was *Clinton v. City of New York*, 524 U.S. 417 (1998).

36. Gregory A. Caldeira and John R. Wright, "The Discuss List: Agenda Building in the Supreme Court," *Law and Society Review* 24 (1990): 813.

37. Walker and Epstein, *Supreme Court*, p. 89.

38. H. W. Perry, "Agenda Setting and Case Selection," in *The American Courts: A Critical Assessment*, ed. John B. Gates and Charles H. Johnson (Washington, DC: CQ Press, 1991), p. 237. Also see Perry's *Deciding to Decide: Agenda Setting in the United States Supreme Court* (Cambridge, MA: Harvard University Press, 1991).

39. U.S. Supreme Court, "The Court and Its Procedures," www.supremecourtus.gov/about/procedures.pdf (accessed 3/17/08).

40. *United States v. Nixon*, 418 U.S. 683 (1974).

41. Lee Epstein, Jeffrey A. Segal, Harold J. Spaeth, and Thomas G. Walker, *The Supreme Court Compendium: Data, Decisions, and Developments*, 3rd ed. (Washington, DC: CQ Press, 2003), Table 7-25.

42. Gregory A. Caldeira and John R. Wright, "*Amicus Curiae* before the Supreme Court: Who Participates, When, and How Much?" *Journal of Politics* 52 (August, 1990): 803.

43. U.S. Supreme Court, Rules of the Supreme Court, adopted March 14, 2005, effective May 2, 2005, Rule 28.7, www.supremecourtus.gov/ctrules/rulesofthecourt.pdf (accessed 7/18/08).

44. Savage, *Guide to the U.S. Supreme Court*, p. 852.

45. U.S. Supreme Court, Argument Transcripts, www.supremecourtus.gov/oral_arguments/argument_transcripts (accessed 7/18/08).

46. Quoted in Savage, *Guide to the U.S. Supreme Court*, p. 854.

47. Forrest Maltzman, James F. Spriggs II, and Paul J. Wahlbeck, *Crafting Law on the Supreme Court: The Collegial Game* (New York: Cambridge University Press, 2000), p. 33.

48. William H. Rehnquist, "Memorandum to the Conference: Policy Regarding Assignments," November 24, 1989, papers of Justice Thurgood Marshall, Library of Congress Manuscript Division, Washington, DC, quoted in Maltzman, Spriggs, and Wahlbeck, *Crafting Law*, pp. 30–31.

49. *Smith v. Allwright*, 321 U.S. 649 (1944).

50. Walker and Epstein, *Supreme Court*, p. 110.

51. Savage, *Guide to the U.S. Supreme Court*, p. 854.

52. Maltzman, Spriggs, and Wahlbeck, *Crafting Law*, p. 51. This specific prediction was for a case that has fifteen *amicus* briefs.

53. Maltzman, Spriggs, and Wahlbeck, *Crafting Law*, pp. 49–50.

54. Quoted in Lee Epstein and Thomas G. Walker, *Constitutional Law for a Changing America*, 5th ed. (Washington, DC: CQ Press, 2004), p. 29.

55. *Maryland v. Craig*, 497 U.S. 836 (1990).

56. Epstein and Walker, *Constitutional Law for a Changing America*, p. 31.

57. Epstein, Segal, Spaeth, and Walker, *Supreme Court Compendium*, Table 6-2.

58. Forrest Maltzman and Paul J. Wahlbeck, "Strategic Considerations and Vote Fluidity on the Burger Court," *American Journal of Political Science* 90 (1996): 581–92; Maltzman, Spriggs, and Wahlbeck, *Crafting Law*.

59. Thomas R. Marshall, *Public Opinion and the Supreme Court* (Boston: Unwin Hyman, 1989), p. 12; as cited in Epstein and Walker, *Constitutional Law for a Changing America*, p. 92.

60. Thomas M. Keck, *The Most Activist Supreme Court in History: The Road to Modern Judicial Conservatism* (Chicago: University of Chicago Press, 2004).

61. Marshall, *Public Opinion*, Table 6-8.

62. Jeffrey Rosen, "Has the Supreme Court Gone Too Far?" *Commentary* 116:3 (October, 2003).

63. Finley Peter Dunne, Paul Green, and Jacques Barzun, *Mr. Dooley in Peace and in War* (1898; repr. Champaign-Urbana, IL: University of Illinois Press, 2001).

64. Robert Dahl, "Decision-Making in a Democracy: The Supreme Court as a National Policy-Maker," *Journal of Public Law* 6 (1957): 279–95, is the classic work on this topic. More recent work challenged Dahl's methods but largely supports that idea that the Court follows the will of the majority.

65. Jeffrey A. Segal, Richard J. Timpone, and Robert M. Howard, "Buyer Beware? Presidential Success through Supreme Court Appointments," *Political Research Quarterly* 53:3 (September, 2000): 557–73; Gregory A. Caldeira and Charles E. Smith Jr., "Campaigning for the Supreme Court: The Dynamics of Public Opinion on the Thomas Nomination," *Political Research Quarterly* 58:3 (August, 1996): 655–81.

66. William Mishler and Reginald S. Sheehan, "The Supreme Court as a Countermajoritarian Institution? The Impact of Public Opinion on Supreme Court Decisions," *American Political Science Review* 87:1 (March, 1993): 87–101.

67. *Roper v. Simmons*, U.S. 03-633 (2005). See Linda Greenhouse, "Supreme Court, 5–4, Forbids Execution in Juvenile Crime," *New York Times*, March 2, 2005, p. A1, for a discussion of this case and Justice Scalia's dissent.

68. David O'Brien, *Storm Center: The Supreme Court in American Politics*, 4th ed. (New York: Norton, 1996).

69. Helmut Norpoth and Jeffrey A. Segal, "Popular Influence in Supreme Court Decisions," *American Political Science Review* 88 (1994): 711–16.

70. *Worcester v. Georgia*, 31 U.S. 515 (1832).

71. *Ex Parte Milligan*, 71 U.S. 2 (1866), *Youngstown Sheet and Tube v. Sawyer*, 343 U.S. 579 (1952), *New York Times v. United States*, 403 U.S. 713 (1971).

72. Linda Greenhouse, "Chief Justice Attacks a Law as Infringing on Judges," *New York Times*, January 1, 2004, p. A1.

73. The seminal case striking down mandatory sentencing was *United States v. Booker*, 543 U.S. 220 (2005). Two of the important subsequent cases are *Kimbrough v. United States*, 128 S. Ct. 558 (2007) and *Spears v. United States*, 129 S. Ct. 840 (2009). For a detailed discussion of cases on this topic, see the Office of General Counsel, "Supreme Court Cases on Sentencing Issues," United States Sentencing Commission (Washington DC; April 2009), www.ussc.gov/training/SUPREME200904.PDF (accessed January 12, 2010).

74. *Foster v. Neilson*, 27 U.S. 253 (1829).

75. *Chicago & Southern Airlines v. Waterman SS Corp*, 333 U.S. 103 (1948).

Challenging Conventional Wisdom

a. Michael Stokes Paulsen, "Judging Judicial Review: Marbury in the Modern Era: The Irrepressible Myth of *Marbury*," *Michigan Law Review* 101 (August, 2003): 2706–43.

b. Robert Lowry Clinton, *Marbury v. Madison and Judicial Review* (Lawrence, KS: University Press of Kansas, 1989).

c. Paulsen, "Judging Judicial Review," p. 2710.

Comparing Ourselves to Others

a. Tom Ginsburg, *Judicial Review in New Democracies: Constitutional Courts in Asian Cases* (New York: Cambridge University Press, 2003), p. 1.

b. "Judicial Review of Parliamentary Legislation: Norway as a European Pioneer," Chief Justice Carsten Smith, The University of London Annual Coffin Memorial Lecture, April 3, 2000, www.hoyesterett.no/artikler/2694.asp.

c. Ginsburg, *Judicial Review in New Democracies*, Table 1.1, 7–8. Also see Arne Mavcic, "Historical Steps in the Development of Systems of Constitutional Review and Particularities of Their Basic Models," for excellent tables on the legal systems of 150 countries, available at www.concourts/tab.

What Do Political Scientists Do?

a. Gerald N. Rosenberg, *The Hollow Hope: Can Courts Bring about Social Change?* 2nd ed. (Chicago: University of Chicago Press, 2008), p. 422.

b. Michael W. McCann, "Casual versus Constitutive Explanations (or, On the Difficulty of Being so Positive . . .)," *Law & Social Inquiry* 21 (1996): 457–82. See Wayne D. Moore's review of *The Hollow Hope* in *Law and Politics Book Review* 18:11 (November, 2008): 1045–54 for a discussion of the central critiques of Rosenberg's book.

CHAPTER 14

1. There are eight commissioners on the Commission on Civil Rights, four appointed by the president and four by Congress. The commissioners serve six-year terms and do not require Senate confirmation, and no more than four members may be of the same political party.

2. Indentured servants were people who could not afford the price of a ticket for passage to the New World. In exchange for transportation, they gave up three to seven years of their freedom. The indentured servants worked in a variety of capacities. Some of them learned a valuable trade, but most of them worked in agriculture, performing tasks similar to those of the slaves who would later replace them.

3. Howard Dodson, "How Slavery Helped Build a World Economy," February 3, 2003, in *Jubilee: The Emergence of African-American Culture* (New York: Schomburg Center for Research in Black Culture, New York City Public Library).

4. John W. Wright, ed., *New York Times 2000 Almanac* (New York: Penguin Reference, 1999), p. 165. Estimates from various online sources are quite a bit higher, averaging about 620,000 deaths.

5. V. O. Key Jr., *Southern Politics in State and Nation* (New York: Knopf, 1949), p. 538. For example, the Louisiana grandfather clause read, "No male person who was on January 1, 1867, or at any date prior thereto, entitled to vote under the Constitution of the United States, wherein he then resided, and no son or grandson of any such person not less than twenty-one years of age at the date of the adoption of this Constitution, . . . shall be denied the right to register and vote in this State by reason of his failure to possess the educational or property qualifications." Grandfather clauses as they applied to voting were ruled unconstitutional in 1915.

6. Chandler Davidson, "The Voting Rights Act: A Brief History," in *Controversies in Minority Voting: The Voting Rights Act in Perspective*, ed. Bernard Grofman and Chandler Davidson (Washington, DC: Brookings Institution, 1992), p. 21.

7. *Cherokee Nation v. Georgia*, 30 U.S. (1831).

8. *United States v. Wong Kim Ark*, 169 U.S. 649 (1898).

9. Institute for Advanced Technology in the Humanities, University of Virginia, Abigail Adams to John Adams, March 31, 1776, http://www.iath.virginia.edu/seminar/unit1/text/adams.htm (accessed 7/30/08).

10. *Bradwell v. Illinois*, 83 U.S. 130 (1873).

11. *Hoyt v. Florida*, 368 U.S. 57 (1961).

12. There are literally hundreds of books and thousands of articles on the subject of racial discrimination. Two recent surveys of research are Matthew Desmond and Mustafa Emirbayer, *Racial Domination, Racial Progress: The Sociology of Race in America* (New York: McGraw Hill, 2010), and Michael K. Brown et al., *Whitewashing Race: The Myth of a Color-Blind Society* (Berkeley, CA: University of California Press, 2003). Several important books on the topic include Tali Mendelberg, *The Race Card: Campaign Strategy, Implicit Messages, and the Norm of Equality* (Princeton, NJ: Princeton University Press, 2001); Paul M. Sniderman and Thomas Piazza, *The Scar of Race* (Cambridge, MA: Belknap Press, 1993); Donald R. Kinder and Lynn M. Sanders, *Divided by Color: Racial Politics and Democratic Ideals* (Chicago: University of Chicago Press, 1996).

13. Helene Cooper, "In Church Visit, Obama Addresses Race, Struggle, and Hope," *New York Times*, January 18, 2010.

14. Davidson, "The Voting Rights Act," p. 22. See U.S. Department of Justice, Civil Rights Division, "About Section 5 of the Voting Rights Act," www.usdoj.gov/crt/voting/sec_5/obj_activ.htm, for a complete list of cases in which the Justice Department has denied "preclearance" of a change in an electoral practice under Section 5 of the Voting Rights Act.

15. United States Commission on Civil Rights, "Voting Irregularities in Florida during the 2000 Presidential Election," June 2001, www.usccr.gov/pubs/vote2000/report/main.htm (accessed 7/30/08).

16. Wendy Weiser and Margaret Chen, "Voter Suppression Incidents, 2008 Analysis," November 3, 2008, www.brennancenter.org/content/resource/voter_suppression_incidents (accessed 1/19/10).

17. U.S. Census Bureau, "Income, Poverty, and Health Insurance Coverage in the United States: 2008," September 2009, www.census.gov/prod/2009pubs/p60-236.pdf, pp. 7, 14 (accessed 9/8/10).

18. For data on Hispanic income figures, U.S. Census Bureau, "Income, Poverty, and Health Insurance Coverage in the United States: 2008"; wealth data are from Federal Reserve System, "2007 Survey of Consumer Finances," May 7, 2009, www.federalreserve.gov/pubs/oss/oss2/2007/scf2007home.html (accessed 9/8/10).

19. Bureau of Labor Statistics, "The Employment Situation," August 6, 2010, www.bls.gov/news.release/pdf/empsit.pdf (accessed 9/8/10).

20. 2009 data from U.S. Census Bureau, "America's Families and Living Arrangements: 2009," Table C3, www.census.gov/population/www/socdemo/hh-fam/cps2009.html (accessed 9/8/10).

21. Stephan Thernstrom and Abigail Thernstrom, *America in Black and White* (New York: Simon and Schuster, 1997), p. 265.

22. Life expectancy and infant mortality rates are from the Centers for Disease Control, www.cdc.gov/NCHS/data/nvsr/nvsr58/nvsr58_19.pdf; maternity mortality rates are from the National Center for Health Statistics, http://mchb.hrsa.gov/mchirc/chusa_04/pages/0409mm.htm (both accessed 3/21/08). Other health data are available from the Department of Health and Human Services, www.hhs.gov.

23. Hundreds of studies have examined these patterns, and, not surprisingly, there are divergent findings. However, most have found differences in sentencing based on race. A meta-analysis of eighty-five studies by Ojmarrh Mitchell and Doris L. MacKenzie funded by the U.S. Department of Justice found, "after taking into account defendant

criminal history and current offense seriousness, African-Americans and Latinos were generally sentenced more harshly than whites." See Mitchell and MacKenzie, "The Relationship between Race, Ethnicity, and Sentencing Outcomes: A Meta-Analysis of Sentencing Research," December 2004, www.ncjrs.gov/pdffiles1/nij/grants/208129.pdf. For government studies of racial profiling, see the Justice Department's "A Resource Guide on Racial Profiling Data Collection Systems," November 2000, www.ncjrs .gov/pdffiles1/bja/184768.pdf. For President Bush's statement on racial profiling, see Department of Justice, "Fact Sheet: Racial Profiling," June 17, 2003, www.usdoj.gov/opa/pr/2003/June/racial_profiling_fact_sheet.pdf. For a GAO study, see "Racial Profiling: Limited Data on Motorist Stops," March 2000, www.gao .gov/new.items/gg00041.pdf. Government statistics on crime may be found on the Federal Bureau of Investigation site at www.fbi.gov. (All documents accessed 3/21/08.)

24. Criminal Justice Information Services Division, Federal Bureau of Investigation, 2006 Hate Crime Statistics, www.fbi.gov/ucr/hc2006/table1.html (accessed 3/21/08).

25. Lucian K. Truscott IV, "The Real Mob at Stonewall," *New York Times*, June 25, 2009, A19.

26. Rosa Parks with James Haskins, *Rosa Parks: My Story* (New York: Dial Books, 1992), p. 116.

27. Clayborne Carson, David J. Garrow, Gerald Gill, Vincent Harding, and Darlene Clark Hine, eds., *The Eyes on the Prize Civil Rights Reader* (New York: Penguin Books, 1997).

28. *Boynton v. Virginia*, 363 U.S. 454 (1960).

29. David Halberstam, *The Children* (New York: Ballantine Books, 1999).

30. Nate Silver, "Tea Party Nonpartisan Attendance Estimates: Now 300,000," April 16, 2009, www.fivethirtyeight.com/2009/04/tea-party-nonpartisan-attendance.html (accessed 1/19/10).

31. *Guinn v. United States*, 238 U.S. 347 (1915); *Smith v. Allwright*, 322 U.S. 718 (1944).

32. *Pearson v. Murray*, 169 Md. 478 (1936).

33. *Missouri ex rel. Gaines v. Canada*, 305 U.S. 377 (1938).

34. *Fisher v. Hurst*, 333 U.S. 147 (1948).

35. *McLaurin v. Oklahoma State Regents of Higher Education*, 339 U.S. 637 (1950).

36. *Sweatt v. Painter*, 339 U.S. 629 (1950).

37. *Brown v. Board of Education*, 347 U.S. 483 (1954).

38. *Brown v. Board of Education (II)*, 349 U.S. 294 (1955).

39. Paul Brest and Sanford Levinson, *Process of Constitutional Decision Making: Cases and Material* (Boston: Little, Brown, 1982), pp. 471–80.

40. *Griffin et al. v. County School Board of Prince Edward County*, 377 U.S. 218 (1964).

41. *Swann v. Charlotte-Mecklenberg Board of Education*, 402 U.S. 1 (1971).

42. *Milliken v. Bradley*, 418 U.S. 717 (1974).

43. *Board of Education of Oklahoma City v. Dowell*, 498 U.S. 237 (1991).

44. *Missouri v. Jenkins*, 515 U.S. 70 (1995).

45. *Parents Involved in Community Schools Inc. v. Seattle School District*, 05-98 (2007); *Meredith v. Jefferson County (Ky.) Board of Education*, 551 U.S. (2007).

46. *Heart of Atlanta Motel, Inc. v. United States*, 379 U.S. 241 (1964).

47. *Katzenbach v. McClung*, 379 U.S. 294 (1964).

48. *Griggs v. Duke Power*, 401 U.S. 424 (1971).

49. *Wards Cove Packing Co. v. Atonio*, 490 U.S. 642 (1989).

50. *Easley v. Cromartie*, 532 U.S. 234 (2001), rehearing denied, 532 U.S. 1076 (2001).

51. *Easley v. Cromartie*, 532 U.S. 1076 (2001).

52. The set-aside case was *Adarand v. Pena* (1995), the Florida case was *Bush v. Gore* (2000), and the California discrimination case was *Circuit City Stores v. Adams* (2001).

53. *Reed v. Reed*, 404 U.S. 71 (1971).

54. *Frontiero v. Richardson*, 411 U.S. 677 (1973).

55. *Craig v. Boren*, 429 U.S. 190 (1976).

56. *Korematsu v. United States*, 323 U.S. 214 (1944).

57. *Rostker v. Goldberg*, 453 U.S. 57 (1981).

58. *Orr v. Orr*, 440 U.S. 268 (1979).

59. *United States v. Virginia*, 518 U.S. 515 (1996).

60. *Johnson v. Transportation Agency of Santa Clara*, 480 U.S. 616 (1987).

61. *Harris v. Forklift Systems*, 510 U.S. 17 (1993).

62. *Grove City College v. Bell*, 465 U.S. 555 (1984).

63. *Ledbetter v. Goodyear Tire & Rubber Co.*, 550 U.S. (2007).

64. Equal Employment Opportunity Commission, "Outback Steakhouse to Pay $19 Million for Sex Bias against Women in 'Glass Ceiling' Suit by EEOC," press release, December 29, 2009, www.eeoc.gov/eeoc/newsroom/release/12-29-09a.cfm (accessed 1/20/10).

65. Women Present Widespread Discrimination at Wal-Mart, press release, April 28, 2003, www.walmartclass.com/staticdata/press_releases/wmcc.html.

66. *Bowers v. Hardwick*, 478 U.S. 186 (1986), rehearing denied, 478 U.S. 1039 (1986).

67. *Hurley v. Irish-American Gay, Lesbian, and Bisexual Group of Boston*, 515 U.S. 557 (1995).

68. *Boy Scouts of America v. Dale*, 530 U.S. 640 (2000).

69. *Romer v. Evans*, 517 U.S. 620 (1996).

70. *Lawrence v. Texas*, 539 U.S. 558 (2003).

71. Drew S. Days III, "Section 5 Enforcement and the Justice Department," in *Controversies in Minority Voting: The Voting Rights Act in Perspective*, ed. Bernard Grofman and Chandler Davidson (Washington, DC: Brookings Institution Press, 1992), p. 52; Frank R. Parker, *Black Votes Count* (Chapel Hill, NC: University of North Carolina Press, 1990), p. 1.

72. Cited in *Congressional Record*, October 22, 1965, 28354.

73. Quoted in Voting Rights Act Extension: Report of the Subcommittee of the Constitution of the Committee on the Judiciary, U.S. Senate, 97th Congress, 2nd session, May 25, 1982, S. Rept. 97-417, 4.

74. Davidson, "The Voting Rights Act," p. 21.

75. *United States v. Morrison*, 529 U.S. 598 (2000).

76. *Board of Trustees of the University of Alabama v. Garrett*, 531 U.S. 356 (2001). However, in *State of Tennessee v. George Lane and Beverly Jones*, 541 U.S. 509 (2004), the Court ruled that the disabled must have access to courthouses.

77. The White House, "Remarks by the Reception Commemorating the Enactment of the Matthew Shepard and James Byrd, Jr. Hate Crimes Prevention Act," October, 28, 2009, www.whitehouse.gov/the-press-office/remarks-president-reception-commemorating-enactment-matthew-shepard-and-James-Byrd (accessed 1/21/10).

78. *New York Times*/CBS poll, December 6–9, 1997. Fifty-nine percent of whites and 82 percent of blacks favored the education programs, while 57 percent of whites but only 23 percent of blacks opposed preferences in hiring and promotion "to make up for past discrimination."

79. The precise wording of the proposition was, "Shall the charter of the City of Houston be amended to end the use of affirmative action for women and minorities in the operation of City of Houston employment and contracting, including ending the current program and any similar programs in the future?"

80. The training program case was *United Steel Workers of America v. Weber*, 443 U.S. 193 (1979); the labor union case was *Sheet Metal Workers v. EEOC*, 478 U.S. 421 (1986); and the Alabama state police case was *U.S. v. Paradise*, 480 U.S. 149 (1987).

81. *Richmond v. J.A. Croson Co.*, 488 U.S. 469 (1989).

82. *Adarand Constructors, Inc. v. Pena*, 515 U.S. 200 (1995).

83. *Ricci v. DeStefano*, 557 U.S. __ 2009.

84. *Regents of Univ. of California v. Bakke*, 438 U.S. 265 (1978).

85. *Grutter v. Bollinger*, 123 S. Ct. 2325 (2003), was the law school case and *Gratz v. Bollinger*, 123 S. Ct. 2411 (2003), was the undergraduate admissions case.

86. In *Bakke*, Justice Lewis Powell was the only member of the Court who held this position, even if it became the basis for all affirmative action programs over the next twenty-five years. Four justices in the *Bakke* decision wanted to get rid of race as a factor in admissions, and another four thought that the "strict scrutiny" standard should not even be applied in this instance.

87. "An Act Providing for the Collection of Data Relative to Traffic Stops," Massachusetts state law, Chapter 228 of the Acts of 2000, www.mass.gov/legis/laws/seslaw00/sl000228.htm (accessed 7/22/08).

What Do Political Scientists Do?

a. Marianne, Bertrand and Sendhil, Mullainathan, "Are Emily and Greg More Employable Than Lakisha and Jamal? A Field Experiment on Labor Market Discrimination," *American Economic Review* 94:4 (September, 2004): 991–1013.

b. Nicholas Valentino, Vincent Hutchings, and Ismail White, "Cues That Matter: How Political Ads Prime Racial Attitudes during Campaigns," *American Political Science Review* 96:1 (2002): 75–90.

c. Roland G. Fryer Jr. and Steven D. Levitt, "The Causes and Consequences of Distinctively Black Names," *Quarterly Journal of Economics* 119:3 (August, 2004): 767–805.

Comparing Ourselves to Others

a. A version of this paragraph appeared in David T. Canon, *Race, Redistricting, and Representation: The Unintended Consequences of Black Majority Districts* (Chicago: University of Chicago Press, 1999), p. 1. Robert Dahl's discussion of "minorities rule" appears in *Preface to Democracy Theory* (Chicago: University of Chicago Press, 1956), pp. 124–51.

b. Data on racial and ethnic minorities are from Andrew Reynolds, "Reserved Seats for National Legislatures: A Research Note," *Legislative Studies Quarterly* 30:2 (May, 2005): 301–10; data on gender are from Pippa Norris, "Increasing Women's Representation in Iraq: Which Strategies Would Work Best?" (unpublished paper, John F. Kennedy School of Government, Harvard University, February 16, 2004).

Challenging Conventional Wisdom

a. Daniel W. Drezner, "Hash of Civilizations," *The New Republic Online*, March 3, 2004, www.danieldrezner.com/policy/hash.htm.

b. All polling data are from PollingReport.com, www.pollingreport.com/immigration.htm.

CHAPTER 15

1. Thomas L. Friedman, *The World Is Flat: A Brief History of the Twenty-First Century* (New York: Farrar, Straus and Giroux, 2005).

2. Ford Corporation, "10 Millionth Vehicle Built at Ford's Saarlouis Plant," July 1, 2005, http://media.ford.com/article_display.cfm?article_id=21100&make_id=92 (accessed 8/5/08).

3. Daniel Yergin and Joseph Stanislaw, *The Commanding Heights: The Battle for the World Economy* (New York: Free Press, 2002), pp. 60–64.

4. The phrase comes from environmental economist E. F. Schumacher's influential book, *Small Is Beautiful: Economics as if People Mattered* (New York: Harper and Row, 1973).

5. Jonathan Rowe and Judith Silverstein, "The GDP Myth: Why 'Growth' Isn't Always a Good Thing," *Washington Monthly* 31:3 (March, 1999).

6. Scott Lanman and Steve Matthews, "Greenspan Concedes to 'Flaw' in His Market Ideology," Bloomberg.com, October 23, 2008, www.bloomberg.com/apps/news?pid=20601087&sid=ah5qh9Up4rIg (accessed 2/12/10).

7. Juann H. Hung, "Recent Shifts in Financing the U.S. Current-Account Deficit," *CBO Economic and Budget Issue Brief* (Washington, DC: Congressional Budget Office, July 12, 2005), www.cbo.gov (accessed 3/15/08).

8. The classic work on the appropriations process in the pre-reform era is Richard F. Fenno's *The Power of the Purse: Appropriations Politics in Congress* (Boston: Little, Brown, 1966). D. Roderick Kiewiet and Mathew D. McCubbins reexamine the appropriations process in the post-reform era and find that the appropriations committees have maintained much of their power; see *The Logic of Delegation: Congressional Parties and the Appropriations Process* (Chicago: University of Chicago Press, 1991).

9. James Sundquist, *The Decline and Resurgence of Congress* (Washington, DC: Brookings Institution Press, 1981), Chapter 8.

10. Action by both houses was required only to restore the more serious "rescissions." For simple deferrals, or postponement of spending, the president's action stood unless either house voted to overrule him (Sundquist, *Decline and Resurgence*, p. 213).

11. The specific provision is paragraph (1)(E) of section 313(b)(1) of the Budget Control Act. James Thurber, "Centralization, Devolution, and Turf Protection in the Congressional Budget Process," in *Congress Reconsidered*, 6th ed., Lawrence C. Dodd and Bruce I. Oppenheimer, ed. (Washington, DC: CQ Press, 1997), pp. 325–46.

12. These figures exclude the Social Security surplus. Including Social Security, the government had a small surplus in 1969. See the Congressional Budget Office's historical budget data, www.cbo.gov/showdoc.cfm?index=18/21&sequence=0. For data before 1962, see the 1981 *Economic Report of the President* (Washington, DC: Government Printing Office, 1981), p. 316.

13. Howard Gleckman, "Pay Go, Pay Gone: AMT Drives Senate Dems to Blink," Tax Policy Center, December 7, 2007, http://taxvox.taxpolicycenter.org/blog/_archives/2007/12/7/3397043.html (accessed 5/30/08).

14. Internal Revenue Service, "Stimulus Payments—It's Not Too Late," www.irs.gov/newsroom/article/0,,id=177937,00.html (accessed 8/5/08).

15. Lori Montgomery, "House Votes to Revive Pay-as-You-Go Budget Rules," *Washington Post*, February 5, 2010, www.washingtonpost.com/wp-dyn/content/article/2010/02/04/AR2010020400354.html (accessed 2/12/10).

16. Sara Murray, "Paper Chased: Budget to Print Budget Is Cut," *Wall Street Journal*, February 5, 2008, p. A4.

17. Office of the United States Trade Representative, "Who We Are," www.ustr.gov/Who_We_Are/Section_Index.html (accessed 8/5/08).

18. National Economic Council, www.whitehouse.gov/nec (accessed 8/5/08).

19. Bradley H. Patterson, *The White House Staff: Inside the West Wing and Beyond* (Washington, DC: Brookings Institution Press, 2000), pp. 88–95.

20. See Charles M. Cameron, *Veto Bargaining: Presidents and the Politics of Negative Power* (New York: Cambridge University Press, 2000), for a general discussion of the strategic elements of issuing veto threats.

21. Board of Governors of the Federal Reserve System, *The Federal Reserve System: Purposes & Functions*, 9th ed., Washington, DC, June 2005, www.federalreserve.gov/pf/pdf/pf_1.pdf, p. 12.

22. See Donald F. Kettl, *Leadership at the Fed* (New Haven, CT: Yale University Press, 1986), for a good general discussion of the Fed.

23. See Federal Research Board, "Membership of the Board of Governors of the Federal Reserve System, 1914," www.federalreserve.gov/bios/boardmembership.htm, for a list of all Federal Reserve Board members (accessed 8/5/08).

24. Federal Reserve Board, "Annual Report 2009, Independent Auditor's Report," www.federalreserve.gov/boarddocs/rptcongress/annual09/sec6/c3.htm (accessed 9/9/10).

25. Neil Irwin, "Senators Critical of Bernanke at Hearing," *Washington Post*, December 4, 2009, www.washingtonpost.com/wp-dyn/content/article/2009/12/03/AR2009120301210.html (accessed 2/12/10).

26. Edward R. Tufte, *Political Control of the Economy* (Princeton, NJ: Princeton University Press, 1978); Douglas Hibbs, "The Partisan Model of Macroeconomic Cycles: More Theory and Evidence for the United States," *Economics and Politics* 6 (1994): 1–23.

27. Jim Granato, "The Effect of Policy-Maker Reputation and Credibility on Public Expectations," *Journal of Theoretical Politics* 8 (1996): 449–70; Irwin L. Morris, *Congress, the President, and the Federal Reserve: The Politics of American Monetary Policy-Making* (Ann Arbor: University of Michigan Press, 2000).

28. Wall Street Journal Blogs, "Bunning Statement on Bernanke: 'You Are the Definition of a Moral Hazard,'" December 3, 2009, http://blogs.wsj.com/economics/2009/12/03/bunning-statement-on-bernanke-you-are-the-definition-of-a-moral-hazard/tab/article/ (accessed 2/12/10).

29. U.S. Department of the Treasury, "Duties and Functions," www.treasury.gov/education/duties (accessed 8/5/08).

30. U.S. Department of the Treasury, "FAQs: Currency: Production and Circulation," www.treasury.gov/education/faq/currency/production.shtml; United States Mint, "Coin Production Figures," www.usmint.gov/about_the_mint/coin_production/index.cfm?action=production_figures (accessed 8/5/08).

31. Zachary A. Goldfarb, David Cho, and Binyamin Appelbaum, "Treasury to Rescue Fannie and Freddie," *Washington Post*, September 7, 2008, p. A1.

32. Peter Baker, "A Professor and a Banker Bury Old Dogma on Markets," *New York Times*, September 21, 2008, p. A1.

33. Renae Merle, "U.S. Stock Markets Soar on Financial Rescue Plan," *Washington Post*, September 19, 2008; Howard Schneider, Neil Irwin, and Binyamin Appelbaum, "Treasury to Temporarily Guarantee Money Market Funds," *Washington Post*, September 19, 2008.

34. Carl Hulse, "Pressure Builds on House after Senate Backs Bailout," *New York Times*, October 1, 2008, p. A1.

35. David M. Herszenhorn, "Bailout Plan Wins Approval; Democrats Vow Tighter Rules," *New York Times*, October 3, 2008, p. A1.

36. "Department of the Treasury, Financial Stability Plan—One Year Later," February 10, 2010, www.financialstability.gov/latest/pr_02102010.html (accessed 2/12/10).

37. Paul Ried, "Three Laws that Caused Obama Midterm Problems, CBS News, November 3, 2010, www.cbsnews.com/stories/2010/11/03/politics/main7020135.shtml (accessed 11/5/10).

38. For example, in his book *Booty Capitalism: The Politics of Banking in the Philippines* (Ithaca, NY: Cornell University Press, 1998), Paul Hutchcroft cites the culture of cronyism and corruption as the main explanation for lagging economic development in the Philippines.

39. John Maynard Keynes, *General Theory of Employment, Interest and Money* (1936; repr. New York: Macmillan, 2007).

40. Robert Dallek, *Flawed Giant: Lyndon Johnson and His Times, 1961–1973* (New York: Oxford University Press, 1998), pp. 71–4.

41. David Shreve, "President John F. Kennedy and the 1964 Tax Cut," Presidential Recordings Project, www.whitehousetapes.org/news/shreve_taxcut_2001.pdf (accessed 4/26/08).

42. Arthur B. Laffer, "The Laffer Curve: Past, Present, and Future," Heritage Foundation Backgrounder #1765, June 1, 2004, www.heritage.org/Research/Taxes/bg1765.cfm (accessed 3/27/08).

43. These figures come from the Congressional Budget Office, "Historical Budget Data," www.cbo.gov (accessed 4/18/08).

44. Office of Management and Budget, "Budget of the United States Government, fiscal year 2011," www.whitehouse.gov/omb/budget/Overview/ (accessed 2/16/10).

45. The "starve the beast" line is usually attributed to David Stockman and his book *The Triumph of Politics: The Inside Story of the Reagan Revolution* (New York: Avon Books, 1986). A Web search for "David Stockman" and "starve the beast" produced 566 hits, including a reference in a *National Review* article: Norman B. Ture, "To Cut and To Please," June 10, 2004, www.nationalreview.com/reagan/ture200406101414.asp. However, we have been unable to find the phrase "starve the beast" in Stockman's book. More recently, smaller-government conservatives such as Grover Norquist have embraced the concept.

46. See the Congressional Budget Office, "Effective Federal Tax Rates," Table 1, www.cbo.gov/ftpdocs/88xx/doc8885/EffectiveTaxRates.shtml (accessed 6/1/08).

47. Congressional Budget Office, "Shares of Federal Tax Liabilities, 2004 and 2005," Table 2 (accessed 6/2/08).

48. The details get a bit more complicated, but this is essentially how money is created. Banks must hold a reserve of 10 percent of all "demand deposits" (which is what economists call checking accounts), so only $90,000 would actually be put into the money stream because the $10,000 reserve would have to come from money that someone deposited in the bank. Also, the money supply would contract as you pay back your loan. The overall effect on the money supply has to take into account the "multiplier effect"—that is, the money you spend from your loan will get spent many times over. The computer store will take your $10,000 and deposit it in its bank, which allows that bank to make more loans, and so on.

49. *Historical Statistics of the United States: Colonial Times to 1970* (Washington, DC: U.S. Department of Commerce, Bureau of the Census, 1975), Table V 20-30, p. 912.

50. Milton Friedman, "The Quantity Theory of Money: A Restatement," in *The Optimum Quantity of Money and Other Essays* (Chicago: Aldine Publishing Co., 1969), p. 52.

51. These figures are hypothetical. In reality, under the Monetary Control Act (MCA) of 1980, the reserve requirement can range from 8 percent to 14 percent for all demand deposits greater than $25 million. In the original law, banks with demand deposits under $25 million only had to have a reserve of 3 percent. The amount that is subject to the lower reserve requirement is increased every year to reflect overall money supply and currently is about $50 million. See Federal Reserve Bank of New York, "Reserve Requirement," www.ny.frb.org/aboutthefed/fedpoint/fed45.html (accessed 8/5/08).

52. In December 2002, the discount rate was effectively discontinued as an active policy tool and was pegged to 1 percent above the targeted FFR (which means that the "discount rate" is oddly named—it really should be called the "premium rate"). December 2002 *Federal Reserve Bulletin* (pp. 482–83). See Donald D. Hester, "U.S. Monetary Policy in the Greenspan Era: 1987–2003," unpublished paper, University of Wisconsin, Madison, November 14, 2003, available at http://ideas.repec.org/p/att/wimass/200323.html (accessed 8/10/08), for an extended discussion of this move.

53. Greenspan made the comment in his July 21, 2005, testimony before Congress. For the full text of his remarks, see "Testimony of Chairman Alan Greenspan," Federal Reserve Board's semiannual Monetary Policy Report to the Congress Before the Committee on Financial Services, U.S. House of Representatives, July 20, 2005, www.federalreserve.gov/boarddocs/hh/2005/july/testimony.htm (accessed 8/5/08).

54. Brian W. Cashell, "The Federal Government Debt: Its Size and Economic Significance," Washington, DC: Congressional Research Service, Report RL31590, March 1, 2005, p. 9.

55. William Greider reports that internal debates between Fed members who wanted to emphasize the money supply and those who wanted to emphasize interest rates started as early as 1982. (See, *Secrets of the Temple: How the Federal Reserve Runs the Country* (New York: Simon and Schuster, 1987), pp. 479–80.)

56. Roger W. Garrison, "Boom, Bust, and the Federal Reserve: Are There Parallels to the 1920s?" St. Louis Discussion Club, April 10, 2003, www.auburn.edu/~garriso/sldc.htm (accessed 8/5/08).

57. Greider, *Secrets of the Temple*, pp. 295–98.

58. Board of Governors of the Federal Reserve System, Credit and Liquidity Programs and the Balance Sheet, www.federalreserve.gov/monetarypolicy/bst_recenttrends.htm (accessed 2/16/10).

59. John B. Taylor, *Economics*, 4th ed. (New York: Houghton Mifflin, 2003), Chapter 10. Some economics textbooks also define regulation of externalities, such as pollution, as economic regulation.

60. *United States v. Microsoft*, 87 F. Supp. 2d 30 (D.D.C. 2000). See Alan Reynolds, *Microsoft Antitrust Appeal: Judge Jackson's "Findings of Fact" Revisited* (Washington, DC: Hudson Institute, 2002), for a detailed discussion of the case.

61. See *Public Interest Group Profiles: 2004–2005* (Washington, DC: CQ Press, 2004) for information on more than 200 public interest groups.

62. See U.S. Environmental Protection Agency, "Pollutants/Toxins," www.epa.gov/ebtpages/pollutants.html, for a complete list of regulated and banned chemicals.

63. Sam Pelzman and Clifford Winston, "Deregulation of Network Industries: What's Next?" AEI-Brookings Joint Center for Regulatory Studies (Washington, DC: Brookings Institution Press, 2000), p. 2, www.aei.brookings.org/admin/authorpdfs/page.php?id=109 (accessed 6/4/08).

64. Samuel P. Huntington, "The Marasmus of the ICC: The Commission, the Railroads, and the Public Interest," in *Public Administration and Policy: Selected Essays*, ed. Peter Woll (New York: Harper and Row, 1966); Harmon Ziegler, *Interest Groups in American Society* (Englewood Cliffs, NJ: Prentice Hall, 1964).

65. Richard A. Posner, "Theories of Economic Regulation," *Bell Journal of Economics and Management Science* 5 (1974): 343.

66. Posner, "Theories of Economic Regulation," p. 343; George Stigler, "Economic Theory of Regulation," *Bell Journal of Economics and Management Science* 2 (1971): 3–21; Sam Peltzman, "Toward a More General Theory of Regulation," *Journal of Law and Economics* 19 (1976): 211–40; Gary S. Becker, "A Theory of Competition Among Pressure Groups for Political Influence," *Quarterly Journal of Economics* 98 (1983): 371–400.

67. David R. Francis, "Losing Patience with U.S. Trade Deficit," *Christian Science Monitor*, July 29, 2004, www.csmonitor.com/2004/0729/p17s01-stgn.html (accessed 4/15/08).

68. Bureau of Economic Analysis, International Economic Accounts, "U.S. Net International Investment Position at Yearend 2009," June 25, 2010, www.bea.gov/newsreleases/international/intinv/2010/intinv09.htm (accessed 9/13/10).

69. David E. Rosenbloom, "Free Trade Is Like Dry Water, Y'All," *New York Times*, December 19, 2004, Week in Review.

70. See Ronald Rogowski, *Commerce and Coalitions* (Princeton, NJ: Princeton University Press, 1986), for the constituency view. James Shoch, *Trading Blows: Party Competition and U.S. Trade Policy in a Globalizing Era* (Chapel Hill, NC: University of North Carolina Press, 2001), pp. 13–19, reviews both explanations.

71. Judith Goldstein, *Ideas, Interests, and American Trade* (Ithaca, NY: Cornell University Press), 1993.

72. David Smick, "If Entire Countries Go Broke, We'll Go with Them," *Washington Post*, October 26, 2008, p. B3.

Challenging Conventional Wisdom

a. David Ricardo, *The Principles of Political Economy and Taxation* (1817). Robert Torrens actually developed the point first in an 1815 essay on the corn trade, but Ricardo usually gets the credit because he explains it more fully.

b. This argument ignores transportation costs and the costs of shifting labor from one industry to another, but its logic is quite powerful. More intuitive, perhaps, is what happens when one nation has a large *absolute* advantage in the cost of production over another. In these situations, if there is free trade, most production of that good will shift to the country that can produce it more cheaply.

c. Suketu Mehta, "A Passage from India," *New York Times*, July 12, 2005, p. A21.

d. Mona Sutphen, "Putting Washington at the Service of the Middle Class," White House Blog, January 27, 2010, www.whitehouse.gov/blog/2010/01/27/putting-washington-service-middle-class (accessed 2/12/10).

What Do Political Scientists Do?

a. Ron Paul, "Why the Fed Likes Independence," Texas Straight Talk Blog, January 11, 2010, www.house.gov/htbin/blog_inc?BLOG,tx14_paul,blog,999,All,Item%20not%20found,ID=100111_3628,TEMPLATE=postingdetail.shtml (accessed 6/25/10).

b. David E. Lewis, *Presidents and the Politics of Agency Design: Political Insulation in the United States Government Bureaucracy, 1946–1997* (Stanford, CA: Stanford University Press, 2003), p. 13.

c. David E. Lewis, *Presidents and the Politics of Agency Design*, p. 161.

You Decide

a. John Tierney, "The Sagebrush Solution," *New York Times*, July 26, 2005, p. A19. Additional information was drawn from www.highcountrynews.org.

b. A very detailed account of this saga may be found in Raymond B. Wrabley Jr., "Managing the Monument: Cows and Conservation in the Grand-Staircase-Escalante National Monument," *Journal of Land, Resources & Environmental* 29:2 (2009): 253–80.

CHAPTER 16

1. John Boehner, "Statement by House GOP Leaders Boehner and McCotter on End-of-Life Treatment Counseling in Democrats' Health Care Legislation," press release, July 23, 2009, http://republican-leader.house.gov/news/DocumentSingle.aspx?DocumentID=139131 (accessed 6/18/2010).

2. Jonathan Cohn, "How They Did It: The Inside Account of Health Care Reform's Triumph," *The New Republic*, June 10, 2010, pp. 14–25.

3. David M. Herszenhorn and Robert Pear, "Final Votes in Congress Cap Battle on Health Bill," *New York Times*, March 25, 2010, p. A1.

4. Herszenhorn and Pear, "Final Votes in Congress."

5. Sari Horwitz and Ben Pershing, "Anger over Health-Care Reform Spurs Rise in Threats against Congress Members," *Washington Post*, April 9, 2010.

6. Theda Skocpol, *Social Policy in the United States: Future Possibilities in Historical Perspective* (Princeton, NJ: Princeton University Press, 1995), p. 37.

7. Franklin D. Roosevelt's second fireside chat on "Government and Modern Capitalism," Washington, DC, September 30, 1934. For the full text, see "The American Presidency Project," John T. Woolley and Gerhard Peters, University of California, Santa Barbara, www.presidency.ucsb.edu/ws/index.php?pid=14636 (accessed 8/8/08).

8. Skocpol, *Social Policy in the United States*, pp. 145–60.

9. David M. Kennedy, *Freedom from Fear: The American People in Depression and War, 1929–1945* (New York: Oxford University Press, 2001); Byron W. Daynes, William Pederson, and Michael P. Riccards, eds., *The New Deal and Public Policy* (New York: St. Martin's Press, 1998).

10. Robert Dallek, *Flawed Giant: Lyndon Johnson and His Times, 1961–1973* (New York: Oxford University Press, 1998); Irving Berstein,

Guns or Butter: The Presidency of Lyndon Johnson (New York: Oxford University Press, 1996).

11. Carmen DeNavas-Walt, Bernadette D. Proctor, and Jessica C. Smith, "Income, Poverty, and Health Insurance Coverage in the United States: 2009," September 2010, www.census.gov/prod/2010pubs/p60-238.pdf, p. 14 (accessed 10/18/10).

12. Larry Bartels, "Inequalities," *New York Times*, April 27, 2008, www.nytimes.com/2008/04/27/magazine/27wwln-idealab-t.html?_r=1&oref=slogin&pagewanted=print (accessed 5/10/08).

13. DeNavas-Walt, Proctor, and Smith, "Income, Poverty, and Healthy Insurance Coverage in the United States: 2009," Table 3.

14. Congressional Budget Office, "Historical Effective Federal Tax Rates: 1979 to 2005," Summary Table 1, p. 6, December 2007 (accessed 8/8/08).

15. "The Forbes 400: The Richest People in America," Forbes.com, September 16, 2010, www.forbes.com/wealth/forbes-400 (accessed 10/18/10).

16. "Changes in U.S. Family Finances from 2004 to 2007: Evidence from the Survey of Consumer Finances," Federal Reserve Bulletin, February 2009, www.federalreserve.gov/pubs/bulletin/2009/pdf/scf09.pdf (accessed 10/18/10).

17. Neil Howe and Philip Longman, "The Next New Deal," *Atlantic Monthly*, April, 1992, pp. 88–99. Somewhat surprisingly, it is difficult to measure accurately how much government money goes to different income groups. The most commonly used census data are notoriously unreliable because wealthy people underreport their income. Tax forms would be useful but researchers do not have access to these. The only comprehensive analysis to overcome this data problem that we are aware of is this CBO study from the 1990s.

18. Housing subsidies for poor people may be found in Department of Housing and Urban Development, "Housing Payments, Summary of Assisted Units and Outlays, 2011 Summary Statement and Initiatives," www.hud.gov/offices/cfo/reports/2011/cjs/Housing_Payments_2011.pdf (accessed 2/18/2010). Tax expenditures on the mortgage interest deduction are in the Joint Committee on Taxation, "Estimates of Federal Tax Expenditures for Fiscal Years 2009–2013," (Washington, DC: Government Printing Office, 2010), pp. 34–35.

19. Eric J. Toder, Benjamin H. Harris, and Katherine Lim, "Distributional Effects of Tax Expenditure," Tax Policy Center, July 21, 2009, www.taxpolicycenter.org/UploadedPDF/411922_expenditures.pdf (accessed 6/17/2010).

20. Dean Baker, *The Conservative Nanny State: How the Wealthy Use the Government to Stay Rich and Get Richer*, May 2006, www.conservativenannystate.org.

21. Chris Edwards and Jeff Patch, "Corporate Welfare," in *Cato Handbook for Policymakers*, 7th ed., Cato Institute, 2009, www.cato.org/pubs/handbook/hb111/hb111-26.pdf.

22. Larry M. Bartels, *Unequal Democracy: The Political Economy of the New Gilded Age* (Princeton, NJ: Princeton University Press, 2008).

23. David Brooks, "The Bursting Point," *New York Times*, September 4, 2005.

24. Joe Soss, *Unwanted Claims: The Politics of Participation in the U.S. Welfare System* (Ann Arbor, MI: University of Michigan Press, 2000).

25. Daniel P. Carpenter, *The Forging of Bureaucratic Autonomy: Reputations, Networks, and Policy Innovation in Executive Agencies, 1862–1928* (Princeton, NJ: Princeton University Press, 2001).

26. Michael Cohen, James March, and Johan Olsen, "A Garbage Can Model of Organizational Choice," *Administrative Science Quarterly* 17 (March, 1972): 1–25; John W. Kingdon, *Agendas, Alternatives, and Public Policies* (Boston: Little, Brown, 1984).

27. Frank R. Baumgartner and Bryan D. Jones, *Agendas and Instability in American Politics* (Chicago: University of Chicago Press, 1993).

28. See William T. Bianco, *Trust: Representatives and Constituents* (Ann Arbor, MI: University of Michigan Press, 1994), Chapter 6, for a discussion of the repeal of the Catastrophic Coverage Act.

29. James Q. Wilson, *Bureaucracy: What Government Agencies Do and Why They Do It* (New York: Basic Books, 1989).

30. See U.S. Department of Agriculture, "USDA01: End the Wool and Mohair Subsidy," http://govinfo.library.unt.edu/npr/library/reports/ag01.html, for information on the pre-1994 policy; and U.S. Department of Agriculture, "2002 Farm Bill, Title 1: Commodities Programs," www.ers.usda.gov/Features/farmbill/titles/titleIcommodities.htm, for the current law (accessed 8/10/08).

31. Paul N. Van de Water and Arloc Sherman, "Social Security Keeps 20 Million Americans Out of Poverty: A State-By-State Analysis," Center on Budget and Policy Priorities, August 11, 2010, www.cbpp.org/cms/?fa=view&id=3260 (accessed 9/16/10).

32. Social Security Administration, Office of Retirement and Disability Policy, and Office of Research, Evaluation, and Statistics, "Fast Facts & Figures about Social Security, 2009," SSA Publication No. 13–11785, July 2009, http://retirement.gov/policy/docs/chartbooks/fast_facts/2009/fast_facts09.pdf (accessed 2/19/10).

33. See the 2008 OASDI Trustees Report, www.ssa.gov/OACT/TR/TR08/II_project.html#wp105643 (accessed 8/10/08).

34. In general, poorer people get back as much as they paid in plus interest much more quickly than wealthier people because of the progressive nature of the benefits. For a study on projected benefits that retirees will receive, see Dean R. Leimer, "Cohort-Specific Measures of Lifetime Social Security Taxes and Benefits," Social Security Administration, Office of Research, Evaluation, and Statistics, December 2007, www.socialsecurity.gov/policy/docs/workingpapers/wp110.pdf (accessed 8/10/08).

35. Social Security Administration, 2010 OASDI Trustees Report, Figure II D4, www.ssa.gov/OACT/TR/2010/trLOF.html (accessed 9/16/10).

36. See Congressional Budget Office, "Menu of Social Security Options," May 25, 2005, www.cbo.gov/ftpdoc.cfm?index=6377&type=1, for a detailed account of the fiscal impact of the various proposals.

37. The life expectancy numbers provided here are for all people. Women have always lived longer than men: in 1940 the difference was 2 years, and in 1990 the difference was 4.3 years. That is, women's life expectancy at age 65 in 1990 was 84.6 and men's was 80.3. Social Security Administration, "Life Expectancy for Social Security," www.ssa.gov/history/lifeexpect.html (accessed 8/10/08).

38. This figure came from a speech by SEC Commissioner Paul R. Carey, "Social Security Privatization," U.S. Securities and Exchange Commission, Washington, DC, January 31, 2001, www.sec.gov/news/speech/spch459.htm.

39. Carmen DeNavas-Walt, Bernadette D. Proctor, and Jessica C. Smith, "Income, Poverty, and Health Insurance Coverage in the United States: 2008," U.S. Census Bureau, September 2009, www.census.gov/prod/2009pubs/p60-236.pdf (accessed 6/18/2010).

40. The data for Europe come from the Organization for Economic Cooperation and Development as cited in Robert Pear, "U.S. Health Care Spending Reaches All-Time High: 15% of GDP," *New York Times*, January 9, 2004, p. 3; the figures for the United States come from Centers for Medicare and Medicaid Services, Office of the Actuary, National Health Statistics Group.

41. Congressional Budget Office, "Updated Estimates of Spending for the Medicare Prescription Drug Program," www.cbo.gov/showdoc.cfm?index=6139&sequence=0 (accessed 8/11/08).

42. Department of Health and Human Services, Centers for Medicare and Medicaid Services, "Brief Summaries of Medicare and Medicaid," www.cms.hhs.gov/MedicaidGenInfo/03_TechnicalSummary.asp (accessed 8/11/08).

43. A complete list of the Federal Medical Assistance Percentages may be found at Department of Health and Human Services, "Federal Financial Participation in State Assistance Expenditures, FY 2009," http://aspe.hhs.gov/health/fmap09.htm (accessed 8/11/08).

44. 2010 Medicare Trustees Report, Washington, DC, August, 2010, pp. 244–45, www.cms.gov/ReportsTrustFunds/tr2010.pdf (accessed 9/16/10).

45. 2010 Medicare Trustees Report, p. 245.

46. Barack Obama, "Remarks by the President to a Joint Session of Congress on Health Care," U.S. Capitol, Washington DC, September 9, 2009, www.whitehouse.gov/the-press-office/remarks-president-a-joint-session-congress-health-care.

47. Peter Grier, "Health Care Reform Bill 101: Who Must Buy Insurance," Christian Science Monitor, March 19, 2010, www.csmonitor.com/USA/Politics/2010/0319/Health-Care-Reform-Bill-101-Who-must-buy-insurance. This article provides an excellent overview of the essential parts of the bill.

48. Congressional Budget Office, "Cost Estimates for H.R. 4872, Reconciliation Act of 2010 (Final Health Care Legislation)," March 20, 2010, www.cbo.gov/doc.cfm?index=11355.

49. Quoted in Stuart Taylor, "Health Care Law Not a Sure Bet in Court," National Journal, March 26, 2010.

50. Richard Cauchi, "State Legislation Challenging Certain Health Reforms, 2010," National Conference of State Legislatures Health Program, June 18, 2010, www.ncsl.org/?tabid=18906 (accessed 6/18/10).

51. Tom Harkin, "The Senate's 'Starter Home' Health Reform," Huffington Post, December 30, 2009, www.huffingtonpost.com/sentom-harkin/the-senates-starter-home_b_407155.html (accessed 6/18/10).

52. Gonzales v. Oregon, 546 U.S. 243 (2006).

53. U.S. Department of Agriculture, "Nutrition Assistance Programs Performance Report, November 2009, US Summary," www.fns.usda.gov/fns/key_data/birdseye-november-2009.pdf (accessed 2/23/10).

54. U.S. Department of Labor, "Unemployment Insurance Chartbook," www.doleta.gov/unemploy/chartbook.cfm, and "Unemployment Insurance Data Summary," http://workforcesecurity.doleta.gov/unemploy/content/data.asp (accessed 2/23/10).

55. Internal Revenue Service, "EITC Awareness Day Fact Sheet," www.irs.gov/pub/irs-utl/eitc_day_fastfacts_011508.pdf (accessed 8/11/08).

56. Internal Revenue Service, "Earned Income Tax Credit," www.irs-eitc.info/SPEC (accessed 2/23/10).

57. Social Security Administration, Office of Retirement and Disability Policy, "SSI Recipients by State and County, 2009," www.socialsecurity.gov/policy/docs/statcomps/ssi_sc/2009/table01.html (accessed 6/17/2010).

58. R. Kent Weaver, Ending Welfare as We Know It (Washington, DC: Brookings Institution Press, 2000).

59. See the analysis of welfare reform by the Center of Budget and Policy Priorities, www.cbpp.org/pubs/tanf.htm, or by the Urban Institute, www.urban.org/toolkit/issues/welfarereform.cfm (accessed 8/18/08).

60. U.S. Department of Education, "Department Overview," www.ed.gov/about/landing.jhtml?src=gu (accessed 11/26/08).

61. U.S. Department of Education, Race to the Top fund, www2.ed.gov/programs/racetothetop/index.html (accessed 2/23/10).

What Do Political Scientists Do?

a. Larry Bartels, Unequal Democracy: The Political Economy of the New Gilded Age (Princeton, NJ: Princeton University Press, 2008), p. 3. The term "Gilded Age" refers to the period of rapid economic growth in the late 19th century, characterized by the "robber barons" of industry and finance. Bartels argues that the recent period of inequality is a New Gilded Age.

b. Bartels, Unequal Democracy, p. ix.

c. Bartels, Unequal Democracy, p. 14.

Comparing Ourselves to Others

a. Willem Adema and Maxime Ladaique, "Net Social Expenditure, 2005 Edition: More Comprehensive Measures of Social Support," OECD Social, Employment, and Migration Working Paper 29, www.oecd.org/dataoecd/56/2/35632106.pdf.

You Decide

a. Alan J. Borsuc, "Vouchers to Pass $100 Million Mark; Increase in Students in a Year Is 2nd-Biggest in Program's History," Journal Sentinel, November 20, 2006, p. 1.

b. Milwaukee Journal Sentinel, "Inside Choice Schools: 15 Years of Vouchers," seven-part series, 2005, www2.jsonline.com/news/choice.

c. John F. Witte, The Market Approach to Education: An Analysis of America's First Voucher Program (Princeton, NJ: Princeton University Press, 2001).

d. Zelman v. Simmons-Harris, 536 U.S. 639 (2002).

Challenging Conventional Wisdom

a. U.S. Department of Health and Human Services, Administration for Children and Families, and Office of Family Assistance, "Caseload Data 1960–1999," www.acf.hhs.gov/programs/ofa/data-reports/caseload/caseload_archive.html (accessed 2/23/10).

b. Quoted in Richard Wolf, "How Welfare Reform Changed America," USA Today, July 18, 2006.

c. Quoted in Joe Soss and Sanford F. Schram, "A Public Transformed? Welfare Reform as Policy Feedback," American Political Science Review 101:1 (February, 2007): 111–27.

CHAPTER 17

1. Kevin Coyne, "In One Town, Intersections of Sacrifice," New York Times, May 27, 2007.

2. Mark Mazzeti, and Eric Schmitt, "C.I.A Missile Strike May Have Killed Pakistan's Taliban Leader," New York Times, August 6, 2009, p. A7.

3. For an example of the isolationist approach, see Justin Raimondo, "Out of Iraq, into Darfur?" American Conservative, June 5, 2006. For a longer exposition of isolationism, see Patrick J. Buchanan, A Republic, Not an Empire, updated ed. (Washington, DC: Regnery Publishing, 2002).

4. Robert O. Keohane, After Hegemony: Cooperation and Discord in the International System (1984; repr. Princeton, NJ: Princeton University Press, 2005).

5. The distinction was first made in E. H. Carr, The Twenty Years' Crisis, 1919–1939: An Introduction to the Study of International Relations (London, UK: Macmillan, 1939). Realism was elaborated as a general theory in Hans Morgenthau, Politics among Nations: The Struggle for Power and Peace (New York: Knopf, 1948). For a general overview, see Jonathan Haslam, No Virtue Like Necessity: Realist Thought in International Relations since Machiavelli (New Haven, CT: Yale University Press, 2002).

6. John J. Mearschimer and Stephen Walt, "Keeping Saddam Hussein in a Box," New York Times, February 2, 2003. Their argument is developed at greater length in "An Unnecessary War," Foreign Policy, January/February 2003. For the theory of offensive realism within the realist paradigm, see John J. Mearsheimer, The Tragedy of Great Power Politics (New York: Norton, 2001).

7. See, for example, Lawrence F. Kaplan, "Regime Change," The New Republic, 228:8 (March, 2003): 21, as well as "Birth of a Bush Doctrine? America's Plans for the Middle East," The Economist, March 1, 2003, p. 46.

8. Michelle Sun, "Woodward Calls War in Iraq Idealist," The Cornell Daily Sun, June 21, 2007.

9. Gilbert Felix, To the Farewell Address: Ideas in Early American Foreign Policy (Princeton, NJ: Princeton University Press, 1961).

10. A synoptic account of the United States as a world power, which takes the story up to the 2003 invasion of Iraq, is Niall Ferguson, Colossus: The Price of America's Empire (New York: Penguin Press, 2004).

11. Samuel Flagg Bemis, *John Quincy Adams and the Foundations of American Foreign Policy* (New York: Knopf, 1949); Ernest R. May, *The Making of the Monroe Doctrine* (Cambridge, MA: Harvard University Press, 1975). The latter stresses domestic political considerations and argues that the Monroe Doctrine was "actually the by-product of an election campaign."

12. Daniel M. Smith, *The Great Departure: The United States and World War I, 1914–1920* (New York: John Wiley and Sons, 1965).

13. Thomas J. Knock, *To End All Wars: Woodrow Wilson and the Quest for a New World Order* (New York: Oxford University Press, 1992).

14. Margaret MacMillan, *Paris 1919: Six Months That Changed the World* (New York: Random House, 2001).

15. John M. Cooper, *Breaking the Heart of the World: Woodrow Wilson and the Fight for the League of Nations* (New York: Cambridge University Press, 2001).

16. John Lewis Gaddis, *Strategies of Containment* (New York: Oxford University Press, 2005).

17. Tony Smith, "Making the World Safe for Democracy in the American Century," *Diplomatic History* 23:2 (1999): 173–88.

18. Winston Churchill, "Sinews of Peace (Iron Curtain)," Westminster College, Fulton, MO, March 5, 1946, available from the Churchill Centre at www.winstonchurchill.org/i4a/pages/index.cfm?pageid=429 (accessed 8/2/08). See also Klaus Larres, *Churchill's Cold War: The Politics of Personal Diplomacy* (New Haven, CT: Yale University Press, 2002).

19. George F. Kennan, "The Sources of Soviet Conduct," *Foreign Affairs* 25:4 (July, 1947): 566–82.

20. Robert L. Beisner, *Dean Acheson: A Life in the Cold War* (New York: Oxford University Press, 2006); Dean Acheson, *Present at the Creation* (New York: Norton, 1969).

21. Michael J. Hogan, *The Marshall Plan: America, Britain, and the Reconstruction of Western Europe* (New York: Cambridge University Press, 1987). See also, Martin Schain, ed., *The Marshall Plan: Fifty Years Later* (New York: Palgrave, 2001).

22. Marc Trachtenberg, *A Constructed Peace: The Making of the European Settlement, 1945–1963* (Princeton, NJ: Princeton University Press, 1999).

23. The balance of military power between NATO and the Warsaw Pact throughout the Cold War is traced in David Miller, *The Cold War: A Military History* (New York: St. Martin's Press, 1998).

24. Robert A. Packenham, *Liberal America and the Third Word* (Princeton, NJ: Princeton University Press, 1973). For an overview, see David P. Forsythe, "Human Rights in U.S. Foreign Policy: Retrospect and Prospect," *Political Science Quarterly* 105:3 (Autumn, 1990): 435–54.

25. Sergei N. Goncharov, John W. Lewis, and Xue Litai, *Uncertain Partners: Stalin, Mao, and the Korean War* (Palo Alto, CA: Stanford University Press, 1999).

26. James A. Bill, *The Eagle and the Lion: The Tragedy of American-Iranian Relations* (New Haven, CT: Yale University Press, 1988).

27. Lawrence Freedman, *Kennedy's Wars: Berlin, Cuba, Laos, and Vietnam* (Oxford, UK: Oxford University Press, 2002).

28. William J. Duiker, *Sacred War: Nationalism and Revolution in a Divided Vietnam* (New York: McGraw-Hill, 1995).

29. Henry Kissinger, *Years of Upheaval* (Boston: Little, Brown, 1982); Jussi Hanhimäki, *The Flawed Architect: Henry Kissinger and American Foreign Policy* (New York: Oxford University Press, 2004).

30. Raymond Garthoff, *Détente and Confrontation: American-Soviet Relations from Nixon to Reagan* (Washington, DC: Brookings Institution Press, 1994).

31. Bill, *The Eagle and the Lion*.

32. Odd Arne Westad, ed., *The Fall of Détente: Soviet-American Relations during the Carter Years* (Oslo, Norway: Scandinavian University Press, 1997).

33. Garthoff, *Détente and Confrontation*.

34. Philip Hanson, *The Rise and Fall of the Soviet Economy* (London, UK: Longman, 2003).

35. "Can Russia Ever Be Secured?" *The Economist*, December 7, 1996, p. 45; Peter Finn, "Antimissile Plan by U.S. Strains Ties with Russia," *Washington Post*, February 21, 2007, p. A10; Matthew Kaminski, "NATO's Chill with Russia Isn't Thawing—Diplomatic Rift Hinders Bid to Involve Moscow in Kosovo Peacekeeping," *Wall Street Journal*, July 2, 1999, p. 1.

36. Francis Fukuyama, *The End of History and the Last Man*, updated ed. (New York: Free Press, 2006).

37. For a summary of American human rights policy, see John W. Dietrich, "U.S. Human Rights Policy in the Post–Cold War Era," *Political Science Quarterly* 121:2 (Summer, 2006): 269–94.

38. Samuel P. Huntington, *The Clash of Civilizations and the Remaking of World Order* (New York: Free Press, 2002).

39. Scott Wilson, "Obama Calls for Fresh Start with Muslims," *Washington Post*, June 5, 2009, p. A1.

40. For descriptions of some of these cross-cultural programs, see U.S. Department of Education, "Programs by Subject: International Education," www.ed.gov/programs/find/subject/index.html?src=ln (accessed 8/2/08).

41. U.S. Department of Agriculture, Foreign Agricultural Service, "Market Development Programs," www.fas.usda.gov/mos/marketdev.asp, and "Issues and Policies," www.fas.usda.gov/issues_policies.asp (both accessed 8/2/08).

42. Louis Fisher, *Presidential War Power* (Lawrence, KS: University Press of Kansas, 2004).

43. Eric Schmitt, "New Teams Connect Dots of Terror Plots," *New York Times*, January 29, 2010, p. A3.

44. Arthur M. Schlesinger, *The Imperial Presidency* (Boston: Houghton Mifflin, 1973).

45. Harold Hongju Koh, "Why the President (Almost) Always Wins in Foreign Affairs: Lessons of the Iran-Contra Affair," *Yale Law Journal* 97:7 (June, 1988): 1255–1342; Joseph T. Stanik, *El Dorado Canyon: Reagan's Undeclared War with Qaddafi* (Annapolis, MD: Naval Institute Press, 2002); Steven V. Roberts, "Capitol Hill Is Sharply Split over the Wisdom of Invading Grenada," *New York Times*, October 26, 1983, p. A22.

46. On Panama, see Stephen Kurkjian, "Bush Used Power as Top Commander for Strike," *Boston Globe*, December 20, 1989, p. 2. On Iraq, see Ronald J. Ostrow, "Legal Experts Split over Bush's Power Policy," *Los Angeles Times*, November 13, 1990, p. 13.

47. Neil A. Lewis, "War Powers: An Old Debate Clinton May Resolve," *New York Times*, May 8, 1993, p. 1.4; Alison Mitchell, "Deadlocked House Denies Support for Air Campaign," *New York Times*, April 29, 1999, p. A1.

48. Terry Moe and William Howell, "Unilateral Action and Presidential Power: A Theory," *Presidential Studies Quarterly* 29:4 (1999): 850–72.

49. Laurie Goering, "Clinton Signs Pacts on Global Warming: President Acts Despite Strong Opposition to the Treaty in the Senate, Which Must Ratify It," *Chicago Tribune*, November 13, 1998, p. 4.

50. David Hoffman and David B. Ottaway, "Panel Drops Covert-Acts Notification; In Compromise, Bush Pledges to Inform Hill in All but Rare Cases," *Washington Post*, October 27, 1989, p. A1.

51. John M. Broder, "Senators Issue Warning on Climate Bill," *New York Times* Green Blog, August 6, 2009, http://greeninc.blogs.nytimes.com/2009/08/06/senators-issue-warning-on-climate-bill/ (accessed 2/12/10).

52. Dahlia Lithwick, "The Enemy Within," *Slate*, June 12, 2008, www.slate.com/id/2193468 (accessed 8/12/08).

53. Somini Sengupta, "As Musharraf's Woes Grow, Enter an Old Rival, Again," *New York Times*, April 6, 2007, p. A3; Leslie Wayne, "Airbus Seeks a Welcome in Alabama," *New York Times*, June 19, 2007, p. C1.

54. American Israel Public Affairs Committee, "What Is AIPAC?," www .aipac.org/about_AIPAC/default.asp (accessed 8/3/08).

55. American Israel Public Affairs Committee, "Legislation and Policy Update," available at http://www.aipac.org/Legislation_and_Policy/ default.asp (accessed 8/3/08).

56. Andrew Jacobs, "China Angered by U.S. Lobbying on Rights," *New York Times*, August 1, 2008.

57. Steven R. Weisman, "U.S. and China Agree to Ease Foreign Investment," *New York Times*, June 19, 2008.

58. Save Darfur, "About Us: Organizational Members," www.savedarfur .org/pages/organizational_members (accessed 8/2/08).

59. Stephanie Strom, "Advocacy Group's Publicity Campaign on Darfur Angers Relief Organizations," *New York Times*, June 2, 2007.

60. See Pew Research Center, "The U.S. Public's Pro-Israel History," July 19, 2006, http://pewresearch.org/pubs/39/the-u.s.-publics-pro-israel-history (accessed 8/2/08).

61. John Harwood, "War-Weary Public Wants Congress to Lead; Poll Shows Desire for Lawmakers to Set Policy Amid Growing Dismay over Iraq, President Bush," *Wall Street Journal*, December 14, 2006, p. A4; E. J. Dionne, "Slowly Sidling to Iraq's Exit; Many GOP Candidates Part Company with Bush," *Washington Post*, August 29, 2006, p. A15.

62. Pew Research Center, "Public Opinion Six Months Later," March 7, 2002, http://people-press.org/commentary/display.php3?AnalysisID=44 (accessed 8/2/08).

63. A directory of NGOs can be found at the Department of Public Information site, Nongovernmental Organization Section, www.un.org/ dpi/ngosection/asp/form.asp (accessed 8/2/08).

64. See Amnesty International, "The Secretive and Illegal U.S. Programme of Rendition," April 5, 2006, www.amnesty.org/en/news-and-updates/feature-stories/secretive-and-illegal-us-programme-of-rendition-20060405 (accessed 8/12/08).

65. See the National Democratic Institute for International Affairs site at www.ndi.org and the International Republican Institute site at www.iri.org.

66. Johanna Neuman and Megan K. Stack, "Americans' Beirut Exodus Underway; Hundreds Are Evacuated by Ship and Helicopter," *Los Angeles Times*, July 20, 2006, p. A10. The Clinton administration resorted to cruise missile attacks five times: three against Iraq (1993, 1996, 1998), one in 1995 against Bosnian Serb forces in the former Yugoslavia, and one against targets in Afghanistan and Sudan in 1998. James Mann, "Foreign Policy of the Cruise Missile," *Los Angeles Times*, December 23, 1998, p. 5.

67. A comprehensive account of the Afghanistan invasion and its aftermath in Barnett R. Rubin, "Saving Afghanistan," *Foreign Affairs* 86:1 (January/February, 2007): 57–78.

68. United States International Trade Commission, Harmonized Tariff Schedule of the United States (2010), Revision 2, www.usitc.gov/docs/ tata/hts/bychapter/1002htsa.pdf (accessed 9/14/10).

69. Tyler Marshall, "Clinton to Nudge China on Rights Reform, Officials Say," *Los Angeles Times*, June 17, 1997, p. 7.

70. Elaine Sciolino, "Call It Aid or a Bribe, It's the Price of Peace," *New York Times*, March 26, 1995, p. 4.3.

71. Colum Lynch, "U.N. Backs Broader Sanctions on Tehran; Security Council Votes to Freeze Some Assets, Ban Arms Exports," *Washington Post*, March 25, 2007, p. A1.

72. William B. Quandt, *Camp David: Peacemaking and Politics* (Washington, DC: Brookings Institution Press, 1986).

73. John Lewis Gaddis, *The Cold War: A New History* (New York: Penguin Press, 2005).

74. David S. Yost, *NATO Transformed: The Alliance's New Roles in International Security* (Washington, DC: United States Institute of Peace Press, 1998).

75. U.S. Department of State, *Treaties in Force*, January 1, 2007, www .state.gov/s/l/treaty/treaties/2007/index.htm (accessed 8/12/08).

76. Lisa L. Martin, "The President and International Commitments: Treaties as Signaling Devices," *Presidential Studies Quarterly* 35:3 (2005): 440–65.

77. Andrew Kohut, "Simply Put, the Public's View Can't Be Put Simply," *Washington Post*, September 29, 2002, p. B5; John B. Judis, "War Resisters," *The American Prospect* 13:18, October 6, 2002, www .prospect.org/cs/articles?article=war_resisters (accessed 9/10/08).

78. P. J. Huffstutter, "A Town Gives until It Hurts," *Los Angeles Times*, November 7, 2003, p. A1.

79. Pew Research Center, "Fewer Americans See Solid Evidence of Global Warming," Oct. 22, 2009, http://people-press.org/report/556/global-warming (accessed 2/17/10).

80. Richard Benedetto, "Poll: Most Support War as a Last Resort," *USA Today*, November 26, 2002, p. A3; Dan Balz and Jim VandeHei, "Democratic Hopefuls Back Bush on Iraq; Gephardt, Lieberman, Edwards Support Launching Preemptive Strike," *Washington Post*, September 14, 2002, p. A4; Jim VandeHei and Juliet Eilperin, "Congress Passes Iraq Resolution; Overwhelming Approval Gives Bush Authority to Attack Unilaterally," *Washington Post*, October 11, 2002, p. A1.

81. Walter Pincus, "U.S. Lacks Specifics on Banned Arms," *Washington Post*, March 16, 2003, p. A17; Michael R. Gordon and Judith Miller, "U.S. Says Hussein Intensifies Quest for A-Bomb Parts," *New York Times*, September 8, 2002, p. 1.1.

82. Bob Drogin, "Iraq Weapons Data Flawed, Congress Told," *Los Angeles Times*, January 29, 2004, p. A1.

83. Adam Clymer, "House Vote on China Trade: The Politics Was Local," *New York Times*, May 27, 2000.

84. Eric Lipton, Eric Schmitt, and Mark Mazetti, "Review of Jet Bomb Plot Shows More Missed Clues," *New York Times*, January 17, 2010, p. A1.

85. Jonathan Weisman, "Democrats to Widen Conflict with Bush; Some on Both Sides See Plans as Risky," *Washington Post*, April 2, 2007, p. A1.

86. For details on the causes, effects, and mitigation of global warming, see the Intergovernmental Panel on Climate Change site at www .ipcc.ch.

87. Thomas C. Schelling, "The Cost of Combating Global Warming," *Foreign Affairs*, November/December 1997.

88. David Victor, *The Collapse of the Kyoto Protocol and the Struggle to Slow Global Warming* (Princeton, NJ: Princeton University Press, 2001).

89. Arch Puddington, "Freedom in the World 2009: Setbacks and Resilience," www.freedomhouse.org/uploads/fiw09/FIW09_ OverviewEssay_Final.pdf.

90. Reuters, "Microsoft, Sun Battle over Indian Programmers," July 8, 2002.

91. See the NightHawk Radiology Services site at www.nighthawkrad.net.

92. For an optimistic review, see Joseph Stiglitz, *Making Globalization Work* (New York: Norton, 2007).

93. Keith Bradsher, "China Finds a Fit with Car Parts: Export Factories Are Gearing Up to Challenge Global Suppliers," *New York Times*, June 7, 2007.

94. Andrew Martin, "FDA Curbs Sale of 5 Seafoods Farmed in China," *New York Times*, June 29, 2007.

95. Joseph Nocera, "The Cufflinks That Went to China," *New York Times*, January 21, 2006; Jodie T. Allen, "NAFTA Math: The Faulty Arithmetic of Job Losses," *Slate*, July 13, 1997, www.slate.com/id/1889 (accessed 8/2/08).

96. Louis Uchitelle, "Retraining, but for What?" *New York Times*, March 26, 2006.

97. William Safire, "On Language: If You Break It . . ." *New York Times Magazine*, October 17, 2004, p. 24.

98. Huntington, *The Clash of Civilizations and the Remaking of World Order*.

99. Pew Research Center, "U.S. Image Up Slightly, but Still Negative," June 23, 2005, pewglobal.org/reports/display.php?ReportID=247 (accessed 8/3/08).

100. Amartya Sen, *Identity and Violence: The Illusion of Destiny* (New York: Norton, 2007); see also Bruce Russett, John R. O'Neal, and Michaelene Cox, "Clash of Civilizations, or Realism and Liberalism Déjà Vu? Some Evidence," *Journal of Peace Research* 5 (2000): 583–608.

101. Mark Mazzetti, "CIA Still Awaiting Rules on Interrogating Suspects," *New York Times*, March 25, 2007, p. 14.

102. Anne Applebaum, "Cold War in a Hot Climate," *Slate*, May 28, 2002, www.slate.com/id/2066250 (accessed 8/3/08).

103. Federation of American Scientists, "Iraq Special Weapons Guide," www.fas.org/nuke/guide/iraq/index.html (accessed 8/2/08).

104. Nicholas Kristof, "Japan Arrests More Suspects in Gas Attack," *New York Times*, July 10, 1995, p. 7.

105. Fred Kaplan, "Let's Talk about Nukes," *Slate*, August 16, 2005, www.slate.com/id/2124544 (accessed 8/3/08).

106. John Mearsheimer and Stephen Walt, "The Israel Lobby and U.S. Foreign Policy," *Middle East Policy* 13 (2006): 29–87.

107. For an insider account, see Dennis Ross, *The Missing Peace: The Inside Story of the Fight for Middle East Peace* (New York: Farrar, Straus and Giroux, 2005).

108. Steven Erlanger, "Divide, Yes, but Conquer, Probably Not," *New York Times*, July 8, 2007.

You Decide

a. See the International Criminal Court site at http://www.icc-cpi.int/home.html; for background on the ICC, see United Nations, UN News Centre, "The International Criminal Court," www.un.org/News/facts/iccfact.htm.

b. Eric Pfanner, "Sudanese Lawyers Receive Guidance for Possible Trials over Darfur," *New York Times*, June 7, 2007; Marlise Simons, "Gambian Defends the International Criminal Court's Initial Focus on Africans," *New York Times*, February 26, 2007.

c. International Criminal Court, "The States Parties to the Rome Statute," June 1, 2008, http://hrw.org/campaigns/icc/ratifications.htm.

d. Thom Shanker and James Dao, "U.S. Might Refuse New Peace Duties without Immunity," *New York Times*, July 3, 2002.

e. David Clark, "U.S to Attend Hague Court Meeting as Observer," Reuters, November 16, 2009, www.reuters.com/article/idUSLG395050 (accessed 2/11/10).

f. Brett D. Schaefer, "Overturning Clinton's Midnight Action on the International Criminal Court," Heritage Foundation Executive Memorandum 708, January 9, 2001, www.heritage.org/Research/InternationalOrganizations/EM708.cfm.

g. Human Rights Watch, "Myths and Facts about the International Criminal Court," http://hrw.org/campaigns/icc/facts.htm.

h. Alan Cowell, "British Soldier Pleads Guilty to War Crime," *New York Times*, September 20, 2006.

i. Michael Lewis, "Military's Opposition to Harsh Interrogation Is Outlined," *New York Times*, July 28, 2005.

Challenging Conventional Wisdom

a. John J. Tkacik Jr., "Does China Pose a Military Threat?" Council on Foreign Relations Online Debate, March 26, 2007, www.cfr.org/publication/12901; as quoted in Economist.com, *Democracy in America*, "Getting Used to China," June 20, 2007, www.economist.com/blogs/democracyinamerica/2007/06/getting_used_to_china.cfm.

b. Andrew Mertha, *The Politics of Piracy: Intellectual Property in Contemporary China* (Ithaca, NY: Cornell University Press, 2007).

c. Wang Jisi, "China's Search for Stability with America," *Foreign Affairs*, September/October 2005, www.foreignaffairs.org/20050901faessay84504/wang-jisi/china-s-search-for-stability-with-america.html.

What Do Political Scientists Do?

a. John Mueller, "Assessing Measures Designed to Protect the Homeland," *Policy Studies Journal*, forthcoming John Mueller, *Overblown: How Politicians, the Terrorism Industry and Other Stoke National Security Fears* (New York: Free Press, 2006).

Credits

TABLES AND FIGURES

Figure 1.2: Robert J. Vanderbei, Map: 2008 Presidential Election, Purple America. Reprinted by permission of Robert J. Vanderbei, Princeton University. **Nuts and Bolts 5.1:** From "Beyond Red vs. Blue: The 2005 Political Typology." Reprinted by permission of The Pew Research Center for the People & the Press. **Table 5.1:** From "American Attitudes Hold Steady in Face of Foreign Crises," August 17, 2006, p. 4. Reprinted by permission of The Pew Research Center for the People & the Press. **Figure 5.3:** Mark Blumenthal, Table from "Economic Stimulus and the Many Faces of Public Opinion," http://www.pollster.com/blogs/economic_stimulus_and_the_many.php. Reprinted with permission. **Table 5.3:** From "Abortion, the Court, and the Public," Oct. 3, 2005, p. 4. Reprinted by permission of The Pew Research Center for the People & the Press. **Tables 5.4 and 5.5:** From "Beyond Red vs. Blue: The 2005 Political Typology." Reprinted by permission of The Pew Research Center for the People & the Press. **Table 5.7:** From "Support for Health Care Principles, Opposition to Package: Mixed Views of Economic Policies and Health Care Reform Persist," Oct. 8, 2009, The Pew Research Center for the People & the Press, a project of the Pew Research Center. Reprinted with permission. **Table 6.1:** From "Key News Audiences Now Blend Online and Traditional Sources: Audience Segments in a Changing News Environment," August 17, 2008, The Pew Research Center for the People & the Press, a project of the Pew Research Center. Reprinted with permission. **Table 6.3:** From "What Americans Know: 1989–2007," April 15, 2007, p. 2. Reprinted by permission of The Pew Research Center for the People & the Press. **Table 6.4:** Pollster.com, Chart: National Job Approval: Pres. Barack Obama, from http://www.pollster.com/polls/us/jobapproval-obama.php. Reprinted with permission. **Table 6.5:** From "Key News Audiences Now Blend Online and Traditional Sources: Audience Segments in a Changing News Environment," August 17, 2008, The Pew Research Center for the People & the Press, a project of the Pew Research Center. Reprinted with permission. **Chapter 6, What Do Political Scientists Do?:** Thomas E. Nelson, Rosalee A. Clawson, and Zoe M. Oxley, two tables from "Media Framing of a Civil Liberties Conflict and Its Effect on Tolerance," *American Political Science Review* Vol. 91, No. 3 (Sept. 1997): 567–83. © 1997 American Political Science Association. Reprinted with the permission of Cambridge University Press. **Figure 7.3:** From "Party Affiliation: What It Is and What It Isn't," Sept. 23, 2004, p. 3. Reprinted by permission of The Pew Research Center for the People & the Press. **Table 7.3:** From "Environment, Immigration, Health Care Slip Down the List: Economy, Jobs Trump All Other Policy Priorities in 2009," Jan. 22, 2009, The Pew Research Center for the People & the Press, a project of the Pew Research Center. Reprinted with permission. **Chapter 8, What Do Political Scientists Do?:** John Sides, two graphs from "Three Myths about Political Independents," http://www.themonkeycage.org/2009/12/three_myths_about_political_in.html. Reprinted by permission of the author. **Table 8.8:** From "Who Votes, Who Doesn't, and Why: Regular Voters, Intermittent Voters, and Those Who Don't," Oct. 16, 2006, p. 1. Reprinted by permission of The Pew Research Center for the People & the Press. **Table 8.9:** Table 5.11 from *The Politics of Congressional Elections*, 6th Edition, by Gary Jacobson. Copyright © 2004. Reprinted by permission of Pearson Education, Inc. **Table 11.1:** From "Once Again, Voters Say: It's the Economy; Bush Reelect Margin Narrows to 45%–43%," Sept. 25, 2003, p. 13. Reprinted by permission of The Pew Research Center for the People & the Press. **Chapter 11, Comparing Ourselves to Others:** Pippa Norris, Table 5.1 from *Driving Democracy: Do Power Sharing Institutions Work?* © Pippa Norris 2008. Reprinted with the permission of Cambridge University Press. **Chapter 12, What Do Political Scientists Do?:** Figure 1 from Jason Webb Yackee and Susan Webb Yackee, "A Bias toward Business? Assessing Interest Group Influence on the U.S. Bureaucracy," *The Journal of Politics* Vol. 68, No. 1 (Feb. 2006): 128–39. Copyright © 2006, Southern Political Science Association. Reprinted with the permission of Cambridge University Press. **Figure 13.5:** Stephen Jessee and Alexander Tahk, Figure "Current Beliefs" from Supreme Court Ideology Project, http://sct.tahk.us/current.html. Reprinted by permission of the authors. **Chapter 15, Comparing Ourselves to Others:** Jack Anderson, Chart "Tax Burden and Spending," *Forbes Magazine*, April 13, 2009. Reprinted by Permission of Forbes Media LLC © 2009. **Table 17.2:** From "Public Wants Proof of Iraqi Weapons Program," Jan. 16, 2003, p. 4. Reprinted by permission of The Pew Research Center for the People & the Press. **Figure 17.3:** Pew Center on Global Climate Change, Fig. 1: "Global Warming Trend Average Surface Warming and Ocean Heat Content" from "Climate Change 101: Overview," January 2009, p. 2. Reprinted by permission of Pew Center on Global Climate Change, www.pewclimate.org.

PHOTOGRAPHS

Page 2: Chase Swift/Corbis; **page 5 (left):** Alaska Dept of Transportation and Public Facilities; **page 5 (right):** Kyle Niemi/US Coast Guard/ZUMA/Corbis; **page 6:** Katie Madonia; **page 8 (left):** U.S. Army Photo by Staff Sgt. Russell Bassett; **page 8 (right):** AP Photo/Houston Chronicle, Brett Coomer; **page 9:** Jupiter Images; **page 11:** AP/Orlin Wagner; **page 12:** AP Photo/Lynne Sladky; **page 13:** Joseph Sohm/Visions of America/Corbis; **page 14:** Charles Ommanney/Getty Images; **page 15:** AP Photo/Craig Lassig; **page 18:** Erin Siegal/Reuters/Landov; **page 19:** Justin Lane/epa/Corbis; **page 20:** Jim Ruymen/UPI/Landov; **page 21:** Flip Schulke/Corbis; **page 22:** Sandy Felsenthal/Corbis; **page 26:** Wally McNamee/Corbis; **page 28:** AP photo/Marta Lavandier; **page 29:** AP/Wide World Photos; **page 34:** Imagno/Getty Images; **page 35:** North Wind Picture Archives; **page 42:** Leonard de Selva/Corbis; **page 44:** Corbis; **page 46:** Karim Sahib/AFP/Getty Images; **page 48:** Kevin Dietsch/UPI/Landov; **page 55:** AP/Alaa Al-Marjani; **page 59:** National Archives/Time Life Pictures/Getty Images; **page 60:** AP Photo/Gary Gardiner; **page 64:** Philip Gould/Corbis; **page 67:** Bettmann/Corbis; **page 69:** Bettmann/Corbis; **page 74:** Wikimedia; **page 76:** Bettmann/Corbis; **page 82:** Karen Bleier/AFP/Getty Images; **page 83:** AP Photo/Chris O'Meara; **page 85:** AP/Will Kincaid; **page 86:** George Frey/Bloomberg/Getty Images; **page 89:** Kevin Maloney/Getty Images; **page 92:** Joshua Adam Nuzzo/US Navy via Getty Images; **page 95:** Justin Sullivan/Getty Images; **page 98:** AP/Wide World Photos; **page 103 (left):** AP Photo; **page 103 (right):** William Thomas Cain/Getty Images; **page 104:** Newscom; **page 111:** Bettmann/Corbis; **page 112:** Hulton Archives/Getty/Newscom; **page 113:** Al Crespo/Sipa Press/Newscom; **page 114:** AP Photo; **page 116:** William Campbell/Sygma/Corbis; **page 118:** Zuma Photos/Newscom; **page 121:** Jana Birchum/Getty Images; **page 123:** Sherry Lavars/MCT/Landov; **page 125:** Getty/Newscom; **page 126:** Jim Morin/

Index

Page numbers in *italics* refer to illustrations. Page numbers in **boldface** refer to figures.

American Society of Newspaper Editors
(ASNE), 210
Americans for Job Security, 228
Americans with Disabilities Act (1990), 82,
82, 87–88, **88**, 90, 534, 542
AmeriCorps program, *601*
amicus curiae, 491, 494, 499
Amish, 102, *103*, 120, 122
Amnesty International, 652, 662
anarchy, anarchists, 7, 8, 33, 107–8, 111
Anderson, John, **286**
Andrade, Leandro, 136
Anglican Church, 54
animal sacrifice, 122
Annapolis Convention, 31, **33**
Annual Economic Report of the President, 569
Ansolabehere, Stephen, 342
Anthony, Susan B., 524
anthrax attacks, 668, 669
Anti-Ballistic Missile Treaty (ABM), 422, **658**
Antifederalist Papers, 468
Antifederalists, 467–68, 511
Constitutional Convention role of, 36, 37,
40, 41, **43**
constitutional opposition by, 44–45, 105
separation of powers and, 49, 71, 80
Appeal, The (Grisham), 481
appeals courts, 477–79, **478**
appointments, judicial:
congressional power over, 47, 48, **48**, 49
executive power of, 47, 48, **48**, 50, 398–
99, 470, 478, 481–86, **483**
political importance of, 48, 50, 87, 399
to Supreme Court, 393, 398–99, 469
appointments, political, 452–53
congressional power over, 49, 60
executive power of, 60, 398–99
in federal bureaucracy, 431
influence of, 40
apportionment, 357
Arab Americans, 520, 551
Arab-Israeli War, 643
Argentina, 54, 405, 656
Argersinger v. Hamlin, **109**
aristocracy, **10**
Aristotle, **10**
Arizona, 72, 131, 270, 276, 279, 357, 538,
550, 610
Arkansas, 90, 521, 543
Arkansas River, 487
armband wearing, as symbolic speech, 496,
496
arms control agreements, 397
Army, U.S., 7, 110, 668
Army Corps of Engineers, U.S., 430, 439
arson, 114
Articles of Confederation:

Constitutional Convention influence of,
29, *36*, 42, 43
duration of, **32**, **33**
economic interpretation of, 35
government organization under, **31**
problems with, 30–32, 37, 39, 44, 68, 70
war powers in, 48
Ashcroft, John, 118, 138–39
Asia, systems of government in, **405**
Asia Foundation, 651
Asian Americans:
civil rights of, 511, 514, 544, 546
voting history of, 20
assassinations, 124–25, *125*, 611, *611*
assisted suicide, 66, 91, 92, 138, 625
Associated Press (AP), 188, 192, 551
astroturf lobbying, 331
AT&T, 129, 318, 336, 541
athletics:
civil rights and, 514, *514*, 537, 541, *541*
regulation and, 434, *434*
Atlanta, Ga., 532, 588
A. T. Massey, 480–81, *481*
attack ads, 280, 283–84, **283**
attack journalism, 211, 212, 214
attitudinalist approach, 497–98
attorney general, 92, 99, 118, 138–39
attorneys, **106**, **109**, 125–26, 132, 134
U.S., firings of, 407, 408, *408*, 452
Atwater v. Lago Vista, 59
Audubon Club, 460
Aum Shinrikyo group, 669
Austin, Tex., 121, *121*
Australia, 68, 447, 607, 642, **657**
Austria, 68, 579, 584, **657**
Automobile Association of America (AAA),
311, 325–26, *326*
automobile industry, 557, *558*, 579
international value of currency and, 590
autonomy, under federalism, 66, 67, 68, 69,
69, 70, 72
Axelrod, David, 416, *416*
Ayers, William, 300

Baby Boom generation, 614, 616, *618*
backbenchers, 245
bail, excessive, **109**
Baker, Howard, 384
Baker, James, 79
Baker v. Carr, 501
Bakke, Allan, 548
Balanced Budget and Emergency Control
Act (1985), 567
balanced budgets, 563–64
balance of payments, 565, 590–93
Baldwin, Tammy, 363–64, *364*, 365, **366**
Bali, 668
Balkans, 397, 638

ballots:
counting of, 265–66
different forms of, 265
see also absentee ballots; voting
Baltimore, Md., 72, 105
Bank of America, 338, **339**, 572
banks, 15, 58–60, **68**, 72–73, **75**, 84, 116,
398, *398*, 430, 562, 570–74, 576,
581–85,
651, 666
federal insuring of deposits in, 562, *563*,
582, *582*
Federal Reserve's role in stabilization of,
570–74, 582–85, 593
in financial crisis of 2008, 347–49, 572–
74, 583, 585, 593, 594, 666
in Great Depression, 582, *582*, 583, 585
lending activity regulation in, 570,
582–84, 585
"runs" on, *582*, 583
Barron v. Baltimore, 74, **75**, 105–6, 107
Bartels, Larry, 604–5
Barwari, Nisreen, *535*
baseball, desegregation of, 514, *514*
Baucus, Max, 597
Bauer, Frederick W., 486
Baumgartner, Frank, 337, 612
Beard, Charles, 35
Bear Stearns, 666
*Before the Next Attack: Preserving Civil
Liberties in an Age of Terrorism*
(Ackerman), 129
Behr, Roy, 248
Beirut, 645
Belarus, 594
Belgium, 69, 447, **579**, **657**
Bell, Sean, 523
BellSouth, 130
benefits, 123
Benjamin, Brent, 480, *481*
Bennett, Robert, 6, 375
Benton v. Maryland, **109**
Berlin Wall, *643*
Bernanke, Ben, 411, 571, *571*, 572, 573, 575,
575, 585
Bernstein, Carl, 198
Berwick, Donald, 399
Best Buy, 289
Better Health Care Together, 330
Bible, 156, **157**
Biden, Joe, 280, *299*, 300, 417
bilateral agreements, 657
Bill of Rights, U.S., 43, **68**, 102, **106**, 196,
511
creation of, 45–46, 57, 104–5
privacy rights in, 137
protections in, 288, 662
public awareness of, 147, *147*

Hussein, Saddam, 69, 143, **145**, 236, 638, 650

Hustler, 117

Hutchings, Vince, 518

hyperinflation, 584, *584*

hypotheses, research and, 10

IBM, 560

Iceland, 447, **579**, 594

Idaho, 302, 388, 395, 534, 536

idealism, 637–40, 641, 659, 662

identity politics, 20–22, 153–54, 156–57, **157**

ideology, 22–24

 federalism and, 90–91, 92

 inconsistency of, 22, 146–47, 148, 150, 179

 polarization of, 164–66, 179, 374

 political conflict as a result of, 13, 164–66, **165**, 573

 public opinion and, 16, 23–24, 145, 148, 149, 151, 152, 164–66

 trade policy influenced by, 592

"I Have a Dream" speech, 517, *517*, 528

IHOP, 538

Illinois, 6, 100, 516

immigration, 21–22, 23, 74, 84, 150, **165**, 176, 224, 245, 251, 275–76, 354, 370, 397, 515, 545, 550–52

 illegal, 550, 552, *552*

 reform debates on, 233, 245, 276–77, 550–51

impeachment, 8, 47, 49, 166, *166*, 387, 425, 444

 of A. Johnson, 425

 of Clinton, 27, 29, 425

 of judges, 503

 pardons and, 406

imperial judiciary, 467

implied powers, 57–60, 67, 73, 74

income:

 immigration and, 551

 inequality of, 602–6, *604*

 political influence of, **157**

 racial divide in, 521

 in South vs. North, 512

 state differences in, **94**

 of women vs. men, 537, **538**, 541

income support, 626–29, **629**

income tax, 57, 59, 395, 430, 579, 580

incumbents, 261

 high reelection rates of, 259–60, **260**, *273*, 274, **287**, 295

 meeting and greeting, 356

 permanent campaign of, 272–74, *273*

 presidential nominations of, 267–68, 272

 retrospective evaluations of, 261, 293, 294, **294**

indecent language, 119

indentured servants, 512

independent agencies, 443, **443**

 number of employees in, 445–46, **445**

independent counsel, 27

Independent Party, 248

independents, 164, **164**, 176, 296–97, *296*

 candidacy of, 240, **259**, 262, **286**

independent voters, 236–37

India, 69, 535, 590, 662, 669, 670

 outsourcing of jobs to, 557, 560

Indiana, 24, 270, 279, 300

individualism, economic, 19

industrialization, 77, 395

industry, 19

infant mortality, 523, 607

Infinity Broadcasting, 191

inflation, 155, 174, 396, *562*, 565, 575, 583, 584, 593, 618

 Misery Index of unemployment and, 561–62, **561**

 prevention of, as economic policy goal, 561–62, 565

informational theory, 378

infrastructure:

 concurrent power over, **68**

 federal authority over, 46, 83

 federal spending on, 6, 9, 18, 94–95, *95*

 state and local spending on, 80, 85

inherent power, 417

initiative, 334–35

In re Oliver 333 U.S. 257, **109**

inside strategies, 327–30, **336**

Intel, 318

intelligence gathering, 100–101, 646, 660, 663

intelligent design, 20, 120

intercontinental railroad, 515, *515*

interest groups, 8, 12, 15, 18, 19, 34, 65, *82*, 95, 124, *133*, 179, 228, 272, 274, 308–45, *308*, *311*, *317*

 campaign ads run by, 279, 281–84, **282**, **283**, 284, 285–86, 311, 331–33, 337

 campaign contributions by, 285–86, **287**, 288, 289, 311, 319, 332–34, 342, 590

 collective action and free riding problems of, 323–27

 definition of, 311

 in European countries, 312, *312*

 factors determining success of, 339–43

 financial expenditures of, 312–17, **313**, 314, 316, **333**, **334**, 337–39, 343

 foreign policy and influence of, 648–49

 as fundamental feature of democracy, 311–12

 funding of, 322, 323

 growth in number of, 312–14, 318, 343

inside lobbying strategies of, 327–30, *329*, 335–36, **336**

leaders or entrepreneurs of, 326

membership size and role in, 320

organizational models of, 318–19

outside lobbying strategies of, *321*, 327, 330–35, **336**

political influence and power of, 276, 309, 311, 321, 337, *337*, 340–41, 342, 589, 649

political parties vs., 311

public opinion and, 16, 20, 157, 309

regulations imposed on, 284–85, 288, 312, 315, 332, 590

resources used by, 321–23

social policy formation and role of, 609, 611–12, 630

staff and revolving door of, 319–20, 323

Supreme Court and, 491, 499

three types of, 317–18

see also lobbying, lobbyists

interest group state, 311

interest rates, 565, 570, 571, *571*, 575, 583, 584, 592, 593

intergovernmental relations, 77

intergovernmental transfers, 69

Interior Department, U.S., **443**, 445, 459, 578, 589

 Endangered Species Act and, 476

Intermediate-Range Nuclear Forces Treaty (INF), **658**

intermediate scrutiny standard, 536

Internal Revenue Code, 285

Internal Revenue Service (IRS), 9, *273*, 332, 430, 444, 455

international aid, 8, 23, 162

 see also foreign aid

International Association of Fire Fighters, 333, **334**

International Atomic Energy Association (IAEA), 653, 669

International Criminal Court (ICC), 638–39, *639*

internationalism, 637, 641

international law, 116, 136

international media, 213

International Monetary Fund (IMF), 69, 529, 641, 651

international organizations, 651–52, 672

International Republican Institute, 652

International Trade Commission, 655

Internet, 17, 119, 126, 160, 190, 193, 213, 300, 314, 586

 fabricated photos on, 195, *195*

 filing of tax returns over, 430

 fund-raising and, 280, 300

 grassroots lobbying on, 331

Supreme Court, U.S. (*continued*)
   rules of access for, 487–88
   on school voucher programs, 610
   separation of powers and, 465, 498–99, 502–3
   "special master" hearings, and, 486–87
   strategic approach to, 498
   strict construction and, 52–53, 496–97, 498, 500
   tenure of justices of, 480
   terror suspects and, 28, 465–66
   2000 election decision of, 28, *28*
   unilateral presidential actions and, 424
   War Powers Resolution and, 401–2
   workload of, 486–87, **487**
   writ of certification and, 488, **490**
   writ of certiorari and, 488, **490**
   writ of mandamus issued by, 470
   see also judicial branch; *specific cases*
surge, in troops, *see* troop surge
surveillance, 28, *29*, 83, 100, 116, 126, *126*, 129–31, 393, 422
   see also spying
surveys, 148, **149**, 651
   interpretation of, 163, 165–66, 168–69
   mass, 158, **159**, 163
   problems with, 146–48, 162–63, **165**, 650
   research and, 11
   techniques of, 160–61
   wording of, 151, 160, **161**, 165, 166–67, 176, 177, 180
   see also polls
suspension of rules, 384
Sweden, 68, **657**
   government spending in, 447, *447*
   tax rates in, 579, **579**
Swift Vets and POWs for Truth, 332
swine flu, 213, **213**
swing states, 270, 300
Swing Vote, 290
Switzerland, 68, 69, 447, **579**, 619, **657**
Syria, 100, 136, 671

Taiwan, 535, 665
"taking the late train," 334
Taliban, 201, 279, 663, 667
talk radio, 191, 193, *193*, 209
Tammany Hall, 230, *230*
Taney, Roger, 74
Tanzania, 644
Target, 289
tariffs, 17, 35, 37, 45, 73, 592, 643, 645, 649, 653, 664
   definition of, 655
TARP, *see* Troubled Asset Relief Program
Tax Day, 529
taxes, tax policy, 447, 558, 568, 572, 661, 672

Articles of Confederation problems with, 30, **31**, 42
Clinton's increase of, 352
concurrent power over, **68**
Constitutional Convention issue of, 36–37, 41, 45, 349
corporate, 580
cuts in, 393, 397, 411, 413, 604
estate, 611
excise, 580
federal authority over, **31**, 46, 59, 69, 70–71, 72–73, 83, 349, 569
fiscal theories on influencing economy with, 576–81, **577**
in foreign countries, 579, **579**
health care programs and, 13, 622, 624
ideological views on, 19, 22
income, 57, 59, 396, 430, 579, 580
local authority over, 67, 91
McCain's work on, 370
marginal tax rate and, 581, **581**
1962 revenue from, **580**
payment for public goods with, 9
payroll, 579, 580–81, 616, **617**, 618, 619, 622
proposed constitutional amendments concerning, **58**
public opinion on, 83, 174, **174**, 362
redistributive, 19, 156, **157**, 578–80, **580**, 581, 593
regressive vs. progressive, 580–81
religious organizations and, 121, 123
Social Security funding and, 616, **617**, 618, 619, 622
standing and, 477
state authority over, 67, **68**, 70–71, 72–73, 86, 93, **93**, 95
and subsidies for wealthy, 603
2006 revenue from, **18**
2008 revenue from, **580**
urban support for raises in, 354
uses for, 17, 67, 113, 578–80, **580**
Tea Party movement, 228, 242, *242*, 301–2, 319, 330, *331*, 529
technology, First Amendment rights and, 496
Telecommunications Act (1996), 190
telegraphs, 188
television, 188–90, 192–94, 215, 314
   campaign ads on, 281–84, *281*, **282**, **283**, 288, 289, 311, 331, 332–33, 334, 337
   comedy shows as news sources on, 200, 202
   corporate ownership in, 190, **191**
   FCC regulations of, 188–90, 587
   framing effects and, 207
   knowledge levels in viewers of, **202**, 203

   nightly news programs on, 192–94, 200, **201**, 202, **202**, 209
   online sites for, 194, **201**
   political bias in, 208–9, **208**
   usage trends in, 200–201, **201**
Temporary Assistance to Needy Families (TANF), 81, 91, 609, 629, **629**
Ten Commandments, 121, *121*
Tennessee, 531
Tennessee Valley Authority, 445
Tenth Amendment, 41, 71, 86–87, *86*, **106**
term limits, **31**, **58**, 59, 90
territorial expansion, Mexican-American war and, 395
terrorism, 8, 27, 28, *29*, 50, 81, 83, 95, 99–101, 112, 114, 116, 126, ,129, 130, *130*, 139, 151–52, **151**, 155, **165**, 173, 635, 637, 638, 643, *644*, 645, 654, 660–61, 663, 668, 669
   "clash of civilizations" as root of, 644, 668
   military tribunals and, 398, 465–66
   restriction of legal rights and, 422, 465–66, 502, 639, 648, 652, 660–61, 668
   undoing presidential actions and, *423*
   see also War on Terror
Terrorist Finance Tracking Program, 116
Texas, 52, 67, 113, 121, 249, 357, 358, 534, *552*
   affirmative action in, 546–47
   annexation of, 395, 422
   desegregation in, 530
   sodomy in, 539
Texas, University of, 548
Theiss-Morse, Elizabeth, 12, 214
Theriault, Sean, 375
thermal imaging devices, 104
Thernstrom, Abigail, 545
Thernstrom, Stephan, 545
Third Amendment, 51, **106**, **109**, 137
third party system, **222**, 223, 224
Thirteenth Amendment, 74, 106, 110, 512, 532
Thomas, Clarence, 52, 87, 466, 497, 498, 499
   original intent perspective of, 497, 498
   Supreme Court appointment of, 482, *482*
Thomas, Timothy, 523
Thompson, Fred, 189
Three-fifths Compromise, 42, 43, 44
"three strikes" law, 136
Thurmond, Strom, 385
Tibet, 665
Time, 192, **208**, *310*
Tinker, Mary Beth, *496*
tobacco subsidies, 389
Tocqueville, Alexis de, 95
Tokyo, 669

Tongass National Forest, *133*
Tonight Show, The, 585
Toomey, Pat, 271
Top Censored Stories, 204
Tories, 29
torture, 28, 50, 100, 101, 393, 398, 400
totalitarianism, 69, 130
Tour de France, 128
Town Hall, 195
town hall meetings, *413*
Toyota, 557
trade, 9, **68**, 403, 569, 572, 590–93
    agreements, 636, 641–42, 643, 653, 655,
        664, 672
    Articles of Confederation and, 30–31
    Constitutional Convention and, 35, 43
    deficits, 565, 590–92, **591**
    executive branch and power over, 569
    free, 362, 396, 397, 592, 594, 640, 655
    international, 477, 569, 579, 590–93,
        594, 635–36, 637, 640, 641–42, 643,
        645, 649, 654–55, **654**, 660, 664,
        664, 670, 671
    most-favored nation status and, 655,
        660
trade associations, 316–17, 326
traffic offenses, **58**, 59, 104, 122, 127
Traficant, James, 373–74
transfer payments, *see* grants
transportation, 67, 76, 82, 353, 398, 587,
    598
    federal spending on, *2*, 4–5, 6, 65, *348*,
        349, 354, 370, 562
Transportation Department, U.S., 398, 430,
    443
    Coast Guard transferred out of, 456,
        456
    number of employees in, 445
Transportation Security Administration,
    U.S., 429, 430, 646
Treasury Department, U.S., **68**, 347, 422,
    438, *438*, 439, **443**, 444, 566, 569,
    570, 571
    economic policies and responsibilities of,
        572–74
    Federal Reserve in cooperation with,
        572–74
    in financial crisis of 2008, 572–74, *572*,
        594
    number of employees in, 445
treaties, 13, 30, 53, **68**, 69, 70, 423, 643,
    646
    definition of, 656
    executive power to negotiate, 48, 49,
        402–3, 405
    fast-track authority for, 402
    as foreign policy tool, 656, 657, 658,
        658

Treaty of Lisbon, 38
Treaty of Versailles, *640*, 641
Treaty on Conventional Forces in Europe
    (CFE), **658**
trespassing, 114
trials, rights concerning, **109**, 115, 116–17,
    125, 127–28, 134
Tribune Company, 190
trickle-down economics, *see* supply-side
    economics
troop surge, 143, 303, 410–12, 666, 667,
    667
Troubled Asset Relief Program (TARP),
    306, 337–39, **339**, 347, 386, *386*,
    398
Truman, Harry S., 129, 199, 272, 424, 502,
    514, 543, 570
Truman Doctrine, 641
trustee, 352
Trustee's Report, 616, 622
trust fund, of Social Security, 616–17, **617**,
    618, *618*
Turkey, **579**, 642
"turkey farms," 452
Tutu, Desmond, 117
Twain, Mark, 360, *360*
Tweed, William "Boss," *230*
Twelfth Amendment, 41, 51–52, 57
Twenty-fifth Amendment, 413, 414
Twenty-first Amendment, 56, 59, *59*, 65
Twenty-second Amendment, 59
Twenty-seventh Amendment, 57, 59
"two presidencies" thesis, 403
Tyco, 475
Tyler, John, 482
tyranny, 29, 44
tyranny of the majority, 8, 37, 46, 84, 93,
    114

Uganda, 136
Ukraine, 594
Underground Railroad, 512
undervotes, 265
unemployment, 155, 173, **174**, *247*, 347, 396,
    409, 522, 560, 565, 568, 574, *574*,
    600
    compensation policies for, 599, 600, 607,
        626, 664
    economic bills passed for reduction of,
        559–60, *559*
    Misery Index of inflation and, 561–62,
        561
Unfunded Mandate Reform Act (1995), 81
unfunded mandates, **79**, 81, 82, 83
unified government, 246
unilateral action (national), 637, 638–39
unilateral action (presidential), 421–25, *422*,
    423, 543, 636, 646

Union Army, *45*, 222, 224
Union League, 513
unions, 67, 225, *225*, 227, 285, 288, 314,
    562, 592, 594, 601
    interest groups and lobbying efforts of,
        317, 325–26, *330*, 333
    OSHA and, 459
unitary executive theory, 422, 424
unitary system, 10, 66, 67, 68, 69, 93
United Kingdom, *see* Great Britain
United Nations (UN), 69, 231, 637, 638–39,
    641, 642, 652, 660, 672
    General Assembly of, 652
    IAEA of, 653, 656, 669
    International Criminal Court of, 638–39,
        639, 672
    Security Council of, 652, 655
United States, international media and,
    213
United States v. Griswold, **109**
United States v. Lopez, **88**, 89, *89*
United States v. Morrison, **88**
United States v. Nixon, 407
universal health care, 607, 620
University of California Regents v. Bakke, 548,
    550
Unorthodox Lawmaking (Sinclair), 379
Unsafe at Any Speed (Nader), 587
urbanization, 77
Uruguay, 592
USA PATRIOT Act (2001), 28, 83, 126,
    126, 232, 329, 28, 128
USA Today, **208**, 328
U.S. Code, 232
U.S. Pacifist Party, 248
U.S. Term Limits v. Thornton, 90, 388
Utah, 263, 610
    national monument in, *422*

Valentino, Nicholas, 518
values, effect on policy of, 135
Van Buren, Martin, 223, 395
Vanguard Investments, 619
variables, research and, 11
Venezuela, 54
verdict, 474
Verizon, 130
vesting clause, 398, 422
veteran-owned businesses, 435
veterans, 155, 429, 559–60, *559*, 599, 630
Veterans Administration, 429
Veterans Affairs Department, U.S., 356,
    442, **443**, 445
veto:
    Articles of Confederation rules for, 30
    in confederal system, 68
    executive power of, 8, 39, 47, 49–50, 379,
        382, 400, 403–4, 423, 570, 646